HALSBURY'S
Laws of England

FIFTH EDITION
2009

Volume 18

This is volume 18 of the Fifth Edition of Halsbury's Laws of England, containing the titles COMPETITION and COMPULSORY ACQUISITION OF LAND.

COMPETITION replaces the Fourth Edition title TRADE, INDUSTRY AND INDUSTRIAL RELATIONS volume 47 (2001 Reissue) Parts 2–6. With the publication of this volume and the accompanying Additional Materials booklet, *Trade, Industry and Industrial Relations*, volume 47 (2001 Reissue) may now be archived.

COMPULSORY ACQUISITION OF LAND replaces the Fourth Edition title COMPULSORY ACQUISITION OF LAND, contained in volume 8(1) (2003 Reissue). That volume should be retained until remaining material is replaced.

For a full list of volumes comprised in a current set of Halsbury's Laws of England please see overleaf.

Fifth Edition volumes:

1 (2008), 2 (2008), 7 (2008), 11 (2009), 12 (2009), 13 (2009), 18 (2009), 39 (2009), 40 (2009), 41 (2009), 48 (2008), 49 (2008), 50 (2008), 54 (2008), 65 (2008), 66 (2009), 67 (2008), 68 (2008), 69 (2009), 72 (2009), 73 (2009), 79 (2008), 93 (2008), 94 (2008), 100 (2009), 101 (2009)

Fourth Edition volumes (bold figures represent reissues):

1(1) (2001 Reissue), 1(2) (2007 Reissue), 2(2), 2(3), 3(1) (2005 Reissue), 3(2) (2002 Reissue), 4(1) (2002 Reissue), 4(2) (2002 Reissue), 4(3), 5(1) (2004 Reissue), 5(2) (2001 Reissue), 5(3) (2008 Reissue), 5(4) (2008 Reissue), 7(1) (2004 Reissue), 7(2) (2004 Reissue), 7(3) (2004 Reissue), 7(4) (2004 Reissue), 8(1) (2003 Reissue), 8(2), 8(3), 9(1), 9(2) (2006 Reissue), 10, 11(1) (2006 Reissue), 11(2) (2006 Reissue), 11(3) (2006 Reissue), 11(4) (2006 Reissue), 12(1), 12(2) (2007 Reissue), 12(3) (2007 Reissue), 13 (2007 Reissue), 14, 15(1) (2006 Reissue), 15(2) (2006 Reissue), 15(3) (2007 Reissue), 15(4) (2007 Reissue), 16(2), 17(2), 18(2), 19(1) (2007 Reissue), 19(2) (2007 Reissue), 19(3) (2007 Reissue), 20(1), 20(2), 21 (2004 Reissue), 22 (2006 Reissue), 23(1), 23(2), 24, 25 (2003 Reissue), 26 (2004 Reissue), 27(1) (2006 Reissue), 27(2) (2006 Reissue), 27(3) (2006 Reissue), 28, 29(2), 30(1), 30(2), 31 (2003 Reissue), 32 (2005 Reissue), 33, 34, 35, 36(1) (2007 Reissue), 36(2), 38 (2006 Reissue), 39(1A), 39(1B), 39(2), 40(1) (2007 Reissue), 40(2) (2007 Reissue), 40(3) (2007 Reissue), 41 (2005 Reissue), 42, 44(1), 44(2), 45(1) (2005 Reissue), 45(2), 46(1), 46(2), 46(3), 48 (2007 Reissue), 49(1) (2005 Reissue), 50 (2005 Reissue), 51, 52

Additional Materials: *Shipping and Water (Pollution)* containing vol 43(2) (Reissue) paras 1135–1369 and vol 49(3) (2004 Reissue) paras 658–746; *Local Government Finance* containing vol 29(1) (Reissue) paras 514–618, 624–634; *Trade, Industry and Industrial Relations* containing vol 47 (2001 Reissue) paras 1–4, 601–1000

Fourth and Fifth Edition volumes:

2008 Consolidated Index (A–E), 2008 Consolidated Index (F–O), 2008 Consolidated Index (P–Z), 2009 Consolidated Table of Statutes, 2009 Consolidated Table of Statutory Instruments, etc, 2009 Consolidated Table of Cases (A–L), 2009 Consolidated Table of Cases (M–Z, ECJ Cases)

August 2009

HALSBURY'S
Laws of England

FIFTH EDITION

LORD MACKAY OF CLASHFERN
Lord High Chancellor of Great Britain
1987–97

Volume 18

2009

Members of the LexisNexis Group worldwide

United Kingdom	LexisNexis, a Division of Reed Elsevier (UK) Ltd, Halsbury House, 35 Chancery Lane, LONDON, WC2A 1EL, and London House, 20–22 East London Street, EDINBURGH, EH7 4BQ
Australia	LexisNexis Butterworths, Chatswood, New South Wales
Austria	LexisNexis Verlag ARD Orac GmbH & Co KG, Vienna
Benelux	LexisNexis Benelux, Amsterdam
Canada	LexisNexis Canada, Markham, Ontario
China	LexisNexis China, Beijing and Shanghai
France	LexisNexis SA, Paris
Germany	LexisNexis Deutschland GmbH Munster
Hong Kong	LexisNexis Hong Kong, Hong Kong
India	LexisNexis India, New Delhi
Italy	Giuffrè Editore, Milan
Japan	LexisNexis Japan, Tokyo
Malaysia	Malayan Law Journal Sdn Bhd, Kuala Lumpur
New Zealand	LexisNexis NZ Ltd, Wellington
Poland	Wydawnictwo Prawnicze LexisNexis Sp, Warsaw
Singapore	LexisNexis Singapore, Singapore
South Africa	LexisNexis Butterworths, Durban
USA	LexisNexis, Dayton, Ohio

FIRST EDITION	*Published in 31 volumes between 1907 and 1917*
SECOND EDITION	*Published in 37 volumes between 1931 and 1942*
THIRD EDITION	*Published in 43 volumes between 1952 and 1964*
FOURTH EDITION	*Published in 56 volumes between 1973 and 1987, with reissues between 1988 and 2008*
FIFTH EDITION	*Commenced in 2008*

A CIP Catalogue record for this book is available from the British Library.

ISBN 13 (complete set, standard binding): 9780406047762

ISBN 13: 9781405738163

ISBN 978-1-4057-3816-3

Typeset by Letterpart Ltd, Reigate, Surrey
Printed in the UK by CPI William Clowes Beccles NR34 7TL
Visit LexisNexis at www.lexisnexis.co.uk

Editor in Chief

THE RIGHT HONOURABLE

LORD MACKAY OF CLASHFERN
LORD HIGH CHANCELLOR OF GREAT BRITAIN

1987–97

Editors of this Volume

TAMSIN CUNDY, MA,
a Solicitor of the Supreme Court

CAROL MARSH, LLB, MA

CLAIRE MASSON, MA,
a Solicitor of the Supreme Court

Sub-editors

GAVIN DILLOW, MA

CLAIRE RAMSBOTTOM, LLB, MSC

Indexer

ALEXANDRA CORRIN, LLB,
of Gray's Inn, Barrister

Managing Editor

CLARE BLANCHARD, BA

Publisher

SIMON HETHERINGTON, LLB

COMPETITION

Consultant Editor

RICHARD WHISH, BA, BCL,

a Solicitor of the Supreme Court;

Professor of Law, King's College, University of London

COMPULSORY ACQUISITION OF LAND

Consultant Editor

JOSEPH HARPER, BA, LLM,

a Bencher of Gray's Inn;

one of Her Majesty's Counsel

The law stated in this volume is in general that in force on 1 July 2009,
although subsequent changes have been included wherever possible.

Any future updating material will be found in the Current Service and annual
Cumulative Supplement to Halsbury's Laws of England.

TABLE OF CONTENTS

HOW TO USE HALSBURY'S LAWS
OF ENGLAND

Volumes

Each text volume of Halsbury's Laws of England contains the law on the titles contained in it as at a date stated at the front of the volume (the operative date).

Information contained in Halsbury's Laws of England may be accessed in several ways.

First, by using the tables of contents.

Each volume contains both a general Table of Contents, and a specific Table of Contents for each title contained in it. From these tables you will be directed to the relevant part of the work.

Readers should note that the current arrangement of titles can be found in the Current Service.

Secondly, by using tables of statutes, statutory instruments, cases or other materials.

If you know the name of the Act, statutory instrument or case with which your research is concerned, you should consult the Consolidated Tables of statutes, cases and so on (published as separate volumes) which will direct you to the relevant volume and paragraph. The Consolidated Tables will indicate if the volume referred to is a Fifth Edition volume.

(Each individual text volume also includes tables of those materials used as authority in that volume.)

Thirdly, by using the indexes.

If you are uncertain of the general subject area of your research, you should go to the Consolidated Index (published as separate volumes) for reference to the relevant volume(s) and paragraph(s). The Consolidated Index will indicate if the volume referred to is a Fifth Edition volume.

(Each individual text volume also includes an index to the material contained therein.)

Additional Materials

The reorganisation of the title scheme of Halsbury's Laws for the Fifth Edition means that from time to time Fourth Edition volumes will be *partially* replaced by Fifth Edition volumes.

In certain instances an Additional Materials softbound book will be issued, in which will be reproduced material which has not yet been replaced by a Fifth Edition title. This will enable users to remove specific Fourth Edition volumes from the shelf and save valuable space pending the replacement of that material in the Fifth Edition. These softbound books are supplied to volumes subscribers free of charge. They continue to form part of the set of Halsbury's Laws Fourth Edition Reissue, and will be updated by the Annual Cumulative Supplement and monthly Noter-up in the usual way.

With the present volume is published Additional Materials: *Trade, Industry and Industrial Relations*. This booklet contains material reproduced from the Fourth Edition (Reissue) title TRADE, INDUSTRY AND INDUSTRIAL RELATIONS volume 47 (2001 Reissue) that has not been included in the Fifth Edition titles EMPLOYMENT or COMPETITION. This material will form the basis of the Fifth Edition title TRADE AND INDUSTRY, which is scheduled for publication at a later date.

Updating publications

The text volumes of Halsbury's Laws should be used in conjunction with the annual Cumulative Supplement and the monthly Noter-Up.

The annual Cumulative Supplement

The Supplement gives details of all changes between the operative date of the text volume and the operative date of the Supplement. It is arranged in the same volume, title and paragraph order as the text volumes. Developments affecting particular points of law are noted to the relevant paragraph(s) of the text volumes. As from the commencement of the Fifth Edition, the Supplement will clearly distinguish between Fourth and Fifth Edition titles.

For narrative treatment of material noted in the Cumulative Supplement, go to the Annual Abridgment volume for the relevant year.

Destination Tables

In certain titles in the annual *Cumulative Supplement*, reference is made to Destination Tables showing the destination of consolidated legislation. Those Destination Tables are to be found either at the end of the titles within the annual *Cumulative Supplement*, or in a separate *Destination Tables* booklet provided from time to time with the *Cumulative Supplement*.

The Noter-Up

The Noter-Up is contained in the Current Service Noter-Up booklet, issued monthly and noting changes since the publication of the annual Cumulative Supplement. Also arranged in the same volume, title and paragraph order as the text volumes, the Noter-Up follows the style of the Cumulative Supplement. As from the commencement of the Fifth Edition, the Noter-Up will clearly distinguish between Fourth and Fifth Edition titles.

For narrative treatment of material noted in the Noter-Up, go to the relevant Monthly Review.

REFERENCES AND ABBREVIATIONS

ACT	Australian Capital Territory
A-G	Attorney General
Admin	Administrative Court
Admlty	Admiralty Court
Adv-Gen	Advocate General
affd	affirmed
affg	affirming
Alta	Alberta
App	Appendix
art	article
Aust	Australia
B	Baron
BC	British Columbia
C	Command Paper (of a series published before 1900)
c	chapter number of an Act
CA	Court of Appeal
CAC	Central Arbitration Committee
CA in Ch	Court of Appeal in Chancery
CB	Chief Baron
CCA	Court of Criminal Appeal
CCR	County Court Rules 1981 (SI 1981/1687) as subsequently amended
CCR	Court for Crown Cases Reserved
C-MAC	Courts-Martial Appeal Court
CO	Crown Office
COD	Crown Office Digest
CPR	Civil Procedure Rules 1998 (SI 1998/3132) as subsequently amended (see the Civil Court Practice)
Can	Canada
Cd	Command Paper (of the series published 1900–18)
Cf	compare
Ch	Chancery Division
ch	chapter
cl	clause

Cm	Command Paper (of the series published 1986 to date)
Cmd	Command Paper (of the series published 1919–56)
Cmnd	Command Paper (of the series published 1956–86)
Comm	Commercial Court
Comr	Commissioner
Court Forms (2nd Edn)	Atkin's Encyclopaedia of Court Forms in Civil Proceedings, 2nd Edn. See note 2 post.
Court Funds Rules 1987	Court Funds Rules 1987 (SI 1987/821) as subsequently amended
DC	Divisional Court
DPP	Director of Public Prosecutions
EAT	Employment Appeal Tribunal
EC	European Community
ECJ	Court of Justice of the European Community
EComHR	European Commission of Human Rights
ECSC	European Coal and Steel Community
ECtHR Rules of Court	Rules of Court of the European Court of Human Rights
EEC	European Economic Community
EFTA	European Free Trade Association
EWCA Civ	Official neutral citation for judgments of the Court of Appeal (Civil Division)
EWCA Crim	Official neutral citation for judgments of the Court of Appeal (Criminal Division)
EWHC	Official neutral citation for judgments of the High Court
Edn	Edition
Euratom	European Atomic Energy Community
Ex Ch	Court of Exchequer Chamber
ex p	ex parte
Fam	Family Division
Fed	Federal
Forms & Precedents (5th Edn)	Encyclopaedia of Forms and Precedents other than Court Forms, 5th Edn. See note 2 post.
GLC	Greater London Council
HC	High Court
HC	House of Commons
HK	Hong Kong
HL	House of Lords
IAT	Immigration Appeal Tribunal
ILM	International Legal Materials

INLR	Immigration and Nationality Law Reports
IRC	Inland Revenue Commissioners
Ind	India
Int Rels	International Relations
Ir	Ireland
J	Justice
JA	Judge of Appeal
Kan	Kansas
LA	Lord Advocate
LC	Lord Chancellor
LCC	London County Council
LCJ	Lord Chief Justice
LJ	Lord Justice of Appeal
LoN	League of Nations
MR	Master of the Rolls
Man	Manitoba
n	note
NB	New Brunswick
NI	Northern Ireland
NS	Nova Scotia
NSW	New South Wales
NY	New York
NZ	New Zealand
OHIM	Office for Harmonisation in the Internal Market
OJ	The Official Journal of the European Community published by the Office for Official Publications of the European Community
Ont	Ontario
P	President
PC	Judicial Committee of the Privy Council
PEI	Prince Edward Island
Pat	Patents Court
q	question
QB	Queen's Bench Division
QBD	Queen's Bench Division of the High Court
Qld	Queensland
Que	Quebec
r	rule
RDC	Rural District Council
RPC	Restrictive Practices Court
RSC	Rules of the Supreme Court 1965 (SI 1965/1776) as subsequently amended

reg	regulation
Res	Resolution
revsd	reversed
Rly	Railway
s	section
SA	South Africa
S Aust	South Australia
SC	Supreme Court
SI	Statutory Instruments published by authority
SR & O	Statutory Rules and Orders published by authority
SR & O Rev 1904	Revised Edition comprising all Public and General Statutory Rules and Orders in force on 31 December 1903
SR & O Rev 1948	Revised Edition comprising all Public and General Statutory Rules and Orders and Statutory Instruments in force on 31 December 1948
SRNI	Statutory Rules of Northern Ireland
STI	Simon's Tax Intelligence (1973–1995); Simon's Weekly Tax Intelligence (1996-current)
Sask	Saskatchewan
Sch	Schedule
Sess	Session
Sing	Singapore
TCC	Technology and Construction Court
TS	Treaty Series
Tanz	Tanzania
Tas	Tasmania
UDC	Urban District Council
UKHL	Official neutral citation for judgments of the House of Lords
UKPC	Official neutral citation for judgments of the Privy Council
UN	United Nations
V-C	Vice-Chancellor
Vict	Victoria
W Aust	Western Australia
Zimb	Zimbabwe

NOTE 1. A general list of the abbreviations of law reports and other sources used in this work can be found at the beginning of the Consolidated Table of Cases.

NOTE 2. Where references are made to other publications, the volume number precedes and the page number follows the name of the publication; eg the reference '12 Forms & Precedents (5th Edn) 44' refers to volume 12 of the Encyclopaedia of Forms and Precedents, page 44.

NOTE 3. An English statute is cited by short title or, where there is no short title, by regnal year and chapter number together with the name by which it is commonly known or a description of its subject matter and date. In the case of a foreign statute, the mode of citation generally follows the style of citation in use in the country concerned with the addition, where necessary, of the name of the country in parentheses.

NOTE 4. A statutory instrument is cited by short title, if any, followed by the year and number, or, if unnumbered, the date.

TABLE OF STATUTES

TABLE OF STATUTORY INSTRUMENTS

TABLE OF CIVIL PROCEDURE

Civil Procedure Rules 1998, SI 1998/3132 (CPR)

Practice Directions supplementing CPR

TABLE OF EUROPEAN
COMMUNITY LEGISLATION

PARA

TABLE OF CASES

PARA

PARA

PARA

PARA

Decisions of the European Court of Justice are listed below numerically. These decisions
are also included in the preceding alphabetical list.

COMPETITION

1. INTRODUCTION

(1) INTRODUCTION AND SCOPE OF THE TITLE

1. Introduction to competition law. The aim of competition law is to protect consumers from the effects of ineffective competition. Such effects include price fixing, resale price maintenance, lack of choice and inefficiency. In order to combat the problem of ineffective competition, competition law seeks to control anti-competitive agreements, abusive behaviour, certain mergers and state interference[1]. In recent years, the common law has been supplanted in most cases by statutory law[2], coupled with European Community legislation[3]. In a small number of cases, the common law decisions on monopolies[4] and restraint of trade[5] remain of importance.

1   See PARA 115 et seq.
2   See in particular the Competition Act 1998 (see PARA 115 et seq) and the Enterprise Act 2002 (see PARA 171 et seq).
3   See PARA 24 et seq.
4   See PARA 361 et seq.
5   See PARA 369 et seq.

2. Scope of the title. This title sets out a brief history of the development of competition law in the United Kingdom[1]. The administrative authorities concerned with the enforcement of competition law are discussed[2]. The provisions of the Competition Act 1998[3] and the Enterprise Act 2002[4] are set out and there is a detailed discussion of the principles of European Community competition law[5]. Finally, the related issues of monopolies and restraint of trade are discussed[6].

1   See PARAS 361–364.
2   See PARAS 5–17.
3   See PARA 115 et seq.
4   See PARA 171 et seq.
5   See PARA 24 et seq.
6   See PARA 361 et seq.

3. Application of domestic competition law to particular agreements and practices. The domestic competition law of the United Kingdom consists of the Enterprise Act 2002, which contains provisions for the control of mergers[1], provides for the making of market investigation references[2] and introduces criminal offences for those involved in cartels[3], and the Competition Act 1998, which prohibits agreements that prevent, restrict or distort competition[4] and the abuse of a dominant position[5].

The Restrictive Trade Practices Act 1976, the Resale Prices Act 1976, the Restrictive Trade Practices Act 1977 and the provisions in the Competition Act 1980 for the investigation of anti-competitive practices were repealed with effect from 1 March 2000[6].

In any case where domestic competition law may be applicable, it is also necessary to consider the possible application of the competition rules contained in Community law[7].

1   See PARAS 172–275.
2   See PARAS 276–318.
3   See PARAS 319–325.
4   See PARAS 116–124.
5   See PARAS 125–128.

6   Competition Act 1998 ss 1, 74(3), Sch 14 Pt I.
7   See PARAS 4, 24 et seq.

4.   European Community law.   The EC Treaty[1] prohibits agreements between undertakings, decisions by associations of undertakings and concerted practices which may affect trade between member states and which have as their object or effect the prevention, restriction or distortion of competition within the common market[2]. In particular, the following agreements are prohibited: (1) those which directly or indirectly fix purchase or selling prices or other trading conditions[3]; (2) those which limit or control production, markets, technical development or investment[4]; (3) those which share markets or sources of supply[5]; (4) those which apply dissimilar conditions to equivalent transactions with other trading parties, thereby placing them at a competitive disadvantage[6]; and (5) those which make the conclusion of contracts subject to the acceptance by other parties of supplementary obligations which, by their nature or according to commercial usage, have no connection with the subject of such contracts[7].

The EC Treaty[8] also prohibits any abuse by one or more undertakings of a dominant position[9] within the common market or in a substantial part of it[10] in so far as it may affect trade between member states[11]. Such abuse may, in particular, consist in: (a) directly or indirectly imposing unfair purchase or selling prices or other unfair trading conditions[12]; (b) limiting production, markets or technical development to the prejudice of consumers[13]; (c) applying dissimilar conditions to equivalent transactions with other trading parties, thereby placing them at a competitive disadvantage[14]; (d) making the concluding of contracts subject to the acceptance by the other parties of supplementary obligations which, by their nature or according to commercial usage, have no connection with the subject of such contracts[15].

Undertakings entrusted by a member state with the operation of services of general economic interest or having the character of a revenue-producing monopoly are subject to the rules of competition contained in the Treaty[16], in so far as the application of such rules does not obstruct the performance, in law or in fact, of the particular tasks assigned to them[17].

Merger control is also regulated by the European Commission[18] where mergers go beyond the national borders of a member state. If the annual turnover of the combined businesses exceeds specified thresholds in terms of global and European sales, the proposed merger must be notified to the European Commission for examination[19]. Below these thresholds, the national competition authorities in the member states may review the merger[20]. The European Commission may also examine mergers which are referred to it from the national competition authorities of the member states[21]. All proposed mergers notified to the Commission are examined to see if they would significantly impede effective competition[22]. If they do not, they are approved unconditionally. If they do, they may be prohibited or approved with conditions[23].

1   See the EC Treaty art 81. As to the EC Treaty (ie the Treaty establishing the European Community (Rome, 25 March 1957; TS 1 (1973); Cmnd 5179)) see PARA 24 note 1. The numbering for the EC Treaty used in this title is as revised by the Treaty of Amsterdam: see PARA 24 note 1. See further PARA 61 et seq.
2   See the EC Treaty art 81(1).
3   EC Treaty art 81(1)(a).
4   EC Treaty art 81(1)(b).
5   EC Treaty art 81(1)(c).
6   EC Treaty art 81(1)(d).

7   EC Treaty art 81(1)(e).
8   See the EC Treaty art 82.
9   As to the meaning of 'dominant position' see PARA 69.
10 As to the meaning of 'substantial part of the common market' see PARA 70.
11 EC Treaty art 82. The examples given in heads (a)–(d) in the text are not exhaustive.
12 EC Treaty art 82(2)(a).
13 EC Treaty art 82(2)(b).
14 EC Treaty art 82(2)(c).
15 EC Treaty art 82(2)(d).
16 This includes in particular the provisions of the EC Treaty art 82: art 86(2).
17 EC Treaty art 86(2). However, the development of trade must not be affected to such an extent
    as would be contrary to the interests of the Community: art 86(2). As to art 86(2) see PARA 27.
18 See EC Council Regulation 139/2004 on the control of concentrations between undertakings
    (the 'EC Merger Regulation') (OJ L24, 29.1.2004, p 1). See further PARA 73 et seq.
19 See the EC Merger Regulation arts 1, 4, 5.
20 See the EC Merger Regulation art 4.
21 See the EC Merger Regulation art 22.
22 See the EC Merger Regulation art 6.
23 See the EC Merger Regulation art 8.

(2) ADMINISTRATIVE AUTHORITIES

(i) The Secretary of State

5.   Government departments and the Secretary of State.   Government
responsibility in relation to competition matters is vested in the Department for
Business, Innovation and Skills ('BIS')[1]. Matters relating to competition were
originally within the general jurisdiction of the Board of Trade[2] and then fell
under the remit of the Department of Trade and Industry[3] before being
transferred to the Department for Business, Enterprise and Regulatory Reform[4]
and then to BIS.

1   In any enactment, 'Secretary of State' means one of Her Majesty's principal Secretaries of State:
    see the Interpretation Act 1978 s 5, Sch 1. In this title, unless the context otherwise requires, the
    Secretary of State referred to is generally to be taken to be the Secretary of State for Business,
    Innovation and Skills. BIS was created on 5 June 2009 by a merger between the Department for
    Business, Enterprise and Regulatory Reform and the Department for Innovation, Universities
    and Skills.
2   As to the Board of Trade see CONSTITUTIONAL LAW AND HUMAN RIGHTS vol 8(2) (Reissue)
    PARA 505.
3   Specialised ministries were established such as those relating to technology, power, science and
    aviation. In 1970 certain powers previously exercised by such ministries were transferred to the
    Secretary of State, which in practice meant the Secretary of State for Trade and Industry, who
    was also empowered to exercise concurrently the powers of the Board of Trade: see the Secretary
    of State for Trade and Industry Order 1970, SI 1970/1537. In 1974 the Department of Trade
    and Industry was divided and its functions transferred en bloc to the Secretary of State and
    distributed by administrative arrangements among the four successor Departments of Trade,
    Industry, Energy and Prices and Consumer Protection: see the Secretary of State (New
    Departments) Order 1974, SI 1974/692; and the Secretary of State for Trade Order 1979,
    SI 1979/578.
        In 1983 the Departments of Trade and of Industry were once again amalgamated to form a
    single department, known as the Department of Trade and Industry, and the functions of the
    Secretary of State for Trade and the Secretary of State for Industry were transferred en bloc to
    the Secretary of State for Trade and Industry: see the Transfer of Functions (Trade and Industry)
    Order 1983, SI 1983/1127.
4   See the Secretaries of State for Children, Schools and Families, for Innovation, Universities and
    Skills and for Business, Enterprise and Regulatory Reform Order 2007, SI 2007/3224, art 11.

(ii) The Office of Fair Trading

6. Establishment and constitution of the Office of Fair Trading. The Office of Fair Trading (the 'OFT') is the United Kingdom's consumer protection and competition authority. The OFT was established as a statutory body corporate on 1 April 2003 by the Enterprise Act 2002[1]. It replaced the Director General of Fair Trading[2], whose functions, property, rights and liabilities were transferred to the OFT[3]. The functions of the OFT are carried out on behalf of the Crown[4].

In managing its affairs the OFT is required to have regard, in addition to any relevant general guidance as to the governance of public bodies, to such generally accepted principles of good corporate governance as it is reasonable to regard as applicable to the OFT[5].

The OFT consists of a chairman and no fewer than four other members, appointed by the Secretary of State[6]. The chairman and other members hold and vacate office in accordance with the terms of their respective appointments[7], and the appointment is for a term not exceeding five years[8]. A person holding office may resign that office by giving notice in writing to the Secretary of State and may be removed from office by the Secretary of State on the ground of incapacity or misbehaviour[9]. A previous appointment as chairman or other member does not affect a person's eligibility for appointment to either office[10].

The OFT must pay to the chairman and other members such remuneration, and such travelling and other allowances, as may be determined by the Secretary of State[11]. The OFT, if required to do so by the Secretary of State, must pay, or pay towards, such pension, allowances or gratuities as may be determined by the Secretary of State to or in respect of a person who holds or has held office as chairman or other member[12]. If, where any person ceases to hold office as chairman or other member, the Secretary of State determines that there are special circumstances which make it right that he should receive compensation, the OFT must pay to him such amount by way of compensation as the Secretary of State may determine[13].

After consulting the chairman, the Secretary of State must appoint a person to act as chief executive of the OFT on such terms and conditions as the Secretary of State may think appropriate[14]. A person appointed as chief executive may not at the same time be chairman[15]. The OFT may, with the approval of the minister for the Civil Service as to numbers and terms and conditions of service, appoint such other staff as it may determine[16].

The members of a committee or sub-committee of the OFT may include persons who are not members of the OFT, and a sub-committee may include persons who are not members of the committee which established it[17].

The OFT may regulate its own procedure, including quorum[18] but must consult the Secretary of State before making or revising its rules and procedures for dealing with conflicts of interest[19].

The application of the seal of the OFT is authenticated by the signature of any member or other person who has been authorised for that purpose by the OFT, whether generally or specially[20]. A document purporting to be duly executed under the seal of the OFT, or signed on its behalf, must be received in evidence and, unless the contrary is proved, be taken to be so executed or signed[21].

Anything authorised or required to be done by the OFT may be done by any member or employee of the OFT who is authorised for that purpose by the OFT, whether generally or specially, and any committee[22] of the OFT which has been so authorised[23].

The OFT has power to do anything which is calculated to facilitate, or is conducive or incidental to, the performance of its functions[24].

Any action taken by or on behalf of the OFT in the exercise of its administrative functions may be investigated by the Parliamentary Commissioner for Administration[25]. Members of the OFT are disqualified for membership of the House of Commons[26] and the Northern Ireland Assembly[27].

1 Enterprise Act 2002 s 1(1).
2 The office of the Director General of Fair Trading was established by the Fair Trading Act 1973 s 1 (repealed).
3 Enterprise Act 2002 s 2(1), (2). Any enactment, instrument or other document passed or made before 1 April 2003 which refers to the Director General of Fair Trading has effect, so far as necessary for the purposes of or in consequence of anything being transferred, as if any reference to the Director were a reference to the OFT: s 2(3).
4 Enterprise Act 2002 s 1(2).
5 Enterprise Act 2002 s 1(4).
6 Enterprise Act 2002 s 1(3), Sch 1 para 1(1). As to the Secretary of State see PARA 5. The Secretary of State must consult the chairman before appointing any other member: Sch 1 para 1(2). The validity of anything done by the OFT is not affected by a vacancy among its members or by a defect in the appointment of a member: Sch 1 para 9.
7 Enterprise Act 2002 Sch 1 para 2(1). The terms of appointment of the chairman and other members are determined by the Secretary of State: Sch 1 para 2(2).
8 Enterprise Act 2002 Sch 1 para 3(1).
9 Enterprise Act 2002 Sch 1 para 3(2).
10 Enterprise Act 2002 Sch 1 para 3(3).
11 Enterprise Act 2002 Sch 1 para 4(1).
12 Enterprise Act 2002 Sch 1 para 4(2).
13 Enterprise Act 2002 Sch 1 para 4(3).
14 Enterprise Act 2002 Sch 1 para 5(1).
15 Enterprise Act 2002 Sch 1 para 5(2), (3).
16 Enterprise Act 2002 Sch 1 para 6. As to the minister for the Civil Service see CONSTITUTIONAL LAW AND HUMAN RIGHTS vol 8(2) (Reissue) PARA 549 et seq.
17 Enterprise Act 2002 Sch 1 para 7.
18 Enterprise Act 2002 Sch 1 para 8(1).
19 Enterprise Act 2002 Sch 1 para 8(2). The OFT must from time to time publish a summary of its rules and procedures for dealing with conflicts of interest: Sch 1 para 8(3).
20 Enterprise Act 2002 Sch 1 para 10(1). This does not apply in relation to any document which is, or is to be, signed in accordance with the law of Scotland: Sch 1 para 10(2).
21 Enterprise Act 2002 Sch 1 para 11.
22 This does not apply to a committee whose members include any person who is not a member or employee of the OFT: Enterprise Act 2002 Sch 1 para 12(2).
23 Enterprise Act 2002 Sch 1 para 12(1).
24 Enterprise Act 2002 Sch 1 para 13. As to the functions of the OFT see PARA 7.
25 See the Parliamentary Commissioner Act 1967 Sch 2 (amended by the Enterprise Act 2002 Sch 1 para 14); and ADMINISTRATIVE LAW vol 1(1) (2001 Reissue) PARA 43. As to the Parliamentary Commissioner for Administration see ADMINISTRATIVE LAW vol 1(1) (2001 Reissue) PARA 41 et seq.
26 See the House of Commons Disqualification Act 1975 Sch 1 Pt II (amended by the Enterprise Act 2002 Sch 1 para 15).
27 See the Northern Ireland Assembly Disqualification Act 1975 Sch 1 Pt 2 (amended by the Enterprise Act 2002 Sch 1 para 16).

7.   General functions of the Office of Fair Trading and annual plan and reports. The Office of Fair Trading (the 'OFT') has the following general functions:

(1)   obtaining, compiling and keeping under review information about matters relating to the carrying out of its functions[1];

(2)   making the public aware of the ways in which competition may benefit

consumers in, and the economy of, the United Kingdom[2] and giving information or advice in respect of matters relating to any of its functions to the public[3];

(3)   making proposals, or giving other information or advice, on matters relating to any of its functions to any minister of the Crown or other public authority, including proposals, information or advice as to any aspect of the law or a proposed change in the law[4];

(4)   promoting good practice in the carrying out of activities which may affect the economic interests of consumers in the United Kingdom[5].

The OFT must, before each financial year, publish an annual plan containing a statement of its main objectives and priorities for the year[6]. For the purposes of public consultation, the OFT must publish a document containing proposals for its annual plan at least two months before publishing the annual plan for any year[7]. The proposal document and annual plan must be laid before Parliament by the OFT[8].

As soon as practicable after the end of each financial year, the OFT must make an annual report to the Secretary of State[9] on its activities and performance during that year[10]. The OFT must lay a copy of each annual report before Parliament and arrange for the report to be published[11].

The OFT may prepare other reports in respect of matters relating to any of its functions and arrange for any such report to be published[12].

1   Enterprise Act 2002 s 5(1). This function is to be carried out with a view to, among other things, ensuring that the OFT has sufficient information to take informed decisions and to carry out its other functions effectively: s 5(2). In carrying out this function the OFT may carry out, commission or support (financially or otherwise) research: s 5(3).

2   As to the meaning of 'United Kingdom' see PARA 401 note 1.

3   Enterprise Act 2002 s 6(1). In carrying out these functions the OFT may: (1) publish educational materials or carry out other educational activities; or (2) support (financially or otherwise) the carrying out by others of such activities or the provision by others of information or advice: s 6(2).

4   Enterprise Act 2002 s 7(1). A minister of the Crown may request the OFT to make proposals or give other information or advice on any matter relating to any of its functions, and the OFT, so far as is reasonably practicable and consistent with its other functions, must comply with the request: s 7(2).

5   Enterprise Act 2002 s 8(1). In carrying out this function the OFT may, without prejudice to the generality of s 8(1), make arrangements for approving consumer codes and may, in accordance with the arrangements, give its approval to or withdraw its approval from any consumer code: s 8(2). 'Consumer code' means a code of practice or other document, however described, intended, with a view to safeguarding or promoting the interests of consumers, to regulate by any means the conduct of persons engaged in the supply of goods or services to consumers (or the conduct of their employees or representatives): s 8(6). Any arrangements under s 8(2) must specify the criteria to be applied by the OFT in determining whether to give approval to or withdraw approval from a consumer code: s 8(3). Any such arrangements may in particular: (1) specify descriptions of consumer code which may be the subject of an application to the OFT for approval (and any such description may be framed by reference to any feature of a consumer code, including the persons who are, or are to be, subject to the code, the manner in which it is, or is to be, operated and the persons responsible for its operation); and (2) provide for the use in accordance with the arrangements of an official symbol intended to signify that a consumer code is approved by the OFT: s 8(4). The OFT must publish any arrangements under s 8(2) in such manner it considers appropriate: s 8(5).

6   Enterprise Act 2002 s 3(1).

7   Enterprise Act 2002 s 3(2).

8   Enterprise Act 2002 s 3(3).

9   As to the Secretary of State see PARA 5.

10   Enterprise Act 2002 s 4(1). The annual report for each year must include: (1) a general survey of developments in respect of matters relating to the OFT's functions; (2) an assessment of the extent to which the OFT's main objectives and priorities for the year (as set out in the annual

plan (see the text to note 6)) have been met; (3) a summary of the significant decisions, investigations or other activities made or carried out by the OFT during the year; (4) a summary of the allocation of the OFT's financial resources to its various activities during the year; and (5) an assessment of the OFT's performance and practices in relation to its enforcement functions: s 4(2).

11 Enterprise Act 2002 s 4(3).
12 Enterprise Act 2002 s 4(4).

8.   Super-complaints to the Office of Fair Trading.   Where a designated consumer body[1] makes a complaint to the Office of Fair Trading (the 'OFT') or another specified regulator[2] that any feature, or combination of features, of a market in the United Kingdom for goods or services[3] is or appears to be significantly harming the interests of consumers[4], then within 90 days[5] after the day on which it receives the complaint, the OFT, or other regulator, must publish a response stating how it proposes to deal with the complaint, and in particular whether it has decided to take any action, or to take no action, in response to the complaint, and if it has decided to take action, what action it proposes to take[6]. The response must state reasons for the proposals[7].

The OFT must issue guidance as to the presentation by the complainant of a reasoned case for the complaint, and may issue such other guidance as appears to it to be appropriate for these purposes[8].

1   'Designated consumer body' means a body designated by the Secretary of State by order: Enterprise Act 2002 s 11(5). An order under s 11 must be made by statutory instrument and is subject to annulment in pursuance of a resolution of either House of Parliament: s 11(8). The Secretary of State: (1) may designate a body only if it appears to him to represent the interests of consumers of any description; and (2) must publish (and may from time to time vary) other criteria to be applied by him in determining whether to make or revoke a designation: s 11(6). 'Consumer' means an individual who is a consumer within the meaning of Pt 4 (ss 131–184): s 11(9)(b). 'Consumer' means any person who is: (a) a person to whom goods are or are sought to be supplied (whether by way of sale or otherwise) in the course of a business carried on by the person supplying or seeking to supply them; or (b) a person for whom services are or are sought to be supplied in the course of a business carried on by the person supplying or seeking to supply them; and who does not receive or seek to receive the goods or services in the course of a business carried on by him: s 183(1). As to the Secretary of State see PARA 5. The following bodies have been designated: the Campaign for Real Ale Limited, the Consumer Council for Water, the Consumers' Association, the General Consumer Council for Northern Ireland, the National Association of Citizens Advice Bureaux and the National Consumer Council: Enterprise Act 2002 (Bodies Designated to make Super-complaints) Order 2004, SI 2004/1517, art 2, Schedule (substituted by SI 2008/2161).
2   The Secretary of State may by order provide that the Enterprise Act 2002 s 11 is to apply to complaints made to a specified regulator in relation to a market of a specified description as it applies to complaints made to the OFT, with such modifications as may be specified: s 205(1). Such an order must be made by statutory instrument, and is subject to annulment in pursuance of a resolution of either House of Parliament: s 205(2). 'Regulator' has the meaning given in the Competition Act 1998 s 54(1) (see PARA 147); and 'specified' means specified in the order: Enterprise Act 2002 s 205(3). The following regulators have been specified for the purposes of super-complaints: the Office of Communications, the Gas and Electricity Markets Authority, the Director General of Electricity Supply for Northern Ireland, the Director General of Gas for Northern Ireland, the Water Services Regulation Authority, the Office of Rail Regulation and the Civil Aviation Authority: Enterprise Act 2002 (Super-complaints to Regulators) Order 2003, SI 2003/1368, art 2, Schedule (amended by the Railways and Transport Safety Act 2003 s 16, Sch 3 para 4; SI 2003/3182; SI 2006/522). As to the regulators see also PARAS 18–22, 147.
3   References to a feature of a market in the United Kingdom for goods or services have the same meaning as if contained in the Enterprise Act 2002 Pt 4 (see PARA 276): s 11(9)(a). As to the meaning of 'United Kingdom' see PARA 401 note 1.
4   Enterprise Act 2002 s 11(1).
5   The Secretary of State may by order substitute any other period: see the Enterprise Act 2002 s 11(4). At the date at which this volume states the law no such order had been made.
6   Enterprise Act 2002 s 11(2).

7 Enterprise Act 2002 s 11(3).
8 Enterprise Act 2002 s 11(7).

(iii) The Competition Commission

9. Constitution of the Commission. The Competition Commission (the 'Commission') is a body corporate[1] having such functions as are conferred on it by or as a result of the Competition Act 1998[2]. The former Monopolies and Mergers Commission was dissolved by the Competition Act 1998 and its functions transferred to the Competition Commission[3].

The Commission consists of members appointed by the Secretary of State to form a panel for the purposes of its general functions[4]. There are also members appointed from specialist panels, namely the utilities (water, electricity, gas and energy code modification appeals) panel, the newspaper panel and the Communications Act panel[5]. A person may be appointed as a member of more than one kind[6]. A person may not be, at the same time, a member of the Commission and a member of the Competition Appeal Tribunal[7]. Each member holds and vacates office in accordance with the terms of his appointment[8] and may not be appointed as a member for more than eight years[9]. Any member may at any time resign by notice in writing to the Secretary of State[10]. The Secretary of State may remove a member on the ground of incapacity or misbehaviour[11]. The validity of the Commission's proceedings is not affected by a defect in the appointment of a member[12].

The Secretary of State must appoint a Chairman of the Commission, and may appoint one or more deputy chairmen, from among the reporting panel members[13].

The Commission has a board known as the Competition Commission Council[14] through which certain of its functions must be exercised[15]. The council may determine its own procedure including, in particular, its quorum[16]. The Chairman, and any person acting as Chairman, has a casting vote on any question being decided by the council[17].

The Secretary of State must pay to the Commission such sums as he considers appropriate to enable it to perform its functions[18]. Provision is made for the payment of such salaries and other remuneration, and pensions, allowances, fees, expenses or gratuities, to members of the Commission, as the Secretary of State may determine[19]. The Commission has a secretary, appointed by the Secretary of State[20], and may appoint such staff as it thinks appropriate[21]. The Commission must keep proper accounts and records[22] and must make an annual report to the Secretary of State[23].

The Commission is not to be regarded as the servant or agent of the Crown or as enjoying any status, privilege or immunity of the Crown[24] and its property is not to be regarded as property of, or held on behalf of, the Crown[25].

In general, the Commission has power to do anything (except borrow money) calculated to facilitate, or incidental or conducive to, the discharge of its functions[26]. The Commission may publish advice and information in relation to any matter connected with the exercise of its functions[27].

Members of the Commission are disqualified for membership of the House of Commons[28] and the Northern Ireland Assembly[29].

1 Competition Act 1998 s 45(1). The application of the Commission's seal must be authenticated by the signature of the secretary or of some other person authorised for the purpose, and a document purporting to be executed under that seal must be received in evidence and taken to be so executed unless the contrary is proved: see s 45(7), Sch 7 para 11.

2 Competition Act 1998 s 45(2).
3 Competition Act 1998 s 45(3). In any enactment, instrument or other document, any reference to the Monopolies and Mergers Commission which has continuing effect is to be read as a reference to the Competition Commission: s 45(4). 'Document' includes information recorded in any form; and 'information' includes estimates and forecasts: s 59(1). As to the power of the Secretary of State to make consequential, supplemental and incidental provision in connection with: (1) the dissolution of the Monopolies and Mergers Commission; and (2) the transfer of its functions, see s 45(5), (6); the Competition Act 1998 (Competition Commission) Transitional, Consequential and Supplemental Provisions Order 1999, SI 1999/506; the Competition Act 1998 (Transitional, Consequential and Supplemental Provisions) Order 2000, SI 2000/311; and the Competition Act 1998 (Consequential and Supplemental Provisions) Order 2000, SI 2000/2031. As to the Secretary of State see PARA 5.
4 Competition Act 1998 Sch 7 para 2(1)(b). Such members are known as 'reporting panel members': Sch 7 para 1. 'General functions' means any functions of the Commission other than functions which are to be discharged by the Council (see the text and note 15): Sch 7 para 1. As to the Commission's general functions see PARAS 10–11. As to the appointment of the reporting panel members on the establishment of the Commission see Sch 7 para 33.
5 See the Competition Act 1998 Sch 7 para 2(1)(c)–(e) (amended by the Utilities Act 2000 s 104(3); the Communications Act 2003 s 406(1), Sch 17 para 153; the Water Act 2003 s 101, Sch 7 para 32(1), Sch 9 Pt 3; and the Enterprise Act 2002 s 185, Sch 11 paras 1, 3(a), (b)). As to the maintenance of panels see the Competition Act 1998 Sch 7 para 22 (amended by the Enterprise Act 2002 Sch 11 paras 1, 12). Such members are known as 'specialist panel members': see the Competition Act 1998 Sch 7 para 1. As to the appointment of the specialist panel members on the establishment of the Commission see the Competition Act 1998 Sch 7 para 34.
6 See the Competition Act 1998 Sch 7 para 2(2), (3) (amended by the Enterprise Act 2002 ss 21, 278(2), Sch 5 paras 1, 7, Sch 11 paras 1, 3(d), (e)).
7 Competition Act 1998 Sch 7 para 2(1A) (added by the Enterprise Act 2002 Sch 11 paras 1, 3(c)).
8 Competition Act 1998 Sch 7 para 6(1).
9 Competition Act 1998 Sch 7 para 6(2) (amended by the Enterprise Act 2002 Sch 11 paras 1, 5(a)). This does not prevent a re-appointment for the purpose only of continuing to act as a member of a group of panel members selected by the Chairman under the Competition Act 1998 Sch 7 para 15 (see PARA 11): Sch 7 para 6(2) (as so amended).
10 Competition Act 1998 Sch 7 para 6(3).
11 Competition Act 1998 Sch 7 para 6(4).
12 Competition Act 1998 Sch 7 para 2(5).
13 See the Competition Act 1998 Sch 7 para 3(1), (2). The Chairman and any deputy chairman may resign office at any time by notice in writing to the Secretary of State: Sch 7 para 3(3). If the Chairman or a deputy chairman ceases to be a member he also ceases to be Chairman or deputy chairman: Sch 7 para 3(4). If the Chairman is absent or unable to act, provision is made for his functions to be performed by a deputy chairman, or if no deputy chairman has been designated so to act, by a member of the Commission designated by the Secretary of State or the Commission: see Sch 7 para 3(5). As to the appointment of the Chairman and deputy chairmen on the establishment of the Commission see Sch 7 paras 31, 32.
14 Competition Act 1998 Sch 7 para 5(1) (amended by the Enterprise Act 2002 ss 185, 278(2), Sch 11 paras 1, 4(a), Sch 26). The council consists of the Chairman of the Commission, any deputy chairmen, any members appointed by the Secretary of State under the Competition Act 1998 Sch 7 para 2(1)(e), such other members as the Secretary of State may appoint and the secretary: Sch 7 para 5(2) (amended by the Enterprise Act 2002 s 21, Sch 5 paras 1, 7(1), (5)(a), Sch 11 paras 1, 4(b), (c)). As to the secretary see the text and note 20. As to the membership of the council on the establishment of the Commission see the Competition Act 1998 Sch 7 para 36.
15 Competition Act 1998 Sch 7 para 5(3) (amended by the Enterprise Act 2002 Sch 5 paras 1, 7(1), 5(b), Sch 26). The functions referred to are those under the Competition Act 1998 Sch 7 paras 3, 7–12 (see the text and notes 1, 13, 18–22). Without prejudice to the question whether any other functions of the Commission are to be so discharged, the functions of the Commission under the Enterprise Act 2002 s 106 (see PARA 255), s 116 (see PARA 265), s 171 (see PARA 311) (and under s 116 as applied for the purposes of references under Pt 4 of that Act by s 176 of that Act (see PARA 315)) are to be discharged by the Council: Competition Act 1998 Sch 7 para 5(3A) (added by the Enterprise Act 2002 Sch 11 paras 1, 4(d)).
16 Competition Act 1998 Sch 7 para 5(4).
17 Competition Act 1998 Sch 7 para 5(5).

18 Competition Act 1998 Sch 7 para 7(1).
19 Competition Act 1998 Sch 7 para 7(2). In certain circumstances, compensation (of such amount as the Secretary of State may determine) may be payable to a person who ceases to be a member otherwise than on the expiry of his term of office: see Sch 7 para 7(3).
20 See the Competition Act 1998 Sch 7 para 9(1). Before appointing a secretary, the Secretary of State must consult the Chairman: Sch 7 para 9(3) (amended by the Enterprise Act 2002 Sch 11 paras 1, 8(a), Sch 26). As to the appointment of the secretary on the establishment of the Commission see the Competition Act 1998 Sch 7 para 35.
21 Competition Act 1998 Sch 7 para 9(4) (amended by the Enterprise Act 2002 Sch 11 paras 1, 8(b)). The approval of the Secretary of State (as to numbers and terms and conditions of service) is required in relation to such appointments: Competition Act 1998 Sch 7 para 9(4) (as so amended).
22 See the Competition Act 1998 Sch 7 para 12.
23 See the Competition Act 1998 Sch 7 para 12A(1) (Sch 7 para 12A added by the Enterprise Act 2002 s 186). The annual report must be made before the end of August next following the financial year to which it relates: Competition Act 1998 Sch 7 para 12A(2) (as so added). The Secretary of State must lay a copy of the annual report before Parliament and arrange for the report to be published: Sch 7 para 12A(3) (as so added).
24 Competition Act 1998 Sch 7 para 13(1).
25 Competition Act 1998 Sch 7 para 13(2).
26 See the Competition Act 1998 Sch 7 para 8 (which is expressed, however, to be subject to the other provisions of Sch 7).
27 Competition Act 1998 Sch 7 para 7A (added by the Enterprise Act 2002 Sch 11 paras 1, 7).
28 See the House of Commons Disqualification Act 1975 Sch 1 Pt II (amended by the Competition Act 1998 Sch 7 para 28).
29 See the Northern Ireland Assembly Disqualification Act 1975 Sch 1 Pt 2 (amended by the Competition Act 1998 Sch 7 para 29).

10. The Commission's principal functions. The Competition Commission investigates and addresses issues of concern that are referred to it by the Office of Fair Trading[1], one of the sectoral regulators[2] or the Secretary of State[3]. There are three areas of concern:

(1) in mergers, where the turnover of the business to be acquired is in excess of £70 million or where the share of supply reached will be more than 25 per cent and where a merger appears likely to lead to a substantial lessening of competition in one or more markets in the United Kingdom[4];

(2) in markets, when it appears that competition may be being prevented, distorted or restricted[5]; and

(3) in regulated sectors, where aspects of the regulatory system may not be operating effectively or to address certain categories of dispute between regulators and regulated companies[6].

The Competition Commission also deals with energy code modification appeals[7], price control appeals[8] and water determinations[9].

1 As to the Office of Fair Trading see PARAS 6–8.
2 As to the sectoral regulators see PARAS 18–22.
3 As to the Secretary of State see PARA 5. The Competition Act 1980 gives the Secretary of State power to make references to the Competition Commission in respect of public bodies and certain other persons (see ss 11, 11A–11D, 12, 16, 17, 19). However, this power has not been exercised for a number of years.
4 See the Enterprise Act 2002 Pt 3 (ss 22–130); and PARA 172 et seq.
5 See the Enterprise Act 2002 Pt 4 (ss 131–184); and PARA 276 et seq.
6 See the Enterprise Act 2002 Pt 8 (ss 210–236); and PARA 339 et seq.
7 Ie under the Energy Act 2004 s 173 (see FUEL AND ENERGY vol 19(1) (2007 Reissue) PARA 733).
8 Ie under the Communications Act 2003 s 193 (see TELECOMMUNICATIONS AND BROADCASTING vol 45(1) (2005 Reissue) PARA 212).
9 Ie under the Water Industry Act 1991 s 12(3)(a) (see WATER AND WATERWAYS vol 100 (2009) PARA 142).

11.   Performance of the Commission's general functions.   When performing its general functions[1] the Competition Commission must do so through a group selected for the purpose by the Chairman[2] except where he is empowered to act on his own[3]. A group must consist of at least three persons, one of whom may be the Chairman[4]. Those persons must generally be reporting panel members or specialist panel members[5]. In selecting the members of the group, the Chairman must comply with any requirement as to its constitution imposed by any enactment applying to specialist panel members[6]. The Chairman must appoint one of the members of a group to act as the chairman of the group[7].

If, during the proceedings of a group:

(1)   a member of the group ceases to be a member of the Commission;

(2)   the Chairman is satisfied that a member of the group will be unable for a substantial period to perform his duties as such; or

(3)   it appears to the Chairman that because of a particular interest of a member of the group it is inappropriate for him to remain in the group,

the Chairman may appoint a replacement[8].

Reporting panel members of the Commission may be invited to attend or otherwise take part in meetings of the group[9].

Subject to any special or general directions given by the Secretary of State[10], each group may determine its own procedure[11]. The Chairman must make rules of procedure in relation to mergers and market references[12].

Apart from certain specified purposes[13], anything done by or in relation to a group in, or in connection with, the performance of functions to be performed by the group is to have the same effect as if done by or in relation to the Commission[14].

The chairman of a group has a casting vote on any question to be decided by the group[15].

1   As to the meaning of 'general functions' see PARA 9 note 4. Power is given to the Secretary of State to make modifications to the Competition Act 1998 s 45(7), Sch 7 Pt II for the purpose of improving the performance by the Commission of its functions: Competition Act 1998 s 45(8) (added by the Enterprise Act 2002 s 278(1), Sch 25 para 38(1), (35)). As to the Secretary of State see PARA 5.

2   As to the Chairman of the Competition Commission see PARA 9.

3   Competition Act 1998 Sch 7 paras 14, 15(1) (amended by the Enterprise Act 2002 s 185, Sch 11 paras 1, 10(1), (2)). While a group is being constituted to perform a particular general function of the Commission, the Chairman may take such steps (falling within that general function) as he considers appropriate to facilitate the work of the group when it has been constituted: Competition Act 1998 Sch 7 para 15(7) (amended by the Enterprise Act 2002 ss 185, 287(2), Sch 11 paras 1, 10(1), (4), Sch 26). The Chairman may exercise the power conferred by the Enterprise Act 2002 s 37(1) (see PARA 185), s 48(1) (see PARA 196) or s 64(1) (see PARA 210) while a group is being constituted to perform a relevant general function of the Commission or, when it has been so constituted, before it has held its first meeting: Competition Act 1998 Sch 7 para 15(8) (added by the Enterprise Act 2002 Sch 11 paras 1, 10(1), (5)).

4   Competition Act 1998 Sch 7 para 15(2).

5   Competition Act 1998 Sch 7 para 15(6), which is expressed to be subject to Sch 7 para 15(2)–(5). As to the meanings of 'reporting panel member' and 'specialist panel member' see PARA 9 notes 4,5.

6   Competition Act 1998 Sch 7 para 15(3).

7   Competition Act 1998 Sch 7 para 16.

8   Competition Act 1998 Sch 7 para 17(1). The Chairman may also at any time appoint any reporting panel member to be an additional member of the group: Sch 7 para 17(2).

9   See the Competition Act 1998 Sch 7 para 18(1). Such a person may not vote, nor have a statement of his dissent included in a report of the group: Sch 7 para 18(2). A group, or a member of a group, is also entitled to consult any member of the Commission with respect to any matter or question with which the group is concerned: Sch 7 para 18(3).

10 No directions have been given under this provision by the Secretary of State; however the Chairman of the Commission publishes Guidance for certain groups on the procedures to be adopted: see PARA 12.

11 Competition Act 1998 Sch 7 para 19(1). In particular, each group may determine: (1) its own quorum; (2) the extent to which persons claiming to be interested in the subject matter of the reference may be present or heard (by themselves or by their representatives), may cross-examine witnesses, or otherwise take part; (3) the extent to which meetings of the group are to be held in public: Sch 7 para 19(2).

Before determining its procedure, the group must have regard to any guidance issued by the Chairman: Sch 7 para 19(3). Before issuing such guidance the Chairman must consult the members of the Commission: Sch 7 para 19(4).

12 See the Competition Act 1998 Sch 7 para 19(5) (added by the Enterprise Act 2002 s 187(2)). As to the rules of procedure see PARA 12.

13 For the purposes of the Enterprise Act 2002 Pt 3 (ss 22–130) (mergers) (see PARA 172 et seq) any decision of a group under s 35(1) or s 36(1) (questions to be decided on non-public interest merger references: see PARA 184) that there is an anti-competitive outcome is to be treated as a decision under that provision that there is not an anti-competitive outcome if the decision is not that of at least two-thirds of the members of the group: Competition Act 1998 Sch 7 para 20(2) (Sch 7 para 20(2) substituted, and Sch 7 para 20(3)–(8) added, by the Enterprise Act 2002 Sch 11 paras 1, 11(1), (3)). For the purposes of the Enterprise Act 2002 Pt 3, if the decision is not that of at least two-thirds of the members of the group: (1) any decision of a group under s 47 (questions to be decided on public interest merger references: see PARA 195) that a relevant merger situation has been created is to be treated as a decision under that provision that no such situation has been created; (2) any decision of a group under s 47 that the creation of a relevant merger situation has resulted, or may be expected to result, in a substantial lessening of competition within any market or markets in the United Kingdom for goods or services is to be treated as a decision under that provision that the creation of that situation has not resulted, or may be expected not to result, in such a substantial lessening of competition; (3) any decision of a group under s 47 that arrangements are in progress or in contemplation which, if carried into effect, will result in the creation of a relevant merger situation is to be treated as a decision under that provision that no such arrangements are in progress or in contemplation; and (4) any decision of a group under s 47 that the creation of such a situation as is mentioned in head (3) may be expected to result in a substantial lessening of competition within any market or markets in the United Kingdom for goods or services is to be treated as a decision under that provision that the creation of that situation may be expected not to result in such a substantial lessening of competition: Competition Act 1998 Sch 7 para 20(3) (as so added). As to the meaning of 'United Kingdom' see PARA 401 note 1.

For the purposes of the Enterprise Act 2002 Pt 3, if the decision is not that of at least two-thirds of the members of the group: (a) any decision of a group under s 63 (questions to be decided on special public interest merger references: see PARA 209) that a special merger situation has been created is to be treated as a decision under that provision that no such situation has been created; and (b) any decision of a group under s 63 that arrangements are in progress or in contemplation which, if carried into effect, will result in the creation of a special merger situation is to be treated as a decision under that provision that no such arrangements are in progress or in contemplation: Competition Act 1998 Sch 7 para 20(4) (as so added).

For the purposes of the Enterprise Act 2002 Pt 4 (ss 131–184) (market investigations), if the decision is not that of at least two-thirds of the members of the group, any decision of a group under s 134 or s 141 (questions to be decided on market investigation references: see PARAS 279, 285) that a feature, or combination of features, of a relevant market prevents, restricts or distorts competition in connection with the supply or acquisition of any goods or services in the United Kingdom or a part of the United Kingdom is to be treated as a decision that the feature or (as the case may be) combination of features does not prevent, restrict or distort such competition: Competition Act 1998 Sch 7 para 20(5) (as so added). Accordingly, for the purposes of the Enterprise Act 2002 Pt 4, a group is to be treated as having decided under s 134 or s 141 that there is no adverse effect on competition if one or more than one decision of the group is to be treated as mentioned in the Competition Act 1998 Sch 7 para 20(5) and there is no other relevant decision of the group: Sch 7 para 20(6) (as so added). 'Relevant decision' means a decision which is not to be treated as mentioned in Sch 7 para 20(5) and which is that a feature, or combination of features, of a relevant market prevents, restricts or distorts competition in connection with the supply or acquisition of any goods or services in the United Kingdom or a part of the United Kingdom: Sch 7 para 20(7) (as so added).

Expressions used in Sch 7 para 20(2)–(7) are to be construed in accordance with the Enterprise Act 2002 Pt 3 or Pt 4, as the case may be: Competition Act 1998 Sch 7 para 20(8) (as so added).

14 Competition Act 1998 Sch 7 para 20(1) (amended by the Enterprise Act 2002 Sch 11 paras 1, 11(1), (2)), which is expressed to be subject to specific provision made by or under other enactments about decisions which are not decisions of at least two-thirds of the members of a group (see the Competition Act 1998 Sch 7 para 20(9) (added by the Enterprise Act 2002 Sch 11 paras 1, 11(1), (3)).

15 Competition Act 1998 Sch 7 para 21.

12. Procedural rules for mergers and market references. The Chairman[1] of the Competition Commission must make rules of procedure in relation to merger reference groups[2], market reference groups[3] and special reference groups[4]. The Chairman must publish the rules in such manner as he considers appropriate for the purpose of bringing them to the attention of those likely to be affected by them[5]. The Chairman must consult the members of the Commission and such other persons as he considers appropriate before making any rules[6]. Rules may make different provision for different cases or different purposes and be varied or revoked by subsequent rules[7]. Subject to any rules made, each merger reference group, market reference group and special reference group may determine its own procedure[8]. In determining how to proceed in accordance with any rules made and in determining its procedure, a group must have regard to any guidance issued by the Chairman[9]. Before issuing any guidance the Chairman must consult the members of the Commission and such other persons as he considers appropriate[10].

Procedural rules may make provision:

(1)   for particular stages of a merger investigation[11], a market investigation[12] or a special investigation[13] to be dealt with in accordance with a timetable and for the revision of that timetable[14];

(2)   as to the documents and information which must be given to a relevant group in connection with a merger investigation, a market investigation or a special investigation[15];

(3)   as to the documents or information which a relevant group[16] must give to other persons in connection with such an investigation[17].

Rules may also make provision:

(a)   as to the quorum of relevant groups[18];

(b)   as to the extent, if any, to which persons interested or claiming to be interested in a matter under consideration which is specified or described in the rules are allowed: (i) to be (either by themselves or by their representatives) present before a relevant group or heard by that group; (ii) to cross-examine witnesses; or (iii) otherwise to take part[19];

(c)   as to the extent, if any, to which sittings of a relevant group are to be held in public[20];

(d)   generally in connection with any matters permitted by rules made under head (b) or head (c) (including, in particular, provision for a record of any hearings)[21];

(e)   for the notification or publication of information in relation to merger investigations, market investigations or special investigations[22]; and

(f)   as to consultation about such investigations[23].

1 As to the Chairman see PARA 9. Further provision about rules is made by the Competition Act 1998 s 45(7), Sch 7A but is not to be taken as restricting the Chairman's powers under Sch 7 para 19A: Sch 7 para 19A(2) (Sch 7 para 19A, Sch 7A added by the Enterprise Act 2002 s 187(3), (4), Sch 12).

2 'Merger reference group' means any group constituted in connection with a reference under the Water Industry Act 1991 s 32 (see WATER AND WATERWAYS vol 100 (2009) PARA 150) or the Enterprise Act 2002 s 22 (see PARA 172), s 33 (see PARA 182), s 45 (see PARA 193) or s 62 (see PARA 208): Competition Act 1998 Sch 7 para 19A(9), Sch 7A para 1 (as added (see note 1); definition amended by the Communications Act 2003 s 406(7), Sch 19(1)).

3 'Market reference group' means any group constituted in connection with a reference under the Enterprise Act 2002 s 131 (see PARA 276) or s 132 (see PARA 277) (including that provision as it has effect by virtue of another enactment): Competition Act 1998 Sch 7 para 19A(9), Sch 7A para 1 (as added: see note 1).

4 Competition Act 1998 Sch 7 para 19A(1) (as added: see note 1). 'Special reference group' means any group constituted in connection with a reference or (in the case of the Financial Services and Markets Act 2000) an investigation under the Competition Act 1980 s 11 (see PARA 10); the Airports Act 1986 s 43 (see AIR LAW vol 2 (2008) PARAS 237–242); the Gas Act 1986 s 24 or s 41E (see FUEL AND ENERGY vol 19(2) (2007 Reissue) PARAS 813, 821); the Electricity Act 1989 s 12 or s 56C (see FUEL AND ENERGY vol 19(2) (2007 Reissue) PARAS 1081, 1089); the Water Industry Act 1991 s 12, s 14 or s 17K (see WATER AND WATERWAYS vol 100 (2009) PARAS 142, 144, 158); the Electricity (Northern Ireland) Order 1992, SI 1992/231 (NI 1), art 15; the Railways Act 1993 s 13 or Schedule 4A (see RAILWAYS, INLAND WATERWAYS AND CROSS-COUNTRY PIPELINES vol 39(1A) (Reissue) PARAS 88, 171 et seq); the Airports (Northern Ireland) Order 1994, SI 1994/426 (NI 1), art 34; the Gas (Northern Ireland) Order 1996, SI 1996/275 (NI 2), art 15; the Postal Services Act 2000 s 15 (see POST OFFICE vol 36(2) (Reissue) PARA 80; the Financial Services and Markets Act 2000 s 162 (see FINANCIAL SERVICES AND INSTITUTIONS vol 48 (2008) PARA 40) or s 306 (see FINANCIAL SERVICES AND INSTITUTIONS vol 49 (2008) PARA 732); the Transport Act 2000 s 12 (see AIR LAW vol 2 (2008) PARA 146); the Communications Act 2003 s 193 (see TELECOMMUNICATIONS AND BROADCASTING vol 45(1) (2005 Reissue) PARA 212); or the Water Services etc (Scotland) Act 2005 (Consequential Provisions and Modifications) Order 2005 art 3: Competition Act 1998 Sch 7 para 19A(9), Sch 7A para 1 (as added (see note 1); definition amended by the Communications Act 2003 Sch 17 para 153(1), (3), Sch 19(1); the Water Act 2003 s 101(1), Sch 8 para 54; SI 2005/3172).

5 Competition Act 1998 Sch 7 para 19A(3) (as added: see note 1). See eg *Competition Commission Rules of Procedure* CC1 (2006).

6 Competition Act 1998 Sch 7 para 19A(4) (as added: see note 1).

7 Competition Act 1998 Sch 7 para 19A(5) (as added: see note 1).

8 Competition Act 1998 Sch 7 para 19A(6) (as added: see note 1).

9 Competition Act 1998 Sch 7 para 19A(7) (as added: see note 1). See eg *Chairman's Guidance to Groups* CC6 (March 2006).

10 Competition Act 1998 Sch 7 para 19A(8) (as added: see note 1).

11 'Merger investigation' means an investigation carried out by a merger reference group in connection with a reference under the Water Industry Act 1991 s 32 (see WATER AND WATERWAYS vol 100 (2009) PARA 150) or the Enterprise Act 2002 s 22, s 33, s 45 or s 62 (see PARAS 172, 182, 193, 208): Competition Act 1998 Sch 7A para 1 (as added: see note 1).

12 'Market investigation' means an investigation carried out by a market reference group in connection with a reference under the Enterprise Act 2002 s 131 or s 132 (see PARAS 276, 277) (including that provision as it has effect by virtue of another enactment): Competition Act 1998 Sch 7A para 1 (as added (see note 1); definition amended by the Communications Act 2003 Sch 19(1)).

13 'Special investigation' means an investigation carried out by a special reference group in connection with a reference under a provision mentioned in any of the enactments contained in the definition of 'special reference group' (see note 4): see the Competition Act 1998 Sch 7A para 1 (as added (see note 1); definition amended by SI 2005/3172).

14 Competition Act 1998 Sch 7A para 2(a) (as added: see note 1). Rules made by virtue of Sch 7A para 2(a), (b) may, in particular, enable or require a relevant group (see note 16) to disregard documents or information given after a particular date: Sch 7A para 3 (as added: see note 1).

15 Competition Act 1998 Sch 7A para 2(b) (as added: see note 1). See note 14.

16 'Relevant group' means a market reference group, merger reference group or special reference group: Competition Act 1998 Sch 7A para 1 (as added: see note 1).

17 Competition Act 1998 Sch 7A para 2(c) (as added: see note 1). Rules made by virtue of Sch 7A para 2(c) may, in particular, make provision for the notification or publication of, and for consultation about, provisional findings of a relevant group: Sch 7A para 4 (as added: see note 1).

18 Competition Act 1998 Sch 7A para 5 (as added: see note 1).

19 Competition Act 1998 Sch 7A para 6(a) (as added: see note 1).

20 Competition Act 1998 Sch 7A para 6(b) (as added: see note 1).
21 Competition Act 1998 Sch 7A para 6(c) (as added: see note 1).
22 Competition Act 1998 Sch 7A para 7(a) (as added: see note 1).
23 Competition Act 1998 Sch 7A para 7(b) (as added: see note 1).

(iv) The Competition Appeal Tribunal

13.   Establishment and constitution of the Competition Appeal Tribunal. The Competition Appeal Tribunal hears appeals and other applications or claims involving competition or economic regulatory issues. It was established under the Enterprise Act 2002 on 1 April 2003[1].

The Tribunal consists of a President[2] appointed by the Lord Chancellor to preside over the Tribunal, members appointed by the Lord Chancellor to form a panel of chairmen[3] and members appointed by the Secretary of State to form a panel of ordinary members[4]. The Tribunal also has a Registrar appointed by the Secretary of State[5]. The expenses of the Tribunal are paid by the Competition Service[6].

The members appointed as President or as chairmen hold and vacate office in accordance with their terms of appointment[7]. However, a person may not be a chairman for more than eight years[8]. The President and the chairmen may resign their offices by notice in writing to the Lord Chancellor[9] and the Lord Chancellor may remove a person from office as President or chairman on the ground of incapacity or misbehaviour[10]. If the President is absent or otherwise unable to act the Lord Chancellor may appoint as acting President any person qualified for appointment as a chairman[11].

Ordinary members also hold and vacate office in accordance with their terms of appointment[12]. A person may not be an ordinary member for more than 8 years[13]. An ordinary member may resign his office by notice in writing to the Secretary of State[14] and the Secretary of State may remove a person from office as an ordinary member on the ground of incapacity or misbehaviour[15].

The Competition Service must pay to the President, the chairmen and the ordinary members such remuneration (whether by way of salaries or fees), and such allowances, as the Secretary of State may determine[16]. The Competition Service, if required to do so by the Secretary of State, must also pay such pension, allowances or gratuities as may be determined by the Secretary of State to or in respect of a person who holds or has held office as President, a chairman or an ordinary member, or make such payments as may be so determined towards provision for the payment of a pension, allowance or gratuities to or in respect of such a person[17].

If, where any person ceases to hold office as President, a chairman or ordinary member, the Secretary of State determines that there are special circumstances which make it right that he should receive compensation, the Competition Service is required pay to him such amount by way of compensation as the Secretary of State may determine[18].

Any staff, office accommodation or equipment required for the Tribunal must be provided by the Competition Service[19].

The President must arrange such training for members of the Tribunal as he considers appropriate[20].

Members of the Tribunal are disqualified for membership of the House of Commons[21] and the Northern Ireland Assembly[22].

1   See the Enterprise Act 2002 s 12(1).

2   A person is not eligible for appointment as President unless: (1) he satisfies the judicial-appointment eligibility condition on a seven-year basis; (2) he is an advocate or solicitor in Scotland of at least seven years' standing; or (3) he is a member of the Bar of Northern Ireland or solicitor of the Supreme Court of Northern Ireland of at least seven years' standing, and he appears to the Lord Chancellor to have appropriate experience and knowledge of competition law and practice: Enterprise Act 2002 s 12(5), Sch 2 para 1(1) (amended by the Tribunals, Courts and Enforcement Act 2007 s 50, Sch 10 para 36(1), (2)). Before appointing an advocate or solicitor in Scotland, the Lord Chancellor must consult the Lord President of the Court of Session: Enterprise Act 2002 Sch 2 para 1(3). As to the judicial-appointment eligibility condition see the Tribunals, Courts and Enforcement Act 2007 ss 50–52; and ADMINISTRATIVE LAW. As to the Lord Chancellor see CONSTITUTIONAL LAW AND HUMAN RIGHTS vol 8(2) (Reissue) PARA 477 et seq.

3   A person is not eligible for appointment as a chairman unless: (1) he satisfies the judicial-appointment eligibility condition on a five-year basis; (2) he is an advocate or solicitor in Scotland of at least five years' standing; or (3) he is a member of the Bar of Northern Ireland or solicitor of the Supreme Court of Northern Ireland of at least five years' standing, and he appears to the Lord Chancellor to have appropriate experience and knowledge (either of competition law and practice or any other relevant law and practice): Enterprise Act 2002 Sch 2 para 1(2) (amended by the Tribunals, Courts and Enforcement Act 2007 Sch 10 para 36(1), (3)). In the Enterprise Act 2002 Sch 2, 'chairman' and 'ordinary member' mean respectively a member of the panel of chairmen, or a member of the panel of ordinary members, appointed under s 12: Sch 2 para 9.

4   Enterprise Act 2002 s 12(2). As to the Secretary of State see PARA 5.

5   Enterprise Act 2002 s 12(3). As to the Registrar see the Competition Appeal Tribunal Rules 2003, SI 2003/1372, r 4.

6   Enterprise Act 2002 s 12(4). As to the Competition Service see PARA 14.

7   Enterprise Act 2002 Sch 2 para 2(1).

8   Enterprise Act 2002 Sch 2 para 2(2). This does not prevent a temporary re-appointment for the purpose of continuing to act as a member of the Tribunal as constituted for the purposes of any proceedings instituted before the end of his term of office: Sch 2 para 2(2).

9   Enterprise Act 2002 Sch 2 para 2(3).

10   Enterprise Act 2002 Sch 2 para 2(4). The Lord Chancellor may remove a person from office as President only with the concurrence of all of the following: (1) the Lord Chief Justice of England and Wales; (2) the Lord President of the Court of Session; (3) the Lord Chief Justice of Northern Ireland: Sch 2 para 2(5) (Sch 2 para 2(5)–(7) added by the Constitutional Reform Act 2005 s 15(1), Sch 4 paras 304, 306). The Lord Chancellor may remove a person from office as chairman only with the concurrence of the appropriate senior judge: Enterprise Act 2002 Sch 2 para 2(6) (as so added). The appropriate senior judge is the Lord Chief Justice of England and Wales, unless: (a) the person to be removed exercises functions wholly or mainly in Scotland, in which case it is the Lord President of the Court of Session; or (b) the person to be removed exercises functions wholly or mainly in Northern Ireland, in which case it is the Lord Chief Justice of Northern Ireland: Sch 2 para 2(7) (as so added).

11   Enterprise Act 2002 Sch 2 para 3.

12   Enterprise Act 2002 Sch 2 para 4(1).

13   Enterprise Act 2002 Sch 2 para 4(2). This does not prevent a temporary re-appointment for the purpose of continuing to act as a member of the Tribunal as constituted for the purposes of any proceedings instituted before the end of his term of office: Sch 2 para 4(2).

14   Enterprise Act 2002 Sch 2 para 4(3).

15   Enterprise Act 2002 Sch 2 para 4(4).

16   Enterprise Act 2002 Sch 2 para 5(1).

17   Enterprise Act 2002 Sch 2 para 5(2).

18   Enterprise Act 2002 Sch 2 para 6.

19   Enterprise Act 2002 Sch 2 para 7.

20   Enterprise Act 2002 Sch 2 para 8.

21   See the House of Commons Disqualification Act 1975 Sch 1 Pt II (amended by the Enterprise Act 2002 Sch 2 para 10).

22   See the Northern Ireland Assembly Disqualification Act 1975 Sch 1 Pt 2 (amended by the Enterprise Act 2002 Sch 2 para 11).

14.   The Competition Service. The Enterprise Act 2002 established a body corporate called the Competition Service[1], the purpose of which is to fund, and provide the Competition Appeal Tribunal[2] with support services, including the provision of staff, accommodation and equipment and any other services which facilitate the carrying out by the Tribunal of its functions[3]. The activities of the Service are not carried out on behalf of the Crown, and its property is not to be regarded as held on behalf of the Crown[4]. The Secretary of State[5] is required to pay to the Service such sums as he considers appropriate to enable it to fund the activities of the Tribunal and to carry out its other activities[6].

The Service consists of the President of the Competition Appeal Tribunal[7], the Registrar of the Competition Appeal Tribunal[8] and one or more members appointed by the Secretary of State after consulting the President[9]. The members are required to choose one of their number to be chairman of the Service[10]. An appointed member holds and vacates office in accordance with the terms of his appointment and is eligible for re-appointment[11].

The Service pays such travelling and other allowances to its members, and such remuneration to any appointed member, as may be determined by the Secretary of State[12]. If required to do so by the Secretary of State, the Service also pays such pension, allowances or gratuities as may be determined by the Secretary of State to or in respect of a person who holds or has held office as an appointed member or makes such payments as may be so determined towards provision for the payment of a pension, allowances or gratuities to or in respect of such a person[13]. If, where any person ceases to hold office as an appointed member, the Secretary of State determines that there are special circumstances which make it right that he should receive compensation, the Service must pay to him such amount by way of compensation as the Secretary of State may determine[14].

The Service may, with the approval of the Secretary of State as to numbers and terms and conditions of service, appoint such staff as it may determine[15].

The Service may regulate its own procedure, including quorum[16]. The validity of anything done by the Service is not affected by a vacancy among its members or by a defect in the appointment of a member[17].

The application of the seal of the Service is authenticated by the signature of any member, or some other person who has been authorised for that purpose by the Service, whether generally or specially[18]. A document purporting to be duly executed under the seal of the Service, or signed on its behalf, must be received in evidence and, unless the contrary is proved, be taken to be so executed or signed[19].

The Service is required to keep proper accounts and records in relation to its accounts and those of the Tribunal[20].

Members of the Service are disqualified for membership of the House of Commons[21] and the Northern Ireland Assembly[22].

1 See the Enterprise Act 2002 s 13(1).
2 As to the establishment and constitution of the Competition Appeal Tribunal see PARA 13.
3 Enterprise Act 2002 s 13(2), (3). The Service has power to do anything which is calculated to facilitate, or is conducive or incidental to, the performance of its functions: s 13(6), Sch 3 para 10. The Secretary of State may make one or more schemes for the transfer to the Service of defined property, rights and liabilities of the Competition Commission, including rights and liabilities relating to contracts of employment: see Sch 3 paras 13–16. As to the Competition Commission see PARA 9.
4 Enterprise Act 2002 s 13(4).
5 As to the Secretary of State see PARA 5.
6 Enterprise Act 2002 s 13(5).
7 As to the President see PARA 13.
8 As to the Registrar see PARA 13.
9 Enterprise Act 2002 Sch 3 para 1(1), (2).

10 Enterprise Act 2002 Sch 3 para 2(1). The first chairman of the Service was designated by the Secretary of State: see Sch 3 para 2(2).
11 Enterprise Act 2002 Sch 3 para 3.
12 Enterprise Act 2002 Sch 3 para 4(1).
13 Enterprise Act 2002 Sch 3 para 4(2).
14 Enterprise Act 2002 Sch 3 para 5.
15 Enterprise Act 2002 Sch 3 para 6(1). The persons to whom the Superannuation Act 1972 s 1 (see CONSTITUTIONAL LAW AND HUMAN RIGHTS vol 8(2) (Reissue) PARA 567) applies include the staff of the Service: Enterprise Act 2002 Sch 3 para 6(2). The Service must pay to the Minister for the Civil Service, at such times as he may direct, such sums as he may determine in respect of any increase attributable to Sch 3 para 6(2) in the sums payable out of money provided by Parliament under the Superannuation Act 1972: Enterprise Act 2002 Sch 3 para 6(3). As to the Minister for the Civil Service see CONSTITUTIONAL LAW AND HUMAN RIGHTS vol 8(2) (Reissue) PARA 550.
16 Enterprise Act 2002 Sch 3 para 7(1).
17 Enterprise Act 2002 Sch 3 para 7(2).
18 Enterprise Act 2002 Sch 3 para 8(1). This does not apply in relation to any document which is, or is to be, signed in accordance with the law of Scotland: Sch 3 para 8(2).
19 Enterprise Act 2002 Sch 3 para 9.
20 Enterprise Act 2002 Sch 3 para 11(1), 12. In performing that duty the Service, in addition to accounts and records relating to its own activities (including the services provided to the Tribunal), must keep separate accounts and separate records in relation to the activities of the Tribunal: Sch 3 para 11(2). The Service must prepare a statement of accounts in respect of each of its financial years and prepare a statement of accounts for the Tribunal for each of its financial years: Sch 3 para 12(1). 'Financial year' means the period of 12 months ending with 31 March: Sch 3 para 12(5). The Service must send copies of the accounts to the Secretary of State and to the Comptroller and Auditor General before the end of August following the financial year to which they relate: Sch 3 para 12(2). As to the Comptroller and Auditor General see CONSTITUTIONAL LAW AND HUMAN RIGHTS vol 8(2) (Reissue) PARA 724. Those accounts must comply with any directions given by the Secretary of State with the approval of the Treasury as to: (1) the information to be contained in them; (2) the manner in which that information is to be presented; and (3) the methods and principles according to which they are to be prepared: Sch 3 para 12(3). The Comptroller and Auditor General must examine, certify and report on each statement of accounts received by him and lay copies of each statement before Parliament: Sch 3 para 12(4).
21 See the House of Commons Disqualification Act 1975 Sch 1 Pt II (amended by the Enterprise Act 2002 Sch 3 para 17).
22 See the Northern Ireland Assembly Disqualification Act 1975 Sch 1 Pt 2 (amended by the Enterprise Act 2002 Sch 3 para 18).

15. Procedure of the Competition Appeal Tribunal. For the purposes of any proceedings before it the Competition Appeal Tribunal consists of a chairman and two other members[1]. The chairman must be the President or a member of the panel of chairmen[2]. The other members may be chosen from either the panel of chairmen or the panel of ordinary members[3]. If the members of the Tribunal as so constituted are unable to agree on any decision, the decision is to be taken by majority vote[4].

A decision of the Tribunal in any proceedings before it must state the reasons for the decision and whether it was unanimous or taken by a majority[5]. The decision must be recorded in a document signed and dated by the chairman of the Tribunal dealing with the proceedings[6].

If a decision of the Tribunal is registered in England and Wales in accordance with rules of court or any practice direction, payment of damages or costs and expenses which are awarded by the decision and any direction given as a result of the decision, may be enforced by the High Court as if the damages, costs or expenses were an amount due in pursuance of a judgment or order of the High Court, or as if the direction were an order of the High Court[7]. Subject to rules of court or any practice direction, a decision of the Tribunal may be registered or recorded for execution (1) for the purpose of enforcing a direction given as a result of the decision, by the Registrar of the Tribunal or a person who was a party to the proceedings; (2) for the purpose of enforcing a decision to award damages, costs or expenses (other than a decision to which head (3) applies), by the person to whom the sum concerned was awarded; and (3) for the purpose of enforcing a decision to award damages which is the subject of an order under the statutory provision relating to claims brought on behalf of consumers[8], by the specified body concerned[9].

1 Enterprise Act 2002 s 14(1). As to the constitution of the Competition Appeal Tribunal see PARA 13. The provisions of s 14 have effect subject to s 14(6), Sch 4 para 18 (consequences of a member of the Tribunal being unable to continue after the proceedings have begun to be heard) (see PARA 16): s 14(5).
2 Enterprise Act 2002 s 14(2). As to the President and the panel of chairmen see PARA 13.
3 Enterprise Act 2002 s 14(3).
4 Enterprise Act 2002 s 14(4).
5 Enterprise Act 2002 Sch 4 para 1(1)(a).
6 Enterprise Act 2002 Sch 4 para 1(1)(b). In preparing the document the Tribunal must have regard to the need for excluding, so far as practicable: (1) information the disclosure of which would in its opinion be contrary to the public interest; (2) commercial information the disclosure of which would or might, in its opinion, significantly harm the legitimate business interests of the undertaking to which it relates; (3) information relating to the private affairs of an individual the disclosure of which would, or might, in its opinion, significantly harm his interests: Sch 4 para 1(2). The Tribunal must also have regard to the extent to which any such disclosure is necessary for the purpose of explaining the reasons for the decision: Sch 4 para 1(3). The President must make such arrangements for the publication of the decisions of the Tribunal as he considers appropriate: Sch 4 para 1(4).
7 Enterprise Act 2002 Sch 4 para 2. If a decision of the Tribunal awards damages, costs or expenses, or results in any direction being given, the decision may be recorded for execution in the Books of Council and Session and is enforceable accordingly: Sch 4 para 3. As to the enforcement of decisions in Northern Ireland see Sch 4 para 5.
8 Ie the Competition Act 1998 s 47B(6) (see PARA 169).
9 Enterprise Act 2002 Sch 4 para 4. A decision of the Tribunal in proceedings under the Competition Act 1998 s 47B (see PARA 169) which: (1) awards damages to an individual in respect of a claim made or continued on his behalf (but is not the subject of an order under s 47B(6)); or (2) awards costs or expenses to an individual in respect of proceedings in respect of a claim made under s 47A (see PARA 168) prior to its being continued on his behalf in the proceedings under s 47B, may only be enforced by the individual concerned with the permission of the High Court or Court of Session: Enterprise Act 2002 Sch 4 para 6. An award of costs or expenses against a specified body in proceedings under the Competition Act 1998 s 47B may not be enforced against any individual on whose behalf a claim was made or continued in those proceedings: Enterprise Act 2002 Sch 4 para 7. In Sch 4 Pt 1 (paras 1–8), any reference to damages includes a reference to any sum of money (other than costs or expenses) which may be awarded in respect of a claim made under the Competition Act 1998 s 47A or included in proceedings under s 47B: Enterprise Act 2002 Sch 4 para 8.

16. Competition Appeal Tribunal rules. The Secretary of State[1] may, after consulting the President[2] and such other persons as he considers appropriate, make Tribunal rules with respect to proceedings before the Competition Appeal Tribunal[3]. Tribunal rules may make provision with respect to matters incidental to or consequential upon appeals provided for by or under any Act to the Court of Appeal or the Court of Session in relation to a decision of the Tribunal[4]. Tribunal rules may specify qualifications for appointment as Registrar[5] and confer functions on the President or the Registrar in relation to proceedings before the Tribunal[6]. They may also contain incidental, supplemental, consequential or transitional provision[7]. The power to make Tribunal rules is exercisable by statutory instrument subject to annulment in pursuance of a resolution of either House of Parliament[8].

Tribunal rules may make different provision for different kinds of proceedings[9]. They may make provision as to the period within which and the manner in which proceedings are to be brought[10]. They may also provide for the Tribunal to reject any proceedings[11] if it considers that the person instituting them does not have a sufficient interest in the decision with respect to which the proceedings are brought, or the document by which he institutes them discloses no valid grounds for bringing them[12]. The rules may also provide for the Tribunal to reject any proceedings if it is satisfied that the person instituting the proceedings has habitually and persistently and without any reasonable ground instituted vexatious proceedings (whether against the same person or against different persons) or made vexatious applications in any proceedings[13]. Tribunal rules must ensure that no proceedings are rejected without giving the parties the opportunity to be heard[14].

Tribunal rules may make provision for the carrying out by the Tribunal of a preliminary consideration of proceedings (a 'pre-hearing review'), which may include provision enabling such powers to be exercised on a pre-hearing review as may be specified in the rules and provision for security and supplemental provision relating to security[15].

Tribunal rules may make provision:

(1) as to the manner in which proceedings are to be conducted, including provision for any hearing to be held in private if the Tribunal considers it appropriate[16];

(2) as to the persons entitled to appear on behalf of the parties[17];

(3) for requiring persons to attend to give evidence and produce documents, and for authorising the administration of oaths to witnesses[18];

(4) as to the evidence which may be required or admitted and the extent to which it should be oral or written[19];

(5) allowing the Tribunal to fix time limits with respect to any aspect of proceedings and to extend any time limit (before or after its expiry)[20];

(6) enabling the Tribunal, on the application of any party or on its own initiative, to order the disclosure between, or the production by, the parties of documents or classes of documents[21];

(7) for the appointment of experts for the purposes of proceedings[22];

(8) for the award of costs or expenses, including allowances payable to persons in connection with attendance before the Tribunal[23];

(9) for taxing or otherwise settling any costs or expenses awarded by the Tribunal or for the enforcement of any order awarding costs or expenses[24].

Tribunal rules may make provision as to the consequences of a member of the Tribunal being unable to continue after part of any proceedings have been heard[25] and may allow the Tribunal to consist of the remaining members for the rest of the proceedings[26].

Tribunal rules may make provision allowing the Tribunal to order that interest is payable on any sum awarded by the Tribunal or on any fees[27] ordered to be paid[28].

Tribunal rules may also make provision as to the withdrawal of proceedings[29], interim orders[30], where to sit for the purposes of proceedings[31], in relation to persons not party to proceedings[32] and as to the transfer of certain claims[33].

1 As to the Secretary of State see PARA 5.
2 As to the President of the Tribunal see PARA 13.

3 Enterprise Act 2002 s 15(1). As to the establishment and constitution of the Tribunal see PARA 13.
4 Enterprise Act 2002 s 15(2).
5 Enterprise Act 2002 s 15(3)(a). See the Competition Appeal Tribunal Rules 2003, SI 2003/1372, r 4. As to the Registrar see PARA 13.
6 Enterprise Act 2002 s 15(3)(b). See the Competition Appeal Tribunal Rules 2003, SI 2003/1372, r 62 (amended by SI 2004/2068). As to proceedings before the Tribunal see PARA 15.
7 Enterprise Act 2002 s 15(3)(c). As to the calculation of time see the Competition Appeal Tribunal Rules 2003, SI 2003/1372, r 64; as to conditional fee arrangements see r 65; as to enforcement of orders see r 66; as to irregularities see r 67; and as to the general power of the Tribunal see r 68.
8 Enterprise Act 2002 s 15(4). In exercise of this power the Secretary of State has made the Competition Appeal Tribunal Rules 2003, SI 2003/1372, and the Competition Appeal Tribunal (Amendment and Communications Act Appeals) Rules 2004, SI 2004/2068. As to the power of the Tribunal under the rules see *Floe Telecom Ltd v Office of Communications* [2006] EWCA Civ 768, [2006] 4 All ER 688.
9 Enterprise Act 2002 s 15(5), Sch 4 para 10. See the Competition Appeal Tribunal Rules 2003, SI 2003/1372, r 3. As to proceedings under the Enterprise Act 2002 see rr 25–29. The provisions of the Enterprise Act 2002 Sch 4 Pt 2 (paras 9–26) (which makes further provision about the rules) has effect, but without prejudice to the generality of s 15(1) (see the text to notes 1–3): s 15(5). In Sch 4, the 'Tribunal', in relation to any proceedings before it, means the Tribunal as constituted (in accordance with s 14 (see PARA 15)) for the purposes of those proceedings: Sch 4 para 9.
10 Enterprise Act 2002 Sch 4 para 11(1). That provision may, in particular: (1) provide for time limits for making claims to which the Competition Act 1998 s 47A (see PARA 168) applies in proceedings under s 47A or s 47B (see PARA 169); (2) provide for the Tribunal to extend the period in which any particular proceedings may be brought; and (3) provide for the form, contents, amendment and acknowledgement of the documents by which proceedings are to be instituted: Enterprise Act 2002 Sch 4 para 11(2). As to the time and manner of commencing appeals see the Competition Appeal Tribunal Rules 2003, SI 2003/1372, rr 8, 9, 13. As to defence see r 14. As to the service of documents on the Tribunal see r 5; and as to the service of documents on other persons see r 63 (amended by SI 2004/2068). As to the Tribunal website see the Competition Appeal Tribunal Rules 2003, SI 2003/1372, r 6. As to the publication of a summary of an appeal see r 15. As to the delivery of the Tribunal's decision see r 54. As to consent orders see r 57. As to appeals from the Tribunal see rr 58, 59.
11 Ie other than proceedings under the Competition Act 1998 s 47A (see PARA 168) or s 47B (see PARA 169). See note 12.
12 Enterprise Act 2002 Sch 4 para 12. Tribunal rules may provide for the Tribunal: (1) to reject the whole of any proceedings under the Competition Act 1998 s 47B (see PARA 169) if it considers that the person bringing the proceedings is not entitled to do so or that the proceedings do not satisfy the requirements of s 47B(1); (2) to reject any claim which is included in proceedings under s 47B if it considers that the claim is not a consumer claim (within the meaning of s 47B(2)) which may be included in such proceedings, or the individual concerned has not consented to its being made or continued on his behalf in such proceedings; or (3) to reject any claim made under s 47A (see PARA 168) or included in proceedings under s 47B if it considers that there are no reasonable grounds for making it: Enterprise Act 2002 Sch 4 para 13. See the Competition Appeal Tribunal Rules 2003, SI 2003/1372, rr 9–11.
13 Enterprise Act 2002 Sch 4 para 14. As to vexatious proceedings see CIVIL PROCEDURE vol 11 (2009) PARAS 244–245.
14 Enterprise Act 2002 Sch 4 para 15.
15 Enterprise Act 2002 Sch 4 para 16(1), (2). 'Provision for security' means provision authorising the Tribunal, in specified circumstances, to order a party to the proceedings, if he wishes to continue to participate in them or to pay a deposit not exceeding such sum as may be specified or calculated in a specified manner: Sch 4 para 16(3)(a). 'Supplemental provision', in relation to security, means provision as to: (1) the manner in which the amount of a deposit is to be determined; (2) the consequences of non-payment of a deposit; (3) the circumstances in which the deposit, or any part of it, may be refunded to the person who paid it or paid to another party to the proceedings: Sch 4 para 16(3)(b).
16 Enterprise Act 2002 Sch 4 para 17(1)(a). The Tribunal may consider it appropriate for a hearing to be held in private because it is considering information the disclosure of which might be contrary to public interest or harm business or personal interests: see Sch 4 paras 1(2), 17(1)(a). As to case management see the Competition Appeal Tribunal Rules 2003, SI 2003/1372, rr 19, 20, 21. As to the failure to comply with directions see r 24. As to the hearing see rr 50–52.

17 Enterprise Act 2002 Sch 4 para 17(1)(b). As to representation see the Competition Appeal Tribunal Rules 2003, SI 2003/1372, r 7.

18 Enterprise Act 2002 Sch 4 para 17(1)(c). As to the summoning or citing of witnesses see the Competition Appeal Tribunal Rules 2003, SI 2003/1372, r 23. A person who without reasonable excuse fails to comply with any requirement imposed by virtue of the Enterprise Act 2002 Sch 4 para 17(1)(c) is guilty of an offence and liable on summary conviction to a fine not exceeding level 3 on the standard scale: Sch 4 para 17(5)(a).

'Standard scale' means the standard scale of maximum fines for summary offences as set out in the Criminal Justice Act 1982 s 37: see the Interpretation Act 1978 s 5, Sch 1 (definition added by the Criminal Justice Act 1988 s 170(1), Sch 15 para 58); and CRIMINAL LAW, EVIDENCE AND PROCEDURE vol 11(4) (2006 Reissue) PARA 1676; MAGISTRATES vol 29(2) (Reissue) PARA 804. At the date at which this volume states the law, the standard scale is as follows: level 1, £200; level 2, £500; level 3, £1,000; level 4, £2,500; level 5, £5,000: Criminal Justice Act 1982 s 37(2) (substituted by the Criminal Justice Act 1991 s 17(1)). As to the determination of the amount of the fine actually imposed, as distinct from the level on the standard scale which it may not exceed, see the Criminal Justice Act 2003 s 164; and CRIMINAL LAW, EVIDENCE AND PROCEDURE vol 11(4) (2006 Reissue) PARA 1678; MAGISTRATES vol 29(2) (Reissue) PARA 807.

19 Enterprise Act 2002 Sch 4 para 17(1)(d). As to evidence see the Competition Appeal Tribunal Rules 2003, SI 2003/1372, r 22. As to requests for confidential treatment of documents see r 53.

20 Enterprise Act 2002 Sch 4 para 17(1)(e).

21 Enterprise Act 2002 Sch 4 para 17(1)(f). As to disclosure see CIVIL PROCEDURE vol 11 (2009) PARA 538 et seq. A person who without reasonable excuse fails to comply with any requirement with respect to the disclosure, production, recovery or inspection of documents which is imposed by virtue of Sch 4 para 17(1)(f) is guilty of an offence and liable on summary conviction to a fine not exceeding level 3 on the standard scale: Sch 4 para 17(5)(b).

22 Enterprise Act 2002 Sch 4 para 17(1)(g).

23 Enterprise Act 2002 Sch 4 para 17(1)(h). Rules under Sch 4 para 17(1)(h) may provide, in relation to a claim made under the Competition Act 1998 s 47A (see PARA 168) which is continued on behalf of an individual in proceedings under s 47B (see PARA 169), for costs or expenses to be awarded to or against that individual in respect of proceedings on that claim which took place before it was included in the proceedings under s 47B: Enterprise Act 2002 Sch 4 para 17(2). Otherwise Tribunal rules may not provide for costs or expenses to be awarded to or against an individual on whose behalf a claim is made or continued in proceedings under the Competition Act 1998 s 47B: Enterprise Act 2002 Sch 4 para 17(3). Tribunal rules may make provision enabling the Tribunal to refer any matter arising in any proceedings (other than proceedings under the Competition Act 1998 s 47A or s 47B) back to the authority that made the decision to which the proceedings relate, if it appears that the matter has not been adequately investigated: Enterprise Act 2002 Sch 4 para 17(4). As to claims for damages see the Competition Appeal Tribunal Rules 2003, SI 2003/1372, Pt IV (rr 30–49) (r 43 amended by SI 2004/2068). As to the award of costs and interest see the Competition Appeal Tribunal Rules 2003, SI 2003/1372, rr 55, 56 (r 55 amended by SI 2004/2068).

24 Enterprise Act 2002 Sch 4 para 17(1)(i). As to costs see CIVIL PROCEDURE vol 12 (2009) PARA 1729 et seq.

25 Enterprise Act 2002 Sch 4 para 18(1).

26 Enterprise Act 2002 Sch 4 para 18(2). The rules may enable the President, if it is the chairman of the Tribunal who is unable to continue: (1) to appoint either of the remaining members to chair the Tribunal; and (2) if that person is not a member of the panel of chairmen, to appoint himself or some other suitably qualified person to attend the proceedings and advise the remaining members on any questions of law arising: Sch 4 para 18(3). A person is 'suitably qualified' if he is, or is qualified for appointment as, a member of the panel of chairmen (see PARA 13): Sch 4 para 18(4).

27 Tribunal rules may provide: (1) for fees to be chargeable in respect of specified costs of proceedings; and (2) for the amount of such costs to be determined by the Tribunal: Sch 4 para 20(1). Any sums received in respect of such fees is to be paid into the Consolidated Fund: Sch 4 para 20(2). As to the Consolidated Fund see CONSTITUTIONAL LAW AND HUMAN RIGHTS vol 8(2) (Reissue) PARA 711 et seq; PARLIAMENT vol 34 (Reissue) PARAS 952–955.

28 Enterprise Act 2002 Sch 4 para 19(1). That provision may include provision as to the circumstances in which such an order may be made and as to the manner in which, and the periods in respect of which, interest is to be calculated and paid: Sch 4 para 19(2).

29 See the Enterprise Act 2002 Sch 4 para 21. Tribunal rules may make provision: (1) preventing a party who has instituted proceedings from withdrawing them without the permission of the Tribunal or, in specified circumstances, the President or the Registrar; (2) for the Tribunal to

grant permission to withdraw proceedings on such conditions as it considers appropriate; (3) enabling the Tribunal to publish any decision which it would have made in any proceedings, had the proceedings not been withdrawn; (4) as to the effect of withdrawal of proceedings; and (5) as to the procedure to be followed if parties to proceedings agree to settle: Sch 4 para 21(1). Tribunal rules may make, in relation to a claim included in proceedings under the Competition Act 1998 s 47B (see PARA 169), any provision which may be made under heads (1)–(3) in relation to the whole proceedings: Enterprise Act 2002 Sch 4 para 21(2). As to withdrawal of an appeal see the Competition Appeal Tribunal Rules 2003, SI 2003/1372, r 12 (amended by SI 2004/2068).

30 See the Enterprise Act 2002 Sch 4 para 22. Tribunal rules may provide for the Tribunal to make an order, on an interim basis: (1) suspending the effect of any decision which is the subject matter of proceedings before it; (2) in the case of an appeal under the Competition Act 1998 s 46 or s 47 (see PARAS 166–167), varying the conditions or obligations attached to an exemption; (3) granting any remedy which the Tribunal would have had power to grant in its final decision: Enterprise Act 2002 Sch 4 para 22(1). Tribunal rules may also make provision giving the Tribunal powers similar to those given to the Office of Fair Trading by the Competition Act 1998 s 35 (see PARA 136): Enterprise Act 2002 Sch 4 para 22(2). As to interim orders see the Competition Appeal Tribunal Rules 2003, SI 2003/1372, r 61.

31 See the Enterprise Act 2002 Sch 4 para 23(1). Tribunal rules may make provision enabling the Tribunal to decide that any proceedings before it are to be treated, for purposes connected with: (1) any appeal from a decision of the Tribunal made in those proceedings; and (2) any other matter connected with those proceedings, as proceedings in England and Wales, Scotland or Northern Ireland (regardless of the decision made as to where to sit for the purposes of Sch 4 para 23(1)): Sch 4 para 23(2). Tribunal rules may provide for each claim made or continued on behalf of an individual in proceedings under the Competition Act 1998 s 47B (see PARA 169) to be treated as separate proceedings: Enterprise Act 2002 Sch 4 para 23(3). As to the forum see the Competition Appeal Tribunal Rules 2003, SI 2003/1372, r 18.

32 See the Enterprise Act 2002 Sch 4 para 24. Tribunal rules may make provision: (1) for a person who is not a party to be joined in any proceedings; (2) for hearing a person who is not a party where, in any proceedings, it is proposed to make an order or give a direction in relation to that person; (3) for proceedings to be consolidated on such terms as the Tribunal thinks appropriate in such circumstances as may be specified: Sch 4 para 24. As to permission to intervene in proceedings see the Competition Appeal Tribunal Rules 2003, SI 2003/1372, r 16 (amended by SI 2004/2068). As to the consolidation of proceedings see the Competition Appeal Tribunal Rules 2003, SI 2003/1372, r 17.

33 See the Enterprise Act 2002 Sch 4 paras 25, 26. Tribunal rules may make provision for the Tribunal to transfer a claim made in proceedings under the Competition Act 1998 s 47A (see PARA 168) to the High Court or a county court in England and Wales or Northern Ireland or the Court of Session or a sheriff court in Scotland: Enterprise Act 2002 Sch 4 para 25. Tribunal rules may make provision in connection with the transfer of any proceedings from such a court to the Tribunal under s 16 (see PARA 17): Sch 4 para 26. As to references to the European Court see the Competition Appeal Tribunal Rules 2003, SI 2003/1372, r 60.

17.   Transfer of certain proceedings to and from the Competition Appeal Tribunal.   The Lord Chancellor[1] may by regulations make provision enabling the court[2] to transfer to the Competition Appeal Tribunal for its determination so much of any proceedings before the court as relates to an infringement issue[3], and to give effect to the determination of that issue by the Tribunal[4]. Regulations may also make such incidental, supplementary, consequential, transitional or saving provision as the Lord Chancellor may consider appropriate[5]. The power to make such regulations is exercisable by statutory instrument subject to annulment in pursuance of a resolution of either House of Parliament[6]. Rules of court may prescribe the procedure to be followed in connection with a transfer to the Tribunal[7].

1   As to the Lord Chancellor see CONSTITUTIONAL LAW AND HUMAN RIGHTS vol 8(2) (Reissue) PARA 477 et seq.
2   'Court' means: (1) the High Court or a county court; or (2) the Court of Session or a sheriff court: Enterprise Act 2002 s 16(6).
3   'Infringement issue' means any question relating to whether or not an infringement of: (1) the Chapter I prohibition (see PARA 116) or the Chapter II prohibition (see PARA 125); or (2) the EC

Treaty art 81 or art 82 (see PARAS 4, 24 et seq), has been or is being committed: Enterprise
Act 2002 s 16(6). As to the EC Treaty (ie the Treaty establishing the European Community
(Rome, 25 March 1957; TS 1 (1973); Cmnd 5179)) see PARA 24 note 1. The numbering for the
EC Treaty used in this title is as revised by the Treaty of Amsterdam: see PARA 24 note 1.

4   Enterprise Act 2002 s 16(1)(a).
5   Enterprise Act 2002 s 16(1)(b).
6   Enterprise Act 2002 s 16(2). See the Act of Sederunt (Ordinary Cause Rules) Amendment
     (Competition Appeal Tribunal) 2004, SSI 2004/350.
7   Enterprise Act 2002 s 16(3). The court may transfer to the Tribunal, in accordance with rules of
     court, so much of any proceedings before it as relates to a claim to which the Competition
     Act 1998 s 47A applies (see PARA 168): Enterprise Act 2002 s 16(4). Rules of court may make
     provision in connection with the transfer from the Tribunal to the High Court or the Court of
     Session of a claim made in proceedings under the Competition Act 1998 s 47A: Enterprise
     Act 2002 s 16(5). See CPR *Practice Direction–Transfer* PD30 para 8.

(v) The Sectoral Regulators

18.   Role of sectoral regulators.   As a result of the demonopolisation and
privatisation of industries, in particular the utilities industries, various
competition issues arose. Firstly, immediately following demonopolisation, the
lack of competition could result in excessive charges being levied and potential
competitors being prevented from entering the market. Second, it was important
to ensure that adequate services were provided. Third, in some industries a
'universal service obligation' was imposed, for example to maintain a water
supply to premises. To deal with these issues, in the United Kingdom detailed
regulatory regimes were established for the privatised industries, namely
telecommunications, gas, electricity, water and rail transport. The regulators are
the Office of Communications[1], the Gas and Electricity Markets Authority[2], the
Water Services Regulation Authority[3] and the Office of Rail Regulation[4].

1   As to the Office of Communications see PARA 19.
2   As to the Gas and Electricity Markets Authority see PARA 20.
3   As to the Water Services Regulation Authority see PARA 21.
4   As to the Office of Rail Regulation see PARA 22.

19.   Office of Communications.   The Office of Communications ('OFCOM')
was established by the Office of Communications Act 2002[1]. It is the principal
duty of OFCOM, in carrying out its functions: (1) to further the interests of
citizens in relation to communications matters; and (2) to further the interests of
consumers in relevant markets, where appropriate by promoting competition[2].
OFCOM also has the duty to ensure: (a) the optimal use for wireless telegraphy
of the electro-magnetic spectrum; (b) the availability throughout the United
Kingdom of a wide range of electronic communications services; (c) the
availability throughout the United Kingdom of a wide range of television and
radio services which (taken as a whole) are both of high quality and calculated to
appeal to a variety of tastes and interests; (d) the maintenance of a sufficient
plurality of providers of different television and radio services; (e) the
application, in the case of all television and radio services, of standards that
provide adequate protection to members of the public from the inclusion of
offensive and harmful material in such services; (f) the application, in the case of
all television and radio services, of standards that provide adequate protection to
members of the public and all other persons from both unfair treatment in
programmes included in such services and unwarranted infringements of privacy
resulting from activities carried on for the purposes of such services[3].

1   See the Office of Communications Act 2002 s 1(1); and TELECOMMUNICATIONS AND
    BROADCASTING vol 45(1) (2005 Reissue) PARA 1 et seq.
2   See the Communications Act 2003 s 3(1); TELECOMMUNICATIONS AND BROADCASTING
    vol 45(1) (2005 Reissue) PARA 16.
3   See the Communications Act 2003 s 3(2); TELECOMMUNICATIONS AND BROADCASTING
    vol 45(1) (2005 Reissue) PARA 16.

20.   Gas and Electricity Markets Authority.   The Gas and Electricity Markets Authority was established by the Utilities Act 2000[1]. The Authority's principal objective when carrying out certain of its functions is to protect the interests of existing and future consumers, wherever appropriate by promoting effective competition between persons engaged in, or in commercial activities connected with, the shipping, transportation or supply of gas conveyed through pipes, and the generation, transmission, distribution or supply of electricity or the provision or use of electricity interconnectors[2].

The Authority has powers under the Competition Act 1998 to investigate suspected anti-competitive activity[3].

1   See the Utilities Act 2000 s 1; and FUEL AND ENERGY vol 19(1) (2007 Reissue) PARA 708.
2   See FUEL AND ENERGY vol 19(1) (2007 Reissue) PARA 708 et seq.
3   See the Competition Act 1998 s 54, Sch 10; and PARA 147.

21.   Water Services Regulation Authority.   The Water Services Regulation Authority ('Ofwat') was established by the Water Act 2003[1] and regulates the regional monopoly water companies. The functions of Ofwat are: (1) to protect the interests of consumers, wherever appropriate by promoting effective competition between persons engaged in, or in commercial activities connected with, the provision of water and sewerage services; (2) to secure that the functions of a water undertaker and of a sewerage undertaker are properly carried out as respects every area of England and Wales; (3) to secure that companies holding appointments as relevant undertakers are able (in particular, by securing reasonable returns on their capital) to finance the proper carrying out of those functions; and (4) to secure that the activities authorised by the licence of a licensed water supplier and any statutory functions imposed on it in consequence of the licence are properly carried out[2].

Ofwat has powers under the Competition Act 1998 to investigate suspected anti-competitive activity[3].

1   See the Water Act 2003 s 34; and WATER AND WATERWAYS vol 100 (2009) PARA 109.
2   See the Water Industry Act 1991 s 2; and WATER AND WATERWAYS vol 100 (2009) PARA 130.
3   See the Competition Act 1998 s 54, Sch 10; and PARA 147.

22.   Office of Rail Regulation.   The Office of Rail Regulation ('ORR') was established by the Railways and Transport Safety Act 2003[1]. The ORR has a duty to exercise its functions in the manner which it considers best calculated: (1) to promote improvements in railway service performance; (2) otherwise to protect the interests of users of railway services; (3) to promote the use of the railway network in Great Britain for the carriage of passengers and goods, and the development of that railway network, to the greatest extent that it considers economically practicable; (4) to contribute to the development of an integrated system of transport of passengers and goods; (5) to contribute to the achievement of sustainable development; (6) to promote efficiency and economy on the part of persons providing railway services; (7) to promote competition in the provision of railway services for the benefit of users of railway services; (8) to promote measures designed to facilitate the making by passengers of journeys which involve use of the services of more than one passenger service operator; (9) to impose on the operators of railway services the minimum restrictions which are consistent with the performance of its functions that are not safety functions; (10) to enable persons providing railway services to plan the future of their businesses with a reasonable degree of assurance[2].

Certain functions of the Office of Fair Trading (the 'OFT')[3] under Part 4 of the Enterprise Act 2002[4], so far as relating to the supply of services relating to railways, are concurrent functions of the ORR and the OFT[5].

The ORR also is entitled to exercise, concurrently with the OFT, the functions of the OFT under the provisions of Part 1 of the Competition Act 1998[6] in connection with: (a) agreements, decisions or concerted practices which may affect trade within the United Kingdom and which have as their object or effect the prevention, restriction or distortion of competition; and (b) conduct amounting to abuse of a dominant market position, so far as they relate to the supply of services relating to railways[7].

1 See the Railways and Transport Safety Act 2003 s 15, Sch 1; and RAILWAYS, INLAND WATERWAYS AND CROSS-COUNTRY PIPELINES vol 39(1A) (Reissue) PARA 47 et seq.
2 See the Railways Act 1993 s 4(1); and RAILWAYS, INLAND WATERWAYS AND CROSS-COUNTRY PIPELINES vol 39(1A) (Reissue) PARA 33.
3 As to the OFT see PARAS 6–8.
4 Ie the Enterprise Act 2002 Pt 4 (ss 131–184) (see PARA 276 et seq).
5 See the Railways Act 1993 s 67(2), (2A); and RAILWAYS, INLAND WATERWAYS AND CROSS-COUNTRY PIPELINES vol 39(1A) (Reissue) PARA 186.
6 Ie the Competition Act 1998 Pt 1 (ss 1–60) (see PARA 115 et seq).
7 See Railways Act 1993 s 67(3); and RAILWAYS, INLAND WATERWAYS AND CROSS-COUNTRY PIPELINES vol 39(1A) (Reissue) PARA 186.

(vi) The European Commission

23. Role of the European Commission. The European Commission has a Directorate specifically responsible for competition policy[1]. Its mission is to enforce the competition rules of the Community Treaties[2] in order to ensure that competition is not distorted and markets operate as efficiently as possible, thereby contributing to the welfare of consumers and to the competitiveness of the European economy. In order to fulfil its objectives, the Directorate General for Competition concentrates on five key areas: (1) the enforcement of competition rules on antitrust, mergers, state infringements and state aid control[3]; (2) sector inquiries and market monitoring[4]; (3) policy development; (4) competition advocacy[5]; and (5) international cooperation[6].

It is usual for proceedings against the European Commission in competition cases to be brought before the Court of First Instance (CFI)[7]. Appeals from the CFI are heard by the European Court of Justice on points of law only[8].

1 Ie the Directorate General for Competition (DG COMP).
2 See PARA 4.
3 See PARA 107 et seq.
4 See PARA 90.
5 Ie actions aimed at influencing regulatory processes to ensure better and pro-competitive regulation.
6 See PARA 34.
7 Ie under the EC Treaty arts 229, 230, 232.
8 See eg Case C-7/95 P *John Deere Ltd v European Commission* [1998] ECR I-3111, [1998] 5 CMLR 311; Case C-551/03 P *General Motors BV v European Commission* [2006] ECR I-3173, [2006] 5 CMLR 1.

2. COMMUNITY ASPECTS OF COMPETITION LAW

(1) INTRODUCTION

(i) Objectives of the European Community

24.   Principles.   The objectives of the European Community are set out in article 2 of the EC Treaty[1] wherein it establishes a common market and an economic and monetary union and by implementing the common policies or activities referred to in articles 3 and 4, aims to promote throughout the Community a harmonious, balanced and sustainable development of economic activities, sustainable and non-inflationary growth, a high level of protection and improvement of the quality of the environment, a high degree of competitiveness and convergence of economic performance, a high level of employment and of social protection, equality between men and women, the raising of the standard of living and quality of life, and economic and social cohesion and solidarity among member states.

The objectives set out in article 2 can be seen as falling into two groups. Firstly, there is the political objective of closer relations between member states; and in the second group, there are the economic objectives of harmonious and sustainable development of economic activities and expansion, increased stability and raising of the standard of living.

Whilst the terms of article 2 lay down the broad objectives of the Community, article 3 of the Treaty sets out the manner in which the objectives are to be achieved. The terms of article 3 can be divided into three groupings. Firstly there are those paragraphs which are the means by which the achievement of an economic union between the member states is to be maintained; secondly those paragraphs which concern the progressive approximation of economic policies; and thirdly those arising from the existence of the European Union[2].

Articles 4 and 5 deal with economic and monetary union and subsidiarity[3]. Article 6 deals with the requirement that regard is to be had to environmental protection in the development of Community policies[4]. Article 7 provides an outline of the institutions to be established under the Treaty, to administer the policies therein enumerated; the institutions mentioned are an Assembly (the European Parliament), a Council, a Commission, a Court of Justice and a Court of Auditors. That article also provides that an Economic and Social Committee and a Committee of the Regions are to assist the Council and the Commission in an advisory capacity[5].

Articles 8 and 9 deal with the establishment of a European Central Bank[6]. Article 10 requires member states to take appropriate measures to ensure the fulfilment of the obligations arising out of the Treaty or from acts of the institutions and to abstain from any measure which could jeopardise the attainment of the objectives of the Treaty[7]. Article 11 provides a framework for an extension of the activities of the Community institutions into other areas agreed on a bilateral basis between member states[8]. Article 12 contains a general prohibition on discrimination on the grounds of nationality although more specific provisions are contained in the later provisions of the Treaty[9].

Article 13 allows the Council to take action to combat discrimination on the basis of sex, racial or ethnic origin, religion or belief, disability, age or sexual orientation[10]. Articles 14 and 15 provide a timetable for the establishment of the internal market[11]. Articles 17 to 22 (Part Two of the Treaty) make provision for citizenship of the European Union[12].

1   Ie the Treaty establishing the European Economic Community (Rome, 25 March 1957; TS 1 (1973); Cmnd 5179) art 2. The European Economic Community was renamed the European Community and the EEC Treaty was renamed the EC Treaty by the Treaty on European Union (the 'Maastricht Treaty') which came into force on 1 November 1993. The articles, titles and sections of the EC Treaty, as amended by the Treaty of Amsterdam (Cmnd 3780), are renumbered in accordance with the table of equivalences set out in the Annex to that Treaty and the new numbering is used in this title.
2   See the EC Treaty art 3.
3   See the EC Treaty arts 4, 5.
4   See the EC Treaty art 6.
5   See the EC Treaty art 7.
6   See the EC Treaty arts 8, 9.
7   See the EC Treaty art 10.
8   See the EC Treaty art 11.
9   See the EC Treaty art 12.
10 See the EC Treaty art 13.
11 See the EC Treaty arts 13–15.
12 See the EC Treaty arts 17–22.

25.   The foundations and policy of the Community.   Part Three of the EC Treaty[1], entitled 'Community Policies' lays down rules aimed at ensuring the establishment of a system of free movement of goods[2], persons[3], services[4], visas, asylum and immigration[5] and of capital[6]. It also provides detailed rules for the establishment of a common agricultural policy[7], rules on transport[8], economic and monetary policy[9], competition[10], taxation[11], approximation of laws[12], employment[13], common commercial policy[14], social policy[15], customs co-operation[16], education[17], vocational training[18], culture[19], public health[20], consumer protection[21], trans-European networks[22], industry[23], economic and social cohesion[24], research and technological development[25], environment[26] and development co-operation[27].

Titles V and VI of Part Three of the Treaty are divided into sections dealing inter alia with common rules on competition[28], tax[29] and approximation of laws[30], economic policy[31], customs co-operation[32], social policy[33] and culture[34].

In Part Three, Title VI, Chapter 1 provides common rules on competition policy applicable to both private and public enterprises within the Community[35] and with rules on state aids[36]. Chapter 2 deals with common tax provisions[37] and rules on the approximation of laws are dealt with in Chapter 3[38].

Titles VII, VIII and IX deal with economic policy[39], employment[40] and with the provision of a common commercial policy[41].

Title XI deals with social policy[42], the establishment of the European Social Fund[43] and education and vocational training[44]. Title XII provides for cultural action[45]. Title XIII deals with public health[46]. Title XIV deals with consumer protection[47]. Title XV deals with trans-European networks[48]. Title XVI deals with industrial policy[49]. Title XVII deals with economic and social cohesion[50]. Title XVIII deals with research and technological development[51]. Title XIX deals with the environment[52]. Title XX deals with development co-operation[53]. Title XXI deals with economic, financial and technical cooperation with third countries[54].

Part Four of the Treaty is concerned with the association of overseas countries and territories[55]. Part Five lays down rules governing the institutions of the Community set up under article 7 of the Treaty[56]. Part Six contains general and final provisions[57].

1 The EC Treaty Pt 3 comprises arts 23–181a. As to the EC Treaty (ie the Treaty establishing the European Community (Rome, 25 March 1957; TS 1 (1973); Cmnd 5179)) see PARA 24 note 1. The numbering for the EC Treaty used in this title is as revised by the Treaty of Amsterdam: see PARA 24 note 1.
2 See the EC Treaty Pt 3 Title I (arts 23–31).
3 See the EC Treaty Pt 3 Title III, Chs 1, 2 (arts 39–48).
4 See the EC Treaty Pt 3 Title III, Ch 3 (art 49–55).
5 See the EC Treaty Pt 3 Title IV (arts 61–69).
6 See the EC Treaty Pt 3 Title III, Ch 4 (arts 56–60).
7 See the EC Treaty Pt 3 Title II (arts 32–38).
8 See the EC Treaty Pt 3 Title V (arts 70–80).
9 See the EC Treaty Pt 3 Title VII (arts 98–124).
10 See the EC Treaty Pt 3 Title VI, Ch 1, Sections 1, 2 (arts 81–89).
11 See the EC Treaty Pt 3 Title VI, Ch 2 (arts 90–93).
12 See the EC Treaty Pt 3 Title VI, Ch 3 (arts 94–97).
13 See the EC Treaty Pt 3 Title VIII (arts 125–130).
14 See the EC Treaty Pt 3 Title IX (arts 131–134).
15 See the EC Treaty Pt 3 Title XI, Chs 1, 2 (arts 136–148).
16 See the EC Treaty Pt 3 Title X (art 135).
17 See the EC Treaty Pt 3 Title XI, Ch 3 art 149.
18 See the EC Treaty Pt 3 Title XI, Ch 3 art 150.
19 See the EC Treaty Pt 3 Title XII (art 151).
20 See the EC Treaty Pt 3 Title XIII (art 152).
21 See the EC Treaty Pt 3 Title XIV (art 153).
22 See the EC Treaty Pt 3 Title XV (arts 154–156).
23 See the EC Treaty Pt 3 Title XVI (art 157).
24 See the EC Treaty Pt 3 Title XVII (art 158–162).
25 See the EC Treaty Pt 3 Title XVIII (arts 163–173).
26 See the EC Treaty Pt 3 Title XIX (arts 174–176).
27 See the EC Treaty Pt 3 Title XX (arts 177–181).
28 See the EC Treaty Pt 3 Title VI, Ch 1, Sections 1, 2 (arts 81–89).
29 See the EC Treaty Pt 3 Title VI, Ch 2 (arts 90–93).
30 See the EC Treaty Pt 3 Title VI, Ch 3 (arts 94–97).
31 See the EC Treaty Pt 3 Titles VII–IX (arts 98–134).
32 See the EC Treaty Pt 3 Title X (art 135).
33 See the EC Treaty Pt 3 Title XI (arts 136–150).
34 See the EC Treaty Pt 3 Title XII (art 151).
35 See the EC Treaty Pt 3 Title VI, Ch 1, Section 1 (arts 81–86).
36 See the EC Treaty Pt 3 Title VI, Ch 1, Section 2 (arts 87–89).
37 See the EC Treaty Pt 3 Title VI, Ch 2 (arts 90–93).
38 See the EC Treaty Pt 3 Title VI, Ch 3 (arts 94–97).
39 See the EC Treaty Pt 3 Title VII, Chs 1–3 (arts 98–115).
40 See the EC Treaty Pt 3 Title VIII (arts 125–130).
41 See the EC Treaty Pt 3 Title IX (arts 131–134).
42 See the EC Treaty Pt 3 Title XI, Ch 1 (arts 136–145).
43 See the EC Treaty Pt 3 Title XI, Ch 2 (arts 146–148).
44 See the EC Treaty Pt 3 Title XI, Ch 3 (arts 149–150).
45 See the EC Treaty Pt 3 Title XII (art 151).
46 See the EC Treaty Pt 3 Title XIII (art 152).
47 See the EC Treaty Pt 3 Title XIV (art 153).
48 See the EC Treaty Pt 3 Title XV (arts 154–156).
49 See the EC Treaty Pt 3 Title XVI (art 157).
50 See the EC Treaty Pt 3 Title XVII (arts 158–162).
51 See the EC Treaty Pt 3 Title XVIII (arts 163–173).
52 See the EC Treaty Pt 3 Title XIX (arts 174–176).
53 See the EC Treaty Pt 3 Title XX (arts 177–181).
54 See the EC Treaty Pt 3 Title XXI (art 181a).

55 See the EC Treaty Pt 4 (arts 182–188).
56 See the EC Treaty Pt 5 (arts 189–280).
57 See the EC Treaty Pt 6 (arts 281–314).

(ii) The Competition Rules within the Treaty Framework

26. Tasks and objectives.   Article 2 of the EC Treaty provides a number of tasks which the Community is to have, including the promotion of a harmonious development of economic activities and the raising of living standards[1]. These objectives can, however, provide no more than a general outline of the role of the Community and article 3 is concerned with some of the areas in which these general objectives are to be ensured[2].

Of these, the most relevant for the purposes of competition law is the requirement that the activities of the Community are to include the institution of a system ensuring that competition in the internal market is not distorted[3]. Whilst this statement merely provides the general aim of the competition policy, it forms the basic tenet of that policy and one that is directly referred to in judgments of the Court of Justice[4].

One of the problems of this requirement, however, is whether the competition which is not to be distorted is that of 'free' competition or that of 'fair' competition; the system cannot maintain both. 'Free' competition assumes a *laissez faire* approach to the problem — letting natural market forces of supply and demand find their own levels and ensuring that the strong will prevail over the weak. 'Fair' competition, on the other hand, implies some control of the market to ensure that it develops in accordance with certain pre-determined norms of business behaviour.

As far as Community competition policy is concerned, the basic approach appears to be that of free competition, whilst having rules, particularly in relation to dominant firms, to ensure that the competitive structure of the market is not irreparably damaged by any use of unfair market behaviour.

1   See the EC Treaty art 2. As to the EC Treaty (ie the Treaty establishing the European Community (Rome, 25 March 1957; TS 1 (1973); Cmnd 5179)) see PARA 24 note 1. The numbering for the EC Treaty used in this title is as revised by the Treaty of Amsterdam: see PARA 24 note 1.
2   See the EC Treaty art 3.
3   See the EC Treaty art 3(g).
4   See eg PARAS 27, 60, 73.

27. Treaty provisions dealing with competition.   In implementation of the objectives of the general requirement concerning competition[1], the EC Treaty contains detailed provisions in articles 81 to 94 indicating the types of behaviour which generally will and will not be permitted.

Articles 81 to 85 contain provisions applicable to private firms aimed at ensuring that the creation of effective conditions of competition is not hindered by the erection of barriers or restrictions by the firms themselves. The maintenance of competition is therefore an essential part of the Community's economic and legal order. Where any question of interpretation of these articles arises, they are to be interpreted in accordance with the general provisions of the Treaty[2]. Articles 81 and 82 cannot be interpreted in such a way that they contradict each other because they serve to achieve the same aim[3].

Government procurement is to be made on the basis of non-discrimination, and article 86 provides in the case of public undertakings and undertakings to which member states grant special or exclusive rights, member states must neither enact nor maintain in force any measure contrary to the rules contained in the Treaty[4] — in effect that public enterprises are to be treated no more favourably than private enterprises[5]. In addition, undertakings entrusted with the operation of services of general economic interest or having the character of a revenue producing monopoly are subject to the rules contained in the Treaty, and in particular to the rules on competition, in so far as the application of such rules does not obstruct the performance, in law or in fact, of the particular tasks assigned to them[6].

Articles 87 to 89 are designed to ensure that competition between firms in different member states is not distorted through the granting of state aids[7].

1   Ie the EC Treaty art 3(g) (see PARA 26). As to the EC Treaty (ie the Treaty establishing the European Community (Rome, 25 March 1957; TS 1 (1973); Cmnd 5179)) see PARA 24 note 1. The numbering for the EC Treaty used in this title is as revised by the Treaty of Amsterdam: see PARA 24 note 1.

2   Ie the EC Treaty arts 2, 3(g): Case 311/85 *Vereniging van Vlaamse Reisbureaus v Sociale Dienst van de Plaatselijke en Gewestelijke Overheidsdiensten* [1987] ECR 3801, [1984] 4 CMLR 213, ECJ. As to the EC Treaty arts 83, 84, which set down certain transitional provisions, see PARA 87.

3   Case 6/72 *Europemballage Corpn and Continental Can Co Inc v EC Commission* [1973] ECR 215, [1973] CMLR 199, ECJ.

4   EC Treaty art 86(1).

5   EC Treaty art 86(1). See EC Commission Decision 89/205 (*Magill TV Guide*) OJ L78, 21.3.89, p 43, [1989] 4 CMLR 757; Joined Cases C-241, 242/91P *Radio Telefis Eireann v EC Commission* [1995] ECR I-743, [1995] 4 CMLR 718, ECJ; EC Commission Decision 90/16 (*Express Delivery Services in the Netherlands*) OJ L10, 12.1.90, p 47. This decision was subsequently annulled by the Court of Justice: see Joined Cases C-48, 66/90 *Netherlands v EC Commission* [1992] ECR I-565, [1993] 5 CMLR 316, ECJ.

6   EC Treaty art 86(2). See e g Joined Cases T-528, 542, 543, 546/93 *Métropole Télévision SA v EC Commission* [1996] ECR II-649, [1996] 5 CMLR 386, CFI (decision to grant exemption under art 81(3) not to be based solely upon a criterion defined by reference to art 86(2)).

7   EC Treaty art 87 provides that, save as otherwise provided in the Treaty, any aid granted by a member state or through state resources in any form whatsoever (for example regional aid, sectoral aid, agricultural aid) which distorts or threatens to distort competition by favouring certain undertakings or the production of certain goods is, in so far as it affects trade between member states, incompatible with the common market. Member states are obliged to keep the Commission informed of state aids which they propose to make: see EC Treaty art 88. See also EC Commission Regulation 800/2008 declaring certain categories of aid compatible with the common market in application of Articles 87 and 88 of the Treaty (OJ L214, 9.8.2008, p 3) (the General Block Exemption Regulation) under which numerous state aid measures are exempted from the obligation to be notified to the Commission.

(iii) Community Law and National Law

28.   The supremacy and direct effect of Community law.   The supremacy of Community law over conflicting rules of national law has been a long-established principle of the Community's legal order. The principles of supremacy[1] and direct applicability[2] of Community law have been affirmed by the European Court of Justice. From a comparatively early stage, articles 81 and 82 of the EC Treaty have been directly effective in the member states[3].

1   See Case 6/64 *Costa v ENEL* [1964] ECR 585 at 593–594, [1964] CMLR 425 at 455–456, ECJ: 'By contrast with ordinary international treaties, the [EC] Treaty has created its own legal system which, on the entry into force of the Treaty, became an integral part of the legal systems of the Member States and which their courts are bound to apply.

      By creating a Community of unlimited duration, having its own institutions, its own personality, its own legal capacity and capacity of representation on the international plane and, more particularly, real powers stemming from a limitation of sovereignty or a transfer of powers from the States to the Community, the Member States have limited their sovereign rights albeit within limited fields and have thus created a body of law which binds both their nationals and themselves ...

The precedence of Community law is confirmed by article [249] whereby a regulation 'shall be binding' and 'directly applicable in all Member States'. This provision, which is subject to no reservation, would be quite meaningless if a State could unilaterally nullify its effects by means of a legislative measure which could prevail over Community law.

It follows from all these observations that the law stemming from the Treaty, an independent source of law, could not, because of its special and original nature, be over-ridden by domestic legal provisions, however framed, without being deprived of its character as Community law and without the legal basis of the Community itself being called into question.

The transfer by the States from the domestic legal system to the Community legal system of the rights and obligations arising under the Treaty carries with it the permanent limitation of their sovereign rights against which a subsequent unilateral act incompatible with the concept of the Community cannot prevail. Consequently article [234] is to be applied regardless of any domestic law, whenever questions relating to the interpretation of the Treaty arise'.

See further Case 14/68 *Wilhelm v Bundeskartellamt* [1969] ECR 1, [1969] CMLR 100, ECJ.

2   See Case 106/77 *Administrazione delle Finanze dello Stato v Simmenthal SpA* [1978] ECR 629 at 643, [1978] 3 CMLR 263 at 282–283, ECJ: 'Direct applicability in such circumstances means that rules of Community law must be fully and uniformly applied in all the Member States from the date of their entering into force and for so long as they continue in force.

These provisions are therefore a direct source of rights and duties for all those affected thereby, whether Member States or individuals, who are parties to legal relationships under Community Law ...

Furthermore, in accordance with the principle of the precedence of Community law, the relationship between the provisions of the Treaty and directly applicable measures of the institutions on the one hand and the national law of the Member States on the other is such that those provisions and measures do not only by their entry into force render automatically inapplicable any conflicting provision of current national law but — in so far as they are an integral part of, and take precedence in, the legal order applicable in the territory of each of the Member States — also preclude the valid adoption of new national legislative measures to the extent to which they would be incompatible with Community provisions'.

3   See eg Case 127/73 *Belgische Radio en Televisie v SV SABAM* [1974] ECR 51, [1974] 2 CMLR 238, ECJ; Case C-453/99 *Courage Ltd v Crehan* [2002] QB 507, [2001] All ER (EC) 886, ECJ.

29.   Enforcement and the Modernisation Regulation.   As from 2004, the Modernisation Regulation requires that, in addition to national competition law, national competition authorities[1] must apply the provisions of article 81 of the EC Treaty to agreements, decisions by associations of undertakings or concerted practices, and of article 82 of the EC Treaty to abuses falling within that article[2].

In any national or Community proceedings for the application of articles 81 and 82 of the Treaty, the burden of proving an infringement of article 81(1) or of article 82 of the Treaty rests on the party or the authority alleging the infringement. The undertaking or association of undertakings claiming the benefit of article 81(3) of the Treaty must bear the burden of proving that the conditions of that paragraph are fulfilled[3].

However, the application of national competition law must not, generally speaking, lead to a stricter prohibition of agreements, decisions by associations of undertakings or concerted practices which may affect trade between member states but which do not restrict competition within the meaning of article 81, or which are permitted by reason of or under the criteria set out in that article[4]. Member states are not otherwise precluded by the Modernisation Regulation from adopting and applying on their territory stricter national laws which prohibit or sanction unilateral conduct engaged in by undertakings[5].

This does not apply when the competition authorities and the courts of the member states apply national merger control laws, and does not preclude the application of provisions of national law that predominantly pursue an objective different from that pursued by articles 81 and 82 of the Treaty[6].

Provisions of the Modernisation Regulation set out the enforcement powers and responsibilities of the Commission, national competition authorities and national courts in the implementation and application of articles 81 and 82. The Commission has the specific powers set out in the Regulation[7], while the national competition authorities have the power to apply articles 81 and 82 in individual cases[8]. Specific provision is made for the co-operation between the Commission and the national competition authorities[9], which has included the formation of a network of public authorities (the European Competition Network) which co-ordinates such co-operation and deals with allocation of work among the Commission and national authorities[10]. In particular, if a national competition authority informs the Commission that it intends to adopt a decision based on EC competition law, the Commission may instead initiate proceedings which has the effect of ending the national process[11]. National competition authorities and national courts cannot make decisions or rulings which are contrary to pre-existing or contemplated decisions of the Commission[12].

National courts also have power to apply articles 81 and 82[13]. It appears from this and the authorities that private enforcement, leading to damages, is available in respect of infringement of those articles[14].

The procedural aspects of the enforcement regime under the Modernisation Regulation are discussed subsequently[15].

1   The designated national competition authorities of the United Kingdom are the Office of Fair Trading and the sectoral regulators: see the Competition Act 1998 and Other Enactments (Amendment) Regulations 2004, SI 2004/1261, reg 3. As to the sectoral regulators see the Competition Act 1998 s 54(1); and PARA 147.
2   EC Council Regulation 1/2003 on the implementation of the rules on competition laid down in Articles 81 and 82 of the Treaty (OJ L1, 4.1.03, p 1) (the 'Modernisation Regulation') art 3(1). As to the EC Treaty (ie the Treaty establishing the European Community (Rome, 25 March 1957; TS 1 (1973); Cmnd 5179)) see PARA 24 note 1. The numbering for the EC Treaty used in this title is as revised by the Treaty of Amsterdam: see PARA 24 note 1.
3   EC Council Regulation 1/2003 (OJ L1, 4.1.03, p 1) art 2.
4   EC Council Regulation 1/2003 (OJ L1, 4.1.03, p 1) art 3(2).
5   EC Council Regulation 1/2003 (OJ L1, 4.1.03, p 1) art 3(2).
6   EC Council Regulation 1/2003 (OJ L1, 4.1.03, p 1) art 3(3). See *Days Healthcare UK Ltd v Pihsiang Machinery Manufacturing Co Ltd* [2006] EWHC 1444 (QB), [2006] 4 All ER 233.
7   See EC Council Regulation 1/2003 (OJ L1, 4.1.03, p 1) art 4. As to those powers see further arts 7–10 (Commission decisions), 17–22 (investigations), 23–24 (penalties).
8   See EC Council Regulation 1/2003 (OJ L1, 4.1.03, p 1) art 5.
9   See EC Council Regulation 1/2003 (OJ L1, 4.1.03, p 1) arts 11–16.
10 See the *Notice on NCA cooperation* OJ [2004] C 101/43.
11 See EC Council Regulation 1/2003 (OJ L1, 4.1.03, p 1) art 11(6).
12 See EC Council Regulation 1/2003 (OJ L1, 4.1.03, p 1) art 16.
13 See EC Council Regulation 1/2003 (OJ L1, 4.1.03, p 1) art 6. Specific provision is made outlining the requisite co-operation between the national courts and the Commission: art 15.
14 See eg Case C-453/99 *Courage Ltd v Crehan* [2002] QB 507, [2001] All ER (EC) 886, ECJ; Case C-295–298/04 *Manfredi v Lloyd Adriatico Assicurazione SpA* [2007] All ER (EC) 27, [2006] ECR I-6619, [2006] CMLR 17, ECJ; *Garden Cottage Foods Ltd v Milk Marketing Board* [1984] AC 130, [1983] 2 All ER 770, HL.
15 See PARA 88 et seq.

(iv) European Economic Area

30.   Competition rules. The competition rules of the European Economic Area ('EEA') Agreement[1] mirror those of the EC Treaty as regards:

(1)   restrictive agreements[2];
(2)   abuse of a dominant position[3];
(3)   mergers[4];
(4)   state aids[5]; and
(5)   public undertakings[6].

Secondary legislation corresponds to the equivalent Community legislation. In addition, the Community notices on competition will apply and equivalent notices have been issued by the EFTA Surveillance Authority, the EEA equivalent in competition matters to the Commission[7].

1   Ie the Agreement on the European Economic Area (Oporto, 2 May 1992; Cm 2073 (OJ L1, 3.1.94, p 3)) as adjusted by the Protocol (Brussels, 17 March 1993; Cm 2183 (OJ L1, 3.1.94, p 572)) (the 'EEA Agreement'). The agreement was implemented in the United Kingdom by the European Economic Area Act 1993 which came into force on 5 November 1993. See also PARA 36. The competition rules comprise EEA Agreement, Pt IV, Chs 1, 2, Protocols 21–27 and Annexes XIV–XVI.
2   See the EEA Agreement art 53.
3   See the EEA Agreement art 54.
4   See the EEA Agreement art 57.
5   See the EEA Agreement arts 61–64.
6   See the EEA Agreement art 59.
7   See Decision of the EFTA Surveillance Authority on the issuing of 10 notices and guidelines in the field of competition (OJ L153, 18.6.94, p 1) which deals with: (1) restrictions ancillary to concentrations; (2) concentrative and co-operative operations; (3) exclusive distribution and purchasing; (4) motor vehicles; (5) commercial agents; (6) co-operation; (7) imports from outside the EEA; (8) sub-contracting; (9) agreements of minor importance; and (10) telecommunications. See also Decision of the EFTA Surveillance Authority on the issuing of three notices in the field of competition (OJ L186, 21.7.94, p 57), dealing with co-operative joint ventures and exclusive supply agreements; Notice on Co-operation between the National Courts and the EFTA Surveillance Authority in applying EEA Agreement arts 53, 54 (OJ C112, 1995, p 7).

31.   Jurisdiction.   Rules exist in the European Economic Area ('EEA') Agreement on the division of responsibility as between the EFTA Surveillance Authority and the Commission[1] but it is only in cases of mixed jurisdiction that the rules are necessary. In most cases it will be the Commission that will have jurisdiction.

Decisions of the Commission applying the EEA competition rules are subject to control and review by the Court of First Instance and the Court of Justice; those of the EFTA Surveillance Authority by the EFTA Court[2].

1   EEA Agreement art 56(1)(a), (c). As to the EEA Agreement see PARA 30 note 1.
2   See eg the Decision of the EFTA Surveillance Authority (OJ L231, 3.9.94, p 1 (as amended)) on state aids annulled by the EFTA Court in Case E-2/94 *Scottish Salmon Growers Association Ltd v EFTA Surveillance Authority* [1995] 1 CMLR 851, EFTA Ct.

(2) COMMON PRINCIPLES

(i) The Relevant Market

32.   The 'relevant market'.   The application and interpretation of competition law is primarily concerned with the exercise of market power; and for the purposes of assessing market power, it is necessary for the relevant market to be ascertainable, in terms of the relevant product market, geographical market and sometimes the temporal market[1].

In December 1997 the Commission published its Notice on the Definition of the Relevant Market for the purposes of Community Competition Law[2].

On a geographical front, the notice states that in determining the relevant market the Commission will generally look at: (1) the distribution of market shares; and (2) price differences. This will then be tested against an analysis of demand characteristics: past evidence of diversion of orders to other areas; basic demand characteristics; views of customers and competitors concerning the boundary of the geographic market; current geographic patterns of purchases of actual customers; trade flows in cases where the number of customers is high; barriers and switching costs, in particular transport costs[3].

On a market front, the notice states that the main purpose of market definition is 'to identify in a systematic way the competitive restraints that the undertakings face' through the identification of those actual competitors who are capable of constraining their behaviour and preventing them from behaving independently of effective competitive pressure. In arriving at this determination, the Commission will consider both the products from which that restraint derives and the geographic market in which it operates. Overall, the notice talks about demand and supply substitution but, interestingly, makes it clear that potential competition is not to be taken into account since the extent to which potential competitors can provide a restraining influence will be very dependent on market entry barriers[4].

1   See e g Case 6/72 *Europemballage Corpn and Continental Can Co Inc v EC Commission* [1973] ECR 215, [1973] CMLR 199, ECJ; Case 27/76 *United Brands Co v EC Commission* [1978] ECR 207, [1978] 1 CMLR 429, ECJ; Case C-234/89 *Delimitis v Henninger Bräu AG* [1991] ECR I-935, [1992] 5 CMLR 210, ECJ.
2   EC Commission Notice on the Definition of the Relevant Market for the purposes of Community Competition Law (OJ C372, 9.12.97, p 5). See also Case 247/86 *Société Alsacienne et Lorraine de Télécommunications et d'Electronique (ALSATEL) v Novasam SA* [1988] ECR 5987, [1990] 4 CMLR 434, ECJ.
3   EC Commission Notice on the Definition of the Relevant Market for the purposes of Community Competition Law (OJ C372, 9.12.97, p 5).
4   EC Commission Notice on the Definition of the Relevant Market for the purposes of Community Competition Law (OJ C372, 9.12.97, p 5).

(ii) Scope of European Competition Law

A. GEOGRAPHICAL

33.   Application within Community territory. The competition rules of the European Community apply in the 27 member states: Austria, Belgium, Bulgaria, Cyprus, Czech Republic, Denmark (but excluding the Faeroe Islands[1] and Greenland[2]), Estonia, Finland, Germany (both what was the Federal Republic as well as what was the German Democratic Republic since 30 October 1990), France (including French Overseas Departments (Reunion, Guadeloupe, Guiana, Martinique and Saint-Pierre-et-Miquelon) but not the dependant overseas territories[3]), Greece, Hungary, Ireland, Italy, Latvia, Lithuania, Luxembourg, Malta, the Netherlands (excluding the Netherlands Antilles), Poland, Portugal (including the Azores and Madeira but not Macao[4]), Romania, Slovenia, Slovakia, Spain (including the Canary Islands, Ceuta and Melilla, which are cities on the Mediterranean coast of Morocco and are autonomous regions of Spain), Sweden and the United Kingdom (including Gibraltar) (although the position of the Channel Islands and the Isle of Man is slightly different[5]). Andorra[6], Monaco[7], San Marino, the Vatican City and the sovereign base areas of the United Kingdom in Cyprus[8] and the member states are almost certainly also covered by the extra-territorial reach of competition rules.

1   EC Treaty art 299 (originally added by the Act of Accession (1972) and applied by the Act of
     Accession of Denmark art 26); Act of Accession (1972), Protocols 2, 4. As to the EC Treaty
     (ie the Treaty establishing the European Community (Rome, 25 March 1957; TS 1 (1973);
     Cmnd 5179)) see PARA 24 note 1. The numbering for the EC Treaty used in this title is as revised
     by the Treaty of Amsterdam: see PARA 24 note 1.
2   Treaty amending, with regard to Greenland, the Treaties establishing the European
     Communities and Protocol on special arrangements for Greenland (Brussels, 13 March 1984;
     EC 19 (1985); Cmnd 9490; OJ L29, 1.2.85, p1).
3   EC Treaty art 299.
4   See Answer to Written Question 401/85 (OJ C251/85, p 26).
5   EC Treaty art 299 (as applied by the Act of Accession (1972) art 26 and Protocol 3 annexed
     thereto).
6   EC Treaty art 299.
7   See Answer to Written Questions 191/78 (OJ C238/78, p 14) and 113/81 (OJ C153/81, p 19).
8   See Answer to Written Question 213/81 (OJ C210/81, p 14).

34.   Extra-territoriality.   In several cases, the Commission has also sought to
exercise its powers under articles 81 and 82 of the EC Treaty[1] against
undertakings from non-member states. The Court of Justice has upheld the
jurisdiction over these undertakings in competition matters subject to the
requirement that the agreement etc in question must have 'affected trade between
member states'[2]. In practice, however, most jurisprudence has been based on the
'economic entity doctrine' rather than on the 'effects doctrine'[3].

The fact that the Commission seeks to exercise jurisdiction over such
companies does not, however, mean that it is able to obtain information from
them and conduct investigations at their premises outside the Community[4].
Where the Commission sends requests for information to an undertaking outside
the Community, the enforcement of such request[5] is a delicate matter normally
dealt with through diplomatic channels. Thus, in one case, the Commission
ordered the undertakings concerned 'to refrain from implementing the notified
arrangements in the [European Community]'[6].

As far as the enforcement of decisions against undertakings outside the
Community is concerned, once a final decision has been taken under article 81 or
82, the Commission will serve that decision at the registered office or place of
business within the Community of the undertaking complained against or of one
of its subsidiaries[7]. For the purposes of Community competition policy the
Commission and the Court of Justice treat groups of undertakings as a single
entity and the strict legal separation of parent and subsidiary is not a concept
that the competition authorities of the Community regard as restricting them in
this matter[8].

Latterly the EC has entered into agreements with other states or groups of
states a purpose of which is to develop international co-operation in the
prevention of anti-competitive practices[9]. Such agreements reduce the need to
apply rules of extra-territoriality.

1   As to the EC Treaty (ie the Treaty establishing the European Community (Rome, 25 March
     1957; TS 1 (1973); Cmnd 5179)) see PARA 24 note 1. The numbering for the EC Treaty used in
     this title is as revised by the Treaty of Amsterdam: see PARA 24 note 1. As to art 81 see PARA 61
     et seq; and as to art 82 see PARA 68 et seq.
2   EC Commission Decision 70/332 (*Kodak*) OJ L147, 7.7.70, p 24, [1970] CMLR D19.
3   EC Commission Decision 69/243 (*Aniline Dyestuffs Cartel*) OJ L195, 7.8.69, p 11, [1969]
     CMLR D23. For a case where the application of the EC Treaty art 81 outside the Community
     was confirmed see Joined Cases 89, 104, 116, 117, 125–129/85 *Ahlström Osakeyhtö v EC
     Commission* [1988] ECR 5193, [1988] 4 CMLR 901, ECJ.
4   Ie under EC Council Regulation 17 of 6 February 1962 (OJ 1962 p 204 (S Edn 1959–1962
     p 87)) art 4, para 2(1).

5   Ie under a decision under EC Council Regulation 17 of 6 February 1962 (OJ 1962 p 204 (S Edn 1959–1962 p 87)) art 11.
6   See EC Commission Decision 91/301 (*ANSAC*) OJ L152, 15.6.91, p 54. This reflected the limits on Community jurisdiction articulated in Joined Cases 89, 104, 116, 117, 125–129/85 *Ahlström Osakeyhtö v EC Commission* [1988] ECR 5193, [1988] 4 CMLR 901, ECJ (the *Woodpulp* case).
7   EC Commission Decision 89/190 (*PVC*) OJ L74, 17.3.89, p 1.
8   EC Commission Decision 69/243 (*Aniline Dyestuffs Cartel*) OJ L195, 7.8.69, p 11, [1969] CMLR D23. See also EC Commission Decision 85/206 (*Aluminium Imports from Eastern Europe*) OJ L92, 30.3.85, p 1; and EC Commission Decision 72/21 (*Continental Can Co*) OJ L7, 8.1.72, p 25, [1972] CMLR D11. See also PARA 61 et seq.
9   See PARA 35 et seq.

35.   Bilateral agreements with non-member states. In addition to the application of the Community rules on competition throughout the member states, the Community has also negotiated a number of bilateral agreements with non-member states in Europe that contain provisions on competition law, a number of which have been superseded by the EEA Agreement[1] or by the accession of the state in question to the EC[2]. These included an association agreement between the Community and Turkey[3].

A trade agreement which contains provisions on competition law was entered into between the Community and Switzerland[4]. Joint committees are established which are responsible for the administration of the agreement but their activity in the sphere of competition has been minimal.

The Commission has applied articles 81 and 82 of the EC Treaty to enterprises established in Switzerland after the conclusion of the trade agreement in question but without applying the agreement[5].

The legal effect of the trade agreements has been unclear but, since a decision of the Court of Justice in 1982, it does appear that the trade agreements, and in particular the competition clauses contained therein, are not directly applicable either in the member states or in such non-member state[6].

1   See PARA 36.
2   Such was the case in relation to Austria, Finland, Greece, Portugal and Sweden. This was also the position in relation to the 'Europe' Agreements made between the EC and Poland, the Czech and Slovak Republics, Hungary, Romania, Bulgaria, Estonia, Lithuania, Latvia and Slovenia.
3   Agreement establishing an Association between the EC and Turkey (OJ 1964 p 3687; OJ C113, 24.12.73, p 2). Competition matters are now largely governed by Decision No 1/95 of the Association Council (1995) between the EU and Turkey on implementing the final phase of the Customs Union (OJ L35, 13.2.1996, p 1). Turkey entered into accession negotiations in 2005.
4   Agreement establishing an Association between the EC and the Swiss Confederation (Brussels, 22 July 1972; OJ L 300, 31.12.72, p 189 (S Edn 1972 (31 December) (1) p 191)).
5   EC Commission Decision 76/642 (*Hoffmann-La Roche (Vitamins)*) OJ L223, 16.8.76, p 27, [1976] 2 CMLR D25.
6   See Case 270/80 *Polydor Ltd v Harlequin Record Shops Ltd* [1982] ECR 329, [1982] 1 CMLR 677, ECJ (the *Polydor* case), which dealt with the Portuguese Trade Agreement.

36.   European Economic Area Agreement. In September 1992 the member states of the European Community and the seven European Free Trade Association ('EFTA') countries (Norway, Sweden, Finland, Austria, Switzerland, Liechtenstein and Iceland) entered into the European Economic Area ('EEA') Agreement[1] to replace the various bilateral free trade agreements which had been entered into. Austria, Finland and Sweden have since become members of the EC. Due to non-ratification, Switzerland remains outside the EEA Agreement.

The EEA Agreement contains provisions mirroring those of the EC Treaty[2] in relation to restrictive agreements[3], abuse of a dominant position[4], mergers[5], state aids[6] and public undertakings[7]. Secondary legislation including that dealing with block exemptions also exists mirroring those of the Community[8].

Like articles 81 and 82 of the EC Treaty, the EEA competition rules have direct effect and can be invoked by individuals before national courts. Their provisions are to be interpreted in accordance with the judgments of the Court of Justice prior to September 1992.

The EEA Agreement sets upon the EFTA Surveillance Authority the responsibility to administer the agreement's competition rules, although a complex set of jurisdictional provisions exists to delimit cases between the European Commission and the Surveillance Authority[9].

1 Ie the Agreement on the European Economic Area (Oporto, 2 May 1992; Cm 2073 (OJ L1, 3.1.94, p 3)) as adjusted by the Protocol (Brussels, 17 March 1993; Cm 2183 (OJ L1, 3.1.94, p 572)) (the 'EEA Agreement'). The agreement was implemented in the United Kingdom by the European Economic Area Act 1993 which came into force on 5 November 1993. The remaining members of EFTA are Norway, Switzerland, Liechtenstein and Iceland.
2 As to the EC Treaty (ie the Treaty establishing the European Community (Rome, 25 March 1957; TS 1 (1973); Cmnd 5179)) see PARA 24 note 1. The numbering for the EC Treaty used in this title is as revised by the Treaty of Amsterdam: see PARA 24 note 1. As to art 81 see PARA 61 et seq; and as to art 82 see PARA 68 et seq.
3 See the EEA Agreement art 53.
4 See the EEA Agreement art 54.
5 See the EEA Agreement art 57.
6 See the EEA Agreement arts 61–64.
7 See the EEA Agreement art 59.
8 See the EEA Agreement art 56, Protocols 21, 23 and 24 and Annex XIV.
9 See PARA 31.

37. The Euro-Mediterranean agreements. The Commission has negotiated agreements with Morocco[1], Tunisia[2], Israel[3], Egypt[4], Algeria[5], Lebanon[6], Jordan[7] and the Palestinian Authority[8], and is negotiating with Syria.

1 See the Euro-Mediterranean Agreement between the EU and Morocco (OJ L70, 18.3.2000, p 2).
2 See the Euro-Mediterranean Agreement between the EU and Tunisia (OJ L97, 30.3.98, p 2).
3 See the Euro-Mediterranean Agreement between the EU and Israel (OJ L147, 21.06.2000, p 3).
4 See the Euro-Mediterranean Agreement establishing an Association between the EU and Egypt (25 June 2001).
5 See the Euro-Mediterranean Agreement establishing an Association between the EU and Algeria (OJ L265, 10.10.2005, p 2).
6 See the Euro-Mediterranean Association Agreement between the EU and Lebanon (OJ L143, 30.05.2006, p 2).
7 See the Euro-Mediterranean Agreement between the EU and Jordan (OJ L129, 15.5.2002, p 3).
8 See the Euro-Mediterranean Interim Association Agreement between the EU and the West Bank and Gaza Strip (OJ L187, 16.7.97, p 3).

38. Partnership and cooperation agreements. Partnership and cooperation agreements have been entered into between the European Community and a number of other countries which cover, amongst other matters, restrictions on competition by undertakings, state aid, public undertakings and undertakings with exclusive rights. Such agreements have been entered into with the following countries: Armenia[1], Azerbaijan[2], Georgia[3], Moldova[4] and Ukraine[5].

1 See the Partnership and Cooperation Agreement between the EU and Armenia (OJ L239, 9.9.99, p 3).
2 See the Partnership and Cooperation Agreement between the EU and Azerbaijan (OJ L246, 17.9.99, p 1).
3 See the Partnership and Cooperation Agreement between the EU and Georgia (OJ L205, 4.8.99, p 3).

4   See the Partnership and Cooperation Agreement between the EU and Moldova (OJ L181, 24.6.98, p 3).
5   See the Partnership and Cooperation Agreement between the EU and Ukraine (OJ L49, 19.2.98, p 3).

39. Stabilisation and association agreements. Relations between the Western Balkan countries and the European Community are governed by the stabilisation and association process which provides a framework in which the countries progress towards closer association with the EU. This framework, amongst other matters, sets out rights and obligations in areas such as competition and state aid rules. Stabilisation and association agreements have been entered into with the following countries: Albania[1], Bosnia and Herzegowina[2], Croatia[3], the former Yugoslav Republic of Macedonia[4] and Montenegro[5] and negotiations are in process with Serbia.

1   Signed on 12 June 2006.
2   Signed on 4 December 2007.
3   Signed in October 2001.
4   Signed in April 2001.
5   Signed on 15 October 2007.

40. Latin and Central American agreements. In Latin and Central America, framework co-operation agreements have been entered into with Mercosur[1], the Andean Community[2], Central American Republics[3] and Argentina[4]. The Commission has concluded a global agreement with Mexico[5] and an association agreement with Chile[6].

1   Mercosur, known as the 'Southern Common Market', was created by the Treaty of Asunción signed by Argentina, Brazil, Paraguay and Uruguay in the Paraguayan capital on 26 March 1991. Chile and Bolivia became associate members in 1996 and 1997 respectively (signed 15 December 1995).
2   OJ C25, 21.1.93. In June 2007 negotiations began on a new agreement which is yet to be concluded.
3   OJ C177, 18.3.93. See also the Political Dialogue and Co-operation Agreement (signed Brussels, 2 October 2003). In 2007 negotiations began on a new agreement which is yet to be concluded.
4   Signed on 2 April 1990 (OJ L295, 26.10.90).
5   See the Economic Partnership, Political Coordination and Cooperation Agreement between the EU and Mexico (OJ L276, 28.10.2000, p 44).
6   See the Association Agreement between the EU and Chile (OJ L352, 30.12.2002, p 3).

41. Agreement with South Africa. In 1999 the Commission concluded a free trade agreement containing provisions on competition and state aid with South Africa[1].

1   See the Agreement on Trade, Development and Cooperation between the EU and South Africa (OJ L311, 4.12.99, p 3).

42. Agreements with the United States of America. In 1991 the Commission concluded a bilateral agreement with the United States of America[1] which was ratified by the Council in 1995 following a decision of the Court of Justice in 1994 that the Commission did not have the competence to enter into the agreement[2].

The purpose of the agreement is to promote co-operation and co-ordination and lessen the possibility or impact of differences between the United States and the European Community in the application of their competition laws. It has specific provisions in relation to notification, exchange of information and co-operation and co-ordination. The agreement contains provisions on confidentiality, but there remains concern that information passed to United States authorities might be used against European companies.

On 4 June 1998 the Community entered into an agreement with the United States on the application of positive comity principles in the enforcement of their competition laws[3]. This agreement elaborates on the principles of positive comity referred to in the 1991 agreement[4] and defines methods for their implementation. Its aim is to enhance the effectiveness of the 1991 agreement in relation to anti-competitive behaviour but it does not apply to mergers.

1 See the EU/US Competition Cooperation Agreement (OJ L132, 15.6.95, p 47).
2 Case C-327/91 *France v EC Commission* [1994] ECR I-3641, [1994] 5 CMLR 517, ECJ. See further PARA 34.
3 See the EU/US Agreement on the application of positive comity principles in the enforcement of their competition laws (OJ L173, 18.6.98, p 28).
4 See note 1.

43.   Agreement with Canada.   On 29 April 1999 the Community entered into an agreement with Canada[1] that provides for a framework of co-operation between the competition authorities of the Community and of Canada[2].

1 See the Agreement between the European Communities and the Government of Canada regarding the application of their competition laws (OJ L175, 10.7.99, p 50).
2 In an exchange of letters made contemporaneously between the Commission and the Government of Canada, it is made clear that, under the agreement, no information may be provided by the Commission, if it were covered by EC Council Regulation 17 of 6 February 1962 (OJ 1962 p 204 (S Edn 1959–1962 p 87)) art 20, without the consent of the source concerned. Equally, Canada will not provide information under the agreement if it could not have been provided in its absence.

44.   Agreement with Japan.   Cooperation with the Japan Fair Trade Commission is based on the Cooperation Agreement signed in July 2003[1]. The Agreement provides for notification of cases under investigation, coordination of enforcement activities and the exchange of information.

1 See the Agreement between the EU and Japan concerning cooperation on anti-competitive activities (OJ L183, 22.7.2003, p 12).

45.   Agreement with the Russian Federation.   Relations with the Russian Federation in the field of competition are primarily governed by the terms of the Partnership and Cooperation Agreement between the EU and the Russian Federation, which entered into force in December 1997[1]. The agreement covers restrictions on competition by undertakings, state aid and monopolies of a commercial character.

1 See the Partnership and Cooperation Agreement between the EU and the Russian Federation (OJ L327, 28.11.97, p 3).

46.   Effect of agreements.   Most of the bilateral agreements between the Commission and other countries contain competition provisions in almost identical terms providing that the following are incompatible with the proper functioning of such agreements:

(1)   all agreements between undertakings, decisions by associations of undertakings and concerted practices between undertakings which have as their object or effect the prevention, restriction or distortion of competition;

(2)   abuse by one or more undertakings of a dominant position in the territories of the Community or of the other signatory as a whole or in a substantial part thereof;

(3)   any official aid which distorts or threatens to distort competition by favouring certain undertakings or the production of certain goods[1].

Their wording is almost identical to that contained in the EC Treaty and in the agreement with Morocco for example, it is provided that:

' ... any practices contrary to this Article shall be assessed on the basis of criteria arising from the application of the rules of Articles [81, 82 and 87] of the [EC Treaty]'[2].

Given that the described practices are not prohibited but merely 'incompatible with the proper functioning of the agreement'[3], it is unlikely that these rules would have direct effect.

1   See eg Euro-Mediterranean Agreement between the EU and Morocco (OJ L70, 18.3.2000, p 2) art 36.
2   See eg Euro-Mediterranean Agreement between the EU and Morocco (OJ L70, 18.3.2000, p 2) art 36(2).
3   See eg Euro-Mediterranean Agreement between the EU and Morocco (OJ L70, 18.3.2000, p 2) art 36(1).

47.   Confidentiality and disclosure.   One of the major issues of concern with each of the co-operation agreements into which the Community has entered[1] is the question of confidentiality and disclosure or sharing of information between regulators in different jurisdictions whose powers of investigation and inquiry may vary dramatically and whose powers (and those of the courts) to impose penalties, fines and damages vary significantly.

Reference has been made above to the side letters in the agreement with Canada[2] and similar declarations have been made for agreements with the United States of America[3]. However, concern remains that despite such undertakings, information may be passed which could be detrimental to the interests of businesses. This concern was reinforced by the statement made by the Commission in its Report to the Council for the period July to December 1996 on the operation of the agreement between the Community and the United States to the effect that the restriction on exchange of information (that it is confidential) curtails the effectiveness of co-operation and that the Commission was investigating the possibility of overcoming the existing obstacles to the exchange of confidential information.

1   See PARA 40 et seq.
2   See PARA 43.
3   See PARA 42.

B. FIELD OF APPLICATION

48.   Extent of coverage.   The EC Treaty is applicable to all types and aspects of economic life[1]. It is, however, concerned only with commercial matters. Nonetheless, non profit-making organisations may fall within the scope of the Community rules if parts of their activities are normal business activities; the competition rules are applicable both to the production of goods and to the provision of services[2]. The competition provisions apply to the agreements and behaviour of undertakings[3], though there are a number exceptions relating to specific fields[4].

The Treaty provisions apply equally to the activities of professional bodies as any other entity or business form[5].

1   As to the EC Treaty (ie the Treaty establishing the European Community (Rome, 25 March 1957; TS 1 (1973); Cmnd 5179)) see PARA 24 note 1.

2   Case 45/85 *Verband der Sachversicherer eV v EC Commission* [1987] ECR 405, [1988]
    4 CMLR 264, ECJ; EC Commission Decision 90/22 *(TEKO)* OJ L13, 17.1.90, p 34; EC
    Commission Decision 90/25 *(Concordato Incendio)* OJ L15, 19.1.90, p 25, [1991] 4 CMLR
    199; *Halifax Building Society (Twenty-first Report on Competition Policy 1991,* Annex III,
    p 335); EC Commission Decision 92/212 *(Eurocheque)* OJ L95, 9.4.92, p 50 (partially annulled
    on other grounds by Joined Cases T-39, 40/92 *Groupement des Cartes Bancaires 'CB' v EC
    Commission* [1994] ECR II-49, CFI); EC Commission Decision 92/521 *(FIFA)* OJ L326,
    12.11.92, p 1.
3   See PARA 59.
4   See PARA 49 et seq.
5   Case C-35/96 *EC Commission v Italy* [1998] ECR I-3851, [1998] 5 CMLR 889, ECJ.
        On 30 January 1995 the Commission took a decision under the EC Treaty art 81 applying
    the competition rules against the Colegio Oficial de Agentes de la Propiedad Industrial (Coapi),
    the professional association of industrial property agents in Spain. All agents practising in Spain
    are members. Such agents give advice to the public, and assist or represent clients in proceedings
    involving industrial property rights. The Commission found that the fixing by the general
    meeting of Coapi of compulsory minimum scales of charges for the cross-border services
    provided by its members constituted an infringement of the EC Treaty art 81. The Commission
    confirmed that the national legal framework, within which such agreements or decisions by
    liberal professions are made, is not relevant to the application of art 81. Even if public
    authorities encourage such behaviour or delegate to an association of undertakings the power to
    fix the prices to be applied by its members, the association's exercise of that power does not fall
    outside the scope of art 81: EC Commission Decision 95/188 *(Colegio Oficial de Agentes de la
    Propiedad Industria (Coapi))* OJ L122, 2.6.95, p 35.

49.   Sport. In July 1998 the Commission issued guidelines on the application
of the Community competition rules to the broadcasting of sports events[1] and in
February 1999 it issued its preliminary conclusions on the application of the
competition rules to sports[2]. This followed a judgment of the Court of Justice on
freedom of movement for professional footballers[3]. In the Commission's opinion,
the principles and legitimate objectives recognised in that case would not be
impaired by the application of the community competition rules. The
compatibility of sporting rules with EC competition law should be examined on
a case-by-case basis in order to establish whether the rule breaches EC
competition law or not[4].

1   See *Competition Policy Newsletter (No 2) 1998.* See, however, EC Commission Decision 00/12
    (Comité Français d'Organisation de la Coupe du Monde de Football 1998) OJ L5, 8.1.2000,
    p 55, where the Commission imposed a fine of only EUR 1,000 against the French organising
    committee for the 1998 football world cup following upon a ticket allocation system which
    favoured applicants with an address in France.
2   EC Commission Press Notice IP (99)133 of 24 February 1999. For a case where the EC Treaty
    arts 81, 82 were held by the English court to have been infringed in relation to the activities of
    a professional snooker players' association see *Hendry v World Professional Billiards and
    Snooker Association* [2001] All ER (D) 71 (Oct). As to the EC Treaty (ie the Treaty establishing
    the European Community (Rome, 25 March 1957; TS 1 (1973); Cmnd 5179)) see PARA 24 note
    1.
3   Case C-415/93 *Union Royale Belge des Sociétés de Football Association ASBL v Bosman* [1996]
    All ER (EC) 97, [1995] ECR I-4921, [1996] 1 CMLR 645, ECJ.
4   See Case C-519/04 P *Meca-Medina v EC Commission* [2006] All ER (EC) 1057, [2006]
    5 CMLR 1023, ECJ.

50.   Nuclear energy. The Euratom Treaty[1] does not contain rules on
competition policy or deal with its implementation and, accordingly, agreements
between undertakings in or relative to matters affecting the provision of atomic
energy and, therefore, within the Euratom Treaty will be dealt with in
accordance with the competition rules contained in the EC Treaty[2].
    The EC Commission has announced a series of initiatives relating to energy
which are designed to create an open market for electricity and other forms of

energy. European Council Directives have now established common rules for the generation, transmission, distribution and supply of electricity[3] and for the internal market in natural gas[4]; and a European Regulation has laid down conditions for access to the network for cross-border exchanges in electricity[5].

1   Ie the Treaty establishing the European Atomic Energy Community (Rome, 25 March 1957; TS 1 (1973); Cmnd 5179).
2   EC Commission Decision 76/249 (*KEWA*) OJ L51, 26.2.76, p 15, [1976] 2 CMLR D15; EC Commission Decision 76/248 (*United Reprocessors*) OJ L51, 26.2.76, p 7, [1976] 2 CMLR D1; EC Commission Decision 91/329 (*Scottish Nuclear*) OJ L178, 6.7.91, p 31. As to the EC Treaty (ie the Treaty establishing the European Community (Rome, 25 March 1957; TS 1 (1973); Cmnd 5179)) see PARA 24 note 1.
3   See European Parliament and EC Council Directive 2003/54 (OJ L176, 15.7.2003, p 37) concerning common rules for the internal market in electricity. In the United Kingdom, that Directive is implemented by certain provisions of the Electricity Act 1989 and by the Electricity (Fuel Mix Disclosure) Regulations 2005, SI 2005/391. See FUEL AND ENERGY vol 19(1) (2007 Reissue) PARA 653.
4   See European Parliament and EC Council Directive 2003/55 (OJ L176, 15.7.2003, p 57) concerning common rules for the internal market in natural gas. In the United Kingdom, that Directive is implemented by certain provisions of the Gas Acts 1986 and 1995, the Petroleum Act 1998, the Utilities Act 2000 and the Energy Act 2004. See FUEL AND ENERGY vol 19(1) (2007 Reissue) PARA 653.
5   See European Parliament and EC Council Regulation 1228/2003 (OJ L176, 15.7.2003, p 1) on conditions for access to the network for cross-border exchanges in electricity. See FUEL AND ENERGY vol 19(1) (2007 Reissue) PARA 653.

51.   Agriculture.   Under the EC Treaty, the rules on competition apply to the production of and trade in agricultural products[1] only to the extent determined by the Council within the prescribed framework[2] and in accordance with the procedure laid down therein, account being taken of the objectives of the Common Agricultural Policy[3]. In implementing these provisions, articles 81 to 86 of the Treaty have been declared applicable to the agricultural sector, subject to certain exceptions to the application of article 81[4].

1   As to agricultural products see the EC Treaty art 32(3), Annex I. As to the EC Treaty (ie the Treaty establishing the European Community (Rome, 25 March 1957; TS 1 (1973); Cmnd 5179)) see PARA 24 note 1.
2   EC Treaty art 36.
3   EC Treaty art 33. As to the objectives of the Common Agricultural Policy see AGRICULTURAL PRODUCTION AND MARKETING vol 1 (2008) PARA 704.
4   See EC Council Regulation 1184/2006 (OJ L214, 4.8.2006, p 7); EC Council Regulation 1234/2007 (OJ L299, 16.11.2007, p 1); and AGRICULTURAL PRODUCTION AND MARKETING vol 1 (2008) PARA 704.

52.   Transport.   In general terms, the competition rules of the EC Treaty[1] apply to the transport sector, by means of regulations enabling the application of articles 81 and 82 to (1) inland transport[2]; (2) maritime transport[3]; and (3) air transport[4]. The procedural rules in the transport sector have been brought into alignment with the general rules of procedure in all sectors by the Modernisation Regulation[5].

1   As to the EC Treaty (ie the Treaty establishing the European Community (Rome, 25 March 1957; TS 1 (1973); Cmnd 5179)) see PARA 24 note 1.
2   See EC Council Regulation 1017/68 (OJ Sp Ed, 1968) 302.
3   See EC Council Regulation 1419/2006 (OJ L269, 28.9.2006, p1) which, together with the Modernisation Regulation, removes previous exemptions from the application of competition rules to maritime transport. In 1986 the Council enacted a regulation on unfair pricing practices in maritime transport: see EC Council Regulation 4057/86 (OJ L378, 31.12.86, p 14). See also *Hyundai Merchant Marine Co* [1988] 1 CMLR 389.

4   See EC Council Regulation 411/2004 (OJ L68, 6.3.2004, p1) which, together with the
    Modernisation Regulation, removes previous exemptions from the application of competition
    rules to air transport. It should be noted that the Commission's power to enforce competition
    law applies to all routes, not just those between airports which are within the European Union.
5   See EC Council Regulation 1/2003 (OJ L1, 4.1.2003, p 1) on the implementation of the rules on
    competition laid down in Articles 81 and 82 of the Treaty (the 'Modernisation Regulation')
    (amended by EC Council Regulation 1419/2006 (OJ L269, 28.9.2006, p 1)). The direct
    applicability of the EC Treaty art 81 to air transport was established by Joined Cases
    209–213/84 *Ministère Public v Asjes* [1986] ECR 1425, [1986] 3 CMLR 173, ECJ; Cases 66/86
    *Ahmed Saeed Flugreisen and Silver Line Reisbüro GmbH v Zentrale zur Bekämpfung
    Unlauteren Wettbewerbs eV* [1989] ECR 803, [1990] 4 CMLR 102, ECJ.

53.   Public undertakings. According to the EC Treaty, public undertakings are
subject to the rules of competition contained in the Treaty, with the exception of
undertakings entrusted with the operation of services of general economic
interest or having the character of a revenue producing monopoly[1]. In fact, this
exception has been very strictly interpreted[2].

1   EC Treaty art 86. For a case where the application of the EC Treaty art 82 was extended by
    art 86, which was also infringed see Case C-18/88 *Régie des Télégraphes et des Téléphones
    (RTT) v GB-Inno-BM-SA* [1991] ECR I-5941, ECJ. As to the EC Treaty (ie the Treaty
    establishing the European Community (Rome, 25 March 1957; TS 1 (1973); Cmnd 5179)) see
    PARA 24 note 1. See also EC Regulation 1370/2007 of the European Parliament and of the
    Council on public passenger transport services by rail and by road (OJ L315, 3.12.2007, p 1). A
    public authority is not a public undertaking, and therefore is not subject to the competition
    rules: see PARA 59.
2   See Case 127/73 *Belgische Radio en Televisie v SV SABAM* [1974] ECR 51, [1974] 2 CMLR
    238, ECJ. See also EC Commission Decision 90/456 (*Courier Services in Spain*) OJ L233,
    28.8.90, p 19, [1991] 4 CMLR 560; Case T-513/93 *Consiglio Nazionale Degli Spedizionieri
    Doganali v EC Commission (Associazione Italiana dei Corrieri Aerei Internazionali intervening)*
    [2000] ECR II-1807, [2000] 3 CMLR 614, CFI (customs agents were 'undertakings'); Case
    C-475/99 *Ambulanz Glöckner v Landkreis Südwestpfalz* [2001] ECR I-8089, [2002] 4 CMLR
    726, ECJ (medical aid organisation entrusted with public ambulance service in Germany).

54.   Arbitration. Even if the parties have provided within their agreement for
some form of binding arbitration, this will not prevent the application of the
rules of articles 81 and 82 of the EC Treaty both to the underlying agreement
and to any settlement proposed by the arbiter[1].

1   See Case C-126/97 *Eco Swiss China Time Ltd v Benetton International NV* [1999] 2 All ER
    (Comm) 44, [1999] ECR I-3055, ECJ. As to the EC Treaty (ie the Treaty establishing the
    European Community (Rome, 25 March 1957; TS 1 (1973); Cmnd 5179)) see PARA 24 note 1.

(iii)   The Concept of Trade between Member States

55.   Introduction. For the EC competition law prohibitions[1] to be invoked the
behaviour must have an appreciable effect on trade between member states[2].
Since the entry into force of the Modernisation Regulation[3], if an agreement or
practice has such effect and the application of those articles is therefore
established, national competition authorities[4] and national courts must apply
those articles in addition to domestic competition law[5].

The question of whether particular behaviour may affect trade between
member states is therefore of first importance, both for establishing whether EC
law or domestic law (or both) is to be applied, and for determining which
authority is to take action. To that end, the Commission has issued guidelines
which set out the basis for answering that question, by reference to the questions
of what amounts to 'trade', whether the behaviour in question 'may affect' trade,
and whether it does so 'appreciably'[6].

1   Ie EC Treaty arts 81, 82. As to the EC Treaty (ie the Treaty establishing the European Community (Rome, 25 March 1957; TS 1 (1973); Cmnd 5179)) see PARA 24 note 1.

2   See EC Treaty arts 81(1), 82(1).

3   Ie EC Council Regulation 1/2003 on the implementation of the rules on competition laid down in Articles 81 and 82 of the Treaty (OJ L1, 4.1.03, p 1) (the 'Modernisation Regulation').

4   As to the national competition authorities see PARA 29 note 1.

5   See EC Council Regulation 1/2003 (OJ L1, 4.1.03, p 1) art 3(1). As to that provision, the separation and sharing of competencies between the Commission and national competition authorities and the circumstances to which it does not apply see PARA 29.

6   See the *Guidelines on inter-state trade* OJ [2004] C101/81.

56. Meaning of 'trade'. The starting point is to determine what the EC Treaty means by 'trade'. The notion is one of more than the purchase and supply of goods; 'trade' encompasses the production and distribution of all types of product, including agricultural products[1]. 'Trade' includes the provision of services of all types, including those of the liberal professions and those provided by state agencies and nationalised industries (under reservation of the fact that article 31 and/or article 86 of the Treaty may be applicable to these activities[2]). It appears that the notion may not extend to certain aspects of the defence and security industries[3].

For article 82, the question of whether the abuse of the dominant position which has been found to exist affects trade between member states will be a question of fact to be determined by examination of the whole circumstances of the case.

The reported cases can be divided into two distinct groups; those where restrictive arrangements were found to exist between undertakings established in two or more member states[4], and those in which the arrangements were between firms in the same member state[5].

1   As to agricultural products see the EC Treaty art 32(3), and Annex I. As to the EC Treaty (ie the Treaty establishing the European Community (Rome, 25 March 1957; TS 1 (1973); Cmnd 5179)) see PARA 24 note 1.

2   See PARA 27.

3   See the EC Treaty art 296.

4   See PARA 57.

5   See PARA 58.

57. Agreements between undertakings in different member states. It is easier to see that trade is more likely to be affected where restrictive arrangements exist between undertakings established in two or more member states than where such arrangements are between firms in the same member state, but trade may be affected in both cases.

The function of the concept of effect on trade is to determine the field of application of the prohibition of article 81 of the EC Treaty, since there is a possibility that the realisation of a single market between member states will be impeded[1]. It is to the extent that the agreement may affect trade between member states that the interference with competition caused by that agreement is caught by the prohibitions, whilst in the converse case it escapes these prohibitions. For this requirement to be fulfilled it must be possible to foresee with a sufficient degree of probability on the basis of a set of objective factors of law or of fact that the agreement in question may have an influence, direct or indirect, actual or potential, on the pattern of trade between member states[2].

The fact that an agreement encourages an increase, even a large one, in the volume of trade between states is not sufficient to exclude the possibility that the agreement may 'affect' such trade[3].

In considering an agreement, it is necessary to consider in particular whether it is capable of bringing about a partitioning of the market in certain products between member states and thus rendering more difficult the interpenetration of trade which the Treaty is intended to create[4].

1 Case 56/65 *Société Technique Minière v Maschinenbau Ulm GmbH* [1966] ECR 235, [1966] CMLR 357, ECJ. As to the EC Treaty (ie the Treaty establishing the European Community (Rome, 25 March 1957; TS 1 (1973); Cmnd 5179)) see PARA 24 note 1.
2 Case 56/65 *Société Technique Minière v Maschinenbau Ulm GmbH* [1966] ECR 235 at 249, [1966] CMLR 357 at 375, ECJ.
3 Joined Cases 56, 58/64 *Etablissements Consten SARL and Grundig-Verkaufs-GmbH v EC Commission* [1966] ECR 299 at 341, [1966] CMLR 418 at 472, ECJ (judgment, para 24).
4 Case 56/65 *Société Technique Minière v Maschinenbau Ulm GmbH* [1966] ECR 235 at 249, [1966] CMLR 357 at 375, ECJ.

58.   Agreements between undertakings in the same member state.   Much of the jurisprudence dealing with agreements between undertakings situated in the same member state concerns the actions of national trade associations. The Commission has considered the practice of rebates calculated on the basis of their total purchases of tiles from German producers; the rebate was cumulative and the wholesalers were, therefore, more likely to purchase their requirements from German producers in order to obtain the most favourable rebate, notwithstanding the fact that imported tiles were, in general, less expensive than German tiles. The Commission considered that such a rebate system was likely to affect trade between member states[1].

Trade will be 'affected' if, but for the existence of the agreement, decision, concerted practice or abuse of the dominant position, it would have developed in a different way from that in which it actually did.

1 EC Commission Decision 71/23 (*German Ceramic Tiles Discount Agreement*) OJ L10, 13.1.71, p 15, [1971] CMLR D6.

(iv) 'Undertakings'

59.   Breadth of the concept of 'undertaking'.   For the purposes of Community anti-trust policy, the notion of 'undertaking' means a legal entity – irrespective of how it is financed – which is involved in any form of economic activity that exists in the world of commerce or manufacture[1]. Hence, the sole trader is caught[2] equally by articles 81 and 82 of the EC Treaty as the multi-national corporation (although the sole trader may fall outside the scope of article 82 through the scope of his activities). Competition policy applies to all economic activity, irrespective of the form under which such activity is conducted[3]. Eurocontrol, which manages air traffic control for a number of member states, was held to exercise prerogatives (control and policing of air space) typical of a public authority. They did not display an economic character justifying the applications of the Treaty's rules on competition[4].

An entity may be acting as an undertaking in carrying out some functions which amount to economic activity, but not when it is engaged in other functions which do not[5].

Entities which are in the same corporate group, such as parents and subsidiaries will not be regarded as separate undertakings (even if they have separate legal personality) if they form what may be considered as a single economic entity, so that agreements between them will not attract the application of the competition rules[6]. Similarly it may be possible to take a decision against the parent company of the entity whose activities are in question, or against the parent and subsidiary jointly, or against a subsidiary of the entity in question, or in the case of commercial agency, against the principal[7].

Certain types of organisation and activities have been excluded from the ambit of the competition rules. Thus an agreement between employers' and employees' representative groups to establish a pension fund was not an 'agreement between undertakings'[8]. However, not all undertakings managing social security systems[9] are excluded from the Treaty rules[10].

Artistic activities are capable of being economic activities sufficient to establish a finding of 'undertaking' in certain cases[11].

By virtue of the nature of the Treaty system, the member states themselves cannot be considered to be 'undertakings' within the meaning of articles 81 and 82[12]. This does not mean, however, that where the member states perform commercial activities through commercial or statutory monopolies, or through governmental or other types of national agency, these organisations will not fall under articles 81 and 82[13].

An employee is not usually considered as an 'undertaking' as he is usually acting on behalf of an undertaking[14]. However, he may become an undertaking if he ceases to pursue the interests of his employer and begins to pursue his own interests[15].

1   Case C-41/90 *Höfner and Elser v Macrotron GmbH* [1991] ECR I-1979, [1993] 4 CMLR 306, ECJ; EC Commission Decision 92/51 (*1990 World Cup Package Tours*) OJ L326, 12.11.92, p 31. It is the activity of offering goods and services in a given market, rather than the business of purchasing, which is the characteristic feature of an economic activity: Case T-319/99 *Federación Nacional de Empresas de Instrumentación Científica, Médica, Técnica y Dental (FENIN) v EC Commission* [2004] All ER (EC) 300, [2003] ECR II-357, CFI. Any activity consisting in offering goods or services on a given market is an economic activity: see Cases C-180/98 to C-184/98 *Pavlov v Stichting Pensioenfonds Medische Specialisten* [2000] ECR I-6451, [2001] 4 CMLR 30, [2000] All ER (D) 1192, ECJ, at para 75. See also Case C-309/99 *Wouters v Algemene Raad van de Nederlandse Orde van Advocaten* [2002] All ER (EC) 193, [2002] ECR I-1577, [2002] 4 CMLR 913.
2   EC Commission Decision 76/29 (*AOIP/Beyrand*) OJ L6, 13.1.76, p 8, [1976] 1 CMLR D14; EC Commission Decision 76/743 (*Reuter/BASF*) OJ L254, 17.9.76, p 40, [1976] 2 CMLR D44; EC Commission Decision 79/86 (*Vaessen/Moris*) OJ L19, 26.1.79, p 32, [1979] 1 CMLR 511; EC Commission Decision 78/516 (*RAI/UNITEL*) OJ L157, 15.6.78, p 39, [1978] 3 CMLR 306; EC Commission Decision 82/897 (*Totecs/Dorcet*) OJ L379, 31.12.82, p 19, [1983] 1 CMLR 412; EC Commission Decision 83/670 (*Nutricia/de Rooij/Zuid-Hollandse Conservenfabriek*) OJ L376, 31.12.83, p 22, [1984] 2 CMLR 165.
3   For an example of a non-profit-making association see EC Commission Decision 90/25 (*Concordato Incendio*) OJ L15, 19.1.90, p 25, [1991] 4 CMLR 199. As to the EC Treaty (ie the Treaty establishing the European Community (Rome, 25 March 1957; TS 1 (1973); Cmnd 5179)) see PARA 24 note 1.
4   Case C-364/92 *SAT Fluggesellschaft mbH v Eurocontrol* [1994] ECR I-43, [1994] 5 CMLR 208, ECJ. See also note 5.
5   See Case T-155/04 *SELEX Sistemi Integrati SpA v EC Commission (Eurocontrol intervening)* [2006] ECR II-4797, [2007] 4 CMLR 372, CFI. The decision was upheld on appeal: Case C-113/07 P *SELEX Sistemi Integrati SpA v EC Commission (Eurocontrol intervening)* [2009] All ER (D) 294 (Mar), ECJ, but the Court of Justice stated that the Court of First Instance had erred in law in deciding that the activities of Eurocontrol under consideration were separable and therefore capable of being economic activity such as to attract the application of the EC Treaty.
6   See eg Case 22/71 *Béguelin Import v GL Import Export* [1971] ECR 949, [1972] CMLR 81, ECJ; Case C-30/87 *Bodson v SA des Pompes Funèbres des Régions Libérés* [1988] ECR 2479, [1989] 4 CMLR 984, ECJ; Case T-102/92 *Viho Europe BV v EC Commission (Parker Pen Ltd intervening)* [1995] ECR-II 17, [1995] 4 CMLR 299, CFI.
7   See eg EC Commission Decision 70/332 (*Kodak*) OJ L147, 7.7.70, p 24, [1970] CMLR D19.
8   See Case C-67/96 *Albany International BV v Stichting Bedrijfspensioenfonds Texieleindustrie* [1999] ECR I-5751, [2000] 4 CMLR 446, ECJ.

9   Joined Cases C-159, 160/91 *Poucet v Assurances Générales de France et Caisse Mutuelle Régionale du Languedoc-Rousillion* [1993] ECR I-637, ECJ. See Joined Cases C-264/01, 306/01, 354/01, 355/01 AOK *Bundesverband v Ichthyol-gesellschaft Cordes, Hermanu & Co* [2004] ECR I-2493, [2004] 4 CMLR 1261, ECJ (non-profit-making public law body which fulfilled exclusively social function was not an undertaking).
10 Case C-244/94 *Fédération Française des Sociétés d'Assurance v Caisse Nationale d'Assurance Vieillesse Mutuelle Agricole* [1995] ECR I-4013, [1996] 4 CMLR 536, ECJ. See also Joined Cases C-264/01, 306/01, 354/01, 355/01 AOK *Bundesverband v Ichthyol-gesellschaft Cordes, Hermanu & Co* [2004] ECR I-2493, [2004] 4 CMLR 1261, ECJ.
11 EC Commission Decision 78/516 (*RAI/UNITEL*) OJ L157, 15.6.78, p 39, [1978] 3 CMLR 306.
12 See, however, *French State/Suralmo* (*Ninth Report on Competition Policy 1980*, point 114) where the Commission considered a patent licence granted by France as falling within the EC Treaty art 81(1).
13 The position of local and regional authorities is probably to be assimilated to that of member states: see Case C-30/87 *Bodson v SA des Pompes Funèbres des Régions Libérés* [1988] ECR 2479, [1989] 4 CMLR 984, ECJ. However, note that under the EC Treaty art 86(2), arts 81 and 82 may be disapplied if they would obstruct the performance of the functions entrusted to the entity in question. See further EC Commission Decision 90/16 (*Express Delivery Services in the Netherlands*) OJ L10, 12.1.90, p 47. This decision was subsequently annulled: see Joined Cases C-48, 66/90 *Netherlands v EC Commission* [1992] ECR I-565, [1993] 5 CMLR 316, ECJ; Case C-18/93 *Corsica Ferries Italia Srl v Corpo dei Piloti del Porto di Genova* [1994] ECR I-1783, ECJ.
14 Joined Cases 40–48/73, 50/73, 54–56/73, 111/73, 113–114/73 *Coöperative verenining Suiker Unie UA v EC Commission* [1975] ECR 1663, [1976] 1 CMLR 295, ECJ.
15 EC Commission Decision 76/743 (*Reuter/BASF*), OJ L254, 17.9.76, p 40, [1976] 2 CMLR D44.

(v) The Interaction between Articles 81 and 82

60.   Overlap.   Although articles 81 and 82 of the EC Treaty are intended to cover different types of anti-competitive activity, there is an inevitable overlap between the two provisions. The Court of Justice has stated that the two articles cannot be interpreted in such a way as to contradict each other because they serve to achieve the same aim[1]. In this connection, it is important to have regard to the provision of the Treaty which provides for the institution of a system ensuring that competition in the common market is not distorted[2].

1   Case 6/72 *Europemballage Corpn and Continental Can Co Inc v EC Commission* [1973] ECR 215, [1973] CMLR 199, ECJ. See also PARAS 26, 73.
2   Ie the EC Treaty art 3(g); see PARA 26. As to the EC Treaty (ie the Treaty establishing the European Community (Rome, 25 March 1957; TS 1 (1973); Cmnd 5179)) see PARA 24 note 1.

(3) PREVENTION, RESTRICTION OR DISTORTION OF COMPETITION

(i) The Prohibition

61.   Agreements between undertakings.   Agreements between undertakings which may affect trade between member states and which have as their object or effect the prevention, restriction or distortion of competition within the common market are prohibited[1]; however, where they affect trade within a member state, without affecting trade between member states, they are likely to violate the domestic law of that state. The form of the agreement is irrelevant; a 'gentleman's agreement' is caught equally with a formally executed contract[2]. It is not relevant to this analysis whether the agreement is between undertakings at the same level on the market (horizontal), or between undertakings at different levels of the market (vertical)[3].

There are no procedural requirements with which an 'agreement' must comply to fall within the meaning of this prohibition. The requirement is merely that the 'agreement' creates rights and obligations between the parties which are capable of enforcement, either by the parties or by some external agency[4]. The fact that one party refuses to sign an undertaking of compliance with a set of rules does not make that set of rules any less an agreement between the issuer of the rules and that latter party if, as a matter of fact, the party refusing to sign carries on his business in a way which would comply with the rules[5]. Where a wholesaler in one member state consents to stop supplying retailers in another member state under strong pressure from a manufacturer, an agreement is constituted notwithstanding that it is against the economic interest of the wholesaler to do so[6]. The Court of Justice has held that the Commission was entitled to treat the common intentions existing between producers both as an agreement between the parties and as concerted practices[7]. Even if an agreement ceases to be in force, it can be caught by the prohibition if it continues to produce effects.

Standard conditions of sale can constitute an agreement between the seller and buyers[8]; however, a unilateral act by a seller probably will not[9].

An agreement between two associations of undertakings falls within the ambit of the prohibition[10] even if the associations are not themselves in a position to compel the enforcement of the obligations contained in the agreement, but have to rely on their constituent undertakings to discharge the obligations incumbent upon the associations[11].

Whilst substantive restrictive practices legislation, particularly the EC Treaty articles 81 and 82, is addressed to undertakings, the question to be considered is the extent to which agreements and concerted practices between legally distinct and separate entities which are economically inter-related, or inter-dependent are to be considered as qualifying for examination under the anti-trust rules[12].

For the intra-undertaking arrangement, rather than the inter-undertaking arrangement, the question is inter alia to whom can the prohibited behaviour in question be imputed? The fact that a subsidiary has a separate legal personality, distinct from that of its parent, is not sufficient to remove the possibility that the behaviour of the subsidiary may be imputed to the parent company[13]. This will be the case where, as a matter of fact, it is established that the subsidiary does not have a distinct autonomous commercial policy, separate from the policy of the parent company[14]. It is when this sufficiency of autonomous behaviour is found lacking that the prohibition may be considered inapplicable to the parent-subsidiary relationship, in that they form a single economic entity[15]. In dismissing a challenge to a decision of the Court of First Instance, the Court of Justice has held that the prohibition does not apply to agreements between companies which are members of the same group[16]. However, the distinction between an agreement caught by the prohibition and an agreement falling outside it is not clear-cut: there is scope for divergence of opinion on whether a particular arrangement falls under the Treaty provision. Even where producers 'form one indivisible system of public supply', this does not mean they form a single economic unit[17].

1   EC Treaty art 81(1). As to the EC Treaty (ie the Treaty establishing the European Community (Rome, 25 March 1957; TS 1 (1973); Cmnd 5179)) see PARA 24 note 1.

2   Case 41/69 *ACF Chemiefarma NV v EC Commission* [1970] ECR 661, ECJ (Quinine Cartel). See also Case 56/89R *Publishers Association v EC Commission* [1989] 2 All ER 1059, [1989] ECR 1693, ECJ. As soon as it is apparent that the object of an agreement is the prevention, restriction or distortion of competition, the actual effect of the agreement is irrelevant: Case T-395/94 *Atlantic Container Line AB (supported by the European Community Shipowners'*

Association ASBL, interveners) v EC Commission (supported by Freight Transport Association Ltd, interveners) [2002] 2 All ER (Comm) 572, [2002] All ER (EC) 684, CFI.
3   As to decisions by associations of undertakings see PARA 62.
4   Case 41/69 *ACF Chemiefarma NV v EC Commission* [1970] ECR 661, ECJ. See EC Commission Decision 96/478 *(Bayer AG/Adalat)* OJ L201, 10.1.96, p 1).
5   EC Commission Decision 88/86 *(Fisher Price/Quaker Oats)* OJ L49, 23.2.88, p 34, [1989] 4 CMLR 553.
6   EC Commission Decision 92/426 *(Viho/Parker Pen)* OJ L233, 15.8.92, p 27.
7   Joined Cases T-1–4, 6–15/89 *Rhône-Poulenc v EC Commission* [1991] ECR II-867, CFI. As to concerted practices see PARA 63.
8   EC Commission Decision 78/163 *(Distillers Co Ltd, Conditions of Sale)* OJ L50, 22.2.78, p 16, [1978] 1 CMLR 400; EC Commission Decision 70/332 *(Kodak)* OJ L147, 7.7.70, p 24, [1970] CMLR D19; EC Commission Decision 87/409 *(Sandoz)* OJ L222, 10.8.87, p 28, [1989] 4 CMLR 628.
9   Joined Cases 25, 26/84 *Ford-Werke AG and Ford of Europe Inc v EC Commission* [1985] ECR 2725, [1985] 3 CMLR 528, ECJ. Signature of a lawful dealership contract does not in itself constitute acquiescence to a later unlawful variation of the contract; the variation is not necessarily, therefore, an agreement: Case T-208/01 *Volkswagen AG v EC Commission* [2004] All ER (EC) 674, [2004] ICR 1197, CFI.
10 EC Commission Decision 69/90 *(European Machine Tool Exhibitions (Cecimo))* OJ L69, 20.3.69, p 13, [1969] CMLR D1; EC Commission Decision 71/337 *(CEMATEX)* OJ L227, 8.10.71, p 26, [1973] CMLR D135; EC Commission Decision 82/371 *(Navewa-Anseau)* OJ L167, 15.6.82, p 39, [1982] 2 CMLR 193 (amended by OJ L325, 20.11.82, p 20). See also Cases T-217/03 and T245/03 *Federation Nationale de la Cooperation Betail and Viande v EC Commission* [2008] 5 CMLR 406.
11 Joined Cases T-1–4, 6–15/89 *Rhône-Poulenc v EC Commission* [1991] ECR II-867, CFI.
12 Case 243/83 *Binon et Cie SA v SA Agence et messageries de la presse* [1985] ECR 2015, [1985] 3 CMLR 800, ECJ.
13 Joined Cases 209–215, 218/78 *Heintz van Landewyck Sàrl v EC Commission* [1980] ECR 3125, [1981] 3 CMLR 134, ECJ. For a consideration of the position where companies cease to be parent and subsidiary see EC Commission Decision 88/84 *(ARG/Unipart)* OJ L45, 18.2.88, p 34, [1988] 4 CMLR 513.
14 EC Commission Decision 85/74 *(Peroxygen Products)* OJ L35, 7.2.85, p 1, [1985] CMLR 481.
15 EC Commission Decision 70/332 *(Kodak)* OJ L147, 7.7.70, p 24, [1970] CMLR D19; EC Commission Decision 69/165 *(Christiani & Nielsen)* OJ L165, 5.7.69, p 12, [1969] CMLR D36.
16 Case C-73/95P *Viho Europe BV v EC Commission* [1997] All ER (EC) 163, [1996] ECR I-5457, [1997] 4 CMLR 419, ECJ.
17 EC Commission Decision 91/50 *(Ijsselcentrale)* OJ L28, 2.2.91, p 32.
    One area of doubt is that of commercial agency, more particularly the overlap between commercial agency (which falls outside the prohibition: see EC Commission Notice (OJ 139, 24.12.62, p 2921)) and the role of the independent trader (which falls within it). Commercial agents exercise no entrepreneurial activity independent of that of their principal; thus, their position is similar to that of the subsidiary discussed above, in that the relations between them and their principal will probably fall outside the scope of the EC Treaty art 81. As to commercial agency see AGENCY vol 1 (2008) PARA 72.

62. **Decisions by associations of undertakings.** Decisions by associations of undertakings which may affect trade between member states, and which have as their object or effect the prevention, restriction or distortion of competition within the common market, are prohibited[1].

The aim is to ensure that undertakings on the market cannot co-ordinate their behaviour with a view to preventing the interplay of free competition. It would be anomalous if undertakings who were unable to co-ordinate their behaviour through restrictive agreements, could do so by entrusting their decision-making in a particular sphere to an association, which could take decisions which would be binding and enforceable against the members of the association[2].

It is not necessary that the association have any particular legal form[3] or, indeed, that it be entitled to any form of legal personality under the relevant national law. It suffices for these purposes that an association exists and has power to take decisions, although such decisions may be reached on an ad hoc basis[4]. The prohibition does not affect the existence of the association as such; it is only its activities with which the authorities are concerned. The Commission has condemned the activities of an association of associations[5].

The decision itself is not required to have any special form. If the association prepares a set of rules or conditions which are adopted as standard terms and conditions by the undertakings which are members of the association, these rules or conditions will be considered as 'decisions' equally with a formal decision or instruction issued to the members of the association[6]. The decision need not be expressed as 'binding' upon the members of the association; the instrument may be merely a recommendation[7] or a suggestion, provided that it can be shown that the members of the association, in fact, always observe such a recommendation or suggestion as if it were in a binding form[8].

1   EC Treaty art 81(1). This is a logical extension of the prohibition of agreements between undertakings: see PARA 61. As to the EC Treaty (ie the Treaty establishing the European Community (Rome, 25 March 1957; TS 1 (1973); Cmnd 5179)) see PARA 24 note 1.
2   EC Commission Decision 93/174 (*International Union of Railways*) OJ L73, 26.3.93, p 38.
3   EC Commission Decision 85/76 (*Milchförderungsfonds*) OJ L35, 7.2.85, p 35, [1985] 3 CMLR 101.
4   EC Commission Decision 69/90 (*European Machine Tool Exhibitions (Cecimo)*) OJ L69, 20.3.69, p 13, [1969] CMLR D1.
5   See EC Commission Decision 92/204 (*Samenwerkende Prijsregelende Organisaties in de Bouwnijverheid*) OJ L92, 7.4.92, p 1.
6   See eg EC Commission Decision 86/499 (*VIFKA*) (OJ L291, 15.10.86 p 46); Case 45/85 *Verband der Sachversicherer eV v EC Commission* [1987] ECR 405, [1988] 4 CMLR 264, ECJ. As to the rules and regulations of a self-regulatory organisation see EC Commission Decisions 85/563—85/566 (OJ L369, 31.12.85 pp 25–34) (*Applications of the London Sugar Futures Market, Cocoa Terminal Market, Rubber Market and Coffee Market*) [1988] 4 CMLR 138–155. A provision made by a national Bar association in order to regulate partnerships between the legal profession and other professions is a decision taken by an association of undertakings for the purposes of the EC Treaty art 81(1): Case C-309/99 *Wouters v Algemene Raad van de Nederlandse Orde van Advocaten (Raad van de Balies van de Europese Gemeenschap intervening)* [2002] All ER (EC) 193, [2002] ECR I-1577, ECJ.
7   Joined Cases 96–102, 104, 105, 108, 110/82 *IAZ International Belgium NV v EC Commission* [1983] ECR 3369, [1984] 3 CMLR 276, ECJ.
8   Case 8/72 *Vereniging van Cementhandelaren v EC Commission* 1972] ECR 977, [1973] CMLR 7, ECJ; Case 45/85 *Verband der Sachversicherer eV v EC Commission* [1987] ECR 405, [1988] 4 CMLR 264, ECJ; EC Commission Decision 96/438 (*Fenex*) OJ L181, 20.7.96, p 28.

63.   Concerted practices.   Also prohibited are concerted practices which may affect trade between member states and which have as their object or effect the prevention, restriction or distortion of competition within the common market[1]. What is required to base a finding of 'concerted practice' is some form of 'agreement' or understanding between the parties; this agreement involves something less than a gentleman's agreement. Irrespective of the type of 'meeting of the minds', each known and wanted co-operation between the parties must be seen as a form of concerted practice[2]. An infringement of article 81 of the EC Treaty may exist where the parties have not set out their understanding but some form of acceptance from each party as to conduct can be inferred[3]. Mere parallelism of behaviour is not sufficient, per se, to permit the supposition of concerted practice. A recommendation does not necessarily represent a type of concerted practice, but a followed recommendation may lead thereto[4]. In this latter case, the supposition of concerted practice can only be based on the uniform conduct of the parties, if there is the necessary mutual understanding.

The Court of Justice has described the concept of a concerted practice as 'a form of co-ordination between undertakings, which, without having been taken to the stage where an agreement properly so-called has been concluded, knowingly substitutes for the risks of competition, practical co-operation between them which leads to conditions of competition which do not correspond to the normal conditions of the market, having regard to the nature of the products, the importance and number of the undertakings as well as the size and nature of the said market. Such practical co-operation amounts to a concerted practice, particularly if it enables the persons concerned to consolidate established positions to the detriment of effective freedom of movement of the products in the common market and of the freedom of consumers to choose their suppliers'[5].

The Court of Justice expressly rejected the submission that the existence of a concerted practice requires the existence of some form of plan between the parties[6]; the essential requirement of Community competition policy is that each trader must set his policy independently of that policy decided upon by his competitors. Although this requirement in no way removes the ability of each firm to adapt its policy intelligently to the way its competitors are behaving, it completely prohibits any contact, direct or indirect, between traders where the object or effect of such contact is to influence the market conduct of either party or to reveal to him market policy or intentions[7].

The Court of Justice has held that the inference by the Commission of concertation from simultaneity of price announcements and the fact that prices were identical was incorrect; such parallel conduct could only be regarded as furnishing proof of concertation if it were the only plausible explanation for such conduct[8].

The Commission has to establish that each participant in a concerted practice participated in the acts which constituted the infringement; each undertaking is liable only to the extent of its participation[9].

Whilst generally, if concertation is established, it will follow that anti-competitive effects will ensue, it is possible for the parties to seek to rebut such a presumption[10].

A unilateral declaration as to future pricing policy is capable of constituting concerted behaviour[11].

1   EC Treaty art 81(1). As to the EC Treaty (ie the Treaty establishing the European Community (Rome, 25 March 1957; TS 1 (1973); Cmnd 5179)) see PARA 24 note 1.
2   Case 48/69 *ICI Ltd v EC Commission* [1972] ECR 619 at 653, 654, [1972] CMLR 557 at 621, 622, ECJ (judgment, paras 51–63).
3   EC Commission Decision 89/93 (*Italian Flat Glass*) OJ L33, 4.2.89, p 44, [1990] 4 CMLR 535; EC Commission Decision 89/190 (*PVC*) OJ L74, 17.3.89, p 1, [1990] 4 CMLR 345; EC Commission Decision 91/299 (*Soda-Ash-Solvay*) OJ L152 15.6.91, p 21.
4   EC Commission Decision 78/760 (*Belgian Tobacco Cartel (Fedetab)*) OJ L224, 15.8.78, p 29, [1978] 3 CMLR 524.
5   Joined Cases 40–48, 50, 54–56, 111, 113, 114/73 *Coöperatieve verening Suiker Unie UA v EC Commission* [1975] ECR 1663 at 1916, [1976] 1 CMLR 295 at 405, ECJ (judgment, para 26).
6   Joined Cases 40–48, 50, 54–56, 111, 113, 114/73 *Coöperatieve verening Suiker Unie UA v EC Commission* [1975] ECR 1663 at 1941–1945, [1976] 1 CMLR 295 at 167–192, ECJ (judgment, paras 167–192).
7   EC Commission Decision 86/398 (*Polypropylene*) OJ L230, 18.8.86, p 1, [1988] 4 CMLR 347.
8   Joined Cases 89, 104, 116, 117, 125–129/85 *Ahlström Osakeyhtö v EC Commission* [1988] ECR 5193, [1988] 4 CMLR 901, ECJ. See also Joined Cases 100–103/80 *Musique Diffusion Française SA v EC Commission* [1983] ECR 1825, [1983] 3 CMLR 221, ECJ.
9   In Joined Cases T-1–4, 6–15/89 *SA Rhône-Poulenc v EC Commission* [1991] ECR II-867, CFI (the Polypropylene case), the Court of First Instance refused to accept collective responsibility as a principle.

10 Case T-41/96 *Bayer AG v EC Commission* [2001] All ER (EC) 1, [2000] ECR II-3383, CFI. In a ruling by the President of the court in that case it appears to be suggested that where there was no written evidence of an agreement to ban exports nor other evidence to suggest that Bayer's wholesalers perceived refusals to supply large orders as sanctions or penalties for not observing an export ban, there was no agreement or concerted practice falling within the EC Treaty art 81(1). In a later decision in 1996, the Commission imposed a fine of ECU 3 million on Bayer for imposing an export ban on a range of medicinal preparations from France and Spain to the United Kingdom: EC Commission Decision 96/478 (*Bayer*) OJ L201, 9.8.96, p 1. As to fines see PARA 107 et seq.

11 Joined Cases T-202, 204, 207/98 *Tate & Lyle plc v EC Commission* [2001] All ER (EC) 839, [2001] ECR II-2035, CFI.

64.   The '*De minimis*' rule. In 2001 the Commission issued a notice[1] (replacing the notice of 1997[2]) dealing with agreements of minor importance which do not fall under the prohibition contained in article 81 of the EC Treaty[3]. This so-called '*De minimis*' notice states that 'this provision is not applicable where the impact of the agreement on intra-Community trade or on competition is not appreciable'. It is acknowledged that agreements between small and medium-sized undertakings[4] are rarely capable of appreciably affecting trade between member states[5].

The Commission holds the view that agreements between undertakings which affect trade between member states do not appreciably restrict competition:

(1)   if the aggregate market share held by the parties to the agreement does not exceed 10 per cent on any of the relevant markets affected by the agreement, where the agreement is made between undertakings which are actual or potential competitors on any of these markets (agreements between competitors)[6]; or

(2)   if the market share held by each of the parties to the agreement does not exceed 15 per cent on any of the relevant markets affected by the agreement, where the agreement is made between undertakings which are not actual or potential competitors on any of these markets (agreements between non-competitors)[7].

In cases where it is difficult to classify the agreement as either an agreement between competitors or an agreement between non-competitors the 10 per cent threshold is applicable[8]. Where there are parallel networks of agreements, the market share threshold is 5 per cent[9].

The notice does not apply to price-fixing or market-sharing agreements and, irrespective of market shares, such agreements will always be prohibited[10].

It has been considered by the Commission that contracts by a brewery with less than 1 per cent of the national market and producing less than 4.4 million gallons of beer per annum limiting supply contracts to 15 years will be considered of minor importance[11].

In cases covered by the notice the Commission will not institute proceedings either upon application or on its own initiative. Where undertakings assume in good faith that an agreement is covered by the notice, the Commission will not impose fines. Although not binding on them, the notice is intended to give guidance to the courts and authorities of the member states in their application of article 81[12].

1   Ie EC Commission Notice on agreements of minor importance which do not appreciably restrict competition under Article 81(1) of the Treaty establishing the European Community (de minimis) (OJ C368, 22.12.2001, p 13).

2   See EC Commission Notice of December 1997 concerning Agreements of Minor Importance (OJ C372, 9.12.97, p 13).

3 Ie the EC Treaty art 81(1). As to the EC Treaty (ie the Treaty establishing the European Community (Rome, 25 March 1957; TS 1 (1973); Cmnd 5179)) see PARA 24 note 1.

4 Ie enterprises which employ fewer than 250 persons and which have an annual turnover not exceeding EUR 50 million, and/or an annual balance sheet total not exceeding EUR 43 million: see EC Commission Recommendation of 6 May 2003 concerning the definition of micro, small and medium-sized enterprises (OJ L124, 20.5.2003, p 36).

5 EC Commission Notice on agreements of minor importance which do not appreciably restrict competition under Article 81(1) of the Treaty establishing the European Community (de minimis) (OJ C368, 22.12.2001, p 13) Pt I para 3.

6 See Commission notice *Guidelines on the applicability of Article 81 of the EC Treaty to horizontal cooperation agreements* (OJ C3, 6.1.2001, para 9).

7 EC Commission Notice on agreements of minor importance which do not appreciably restrict competition under Article 81(1) of the Treaty establishing the European Community (de minimis) (OJ C368, 22.12.2001, p 13) Pt II para 7.

8 EC Commission Notice on agreements of minor importance which do not appreciably restrict competition under Article 81(1) of the Treaty establishing the European Community (de minimis) (OJ C368, 22.12.2001, p 13) Pt II para 7.

9 EC Commission Notice on agreements of minor importance which do not appreciably restrict competition under Article 81(1) of the Treaty establishing the European Community (de minimis) (OJ C368, 22.12.2001, p 13) Pt II para 8.

10 These are the so-called 'hardcore restrictions': see EC Commission Notice on agreements of minor importance which do not appreciably restrict competition under Article 81(1) of the Treaty establishing the European Community (de minimis) (OJ C368, 22.12.2001, p 13) Pt II para 11.

11 OJ 1992, C121/2.

12 EC Commission Notice on agreements of minor importance which do not appreciably restrict competition under Article 81(1) of the Treaty establishing the European Community (de minimis) (OJ C368, 22.12.2001, p 13) Pt I para 4.

(ii) Nullity

65. Automatic nullity. Any agreement falling within the prohibition contained in article 81 of the EC Treaty[1] is automatically void[2]. The Court of Justice has held that this provision renders agreements and decisions prohibited pursuant thereto automatically void and such nullity is therefore capable of having a bearing on all the effects, either past or future, of the agreement or decision. Consequently, the nullity provided for is of retrospective effect[3].

Where voidness follows from an infringement of art 81 of the EC Treaty, it is possible to sever the offending provisions of the contract from the rest of its terms[4] in accordance with the domestic law of each member state[5].

However, the courts have not been sympathetic to attempts to use the provisions of competition law to avoid contractual obligations[6].

1 Ie the EC Treaty art 81(1): see PARAS 61–64. As to the EC Treaty (ie the Treaty establishing the European Community (Rome, 25 March 1957; TS 1 (1973); Cmnd 5179)) see PARA 24 note 1.

2 EC Treaty art 81(2). See Case C-126/97 *Eco Swiss China Time Ltd v Benetton International NV* [1999] ECR I-3055, [2000] 5 CMLR 816.

3 Case 48/72 *Brasserie de Haecht SA v Wilkin-Janssen* [1973] ECR 77, [1973] CMLR 287, ECJ. In that case, the Court of Justice was asked whether the nullity of agreements exempted from notification was deemed to take effect from the date when one of the contracting parties brought proceedings for nullity or merely from the date of the judgment of the court or decision of the Commission which established it. It should be noted that the nullity cannot have effect prior to 1 January 1958.

4 See Case 56/65 *Société Technique Minière v Maschinenbau Ulm GmbH* [1966] ECR 235, [1966] CMLR 357.

5 See Case 319/82 *Société de Vente de Ciments et Betons de L'Est SA v Kerpen and Kerpen GmbH & Co KG* [1983] ECR 4173, [1985] 1 CMLR 511, ECJ. The English courts have dealt with this issue in eg *Chemidus Wavin Ltd v Société pour la Transformation et l'Exploitation des Résines Industrielles SA* [1978] 3 CMLR 514, [1977] FSR 181, CA; *Inntrepreneur Estates Ltd v Mason* [1993] 2 CMLR 293, [1993] 2 EGLR 189.

6   See *Panayiotou v Sony Music Entertainment (UK) Ltd* [1994] Ch 142, [1994] 1 All ER 755; *Lloyd's v Clementson* [1995] 1 CMLR 693, [1995] 43 LS Gaz R 26; *Marchant & Eliot Underwriting Ltd v Higgins* [1996] 1 Lloyd's Rep 313 (affd [1996] 3 CMLR 349, [1996] 2 Lloyd's Rep 31, CA).

(iii) Exemption

66. Individual exemption. The EC Treaty provides that the prohibition contained in article 81 may be declared inapplicable in certain circumstances[1] and contains two positive conditions, satisfaction of which enable it to be invoked, and two negative conditions, which must not be found for exemption to be granted.

The two positive conditions, at least one of which must be satisfied, are:

(1)   the improvement of the production or distribution of goods; and

(2)   the promotion of technical and economic progress[2].

In addition, in both cases, the agreement, decision or concerted practice must allow consumers a fair share of the resultant benefit[3]. The Commission seems to interpret this as meaning lower prices (as opposed to other less measurable benefits)[4]. The arrangement must satisfy two negative criteria, namely:

(a)   it must not impose on the undertakings concerned restrictions which are not indispensable to the attainment of the positive objective stated above (and this means that there is no less restrictive means of achieving the same object)[5]; and

(b)   it must not afford such undertakings the possibility of eliminating competition in respect of a substantial part of the products in question[6].

These negative criteria are not alternatives and each must be absolute. The rules for exemptions are stated in the Treaty and procedural provisions are contained in the Modernisation Regulation[7].

The Modernisation Regulation removed the system of notification for individual exemptions as from 1 May 2004. Prior to this, the Commission was inundated with agreements awaiting exemption which resulted in long delays for the undertakings concerned and also diverted the resources of the Commission from curbing more serious infringements of competition law[8]. The Modernisation Regulation introduced the system of self-assessment of the application of article 81 with the onus now on undertakings to ensure compliance[9].

1   EC Treaty art 81(3). As to the EC Treaty (ie the Treaty establishing the European Community (Rome, 25 March 1957; TS 1 (1973); Cmnd 5179)) see PARA 24 note 1. As to the prohibition and the automatic nullity of agreements, decisions and practices which infringe it see art 81(1), (2); and PARAS 61, 65.

2   EC Treaty art 81(3).

3   EC Treaty art 81(3).

4   EC Commission Decision 82/123 (*VBBB/VBVB*) OJ L54, 25.2.82, p 36, [1982] 2 CMLR 344.

5   EC Treaty art 81(3)(a). See eg EC Commission Decision 76/172 (*Bayer/Gist-Brocades*) OJ L30, 5.2.76 p 13, [1976] 1 CMLR D98; EC Commission Decision 86/405 (*Optical Fibres*) OJ L236, 22.8.86 p 30; EC Commission Decision 93/126 (*Jahrhundertvertrag*) OJ L50, 2.3.93, p 14.

6   EC Treaty art 81(3)(b). See eg EC Commission Decision 84/381 (*Carlsberg*) OJ L207, 2.8.84, p 26, [1985] 1 CMLR 735.

7   Ie EC Council Regulation 1/2003 on the implementation of the rules on competition laid down in Articles 81 and 82 of the Treaty (OJ L1, 4.1.2003, p 1) (the 'Modernisation Regulation').

8   See EC Council Regulation 1/2003 (OJ L1, 4.1.2003, p 1) recital 3.

9   See EC Council Regulation 1/2003 (OJ L1, 4.1.2003, p 1) art 1.

67. Group exemption. From the start of 1963, when the Commission was processing the many thousands of notifications and requests for negative clearances which had been sent to it[1], it appeared to it that the best way to deal with these notifications, most of which dealt with the same legal problems, would be by way of a block exemption covering all agreements of a particular type, provided that certain stated criteria were met.

The method of such exemption was to be that an enabling regulation was to be passed by the Council allowing the Commission, after it had gained sufficient expertise and experience through the examination of particular cases and the issue of individual decisions, to state what provisions could be permitted and exemptions granted, and thereafter to issue an exemption regulation covering a particular type of agreement. Such regulations of the Council and of the Commission rest solely on articles 81 and 83 of the EC Treaty[2] and therefore must follow the procedure laid down in those articles.

The EC Council has provided that any exempting regulation adopted by the Commission should define the categories of agreement to which the exemption applied, and in particular should specify restrictions or clauses which must not appear in the agreement and those conditions which must be contained in the agreement or other conditions which must be satisfied for the exemption to be available. The exemption was to be for a specific period and it was to be available retrospectively to agreements in respect of which the parties had amended the provisions within three months of the Commission regulation so that the agreement would comply with the requirements for exemption under its provisions[3].

Group exemptions have been made available to vertical agreements in general[4], including concerted practices[5] and motor vehicles[6]. Group exemptions have also been made available to horizontal agreements[7], including specialisation agreements[8] and research and development agreements[9]. Licensing agreements for the transfer of technology are also the subject of a group exemption[10].

A regulation in the maritime sector[11] in relation to consortium agreements in cargo liner shipping was enacted in 1995 and renewed in 2000[12] and in May 1996 the Commission authorised a series of consortium agreements[13] under that regulation. Although the Commission has power to publish block exemptions in the air transport sector[14], none are currently in force[15].

1 Ie under EC Council Regulation 17 of 6 February 1962 (OJ 1962 p 204 (S Edn 1959–62 p 87)). See now EC Council Regulation 1/2003 on the implementation of the rules on competition laid down in Articles 81 and 82 of the Treaty (OJ L1, 4.1.2003, p 1) (the 'Modernisation Regulation').

2 See PARA 61 et seq. As to the EC Treaty (ie the Treaty establishing the European Community (Rome, 25 March 1957; TS 1 (1973); Cmnd 5179)) see PARA 24 note 1.

3 EC Council Regulation 19/65 (OJ L36, 6.3.65, p 533 (S Edn 1965–66 p 35)). See also note 1. See also EC Council Regulation 1215/1999 (OJ L148, 15.6.99, p 1).

4 See EC Council Regulation 19/65 (OJ L36, 6.3.65, p 533 (S Edn 1965–66 p 35)).

5 EC Commission Regulation 2790/99 (OJ L336, 29.12.99, p 21).

6 EC Commission Regulation 1400/2002 (OJ L203, 1.8.2002, p 30). See also Case 10/86 *VAG France v Etablissements Magne SA* [1986] ECR 4071, [1988] 4 CMLR 98; and the decisions in Case T-23/90 *Automobiles Peugot SA v EC Commission* [1991] ECR II-653, [1993] 5 CMLR 540, CFI; and Case T-9/92 *Automobiles Peugot SA v EC Commission* [1993] ECR II-493, [1995] 5 CMLR 696, CFI (confirmed in Case C-322/93 *Automobiles Peugot SA v EC Commission* [1994] ECR I-2727, ECJ).

7 See EC Council Regulation 2821/71 (OJ L285, 29.12.71, p 46).

8 See EC Commission Regulation 2658/2000 (OJ L304, 5.12.2000, p 3).

9 See EC Commission Regulation 2659/2000 (OJ L304, 5.12.2000, p 7).

10 See EC Commission Regulation 772/2004 (OJ L123, 27.04.2004, p 11). See also EC Commission NoticeGuidelines on the application of Article 81 of the EC Treaty to technology transfer agreements (OJ C101, 27.04.2004, p 2).

11 A block exemption for liner conferences (see EC Council Regulation 4056/86 (OJ L378, 31.12.86, p 4)) was abolished in 2006 (see EC Council Regulation 1419/2006 (OJ L269, 28.9.2006, p 1)).

12 See EC Commission Regulation 870/95 (OJ L89, 20.4.95, p 7) (made under EC Council Regulation 479/92 (OJ L55, 25.2.92, p 3)). See now EC Commission Regulation 823/00 (OJ L100, 20.4.2000, p 24).

13 *St Lawrence Cooordinated Service* EC Commission Press Release IP (96)400 of 8 May 1996; *East Africa Container Service* (*Twenty-third Report on Competition Policy 1993*, point 230); *Joint Mediterranean Canada Service* 2 April 1996; *Joint Pool Agreement* 5 March 1997.

14 See EC Council Regulation 3976/87 (OJ L374, 31.12.87, p 9).

15 The applicable procedural regime for air transport is now that of the Modernisation Regulation (see note 1) together with EC Council Regulation 411/2004 (OJ L68, 6.3.2004, p 1).

(4) ABUSE OF A DOMINANT POSITION

68.   Prohibition of abuse of a dominant position. The EC Treaty[1] prohibits any abuse by one or more undertakings of a dominant position[2] within the common market or in a substantial part of it[3] in so far as it may affect trade between member states[4]. The Treaty itself gives examples of what constitutes abuse[5], though it does not provide an exhaustive list[6].

Undertakings entrusted by a member state with the operation of services of general economic interest or having the character of a revenue-producing monopoly are subject to the rules of competition contained in the Treaty[7], in so far as the application of such rules does not obstruct the performance, in law or in fact, of the particular tasks assigned to them[8].

For the EC Treaty article 82[9] to be applicable, an undertaking or undertakings must have abused their dominant position within the common market or a substantial part of it, and the abuse must be likely to have an effect on trade between member states. The concepts of 'undertakings' and 'an effect on trade between member states' have already been discussed in the context of article 81[10]. In relation to article 82, it is also necessary to consider the following points: (1) what is meant by a dominant position[11]; (2) whether that position is held in a substantial part of the common market[12]; and (3) what behaviour is likely to be characterised as abusive[13].

1 See the EC Treaty art 82, which is directly applicable in member states (see PARA 28). As to the EC Treaty (ie the Treaty establishing the European Community (Rome, 25 March 1957; TS 1 (1973); Cmnd 5179)) see PARA 24 note 1.

2 As to the meaning of 'dominant position' see PARA 69.

3 As to the meaning of 'substantial part of the common market' see PARA 70.

4 EC Treaty art 82.

5 See PARA 71.

6 See Case 6/72 *Europemballage Corpn and Continental Can Co Inc v EC Commission* [1973] ECR 215, [1973] CMLR 199, ECJ.

7 This includes in particular the provisions of the EC Treaty art 82: art 86(2).

8 EC Treaty art 86(2). However, the development of trade must not be affected to such an extent as would be contrary to the interests of the Community: art 86(2). As to art 86(2) see PARA 27. Note that the Court of Justice has held that art 82 applies only to anti-competitive conduct engaged in by companies on their own initiative, not anti-competitive conduct required of the companies by national legislation: see Joined Cases C-359, 379/95P *EC Commission and France v Ladbroke Racing Ltd* [1997] ECR I-6265, [1998] 4 CMLR 27, ECJ.

9 See the text and notes 1–4.

10 See PARAS 55 et seq, 59.

11 See PARA 69.

12 See PARA 70.

13 See PARA 71.

69.   Dominant position.   The EC Treaty article 82[1] does not define 'dominant position' or lay down any criteria that must be satisfied. It is necessary to look to the judgments of the courts and the decisions of the European Commission to determine the factors that can lead to a finding of dominance.

The European Court of Justice has described a dominant position as a position of economic strength enjoyed by an undertaking which enables it to prevent effective competition being maintained on the relevant market by affording it the power to behave to an appreciable extent independently of its competitors, its customers and ultimately of its consumers. Such a position does not preclude some competition, which it does where there is a monopoly or a quasi-monopoly, but enables the undertaking which profits by it, if not to determine, at least to have an appreciable influence on the conditions under which that competition will develop, and in any case to act largely in disregard of it so long as such conduct does not operate to its detriment[2]. There are two elements to the definition: the capacity to prevent effective competition; and having the power to behave independently[3].

It has been established that article 82 covers both the buying and selling sides of the market[4].

The market share of an undertaking is not the only factor which must be taken into account when assessing market power, although very large shares may be evidence of the existence of a dominant position[5]. There is a rebuttable presumption of dominance where an undertaking has a market share of 50 per cent or more[6]. It is possible to have a dominant position with a market share of less than 50 per cent[7].

As well as market share, other factors in determining market power are barriers to expansion and entry[8] faced by competitors such as statutory monopolies[9] or other legal regulation[10], intellectual property rights[11], technological superiority[12], economies of scale[13], access to financial resources[14], vertical integration and other vertical arrangements[15], access to raw materials and other resources[16], advertising and product differentiation[17], the maturity of the market[18], economic performance[19], market conduct[20], predatory pricing[21] and relationships with customers and competitors[22]. Countervailing buyer power (that is, the extent to which its customers are able to constrain an allegedly dominant undertaking) is also a factor to be considered[23].

It is possible for two or more undertakings to be collectively dominant if they are linked in such a way that they adopt the same conduct on the market[24], or present themselves or act together as a collective entity[25]; however, cases of abuse of collective dominance are rare.

A dominant position can exist only in relation to a relevant market and the delimitation of that market is of essential importance[26]. The relevant market consists of not only the product or services market[27], but also the temporal and geographical market[28].

1   As to the EC Treaty (ie the Treaty establishing the European Community (Rome, 25 March 1957; TS 1 (1973); Cmnd 5179)) see PARA 24 note 1. See also PARA 68.

2   See Case 85/76 *Hoffmann-La Roche & Co AG v EC Commission* [1979] ECR 461, [1979] 3 CMLR 211, ECJ. See also Case 27/76 *United Brands Co v EC Commission* [1978] ECR 207, [1978] 1 CMLR 429, ECJ, which lays down a similar test.

3   The connection between the two elements is unclear. It has been suggested that the essential issue is the ability to act independently: see Case 85/76 *Hoffmann-La Roche & Co AG v EC Commission* [1979] ECR 461, [1979] 3 CMLR 211, ECJ.

4   See eg Case C-95/04 *British Airways plc v EC Commission* [2007] ECR I-2331, [2007] 4 CMLR 982.

5   See Case 85/76 *Hoffmann-La Roche & Co AG v EC Commission* [1979] ECR 461, [1979] 3 CMLR 211, ECJ. As to the calculation of market shares see EC Commission Notice on the Definition of the Relevant Market for the purposes of Community Competition Law (OJ C372, 9.12.97, p 5); and PARA 32.

6   This presumption was laid down in Case 62/86 *AKZO Chemie BV v EC Commission* [1991] ECR I-3359, [1993] 5 CMLR 215, ECJ. Where the presumption is established, the undertaking concerned has the burden of showing that it is not dominant.

7   See Case 27/76 *United Brands Co v EC Commission* [1978] ECR 207, [1978] 1 CMLR 429, ECJ (undertaking with a market share of 40–45% was dominant); EC Commission Decision 2000/74 (*British Airways/Virgin*) OJ [2000] L30, 4.2.2000, p 1, [2000] 4 CMLR 999; and in further stages Case T-219/99 *British Airways v EC Commission* [2003] ECR II-5917, [2004] 4 CMLR 1008, CFI; Case C-95/04 P *British airways plc v EC Commission* [2007] ECR I-2331, [2007] 4 CMLR 982, ECJ (39.7% share was dominant where the competitors' market shares were relatively low and there were other factors indicating dominance, and despite the fact that the share held by the particular undertaking was in decline).

8   In 2005 the Directorate-General for Competition issued a *Discussion Paper on the Application of article 82 of the Treaty to Exclusionary Abuses*, 19 December 2005; and in 2009 the Commission issued the *Communication from the Commission — Guidance on the Commission's enforcement priorities in applying Article 82 of the EC Treaty to abusive exclusionary conduct by dominant undertakings* (OJ C45, 24.2.2009, p 7). Those papers give an indication of the kinds of factor likely in future to be relevant in considering whether there are barriers to entry or expansion in any given case. The list in the text and notes below is drawn from decisions of the ECJ, the CFI or the EC Commission, and the papers mentioned above draw largely from the such decisions.

9   See eg Case 26/75 *General Motors Continental NV v EC Commission* [1975] ECR 1367, [1976] 1 CMLR 95; Case 226/84 *British Leyland plc v EC Commission* [1986] ECR 3263, [1987] 1 CMLR 185; Case 311/84 *Centre Belge d'Etudes de Marché-Télémarketing v CLT* [1985] ECR 3261, [1986] 2 CMLR 558.

10 See EC Commission Decision 89/113 (*Decca Navigator System*) OJ L43, 15.2.89, p 27, [1990] 4 CMLR 627.

11 Ownership of intellectual property rights does not necessarily put the owner into a dominant position (see Case 24/67 *Parke, Davis & Co v Probel* [1968] ECR 55, [1968] CMLR 47; Case 40/70 *Sirena v Eda* [1971] ECR 69, [1971] CMLR 260; Case 78/70 *Deutsche Grammophon v Metro* [1971] ECR 487, [1971] CMLR 631; Cases C-241–242/91P *RTE and ITP v EC Commission* [1995] ECR I-743, [1995] 4 CMLR 718) but may be a significant factor (see eg Case T-30/89 *Hilti AG v EC Commission* [1991] ECR II-1439, [1992] 4 CMLR 16; confirmed on appeal Case C-53/92P *Hilti AG v EC Commission* [1994] ECR I-667, [1994] 4 CMLR 614; EC Commission Decision 88/501 (*Tetra Pak*) OJ L272, 4.10.88, p 27, [1990] 4 CMLR 47).

12 The European Court of Justice has held that a position of technological superiority allows an undertaking an advantage in terms of product development: see eg Case 85/76 *Hoffmann-La Roche & Co AG v EC Commission* [1979] ECR 461, [1979] 3 CMLR 211; Case 27/76 *United Brands v EC Commission* [1978] ECR 207, [1978] 1 CMLR 429.

13 Ie the relation of costs of production to the size of the market. See eg Case 27/76 *United Brands Co v EC Commission* [1978] ECR 207, [1978] 1 CMLR 429, ECJ; EC Commission Decision 89/22 (*BPB Industries plc*) OJ L10, 13.1.89, p 50, [1989] 4 CMLR 84.

14 See Case 85/76 *Hoffmann-La Roche & Co AG v EC Commission* [1979] ECR 461, [1979] 3 CMLR 211; Case 27/76 *United Brands v EC Commission* [1978] ECR 207, [1978] 1 CMLR 429. See also EC Commission Decision 72/21 (*Continental Can Co*) OJ L7, 8.1.72, p 25, [1972] CMLR D11.

15 See Case 27/76 *United Brands v EC Commission* [1978] ECR 207, [1978] 1 CMLR 429; EC Commission Decision 89/22 (*BPB Industries plc*) OJ L10, 13.1.89, p 50, [1989] 4 CMLR 84.

16 See eg EC Commission Decision 89/22 (*BPB Industries plc*) OJ L10, 13.1.89, p 50, [1989] 4 CMLR 84 (undertaking controlled virtually all the deposits of gypsum in Great Britain); EEC Commission Decision 91/299 (*Soda-ash/Solvay*) OJ L152, 15.6.91, p 21, (undertaking was the largest producer of the raw material (salt) in the Community).

17 See eg Case 27/76 *United Brands v EC Commission* [1978] ECR 207, [1978] 1 CMLR 429 (bananas were repeatedly advertised as superior to other brands). See also Case 322/81 *Nederlandsche Banden-Industrie Michelin v EC Commission* [1983] ECR 3461, [1985] 1 CMLR 282; EC Commission Decision 93/252 (*Wilkinson Sword/Gillette*) OJ L116, 12.5.93, p 21.

18 Where the market is mature new entrants may be discouraged from entering it: see eg EC Commission Decision 88/501 (*Tetra Pak*) OJ L272, 4.10.88, p 27, [1990] 4 CMLR 47.

19 See Case 85/76 *Hoffmann-La Roche & Co AG v EC Commission* [1979] ECR 461, [1979] 3 CMLR 211.
20 Ie looking at the undertaking's commercial behaviour as an indicator of dominance: see EEC Commission Decision 91/299 (*Soda-ash/Solvay*) OJ L152, 15.6.91, p 21; Case T-30/89 *Hilti AG v EC Commission* [1991] ECR II-1439, [1992] 4 CMLR 16 (confirmed on appeal Case C-53/92P *Hilti AG v EC Commission* [1994] ECR I-667, [1994] 4 CMLR 614).
21 Ie reducing prices to drive competitors from the market. See eg EC Commission Decision 88/518 (*Napier Brown/British Sugars*) OJ L284, 19.10.89, p 41, [1990] 4 CMLR 196; Case 85/76 *Hoffmann-La Roche & Co AG v EC Commission* [1979] ECR 461, [1979] 3 CMLR 211.
22 See eg EEC Commission Decision 91/299 (*Soda-ash/Solvay*) OJ L152, 15.6.91, p 21.
23 See the Directorate-General for Competition *Discussion Paper on the Application of article 82 of the Treaty to Exclusionary Abuses*, 19 December 2005; and the *Communication from the Commission — Guidance on the Commission's enforcement priorities in applying Article 82 of the EC Treaty to abusive exclusionary conduct by dominant undertakings* (OJ C45, 24.2.2009, p 7); and Case T-228/97 *Irish Sugar v EC Commission* [2000] All ER (EC) 198, [1999] ECR II-2969, CFI.
24 See Case C-393/92 *Gemeente Alemo v NV Energiebedrijf IJsselmij* [1994] ECR I-1477; elaborating on the principle stated in EEC Commission Decision 89/93 (*Italian Flat Glass*) OJ L33, 4.2.89, p 44, [1990] 4 CMLR 535. See further Case T-342/99 *Airtours plc v EC Commission* [2002] ECR II-2585, [2002] 5 CMLR 317.
25 Case T-193/02 *Laurent Piau v EC Commission* [2005] ECR II-209, [2005] 5 CMLR 42, CFI.
26 See Case 6/72 *Europemballage Corpn and Continental Can Co Inc v EC Commission* [1973] ECR 215, [1973] CMLR 199, ECJ.
27 The relevant product market has been discussed in eg Case 322/81 *Nederlandsche Banden-Industrie Michelin v EC Commission* [1983] ECR 3461, [1985] 1 CMLR 282; Case 85/76 *Hoffmann-La Roche & Co AG v EC Commission* [1979] ECR 461, [1979] 3 CMLR 211, ECJ; Case 6/72 *Europemballage Corpn and Continental Can Co Inc v EC Commission* [1973] ECR 215, [1973] CMLR 199, ECJ.
28 See EC Commission Notice on the Definition of the Relevant Market for the purposes of Community Competition Law (OJ C372, 9.12.97, p 5). The concept of the relevant market has been discussed in relation to the EC Treaty art 81 (see PARA 32).

70.   Substantial part of the common market.   Article 82[1] does not apply unless the dominant position[2] is held in the whole or a substantial part of the common market[3]. It is a question of fact in each case which cannot be determined solely on a geographical basis. The pattern and volume of the production and consumption of the product as well as the habits and economic opportunities of vendors and purchasers must be considered[4]. A substantial part cannot be determined solely by looking at the percentage of the common market involved[5]. A member state has been held to be a substantial part of the common market[6], as has a part of a member state[7].

1   See the EC Treaty art 82; and PARA 68. As to the EC Treaty (ie the Treaty establishing the European Community (Rome, 25 March 1957; TS 1 (1973); Cmnd 5179)) see PARA 24 note 1. This is a separate issue from determining the relevant market (see PARA 69 text and notes 26–28).
2   See PARA 69.
3   See the EC Treaty art 82; and PARA 69.
4   See Joined Cases 40–48, 50, 54–56, 111, 113, 114/73 *Coöperatieve verening Suiker Unie UA v EC Commission* [1975] ECR 1663, [1976] 1 CMLR 295, ECJ.
5   Such an approach has been criticised: see Case 77/77 *Benzine en Petroleum Handelsmaatschappij BV v EC Commission* [1978] ECR 1513, [1978] 3 CMLR 174, ECJ.
6   See Joined Cases 40–48, 50, 54–56, 111, 113, 114/73 *Coöperatieve verening Suiker Unie UA v EC Commission* [1975] ECR 1663, [1976] 1 CMLR 295, ECJ; Case 26/75 *General Motors Continental NV v EC Commission* [1975] ECR 1367, [1976] 1 CMLR 95, ECJ; Case 322/81 *Nederlandsche Banden-Industrie Michelin v EC Commission* [1983] ECR 3461, [1985] 1 CMLR 282.
7   See Joined Cases 40–48, 50, 54–56, 111, 113, 114/73 *Coöperatieve verening Suiker Unie UA v EC Commission* [1975] ECR 1663, [1976] 1 CMLR 295, ECJ; Case 22/78 *Hugin Kassaregister AB v EC Commission* [1979] ECR 1869, [1979] 3 CMLR 345, ECJ. In some

cases, a particular place has been held to be a substantial part of the common market: see eg *B & I Line plc v Sealink Harbours Ltd and Sealink Stena Ltd* [1992] 5 CMLR 255 (port of Holyhead); EC Commission Decision 98/190 (*KLM Royal Dutch Airlines NV v Flughafen Frankfurt/Main AG*) OJ L72, 11.3.98, p 30, [1998] 4 CMLR 779 (Frankfurt Airport).

71. Abusive behaviour. It is not a contravention of EC competition law simply that an undertaking is dominant in the whole or part of the common market[1]. For an offence to be committed, the undertaking must have abused the position of dominance[2].

A number of examples of abusive behaviour are given in article 82, namely:

(1)   directly or indirectly imposing unfair purchase or selling prices or other unfair trading conditions[3];

(2)   limiting production, markets or technical development to the prejudice of consumers[4];

(3)   applying dissimilar conditions to equivalent transactions with other trading parties, thereby placing them at a competitive disadvantage[5]; and

(4)   making the conclusion of contracts subject to the acceptance by the other parties of supplementary obligations which, by their nature or according to commercial usage, have no connection with the subject of such contracts[6].

The term 'abuse' may also cover practices which affect the structure of the market and so affect competition[7]. The categories of abuse are not closed and may include conduct that would be unexceptionable in a non-dominant firm.

A distinction is drawn between exploitative abuses, that is to say the exploiting of customers by reducing output and increasing prices, and exclusionary abuses, that is to say behaviour aimed at reducing competition. The European Commission gives priority to exclusionary abuses which are liable to have harmful effects on consumers, the most common of which are exclusive dealing, rebates, tying and bundling, predatory practices, refusal to supply and margin squeeze[8].

1   See the EC Treaty art 82; and PARAS 69–70. As to the EC Treaty (ie the Treaty establishing the European Community (Rome, 25 March 1957; TS 1 (1973); Cmnd 5179)) see PARA 24 note 1.
2   See the EC Treaty art 82; and PARA 69. A dominant undertaking owes a special responsibility to the competitive process: see Case 322/81 *Nederlandsche Banden-Industrie Michelin v EC Commission* [1983] ECR 3461, [1985] 1 CMLR 282. 'Superdominant' undertakings (ie undertakings whose dominance approaches monopoly) owe a greater responsibility: see Cases C-395–396/96P *Compagnie Maritime Belge Transports SA v EC Commission* [2000] All ER (EC) 385, [2000] ECR I-1365, ECJ.
3   EC Treaty art 82(a). See Case T-340/03 *France Télécom SA (formerly Wanadoo Interactive SA) v EC Commission* [2008] All ER (EC) 677, [2007] 4 CMLR 919, CFI (evidence of predatory pricing amounted to abuse of dominant position).
4   EC Treaty art 82(b).
5   EC Treaty art 82(c).
6   EC Treaty art 82(d).
7   See EC Commission Decision 72/21 (*Continental Can Co*) OJ L7, 8.1.72, p 25, [1972] CMLR D11; Case 322/81 *Nederlandsche Banden-Industrie Michelin v EC Commission* [1983] ECR 3461, [1985] 1 CMLR 282; Case 85/76 *Hoffmann-La Roche & Co AG v EC Commission* [1979] ECR 461, [1979] 3 CMLR 211.
8   See *Communication from the Commission — Guidance on the Commission's enforcement priorities in applying Article 82 of the EC Treaty to abusive exclusionary conduct by dominant undertakings* (OJ C45, 24.2.2009, p 7).

72. Defences. If a dominant undertaking[1] can show that its conduct can be objectively justified then the conduct will not be held to be an abuse[2]. This concept has been applied to distinguish legitimate commercial behaviour from abusive conduct aimed at weakening the competition[3].

The European Commission has stated that in the enforcement of article 82[4], it will examine claims put forward by a dominant undertaking that its conduct is justified. A dominant undertaking may do so either by demonstrating that its conduct is objectively necessary or by demonstrating that its conduct produces substantial efficiencies which outweigh any anticompetitive effects on consumers. In this context, the Commission will assess whether the conduct in question is indispensable and proportionate to the goal allegedly pursued by the dominant undertaking[5].

1 See PARA 69.
2 As to abusive behaviour see PARA 71.
3 See eg Case 311/84 *Centre Belge d'Etudes de Marché-Télémarketing v CLT* [1985] ECR 3261, [1986] 2 CMLR 558. Tie-in provisions were found to have no objective justification in EC Commission Decision 88/138 (*Hilti*) OJ L65, 11.3.88, p 19, [1989] 4 CMLR 677; and EC Commission Decision 92/163 (*Tetra Pak II*) (upheld in Case T-83/91 *Tetra Pak International SA v EC Commission* [1994] ECR II-755, [1997] 4 CMLR 726, CFI).
4 See the EC Treaty art 82; and PARAS 69–70. As to the EC Treaty (ie the Treaty establishing the European Community (Rome, 25 March 1957; TS 1 (1973); Cmnd 5179)) see PARA 24 note 1.
5 See *Communication from the Commission — Guidance on the Commission's enforcement priorities in applying Article 82 of the EC Treaty to abusive exclusionary conduct by dominant undertakings* (OJ C45, 24.2.2009, p 7) paras 28–31.

(5) MERGER CONTROL

(i) Control by the Merger Regulation

73. Concentration. Until 1990 article 82 of the EC Treaty[1] operated to some degree to govern the control concentrations and mergers under EC competition law[2]. However, the point ceased to be of practical importance when a distinct regime for the control of mergers was introduced by the adoption of the Merger Control Regulation[3].

In 2004 the Merger Control Regulation was itself replaced by the Merger Regulation[4].

1 See the EC Treaty art 82; and PARA 68. As to the EC Treaty (ie the Treaty establishing the European Community (Rome, 25 March 1957; TS 1 (1973); Cmnd 5179)) see PARA 24 note 1.
2 See Case 6/72 *Europemballage Corpn and Continental Can Co Inc v EC Commission* [1973] ECR 215, [1973] CMLR 199, ECJ, where the court held that some merger activity could be controlled under art 82.
3 Ie EC Council Regulation 4064/89 (OJ L395, 30.12.89, p 1) (the 'Merger Control Regulation').
4 Ie EC Council Regulation 139/2004 on the control of concentrations between undertakings (OJ L24, 29.1.2004, p 1) (the 'Merger Regulation'). See PARA 74.

74. The Merger Regulation. A Council regulation on the control of concentration between undertakings (the 'Merger Regulation')[1] came into force on 1 May 2004.

The regulation contains extensive provisions to deal with concentration. A concentration is deemed to arise where a change of control on a lasting basis results from the merger of two or more previously independent undertakings or the acquisition, by persons already controlling one undertaking, of direct or indirect control of other undertakings[2]. The regulation covers concentrations with a Community dimension where:

(1) the combined aggregate worldwide turnover of all the undertakings concerned is more than EUR 5,000 million; and

(2)   the aggregate Community-wide turnover of each of at least two of the undertakings concerned is more than EUR 250 million,

unless each of the undertakings concerned achieves more than two-thirds of its aggregate Community-wide turnover within one and the same member state[3].

A concentration that does not meet these thresholds may nevertheless have a Community dimension where:

(a)   the combined aggregate worldwide turnover of all the undertakings concerned is more than EUR 2500 million;

(b)   in each of at least three member states, the combined aggregate turnover of all the undertakings concerned is more than EUR 100 million;

(c)   in each of at least three member states included for the purpose of head (b), the aggregate turnover of each of at least two of the undertakings concerned is more than EUR 25 million; and

(d)   the aggregate Community-wide turnover of each of at least two of the undertakings concerned is more than EUR 100 million,

unless each of the undertakings concerned achieves more than two-thirds of its aggregate Community-wide turnover within one and the same member state[4].

A concentration between foreign entities that has anti-competitive effects within the Community will fall within the scope of the regulation provided that the turnover thresholds set out above are satisfied[5]. A concentration which would significantly impede effective competition, in the common market or in a substantial part of it, in particular as a result of the creation or strengthening of a dominant position, is incompatible with the common market[6].

Concentrations are appraised by the Commission with a view to establishing whether or not they are compatible with the common market, taking into account the need to maintain and develop effective competition within the common market, and the market position of the undertakings concerned and their economic and financial power[7].

The regulation provides for:

(i)   mandatory prior notification of all concentrations that satisfy the regulation's turnover requirements[8];

(ii)   a mandatory suspensory period during which the concentration may not be implemented until the Commission has adopted a final decision unless a specific individual derogation is granted[9];

(iii) fines of up to 10 per cent of the annual turnover of the companies concerned for a failure to notify, for implementation of the concentration in the suspensory period or following a determination that the concentration is incompatible with the common market[10]; and

(iv)   a review procedure by the Court of Justice[11].

1   Ie EC Council Regulation 139/2004 on the control of concentrations between undertakings (OJ L24, 29.1.2004, p 1) (the 'Merger Regulation'). See also EC Commission Regulation 802/2004 implementing EC Council Regulation 139/2004 and its annexes (OJ L133, 30.04.2004, p 1) (the 'Implementing Regulation'). The Merger Regulation replaced EC Council Regulation 4064/89 (OJ L395, 30.12.89, p 1) (the 'Merger Control Regulation'). As to the application of EC Council Regulation 139/2004 (OJ L24, 29.1.2004, p 1) generally see art 21.

2   EC Council Regulation 139/2004 (OJ L24, 29.1.2004, p 1) art 3(1). Control may be taken by purchase of securities or assets, by contract or by any other means: art 3(1). The creation of a joint venture constitutes a concentration: see art 3(4). As to when concentrations are not deemed to arise see art 3(5).

3   EC Council Regulation 139/2004 (OJ L24, 29.1.2004, p 1) art 1(2). As to the calculation of turnover see art 5. As to the EC Treaty (ie the Treaty establishing the European Community (Rome, 25 March 1957; TS 1 (1973); Cmnd 5179)) see PARA 24 note 1.

4   EC Council Regulation 139/2004 (OJ L24, 29.1.2004, p 1) art 1(3).

5 See Case T-102/96 *Gencor Ltd v EC Commission* [1997] ECR II-879, [1997] 5 CMLR 290, [1998] 1 CMLR 142, [1999] All ER (EC) 289, CFI.
6 EC Council Regulation 139/2004 (OJ L24, 29.1.2004, p 1) art 2(3).
7 See EC Council Regulation 139/2004 (OJ L24, 29.1.2004, p 1) art 2.
8 EC Council Regulation 139/2004 (OJ L24, 29.1.2004, p 1) art 4(1). Failure to comply with the notification requirements may result in the undertakings being fined: art 14. See eg EC Commission Decision 1999/459 (*A P Møller*) OJ L183, 16.7.99, p 29 in which an undertaking was fined EUR 219,000 for failing to notify and for putting into effect three concentrations. As to fines see PARA 107 et seq.
9 EC Council Regulation 139/2004 (OJ L24, 29.1.2004, p 1) art 7.
10 EC Council Regulation 139/2004 (OJ L24, 29.1.2004, p 1) art 14.
11 EC Council Regulation 139/2004 (OJ L24, 29.1.2004, p 1) art 16.

75. Supplementary notices. The Commission has issued a number of notices supplemental to or interpretative of the Merger Regulation[1] dealing with: jurisdiction[2]; simplified procedure[3]; case referrals[4]; non-horizontal guidelines[5]; horizontal guidelines[6]; relevant market[7]; remedies[8]; ancillary restraints[9]; the role of the hearing officer[10]; access to file[11]; and abandonment of concentrations[12].

1 Ie EC Council Regulation 139/2004 (OJ L24, 29.1.2004, p 1). See PARA 74.
2 See Commission Consolidated Jurisdictional Notice under EC Council Regulation 139/2004 on the control of concentrations between undertakings (OJ C95, 16.4.2008, p 1).
3 See Commission Notice on a simplified procedure for treatment of certain concentrations under EC Council Regulation 139/2004 (OJ C56, 5.3.2005, p 32).
4 See Commission Notice on Case Referral in respect of concentrations (OJ C56, 5.3.2005, p 2).
5 See Guidelines on the assessment of non-horizontal mergers under the Council Regulation on the control of concentrations between undertakings (OJ C265, 18.10.2008, p 6).
6 See Guidelines on the assessment of horizontal mergers under the Council Regulation on the control of concentrations between undertakings (OJ C31, 5.2.2004, p 5).
7 See Commission notice on the definition of the Relevant Market for the purposes of Community competition law (OJ C372, 9.12.97, p 5).
8 See Commission Notice on remedies acceptable under EC Council Regulation 139/2004 and under EC Commission Regulation 802/2004 (OJ C267, 22.10.2008, p 1).
9 See Commission Notice on restrictions directly related and necessary to concentrations (OJ C56, 5.3.2005, p 24).
10 See Commission Decision 2001/462 of 23 May 2001 on the terms of reference of hearing officers in certain competition proceedings (OJ L162, 19.6.2001, p 21).
11 See Commission Notice on the rules for access to the Commission file in cases pursuant to Articles 81 and 82 of the EC Treaty, Articles 53, 54 and 57 of the EEA Agreement and EC Council Regulation 139/2004 (OJ C325, 22.12.2005, p 7).
12 See DG Competition Information note on EC Council Regulation 139/2004 art 6(1)(c) 2nd sentence (abandonment of concentrations).

(ii) Procedural Aspects of Merger Control

76. Notification of concentrations. Concentrations with a Community dimension[1] must be notified to the Commission prior to their implementation and following the conclusion of the agreement, the announcement of the public bid, or the acquisition of a controlling interest[2]. Notification may also be made where the undertakings concerned demonstrate to the Commission a good faith intention to conclude an agreement or, in the case of a public bid, where they have publicly announced an intention to make such a bid, provided that the intended agreement or bid would result in a concentration with a Community dimension[3].

The Commission must publish the fact of the notification, at the same time indicating the names of the undertakings concerned, their country of origin, the nature of the concentration and the economic sectors involved[4].

Prior to the notification of a concentration, the parties involved may inform the Commission, by means of a reasoned submission, that the concentration may significantly affect competition in a market within a member state which presents all the characteristics of a distinct market and should therefore be examined, in whole or in part, by that member state[5]. The relevant member state then has 15 working days to express disagreement, following which it is deemed to have agreed[6]. The Commission then has 25 working days to decide whether to refer the matter to the member state to be decided according to that state's national competition law[7].

Where a case does not have a community dimension and is capable of being reviewed under the national competition laws of at least three member states, the parties involved may request that the concentration be examined by the Commission[8]. One or more member states may request the Commission to examine any concentration that does not have a community dimension but affects trade between member states and threatens to significantly affect competition within the territory of the member state or states making the request[9].

1   See PARA 74.

2   EC Council Regulation 139/2004 on the control of concentrations between undertakings (OJ L24, 29.1.2004, p 1) (the 'Merger Regulation') art 4(1). A concentration which consists of a merger or in the acquisition of joint control must be notified jointly by the parties to the merger or by those acquiring joint control as the case may be; and in all other cases, the notification must be effected by the person or undertaking acquiring control of the whole or parts of one or more undertakings: art 4(2). As to the fines payable for failure to notify and for incorrect notification see arts 14, 15, 16.

3   EC Council Regulation 139/2004 (OJ L24, 29.1.2004, p 1) art 4(1).

4   EC Council Regulation 139/2004 (OJ L24, 29.1.2004, p 1) art 4(3). The Commission must take account of the legitimate interest of undertakings in the protection of their business secrets: art 4(3).

5   EC Council Regulation 139/2004 (OJ L24, 29.1.2004, p 1) art 4(4).

6   EC Council Regulation 139/2004 (OJ L24, 29.1.2004, p 1) art 4(4).

7   EC Council Regulation 139/2004 (OJ L24, 29.1.2004, p 1) art 4(4).

8   EC Council Regulation 139/2004 (OJ L24, 29.1.2004, p 1) art 4(5). In such a case any of the member states concerned may express its disagreement within 15 working days. If no disagreement is expressed, the Commission has exclusive jurisdiction over the matter: see art 4(5).

9   See EC Council Regulation 139/2004 (OJ L24, 29.1.2004, p 1) art 22.

77. Examination of the notification and initiation of proceedings. The Commission must examine the notification as soon as it is received[1]. Where it concludes that the concentration notified does not fall within the scope of the Merger Regulation, it must record that finding by means of a decision[2]. Where it finds that the concentration notified, although falling within the scope of the Regulation, does not raise serious doubts as to its compatibility with the common market, it must decide not to oppose it and must declare that it is compatible with the common market[3]. Where the Commission finds that the concentration notified falls within the scope of the Merger Regulation and raises serious doubts as to its compatibility with the common market, it must decide to initiate proceedings[4]. Where the Commission finds that, following modification by the undertakings concerned, a notified concentration no longer raises serious doubts, it must declare the concentration compatible with the common market[5]. The Commission may revoke a decision where the decision is based on incorrect information for which one of the undertakings is responsible or where it has been obtained by deceit, or the undertakings concerned commit a breach of an obligation attached to the decision[6].

The Commission must notify its decision to the undertakings concerned and the competent authorities of the member states without delay[7].

1   EC Council Regulation 139/2004 on the control of concentrations between undertakings (OJ L24, 29.1.2004, p 1) (the 'Merger Regulation') art 6(1). As to the notification see PARA 76. As to the Merger Regulation see further PARA 74.
2   EC Council Regulation 139/2004 (OJ L24, 29.1.2004, p 1) art 6(1)(a).
3   EC Council Regulation 139/2004 (OJ L24, 29.1.2004, p 1) art 6(1)(b). A decision declaring a concentration compatible is deemed to cover restrictions directly related and necessary to the implementation of the concentration: art 6(1). The Commission may attach to its decision under art 6(1)(b) conditions and obligations intended to ensure that the undertakings concerned comply with the commitments they have entered into vis-à-vis the Commission with a view to rendering the concentration compatible with the common market: art 6(2).
4   EC Council Regulation 139/2004 (OJ L24, 29.1.2004, p 1) art 6(1)(c). Without prejudice to art 9 (see PARA 80), such proceedings are to be closed by means of a decision as provided for in art 8(1)–(4) (see PARA 79), unless the undertakings concerned have demonstrated to the satisfaction of the Commission that they have abandoned the concentration: art 6(1)(c).
5   EC Council Regulation 139/2004 (OJ L24, 29.1.2004, p 1) art 6(2).
6   EC Council Regulation 139/2004 (OJ L24, 29.1.2004, p 1) art 6(3), (4). As to time limits see art 10.
7   EC Council Regulation 139/2004 (OJ L24, 29.1.2004, p 1) art 6(5).

78.   Suspension of concentrations.   A concentration with a Community dimension[1], or which is to be examined by the Commission[2], must not be implemented either before its notification[3] or until it has been declared compatible with the common market[4]. This prohibition does not prevent the implementation of a public bid or of a series of transactions in securities including those convertible into other securities admitted to trading on a market such as a stock exchange, by which control is acquired from various sellers, provided that: (1) the concentration is notified to the Commission without delay; and (2) the acquirer does not exercise the voting rights attached to the securities in question or does so only to maintain the full value of its investments based on a derogation granted by the Commission[5].

The prohibition has no effect on the validity of transactions in securities including those convertible into other securities admitted to trading on a market such as a stock exchange, unless the buyer and seller knew or ought to have known that the transaction was carried out in contravention of the prohibition[6].

1   See PARA 74.
2   Ie pursuant to EC Council Regulation 139/2004 on the control of concentrations between undertakings (OJ L24, 29.1.2004, p 1) (the 'Merger Regulation') art 4(5) (see PARA 76). As to the Merger Regulation see further PARA 74.
3   See PARA 76.
4   EC Council Regulation 139/2004 (OJ L1, 4.1.2003, p 1) art 7(1). A declaration may be made pursuant to a decision under art 6(1)(b), 8(1) or 8(2), or on the basis of a presumption according to art 10(6). As to the fine payable for implementing a concentration in breach of art 7 see arts 14, 15, 16.
5   EC Council Regulation 139/2004 (OJ L24, 29.1.2004, p 1) art 7(2). As to the Commission's power to grant a derogation see art 7(3).
6   EC Council Regulation 139/2004 (OJ L1, 4.1.2003, p 1) art 7.

79.   Powers of decision of the Commission.   Where the Commission finds that a notified concentration[1] would not significantly impede effective competition in the common market[2] or contributes to improving the production or distribution of goods or to promoting technical or economic progress while allowing consumers a fair share of the resulting benefit[3], it must issue a decision declaring the concentration compatible with the common market[4]. Where the Commission finds that a concentration does not fulfil these criteria, it must issue a decision declaring the concentration is incompatible with the common market[5].

Where the Commission finds that a concentration has already been implemented and that concentration has been declared incompatible with the common market, or has been implemented in contravention of a condition, the Commission may require the undertakings concerned to dissolve the concentration, in particular through the dissolution of the merger or the disposal of all the shares or assets acquired, so as to restore the situation prevailing prior to the implementation of the concentration, or order any other appropriate measure to ensure the concentration is dissolved[6]. The Commission may take interim measures to restore or maintain conditions of effective competition where necessary[7].

The Commission may revoke a decision where the declaration of compatibility is based on incorrect information for which one of the undertakings is responsible or where it has been obtained by deceit, or the undertakings concerned commit a breach of an obligation attached to the decision[8].

The Commission must notify its decision to the undertakings concerned and the competent authorities of the member states without delay[9].

1   See PARA 76. This provision also applies where satisfactory modification has been made to a notified concentration: see EC Council Regulation 139/2004 on the control of concentrations between undertakings (OJ L24, 29.1.2004, p 1) (the 'Merger Regulation') art 8(2). As to the Merger Regulation see further PARA 74.
2   Ie fulfils the criterion laid down in EC Council Regulation 139/2004 (OJ L24, 29.1.2004, p 1) art 2(2).
3   Ie fulfils the criteria laid down in the EC Treaty art 81(3). As to the EC Treaty (ie the Treaty establishing the European Community (Rome, 25 March 1957; TS 1 (1973); Cmnd 5179)) see PARA 24 note 1.
4   EC Council Regulation 139/2004 (OJ L24, 29.1.2004, p 1) art 8(1). A decision declaring a concentration compatible is deemed to cover restrictions directly related and necessary to the implementation of the concentration: art 8(1). As to time limits see art 10. As to the application of time limits see art 8(7).
5   EC Council Regulation 139/2004 (OJ L24, 29.1.2004, p 1) art 8(3).
6   EC Council Regulation 139/2004 (OJ L24, 29.1.2004, p 1) art 8(4). In circumstances where restoration of the situation prevailing before the implementation of the concentration is not possible through dissolution of the concentration, the Commission may take any other measure appropriate to achieve such restoration as far as possible: art 8(4).
7   See EC Council Regulation 139/2004 (OJ L24, 29.1.2004, p 1) art 8(5).
8   EC Council Regulation 139/2004 (OJ L24, 29.1.2004, p 1) art 8(6).
9   EC Council Regulation 139/2004 (OJ L24, 29.1.2004, p 1) art 8(8).

80.   Referral to the competent authorities of the member states.   The Commission may, by means of a decision notified without delay to the undertakings concerned and the competent authorities of the other member states, refer a notified concentration[1] to the competent authorities of the member state concerned[2]. Within 15 working days of the date of receipt of the copy of the notification, a member state, on its own initiative or upon the invitation of the Commission, may inform the Commission, which must inform the undertakings concerned, that: (1) a concentration threatens to affect significantly competition in a market within that member state, which presents all the characteristics of a distinct market; or (2) a concentration affects competition in a market within that member state, which presents all the characteristics of a distinct market and which does not constitute a substantial part of the common market[3]. If the Commission considers that there is such a distinct market and that such a threat exists, it must either deal with the case itself, or refer the whole or part of the case to the competent authorities of the member state concerned to be dealt with under that state's national competition law[4]. The competent authority must decide upon the case without undue delay and must inform the undertakings concerned within 45 days[5]. The member state concerned may take only the measures strictly necessary to safeguard or restore effective competition on the market concerned[6].

1 See PARA 76.
2 EC Council Regulation 139/2004 on the control of concentrations between undertakings (OJ L24, 29.1.2004, p 1) (the 'Merger Regulation') art 9(1). As to the Merger Regulation see further PARA 74.
3 EC Council Regulation 139/2004 (OJ L24, 29.1.2004, p 1) art 9(2).
4 EC Council Regulation 139/2004 (OJ L24, 29.1.2004, p 1) art 9(3). As to the relevant time limits see arts 9(4), (5), 10. As to the geographical area see art 9(7). As to appeals by the member state to the Court of Justice see art 9(9).
5 See EC Council Regulation 139/2004 (OJ L24, 29.1.2004, p 1) art 9(6).
6 EC Council Regulation 139/2004 (OJ L24, 29.1.2004, p 1) art 9(8).

81. Requests for information. The Commission may, by simple request or by decision, require the persons carrying out a concentration[1] as well as undertakings and associations of undertakings, governments and competent authorities of member states, to provide all necessary information[2]. When requiring information, the Commission must state the legal basis and the purpose of the request, specify the information required and the time limits that apply and indicate the penalties for failure to comply[3]. The owners of the undertakings or their representatives and, in the case of legal persons, companies or firms, or associations having no legal personality, the persons authorised to represent them by law or by their constitution, must supply the information requested on behalf of the undertaking concerned[4]. The Commission must without delay forward a copy of any decision taken to the competent authorities of the member state in whose territory the residence of the person or the seat of the undertaking or association of undertakings is situated, and to the competent authority of the member state whose territory is affected[5].

The Commission may interview any natural or legal person who consents to be interviewed for the purpose of collecting information relating to the subject matter of an investigation[6]. At the beginning of the interview, which may be conducted by telephone or other electronic means, the Commission must state the legal basis and the purpose of the interview[7].

1 See PARAS 74, 76.
2 EC Council Regulation 139/2004 on the control of concentrations between undertakings (OJ L24, 29.1.2004, p 1) (the 'Merger Regulation') art 11(1). As to the Merger Regulation see further PARA 74.
3 EC Council Regulation 139/2004 (OJ L24, 29.1.2004, p 1) art 11(2), (3). Where the requirement to provide information is made by decision, the Commission must inform the person of the right to have the decision reviewed by the Court of Justice: art 11(3). As to the fines payable for the supply of misleading, incomplete or incorrect information see arts 14, 15, 16.
4 EC Council Regulation 139/2004 (OJ L24, 29.1.2004, p 1) art 11(4). Persons duly authorised to act may supply the information on behalf of their clients but the clients remain fully responsible if the information supplied is incomplete, incorrect or misleading: art 11(4).
5 EC Council Regulation 139/2004 (OJ L24, 29.1.2004, p 1) art 11(5). At the specific request of the competent authority of a member state, the Commission must also forward to that authority copies of simple requests for information relating to a notified concentration: art 11(5).

6   EC Council Regulation 139/2004 (OJ L24, 29.1.2004, p 1) art 11(7). Where an interview is not conducted on the premises of the Commission or by telephone or other electronic means, the Commission must inform in advance the competent authority of the member state in whose territory the interview takes place; if the competent authority so requests, officials of that authority may assist the officials and other persons authorised by the Commission to conduct the interview: art 11(7).
7   EC Council Regulation 139/2004 (OJ L24, 29.1.2004, p 1) art 11(7).

82.   Powers of inspection. The Commission may conduct all necessary inspections of undertakings and associations of undertakings[1]. The officials and other accompanying persons authorised by the Commission to conduct an inspection have the power:

(1)   to enter any premises, land and means of transport of undertakings and associations of undertakings;
(2)   to examine the books and other records related to the business, irrespective of the medium on which they are stored;
(3)   to take or obtain in any form copies of or extracts from such books or records;
(4)   to seal any business premises and books or records for the period and to the extent necessary for the inspection;
(5)   to ask any representative or member of staff of the undertaking or association of undertakings for explanations on facts or documents relating to the subject matter and purpose of the inspection and to record the answers[2].

At the request of the Commission, the competent authorities of the member states must undertake the inspections which the Commission considers to be necessary[3].

Undertakings are required to submit to inspections ordered by decision of the Commission[4]. Where an undertaking opposes an inspection, the member state must provide any necessary assistance to the Commission officials, including police assistance[5]. If a warrant is required, the national judicial authority must ensure that the Commission decision is authentic and that the coercive measures envisaged are neither arbitrary nor excessive having regard to the subject matter of the inspection[6].

1   EC Council Regulation 139/2004 on the control of concentrations between undertakings (OJ L24, 29.1.2004, p 1) (the 'Merger Regulation') art 13(1). As to the Merger Regulation see further PARA 74.
2   EC Council Regulation 139/2004 (OJ L24, 29.1.2004, p 1) art 13(2). Officials must produce a written authorisation for the inspection showing the penalties for failure to comply: see art 13(3). As to the fines payable see arts 14, 15, 16.
3   EC Council Regulation 139/2004 (OJ L24, 29.1.2004, p 1) art 12(1). Such inspections must be carried out in accordance with the member state's national law: art 12(1). If so requested by the Commission or by the competent authority of the member state within whose territory the inspection is to be conducted, officials and other accompanying persons authorised by the Commission may assist the officials of the authority concerned: art 12(2). The officials of the authority concerned have the powers set out in heads (1)–(5) in the text: see art 12(5).
4   See EC Council Regulation 139/2004 (OJ L24, 29.1.2004, p 1) art 13(4).
5   See EC Council Regulation 139/2004 (OJ L24, 29.1.2004, p 1) art 13(6), (7).
6   EC Council Regulation 139/2004 (OJ L24, 29.1.2004, p 1) art 13(8). The national judicial authority may ask the Commission for detailed explanations relating to the subject matter of the inspection but it may not call into question the necessity for the inspection nor demand that it be provided with the information in the Commission's file; the lawfulness of the Commission's decision is subject to review only by the Court of Justice: art 13(8).

83.   Professional secrecy. Information acquired[1] by the Commission is to be used only for the purposes of the relevant request, investigation or hearing[2]. The

Commission and the competent authorities of the member states, their officials and other servants and other persons working under the supervision of these authorities as well as officials and civil servants of other authorities of the member states must not disclose information they have acquired[3] of the kind covered by the obligation of professional secrecy[4]. These prohibitions do not prevent publication of general information or of surveys which do not contain information relating to particular undertakings or associations of undertakings[5].

1 Ie as the result of the application of EC Council Regulation 139/2004 on the control of concentrations between undertakings (OJ L24, 29.1.2004, p 1) (the 'Merger Regulation'). As to the Merger Regulation see further PARA 74.
2 EC Council Regulation 139/2004 (OJ L24, 29.1.2004, p 1) art 17(1).
3 See note 1.
4 EC Council Regulation 139/2004 (OJ L24, 29.1.2004, p 1) art 17(2). Privilege may extend to documents which have not been sent to a lawyer but have been drafted for that purpose: Cases T-125/03 and T-253/03 *Akzo Nobel Chemicals Ltd v EC Commission* [2008] All ER (EC) 1, [2008] 4 CMLR 97, CFI.
5 EC Council Regulation 139/2004 (OJ L24, 29.1.2004, p 1) art 17(3).

84. Hearing of the parties and of third persons. Before taking certain decisions[1], the Commission is required to give the persons, undertakings and associations of undertakings concerned the opportunity, at every stage of the procedure up to the consultation of the Advisory Committee, of making known their views on the objections against them[2]. The Commission must base its decision only on objections on which the parties have been able to submit their observations[3]. The rights of the defence must be fully respected in the proceedings[4]. Access to the file must be open at least to the parties directly involved, subject to the legitimate interest of undertakings in the protection of their business secrets[5].

In so far as the Commission or the competent authorities of the member states deem it necessary, they may also hear other natural or legal persons[6]. Natural or legal persons showing a sufficient interest and especially members of the administrative or management bodies of the undertakings concerned or the recognised representatives of their employees are entitled, upon application, to be heard[7].

1 Ie as provided for in EC Council Regulation 139/2004 on the control of concentrations between undertakings (OJ L24, 29.1.2004, p 1) (the 'Merger Regulation') art 6(3), art 7(3), art 8(2)–(6) and arts 14 and 15 (see PARA 77 et seq). As to the Merger Regulation see further PARA 74.
2 EC Council Regulation 139/2004 (OJ L24, 29.1.2004, p 1) art 18(1). However, a decision pursuant to arts 7(3), 8(5) may be taken provisionally, without the persons, undertakings or associations of undertakings concerned being given the opportunity to make known their views beforehand, provided that the Commission gives them that opportunity as soon as possible after having taken its decision: art 18(2). As to the Advisory Committee see PARA 85.
3 EC Council Regulation 139/2004 (OJ L24, 29.1.2004, p 1) art 18(3).
4 EC Council Regulation 139/2004 (OJ L24, 29.1.2004, p 1) art 18(3).
5 EC Council Regulation 139/2004 (OJ L24, 29.1.2004, p 1) art 18(3).
6 EC Council Regulation 139/2004 (OJ L24, 29.1.2004, p 1) art 18(4).
7 EC Council Regulation 139/2004 (OJ L24, 29.1.2004, p 1) art 18(4).

85. Liaison with the authorities of the member states. The Commission must transmit to the competent authorities of the member states copies of notifications[1] within three working days and, as soon as possible, copies of the most important documents lodged with or issued by the Commission[2]. Such documents must include commitments offered by the undertakings concerned to the Commission with a view to rendering the concentration compatible with the common market[3]. The Commission must carry out any procedures in close and constant liaison with the competent authorities of the member states, which may express their views upon those procedures[4].

An Advisory Committee on concentrations must be consulted before certain decisions are taken[5]. The Advisory Committee consists of representatives of the competent authorities of the member states. Each member state must appoint one or two representatives; if unable to attend, they may be replaced by other representatives. At least one of the representatives of a member state must be competent in matters of restrictive practices and dominant positions[6]. Consultation takes place at a joint meeting convened at the invitation of and chaired by the Commission. A summary of the case, together with an indication of the most important documents and a preliminary draft of the decision to be taken for each case considered, is sent with the invitation. The meeting takes place not less than ten working days after the invitation has been sent. The Commission may in exceptional cases shorten that period as appropriate in order to avoid serious harm to one or more of the undertakings concerned by a concentration[7]. The Advisory Committee delivers an opinion on the Commission's draft decision, if necessary by taking a vote. The Advisory Committee may deliver an opinion even if some members are absent and unrepresented. The opinion is delivered in writing and appended to the draft decision. The Commission must take the utmost account of the opinion delivered by the Committee and must inform the Committee of the manner in which its opinion has been taken into account[8]. The Commission must communicate the opinion of the Advisory Committee, together with the decision, to the addressees of the decision. It must make the opinion public together with the decision, having regard to the legitimate interest of undertakings in the protection of their business secrets[9].

1 See PARA 76.
2 EC Council Regulation 139/2004 on the control of concentrations between undertakings (OJ L24, 29.1.2004, p 1) (the 'Merger Regulation') art 19(1). As to the Merger Regulation see further PARA 74.
3 EC Council Regulation 139/2004 (OJ L24, 29.1.2004, p 1). See PARAS 77, 79.
4 EC Council Regulation 139/2004 (OJ L24, 29.1.2004, p 1) art 19(2).
5 EC Council Regulation 139/2004 (OJ L24, 29.1.2004, p 1) art 19(3). This applies to any decision taken pursuant to arts 8(1)–(6), 14, 15, with the exception of provisional decisions taken in accordance with art 18(2) (see PARA 79 et seq).
6 EC Council Regulation 139/2004 (OJ L24, 29.1.2004, p 1) art 19(4).
7 EC Council Regulation 139/2004 (OJ L24, 29.1.2004, p 1) art 19(5).
8 EC Council Regulation 139/2004 (OJ L24, 29.1.2004, p 1) art 19(6).
9 EC Council Regulation 139/2004 (OJ L24, 29.1.2004, p 1) art 19(7).

86. Publication of decisions. The Commission is required to publish the decisions which it takes[1], together with the opinion of the Advisory Committee[2], in the Official Journal of the European Union[3]. The publication must state the names of the parties and the main content of the decision; it must have regard to the legitimate interest of undertakings in the protection of their business secrets[4].

1 Ie pursuant to EC Council Regulation 139/2004 on the control of concentrations between undertakings (OJ L24, 29.1.2004, p 1) (the 'Merger Regulation') arts 8(1)–(6), 14, 15 with the exception of provisional decisions taken in accordance with art 18(2) (see PARA 79 et seq). As to the Merger Regulation see further PARA 74.
2 See PARA 85.
3 EC Council Regulation 139/2004 (OJ L24, 29.1.2004, p 1) art 20(1).
4 EC Council Regulation 139/2004 (OJ L24, 29.1.2004, p 1) art 20(2).

(6) PROCEDURAL ASPECTS TO THE ENFORCEMENT OF ARTICLES 81 AND 82

(i) National Authorities and the Commission

87. Legislative powers. Within three years of the entry into force of the EC Treaty, the Council was to adopt appropriate regulations to give effect to the principles set out in articles 81 and 82[1]. Until the entry into force of such provisions, the authorities of the member states were to rule on the admissibility of agreements and decisions and on concerted practice and on abuse of the dominant position in accordance with the law of their country and the provisions of articles 81 and 82[2]. In fact, there were no decisions taken by member states during the transitional period and with the enactment of Regulation 17 of 1962[3], it was no longer possible for member states to rely on these powers, other than in relation to sea and air transport and in these areas such a possibility was removed by regulations passed in 1986[4], 1987[5], 2004[6] and 2006[7].

Without prejudice to the power of member states to rule on the admissibility of decisions, agreements and practices[8], the Commission must ensure the application of the principles laid down in articles 81 and 82. On application by a member state or on its own initiative, and in co-operation with the competent authorities in the member states (who must give it their assistance), the Commission must investigate cases of suspected infringement of these principles. If it finds that there has been an infringement, it must propose appropriate measures to bring it to an end[9].

In 2003, a new procedure was put into place by the Modernisation Regulation[10]. This replaced the previous system with a directly applicable system in which the competition authorities and courts of the member states have the power to apply articles 81 and 82 of the EC Treaty in full[11].

1 EC Treaty art 83. As to the EC Treaty (ie the Treaty establishing the European Community (Rome, 25 March 1957; TS 1 (1973); Cmnd 5179)) see PARA 24 note 1.
2 EC Treaty art 84.
3 Ie EC Council Regulation 17 of 6 February 1962 (OJ 1962 p 204; (S Edn 1959–1962 p 87)) art 4, para 2(1).
4 EC Council Regulation 4056/86 (OJ L378, 31.12.86, p 4).
5 EC Council Regulation 3976/87 (OJ L374, 31.12.87, p 9).
6 EC Council Regulation 411/2004 (OJ L68, 6.3.2004, p 1).
7 EC Council Regulation 1419/2006 (OJ L269 28.9.2006 p 1).
8 Ie under the EC Treaty art 84 (see the text and note 2).
9 EC Treaty art 85(1). If the infringement is not brought to an end, the Commission must record such infringement of the principles in a reasoned decision; it may publish its decision and authorise member states to take the measures, the conditions and details of which it must determine, needed to remedy the situation: art 85(2).
10 Ie EC Council Regulation 1/2003 on the implementation of the rules on competition laid down in Articles 81 and 82 of the Treaty (OJ L1, 4.1.2003, p 1).
11 See EC Council Regulation 1/2003 (OJ L1, 4.1.2003, p 1) arts 5, 6.

88. Jurisdiction and liaison. The Commission must transmit copies of the most important documents lodged therewith to the competent authorities of the member states[1]. The competition authorities and the national courts of the member states have the power to apply articles 81 and 82 of the Treaty in individual cases[2]. The competition authorities of the member states must inform the Commission in writing before or without delay after commencing the first formal investigative measure[3]. The Commission and the competition authorities of the member states have the power to provide one another with and use in evidence any matter of fact or of law, including confidential information[4]. Where competition authorities of two or more member states have received a complaint or are acting on their own initiative against the same agreement, decision of an association or practice, the fact that one authority is dealing with the case is sufficient grounds for the others to suspend the proceedings before them or to reject the complaint, and the Commission may likewise reject a complaint on the ground that a competition authority of a member state is dealing with the case[5]. Where a competition authority of a member state or the Commission has received a complaint against an agreement, decision of an association or practice which has already been dealt with by another competition authority, it may reject it[6].

1   EC Council Regulation 1/2003 on the implementation of the rules on competition laid down in Articles 81 and 82 of the Treaty (OJ L1, 4.1.2003, p 1) (the 'Modernisation Regulation') art 11(2). As to the right of an individual lawyer to see copies of replies which the European Commission had given to member state courts who asked for information about the application and interpretation of various aspects of EC Competition rules see Joined Cases C-174/98P and C-189/98P *Netherlands v EC Commission* [2000] ECR 1, [2002] 1 CMLR 457, sub nom *Van der Wal (supported by Kingdom of The Netherlands, intervener) v EC Commission* (2000) Times, 22 February, ECJ.
2   See EC Council Regulation 1/2003 (OJ L1, 4.1.2003, p 1) arts 5, 6. As to the EC Treaty (ie the Treaty establishing the European Community (Rome, 25 March 1957; TS 1 (1973); Cmnd 5179)) see PARA 24 note 1.
3   See EC Council Regulation 1/2003 (OJ L1, 4.1.2003, p 1) art 11(3).
4   See EC Council Regulation 1/2003 (OJ L1, 4.1.2003, p 1) art 12.
5   See EC Council Regulation 1/2003 (OJ L1, 4.1.2003, p 1) art 13(1).
6   See EC Council Regulation 1/2003 (OJ L1, 4.1.2003, p 1) art 13(2).

89.   The Advisory Committee on Restrictive Practices and Dominant Positions.   Before it makes a decision as to the infringement of the EC Treaty article 81 or article 82[1], the Commission is required to consult the Advisory Committee on Restrictive Practices and Dominant Positions, which is composed of representatives of the competition authorities of the member states[2]. The Commission must take the utmost account of the opinion delivered by the Advisory Committee[3].

1   As to the EC Treaty (ie the Treaty establishing the European Community (Rome, 25 March 1957; TS 1 (1973); Cmnd 5179)) see PARA 24 note 1.
2   EC Council Regulation 1/2003 on the implementation of the rules on competition laid down in Articles 81 and 82 of the Treaty (OJ L1, 4.1.2003, p 1) (the 'Modernisation Regulation') art 14(1), (2).
3   EC Council Regulation 1/2003 (OJ L1, 4.1.2003, p 1) art 14(5).

90.   Sector inquiries.   The Commission may conduct inquiries into any economic sector and in that regard may request undertakings in the sector concerned to supply the information necessary for the Commission's investigation[1]. The Commission may in particular request the undertaking concerned to communicate to it all agreements, decisions and concerted practices[2]. The Commission may publish a report on the results of its inquiry into particular sectors of the economy or particular types of agreements across various sectors and invite comments from interested parties[3]. Recent sector inquiries have been carried out in relation to business insurance[4], retail banking[5] and gas and electricity[6] amongst others.

1   EC Council Regulation 1/2003 on the implementation of the rules on competition laid down in Articles 81 and 82 of the Treaty (OJ L1, 4.1.2003, p 1) (the 'Modernisation Regulation') art 17(1).

2 EC Council Regulation 1/2003 (OJ L1, 4.1.2003, p 1) art 17(1). As to concerted practices see PARA 63.
3 EC Council Regulation 1/2003 (OJ L1, 4.1.2003, p 1) art 17(1).
4 See *Communication from the Commission to the European Parliament, the Council, the European Economic and Social Committee and the Committee of the Regions – Sector Inquiry under Article 17 of Regulation (EC) No 1/2003 on business insurance* (COM/2007/0556).
5 See *Communication from the Commission – Sector Inquiry under Article 17 of EC Regulation 1/2003 on retail banking* (COM/2007/0033).
6 See *Communication from the Commission – Inquiry pursuant to Article 17 of EC Regulation 1/2003 into the European gas and electricity sectors* (COM/2006/0851).

(ii) Administrative Procedure

91. Requests for information. The Commission may, by simple request or by decision, require undertakings and associations of undertakings to provide all necessary information[1]. When requiring information, the Commission must state the legal basis and the purpose of the request, specify the information required and the time limits that apply and indicate the penalties for failure to comply[2]. The owners of the undertakings or their representatives and, in the case of legal persons, companies or firms, or associations having no legal personality, the persons authorised to represent them by law or by their constitution, must supply the information requested on behalf of the undertaking concerned[3]. The Commission must without delay forward a copy of any decision taken to the competent authorities of the member state in whose territory the seat of the undertaking or association of undertakings is situated, and to the competent authority of the member state whose territory is affected[4].

The Commission may interview any natural or legal person who consents to be interviewed for the purpose of collecting information relating to the subject matter of an investigation[5].

1 EC Council Regulation 1/2003 on the implementation of the rules on competition laid down in Articles 81 and 82 of the Treaty (OJ L1, 4.1.2003, p 1) (the 'Modernisation Regulation') art 18(1). As to the Modernisation Regulation see further PARA 29.
2 EC Council Regulation 1/2003 (OJ L1, 4.1.2003, p 1) art 18(2), (3). Where the requirement to provide information is made by decision, the Commission must inform the person of the right to have the decision reviewed by the Court of Justice: art 18(3). As to the fines payable for the supply of misleading, incomplete or incorrect information see arts 23, 24.
3 EC Council Regulation 1/2003 (OJ L1, 4.1.2003, p 1) art 18(4). Lawyers duly authorised to act may supply the information on behalf of their clients but the clients remain fully responsible if the information supplied is incomplete, incorrect or misleading: art 18(4).
4 EC Council Regulation 1/2003 (OJ L1, 4.1.2003, p 1) art 18(5).
5 EC Council Regulation 1/2003 (OJ L1, 4.1.2003, p 1) art 19(1). Where an interview is conducted on the premises of an undertaking the Commission must inform the competent authority of the member state in whose territory the interview takes place; if the competent authority so requests, officials of that authority may assist the officials and other persons authorised by the Commission to conduct the interview: art 19(2).

92. Powers of inspection. The Commission may conduct all necessary inspections of undertakings and associations of undertakings[1]. The officials and other accompanying persons authorised by the Commission to conduct an inspection have the power:

(1) to enter any premises, land and means of transport of undertakings and associations of undertakings;

(2) to examine the books and other records related to the business, irrespective of the medium on which they are stored;

(3) to take or obtain in any form copies of or extracts from such books or records;

(4)   to seal any business premises and books or records for the period and to the extent necessary for the inspection;

(5)   to ask any representative or member of staff of the undertaking or association of undertakings for explanations on facts or documents relating to the subject matter and purpose of the inspection and to record the answers[2].

At the request of the Commission, the competent authorities of the member states must undertake the inspections which the Commission considers to be necessary[3].

Undertakings are required to submit to inspections ordered by decision of the Commission[4]. Where an undertaking opposes an inspection, the member state must provide any necessary assistance to the Commission officials, including police assistance[5]. If a warrant is required, the national judicial authority must ensure that the Commission decision is authentic and that the coercive measures envisaged are neither arbitrary nor excessive having regard to the subject matter of the inspection[6].

Provision is made for the inspection of other premises, land or means of transport (including the homes of directors and staff of the undertaking concerned) with due prior authorisation[7].

1   EC Council Regulation 1/2003 on the implementation of the rules on competition laid down in Articles 81 and 82 of the Treaty (OJ L1, 4.1.2003, p 1) (the 'Modernisation Regulation') art 20(1). As to the Modernisation Regulation see further PARA 29.
2   EC Council Regulation 1/2003 (OJ L1, 4.1.2003, p 1) art 20(2). Officials must produce a written authorisation for the inspection showing the penalties for failure to comply: see art 20(3). As to the fines payable see arts 23–26.
3   EC Council Regulation 1/2003 (OJ L1, 4.1.2003, p 1) art 22(2). Such inspections must be carried out in accordance with the member state's national law: art 22(2). If so requested by the Commission or by the competent authority of the member state within whose territory the inspection is to be conducted, officials and other accompanying persons authorised by the Commission may assist the officials of the authority concerned: art 20(5). The officials of the authority concerned have the powers set out in heads (1)–(5) in the text: see art 20(5).
4   See EC Council Regulation 1/2003 (OJ L1, 4.1.2003, p 1) art 20(4).
5   EC Council Regulation 1/2003 (OJ L1, 4.1.2003, p 1) art 20(6), (7).
6   EC Council Regulation 1/2003 (OJ L1, 4.1.2003, p 1) art 20(8). The national judicial authority may ask the Commission for detailed explanations relating to the subject matter of the inspection but it may not call into question the necessity for the inspection nor demand that it be provided with the information in the Commission's file; the lawfulness of the Commission's decision is subject to review only by the Court of Justice: see art 20(8).
7   See EC Council Regulation 1/2003 (OJ L1, 4.1.2003, p 1) art 21.

93.   Professional secrecy.   Information collected in relation to competition proceedings[1] may be used only for the purpose for which it was acquired[2]. Without prejudice to the permitted exchange and use of information between the Commission and the competition authorities of the member states, their officials, servants and other persons working under the supervision of these authorities as well as officials and civil servants of other authorities of the member states must not disclose information acquired or exchanged by them[3] and of the kind covered by the obligation of professional secrecy[4]. This obligation also applies to all representatives and experts of member states attending meetings of the Advisory Committee[5].

1   Ie information collected pursuant to EC Council Regulation 1/2003 on the implementation of the rules on competition laid down in Articles 81 and 82 of the Treaty (OJ L1, 4.1.2003, p 1) arts 17–22.
2   EC Council Regulation 1/2003 (OJ L1, 4.1.2003, p 1) art 28(1).
3   See note 1.

4   EC Council Regulation 1/2003 (OJ L1, 4.1.2003, p 1) art 28(2). Privilege may extend to
     documents which have not been sent to a lawyer but have been drafted for that purpose: Cases
     T-125/03 and T-253/03 *Akzo Nobel Chemicals Ltd v EC Commission* [2008] All ER (EC) 1,
     [2008] 4 CMLR 97, CFI.
5   EC Council Regulation 1/2003 (OJ L1, 4.1.2003, p 1) art 28(2). The Advisory Committee meets
     pursuant to art 14 (see PARA 89).

**94.   Statement of objection and hearing of the parties, complainants and
others.**   Before taking decisions relating to infringements, interim measures or
fines[1], the Commission must give the undertakings or associations of
undertakings which are the subject of the proceedings conducted by the
Commission the opportunity of being heard on the matters to which the
Commission has taken objection. The Commission must base its decisions only
on objections on which the parties concerned have been able to comment.
Complainants must be associated closely with the proceedings[2].

The Commission must inform the parties concerned of the objections raised
against them in a statement of objections which must be notified in writing to
each of the parties against whom objections are raised[3]. It is essential that the
Commission serves a statement of objection on the parties in sufficient detail to
enable them to ascertain the nature of the complaint against them and the
matters on which the Commission has based its initial views[4]. It is not necessary
that all the information necessary for the undertaking to be made aware of the
case against it is disclosed in the initial statement of objection, as long as the
details necessary for the undertaking's defence are supplied in the course of the
administrative procedure and the undertaking concerned has an opportunity to
rebut any fact produced which is contrary to its interests. The mere fact that a
statement of objection has been made does not prevent the Commission from
continuing its investigations; equally, the statement does not require to be
particularly detailed, provided it indicates the essential facts on which the
Commission bases its case. Whilst the Commission is required to provide reasons
for its decision (if it ultimately reaches a formal decision), it does not require to
refute all the arguments adduced during administrative procedures[5]. The
statement of objection must not be ambiguous, but must set out clearly the
intention and effect of the action for breach of the rules of competition[6].

Neither the initiation of a procedure, nor a statement of objection, may be
considered by its nature and the legal effects which it produces as being a
'decision' which is capable of being challenged in an action for a declaration that
it is void[7]. In the context of an administrative procedure, they are procedural
measures adopted preparatory to the decision that represents their culmination.

The rights of defence of the parties concerned must be fully respected in the
proceedings. They are entitled to have access to the Commission's file, subject to
the legitimate interest of undertakings in the protection of their business secrets.
The right of access to the file does not extend to confidential information and
internal documents of the Commission or the competition authorities of the
member states. In particular, the right of access does not extend to
correspondence between the Commission and the competition authorities of the
member states, or between the latter. However, nothing in these provisions
prevents the Commission from disclosing and using information necessary to
prove an infringement[8].

If the Commission considers it necessary, it may also hear other natural or
legal persons. Applications to be heard on the part of such persons, where they

show a sufficient interest, must be granted. The competition authorities of the member states may also ask the Commission to hear other natural or legal persons[9].

Where the Commission intends to adopt a decision relating to commitments or making a finding of inapplicability[10], it must publish a concise summary of the case and the main content of the commitments or of the proposed course of action. Interested third parties may submit their observations within a time limit which is fixed by the Commission in its publication and which may not be less than one month. Regard must be had to the legitimate interest of undertakings in the protection of their business secrets[11].

1   Ie as provided for in EC Council Regulation 1/2003 on the implementation of the rules on competition laid down in Articles 81 and 82 of the Treaty (OJ L1, 4.1.2003, p 1) arts 7, 8, 23 and 24(2).
2   EC Council Regulation 1/2003 (OJ L1, 4.1.2003, p 1) art 27(1).
3   See EC Commission Regulation 773/2004 (OJ L123, 27.4.2004, p 18) art 10.
4   See Case T-221/95 *Endemol Entertainment Holding BV v EC Commission* [1999] All ER (EC) 385, [1999] 5 CMLR 611, CFI (right of businesses to have their business secrets protected had to be balanced against safeguarding rights of defence; Commission could be required to reconcile opposing interests by preparing non-confidential versions of documents containing business secrets or other sensitive information).
5   Case 41/69 *ACF Chemiefarma NV v EC Commission* [1970] ECR 661, ECJ (Quinine Cartel).
6   Joined Cases T-25, 26, 30–32, 34–39, 42–46, 48, 50–65, 68–71, 87, 88, 103, 104/95 *Cimenteries CBR SA v EC Commission* [2000] ECR II-491, [2000] 5 CMLR 204, CFI.
7   Case 60/81 *International Business Machines Corpn v EC Commission* [1981] ECR 2639, [1981] 3 CMLR 635, ECJ. See also Case C-413/06 *Bertelsmann AG v Independent Music Publishers and Labels Association* [2008] 5 CMLR 1073, [2008] All ER (D) 151 (Jul) (ECJ: Grand Chamber).
8   EC Council Regulation 1/2003 (OJ L1, 4.1.2003, p 1) art 27(2).
9   EC Council Regulation 1/2003 (OJ L1, 4.1.2003, p 1) art 27(3).
10 Ie pursuant to EC Council Regulation 1/2003 (OJ L1, 4.1.2003, p 1) art 9 or art 10.
11 EC Council Regulation 1/2003 (OJ L1, 4.1.2003, p 1) art 27(4).

95.   Service. The Commission is required to inform undertakings in writing of the objections raised against them and only to deal in its decisions with those objections raised against undertakings in respect of which they have been afforded the opportunity of making known their views[1]. There is no particular method by which the complaint is to be brought to the attention of the undertaking concerned, and posting the statement to an undertaking outside the Community can still constitute effective service[2]. It has been held that the fact that the notification did not comply with the law of the state where the undertaking was established did not affect the service of the document as far as Community law was concerned, because the undertaking had received it and had thus an opportunity of making known its views[3].

1   See EC Commission Regulation 773/2004 (OJ L123, 27.4.2004, p 18) art 10. See also Case T-221/95 *Endemol Entertainment Holding BV v EC Commission* [1999] All ER (EC) 385, [1999] 5 CMLR 611, CFI.
2   Case 52/69 *JR Geigy AG v EC Commission* [1972] ECR 787, [1972] CMLR 557, ECJ.
3   Case 52/69 *JR Geigy AG v EC Commission* [1972] ECR 787, [1972] CMLR 557, ECJ. See also Case 53/69 *Sandoz AG v EC Commission* [1972] ECR 845, [1972] CMLR 557, ECJ.

96.   Hearings. The Commission has set out the procedures to be followed in a hearing to afford an undertaking an opportunity to reply to a statement of objections[1]. This procedure distinguishes between parties to whom the Commission has addressed objections[2] and other interested parties[3], provides for the recording of statements made at oral hearings, and for tape recording to replace written minutes[4]. The procedures set out in the regulation apply in all competition cases other than mergers[5].

1   See EC Commission Regulation 773/2004 (OJ L123, 27.4.2004, p 18) arts 11–14.
      As to access to the Commission's administrative file see PARA 101. As to the EC Treaty (ie the Treaty establishing the European Community (Rome, 25 March 1957; TS 1 (1973); Cmnd 5179)) see PARA 24 note 1.

2   See EC Commission Regulation 773/2004 (OJ L123, 27.4.2004, p 18) arts 11, 12.

3   See EC Commission Regulation 773/2004 (OJ L123, 27.4.2004, p 18) art 13.

4   See EC Commission Regulation 773/2004 (OJ L123, 27.4.2004, p 18) art 13(8).
5   See PARA 74.

97.   The Hearing Officer.   Following its *Eleventh Report on Competition Policy*[1], the Commission appointed a Hearing Officer to ensure hearings are properly conducted and to contribute to the objectivity of the hearing itself and of any decision taken subsequently. The Hearing Officer is to seek to ensure in particular that in the preparation of draft Commission decisions in competition cases due account is taken of all relevant facts, whether favourable or unfavourable to the parties concerned, and to see that the rights of the defence are respected, taking account of the need for effective application of the competition rules in accordance with the regulations in force under principles laid down by the Court of Justice[2].

It has been stated that the report of the Hearing Officer does not require to be passed either to the Advisory Committee[3] or to the Commission; the report is not one which the Commission was required to obtain when taking a decision pursuant to article 81 of the EC Treaty[4].

In 1994 the Commission extended the terms of reference of the Hearing Officer by delegating to him the right to take decisions concerning the right to a hearing and on access to the Commission's file on the matter[5].

In May 2001, the Commission further strengthened the role of the Hearing Officer by attaching him directly to the Competition Commissioner; his report will be made available to the parties and will be published in the *Official Journal* with the final decision, improving transparency in the decision making process[6].

Oral hearings are to be conducted by a Hearing Officer in full independence[7].

1   See *Eleventh Report on Competition Policy 1981*, point 26.

2   EC Commission Notice on Procedures for applying the Competition Rules (OJ C251, 25.9.82, p 2); Terms of Reference in *Thirteenth Report on Competition Policy 1983*, pp 273, 274. It should be noted that there had only been one case in which a decision had been annulled because the Commission introduced into a formal decision a matter which was not raised at the hearing stage: see Case 17/74 *Transocean Marine Paint Association v EC Commission* [1974] ECR 1063, [1974] 2 CMLR 459, ECJ.
3   As to the Advisory Committee see PARA 372.

4   Joined Cases T-1–4, 6–8/89 *Rhône-Poulenc SA v EC Commission* [1990] ECR II-637, [1991] ECR II-867, CFI. As to the EC Treaty (ie the Treaty establishing the European Community (Rome, 25 March 1957; TS 1 (1973); Cmnd 5179)) see PARA 24 note 1.

5   EC Commission Decision 94/810 (OJ L330, 21.12.94, p 67). It is also believed that the Commission has approved a notice (to be published) dealing with parties' access to the Commission's file: See EC Commission Press Release IP (94)957 of 19 October 1994. As to the file see PARA 388.

6   EC Commission Press Release IP (01)736 of 23 May 2001.

7   See EC Commission Regulation 773/2004 (OJ L123, 27.4.2004, p 18) art 14.

98.   Notification of decisions.   Decisions must be notified to the persons to whom they are addressed, and take effect upon such notification[1]. Irregularities in the procedure of notification of the decision are external to the legal act and therefore cannot vitiate it[2].

A decision is properly notified within the meaning of the EC Treaty if it reaches the addressee and puts the latter in a position to take cognisance of it[3]. It does not appear essential that notification is made in any particular way, or indeed that notification is made directly to the undertaking in question, although this would be the normal procedure[4].

1   EC Treaty art 254. As to the EC Treaty (ie the Treaty establishing the European Community (Rome, 25 March 1957; TS 1 (1973); Cmnd 5179)) see PARA 24 note 1.
2   Case 48/69 *Imperial Chemical Industries Ltd v EC Commission* [1972] ECR 619, [1972] CMLR 557, ECJ. In that case, a decision taken against ICI in the United Kingdom (which at that time was not a member of the Community) was notified by sending a copy of the decision to its German subsidiary which, ICI maintained, did not have authority to accept service on its behalf. In addition, under German law, such a subsidiary was under no obligation to bring the documents in question to ICI's notice. However, in that case, it was apparent that ICI had complete knowledge of the text of the decision and availed itself of the opportunity within the time limits provided in the decision to raise an action for its annulment: Case 48/69 *Imperial Chemical Industries Ltd v EC Commission* at 652, 620, ECJ (judgment, para 42).
3   Case 6/72 *Europemballage Corpn and Continental Can Co Inc v EC Commission* [1973] ECR 215 at 241, [1973] CMLR 199 at 221, ECJ (judgment, para 10).
4   Cf the procedure for service of a statement of objections (see PARA 95).

99.   Publicity.   The Commission is required to publish the decisions which it takes in respect of infringement of article 81 or article 82 of the EC Treaty[1] and in respect of penalties for breach[2]. The publication must state the names of the parties and the main content of the decision, including any penalties imposed[3]. Regard must be had to the legitimate interest of undertakings in the protection of their business secrets[4].

The fact that the Commission had issued a press release at the time a statement of objection was issued, and before the undertakings concerned had an opportunity to defend their position, did not vitiate the legality of the decision which was ultimately taken[5].

1   See PARAS 61–68. As to the EC Treaty (ie the Treaty establishing the European Community (Rome, 25 March 1957; TS 1 (1973); Cmnd 5179)) see PARA 24 note 1.
2   EC Council Regulation 1/2003 on the implementation of the rules on competition laid down in Articles 81 and 82 of the Treaty (OJ L1, 4.1.2003, p 1) (the 'Modernisation Regulation') art 30(1).
3   EC Council Regulation 1/2003 (OJ L1, 4.1.2003, p 1) art 30(2).
4   EC Council Regulation 1/2003 (OJ L1, 4.1.2003, p 1) art 30(2).
5   Joined Cases 40–48, 50, 54–56, 111, 113, 114/73 *Coöperatieve vereniging Suiker Unie UA v EC Commission* [1975] ECR 1663, [1976] 1 CMLR 295, ECJ. The Court of Justice suggested in its judgment that the action by the Commission in making such a press release was not free from criticism: Joined Cases 40–48, 50, 54–56, 111, 113, 114/73 *Coöperatieve vereniging Suiker Unie UA v EC Commission* at 1927, 413, ECJ (judgment paras 89–93).

100.   Reasoning.   The Commission is required to state the reasons on which its decision is based[1], enumerating the facts forming the legal basis of the measure and the considerations which led it to adopt that decision[2]. Nevertheless, the Commission is not required to discuss all the issues of fact and of law which may have been touched on by every interested person in the course of the administrative procedure.

With regard more particularly to decisions imposing a fine, it appears that the statement of reasons is to be considered sufficient if it indicates clearly and coherently the considerations of fact and of law on the basis of which the fine has been imposed on the parties concerned in such a way as to acquaint both the latter and the Court of Justice with the essential factors of the Commission's reasoning[3].

1   EC Treaty art 253. As to the EC Treaty (ie the Treaty establishing the European Community (Rome, 25 March 1957; TS 1 (1973); Cmnd 5179)) see PARA 24 note 1.

2   As to the extent of the duty to give reasons see Case 73/74 *Groupement des Fabricants de Papiers Peints de Belgique v EC Commission* [1975] ECR 1491 at 1514, [1976] 1 CMLR 589 at 614, ECJ.

3   Thus in Case 41/69 *ACF Chemiefarma NV v EC Commission* [1970] ECR 661 at 683, 684, ECJ (Quinine Cartel) (judgment, paras 22–30), it was held that the Commission did not infringe an essential procedural requirement by omitting from the reasons for its decision factors which it, rightly or wrongly, considered irrelevant to the proceedings. However, in Case T-61/89 *Dansk Pelsdyravlerforening v EC Commission* [1992] ECR II-1931, CFI, a decision of the Commission dealing with concerted practices was in part annulled on the ground that the reasoning of the decision was not sufficiently precise.

101.   The administrative file.   If so requested, the Commission must grant access to the file to the parties to whom it has addressed a statement of objections[1]. The right of access to the file does not extend to business secrets, other confidential information and internal documents of the Commission or of the competition authorities of the member states[2]. Nor does it extend to correspondence between the Commission and the competition authorities of the member states or between the latter where such correspondence is contained in the file of the Commission[3]. However, this does not prevent the Commission from disclosing and using information necessary to prove an infringement of article 81 or 82 of the EC Treaty[4]. Documents obtained through access to the file pursuant to these provisions may only be used for the purposes of judicial or administrative proceedings for the application of articles 81 and 82 of the EC Treaty[5].

The Court of First Instance has rejected a decision by the Commission to deny access to documents that contained information or trade secrets of the applicants or third parties unless the persons concerned continued to assert the claim that the information was confidential. Each document was then to be considered to determine whether its age, nature and relevance to the matter in hand justified continuing confidentiality. In addition, for the Commission's internal documents, there is no general rule of administrative confidentiality; access to each document has to be balanced against the requirements of judicial supervision and the rights of the defence[6].

In 2005 the Commission published a notice laying down new internal rules for access to the file, and concerned with the extent of the right of access; and practical procedures for the exercise of the right[7].

1   EC Commission Regulation 773/2004 (OJ L123, 27.4.2004, p 18) art 15(1). Access is to be granted after the notification of the statement of objections: art 15(1). As to the statement of objections see PARA 94. See Case T-7/89 *Hercules Chemicals NV SA v EC Commission* [1991] ECR II-1711, [1992] 4 CMLR 84, CFI. As to the procedure for allowing the addressees of a statement of objections to examine evidence in the Commission's files, so that they are able properly to defend themselves against the objections raised, see Case T-221/95 *Endemol Entertainment Holding BV v European Commission* [1999] All ER (EC) 385, [1999] 5 CMLR 611, CFI; and Joined Cases T-25, 26, 30–32, 34–39, 42–46, 48, 50–65, 68–71, 87, 88, 103, 104/95 *Cimenteries CBR SA v EC Commission* [2000] ECR II-491, [2000] 5 CMLR 204, CFI.

2   EC Commission Regulation 773/2004 (OJ L123, 27.4.2004, p 18) art 15(2).

3   EC Commission Regulation 773/2004 (OJ L123, 27.4.2004, p 18) art 15(2).

4　EC Commission Regulation 773/2004 (OJ L123, 27.4.2004, p 18) art 15(3). As to the EC Treaty (ie the Treaty establishing the European Community (Rome, 25 March 1957; TS 1 (1973); Cmnd 5179)) see PARA 24 note 1.

5　EC Commission Regulation 773/2004 (OJ L123, 27.4.2004, p 18) art 15(4).

6　Joined Cases T-134, 136–138, 141, 145, 147, 148, 151, 156, 157/94 *NMH Stahlwerke GmbH v EC Commission* [1996] ECR II-537, [1997] 5 CMLR 227, CFI (interim ruling) (the 'Steel Beams' case). See also Case T-30/91 *Solvay SA v EC Commission* [1995] ECR II-1775, [1996] 5 CMLR 57, CFI.

7　EC Notice on the rules for access to the Commission file in cases pursuant to Articles 81 and 82 of the EC Treaty, Articles 53, 54 and 57 of the EEA Agreement and Council Regulation (EC) No 139/2004 (OJ C325, 22.12.05, p 7).

102.　Limitation of actions.　Provision is made that the power of the Commission to impose fines or periodic penalties[1] is subject to limitation periods of three years in the case of infringements of provisions concerning requests for information or the conduct of inspections, and of five years in the case of all other infringements[2]. Time begins to run on the day on which the infringement is committed, and in the case of continuing or repeated infringements, time begins to run on the day on which the infringement ceases[3].

The limitation period is interrupted by any action of the Commission or by the competition authority of a member state for the purpose of the investigation or proceedings in respect of an infringement. Each interruption starts time running afresh, but the limitation period expires at the latest on the day on which a period equal to twice the limitation period has elapsed without the Commission having imposed a fine or a penalty[4].

Proceedings before the Court of Justice suspend the limitation period[5]. The power of the Commission to enforce decisions imposing fines, penalties or periodic payments is subject to a five-year limitation period[6].

1　Ie under EC Council Regulation 1/2003 on the implementation of the rules on competition laid down in Articles 81 and 82 of the Treaty (OJ L1, 4.1.2003, p 1) (the 'Modernisation Regulation') arts 23, 24. See PARA 107.

2　EC Council Regulation 1/2003 (OJ L1, 4.1.2003, p 1) art 25(1).

3　EC Council Regulation 1/2003 (OJ L1, 4.1.2003, p 1) art 25(2). See also Case 243/83 *Binon et Cie SA v SA Agence et messageries de la presse* [1985] ECR 2015, [1985] 3 CMLR 800, ECJ.

4　EC Council Regulation 1/2003 (OJ L1, 4.1.2003, p 1) art 25(3), (5).

5　EC Council Regulation 1/2003 (OJ L1, 4.1.2003, p 1) art 25(3), (6).

6　See EC Council Regulation 1/2003 (OJ L1, 4.1.2003, p 1) art 26.

(iii)　Interim Measures by the Commission

103.　Power to take interim measures.　In cases of urgency due to the risk of serious and irreparable damage to competition, the Commission, acting on its own initiative may by decision, on the basis of a prima facie finding of infringement, order interim measures[1]. Such a decision applies for a specified period of time and may be renewed in so far as this is necessary and appropriate[2].

1　EC Council Regulation 1/2003 on the implementation of the rules on competition laid down in Articles 81 and 82 of the Treaty (OJ L1, 4.1.2003, p 1) (the 'Modernisation Regulation') art 8(1).

2　EC Council Regulation 1/2003 (OJ L1, 4.1.2003, p 1) art 8(2).

(iv)　Final Decisions of the Commission

104.　Termination of infringement.　Where the Commission finds that there is an infringement of article 81 or 82 of the EC Treaty, it may by decision require the undertakings concerned to bring such infringement to an end[1]. For this purpose, it may impose on them any behavioural or structural remedies which are proportionate to the infringement committed and necessary to bring the infringement effectively to an end. Structural remedies can only be imposed either where there is no equally effective behavioural remedy or where any equally effective behavioural remedy would be more burdensome for the undertaking concerned than the structural remedy. If the Commission has a legitimate interest in doing so, it may also find that an infringement has been committed in the past[2]. The Commission may also take interim decisions[3].

1   EC Council Regulation 1/2003 on the implementation of the rules on competition laid down in Articles 81 and 82 of the Treaty (OJ L1, 4.1.2003, p 1) (the 'Modernisation Regulation') art 7(1). As to the EC Treaty (ie the Treaty establishing the European Community (Rome, 25 March 1957; TS 1 (1973); Cmnd 5179)) see PARA 24 note 1.
2   EC Council Regulation 1/2003 (OJ L1, 4.1.2003, p 1) art 7(1).
3   See PARA 103.

105.   Guidance letters.   Where cases give rise to genuine uncertainty because they present novel or unresolved questions for the application of articles 81 and 82 of the EC Treaty[1], individual undertakings may wish to seek informal guidance from the Commission. Where it considers it appropriate and subject to its enforcement priorities, the Commission may provide such guidance on novel questions concerning the interpretation of article 81 or 82 in a written guidance letter[2].

1   As to the EC Treaty (ie the Treaty establishing the European Community (Rome, 25 March 1957; TS 1 (1973); Cmnd 5179)) see PARA 24 note 1.
2   See Commission Notice on informal guidance relating to novel questions concerning Articles 81 and 82 of the EC Treaty that arise in individual cases (guidance letters) (OJ C101, 27.4.2004, p 78). Guidance letters are not Commission decisions and do not bind member states' competition authorities or courts although it is open to them to take account of guidance letters issued by the Commission as they see fit in the context of a case: see PARA 25.

106.   Commitments.   Where the Commission intends to adopt a decision requiring that an infringement be brought to an end and the undertakings concerned offer commitments to meet the concerns expressed to them by the Commission in its preliminary assessment, the Commission may by decision make those commitments binding on the undertakings[1]. Such a decision may be adopted for a specified period and must conclude that there are no longer grounds for action by the Commission[2].

The Commission may, upon request or on its own initiative, reopen the proceedings where there has been a material change in any of the facts on which the decision was based; where the undertakings concerned act contrary to their commitments; or where the decision was based on incomplete, incorrect or misleading information provided by the parties[3].

1   EC Council Regulation 1/2003 on the implementation of the rules on competition laid down in Articles 81 and 82 of the Treaty (OJ L1, 4.1.2003, p 1) (the 'Modernisation Regulation') art 9(1). As to the EC Treaty (ie the Treaty establishing the European Community (Rome, 25 March 1957; TS 1 (1973); Cmnd 5179)) see PARA 24 note 1.
2   EC Council Regulation 1/2003 (OJ L1, 4.1.2003, p 1) art 9(1).
3   EC Council Regulation 1/2003 (OJ L1, 4.1.2003, p 1) art 9(2).

(v) Sanctions and Penalties

107.   Fines and periodic penalty payments in general.   The Commission may by decision impose a fine not exceeding 1 per cent of total turnover in the previous business year on undertakings for supplying incorrect or misleading information intentionally or negligently[1]. The Commission may also by decision impose fines of up to 10 per cent of the turnover in the previous business year on undertakings where, either intentionally or negligently they infringe article 81 or article 82 of the EC Treaty[2], or they contravene a decision ordering interim measures[3], or they fail to comply with a commitment made binding by a decision[4].

In fixing the amount of the fine, regard is to be had both to the gravity and to the duration of the infringement[5].

Decisions to impose such fines are not of the nature of criminal law[6].

In addition to the fines under the provisions described above, the Commission is further empowered to impose periodic penalty payments not exceeding 5 per cent of the average daily turnover in the preceding business year per day, calculated from a date appointed by the decision, in order to compel undertakings:

(1)   to put an end to any infringement of article 81 or 82 in accordance with a decision taken by the Commission[7];

(2)   to comply with a decision ordering interim measures[8];

(3)   to comply with a commitment made binding by a decision[9];

(4)   to supply complete and correct information which has been requested by a decision[10];

(5)   to submit to an investigation which is ordered by a decision[11].

Where the undertakings or associations of undertakings have satisfied the obligation which the periodic penalty payment was intended to enforce, the Commission may fix the definitive amount of the periodic penalty payment at a figure lower than that which would arise under the original decision[12].

1   See EC Council Regulation 1/2003 on the implementation of the rules on competition laid down in Articles 81 and 82 of the Treaty (OJ L1, 4.1.2003, p 1) (the 'Modernisation Regulation') art 23(1).

2   As to the EC Treaty (ie the Treaty establishing the European Community (Rome, 25 March 1957; TS 1 (1973); Cmnd 5179)) see PARA 24 note 1.

3   Ie under EC Council Regulation 1/2003 (OJ L1, 4.1.2003, p 1) art 8 (see PARA 103).

4   EC Council Regulation 1/2003 (OJ L1, 4.1.2003, p 1) art 23(2). A commitment is made binding under art 9 (see PARA 106). See Guidelines on the method of setting fines imposed pursuant to Article 23(2)(a) of Regulation No 1/2003 (OJ C210, 1.9.2006, p 2).

5   EC Council Regulation 1/2003 (OJ L1, 4.1.2003, p 1) art 23(3). As to when an undertaking is insolvent see art 23(4).

6   EC Council Regulation 1/2003 (OJ L1, 4.1.2003, p 1) art 23(5).

7   Ie under EC Council Regulation 1/2003 (OJ L1, 4.1.2003, p 1) art 7 (see PARA 104).

8   Ie under EC Council Regulation 1/2003 (OJ L1, 4.1.2003, p 1) art 8 (see PARA 103).

9   Ie under EC Council Regulation 1/2003 (OJ L1, 4.1.2003, p 1) art 9 (see PARA 106).

10   Ie under EC Council Regulation 1/2003 (OJ L1, 4.1.2003, p 1) art 17 or art 18(3) (see PARAS 90–91).

11   EC Council Regulation 1/2003 (OJ L1, 4.1.2003, p 1) art 24(1). An investigation is ordered under art 20 (see PARA 92).

12   EC Council Regulation 1/2003 (OJ L1, 4.1.2003, p 1) art 24(2). Article 23(4) applies correspondingly: art 24(2).

108.   Immunity from fines or reduction of fines in cartel cases.   By the terms of a notice published by the Commission in 2006[1], the following conditions must be fulfilled before immunity from or reduction of fines may be granted:

(1)   the undertaking disclosing its participation in an alleged cartel affecting the Community must be the first to submit information and evidence which in the Commission's view will enable it to carry out a targeted

inspection in connection with the alleged cartel or find an infringement of article 81 of the EC Treaty[2] in connection with the alleged cartel[3];

(2)   for the Commission to be able to carry out such a targeted inspection, the undertaking must provide the Commission with detailed information and evidence, to the extent that this, in the Commission's view, would not jeopardize the inspections[4];

(3)   the undertaking must cooperate genuinely, fully, on a continuous basis and expeditiously from the time it submits its application throughout the Commission's administrative procedure[5];

(4)   the undertaking must end its involvement in the alleged cartel immediately following its application, except for what would, in the Commission's view, be reasonably necessary to preserve the integrity of the inspections[6];

(5)   when contemplating making its application to the Commission, the undertaking must not have destroyed, falsified or concealed evidence of the alleged cartel nor disclosed the fact or any of the content of its contemplated application, except to other competition authorities[7].

An undertaking which took steps to coerce other undertakings to join the cartel or to remain in it is not eligible for immunity from fines but it may still qualify for a reduction of fines if it fulfils the relevant requirements and meets all the conditions therefor[8].

Undertakings disclosing their participation in an alleged cartel affecting the Community that do not meet the above conditions may be eligible to benefit from a reduction of any fine that would otherwise have been imposed[9]. In order to qualify, an undertaking must provide the Commission with evidence of the alleged infringement which represents significant added value with respect to the evidence already in the Commission's possession and must meet the conditions set out in heads (3) to (5) above[10].

The European Commission has introduced a settlement procedure for cartels to allow the Commission to settle cartel cases through a simplified procedure. Under this procedure, parties, having seen the evidence in the Commission file, choose to acknowledge their involvement in the cartel and their liability for it. In return for this acknowledgement, the Commission can reduce the fine imposed on the parties by 10 per cent[11].

1   Ie EC Commission Notice on Immunity from fines and reduction of fines in cartel cases (OJ C298, 8.12.2006, p 17).
2   As to the EC Treaty (ie the Treaty establishing the European Community (Rome, 25 March 1957; TS 1 (1973); Cmnd 5179)) see PARA 24 note 1.
3   EC Commission Notice on Immunity from fines and reduction of fines in cartel cases (OJ C298, 8.12.2006, p 17) para 8.
4   See EC Commission Notice on Immunity from fines and reduction of fines in cartel cases (OJ C298, 8.12.2006, p 17) para 9.
5   See EC Commission Notice on Immunity from fines and reduction of fines in cartel cases (OJ C298, 8.12.2006, p 17) para 12(a).
6   See EC Commission Notice on Immunity from fines and reduction of fines in cartel cases (OJ C298, 8.12.2006, p 17) para 12(b).
7   See EC Commission Notice on Immunity from fines and reduction of fines in cartel cases (OJ C298, 8.12.2006, p 17) para 12(c).
8   See EC Commission Notice on Immunity from fines and reduction of fines in cartel cases (OJ C298, 8.12.2006, p 17) para 13.
9   See EC Commission Notice on Immunity from fines and reduction of fines in cartel cases (OJ C298, 8.12.2006, p 17) para 23.
10   See EC Commission Notice on Immunity from fines and reduction of fines in cartel cases (OJ C298, 8.12.2006, p 17) paras 24–26.
11   See EC Commission Regulation 622/2008 (OJ L171, 1.7.2008, p 3).

109. Guidelines on setting fines. The Commission has published guidelines on the method of setting fines in competition law cases[1]. Guidance is given as to method of determining the basic amount of the fine[2], aggravating circumstances[3] and mitigating circumstances[4] which are to be taken into account, and the application of the Notice on Immunity from fines and reduction of fines in cartel cases[5].

The Commission will pay particular attention to the need to ensure that fines have a sufficiently deterrent effect; to that end, it may increase the fine to be imposed on undertakings which have a particularly large turnover beyond the sales of goods or services to which the infringement relates[6]. The Commission will also take into account the need to increase the fine in order to exceed the amount of gains improperly made as a result of the infringement where it is possible to estimate that amount[7].

The final amount of the fine must not, in any event, exceed 10 per cent of the total turnover in the preceding business year of the undertaking or association of undertakings participating in the infringement[8].

The Commission will apply the leniency rules in line with the conditions set out in the applicable notice[9].

In exceptional cases, the Commission may, upon request, take account of the undertaking's inability to pay in a specific social and economic context. It will not base any reduction granted for this reason in the fine on the mere finding of an adverse or loss-making financial situation. A reduction could be granted solely on the basis of objective evidence that imposition of the fine as provided for in the Guidelines would irretrievably jeopardise the economic viability of the undertaking concerned and cause its assets to lose all their value[10].

The Commission may, in certain cases, impose a symbolic fine and the justification for imposing such a fine should be given in its decision[11].

The guidelines present the general methodology for the setting of fines but the particularities of a given case or the need to achieve deterrence in a particular case may justify departing from such methodology or from the limits specified[12].

1   See Guidelines on the method of setting fines imposed pursuant to Article 23(2)(a) of Regulation No 1/2003 (OJ C210, 1.9.2006, p 2).

2   As to the basic amount see PARA 110.

3   As to aggravating circumstances see PARA 111.

4   As to mitigating circumstances see PARA 112.

5   See EC Commission Notice on Immunity from fines and reduction of fines in cartel cases (OJ C298, 8.12.2006, p 17); and PARA 108.

6   Guidelines on the method of setting fines imposed pursuant to Article 23(2)(a) of Regulation No 1/2003 (OJ C210, 1.9.2006, p 2) para 30.

7   Guidelines on the method of setting fines imposed pursuant to Article 23(2)(a) of Regulation No 1/2003 (OJ C210, 1.9.2006, p 2) para 31.

8   Guidelines on the method of setting fines imposed pursuant to Article 23(2)(a) of Regulation No 1/2003 (OJ C210, 1.9.2006, p 2) para 32.

9   Guidelines on the method of setting fines imposed pursuant to Article 23(2)(a) of Regulation No 1/2003 (OJ C210, 1.9.2006, p 2) para 34. See EC Commission Notice on Immunity from fines and reduction of fines in cartel cases (OJ C298, 8.12.2006, p 17); and PARA 108.

10 Guidelines on the method of setting fines imposed pursuant to Article 23(2)(a) of Regulation No 1/2003 (OJ C210, 1.9.2006, p 2) para 35.

11 Guidelines on the method of setting fines imposed pursuant to Article 23(2)(a) of Regulation No 1/2003 (OJ C210, 1.9.2006, p 2) para 36.

12 Guidelines on the method of setting fines imposed pursuant to Article 23(2)(a) of Regulation No 1/2003 (OJ C210, 1.9.2006, p 2) para 37.

110.   The basic amount. The Commission's guidelines on the method of setting fines[1] provide that the basic amount is to be set by reference to the value of sales applying the following methodology:

(1)   in calculating the value of sales:

   (a)   in determining the basic amount of the fine to be imposed, the Commission will take the value of the undertaking's sales of goods or services to which the infringement directly or indirectly relates in the relevant geographic area within the EEA and will normally take the sales made by the undertaking during the last full business year of its participation in the infringement (hereafter 'value of sales'):

   (b)   where the infringement by an association of undertakings relates to the activities of its members, the value of sales will generally correspond to the sum of the value of sales by its members;

   (c)   in determining the value of sales by an undertaking, the Commission will take that undertaking's best available figures;

   (d)   where the figures made available by an undertaking are incomplete or not reliable, the Commission may determine the value of its sales on the basis of the partial figures it has obtained and/or any other information which it regards as relevant and appropriate;

   (e)   the value of sales will be determined before VAT and other taxes directly related to the sales;

   (f)   where the geographic scope of an infringement extends beyond the EEA (for example worldwide cartels), the relevant sales of the undertakings within the EEA may not properly reflect the weight of each undertaking in the infringement, in particular with worldwide market-sharing arrangements; in such circumstances, in order to reflect both the aggregate size of the relevant sales within the EEA and the relative weight of each undertaking in the infringement, the Commission may assess the total value of the sales of goods or services to which the infringement relates in the relevant geographic area (wider than the EEA), may determine the share of the sales of each undertaking party to the infringement on that market and may apply this share to the aggregate sales within the EEA of the undertakings concerned. The result will be taken as the value of sales for the purpose of setting the basic amount of the fine[2];

(2)   in determining the basic amount of the fine:

   (a)   the basic amount of the fine will be related to a proportion of the value of sales, depending on the degree of gravity of the infringement, multiplied by the number of years of infringement;

   (b)   the assessment of gravity will be made on a case-by-case basis for all types of infringement, taking account of all the relevant circumstances of the case;

   (c)   as a general rule, the proportion of the value of sales taken into account will be set at a level of up to 30 per cent of the value of sales;

   (d)   in order to decide whether the proportion of the value of sales to be considered in a given case should be at the lower end or at the higher end of that scale, the Commission will have regard to a number of factors, such as the nature of the infringement, the combined market share of all the undertakings concerned, the geographic scope of the infringement and whether or not the infringement has been implemented;

(e)   horizontal price-fixing, market-sharing and output-limitation agreements, which are usually secret, are, by their very nature, among the most harmful restrictions of competition and, as a matter of policy, they will be heavily fined. Therefore, the proportion of the value of sales taken into account for such infringements will generally be set at the higher end of the scale;

(f)   in order to take fully into account the duration of the participation of each undertaking in the infringement, the amount determined on the basis of the value of sales will be multiplied by the number of years of participation in the infringement. Periods of less than six months will be counted as half a year; periods longer than six months but shorter than one year will be counted as a full year;

(g)   in addition, irrespective of the duration of the undertaking's participation in the infringement, the Commission will include in the basic amount a sum of between 15 per cent and 25 per cent of the value of sales in order to deter undertakings from even entering into horizontal price-fixing, market-sharing and output-limitation agreements. The Commission may also apply such an additional amount in the case of other infringements. For the purpose of deciding the proportion of the value of sales to be considered in a given case, the Commission will have regard to a number of factors, in particular those referred in head (2)(d);

(h)   where the value of sales by undertakings participating in the infringement is similar but not identical, the Commission may set for each of them an identical basic amount and moreover, in determining the basic amount of the fine, the Commission will use rounded figures[3].

1   Guidelines on the method of setting fines imposed pursuant to Article 23(2)(a) of Regulation No 1/2003 (OJ C210, 1.9.2006, p 2).

2   Guidelines on the method of setting fines imposed pursuant to Article 23(2)(a) of Regulation No 1/2003 (OJ C210, 1.9.2006, p 2) paras 12–18.

3   Guidelines on the method of setting fines imposed pursuant to Article 23(2)(a) of Regulation No 1/2003 (OJ C210, 1.9.2006, p 2) paras 19–26.

111. Aggravating circumstances. The Commission's guidelines on the method of setting fines[1] provide that the basic amount may be increased where the Commission finds that there are aggravating circumstances, such as:

(1)   where an undertaking continues or repeats the same or a similar infringement after the Commission or a national competition authority has made a finding that the undertaking infringed article 81 or 82 of the EC Treaty[2] and the basic amount will be increased by up to 100 per cent for each such infringement established;

(2)   refusal to cooperate with or obstruction of the Commission in carrying out its investigations;

(3)   role of leader in, or instigator of, the infringement; the Commission will also pay particular attention to any steps taken to coerce other undertakings to participate in the infringement and/or any retaliatory

measures taken against other undertakings with a view to enforcing the practices constituting the infringement[3].

1   Ie Guidelines on the method of setting fines imposed pursuant to Article 23(2)(a) of Regulation No 1/2003 (OJ C210, 1.9.2006, p 2).
2   As to the EC Treaty (ie the Treaty establishing the European Community (Rome, 25 March 1957; TS 1 (1973); Cmnd 5179)) see PARA 24 note 1.
3   Guidelines on the method of setting fines imposed pursuant to Article 23(2)(a) of Regulation No 1/2003 (OJ C210, 1.9.2006, p 2) para 28.

112. Mitigating circumstances. The Commission's guidelines on the method of setting fines[1] provide that the basic amount[2] may be reduced where the Commission finds that mitigating circumstances exist, such as:

(1)   where the undertaking concerned provides evidence that it terminated the infringement as soon as the Commission intervened: this will not apply to secret agreements or practices (in particular, cartels[3]);

(2)   where the undertaking provides evidence that the infringement has been committed as a result of negligence;

(3)   where the undertaking provides evidence that its involvement in the infringement is substantially limited and thus demonstrates that, during the period in which it was party to the offending agreement, it actually avoided applying it by adopting competitive conduct in the market: the mere fact that an undertaking participated in an infringement for a shorter duration than others will not be regarded as a mitigating circumstance since this will already be reflected in the basic amount;

(4)   where the undertaking concerned has effectively cooperated with the Commission outside the scope of the Leniency Notice[4] and beyond its legal obligation to do so;

(5)   where the anti-competitive conduct of the undertaking has been authorised or encouraged by public authorities or by legislation[5].

1   Ie Guidelines on the method of setting fines imposed pursuant to Article 23(2)(a) of Regulation No 1/2003 (OJ C210, 1.9.2006, p 2).
2   See PARA 110.
3   See PARAS 108–109.
4   Ie EC Commission Notice on Immunity from fines and reduction of fines in cartel cases (OJ C298, 8.12.2006, p 17) (see PARA 108).
5   Guidelines on the method of setting fines imposed pursuant to Article 23(2)(a) of Regulation No 1/2003 (OJ C210, 1.9.2006, p 2) para 29.

113. More than one penalty on the same facts. Although the Community and the member states have an obligation to take into account previous penalties imposed for the same set of facts[1], this principle cannot apply in cases of a clash between penalties imposed under Community law and the laws of non-member states. Although the facts giving rise to the fines might be the same, the fact that the penalties were imposed for infringements of two separate sets of rules means that there can be no question of set-off between the two penalties imposed[2].

1   As to the rule, now known as 'ne bis in idem', see Case 14/68 *Wilhelm v Bundeskartellamt* [1969] ECR 1, [1969] CMLR 100, ECJ.
2   See Case T-59/02 *Archer Daniels Midland Co v EC Commission* [2006] ECR II-3627, [2006] 5 CMLR 1528, CFI; upheld on appeal, [2009] All ER (D) 225, ECJ.

(vi) Judicial Review

114. Powers of the Court of Justice. The Court of Justice has unlimited jurisdiction to review decisions whereby the Commission has fixed a fine or periodic penalty payment. It may cancel, reduce or increase the fine or periodic penalty payment imposed[1]. Article 230 of the Treaty, which is the basis for judicial review by the Court of Justice of acts of the Council and Commission, provides the basis for actions for annulment of all Commission decisions in the field of competition law. Article 232 provides for the right to make an application in respect of a failure to act by the Commission. Proceedings brought before the Court of Justice do not have suspensory effect, although the court may, if it considers the circumstances so require, order that application of the contested act be suspended[2]. The Court of Justice may, in any cases before it, prescribe any necessary interim measures[3].

The Commission has issued a statement[4] reminding parties that even if an appeal were to be made against a Commission decision, this does not have suspensory effect and the parties are required to refrain from the conduct condemned until the appeal is successful or the decision is suspended[5].

Only the operative parts of a decision are capable of being contested[6].

The Court of Justice has held that the only parties who can benefit from a court ruling annulling a Commission decision are parties actually joined in the case before the court. A party who was subject to the original decision but had not challenged it before the Court of First Instance or Court of Justice cannot benefit from any order annulling the decision; as nothing has been decided in relation to those undertakings the original decision remains binding on them[7]. Under article 230 of the EC Treaty any Commission decision not challenged within the time limit specified becomes definitive against the addressee. It would be contrary to the principle of legal certainty if decisions against one party could be challenged outside that time limit by the mere fact that an addressee of an identical decision had sought to challenge that latter decision[8].

1   EC Council Regulation 1/2003 on the implementation of the rules on competition laid down in Articles 81 and 82 of the Treaty (OJ L1, 4.1.2003, p 1) (the 'Modernisation Regulation') art 31. As to the EC Treaty (ie the Treaty establishing the European Community (Rome, 25 March 1957; TS 1 (1973); Cmnd 5179)) see PARA 24 note 1.
2   EC Treaty art 242. See eg Case T-41/96R *Bayer AG v EC Commission* [1996] ECR II-381, [1996] 5 CMLR 290, CFI, in which the President of the court suspended the enforcement of a fine of ECU 3 million on Bayer on the basis that there was a prima facie case for appeal and also that Bayer would suffer serious and irreparable harm. In the 'PVC' cases, the Court of First Instance dismissed actions brought by PVC producers on the basis that, due to procedural irregularities, the Commission measure being challenged was non-existent: Joined Cases T-79, 84–86, 89, 91, 92, 96, 98, 102, 104/89 *BASF AG v EC Commission* [1992] ECR II-315, [1992] 4 CMLR 357, CFI.
3   EC Treaty art 243.
4   This statement was issued following EC Commission Decision 92/204 (*Samenwerkende Prijsregelende Organisaties in de Bouwnijverheid*) OJ L92, 7.4.92, p 1.
5   EC Commission Press Release IP (92)195 of 17 March 1992.
6   *Elopak/Metal Box-Odin* EC Commission Notice (OJ C215, 30.8.87, p 3).
7   Case C-310/97P *EC Commission v AssiDomän Kraft Products AB* [1999] All ER (EC) 737, [1999] ECR I-5363, ECJ.
8   Case C-310/97P *EC Commission v AssiDomän Kraft Products AB* [1999] All ER (EC) 737, [1999] ECR I-5363, ECJ (judgment, para 63).

3. THE COMPETITION ACT 1998

(1) INTRODUCTION

115. The Chapter I and Chapter II prohibitions. The Competition Act 1998, which entered fully into force on 1 March 2000, makes provision for the strengthening of United Kingdom competition law by the introduction of two principal prohibitions, the Chapter I prohibition[1] and the Chapter II prohibition[2]. The prohibitions are closely modelled on provisions of European Community law[3], and provision is made for the prohibitions to be interpreted consistently with European competition law[4]. The Restrictive Trade Practices Act 1976, the Resale Prices Act 1976 and the Restrictive Trade Practices Act 1977, which formerly applied to agreements restrictive of competition, have been repealed and are replaced by the Chapter I prohibition[5]. The provisions in the Competition Act 1980 for the control of anti-competitive practices[6] have been repealed and replaced by the Chapter II prohibition[7]. The Competition Act 1998 has been substantially amended to implement the provisions of the EC Competition Regulation[8].

The Office of Fair Trading has published numerous Guidelines on the operation of the Act[9].

1 See the Competition Act 1998 s 2. As to the Chapter I prohibition see PARAS 116–124.
2 See the Competition Act 1998 s 18. As to the Chapter II prohibition see PARAS 125–128.
3 Ie the EC Treaty arts 81, 82 (see PARAS 61 et seq, 68 et seq). As to the EC Treaty (ie the Treaty establishing the European Community (Rome, 25 March 1957; TS 1 (1973); Cmnd 5179)) see PARA 24 note 1. The numbering for the EC Treaty used in this title is as revised by the Treaty of Amsterdam: see PARA 24 note 1.
4 See the Competition Act 1998 s 60; and PARA 150.
5 See the Competition Act 1998 s 1.
6 Ie the Competition Act 1980 ss 2–10 (repealed).
7 Competition Act 1998 s 17.
8 Ie EC Council Regulation 1/2003 on the implementation of the rules on competition laid down in Articles 81 and 82 of the Treaty (OJ L1, 4.1.03, p 1) (the 'Modernisation Regulation'). The amendments to the Competition Act 1998 are made by the Competition Act 1998 and Other Enactments (Amendment) Regulations 2004, SI 2004/1261.
9 Provision is made for the preparation and publication of 'advice and information' by the Competition Act 1998 s 52: see PARA 145. Relevant Guidelines are referred to in the following paragraphs. As to the Office of Fair Trading see PARAS 6–8.

(2) THE CHAPTER I PROHIBITION

116. Prohibited agreements. Agreements between undertakings, decisions by associations of undertakings or concerted practices which: (1) may affect trade within the United Kingdom[1]; and (2) have as their object or effect the prevention, restriction or distortion of competition within the United Kingdom, are prohibited unless they are exempt in accordance with the provisions of Part I of the Competition Act 1998[2]. The above provision applies, in particular, to agreements, decisions or practices which: (a) directly or indirectly fix purchase or selling prices or any other trading conditions[3]; (b) limit or control production, markets, technical development or investment[4]; (c) share markets or sources of supply[5]; (d) apply dissimilar conditions to equivalent transactions with other trading parties, thereby placing them at a competitive disadvantage[6]; or (e) make the conclusion of contracts subject to acceptance by the other parties of supplementary obligations which, by their nature or according to commercial usage, have no connection with the subject of such contracts[7]. This prohibition is referred to as the 'Chapter I prohibition'[8]. The Chapter I prohibition does not apply to certain excluded agreements[9]. The Chapter I prohibition applies only if the agreement, decision or practice is, or is intended to be, implemented in the United Kingdom[10]. Any agreement or decision which is prohibited by the Chapter I prohibition is void[11]. A provision of Part I of the Competition Act 1998 which is expressed to apply to, or in relation to, an agreement is to be read as applying equally to, or in relation to, a decision by an association of undertakings or a concerted practice (but with any necessary modifications)[12].

Guidance on the operation of the Chapter I prohibition can be found in the Guidelines of the Office of Fair Trading[13]. The following examples that might appreciably restrict competition are given in the Guidelines: agreements which have the object or effect of directly or indirectly fixing prices, fixing trading conditions, sharing markets, limiting or controlling production or investment, collusive tendering (bid-rigging), joint purchasing or selling, sharing information, exchanging price information, exchanging non-price information, restricting advertising or setting technical or design standards[14].

1   In the Competition Act 1998 s 2, 'United Kingdom' means, in relation to an agreement which operates or is intended to operate only in a part of the United Kingdom, that part: s 2(7). As to the meaning of 'United Kingdom' generally see PARA 401 note 1.
2   Competition Act 1998 s 2(1). Part I of the Competition Act 1998 comprises ss 1–60. See e g _Institute of Independent Insurance Brokers v Director General of Fair Trading_ [2001] All ER (D) 58 (Sep), Competition Commission Appeal Tribunal.
    For decisions of the EC Commission and the European Court of Justice on the corresponding provisions of European Community law see PARAS 24 et seq, 61 et seq. As to the duty to interpret the provisions of the Competition Act 1998 in a manner consistent with European Community law and the decisions of the European Court of Justice see s 60; and PARA 150. For a decision in which the relevant provisions both of the EC Treaty and the Competition Act 1998 were considered see _Hendry v World Professional Billiards and Snooker Association_ [2001] All ER (D) 71 (Oct). As to the EC Treaty (ie the Treaty establishing the European Community (Rome, 25 March 1957; TS 1 (1973); Cmnd 5179)) see PARA 24 note 1.
3   Competition Act 1998 s 2(2)(a).
4   Competition Act 1998 s 2(2)(b).
5   Competition Act 1998 s 2(2)(c).
6   Competition Act 1998 s 2(2)(d).
7   Competition Act 1998 s 2(2)(e).
8   Competition Act 1998 ss 2(8), 59(1).
9   See PARA 117.
10 Competition Act 1998 s 2(3).
11 Competition Act 1998 s 2(4).
12 Competition Act 1998 s 2(5), which, however, does not apply where the context otherwise requires: s 2(6).
13 See OFT Guideline 401 _Agreements and concerted practices_ (December 2004). See also, in particular, OFT Guideline 403 _Market Definition_ (December 2004); OFT Guideline 408 _Trade Associations, Professional Bodies and Self-Regulating Bodies_ (December 2004); OFT Guideline 419 _Vertical Agreements_ (December 2004); OFT Guideline 420 _Land Agreements_ (December 2004).
14 See OFT Guideline 401 _Agreements and concerted practices_ (December 2004) para 3.

117.   Excluded agreements: introductory. The Chapter I prohibition[1] does not apply in any of the cases in which it is excluded by or as a result of certain specified provisions[2]; these provisions relate to mergers and concentrations[3], competition scrutiny under other enactments[4]; and planning obligations and other general exclusions[5].

Provision is made for amendment to be made by the Secretary of State to these exclusions[6].

The fact that to a limited extent the Chapter I prohibition does not apply to an agreement, because of an exclusion provided by or under Part I of the Competition Act 1998[7] or any other enactment, does not require those provisions of the agreement to which the exclusion relates to be disregarded when considering whether the agreement infringes the prohibition for other reasons[8].

Provision is also made, and has been exercised, for the exclusion of vertical and land agreements from the Chapter I prohibition[9].

1 As to the meaning of 'Chapter I prohibition' see PARA 116.
2 See the Competition Act 1998 s 3(1).
3 See the Competition Act 1998 s 3(1)(a), Sch 1; and PARA 118.
4 See the Competition Act 1998 s 3(1)(b), Sch 2; and PARA 119.
5 See the Competition Act 1998 s 3(1)(c), Sch 3; and PARA 120.
6 See PARAS 118, 120. As to the Secretary of State see PARA 5.
7 Ie the Competition Act 1998 Pt 1 (ss 1–60).
8 Competition Act 1998 s 59(2).
9 See PARA 142.
   For decisions of the EC Commission and the European Court of Justice on the provisions of European Community law corresponding to those of the Competition Act 1998 see PARA 24 et seq. As to the duty to interpret the provisions of the Competition Act 1998 in a manner consistent with European Community law and the decisions of the European Court of Justice see s 60; and PARA 150.

118. Excluded agreements: mergers and concentrations. To the extent to which an agreement (either on its own or when taken together with another agreement) results, or if carried out would result, in any two enterprises ceasing to be distinct enterprises[1], the Chapter I prohibition[2] does not apply to the agreement[3].

This exclusion does not apply to a particular agreement if the Office of Fair Trading (the 'OFT')[4] gives a direction to that effect[5]. If the OFT is considering whether to give such a direction, it may by notice in writing require any party to the agreement in question to give the OFT such information in connection with the agreement as it may require[6]; if at the end of such period as may be specified[7] a person[8] has failed, without reasonable excuse, to comply with such a requirement, the OFT may give a direction as described above[9]. The OFT may also give such a direction if: (1) it considers that the agreement will, if not excluded, infringe the Chapter I prohibition; and (2) the agreement is not a protected agreement[10]. The OFT may only give a direction in either of the circumstances described above[11].

To the extent to which an agreement (either on its own or when taken together with another agreement) gives rise to, or would if carried out give rise to, a concentration[12], the Chapter I prohibition does not apply to the agreement if the EC Merger Regulation[13] gives the European Commission[14] exclusive jurisdiction in the matter[15].

1 Ie for the purposes of the Enterprise Act 2002 Pt 3 (ss 22–130): see in particular PARA 176.
2 As to the Chapter I prohibition see PARA 116.
3 Competition Act 1998 s 3(1)(a), Sch 1 para 1(1) (amended by the Enterprise Act 2002 s 278(1), Sch 25 para 38(1), (50)(a)(i)). This exclusion extends to any provision directly related and necessary to the implementation of the merger provisions: Competition Act 1998 Sch 1 para 1(2). 'Merger provisions' means the provisions of the agreement which cause, or if carried out would cause, the agreement to have the result of two enterprises ceasing to be distinct enterprises: Sch 1 para 1(3). The Enterprise Act 2002 s 26 (see PARA 176) applies with modifications for the purpose of this provision: Competition Act 1998 Sch 1 para 1(4) (amended by the Enterprise Act 2002 Sch 25 para 38(1), (50)(a)(ii)).

The Secretary of State may at any time by order amend the Competition Act 1998 Sch 1, with respect to the Chapter I prohibition, by: (1) providing for one or more additional exclusions; or (2) amending or removing any provision (whether or not it has been added by an order under this provision): s 3(2). Such an order may include provision (similar to that made with respect to any other exclusion provided by Sch 1) for the exclusion concerned to cease to apply to a particular agreement: s 3(5).

For decisions of the EC Commission and the European Court of Justice on the provisions of European Community law corresponding to those of the Competition Act 1998 see PARA 24 et seq, and particularly PARA 73 et seq. As to the duty to interpret the provisions of the Competition Act 1998 in a manner consistent with European Community law and the decisions of the European Court of Justice see s 60; and PARA 150.

4 As to the OFT see PARAS 6–8.

5 Competition Act 1998 Sch 1 para 4(1) (amended by the Enterprise Act 2002 s 278(1), Sch 25 para 38(1), (50)(c)(i)). Such a direction must be in writing, and may be made so as to have effect from a date specified in the direction (which may not be earlier than the date on which it is given): Competition Act 1998 Sch 1 para 4(7).

6 Competition Act 1998 Sch 1 para 4(2) (amended by the Enterprise Act 2002 s 278(1), Sch 25 para 38(1), (50)(c)(ii)). As to the meaning of 'information' see PARA 9 note 3.

7 Ie specified in rules under the Competition Act 1998 s 51 (see PARA 144).

8 'Person' includes any undertaking, in addition to the meaning given by the Interpretation Act 1978 (see STATUTES vol 44(1) (Reissue) PARA 1382): Competition Act 1998 s 59(1).

9 Competition Act 1998 Sch 1 para 4(4) (amended by the Enterprise Act 2002 s 278(1), Sch 25 para 38(1), (50)(c)(i)).

10 Competition Act 1998 Sch 1 para 4(5) (amended by the Enterprise Act 2002 s 278(1), Sch 25 para 38(1), (50)(c)(i); and by SI 2004/1261).

An agreement is a protected agreement for this purpose if: (1) the OFT or the Secretary of State has published its or his decision not to make a merger reference to the Competition Commission under the Enterprise Act 2002 s 22 (see PARA 172), s 33 (see PARA 182), s 45 (see PARA 193) or s 62 (see PARA 208) in connection with the agreement; (2) the OFT or the Secretary of State has made a merger reference to the Competition Commission under s 22, 33, 45 or 62 in connection with the agreement and the Commission has found that the agreement has given rise to, or would if carried out give rise to, a relevant merger situation (see PARA 173) or a special merger situation (see PARA 204); (3) the agreement does not fall within head (1) or head (2) but has given rise to, or would if carried out give rise to, enterprises to which it relates being regarded under s 26 (see PARA 176) as ceasing to be distinct enterprises (otherwise than as the result of s 26(3) or (4)(b)); or (4) the OFT has made a merger reference to the Competition Commission under the Water Industry Act 1991 s 32 (see WATER AND WATERWAYS vol 100 (2009) PARAS 150–151) in connection with the agreement and the Commission has found that the agreement has given rise to, or would if carried out give rise to, a merger of the kind to which that provision applies: Competition Act 1998 Sch 1 para 5 (amended by the Enterprise Act 2002 Sch 25 para 38(1), (50)(d)). As to the Secretary of State see PARA 5.

11 Competition Act 1998 Sch 1 para 4(3) (amended by the Enterprise Act 2002 Sch 25 para 38(1), (50)(c)(i)).

12 'Concentration' means a concentration with a Community dimension within the meaning of the Merger Regulation arts 1, 3 (as to which see note 13): Competition Act 1998 Sch 1 para 6(3). As to concentrations see PARA 73 et seq.

13 Ie EC Council Regulation 139/2004 (OJ L24, 29.1.2004, p 1) (the 'EC Merger Regulation') (see PARA 74).

14 See PARA 123 note 2.

15 Competition Act 1998 Sch 1 para 6(1).

119. Excluded agreements: competition scrutiny under other enactments. The Chapter I prohibition[1] does not apply in any of the cases in which it is excluded by or as a result of certain enactments which provide for competition scrutiny under enactments other than the Competition Act 1998[2].

The exclusions referred to above relate to:

(1) self-regulating organisations, investment exchanges and clearing houses, and professional bodies and investment business, under the Financial Services Act 1986[3];

(2) agreements relating to Channel 3 news provision, under the Broadcasting Act 1990[4];

(3) networking arrangements[5];

(4) provisions of the Financial Services and Markets Act 2000[6].

1 As to the Chapter I prohibition see PARA 116.

2 See the Competition Act 1998 s 3(1)(b); the enactments are mainly those listed in Sch 2 (see the text and notes 3–6), but other enactments may themselves provide for exclusion from the Chapter I prohibition: see e g the text and note 6.

3 The Competition Act 1998 Sch 2 para 1(2), (4) substituted the Financial Services Act 1986 ss 125, 127 (repealed); see now the Financial Services and Markets Act 2000 s 164 (see FINANCIAL SERVICES AND INSTITUTIONS vol 48 (2008) PARA 42) and s 311 (see FINANCIAL SERVICES AND INSTITUTIONS vol 49 (2008) PARA 736).

4 See the Broadcasting Act 1990 s 194A(2)–(11) (substituted by the Competition Act 1998 Sch 2 para 4(2)); and TELECOMMUNICATIONS AND BROADCASTING vol 45(1) (2005 Reissue) PARA 380.

5 Ie networking arrangements under the Communications Act 2003 s 291 (see TELECOMMUNICATIONS AND BROADCASTING vol 45(1) (2005 Reissue) PARA 279): Competition Act 1998 Sch 2 para 5 (amended by the Communications Act 2003 ss 291(3), (4), 371(6)).

6 See the Financial Services and Markets Act 2000 s 164 (see FINANCIAL SERVICES AND INSTITUTIONS vol 48 (2008) PARA 42) and s 311 (see FINANCIAL SERVICES AND INSTITUTIONS vol 49 (2008) PARA 736).

120. Excluded agreements: general exclusions. The Chapter I prohibition[1] does not apply in any of the cases in which it is excluded by or as a result of provisions of the Competition Act 1998 which make exclusions of a general nature[2].

The exclusions referred to above relate to:

(1) planning obligations[3];

(2) EEA regulated markets[4];

(3) services of general economic interest or having the character of a revenue-producing monopoly[5];

(4) agreements made in order to comply with legal requirements[6];

(5) avoidance of conflict with international obligations[7];

(6) exceptional and compelling reasons of public policy[8];

(7) coal and steel[9];

(8) agricultural products[10].

1 As to the Chapter I prohibition see PARA 116.

2 Competition Act 1998 s 3(1)(c). The exclusions are set out in Sch 3: see the text and notes 3–10. The Secretary of State may at any time by order amend Sch 3, with respect to the Chapter I prohibition, by: (1) providing for one or more additional exclusions; or (2) amending or removing any provision added by an order under this provision, or included in Sch 3 para 1, 2, 8 or 9: s 3(3). The power under s 3(3) to provide for an additional exclusion may be exercised only if it appears to the Secretary of State that agreements which fall within the additional exclusion: (a) do not in general have an adverse effect on competition; or (b) are, in general, best considered under Chapter II (see PARAS 125–128) or the Enterprise Act 2002 (see PARA 171 et seq): Competition Act 1998 s 3(4) (amended by the Enterprise Act 2002 s 278(1), Sch 25 para 38(1), (2)). Such an order may include provision (similar to that made with respect to any other exclusion provided by the Competition Act 1998 Sch 3) for the exclusion concerned to cease to apply to a particular agreement: s 3(5). Schedule 3 also gives the Secretary of State power to exclude agreements from the Chapter I prohibition in certain circumstances: s 3(6). As to the Secretary of State see PARA 5.

3 See the Competition Act 1998 Sch 3 para 1. 'Planning obligation' means a planning obligation for the purposes of the Town and Country Planning Act 1990 s 106 (see TOWN AND COUNTRY PLANNING vol 46(1) (Reissue) PARAS 244, 245): Competition Act 1998 Sch 3 para 1(2).

4 See the Competition Act 1998 Sch 3 para 3 (amended by SI 2007/126). 'EEA regulated market' means a market which: (1) is listed by an EEA state other than the United Kingdom pursuant to EC Directive 2004/39 of the European Parliament and Council on markets in financial

instruments (OJ L145, 30.4.2004, p 1) art 47; and (2) operates without any requirement that a person dealing on the market should have a physical presence in the EEA state from which any trading facilities are provided or on any trading floor that the market may have; 'EEA state' means a state which is a contracting party to the EEA Agreement (see PARA 123 note 2): Competition Act 1998 Sch 3 para 3(5) (as so amended).

5   See the Competition Act 1998 Sch 3 para 4.

6   See the Competition Act 1998 Sch 3 para 5.

7   See the Competition Act 1998 Sch 3 para 6. Exclusion under this head is by order of the Secretary of State, and may relate to a particular agreement or agreements of a particular description: see Sch 3 para 6(1). The order may provide for exclusion only in specified circumstances: see Sch 3 para 6(2). It may also provide that the Chapter I prohibition is to be deemed never to have applied: see Sch 3 para 6(3).

8   See the Competition Act 1998 Sch 3 para 7. Exclusion under this head is by order of the Secretary of State, and may relate to a particular agreement or agreements of a particular description: see Sch 3 para 7(1). The order may provide for exclusion only in specified circumstances: see Sch 3 para 7(2). It may also provide that the Chapter I prohibition is to be deemed never to have applied: see Sch 3 para 7(3). See the Competition Act 1998 (Public Policy Exclusion) Order 2006, SI 2006/605; the Competition Act 1998 (Public Policy Exclusion) Order 2007, SI 2007/1896; and the Competition Act 1998 (Public Policy Exclusion) Order 2008, SI 2008/1820.

9   See the Competition Act 1998 Sch 3 para 8.

10 See the Competition Act 1998 Sch 3 para 9 (amended by the Enterprise Act 2002 s 278(1), Sch 25 para 38(1), (51); and SI 2004/1261). This exclusion applies to an agreement to the extent to which it relates to production of or trade in an agricultural product and: (1) forms an integral part of a national market organisation; (2) is necessary for the attainment of the objectives set out in the EC Treaty art 33; or (3) is an agreement of farmers or farmers' associations (or associations of such associations) belonging to a single member state which concerns the production or sale of agricultural products, or the use of joint facilities for the storage, treatment or processing of agricultural products, and under which there is no obligation to charge identical prices: see the Competition Act 1998 Sch 3 para 9(1). As to the EC Treaty (ie the Treaty establishing the European Community (Rome, 25 March 1957; TS 1 (1973); Cmnd 5179)) see PARA 24 note 1. The numbering for the EC Treaty used in this title is as revised by the Treaty of Amsterdam: see PARA 24 note 1.

121.   Block exemptions.   If agreements which fall within a particular category of agreement are, in the opinion of the Office of Fair Trading (the 'OFT')[1], likely to be exempt agreements[2], the OFT may recommend that the Secretary of State make an order specifying that category for the purposes of this provision[3]. The Secretary of State may make an order ('a block exemption order') giving effect to such a recommendation in the form in which the recommendation is made, or subject to such modifications as he considers appropriate[4]. An agreement which falls within a category specified[5] in a block exemption order is exempt from the Chapter I prohibition[6]. An exemption under this provision is referred to in Part I of the Competition Act 1998 as a 'block exemption'[7].

A block exemption order may impose conditions or obligations subject to which a block exemption is to have effect[8]. A block exemption order may provide:

(1)   that breach of a condition imposed by the order has the effect of cancelling the block exemption in respect of an agreement[9];

(2)   that if there is a failure to comply with an obligation imposed by the order, the OFT may, by notice in writing, cancel the block exemption in respect of the agreement[10];

(3)   that if the OFT considers that a particular agreement is not an exempt agreement[11], it may cancel the block exemption in respect of that agreement[12].

A block exemption order may provide that the order is to cease to have effect at the end of a specified period[13]. A block exemption order may provide for a block exemption to have effect from a date earlier than that on which the order is made[14].

If, in the opinion of the OFT, it is appropriate to vary or revoke a block exemption order it may make a recommendation to that effect to the Secretary of State[15]. Before exercising his power to vary or revoke a block exemption order (in a case where no such recommendation has been made), the Secretary of State must inform the OFT of the proposed variation or revocation; and take into account any comments made by the OFT[16].

One block exemption has been made by the Secretary of State, in relation to public transport ticketing schemes[17].

1 As to the OFT see PARAS 6–8.
2 'Exempt agreement' means an agreement which is exempt from the Chapter I prohibition as a result of the Competition Act 1998 s 9 (see PARA 122): s 6(8) (substituted by SI 2004/1261). As to the Chapter I prohibition see PARA 116.
3 Competition Act 1998 s 6(1) (amended by the Enterprise Act 2002 s 278(1), Sch 25 para 38(1), (5)(a); and SI 2004/1261). As to the Secretary of State see PARA 5. Before making a recommendation under the Competition Act 1998 s 6(1), the OFT must publish details of its proposed recommendation in such a way as it thinks most suitable for bringing it to the attention of those likely to be affected, and consider any representations about it which are made to it: s 8(1) (amended by the Enterprise Act 2002 Sch 25 para 38(1), (7)).
    For decisions of the EC Commission and the European Court of Justice on the provisions of European Community law corresponding to those of the Competition Act 1998 see PARA 24 et seq, and particularly PARA 67. As to the duty to interpret the provisions of the Competition Act 1998 in a manner consistent with European Community law and the decisions of the European Court of Justice see s 60; and PARA 150.
4 Competition Act 1998 s 6(2). If the Secretary of State proposes to give effect to such a recommendation subject to modifications, he must inform the OFT of the proposed modifications and take into account any comments made by the OFT: s 8(2) (amended by the Enterprise Act 2002 Sch 25 para 38(1), (7)(a)).
5 'Specified' means specified in a block exemption order: Competition Act 1998 s 6(8) (substituted by SI 2004/1261).
6 Competition Act 1998 s 6(3).
7 Competition Act 1998 s 6(4).
8 Competition Act 1998 s 6(5).
9 Competition Act 1998 s 6(6)(a).
10 Competition Act 1998 s 6(6)(b) (amended by the Enterprise Act 2002 Sch 25 para 38(1), (5)).
11 See note 2.
12 Competition Act 1998 s 6(6)(c) (amended by the Enterprise Act 2002 Sch 25 para 38(1), (5)).
13 Competition Act 1998 s 6(7).
14 Competition Act 1998 s 8(6).
15 Competition Act 1998 s 8(3) (amended by the Enterprise Act 2002 Sch 25 para 38(1), (7)). The Competition Act 1998 s 8(1) (see note 3) also applies to any proposed recommendation under s 8(3): s 8(4).
16 Competition Act 1998 s 8(5) (amended by the Enterprise Act 2002 Sch 25 para 38(1), (7)).
17 See the Competition Act 1998 (Public Transport Ticketing Schemes Block Exemption) Order 2001, SI 2001/319 (amended by SI 2005/3347).

122. Exempt agreements. An agreement is exempt from the Chapter I prohibition[1] if it contributes to improving production or distribution, or promoting technical or economic progress, while allowing consumers a fair share of the resulting benefit[2]. The agreement must not impose on the undertakings concerned restrictions which are not indispensable to the attainment of those objectives, or afford the undertakings concerned the possibility of eliminating competition in respect of a substantial part of the products in question[3].

In any proceedings in which it is alleged that the Chapter I prohibition is being or has been infringed by an agreement, any undertaking or association of undertakings claiming that the agreement is exempt bears the burden of proving that the above conditions are satisfied[4].

1   As to the Chapter I prohibition see PARA 116.
2   Competition Act 1998 s 9(1)(a) (s 9 substituted by SI 2004/1261).
3   Competition Act 1998 s 9(1)(b) (as substituted: see note 2).
4   Competition Act 1998 s 9(2) (as substituted: see note 2).

123.   Parallel exemptions.   An agreement is exempt from the Chapter I prohibition[1] if it is exempt from the Community prohibition[2] by virtue of a Regulation or because of a decision of the European Commission under the EC Competition Regulation[3]. An agreement is exempt from the Chapter I prohibition if it does not affect trade between member states but otherwise falls within a category of agreement which is exempt from the Community prohibition by virtue of a Regulation[4]. An exemption from the Chapter I prohibition under this provision is known[5] as a 'parallel exemption'[6].

A parallel exemption takes effect on the date on which the relevant exemption from the Community prohibition takes effect (or, as the case may be[7], would take effect if the agreement in question affected trade between member states)[8]. It ceases to have effect if the relevant exemption from the Community prohibition ceases to have effect, or on being cancelled as described below[9].

In such circumstances and manner as may be specified[10], the Office of Fair Trading (the 'OFT')[11] may: (1) impose conditions or obligations subject to which a parallel exemption is to have effect[12]; (2) vary or remove any such condition or obligation[13]; (3) impose one or more additional conditions or obligations[14]; or (4) cancel the exemption[15]. In such circumstances as may be specified[16], the date from which cancellation of an exemption is to take effect may be earlier than the date on which notice of cancellation is given[17]. Breach of a condition imposed by the OFT has the effect of cancelling the exemption[18]. In exercising its powers, the OFT may require any person who is a party to the agreement in question to give it such information as it may require[19].

1   As to the Chapter I prohibition see PARA 116.
2   In the Competition Act 1998 s 10, 'Community prohibition' means the prohibition contained in (1) the EC Treaty art 81(1); (2) any corresponding provision replacing, or otherwise derived from, that provision; (3) such other Regulation as the Secretary of State may by order specify: Competition Act 1998 s 10(10) (amended by SI 2004/1261). 'Regulation' means a Regulation adopted by the European Commission or by the Council of the European Union: Competition Act 1998 ss 10(10), 59(1). As to the EC Treaty (ie the Treaty establishing the European Community (Rome, 25 March 1957; TS 1 (1973); Cmnd 5179)) see PARA 24 note 1. The numbering for the EC Treaty used in this title is as revised by the Treaty of Amsterdam: see PARA 24 note 1.
    For the purpose of the Competition Act 1998 s 10, references to an agreement being exempt from the Community prohibition are to be read as including references to the prohibition being inapplicable to the agreement by virtue of a Regulation (other than EC Council Regulation 1/2003 on the implementation of the rules on competition laid down in Articles 81 and 82 of the Treaty (OJ L1, 4.1.03, p 1) (the 'Modernisation Regulation')) or a decision by the European Commission: Competition Act 1998 s 10(9) (amended by SI 2004/1261).
    The Competition Act 1998 s 10 has effect in relation to the prohibition contained in the EEA Agreement art 53 para 1 (and the EFTA Surveillance Authority) as it has effect in relation to the Community prohibition (and the Commission) subject to any modifications which the Secretary of State may by order prescribe: Competition Act 1998 s 10(11). 'EEA Agreement' means the Agreement on the European Economic Area (Oporto, 2 May 1992 (Cm 2073; OJ L1, 3.1.94, p 3)) as it has effect for the time being: Competition Act 1998 s 59(1).

As to the Secretary of State see PARA 5. As to the power to make subordinate legislation under the Competition Act 1998 see PARA 163.

3   Competition Act 1998 s 10(1) (amended by SI 2004/1261). As to the EC Competition Regulation see note 2.

4   Competition Act 1998 s 10(2).

5   Ie in the Competition Act 1998 Pt I (ss 1–60).

6   Competition Act 1998 ss 10(3), 59(1).

7   Ie in the case of a parallel exemption under the Competition Act 1998 s 10(2) (see the text to note 4).

8   Competition Act 1998 s 10(4)(a).

9   Competition Act 1998 s 10(4)(b). As to cancellation see s 10(5), (7); and the text and notes 11–15, 18.

10 Ie in rules made under the Competition Act 1998 s 51 (see PARA 144). See the Competition Act 1998 (Office of Fair Trading's Rules) Order 2004, SI 2004/2751, Schedule r 12.

11 Competition Act 1998 s 10(5) (amended by the Enterprise Act 2002 s 278(1), Sch 25 para 38(1), (8)). As to the OFT see PARAS 6–8.

12 Competition Act 1998 s 10(5)(a).

13 Competition Act 1998 s 10(5)(b).

14 Competition Act 1998 s 10(5)(c).

15 Competition Act 1998 s 10(5)(d).

16 See note 10.

17 Competition Act 1998 s 10(6).

18 Competition Act 1998 s 10(7) (amended by the Enterprise Act 2002 Sch 25 para 38(1), (8)).

19 Competition Act 1998 s 10(8) (amended by the Enterprise Act 2002 Sch 25 para 38(1), (8)). For the purposes of the Competition Act 1998 Pt I, the power to require information, in relation to information recorded otherwise than in a legible form, includes power to require a copy of it in a legible form: s 59(3). Any power conferred on the OFT by Pt I to require information includes power to require any document which it believes may contain that information: s 59(4) (amended by the Enterprise Act 2002 Sch 25 para 38(1), (44)). As to the meaning of 'person' see PARA 118 note 8. As to the meaning of 'information' see PARA 9 note 3.

124.   Exemption for certain other agreements.   The fact that a ruling may be given by virtue of the EC Treaty[1] on the question whether or not agreements of a particular kind are prohibited by the Treaty[2] does not prevent such agreements from being subject to the Chapter I prohibition[3]. However, the Secretary of State[4] may by regulations make such provision as he considers appropriate for the purpose of granting an exemption from the Chapter I prohibition, in prescribed circumstances, in respect of such agreements[5].

The circumstances in which agreements in relation to which a ruling may be given by virtue of the Treaty are exempt from the Chapter I prohibition are that the Office of Fair Trading (the 'OFT')[6] has not found that an agreement which would otherwise benefit from such an exemption has effects in the United Kingdom[7], or a part of it, which are incompatible with the criteria laid down[8] for exempt agreements[9].

An exemption under these provisions takes effect on the date on which the relevant exemption from the Community prohibition takes effect[10]. However, it may, if the OFT considers it appropriate and so determines, take effect from a date specified by the OFT which is earlier than the date on which the exemption from the Community prohibition takes effect[11]. It ceases to have effect on the date on which the relevant exemption from the Community prohibition otherwise ceases to have effect or a finding is made by the OFT that the agreement to which the relevant exemption relates has effects in the United Kingdom, or a part of it, which are incompatible with the criteria for exempt agreements[12].

1   Ie the EC Treaty art 84. As to the EC Treaty (ie the Treaty establishing the European Community (Rome, 25 March 1957; TS 1 (1973); Cmnd 5179)) see PARA 24 note 1. The numbering for the EC Treaty used in this title is as revised by the Treaty of Amsterdam: see PARA 24 note 1.
2   Ie by the EC Treaty art 81(1). See further PARA 123 note 2.
3   Competition Act 1998 s 11(1) (amended by SI 2004/1261). As to the Chapter I prohibition see PARA 116.
4   As to the Secretary of State see PARA 5.
5   Competition Act 1998 s 11(2). An exemption from the Chapter I prohibition by virtue of such regulations is referred to in Pt I (ss 1–60) as a 'section 11 exemption': ss 11(3), 59(1). As to the power to make subordinate legislation under the Competition Act 1998 see PARA 163.
6   As to the OFT see PARAS 6–8.
7   As to the meaning of 'United Kingdom' see PARA 401 note 1.
8   Ie in the Competition Act 1998 s 9 (see PARA 122).
9   Competition Act 1998 (Section 11 Exemption) Regulations 2001, SI 2001/2993, reg 3(1) (amended by SI 2007/1846). The OFT may not make such a finding otherwise than in the manner specified in what is now the Competition Act 1998 (Office of Fair Trading's Rules) Order 2004, SI 2004/2751, Schedule r 12: see the Competition Act 1998 (Section 11 Exemption) Regulations 2001, SI 2001/2993, reg 3(4).
10 Competition Act 1998 (Section 11 Exemption) Regulations 2001, SI 2001/2993, reg 3(2)(a).
11 Competition Act 1998 (Section 11 Exemption) Regulations 2001, SI 2001/2993, reg 3(3).
12 Competition Act 1998 (Section 11 Exemption) Regulations 2001, SI 2001/2993, reg 3(2)(b) (amended by SI 2007/1846).

(3) THE CHAPTER II PROHIBITION

125.   The prohibition.   Any conduct on the part of one or more undertakings which amounts to the abuse of a dominant position[1] in a market is prohibited if it may affect trade within the United Kingdom[2]. Conduct may, in particular, constitute such an abuse if it consists in[3]:

(1)   directly or indirectly imposing unfair purchase or selling prices or other unfair trading conditions[4];

(2)   limiting production, markets or technical development to the prejudice of consumers[5];

(3)   applying dissimilar conditions to equivalent transactions with other trading parties, thereby placing them at a competitive disadvantage[6];

(4)   making the conclusion of contracts subject to acceptance by the other parties of supplementary obligations which, by their nature or according to commercial usage, have no connection with the subject of the contracts[7].

This prohibition is referred to as the 'Chapter II prohibition'[8]. The Chapter II prohibition does not apply to certain excluded cases[9].

The Office of Fair Trading (the 'OFT')[10] has published numerous Guidelines on the operation of the Act[11].

1   In the Competition Act 1998 s 18, 'dominant position' means a dominant position within the United Kingdom: s 18(3). 'United Kingdom' means the United Kingdom or any part of it: s 18(3). As to the meaning of 'United Kingdom' see PARA 401 note 1.
    For decisions of the EC Commission and the European Court of Justice on the provisions of European Community law corresponding to those of the Competition Act 1998 see PARA 24 et seq, and particularly PARA 68 et seq. As to the duty to interpret the provisions of the Competition Act 1998 in a manner consistent with European Community law and the decisions of the European Court of Justice see s 60; and PARA 150. For a decision in which the relevant provisions both of the EC Treaty and the Competition Act 1998 were considered see *Hendry v World Professional Billiards and Snooker Association* [2001] All ER (D) 71 (Oct) (abuse of dominant position by governing body of sport: see PARA 49). There must be an element of abusive behaviour in order to establish an abuse of a dominant position: *Getmapping plc v*

Ordnance Survey [2002] EWHC 1089 (Ch), [2003] ICR 1 (use of funds acquired as a result of
a position of dominance in one market in order to enter another market at advantage not an
automatic abuse).
2 Competition Act 1998 s 18(1).
3 Competition Act 1998 s 18(2).
4 Competition Act 1998 s 18(2)(a).
5 Competition Act 1998 s 18(2)(b).
6 Competition Act 1998 s 18(2)(c).
7 Competition Act 1998 s 18(2)(d).
8 Competition Act 1998 ss 18(4), 59(1).
9 See PARA 126.
10 As to the Office of Fair Trading see PARAS 6–8.
11 See in particular OFT Guideline 402 *Abuse of a Dominant Position* (December 2004); OFT
Guideline 403 *Market Definition* (December 2004); OFT Guideline 414a *Assessment of
Conduct* (April 2004); OFT Guideline 415 *Assessment of Market Power* (December 2004).

126. Excluded cases: introductory. The Chapter II prohibition[1] does not
apply in any of the cases in which it is excluded by or as a result of certain
specified provisions[2]; these provisions relate to mergers and concentrations[3] and
general exclusions[4]. The Financial Services and Markets Act 2000 provides for
further exclusions from the Chapter II prohibition[5].

Provision is made for amendment to be made by the Secretary of State to these
exclusions[6].

1 As to the Chapter II prohibition see PARA 125.
2 Competition Act 1998 s 19(1).
3 Competition Act 1998 s 19(1), Sch 1.
4 Competition Act 1998 Sch 3. The exclusions provided for by this Schedule consist of services of
general economic interest (see Sch 3 para 4); compliance with legal requirements (see Sch 3
para 5); avoidance of conflict with international obligations (see Sch 3 para 6); public policy (see
Sch 3 para 7); and coal and steel (see Sch 3 para 8).
5 See PARA 117 text and note 4.
6 See PARAS 127–128.

127. Excluded cases: mergers and concentrations. To the extent to which
conduct (either on its own or when taken together with other conduct) results in
any two enterprises ceasing to be distinct enterprises[1], or is directly related and
necessary to the attainment of that result, the Chapter II prohibition[2] does not
apply to that conduct[3].

To the extent to which conduct (either on its own or when taken together with
other conduct) gives rise to, or would if pursued give rise to, a concentration[4],
the Chapter II prohibition does not apply to the conduct if the EC Merger
Regulation[5] gives the European Commission[6] exclusive jurisdiction in the
matter[7].

1 Ie for the purposes of the Enterprise Act 2002 Pt 3 (ss 22–130): see PARA 176.
2 As to the Chapter II prohibition see PARA 125.
3 Competition Act 1998 s 19(1)(a), Sch 1 para 2(1) (amended by the Enterprise Act 2002
s 278(1), Sch 25 para 38(1), (50)(b)(i)). The Enterprise Act 2002 s 26 (see PARA 176) applies
with modifications for the purpose of this provision: Competition Act 1998 Sch 1 paras 1(4),
2(2) (amended by the Enterprise Act 2002 Sch 25 para 38(1), (50)(b)(ii)).
   The Secretary of State may at any time by order amend the Competition Act 1998 Sch 1,
with respect to the Chapter II prohibition, by: (1) providing for one or more additional
exclusions; or (2) amending or removing any provision (whether or not it has been added by an
order under this provision): s 19(2). As to the power to make subordinate legislation under the
Competition Act 1998 see PARA 163.
   For decisions of the EC Commission and the European Court of Justice on the provisions of
European Community law corresponding to those of the Competition Act 1998 see PARA 24 et
seq, and particularly PARA 73 et seq. As to the duty to interpret the provisions of the

Competition Act 1998 in a manner consistent with European Community law and the decisions of the European Court of Justice see s 60; and PARA 150.

4   As to the meaning of 'concentration' see PARA 118 note 12.
5   Ie EC Council Regulation 139/2004 (OJ L24, 29.1.2004, p 1) (the 'EC Merger Regulation') (see PARA 74).
6   See PARA 123 note 2.
7   Competition Act 1998 Sch 1 para 6(2).

128.   Excluded cases: general exclusions.   The Chapter II prohibition[1] does not apply in any of the cases in which it is excluded by or as a result of provisions of the Competition Act 1998 which make exclusions of a general nature[2].

The exclusions referred to above relate to:

(1)   services of general economic interest or having the character of a revenue-producing monopoly[3];
(2)   conduct engaged in in order to comply with legal requirements[4];
(3)   avoidance of conflict with international obligations[5];
(4)   exceptional and compelling reasons of public policy[6];
(5)   coal and steel[7].

1   As to the Chapter II prohibition see PARA 125.
2   Competition Act 1998 s 19(1)(b). The exclusions are set out in Sch 3 (see the text and notes 3–7).
3   See the Competition Act 1998 Sch 3 para 4.
4   See the Competition Act 1998 Sch 3 para 5.
5   See the Competition Act 1998 Sch 3 para 6. Exclusion under this head is by order of the Secretary of State, which may provide for exclusion only in specified circumstances: see Sch 3 para 6(4). It may also provide that the Chapter II prohibition is to be deemed never to have applied: see Sch 3 para 6(5). As to the Secretary of State see PARA 5.
6   See the Competition Act 1998 Sch 3 para 7. Exclusion under this head is by order of the Secretary of State, which may provide for exclusion only in specified circumstances: see Sch 3 para 7(4). It may also provide that the Chapter II prohibition is to be deemed never to have applied: see Sch 3 para 7(5).
7   See the Competition Act 1998 Sch 3 para 8.
    The Secretary of State may at any time by order amend Sch 3 para 8 with respect to the Chapter II prohibition: s 19(3). Schedule 3 also gives the Secretary of State power to provide that the Chapter II prohibition is not to apply in certain circumstances: s 19(4). As to the power to make subordinate legislation under the Competition Act 1998 see PARA 163.

(4) INVESTIGATION BY THE OFFICE OF FAIR TRADING

129.   Power of the Office of Fair Trading to investigate.   The Office of Fair Trading (the 'OFT')[1] may conduct an investigation in any of the following cases[2]:

(1)   where there are reasonable grounds for suspecting that there is an agreement which may affect trade within the United Kingdom[3] and which has as its object or effect the prevention, restriction or distortion of competition within the United Kingdom[4];
(2)   where there are reasonable grounds for suspecting that there is an agreement which may affect trade between member states and which has as its object or effect the prevention, restriction or distortion of competition within the European Community[5];
(3)   where there are reasonable grounds for suspecting that the Chapter II prohibition[6] has been infringed[7];
(4)   where there are reasonable grounds for suspecting that the prohibition on abuse of a dominant position in the EC Treaty[8] has been infringed[9];
(5)   where there are reasonable grounds for suspecting that, at some time in the past, there was an agreement which at that time may have affected

trade within the United Kingdom and had as its object or effect the prevention, restriction or distortion of competition within the United Kingdom[10];

(6)   where there are reasonable grounds for suspecting that, at some time in the past, there was an agreement which at that time may have affected trade between member states and had as its object or effect the prevention, restriction or distortion of competition within the European Community[11].

The OFT has published guidance on investigations[12].

For the purposes of an investigation, the OFT may, by notice in writing, require any person to produce to it a specified[13] document, or to provide it with specified information, which it considers relates to any matter relevant to the investigation[14]. The notice must indicate the subject matter and purpose of the investigation and the nature of the offences created by failure to comply with the notice[15]. The OFT may also specify in the notice the time and place at which any document is to be produced or any information is to be provided and the manner and form in which it is to be produced or provided[16].

1   As to the OFT see PARAS 6–8.
2   Competition Act 1998 s 25(1) (s 25 substituted by SI 2004/1261).
3   As to the meaning of 'United Kingdom' see PARA 401 note 1.
4   Competition Act 1998 s 25(2) (as substituted: see note 2). Section 25(2) does not permit an investigation to be conducted in relation to an agreement if the OFT: (1) considers that the agreement is exempt from the Chapter I prohibition as a result of a block exemption or a parallel exemption; and (2) does not have reasonable grounds for suspecting that the circumstances may be such that it could exercise its power to cancel the exemption: s 25(8) (as substituted: see note 2). As to the Chapter I prohibition see PARA 116. As to the meaning of 'block exemption' see PARA 121; and as to the meaning of 'parallel exemption' see PARA 123.
5   Competition Act 1998 s 25(3) (as substituted: see note 2). Section 25(3) does not permit an investigation to be conducted if the OFT: (1) considers that the agreement is an agreement to which the prohibition in the EC Treaty art 81(1) (see PARA 61 et seq) is inapplicable by virtue of a regulation of the European Commission (the 'relevant regulation'); and (2) does not have reasonable grounds for suspecting that the conditions set out in EC Council Regulation 1/2003 on the implementation of the rules on competition laid down in Articles 81 and 82 of the Treaty (OJ L1, 4.1.03, p 1) (the 'Modernisation Regulation') art 29(2) for the withdrawal of the benefit of the relevant regulation may be satisfied in respect of that agreement: Competition Act 1998 s 25(9) (as substituted: see note 2). As to the EC Treaty (ie the Treaty establishing the European Community (Rome, 25 March 1957; TS 1 (1973); Cmnd 5179)) see PARA 24 note 1. The numbering for the EC Treaty used in this title is as revised by the Treaty of Amsterdam: see PARA 24 note 1.
6   As to the Chapter II prohibition see PARA 125.
7   Competition Act 1998 s 25(4) (as substituted: see note 2).
8   Ie the EC Treaty art 82 (see PARA 68).
9   Competition Act 1998 s 25(5) (as substituted: see note 2).
10 Competition Act 1998 s 25(6) (as substituted: see note 2). Section 25(6) does not permit an investigation to be conducted in relation to any agreement if the OFT considers that, at the time in question, the agreement was exempt from the Chapter I prohibition as a result of a block exemption or a parallel exemption: s 25(10) (as substituted: see note 2). It is immaterial for the purposes of s 25(6) or s 25(7) (see head (6) in the text) whether the agreement in question remains in existence: s 25(12) (as substituted: see note 2).
11 Competition Act 1998 s 25(7) (as substituted: see note 2). Section 25(7) does not permit an investigation to be conducted in relation to any agreement if the OFT considers that, at the time in question, the agreement was an agreement to which the prohibition in the EC Treaty art 81(1) (see PARA 61 et seq) was inapplicable by virtue of a regulation of the European Commission: Competition Act 1998 s 25(11) (as substituted: see note 2). See also note 10.
12 See OFT 404 *Powers of investigation* (December 2004).
13 'Specified' means: (1) specified, or described, in the notice; or (2) falling within a category which is specified, or described, in the notice: Competition Act 1998 s 26(4).

14 Competition Act 1998 s 26(1), (2) (s 26(1) amended by the Enterprise Act 2002 s 278(1), Sch 25 para 38(1), (20)(a); and SI 2004/1261). The power to require a person to produce a document includes power: (1) if the document is produced, to take copies of it or extracts from it or to require him, or any person who is a present or past officer of his, or is or was at any time employed by him, to provide an explanation of the document; (2) if the document is not produced, to require him to state, to the best of his knowledge and belief, where it is: Competition Act 1998 s 26(6). See also the Competition Act 1998 (Office of Fair Trading's Rules) Order 2004, SI 2004/2751, art 2, Schedule r 3 (legal advice during investigations and inspections).
15 Competition Act 1998 s 26(3). The offences are those created by ss 42–44 (see PARAS 140–141).
16 Competition Act 1998 s 26(5) (amended by the Enterprise Act 2002 s 278(1), Sch 25 para 38(1), (20)(b)).

130.   Power to enter business premises without a warrant.   Any officer of the Office of Fair Trading (the 'OFT')[1] who is authorised in writing by the OFT to do so (an 'investigating officer') may enter any business premises[2] in connection with an investigation[3]. No investigating officer is to enter any premises in the exercise of his powers under these provisions unless he has given to the occupier of the premises a written notice[4] which:

(1)   gives at least two working days' notice of the intended entry[5];
(2)   indicates the subject matter and purpose of the investigation[6]; and
(3)   indicates the nature of certain offences created by failure to comply[7].

An investigating officer entering any premises under these provisions may:

(a)   take with him such equipment as appears to him to be necessary[8];
(b)   require any person on the premises (i) to produce any document which he considers relates to any matter relevant to the investigation; and (ii) if the document is produced, to provide an explanation of it[9];
(c)   require any person to state, to the best of his knowledge and belief, where any such document is to be found[10];
(d)   take copies of, or extracts from, any document which is produced[11];
(e)   require any information which is stored in any electronic form and is accessible from the premises and which the investigating officer considers relates to any matter relevant to the investigation, to be produced in a form (i) in which it can be taken away; and (ii) in which it is visible and legible or from which it can readily be produced in a visible and legible form[12];
(f)   take any steps which appear to be necessary for the purpose of preserving or preventing interference with any document which he considers relates to any matter relevant to the investigation[13].

A reasonable period may be allowed for an occupier's legal adviser to arrive at the premises before an investigation continues[14].

1 As to the OFT see PARAS 6–8.
2 'Business premises' means premises (or any part of premises) not used as a dwelling: Competition Act 1998 s 27(6) (added by SI 2004/1261). 'Premises' includes any land or means of transport: Competition Act 1998 s 59(1) (definition substituted by SI 2004/1261). As to the meaning of 'document' see PARA 9 note 3.
3 Competition Act 1998 s 27(1) (amended by the Enterprise Act 2002 s 278(1), Sch 25 para 38(1), (21)(a); and SI 2004/1261). In certain circumstances the officer may be required to produce evidence of his authorisation and certain other information: see note 4. As to corresponding powers conferred by European Community law see PARA 82.
4 Competition Act 1998 s 27(2). This requirement does not apply: (1) if the OFT has a reasonable suspicion that the premises are, or have been, occupied by (a) a party to an agreement which it is investigating under s 25 (see PARA 129); or (b) an undertaking the conduct of which it is investigating under s 25 (see PARA 129); or (2) if the investigating officer has taken all such steps as are reasonably practicable to give notice but has not been able to do so: s 27(3) (amended by the Enterprise Act 2002 Sch 25 para 38(1), (21)(a), (b); and SI 2004/1261). In a case falling

within the Competition Act 1998 s 27(3), the power of entry conferred by s 27(1) is to be exercised by the investigating officer on production of: (i) evidence of his authorisation; and (ii) a document containing the information referred to in s 27(2)(b) and (c) (see heads (2) and (3) in the text): s 27(4).

5   Competition Act 1998 s 27(2)(a). 'Working day' means a day which is not Saturday, Sunday, Christmas Day, Good Friday or a day which is a bank holiday under the Banking and Financial Dealings Act 1971 in any part of the United Kingdom: Competition Act 1998 s 59(1) (definition added by SI 2004/1261).
6   Competition Act 1998 s 27(2)(b).
7   Competition Act 1998 s 27(2)(c). The offences are those created by ss 42–44 (see PARAS 140–141).
8   Competition Act 1998 s 27(5)(a).
9   Competition Act 1998 s 27(5)(b).
10 Competition Act 1998 s 27(5)(c).
11 Competition Act 1998 s 27(5)(d).
12 Competition Act 1998 s 27(5)(e) (amended by the Criminal Justice and Police Act 2001 s 70, Sch 2 para 21(a), (b)). As to the meaning of 'information' see PARA 9 note 3.
13 Competition Act 1998 s 27(5)(f) (added by SI 2004/1261).
14 See the Competition Act 1998 (Office of Fair Trading's Rules) Order 2004, SI 2004/2751, art 2, Schedule r 3.

131.   Power to enter business or domestic premises under a warrant.   On an application made by the Office of Fair Trading (the 'OFT')[1] to the court[2] in accordance with rules of court, a judge may issue a warrant[3] if he is satisfied that:

(1)   there are reasonable grounds for suspecting that there are on any business premises[4] or domestic premises[5] documents[6] the production of which has been required in connection with an investigation[7], and which have not been produced as required[8];

(2)   there are reasonable grounds for suspecting that there are on any business premises or domestic premises documents which the OFT has power to require to be produced[9], and that if the documents were required to be produced, they would not be produced but would be concealed, removed, tampered with or destroyed[10]; or

(3)   in relation to business premises only, an investigating officer[11] has attempted to enter premises in the exercise of his power to enter without a warrant[12] but has been unable to do so and that there are reasonable grounds for suspecting that there are on the premises documents the production of which could have been required[13].

A warrant under these provisions must authorise a named officer of the OFT, and any other of the OFT's officers whom the OFT has authorised in writing to accompany the named officer[14]:

(a)   to enter the premises specified in the warrant, using such force as is reasonably necessary for the purpose[15];

(b)   to search the premises and take copies of, or extracts from, any document appearing to be of a kind in respect of which the application was granted (the 'relevant kind')[16];

(c)   to take possession of any documents appearing to be of the relevant kind if (i) such action appears to be necessary for preserving the documents or preventing interference with them; or (ii) it is not reasonably practicable to take copies of the documents on the premises[17];

(d)   to take any other steps which appear to be necessary for preserving the documents or preventing interference with them[18];

(e)   to require any person to provide an explanation of any document appearing to be of the relevant kind or to state, to the best of his knowledge and belief, where it may be found[19];

(f)   to require any information which is stored in any electronic form and is accessible from the premises and which the named officer considers relates to any matter relevant to the investigation, to be produced in a form (i) in which it can be taken away; and (ii) in which it is visible and legible or from which it can readily be produced in a visible and legible form[20].

The warrant must indicate the subject matter and purpose of the investigation, and the nature of certain offences created by failure to comply[21].

Any person entering premises by virtue of a warrant may take with him such equipment as appears to him to be necessary[22]. On leaving any premises which he has entered by virtue of a warrant, the named officer must, if the premises are unoccupied or the occupier is temporarily absent, leave them as effectively secured as he found them[23]. A warrant continues in force until the end of the period of one month beginning with the day on which it is issued[24].

If there is no one at the premises when the named officer proposes to execute the warrant he must, before executing it, take such steps as are reasonable in all the circumstances to inform the occupier[25] of the intended entry, and if the occupier is informed, afford him or his legal or other representative a reasonable opportunity to be present when the warrant is executed[26].

1   As to the OFT see PARAS 6–8.
2   'Court' means, in England and Wales, the High Court: Competition Act 1998 s 59(1).
3   Competition Act 1998 s 28(1) (amended by the Enterprise Act 2002 s 278(1), Sch 25 para 38(1), (22)(a)); Competition Act 1998 s 28A(1) (added by SI 2004/1261). The powers conferred by the Competition Act 1998 ss 28, 28A are to be exercised on production of a warrant issued thereunder: s 29(2) (amended by SI 2004/1261).
4   As to the meaning of 'business premises' see PARA 130 note 2; definition applied by the Competition Act 1998 s 28(8) (added by SI 2004/1261).
5   'Domestic premises' means premises (or any part of premises) that are used as a dwelling and are: (1) premises also used in connection with the affairs of an undertaking or association of undertakings; or (2) premises where documents relating to the affairs of an undertaking or association of undertakings are kept: Competition Act 1998 s 28A(9) (added by SI 2004/1261).
6   As to the meaning of 'document' see PARA 9 note 3.
7   Ie required under the Competition Act 1998 s 26 or s 27 (see PARAS 129–130).
8   Competition Act 1998 ss 28(1)(a), 28A(1)(a) (s 28(1)(a) amended, and s 28A(1)(a) added, by SI 2004/1261).
9   Ie under the Competition Act 1998 s 26 (see PARA 129).
10   Competition Act 1998 s 28(1)(b) (s 28(1)(b) amended by the Enterprise Act 2002 Sch 25 para 38(1), (22)(a); and SI 2004/1261); Competition Act 1998 s 28A(1)(b) (added by SI 2004/1261). If, in the case of a warrant under head (2) in the text, the judge is satisfied that it is reasonable to suspect that there are also on the premises other documents relating to the investigation concerned, the warrant must also authorise action mentioned in the Competition Act 1998 ss 28(2), 28A(2) to be taken in relation to any such document: ss 28(3), 28A(3) (added by SI 2004/1261).
11   As to the meaning of 'investigating officer' see PARA 130.
12   Ie his power under the Competition Act 1998 s 27 (see PARA 130).
13   Competition Act 1998 s 28(1)(c).
14   Competition Act 1998 s 28(2) (amended by the Enterprise Act 2002 Sch 25 para 38(1), (22)(b)); Competition Act 1998 s 28A(2) (added by SI 2004/1261). A warrant may authorise persons specified in the warrant to accompany the named officer who is executing it: Competition Act 1998 s 28(3A) (added by the Enterprise Act 2002 s 203(1), (2)); Competition Act 1998 s 28A(4) (added by SI 2004/1261).
15   Competition Act 1998 ss 28(2)(a), 28A(2)(a) (added by SI 2004/1261). See the Competition Act 1998 (Office of Fair Trading's Rules) Order 2004, SI 2004/2751, art 2, Schedule r 3. The rights to enter and search premises under the Competition Act 1998 do not infringe the rights to a fair trial and respect for private life under the Convention for the Protection of Human Rights

and Fundamental Freedoms (Rome, 4 November 1950; TS 71 (1953) Cmd 8969) arts 6, 8: *Office of Fair Trading v X* [2003] EWHC 1042 (Comm), [2003] 2 All ER (Comm) 183, [2004] ICR 105.

16 Competition Act 1998 ss 28(2)(b), 28A(2)(b) (added by SI 2004/1261).

17 Competition Act 1998 ss 28(2)(c), 28A(2)(c) (added by SI 2004/1261). Any document of which possession is taken under head (c) in the text may be retained for a period of three months: Competition Act 1998 ss 28(7), 28A(8) (added by SI 2004/1261).

18 Competition Act 1998 ss 28(2)(d), 28A(2)(d) (added by SI 2004/1261).

19 Competition Act 1998 ss 28(2)(e), 28A(2)(e) (added by SI 2004/1261).

20 Competition Act 1998 s 28(2)(f) (amended by the Criminal Justice and Police Act 2001 s 70, Sch 2 Pt 2 para 21); Competition Act 1998 s 28A(2)(f) (added by SI 2004/1261). As to the meaning of 'information' see PARA 9 note 3.

21 See the Competition Act 1998 s 29(1) (amended by SI 2004/1261), which refers to offences created by the Competition Act 1998 ss 42–44 (see PARAS 140–141).

22 Competition Act 1998 ss 28(4), 28A(5) (added by SI 2004/1261).

23 Competition Act 1998 ss 28(5), 28A(6) (added by SI 2004/1261).

24 Competition Act 1998 ss 28(6), 28A(7) (added by SI 2004/1261).

25 'Occupier', in relation to any premises, means a person whom the named officer reasonably believes is the occupier of those premises: Competition Act 1998 s 29(5).

26 Competition Act 1998 s 29(3). If the named officer is unable to inform the occupier of the intended entry he must, when executing the warrant, leave a copy of it in a prominent place on the premises: s 29(4).

132.   Privileged communications and use of statements.   A person[1] will not be required, under any provision of Part I of the Competition Act 1998[2], to produce or disclose a privileged communication[3].

A statement made by a person in response to a requirement imposed in connection with an investigation[4] may not be used in evidence against him on a prosecution for a cartel offence[5] unless, in the proceedings: (1) in giving evidence, he makes a statement inconsistent with it; and (2) evidence relating to it is adduced, or a question relating to it is asked, by him or on his behalf[6].

1 As to the meaning of 'person' see PARA 118 note 8.

2 Ie the Competition Act 1998 ss 1–60.

3 Competition Act 1998 s 30(1). 'Privileged communication' means a communication: (1) between a professional legal adviser and his client; or (2) made in connection with, or in contemplation of, legal proceedings and for the purposes of those proceedings, which in proceedings in the High Court would be protected from disclosure on grounds of legal professional privilege: s 30(2). See CIVIL PROCEDURE vol 11 (2009) PARA 558 et seq.

For decisions of the EC Commission and the European Court of Justice on the provisions of European Community law corresponding to those of the Competition Act 1998 see PARA 24 et seq, particularly PARA 93. As to the duty to interpret the provisions of the Competition Act 1998 in a manner consistent with European Community law and the decisions of the European Court of Justice see s 60; and PARA 150.

4 Ie by virtue of any of the Competition Act 1998 ss 26–28A (see PARAS 129–131).

5 Ie an offence under the Enterprise Act 2002 s 188 (see PARA 319).

6 Competition Act 1998 s 30A (added by the Enterprise Act 2002 s 198; and amended by SI 2004/1261).

133.   Decisions following an investigation.   If, as the result of an investigation[1], the Office of Fair Trading (the 'OFT')[2] proposes to make a decision: (1) that the Chapter I prohibition[3] has been infringed; (2) that the Chapter II prohibition[4] has been infringed; (3) that the prohibition against restriction or distortion of competition in the EC Treaty[5] has been infringed; or (4) that the prohibition against abuse of a dominant position[6] in the EC Treaty[7], the OFT must give written notice to the person[8] (or persons) likely to be affected by the proposed decision and give that person (or those persons) an opportunity to make representations[9].

1 See PARA 129.
2 As to the OFT see PARAS 6–8.
3 As to the Chapter I prohibition see PARA 116.
4 As to the Chapter II prohibition see PARA 125.
5 Ie the EC Treaty art 81 (see PARA 61 et seq). As to the EC Treaty (ie the Treaty establishing the European Community (Rome, 25 March 1957; TS 1 (1973); Cmnd 5179)) see PARA 24 note 1. The numbering for the EC Treaty used in this title is as revised by the Treaty of Amsterdam: see PARA 24 note 1.
6 Ie the EC Treaty art 82 (see PARA 68 et seq).
7 Competition Act 1998 s 31(1) (substituted by SI 2004/1261).
8 As to the meaning of 'person' see PARA 118 note 8.
9 Competition Act 1998 s 31(2) (substituted by SI 2004/1261).

134. Commitments. Where the Office of Fair Trading (the 'OFT')[1] has begun an investigation[2] but has not made a decision as to infringement[3], then for the purposes of addressing the competition concerns it has identified, the OFT may accept from such person[4] (or persons) concerned as it considers appropriate commitments to take such action (or refrain from taking such action) as it considers appropriate[5]. At any time when commitments are in force the OFT may accept from the person (or persons) who gave the commitments: (1) a variation of them if it is satisfied that the commitments as varied will address its current competition concerns; (2) commitments in substitution for them if it is satisfied that the new commitments will address its current competition concerns[6]. Commitments come into force when accepted, and may be released by the OFT where it is requested to do so by the person (or persons) who gave the commitments or it has reasonable grounds for believing that the relevant competition concerns no longer arise[7].

If the OFT has accepted commitments, and has not released them, the OFT must not continue the investigation, make a decision regarding infringement[8] or give a direction[9], in relation to the agreement or conduct which was the subject of the investigation[10]. This provision does not prevent the OFT from taking any action in relation to competition concerns which are not addressed by commitments accepted by it[11]. This provision also does not prevent the OFT from continuing the investigation, making a decision, or giving a direction where: (a) it has reasonable grounds for believing that there has been a material change of circumstances since the commitments were accepted; (b) it has reasonable grounds for suspecting that a person has failed to adhere to one or more of the terms of the commitments; or (c) it has reasonable grounds for suspecting that information which led it to accept the commitments was incomplete, false or misleading in a material particular[12].

Where the OFT is reviewing or has reviewed the effectiveness of commitments accepted, it must, if requested to do so by the Secretary of State[13], prepare a report of its findings[14].

The OFT must prepare and publish guidance as to the circumstances in which it may be appropriate to accept commitments[15]. The OFT may at any time alter the guidance[16] and, if the guidance is altered, the OFT must publish it as altered[17]. No guidance is to be published without the approval of the Secretary of State[18]. The OFT may, after consulting the Secretary of State, choose how it publishes its guidance[19]. If the OFT is preparing or altering guidance it must consult such persons as it considers appropriate[20]. If the proposed guidance or alteration relates to a matter in respect of which a regulator[21] exercises concurrent jurisdiction, those consulted must include that regulator[22]. When exercising its discretion to accept commitments, the OFT must have regard to the guidance for the time being in force[23].

If a person from whom the OFT has accepted commitments fails without reasonable excuse to adhere to the commitments (and has not been released from them), the OFT may apply to the court[24] for an order: (i) requiring the defaulter to make good his default within a time specified in the order; or (ii) if the commitments relate to anything to be done in the management or administration of an undertaking, requiring the undertaking or any of its officers to do it[25].

1 As to the OFT see PARAS 6–8.
2 Ie under the Competition Act 1998 s 25 (see PARA 129).
3 Ie a decision under s 31(2) (see PARA 133).
4 As to the meaning of 'person' see PARA 118 note 8.
5 Competition Act 1998 s 31A(1), (2) (ss 31A–31E added by SI 2004/1261). As to the procedural requirements for the acceptance, variation and release of commitments see the Competition Act 1998 s 31A(5), Sch 6A (added by SI 2004/1261).
6 Competition Act 1998 s 31A(3) (as added: see note 5).
7 Competition Act 1998 s 31A(4) (as added: see note 5).
8 Ie under the Competition Act 1998 s 31(2) (see PARA 133).
9 Ie under the Competition Act 1998 s 35 (see PARA 136).
10 Competition Act 1998 s 31B(1), (2) (as added: see note 5), which is expressed to be subject to s 31B(3), (4) (see the text and notes 11–12).
11 Competition Act 1998 s 31B(3) (as added: see note 5).
12 Competition Act 1998 s 31B(4) (as added: see note 5). If, pursuant to s 31B(4), the OFT makes a decision or gives a direction the commitments are to be treated as released from the date of that decision or direction: s 31B(5) (as added: see note 5).
13 As to the Secretary of State see PARA 5.
14 Competition Act 1998 s 31C(1) (as added: see note 5). The OFT must give any report prepared by it to the Secretary of State and publish the report: s 31C(2) (as added: see note 5).
15 Competition Act 1998 s 31D(1) (as added: see note 5). See OFT Guideline 407 *Enforcement* (December 2004).
16 Competition Act 1998 s 31D(2) (as added: see note 5).
17 Competition Act 1998 s 31D(3) (as added: see note 5).
18 Competition Act 1998 s 31D(4) (as added: see note 5).
19 Competition Act 1998 s 31D(5) (as added: see note 5).
20 Competition Act 1998 s 31D(6) (as added: see note 5).
21 As to the meaning of 'regulator' see PARA 147.
22 Competition Act 1998 s 31D(7) (as added: see note 5).
23 Competition Act 1998 s 31D(8) (as added: see note 5).
24 As to the meaning of 'court' see PARA 131 note 2.
25 Competition Act 1998 s 31E(1) (as added: see note 5). An order of the court may provide for all the costs of, or incidental to, the application for the order to be borne by: (1) the person in default; or (2) any officer of an undertaking who is responsible for the default: s 31E(2) (as added: see note 5).

(5) ENFORCEMENT

135. Directions. If the Office of Fair Trading (the 'OFT')[1] has made a decision that an agreement infringes the Chapter I prohibition[2] or that it infringes the prohibition against restriction or distortion of competition in the EC Treaty[3], it may give to such person[4] or persons as it considers appropriate such directions as it considers appropriate to bring the infringement to an end[5]. A direction under this provision may, in particular, include provision requiring the parties to the agreement to modify the agreement, or requiring them to terminate the agreement[6]. A direction under this provision must be given in writing[7].

If the OFT has made a decision that conduct infringes the Chapter II prohibition[8] or infringes the prohibition against abuse of a dominant position in the EC Treaty[9], it may give to such person or persons as it considers appropriate such directions as it considers appropriate to bring the infringement to an end[10]. A direction under this provision may, in particular, include provision requiring the person concerned to modify the conduct in question, or requiring him to cease that conduct[11]. A direction under this provision must be given in writing[12].

If a person fails, without reasonable excuse, to comply with a direction under either of the provisions described above[13], the OFT may apply to the court[14] for an order[15]:

(1)   requiring the defaulter to make good his default within a time specified in the order[16]; or

(2)   if the direction related to anything to be done in the management or administration of an undertaking, requiring the undertaking or any of its officers[17] to do it[18].

Provision is made in the OFT's Rules in relation to directions[19]. The OFT has published guidance on enforcement[20].

1   As to the OFT see PARAS 6–8.
2   As to the Chapter I prohibition see PARA 116.
3   Ie the EC Treaty art 81(1) (see PARA 61 et seq). As to the EC Treaty (ie the Treaty establishing the European Community (Rome, 25 March 1957; TS 1 (1973); Cmnd 5179)) see PARA 24 note 1. The numbering for the EC Treaty used in this title is as revised by the Treaty of Amsterdam: see PARA 24 note 1.
4   As to the meaning of 'person' see PARA 118 note 8.
5   Competition Act 1998 s 32(1) (amended by the Enterprise Act 2002 s 278(1), Sch 25 para 38(1), (24)(a); and SI 2004/1261).
     For decisions of the EC Commission and the European Court of Justice on the provisions of European Community law corresponding to those of the Competition Act 1998 see PARA 24 et seq. As to the duty to interpret the provisions of the Competition Act 1998 in a manner consistent with European Community law and the decisions of the European Court of Justice see s 60; and PARA 150.
6   Competition Act 1998 s 32(3).
7   Competition Act 1998 s 32(4).
8   As to the Chapter II prohibition see PARA 125.
9   Ie the EC Treaty art 82 (see PARA 68 et seq).
10 Competition Act 1998 s 33(1) (amended by the Enterprise Act 2002 Sch 25 para 38(1), (25)(a); and SI 2004/1261).
11 Competition Act 1998 s 33(3).
12 Competition Act 1998 s 33(4).
13 Ie a direction given under the Competition Act 1998 s 32 or s 33 (see the text and notes 1–12).
14 As to the meaning of 'court' see PARA 131 note 2.
15 Competition Act 1998 s 34(1) (amended by the Enterprise Act 2002 Sch 25 para 38(1), (26)).
16 Competition Act 1998 s 34(1)(a).
17 'Officer', in relation to a body corporate, includes a director, manager or secretary: Competition Act 1998 s 59(1).
18 Competition Act 1998 s 34(1)(b). An order of the court under s 34(1) may provide for all of the costs of, or incidental to, the application for the order to be borne by the person in default or any officer of an undertaking who is responsible for the default: s 34(2).
19 See the Competition Act 1998 (Office of Fair Trading's Rules) Order 2004, SI 2004/2751, Schedule r 8. As to such rules generally see PARA 144.
20 See OFT Guideline 407 *Enforcement* (December 2004).

136.   Interim measures. If the Office of Fair Trading[1] has begun an investigation[2] which it has power to conduct and has not completed it[3], it may, if it considers that it is necessary for it to act as a matter of urgency for the purpose: (1) of preventing serious, irreparable damage to a particular person or category of person; or (2) of protecting the public interest, give such directions as it considers appropriate for that purpose[4].

Before giving such a direction, the OFT must give written notice to the person (or persons) to whom it proposes to give the direction, and give that person (or each of them) an opportunity to make representations[5].

A direction given may, if the circumstances permit, be replaced either by a direction in relation to agreements or conduct[6], or by commitments accepted by the OFT[7].

Further provision is made in relation to interim measures by the OFT's Rules[8].

1 As to the OFT see PARAS 6–8.

2 Ie under the Competition Act 1998 s 25 (see PARA 129).

3 Competition Act 1998 s 35(1) (substituted by SI 2004/1261). In the case of an investigation conducted by virtue of the Competition Act 1998 s 25(2) or s 25(6) (see PARA 129), s 35 does not apply if a person has produced evidence to the OFT in connection with the investigation that satisfies it on the balance of probabilities that, in the event of it reaching the basic infringement conclusion, it would also reach the conclusion that the suspected agreement is exempt from the Chapter I prohibition as a result of s 9(1) (see PARA 122): s 35(8) (added by SI 2004/1261). For this purpose, the 'basic infringement conclusion' is the conclusion that there is an agreement which: (1) may affect trade within the United Kingdom; and (2) has as its object or effect the prevention, restriction or distortion of competition within the United Kingdom: Competition Act 1998 s 35(8) (as so added). As to the Chapter I prohibition see PARA 116. As to the meaning of 'person' see PARA 118 note 8. As to the meaning of 'United Kingdom' see PARA 401 note 1.
  In the case of an investigation conducted by virtue of s 25(3) or s 25(7) (see PARA 129), s 35 does not apply if a person has produced evidence to the OFT in connection with the investigation that satisfies it on the balance of probabilities that, in the event of it reaching the basic infringement conclusion, it would also reach the conclusion that the suspected agreement is an agreement to which the prohibition in the EC Treaty art 81(1) (see PARA 61 et seq) is inapplicable because the agreement satisfies the conditions in art 81(3): Competition Act 1998 s 35(9) (added by SI 2004/1261). For this purpose, the 'basic infringement conclusion' is the conclusion that there is an agreement which: (a) may affect trade between member states; and (b) has as its object or effect the prevention, restriction or distortion of competition within the Community: Competition Act 1998 s 35(9) (as so added). As to the EC Treaty (ie the Treaty establishing the European Community (Rome, 25 March 1957; TS 1 (1973); Cmnd 5179)) see PARA 24 note 1. The numbering for the EC Treaty used in this title is as revised by the Treaty of Amsterdam: see PARA 24 note 1.

4 Competition Act 1998 s 35(2) (amended by the Enterprise Act 2002 s 278(1), Sch 25 para 38(1), (27); and SI 2004/1261). In the cases mentioned in the Competition Act 1998 s 25(2), (3), (6) and (7) (see PARA 129), s 32(3) and s 34 (see PARA 135) also apply to directions given under s 35: s 35(6) (amended by SI 2004/1261). In the cases mentioned in the Competition Act 1998 s 25(4) and (5) (see PARA 129), s 33(3) and s 34 (see PARA 135) also apply to directions given under s 35: s 35(7) (amended by SI 2004/1261).
  For decisions of the EC Commission and the European Court of Justice on the provisions of European Community law corresponding to those of the Competition Act 1998 see PARA 24 et seq. As to the duty to interpret the provisions of the Competition Act 1998 in a manner consistent with European Community law and the decisions of the European Court of Justice see s 60; and PARA 150.

5 Competition Act 1998 s 35(3) (amended by the Enterprise Act 2002 Sch 25 para 38(1), (27)). Such a notice must indicate the nature of the direction which the OFT is proposing to give and its reasons for wishing to give it: Competition Act 1998 s 35(4) (amended by the Enterprise Act 2002 Sch 25 para 38(1), (27)).

6 Ie under the Competition Act 1998 s 32 or (as appropriate) s 33 (see PARA 135).

7 Competition Act 1998 s 35(5) (substituted by SI 2004/1261). Otherwise, the direction has effect while the Competition Act 1998 s 35 applies: s 35(5) (as so substituted). Commitments are accepted under s 31A (see PARA 134).

8 See the Competition Act 1998 (Office of Fair Trading's Rules) Order 2004, SI 2004/2751, Schedule r 9. As to such rules generally see PARA 144.

137. Penalties. On making a decision that an agreement has infringed the Chapter I prohibition[1] or the prohibition against restriction or distortion of competition in the EC Treaty[2], the Office of Fair Trading (the 'OFT')[3] may require an undertaking which is a party to the agreement to pay the OFT a penalty in respect of the infringement[4]. On making a decision that conduct has infringed the Chapter II prohibition[5] or the prohibition against abuse of a dominant position in the EC Treaty[6], the OFT may require the undertaking concerned to pay the OFT a penalty in respect of the infringement[7]. The OFT may impose a penalty on an undertaking only if the OFT is satisfied that the infringement has been committed intentionally or negligently by the undertaking[8].

Notice of any such penalty must be in writing, and must specify the date before which the penalty is required to be paid[9]. No such penalty fixed by the OFT may exceed 10 per cent of the turnover of the undertaking (determined in accordance with such provisions as may be specified in an order made by the Secretary of State)[10]. Any sums received by the OFT are to be paid into the Consolidated Fund[11].

If the specified date[12] in a penalty notice has passed and: (1) the period during which an appeal against the imposition, or amount, of the penalty may be made has expired without an appeal having been made; or (2) such an appeal has been made and determined, the OFT may recover from the undertaking, as a civil debt due to the OFT, any amount payable under the penalty notice which remains outstanding[13].

The OFT must prepare and publish guidance as to the appropriate amount of any penalty under Part I of the Competition Act 1998[14]. When setting the amount of such a penalty, the OFT must have regard to the guidance for the time being in force[15]. The OFT may at any time alter the guidance[16], and if the guidance is altered, the OFT must publish it as altered[17]. No guidance may be so published without the approval of the Secretary of State[18]. If the OFT is preparing or altering guidance it must consult such persons as it considers appropriate[19]. If the proposed guidance or alteration relates to a matter in respect of which a regulator[20] exercises concurrent jurisdiction, those consulted must include that regulator[21].

If a penalty or a fine has been imposed by the European Commission, or by a court or other body in another member state, in respect of an agreement or conduct, the OFT, an appeal tribunal[22] or the appropriate court[23] must take that penalty or fine into account when setting the amount of a penalty under Part I of the Competition Act 1998 in relation to that agreement or conduct[24].

1 As to the Chapter I prohibition see PARA 116.
2 Ie the EC Treaty art 81(1) (see PARA 61 et seq). As to the EC Treaty (ie the Treaty establishing the European Community (Rome, 25 March 1957; TS 1 (1973); Cmnd 5179)) see PARA 24 note 1. The numbering for the EC Treaty used in this title is as revised by the Treaty of Amsterdam: see PARA 24 note 1.
3 As to the OFT see PARAS 6–8.

4 Competition Act 1998 s 36(1) (amended by the Enterprise Act 2002 s 278(1), Sch 25 para 38(1), (28)(a); and SI 2004/1261). The Competition Act 1998 s 36(1) is subject to s 39 (see PARA 138) and does not apply in relation to a decision that an agreement has infringed the Chapter I prohibition if the OFT is satisfied that the undertaking acted on the reasonable assumption that s 39 gave it immunity in respect of the agreement: s 36(4) (amended by the Enterprise Act 2002 Sch 25 para 38(1), (28)(a); and SI 2004/1261).
   For decisions of the EC Commission and the European Court of Justice on the provisions of European Community law corresponding to those of the Competition Act 1998 see PARA 24 et seq, particularly PARA 107 et seq. As to the duty to interpret the provisions of the Competition

Act 1998 in a manner consistent with European Community law and the decisions of the European Court of Justice see s 60; and PARA 150.

5   As to the Chapter II prohibition see PARA 125.

6   Ie the EC Treaty art 82 (see PARA 68 et seq).

7   Competition Act 1998 s 36(2) (amended by the Enterprise Act 2002 Sch 25 para 38(1), (28)(a), (b); and SI 2004/1261). The Competition Act 1998 s 36(2) is subject to s 40 (see PARA 139) and does not apply in relation to a decision that conduct has infringed the Chapter II prohibition if the OFT is satisfied that the undertaking acted on the reasonable assumption that s 40 gave it immunity in respect of the conduct: s 36(5) (amended by the Enterprise Act 2002 Sch 25 para 38(1), (28)(a); and SI 2004/1261).

8   Competition Act 1998 s 36(3) (amended by the Enterprise Act 2002 Sch 25 para 38(1), (28)(a), (c)).

9   Competition Act 1998 s 36(6). The date specified must not be earlier than the end of the period within which an appeal against the notice may be brought under s 46 (see PARA 166): s 36(7).

10 Competition Act 1998 s 36(8) (amended by the Enterprise Act 2002 Sch 25 para 38(1), (28)(a)). See the Competition Act 1998 (Determination of Turnover for Penalties) Order 2000, SI 2000/309 (amended by SI 2004/1259). As to the Secretary of State see PARA 5.

11 Competition Act 1998 s 36(9) (amended by the Enterprise Act 2002 Sch 25 para 38(1), (28)(a)). As to the Consolidated Fund see CONSTITUTIONAL LAW AND HUMAN RIGHTS vol 8(2) (Reissue) PARA 711.

12 For these purposes 'specified date' means the date specified in the penalty notice: Competition Act 1998 s 37(2). 'Penalty notice' means a notice given under s 36 (see the text and notes 1–11): s 37(2).

13 Competition Act 1998 s 37(1) (amended by the Enterprise Act 2002 Sch 25 para 38(1), (29)).

14 Competition Act 1998 s 38(1) (amended by the Enterprise Act 2002 Sch 25 para 38(1), (30)). See OFT Guideline 423 OFT's *Guidance as to the Appropriate Amount of a Penalty* (December 2004). Part I of the Competition Act 1998 consists of ss 1–60. The guidance must include provision about the circumstances in which, in determining a penalty under Pt I, the OFT may take into account effects in another member state of the agreement or conduct concerned: s 38(1A) (added by SI 2004/1261). The OFT may, after consulting the Secretary of State, choose how it publishes its guidance: Competition Act 1998 s 38(5) (amended by the Enterprise Act 2002 Sch 25 para 38(1), (30)).

15 Competition Act 1998 s 38(8) (amended by the Enterprise Act 2002 Sch 25 para 38(1), (30)).

16 Competition Act 1998 s 38(2) (amended by the Enterprise Act 2002 Sch 25 para 38(1), (30)).

17 Competition Act 1998 s 38(3) (amended by the Enterprise Act 2002 Sch 25 para 38(1), (30)).

18 Competition Act 1998 s 38(4).

19 Competition Act 1998 s 38(6) (amended by the Enterprise Act 2002 Sch 25 para 38(1), (30)).

20 As to the meaning of 'regulator' see PARA 147.

21 Competition Act 1998 s 38(7).

22 See PARA 166.

23 For these purposes, 'appropriate court' means, in relation to England and Wales, the Court of Appeal or the House of Lords: Competition Act 1998 s 38(10). As from 1 October 2009, the reference to the House of Lords is replaced with a reference to the Supreme Court: see s 38(10) (prospectively amended by the Constitutional Reform Act 2005 s 40(4), Sch 9 para 65(1), (2)).

24 Competition Act 1998 s 38(9).

138.   Immunity from penalties for small agreements.   A party to a small agreement is immune from being required to pay a penalty[1] for infringing the Chapter I prohibition[2]. However, the Office of Fair Trading (the 'OFT')[3] may make a decision withdrawing that immunity[4] if, having investigated the agreement, and as a result of its investigation, it considers that the agreement is likely to infringe the Chapter I prohibition[5]. The OFT must give each of the parties in respect of which immunity is withdrawn written notice of its decision to withdraw the immunity[6].

For these purposes, an agreement is a small agreement if it falls within a category prescribed for the purpose, but is not a price fixing agreement[7]. The criteria by reference to which a category of agreement is prescribed may, in particular, include: (1) the combined turnover of the parties to the agreement (determined in accordance with prescribed provisions); and (2) the share of the market affected by the agreement (determined in that way)[8].

1 Ie under the Competition Act 1998 s 36(1) (see PARA 137), so far as that provision relates to decision about infringement of the Chapter I prohibition.
2 Competition Act 1998 s 39(3) (amended by the Enterprise Act 2002 s 278(1), Sch 25 para 38(1), (31); and SI 2004/1261). As to the Chapter I prohibition see PARA 116.
3 As to the OFT see PARAS 6–8.
4 Competition Act 1998 s 39(3) (as amended: see note 2).
5 Competition Act 1998 s 39(4) (amended by the Enterprise Act 2002 Sch 25 para 38(1), (31)). A decision under the Competition Act 1998 s 39(4) takes effect on such date (the 'withdrawal date') as may be specified in the decision: s 39(6). The withdrawal date must be a date after the date on which the decision is made: s 39(7). In determining the withdrawal date, the OFT must have regard to the amount of time which the parties are likely to require in order to secure that there is no further infringement of the Chapter I prohibition with respect to the agreement: s 39(8) (amended by the Enterprise Act 2002 Sch 25 para 38(1), (31)).
   As to the *de minimis* rule applied by the European Commission and the European Court of Justice in relation to agreements of minor importance see PARA 64. As to the duty to interpret the provisions of the Competition Act 1998 in a manner consistent with European Community law and the decisions of the European Court of Justice see the Competition Act 1998 s 60; and PARA 150.
6 Competition Act 1998 s 39(5) (amended by the Enterprise Act 2002 Sch 25 para 38(1), (31)).
7 Competition Act 1998 s 39(1). 'Price fixing agreement' means an agreement which has as its object or effect, or one of its objects or effects, restricting the freedom of a party to the agreement to determine the price to be charged (otherwise than as between that party and another party to the agreement) for the product, service or other matter to which the agreement relates: s 39(9).
8 Competition Act 1998 s 39(2). See the Competition Act 1998 (Small Agreements and Conduct of Minor Significance) Regulations 2000, SI 2000/262 (amended by SI 2000/2952; SI 2004/3379; SI 2006/3221; SI 2007/3253). As to the power to make subordinate legislation under the Competition Act 1998 see PARA 163.

139.   Immunity from penalties for conduct of minor significance.   A person[1] is immune from being required to pay a penalty[2] for infringing the Chapter II prohibition[3] if his conduct is conduct of minor significance[4]. However, the Office of Fair Trading (the 'OFT')[5] may make a decision withdrawing that immunity if, having investigated conduct of minor significance, and as a result of its investigation, it considers that the conduct is likely to infringe the Chapter II prohibition[6]. The OFT must give the person, or persons, whose immunity has been withdrawn written notice of its decision to withdraw the immunity[7].

For these purposes, conduct is conduct of minor significance if it falls within a category prescribed for the purposes of these provisions[8]. The criteria by reference to which a category is prescribed may, in particular, include: (1) the turnover of the person whose conduct it is (determined in accordance with prescribed provisions); (2) the share of the market affected by the conduct (determined in that way)[9].

1 As to the meaning of 'person' see PARA 118 note 8.
2 Ie under the Competition Act 1998 s 36(2) (see PARA 137) so far as that provision relates to decisions about infringement of the Chapter II prohibition.
3 As to the Chapter II prohibition see PARA 125.
4 Competition Act 1998 s 40(3) (amended by the Enterprise Act 2002 s 278(1), Sch 25 para 38(1), (32)(a); and SI 2004/1261). See also PARA 138 note 5.
5 As to the OFT see PARAS 6–8.
6 Competition Act 1998 s 40(4) (amended by the Enterprise Act 2002 Sch 25 para 38(1), (32)(b)). A decision under the Competition Act 1998 s 40(4) takes effect on such date (the 'withdrawal date') as may be specified in the decision: s 40(6). The withdrawal date must be a date after the date on which the decision is made: s 40(7). In determining the withdrawal date, the OFT must have regard to the amount of time which the person or persons affected are likely to require in

order to secure that there is no further infringement of the Chapter II prohibition: s 40(8) (amended by the Enterprise Act 2002 Sch 25 para 38(1), (32)(a)).

7   Competition Act 1998 s 40(5) (amended by the Enterprise Act 2002 Sch 25 para 38(1), (32)(a)).
8   Competition Act 1998 s 40(1).
9   Competition Act 1998 s 40(2). See the Competition Act 1998 (Small Agreements and Conduct of Minor Significance) Regulations 2000, SI 2000/262 (amended by SI 2000/2952; SI 2004/3379; SI 2006/3221; SI 2007/3253). As to the power to make subordinate legislation under the Competition Act 1998 see PARA 163.

(6) OFFENCES

140. Offences relating to investigations. A person[1] is guilty of an offence if he fails to comply with a requirement imposed on him under provisions relating to the power of the Office of Fair Trading (the 'OFT')[2] to conduct investigations[3]. If a person is charged with such an offence in respect of a requirement to produce a document[4], it is a defence for him to prove that the document was not in his possession or under his control, and that it was not reasonably practicable for him to comply with the requirement[5]. If a person is charged with an offence in respect of a requirement: (1) to provide information[6]; (2) to provide an explanation of a document; or (3) to state where a document is to be found, it is a defence for him to prove that he had a reasonable excuse for failing to comply with the requirement[7].

A person is guilty of an offence if he intentionally obstructs an officer acting in the exercise of his power to enter business premises without a warrant[8].

A person guilty of one of the offences described above is liable on summary conviction to a fine not exceeding the statutory maximum[9], or on conviction on indictment to a fine[10].

A person who intentionally obstructs an officer in the exercise of his powers under a warrant[11] is guilty of an offence and liable on summary conviction to a fine not exceeding the statutory maximum, or on conviction on indictment to imprisonment for a term not exceeding two years or to a fine or to both[12].

A person is guilty of an offence if, having been required to produce a document[13]: (a) he intentionally or recklessly destroys or otherwise disposes of it, falsifies it or conceals it; or (b) he causes or permits its destruction, disposal, falsification or concealment[14]. A person guilty of this offence is liable on summary conviction to a fine not exceeding the statutory maximum, or on conviction on indictment to imprisonment for a term not exceeding two years or to a fine or to both[15].

1   As to the meaning of 'person' see PARA 118 note 8. As to the commission of offences by bodies corporate see the Competition Act 1998 s 72; and PARA 164.
2   As to the OFT see PARAS 6–8.
3   Competition Act 1998 s 42(1) (amended by SI 2004/1261). The provisions referred to are the Competition Act 1998 s 26, 27, 28 or 28A (see PARAS 129–131). Failure to comply with a requirement imposed under s 26 or s 27 is not an offence if the person imposing the requirement has failed to act in accordance with that provision: s 42(4).
4   As to the meaning of 'document' see PARA 9 note 3.
5   Competition Act 1998 s 42(2).
6   As to the meaning of 'information' see PARA 9 note 3.
7   Competition Act 1998 s 42(3).
8   Competition Act 1998 s 42(5). The power referred to is conferred by s 27 (see PARA 130).
9   The 'statutory maximum', with reference to a fine or penalty on summary conviction for an offence, is the prescribed sum within the meaning of the Magistrates' Courts Act 1980 s 32: see the Interpretation Act 1978 s 5, Sch 1 (definition added by the Criminal Justice Act 1988 s 170(1), Sch 15 para 58); and CRIMINAL LAW, EVIDENCE AND PROCEDURE vol 11(4) (2006 Reissue) PARA 1674; MAGISTRATES vol 29(2) (Reissue) PARA 804. The 'prescribed sum' means

£5,000 or such sum as is for the time being substituted in this definition by order under the Magistrates' Courts Act 1980 s 143(1): see s 32(9) (amended by the Criminal Justice Act 1991 s 17(2)); and CRIMINAL LAW, EVIDENCE AND PROCEDURE vol 11(4) (2006 Reissue) PARA 1675; MAGISTRATES vol 29(2) (Reissue) PARA 804.

10 Competition Act 1998 s 42(6).
11 Ie a warrant issued under the Competition Act 1998 s 28 or s 28A (see PARA 131).
12 Competition Act 1998 s 42(7) (amended by SI 2004/1261).
13 Ie required under the Competition Act 1998 s 26, s 27, s 28 or s 28A (see PARAS 129–131).
14 Competition Act 1998 s 43(1) (amended by SI 2004/1261).
15 Competition Act 1998 s 43(2).

141. False or misleading information. If information is provided by a person[1] to the Office of Fair Trading (the 'OFT')[2] in connection with any function of the OFT under Part I of the Competition Act 1998[3], that person is guilty of an offence if: (1) the information is false or misleading in a material particular; and (2) he knows that it is or is reckless as to whether it is[4]. A person who (a) provides any information to another person, knowing the information to be false or misleading in a material particular; or (b) recklessly provides any information to another person which is false or misleading in a material particular, knowing that the information is to be used for the purpose of providing information to the OFT in connection with any of its functions under Part I of the Competition Act 1998, is guilty of an offence[5].

1 As to the meaning of 'person' see PARA 118 note 8. As to the commission of offences by bodies corporate see the Competition Act 1998 s 72; and PARA 164.
2 As to the OFT see PARAS 6–8.
3 Ie the Competition Act 1998 ss 1–60.
4 Competition Act 1998 s 44(1) (amended by the Enterprise Act 2002 s 278(1), Sch 25 para 38(1), (34)).
5 Competition Act 1998 s 44(2) (amended by the Enterprise Act 2002 Sch 25 para 38(1), (34)). A person guilty of one of the offences described above is liable on summary conviction to a fine not exceeding the statutory maximum, and on conviction on indictment to imprisonment for a term not exceeding two years or to a fine or to both: Competition Act 1998 s 44(3). As to the statutory maximum see PARA 140 note 9.

(7) LAND AGREEMENTS

142. Provision for the exclusion or exemption of vertical and land agreements. The Secretary of State[1] may by order provide for any provision of Part I of the Competition Act 1998[2] to apply in relation to: (1) vertical agreements[3]; or (2) land agreements[4], with such modifications as may be prescribed[5]. An order may, in particular, provide for exclusions or exemptions, or otherwise provide for prescribed provisions not to apply, in relation to: (a) vertical agreements, or land agreements, in general; or (b) vertical agreements, or land agreements, of any prescribed description[6]. An order may empower the Office of Fair Trading (the 'OFT')[7] to give directions to the effect that in prescribed circumstances an exclusion, exemption or modification is not to apply (or is to apply in a particular way) in relation to an individual agreement[8]. Pursuant to this provision the Secretary of State has excluded certain land agreements from the Chapter I prohibition[9].

1 As to the Secretary of State see PARA 5.
2 Ie the Competition Act 1998 ss 1–60.
3 'Vertical agreement' has such meaning as may be prescribed by an order: Competition Act 1998 s 50(5). At the date at which this volume states the law no such order had been made. All vertical agreements, apart from those imposing minimum or fixed resale prices, were excluded

from the Chapter I prohibition until 30 April 2005 (see the Competition Act 1998 (Land and Vertical Agreements Exclusion) Order 2000, SI 2000/310 (revoked)).
4   'Land agreement' has such meaning as may be prescribed by an order: Competition Act 1998 s 50(5). See PARA 143.
5   Competition Act 1998 s 50(1). As to the power to make subordinate legislation under the Competition Act 1998 see PARA 163.
      For decisions of the European Commission and the European Court of Justice on the provisions of European Community law corresponding to those of the Competition Act 1998 see PARA 24 et seq. As to the duty to interpret the provisions of the Competition Act 1998 in a manner consistent with European Community law and the decisions of the European Court of Justice see s 60; and PARA 150.
6   Competition Act 1998 s 50(2). Section 50(2) is not to be read as limiting the powers conferred by s 71 (see PARA 163): s 50(4).
7   As to the OFT see PARAS 6–8.
8   Competition Act 1998 s 50(3) (amended by the Enterprise Act 2002 s 278(1), Sch 25 para 38(1), (37)). The Competition Act 1998 s 50(3) is not to be read as limiting the powers conferred by s 71 (see PARA 163): s 50(4).
9   See the Competition Act 1998 (Land Agreements Exclusion and Revocation) Order 2004, SI 2004/1260; and PARA 143. As to the Chapter I prohibition see PARA 116.

143.   Exclusion of land agreements. The Chapter I prohibition[1] does not apply to an agreement to the extent that it is a land agreement[2], that is to say an agreement between undertakings which creates, alters, transfers or terminates an interest in land[3], or an agreement to enter into such an agreement, together with certain obligations and restrictions[4]. Power is given to the Office of Fair Trading (the 'OFT')[5] to withdraw the benefit of the exclusion for land agreements[6].
   The OFT has published guidance on land agreements[7].

1   As to the Chapter I prohibition see PARA 116.
2   Competition Act 1998 (Land Agreements Exclusion and Revocation) Order 2004, SI 2004/1260, art 4.
3   'Interest in land' includes any estate, interest, easement, servitude or right in or over land (including any interest or right created by a licence); and 'land' includes buildings and other structures and land covered with water: Competition Act 1998 (Land Agreements Exclusion and Revocation) Order 2004, SI 2004/1260, art 3.
4   See the Competition Act 1998 (Land Agreements Exclusion and Revocation) Order 2004, SI 2004/1260, art 3. The obligations and restrictions referred to in the text are contained in art 5.
5   As to the OFT see PARAS 6–8.
6   See the Competition Act 1998 (Land Agreements Exclusion and Revocation) Order 2004, SI 2004/1260, art 6. The exclusion does not apply to a land agreement to the extent that it takes effect between the same parties and is to the like object or effect as an agreement in relation to which the exclusion has been withdrawn pursuant to art 6: see art 7.
7   See OFT Guideline 420 *Land Agreements* (December 2004).

(8)   OFFICE OF FAIR TRADING'S RULES AND ADVICE; DEFAMATION

144.   Rules. The Office of Fair Trading (the 'OFT')[1] may make such rules about procedural and other matters in connection with the carrying into effect of the provisions of Part I of the Competition Act 1998[2] as it considers appropriate[3]. If the OFT is preparing rules it must consult such persons as it considers appropriate[4]. If the proposed rules relate to a matter in respect of which a regulator[5] exercises concurrent jurisdiction, those consulted must include that regulator[6]. No rule made by the OFT is to come into operation until it has been approved by an order made by the Secretary of State[7]. The Secretary of State may approve any rule made by the OFT: (1) in the form in which it is submitted; or (2) subject to such modifications as he considers appropriate[8]. If the Secretary of State proposes to approve a rule subject to modifications he must inform the OFT of the proposed modifications and take into account any comments made by the OFT[9]. The Secretary of State may, after consulting the OFT, by order vary or revoke any rules made under these provisions[10]. If the Secretary of State considers that rules should be made with respect to a particular matter he may direct the OFT to exercise its powers and make rules about that matter[11].

Pursuant to these powers the Secretary of State has approved the OFT's Rules[12].

1   As to the OFT see PARAS 6–8.
2   Ie the Competition Act 1998 ss 1–60.
3   Competition Act 1998 s 51(1) (amended by the Enterprise Act 2002 s 278(1), Sch 25 para 38(1), (38)(a)). In particular, provision can be made by such rules in relation to decisions (Competition Act 1998 Sch 9 para 5 (amended by the Enterprise Act 2002 Sch 25 para 38(1), (55); and SI 2004/1261)); block exemptions (Competition Act 1998 Sch 9 para 8 (substituted by SI 2004/1261)); parallel exemptions (Competition Act 1998 Sch 9 para 9 (amended by the Enterprise Act 2002 Sch 25 para 38(1), (55)); section 11 exemptions (see PARA 124) (Competition Act 1998 Sch 9 para 10); directions withdrawing exclusions (Sch 9 para 11 (amended by the Enterprise Act 2002 Sch 25 para 38(1), (55); and SI 2004/1261)); disclosure of information (Competition Act 1998 Sch 9 para 12 (amended by the Enterprise Act 2002 Sch 25 para 38(1), (55))); applications under the Competition Act 1998 s 47 (see PARA 167) (Sch 9 para 13 (amended by the Enterprise Act 2002 Sch 25 para 38(1), (55)); and enforcement (Competition Act 1998 Sch 9 para 14 (amended by the Enterprise Act 2002 Sch 25 para 38(1), (55); and SI 2004/1261)). The OFT's powers under the Competition Act 1998 s 51 may not be taken to be restricted by Sch 9: s 51(2) (amended by the Enterprise Act 2002 Sch 25 para 38(1), (38)(b)).
4   Competition Act 1998 s 51(3) (amended by the Enterprise Act 2002 Sch 25 para 38(1), (38)(c)).
5   As to the meaning of 'regulator' see PARA 147.
6   Competition Act 1998 s 51(4).
7   Competition Act 1998 s 51(5) (amended by the Enterprise Act 2002 Sch 25 para 38(1), (38)(d)). The Competition Act 1998 s 51(5)–(7) applies also to any alteration of the rules made by the OFT: s 51(8) (amended by the Enterprise Act 2002 Sch 25 para 38(1), (38)(d)). As to the Secretary of State see PARA 5. As to the power to make subordinate legislation under the Competition Act 1998 see PARA 163.
8   Competition Act 1998 s 51(6) (amended by the Enterprise Act 2002 Sch 25 para 38(1), (38)(d)). See also note 7.
9   Competition Act 1998 s 51(7) (amended by the Enterprise Act 2002 Sch 25 para 38(1), (38)(d)). See also note 7.
10 Competition Act 1998 s 51(9) (amended by the Enterprise Act 2002 Sch 25 para 38(1), (38)(d)).
11 Competition Act 1998 s 51(10) (amended by the Enterprise Act 2002 Sch 25 para 38(1), (38)(e)).
12 See the Competition Act 1998 (Office of Fair Trading's Rules) Order 2004, SI 2004/2751.

145.   Advice and information.   The Office of Fair Trading (the 'OFT')[1] has published general advice and information[2] about: (1) the application of the Chapter I prohibition[3] and the Chapter II prohibition[4], and the enforcement of those prohibitions[5]; and (2) the application of the prohibitions on restriction or distortion of competition and abuse of a dominant position in the EC Treaty[6], and the enforcement by it of those prohibitions[7]. The OFT may at any time publish revised, or new, advice or information[8]. Advice and information published under these provisions must be prepared with a view to: (a) explaining provisions of Part I of the Competition Act 1998[9] to persons who are likely to be affected by them; and (b) indicating how the OFT expects such provisions to operate[10]. Any advice or information published by the OFT is to be published in such form and in such manner as it considers appropriate[11]. If the OFT is preparing any advice or information it must consult such persons as it considers appropriate[12]. If the proposed advice or information relates to a matter in respect of which a regulator[13] exercises concurrent jurisdiction, those consulted must include that regulator[14]. In preparing any advice or information about a matter in respect of which he may exercise functions under Part I of the Competition Act 1998, a regulator must consult: (i) the OFT; (ii) the other regulators; and (iii) such other persons as he considers appropriate[15].

1 As to the OFT see PARAS 6–8.
2 Pursuant to the Competition Act 1998 s 52(1); the Guidelines published under this provision can be accessed on the OFT's website http://www.oft.gov.uk.
3 As to the Chapter I prohibition see PARA 116.
4 As to the Chapter II prohibition see PARA 125.
5 The requirement to publish such advice and information is imposed by the Competition Act 1998 s 52(1).
6 Ie the EC Treaty art 81 (see PARA 61 et seq) and art 82 (see PARA 68 et seq). As to the EC Treaty (ie the Treaty establishing the European Community (Rome, 25 March 1957; TS 1 (1973); Cmnd 5179)) see PARA 24 note 1. The numbering for the EC Treaty used in this title is as revised by the Treaty of Amsterdam: see PARA 24 note 1.
7 Competition Act 1998 s 52(1A) (added by SI 2004/1261).
8 Competition Act 1998 s 52(2) (amended by the Enterprise Act 2002 s 278(1), Sch 25 para 38(1), (39)(a)).
9 Ie the Competition Act 1998 ss 1–60.
10 Competition Act 1998 s 52(3) (amended by the Enterprise Act 2002 Sch 25 para 38(1), (39)(a)). Advice (or information) published by virtue of head (b) in the text may include advice (or information) about the factors which the OFT may take into account in considering whether, and if so how, to exercise a power conferred on it by the Competition Act 1998 Ch I (ss 1–11), Ch II (ss 17–19) or Ch III (ss 25–44): s 52(4) (amended by the Enterprise Act 2002 Sch 25 para 38(1), (39)(b)).
11 Competition Act 1998 s 52(5) (amended by the Enterprise Act 2002 Sch 25 para 38(1), (39)(c)).
12 Competition Act 1998 s 52(6) (amended by the Enterprise Act 2002 Sch 25 para 38(1), (39)(d)).
13 As to the meaning of 'regulator' see PARA 147.
14 Competition Act 1998 s 52(7).
15 Competition Act 1998 s 52(8) (amended by the Enterprise Act 2002 Sch 25 para 38(1), (39)(e)).

146. Defamation. For the purposes of the law relating to defamation, absolute privilege attaches to any advice, guidance, notice or direction given, or decision made, by the Office of Fair Trading (the 'OFT')[1] in the exercise of any of its functions under Part I of the Competition Act 1998[2].

1 As to the OFT see PARAS 6–8.
2 Competition Act 1998 s 57 (amended by the Enterprise Act 2002 s 278(1), Sch 25 para 38(1), 42). Part I of the Act consists of ss 1–60. As to defamation generally see LIBEL AND SLANDER.

(9) SECTORAL REGULATORS

147. Concurrent powers of the sectoral regulators. In Part I of the Competition Act 1998[1] 'regulator' means:
(1) the Office of Communications[2];
(2) the Gas and Electricity Markets Authority[3];
(3) the Director General of Electricity Supply for Northern Ireland[4];
(4) the Water Services Regulation Authority[5];
(5) the Office of Rail Regulation[6];
(6) the Director General of Gas for Northern Ireland[7];
(7) the Civil Aviation Authority[8].
Functions of the Office of Fair Trading (the 'OFT')[9] under Part I of the Competition Act 1998 are exercisable concurrently by the regulators[10]. The Secretary of State[11] may make regulations[12] for the purpose of co-ordinating the performance of functions under Part I of the Competition Act 1998 ('Part I

functions') which are exercisable concurrently by two or more competent persons[13] as a result of any enactment, including any subordinate legislation, whenever passed or made[14]. The regulations may, in particular, make provision:

(a) as to the procedure to be followed by competent persons when determining who is to exercise Part I functions in a particular case[15];

(b) as to the steps which must be taken before a competent person exercises, in a particular case, such Part I functions as may be prescribed[16];

(c) as to the procedure for determining, in a particular case, questions arising as to which competent person is to exercise Part I functions in respect of the case[17];

(d) for Part I functions in a particular case to be exercised jointly (i) by the OFT and one or more regulators; or (ii) by two or more regulators, and as to the procedure to be followed in such cases[18];

(e) as to the circumstances in which the exercise by a competent person of such Part I functions as may be prescribed is to preclude the exercise of such functions by another such person[19];

(f) for cases in respect of which Part I functions are being, or have been, exercised by a competent person to be transferred to another such person[20];

(g) for the person exercising Part I functions in a particular case (i) to appoint another competent person to exercise Part I functions on his behalf in relation to the case; or (ii) to appoint officers of that other person (with the latter's consent) to act as officers of the first named person in relation to the case[21];

(h) for notification as to who is exercising Part I functions in respect of a particular case[22].

Guidance has been published on the concurrent powers of the OFT and the regulators[23].

1 Ie the Competition Act 1998 ss 1–60.
2 Competition Act 1998 s 54(1)(a) (substituted by the Communications Act 2003 s 371(5)(a)). See PARA 19.
3 Competition Act 1998 s 54(1)(b) (substituted by the Enterprise Act 2002 s 278(1), Sch 25 para 38(1), (41)(a)). See PARA 20.
4 Competition Act 1998 s 54(1)(c) (substituted by the Enterprise Act 2002 Sch 25 para 38(1), (41)(a)).
5 Competition Act 1998 s 54(1)(d) (substituted by the Water Act 2003 s 101(1), Sch 7 para 32(1), (2)). See PARA 21.
6 Competition Act 1998 s 54(1)(e) (substituted by the Railways and Transport Safety Act 2003 s 16(5), Sch 2 para 19(p)). See PARA 22.
7 Competition Act 1998 s 54(1)(f) (substituted by the Enterprise Act 2002 Sch 25 para 38(1), (41)(a)).
8 Competition Act 1998 s 54(1)(g) (substituted by the Enterprise Act 2002 Sch 25 para 38(1), (41)(a)). See PARA 342 note 20.
9 As to the OFT see PARAS 6–8.
10 See the Competition Act 1998 s 54(2), Sch 10 Pt II (s 54(2) amended by the Enterprise Act 2002 Sch 25 para 38(1), (41)(b); the Competition Act 1998 Sch 10 Pt II amended by the Utilities Act 2000 s 108, Sch 8, the Enterprise Act 2002 Sch 26, the Communications Act 2003 s 406(7), Sch 19(1), the Water Act 2003 s 101, Sch 7 para 32(1), (4)(a) and the Railways and Transport Safety Act 2003 s 16(4), (5), Sch 3 para 4), which makes amendments to a number of other enactments in order to give effect to such concurrency. Minor and consequential amendments in connection with the regulators' competition functions are also made: see the Competition Act 1998 s 54(3), Sch 10 Pt IV (amended by the Transport Act 2000 s 274, Sch 31 Pt IV, the Enterprise Act 2002 Sch 26, the Communications Act 2003 Sch 19(1), the Water Act 2003 Sch 7 para 32(1), (4)(b), Sch 9 Pt 3 and SI 2003/1398).
11 As to the Secretary of State see PARA 5.

12 For the regulations made in pursuance of this power see the Competition Act 1998 (Concurrency) Regulations 2004, SI 2004/1077. As to the power to make subordinate legislation under the Competition Act 1998 see PARA 163.
13 'Competent person' means the OFT or any of the regulators: Competition Act 1998 s 54(7) (amended by the Enterprise Act 2002 Sch 25 para 38(1), (41)(b)).
14 Competition Act 1998 s 54(4) (amended by SI 2004/1261). 'Subordinate legislation' has the same meaning as in the Interpretation Act 1978 s 21(1) (see STATUTES vol 44(1) (Reissue) PARA 1381) and includes an instrument made under an Act of the Scottish Parliament and Northern Ireland legislation: Competition Act 1998 s 54(8) (added by SI 2004/1261).
15 Competition Act 1998 s 54(5)(a).
16 Competition Act 1998 s 54(5)(b).
17 Competition Act 1998 s 54(5)(c). Provision made under this head may provide for questions to be referred to and determined by the Secretary of State or by such other person as may be prescribed: s 54(6).
18 Competition Act 1998 s 54(5)(d) (amended by the Enterprise Act 2002 Sch 25 para 38(1), (41)(b)).
19 Competition Act 1998 s 54(5)(e).
20 Competition Act 1998 s 54(5)(f).
21 Competition Act 1998 s 54(5)(g).
22 Competition Act 1998 s 54(5)(h).
23 See OFT Guideline 405 *Concurrent Application to Regulated Industries* (December 2004).

(10) FINDINGS OF FACT AND INFRINGEMENT

148. Office of Fair Trading's findings bind the parties. Unless the court[1] directs otherwise, a finding of fact made by the Office of Fair Trading (the 'OFT')[2] in the course of conducting an investigation[3] which is relevant to an issue arising in Part I proceedings[4] is binding on the parties if: (1) the time for bringing an appeal[5] in respect of the finding has expired and the relevant party[6] has not brought such an appeal; or (2) the decision of the Competition Appeal Tribunal[7] on such an appeal has confirmed the finding[8]. Rules of court may make provision in respect of assistance to be given by the OFT to the court in Part I proceedings[9].

1 As to the meaning of 'court' see PARA 131 note 2.
2 As to the OFT see PARAS 6–8.
3 As to investigations see PARA 129.
4 'Part I proceedings' means proceedings brought otherwise that by the OFT: (1) in respect of an alleged infringement of the Chapter I prohibition or of the Chapter II prohibition; or (2) in respect of an alleged infringement of the prohibitions in the EC Treaty art 81(1) (see PARA 61 et seq) or art 82 (see PARA 68 et seq): Competition Act 1998 s 58(2) (definition substituted by SI 2004/1261). As to the Chapter I prohibition see PARA 116. As to the Chapter II prohibition see PARA 125. As to the EC Treaty (ie the Treaty establishing the European Community (Rome, 25 March 1957; TS 1 (1973); Cmnd 5179)) see PARA 24 note 1. The numbering for the EC Treaty used in this title is as revised by the Treaty of Amsterdam: see PARA 24 note 1.
5 Ie under the Competition Act 1998 s 46 or s 47 (see PARAS 166–167).
6 'Relevant party' means: (1) in relation to the Chapter I prohibition or the prohibition in the EC Treaty art 81(1), a party to the agreement which is alleged to have infringed the prohibition; and (2) in relation to the Chapter II prohibition or the prohibition in the EC Treaty art 82, the undertaking whose conduct is alleged to have infringed the prohibition: Competition Act 1998 s 58(2) (definition amended by SI 2004/1261).
7 As to the Competition Appeal Tribunal see PARAS 13–17.
8 Competition Act 1998 s 58(1), (2) (s 58(1) amended by the Enterprise Act 2002 ss 21, 278(1), Sch 5 paras 1, 5(a), (b), Sch 25 para 38(1), (43)(a), (b) and by SI 2004/1261; the Competition Act 1998 s 58(2) amended by SI 2004/1261).
9 Competition Act 1998 s 58(3) (amended by the Enterprise Act 2002 Sch 25 para 38(1), (43)(a)).

149. Findings of infringements. Where there are proceedings before the court[1] in which damages or any other sum of money is claimed in respect of an infringement of the Chapter I prohibition[2], the Chapter II prohibition[3], the prohibition on restriction or distortion of competition in the EC Treaty[4] or the prohibition on abuse of a dominant position in the EC Treaty[5] then, in such proceedings, the court is bound by the decisions of the Office of Fair Trading (the 'OFT')[6] or the Competition Appeal Tribunal[7] that there has been an infringement[8], once any period available for further appeal has elapsed[9].

1 As to the meaning of 'court' see PARA 131 note 2.
2 As to the Chapter I prohibition see PARA 116.
3 As to the Chapter II prohibition see PARA 125.
4 Ie the EC Treaty art 81 (see PARA 61 et seq). As to the EC Treaty (ie the Treaty establishing the European Community (Rome, 25 March 1957; TS 1 (1973); Cmnd 5179)) see PARA 24 note 1. The numbering for the EC Treaty used in this title is as revised by the Treaty of Amsterdam: see PARA 24 note 1.
5 Ie the EC Treaty art 82 (see PARA 68 et seq).
6 As to the OFT see PARAS 6–8.
7 As to the Competition Appeal Tribunal see PARAS 13–17.
8 See the Competition Act 1998 s 58A(3) (added by the Enterprise Act 2002 s 20(1)).
9 Competition Act 1998 s 58A(1), (2) (added by the Enterprise Act 2002 s 20(1)). The periods available are: (1) in the case of a decision of the OFT, the period during which an appeal may be made to the Tribunal under the Competition Act 1998 s 46 or s 47 (see PARAS 166–167); (2) in the case of a decision of the Tribunal, the period during which a further appeal may be made under s 49 (see PARA 170); (3) in the case of any decision which is the subject of a further appeal, the period during which an appeal may be made to the House of Lords from a decision on the further appeal; and, where any appeal mentioned in head (1), (2) or (3) is made, the period specified includes the period before the appeal is determined: s 58A(4) (added by the Enterprise Act 2002 s 20(1); and amended by SI 2007/1846). As from 1 October 2009, the Competition Act 1998 s 58A(4) is amended by the Constitutional Reform Act 2005 s 40(4), Sch 9 para 65(1), (4) to replace the reference to the House of Lords with a reference to the Supreme Court.

(11) PRINCIPLES TO BE APPLIED IN DETERMINING QUESTIONS

150. Consistency with European Community law. Provision is made to ensure that so far as is possible (having regard to any relevant differences between the provisions concerned), questions arising under Part I of the Competition Act 1998[1] in relation to competition within the United Kingdom are dealt with in a manner which is consistent with the treatment of corresponding questions arising in Community law in relation to competition within the Community[2]. At any time when the court[3] determines a question arising under Part I of the Competition Act 1998, it must act (so far as is compatible with the provisions of Part I and whether or not it would otherwise be required to do so) with a view to securing that there is no inconsistency between: (1) the principles applied, and decision reached, by the court in determining that question; and (2) the principles laid down by the EC Treaty[4] and the European Court[5], and any relevant decision[6] of that Court, as applicable at that time in determining any corresponding question arising in Community law[7]. The court must, in addition, have regard to any relevant decision or statement of the European Commission[8].

The provisions described above also apply to the Office of Fair Trading (the 'OFT')[9], and to any person acting on behalf of the OFT, in connection with any matter arising under Part I of the Competition Act 1998[10].

1 Ie the Competition Act 1998 ss 1–60.
2 Competition Act 1998 s 60(1).

3   In the Competition Act 1998 s 60(2), (3), 'court' means any court or tribunal: s 60(5).
4   As to the EC Treaty (ie the Treaty establishing the European Community (Rome, 25 March 1957; TS 1 (1973); Cmnd 5179)) see PARA 24 note 1.
5   'European Court' means the Court of Justice of the European Communities and includes the Court of First Instance: Competition Act 1998 s 59(1).
6   In head (2) in the text and the Competition Act 1998 s 60(3) (see the text and note 8), 'decision' includes a decision as to: (1) the interpretation of any provision of Community law; (2) the civil liability of an undertaking for harm caused by its infringement of Community law: s 60(6).
7   Competition Act 1998 s 60(2).
8   Competition Act 1998 s 60(3). As to the meanings of 'court' and 'decision' for these purposes see notes 3, 6.
9   As to the OFT see PARAS 6–8.
10 Competition Act 1998 s 60(4) (amended by the Enterprise Act 2002 s 278(1), Sch 25 para 38(1), (45)).

(12) INSPECTIONS ON BEHALF OF THE EUROPEAN COMMISSION OR ANOTHER MEMBER STATE

(i) Inspections on behalf of the European Commission

151. Power to enter business premises: European Commission inspections. A judge of the High Court must issue a warrant if satisfied, on an application made to the High Court in accordance with rules of court by the Office of Fair Trading (the 'OFT')[1], that the European Commission has ordered an inspection of business premises[2], that inspection is being, or is likely to be, obstructed and the measures that would be authorised by the warrant are neither arbitrary nor excessive having regard to the subject matter of the inspection[3].

A European Commission investigation is being obstructed if: (1) a Commission official[4], exercising his power in accordance with the provision under which the investigation is being conducted[5], has attempted to enter any business premises[6] but has been unable to do so[7]; and (2) there are reasonable grounds for suspecting that there are on any business premises books or records[8] which the Commission official has power to examine[9]. A Commission investigation is also being obstructed if there are reasonable grounds for suspecting that there are on any business premises books or records the production of which has been required by a Commission official exercising his power in accordance with the provision under which the investigation is being conducted[10] and which have not been produced as required[11]. A Commission investigation is likely to be obstructed if: (a) there are reasonable grounds for suspecting that there are on any business premises books or records which a Commission official has power to examine; and (b) there are also reasonable grounds for suspecting that, if the Commission official attempted to exercise his power to examine any of the books or records, they would not be produced but would be concealed, removed, tampered with or destroyed[12].

A warrant[13] issued under the provisions described above authorises a named officer of the OFT and any other OFT officer[14], or Commission official, accompanying the named officer: (i) to enter any business premises specified in the warrant using such force as is reasonably necessary for the purpose; (ii) to search for books and records which a Commission official has power to examine, using such force as is reasonably necessary for the purpose; (iii) to take or obtain copies of or extracts from such books and records; and (iv) to seal the premises, any part of the premises or any books or records which a Commission official has power to seal, for the period and to the extent necessary for the inspection[15]. Any person entering any premises by virtue of a warrant may take with him such equipment as appears to him to be necessary[16]. If there is no one at the premises when the officer named in the warrant proposes to execute it he must, before executing it, take such steps as are reasonable in all the circumstances to inform the occupier[17] of the intended entry, and if the occupier is informed, afford him or his legal or other representative a reasonable opportunity to be present when the warrant is executed[18]. On leaving any premises entered by virtue of the warrant the named officer must, if the premises are unoccupied or the occupier is temporarily absent, leave them as effectively secured as he found them[19]. A warrant continues in force until the end of the period of one month beginning with the day on which it is issued[20].

1 As to the OFT see PARAS 6–8.
2 Ie an inspection under EC Council Regulation 1/2003 on the implementation of the rules on competition laid down in Articles 81 and 82 of the Treaty (OJ L1, 4.1.03, p 1) (the 'Modernisation Regulation') art 20 (an 'Article 20 inspection'). See PARA 92. As to the EC Treaty (ie the Treaty establishing the European Economic Community, Rome, 25th March 1957) see PARA 24 note 1. The numbering for the EC Treaty used in this title is as revised by the Treaty of Amsterdam: see PARA 24 note 1. As to investigations by the European Commission see PARA 82 et seq.
3 Competition Act 1998 s 62(1) (amended by the Enterprise Act 2002 s 278(1), Sch 25 para 38(1), (47)(a); and SI 2004/1261).
4 'Commission official' means any of the persons authorised by the Commission to conduct the Article 20 inspection: Competition Act 1998 s 62(10) (added by SI 2004/1261).
5 Ie in accordance with EC Competition Regulation art 20(3).
6 'Business premises' means any premises of an undertaking or association of undertakings which a Commission official has under Article 20 of the EC Competition Regulation power to enter in the course of the Article 20 inspection: Competition Act 1998 s 62(10) (added by SI 2004/1261). The reference in the definition of 'business premises' to Article 20 of the EC Competition Regulation does not include a reference to that Article as applied by Article 21 of that Regulation: Competition Act 1998 s 62(11) (added by SI 2004/1261). 'Premises' includes any land or any means of transport: Competition Act 1998 s 61 (substituted by SI 2004/1261).
7 Competition Act 1998 s 62(2)(a) (amended by SI 2004/1261).
8 'Books and records' includes books and records stored on any medium: Competition Act 1998 s 61 (substituted by SI 2004/1261).
9 Competition Act 1998 s 62(2)(b) (amended by SI 2004/1261).
10 Ie under EC Competition Regulation art 20(3).
11 Competition Act 1998 s 62(3) (amended by SI 2004/1261).
12 Competition Act 1998 s 62(4) (amended by SI 2004/1261).
13 Ie a warrant issued under the Competition Act 1998 s 62. A warrant must indicate the subject matter and purpose of the inspection, and the nature of the offence created by s 65 (see PARA 154): s 64(1) (amended by SI 2004/1261).
14 'OFT officer' means any officer of the OFT whom the OFT has authorised in writing to accompany the named officer: Competition Act 1998 s 62(10) (added by SI 2004/1261).
15 Competition Act 1998 s 62(5) (substituted by SI 2004/1261). The powers conferred by s 62 are to be exercised on production of a warrant issued under that provision: Competition Act 1998 s 62(2). A warrant may authorise persons specified in the warrant to accompany the named officer who is executing it: s 62(5A) (added by the Enterprise Act 2002 s 203(1), (3)).
16 Competition Act 1998 s 62(6).
17 'Occupier', in relation to any premises, means a person whom the named officer reasonably believes is the occupier of those premises: Competition Act 1998 s 64(5).
18 Competition Act 1998 s 64(3), (5) (amended by SI 2004/1261). If the named officer is unable to inform the occupier of the intended entry he must, when executing the warrant, leave a copy of it in a prominent place on the premises: Competition Act 1998 s 64(4).
19 Competition Act 1998 s 62(7).
20 Competition Act 1998 s 62(8).

152.   Power to enter non-business premises: European Commission inspections. A judge of the High Court must issue a warrant if satisfied, on an application made to the High Court in accordance with the rules of court by the

Office of Fair Trading (the 'OFT')[1], that the European Commission has ordered an inspection of non-business premises[2], and the measures that would be authorised by the warrant are neither arbitrary nor excessive having regard in particular to the following matters[3]: (1) the seriousness of the suspected infringement of the prohibition on restriction or distortion of competition in the EC Treaty[4] or the prohibition on abuse of a dominant position in the EC Treaty[5]; (2) the importance of the evidence sought; (3) the involvement of the undertaking or association of undertakings concerned; and (4) whether it is reasonably likely that business books and records[6] relating to the subject matter of the inspection are kept on the non-business premises that would be specified in the warrant[7].

A warrant under the above provisions authorises a named officer of the OFT and any other OFT officer[8], or Commission official[9], accompanying the named officer to enter any non-business premises specified in the warrant[10]. A warrant may authorise a named officer of the OFT and any other OFT officer, or Commission official, accompanying the named officer to search for books or records which a Commission official has power to examine[11]. A warrant may authorise a named officer of the OFT and any other OFT officer, or Commission official, accompanying the named officer to take or obtain copies of books or records of which a Commission official has power to take or obtain copies[12]. A warrant may authorise persons specified in the warrant to accompany the named officer who is executing it[13]. Any person entering any premises by virtue of a warrant may take with him such equipment as appears to him to be necessary[14].

If there is no one at the premises when the officer named in the warrant proposes to execute it he must, before executing it, take such steps as are reasonable in all the circumstances to inform the occupier[15] of the intended entry, and if the occupier is informed, afford him or his legal or other representative a reasonable opportunity to be present when the warrant is executed[16]. On leaving any premises entered by virtue of a warrant the named officer must, if the premises are unoccupied or the occupier is temporarily absent, leave them as effectively secured as he found them[17]. A warrant continues in force until the end of the period of one month beginning with the day on which it is issued[18].

1 As to the OFT see PARAS 6–8.
2 Ie an inspection under EC Council Regulation 1/2003 on the implementation of the rules on competition laid down in Articles 81 and 82 of the Treaty (OJ L1, 4.1.03, p 1) (the 'Modernisation Regulation') art 21 (an 'Article 21 inspection'). See PARA 92. As to the EC Treaty (ie the Treaty establishing the European Economic Community, Rome, 25th March 1957) see PARA 24 note 1. The numbering for the EC Treaty used in this title is as revised by the Treaty of Amsterdam: see PARA 24 note 1. As to investigations by the European Commission see PARA 82 et seq. 'Non-business premises' means any premises to which a decision of the European Commission ordering the Article 21 inspection relates: Competition Act 1998 s 62A(12) (added by SI 2004/1261). As to the meaning of 'premises' see PARA 151 note 6.
3 Competition Act 1998 s 62A(1) (added by SI 2004/1261).
4 Ie the EC Treaty art 81 (see PARA 61 et seq).
5 Ie the EC Treaty art 82 (see PARA 68 et seq).
6 As to the meaning of 'books and records' see PARA 151 note 8.
7 Competition Act 1998 s 62A(2) (added by SI 2004/1261).
8 'OFT officer' means any officer of the OFT whom the OFT has authorised in writing to accompany the named officer: Competition Act 1998 s 62A(12) (added by SI 2004/1261).
9 'Commission official' means any of the persons authorised by the European Commission to conduct the Article 21 inspection: Competition Act 1998 s 62A(12) (added by SI 2004/1261).
10 Competition Act 1998 s 62A(3) (added by SI 2004/1261). A warrant may authorise the use, for either or both of the purposes mentioned in the Competition Act 1998 s 62A(3) and (4), of such force as is reasonably necessary: s 62A(6) (added by SI 2004/1261). A warrant must indicate the subject matter and purpose of the inspection, and the nature of the offence created by the

Competition Act 1998 s 65 (see PARA 154): s 64(1) (amended by SI 2004/1261). The powers conferred by the Competition Act 1998 s 62A are to be exercised on production of a warrant issued under that provision: s 64(2) (amended by SI 2004/1261).
11 Competition Act 1998 s 62A(4) (added by SI 2004/1261). See note 10.
12 Competition Act 1998 s 62A(5) (added by SI 2004/1261).
13 Competition Act 1998 s 62A(7) (added by SI 2004/1261).
14 Competition Act 1998 s 62A(8) (added by SI 2004/1261).
15 'Occupier', in relation to any premises, means a person whom the named officer reasonably believes is the occupier of those premises: Competition Act 1998 s 64(5).
16 Competition Act 1998 s 64(3), (5) (amended by SI 2004/1261). If the named officer is unable to inform the occupier of the intended entry he must, when executing the warrant, leave a copy of it in a prominent place on the premises: Competition Act 1998 s 64(4).
17 Competition Act 1998 s 62A(9) (added by SI 2004/1261).
18 Competition Act 1998 s 62A(10) (added by SI 2004/1261).

153.   Power to enter premises: Office of Fair Trading's inspection at the request of the European Commission. A judge of the High Court must issue a warrant if satisfied, on an application made to the High Court in accordance with rules of court by the Office of Fair Trading (the 'OFT')[1], that: (1) the European Commission has requested the OFT to conduct an inspection[2] which the Commission has ordered[3]; (2) the inspection is being, or is likely to be, obstructed; and (3) the measures that would be authorised by the warrant are neither arbitrary nor excessive having regard to the subject matter of the inspection[4].

An inspection is being obstructed if: (a) an authorised officer[5] of the OFT has attempted to enter any business premises[6] but has been unable to do so; (b) the officer has produced his authorisation to the undertaking, or association of undertakings, concerned; and (c) there are reasonable grounds for suspecting that there are on any business premises books or records[7] which the officer has power to examine[8]. An inspection is also being obstructed if: (i) there are reasonable grounds for suspecting that there are on business premises books or records which an authorised officer of the OFT has power to examine; (ii) the officer has produced his authorisation to the undertaking, or association of undertakings, and has required production of the books or records; and (iii) the books and records have not been produced as required[9]. An inspection is likely to be obstructed if there are reasonable grounds for suspecting that there are on any business premises books or records which an authorised officer of the OFT has power to examine, and there are also reasonable grounds for suspecting that, if the officer attempted to exercise his power to examine any of the books or records, they would not be produced but would be concealed, removed, tampered with or destroyed[10].

A warrant under the above provisions authorises a named authorised officer of the OFT, any other authorised officer of the OFT, or Commission official[11], accompanying the named authorised officer[12]: (A) to enter any business premises specified in the warrant using such force as is reasonably necessary for the purpose; (B) to search for books and records which an authorised officer of the OFT has power to examine, using such force as is reasonably necessary for the purpose; (C) to take or obtain copies of or extracts from such books and records; and (D) to seal the premises, any part of the premises or any books or records with any authorised officer of the OFT has power to seal, for the period and to the extent necessary for the inspection[13]. Any person entering any premises by virtue of a warrant may take with him such equipment as appears to him to be necessary[14]. If there is no one at the premises when the officer named in the warrant proposes to execute it he must, before executing it, take such steps as are reasonable in all the circumstances to inform the occupier[15] of the intended entry, and if the occupier is informed, afford him or his legal or other representative a reasonable opportunity to be present when the warrant is executed[16]. On leaving any premises which he has entered by virtue of the warrant the named authorised officer must, if the premises are unoccupied or the occupier is temporarily absent, leave them as effectively secured as he found them[17]. A warrant continues in force until the end of the period of one month beginning with the day on which it is issued[18].

1 As to the OFT see PARAS 6–8.
2 Ie an inspection under EC Council Regulation 1/2003 on the implementation of the rules on competition laid down in Articles 81 and 82 of the Treaty (OJ L1, 4.1.03, p 1) (the 'Modernisation Regulation') art 22(2) (an 'Article 22(2) inspection'). See PARA 92. As to the EC Treaty (ie the Treaty establishing the European Economic Community, Rome, 25th March 1957) see PARA 24 note 1. The numbering for the EC Treaty used in this title is as revised by the Treaty of Amsterdam: see PARA 24 note 1. As to investigations by the European Commission see PARA 82 et seq.
3 Ie by a decision under the EC Competition Regulation art 20(4).
4 Competition Act 1998 s 63(1) (amended by the Enterprise Act 2002 s 278(1), Sch 25 para 38(1), (48)(a); and SI 2004/1261).
5 'Authorised officer of the OFT' means any officer of the OFT to whom an authorisation has been given: Competition Act 1998 s 62B(2) (added by SI 2004/1261). 'Authorisation' means an authorisation given in writing by the OFT which: (1) identifies the officer; (2) indicates the subject matter and purpose of the investigation; and (3) draws attention to any penalties which a person may incur under the EC Competition Regulation in connection with the inspection: Competition Act 1998 s 62B(2) (added by SI 2004/1261). For the purposes of an Article 22(2) inspection, an authorised officer of the OFT has the powers specified in EC Competition Regulation art 20(2): Competition Act 1998 s 62B(1) (added by SI 2004/1261).
6 'Business premises' means any premises of an undertaking or association of undertakings which an authorised officer of the OFT has power to enter in the course of the Article 22(2) inspection: Competition Act 1998 s 63(10) (added by SI 2004/1261). As to the meaning of 'premises' see PARA 151 note 6.
7 As to the meaning of 'books and records' see PARA 151 note 8.
8 Competition Act 1998 s 63(2) (amended by the Enterprise Act 2002 Sch 25 para 38(1), (48)(b); and SI 2004/1261).
9 Competition Act 1998 s 63(3) (amended by the Enterprise Act 2002 Sch 25 para 38(1), (48)(b); and SI 2004/1261).
10 Competition Act 1998 s 63(4) (amended by the Enterprise Act 2002 Sch 25 para 38(1), (48)(b); and SI 2004/1261).
11 'Commission official' means any person authorised by the European Commission to assist with the Article 22(2) inspection: Competition Act 1998 s 63(10) (added by SI 2004/1261).
12 A warrant under the Competition Act 1998 s 63 may authorise persons specified in the warrant to accompany the named authorised officer who is executing it: s 63(5A) (added by the Enterprise Act 2002 s 203(1), (4)).
13 Competition Act 1998 s 63(5) (substituted by SI 2004/1261). A warrant must indicate the subject matter and purpose of the investigation, and the nature of the offence created by s 65 (see PARA 154): s 64(1). The powers conferred by s 63 are to be exercised on production of a warrant issued under that provision: s 64(2).
14 Competition Act 1998 s 63(6).
15 'Occupier', in relation to any premises, means a person whom the named officer reasonably believes is the occupier of those premises: Competition Act 1998 s 64(5).
16 Competition Act 1998 s 64(3), (5). If the named officer is unable to inform the occupier of the intended entry he must, when executing the warrant, leave a copy of it in a prominent place on the premises: s 64(4).
17 Competition Act 1998 s 63(7) (amended by SI 2004/1261).
18 Competition Act 1998 s 63(8).

154. Offences. A person is guilty of an offence if he intentionally obstructs any person in the exercise of his powers under a warrant issued for the purposes of a European Commission inspection or an inspection by the Office of Fair

Trading at the request of the Commission[1]. A person guilty of such an offence is liable on summary conviction to a fine not exceeding the statutory maximum[2], or on conviction on indictment to imprisonment for a term not exceeding two years or to a fine or to both[3].

1 Competition Act 1998 s 65(1) (amended by SI 2004/1261). Such warrants are issued under the Competition Act 1998 s 62 (Commission inspections of business premises) (see PARA 151), s 62A (Commission inspections of non-business premises) (see PARA 152) or s 63 (OFT's inspections of business premises) (see PARA 153). As to offences by bodies corporate see s 72; and PARA 164. As to the Office of Fair Trading see PARAS 6–8.
2 As to the statutory maximum see PARA 140 note 9.
3 Competition Act 1998 s 65(2).

155. Privileged communications and use of statements in prosecution. A person may not be required, in connection with an inspection by the Office of Fair Trading[1] at the request of the European Commission[2], to produce or disclose a privileged communication[3]. A privileged communication is: (1) a communication between a professional legal adviser and his client; or (2) made in connection with, or in contemplation of, legal proceedings and for the purposes of those proceedings, which in proceedings in the High Court would be protected from disclosure on grounds of legal professional privilege[4].

A statement made by a person in connection with such an inspection[5] may not be used in evidence against him on a prosecution for a cartel offence[6] unless, in the proceedings: (a) in giving evidence, he makes a statement inconsistent with it; and (b) evidence relating to it is adduced, or a question relating to it is asked, by him or on his behalf[7].

1 As to the Office of Fair Trading see PARAS 6–8.
2 Ie by virtue of any provision of the Competition Act 1998 s 62B or s 63 (see PARA 153).
3 Competition Act 1998 s 65A(1) (added by SI 2004/1261).
4 Competition Act 1998 s 65A(2) (added by SI 2004/1261). As to legal professional privilege see LEGAL PROFESSIONS vol 65 (2008) PARA 719; LEGAL PROFESSIONS vol 66 (2009) PARA 1146.
5 Ie in response to a requirement imposed by virtue of the Competition Act 1998 s 62B or s 63 (see PARA 153).
6 Ie an offence under the Enterprise Act 2002 s 188 (see PARA 319).
7 Competition Act 1998 s 65B (added by SI 2004/1261).

(ii) Investigations by the Office of Fair Trading on behalf of the Competition Authority of another Member State

156. Power to conduct an investigation. In any of the following cases, the Office of Fair Trading (the 'OFT')[1] may conduct an investigation on behalf of and for the account of the competition authority of another member state[2]:

(1) where there are reasonable grounds for suspecting that there is an agreement[3] which may affect trade between member states and has as its object or effect the prevention, restriction or distortion of competition within the European Community[4];

(2) where there are reasonable grounds for suspecting that the prohibition on abuse of a dominant position in the EC Treaty[5] has been infringed[6];

(3) where there are reasonable grounds for suspecting that, at some time in the past, there was an agreement which at that time may have affected trade between member states and had as its object or effect the prevention, restriction or distortion of competition within the European Community[7].

1 As to the OFT see PARAS 6–8.

2   Ie an investigation pursuant to EC Council Regulation 1/2003 on the implementation of the
     rules on competition laid down in Articles 81 and 82 of the Treaty (OJ L1, 4.1.03, p 1) (the
     'Modernisation Regulation') art 22(1) (an 'Article 22(1) investigation'). See PARA 92. As to the
     EC Treaty (ie the Treaty establishing the European Economic Community, Rome, 25th March
     1957) see PARA 24 note 1. The numbering for the EC Treaty used in this title is as revised by the
     Treaty of Amsterdam: see PARA 24 note 1. 'Competition authority of another member state'
     means a competition authority designated as such under the EC Competition Regulation art 35
     by a member state other than the United Kingdom: Competition Act 1998 s 65C(1) (added by
     SI 2004/1261). As to the meaning of 'United Kingdom' see PARA 401 note 1.
3   A provision of the Competition Act 1998 Pt IIA (ss 65C–65N) which is expressed to apply to, or
     in relation to, an agreement is to be read as applying equally to, or in relation to, a decision by
     an association of undertakings or a concerted practice: s 65D(6) (added by SI 2004/1261).
4   Competition Act 1998 s 65D(1), (2) (added by SI 2004/1261).
5   Ie the EC Treaty art 82 (see PARA 68 et seq).
6   Competition Act 1998 s 65D(1), (3) (added by SI 2004/1261).
7   Competition Act 1998 s 65D(1), (4) (added by SI 2004/1261). It is immaterial whether the
     agreement in question remains in existence: Competition Act 1998 s 65D(5) (added by
     SI 2004/1261).

157. Power when conducting investigations. For the purposes of an
investigation on behalf of and for the account of the competition authority of
another member state[1], the Office of Fair Trading (the 'OFT')[2] may require any
person to produce[3] to it a specified[4] document[5], or to provide it with specified
information[6], which it considers relates to any matter relevant to the
investigation[7]. The power is to be exercised by a notice in writing[8] and the notice
must indicate the subject matter and purpose of the investigation and the nature
of the offences created[9].

The OFT may also specify in the notice: (1) the time and place at which any
document is to be produced or any information is to be provided; and (2) the
manner and form in which it is to be produced or provided[10].

1   Ie an investigation pursuant to EC Council Regulation 1/2003 on the implementation of the
     rules on competition laid down in Articles 81 and 82 of the Treaty (OJ L1, 4.1.03, p 1) (the
     'Modernisation Regulation') art 22(1) (an 'Article 22(1) investigation'). See PARA 156. As to the
     EC Treaty (ie the Treaty establishing the European Economic Community, Rome, 25th March
     1957) see PARA 24 note 1. The numbering for the EC Treaty used in this title is as revised by the
     Treaty of Amsterdam: see PARA 24 note 1. As to the meaning of 'Competition authority of
     another member state' see PARA 156 note 2.
2   As to the OFT see PARAS 6–8.
3   The power to require a person to produce a document includes power: (1) if the document is
     produced (a) to take copies of it or extracts from it; (b) to require him, or any person who is a
     present or past officer of his, or is or was at any time employed by him, to provide an
     explanation of the document; and (2) if the document is not produced, to require him to state, to
     the best of his knowledge and belief, where it is: Competition Act 1998 s 65E(6) (added by
     SI 2004/1261).
4   'Specified' means: (1) specified, or described, in the notice; or (2) falling within a category which
     is specified, or described, in the notice: Competition Act 1998 s 65E(4) (added by
     SI 2004/1261).
5   As to the meaning of 'document' see PARA 9 note 3; definition applied by the Competition
     Act 1998 s 65C(2) (added by SI 2004/1261).
6   As to the meaning of 'information' see PARA 9 note 3; definition applied by the Competition
     Act 1998 s 65C(2) (added by SI 2004/1261).
7   Competition Act 1998 s 65E(1) (added by SI 2004/1261). For the purposes of the Competition
     Act 1998 Pt IIA (ss 65C–65N), the power to require information, in relation to information
     recorded otherwise than in a legible form, includes power to require a copy of it in a legible
     form: s 65C(3) (added by SI 2004/1261). Any power conferred on the OFT by the Competition
     Act 1998 Pt IIA to require information includes power to require any document which it
     believes may contain that information: s 65C(4) (added by SI 2004/1261).
8   Competition Act 1998 s 65E(2) (added by SI 2004/1261).

9   Competition Act 1998 s 65E(3) (added by SI 2004/1261). The offences are those created by the
     Competition Act 1998 ss 65L–65N (see PARA 161).
10   Competition Act 1998 s 65E(5) (added by SI 2004/1261).

158.   Power to enter business premises without a warrant. Any officer of the
Office of Fair Trading (the 'OFT')[1] who is authorised in writing by the OFT to
do so (an 'investigating officer') may enter any business premises[2] in connection
with an investigation on behalf of and for the account of the competition
authority of another member state[3].

No investigating officer is to enter any premises in the exercise of these
powers unless he has given to the occupier of the premises a written notice which
gives at least two working days'[4] notice of the intended entry, indicates the
subject matter and purpose of the investigation and indicates the nature of the
offences created[5]. This requirement does not apply if the OFT has a reasonable
suspicion that the premises are, or have been, occupied by a party to an
agreement which it is investigating[6] or an undertaking the conduct of which it is
investigating[7]. It also does not apply if the investigating officer has taken all such
steps as are reasonably practicable to give notice but has not been able to do so[8].
Where notice has not been given[9], the power of entry is to be exercised by the
investigating officer on production of evidence of his authorisation and a
document indicating the subject matter and purpose of the investigation and the
nature of the offences created[10].

An investigating officer entering any premises under the above provisions
may:

(1)   take with him such equipment as appears to him to be necessary[11];

(2)   require any person on the premises to produce any document[12] which
       he considers relates to any matter relevant to the investigation and, if
       the document is produced, to provide an explanation of it[13];

(3)   require any person to state, to the best of his knowledge and belief,
       where any such document is to be found[14];

(4)   take copies of, or extracts from, any document which is produced[15];

(5)   require any information which is stored in any electronic form and is
       accessible from the premises and which the investigating officer
       considers relates to any matter relevant to the investigation, to be
       produced in a form in which it can be taken away, and in which it is
       visible and legible or from which it can readily be produced in a visible
       and legible form[16];

(6)   take any steps which appear to be necessary for the purpose of
       preserving or preventing interference with any document which he
       consider relates to any matter relevant to the investigation[17].

1   As to the OFT see PARAS 6–8.

2   'Business premises' means premises (or any part of premises) not used as a dwelling:
     Competition Act 1998 s 65F(6) (added by SI 2004/1261). As to the meaning of 'premises' see
     PARA 130 note 2; definition applied by the Competition Act 1998 s 65C(2) (added by
     SI 2004/1261).

3   Competition Act 1998 s 65F(1) (added by SI 2004/1261). Such an investigation is one pursuant
     to EC Council Regulation 1/2003 on the implementation of the rules on competition laid down
     in Articles 81 and 82 of the Treaty (OJ L1, 4.1.03, p 1) (the 'Modernisation Regulation')
     art 22(1) (an 'Article 22(1) investigation'). See PARA 156. As to the EC Treaty (ie the Treaty
     establishing the European Economic Community, Rome, 25th March 1957) see PARA 24 note 1.
     The numbering for the EC Treaty used in this title is as revised by the Treaty of Amsterdam: see
     PARA 24 note 1. As to the meaning of 'Competition authority of another member state' see PARA
     156 note 2.

4   As to the meaning of 'working day' see PARA 130 note 5; definition applied by the Competition
    Act 1998 s 65C(2) (added by SI 2004/1261).
5   Competition Act 1998 s 65F(2) (added by SI 2004/1261). The offences are those created by the
    Competition Act 1998 ss 65L–65N (see PARA 161).
6   Ie under the Competition Act 1998 s 65D (see PARA 156).
7   Competition Act 1998 s 65F(3)(a) (added by SI 2004/1261). See note 6.
8   Competition Act 1998 s 65F(3)(b) (added by SI 2004/1261).
9   Ie in a case falling within the Competition Act 1998 s 65F(3) (see the text and notes 6–8).
10 Competition Act 1998 s 65F(4) (added by SI 2004/1261).
11 Competition Act 1998 s 65F(5)(a) (added by SI 2004/1261).
12 As to the meaning of 'document' see PARA 9 note 3; definition applied by the Competition
    Act 1998 s 65C(2) (added by SI 2004/1261).
13 Competition Act 1998 s 65F(5)(b) (added by SI 2004/1261). As to the power to require
    information see PARA 157 note 7.
14 Competition Act 1998 s 65F(5)(c) (added by SI 2004/1261).
15 Competition Act 1998 s 65F(5)(d) (added by SI 2004/1261).
16 Competition Act 1998 s 65F(5)(e) (added by SI 2004/1261).
17 Competition Act 1998 s 65F(5)(f) (added by SI 2004/1261).

159. Power to enter business or domestic premises under a warrant. On an application made by the Office of Fair Trading (the 'OFT')[1] to the court[2] in accordance with rules of court, a judge may issue a warrant[3] if he is satisfied that: (1) there are reasonable grounds for suspecting that there are on any business premises[4] or domestic premises[5] documents[6] the production of which has been required[7] and which have not been produced as required[8]; (2) there are reasonable grounds for suspecting that there are on any business premises or domestic premises documents which the OFT has power[9] to require to be produced and if the documents were required to be produced, they would not be produced but would be concealed, removed, tampered with or destroyed[10]; or, in relation to business premises only, (3) an investigating officer[11] has attempted to enter premises in the exercise of his powers to enter business premises without a warrant[12] but has been unable to do so and that there are reasonable grounds for suspecting that there are on the premises documents the production of which could have been required under that power[13].

A warrant under the above provisions authorises a named officer of the OFT and any other of its officers whom the OFT has authorised in writing to accompany the named officer:

(a)   to enter the premises specified in the warrant, using such force as is reasonably necessary for the purpose[14];
(b)   to search the premises and take copies of, or extracts from, any document appearing to be of a kind in respect of which the application was granted (the 'relevant kind')[15];
(c)   to take possession of any documents appearing to be of the relevant kind if such action appears to be necessary for preserving the documents or preventing interference with them or it is not reasonably practicable to take copies of the documents on the premises[16];
(d)   to take any other steps which appear to be necessary for preserving the documents or preventing interference with them[17];
(e)   to require any person to provide an explanation of any document appearing to be of the relevant kind or to state, to the best of his knowledge and belief, where it may be found[18];
(f)   to require any information which is stored in any electronic form and is accessible from the premises and which the named officer considers relates to any matter relevant to the investigation, to be produced in a

form in which it can be taken away, and in which it is visible and legible or from which it can readily be produced in a visible and legible form[19].

A warrant may authorise persons specified in the warrant to accompany the named officer who is executing it[20]. Any person entering premises by virtue of a warrant may take with him such equipment as appears to him to be necessary[21].

If there is no one at the premises when the officer named in the warrant proposes to execute the warrant he must, before executing it, take such steps as are reasonable in all the circumstances to inform the occupier[22] of the intended entry and, if the occupier is informed, afford him or his legal or other representative a reasonable opportunity to be present when the warrant is executed[23]. If the named officer is unable to inform the occupier of the intended entry he must, when executing the warrant, leave a copy of it in a prominent place on the premises[24].

On leaving any premises which he has entered by virtue of a warrant, the named officer must, if the premises are unoccupied or the occupier is temporarily absent, leave them as effectively secured as he found them[25].

A warrant under the above provisions continues in force until the end of the period of one month beginning with the day on which it is issued[26].

1   As to the OFT see PARAS 6–8.
2   As to the meaning of 'court' see PARA 131 note 2; definition applied by the Competition Act 1998 s 65C(2) (added by SI 2004/1261).
3   A warrant issued under the Competition Act 1998 ss 65G, 65H must indicate: (1) the subject matter of the investigation; (2) the nature of the offences created by ss 65L–65N (see PARA 161): s 65I(1) (added by SI 2004/1261). The powers conferred by the Competition Act 1998 ss 65G, 65H are to be exercised on production of a warrant issued under that provision: s 65I(2) (added by SI 2004/1261).
4   'Business premises' means premises (or any part of premises) not used as a dwelling: Competition Act 1998 s 65F(6); definition applied by s 65G(9) (both added by SI 2004/1261). As to the meaning of 'premises' see PARA 130 note 2; definition applied by the Competition Act 1998 s 65C(2) (added by SI 2004/1261).
5   'Domestic premises' means premises (or any part of premises) that are used as a dwelling and are: (1) premises also used in connection with the affairs of an undertaking or association of undertakings; or (2) premises where documents relating to the affairs of an undertaking or association of undertakings are kept: Competition Act 1998 s 65H(9) (added by SI 2004/1261).
6   As to the meaning of 'document' see PARA 9 note 3; definition applied by the Competition Act 1998 s 65C(2) (added by SI 2004/1261).
7   Ie required under the Competition Act 1998 s 65E or s 65F (see PARAS 157–158).
8   Competition Act 1998 ss 65G(1)(a), 65H(1)(a) (both added by SI 2004/1261).
9   Ie under the Competition Act 1998 s 65E (see PARA 157).
10 Competition Act 1998 ss 65G(1)(b), 65H(1)(b) (both added by SI 2004/1261). If, in the case of a warrant under the Competition Act 1998 ss 65G(1)(b), 65H(1)(b), the judge is satisfied that it is reasonable to suspect that there are also on the premises other documents relating to the investigation concerned, the warrant must also authorise action mentioned in ss 65G(2), 65H(2) (see heads (a)–(f) in the text) to be taken in relation to any such document: ss 65G(3), 65H(3) (both added by SI 2004/1261).
11 As to the investigating officer see PARA 158.
12 Ie under the Competition Act 1998 s 65F (see PARA 158).
13 Competition Act 1998 s 65G(1)(c) (added by SI 2004/1261).
14 Competition Act 1998 ss 65G(2)(a), 65H(2)(a) (both added by SI 2004/1261).
15 Competition Act 1998 ss 65G(2)(b), 65H(2)(b) (both added by SI 2004/1261).
16 Competition Act 1998 ss 65G(2)(c), 65H(2)(c) (both added by SI 2004/1261). Any document of which possession is taken may be retained for a period of three months: Competition Act 1998 ss 65G(8), 65H(8) (both added by SI 2004/1261).
17 Competition Act 1998 ss 65G(2)(d), 65H(2)(d) (both added by SI 2004/1261).
18 Competition Act 1998 ss 65G(2)(e), 65H(2)(e) (both added by SI 2004/1261).
19 Competition Act 1998 ss 65G(2)(f), 65H(2)(f) (both added by SI 2004/1261).
20 Competition Act 1998 ss 65G(4), 65H(4) (both added by SI 2004/1261).
21 Competition Act 1998 ss 65G(5), 65H(5) (both added by SI 2004/1261).

22 'Occupier', in relation to any premises, means a person whom the named officer reasonably
   believes is the occupier of those premises: Competition Act 1998 s 65I(5) (added by
   SI 2004/1261).
23 Competition Act 1998 s 65I(3), (5) (added by SI 2004/1261).
24 Competition Act 1998 s 65I(4) (added by SI 2004/1261).
25 Competition Act 1998 ss 65G(6), 65H(6) (both added by SI 2004/1261).
26 Competition Act 1998 ss 65G(7), 65H(7) (both added by SI 2004/1261).

160. Privileged communications and use of statements in prosecution. A
person may not be required, in connection with an investigation[1] by the Office of
Fair Trading[2], to produce or disclose a privileged communication[3]. A privileged
communication is: (1) a communication between a professional legal adviser and
his client; or (2) made in connection with, or in contemplation of, legal
proceedings and for the purposes of those proceedings, which in proceedings in
the High Court would be protected from disclosure on grounds of legal
professional privilege[4].

A statement made by a person in connection with such an investigation[5] may
not be used in evidence against him on a prosecution for a cartel offence[6] unless,
in the proceedings: (a) in giving evidence, he makes a statement inconsistent with
it; and (b) evidence relating to it is adduced, or a question relating to it is asked,
by him or on his behalf[7].

1 Ie under any provision of the Competition Act 1998 Pt IIA (ss 65C–65N).
2 As to the Office of Fair Trading see PARAS 6–8.
3 Competition Act 1998 s 65J(1) (added by SI 2004/1261).
4 Competition Act 1998 s 65J(2) (added by SI 2004/1261). As to legal professional privilege see
  LEGAL PROFESSIONS vol 65 (2008) PARA 719; LEGAL PROFESSIONS vol 66 (2009) PARA 1146.
5 Ie in response to a requirement imposed by virtue of any of the Competition Act 1998
  ss 65E–65H (see PARAS 157–159).
6 Ie an offence under the Enterprise Act 2002 s 188 (see PARA 319).
7 Competition Act 1998 s 65J (added by SI 2004/1261).

161. Offences in relation to investigations. A person is guilty of an offence if
he fails to comply with a requirement imposed on him in relation to an
investigation by the Office of Fair Trading (the 'OFT')[1] conducted on behalf of a
competition authority of another member state[2].

If a person is charged with an offence in respect of a requirement to produce a
document[3], it is a defence for him to prove that the document was not in his
possession or under his control and that it was not reasonably practicable for
him to comply with the requirement[4].

If a person is charged with an offence in respect of a requirement: (1) to
provide information[5]; (2) to provide an explanation of a document; or (3) to
state where a document is to be found, it is a defence for him to prove that he
had a reasonable excuse for failing to comply with the requirement[6].

Failure to comply with a requirement to provide documents or information[7] is
not an offence if the person imposing the requirement has failed to act in
accordance with the statutory requirements[8].

A person is guilty of an offence if he intentionally obstructs an officer acting in
the exercise of his powers to enter business premises without a warrant[9].

A person is guilty of an offence if, having been required to produce a
document[10], he intentionally or recklessly destroys or otherwise disposes of it,
falsifies it or conceals it, or he causes or permits its destruction, disposal,
falsification or concealment[11].

If information is provided by a person to the OFT in connection with any
function of the OFT relating to its power to conduct investigations[12], that person

is guilty of an offence if the information is false or misleading in a material particular and he knows that it is or is reckless as to whether it is[13]. A person who: (a) provides any information to another person, knowing the information to be false or misleading in a material particular; or (b) recklessly provides any information to another person which is false or misleading in a material particular, knowing that the information is to be used for the purpose of providing information to the OFT[14], is guilty of an offence[15].

1   As to the OFT see PARAS 6–8.
2   Competition Act 1998 s 65L(1) (added by SI 2004/1261). Such a requirement may be imposed under the Competition Act 1998 s 65E, 65F, 65G or s 65H (see PARAS 157–159). A person guilty of an offence under s 65L(1) is liable: (1) on summary conviction, to a fine not exceeding the statutory maximum; (2) on conviction on indictment, to a fine: s 65L(6) (added by SI 2004/1261). As to the statutory maximum see PARA 140 note 9. A person who intentionally obstructs an officer in the exercise of his powers under a warrant issued under the Competition Act 1998 s 65G or s 65H (see PARA 159) is guilty of an offence and liable: (a) on summary conviction, to a fine not exceeding the statutory maximum; (b) on conviction on indictment, to imprisonment for a term not exceeding two years or to a fine or to both: s 65L(7) (added by SI 2004/1261).
3   As to the meaning of 'document' see PARA 9 note 3; definition applied by the Competition Act 1998 s 65C(2) (added by SI 2004/1261).
4   Competition Act 1998 s 65L(2) (added by SI 2004/1261).
5   As to the meaning of 'information' see PARA 9 note 3; definition applied by the Competition Act 1998 s 65C(2) (added by SI 2004/1261).
6   Competition Act 1998 s 65L(3) (added by SI 2004/1261).
7   Ie imposed under the Competition Act 1998 s 65E or s 65F (see PARAS 157–158).
8   Competition Act 1998 s 65L(4) (added by SI 2004/1261).
9   Competition Act 1998 s 65L(5) (added by SI 2004/1261). The power to enter business premises without a warrant is set out in the Competition Act 1998 s 65F (see PARA 158). A person guilty of an offence under s 65L(5) is liable: (1) on summary conviction, to a fine not exceeding the statutory maximum; (2) on conviction on indictment, to a fine: s 65L(6) (added by SI 2004/1261).
10   Ie under the Competition Act 1998 s 65E, 65F, 65G or s 65H (see PARAS 157–159).
11   Competition Act 1998 s 65M(1) (added by SI 2004/1261). A person guilty of such an offence is liable: (1) on summary conviction, to a fine not exceeding the statutory maximum; (2) on conviction on indictment, to imprisonment for a term not exceeding two years or to a fine or to both: Competition Act 1998 s 65M(2) (added by SI 2004/1261).
12   Ie in connection with any function of the OFT under the Competition Act 1998 Pt IIA (see PARAS 156–160).
13   Competition Act 1998 s 65N(1) (added by SI 2004/1261). A person guilty of such an offence is liable: (1) on summary conviction, to a fine not exceeding the statutory maximum; (2) on conviction on indictment, to imprisonment for a term not exceeding two years or to a fine or to both: Competition Act 1998 s 65N(3) (added by SI 2004/1261).
14   Ie in connection with any of its functions under the Competition Act 1998 Pt IIA (see PARAS 156–160).
15   Competition Act 1998 s 65N(2) (added by SI 2004/1261). A person guilty of such an offence is liable: (1) on summary conviction, to a fine not exceeding the statutory maximum; (2) on conviction on indictment, to imprisonment for a term not exceeding two years or to a fine or to both: Competition Act 1998 s 65N(3) (added by SI 2004/1261).

(iii) Office of Fair Trading's Rules in relation to Inspections

162.   Procedural rules in relation to inspections and investigations. The Office of Fair Trading (the 'OFT')[1] may make such rules about procedural and other matters in connection with the carrying into effect of the provisions relating to inspections and investigations[2] as it considers appropriate[3]. If the OFT is preparing any rules it must consult such persons as it considers appropriate[4]. No rule made by the OFT is to come into operation until it has been approved by an order made by the Secretary of State[5]. The Secretary of State may approve any rule made by the OFT in the form in which it is submitted, or subject to such modifications as he considers appropriate[6]. The Secretary of State may, after consulting the OFT, by order vary or revoke any rules made under this provision[7].

If the Secretary of State considers that rules should be made with respect to a particular matter he may direct the OFT to exercise its powers and make rules about that matter[8].

1   As to the OFT see PARAS 6–8.
2   Ie the provisions of the Competition Act 1998 Pt II (ss 61–65B) and Pt IIA (ss 65C–65N).
3   Competition Act 1998 s 75A(1) (added by SI 2004/1261). See the Competition Act 1998 (Office of Fair Trading's Rules) Order 2004, SI 2004/2751.
4   Competition Act 1998 s 75A(2) (added by SI 2004/1261).
5   Competition Act 1998 s 75A(3) (added by SI 2004/1261). As to the Secretary of State see PARA 5.
6   Competition Act 1998 s 75A(4) (added by SI 2004/1261). If the Secretary of State proposes to approve a rule subject to modifications he must inform the OFT of the proposed modifications and take into account any comments made by the OFT: Competition Act 1998 s 75A(5) (added by SI 2004/1261). The provisions of the Competition Act 1998 s 75A(3)–(5) apply also to any alteration of the rules made by the OFT: s 75A(6) (added by SI 2004/1261).
7   Competition Act 1998 s 75A(7) (added by SI 2004/1261).
8   Competition Act 1998 s 75A(8) (added by SI 2004/1261).

(13) MISCELLANEOUS PROVISIONS

163. Regulations, orders and rules. Any power to make regulations or orders which is conferred by the Competition Act 1998 is exercisable by statutory instrument[1]. Any statutory instrument made under the Competition Act 1998 may: (1) contain such incidental, supplemental, consequential and transitional provision as the Secretary of State[2] considers appropriate; and (2) make different provision for different cases[3].

1   Competition Act 1998 s 71(1). No order may be made under s 3 (see PARA 117), s 19 (see PARA 126), s 36(8) (see PARA 137), s 45(8) (see PARA 11) or s 50 (see PARA 142), unless a draft of the order has been laid before Parliament and approved by a resolution of each House: s 71(4) (amended by the Enterprise Act 2002 s 278(1), Sch 25 para 38(1), (49)). Any statutory instrument made under the Competition Act 1998, apart from one made under any of the provisions mentioned in s 71(4), or under s 76(3) (commencement), is subject to annulment by a resolution of either House of Parliament: s 71(5). The power to make rules under s 48 is also exercisable by statutory instrument, and accordingly s 71(3), (5) applies: see s 71(2).
2   As to the Secretary of State see PARA 5.
3   Competition Act 1998 s 71(3).

164. Offences by bodies corporate etc. If an offence[1] committed by a body corporate is proved (1) to have been committed with the consent or connivance of an officer[2]; or (2) to be attributable to any neglect on his part, the officer as well as the body corporate is guilty of the offence and liable to be proceeded against and punished accordingly[3].

1   This applies to any offence under any of the Competition Act 1998 ss 42–44 (see PARAS 140–141), s 65 (see PARA 154) or ss 65L–65N (see PARA 161): s 72(1) (amended by SI 2004/1261).
2   For these purposes 'officer', in relation to a body corporate, means a director, manager, secretary or other similar officer of the body, or a person purporting to act in any such capacity: Competition Act 1998 s 72(3).
3   Competition Act 1998 s 72(2). If the affairs of a body corporate are managed by its members, s 72(2) applies in relation to the acts and defaults of a member in connection with his functions of management as if he were a director of the body corporate: s 72(4).

165. Crown application. Any provision made by or under the Competition Act 1998 binds the Crown[1] except that:

(1)   the Crown is not criminally liable as a result of any such provision[2];

(2)   the Crown is not liable for any penalty under any such provision[3]; and

(3)   nothing in the Act affects Her Majesty in her private capacity[4].

If an investigation is conducted by the Office of Fair Trading (the 'OFT')[5] in respect of an agreement[6] where none of the parties is the Crown or a person in the public service of the Crown, or in respect of conduct[7] otherwise than by the Crown or such a person then: (a) the power to enter business premises without a warrant[8] may not be exercised in relation to land which is occupied by a government department, or otherwise for purposes of the Crown, without the written consent of the appropriate person[9]; and (b) provision relating to the power to enter business or domestic premises under a warrant[10] does not apply in relation to land so occupied[11]. Provisions relating to the power to enter premises with respect to European Commission investigations[12] do not apply in relation to land which is occupied by a government department, or otherwise for purposes of the Crown, unless the matter being investigated is an agreement to which the Crown or a person in the service of the Crown is a party, or conduct by the Crown or such a person[13]. If the Secretary of State certifies that it appears to him to be in the interests of national security that powers of entry[14] should not be exercisable in relation to premises held or used by or on behalf of the Crown and which are specified in the certificate, those powers are not exercisable in relation to those premises[15].

1   Competition Act 1998 s 73(1). Any amendment, repeal or revocation made by the Competition Act 1998 binds the Crown to the extent that the enactment amended, repealed or revoked binds the Crown: s 73(9).

2   Competition Act 1998 s 73(1)(a). Head (1) in the text does not affect the application of any provision of the Act in relation to persons in the public service of the Crown: s 73(2).

3   Competition Act 1998 s 73(1)(b).

4   Competition Act 1998 s 73(1)(c). Head (3) in the text is to be interpreted as if the Crown Proceedings Act 1947 s 38(3) (interpretation of references in that Act to Her Majesty in her private capacity: see CROWN PROCEEDINGS AND CROWN PRACTICE vol 12(1) (Reissue) PARA 103) were contained in the Competition Act 1998: s 73(3).

5   Ie under the Competition Act 1998 s 25 (see PARA 129) or s 65D (see PARA 156). As to the OFT see PARAS 6–8.

6   In the Competition Act 1998 s 73(4), (6), 'agreement' includes a suspected agreement and is to be read as applying equally to, or in relation to, a decision by an association of undertakings or a concerted practice: s 73(6A) (added by SI 2004/1261).

7   In the Competition Act 1998 s 73(4), (6), 'conduct' includes suspected conduct: s 73(6A) (added by SI 2004/1261).

8   Ie under the Competition Act 1998 s 27 (see PARA 130) or (as the case may be) s 65F (see PARA 158).

9   Competition Act 1998 s 73(4)(a) (substituted by SI 2004/1261). In any case in which such consent is required, the person who is the appropriate person in relation to that case is to be determined in accordance with regulations made by the Secretary of State: Competition Act 1998 s 73(5). For that purpose 'appropriate person' means: (1) in relation to any land which is occupied by a government department, that department; and (2) in relation to any other land which is otherwise occupied for purposes of the Crown, the person occupying the land for such purposes: Competition Act 1998 (Definition of Appropriate Person) Regulations 1999, SI 1999/2282, reg 2. As to the power to make subordinate legislation under the Competition Act 1998 see PARA 163. As to the Secretary of State see PARA 5.

10   Ie under a warrant issued by virtue of the Competition Act 1998 ss 28, 28A (see PARA 131), ss 65G, 65H (see PARA 159).

11   Competition Act 1998 s 73(4)(b) (substituted by SI 2004/1261).

12   Ie the Competition Act 1998 ss 62, 62A, 63 (see PARAS 151–153).

13   Competition Act 1998 s 73(6) (amended by SI 2004/1261). See notes 6, 7.

14 Ie powers conferred by the Competition Act 1998 s 27 (see PARA 130) or s 65F (see PARA 158), or that may be conferred by a warrant under ss 28, 28A (see PARA 131), ss 62, 62A, 63, 65G or s 65H (see PARAS 151, 152, 153, 159).
15 Competition Act 1998 s 73(8) (amended by SI 2004/1261).

(14) APPEALS TO THE COMPETITION APPEAL TRIBUNAL

166. Appealable decisions. Any party to an agreement in respect of which the Office of Fair Trading (the 'OFT')[1] has made a decision[2] may appeal to the Competition Appeal Tribunal[3] against, or with respect to, the decision[4]. Any person[5] in respect of whose conduct the OFT has made a decision may appeal to the Tribunal against, or with respect to, the decision[6]. Except in the case of an appeal against the imposition, or the amount, of a penalty[7], the making of an appeal under the provisions described above does not suspend the effect of the decision to which the appeal relates[8].

The Tribunal must determine the appeal[9] on the merits by reference to the grounds of appeal set out in the notice of appeal[10]. The Tribunal may confirm or set aside the decision which is the subject of the appeal, or any part of it[11], and may:

(1) remit the matter to the OFT[12];

(2) impose or revoke, or vary the amount of, a penalty[13];

(3) give such directions, or take such other steps, as the OFT could itself have given or taken[14]; or

(4) make any other decision which the OFT could itself have made[15].

Any decision of the Tribunal on an appeal has the same effect, and may be enforced in the same manner, as a decision of the OFT[16]. If the Tribunal confirms the decision which is the subject of the appeal it may nevertheless set aside any finding of fact on which the decision was based[17].

In relation to an appeal regarding commitments[18], the Tribunal must, by reference to the grounds of appeal set out in the notice of appeal, determine the appeal by applying the same principles as would be applied by a court on an application for judicial review[19]. The Tribunal may: (a) dismiss the appeal or quash the whole or part of the decision to which it relates; and (b) where it quashes the whole or part of that decision, remit the matter back to the OFT with a direction to reconsider and make a new decision in accordance with the ruling of the Tribunal[20].

Proceedings in the High Court should be stayed when an appeal to the Tribunal is pending[21].

1 As to the OFT see PARAS 6–8.
2 In this provision, 'decision' means a decision of the OFT:
    (1) as to whether the Chapter I prohibition has been infringed (see PARA 116);
    (2) as to whether the prohibition in the EC Treaty art 81(1) has been infringed (see PARA 61 et seq);
    (3) as to whether the Chapter II prohibition has been infringed (see PARA 125);
    (4) as to whether the prohibition in the EC Treaty art 82 has been infringed (see PARA 68 et seq);
    (5) cancelling a block or parallel exemption (see PARAS 121, 123);
    (6) withdrawing the benefit of a regulation of the European Commission pursuant to the EC Council Regulation 1/2003 on the implementation of the rules on competition laid down in Articles 81 and 82 of the Treaty (OJ L1, 4.1.03, p 1) (the 'Modernisation Regulation') art 29(2) (see PARA 29);
    (7) not releasing commitments pursuant to a request made under the Competition Act 1998 s 31A(4)(b)(i) (see PARA 134);
    (8) releasing commitments under s 31A(4)(b)(ii) (see PARA 134);

(9)   as to the imposition of any penalty under s 36 or as to the amount of any such penalty (see PARA 137),

and includes a direction given under s 32, s 33 or s 35 (see PARAS 135–136) and such other decisions under Pt I (ss 1–60) as may be prescribed: s 46(3) (substituted by SI 2004/1261). As to the EC Treaty (ie the Treaty establishing the European Community (Rome, 25 March 1957; TS 1 (1973); Cmnd 5179)) see PARA 24 note 1. The numbering for the EC Treaty used in this title is as revised by the Treaty of Amsterdam: see PARA 24 note 1.

Three further appealable decisions have been prescribed by the Competition Act 1998 (Appealable Decisions and Revocation of Notification of Excluded Agreements) Regulations 2004, SI 2004/1078, reg 2, namely:

(a)   a decision of the OFT imposing conditions or obligations subject to which a parallel exemption is to have effect;

(b)   a decision of the OFT imposing one or more additional conditions or obligations subject to which a parallel exemption is to have effect; and

(c)   a decision of the OFT varying or removing any such condition or obligation.

As to the Chapter I prohibition see PARA 116. As to the Chapter II prohibition see PARA 125. Where no view has been expressed on the question whether there has been an infringement of the Chapter II prohibition, there is no appealable decision: *Independent Water Co Ltd v Water Services Regulation Authority* [2007] CAT 6, [2007] All ER (D) 264 (Jan).

3   As to the Competition Appeal Tribunal see PARAS 13–17.

4   Competition Act 1998 s 46(1) (amended by the Enterprise Act 2002 ss 21, 278(1), Sch 5 paras 1, 2(a), Sch 25 para 38(1), (36)). An appeal to the Competition Appeal Tribunal must be made by sending a notice of appeal to it within the specified period: Competition Act 1998 s 46(5), Sch 8 para 2(1) (amended by the Enterprise Act 2002 Sch 5 paras 1, 8(1), (3)(a)). The notice of appeal must set out the grounds of appeal in sufficient detail to indicate: (1) under which provision of the Competition Act 1998 the appeal is brought; (2) to what extent (if any) the appellant contends that the decision against, or with respect to which, the appeal is brought was based on an error of fact or was wrong in law; and (3) to what extent (if any) the appellant is appealing against the OFT's exercise of its discretion in making the disputed decision: Sch 8 para 2(2) (amended by the Enterprise Act 2002 Sch 25 para 38(1), (54)(b)). The Tribunal may give an appellant leave to amend the grounds of appeal identified in the notice of appeal: Competition Act 1998 Sch 8 para 2(3) (amended by the Enterprise Act 2002 Sch 5 paras 1, 8(1), (3)(b)). In the Competition Act 1998 Sch 8 para 2, references to the Tribunal are to the Tribunal as constituted (in accordance with the Enterprise Act 2002 s 14 (see PARA 15)) for the purposes of the proceedings in question: Competition Act 1998 Sch 8 para 2(4) (added by the Enterprise Act 2002 Sch 5 paras 1, 8(1), (3)(c)). Nothing in the Competition Act 1998 Sch 8 para 2 restricts the power under the Enterprise Act 2002 s 15 (Tribunal rules) (see PARA 16) to make provision as to the manner of instituting proceedings before the Tribunal: Competition Act 1998 Sch 8 para 2(5) (added by the Enterprise Act 2002 Sch 5 paras 1, 8(1), (3)(c)).

5   As to the meaning of 'person' see PARA 118 note 8.

6   Competition Act 1998 s 46(2) (amended by the Enterprise Act 2002 Sch 5 paras 1, 2(a), Sch 25 para 38(1), (36)).

7   As to penalties see the Competition Act 1998 ss 36–40 (see PARAS 137–139).

8   Competition Act 1998 s 46(4).

9   The provisions in the Competition Act 1998 Sch 8 para 3 apply to any appeal under s 46 or s 47 (see PARA 167) other than: (1) an appeal under s 46 against, or with respect to, a decision of the kind specified in s 46(3)(g) or (h) (see note 2 heads (7), (8)); and (2) an appeal under s 47(1)(b) or (c) (see PARA 167): Sch 8 para 3(A1) (added by SI 2004/1261).

10   Competition Act 1998 Sch 8 para 3(1) (amended by the Enterprise Act 2002 Sch 5 paras 1, 8(1), (4)).

11   Competition Act 1998 Sch 8 para 3(2) (amended by the Enterprise Act 2002 Sch 5 paras 1, 8(1), (4)).

12   Competition Act 1998 Sch 8 para 3(2)(a) (amended by the Enterprise Act 2002 Sch 25 paras 38(1), 54(a)).

13   Competition Act 1998 Sch 8 para 3(2)(b).

14   Competition Act 1998 Sch 8 para 3(2)(d) (amended by the Enterprise Act 2002 Sch 25 paras 38(1), 54(a), (c)).

15   Competition Act 1998 Sch 8 para 3(2)(e) (amended by the Enterprise Act 2002 Sch 25 paras 38(1), 54(a), (c)). See *VIP Communications Ltd v Office of Communications (T-Mobile (UK) Ltd intervening)* [2007] CAT 3, [2007] All ER (D) 138 (Jan).

16   Competition Act 1998 Sch 8 para 3(3) (amended by the Enterprise Act 2002 Sch 5 paras 1, 8(1), (4), Sch 25 paras 38(1), 54(a), (c)).

17 Competition Act 1998 Sch 8 para 3(4) (amended by the Enterprise Act 2002 Sch 5 paras 1, 8(1), (4)).
18 Ie any appeal under the Competition Act 1998 s 46 against, or with respect to, a decision of the kind specified in s 46(3)(g) or (h) (see note 2 heads (7), (8)), and any appeal under s 47(1)(b) or (c) (see PARA 167).
19 Competition Act 1998 Sch 8 para 3A(1), (2) (added by SI 2004/1261). As to judicial review see ADMINISTRATIVE LAW vol 1(1) (2001 Reissue) PARA 58 et seq.
20 Competition Act 1998 Sch 8 para 3A(3) (added by SI 2004/1261).
21 *Synstar Computer Services (UK) Ltd v ICL (Sorbus) Ltd* [2002] ICR 112, [2001] All ER (D) 360 (Mar).

167. Third party appeals. A person[1] who is not a party to an agreement respecting which a decision has been made, or who is not a person in respect of whose conduct a decision has been made[2] may appeal to the Competition Appeal Tribunal[3] with respect to certain decisions[4] of the Office of Fair Trading (the 'OFT')[5]. It is a question of fact whether an appealable decision has been taken; whether a decision has been taken is a question of substance, not form and may have been made either expressly or by necessary implication[6].

A person may make such an appeal only if the Tribunal considers that he has a sufficient interest in the decision with respect to which the appeal is made, or that he represents persons who have such an interest[7].

The making of an appeal does not suspend the effect of the decision to which the appeal relates[8].

1 As to the meaning of 'person' see PARA 118 note 8.
2 Ie a person who does not fall within the Competition Act 1998 s 46(1) or (2) (see PARA 166).
3 As to the Competition Appeal Tribunal see PARAS 13–17.
4 Ie one of the following decisions (see the Competition Act 1998 s 47(1)(a)–(f) (substituted by SI 2004/1261)):
    (1) a decision falling within s 46(3)(a)–(f) (see PARA 166 note 2, heads (1)–(6));
    (2) a decision falling within s 46(3)(g) (see PARA 166 note 2, head (7));
    (3) a decision of the OFT to accept or release commitments under s 31A (see PARA 134), or to accept a variation of such commitments other than a variation which is not material in any respect;
    (4) a decision of the OFT to make directions under s 35 (see PARA 136);
    (5) a decision of the OFT not to make directions under s 35; or
    (6) such other decision of the OFT under Pt I (ss 1–60) as may be prescribed.
    Three further appealable decisions have been prescribed by the Competition Act 1998 (Appealable Decisions and Revocation of Notification of Excluded Agreements) Regulations 2004, SI 2004/1078, reg 2, namely:
    (a) a decision of the OFT imposing conditions or obligations subject to which a parallel exemption is to have effect;
    (b) a decision of the OFT imposing one or more additional conditions or obligations subject to which a parallel exemption is to have effect; and
    (c) a decision of the OFT varying or removing any such condition or obligation.
    As to the power to make subordinate legislation under the Competition Act 1998 see PARA 163.
5 Competition Act 1998 s 47(1) (substituted by SI 2004/1261). As to the OFT see PARAS 6–8.
6 See *Claymore Dairies Ltd v Director General of Fair Trading (Robert Wiseman Dairies plc intervening)* [2003] All ER (D) 357 (Mar), CCAT; *Freeserve.com plc v Director General of Telecommunications (BT Group plc intervening)* [2002] All ER (D) 152 (Nov), CCAT.
7 Competition Act 1998 s 47(2) (substituted by the Enterprise Act 2002 s 17).
8 Competition Act 1998 s 47(3) (substituted by the Enterprise Act 2002 s 17).

168. Monetary claims before the Competition Appeal Tribunal. In relation to any claim for damages, or any other claim for a sum of money, which a person[1] who has suffered loss or damage as a result of the infringement of a relevant prohibition[2] may make in civil proceedings brought in any part of the United Kingdom[3], the following provisions apply[4].

For the purpose of identifying claims which may be made in civil proceedings, any limitation rules that would apply in such proceedings are to be disregarded[5]. Such a claim may be made in proceedings brought before the Competition Appeal Tribunal[6]. No claim may be made in such proceedings until a decision[7] has established that the relevant prohibition in question has been infringed[8]. A claim may also not be made otherwise than with the permission of the Tribunal, during any specified period[9] which relates to that decision[10].

In determining a claim, the Tribunal is bound by any decision[11] which establishes that the prohibition in question has been infringed[12].

The right to make a claim in proceedings before the Tribunal does not affect the right to bring any other proceedings in respect of the claim[13].

1 As to the meaning of 'person' see PARA 118 note 8.
2 'Relevant prohibition' means any of the following (see the Competition Act 1998 s 47A(2) (added by the Enterprise Act 2002 s 18(1))):
    (1) the Chapter I prohibition (see PARA 116);
    (2) the Chapter II prohibition (see PARA 125);
    (3) the prohibition in the EC Treaty art 81(1) (see PARA 61 et seq);
    (4) the prohibition in the EC Treaty art 82 (see PARA 68 et seq).
    As to the EC Treaty (ie the Treaty establishing the European Community (Rome, 25 March 1957; TS 1 (1973); Cmnd 5179)) see PARA 24 note 1. The numbering for the EC Treaty used in this title is as revised by the Treaty of Amsterdam: see PARA 24 note 1.
3 As to the meaning of 'United Kingdom' see PARA 401 note 1.
4 Competition Act 1998 s 47A(1) (added by the Enterprise Act 2002 s 18(1)).
5 Competition Act 1998 s 47A(3) (added by the Enterprise Act 2002 s 18(1)). See LIMITATION PERIODS vol 68 (2008) PARA 915 et seq.
6 Competition Act 1998 s 47A(4) (added by the Enterprise Act 2002 s 18(1)). The making of such a claim is subject to the provisions of the Competition Act 1998 and Tribunal rules: s 47A(4) (as so added). As to the Competition Appeal Tribunal see PARAS 13–17. As to time limits for making claims see PARA 16; and as to the enforcement of decisions of the Tribunal see PARA 15.
7 The decisions which may be relied on for the purposes of proceedings under the Competition Act 1998 s 47A are (see s 47A(6) (added by the Enterprise Act 2002 s 18(1))):
    (1) a decision of the Office of Fair Trading (the 'OFT') that the Chapter I prohibition (see PARA 116) or the Chapter II prohibition (see PARA 125) has been infringed;
    (2) a decision of the OFT that the prohibition in the EC Treaty art 81(1) (see PARA 61 et seq) or art 82 (see PARA 68 et seq) has been infringed;
    (3) a decision of the Tribunal (on an appeal from a decision of the OFT) that the Chapter I prohibition, the Chapter II prohibition or the prohibition in the EC Treaty art 81(1) or art 82 has been infringed; or
    (4) a decision of the European Commission that the prohibition in the EC Treaty art 81(1) or art 82 has been infringed.
8 Competition Act 1998 s 47A(5)(a) (added by the Enterprise Act 2002 s 18(1)).
9 The periods during which proceedings in respect of a claim made in reliance on a decision mentioned in the Competition Act 1998 s 47A(6)(a), (b) or (c) (see note 7 heads (1)–(3)) may not be brought without permission are: (1) in the case of a decision of the OFT, the period during which an appeal may be made to the Tribunal under s 46 or s 47 (see PARAS 166–167); (2) in the case of a decision of the OFT which is the subject of an appeal mentioned in head (1) above, the period following the decision of the Tribunal on the appeal during which a further appeal may be made under s 49 (see PARA 170); (3) in the case of a decision of the Tribunal mentioned in s 47A(6)(c) (see note 7 head (3)), the period during which a further appeal may be made under s 49 (see PARA 170); (4) in the case of any decision which is the subject of a further appeal, the period during which an appeal may be made to the House of Lords from a decision on the further appeal; and, where any appeal mentioned in head (1), (2), (3) or (4) above is made, the period specified includes the period before the appeal is determined: s 47A(7) (added by the Enterprise Act 2002 s 18(1); and amended by SI 2007/1846). As from 1 October 2009, the reference to the House of Lords is replaced by a reference to the Supreme Court: see the Competition Act 1998 s 47A(7) (prospectively amended by the Constitutional Reform Act 2005 s 40(4), Sch 9 Pt 1).
    The periods during which proceedings in respect of a claim made in reliance on a decision or finding of the European Commission may not be brought without permission are: (a) the period during which proceedings against the decision or finding may be instituted in the European

Court; and (b) if any such proceedings are instituted, the period before those proceedings are determined: Competition Act 1998 s 47A(8) (added by the Enterprise Act 2002 s 18(1)). See *BCL Old Co Ltd v BASF SE* [2009] EWCA Civ 434, [2009] All ER (D) 212 (May).

10 Competition Act 1998 s 47A(5)(b) (added by the Enterprise Act 2002 s 18(1)).
11 Ie any decision mentioned in the Competition Act 1998 s 47A(6) (see note 7).
12 Competition Act 1998 s 47A(9) (added by the Enterprise Act 2002 s 18(1)).
13 Competition Act 1998 s 47A(10) (added by the Enterprise Act 2002 s 18(1)).

169. Claims brought on behalf of consumers. A specified body[1] may bring proceedings before the Competition Appeal Tribunal[2] which comprise consumer claims[3] made or continued on behalf of at least two individuals[4]. A consumer claim may be included in such proceedings if it is: (1) a claim made in the proceedings on behalf of the individual concerned by the specified body; or (2) a claim made by the individual concerned[5] which is continued in the proceedings on his behalf by the specified body; and such a claim may only be made or continued in the proceedings with the consent of the individual concerned[6]. The consumer claims included in such proceedings must all relate to the same infringement[7].

Any damages or other sum (not being costs or expenses) awarded in respect of a consumer claim included in proceedings under the provisions set out above must be awarded to the individual concerned; but the Tribunal may, with the consent of the specified body and the individual, order that the sum awarded must be paid to the specified body (acting on behalf of the individual)[8].

1 'Specified' means specified in an order made by the Secretary of State, in accordance with criteria to be published by the Secretary of State for these purposes: Competition Act 1998 s 47B(9) (added by the Enterprise Act 2002 s 19). As to the Secretary of State see PARA 5. An application by a body to be specified in an order is to be made in a form approved by the Secretary of State for the purpose: Competition Act 1998 s 47B(10) (added by the Enterprise Act 2002 s 19). The Consumers' Association is specified for these purposes: see the Specified Body (Consumer Claims) Order 2005, SI 2005/2365, art 2. As to the Consumers' Association see PARA 342 note 9.
2 As to the Competition Appeal Tribunal see PARAS 13–17.
3 'Consumer claim' means a claim to which the Competition Act 1998 s 47A applies (see PARA 168) which an individual has in respect of an infringement affecting (directly or indirectly) goods or services to which: (1) the individual received, or sought to receive, otherwise than in the course of a business carried on by him (notwithstanding that he received or sought to receive them with a view to carrying on a business); and (2) were, or would have been, supplied to the individual (in the case of goods whether by way of sale or otherwise) in the course of a business carried on by the person who supplied or would have supplied them: s 47B(7) (added by the Enterprise Act 2002 s 19). A business includes: (a) a professional practice; (b) any other undertaking carried on for gain or reward; (c) any undertaking in the course of which goods or services are supplied otherwise than free of charge: Competition Act 1998 s 47B(8) (added by the Enterprise Act 2002 s 19).
4 Competition Act 1998 s 47B(1) (added by the Enterprise Act 2002 s 19), which is expressed to be subject to the provisions of the Competition Act 1998 and Tribunal rules. As to time limits for making claims see PARA 16; and as to the enforcement of decisions of the Tribunal see PARA 15.
5 Ie a claim made under the Competition Act 1998 s 47A (see PARA 168).
6 Competition Act 1998 s 47B(3) (added by the Enterprise Act 2002 s 19). The provisions of the Competition Act 1998 s 47A(5)–(10) (see PARA 168) apply to a consumer claim included in proceedings under s 47B as they apply to a claim made in proceedings under s 47A: s 47B(5) (added by the Enterprise Act 2002 s 19).
7 Competition Act 1998 s 47B(4) (added by the Enterprise Act 2002 s 19).
8 Competition Act 1998 s 47B(6) (added by the Enterprise Act 2002 s 19).

170. Further appeals. An appeal lies to the Court of Appeal[1]: (1) from a decision of the Competition Appeal Tribunal[2] as to the amount of a penalty[3]; (2) from a decision of the Tribunal as to the award of damages or other sum in respect of a monetary claim before the Tribunal[4] or included in proceedings brought on behalf of consumers[5] (other than a decision on costs or expenses) or as to the amount of any such damages or other sum; and (3) on a point of law arising from any other decision of the Tribunal on an appeal[6]. An appeal may be brought by a party to the proceedings before the Tribunal or by a person who has a sufficient interest in the matter[7]. An appeal requires the permission of the Tribunal or the Court of Appeal[8].

1 See the Competition Act 1998 s 49(3) (substituted by the Enterprise Act 2002 s 21, Sch 5 paras 1, 4).
2 As to the Competition Appeal Tribunal see PARAS 13–17.
3 Ie under the Competition Act 1998 s 36 (see PARA 137). As to penalties see ss 36–41; and PARAS 137–139.
4 Ie made in proceedings under the Competition Act 1998 s 47A (see PARA 168).
5 Ie under the Competition Act 1998 s 47B (see PARA 169).
6 Competition Act 1998 s 49(1) (substituted by the Enterprise Act 2002 Sch 5 paras 1, 4). An appeal is made under the Competition Act 1998 s 46 or s 47 (see PARAS 166–167).
7 Competition Act 1998 s 49(2)(a) (substituted by the Enterprise Act 2002 Sch 5 paras 1, 4).
8 Competition Act 1998 s 49(2)(b) (substituted by the Enterprise Act 2002 Sch 5 paras 1, 4).

4. THE ENTERPRISE ACT 2002

(1) INTRODUCTION

171.   The Enterprise Act 2002. The Enterprise Act 2002 implemented the Government's intention to give more independence to the competition authorities, to reform the bankruptcy laws and to tackle trading practices that harm consumers[1].

Part 1 of the Enterprise Act 2002 establishes the Office of Fair Trading (the 'OFT')[2], sets out its general functions, and provides for arrangements for making super-complaints to the OFT[3]. Part 2 establishes and makes provisions for proceedings before the Competition Appeal Tribunal[4]. Part 3 provides for a new merger regime, the definition of a qualifying merger and the duty of the OFT to make references to the Competition Commission[5]; the determination of references; the procedures that relate to certain public interest cases and other special cases; powers of enforcement; undertakings and orders; and various supplementary matters, such as information and publicity requirements and powers to require information[6]. Part 4 makes provision for market investigations and sets out the power of the OFT and the Secretary of State[7] to make references to the Competition Commission, and how the Commission should report on the references. It provides for particular arrangements to apply in public interest cases, and also covers powers of enforcement and various supplementary matters[8]. Part 5 contains provisions relating to the Competition Commission, and provides for its rules of procedure[9]. Part 6 is concerned with cartel offences[10]. Part 7 deals with miscellaneous competition provisions, including powers to disqualify directors who engage in serious competition breaches[11]. There is also specific provision allowing changes to be made in the light of reform of Community competition law[12]. Part 8 sets out procedures for enforcing certain consumer legislation[13]. Part 9 governs the disclosure of information held by public authorities[14]. Part 10 introduces a new insolvency regime for company administration restricting the future use of administrative receivership; abolishes Crown preference; establishes a new regime for the insolvency of individuals; and makes changes to the operation of the Insolvency Services Account[15]. Supplementary provisions are contained in Part 11[16], including the power of the Secretary of State to provide financial assistance of consumer purposes[17] and financial provision generally[18].

1   See the White Papers *'Productivity and Enterprise: A World Class Competition Regime'* (Cm 5233) (July 2001), *'Productivity and Enterprise: Insolvency – A Second Chance'* (Cm 5234) (July 2001) and *'Modern Markets: Confident Consumers'* (Cm 4410) (July 1999).
2   As to the OFT see PARAS 6–8.
3   See the Enterprise Act 2002 Pt 1 (ss 1–11); and PARAS 6–8.
4   See the Enterprise Act 2002 Pt 2 (ss 12–21); and PARAS 13–17.
5   As to the Competition Commission see PARAS 9–12.
6   See the Enterprise Act 2002 Pt 3 (ss 22–130); and PARAS 172–275. The provisions of Pt 3 are modified in relation to mergers and merger references of water enterprises: see the Water Mergers (Modification of Enactments) Regulations 2004, SI 2004/3202; and WATER AND WATERWAYS vol 100 (2009) PARA 151. See also the disapplication of the Enterprise Act 2002 Pt 3 by the Bradford & Bingley plc Transfer of Securities and Property etc Order 2008, SI 2008/2546, art 40.
7   As to the Secretary of State see PARA 5.
8   See the Enterprise Act 2002 Pt 4 (ss 131–184); and PARAS 276–318.
9   See the Enterprise Act 2002 Pt 5 (ss 185–187); and PARAS 9–12.
10 See the Enterprise Act 2002 Pt 6 (ss 188–202); and PARAS 319–325.

11 See the Enterprise Act 2002 Pt 7 (ss 203–209). See further the Company Directors Disqualification Act 1986 ss 9A–9E (added by the Enterprise Act 2002 s 204); and COMPANIES vol 7(2) (2004 Reissue) PARAS 1705–1708.

12 The Secretary of State may by regulations make such modifications of the Competition Act 1998 as he considers appropriate for the purpose of eliminating or reducing any differences between: (1) the domestic provisions of the Competition Act 1998; and (2) European Community competition law, which result (or would otherwise result) from a relevant Community instrument made after the passing of the Enterprise Act 2002 (ie 7 November 2002): s 209(1). 'The domestic provisions of the Competition Act 1998' means the provisions of that Act so far as they do not implement or give effect to a relevant Community instrument; 'European Community competition law' includes any Act or subordinate legislation so far as it implements or gives effect to a relevant Community instrument; and 'relevant Community instrument' means a regulation or directive under the EC Treaty art 83: Enterprise Act 2002 s 209(2). As to the EC Treaty (ie the Treaty establishing the European Community (Rome, 25 March 1957; TS 1 (1973); Cmnd 5179)) see PARA 24 note 1. The Secretary of State may by regulations repeal or otherwise modify any provision of an Act (other than the Competition Act 1998) which excludes any matter from the Chapter I prohibition or the Chapter II prohibition (see PARA 115): Enterprise Act 2002 s 209(3). The power under s 209(3) may not be exercised before the power under s 209(1) has been exercised nor may it be used so as to extend the scope of any exclusion that is not being removed by the regulations: s 209(4). Regulations under s 209 may confer power to make subordinate legislation, may make such consequential, supplementary, incidental, transitory, transitional or saving provision as the Secretary of State considers appropriate (including provision modifying any Act or subordinate legislation) and may make different provision for different cases or circumstances: s 209(5). The power to make regulations under s 209 is exercisable by statutory instrument: s 209(6). No regulations may be made under s 209 unless a draft of them has been laid before and approved by a resolution of each House of Parliament: s 209(7). The restriction on powers to legislate in the European Communities Act 1972 Sch 2 para 1(1)(c) does not apply to regulations which implement or give effect to a relevant Community instrument made after 7 November 2002: Enterprise Act 2002 s 209(8). At the date at which this volume states the law no such regulations had been made.

13 See the Enterprise Act 2002 Pt 8 (ss 210–236); and PARAS 339–360.

14 See the Enterprise Act 2002 Pt 9 (ss 237–247); and PARAS 326–335.

15 See the Enterprise Act 2002 Pt 10 (ss 248–272), which replaces the Insolvency Act 1986 Pt II; and COMPANY AND PARTNERSHIP INSOLVENCY vol 7(3) (2004 Reissue) PARA 213 et seq.

16 See the Enterprise Act 2002 Pt 11 (ss 273–281).

17 The Secretary of State may give financial assistance to any person for the purpose of assisting: (1) activities which the Secretary of State considers are of benefit to consumers; or (2) the provision of (a) advice or information about consumer matters; (b) educational materials relating to consumer matters; or (c) advice or information to the Secretary of State in connection with the formulation of policy in respect of consumer matters: Enterprise Act 2002 s 274.

18 There is to be paid out of money provided by Parliament: (1) any expenditure incurred by the OFT, the Secretary of State, any other minister of the Crown or a government department by virtue of the Enterprise Act 2002; and (2) any increase attributable to the Enterprise Act 2002 in the sums payable out of money so provided by virtue of any other Act: Enterprise Act 2002 s 275.

(2) MERGERS

(i) Duty to make References

A. COMPLETED MERGERS

172. Duty to make references. The Office of Fair Trading (the 'OFT')[1] must make a reference to the Competition Commission[2] if the OFT believes that it is or may be the case that: (1) a relevant merger situation[3] has been created[4]; and (2) the creation of that situation has resulted, or may be expected to result, in a substantial lessening of competition within any market or markets in the United Kingdom[5] for goods or services[6].

The OFT may decide not to make a reference if it believes that the market concerned is not, or the markets concerned are not, of sufficient importance to justify the making of a reference to the Commission[7], or any relevant customer benefits[8] in relation to the creation of the relevant merger situation concerned outweigh the substantial lessening of competition concerned and any adverse effects of the substantial lessening of competition concerned[9].

No reference is to be made by the OFT if:

(a)   an undertaking or merger notice has been given[10];

(b)   the OFT is considering whether to accept undertakings[11] instead of making such a reference[12];

(c)   the relevant merger situation concerned is being, or has been, dealt with in connection with a reference of an anticipated merger[13];

(d)   an intervention notice[14] is in force in relation to the matter or the matter to which such a notice relates has been finally determined[15];

(e)   the European Commission is considering a request made, in relation to the matter concerned, by the United Kingdom (whether alone or with others)[16], is proceeding with the matter in pursuance of such a request or has dealt with the matter in pursuance of such a request[17]; or

(f)   a reasoned submission requesting referral to the European Commission has been submitted[18] to the European Commission[19].

A reference must, in particular, specify the enactment[20] under which it is made and the date on which it is made[21]. Specific provision is made regarding the primacy of Community law in relation to such references[22].

1   As to the OFT see PARAS 6–8. As to the power of the Secretary of State to give an intervention notice to the OFT see PARAS 189, 204. As to the Secretary of State see PARA 5.
2   As to the Competition Commission see PARAS 9–12.
3   See PARA 173.
4   The references to the creation of a relevant merger situation are to be construed in accordance with the Enterprise Act 2002 s 23 (see PARA 173): s 22(5).
5   In the Enterprise Act 2002 Pt 3 (ss 22–130), 'market in the United Kingdom' includes: (1) so far as it operates in the United Kingdom or a part of the United Kingdom, any market which operates there and in another country or territory or in a part of another country or territory; and (2) any market which operates only in a part of the United Kingdom; and references to a market for goods or services include references to a market for goods and services: ss 22(6), 130. As to the meaning of 'United Kingdom' see PARA 401 note 1. 'Goods' includes buildings and other structures, and also includes ships, aircraft and hovercraft: ss 129(1), 130. 'Supply', in relation to the supply of goods, includes supply by way of sale, lease, hire or hire-purchase, and, in relation to buildings or other structures, includes the construction of them by a person for another person: ss 129(1), 130. References in Pt 3 to the supply of services are to be construed in accordance with s 128; and references in Pt 3 to a market for services and other related expressions are to be construed accordingly: ss 128(1), 130. The supply of services does not include the provision of services under a contract of service or of apprenticeship whether it is express or implied and (if it is express) whether it is oral or in writing: s 128(2). The supply of services includes: (a) performing for gain or reward any activity other than the supply of goods; (b) rendering services to order; (c) the provision of services by making them available to potential users: s 128(3). The supply of services includes making arrangements for the use of computer software or for granting access to data stored in any form which is not readily accessible: s 128(4). The supply of services includes making arrangements by means of a relevant agreement (within the meaning of the Telecommunications Act 1984 Sch 2 para 29 (see TELECOMMUNICATIONS AND BROADCASTING vol 45(1) (2005 Reissue) PARA 155)) for sharing the use of telecommunications apparatus: Enterprise Act 2002 s 128(5) (amended by the Communications Act 2003 s 406(1), Sch 17 para 174(1), (3)). The supply of services includes permitting or making arrangements to permit the use of land in such circumstances as the Secretary of State may by order specify: Enterprise Act 2002 s 128(6). In exercise of this power, the Secretary of State has made the Enterprise Act 2002 (Supply of Services) Order 2003, SI 2003/1594.

6   Enterprise Act 2002 s 22(1). The decision of the OFT not to refer a merger can be challenged: see eg Case 1023/4/1/03 *IBA Health Ltd v Office of Fair Trading* [2003] CAT 27, [2004] CompAR 235; on appeal *Office of Fair Trading v IBA Health Ltd* [2004] EWCA Civ 142, [2004] 4 All ER 1103, [2004] All ER (D) 312 (Feb) (a case under the Enterprise Act 2002 s 33 (reference of anticipated mergers (see PARA 182))).

7   Enterprise Act 2002 s 22(2)(a). See eg OFT Press Release 16/08, 4 February 2008.

8   The reference to relevant consumer benefits is to be construed in accordance with the Enterprise Act 2002 s 30 (see PARA 180): s 22(5).

9   Enterprise Act 2002 s 22(2)(b).

10 Enterprise Act 2002 s 22(3)(a) (amended by the Communications Act 2003 s 406(7), Sch 19(1)). For this purpose, an undertaking may be given under the Enterprise Act 2002 s 74(1) (see PARA 218) or Sch 7 para 4 (see PARA 229) and a merger notice may be given under s 96(3) (see PARA 250).

11 Ie under the Enterprise Act 2002 s 73 (see PARA 217).

12 Enterprise Act 2002 s 22(3)(b).

13 Enterprise Act 2002 s 22(3)(c). A reference of anticipated merger is made under s 33 (see PARA 182).

14 Ie a notice under the Enterprise Act 2002 s 42(2) (see PARA 189).

15 Enterprise Act 2002 s 22(3)(d) (amended by SI 2004/1079). A notice under the Enterprise Act 2002 s 42(2) (see PARA 189) is determined under Pt 3 Ch 2 (ss 42–58A) (see PARA 189 et seq) otherwise than in circumstances in which a notice is then given to the OFT under s 56(1) (see PARA 202). The reference to a matter to which a notice under s 42(2) relates being finally determined under Ch 2 is to be construed in accordance with s 43(4), (5) (see PARA 190): s 22(5).

16 Ie under EC Council Regulation 139/2004 (OJ L24, 29.1.2004, p 1) (the 'EC Merger Regulation') art 22(1) (see PARA 76).

17 Enterprise Act 2002 s 22(3)(e) (amended by SI 2004/1079).

18 Ie under the EC Merger Regulation art 4(5) (see PARA 76).

19 Enterprise Act 2002 s 22(3)(f) (added by SI 2004/1079). This provision ceases to apply if the OFT is informed that a member state competent to examine the concentration under its national competition law has, within the time permitted by the EC Merger Regulation art 4(5), expressed its disagreement as regards the request to refer the case to the European Commission; and this provision is to be construed in accordance with that Regulation: Enterprise Act 2002 s 22(3A) (added by SI 2004/1079).

20 'Enactment' includes an Act of the Scottish Parliament, Northern Ireland legislation and an enactment comprised in subordinate legislation, and includes an enactment whenever passed or made: Enterprise Act 2002 ss 129(1), 130. 'Subordinate legislation' has the same meaning as in the Interpretation Act 1978 (see STATUTES vol 44(1) (Reissue) PARA 1232) and also includes an instrument made under an Act of the Scottish Parliament and an instrument made under Northern Ireland legislation: Enterprise Act 2002 ss 129(1), 130.

21 Enterprise Act 2002 s 22(4).

22 'Community law' means (1) all the rights, powers, liabilities, obligations and restrictions from time to time created or arising by or under the Community Treaties; and (2) all the remedies and procedures from time to time provided for by or under the Community Treaties: Enterprise Act 2002 s 129(1). The duty to make a reference under the Enterprise Act 2002 s 22 applies in a case in which the relevant enterprises ceased to be distinct enterprises at a time or in circumstances not falling within s 24 (see PARA 174) if the following condition is satisfied: s 122(3). The condition is that, because of the EC Merger Regulation or anything done under or in accordance with it, the reference could not have been made earlier than four months before the date on which it is to be made: see Enterprise Act 2002 s 122(4), (5).

173.   Relevant merger situations. For the purposes of the statutory provisions relating to mergers[1], a relevant merger situation has been created if two or more enterprises[2] have ceased to be distinct enterprises[3] at a specified time or in specified circumstances[4] and the value of the turnover in the United Kingdom[5] of the enterprise being taken over exceeds £70 million[6].

A relevant merger situation has also been created if two or more enterprises have ceased to be distinct enterprises at a specified time or in specified circumstances[7] and, as a result, one or both of the following conditions prevails or prevails to a greater extent[8]. The first condition is that, in relation to the supply of goods[9] of any description, at least one-quarter[10] of all the goods of that description which are supplied in the United Kingdom, or in a substantial part of the United Kingdom are supplied by one and the same person or are supplied to one and the same person, or are supplied by the persons by whom the enterprises concerned are carried on, or are supplied to those persons[11]. The second condition is that, in relation to the supply of services of any description, the supply of services of that description in the United Kingdom, or in a substantial part of the United Kingdom, is to the extent of at least one-quarter, supply by one and the same person, or supply for one and the same person or supply by the persons by whom the enterprises concerned are carried on, or supply for those persons[12].

In relation to the duty to make references[13], the question whether a relevant merger situation has been created is to be determined immediately before the time when the reference has been, or is to be, made[14].

1 Ie the Enterprise Act 2002 Pt 3 (ss 22–130).
2 'Enterprise' means the activities, or part of the activities, of a business: Enterprise Act 2002 ss 129(1), 130. 'Business' includes a professional practice and includes any other undertaking which is carried on for gain or reward or which is an undertaking in the course of which goods or services are supplied otherwise than free of charge: ss 129(1), 130. As to the meanings of 'goods', 'supply of goods' and 'supply of services' see PARA 172 note 5. See also note 9.
3 As to enterprises ceasing to be distinct enterprises see PARA 176.
4 Ie time limits and circumstances falling within the Enterprise Act 2002 s 24 (see PARA 174).
5 As to the meaning of 'United Kingdom' see PARA 401 note 1.
6 Enterprise Act 2002 s 23(1). As to the turnover test see PARA 178.
7 Enterprise Act 2002 s 23(2)(a). See note 4.
8 Enterprise Act 2002 s 23(2)(b). The Secretary of State may by order amend or replace the conditions which determine for the purposes of Pt 3 whether a relevant merger situation has been created: s 123(1). As to the Secretary of State see PARA 5. The Secretary of State is not permitted to exercise this power to amend or replace the conditions mentioned in s 23(1) (see the text to notes 1–6) or to amend or replace the condition mentioned in s 23(2)(a) (see the text and note 7): s 123(2). In exercising his power to amend or replace the condition mentioned in s 23(2)(b) or any condition which for the time being applies instead of it, the Secretary of State must, in particular, have regard to the desirability of ensuring that any amended or new condition continues to operate by reference to the degree of commercial strength which results from the enterprises concerned having ceased to be distinct: s 123(3). Before making such an order, the Secretary of State must consult the Office of Fair Trading (the 'OFT') and the Competition Commission: s 123(4). As to the OFT see PARAS 6–8; and as to the Competition Commission see PARAS 9–12. An order may provide for the delegation of functions to the decision-making authority: s 123(5). 'Decision-making authority' means: (1) in the case of a reference or possible reference under s 22 (see PARA 172) or s 33 (see PARA 182), the OFT or (as the case may be) the Competition Commission; and (2) in the case of a notice or possible notice from the Secretary of State under s 42(2) (see PARA 189) or s 59(2) (see PARA 204) or a reference or possible reference under s 45 (see PARA 193) or s 62 (see PARA 208), the OFT, the Commission or the Secretary of State: s 22(7).
9 References in the Enterprise Act 2002 s 23(3), (4) to the supply of goods or services, in relation to goods or services of any description which are the subject of different forms of supply, are to be construed in whichever of the following ways the decision-making authority considers appropriate: (1) as references to any of those forms of supply taken separately; (2) as references to all those forms of supply taken together; or (3) as references to any of those forms of supply taken in groups: s 23(6). For the purposes of s 23(6), the decision-making authority may treat goods or services as being the subject of different forms of supply whenever: (a) the transactions concerned differ as to their nature, their parties, their terms or their surrounding circumstances; and (b) the difference is one which, in the opinion of the decision-making authority, ought for the purposes of that provision to be treated as a material difference: s 23(7). The criteria for deciding when goods or services can be treated, for these purposes, as goods or services of a separate description are to be such as in any particular case the decision-making authority considers appropriate in the circumstances of that case: s 23(8).
10 For the purpose of deciding whether the proportion of one-quarter mentioned in the Enterprise Act 2002 s 23(3), (4) is fulfilled with respect to goods or services of any description, the

decision-making authority must apply such criterion (whether value, cost, price, quantity, capacity, number of workers employed or some other criterion, of whatever nature), or such combination of criteria, as the decision-making authority considers appropriate: s 23(5).

11 Enterprise Act 2002 s 23(3).
12 Enterprise Act 2002 s 23(4). See also note 10.
13 Ie for the purposes of the Enterprise Act 2002 Pt 3 Ch 1 (ss 22–41).
14 Enterprise Act 2002 s 23(9)(b). In the case of a reference which is treated as having been made under s 22 (see PARA 172) by virtue of s 37(2) (see PARA 185), the question whether a relevant merger situation has been created is to be determined as at such time as the Competition Commission may determine: s 23(9)(a).

174. Time limits and prior notice. For the purpose of deciding on relevant merger situations[1], two or more enterprises have ceased to be distinct enterprises[2] at a time or in circumstances falling within the following provisions if the two or more enterprises ceased to be distinct enterprises before the day on which the reference relating to them is to be made and did so not more than four months before that day[3]. They also cease to be distinct enterprises if notice[4] of material facts about the arrangements or transactions under or in consequence of which the enterprises have ceased to be distinct enterprises has not been given correctly[5]. Notice of material facts is given correctly if: (1) it is given to the Office of Fair Trading (the 'OFT')[6] prior to the entering into of the arrangements or transactions concerned or the facts are made public[7] prior to the entering into of those arrangements or transactions; or (2) it is given to the OFT, or the facts are made public, more than four months before the day on which the reference is to be made[8].

1 Ie for the purposes of the Enterprise Act 2002 s 23 (see PARA 173).
2 As to the meaning of 'enterprise' see PARA 173 note 2. As to enterprises ceasing to be distinct see PARA 176.
3 Enterprise Act 2002 s 24(1)(a). As to the extension of time limits see PARA 175.
4 For this purpose, 'notice' includes notice which is not in writing: Enterprise Act 2002 s 24(3).
5 Enterprise Act 2002 s 24(1)(b).
6 As to the OFT see PARAS 6–8.
7 'Made public' means so publicised as to be generally known or readily ascertainable: Enterprise Act 2002 s 24(3).
8 Enterprise Act 2002 s 24(2).

175. Extension of time limits. The Office of Fair Trading (the 'OFT')[1] and the persons carrying on the enterprises which have or may have ceased to be distinct enterprises[2] may agree to extend by no more than 20 days the four month time limit for determining the matter[3].

The OFT may by notice[4] to the persons carrying on the enterprises which have or may have ceased to be distinct enterprises extend the four month period[5] if it considers that any of those persons has failed to provide, within the period stated in a notice[6] and in the manner authorised or required, information requested of him in that notice[7]. Such an extension is for the period beginning with the end of the period within which the information is to be provided and which is stated in the notice[8] and ending with the provision of the information to the satisfaction of the OFT or, if earlier, the cancellation by the OFT of the extension[9].

The OFT may by notice to the persons carrying on the enterprises which have or may have ceased to be distinct enterprises extend the four month period if it is seeking undertakings from any of those persons[10]. The OFT may also by notice to such persons extend the four month period if the European Commission is considering a request made, in relation to the matter concerned, by the United

Kingdom[11], whether alone or with others, for referral to the Commission[12], but is not yet proceeding with the matter in pursuance of such a request[13].

Where the four month period is extended or further extended by virtue of the provisions set out above in relation to a particular case, any reference to that period[14] has effect in relation to that case as if it were a reference to a period equivalent to the aggregate of the period being extended and the period of the extension, whether or not those periods overlap in time[15].

1　As to the OFT see PARAS 6–8.
2　As to the meaning of 'enterprise' see PARA 173 note 2. As to enterprises ceasing to be distinct see PARA 176. The Secretary of State may make regulations for the purposes of the Enterprise Act 2002 s 25: s 32(1). At the date at which this volume states the law no such regulations had been made. Regulations may provide that a person is, or is not, to be treated, in such circumstances as may be specified in the regulations, as acting on behalf of a person carrying on an enterprise which has or may have ceased to be a distinct enterprise: s 32(1), (2)(e).
3　Enterprise Act 2002 s 25(1). The four month time limit is that mentioned in s 24(1)(a) or s 24(2)(b) (see PARA 174). No more than one extension is possible under s 25(1): s 25(12).
　　In determining for the purposes of s 25(1), (5)(b) (see note 10 head (2)), s 32(3) (see note 7) any period which is expressed in the enactment concerned as a period of days or number of days no account is to be taken of Saturday, Sunday, Good Friday and Christmas Day and any day which is a bank holiday in England and Wales: s 32(4).
4　'Notice' means notice in writing: Enterprise Act 2002 ss 129(1), 130.
5　See note 3.
6　Ie a notice under the Enterprise Act 2002 s 31 (see PARA 181).
7　Enterprise Act 2002 s 25(2). A notice under s 25(2) must be given within five days of the end of the period within which the information is to be provided and which is stated in the notice under s 31 (see PARA 181) and must inform the person to whom it is addressed of the OFT's opinion as mentioned in s 25(2) and the OFT's intention to extend the period for considering whether to make a reference: s 32(3).
8　See note 6.
9　Enterprise Act 2002 s 25(3). Regulations may: (1) provide for the manner in which any information requested by the OFT under s 31 (see PARA 181) is authorised or required to be provided, and the time at which such information is to be treated as provided (including the time at which it is to be treated as provided to the satisfaction of the OFT for the purposes of s 25(3)); (2) provide for the persons carrying on the enterprises which have or may have ceased to be distinct enterprises to be informed, in circumstances in which s 25(3) applies (a) of the fact that the OFT is satisfied as to the provision of the information requested by it or (as the case may be) of the OFT's decision to cancel the extension; and (b) of the time at which the OFT is to be treated as so satisfied or (as the case may be) of the time at which the cancellation is to be treated as having effect: s 32(1), (2)(b).
10　Enterprise Act 2002 s 25(4). Undertakings in lieu of references are sought under s 73 (see PARA 217). An extension under s 25(4) is for the period beginning with the receipt of the notice under that provision and ending with the earliest of the following events: (1) the giving of the undertakings concerned; (2) the expiry of the period of ten days beginning with the first day after the receipt by the OFT of a notice from the person who has been given a notice under s 25(4) and from whom the undertakings are being sought stating that he does not intend to give the undertakings; or (3) the cancellation by the OFT of the extension: s 25(5). See note 3. Regulations may provide for the persons carrying on the enterprises which have or may have ceased to be distinct enterprises to be informed, in circumstances in which s 25(5) applies, of the OFT's decision to cancel the extension and of the time at which the cancellation is to be treated as having effect: s 32(1), (2)(c). Regulations may also provide for the time at which any notice under s 25(4), (5)(b) (see head (2)), (6) or (8) (see note 13) is to be treated as received: s 32(1), (2)(d).
11　As to the meaning of 'United Kingdom' see PARA 401 note 1.
12　Ie under EC Council Regulation 139/2004 (OJ L24, 29.1.2004, p 1) (the 'EC Merger Regulation') (see PARA 74).
13　Enterprise Act 2002 s 25(6) (amended by SI 2004/1079). An extension under the Enterprise Act 2002 s 25(6) is for the period beginning with the receipt of the notice under that provision and ending with the receipt of a notice given by the OFT to inform the persons carrying on the enterprises which have or may have ceased to be distinct enterprises of the completion by the European Commission of its consideration of the request of the United Kingdom: s 25(7), (8).

14 Ie in the Enterprise Act 2002 s 24 (see PARA 174) or s 25(1)–(8) (see the text and notes 1–13).

15 Enterprise Act 2002 s 25(9). However, where: (1) the four month period is further extended; (2) the further extension and at least one previous extension is made under one or more of s 25(2), (4) and (6); and (3) the same days or fractions of days are included in or comprise the further extension and are included in or comprise at least one such previous extension then, in calculating the period of the further extension, any days or fractions of days of the kind mentioned in head (3) are to be disregarded: s 25(10), (11).

176. Enterprises ceasing to be distinct enterprises.

For the purposes of deciding on relevant merger situations[1], any two enterprises cease to be distinct enterprises[2] if they are brought under common ownership or common control, whether or not the business to which either of them formerly belonged continues to be carried on under the same or different ownership or control[3].

Enterprises are, in particular, treated as being under common control if they are: (1) enterprises of interconnected bodies corporate; (2) enterprises carried on by two or more bodies corporate of which one and the same person or group of persons has control; or (3) an enterprise carried on by a body corporate and an enterprise carried on by a person or group of persons having control of that body corporate[4].

A person or group of persons able, directly or indirectly, to control or materially to influence the policy of a body corporate, or the policy of any person in carrying on an enterprise but without having a controlling interest in that body corporate or in that enterprise, may, for these purposes, be treated as having control of it[5]. Associated persons[6], and any bodies corporate[7] which they or any of them control, are to be treated as one person for the purpose of deciding whether any two enterprises have been brought under common ownership or common control[8].

1 Ie for the purposes of the Enterprise Act 2002 s 23 (see PARA 173).

2 As to the meaning of 'enterprise' see PARA 173 note 2. As to when enterprises cease to be distinct see PARA 177.

3 Enterprise Act 2002 s 26(1). For the purposes of s 26(1), in so far as it relates to bringing two or more enterprises under common control, a person or group of persons may be treated as bringing an enterprise under his or their control if: (1) being already able to control or materially to influence the policy of the person carrying on the enterprise, that person or group of persons acquires a controlling interest in the enterprise or, in the case of an enterprise carried on by a body corporate, acquires a controlling interest in that body corporate; or (2) being already able materially to influence the policy of the person carrying on the enterprise, that person or group of persons becomes able to control that policy: s 26(4).

4 Enterprise Act 2002 s 26(2).

5 Enterprise Act 2002 s 26(3).

6 For this purpose: (1) any individual and that individual's spouse, civil partner or partner and any relative, or spouse, civil partner or partner of a relative, of that individual or of that individual's spouse, civil partner or partner; (2) any person in his capacity as trustee of a settlement and the settlor or grantor and any person associated with the settlor or grantor; (3) persons carrying on business in partnership and the spouse, civil partner or partner and relatives of any of them; or (4) two or more persons acting together to secure or exercise control of a body of persons corporate or unincorporate or to secure control of any enterprise or assets, are to be regarded as associated with one another: Enterprise Act 2002 s 127(4) (amended by the Civil Partnership Act 2004 s 261(1), Sch 27 para 168). 'Relative' means a brother, sister, uncle, aunt, nephew, niece, lineal ancestor or descendant (the stepchild of any person, or anyone adopted by a person, whether legally or otherwise, as his child being regarded as a relative or taken into account to trace a relationship in the same way as that person's child); and references to a spouse, civil partner or partner includes a former spouse, civil partner or partner: Enterprise Act 2002 s 127(6) (amended by the Civil Partnership Act 2004 Sch 27 para 168).

A reference under the Enterprise Act 2002 s 22 (see PARA 172), s 33 (see PARA 182), s 45 (see PARA 193) or s 62 (see PARA 208) (whether or not made by virtue of s 127) may be framed so as to exclude from consideration, either altogether or for a specified purpose or to a specified extent, any matter which would otherwise not have been taken into account on that reference: s 127(3).

7   The reference in the text to bodies corporate which associated persons control is to be construed in accordance with the Enterprise Act 2002 s 26(3), (4) (see the text and notes 3, 5): s 127(5).

8   Enterprise Act 2002 s 127(1)(a). This does not exclude from s 26 (see the text and notes 1–5) any case which would otherwise fall within that provision: s 127(2).

177.   Time when enterprises cease to be distinct.   In relation to any arrangements or transaction not having immediate effect or having immediate effect only in part but under or in consequence of which any two enterprises cease to be distinct enterprises[1], the time when the parties to any such arrangements or transaction become bound to such extent as will result, on effect being given to their obligations, in the enterprises ceasing to be distinct enterprises is taken to be the time at which the two enterprises cease to be distinct enterprises[2]. Accordingly, no account is to be taken of any option or other conditional right until the option is exercised or the condition is satisfied[3].

Where there are successive events: (1) which occur within a period of two years under or in consequence of the same arrangements or transaction, or successive arrangements or transactions between the same parties or interests; and (2) by virtue of each of which, under or in consequence of the arrangements or the transaction or transactions concerned, any enterprises cease as between themselves to be distinct enterprises[4], the decision-making authority[5] may, for the purposes of a reference, treat the successive events as having occurred simultaneously on the date on which the latest of them occurred[6]. The decision-making authority may treat such arrangements or transactions as the decision-making authority considers appropriate as arrangements or transactions between the same interests[7].

1   As to the meaning of 'enterprise' see PARA 173 note 2. As to enterprises ceasing to be distinct see PARA 176.

2   Enterprise Act 2002 s 27(1), (2). The provisions of s 27(1)–(3) are subject to s 27(5)–(8) (see the text and notes 4–7) and s 29 (see PARA 179): s 27(4).

3   See the Enterprise Act 2002 s 27(3). See note 2.

4   Enterprise Act 2002 s 27(6).

5   As to the meaning of 'decision-making authority' see PARA 173 note 8.

6   Enterprise Act 2002 s 27(5).

7   Enterprise Act 2002 s 27(7). In deciding whether it is appropriate to treat arrangements or transactions as arrangements or transactions between the same interests the decision-making authority must, in particular, have regard to the persons substantially concerned in the arrangements or transactions concerned: s 27(8).

178.   Turnover test.   For the purposes of determining relevant merger situations[1] the value of the turnover in the United Kingdom[2] of the enterprise[3] being taken over is to be determined by taking the total value of the turnover in the United Kingdom of the enterprises which cease to be distinct enterprises[4] and deducting: (1) the turnover in the United Kingdom of any enterprise which continues to be carried on under the same ownership and control; or (2) if no enterprise continues to be carried on under the same ownership and control, the turnover in the United Kingdom which, of all the turnovers concerned, is the turnover of the highest value[5].

The turnover in the United Kingdom of an enterprise is be determined in accordance with such provisions as may be specified in an order made by the Secretary of State[6]. An order may, in particular, make provision as to: (a) the amounts which are, or which are not, to be treated as comprising an enterprise's turnover; (b) the date or dates by reference to which an enterprise's turnover is to be determined; (c) the connection with the United Kingdom by virtue of which an enterprise's turnover is turnover in the United Kingdom[7]. An order may, in particular, make provision enabling the decision-making authority[8] to determine matters of a description specified in the order[9].

The Office of Fair Trading (the 'OFT')[10] must keep under review the sum set[11] for the value of turnover and from time to time advise the Secretary of State as to whether the sum is still appropriate[12]. The Secretary of State may by order alter the sum[13].

1   Ie for the purposes of the Enterprise Act 2002 s 23 (see PARA 173).
2   As to the meaning of 'United Kingdom' see PARA 401 note 1.
3   As to the meaning of 'enterprise' see PARA 173 note 2.
4   As to enterprises ceasing to be distinct see PARA 176.
5   Enterprise Act 2002 s 28(1).
6   Enterprise Act 2002 s 28(2). This determination applies for the purposes of Pt 3 (ss 22–130) (other than s 121(4)(c)(ii) (see PARA 272)). As to the Secretary of State see PARA 5.
7   Enterprise Act 2002 s 28(3). See the Enterprise Act 2002 (Merger Fees and Determination of Turnover) Order 2003, SI 2003/1370, art 11 (amended by SI 2004/3204).
8   As to the meaning of 'decision-making authority' see PARA 173 note 8.
9   Enterprise Act 2002 s 28(4). This may include any of the matters mentioned in heads (a)–(c) in the text: s 28(4).
10 As to the OFT see PARAS 6–8.
11 Ie the sum mentioned in the Enterprise Act 2002 s 23(1)(b) (see PARA 173).
12 Enterprise Act 2002 s 28(5).
13 Enterprise Act 2002 s 28(6).

179. Obtaining control by stages. Where an enterprise[1] is brought under the control[2] of a person or group of persons in the course of a series of two or more transactions which (1) enable that person or group of persons directly or indirectly to control or materially to influence the policy of any person carrying on the enterprise or to do so to a greater degree or is a direct or indirect step towards doing so[3]; or (2) by virtue of which that person or group of persons acquires a controlling interest in the enterprise or, where the enterprise is carried on by a body corporate, in that body corporate[4], then those transactions may, if the decision-making authority[5] considers it appropriate, be treated for the purposes of a reference as having occurred simultaneously on the date on which the latest of them occurred[6].

Where the period within which a series of transactions occurs exceeds two years, the transactions that may be treated as having occurred simultaneously are any of those transactions that occur within a period of two years[7]. In determining the time at which any transaction occurs, no account is to be taken of any option or other conditional right until the option is exercised or the condition is satisfied[8].

1   As to the meaning of 'enterprise' see PARA 173 note 2.
2   The provisions of the Enterprise Act 2002 s 26(2)–(4) and s 127(1), (2), (4)–(6) (see PARA 176) apply for these purposes to determine: (1) whether an enterprise is brought under the control of a person or group of persons; and (2) whether a transaction is one to which s 29(2) applies (see the text and notes 4–6), as they apply for the purposes of s 26 to determine whether enterprises are brought under common control: s 29(5).
3   Enterprise Act 2002 s 29(2)(a).
4   Enterprise Act 2002 s 29(2)(b). Where a series of transactions includes a transaction falling within s 29(2)(b), any transaction occurring after the occurrence of that transaction is to be disregarded for the purposes of s 29(1): s 29(3).
5   As to the meaning of 'decision-making authority' see PARA 173 note 8.
6   Enterprise Act 2002 s 29(1), (2).

7   Enterprise Act 2002 s 29(4).
8   Enterprise Act 2002 s 29(6).

180.   Relevant customer benefits.   For the purposes of the provisions relating to the referral of mergers[1], a benefit is a relevant customer benefit if it is a benefit to relevant customers[2] in the form of lower prices, higher quality or greater choice of goods[3] or services in any market in the United Kingdom[4], whether or not the market or markets in which the substantial lessening of competition concerned has, or may have, occurred or, as the case may be, may occur[5], or in the form of greater innovation in relation to such goods or services[6]. In addition, it is necessary that the decision-making authority[7] believes either: (1) the benefit has accrued as a result of the creation of the relevant merger situation concerned or may be expected to accrue within a reasonable period as a result of the creation of that situation and the benefit was, or is, unlikely to accrue without the creation of that situation or a similar lessening of competition[8]; or (2) that the benefit may be expected to accrue within a reasonable period as a result of the creation of the relevant merger situation concerned and the benefit is unlikely to accrue without the creation of that situation or a similar lessening of competition[9].

1   Ie for the purposes of the Enterprise Act 2002 Pt 3 (ss 22–130) (see PARAS 172–179, 181 et seq).
2   'Relevant customers' means: (1) customers of any person carrying on an enterprise which, in the creation of the relevant merger situation concerned, has ceased to be, or (as the case may be) will cease to be, a distinct enterprise; (2) customers of such customers; and (3) any other customers in a chain of customers beginning with the customers mentioned in head (1); and 'customers' includes future customers: Enterprise Act 2002 s 30(4). As to the meaning of 'enterprise' see PARA 173 note 2. As to enterprises ceasing to be distinct see PARA 176. 'Customer' includes a customer who is not a consumer: ss 129(1), 130. 'Consumer' means any person who is: (a) a person to whom goods are or are sought to be supplied (whether by way of sale or otherwise) in the course of a business carried on by the person supplying or seeking to supply them; or (b) a person for whom services are or are sought to be supplied in the course of a business carried on by the person supplying or seeking to supply them; and who does not receive or seek to receive the goods or services in the course of a business carried on by him: ss 129(1), 130.
3   As to the meaning of 'goods' see PARA 172 note 5.
4   As to the meaning of 'market in the United Kingdom' see PARA 172 note 5. As to the meaning of 'United Kingdom' see PARA 401 note 1.
5   Enterprise Act 2002 s 30(1)(a).
6   Enterprise Act 2002 s 30(1)(b).
7   As to the meaning of 'decision-making authority' see PARA 173 note 8.
8   Enterprise Act 2002 s 30(1)(b)(i), (2). The decision-making authority must hold this belief in the case of a reference or possible reference under s 22 (see PARA 172) or s 45(2) (see PARA 193).
9   Enterprise Act 2002 s 30(1)(b)(ii), (3). The decision-making authority must hold this belief in the case of a reference or possible reference under s 33 (see PARA 182) or s 45(4) (see PARA 193).

181.   Information powers in relation to completed mergers.   The Office of Fair Trading (the 'OFT')[1] may by notice[2] to any of the persons carrying on the enterprises[3] which have or may have ceased to be distinct enterprises[4] request him to provide the OFT with such information as the OFT may require for the purpose of deciding whether to make a reference to the Competition Commission[5]. The notice must state the information required, the period within which the information is to be provided and the possible consequences of not providing the information within the stated period and in the authorised or required manner[6].

1   As to the OFT see PARAS 6–8.
2   As to the meaning of 'notice' see PARA 175 note 4.
3   As to the meaning of 'enterprise' see PARA 173 note 2.
4   As to enterprises ceasing to be distinct see PARA 176.

5   Enterprise Act 2002 s 31(1). A reference is made under s 22 (see PARA 172). As to the
    Competition Commission see PARAS 9–12. The Secretary of State may make regulations for the
    purposes of s 31: see s 32(1); and PARA 175. At the date at which this volume states the law no
    such regulations had been made.
6   Enterprise Act 2002 s 31(2).

B. ANTICIPATED MERGERS

182.   Duty to make references.   The Office of Fair Trading (the 'OFT')[1] must
make a reference to the Competition Commission[2] if the OFT believes that it is
or may be the case that: (1) arrangements are in progress or in contemplation
which, if carried into effect, will result in the creation of a relevant merger
situation[3]; and (2) the creation of that situation may be expected to result in a
substantial lessening of competition within any market or markets in the United
Kingdom[4] for goods[5] or services[6]. However, the OFT may decide not to make a
reference if it believes that the market concerned is not, or the markets concerned
are not, of sufficient importance to justify the making of a reference to the
Commission[7], the arrangements concerned are not sufficiently far advanced, or
are not sufficiently likely to proceed, to justify the making of a reference to the
Commission[8] or any relevant customer benefits[9] in relation to the creation of the
relevant merger situation[10] concerned outweigh the substantial lessening of
competition concerned and any adverse effects of the substantial lessening of
competition concerned[11]. In addition, a reference may be prohibited by statute[12].

A reference must, in particular, specify the enactment under which it is made
and the date on which it is made[13].

The Secretary of State[14] may make further provision by order in relation to
arrangements which are in progress or contemplation[15].

1   As to the OFT see PARAS 6–8.
2   As to the Competition Commission see PARAS 9–12.
3   Enterprise Act 2002 s 33(1)(a). As to the meaning of 'relevant merger situation' see PARA 173.
4   As to the meaning of 'market in the United Kingdom' see PARA 172 note 5. As to the meaning of
    'United Kingdom' see PARA 401 note 1.
5   As to the meaning of 'goods' see PARA 172 note 5.
6   Enterprise Act 2002 s 33(1)(b).
7   Enterprise Act 2002 s 33(2)(a).
8   Enterprise Act 2002 s 33(2)(b).
9   As to the meaning of 'relevant customer benefits' see PARA 180.
10 As to the meaning of 'relevant merger situation' see PARA 173.
11 Enterprise Act 2002 s 33(2)(c).
12 See the Enterprise Act 2002 s 33(3) (amended by the Communications Act 2003 s 406(7),
    Sch 19(1); and SI 2004/1079), which provides that no reference may be made if:
    (1)   the making of the reference is prevented by the Enterprise Act 2002 s 74(1) (see PARA
          218) or s 96(3) (see PARA 250) or Sch 7 para 4 (see PARA 229);
    (2)   the OFT is considering whether to accept undertakings under s 73 (see PARA 217)
          instead of making such a reference;
    (3)   the arrangements concerned are being, or have been, dealt with in connection with a
          reference made under s 22 (see PARA 172);
    (4)   an intervention notice under s 42(2) (see PARA 189) is in force in relation to the matter
          or the matter to which such a notice relates has been finally determined under the
          provisions relating to public interest cases (ie Pt 3 Ch 2 (ss 42–58A)) otherwise than in
          circumstances in which a notice is then given to the OFT under s 56(1) (see PARA 202);
    (5)   the European Commission is considering a request made, in relation to the matter
          concerned, by the United Kingdom (whether alone or with others) under EC Council
          Regulation 139/2004 (OJ L24, 29.1.2004, p 1) (the 'EC Merger Regulation') art 22(1)
          (see PARA 74), is proceeding with the matter in pursuance of such a request or has dealt
          with the matter in pursuance of such a request; or

(6) a reasoned submission requesting referral to the European Commission has been submitted to the European Commission under the EC Merger Regulation art 4(5).
Head (6) ceases to apply if the OFT is informed that a member state competent to examine the concentration under its national competition law has, within the time permitted by the EC Merger Regulation art 4(5), expressed its disagreement as regards the request to refer the case to the European Commission; and this provision is to be construed in accordance with that Regulation: Enterprise Act 2002 s 33(3A) (added by SI 2004/1079).
13 Enterprise Act 2002 s 33(4).
14 As to the Secretary of State see PARA 5.
15 See the Enterprise Act 2002 s 34. The Secretary of State may by order make such provision as he considers appropriate about the operation of s 27 (see PARA 177) and s 29 (see PARA 179) in relation to references under Pt 3 (ss 22–130) which relate to arrangements which are in progress or in contemplation or in relation to notices under s 42(2) (see PARA 189), s 59(2) (see PARA 204) or s 67(2) (see PARA 213) which relate to such arrangements: s 34(1). Such an order may, in particular, provide for s 27(5)–(8) (see PARA 177) and s 29 (see PARA 179) to apply with modifications in relation to such references or notices or in relation to particular descriptions of such references or notices: s 34(2)(a). Such an order may also enable particular descriptions of events, arrangements or transactions which have already occurred: (1) to be taken into account for the purposes of deciding whether to make such references or such references of a particular description or whether to give such notices or such notices of a particular description; (2) to be dealt with under such references or such references of a particular description or under such notices or such notices of a particular description: s 34(2)(b).
In exercise of this power, the Secretary of State has made the Enterprise Act 2002 (Anticipated Mergers) Order 2003, SI 2003/1595.

C. CASES REFERRED BY THE EUROPEAN COMMISSION

183. Duty of the Office of Fair Trading where case referred by the European Commission. If the European Commission has by a decision referred the whole or part of a case to the Office of Fair Trading (the 'OFT')[1], or is deemed to have taken such a decision, unless an intervention notice[2] is in force in relation to that case[3], then before the end of the preliminary assessment period[4], the OFT must decide whether to make a reference to the Commission[5] and must inform the persons carrying on the enterprises[6] concerned by notice[7] of that decision and of the reasons for it[8].

The OFT may by notice[9] to any of the persons carrying on the enterprises concerned request him to provide the OFT with such information as the OFT may require for the purpose of making a decision[10].

The OFT may decide not to make a reference on the basis that it is considering whether to seek or accept undertakings[11] instead of making a reference, but a decision taken on that basis does not prevent the OFT from making a reference in the event of no such undertakings being offered or accepted[12].

If the OFT has imposed a requirement to provide information[13] and it considers that the person on whom that requirement was imposed has failed to comply with it, the OFT may, by notice to the persons carrying on the enterprises concerned, extend the preliminary assessment period[14].

1 Ie under EC Council Regulation 139/2004 (OJ L24, 29.1.2004, p 1) (the 'EC Merger Regulation') art 4(4) or art 9 (see PARA 74). As to the OFT see PARAS 6–8.
2 As to intervention notices see PARA 189.
3 Enterprise Act 2002 s 34A(1) (ss 34A, 34B added by SI 2004/1079).
4 'Preliminary assessment period' means the period of 45 working days beginning with the day after the day on which the decision of the European Commission to refer the case is taken (or is deemed to have been taken): Enterprise Act 2002 s 34A(4) (as added: see note 3). 'Working day' means any day which is not a Saturday, a Sunday or a day which is a European Commission holiday (as published in the Official Journal of the European Communities before the beginning of the year in which it occurs): Enterprise Act 2002 s 34A(4) (as so added).

5 Enterprise Act 2002 s 34A(2)(a) (as added: see note 3). A reference is made to the Commission under s 22 (see PARA 172) or s 33 (see PARA 182).
6 As to the meaning of 'enterprise' see PARA 173 note 2.
7 As to the meaning of 'notice' see PARA 175 note 4.
8 Enterprise Act 2002 s 34A(2)(b) (as added: see note 3).
9 The notice must state: (1) the information required; (2) the period within which the information is to be provided; (3) the manner (if any) in which the information is required to be provided; and (4) the possible consequences (a) of not providing the information within the stated period; and (b) if a manner for its provision is stated in the notice, of not providing it in that manner: Enterprise Act 2002 s 34B(2) (as added: see note 3).
10 Enterprise Act 2002 s 34B(1) (as added: see note 3).
11 Ie under the Enterprise Act 2002 s 73 (see PARA 217).
12 Enterprise Act 2002 s 34A(3) (as added: see note 3).
13 Ie under the Enterprise Act 2002 s 34B (see the text and notes 9–10).
14 Enterprise Act 2002 s 34A(5) (as added: see note 3). The period of an extension under s 34A(5): (1) begins with the end of the period within which the requirement under s 34B could be complied with (see the text and notes 9–10); and (2) ends with the earlier of either compliance with the requirement to the satisfaction of the OFT or cancellation by the OFT of the extension: s 34A(6) (as added: see note 3). A notice under s 34A(6) must be given within five working days of the end of the period mentioned in head (1), and must inform the person to whom it is addressed that the OFT is of the opinion that the requirement to provide information has not been complied with and that it intends to extend the preliminary assessment period: s 34A(7) (as added: see note 3).

D. DETERMINATION OF REFERENCES

184.   Questions to be decided in relation to completed and anticipated mergers.   The Competition Commission[1], on a reference in relation to a completed merger or an anticipated merger[2], must decide whether a relevant merger situation[3] has been created, or (in relation to an anticipated merger) whether arrangements are in progress or in contemplation which, if carried into effect, will result in the creation of a relevant merger situation, and, if so, whether the creation of that situation has resulted, or may be expected to result, in a substantial lessening of competition within any market or markets in the United Kingdom[4] for goods or services[5].

The Commission may decide if there is an anti-competitive outcome in relation to a merger. There is an anti-competitive outcome if: (1) a relevant merger situation has been created and the creation of that situation has resulted, or may be expected to result, in a substantial lessening of competition within any market or markets in the United Kingdom for goods or services[6]; or (2) arrangements are in progress or in contemplation which, if carried into effect, will result in the creation of a relevant merger situation and the creation of that situation may be expected to result in a substantial lessening of competition within any market or markets in the United Kingdom for goods or services[7].

If the Commission has decided on a reference that there is an anti-competitive outcome, it must decide the following additional questions[8]:

(a)   whether action[9] should be taken by it[10] for the purpose of remedying, mitigating or preventing the substantial lessening of competition concerned or any adverse effect which has resulted from, or may be expected to result from, the substantial lessening of competition[11];

(b)   whether it should recommend the taking of action by others for the purpose of remedying, mitigating or preventing the substantial lessening of competition concerned or any adverse effect which has resulted from, or may be expected to result from, the substantial lessening of competition[12]; and

(c)   in either case, if action should be taken, what action should be taken and what is to be remedied, mitigated or prevented[13].

In deciding these questions the Commission must, in particular, have regard to the need to achieve as comprehensive a solution as is reasonable and practicable to the substantial lessening of competition and any adverse effects resulting from it[14]. The Commission may, in particular, have regard to the effect of any action on any relevant customer benefits[15] in relation to the creation of the relevant merger situation concerned[16].

1   As to the Competition Commission see PARAS 9–12. As to decisions of the Commission under the Enterprise Act 2002 ss 35(1), 36(1) see PARA 11 note 13.
2   A completed merger is referred under the Enterprise Act 2002 s 22 (see PARA 172) and an anticipated merger under s 33 (see PARA 182). In relation to the question whether a relevant merger situation has been created, a reference under s 22 or s 33 may be framed so as to require the Commission to exclude from consideration s 23(1) or s 23(2) (see PARA 173) or one of those provisions if the Commission finds that the other is satisfied: ss 35(6), 36(5). In relation to the question whether any such result as is mentioned in s 23(2)(b) has arisen (see PARA 173), a reference under s 22 or s 33 may be framed so as to require the Commission to confine its investigation to the supply of goods or services in a part of the United Kingdom specified in the reference: ss 35(7), 36(6). As to the meanings of 'goods' and 'supply of services' see PARA 172 note 5. As to the meaning of 'United Kingdom' see PARA 401 note 1.
3   As to the meaning of 'relevant merger situation' see PARA 173.
4   As to the meaning of 'market in the United Kingdom' see PARA 172 note 5.
5   Enterprise Act 2002 ss 35(1), 36(1), which are expressed to be subject to ss 35(6), (7), 36(5), (6) (see note 2) and s 127(3) (see PARA 176). As to the meaning of 'market for goods or services' see PARA 172 note 5.
6   Enterprise Act 2002 s 35(2)(a).
7   Enterprise Act 2002 s 35(2)(b).
8   Enterprise Act 2002 ss 35(3), 36(2).
9   'Action' includes omission; and references to the taking of action include references to refraining from action: Enterprise Act 2002 ss 129(1), 130.
10   Ie under the Enterprise Act 2002 s 41(2) (see PARA 188).
11   Enterprise Act 2002 ss 35(3)(a), 36(2)(a).
12   Enterprise Act 2002 ss 35(3)(b), 36(2)(b).
13   Enterprise Act 2002 ss 35(3)(c), 36(2)(c).
14   Enterprise Act 2002 ss 35(4), 36(3).
15   As to the meaning of 'relevant customer benefit' see PARA 180.
16   Enterprise Act 2002 ss 35(5), 36(4).

185. Cancellation and variation of references. The Competition Commission[1] must cancel a reference of an anticipated merger[2] if it considers that the proposal to make arrangements of the kind mentioned in the reference has been abandoned[3].

The Commission may, if it considers that doing so is justified by the facts (including events occurring on or after the making of the reference concerned), treat a reference of a completed merger as if it had been a reference of an anticipated merger and vice versa[4]. Where the Commission treats a reference in this way, any interim undertaking[5] or interim order[6] which is in force, continues in force as if it had been made in relation to the reference as so treated and the undertaking or order concerned may be varied, superseded, released or revoked accordingly[7].

The OFT may at any time vary a reference after consulting the Commission[8]. However, no variation by the OFT is capable of altering the period within which the report of the Commission[9] is to be prepared and published[10].

1   As to the Competition Commission see PARAS 9–12.
2   Ie a reference under the Enterprise Act 2002 s 33 (see PARA 182).
3   Enterprise Act 2002 s 37(1).

4   See the Enterprise Act 2002 s 37(2). This allows the Commission to treat a reference made under
    s 22 (see PARA 172) or s 33 (see PARA 182) as if it had been made under s 33 or (as the case may
    be) s 22; and, in such cases, references in Pt 3 (ss 22–130) to references under those provisions,
    so far as may be necessary, must be construed accordingly: s 37(2). Where, by virtue of s 37(2),
    the Commission treats a reference made under s 22 or s 33 as if it had been made under s 33 or
    (as the case may be) s 22, ss 77–81 (interim restrictions and powers: see PARAS 221–224), in
    particular, apply as if the reference had been made under s 33 or (as the case may be) s 22
    instead of under s 22 or s 33: s 37(3).
5   Ie an undertaking accepted under the Enterprise Act 2002 s 80 (see PARA 223).
6   Ie an order made under the Enterprise Act 2002 s 81 (see PARA 224).
7   Enterprise Act 2002 s 37(4), (5).
8   Enterprise Act 2002 s 37(6), (7). The Commission need not be consulted if it has requested the
    variation concerned: s 37(8).
9   Ie the report of the Commission under the Enterprise Act 2002 s 38 (see PARA 186).
10 Enterprise Act 2002 s 37(9).

186.   Investigations and reports on references.   The Competition Commission[1]
must prepare and publish[2] a report on a reference in relation to a merger or an
anticipated merger[3] within 24 weeks beginning with the date of the reference
concerned[4].

The report, in particular, must contain: (1) the decisions of the Commission
on the questions which it is required to answer[5]; (2) its reasons for its decisions[6];
and (3) such information as the Commission considers appropriate for
facilitating a proper understanding of those questions and of its reasons for its
decisions[7].

The Commission must carry out such investigations as it considers
appropriate for the purposes of preparing the report[8]. At the same time as a
report is published, the Commission must give it to the Office of Fair Trading
(the 'OFT')[9].

1   As to the Competition Commission see PARAS 9–12.
2   Any duty to publish which is imposed on a person by the Enterprise Act 2002 Pt 3 (ss 22–130),
    unless the context otherwise requires, is to be construed as a duty on that person to publish in
    such manner as he considers appropriate for the purpose of bringing the matter concerned to the
    attention of those likely to be affected by it: s 129(4).
3   Ie a reference under the Enterprise Act 2002 s 22 (see PARA 172) or s 33 (see PARA 182).
4   Enterprise Act 2002 ss 38(1), 39(1). As to the extension of the period see PARA 187.
5   Enterprise Act 2002 s 38(2)(a). The Commission is required to answer questions by virtue of
    s 35 or s 36 (see PARA 184).
6   Enterprise Act 2002 s 38(2)(b).
7   Enterprise Act 2002 s 38(2)(c).
8   Enterprise Act 2002 s 38(3).
9   Enterprise Act 2002 s 38(4). As to the OFT see PARAS 6–8.

187.   Time limits for investigations and reports.   The Competition
Commission[1] must prepare and publish its report on a merger reference[2] within
the period of 24 weeks beginning with the date of the reference concerned[3]. The
Commission may extend, by no more than eight weeks, the period within which
a report is to be prepared and published if it considers that there are special
reasons why the report cannot be prepared and published within that period[4].
The Commission may also extend the period within which a report is to be
prepared and published if it considers that a relevant person[5] has failed, whether
with or without a reasonable excuse, to comply with any requirement of a notice
for attendance of witnesses or production of documents[6]. An extension comes
into force when published[7]. An extension for failure to comply with a notice
continues in force until the person concerned provides the information or
documents to the satisfaction of the Commission or, as the case may be, appears

as a witness in accordance with the requirements of the Commission or the
Commission publishes its decision to cancel the extension[8].

1   As to the Competition Commission see PARAS 9–12.

2   Ie a report under the Enterprise Act 2002 s 38 (see PARA 186).

3   Enterprise Act 2002 s 39(1). References in Pt 3 (ss 22–130) to the date of a reference are to be
     construed as references to the date specified in the reference as the date on which it is made:
     s 39(9). The provisions of s 39 are subject to s 40: s 39(10). The Secretary of State may by order
     amend s 39 so as to alter the period of 24 weeks mentioned in s 39(1) or any period for the time
     being mentioned in substitution for that period, provided that the period does not exceed 24
     weeks: s 40(8)(a), (9) (s 40(8), (9) amended by SI 2004/1079). As to the Secretary of State see
     PARA 5. An order under the Enterprise Act 2002 s 40(8) does not affect any period of time
     within which the Commission is under a duty to prepare and publish its report under s 38 if the
     Commission is already under that duty in relation to that reference when the order is made:
     s 40(10). Before making an order under s 40(8) the Secretary of State must consult the
     Commission and such other persons as he considers appropriate: s 40(11).

4   Enterprise Act 2002 s 39(3). The Secretary of State may by order amend s 39 so as to alter the
     period of eight weeks mentioned in s 39(3) or any period for the time being mentioned in
     substitution for that period, provided that the period does not exceed eight weeks: s 40(8)(c), (9)
     (as amended: see note 3). See also note 3. A period extended under s 39(3) may also be extended
     under s 39(4) (see the text to notes 5–6) and a period extended under s 39(4) may also be
     extended under s 39(3): s 40(3). No more than one extension is possible under s 39(3): s 40(4).
        Where a period within which a report under s 38 (see PARA 186) is to be prepared and
     published is extended or further extended under s 39(3) or (4), the period as extended or (as the
     case may be) further extended is calculated by taking the period being extended and adding to it
     the period of the extension (whether or not those periods overlap in time): s 40(5). Where: (1)
     the period within which the report under s 38 is to be prepared and published is further
     extended; (2) the further extension and at least one previous extension is made under s 39(4);
     and (3) the same days or fractions of days are included in or comprise the further extension and
     are included in or comprise at least one such previous extension then, in calculating the period
     of the further extension, any days or fractions of days of the kind mentioned in head (3) are to
     be disregarded: s 40(6), (7).

5   'Relevant person' means: (1) any person carrying on any of the enterprises concerned; (2) any
     person who (whether alone or as a member of a group) owns or has control of any such person;
     or (3) any officer, employee or agent of any person mentioned in head (1) or head (2): Enterprise
     Act 2002 s 39(5). For the purposes of s 39(5) a person or group of persons able, directly or
     indirectly, to control or materially to influence the policy of a body of persons corporate or
     unincorporate, but without having a controlling interest in that body of persons, may be treated
     as having control of it: s 39(6).

6   Enterprise Act 2002 s 39(4). See also note 4. A notice for attendance of witnesses or production
     of documents is given under s 109 (see PARA 259).

7   Enterprise Act 2002 s 39(7). An extension is published under s 107 (see PARA 257). As to the
     meaning of 'publish' see PARA 186 note 2.

8   Enterprise Act 2002 s 39(8). The Secretary of State may make regulations for the purposes of
     s 39(8): s 40(12). The regulations may, in particular: (1) provide for the time at which
     information or documents are to be treated as provided (including the time at which they are to
     be treated as provided to the satisfaction of the Commission for the purposes of s 39(8)); (2)
     provide for the time at which a person is to be treated as appearing as a witness (including the
     time at which he is to be treated as appearing as a witness in accordance with the requirements
     of the Commission for the purposes of s 39(8)); (3) provide for the persons carrying on the
     enterprises which have or may have ceased to be, or may cease to be, distinct enterprises to be
     informed, in circumstances in which s 39(8) applies, of the fact that (a) the Commission is
     satisfied as to the provision of the information or documents required by it; or (b) the person
     concerned has appeared as a witness in accordance with the requirements of the Commission;
     (4) provide for the persons carrying on the enterprises which have or may have ceased to be, or
     may cease to be, distinct enterprises to be informed, in circumstances in which s 39(8) applies, of
     the time at which the Commission is to be treated as satisfied as mentioned in head (3)(a) or the
     person concerned is to be treated as having appeared as mentioned in head (3)(b): s 40(13). As
     to the meaning of 'enterprise' see PARA 173 note 2. As to enterprises ceasing to be distinct see
     PARA 176. At the date at which this volume states the law no such regulations had been made.

188. Duty to remedy effects of completed or anticipated mergers. Where a report of the Competition Commission[1] has been prepared and published[2] within the permitted period[3] and contains the decision that there is an anti-competitive outcome[4], the Commission must take such action[5] as it considers to be reasonable and practicable to remedy, mitigate or prevent the substantial lessening of competition concerned and to remedy, mitigate or prevent any adverse effects which have resulted from, or may be expected to result from, the substantial lessening of competition[6].

In making its decision, the Commission, in particular, must have regard to the need to achieve as comprehensive a solution as is reasonable and practicable to the substantial lessening of competition and any adverse effects resulting from it[7]. The Commission may, in particular, have regard to the effect of any action on any relevant customer benefits[8] in relation to the creation of the relevant merger situation[9] concerned[10].

1 As to the Competition Commission see PARAS 9–12.
2 Ie under the Enterprise Act 2002 s 38 (see PARA 186). As to the meaning of 'publish' see PARA 186 note 2.
3 Ie the period permitted by the Enterprise Act 2002 s 39 (see PARA 187).
4 Enterprise Act 2002 s 41(1). As to the meaning of 'anti-competitive outcome' see PARA 184.
5 Ie under the Enterprise Act 2002 s 82 (final undertakings: see PARA 225) or s 84 (final orders: see PARA 226). As to the meaning of 'action' see PARA 184 note 9.
6 Enterprise Act 2002 s 41(2). The decision of the Commission under s 41(2) must be consistent with its decisions as included in its report by virtue of s 35(3) or (as the case may be) s 36(2) (see PARA 184) unless there has been a material change of circumstances since the preparation of the report or the Commission otherwise has a special reason for deciding differently: s 41(3).
7 Enterprise Act 2002 s 41(4).
8 As to the meaning of 'relevant customer benefit' see PARA 180.
9 As to the meaning of 'relevant merger situation' see PARA 173.
10 Enterprise Act 2002 s 41(5).

(ii) Public Interest Cases

A. POWER TO MAKE REFERENCES

189. Intervention by the Secretary of State. Where: (1) the Secretary of State[1] has reasonable grounds for suspecting that it is or may be the case that a relevant merger situation[2] has been created or that arrangements are in progress or in contemplation which, if carried into effect, will result in the creation of a relevant merger situation[3]; (2) no reference of a completed or anticipated merger[4] has been made in relation to the relevant merger situation concerned[5]; (3) no decision has been made not to make such a reference[6]; and (4) no reference is prevented from being made by statute[7] or by Community law or anything done under or in accordance with it[8], then the Secretary of State may give an intervention notice to the Office of Fair Trading (the 'OFT')[9] if he believes that it is or may be the case that one or more than one public interest consideration[10] is relevant to a consideration of the relevant merger situation concerned[11]. No more than one intervention notice may be given in relation to the same relevant merger situation[12].

Where the Secretary of State has given an intervention notice mentioning a public interest consideration which, at that time, is not finalised[13], he must, as soon as practicable, take such action[14] as is within his power to ensure that it is finalised[15].

Specific provision is made regarding the primacy of Community law in relation to such references[16].

1   As to the Secretary of State see PARA 5.
2   As to the meaning of 'relevant merger situation' see PARA 173.
3   Enterprise Act 2002 s 42(1)(a). For the purposes of deciding whether a relevant merger situation
    has been created or whether arrangements are in progress or in contemplation which, if carried
    into effect, will result in the creation of a relevant merger situation, ss 23–32 (see PARAS
    173–181) (read together with s 34 (see PARA 182)) apply for the purposes of Pt 3 Ch 2
    (ss 42–58A) as they do for the purposes of Pt 3 Ch 1 (ss 22–41) with the amendments made by
    s 42(6): see s 42(5), (6).
4   Ie under the Enterprise Act 2002 s 22 (see PARA 172) or s 33 (see PARA 182).
5   Enterprise Act 2002 s 42(1)(b).
6   Enterprise Act 2002 s 42(1)(c). This does not include a decision made by virtue of s 33(2)(b) (see
    PARA 182) or a decision to accept undertakings under s 73 (see PARA 217) instead of making
    such a reference: s 42(1)(c).
7   Ie under the Enterprise Act 2002 s 22 (see PARA 172) or s 33 (see PARA 182) by virtue of
    s 22(3)(a) or (e) or (as the case may be) s 33(3)(a) or (e).
8   Enterprise Act 2002 s 42(1)(d). See further PARA 24 et seq.
9   As to the OFT see PARAS 6–8.
10 For the purposes of the Enterprise Act 2002 Pt 3 (ss 22–130), a public interest consideration is
    a consideration which, at the time of the giving of the intervention notice concerned, is specified
    in s 58 (see PARA 203) or is not so specified but, in the opinion of the Secretary of State, ought
    to be so specified: s 42(3).
11 Enterprise Act 2002 s 42(2). In Pt 3 such a notice is an 'intervention notice': ss 42(2), 130. As to
    intervention notices see PARA 190. No reference may be made under s 22 (see PARA 172) or s 33
    (see PARA 182) if an intervention notice is in force in relation to the matter or the matter to
    which such a notice relates has been finally determined under Pt 3 Ch 2 (ss 42–58A) otherwise
    than in circumstances in which a notice is then given to the OFT under s 56(1) (see PARA 202):
    see ss 22(3)(d), 33(3)(d).
12 Enterprise Act 2002 s 42(4).
13 For the purposes of the Enterprise Act 2002 Pt 3, a public interest consideration is finalised if:
    (1) it is specified in s 58 (see PARA 203) otherwise than by virtue of an order under s 58(3); or (2)
    it is specified in s 58 by virtue of an order under s 58(3) and the order providing for it to be so
    specified has been laid before, and approved by, Parliament in accordance with s 124(7) (see
    PARA 273) and within the period mentioned in that provision: s 42(8).
14 As to the meaning of 'action' see PARA 184 note 9.
15 Enterprise Act 2002 s 42(7).
16 As to the meaning of 'Community law' see PARA 172 note 22. The power to give an intervention
    notice under s 42 applies in a case in which the relevant enterprises ceased to be distinct
    enterprises at a time or in circumstances not falling within s 24 (see PARA 174) if the following
    condition is satisfied: s 122(3). The condition is that, because of EC Council
    Regulation 139/2004 (OJ L24, 29.1.2004, p 1) (the 'EC Merger Regulation') or anything done
    under or in accordance with it, the reference under the Enterprise Act 2002 s 22 to which the
    intervention notice relates, could not have been made earlier than four months before the date
    on which it is to be made: see s 122(4), (5).

190. Intervention notices. An intervention notice[1] must state: (1) the relevant
merger situation[2] concerned[3]; (2) the public interest consideration[4] or
considerations which are, or may be, relevant to a consideration of the relevant
merger situation concerned[5]; and (3) where any public interest consideration
concerned is not finalised[6], the proposed timetable for finalising it[7].

Where the Secretary of State believes that it is or may be the case that two or
more public interest considerations are relevant to a consideration of the relevant
merger situation concerned, he may decide not to mention in the intervention
notice such of those considerations as he considers appropriate[8].

An intervention notice comes into force when it is given and ceases to be in
force when the matter to which it relates is finally determined[9]. For this purpose,
a matter to which an intervention notice relates is finally determined if:

(a)   the time within which the Office of Fair Trading (the 'OFT')[10] or, if
       relevant, the Office of Communications ('OFCOM')[11] is to report to the
       Secretary of State[12] has expired and no such report has been made[13];

(b)   the Secretary of State decides to accept an undertaking or group of undertakings[14] instead of making a reference to the Competition Commission[15];

(c)   the Secretary of State otherwise decides not to make a reference to the Commission[16];

(d)   the Commission cancels such a reference[17];

(e)   the time within which the Commission is to prepare a report[18] and give it to the Secretary of State has expired and no such report has been prepared and given to the Secretary of State[19];

(f)   the time within which the Secretary of State is to make and publish[20] a decision[21] has expired and no such decision has been made and published[22];

(g)   the Secretary of State decides[23] to make no finding at all in the matter[24];

(h)   the Secretary of State otherwise decides[25] not to make an adverse public interest finding[26];

(i)   the Secretary of State decides[27] to make an adverse public interest finding but decides neither to accept an undertaking[28] nor to make an enforcement order[29]; or

(j)   the Secretary of State decides[30] to make an adverse public interest finding and accepts an undertaking[31] or makes an enforcement order[32].

The time when a matter to which an intervention notice relates is finally determined is either the expiry of the time concerned[33], the acceptance of the undertaking or group of undertakings concerned[34], the making of the decision concerned[35], the making of the decision neither to accept an undertaking nor to make an order[36], or the acceptance of the undertaking concerned or (as the case may be) the making of the order concerned[37].

1   As to the power of the Secretary of State to make intervention notices see PARA 189. As to the meaning of 'intervention notice' see PARA 189 note 11. As to the Secretary of State see PARA 5.
2   As to the meaning of 'relevant merger situation' see PARA 173; and see PARA 189 note 3.
3   Enterprise Act 2002 s 43(1)(a).
4   As to the meaning of 'public interest consideration' see PARA 189 note 10.
5   Enterprise Act 2002 s 43(1)(b).
6   As to the meaning of 'public interest consideration being finalised' see PARA 189 note 13.
7   Enterprise Act 2002 s 43(1)(c).
8   Enterprise Act 2002 s 43(2).
9   Enterprise Act 2002 s 43(3).
10 As to the OFT see PARAS 6–8.
11 As to OFCOM see PARA 19.
12 Ie under the Enterprise Act 2002 s 44 (see PARA 191) or (as the case may be) s 44A (see PARA 192).
13 Enterprise Act 2002 s 43(4)(a), (6).
14 Ie under the Enterprise Act 2002 Sch 7 para 3 (see PARA 229).
15 Enterprise Act 2002 s 43(4)(b). A reference to the Competition Commission is made under s 45 (see PARA 193). As to the Competition Commission see PARAS 9–12.
16 Enterprise Act 2002 s 43(4)(c).
17 Enterprise Act 2002 s 43(4)(d). The Commission may cancel such a reference under s 48(1) (see PARA 196) or s 53(1) (see PARA 199).
18 Ie under the Enterprise Act 2002 s 50 (see PARA 198).
19 Enterprise Act 2002 s 43(4)(e).
20 As to the meaning of 'publish' see PARA 186 note 2.
21 Ie under the Enterprise Act 2002 s 54(2) (see PARA 200).
22 Enterprise Act 2002 s 43(4)(f).
23 Ie under the Enterprise Act 2002 s 54(2) (see PARA 200).
24 Enterprise Act 2002 s 43(4)(g).
25 Ie under the Enterprise Act 2002 s 54(2) (see PARA 200).
26 Enterprise Act 2002 s 43(4)(h). As to adverse public interest findings see PARA 200.

27 Ie under the Enterprise Act 2002 s 54(2) (see PARA 200).
28 Ie under the Enterprise Act 2002 Sch 7 para 9 (see PARA 231).
29 Enterprise Act 2002 s 43(4)(i). An enforcement order is made under Sch 7 para 11 (see PARA 231).
30 Ie under the Enterprise Act 2002 s 54(2) (see PARA 200).
31 Ie under the Enterprise Act 2002 Sch 7 para 9 (see PARA 231).
32 Enterprise Act 2002 s 43(4)(j). An enforcement order is made under Sch 7 para 11 (see PARA 231).
33 Ie in a case falling within head (a), (e) or (f) in the text.
34 Ie in a case falling within head (b) in the text.
35 Ie in a case falling within head (c), (d), (g) or (h) in the text.
36 Ie in a case falling within head (i).
37 Enterprise Act 2002 s 43(5)(a)–(e). The acceptance of the undertaking or making of the order concerned applies to a case falling within head (j) in the text.

191. Investigation and report by the Office of Fair Trading. Where the Secretary of State[1] has given an intervention notice[2] in relation to a relevant merger situation[3], the Office of Fair Trading (the 'OFT')[4], within such period as the Secretary of State may require, must give a report to the Secretary of State in relation to the case[5]. The report must contain advice from the OFT on the considerations relevant to the making of a reference of a merger[6] which are also relevant to the Secretary of State's decision as to whether to make a reference to the Competition Commission[7]. The report must also contain a summary of any representations about the case which have been received by the OFT and which relate to any public interest consideration[8] mentioned in the intervention notice concerned (other than a media public interest consideration[9]) and which is or may be relevant to the Secretary of State's decision as to whether to make a reference to the Commission[10]. The report, in particular, must include decisions as to whether the OFT believes that it is, or may be, the case that:

(1) a relevant merger situation has been created or arrangements are in progress or in contemplation which, if carried into effect, will result in the creation of a relevant merger situation[11];

(2) the creation of that situation has resulted, or may be expected to result, in a substantial lessening of competition within any market or markets in the United Kingdom[12] for goods or services[13];

(3) the market or markets concerned would not be of sufficient importance to justify the making of a reference to the Commission[14];

(4) in the case of arrangements which are in progress or in contemplation, the arrangements are not sufficiently far advanced, or not sufficiently likely to proceed, to justify the making of such a reference[15];

(5) any relevant customer benefits[16] in relation to the creation of the relevant merger situation concerned outweigh the substantial lessening of competition and any adverse effects of the substantial lessening of competition[17]; or

(6) it would be appropriate to deal with the matter (disregarding any public interest considerations mentioned in the intervention notice concerned) by way of undertakings[18].

If the OFT believes that it is or may be the case that it would be appropriate to deal with the matter (disregarding any public interest considerations mentioned in the intervention notice concerned) by way of undertakings[19], the report must contain descriptions of the undertakings which the OFT believes are, or may be, appropriate[20].

The report may, in particular, contain a summary of any representations about the case which have been received by the OFT and which relate to any media public interest consideration mentioned in the intervention notice concerned and which is or may be relevant to the Secretary of State's decision as to whether to make a reference to the Commission[21]. The report may also include advice and recommendations on any public interest consideration mentioned in the intervention notice concerned and which is or may be relevant to the Secretary of State's decision as to whether to make a reference to the Commission[22].

The Secretary of State may exclude a matter from the report if he considers the publication of the matter would be inappropriate[23].

1　As to the Secretary of State see PARA 5.
2　As to intervention notices see PARA 190.
3　As to the meaning of 'relevant merger situation' see PARA 173; and see PARA 189 note 3.
4　As to the OFT see PARAS 6–8.
5　Enterprise Act 2002 s 44(1), (2). The OFT must carry out such investigations as it considers appropriate for the purposes of producing the report: s 44(7).
6　Ie under the Enterprise Act 2002 s 22 (see PARA 172) or s 33 (see PARA 182).
7　Enterprise Act 2002 s 44(3)(a). A reference to the Competition Commission is made under s 45 (see PARA 193). As to the Competition Commission see PARAS 9–12.
8　As to the meaning of 'public interest consideration' see PARA 189 note 10.
9　In the Enterprise Act 2002 Pt 3 (ss 22–130), 'media public interest consideration' means any consideration which, at the time of the giving of the intervention notice concerned, is specified in s 58(2A)–(2C) (see PARA 203) or, in the opinion of the Secretary of State, is concerned with broadcasting or newspapers and ought to be specified in s 58 (see PARA 203): ss 44(8), 130 (s 44(8)–(11) added by the Communications Act 2003 s 376(3)). 'Broadcasting' means the provision of services the provision of which: (1) is required to be licensed under the Broadcasting Act 1990 Pt 1 (ss 3–71) or Pt 3 (ss 85–126) or the Broadcasting Act 1996 Pt 1 (ss 1–39) or Pt 2 (ss 40–72) (see TELECOMMUNICATIONS AND BROADCASTING vol 45(1) (2005 Reissue) PARA 261 et seq); or (2) would be required to be so licensed if provided by a person subject to licensing under the Part in question: Enterprise Act 2002 s 44(9) (as so added). 'Newspaper' means a daily, Sunday or local (other than daily or Sunday) newspaper circulating wholly or mainly in the United Kingdom or in a part of the United Kingdom: s 44(10) (as so added). The Secretary of State may by order amend s 44(9), (10): s 44(11) (as so added). At the date at which this volume states the law no such order had been made.
10　Enterprise Act 2002 s 44(3)(b) (amended by the Communications Act 2003 s 376(1)).
11　Enterprise Act 2002 s 44(4)(a).
12　As to the meaning of 'market in the United Kingdom' see PARA 172 note 5. As to the meaning of 'United Kingdom' see PARA 401 note 1.
13　Enterprise Act 2002 s 44(4)(b). As to the meanings of 'market for goods or services' and 'goods' see PARA 172 note 5.
14　Enterprise Act 2002 s 44(4)(c). A reference to the Commission is made under s 22 (see PARA 172) or s 33 (see PARA 182).
15　Enterprise Act 2002 s 44(4)(d).
16　As to the meaning of 'relevant customer benefit' see PARA 180.
17　Enterprise Act 2002 s 44(4)(e).
18　Enterprise Act 2002 s 44(4)(f). Undertakings are given under Sch 7 para 3 (see PARA 229).
19　Ie under the Enterprise Act 2002 Sch 7 para 3 (see PARA 229).
20　Enterprise Act 2002 s 44(5).
21　Enterprise Act 2002 s 44(5A) (added by the Communications Act 2003 s 376(2)). A reference is made to the Commission under s 45 (see PARA 193).
22　Enterprise Act 2002 s 44(6).
23　See the Enterprise Act 2002 s 118(1)(a), (2). The OFT must advise the Secretary of State as to any matters which it considers should be excluded: s 118(4). In deciding what is inappropriate, the Secretary of State must have regard to the considerations mentioned in s 244 (see PARA 334): s 118(3). References in s 38(4) (see PARA 186) and s 107(11) (see PARA 257) to the giving or laying of a report of the Commission are to be construed as references to the giving or laying of the report as published: s 118(5).

192.　Additional investigation and report by the Office of Communications in relation to media mergers.　Where the Secretary of State[1] has given an intervention notice[2] in relation to a relevant merger situation[3] and the

intervention notice mentions any media public interest consideration[4], then the Office of Communications ('OFCOM')[5], within such period as the Secretary of State may require, must give a report to the Secretary of State on the effect of the consideration or considerations concerned on the case[6]. The report must contain advice and recommendations on any media public interest consideration mentioned in the intervention notice concerned and which is or may be relevant to the Secretary of State's decision as to whether to make a reference to the Competition Commission[7]. The report must also contain a summary of any representations about the case which have been received by OFCOM and which relate to any such consideration[8].

The Secretary of State may exclude a matter from the report if he considers the publication of the matter would be inappropriate[9].

1   As to the Secretary of State see PARA 5.
2   As to intervention notices see PARA 190.
3   As to the meaning of 'relevant merger situation' see PARA 173; and see PARA 189 note 3.
4   As to the meaning of 'media public interest consideration' see PARA 191 note 9.
5   As to OFCOM see PARA 19.
6   Enterprise Act 2002 s 44A(1), (2) (s 44A added by the Communications Act 2003 s 377). OFCOM must carry out such investigations as they consider appropriate for the purposes of producing the report: Enterprise Act 2002 s 44A(4) (as so added).
7   Enterprise Act 2002 s 44A(3)(a) (as added: see note 6). A reference to the Competition Commission is made under s 45 (see PARA 193). As to the Competition Commission see PARAS 9–12.
8   Enterprise Act 2002 s 44A(3)(b) (as added: see note 6).
9   See the Enterprise Act 2002 s 118(1)(aa), (2) (s 118(1)(aa) added by the Communications Act 2003 s 389(1), Sch 16 para 21). The OFT must advise the Secretary of State as to any matters which it considers should be excluded: Enterprise Act 2002 s 118(4). In deciding what is inappropriate, the Secretary of State must have regard to the considerations mentioned in s 244 (see PARA 334): s 118(3). References in s 38(4) (see PARA 186) and s 107(11) (see PARA 257) to the giving or laying of a report of the Commission are to be construed as references to the giving or laying of the report as published: s 118(5).

193. Power of the Secretary of State to refer a matter to the Competition Commission.

Where the Secretary of State[1] has given an intervention notice[2] in relation to a relevant merger situation[3] and has received a report of the Office of Fair Trading (the 'OFT')[4], and any report of the Office of Communications ('OFCOM')[5] which is required[6] in relation to the matter[7], then the Secretary of State may make a reference to the Competition Commission[8] if he believes that it is or may be the case that one of the following situations applies:

(1)   a relevant merger situation has been created[9]; and

   (a)   the creation of that situation has resulted, or may be expected to result, in a substantial lessening of competition within any market or markets in the United Kingdom[10] for goods or services[11];

   (b)   one or more than one public interest consideration[12] mentioned in the intervention notice is relevant to a consideration of the relevant merger situation concerned[13]; and

   (c)   taking account only of the substantial lessening of competition and the relevant public interest consideration or considerations concerned, the creation of that situation operates or may be expected to operate against the public interest[14];

(2)   a relevant merger situation has been created[15]; and

   (a)   the creation of that situation has not resulted, and may be expected not to result, in a substantial lessening of competition within any market or markets in the United Kingdom for goods or services[16];

(b)   one or more than one public interest consideration mentioned in the intervention notice is relevant to a consideration of the relevant merger situation concerned[17]; and

(c)   taking account only of the relevant public interest consideration or considerations concerned, the creation of that situation operates or may be expected to operate against the public interest[18];

(3)   arrangements are in progress or in contemplation which, if carried into effect, will result in the creation of a relevant merger situation[19]; and

(a)   the creation of that situation may be expected to result in a substantial lessening of competition within any market or markets in the United Kingdom for goods or services[20];

(b)   one or more than one public interest consideration mentioned in the intervention notice is relevant to a consideration of the relevant merger situation concerned[21]; and

(c)   taking account only of the substantial lessening of competition and the relevant public interest consideration or considerations concerned, the creation of the relevant merger situation may be expected to operate against the public interest[22];

(4)   arrangements are in progress or in contemplation which, if carried into effect, will result in the creation of a relevant merger situation[23]; and

(a)   the creation of that situation may be expected not to result in a substantial lessening of competition within any market or markets in the United Kingdom for goods or services[24];

(b)   one or more than one public interest consideration mentioned in the intervention notice is relevant to a consideration of the relevant merger situation concerned[25]; and

(c)   taking account only of the relevant public interest consideration or considerations concerned, the creation of the relevant merger situation may be expected to operate against the public interest[26].

The Secretary of State, in deciding whether to make a reference must accept the decisions of the OFT included in its report[27] and any descriptions of undertakings the OFT believes are appropriate[28].

Where the decision to make a reference is made at any time on or after the end of the period of 24 weeks beginning with the giving of the intervention notice concerned, the Secretary of State, in deciding whether to make such a reference, must disregard any public interest consideration which is mentioned in the intervention notice but which has not been finalised before the end of that period[29]. Where the decision to make a reference in the situations described in head (1) or head (3) is made at any time before the end of the period of 24 weeks beginning with the giving of the intervention notice concerned, the Secretary of State, in deciding whether to make such a reference, must disregard any public interest consideration which is mentioned in the intervention notice but which has not been finalised if its effect would be to prevent, or to help to prevent, an anti-competitive outcome[30] from being adverse to the public interest[31].

A reference must, in particular, specify the statutory provision under which it is made[32], the date on which it is made[33] and the public interest consideration or considerations mentioned in the intervention notice concerned which the Secretary of State is not under a duty to disregard[34] and which he believes are or may be relevant to a consideration of the relevant merger situation concerned[35].

Specific provision is made regarding the primacy of Community law in relation to such references[36].

1   As to the Secretary of State see PARA 5.
2   As to intervention notices see PARA 190.
3   As to the meaning of 'relevant merger situation' see PARA 173; and see PARA 189 note 3.
4   As to the OFT see PARAS 6–8. A report is made under the Enterprise Act 2002 s 44 (see PARA 191).
5   As to OFCOM see PARA 19.
6   Ie required by virtue of the Enterprise Act 2002 s 44A (see PARA 192).
7   Enterprise Act 2002 s 45(1) (amended by the Communications Act 2003 s 389(1), Sch 16 para 9).
8   As to the Competition Commission see PARAS 9–12. No reference may be made under the Enterprise Act 2002 s 45 if: (1) the making of the reference is prevented by s 74(1) (see PARA 218) or s 96(3) (see PARA 250) or Sch 7 para 4 (see PARA 229); (2) the European Commission is considering a request made, in relation to the matter concerned, by the United Kingdom (whether alone or with others) under EC Council Regulation 139/2004 (OJ L24, 29.1.2004, p 1) (the 'EC Merger Regulation') art 22(1) (see PARA 74), is proceeding with the matter in pursuance of such a request or has dealt with the matter in pursuance of such a request; or (3) a reasoned submission requesting referral to the European Commission has been submitted to the European Commission under the EC Merger Regulation art 4(5): Enterprise Act 2002 ss 45(7), 46(1) (amended by the Communications Act 2003 s 406(7), Sch 19(1); and SI 2004/1079). Head (3) above ceases to apply if the Secretary of State is informed that a member state competent to examine the concentration under its national competition law has, within the time permitted by the EC Merger Regulation art 4(5), expressed its disagreement as regards the request to refer the case to the European Commission; and the Enterprise Act 2002 s 46(1A) is to be construed in accordance with the EC Merger Regulation: Enterprise Act 2002 s 46(1A) (added by SI 2004/1079).
9   Enterprise Act 2002 s 45(2)(a).
10 As to the meaning of 'market in the United Kingdom' see PARA 172 note 5. As to the meaning of 'United Kingdom' see PARA 401 note 1.
11 Enterprise Act 2002 s 45(2)(b). As to the meanings of 'market for goods or services' and 'goods' see PARA 172 note 5.
12 As to the meaning of 'public interest consideration' see PARA 189 note 10.
13 Enterprise Act 2002 s 45(2)(c).
14 Enterprise Act 2002 s 45(2)(d).
15 Enterprise Act 2002 s 45(3)(a).
16 Enterprise Act 2002 s 45(3)(b).
17 Enterprise Act 2002 s 45(3)(c).
18 Enterprise Act 2002 s 45(3)(d).
19 Enterprise Act 2002 s 45(4)(a).
20 Enterprise Act 2002 s 45(4)(b).
21 Enterprise Act 2002 s 45(4)(c).
22 Enterprise Act 2002 s 45(4)(d).
23 Enterprise Act 2002 s 45(5)(a).
24 Enterprise Act 2002 s 45(5)(b).
25 Enterprise Act 2002 s 45(5)(c).
26 Enterprise Act 2002 s 45(5)(d).
27 Ie by virtue of the Enterprise Act 2002 s 44(4) (see PARA 191).
28 Enterprise Act 2002 s 46(2). The undertakings are those as mentioned in s 44(5) (see PARA 191).
29 Enterprise Act 2002 s 46(3).
30 For the purposes of the Enterprise Act 2002 Pt 3 Ch 2 (ss 42–58A), any anti-competitive outcome is to be treated as being adverse to the public interest unless it is justified by one or more than one public interest consideration which is relevant: s 45(6). As to the meaning of 'anti-competitive outcome' generally see PARA 184.
31 Enterprise Act 2002 s 46(4). The Secretary of State may, however, if he believes that there is a realistic prospect of the public interest consideration being finalised within the period of 24 weeks beginning with the giving of the intervention notice concerned, delay deciding whether to make the reference concerned until the public interest consideration is finalised or, if earlier, the period expires: s 46(5).
32 Enterprise Act 2002 s 46(6)(a).
33 Enterprise Act 2002 s 46(6)(b).

34   Ie by virtue of the Enterprise Act 2002 s 46(3) (see the text to note 29).

35   Enterprise Act 2002 s 46(6)(c).

36   As to the meaning of 'Community law' see PARA 172 note 22. The power to make a reference under the Enterprise Act 2002 s 45(2) or s 45(3) applies in a case in which the relevant enterprises ceased to be distinct enterprises at a time or in circumstances not falling within s 24 (see PARA 174) if the following condition is satisfied: s 122(3). The condition is that, because of the EC Merger Regulation or anything done under or in accordance with it, the reference could not have been made earlier than four months before the date on which it is to be made: see s 122(4), (5).

B. CASES REFERRED BY THE EUROPEAN COMMISSION

194.   Cases referred when an intervention notice is in force. If the European Commission has by a decision referred the whole or part of a case to the Office of Fair Trading (the 'OFT')[1], or is deemed to have taken such a decision, and an intervention notice[2] is in force in relation to that case[3] then, before the end of the preliminary assessment period[4], the Secretary of State[5] must decide whether to make a reference to the Competition Commission[6] and inform the persons carrying on the enterprises[7] concerned by notice of that decision and of the reasons for it[8].

The OFT may by notice[9] to any of the persons carrying on the enterprises concerned request him to provide the OFT with such information as the OFT may require for the purpose of enabling the Secretary of State to make the decision[10]. The Secretary of State may also by notice to any of the persons carrying on the enterprises concerned request him to provide the Secretary of State with such information as he may require for the purpose of enabling him to make the decision[11].

If the OFT or the Secretary of State has imposed a requirement to provide information and it or he considers that the person on whom that requirement was imposed has failed to comply with it, the OFT or the Secretary of State may, by notice[12] to the persons carrying on the enterprises concerned, extend the preliminary assessment period[13].

1   As to the OFT see PARAS 6–8. A reference is made under EC Council Regulation 139/2004 (OJ L24, 29.1.2004, p 1) (the 'EC Merger Regulation') art 4(4) or art 9 (see PARA 74).

2   As to the meaning of 'intervention notice' see PARA 189 note 11.

3   Enterprise Act 2002 s 46A(1) (ss 46A–46C added by SI 2004/1079).

4   'Preliminary assessment period' means the period of 45 working days beginning with the day after the day on which the decision of the European Commission to refer the case is taken (or is deemed to have been taken); and 'working day' means any day which is not a Saturday, a Sunday or a day which is a European Commission holiday (as published in the Official Journal of the European Communities before the beginning of the year in which it occurs): Enterprise Act 2002 s 46A(4) (as added: see note 3).

5   As to the Secretary of State see PARA 5.

6   Ie under the Enterprise Act 2002 s 45 (see PARA 193). As to the Competition Commission see PARAS 9–12. The Secretary of State may decide not to make a reference on the basis that he is considering whether to seek or accept undertakings under Sch 7 para 3 (see PARA 229) instead of making a reference; but a decision taken on that basis does not prevent the Secretary of State from making a reference under s 45 (see PARA 193) in the event of no such undertakings being offered or accepted: s 46A(3) (as added: see note 3).

7   As to the meaning of 'enterprise' see PARA 173 note 2.

8   Enterprise Act 2002 s 46A(2) (as added: see note 3).

9   As to the meaning of 'notice' see PARA 175 note 4. A notice under the Enterprise Act 2002 s 46C(1) or (2) (see the text to note 11) must state: (1) the information required; (2) the period within which the information is to be provided; (3) the manner (if any) in which the information is required to be provided; and (4) the possible consequences of not providing the information within the stated period and, if a manner for its provision is stated in the notice, of not providing it in that manner: s 46C(3) (as added: see note 3).

10   Enterprise Act 2002 s 46C(1) (as added: see note 3).

11   Enterprise Act 2002 s 46C(2) (as added: see note 3).

12   A notice under the Enterprise Act 2002 s 46C must be given within five working days of the end of the period within which the requirement could be complied with, and inform the person to whom it is addressed that the OFT or the Secretary of State is of the opinion that the person had failed to comply with the requirement and that it or he intends to extend the preliminary assessment period: s 46B(4) (as added: see note 3).

13   Enterprise Act 2002 s 46B(1), (2) (as added: see note 3). The period of an extension begins with the end of the period within which the requirement under s 46C could be complied with (see the text to notes 9–11) and ends with the earlier of either compliance with the requirement to the satisfaction of the OFT or the Secretary of State or cancellation by the OFT or the Secretary of State of the extension: s 46B(3) (as added: see note 3).

C.   REPORTS ON REFERENCES

195.   Questions to be decided on references to the Competition Commission.
On a reference by the Secretary of State[1], the Competition Commission[2] must decide whether a relevant merger situation[3] has been created[4]. If the Commission decides that such a situation has been created, it must also decide the following additional questions:

(1)   where the Secretary of State believes that it may be the case that the creation of the relevant merger situation has resulted in a substantial lessening of competition within any market or markets in the United Kingdom for goods or services[5], whether: (a) the creation of that situation has resulted, or may be expected to result, in a substantial lessening of competition within any market or markets in the United Kingdom for goods or services; and (b) whether, taking account only of any substantial lessening of competition and the admissible public interest consideration[6] or considerations concerned, the creation of that situation operates or may be expected to operate against the public interest[7];

(2)   where the Secretary of State believes that the creation of the relevant merger situation has not resulted in a substantial lessening of competition[8], whether, taking account only of the admissible public interest consideration[9] or considerations concerned, the creation of that situation operates or may be expected to operate against the public interest[10];

(3)   where the Secretary of State believes that arrangements are in progress which could lead to a relevant merger situation[11], whether arrangements are in progress or in contemplation which, if carried into effect, will result in the creation of a relevant merger situation[12];

(4)   if the Commission decides that such arrangements are in progress or in contemplation: (a) whether the creation of that situation may be expected to result in a substantial lessening of competition within any market or markets in the United Kingdom for goods or services; and (b) whether, taking account only of any substantial lessening of competition and the admissible public interest consideration or considerations concerned, the creation of that situation may be expected to operate against the public interest[13];

(5)   if the Commission decides that arrangements are in progress or in contemplation which, if carried into effect, will result in the creation of a relevant merger situation, whether, taking account only of the

admissible public interest consideration or considerations concerned, the creation of that situation may be expected to operate against the public interest[14];

(6) if the Commission has decided that the creation of a relevant merger situation operates or may be expected to operate against the public interest: (a) whether enforcement action[15] should be taken by the Secretary of State[16] for the purpose of remedying, mitigating or preventing any of the effects adverse to the public interest which have resulted from, or may be expected to result from, the creation of the relevant merger situation; (b) whether the Commission should recommend the taking of other action by the Secretary of State or action by persons other than itself and the Secretary of State for the purpose of remedying, mitigating or preventing any of the effects adverse to the public interest which have resulted from, or may be expected to result from, the creation of the relevant merger situation; and (c) in either case, if action should be taken, what action should be taken and what is to be remedied, mitigated or prevented[17].

Where the Commission has decided that there is or will be a substantial lessening of competition within any market or markets in the United Kingdom for goods or services, it must also decide separately the following questions[18]: (i) whether action should be taken by it[19] for the purpose of remedying, mitigating or preventing the substantial lessening of competition concerned or any adverse effect which has resulted from, or may be expected to result from, the substantial lessening of competition; (ii) whether the Commission should recommend the taking of action by other persons for the purpose of remedying, mitigating or preventing the substantial lessening of competition concerned or any adverse effect which has resulted from, or may be expected to result from, the substantial lessening of competition; and (iii) in either case, if action should be taken, what action should be taken and what is to be remedied, mitigated or prevented[20].

In deciding whether action need be taken[21], the Commission, in particular, must have regard to the need to achieve as comprehensive a solution as is reasonable and practicable to the adverse effects to the public interest or to the substantial lessening of competition and any adverse effects resulting from it[22].

1 Ie on a reference under the Enterprise Act 2002 s 45(2) or (3) (see PARA 193 heads (1) and (2)). As to the Secretary of State see PARA 5.
2 As to the Competition Commission see PARAS 9–12.
3 As to the meaning of 'relevant merger situation' see PARA 173; and see PARA 189 note 3.
4 Enterprise Act 2002 s 47(1).
5 Ie a reference under the Enterprise Act 2002 s 45(2) (see PARA 193 head (1)). As to the meaning of 'market in the United Kingdom' see PARA 172 note 5; as to the meaning of 'United Kingdom' see PARA 401 note 1; and as to the meanings of 'market for goods or services' and 'goods' see PARA 172 note 5.
6 As to the meaning of 'public interest consideration' see PARA 189 note 10.
7 Enterprise Act 2002 s 47(2). As to decisions made by the Commission under s 47 see PARA 11 note 13.
8 Ie a reference under the Enterprise Act 2002 s 45(3) (see PARA 193 head (2)).
9 'Admissible public interest consideration' means any public interest consideration which is specified in the reference under the Enterprise Act 2002 s 45 (see PARA 193) and which the Commission is not under a duty to disregard: s 47(11).
10 Enterprise Act 2002 s 47(3).
11 Ie a reference under the Enterprise Act 2002 s 45(4) or (5) (see PARA 193 heads (3), (4)).
12 Enterprise Act 2002 s 47(4).
13 Enterprise Act 2002 s 47(5).
14 Enterprise Act 2002 s 47(6).
15 As to the meaning of 'action' see PARA 184 note 9.

16 Ie under the Enterprise Act 2002 s 55 (see PARA 201).
17 Enterprise Act 2002 s 47(7).
18 Ie on the assumption that it is proceeding as mentioned in the Enterprise Act 2002 s 56(6) (see PARA 202).
19 Ie under the Enterprise Act 2002 s 41 (see PARA 188).
20 Enterprise Act 2002 s 47(8).
21 Ie in deciding the questions mentioned in the Enterprise Act 2002 s 47(7), (8) (see the text to notes 15–20).
22 Enterprise Act 2002 s 47(9). In deciding the questions mentioned in s 47(7), (8) (see the text to notes 15–20) in a case where it has decided that there is or will be a substantial lessening of competition, the Commission may, in particular, have regard to the effect of any action on any relevant customer benefits in relation to the creation of the relevant merger situation concerned: s 47(10). As to the meaning of 'relevant customer benefit' see PARA 180.

196. Cases where references or certain questions need not be decided. The Competition Commission[1] must cancel a reference from the Secretary of State[2] if it considers that the proposal to make arrangements which will result in the creation of a relevant merger situation[3] has been abandoned[4].

In relation to the question whether a relevant merger situation has been created or the question whether a relevant merger situation will be created, a reference may be framed so as to require the Commission to exclude from consideration the turnover test[5] or the share of supply test[6] or one of those tests if the Commission finds that the other is satisfied[7]. In relation to the share of supply test, a reference may be framed so as to require the Commission to confine its investigation to the supply of goods or services[8] in a part of the United Kingdom[9] specified in the reference[10].

1 As to the Competition Commission see PARAS 9–12.
2 Ie under the Enterprise Act 2002 s 45(4), (5) (see PARA 193). As to the Secretary of State see PARA 5.
3 As to the meaning of 'relevant merger situation' see PARA 173; and see PARA 189 note 3.
4 Enterprise Act 2002 s 48(1).
5 Ie the Enterprise Act 2002 s 23(1) (see PARA 173).
6 Ie the Enterprise Act 2002 s 23(2) (see PARA 173).
7 See the Enterprise Act 2002 s 48(2).
8 As to the meanings of 'goods', 'supply of goods' and 'supply of services' see PARA 172 note 5.
9 As to the meaning of 'United Kingdom' see PARA 401 note 1.
10 Enterprise Act 2002 s 48(3).

197. Variation of references. The Competition Commission[1] may, if it considers that doing so is justified by the facts (including events occurring on or after the making of the reference concerned), treat a reference by the Secretary of State[2] of a relevant merger situation[3] as if it were a reference of an anticipated merger or vice versa[4]. In the event of such treatment, any undertaking or order[5] in force in relation to the reference before that treatment continues in force and may be varied, superseded, released or revoked accordingly[6].

The Secretary of State may at any time, after consulting the Commission, vary a reference[7]. However, no variation by the Secretary of State is capable of altering the public interest consideration[8] or considerations specified in the reference or the period[9] within which the report of the Commission[10] is to be prepared and given to the Secretary of State[11].

1 As to the Competition Commission see PARAS 9–12.
2 As to the Secretary of State see PARA 5.
3 As to the meaning of 'relevant merger situation' see PARA 173; and see PARA 189 note 3.
4 Enterprise Act 2002 s 49(1). Accordingly, the Commission may treat: (1) a reference made under s 45(2) or (3) (see PARA 193 heads (1), (2)) as if it had been made under s 45(4) or (5) (see PARA 193 heads (3), (4)); or (2) a reference made under s 45(4) or (5) as if it had been made under

s 45(2) or (3); and, in such cases, references in Pt 3 (ss 22–130) to references under those enactments, so far as may be necessary, are to be construed accordingly: s 49(1).

Where the Commission treats a reference made under s 45(2) or (3) as if it had been made under s 45(4) or (5), Sch 7 paras 1, 2, 7 and 8 (see PARAS 228, 230), in particular, apply as if the reference had been made under s 45(4) or (5) instead of under s 45(2) or (3): s 49(2). Where the Commission treats a reference made under s 45(4) or (5) as if it had been made under s 45(2) or (3), Sch 7 paras 1, 2, 7 and 8, in particular, apply as if the reference had been made under s 45(2) or (3) instead of under s 45(4) or (5): s 49(3).

5   Ie any undertaking accepted under the Enterprise Act 2002 Sch 7 para 1 and any order made under Sch 7 para 2 (see PARA 228): s 49(4).
6   Enterprise Act 2002 s 49(5).
7   Enterprise Act 2002 s 49(6), (7). The Secretary of State need not consult the Commission if the Commission has requested the variation concerned: s 49(8).
8   As to the meaning of 'public interest consideration' see PARA 189 note 10.
9   Ie the period permitted by the Enterprise Act 2002 s 51 (see PARA 144).
10   Ie the report required by the Enterprise Act 2002 s 50 (see PARA 198).
11   Enterprise Act 2002 s 49(9).

198.   Investigations and reports on references. The Competition Commission[1] is required to prepare a report on a reference from the Secretary of State[2] and give it to the Secretary of State within the period of 24 weeks[3] beginning with the date of the reference concerned[4]. The report, in particular, must contain: (1) the decisions of the Commission on the questions which it is required to answer[5]; (2) its reasons for its decisions[6]; and (3) such information as the Commission considers appropriate for facilitating a proper understanding of those questions and of its reasons for its decisions[7]. The Commission may carry out such investigations as it considers appropriate for the purpose of producing its report[8].

The Commission may extend, by no more than eight weeks[9], the period within which the report is to be prepared and given to the Secretary of State if it considers that there are special reasons why the report cannot be prepared and given to the Secretary of State within that period[10]. The Commission may also extend the period within which the report is to be prepared and given to the Secretary of State if it considers that a relevant person[11] has failed, whether with or without a reasonable excuse, to comply with any requirement of a notice[12] to attend as a witness or produce documents[13]. An extension comes into force when published[14], and continues in force until the person concerned provides the information or documents to the satisfaction of the Commission or, as the case may be, appears as a witness in accordance with the requirements of the Commission or the Commission publishes its decision to cancel the extension[15].

1   As to the Competition Commission see PARAS 9–12.
2   Ie a reference under the Enterprise Act 2002 s 45 (see PARA 193). As to the Secretary of State see PARA 5.
3   After consulting the Commission and such other persons as he considers appropriate, the Secretary of State may by order amend the Enterprise Act 2002 s 51 so as to alter the period of 24 weeks or any period for the time being mentioned in substitution for that period, provided the altered period does not exceed 24 weeks: s 52(8)(a), (9), (11) (s 52(9) amended by SI 2004/1079). At the date at which this volume states the law no such order had been made. An order under the Enterprise Act 2002 s 52(8) does not affect any period of time within which the Commission is under a duty to prepare and give to the Secretary of State its report under s 50 in relation to a reference under s 45 (see PARA 193) if the Commission is already under that duty in relation to that reference when the order is made: s 52(10).
4   Enterprise Act 2002 ss 50(1), 51(1). Where the report relates to a reference under s 45 which has been made after a report of the Office of Communications ('OFCOM') under s 44A (see PARA 192), the Commission must give a copy of its report (whether or not published) to OFCOM: s 50(2A) (added by the Communications Act 2003 s 389(1), Sch 16 para 10).

5   Enterprise Act 2002 s 50(2)(a). The Commission is required to answer questions by virtue of s 47 (see PARA 195).
6   Enterprise Act 2002 s 50(2)(b).
7   Enterprise Act 2002 s 50(2)(c).
8   Enterprise Act 2002 s 50(3).
9   After consulting the Commission and such other persons as he considers appropriate, the Secretary of State may by order amend the Enterprise Act 2002 s 51 so as to alter the period of eight weeks or any period for the time being mentioned in substitution for that period, provided the altered period does not exceed eight weeks: s 52(8)(c), (9), (11) (s 52(9) amended by SI 2004/1079). At the date at which this volume states the law no such order had been made. See also note 4.
10 Enterprise Act 2002 s 51(3). A period extended under s 51(3) may also be extended under s 51(4) (see the text to note 13) and a period extended under s 51(4) may also be extended under s 51(3): ss 51(9), 52(3). No more than one extension is possible under s 51(3): s 52(4). Where a period within which a report under s 50 is to be prepared and given to the Secretary of State is extended or further extended under s 51(3) or (4), the period as extended or (as the case may be) further extended is calculated by taking the period being extended and adding to it the period of the extension (whether or not those periods overlap in time): s 52(5).
11 'Relevant person' means: (1) any person carrying on any of the enterprises concerned; (2) any person who (whether alone or as a member of a group) owns or has control of any such person; or (3) any officer, employee or agent of any person mentioned in head (1) or head (2): Enterprise Act 2002 s 51(5). A person or group of persons able, directly or indirectly, to control or materially to influence the policy of a body of persons corporate or unincorporate, but without having a controlling interest in that body of persons, may be treated as having control of it: s 51(6).
12 Ie under the Enterprise Act 2002 s 109 (see PARA 259).
13 Enterprise Act 2002 s 51(4). See note 8. Where: (1) the period within which the report under s 50 is to be prepared and given to the Secretary of State is further extended; (2) the further extension and at least one previous extension is made under s 51(4); and (3) the same days or fractions of days are included in or comprise the further extension and are included in or comprise at least one such previous extension then, in calculating the period of the further extension, any days or fractions of days of the kind mentioned in head (3) are to be disregarded: s 52(6), (7).
14 Enterprise Act 2002 s 51(7). The extension is published under s 107 (see PARA 257).
15 Enterprise Act 2002 s 51(8). The Secretary of State may make regulations for the purposes of s 51(8): s 52(12). The regulations may, in particular: (1) provide for the time at which information or documents are to be treated as provided (including the time at which they are to be treated as provided to the satisfaction of the Commission for the purposes of s 51(8)); (2) provide for the time at which a person is to be treated as appearing as a witness (including the time at which he is to be treated as appearing as a witness in accordance with the requirements of the Commission for the purposes of s 51(8)); (3) provide for the persons carrying on the enterprises which have or may have ceased to be, or may cease to be, distinct enterprises to be informed, in circumstances in which s 51(8) applies, of the fact that the Commission is satisfied as to the provision of the information or documents required by it or the person concerned has appeared as a witness in accordance with the requirements of the Commission; (4) provide for the persons carrying on the enterprises which have or may have ceased to be, or may cease to be, distinct enterprises to be informed, in circumstances in which s 51(8) applies, of the time at which the Commission is to be treated as satisfied as mentioned in head (3) above or the person concerned is to be treated as having appeared as mentioned in head (3) above: s 52(13). At the date at which this volume states the law no such regulations had been made. As to enterprises ceasing to be distinct see PARA 176.

199. Restrictions on action where public interest considerations not finalised.

The Competition Commission[1] must cancel a reference from the Secretary of State[2] if: (1) the intervention notice[3] concerned mentions a public interest consideration[4] which was not finalised[5] on the giving of that notice or public interest considerations which, at that time, were not finalised[6]; (2) no other public interest consideration is mentioned in the notice[7]; (3) at least 24 weeks has elapsed since the giving of the notice[8]; and (4) the public interest consideration mentioned in the notice has not been finalised within that period of 24 weeks or (as the case may be) none of the public interest considerations mentioned in the notice has been finalised within that period of 24 weeks[9].

Where a reference to the Commission by the Secretary of State specifies a public interest consideration which has not been finalised before the making of the reference, the Commission must not give its report to the Secretary of State[10] in relation to that reference unless the period of 24 weeks beginning with the giving of the intervention notice concerned has expired or the public interest consideration concerned has been finalised[11].

In reporting on certain questions[12], the Commission must disregard any public interest consideration which has not been finalised before the giving of the report[13] or which was not finalised on the giving of the intervention notice concerned and has not been finalised within the period of 24 weeks beginning with the giving of the notice concerned[14].

The provisions set out above are without prejudice to the power of the Commission to carry out investigations in relation to any public interest consideration to which it might be able to have regard in its report[15].

1   As to the Competition Commission see PARAS 9–12.
2   Ie under the Enterprise Act 2002 s 45 (see PARA 193). As to the Secretary of State see PARA 5.
3   As to the meaning of 'intervention notice' see PARA 189 note 11.
4   As to the meaning of 'public interest consideration' see PARA 189 note 10.
5   As to the meaning of 'public interest consideration being finalised' see PARA 189 note 13.
6   Enterprise Act 2002 s 53(1)(a).
7   Enterprise Act 2002 s 53(1)(b).
8   Enterprise Act 2002 s 53(1)(c).
9   Enterprise Act 2002 s 53(1)(d).
10 Ie under the Enterprise Act 2002 s 50 (see PARA 198).
11 Enterprise Act 2002 s 53(2) (amended by SI 2004/1079).
12 Ie any of the questions mentioned in the Enterprise Act 2002 s 47(2)(b), (3), (5)(b), (6), (7) (see PARA 195).
13 Enterprise Act 2002 s 53(3).
14 Enterprise Act 2002 s 53(4).
15 Enterprise Act 2002 s 53(5).

D. DECISIONS OF THE SECRETARY OF STATE

200.   Decisions of the Secretary of State in public interest cases.   Where the Secretary of State[1] has received a report of the Competition Commission[2] in relation to a relevant merger situation[3], the Secretary of State must decide whether to make an adverse public interest finding[4] in relation to the relevant merger situation[5] and whether to make no finding at all in the matter[6]. The Secretary of State may make no finding at all in the matter only if he decides that there is no public interest consideration which is relevant to a consideration of the relevant merger situation concerned[7]. The Secretary of State must make and publish[8] his decision within the period of 30 days[9] beginning with the receipt of the report of the Commission[10].

1   As to the Secretary of State see PARA 5.
2   Ie under the Enterprise Act 2002 s 50 (see PARA 198). As to the Competition Commission see PARAS 9–12.
3   As to the meaning of 'relevant merger situation' see PARA 173; and see PARA 189 note 3.
4   For the purposes of the Enterprise Act 2002 Pt 3 (ss 22–130) the Secretary of State makes an adverse public interest finding in relation to a relevant merger situation if, in relation to that situation, he decides: (1) in connection with a reference to the Commission under s 45(2), that it is the case as mentioned in s 45(2)(a)–(d) (see PARA 193 head (1)(a)–(d)) or s 45(3) (see PARA 193 head (2)); (2) in connection with a reference to the Commission under s 45(3), that it is the case as mentioned in s 45(3)(a)–(d) (see PARA 193 head (2)(a)–(d)); (3) in connection with a reference

to the Commission under s 45(4), that it is the case as mentioned in s 45(4)(a)–(d) (see PARA 193 head (3)(a)–(d)) or s 45(5); and (4) in connection with a reference to the Commission under s 45(5), that it is the case as mentioned in s 45(5)(a)–(d) (see PARA 193 head (4)(a)–(d)): s 54(3). See note 6.

5   In deciding whether to make an adverse public interest finding under the Enterprise Act 2002 s 54(2), the Secretary of State must accept: (1) in connection with a reference to the Commission under s 45(2) or (4) (see PARA 193 heads (1), (3)), the decision of the report of the Commission under s 50 (see PARA 198) as to whether there is an anti-competitive outcome; and (2) in connection with a reference to the Commission under s 45(3) or (5) (see PARA 193 heads (2), (4)), the decision of the report of the Commission under s 50 as to whether a relevant merger situation has been created or (as the case may be) arrangements are in progress or in contemplation which, if carried into effect, will result in the creation of a relevant merger situation, and the decision of the report of the Office of Fair Trading (the 'OFT') under s 44 (see PARA 191) as to the absence of a substantial lessening of competition: s 54(7). As to the OFT see PARAS 6–8.

6   Enterprise Act 2002 s 54(1), (2). In making a decision under s 54(2)–(4) (see note 4, and the text to note 7), the Secretary of State must disregard any public interest consideration not specified in the reference under s 45 (see PARA 193) and any public interest consideration disregarded by the Commission for the purposes of its report: s 54(6). As to the meaning of 'public interest consideration' see PARA 189 note 10.

7   Enterprise Act 2002 s 54(4). See note 6.

8   As to the meaning of 'publish' see PARA 186 note 2.

9   In determining the period of 30 days no account must be taken of Saturday, Sunday, Good Friday and Christmas Day, and any day which is a bank holiday in England and Wales: Enterprise Act 2002 s 54(8).

10 Enterprise Act 2002 s 54(5).

201.   Enforcement action by the Secretary of State. Where the Secretary of State[1] has decided[2] to make an adverse public interest finding[3] in relation to a relevant merger situation[4] and has published[5] his decision within the period so required[6], then the Secretary of State may take such action[7] as he considers to be reasonable and practicable to remedy, mitigate or prevent any of the effects adverse to the public interest which have resulted from, or may be expected to result from, the creation of the relevant merger situation concerned[8]. In making the decision, the Secretary of State, in particular, must have regard to the report of the Competition Commission[9]. In any case of a substantial lessening of competition, the Secretary of State may, in particular, have regard to the effect of any action on any relevant customer benefits[10] in relation to the creation of the relevant merger situation concerned[11].

1   As to the Secretary of State see PARA 5.
2   Ie under the Enterprise Act 2002 s 54(2) within the period required by s 54(5) (see PARA 200).
3   As to the meaning of 'adverse public interest finding' see PARA 200 note 4.
4   As to the meaning of 'relevant merger situation' see PARA 173; and see PARA 189 note 3.
5   As to the meaning of 'publish' see PARA 186 note 2.
6   Enterprise Act 2002 s 55(1).
7   Ie under the Enterprise Act 2002 Sch 7 para 9 or 11 (see PARA 227). As to the meaning of 'action' see PARA 184 note 9.
8   Enterprise Act 2002 s 55(2).
9   Enterprise Act 2002 s 55(3). The report of the Competition Commission is made under s 50 (see PARA 198). As to the Competition Commission see PARAS 9–12.
10 As to the meaning of 'relevant customer benefit' see PARA 180.
11 Enterprise Act 2002 s 55(4).

202.   Cessation of intervention on public interest grounds. Where the Secretary of State[1] decides not to make a reference to the Competition Commission[2] on the ground that no public interest consideration[3] to which he is able to have regard is relevant to a consideration of the relevant merger situation[4] concerned, he must by notice[5] require the Office of Fair Trading (the

'OFT')[6] to deal with the matter otherwise than as a public interest case[7]. Where a notice is given to the OFT in these circumstances, the OFT must decide whether to make a merger reference[8].

Where the Commission cancels[9] a reference from the Secretary of State[10] where a public interest consideration is not finalised and the report of the OFT[11] contains the decision that it is or may be the case that there is an anti-competitive outcome[12] in relation to the relevant merger situation concerned, the Commission may proceed with the matter as a public interest case[13] as if a merger reference[14] had been made to it by the OFT[15].

Where the Secretary of State decides to make no finding at all in the matter[16] in connection with a reference to the Commission[17], the Commission must proceed[18] as if a merger reference[19] had been made to it instead of a public interest case reference[20].

1   As to the Secretary of State see PARA 5.
2   Ie under the Enterprise Act 2002 s 45 (see PARA 193). As to the Competition Commission see PARAS 9–12.
3   As to the meaning of 'public interest consideration' see PARA 189 note 10.
4   As to the meaning of 'relevant merger situation' see PARA 173; and see PARA 189 note 3.
5   As to the meaning of 'notice' see PARA 175 note 4.
6   As to the OFT see PARAS 6–8.
7   Enterprise Act 2002 s 56(1).
8   Enterprise Act 2002 s 56(2). A merger reference is made under s 22 (see PARA 172) or s 33 (see PARA 182). Any time-limits in relation to the Secretary of State's decision whether to make a reference to the Commission under s 45 (see PARA 193) (including any remaining powers of extension) apply in relation to the decision of the OFT whether to make a reference under s 22 or s 33: s 56(2).
9   Ie under the Enterprise Act 2002 s 53(1) (see PARA 199).
10 Ie under the Enterprise Act 2002 s 45 (see PARA 193).
11 Ie under the Enterprise Act 2002 s 44 (see PARA 191).
12 As to the meaning of 'anti-competitive outcome' see PARA 184.
13 Ie under the Enterprise Act 2002 Pt 3 Ch 2 (ss 42–58A).
14 Ie under the Enterprise Act 2002 s 22 (see PARA 172) or s 33 (see PARA 182).
15 Enterprise Act 2002 s 56(3). In proceeding by virtue of s 56(3) to prepare and publish a report under s 38 (see PARA 186), the Commission must proceed as if: (1) the reference under s 22 (see PARA 172) or s 33 (see PARA 182) had been made at the same time as the reference under s 45 (see PARA 193); (2) the timetable for preparing and giving its report under s 50 (including any remaining powers of extension and as extended by an additional period of 20 days) (see PARA 198) were the timetable for preparing and publishing its report under s 38; and (3) in relation to the question whether a relevant merger situation has been created or the question whether arrangements are in progress or in contemplation which, if carried into effect, will result in the creation of a relevant merger situation, the Commission were confined to the questions on the subject to be investigated by it under s 47 (see PARA 195): s 56(4). In determining the period of 20 days mentioned in s 56(4) no account is to be taken of Saturday, Sunday, Good Friday and Christmas Day and any day which is a bank holiday in England and Wales: s 56(5).
    Where the Commission becomes under a duty to proceed as mentioned in s 56(3) or (6) (see the text to notes 16–20), references in Pt 3 (ss 22–130) to references under s 22 (see PARA 172) and s 33 (see PARA 182), so far as may be necessary, are to be construed accordingly; and, in particular, ss 77–81 (see PARAS 221–224) apply as if a reference has been made to the Commission by the OFT under s 22 or (as the case may be) s 33: s 56(8).
16 Ie under the Enterprise Act 2002 s 54(2) (see PARA 200).
17 Ie under the Enterprise Act 2002 s 45(2) or (4) (see PARA 193 heads (1), (3)).
18 Ie under the Enterprise Act 2002 Pt 3.
19 Ie under the Enterprise Act 2002 s 22 (see PARA 172) or s 33 (see PARA 182).
20 Enterprise Act 2002 s 56(6). The Commission must also proceed as if its report to the Secretary of State under s 50 (see PARA 198) had been prepared and published by it under s 38 (see PARA 186) within the period permitted by s 39 (see PARA 187): s 56(6). In relation to proceedings by virtue of s 56(6), the reference in s 41(3) to decisions of the Commission as included in its report by virtue of s 35(3) or s 36(2) (see PARA 184) is to be construed as a reference to decisions which were included in the report of the Commission by virtue of s 47(8) (see PARA 195): s 56(7).

E. NATIONAL SECURITY

203. Duty to inform the Secretary of State. The Office of Fair Trading (the 'OFT')[1], in considering whether to make a merger reference[2], must bring to the attention of the Secretary of State[3] any case which it believes raises any national security consideration[4] unless it believes that the Secretary of State would consider any such consideration immaterial in the context of the particular case[5].

The interests of national security[6] are specified as follows[7]:

(1) the need for accurate presentation of news and free expression of opinion in newspapers[8];

(2) the need for, to the extent that it is reasonable and practicable, a sufficient plurality of views in newspapers in each market for newspapers in the United Kingdom[9] or a part of the United Kingdom[10];

(3) the need, in relation to every different audience in the United Kingdom or in a particular area or locality of the United Kingdom, for there to be a sufficient plurality of persons with control of the media enterprises[11] serving that audience[12];

(4) the need for the availability throughout the United Kingdom of a wide range of broadcasting[13] which, taken as a whole, is both of high quality and calculated to appeal to a wide variety of tastes and interests[14];

(5) the need for persons carrying on media enterprises, and for those with control of such enterprises, to have a genuine commitment to the attainment in relation to broadcasting of the programme and fairness standards objectives[15]; and

(6) the interest of maintaining the stability of the UK financial system[16].

The Secretary of State may by order modify these provisions for the purpose of specifying a new consideration or removing or amending any consideration which is for the time being specified[17]. Such an order may, in particular, provide for a consideration to be specified for a particular purpose or purposes or for all purposes[18]. An order may apply in relation to cases under consideration by the OFT, OFCOM, the Commission or the Secretary of State before the making of the order as well as cases under consideration on or after the making of the order[19].

1 As to the OFT see PARAS 6–8.
2 Ie under the Enterprise Act 2002 s 22 (see PARA 172) or s 33 (see PARA 182).
3 As to the Secretary of State see PARA 5.
4 Ie any consideration specified in the Enterprise Act 2002 s 58 (see the text and notes 7–19).
5 Enterprise Act 2002 s 57(1).
6 'National security' includes public security; and 'public security' has the same meaning as in EC Council Regulation 139/2004 (OJ L24, 29.1.2004, p 1) (the 'EC Merger Regulation') art 21(4) (see PARA 74): Enterprise Act 2002 s 58(2) (amended by SI 2004/1079).
7 Enterprise Act 2002 s 58(1).
8 Enterprise Act 2002 s 58(2A) (s 58(2A)–(2C) added by the Communications Act 2003 s 375(1)).
9 As to the meaning of 'United Kingdom' see PARA 401 note 1.
10 Enterprise Act 2002 s 58(2B) (as added: see note 8).
11 An enterprise is a media enterprise if it consists in or involves broadcasting: Enterprise Act 2002 s 58A(1) (s 58A added by the Communications Act 2003 s 375(2)). In the case of a merger situation in which at least one of the enterprises ceasing to be distinct consists in or involves broadcasting, the references in the Enterprise Act 2002 s 58(2C)(a) (see head (3) in the text) or s 58A to media enterprises include references to newspaper enterprises: s 58A(2) (as so added). As to enterprises ceasing to be distinct see PARA 176. In Pt 3 (ss 22–130), 'newspaper enterprise' means an enterprise consisting in or involving the supply of newspapers: s 58A(3) (as so added). As to the meaning of 'newspaper' see PARA 191 note 9.
    Wherever in a merger situation two media enterprises serving the same audience cease to be distinct, the number of such enterprises serving that audience is assumed to be more immediately

before they cease to be distinct than it is afterwards: s 58A(4) (as so added). For the purposes of s 58, where two or more media enterprises would fall to be treated as under common ownership or common control for the purposes of s 26 (see PARA 176) or are otherwise in the same ownership or under the same control, they are to be treated (subject to s 58A(4)) as all under the control of only one person: s 58A(5) (as so added). A reference in s 58 or s 58A to an audience is to be construed in relation to a media enterprise in whichever of the following ways the decision-making authority considers appropriate: (1) as a reference to any one of the audiences served by that enterprise, taking them separately; (2) as a reference to all the audiences served by that enterprise, taking them together; (3) as a reference to a number of those audiences taken together in such group as the decision-making authority considers appropriate; or (4) as a reference to a part of anything that could be taken to be an audience under any of heads (1)–(3): s 58A(6) (as so added). The criteria for deciding who can be treated for this purpose as comprised in an audience, or as comprised in an audience served by a particular service is such as the decision-making authority considers appropriate in the circumstances of the case, and may allow for persons to be treated as members of an audience if they are only potentially members of it: s 58A(7) (as so added). 'Audience' includes readership: s 58A(8) (as so added). As to the meaning of 'decision-making authority' see PARA 173 note 8.

The power under s 58(3) to modify s 58 (see the text and note 17) includes power to modify s 58A: s 58A(9) (as so added).

12   Enterprise Act 2002 s 58(2C)(a) (as added: see note 8). Associated persons, and any bodies corporate which they or any of them control, are to be treated as one person for the purposes of s 58(2C): s 127(1)(aa) (added by the Communications Act 2003 s 375(3)). See PARA 176.

13   As to the meaning of 'broadcasting' see PARA 191 note 9.

14   Enterprise Act 2002 s 58(2C)(b) (as added: see note 8).

15   Enterprise Act 2002 s 58(2C)(c) (as added: see note 8). The standards objectives are those set out in the Communications Act 2003 s 319 (see TELECOMMUNICATIONS AND BROADCASTING vol 45(1) (2005 Reissue) PARA 289.

16   Enterprise Act 2002 s 58(2D) (added by SI 2008/2645). This does not include the interest of maintaining the stability of the UK financial system for the purposes of European mergers (see the Enterprise Act 2002 ss 67, 68; and PARAS 213–214) or references made, or deemed to be made, by the European Commission to the OFT under EC Council Regulation 139/2004 (OJ L24, 29.1.2004, p 1) (the 'EC Merger Regulation') art 4(4) or 9 (see PARA 74).

17   Enterprise Act 2002 s 58(3). In exercise of this power, the Secretary of State has made the Enterprise Act 2002 (Specification of Additional Section 58 Consideration) Order 2008, SI 2008/2645.

The OFT, the Office of Communications ('OFCOM') and the Competition Commission must bring to the attention of the Secretary of State any representations about exercising his powers under the Enterprise Act 2002 s 58(3) which have been made to the OFT, OFCOM or the Commission: s 57(2). As to OFCOM see PARA 19. As to the Competition Commission see PARAS 9–12.

18   Enterprise Act 2002 s 58(4)(a).

19   Enterprise Act 2002 s 58(4)(b).

(iii) Other Special Cases

A. SPECIAL PUBLIC INTEREST CASES

204.   Intervention by the Secretary of State in special public interest cases.
Where the Secretary of State[1] has reasonable grounds for suspecting that it is or may be the case that a special merger situation has been created or arrangements are in progress or in contemplation which, if carried into effect, will result in the creation of a special merger situation[2], then the Secretary of State may give a special intervention notice to the Office of Fair Trading (the 'OFT')[3] if he believes that it is or may be the case that one or more than one national security consideration[4] is relevant to a consideration of the special merger situation concerned[5].

A special merger situation has been created if:
(1)   no relevant merger situation has been created as the enterprise[6] does not

pass the turnover test[7] or the share of supply test[8] but a relevant merger situation would otherwise have been created[9]; and

(2)   immediately before the enterprises concerned ceased to be distinct:

(a)   at least one of the enterprises concerned was carried on in the United Kingdom[10] or by or under the control of a body corporate incorporated in the United Kingdom and a person carrying on one or more of the enterprises concerned was a relevant government contractor[11];

(b)   in relation to the supply of newspapers[12] of any description[13], at least one-quarter[14] of all the newspapers of that description which were supplied in the United Kingdom, or in a substantial part of the United Kingdom, were supplied by the person or persons by whom one of the enterprises concerned was carried on[15]; or

(c)   in relation to the provision of broadcasting[16] of any description, at least one-quarter of all broadcasting of that description provided in the United Kingdom, or in a substantial part of the United Kingdom, was provided by the person or persons by whom one of the enterprises concerned was carried on[17].

No more than one special intervention notice may be given in relation to the same special merger situation[18].

1   As to the Secretary of State see PARA 5.
2   Enterprise Act 2002 s 59(1).
3   As to the OFT see PARAS 6–8.
4   Ie a consideration specified in the Enterprise Act 2002 s 58 (see PARA 203).
5   Enterprise Act 2002 s 59(2). As to special intervention notices see PARA 205.
6   As to the meaning of 'enterprise' see PARA 173 note 2.
7   As to the turnover test see the Enterprise Act 2002 s 23(1)(b); and PARAS 173, 178.
8   As to the share of supply test see the Enterprise Act 2002 s 23(2)(b); and PARA 173.
9   Enterprise Act 2002 s 59(3)(a), (3A) (s 59(3) substituted, and s 59(3A)–(3D) added, by the Communications Act 2003 s 378(1)). For the purposes of deciding whether a relevant merger situation has been created or whether arrangements are in progress or in contemplation which, if carried into effect, will result in the creation of a relevant merger situation, the Enterprise Act 2002 ss 23–32 (read together with s 34) (see PARAS 173–182) apply for the purposes of Pt 3 Ch 3 (ss 59–70) as they do for the purposes of Pt 3 Ch 1 (ss 22–41) with certain modifications: see s 59(5), (6).
10 As to the meaning of 'United Kingdom' see PARA 401 note 1.
11 Enterprise Act 2002 s 59(3)(b)(i), (3B) (as substituted and added: see note 9). 'Relevant government contractor' means: (1) a government contractor who has been notified by or on behalf of the Secretary of State of information, documents or other articles relating to defence and of a confidential nature which the government contractor or an employee of his may hold or receive in connection with being such a contractor and whose notification has not been revoked by or on behalf of the Secretary of State; or (2) a former government contractor who was so notified when he was a government contractor and whose notification has not been revoked by or on behalf of the Secretary of State: s 59(8). 'Defence' has the same meaning as in the Official Secrets Act 1989 s 2 (see CRIMINAL LAW, EVIDENCE AND PROCEDURE vol 11(1) (2006 Reissue) PARA 484); and 'government contractor' has the same meaning as in the Official Secrets Act 1989 (see CRIMINAL LAW, EVIDENCE AND PROCEDURE vol 11(1) (2006 Reissue) PARA 483) and includes any sub-contractor of a government contractor, any sub-contractor of that sub-contractor and any other sub-contractor in a chain of sub-contractors which begins with the sub-contractor of the government contractor: Enterprise Act 2002 s 59(9).
12 As to the meaning of 'newspaper' see PARA 191 note 9. References in the Enterprise Act 2002 s 59(3C) to the supply of newspapers, in relation to newspapers of any description which are the subject of different forms of supply, is to be construed in whichever of the following ways the decision-making authority considers appropriate: (1) as references to any of those forms of supply taken separately; (2) as references to all those forms of supply taken together; or (3) as references to any of those forms of supply taken in groups: s 59A(2) (s 59A added by the Communications Act 2003 s 378(3)). As to the meaning of 'decision-making authority' see PARA 173 note 8. For these purposes, the decision-making authority may treat newspapers as being

the subject of different forms of supply whenever: (a) the transactions concerned differ as to their nature, their parties, their terms or their surrounding circumstances; and (b) the difference is one which, in the opinion of the decision-making authority, ought for these purposes to be treated as a material difference: Enterprise Act 2002 s 59A(3) (as so added).

13 The criteria for deciding when newspapers or broadcasting can be treated, for the purposes of the Enterprise Act 2002 s 59, as newspapers or broadcasting of a separate description is to be such as in any particular case the decision-making authority considers appropriate in the circumstances of that case: s 59A(6) (as added: see note 12).

14 For the purpose of deciding whether the proportion of one-quarter mentioned in the Enterprise Act 2002 s 59(3C), (3D) is fulfilled with respect to newspapers of any description, or broadcasting of any description, the decision-making authority must apply such criterion (whether value, cost, price, quantity, capacity, number of workers employed or some other criterion, of whatever nature), or such combination of criteria, as the decision-making authority considers appropriate: s 59A(1) (as added: see note 12).

15 Enterprise Act 2002 s 59(3)(b)(ii), (3C) (as substituted and added: see note 9). The Secretary of State may by order amend the conditions mentioned in s 59(3)(b)(ii), (iii) (see head (2)(c) in the text): s 59(6A) (added by the Communications Act 2003 s 378(2)). At the date at which this volume states the law no such order had been made.

16 As to the meaning of 'broadcasting' see PARA 191 note 9. References to the provision of broadcasting, in relation to broadcasting of any description which is the subject of different forms of provision, are to be construed in whichever of the following ways the decision-making authority considers appropriate: (1) as references to any of those forms of provision taken separately; (2) as references to all those forms of provision taken together; or (3) as references to any of those forms of provision taken in groups: Enterprise Act 2002 s 59A(4) (as added: see note 12). The decision-making authority may treat broadcasting as being the subject of different forms of provision whenever: (a) the transactions concerned differ as to their nature, their parties, their terms or their surrounding circumstances; and (b) the difference is one which, in the opinion of the decision-making authority, ought for these purposes to be treated as a material difference: s 59A(5) (as added: see note 12). 'Provision' and cognate expressions have the same meaning in relation to broadcasting as in the Communications Act 2003 Pt 3 (ss 198–362) (see TELECOMMUNICATIONS AND BROADCASTING vol 45(1) (2005 Reissue) PARA 312), subject to the Enterprise Act 2002 s 59A(4), (5): s 59A(7) (as added: see note 12).

17 Enterprise Act 2002 s 59(3)(b)(iii), (3D) (as substituted and added: see note 9). See notes 14, 15.

18 Enterprise Act 2002 s 59(7).

205. Special intervention notices. A special intervention notice[1] must state the special merger situation[2] concerned and the national security considerations[3] which are, or may be, relevant to the special merger situation concerned[4].

Where the Secretary of State[5] believes that it is or may be the case that two or more national security considerations are relevant to a consideration of the special merger situation concerned, he may decide not to mention in the special intervention notice such of those considerations as he considers appropriate[6].

A special intervention notice comes into force when it is given and ceases to be in force when the matter to which it relates is finally determined[7].

1 Ie a notice given under the Enterprise Act 2002 s 59 (see PARA 204).
2 As to the meaning of 'special merger situation' see PARA 204.
3 Ie the consideration specified in the Enterprise Act 2002 s 58 (see PARA 203).
4 Enterprise Act 2002 s 60(1).
5 As to the Secretary of State see PARA 5.
6 Enterprise Act 2002 s 60(2).
7 Enterprise Act 2002 s 60(3). For the purposes of Pt 3 (ss 22–130), a matter to which a special intervention notice relates is finally determined under Pt 3 Ch 3 (ss 59–70) if:
   (1) the time within which the Office of Fair Trading (the 'OFT') or, if relevant, the Office of Communications ('OFCOM') is to report to the Secretary of State under s 61 or (as the case may be) s 61A (see PARAS 206–207) has expired and no such report has been made (s 60(4)(a));
   (2) the Secretary of State decides to accept an undertaking or group of undertakings under Sch 7 para 3 (see PARA 229) instead of making a reference under s 62 (see PARA 208) (s 60(4)(b));

(3)   the Secretary of State otherwise decides not to make a reference under s 62 (see PARA
       208) (s 60(4)(c));
(4)   the Competition Commission cancels such a reference under s 64(1) (see PARA 210)
       (s 60(4)(d));
(5)   the time within which the Commission is to prepare a report under s 65 (see PARA 211)
       and give it to the Secretary of State has expired and no such report has been prepared
       and given to the Secretary of State (s 60(4)(e));
(6)   the time within which the Secretary of State is to make and publish a decision under
       s 66(2) (see PARA 212) has expired and no such decision has been made and published
       (s 60(4)(f));
(7)   the Secretary of State decides under s 66(2) otherwise than as mentioned in s 66(5) (see
       PARA 212) (s 60(4)(g));
(8)   the Secretary of State decides under s 66(2) as mentioned in s 66(5) (see PARA 212) but
       decides neither to accept an undertaking under Sch 7 para 9 nor to make an order
       under Sch 7 para 11 (see PARA 231) (s 60(4)(h)); or
(9)   the Secretary of State decides under s 66(2) as mentioned in s 66(5) (see PARA 212) and
       accepts an undertaking under Sch 7 para 9 or makes an order under Sch 7 para 11 (see
       PARA 231) (s 60(4)(i)).

For the purposes of Pt 3, the time when a matter to which a special intervention notice
relates is finally determined under Pt 3 Ch 3 is: (a) in a case falling within head (1), (5) or (6),
the expiry of the time concerned; (b) in a case falling within head (2), the acceptance of the
undertaking or group of undertakings concerned; (c) in a case falling within head (3), (4) or (7),
the making of the decision concerned; (d) in a case falling within head (8), the making of the
decision neither to accept an undertaking under Sch 7 para 9 nor to make an order under Sch 7
para 11; and (e) in a case falling within head (9), the acceptance of the undertaking concerned or
(as the case may be) the making of the order concerned: s 60(5).

206.   Initial investigation and report by the Office of Fair Trading.   Where the
Secretary of State[1] has given a special intervention notice[2] in relation to a special
merger situation[3], the Office of Fair Trading (the 'OFT')[4], within such period as
the Secretary of State may require, must give a report to the Secretary of State in
relation to the case[5].

The report must contain: (1) advice from the OFT on the considerations
relevant to the making of a merger reference[6] which are also relevant to the
Secretary of State's decision as to whether to make a special merger reference to
the Competition Commission[7]; and (2) a summary of any representations about
the case which have been received by the OFT and which relate to any
consideration mentioned in the special intervention notice concerned[8] and which
is or may be relevant to the Secretary of State's decision as to whether to make a
reference to the Commission[9]. The report must include a decision as to whether
the OFT believes[10] that it is, or may be, the case that a special merger situation
has been created or arrangements are in progress or in contemplation which, if
carried into effect, will result in the creation of a special merger situation[11]. The
report may, in particular, contain a summary of any representations about the
case which have been received by the OFT and which relate to any consideration
which is mentioned in the special intervention notice concerned and, at the time
of the giving of that notice, was specified as a national security consideration[12]
and is or may be relevant to the Secretary of State's decision as to whether to
make a reference to the Commission[13]. The report may also, in particular,
include advice and recommendations on any consideration mentioned in the
special intervention notice concerned and which is or may be relevant to the
Secretary of State's decision as to whether to make a reference to the
Commission[14].

The OFT must carry out such investigations as it considers appropriate for the
purposes of producing the report[15].

The Secretary of State may exclude a matter from the report if he considers the publication of the matter would be inappropriate[16].

1 As to the Secretary of State see PARA 5.
2 Ie a notice given under the Enterprise Act 2002 s 59 (see PARA 204).
3 Enterprise Act 2002 s 61(1). As to the meaning of 'special merger situation' see PARA 204.
4 As to the OFT see PARAS 6–8.
5 Enterprise Act 2002 s 61(2).
6 Ie a reference under the Enterprise Act 2002 s 22 (see PARA 172) or s 33 (see PARA 182).
7 Enterprise Act 2002 s 61(3)(a). A special merger reference by the Secretary of State to the Competition Commission is made under s 62 (see PARA 208). As to the Competition Commission see PARAS 9–12.
8 This does not include a national security consideration which, at the time of the giving of the notice, was specified in the Enterprise Act 2002 s 58(2A)–(2C) (see PARA 203): s 61(3)(b) (amended by the Communications Act 2003 s 379(1), (2)).
9 Enterprise Act 2002 s 61(3)(b) (as amended: see note 8).
10 Ie disregarding the issue of whether a person carrying on one of the enterprises concerned was a government contractor: see the Enterprise Act 2002 s 59(3B)(b).
11 Enterprise Act 2002 s 61(4) (amended by the Communications Act 2003 s 379(1), (3)).
12 Ie specified in the Enterprise Act 2002 s 58(2A)–(2C) (see PARA 203).
13 Enterprise Act 2002 s 61(4A) (added by the Communications Act 2003 s 379(1), (4)).
14 Enterprise Act 2002 s 61(5).
15 Enterprise Act 2002 s 61(6).
16 See the Enterprise Act 2002 s 118(1)(a), (2). The OFT must advise the Secretary of State as to any matters which it considers should be excluded: s 118(4). In deciding what is inappropriate, the Secretary of State must have regard to the considerations mentioned in s 244 (see PARA 334): s 118(3). References in s 38(4) (see PARA 186) and s 107(11) (see PARA 257) to the giving or laying of a report of the Commission are to be construed as references to the giving or laying of the report as published: s 118(5).

207.   Investigation and report by the Office of Communications in relation to media mergers.   Where the Secretary of State[1] has given a special intervention notice[2] in relation to a special merger situation[3] and the special intervention notice mentions any national security consideration which, at the time of the giving of the notice, was specified in relation to media mergers[4], the Office of Communications ('OFCOM')[5], within such period as the Secretary of State may require, must give a report to the Secretary of State on the effect of the consideration or considerations concerned on the case[6].

The report must contain advice and recommendations on any consideration which is mentioned in the special intervention notice concerned and, at the time of the giving of that notice, was specified in relation to media mergers[7] and is or may be relevant to the Secretary of State's decision as to whether to make a reference to the Competition Commission[8]. The report must also contain a summary of any representations about the case which have been received by OFCOM and which relate to any such consideration[9].

OFCOM must carry out such investigations as they consider appropriate for the purposes of producing the report[10].

The Secretary of State may exclude a matter from the report if he considers the publication of the matter would be inappropriate[11].

1 As to the Secretary of State see PARA 5.
2 Ie a notice given under the Enterprise Act 2002 s 59 (see PARA 204).
3 Enterprise Act 2002 s 61A(1)(a) (s 61A added by the Communications Act 2003 s 380). As to the meaning of 'special merger situation' see PARA 204.
4 Enterprise Act 2002 s 61A(1)(b) (as added: see note 3). A national security consideration is specified in s 58(2A)–(2C) (see PARA 203).
5 As to OFCOM see PARA 19.
6 Enterprise Act 2002 s 61A(2) (as added: see note 3).

7　Enterprise Act 2002 s 61A(3)(a)(i) (as added: see note 3).
8　Enterprise Act 2002 s 61A(3)(a)(ii) (as added: see note 3).
9　Enterprise Act 2002 s 61A(3)(b) (as added: see note 3).
10　Enterprise Act 2002 s 61A(4) (as added: see note 3).
11　See the Enterprise Act 2002 s 118(1)(aa), (2) (s 118(1)(aa) added by the Communications Act 2003 s 389(1), Sch 16 para 21). The OFT must advise the Secretary of State as to any matters which it considers should be excluded: Enterprise Act 2002 s 118(4). In deciding what is inappropriate, the Secretary of State must have regard to the considerations mentioned in s 244 (see PARA 334): s 118(3). References in s 38(4) (see PARA 186) and s 107(11) (see PARA 257) to the giving or laying of a report of the Commission are to be construed as references to the giving or laying of the report as published: s 118(5).

208. Power of Secretary of State to refer the matter. Where the Secretary of State[1] has given a special intervention notice[2] in relation to a special merger situation[3] and has received a report of the Office of Fair Trading the 'OFT'[4] and any report of the Office of Communications ('OFCOM')[5] which is required in relation to the matter[6], the Secretary of State may make a reference to the Competition Commission[7] if he believes that it is or may be the case that: (1) a special merger situation has been created[8]; (2) one or more than one consideration mentioned in the special intervention notice is relevant to a consideration of the special merger situation concerned[9]; and (3) taking account only of the relevant consideration or considerations concerned, the creation of that situation operates or may be expected to operate against the public interest[10].

The Secretary of State may also make a reference to the Commission if he believes that it is or may be the case that: (a) arrangements are in progress or in contemplation which, if carried into effect, will result in the creation of a special merger situation[11]; (b) one or more than one consideration mentioned in the special intervention notice is relevant to a consideration of the special merger situation concerned[12]; and (c) taking account only of the relevant consideration or considerations concerned, the creation of that situation may be expected to operate against the public interest[13].

No reference may be made to the Commission if the Secretary of State has accepted an undertaking in relation to the special merger situation[14].

The Secretary of State, in deciding whether to make a reference to the Commission, must accept the decision of the OFT included in its report as to whether a special merger situation has been created or is in contemplation[15].

A reference by the Secretary of State must, in particular, specify the statutory provision under which it is made, the date on which it is made and the consideration or considerations mentioned in the special intervention notice which the Secretary of State believes are, or may be, relevant to a consideration of the special merger situation concerned[16].

1　As to the Secretary of State see PARA 5.
2　Ie a notice given under the Enterprise Act 2002 s 59 (see PARA 204).
3　Enterprise Act 2002 s 62(1)(a). As to the meaning of 'special merger situation' see PARA 204.
4　Ie under the Enterprise Act 2002 s 61 (see PARA 206). As to the OFT see PARAS 6–8.
5　Ie under the Enterprise Act 2002 s 61A (see PARA 207). As to OFCOM see PARA 19.
6　Enterprise Act 2002 s 62(1)(b) (amended by the Communications Act 2003 s 389(1), Sch 16 para 14).
7　As to the Competition Commission see PARAS 9–12.
8　Enterprise Act 2002 s 62(2)(a).
9　Enterprise Act 2002 s 62(2)(b).
10　Enterprise Act 2002 s 62(2)(c).
11　Enterprise Act 2002 s 62(3)(a).
12　Enterprise Act 2002 s 62(3)(b).

13 Enterprise Act 2002 s 62(3)(c).
14 Enterprise Act 2002 s 62(4) (amended by the Communications Act 2003 s 406(7), Sch 19(1)). In
     such case the reference is prevented by the Enterprise Act 2002 Sch 7 para 4 (see PARA 229).
15 Enterprise Act 2002 s 62(5). The decision of the OFT on this matter is under s 61(4) (see PARA
     206).
16 Enterprise Act 2002 s 62(6).

209. Questions to be decided on references of special merger situations. The
Competition Commission[1], on a reference from the Secretary of State[2], must
decide whether a special merger situation[3] has been created[4], or whether
arrangements are in progress or in contemplation which, if carried into effect,
will result in the creation of a special merger situation[5].

If the Commission decides that a special merger situation has been created or
that arrangements are in progress or in contemplation which, if carried into
effect, will result in the creation of a special merger situation, it must then decide
whether, taking account only of the consideration or considerations mentioned in
the reference, the creation of that situation operates or may be expected to
operate against the public interest[6].

If the Commission has decided that the creation of a special merger situation
operates or may be expected to operate against the public interest, it must then
decide the following additional questions[7]:

(1) whether enforcement action[8] should be taken by the Secretary of State
     for the purpose of remedying, mitigating or preventing any of the effects
     adverse to the public interest which have resulted from, or may be
     expected to result from, the creation of the special merger situation
     concerned[9];
(2) whether the Commission should recommend the taking of other
     action[10] by the Secretary of State or action by persons other than itself
     and the Secretary of State for the purpose of remedying, mitigating or
     preventing any of the effects adverse to the public interest which have
     resulted from, or may be expected to result from, the creation of the
     special merger situation concerned[11]; and
(3) in either case, if action should be taken, what action should be taken
     and what is to be remedied, mitigated or prevented[12].

1   As to the Competition Commission see PARAS 9–12.
2   Ie under the Enterprise Act 2002 s 62(2) or s 62(3) (see PARA 208). As to the Secretary of State
     see PARA 5.
3   As to the meaning of 'special merger situation' see PARA 204.
4   Enterprise Act 2002 s 63(1).
5   Enterprise Act 2002 s 63(2).
6   Enterprise Act 2002 s 63(3).
7   Enterprise Act 2002 s 63(4).
8   Ie under the Enterprise Act 2002 s 66 (see PARA 212).
9   Enterprise Act 2002 s 63(4)(a).
10 As to the meaning of 'action' see PARA 184 note 9.
11 Enterprise Act 2002 s 63(4)(b).
12 Enterprise Act 2002 s 63(4)(c).

210. Cancellation and variation of references. The Competition Commission[1]
must cancel a reference of an anticipated special merger situation[2] if it considers
that the proposal to make arrangements that will result in a special merger
situation has been abandoned[3].

The Commission may, if it considers that doing so is justified by the facts
(including events occurring on or after the making of the reference concerned),

treat a reference of a special merger situation as if it were a reference of an anticipated special merger situation and vice versa[4]. Where the Commission treats a reference in this way, any undertaking[5] or order[6] which is in force, continues in force as if it had been made in relation to the reference as so treated and the undertaking or order concerned may be varied, superseded, released or revoked accordingly[7].

The Secretary of State may at any time vary a reference after consulting the Commission[8]. However, no variation by the Secretary of State is capable of altering the consideration or considerations specified in the reference or the period within which the report of the Commission[9] is to be prepared and given to the Secretary of State[10].

1   As to the Competition Commission see PARAS 9–12.
2   Ie a reference under the Enterprise Act 2002 s 62(3) (see PARA 208). As to the meaning of 'special merger situation' see PARA 204.
3   Enterprise Act 2002 s 64(1).
4   Enterprise Act 2002 s 64(2). The Commission may treat a reference made under s 62(2) or s 62(3) (see PARA 208) as if it had been made under s 62(3) or (as the case may be) s 62(2); and, in such cases, references in Pt 3 (ss 22–130) to references under those enactments, so far as may be necessary, are to be construed accordingly: s 64(2). Where, by virtue of s 64(2), the Commission treats a reference made under s 62(2) or s 62(3) as if it had been made under s 62(3) or (as the case may be) s 62(2), Sch 7 paras 1, 2, 7, 8 (undertakings: see PARAS 228, 230), in particular, apply as if the reference had been made under s 62(3) or (as the case may be) s 62(2) instead of under s 62(2) or s 62(3): s 64(3).
5   Ie any undertaking accepted under the Enterprise Act 2002 Sch 7 para 1 (see PARA 228).
6   Ie any order made under the Enterprise Act 2002 Sch 7 para 2 (see PARA 228).
7   Enterprise Act 2002 s 64(4), (5).
8   Enterprise Act 2002 s 64(6), (7). The Secretary of State need not consult the Commission if the Commission had requested the variation concerned: s 64(8). As to the Secretary of State see PARA 5.
9   Ie under the Enterprise Act 2002 s 65 (see PARA 211).
10 Enterprise Act 2002 s 64(9).

211. Investigations and reports on references. The Competition Commission[1] must prepare a report on a reference of a special merger situation[2] and give it to the Secretary of State[3] within the period of 24 weeks beginning with the date of the reference concerned[4].

The report, in particular, must contain the decisions of the Commission on the questions to be decided on a reference[5], its reasons for its decisions and such information as the Commission considers appropriate for facilitating a proper understanding of those questions and of its reasons for its decisions[6].

Where the report relates to a reference which has been made after a report of the Office of Communications ('OFCOM')[7], the Commission must give a copy of its report, whether or not published, to OFCOM[8].

The Commission must carry out such investigations as it considers appropriate for the purpose of producing the report[9].

1   As to the Competition Commission see PARAS 9–12.
2   Ie a reference under the Enterprise Act 2002 s 62 (see PARA 208). As to the meaning of 'special merger situation' see PARA 204.
3   As to the Secretary of State see PARA 5.
4   Enterprise Act 2002 s 65(1), (3). The provisions of s 51 and s 52 (time limits: see PARA 198) (but not s 53 (see PARA 199)) apply for the purposes of a report under s 65 as they apply for the purposes of a report under s 50: s 65(3).
5   Ie the questions the Commission is required to answer by virtue of the Enterprise Act 2002 s 63 (see PARA 209).
6   Enterprise Act 2002 s 65(2).
7   Ie a report under the Enterprise Act 2002 s 61A (see PARA 207). As to OFCOM see PARA 19.

8   Enterprise Act 2002 s 65(2A) (added by the Communications Act 2003 s 389(1), Sch 16 para 15).

9   Enterprise Act 2002 s 65(4).

212.   Decision and enforcement action by the Secretary of State.   Where the Secretary of State[1] has received a report of the Competition Commission[2] in relation to a special merger situation[3], the Secretary of State must decide if a special merger situation has been created or is anticipated and, if so, if the creation of that situation operates or may be expected to operate against the public interest[4].

The Secretary of State must make and publish[5] his decision within the period of 30 days beginning with the receipt of the report of the Commission[6].

In making his decisions, the Secretary of State must accept the decisions of the report of the Commission[7] as to whether a special merger situation has been created or whether arrangements are in progress or in contemplation which, if carried into effect, will result in the creation of a special merger situation[8].

Where the Secretary of State has decided that:

(1)   a special merger situation has been created or arrangements are in progress or in contemplation which, if carried into effect, will result in the creation of a special merger situation[9];

(2)   at least one consideration which is mentioned in the special intervention notice[10] concerned is relevant to a consideration of the special merger situation concerned[11]; and

(3)   taking account only of the relevant consideration or considerations concerned, the creation of that situation operates or may be expected to operate against the public interest[12],

and has so decided, and published his decision[13], then the Secretary of State may take such action[14] as he considers to be reasonable and practicable to remedy, mitigate or prevent any of the effects adverse to the public interest which have resulted from, or may be expected to result from, the creation of the special merger situation concerned[15].

1   As to the Secretary of State see PARA 5.
2   Ie under the Enterprise Act 2002 s 65 (see PARA 211). As to the Competition Commission see PARAS 9–12.
3   Enterprise Act 2002 s 66(1). As to the meaning of 'special merger situation' see PARA 204.
4   Enterprise Act 2002 s 66(2). The Secretary of State must decide the questions which the Commission is required to decide by virtue of s 63(1)–(3) (see PARA 209).
5   As to the meaning of 'publish' see PARA 186 note 2.
6   Enterprise Act 2002 s 66(3). In determining the period of 30 days no account is to be taken of Saturday, Sunday, Good Friday and Christmas Day and any day which is a bank holiday in England and Wales: ss 54(8), 66(3).
7   Ie under the Enterprise Act 2002 s 65 (see PARA 211).
8   Enterprise Act 2002 s 66(4).
9   Enterprise Act 2002 s 66(5)(a).
10   As to the meaning of 'special intervention notice' see PARA 204.
11   Enterprise Act 2002 s 66(5)(b).
12   Enterprise Act 2002 s 66(5)(c).
13   Ie within the period required by the Enterprise Act 2002 s 66(3) (see the text and notes 5–6).
14   Ie under the Enterprise Act 2002 Sch 7 para 9 or 11 (see PARA 231).
15   Enterprise Act 2002 s 66(6). In making a decision under s 66(6), the Secretary of State, in particular, must have regard to the report of the Commission under s 65 (see PARA 211): s 66(7).

B. EUROPEAN MERGERS

213. Intervention to protect legitimate interests. Where (1) the Secretary of State[1] has reasonable grounds for suspecting that it is or may be the case that a relevant merger situation[2] has been created or that arrangements are in progress or in contemplation which, if carried into effect, will result in the creation of a relevant merger situation[3], and a concentration with a Community dimension[4], or a part of such a concentration, has thereby arisen or will thereby arise[5]; (2) a reference is prevented from being made[6] in relation to the relevant merger situation concerned (whether or not there would otherwise have been a duty to make such a reference) by virtue of Community law or anything done under or in accordance with it[7]; and (3) the Secretary of State is considering whether to take appropriate measures to protect legitimate interests[8], then the Secretary of State may give a European intervention notice to the Office of Fair Trading (the 'OFT')[9] if he believes that it is or may be the case that one or more than one public interest consideration[10] is relevant to a consideration of the relevant merger situation concerned[11].

A European intervention notice must state the relevant merger situation concerned, the public interest consideration or considerations which are, or may be, relevant to a consideration of the relevant merger situation concerned and, where any public interest consideration concerned is not finalised[12], the proposed timetable for finalising it[13].

Where the Secretary of State believes that it is or may be the case that two or more public interest considerations are relevant to a consideration of the relevant merger situation concerned, he may decide not to mention in the intervention notice such of those considerations as he considers appropriate[14].

1 As to the Secretary of State see PARA 5.
2 As to the meaning of 'relevant merger situation' see PARA 173.
3 For the purposes of deciding whether a relevant merger situation has been created or whether arrangements are in progress or in contemplation which, if carried into effect, will result in the creation of a relevant merger situation, the Enterprise Act 2002 ss 23–32 (read together with s 34) (see PARAS 173–182) apply for the purposes of s 67 as they do for the purposes of Pt 3 Ch 1 (ss 22–41), subject to certain modifications: see s 67(7), (8).
4 A concentration has a Community dimension where: (1) the combined aggregate worldwide turnover of all the undertakings concerned is more than EUR 5000 million; and (2) the aggregate Community-wide turnover of each of at least two of the undertakings concerned is more than EUR 250 million, unless each of the undertakings concerned achieves more than two-thirds of its aggregate Community-wide turnover within one and the same member state; and a concentration that does not meet these thresholds has a Community dimension where: (a) the combined aggregate worldwide turnover of all the undertakings concerned is more than EUR 2500 million; (b) in each of at least three member states, the combined aggregate turnover of all the undertakings concerned is more than EUR 100 million; (c) in each of at least three member states included for the purpose of head (b), the aggregate turnover of each of at least two of the undertakings concerned is more than EUR 25 million; and (d) the aggregate Community-wide turnover of each of at least two of the undertakings concerned is more than EUR 100 million, unless each of the undertakings concerned achieves more than two-thirds of its aggregate Community-wide turnover within one and the same member state: see EC Council Regulation 139/2004 (OJ L24, 29.1.2004, p 1) (the 'EC Merger Regulation') art 1(2), (3); definition applied by the Enterprise Act 2002 s 67(1)(a)(ii). As to the EC Merger Regulation see further PARA 74.
5 Enterprise Act 2002 s 67(1)(a) (amended by SI 2004/1079).
6 Ie under the Enterprise Act 2002 s 22 (see PARA 172) or s 33 (see PARA 182).
7 Enterprise Act 2002 s 67(1)(b) (amended by the Communications Act 2003 ss 389(1), 406(7), Sch 16 para 16, Sch 19(1)).
8 Enterprise Act 2002 s 67(1)(c) (amended by SI 2004/1079). The protection of legitimate interests is as permitted by the EC Merger Regulation art 21(4) (see PARA 74).
9 As to the OFT see PARAS 6–8.

10 As to the meaning of 'public interest consideration' see PARA 189 note 10; definition applied by the Enterprise Act 2002 s 67(9).
11 Enterprise Act 2002 s 67(2). No more than one European intervention notice may be given in relation to the same relevant merger situation: s 67(5).
12 As to the meaning of 'public interest consideration being finalised' see PARA 189 note 13.
13 Enterprise Act 2002 s 67(3). Where the Secretary of State has given a European intervention notice mentioning a public interest consideration which, at that time, is not finalised, he must, as soon as practicable, take such action as is within his power to ensure that it is finalised: s 67(6).
14 Enterprise Act 2002 s 67(4).

214. Scheme for protecting legitimate interests. The Secretary of State[1] may by order provide for the taking of action, where a European intervention notice[2] has been given, to remedy, mitigate or prevent effects adverse to the public interest which have resulted from, or may be expected to result from, the creation of a European relevant merger situation[3].

A European relevant merger situation is a relevant merger situation[4]:

(1) which has been created or will be created if arrangements which are in progress or in contemplation are carried into effect[5];

(2) by virtue of which a concentration with a Community dimension[6], or a part of such a concentration, has arisen or will arise[7]; and

(3) in relation to which a reference was prevented from being made[8] (whether or not there would otherwise have been a duty to make such a reference) by virtue of Community law or anything done under or in accordance with it[9].

Provision made by the Secretary of State must include provision ensuring that considerations which are not public interest considerations[10] mentioned in the European intervention notice concerned may not be taken into account in determining whether anything operates, or may be expected to operate, against the public interest[11]. Provision must also be made for: (a) applying with modifications the statutory provisions relating to the duty to make references[12] for the purposes of deciding whether a relevant merger situation has been created or whether arrangements are in progress or in contemplation which, if carried into effect, will result in the creation of a relevant merger situation[13]; (b) requiring the Office of Fair Trading (the 'OFT')[14] to make a report to the Secretary of State before a reference is made[15]; (c) enabling the Secretary of State to make a reference to the Competition Commission[16]; (d) requiring the Commission to investigate and report to the Secretary of State on such a reference[17]; and (e) enabling the taking of interim and final enforcement action[18].

An order may include provision (including provision for the creation of offences and penalties, the payment of fees and the delegation of functions) corresponding to any provision made in, or in connection with, intervention notices[19] or special intervention notices[20] and the cases to which they relate[21].

1 As to the Secretary of State see PARA 5.
2 See PARA 213.
3 Enterprise Act 2002 s 68(1). In exercise of this power, the Secretary of State has made the Enterprise Act 2002 (Protection of Legitimate Interests) Order 2003, SI 2003/1592.
4 As to the meaning of 'relevant merger situation' see PARA 173.
5 Enterprise Act 2002 s 68(2)(a).
6 See PARA 213 note 4; definition applied by the Enterprise Act 2002 s 68(2)(b) (amended by SI 2004/1079).
7 Enterprise Act 2002 s 68(2)(b) (as amended: see note 6).
8 Ie under the Enterprise Act 2002 s 22 (see PARA 172) or s 33 (see PARA 182).
9 Enterprise Act 2002 s 68(2)(c) (amended by the Communications Act 2003 s 389(1), Sch 16 para 17(b)).
10 As to the meaning of 'public interest consideration' see PARA 189 note 10.

11 Enterprise Act 2002 s 68(3).
12 Ie the Enterprise Act 2002 ss 23–32 (see PARAS 173–181).
13 Enterprise Act 2002 s 68(4)(a).
14 As to the OFT see PARAS 6–8.
15 Enterprise Act 2002 s 68(4)(b).
16 Enterprise Act 2002 s 68(4)(c). As to the Competition Commission see PARAS 9–12.
17 Enterprise Act 2002 s 68(4)(d).
18 Enterprise Act 2002 s 68(4)(e).
19 As to the meaning of 'intervention notice' see PARA 189 note 11.
20 As to the meaning of 'special intervention notice' see PARA 204.
21 Enterprise Act 2002 s 68(5).

(iv) Enforcement

A. POWERS EXERCISABLE BEFORE REFERENCES

215. Initial undertakings in relation to completed mergers. Where the Office of Fair Trading (the 'OFT')[1] is considering whether to make a reference of a completed merger[2], the OFT may, for the purpose of preventing pre-emptive action[3], accept from such of the parties concerned as it considers appropriate undertakings to take such action as it considers appropriate[4]. No undertaking may be accepted unless the OFT has reasonable grounds for suspecting that it is or may be the case that a relevant merger situation[5] has been created[6].

An undertaking comes into force when accepted[7]. It may be varied or superseded by another undertaking[8] and it may be released by the OFT[9].

An undertaking which is in force in relation to a possible reference or reference of a completed merger and which has not been adopted[10] ceases to be in force if an initial enforcement order[11] or an interim order[12] comes into force in relation to that reference or an order in relation to public interest cases[13] comes into force in relation to the matter[14]. An undertaking, if it has not previously ceased to be in force and if it has not been adopted[15], ceases to be in force: (1) where the OFT has decided to make the merger reference concerned[16], at the end of the period of seven days beginning with the making of the reference[17]; (2) where the OFT has decided to accept an undertaking[18] instead of making that reference, on the acceptance of that undertaking[19]; (3) where an intervention notice is in force, at the end of the period of seven days beginning with the giving of that notice[20]; and (4) where the OFT has otherwise decided not to make the merger reference concerned, on the making of that decision[21].

The OFT, as soon as reasonably practicable, must consider any representations received by it in relation to varying or releasing an undertaking[22].

1 As to the OFT see PARAS 6–8.
2 Ie under the Enterprise Act 2002 s 22 (see PARA 172).
3 'Pre-emptive action' means action which might prejudice the reference concerned or impede the taking of any action under the Enterprise Act 2002 Pt 3 (ss 22–130) which may be justified by the Competition Commission's decisions on the reference: s 71(8). As to the meaning of 'action' see PARA 184 note 9. As to the Competition Commission see PARAS 9–12.
4 Enterprise Act 2002 s 71(1), (2). The provision which may be contained in an enforcement undertaking is not limited to the provision which is permitted by Sch 8 (see PARA 232): s 89(1). In Pt 3, 'enforcement undertaking' means an undertaking under s 71, s 73 (see PARA 217), s 80 (see PARA 223) or s 82 (see PARA 225) or under Sch 7 para 1, 3 or 9 (see PARAS 228–229, 231): s 89(2).
5 As to the meaning of 'relevant merger situation' see PARA 173.
6 Enterprise Act 2002 s 71(3).
7 Enterprise Act 2002 s 71(4)(a).

8   Enterprise Act 2002 s 71(4)(b).
9   Enterprise Act 2002 s 71(4)(c).
10 Ie under the Enterprise Act 2002 s 80 (see PARA 223) or Sch 7 para 1 (see PARA 228).
11 Ie an order under the Enterprise Act 2002 s 72 (see PARA 216).
12 Ie an order under the Enterprise Act 2002 s 81 (see PARA 224).
13 Ie an order under the Enterprise Act 2002 Sch 7 para 2 (see PARA 228).
14 Enterprise Act 2002 s 71(5).
15 See note 10.
16 Ie a reference under the Enterprise Act 2002 s 22 (see PARA 172).
17 Enterprise Act 2002 s 71(6)(a).
18 Ie under the Enterprise Act 2002 s 73 (see PARA 217).
19 Enterprise Act 2002 s 71(6)(b).
20 Enterprise Act 2002 s 71(6)(c).
21 Enterprise Act 2002 s 71(6)(d).
22 Enterprise Act 2002 s 71(7).

216.   Initial enforcement orders in relation to completed mergers. Where the Office of Fair Trading (the 'OFT')[1] is considering whether to make a reference of a completed merger[2], the OFT may by order, for the purpose of preventing pre-emptive action[3]:

(1)   prohibit or restrict the doing of things which the OFT considers would constitute pre-emptive action[4];
(2)   impose on any person concerned obligations as to the carrying on of any activities or the safeguarding of any assets[5];
(3)   provide for the carrying on of any activities or the safeguarding of any assets either by the appointment of a person to conduct or supervise the conduct of any activities (on such terms and with such powers as may be specified or described in the order) or in any other manner[6];
(4)   require any person to supply information to the relevant authority or to the OFT and provide for the publication of that information, by the person who has received it[7].

No order may be made unless the OFT has reasonable grounds for suspecting that it is or may be the case that a relevant merger situation[8] has been created and pre-emptive action is in progress or in contemplation[9].

An order comes into force at such time as is determined by or under the order and may be varied or revoked by another order[10].

An order which is in force in relation to a possible reference or a merger reference[11] and has not been adopted[12] ceases to be in force if an undertaking[13] comes into force in relation to that reference or in relation to the matter[14].

An order, if it has not previously ceased to be in force and if it is not adopted[15], ceases to be in force: (a) where the OFT has decided to make the merger reference concerned[16], at the end of the period of seven days beginning with the making of the reference[17]; (b) where the OFT has decided to accept an undertaking[18] instead of making that reference, on the acceptance of that undertaking[19]; (c) where an intervention notice[20] is in force, at the end of the period of seven days beginning with the giving of that notice[21]; and (d) where the OFT has otherwise decided not to make the merger reference concerned, on the making of that decision[22].

The OFT, as soon as reasonably practicable, must consider any representations received by it in relation to varying or revoking such an order[23].

1   As to the OFT see PARAS 6–8.
2   Ie under the Enterprise Act 2002 s 22 (see PARA 172).
3   Enterprise Act 2002 s 72(1), (2). As to the meaning of 'pre-emptive action' see PARA 215 note 3.
4   Enterprise Act 2002 s 72(2)(a).

5 Enterprise Act 2002 s 72(2)(b).
6 Enterprise Act 2002 s 72(2)(c).
7 Enterprise Act 2002 s 72(2)(d), Sch 8 para 19.
8 As to the meaning of 'relevant merger situation' see PARA 173.
9 Enterprise Act 2002 s 72(3).
10 Enterprise Act 2002 s 72(4).
11 Ie under the Enterprise Act 2002 s 22 (see PARA 172).
12 Ie under the Enterprise Act 2002 s 81 (see PARA 224) or Sch 7 para 2 (see PARA 228).
13 Ie an undertaking under the Enterprise Act 2002 s 71 (see PARA 215), s 80 (see PARA 223) or Sch 7 para 2 (see PARA 228).
14 Enterprise Act 2002 s 72(5).
15 See note 12.
16 Ie under the Enterprise Act 2002 s 22 (see PARA 172).
17 Enterprise Act 2002 s 72(6)(a).
18 Ie under the Enterprise Act 2002 s 73 (see PARA 217).
19 Enterprise Act 2002 s 72(6)(b).
20 As to the meaning of 'intervention notice' see PARA 189 note 11.
21 Enterprise Act 2002 s 72(6)(c).
22 Enterprise Act 2002 s 72(6)(d).
23 Enterprise Act 2002 s 72(7).

217. Undertakings in lieu of references. If the Office of Fair Trading (the 'OFT')[1] considers that it is under a duty to make a merger reference[2] it may, instead of making such a reference and for the purpose of remedying, mitigating or preventing the substantial lessening of competition concerned or any adverse effect which has or may have resulted from it or may be expected to result from it, accept from such of the parties concerned as it considers appropriate undertakings to take such action[3] as it considers appropriate[4].

In proceeding in this way, the OFT, in particular, must have regard to the need to achieve as comprehensive a solution as is reasonable and practicable to the substantial lessening of competition and any adverse effects resulting from it[5]. The OFT may, in particular, have regard to the effect of any action on any relevant customer benefits[6] in relation to the creation of the relevant merger situation[7] concerned[8].

An undertaking comes into force when accepted[9]. It may be varied or superseded by another undertaking[10] and may be released by the OFT[11]. An undertaking which is in force in relation to a relevant merger situation ceases to be in force if an order comes into force[12] in relation to that undertaking[13].

The OFT, as soon as reasonably practicable, must consider any representations received by it in relation to varying or releasing an undertaking[14].

1 As to the OFT see PARAS 6–8.
2 Ie under the Enterprise Act 2002 s 22 (see PARA 172) or s 33 (see PARA 182). The operation of s 22(3)(b) or (as the case may be) s 33(3)(b) must be disregarded but account must be taken of the power of the OFT under s 22(2) or (as the case may be) s 33(2) to decide not to make such a reference: s 73(1).
3 As to the meaning of 'action' see PARA 184 note 9.
4 Enterprise Act 2002 s 73(1), (2).
5 Enterprise Act 2002 s 73(3).
6 As to the meaning of 'relevant customer benefit' see PARA 180.
7 As to the meaning of 'relevant merger situation' see PARA 173.
8 Enterprise Act 2002 s 73(4).
9 Enterprise Act 2002 s 73(5)(a).
10 Enterprise Act 2002 s 73(5)(b).
11 Enterprise Act 2002 s 73(5)(c).
12 Ie under the Enterprise Act 2002 s 75 (see PARA 219) or s 76 (see PARA 220).

13 Enterprise Act 2002 s 73(6).
14 Enterprise Act 2002 s 73(7).

218.   Effect of undertakings. The relevant authority[1] is not permitted to make a reference[2] in relation to the creation of a relevant merger situation[3] if the Office of Fair Trading (the 'OFT') has accepted an undertaking or group of undertakings[4] and the relevant merger situation is the situation by reference to which the undertaking or group of undertakings was accepted[5].

The making of a reference is not prevented if material facts about relevant arrangements or transactions, or relevant proposed arrangements or transactions[6], were not notified, whether in writing or otherwise, to the OFT or made public[7] before any undertaking concerned was accepted[8].

1   'Relevant authority' means: (1) in relation to a possible reference under the Enterprise Act 2002 s 22 (see PARA 172) or s 33 (see PARA 182), the Office of Fair Trading (the 'OFT'); and (2) in relation to a possible reference under s 45 (see PARA 193), the Secretary of State: s 74(5). As to the OFT see PARAS 6–8. As to the Secretary of State see PARA 5.
2   Ie a reference under the Enterprise Act 2002 under s 22 (see PARA 172), s 33 (see PARA 182) or s 45 (see PARA 193).
3   As to the meaning of 'relevant merger situation' see PARA 173.
4   Ie under the Enterprise Act 2002 s 73 (see PARA 217).
5   Enterprise Act 2002 s 74(1).
6   Arrangements or transactions, or proposed arrangements or transactions, are relevant if they are the ones in consequence of which the enterprises concerned ceased or may have ceased, or may cease, to be distinct enterprises: Enterprise Act 2002 s 74(3). As to the meaning of 'enterprise' see PARA 173 note 2. As to enterprises ceasing to be distinct enterprises see PARA 176.
7   'Made public' means so publicised as to be generally known or readily ascertainable: Enterprise Act 2002 s 74(4).
8   Enterprise Act 2002 s 74(2).

219.   Order-making powers where undertakings not fulfilled. Where the Office of Fair Trading (the 'OFT')[1] considers that an undertaking accepted by it[2] has not been, is not being or will not be fulfilled[3] or, in relation to an undertaking accepted by it, information which was false or misleading in a material respect was given to the OFT by the person giving the undertaking before the OFT decided to accept the undertaking[4], then the OFT may, for the purpose of remedying, mitigating or preventing the substantial lessening of competition[5], make an order[6]. In making such an order, the OFT, in particular, must have regard to the need to achieve as comprehensive a solution as is reasonable and practicable to the substantial lessening of competition and any adverse effects resulting from it and may have regard to the effect of any action[7] on any relevant customer benefits[8] in relation to the creation of the relevant merger situation[9] concerned[10].

An order may contain anything permitted by an enforcement order[11] and such supplementary, consequential or incidental provision as the OFT considers appropriate[12]. An order comes into force at such time as is determined by or under the order[13]. It may contain provision which is different from the provision contained in the undertaking concerned[14] and may be varied or revoked by another order[15]. The OFT, as soon as reasonably practicable, must consider any representations received by it in relation to varying or revoking an order[16].

1   As to the OFT see PARAS 6–8.
2   Ie under the Enterprise Act 2002 s 73 (see PARA 217).
3   Enterprise Act 2002 s 75(1)(a).
4   Enterprise Act 2002 s 75(1)(b).
5   Ie for any of the purposes mentioned in the Enterprise Act 2002 s 73(2) (see PARA 217).
6   Enterprise Act 2002 s 75(2).

7   As to the meaning of 'action' see PARA 184 note 9.
8   As to the meaning of 'relevant customer benefit' see PARA 180.
9   As to the meaning of 'relevant merger situation' see PARA 173.
10 Enterprise Act 2002 s 75(3), applying s 73(3), (4).
11 Ie anything permitted by the Enterprise Act 2002 Sch 8 (see PARA 232).
12 Enterprise Act 2002 s 75(4). The order or any explanatory material accompanying the order
    must state: (1) the actions that the persons or description of persons to whom the order is
    addressed must do or (as the case may be) refrain from doing; (2) the date on which the order
    comes into force; (3) the possible consequences of not complying with the order; and (4) the
    statutory provision under which a review can be sought in relation to the order: s 88(1), (2).
13 Enterprise Act 2002 s 75(5)(a).
14 Enterprise Act 2002 s 75(5)(b).
15 Enterprise Act 2002 s 75(5)(c).
16 Enterprise Act 2002 s 75(6).

220.   Supplementary interim order-making power.   Where the Office of Fair
Trading (the 'OFT')[1] or the Competition Commission[2] has the power[3] in relation
to a particular undertaking to make an order because undertakings have not
been fulfilled and it intends to make such an order[4], then the OFT or (as the case
may be) the Commission may, for the purpose of preventing any action[5] which
might prejudice the making of that order, make an interim order[6]. However, no
such interim order[7] may be made unless the OFT or (as the case may be) the
Commission has reasonable grounds for suspecting that it is or may be the case
that action which might prejudice the making of the original order[8] is in progress
or in contemplation[9].
    An interim order may:
(1)   prohibit or restrict the doing of things which the OFT or (as the case
        may be) the Commission considers would prejudice the making of the
        original order[10];
(2)   impose on any person concerned obligations as to the carrying on of any
        activities or the safeguarding of any assets[11];
(3)   provide for the carrying on of any activities or the safeguarding of any
        assets either by the appointment of a person to conduct or supervise the
        conduct of any activities (on such terms and with such powers as may
        be specified or described in the order) or in any other manner[12];
(4)   require any person to supply information to the relevant authority (and
        where the OFT is not the relevant authority, to the OFT itself) and
        provide for the publication of that information[13].
    An interim order comes into force at such time as is determined by or under
the order[14]. It may be varied or revoked by another order[15], and the OFT or (as
the case may be) the Commission must consider any representations received by
it in relation to varying or revoking an interim order as soon as reasonably
practicable[16].

1   As to the OFT see PARAS 6–8.
2   As to the Competition Commission see PARAS 9–12.
3   Ie where the OFT has power to make an order under the Enterprise Act 2002 s 75 (see PARA
    219) or where the Commission has power to make an order under s 83 (see PARA 225).
4   Enterprise Act 2002 s 76(1).
5   As to the meaning of 'action' see PARA 184 note 9.
6   Enterprise Act 2002 s 76(2).
7   Ie under the Enterprise Act 2002 s 76(2).
8   Ie the order made under the Enterprise Act 2002 s 75 or s 83 as the case may be.
9   Enterprise Act 2002 s 76(3).
10 Enterprise Act 2002 s 76(4)(a). See note 8.
11 Enterprise Act 2002 s 76(4)(b).
12 Enterprise Act 2002 s 76(4)(c).

13 Enterprise Act 2002 ss 76(4)(d), Sch 8 para 19.
14 Enterprise Act 2002 s 76(5)(a). An order under s 76(2), if it has not previously ceased to be in force, ceases to be in force on (1) the coming into force of an order under s 75 or (as the case may be) s 83 in relation to the undertaking concerned; or (2) the making of the decision not to proceed with such an order: s 76(6).
15 Enterprise Act 2002 s 76(5)(b).
16 Enterprise Act 2002 s 76(7).

B. INTERIM RESTRICTIONS AND POWERS

221. Restrictions on certain dealings in relation to completed mergers. Where a reference has been made in relation to a completed merger[1] by the Office of Fair Trading (the 'OFT')[2] to the Competition Commission[3] but has not been finally determined[4], and no undertakings to prevent pre-emptive action[5] are in force in relation to the relevant merger situation[6] concerned and no initial enforcement orders[7] are in force in relation to that situation, there are restrictions on certain dealings[8].

In particular, no relevant person[9] may, without the consent of the Commission[10] (1) complete any outstanding matters in connection with any arrangements which have resulted in the enterprises[11] concerned ceasing to be distinct enterprises[12]; (2) make any further arrangements in consequence of that result (other than arrangements which reverse that result)[13]; or (3) transfer the ownership or control of any enterprises to which the reference relates[14]. No relevant person may, without the consent of the Commission, assist in any of the activities mentioned in heads (1) to (3)[15]. However, these prohibitions[16] do not apply in relation to anything which the person concerned is required to do by virtue of any enactment[17].

The prohibitions described above[18] apply to a person's conduct outside the United Kingdom[19] if (and only if) he is (a) a United Kingdom national; (b) a body incorporated under the law of the United Kingdom or of any part of the United Kingdom; or (c) a person carrying on business in the United Kingdom[20].

1 Ie under the Enterprise Act 2002 s 22 (see PARA 172).
2 As to the OFT see PARAS 6–8.
3 As to the Competition Commission see PARAS 9–12.
4 The time when a reference under the Enterprise Act 2002 s 22 (see PARA 172) or s 33 (see PARA 182) is finally determined is as follows: (1) if the reference is cancelled under s 37(1) (see PARA 185), it is the making of the decision concerned (see s 79(1)(a), (2)(a)); (2) if the time within which the Commission is to prepare and publish a report under s 38 (see PARA 186) in relation to the reference has expired and no such report has been prepared and published, then it is the expiry of the time concerned (s 79(1)(b), (2)(b)); (3) if the report of the Commission under s 38 contains the decision that there is not an anti-competitive outcome, then it is the publication of the report (s 79(1)(c), (2)(c)); (4) if the report of the Commission under s 38 contains the decision that there is an anti-competitive outcome and the Commission has decided under s 41(2) (see PARA 188) neither to accept an undertaking under s 82 (see PARA 225) nor to make an order under s 84 (see PARA 226), then it is the making of the decision under s 41(2) (s 79(1)(d), (2)(d)); (5) if the report of the Commission under s 38 contains the decision that there is an anti-competitive outcome and the Commission has decided under s 41(2) to accept an undertaking under s 82 or to make an order under s 84, then it is the acceptance of the undertaking concerned or (as the case may be) the making of the order concerned (s 79(1)(e), (2)(e)).
5 Ie undertakings under the Enterprise Act 2002 s 71 (see PARA 215) or s 80 (see PARA 223).
6 As to the meaning of 'relevant merger situation' see PARA 173.
7 Ie orders under the Enterprise Act 2002 s 72 (see PARA 216) or s 81 (see PARA 224).
8 Enterprise Act 2002 s 77(1).
9 For these purposes, 'relevant person' means: (1) any person who carries on any enterprise to which the reference relates or who has control of any such enterprise; (2) any subsidiary of any

person falling within head (1); or (3) any person associated with any person falling within head (1) or any subsidiary of any person so associated: Enterprise Act 2002 s 77(8).

10 The consent of the Commission under the Enterprise Act 2002 s 77(2) or s 77(3) may be general or special and may be revoked by the Commission: s 77(5)(a)(b). The consent must be published in such manner as the Commission considers appropriate for the purpose of bringing it to the attention of any person entitled to the benefit of it (s 77(5)(c)), but this does not apply if the Commission considers that publication is not necessary for that purpose (s 77(6)).

11 As to the meaning of 'enterprise' see PARA 173 note 2.

12 Enterprise Act 2002 s 77(2)(a). As to enterprises ceasing to be distinct see PARA 176.

13 Enterprise Act 2002 s 77(2)(b).

14 Enterprise Act 2002 s 77(2)(c). A reference to a person carrying on or having control of any enterprise includes a group of persons carrying on or having control of an enterprise and any member of such a group: s 79(7). Sections 26(2)–(4), 127(1), (2), (4)–(6) (see PARA 176) apply for the purposes of s 77 to determine whether any person or group of persons has control of any enterprise and whether persons are associated as they apply for the purposes of s 26 to determine whether enterprises are brought under common control: s 79(8). As to whether a company is a subsidiary of an individual or of a group of persons see the Companies Act 2006 ss 1159, 1160 (see COMPANIES); applied by the Enterprise Act 2002 s 79(9); Companies Act 2006 s 1297.

15 Enterprise Act 2002 s 77(3). As to the consent of the Commission see note 10.

16 Ie those prohibitions in the Enterprise Act 2002 s 77(2), (3): see the text and notes 9–15.

17 Enterprise Act 2002 s 77(4).

18 See note 16.

19 As to the meaning of 'United Kingdom' see PARA 401 note 1.

20 Enterprise Act 2002 s 77(7).

222. Restrictions on certain share dealings in relation to anticipated mergers.
Where a reference has been made[1] by the Office of Fair Trading (the 'OFT')[2] to the Competition Commission[3] in relation to an anticipated merger and no undertakings to prevent pre-emptive action[4] are in force in relation to the relevant merger situation[5] concerned and no initial enforcement orders[6] are in force in relation to that situation, there are restrictions on certain dealings[7].

No relevant person[8] may, without the consent of the Commission[9], directly or indirectly acquire during the relevant period[10] an interest in shares in a company[11] if any enterprise[12] to which the reference relates is carried on by or under the control of that company[13].

This prohibition applies to a person's conduct outside the United Kingdom[14] if (and only if) he is (1) a United Kingdom national; (2) a body incorporated under the law of the United Kingdom or of any part of the United Kingdom; or (3) a person carrying on business in the United Kingdom[15].

1 Ie under the Enterprise Act 2002 s 33 (see PARA 182).

2 As to the OFT see PARAS 6–8.

3 As to the Competition Commission see PARAS 9–12.

4 Ie undertakings under the Enterprise Act 2002 s 80 (see PARA 223).

5 As to the meaning of 'relevant merger situation' see PARA 173.

6 Ie orders under the Enterprise Act 2002 s 81 (see PARA 224).

7 Enterprise Act 2002 s 78(1).

8 For these purposes, 'relevant person' means: (1) any person who carries on any enterprise to which the reference relates or who has control of any such enterprise; (2) any subsidiary of any person falling within head (1); or (3) any person associated with any person falling within head (1) or any subsidiary of any person so associated: Enterprise Act 2002 s 78(6).

9 The consent of the Commission under the Enterprise Act 2002 s 78(2) may be general or special and may be revoked by the Commission: s 78(3)(a), (b). The consent must be published in such manner as the Commission considers appropriate for bringing it to the attention of any person entitled to the benefit of it (s 78(3)(c)), but this does not apply if the Commission considers that publication is not necessary for that purpose (s 78(4)).

10 'Relevant period' means the period beginning with the making of the reference concerned and ending when the reference is finally determined: Enterprise Act 2002 s 78(6). As to when a reference under s 33 is finally determined see PARA 221 note 4.

11 The circumstances in which a person acquires an interest in shares include those where: (1) he enters into a contract to acquire the shares (whether or not for cash); (2) he is not the registered holder but acquires the right to exercise, or to control the exercise of, any right conferred by the holding of the shares; or (3) he either acquires a right to call for delivery of the shares to himself or to his order or to acquire an interest in the shares, or he assumes an obligation to acquire such an interest: Enterprise Act 2002 s 79(3). The circumstances in which a person acquires a right mentioned in heads (1)–(3) include those where he acquires a right, or assumes an obligation, whose exercise or fulfilment would give him that right (s 79(5)(a)), but they do not include those where he is appointed as proxy to vote at a specified meeting of a company or of any class of its members or at any adjournment of the meeting or he is appointed by a corporation to act as its representative at any meeting of the company or of any class of its members (s 79(5)(b)). The circumstances in which a person acquires an interest in shares do not, however, include those where he acquires an interest in pursuance of an obligation assumed before the publication by the OFT of the reference concerned: s 79(4). The references to rights and obligations in s 79(3)–(5) include conditional rights and conditional obligations: s 79(6). 'Company' includes any body corporate; and 'share' means share in the capital of a company, and includes stock: s 78(6).

12 As to the meaning of 'enterprise' see PARA 173 note 2.

13 Enterprise Act 2002 s 78(2). A reference to a person carrying on or having control of any enterprise includes a group of persons carrying on or having control of an enterprise and any member of such a group: s 79(7). Sections 26(2)–(4), 127(1), (2), (4)–(6) (see PARAS 176) apply for the purposes of s 77 to determine whether any person or group of persons has control of any enterprise and whether persons are associated as they apply for the purposes of s 26 to determine whether enterprises are brought under common control: s 79(8). As to whether a company is a subsidiary of an individual or of a group of persons see the Companies Act 2006 ss 1159, 1160 (see COMPANIES); applied by the Enterprise Act 2002 s 79(9); Companies Act 2006 s 1297.

14 As to the meaning of 'United Kingdom' see PARA 401 note 1.

15 Enterprise Act 2002 s 78(5).

223. Interim undertakings. Where a reference has been made by the Office of Fair Trading (the 'OFT')[1] to the Competition Commission[2] in relation to a completed merger[3] or an anticipated merger[4] but is not finally determined[5], then the Commission may, for the purpose of preventing pre-emptive action[6], accept from such of the parties concerned as it considers appropriate undertakings to take such action as it considers appropriate[7]. The Commission may also, for the purpose of preventing pre-emptive action, adopt an initial undertaking in relation to a completed merger accepted by the OFT[8] if the undertaking is still in force when the Commission adopts it[9].

1 As to the OFT see PARAS 6–8.
2 As to the Competition Commission see PARAS 9–12.
3 Ie a reference under the Enterprise Act 2002 s 22 (see PARA 172).
4 Ie a reference under the Enterprise Act 2002 s 33 (see PARA 182).
5 As to when a reference under s 22 or s 33 is finally determined see PARA 221 note 4.
6 For the purposes of the Enterprise Act 2002 ss 80, 81, 'pre-emptive action' means action which might prejudice the reference concerned or impede the taking of any action under Pt 3 (ss 22–130) which may be justified by the Commission's decisions on the reference: s 80(10). As to the meaning of 'action' see PARA 184 note 9.
7 Enterprise Act 2002 s 80(1), (2). As to undertakings see note 9.
8 Ie under the Enterprise Act 2002 s 71 (see PARA 215).
9 Enterprise Act 2002 s 80(3). An undertaking adopted under s 80(3): (1) continues in force, in accordance with its terms, when adopted; (2) may be varied or superseded by an undertaking under s 80; and (3) may be released by the Commission: s 80(4). Any other undertaking under s 80: (a) comes into force when accepted; (b) may be varied or superseded by another undertaking; and (c) may be released by the Commission: s 80(5). References in Pt 3 to undertakings under s 80 include, unless the context otherwise requires, references to undertakings adopted under s 80; and references to the acceptance or giving of undertakings under s 80 are to be construed accordingly: s 80(6). An undertaking which is in force under s 80 in relation to a reference under s 22 or s 33 ceases to be in force if an order under s 81 (see PARA 224) comes into force in relation to that reference: s 80(7). An undertaking under s 80, if it has

not previously ceased to be in force, ceases to be in force when the reference under s 22 or s 33 is finally determined: s 80(8); and see note 5. The Commission must, as soon as reasonably practicable, consider any representations received by it in relation to varying or releasing an undertaking under s 80: s 80(9).

224. Interim orders. Where a reference has been made by the Office of Fair Trading (the 'OFT')[1] to the Competition Commission[2] in relation to a completed merger[3] or an anticipated merger[4] but is not finally determined[5], then the Commission may by order, for the purpose of preventing pre-emptive action[6]:

(1)   prohibit or restrict the doing of things which the Commission considers would constitute pre-emptive action[7];

(2)   impose on any person concerned obligations as to the carrying on of any activities or the safeguarding of any assets[8];

(3)   provide for the carrying on of any activities or the safeguarding of any assets either by the appointment of a person to conduct or supervise the conduct of any activities (on such terms and with such powers as may be specified or described in the order) or in any other manner[9];

(4)   require any person to supply information to the relevant authority (and where the OFT is not the relevant authority, to the OFT itself) and provide for the publication of that information[10].

The Commission may also, for the purpose of preventing pre-emptive action, adopt an initial enforcement order made by the OFT in relation to a completed merger[11] if the order is still in force when the Commission adopts it[12].

1   As to the OFT see PARAS 6–8.
2   As to the Competition Commission see PARAS 9–12.
3   Ie a reference under the Enterprise Act 2002 s 22 (see PARA 172).
4   Ie a reference under the Enterprise Act 2002 s 33 (see PARA 182).
5   Enterprise Act 2002 s 81(1). As to when a reference under s 22 or s 33 is finally determined see PARA 221 note 4.
6   As to the meaning of 'pre-emptive action' see PARA 223 note 6.
7   Enterprise Act 2002 s 81(2)(a).
8   Enterprise Act 2002 s 81(2)(b).
9   Enterprise Act 2002 s 81(2)(c).
10 Enterprise Act 2002 s 81(2)(d), Sch 8 para 19.
11 Ie under the Enterprise Act 2002 s 72 (see PARA 216).
12 Enterprise Act 2002 s 81(3). An order adopted under s 81(3): (1) continues in force, in accordance with its terms, when adopted; and (2) may be varied or revoked by an order under s 81: s 81(4). Any other order under s 81: (a) comes into force at such time as is determined by or under the order; and (b) may be varied or revoked by another order: s 81(5). References in Pt 3 to orders under s 81, unless the context otherwise requires, include references to orders adopted under s 81; and references to the making of orders under s 81 are to be construed accordingly: s 81(6). An order which is in force under s 81 in relation to a reference under s 22 or s 33 ceases to be in force if an undertaking under s 80 (see PARA 223) comes into force in relation to that reference: s 81(7). An order under s 81, if it has not previously ceased to be in force, ceases to be in force when the reference under s 22 or s 33 is finally determined: s 81(8); and see note 5. The Commission must, as soon as reasonably practicable, consider any representations received by it in relation to varying or revoking an order under s 81: s 81(9).

C. FINAL POWERS

225. Final undertakings. Where a report of the Competition Commission[1] has been prepared and published[2] and contains the decision that there is an anti-competitive outcome[3], the Commission must take such action[4] as it considers to be reasonable and practicable (1) to remedy, mitigate or prevent the substantial lessening of competition concerned; and (2) to remedy, mitigate or prevent any adverse effects which have resulted from, or may be expected to result from, the substantial lessening of competition[5]. The Commission may therefore[6], accept, from such persons as it considers appropriate, undertakings to take action specified or described in the undertakings[7].

Where the Commission considers that (a) such an undertaking[8] has not been, is not being or will not be fulfilled; or (b) in relation to such an undertaking accepted by it, information which was false or misleading in a material respect was given to the Commission or the Office of Fair Trading (the 'OFT')[9] by the person giving the undertaking before the Commission decided to accept the undertaking[10], then the Commission may make an order[11] to remedy, mitigate or prevent the substantial lessening of competition concerned and to remedy, mitigate or prevent any adverse effects which have resulted from, or may be expected to result from, the substantial lessening of competition[12].

1   As to the Competition Commission see PARAS 9–12.
2   Ie under the Enterprise Act 2002 s 38 (see PARA 186) within the period permitted by s 39 (see PARA 187).
3   See the Enterprise Act 2002 s 41(1); and PARA 188.
4   Ie under the Enterprise Act 2002 s 82 (see notes 6–7) or s 84 (see PARA 226).
5   See the Enterprise Act 2002 s 41(2); and PARA 188.
6   Ie in accordance with the Enterprise Act 2002 s 41 (see PARA 188).

7   Enterprise Act 2002 s 82(1). An undertaking under s 82: (1) comes into force when accepted; (2) may be varied or superseded by another undertaking; and (3) may be released by the Commission: s 82(2). An undertaking which is in force under s 82 in relation to a reference under s 22 (see PARA 172) or s 33 (see PARA 182) ceases to be in force if an order under s 76(1)(b) (see PARA 220) or s 83 (see the text and notes 8–12) comes into force in relation to the subject-matter of the undertaking: s 82(3). No undertaking may be accepted under s 82 in relation to a reference under s 22 or s 33 if an order has been made under s 76(1)(b) or s 83 in relation to the subject-matter of the undertaking, or s 84 (see PARA 226) in relation to that reference: s 82(4). The Commission must, as soon as reasonably practicable, consider any representations received by it in relation to varying or releasing an undertaking under s 82: s 82(5).

8   Ie an undertaking accepted by it under the Enterprise Act 2002 s 82: see the text and notes 6–7.
9   As to the OFT see PARAS 6–8.

10 Enterprise Act 2002 s 83(1).

11 An order under the Enterprise Act 2002 s 83 may contain anything permitted by Sch 8 (see PARAS 232–239) as well as such supplementary, consequential or incidental provision as the Commission considers appropriate: s 83(4). The order or any explanatory material accompanying the order must state: (1) the actions that the persons or description of persons to whom the order is addressed must do or (as the case may be) refrain from doing; (2) the date on which the order comes into force; (3) the possible consequences of not complying with the order; and (4) the statutory provision under which a review can be sought in relation to the order: s 88(1), (2). The order comes into force at such time as is determined by or under the order, and may contain provision which is different from the provision contained in the undertaking concerned: s 83(5)(a), (b). It may be varied or revoked by another order (s 83(5)(c)), but only if the OFT advises that such a variation or revocation is appropriate by reason of a change of circumstances (s 83(6)).
12 Enterprise Act 2002 ss 41(2), 83(2). Section 41(3)–(5) (see PARA 188) applies for the purposes of s 83(2) as it applies for the purposes of s 41(2): s 83(3).

226.   Final orders. Where a report of the Competition Commission[1] has been prepared and published[2] and contains the decision that there is an anti-competitive outcome[3], the Commission must take such action[4] as it considers to be reasonable and practicable (1) to remedy, mitigate or prevent the substantial lessening of competition concerned; and (2) to remedy, mitigate or prevent any adverse effects which have resulted from, or may be expected to result from, the substantial lessening of competition[5]. In these circumstances the Commission may[6] make a final order[7]. However, no such order may be made in relation to a reference in relation to a completed merger[8] or an anticipated merger[9] if a final undertaking has been accepted[10] in relation to that reference[11].

1 As to the Competition Commission see PARAS 9–12.
2 Ie under the Enterprise Act 2002 s 38 (see PARA 186) within the period permitted by s 39 (see PARA 187).
3 See the Enterprise Act 2002 s 41(1); and PARA 188.
4 Ie under the Enterprise Act 2002 s 82 (see PARA 225) or s 84.
5 See the Enterprise Act 2002 s 41(2); and PARA 188.
6 Ie in accordance with the Enterprise Act 2002 s 41 (see PARA 188).
7 Enterprise Act 2002 s 84(1). An order under s 84 may contain anything permitted by Sch 8 (see PARAS 232–239) as well as such supplementary, consequential or incidental provision as the Commission considers appropriate: s 84(2). The order or any explanatory material accompanying the order must state: (1) the actions that the persons or description of persons to whom the order is addressed must do or (as the case may be) refrain from doing; (2) the date on which the order comes into force; (3) the possible consequences of not complying with the order; and (4) the statutory provision under which a review can be sought in relation to the order: s 88(1), (2). The order comes into force at such time as is determined by or under the order, and may be varied or revoked by another order: s 84(3). However, no such order may be varied or revoked under s 84 unless the OFT advises that such a variation or revocation is appropriate by reason of a change of circumstances: s 84(4).
8 Ie under the Enterprise Act 2002 s 22 (see PARA 172).
9 Ie under the Enterprise Act 2002 s 33 (see PARA 182).
10 Ie under the Enterprise Act 2002 s 82 (see PARA 225).
11 Enterprise Act 2002 s 84(5).

D. PUBLIC INTEREST AND SPECIAL PUBLIC INTEREST CASES

227. Enforcement regime for public interest and special public interest cases. The Enterprise Act 2002 sets out the enforcement regime for public interest and special public interest cases[1]. The enforcement regime covers pre-emptive undertakings and orders[2], undertakings in lieu of certain references[3], the statutory restrictions following those references[4], and final undertakings and orders[5]. The Office of Fair Trading (the 'OFT')[6] may advise the Secretary of State[7] in relation to the taking by him of such enforcement action[8].

1 The enforcement regime is set out in the Enterprise Act 2002 Sch 7: see s 85(1).
2 See the Enterprise Act 2002 Sch 7 paras 1, 2; and PARA 228.
3 Ie undertakings in lieu of references under the Enterprise Act 2002 s 45 (see PARA 193) or s 62 (see PARA 208): see Sch 7 paras 3–6; and PARA 229.
4 See the Enterprise Act 2002 Sch 7 paras 7, 8; and PARA 230.
5 See the Enterprise Act 2002 Sch 7 paras 9–11; and PARA 231.
6 As to the OFT see PARAS 6–8.
7 As to the Secretary of State see PARA 5.
8 Enterprise Act 2002 s 85(2).

228. Enforcement provisions relating to pre-emptive undertakings and orders. Where an intervention notice[1] or a special intervention notice[2] is in force, the Secretary of State[3] may, for the purpose of preventing pre-emptive action[4], accept from such of the parties concerned as he considers appropriate undertakings to take such action as he considers appropriate[5]. Where an intervention notice is in force, the Secretary of State may, for the purpose of preventing pre-emptive action, adopt an undertaking accepted by the OFT[6] if the undertaking is still in force when the Secretary of State adopts it[7].

Where an intervention notice or special intervention notice is in force[8], the Secretary of State or the OFT may by order, for the purpose of preventing pre-emptive action:

(1) prohibit or restrict the doing of things which the Secretary of State or (as the case may be) the OFT considers would constitute pre-emptive action[9];

(2) impose on any person concerned obligations as to the carrying on of any activities or the safeguarding of any assets[10];

(3) provide for the carrying on of any activities or the safeguarding of any assets either by the appointment of a person to conduct or supervise the conduct of any activities (on such terms and with such powers as may be specified or described in the order) or in any other manner[11]; and

(4) require any person to supply information to the relevant authority, or (where the OFT is not the relevant authority) require any person to supply information to the OFT, and provide for the publication, by the person who has received such information, of that information[12].

Where an intervention notice is in force[13], the Secretary of State or the OFT may, for the purpose of preventing pre-emptive action, adopt an order made by the OFT[14] if the order is still in force when the Secretary of State or (as the case may be) the OFT adopts it[15].

1   As to the meaning of 'intervention notice' see PARA 189 note 11.
2   As to the meaning of 'special intervention notice' see PARA 204.
3   As to the Secretary of State see PARA 5.
4   For these purposes, 'pre-emptive action' means action which might prejudice the reference or possible reference concerned under the Enterprise Act 2002 s 45 (see PARA 193) or (as the case may be) s 62 (see PARA 208) or impede the taking of any action under Pt 3 which may be justified by the Secretary of State's decisions on the reference: Sch 7 para 1(12).
5   Enterprise Act 2002 Sch 7 para 1(1), (2). See note 7.
6   Ie an undertaking under the Enterprise Act 2002 s 71 (see PARA 215).
7   Enterprise Act 2002 Sch 7 para 1(3), (4). An undertaking adopted under Sch 7 para 1(4) continues in force, in accordance with its terms, when adopted: Sch 7 para 1(5)(a). It may be varied or superseded by an undertaking under Sch 7 para 1 and it may be released by the Secretary of State: Sch 7 para 1(5)(b), (c). Any other undertaking under Sch 7 para 1 comes into force when accepted, and may be varied or superseded by another undertaking, and may be released by the Secretary of State: Sch 7 para 1(6).
    References in Pt 3 to undertakings under Sch 7 para 1, unless the context otherwise requires, include references to undertakings adopted under Sch 7 para 1; and references to the acceptance or giving of undertakings under Sch 7 para 1 are to be construed accordingly: Sch 7 para 1(7). An undertaking which is in force under Sch 7 para 1 in relation to a reference or possible reference under s 45 (see PARA 193) or (as the case may be) s 62 (see PARA 208) ceases to be in force if an order under Sch 7 para 2 or an undertaking under Sch 7 para 3 comes into force in relation to that reference: Sch 7 para 1(8). An undertaking under Sch 7 para 1, if it has not previously ceased to be in force, ceases to be in force when the intervention notice concerned or (as the case may be) special intervention notice concerned ceases to be in force: Sch 7 para 1(9).
    No undertaking may be accepted by the Secretary of State under Sch 7 para 1 before the making of a reference under s 45 or (as the case may be) s 62 unless the undertaking relates to a relevant merger situation which has been, or may have been, created or (as the case may be) a special merger situation which has been, or may have been, created: Sch 7 para 1(10). As to the meaning of 'relevant merger situation' see PARA 173. The Secretary of State must, as soon as reasonably practicable, consider any representations received by him in relation to varying or releasing an undertaking under Sch 7 para 1: Sch 7 para 1(11).
8   Enterprise Act 2002 Sch 7 para 2(1).
9   Enterprise Act 2002 Sch 7 para 2(2)(a).
10 Enterprise Act 2002 Sch 7 para 2(2)(b).
11 Enterprise Act 2002 Sch 7 para 2(2)(c).
12 Enterprise Act 2002 Sch 7 para 2(2)(d), Sch 8 para 19; and see PARA 236.
13 Enterprise Act 2002 Sch 7 para 2(3).
14 Ie under the Enterprise Act 2002 s 72 (see PARA 216).
15 Enterprise Act 2002 Sch 7 para 2(4). An order adopted under Sch 7 para 2(4) continues in force, in accordance with its terms, when adopted, and may be varied or revoked by an order under

Sch 7 para 2: Sch 7 para 2(5). Any other order under Sch 7 para 2 comes into force at such time as is determined by or under the order, and may be varied or revoked by another order: Sch 7 para 2(6).

References in Pt 3 to orders under Sch 7 para 2, unless the context otherwise requires, include references to orders adopted under Sch 7 para 2; and references to the making of orders under Sch 7 para 2 are to be construed accordingly: Sch 7 para 2(7). An order which is in force under Sch 7 para 2 in relation to a reference or possible reference under s 45 or (as the case may be) s 62 ceases to be in force if an undertaking under Sch 7 para 1 or Sch 7 para 3 comes into force in relation to that reference: Sch 7 para (8). An order under Sch 7 para 2, if it has not previously ceased to be in force, ceases to be in force when the intervention notice concerned or (as the case may be) special intervention notice concerned ceases to be in force: Sch 7 para 2(9).

No order may be made by the Secretary of State or the OFT under Sch 7 para 2 before the making of a reference under s 45 or (as the case may be) s 62 unless the order relates to a relevant merger situation which has been, or may have been, created or (as the case may be) a special merger situation which has been, or may have been, created: Sch 7 para 2(10). The Secretary of State or (as the case may be) the OFT must, as soon as reasonably practicable, consider any representations received by that person in relation to varying or revoking an order under Sch 7 para 2: Sch 7 para 2(11).

229.   Enforcement provisions relating to undertakings in lieu of references to the Competition Commission.   If the Secretary of State[1] has power to make a reference to the Competition Commission[2] and otherwise intends to make such a reference[3], then he may, instead of making such a reference and for the purpose of remedying, mitigating or preventing any of the effects adverse to the public interest which have or may have resulted, or which may be expected to result, from the creation of the relevant merger situation[4] concerned or (as the case may be) the special merger situation[5] concerned, accept from such of the parties concerned as he considers appropriate undertakings to take such action as he considers appropriate[6].

The relevant authority[7] must not make a reference to the Commission[8] in relation to the creation of a relevant merger situation or (as the case may be) a reference[9] in relation to the creation of a special merger situation if the Secretary of State has accepted an undertaking[10] or group of undertakings as described above and the relevant merger situation or (as the case may be) the special merger situation is the situation by reference to which the undertaking or group of undertakings was accepted[11]. However, this does not prevent the making of a reference if material facts about relevant arrangements or transactions, or relevant proposed arrangements or transactions, were not notified[12] to the Secretary of State or the Office of Fair Trading (the 'OFT') or made public before any undertaking concerned was accepted[13].

Where the Secretary of State considers that an undertaking accepted by him[14] has not been, is not being or will not be fulfilled, or where in relation to an undertaking accepted by him information which was false or misleading in a material respect was given to him or the OFT by the person giving the undertaking before he decided to accept the undertaking[15], then the Secretary of State may make an order for the purpose of remedying, mitigating or preventing any of the effects adverse to the public interest which have or may have resulted, or which may be expected to result, from the creation of the relevant merger situation concerned or (as the case may be) the special merger situation concerned[16]. Where the Secretary of State has the power to make such an order[17] in relation to a particular undertaking and intends to make such an order, or where he has the power to make a final order[18] in relation to a particular undertaking and intends to make such an order[19], then he may, for the purpose of preventing any action which might prejudice the making of that order, make another order[20]. This order may:

(1) prohibit or restrict the doing of things which the Secretary of State considers would prejudice the making of the original order[21];

(2) impose on any person concerned obligations as to the carrying on of any activities or the safeguarding of any assets[22];

(3) provide for the carrying on of any activities or the safeguarding of any assets either by the appointment of a person to conduct or supervise the conduct of any activities (on such terms and with such powers as may be specified or described in the order) or in any other manner[23];

(4) require any person to supply information to the relevant authority, or where the OFT is not the relevant authority, require any person to supply information to the OFT, and provide for the publication, by the person who has received information, of that information[24].

1 As to the Secretary of State see PARA 5.
2 Ie under the Enterprise Act 2002 s 45 (see PARA 193) or s 62 (see PARA 208). As to the Competition Commission see PARAS 9–12.
3 Enterprise Act 2002 Sch 7 para 3(1).
4 As to the meaning of 'relevant merger situation' see PARA 173.
5 As to the meaning of 'special merger situation' see PARA 204.
6 Enterprise Act 2002 Sch 7 para 3(2). In proceeding under Sch 7 para 3(2), the Secretary of State must, in particular: (1) accept the decisions of the OFT included in its report under s 44 so far as they relate to the matters mentioned in s 44(4), (5) (see PARA 191); or (2) (as the case may be) accept the decisions of the OFT included in its report under s 61 so far as they relate to the matters mentioned in s 61(3)(a), (4) (see PARA 206): Sch 7 para 3(3). As to the Office of Fair Trading (the 'OFT') see PARAS 6–8. In proceeding under Sch 7 para 3(2) in relation to an anti-competitive outcome, the Secretary of State may, in particular, have regard to the effect of any action on any relevant customer benefits in relation to the creation of the relevant merger situation concerned: Sch 7 para 3(4). As to the meaning of 'anti-competitive outcome' see PARA 184. As to the meaning of 'action' see PARA 184 note 9. As to the meaning of 'relevant customer benefit' see PARA 180.
   No undertaking may be accepted by the Secretary of State under Sch 7 para 3 in connection with a possible reference under s 45 (see PARA 193) if a public interest consideration mentioned in the intervention notice concerned has not been finalised and the period of 24 weeks beginning with the giving of that notice has not expired: Sch 7 para 3(5). As to the meaning of 'public interest consideration' see PARA 189 note 10. As to the meaning of 'intervention notice' see PARA 189 note 11. The Secretary of State may delay making a decision as to whether to accept any such undertaking (and any related decision as to whether to make a reference under s 45) if he considers that there is a realistic prospect of the public interest consideration being finalised within the period of 24 weeks beginning with the giving of the intervention notice concerned: Sch 7 para 3(6). However, such a delay must not extend beyond (a) the time when the public interest consideration is finalised; or (b) if earlier, the expiry of that 24 week period: Sch 7 para 3(7).
   An undertaking under Sch 7 para 3 comes into force when accepted and may be varied or superseded by another undertaking or may be released by the Secretary of State: Sch 7 para 3(8). The Secretary of State must, as soon as reasonably practicable, consider any representations received by him in relation to varying or releasing an undertaking: Sch 7 para 3(10). An undertaking under Sch 7 para 3 which is in force in relation to a relevant merger situation or (as the case may be) a special merger situation ceases to be in force if an order comes into force under Sch 7 para 5 or para 6 (see the text and notes 14–24) in relation to that undertaking: Sch 7 para 3(9).
7 For these purposes, 'relevant authority' means (1) in relation to a possible reference under s 22 (see PARA 172) or s 33 (see PARA 182), the OFT; and (2) in relation to a possible reference under s 45 (see PARA 193) or s 62 (see PARA 208), the Secretary of State: Enterprise Act 2002 Sch 7 para 4(2).
8 Ie a reference under the Enterprise Act 2002 s 22, s 33 or s 45 (see PARAS 172, 182, 193).
9 Ie under the Enterprise Act 2002 s 62 (see PARA 208).
10 Ie under the Enterprise Act 2002 Sch 7 para 3.
11 Enterprise Act 2002 Sch 7 para 4(1).
12 Ie whether in writing or otherwise: see Sch 7 para 4(3).

13 Enterprise Act 2002 Sch 7 para 4(3). Arrangements or transactions, or proposed arrangements or transactions, are relevant if they are the ones in consequence of which the enterprises concerned ceased or may have ceased, or may cease, to be distinct enterprises: Sch 7 para 4(4). The reference to 'made public' means so publicised as to be generally known or readily ascertainable: Sch 7 para 4(5).

14 Ie an undertaking under the Enterprise Act 2002 Sch 7 para 3: see the text and notes 1–6.

15 Enterprise Act 2002 Sch 7 para 5(1).

16 Enterprise Act 2002 Sch 7 paras 3(2), 5(2). Schedule 7 para 3(3), (4) (see note 6) is also applicable for the purposes of Sch 7 para 5(2): Sch 7 para 5(3). An order under Sch 7 para 5(2) may contain anything permitted by Sch 8 (see PARAS 232–239), as well as such supplementary, consequential or incidental provision as the Secretary of State considers appropriate: Sch 7 para 5(4). The order or any explanatory material accompanying the order must state: (1) the actions that the persons or description of persons to whom the order is addressed must do or (as the case may be) refrain from doing; (2) the date on which the order comes into force; (3) the possible consequences of not complying with the order; and (4) the statutory provision under which a review can be sought in relation to the order: s 88(1), (2). Such an order comes into force at such time as is determined by or under the order, and it may contain provision which is different from the provision contained in the undertaking concerned: Sch 7 para 5(5). No order may be varied or revoked under Sch 7 para 5 unless the OFT advises that such a variation or revocation is appropriate by reason of a change of circumstances: Sch 7 para 5(6).

17 Ie under the Enterprise Act 2002 Sch 7 para 5.

18 Ie under the Enterprise Act 2002 Sch 7 para 10 (see PARA 231).

19 Enterprise Act 2002 Sch 7 para 6(1).

20 Enterprise Act 2002 Sch 7 para 6(2). No order may be made under Sch 7 para 6(2) unless the Secretary of State has reasonable grounds for suspecting that it is or may be the case that action which might prejudice the making of the order under Sch 7 para 5 or (as the case may be) Sch 7 para 10 is in progress or in contemplation: Sch 7 para 6(3). An order under Sch 7 para 6 comes into force at such time as is determined by or under the order: Sch 7 para 6(5). Such an order, if it has not previously ceased to be in force, ceases to be in force on (1) the coming into force of an order under Sch 7 para 5 or (as the case may be) Sch 7 para 10 in relation to the undertaking concerned; or (2) the making of the decision not to proceed with such an order: Sch 7 para 6(6). The Secretary of State must, as soon as reasonably practicable, consider any representations received by him in relation to varying or revoking an order under Sch 7 para 6: Sch 7 para 6(7).

21 Enterprise Act 2002 Sch 7 para 6(4)(a). The reference in the text to the original order is a reference to the order under Sch 7 para 5 or Sch 7 para 10.

22 Enterprise Act 2002 Sch 7 para 6(4)(b).

23 Enterprise Act 2002 Sch 7 para 6(4)(c).

24 Enterprise Act 2002 Sch 7 para 6(4)(d), Sch 8 para 19.

230.   Statutory restrictions following certain references to the Competition Commission.   Where the Secretary of State[1] has made a certain reference[2] to the Competition Commission[3] but it has not been finally determined[4], and no pre-emptive undertakings[5] are in force in relation to the relevant merger situation concerned[6] or (as the case may be) the special merger situation[7] concerned and no pre-emptive orders[8] are in force in relation to that situation[9], then no relevant person[10] may, without the consent of the Secretary of State[11]:

(1)   complete any outstanding matters in connection with any arrangements which have resulted in the enterprises concerned ceasing to be distinct enterprises[12];

(2)   make any further arrangements in consequence of that result (other than arrangements which reverse that result)[13]; or

(3)   transfer the ownership or control of any enterprises to which the reference relates[14].

Nor may any relevant person, without the consent of the Secretary of State, assist in any of the activities mentioned in heads (1) to (3)[15]. These prohibitions do not, however, apply in relation to anything which the person concerned is required to do by virtue of any enactment[16]. They apply to a person's conduct outside the United Kingdom if (and only if) he is a United Kingdom national, or a body incorporated under the law of the United Kingdom or of any part of the United Kingdom, or a person carrying on business in the United Kingdom[17].

Where a certain reference has been made[18] and no pre-emptive undertakings[19] are in force in relation to the relevant merger situation concerned or (as the case may be) special merger situation concerned and no pre-emptive orders[20] are in force in relation to that situation[21], then no relevant person[22] may, without the consent of the Secretary of State[23], directly or indirectly acquire during the relevant period[24] an interest in shares in a company[25] if any enterprise to which the reference relates is carried on by or under the control of that company[26]. This prohibition applies to a person's conduct outside the United Kingdom if (and only if) he is a United Kingdom national, or a body incorporated under the law of the United Kingdom or of any part of the United Kingdom, or a person carrying on business in the United Kingdom[27].

1   As to the Secretary of State see PARA 5.
2   Ie a reference has been made under the Enterprise Act 2002 s 45(2) or s 45(3) (see PARA 193) or 62(2) (see PARA 208).
3   As to the Competition Commission see PARAS 9–12.
4   The time when a reference under the Enterprise Act 2002 s 45(2) or s 45(3) is finally determined is as follows: (1) when the time within which the Commission is to prepare a report under s 50 in relation to the reference and give it to the Secretary of State has expired and no such report has been so prepared and given, then it is the expiry of the time concerned (Sch 7 para 7(8)(a), (10)(a)); (2) when the Commission decides to cancel the reference under s 53(1), then it is the making of the decision concerned (Sch 7 para 7(8)(b), 7(10)(b)); (3) when the time within which the Secretary of State is to make and publish a decision under s 54(2) has expired and no such decision has been made and published, then it is the expiry of the time concerned (Sch 7 para 7(8)(c), (10)(a)); (4) when the Secretary of State decides under s 54(2) to make no finding at all in the matter, then it is the making of the decision concerned (Sch 7 para 7(8)(d), (10)(b)); (5) when the Secretary of State otherwise decides under s 54(2) not to make an adverse public interest finding, then it is the making of the decision concerned (Sch 7 para 7(8)(e), (10)(b)); (6) when the Secretary of State decides under s 54(2) to make an adverse public interest finding but decides neither to accept an undertaking under Sch 7 para 9 nor to make an order under Sch 7 para 11, then it is the making of the decision neither to accept an undertaking under Sch 7 para 9 nor to make an order under Sch 7 para 11 (Sch 7 para 7(8)(f), (10)(c)); or (7) when the Secretary of State decides under s 54(2) to make an adverse public interest finding and accepts an undertaking under Sch 7 para 9 or makes an order under Sch 7 para 11, then it is the acceptance of the undertaking concerned or (as the case may be) the making of the order concerned (Sch 7 para 7(8)(g), (10)(d)).
      The time when a reference under s 62(2) is finally determined is as follows: (a) when the time within which the Commission is to prepare a report under s 65 in relation to the reference and give it to the Secretary of State has expired and no such report has been so prepared and given, then it is the expiry of the time concerned (Sch 7 para 7(9)(a), (10)(a)); (b) when the time within which the Secretary of State is to make and publish a decision under s 66(2) has expired and no such decision has been made and published, then it is the expiry of the time concerned (Sch 7 para 7(9)(b), (10)(a)); (c) when the Secretary of State decides under s 66(2) otherwise than as mentioned in s 66(5), then it is the making of the decision concerned (Sch 7 para 7(9)(c), (10)(b)); (d) when the Secretary of State decides under s 66(2) as mentioned in s 66(5) but decides neither to accept an undertaking under Sch 7 para 9 nor to make an order under Sch 7 para 11, then it is the making of the decision neither to accept an undertaking under Sch 7 para 9 nor to make an order under Sch 7 para 11 (Sch 7 para 7(9)(d), (10)(c)); or (e) when the Secretary of State decides under s 66(2) as mentioned in s 66(5) and accepts an undertaking under Sch 7 para 9 or makes an order under Sch 7 para 11, then it is the acceptance of the undertaking concerned or (as the case may be) the making of the order concerned (Sch 7 para 7(9)(e), (10)(d)). Section 79 (see PARA 222) applies to Sch 7 para 7 with modifications: see Sch 7 para 8(10), (11).
5   Ie under the Enterprise Act 2002 Sch 7 para 1 (see PARA 228).
6   As to the meaning of 'relevant merger situation' see PARA 173.
7   As to the meaning of 'special merger situation' see PARA 204.
8   Ie under the Enterprise Act 2002 Sch 7 para 2 (see PARA 228).
9   Enterprise Act 2002 Sch 7 para 7(1).

10 For these purposes, 'relevant person' means: (1) any person who carries on any enterprise to which the reference relates or who has control of any such enterprise; (2) any subsidiary of any person falling within head (1); or (3) any person associated with any person falling within head (1) or any subsidiary of any person so associated: Enterprise Act 2002 Sch 7 para 7(11).

11 The consent of the Secretary of State under the Enterprise Act 2002 Sch 7 para 7(2) or Sch 7 para 7(3) may be general or specific and may be revoked by the Secretary of State: Sch 7 para 7(5)(a), (b). It must be published in such manner as the Secretary of State considers appropriate for bringing it to the attention of any person entitled to the benefit of it (Sch 7 para 7(5)(c)), but not if the Secretary of State considers that publication is not necessary for that purpose (Sch 7 para 7(6)).

12 Enterprise Act 2002 Sch 7 para 7(2)(a). As to enterprises ceasing to be distinct see PARA 176.

13 Enterprise Act 2002 Sch 7 para 7(2)(b).

14 Enterprise Act 2002 Sch 7 para 7(2)(c).

15 Enterprise Act 2002 Sch 7 para 7(3). As to the consent of the Secretary of State see note 23.

16 Enterprise Act 2002 Sch 7 para 7(4).

17 Enterprise Act 2002 Sch 7 para 7(7).

18 Ie a reference has been made under the Enterprise Act 2002 s 45(4) or s 45(5) (see PARA 193) or s 62(3) (see PARA 208).

19 Ie under the Enterprise Act 2002 Sch 7 para 1 (see PARA 228).

20 Ie under the Enterprise Act 2002 Sch 7 para 2 (see PARA 228).

21 Enterprise Act 2002 Sch 7 para 8(1).

22 For these purposes, 'relevant person' means: (1) any person who carries on any enterprise to which the reference relates or who has control of any such enterprise; (2) any subsidiary of any person falling within head (1); or (3) any person associated with any person falling within head (1) or any subsidiary of any person so associated: Enterprise Act 2002 Sch 7 para 8(6).

23 The consent of the Secretary of State under the Enterprise Act 2002 Sch 7 para 8(3) may be general or specific and may be revoked by the Secretary of State: Sch 7 para 8(3)(a), (b). It must be published in such manner as the Secretary of State considers appropriate for bringing it to the attention of any person entitled to the benefit of it (Sch 7 para 8(3)(c)), but not if the Secretary of State considers that publication is not necessary for that purpose (Sch 7 para 8(4)).

24 'Relevant period' means the period beginning with the publication of the decision of the Secretary of State to make the reference concerned and ending when the reference is finally determined: Enterprise Act 2002 Sch 7 para 8(6). The time when a reference under s 45(4) or s 45(5) is finally determined is as follows: (1) when the Commission cancels the reference under s 48(1) or s 53(1), then it is the making of the decision concerned (Sch 7 para 8(7)(a), (9)(a)); (2) when the time within which the Commission is to prepare a report under s 50 in relation to the reference and give it to the Secretary of State has expired and no such report has been so prepared and given, then it is the expiry of the time concerned (Sch 7 para 8(7)(b), (9)(b)); (3) when the time within which the Secretary of State is to make and publish a decision under s 54(2) has expired and no such decision has been made and published, then it is the expiry of the time concerned (Sch 7 para 8(7)(c), (9)(b)); (4) when the Secretary of State decides under s 54(2) to make no finding at all in the matter, then it is the making of the decision concerned (Sch 7 para 8(7)(d), (9)(a)); (5) when the Secretary of State otherwise decides under s 54(2) not to make an adverse public interest finding, then it is the making of the decision concerned (Sch 7 para 8(7)(e), (9)(a)); (6) when the Secretary of State decides under s 54(2) to make an adverse public interest finding but decides neither to accept an undertaking under Sch 7 para 9 nor to make an order under Sch 7 para 11, then it is the making of the decision neither to accept an undertaking under Sch 7 para 9 nor to make an order under Sch 7 para 11 (Sch 7 para 8(7)(f), (9)(c)); or (7) when the Secretary of State decides under s 54(2) to make an adverse public interest finding and accepts an undertaking under Sch 7 para 9 or makes an order under Sch 7 para 11, then it is the acceptance of the undertaking concerned or (as the case may be) the making of the order concerned (Sch 7 para 8(7)(g), (9)(d)).

The time when a reference under s 62(3) is finally determined is as follows: (a) when the Commission cancels the reference under s 64(1), then it is the making of the decision concerned (Sch 7 para 8(8)(a), (9)(a)); (b) when the time within which the Commission is to prepare a report under s 65 in relation to the reference and give it to the Secretary of State has expired and no such report has been so prepared and given, then it is the expiry of the time concerned (Sch 7 para 8(8)(b), (9)(b)); (c) when the time within which the Secretary of State is to make and publish a decision under s 66(2) has expired and no such decision has been made and published, then it is the expiry of the time concerned (Sch 7 para 8(8)(c), (9)(b)); (d) when the Secretary of State decides under s 66(2) otherwise than as mentioned in s 66(5), then it is the making of the decision concerned (Sch 7 para 8(8)(d), (9)(a)); (e) when the Secretary of State decides under s 66(2) as mentioned in s 66(5) but decides neither to accept an undertaking under Sch 7 para 9 nor to make an order under Sch 7 para 11, then it is the making of the decision neither to accept an undertaking under Sch 7 para 9 nor to make an order under Sch 7 para 11 (Sch 7 para 8(8)(e), (9)(c)); or (f) when the Secretary of State decides under s 66(2) as mentioned in s 66(5) and accepts an undertaking under Sch 7 para 9 or makes an order under Sch 7 para 11, then it is the acceptance of the undertaking concerned or (as the case may be) the making of the order concerned (Sch 7 para 8(8)(f), (9)(d)). Section 79 (see PARA 221) applies to Sch 7 para 8 with modifications: see Sch 7 para 8(10), (11).

25 For these purposes, 'company' includes any body corporate; and 'share' means share in the capital of a company, and includes stock: Enterprise Act 2002 Sch 7 para 8(6).
26 Enterprise Act 2002 Sch 7 para 8(2).
27 Enterprise Act 2002 Sch 7 para 8(5).

231. Enforcement provisions relating to final undertakings and orders. Where the Secretary of State[1] has decided[2] to make an adverse public interest finding[3] in relation to a relevant merger situation[4] and has published his decision within the period so required[5], he may take such of the following action as he considers to be reasonable and practicable to remedy, mitigate or prevent any of the effects adverse to the public interest which have resulted from, or may be expected to result from, the creation of the relevant merger situation concerned[6]. Similarly, where the Secretary of State has decided and published his decision that:

(1) a special merger situation[7] has been created or arrangements are in progress or in contemplation which, if carried into effect, will result in the creation of a special merger situation[8];

(2) at least one consideration which is mentioned in the special intervention notice[9] concerned is relevant to a consideration of the special merger situation concerned[10]; and

(3) taking account only of the relevant consideration or considerations concerned, the creation of that situation operates or may be expected to operate against the public interest[11],

he may take such of the following action as he considers to be reasonable and practicable to remedy, mitigate or prevent any of the effects adverse to the public interest which have resulted from, or may be expected to result from, the creation of the special merger situation concerned[12].

The action which the Secretary of State may take is as follows. He may[13] accept, from such persons as he considers appropriate, undertakings to take action[14] specified or described in the undertakings[15]. Alternatively, he may make an order[16].

Where the Secretary of State considers that (1) an undertaking so accepted by him has not been, is not being or will not be fulfilled[17]; or (2) in relation to an undertaking so accepted by him, information which was false or misleading in a material respect was given to him or the Office of Fair Trading (the 'OFT')[18] by the person giving the undertaking before he decided to accept the undertaking[19], then the Secretary of State may, in order to remedy, mitigate or prevent any of the effects adverse to the public interest which have resulted from, or may be expected to result from, the creation of the relevant merger situation concerned[20], make an order[21].

1 As to the Secretary of State see PARA 5.
2 Ie under the Enterprise Act 2002 s 54(2) within the period required by s 54(5) (see PARA 200).
3 As to the meaning of 'adverse public interest finding' see PARA 200 note 4.
4 As to the meaning of 'relevant merger situation' see PARA 173.
5 Enterprise Act 2002 s 55(1).
6 Enterprise Act 2002 s 55(2).
7 As to the meaning of 'special merger situation' see PARA 204.
8 Enterprise Act 2002 s 66(5)(a).

9 As to the meaning of 'special intervention notice' see PARA 204.

10 Enterprise Act 2002 s 66(5)(b).

11 Enterprise Act 2002 s 66(5)(c).

12 Enterprise Act 2002 s 66(6).

13 Ie in accordance with the Enterprise Act 2002 s 55 (see PARA 201) or (as the case may be) s 66(5)–(7) (see PARA 212).

14 As to the meaning of 'action' see PARA 184 note 9.

15 Enterprise Act 2002 Sch 7 para 9(1). An undertaking under Sch 7 para 9 comes into force when accepted and it may be varied or superseded by another undertaking, and may be released by the Secretary of State: Sch 7 para 9(2). An undertaking which is in force under Sch 7 para 9 in relation to a reference under s 45 (see PARA 193) or s 62 (see PARA 208) ceases to be in force if an order under Sch 7 para 6(1)(b) (see PARA 229) or Sch 7 para 10 comes into force in relation to the subject-matter of the undertaking: Sch 7 para 9(3). No undertaking is to be accepted under Sch 7 para 9 in relation to a reference under s 45 or s 62 if an order has been made under (1) Sch 7 para 6(1)(b) or Sch 7 para 10 in relation to the subject-matter of the undertaking; or (2) Sch 7 para 11 in relation to that reference: Sch 7 para 9(4). The Secretary of State must, as soon as reasonably practicable, consider any representations received by him in relation to varying or releasing an undertaking under Sch 7 para 9: Sch 7 para 9(5).

16 Enterprise Act 2002 Sch 7 para 11(1). An order under Sch 7 para 11 may contain anything permitted by Sch 8, as well as such supplementary, consequential or incidental provision as the Secretary of State considers appropriate: Sch 7 para 11(2). The order or any explanatory material accompanying the order must state: (1) the actions that the persons or description of persons to whom the order is addressed must do or (as the case may be) refrain from doing; (2) the date on which the order comes into force; (3) the possible consequences of not complying with the order; and (4) the statutory provision under which a review can be sought in relation to the order: s 88(1), (2). An order under Sch 7 para 11 comes into force at such time as is determined by or under the order: Sch 7 para 11(3). No order may be made under Sch 7 para 11 in relation to a reference under s 45 or (as the case may be) s 62 if an undertaking has been accepted under Sch 7 para 9 in relation to that reference: Sch 7 para 11(4). No order may be varied or revoked under Sch 7 para 11 unless the OFT advises that such a variation or revocation is appropriate by reason of a change of circumstances: Sch 7 para 11(5).

17 Enterprise Act 2002 Sch 7 para 10(1)(a).

18 As to the OFT see PARAS 6–8.

19 Enterprise Act 2002 Sch 7 para 10(1)(b).

20 See the Enterprise Act 2002 ss 55(2), 66(6) (see PARAS 201, 212).

21 Enterprise Act 2002 Sch 7 para 10(2). Section 55(3), (4) (see PARA 201) or (as the case may be) s 66(7) (see PARA 212) applies for these purposes: Sch 7 para 10(3). An order under Sch 7 para 10 may contain anything permitted by Sch 8 (see PARAS 232–239), as well as such supplementary, consequential or incidental provision as the Secretary of State considers appropriate: Sch 7 para 10(4). The order or any explanatory material accompanying the order must state: (1) the actions that the persons or description of persons to whom the order is addressed must do or (as the case may be) refrain from doing; (2) the date on which the order comes into force; (3) the possible consequences of not complying with the order; and (4) the statutory provision under which a review can be sought in relation to the order: s 88(1), (2). An order under Sch 7 para 10 comes into force at such time as is determined by or under the order, and it may contain provision which is different from the provision contained in the undertaking concerned: Sch 7 para 10(5). No order may be varied or revoked under Sch 7 para 10 unless the OFT advises that such a variation or revocation is appropriate by reason of a change of circumstances: Sch 7 para 10(6).

E. UNDERTAKINGS AND ORDERS

232.   Enforcement orders. The Enterprise Act 2002 contains provisions relating to enforcement orders[1], and specifies what provision may be made in such orders[2].

An enforcement order may extend to a person's conduct outside the United Kingdom[3] if (and only if) he is a United Kingdom national, a body incorporated under the law of the United Kingdom or of any part of the United Kingdom, or a person carrying on business in the United Kingdom[4]. Nothing in an enforcement order has effect so as to (1) cancel or modify conditions in licences granted under a patent[5] or a European patent (UK) or in respect of a design registered under the Registered Designs Act 1949 by the proprietor of the patent or design[6]; or (2) require an entry to be made in the register of patents or the register of designs to the effect that licences under such a patent or such a design are to be available as of right[7]. An enforcement order may prohibit the performance of an agreement already in existence when the order is made[8].

An order, as well as making provision in relation to all cases to which it may extend, may make provision in relation to those cases subject to specified exceptions, or any particular case or class of case[9]. An order may, in relation to the cases in relation to which it applies, make the full provision which may be made by it or any less provision (whether by way of exception or otherwise)[10]. An order may make provision for matters to be determined under the order[11], and it may make different provision for different cases or classes of case or different purposes and make such transitional, transitory or saving provision as the person making it considers appropriate[12].

An order which may prohibit the doing of anything (or the refraining from doing anything) may in particular[13] prohibit the doing of that thing (or the refraining from doing of it) except to such extent and in such circumstances as may be provided by or under the order[14].

1   For these purposes, 'enforcement order' means an order made under the Enterprise Act 2002 s 72 (see PARA 216), s 75 (see PARA 219), s 76 (see PARA 220), s 81 (see PARA 224), s 83 (see PARA 225) or s 84 (see PARA 226) or under Sch 7 para 2 (see PARA 228), Sch 7 paras 5, 6 (see PARA 229), Sch 7 para 10 or 11 (see PARA 231): see s 86(6).
2   See the Enterprise Act 2002 s 86(4), Sch 8. As to the provisions which may be included in enforcement orders see PARAS 233–239. Schedule 8 applies in relation to such orders, and to such extent, as is provided by Pt 3 and Pt 4 and any other enactment (and references in Sch 8 to an order are to be construed accordingly): Sch 8 para 1. The Secretary of State may by order made by statutory instrument modify Sch 8: see s 206. As to the Secretary of State see PARA 5.
3   As to the meaning of 'United Kingdom' see PARA 401 note 1.
4   Enterprise Act 2002 s 86(1).
5   Ie a patent granted under the Patents Act 1977 (see PATENTS AND REGISTERED DESIGNS).
6   Enterprise Act 2002 s 86(2)(a).
7   Enterprise Act 2002 s 86(2)(b).
8   Enterprise Act 2002 s 86(3).
9   Enterprise Act 2002 Sch 8 para 21(1).
10 Enterprise Act 2002 Sch 8 para 21(2).
11 Enterprise Act 2002 Sch 8 para 21(3).
12 Enterprise Act 2002 Sch 8 para 21(4).
13 Ie by virtue of the Enterprise Act 2002 Sch 8 para 21(2): see the text and note 10.
14 Enterprise Act 2002 Sch 8 para 22(1). Any such order may, in particular, prohibit the doing of that thing (or the refraining from doing of it) without the agreement of the relevant authority or another person, or by or in relation to a person who has not been approved by the relevant authority or another person: Sch 8 para 22(2).

233.   General restrictions on conduct. An order[1] may prohibit the making or performance of an agreement, or require any party to an agreement to terminate the agreement[2]. However, such an order may not prohibit the making or performance of an agreement, or require any person to terminate an agreement so far as, if made, the agreement would relate, or (as the case may be) so far as the agreement relates, to the terms and conditions of employment of any workers or to the physical conditions in which any workers are required to work[3].

An order may prohibit the withholding from any person of any goods or services, or any orders for any such goods or services[4]. An order may prohibit requiring as a condition of the supply of goods or services to any person: (1) the buying of any goods; (2) the making of any payment in respect of services other than the goods or services supplied; (3) the doing of any other such matter or the refraining from doing anything mentioned in head (1) or (2) or any other such matter[5].

An order may prohibit: (a) discrimination between persons in the prices charged for goods or services; (b) anything which the relevant authority considers to be such discrimination; (c) procuring others to do anything which is such discrimination or which the relevant authority considers to be such discrimination[6]. An order may prohibit: (i) giving, or agreeing to give in other ways, any preference in respect of the supply of goods or services or in respect of the giving of orders for goods or services; (ii) giving, or agreeing to give in other ways, anything which the relevant authority considers to be a preference in respect of the supply of goods or services or in respect of the giving of orders for goods or services; (iii) procuring others to do anything mentioned in head (i) or (ii)[7].

An order may prohibit charging, for goods or services supplied, prices differing from those in any published list or notification, as well as doing anything which the relevant authority considers to be charging such prices[8]. An order may regulate the prices to be charged for any goods or services[9], but not unless the relevant report in relation to the matter concerned identifies the prices charged for the goods or services as requiring remedial action[10].

An order may prohibit the exercise of any right to vote exercisable by virtue of the holding of any shares, stock or securities[11].

1   As to the orders to which the Enterprise Act 2002 Sch 8 applies see PARA 232 notes 1, 2.
2   Enterprise Act 2002 Sch 8 para 2(1).
3   Enterprise Act 2002 Sch 8 para 2(2).
4   Enterprise Act 2002 Sch 8 para 3(1). The references to withholding include references to: (1) agreeing or threatening to withhold; and (2) procuring others to withhold or to agree or threaten to withhold: Sch 8 para 3(2).
5   Enterprise Act 2002 Sch 8 para 4.
6   Enterprise Act 2002 Sch 8 para 5. For the purposes of Sch 8, the 'relevant authority' means: (1) in the case of an order to be made by the Office of Fair Trading (the 'OFT'), the OFT; (2) in the case of an order to be made by the Competition Commission, the Commission; and (3) in the case of an order to be made by the Secretary of State, the Secretary of State: Sch 8 para 24. As to the OFT see PARAS 6–8. As to the Competition Commission see PARAS 9–12. As to the Secretary of State see PARA 5.
7   Enterprise Act 2002 Sch 8 para 6.
8   Enterprise Act 2002 Sch 8 para 7.
9   Enterprise Act 2002 Sch 8 para 8(1).
10 Enterprise Act 2002 Sch 8 para 8(2). 'Relevant report' means the report of the Competition Commission which is required by the enactment concerned before an order can be made under Sch 8: Sch 8 para 8(3). As to the Competition Commission see PARAS 9–12.
11 Enterprise Act 2002 Sch 8 para 9.

234. General obligations to be performed. An order[1] may require a person to supply goods or services or to do anything which the relevant authority considers appropriate to facilitate the provision of goods or services[2]. An order may require a person who is supplying, or is to supply, goods or services to supply such goods or services to a particular standard or in a particular manner or to do anything which the relevant authority considers appropriate to facilitate the provision of such goods or services to that standard or in that manner[3]. An order may also require any activities to be carried on separately from any other activities[4].

1   As to the orders to which the Enterprise Act 2002 Sch 8 applies see PARA 232 notes 1, 2.

2 Enterprise Act 2002 Sch 8 para 10(1). As to the meaning of 'relevant authority' see PARA 233 note 6.
3 Enterprise Act 2002 Sch 8 para 10(2).
4 Enterprise Act 2002 Sch 8 para 11.

235. Acquisitions and divisions. An order[1] may prohibit or restrict: (1) the acquisition by any person of the whole or part of the undertaking or assets of another person's business; (2) the doing of anything which will or may result in two or more bodies corporate becoming interconnected bodies corporate[2]. An order may require that if an acquisition of the kind mentioned in head (1) is made, or anything is done which results in two or more bodies corporate becoming interconnected bodies corporate, the persons concerned or any of them must observe any prohibitions or restrictions imposed by or under the order[3].

An order may provide for the division of any business (whether by the sale of any part of the undertaking or assets or otherwise)[4], and the division of any group of interconnected bodies corporate[5]. Such an order may contain such provision as the relevant authority considers appropriate to effect or take account of the division, including, in particular, provision as to:

(a) the transfer or creation of property, rights, liabilities or obligations[6];
(b) the number of persons to whom the property, rights, liabilities or obligations are to be transferred or in whom they are to be vested[7];
(c) the time within which the property, rights, liabilities or obligations are to be transferred or vested[8];
(d) the adjustment of contracts (whether by discharge or reduction of any liability or obligation or otherwise)[9];
(e) the creation, allotment, surrender or cancellation of any shares, stock or securities[10];
(f) the formation or winding up of any company or other body of persons corporate or unincorporate[11];
(g) the amendment of the memorandum and articles or other instruments regulating any such company or other body of persons[12];
(h) the extent to which, and the circumstances in which, provisions of the order affecting a company or other body of persons corporate or unincorporate in its share capital, constitution or other matters may be altered by the company or other body of persons concerned[13];
(i) the registration of the order under any enactment by a company or other body of persons corporate or unincorporate which is affected by it as mentioned in head (h)[14];
(j) the continuation, with any necessary change of parties, of any legal proceedings[15];
(k) the approval by the relevant authority or another person of anything required by virtue of the order to be done or of any person to whom anything is to be transferred, or in whom anything is to be vested, by virtue of the order[16]; or
(l) the appointment of trustees or other persons to do anything on behalf of another person which is required of that person by virtue of the order or to monitor the doing by that person of any such thing[17].

1 As to the orders to which the Enterprise Act 2002 Sch 8 applies see PARA 232 notes 1, 2.
2 Enterprise Act 2002 Sch 8 para 12(1). See note 3.
3 Enterprise Act 2002 Sch 8 para 12(2). Schedule 8 para 12 also applies to any result consisting in two or more enterprises ceasing to be distinct enterprises (other than any result consisting in two or more bodies corporate becoming interconnected bodies corporate): Sch 8 para 12(3).

4 For these purposes, all the activities carried on by way of business by any one person or by any two or more interconnected bodies corporate may be treated as a single business: Enterprise Act 2002 Sch 8 para 13(2). As to the references in Sch 8 para 13 to the division of a business as mentioned in the text see Sch 8 para 14.
5 Enterprise Act 2002 Sch 8 para 13(1).
6 Enterprise Act 2002 Sch 8 para 13(3)(a). As to the meaning of 'relevant authority' see PARA 233 note 6.
7 Enterprise Act 2002 Sch 8 para 13(3)(b).
8 Enterprise Act 2002 Sch 8 para 13(3)(c).
9 Enterprise Act 2002 Sch 8 para 13(3)(d).
10 Enterprise Act 2002 Sch 8 para 13(3)(e).
11 Enterprise Act 2002 Sch 8 para 13(3)(f).
12 Enterprise Act 2002 Sch 8 para 13(3)(g).
13 Enterprise Act 2002 Sch 8 para 13(3)(h).
14 Enterprise Act 2002 Sch 8 para 13(3)(i).
15 Enterprise Act 2002 Sch 8 para 13(3)(j).
16 Enterprise Act 2002 Sch 8 para 13(3)(k).
17 Enterprise Act 2002 Sch 8 para 13(3)(l).

236. Supply and publication of information. An order[1] may require a person supplying goods or services to publish a list of prices or otherwise notify prices[2]. Such an order may also require or prohibit the publication or other notification of further information[3].

An order may prohibit any person from notifying (whether by publication or otherwise) to persons supplying goods or services prices recommended or suggested as appropriate to be charged by those persons for those goods or services[4].

An order may require a person supplying goods or services to publish: (1) accounting information in relation to the supply of the goods or services; (2) information in relation to the quantities of goods or services supplied; (3) information in relation to the geographical areas in which they are supplied[5].

An order may require any person to supply information to the relevant authority[6]. Where the Office of Fair Trading (the 'OFT') is not the relevant authority, an order may require any person to supply information to the OFT[7]. An order may provide for the publication of that information, by the person who has received it[8].

1 As to the orders to which the Enterprise Act 2002 Sch 8 applies see PARA 232 notes 1, 2.
2 Enterprise Act 2002 Sch 8 para 15(1). An order made by virtue of Sch 8 para 15 may provide for the manner in which information is to be published or otherwise notified: Sch 8 para 18.
3 Enterprise Act 2002 Sch 8 para 15(2). References in Sch 8 to the notification of prices or other information are not limited to the notification in writing of prices or other information: Sch 8 para 23.
4 Enterprise Act 2002 Sch 8 para 16.
5 Enterprise Act 2002 Sch 8 para 17(1). 'Accounting information', in relation to a supply of goods or services, means information as to: (1) the costs of the supply, including fixed costs and overheads; (2) the manner in which fixed costs and overheads are calculated and apportioned for accounting purposes of the supplier; and (3) the income attributable to the supply: Sch 8 para 17(2). An order made by virtue of Sch 8 para 17 may provide for the manner in which information is to be published or otherwise notified: Sch 8 para 18.
6 Enterprise Act 2002 Sch 8 para 19(a). As to the meaning of 'relevant authority' see PARA 233 note 6.
7 Enterprise Act 2002 Sch 8 para 19(b). As to the OFT see PARAS 6–8.
8 See the Enterprise Act 2002 Sch 8 para 19(c).

237.   National security. An order[1] may make such provision as the person making the order considers to be appropriate in the interests of national security[2]. Such provision may, in particular, include provision requiring a person to do, or not to do, particular things[3].

1   As to the orders to which the Enterprise Act 2002 Sch 8 applies see PARA 232 notes 1, 2.
2   Enterprise Act 2002 Sch 8 para 20(1). As to the interests of national security see s 58(1); and PARA 203.
3   Enterprise Act 2002 Sch 8 para 20(2).

238.   Newspaper mergers. Where an order is to be made following the giving of:

    (1)   an intervention notice which mentions a newspaper public interest consideration[1];

    (2)   an intervention notice which mentions any other media public interest consideration in relation to a relevant merger situation in which one of the enterprises ceasing to be distinct is a newspaper enterprise[2];

    (3)   a special intervention notice which mentions a certain specified consideration[3]; or

    (4)   a special intervention notice which, in relation to a special merger situation in which one of the enterprises ceasing to be distinct is a newspaper enterprise, mentions a certain specified consideration[4],

and the consideration concerned is still relevant[5], then the order may make such provision as the person making the order considers to be appropriate in all circumstances of the case[6]. Such provision may, in particular, include provision requiring a person to do, or not to do, particular things[7]. It may, in particular, include provision: (a) altering the constitution of a body corporate (whether in connection with the appointment of directors, the establishment of an editorial board or otherwise)[8]; (b) requiring the agreement of the relevant authority or another person before the taking of particular action (including the appointment or dismissal of an editor, journalists or directors or acting as a shadow director)[9]; (c) attaching conditions to the operation of a newspaper[10]; (d) prohibiting consultation or co-operation between subsidiaries[11].

1   Enterprise Act 2002 Sch 8 para 20A(1)(a)(i) (Sch 8 para 20A added by the Communications Act 2003 s 387). Schedule 8 para 20A is without prejudice to the operation of the other paragraphs of Sch 8 in relation to the order concerned: Sch 8 para 20A(6) (as so added). As to the meaning of 'intervention notice' see PARA 189 note 11. For these purposes, 'newspaper public interest consideration' means a media public interest consideration other than one which is such a consideration by virtue of s 58(2C), or by virtue of having been, in the opinion of the Secretary of State, concerned with broadcasting and a consideration that ought to have been specified in s 58 (see PARA 203): Sch 8 para 20A(5) (as so added). As to the meaning of 'public interest consideration' see PARA 189 note 10. As to the meaning of 'newspaper' see PARA 191 note 9.
2   Enterprise Act 2002 Sch 8 para 20A(1)(a)(ii) (as added: see note 1). As to the meaning of 'media public interest consideration' see PARA 191 note 9. As to the meaning of 'relevant merger situation' see PARA 173. As to the meaning of 'newspaper enterprise' see PARA 203 note 11.
3   Enterprise Act 2002 Sch 8 para 20A(1)(a)(iii) (as added: see note 1). The text refers to a consideration specified in s 58(2A) or (2B) (see PARA 203). As to the meaning of 'special intervention notice' see PARA 204.
4   Enterprise Act 2002 Sch 8 para 20A(1)(a)(iv) (as added: see note 1). The text refers to a consideration specified in s 58(2C) (see PARA 203). As to the meaning of 'special merger situation' see PARA 204.
5   Enterprise Act 2002 Sch 8 para 20A(1)(b) (as added: see note 1).
6   Enterprise Act 2002 Sch 8 para 20A(2) (as added: see note 1).
7   Enterprise Act 2002 Sch 8 para 20A(3) (as added: see note 1).
8   Enterprise Act 2002 Sch 8 para 20A(4)(a) (as added: see note 1).

9 Enterprise Act 2002 Sch 8 para 20A(4)(b) (as added: see note 1). As to the meaning of 'relevant authority' see PARA 233 note 6.
10 Enterprise Act 2002 Sch 8 para 20A(4)(c) (as added: see note 1).
11 Enterprise Act 2002 Sch 8 para 20A(4)(d) (as added: see note 1).

239. Maintaining the stability of the UK financial system. An enforcement order in a case relating to the stability of the UK financial system[1] may make such provision as the person making the order considers to be appropriate in the interest of maintaining the stability of the UK financial system[2]. Such provision may, in particular, include provision requiring a person to do, or not to do, particular things[3].

1 The Enterprise Act 2002 Sch 8 para 20B applies for the purposes of a relevant order under Sch 7 para 5, 10 or 11 (see PARAS 229, 231) but not for any other purposes of Pt 3 or Pt 4 or any other enactment: Sch 8 para 20B(1) (Sch 8 para 20B added by SI 2008/2645). 'Relevant order' means an order: (1) which is to be made following the giving of an intervention notice or special intervention notice which mentions the consideration specified in the Enterprise Act 2002 s 58(2D) (including, in the case of a notice given before the consideration was so specified, an intervention notice which mentions the consideration as a consideration which ought to be specified in s 58 (see PARA 203)); and (2) to which the consideration is still relevant: Sch 8 para 20B(5) (as so added). As to the meaning of 'intervention notice' see PARA 189 note 11. As to the meaning of 'special intervention notice' see PARA 204.
2 Enterprise Act 2002 Sch 8 para 20B(2) (as added: see note 1). Schedule 8 para 20B is without prejudice to the operation of the other paragraphs of Sch 8 in relation to the order: Sch 8 para 20B(4) (as so added).
3 Enterprise Act 2002 Sch 8 para 20B(3) (as added: see note 1).

240. Delegated power of directions. An enforcement order may authorise the person making the order to give certain directions to a person specified in the directions, or to the holder for the time being of a specified office in any body of persons corporate or unincorporate[1]. The directions which may be made are directions to take specified action for the purpose of carrying out, or ensuring compliance with, the enforcement order concerned, or to do, or refrain from doing, anything specified or described in the order which the person might be required by that order to do or refrain from doing[2]. An enforcement order may authorise the person making the order to vary or revoke any directions so given[3].

The court[4] may by order require any person who has failed to comply with any such directions to comply with them, or otherwise remedy his failure, within such time as may be specified in the order[5]. Where the directions related to anything done in the management or administration of a body of persons corporate or unincorporate, the court may by order require the body of persons concerned or any officer of it to comply with the directions, or otherwise remedy the failure to comply with them, within such time as may be specified in the order[6]. Such court orders[7] are made on the application of the person authorised[8] to give the directions concerned[9], and they may provide for all the costs or expenses of, or incidental to, the application for the order to be met by any person in default or by any officers of a body of persons corporate or unincorporate who are responsible for its default[10].

1 Enterprise Act 2002 s 87(1). As to the meaning of 'enforcement order' see PARA 232 note 1.
2 Enterprise Act 2002 s 87(2).
3 Enterprise Act 2002 s 87(3).
4 For these purposes 'court' means, in relation to England and Wales or Northern Ireland, the High Court: Enterprise Act 2002 s 87(8).
5 Enterprise Act 2002 s 87(4).
6 Enterprise Act 2002 s 87(5).
7 Ie an order under the Enterprise Act 2002 s 87(4) or s 87(5).

8   Ie authorised by virtue of the Enterprise Act 2002 s 87.

9   Enterprise Act 2002 s 87(6).

10 Enterprise Act 2002 s 87(7).

241.   Procedural requirements for certain undertakings and orders. The Enterprise Act 2002 sets out the procedure for accepting certain enforcement undertakings and for the making and termination of certain enforcement orders[1]. Before accepting such an undertaking[2] or making such an order[3], the relevant authority (whether it be the Office of Fair Trading (the 'OFT')[4], the Competition Commission[5] or the Secretary of State[6]) must give notice of the proposed undertaking or order[7], and must consider any representations made in accordance with the notice and not withdrawn[8]. The relevant authority may not accept the undertaking with modifications or (as the case may be) make the order with modifications unless the relevant authority gives notice of the proposed modifications, and considers any representations made in accordance with the notice and not withdrawn[9]. If, after giving notice[10], the relevant authority decides not to accept the undertaking concerned or (as the case may be) make the order concerned, and also not to proceed[11], then the relevant authority must give notice of that decision[12]. As soon as practicable after accepting an undertaking[13] or (as the case may be) making an order[14], the relevant authority must (except in the case of an order which is a statutory instrument) serve a copy of the undertaking on any person by whom it is given or (as the case may be) serve a copy of the order on any person identified in the order as a person on whom a copy of the order should be served, and must also publish the undertaking or (as the case may be) the order[15].

Where the relevant authority is proposing to release a certain undertaking[16] or revoke a certain order[17], it must, before doing so, give notice of the proposed release or (as the case may be) revocation, and also consider any representations made in accordance with the notice and not withdrawn[18]. As soon as practicable after releasing the undertaking or making the revoking order, the relevant authority must (except in the case of an order which is a statutory instrument) serve a copy of the release of the undertaking on the person who gave the undertaking or (as the case may be) serve a copy of the revoking order on any person identified in the order being revoked as a person on whom a copy of that order should be served, and must also publish the release or (as the case may be) the revoking order[19].

The relevant authority may dispense with any or all of these requirements[20] if the relevant authority considers that the relevant authority has special reasons for doing so[21].

1   Enterprise Act 2002 s 90. The procedure is set out in Sch 10 (see the text and notes 2–21). As to the meaning of 'enforcement undertaking' see PARA 215 note 4. As to the meaning of 'enforcement order' see PARA 232 note 1.

2   Ie any undertaking under the Enterprise Act 2002 s 73 (see PARA 217) or s 82 (see PARA 225) or Sch 7 para 3 (see PARA 229) or Sch 7 para 9 (see PARA 231) (other than an undertaking under the enactment concerned which varies an undertaking under that enactment but not in any material respect): Sch 10 para 1(a).

3   Ie any order under the Enterprise Act 2002 s 75 (see PARA 219), s 83 (see PARA 225) or s 84 (see PARA 226) or Sch 7 para 5 (see PARA 229), Sch 7 para 10 or 11 (see PARA 231) (other than an order under the enactment concerned which is a revoking order of the kind dealt with by Sch 10 paras 6–8): Sch 7 para 1(b).

4   As to the OFT see PARAS 6–8.

5   As to the Competition Commission see PARAS 9–12.

6   As to the Secretary of State see PARA 5.

7   Enterprise Act 2002 Sch 10 para 2(1)(a). The notice must state: (1) that the relevant authority proposes to accept the undertaking or (as the case may be) make the order; (2) the purpose and effect of the undertaking or (as the case may be) order; (3) the situation that the undertaking or (as the case may be) order is seeking to deal with; (4) any other facts which the relevant authority considers justify the acceptance of the undertaking or (as the case may be) the making of the order; (5) a means of gaining access to an accurate version of the proposed undertaking or (as the case may be) order at all reasonable times; and (6) the period (not less than 15 days starting with the date of publication of the notice in the case of an undertaking and not less than 30 days starting with that date in the case of an order) within which representations may be made in relation to the proposed undertaking or (as the case may be) order: Sch 10 para 2(2). The notice must be given, in the case of a proposed order, by serving on any person identified in the order as a person on whom a copy of the order should be served a copy of the notice and a copy of the proposed order; and, in every case, by publishing the notice: Sch 10 para 2(3).

8   Enterprise Act 2002 Sch 10 para 2(1)(b).

9   Enterprise Act 2002 Sch 10 para 2(4). The notice must state: (1) the proposed modifications; (2) the reasons for them; and (3) the period (not less than seven days starting with the date of the publication of the notice under Sch 10 para 2(4)) within which representations may be made in relation to the proposed modifications: Sch 10 para 2(5). The notice must be given, in the case of a proposed order, by serving a copy of the notice on any person identified in the order as a person on whom a copy of the order should be served; and, in every case, by publishing the notice: Sch 10 para 2(6).
      The requirements of Sch 10 para 2(4) (and those of Sch 10 para 2(1)) do not apply if the relevant authority has already given notice under Sch 10 para 2(1) but not Sch 10 para 2(4) in relation to the proposed undertaking or order, and considers that the modifications which are now being proposed are not material in any respect: Sch 10 para 5(1). The requirements of Sch 10 para 2(4) (and those of Sch 10 para 2(1)) do not apply if the relevant authority has already given notice under Sch 10 para 2(1) and Sch 10 para 2(4) in relation to the matter concerned, and considers that the further modifications which are now being proposed do not differ in any material respect from the modifications in relation to which notice was last given under Sch 10 para 2(4): Sch 10 para 5(2).

10   Ie under the Enterprise Act 2002 Sch 10 para 2(1) or Sch 10 para 2(4).

11   Ie by virtue of the Enterprise Act 2002 Sch 10 para 5.

12   Enterprise Act 2002 Sch 10 para 3(1). The notice must be given, in the case of a proposed order, by serving a copy of the notice on any person identified in the order as a person on whom a copy of the order should be served; and, in every case, by publishing the notice: Sch 10 para 3(2).

13   See note 2.

14   See note 3.

15   Enterprise Act 2002 Sch 10 para 4.

16   Ie any undertaking under the Enterprise Act 2002 s 73 (see PARA 217) or s 82 (see PARA 225) or Sch 7 para 3 (see PARA 229) or Sch 7 para 9 (see PARA 231) (other than in connection with accepting an undertaking under the enactment concerned which varies or supersedes an undertaking under that enactment): Sch 10 para 6(a).

17   Ie any order under the Enterprise Act 2002 s 75 (see PARA 219), s 83 (see PARA 225) or s 84 (see PARA 226) or Sch 7 para 5 (see PARA 229), Sch 7 para 10 or 11 (see PARA 231) (other than in connection with making an order under the enactment concerned which varies or supersedes an order under that enactment): Sch 10 para 6(b).

18   Enterprise Act 2002 Sch 10 para 7(1). The notice must state: (1) the fact that a release or (as the case may be) revocation is proposed; (2) the reasons for it; and (3) the period (not less than 15 days starting with the date of publication of the notice in the case of an undertaking and not less than 30 days starting with that date in the case of an order) within which representations may be made in relation to the proposed release or (as the case may be) revocation: Sch 10 para 7(2). If after giving the notice the relevant authority decides not to proceed with the release or (as the case may be) the revocation, the relevant authority must give notice of that decision: Sch 10 para 7(3). A notice under Sch 10 para 7(1) or Sch 10 para 7(3) must be given by: (a) serving a copy of the notice on the person who gave the undertaking which is being released or (as the case may be) on any person identified in the order being revoked as a person on whom a copy of the order should be served; and (b) publishing the notice: Sch 10 para 7(4).

19   Enterprise Act 2002 Sch 10 para 8.

20   Ie the requirements of the Enterprise Act 2002 Sch 10 (see the text and notes 1–19).

21   Enterprise Act 2002 Sch 10 para 9.

242.   Register of undertakings and orders. The Office of Fair Trading (the 'OFT') is under a duty to compile and maintain a register of undertakings and orders[1] in such form as it considers appropriate[2]. It must ensure that the following matters are entered in the register: (1) the provisions of any enforcement undertaking accepted under Part 3 of the Enterprise Act 2002[3]; (2) the provisions of any enforcement order made under that Part[4]; (3) the details of any variation, release or revocation of such an undertaking or order[5]; and (4) the details of consents given by the Competition Commission[6] or by the Secretary of State[7]. However, the duty to include such matters does not extend to anything of which the OFT is unaware[8]. The Commission and the Secretary of State must inform the OFT of any matters which are to be included in the register and which relate to enforcement undertakings accepted by them, enforcement orders made by them or consents given by them[9].

The OFT must ensure that the contents of the register are available to the public[10], and if requested by any person to do so (and subject to such reasonable fees (if any) as the OFT may determine), the OFT must supply the person concerned with a certified copy of the register or of an extract from it[11].

1 Enterprise Act 2002 s 91(1). As to the OFT see PARAS 6–8.
2 Enterprise Act 2002 s 91(2).
3 Enterprise Act 2002 s 91(3)(a). As to the meaning of 'enforcement undertaking' see PARA 215 note 4.
4 Enterprise Act 2002 s 91(3)(b). As to the meaning of 'enforcement order' see PARA 232 note 1.
5 Enterprise Act 2002 s 91(3)(c).
6 Ie under the Enterprise Act 2002 s 77(2), (3) or s 78(2): see s 91(3)(d). As to the Competition Commission see PARAS 9–12.
7 Ie under the Enterprise Act 2002 Sch 7 para 7(2), (3) or Sch 7 para 8(2): see s 91(3)(d). As to the Secretary of State see PARA 5.
8 Enterprise Act 2002 s 91(4).
9 Enterprise Act 2002 s 91(5).
10 The contents must be available to the public during (as a minimum) such hours as may be specified in an order made by the Secretary of State, and subject to such reasonable fees (if any) as the OFT may determine: Enterprise Act 2002 s 91(6).
11 Enterprise Act 2002 s 91(7).

F. ENFORCEMENT FUNCTIONS OF THE OFFICE OF FAIR TRADING

243.   Duty to monitor undertakings and orders. The Office of Fair Trading (the 'OFT')[1] must keep under review (1) the carrying out of any enforcement undertaking or any enforcement order[2]; and (2) compliance with statutory prohibitions[3]. The OFT must, in particular, from time to time consider whether an enforcement undertaking or enforcement order has been or is being complied with[4]. It must also consider whether, by reason of any change of circumstances, an enforcement undertaking is no longer appropriate and whether one or more of the parties to it can be released from it or whether it needs to be varied or to be superseded by a new enforcement undertaking[5]. It also has a duty to consider whether, by reason of any change of circumstances, an enforcement order is no longer appropriate and needs to be varied or revoked[6].

The OFT must give the Competition Commission[7] or (as the case may be) the Secretary of State[8] such advice as it considers appropriate in relation to:

(a)   any possible variation or release by the Commission or (as the case may be) the Secretary of State of an enforcement undertaking accepted by it or (as the case may be) him[9];

(b)   any possible new enforcement undertaking to be accepted by the Commission or (as the case may be) the Secretary of State so as to supersede another enforcement undertaking given to the Commission or (as the case may be) the Secretary of State[10];

(c)   any possible variation or revocation by the Commission or (as the case may be) the Secretary of State of an enforcement order made by the Commission or (as the case may be) the Secretary of State[11];

(d)   any possible enforcement undertaking to be accepted by the Commission or (as the case may be) the Secretary of State instead of an enforcement order or any possible enforcement order to be made by the Commission or (as the case may be) the Secretary of State instead of an enforcement undertaking[12];

(e)   the enforcement[13] of any enforcement undertaking or enforcement order[14]; or

(f)   the enforcement[15] of statutory prohibitions[16].

The OFT must take such action as it considers appropriate in relation to: (i) any possible variation or release by it of an enforcement undertaking accepted by it[17]; (ii) any possible new enforcement undertaking to be accepted by it so as to supersede another enforcement undertaking given to it[18]; (iii) any possible variation or revocation by it of an enforcement order made by it[19]; (iv) any possible enforcement undertaking to be accepted by it instead of an enforcement order or any possible enforcement order to be made by it instead of an enforcement undertaking[20]; (v) the enforcement by it[21] of any enforcement undertaking or enforcement order[22]; or (vi) the enforcement by it[23] of statutory prohibitions[24].

The OFT must keep under review the effectiveness of enforcement undertakings accepted under Part 3 of the Enterprise Act 2002[25] and enforcement orders made under that Part[26], and must, whenever requested to do so by the Secretary of State and otherwise from time to time, prepare a report of its findings in this respect[27].

1   As to the OFT see PARAS 6–8.
2   Enterprise Act 2002 s 92(1)(a). As to the meaning of 'enforcement undertaking' see PARA 215 note 4. As to the meaning of 'enforcement order' see PARA 232 note 1.
3   Enterprise Act 2002 s 92(1)(b). This refers to the prohibitions in s 77(2), (3) (see PARA 221), s 78(2) (see PARA 222), Sch 7 paras 7(2), (3), 8(2) (see PARA 230).
4   Enterprise Act 2002 s 92(2)(a).
5   Enterprise Act 2002 s 92(2)(b).
6   Enterprise Act 2002 s 92(2)(c).
7   As to the Competition Commission see PARAS 9–12.
8   As to the Secretary of State see PARA 5.
9   Enterprise Act 2002 s 92(3)(a).
10 Enterprise Act 2002 s 92(3)(b).
11 Enterprise Act 2002 s 92(3)(c).
12 Enterprise Act 2002 s 92(3)(d).
13 Ie by virtue of the Enterprise Act 2002 s 94(6)–(8) (see PARA 245).
14 Enterprise Act 2002 s 92(3)(e).
15 Ie by virtue of the Enterprise Act 2002 s 95(4), (5) (see PARA 245).
16 Enterprise Act 2002 s 92(3)(f). As to the prohibitions see note 3.
17 Enterprise Act 2002 s 92(4)(a).
18 Enterprise Act 2002 s 92(4)(b).
19 Enterprise Act 2002 s 92(4)(c).
20 Enterprise Act 2002 s 92(4)(d).
21 Ie by virtue of the Enterprise Act 2002 s 94(6) (see PARA 245).
22 Enterprise Act 2002 s 92(4)(e).
23 Ie by virtue of the Enterprise Act 2002 s 95(4), (5) (see PARA 245).
24 Enterprise Act 2002 s 92(4)(f). As to the prohibitions see note 3.
25 Ie the Enterprise Act 2002 Pt 3 (ss 22–130).
26 Enterprise Act 2002 s 92(5).

27 Enterprise Act 2002 s 92(6). The OFT must give any report prepared by it under s 92(6) to the Commission, with a copy to the Secretary of State, and must also publish it: s 92(7).

244.   Further role in relation to undertakings and orders. Where the relevant authority (whether it be the Competition Commission[1] or the Secretary of State[2]) is considering whether to accept certain undertakings[3], it may require the Office of Fair Trading (the 'OFT')[4] to consult with such persons as the relevant authority considers appropriate with a view to discovering whether they will offer undertakings which the relevant authority would be prepared to accept[5]. The relevant authority may require the OFT to report to the relevant authority on the outcome of the OFT's consultations within such period as the relevant authority may require[6].

These powers conferred on the relevant authority[7] are without prejudice to the power of the relevant authority to consult the persons concerned itself[8]. If asked by the relevant authority for advice in relation to the taking of enforcement action (whether or not by way of undertaking) in a particular case, the OFT must give such advice as it considers appropriate[9].

1 As to the Competition Commission see PARAS 9–12.
2 As to the Secretary of State see PARA 5.
3 Ie (1) where the Commission is considering whether to accept undertakings under the Enterprise Act 2002 s 80 (see PARA 223) or s 82 (see PARA 225); or (2) the Secretary of State is considering whether to accept undertakings under Sch 7 para 1, 3 or 9 (see PARAS 228, 229, 231 respectively): s 93(1).
4 As to the OFT see PARAS 6–8.
5 Ie under the Enterprise Act 2002 s 80 or s 82 or (as the case may be) Sch 7 para 1, 3 or 9: s 93(2); and see note 3.
6 Enterprise Act 2002 s 93(3). This report must, in particular, contain advice from the OFT as to whether any undertakings offered should be accepted by the relevant authority under s 80 or s 82 or (as the case may be) Sch 7 para 1, 3 or 9 (see note 3): s 93(4).
7 Ie the powers conferred by the Enterprise Act 2002 s 93(1)–(4) (see the text and notes 1–6).
8 Enterprise Act 2002 s 93(5).
9 Enterprise Act 2002 s 93(6).

G. RIGHTS TO ENFORCE

245.   Enforcement undertakings and orders. Any person to whom an enforcement undertaking[1] or enforcement order[2] relates has a duty to comply with it[3]. This duty is owed to any person who may be affected by a contravention of the undertaking or (as the case may be) order[4]. Any breach of the duty which causes such a person to sustain loss or damage is actionable by him[5]. However, in any such proceedings brought against a person to whom an enforcement undertaking or an enforcement order relates it is a defence for that person to show that he took all reasonable steps and exercised all due diligence to avoid contravening the undertaking or (as the case may be) order[6].

Compliance with an enforcement undertaking or an enforcement order is also enforceable by civil proceedings brought by the Office of Fair Trading (the 'OFT')[7] for an injunction or for interdict or for any other appropriate relief or remedy[8]. Compliance with certain undertakings and orders[9] is also enforceable by civil proceedings brought by the Competition Commission[10] or the Secretary of State[11] for an injunction or for interdict or for any other appropriate relief or remedy[12].

1 As to the meaning of 'enforcement undertaking' see PARA 215 note 4.
2 As to the meaning of 'enforcement order' see PARA 232 note 1.
3 Enterprise Act 2002 s 94(1), (2).

4   Enterprise Act 2002 s 94(3).
5   Enterprise Act 2002 s 94(4).
6   Enterprise Act 2002 s 94(5).
7   As to the OFT see PARAS 6–8.
8   Enterprise Act 2002 s 94(6). Section 94(6) does not prejudice any right that a person may have by virtue of s 94(4) to bring civil proceedings for contravention or apprehended contravention of an enforcement undertaking or an enforcement order: s 94(9).
9   Ie compliance with an undertaking under the Enterprise Act 2002 s 80 (see PARA 223) or s 82 (see PARA 225), an order made by the Competition Commission under s 76 (see PARA 220) or an order under s 81 (see PARA 224), s 83 (see PARA 225) or s 84 (see PARA 226) is enforceable by civil proceedings brought by the Commission: s 94(7). Compliance with an undertaking under Sch 7 para 1, 3 or 9, an order made by the Secretary of State under Sch 7 para 2 or an order under Sch 7 para 5, 6, 10 or 11, is enforceable by civil proceedings brought by the Secretary of State: s 94(8).
10 As to the Competition Commission see PARAS 9–12.
11 As to the Secretary of State see PARA 5.
12 Enterprise Act 2002 s 94(7), (8). Section 94(7), (8) does not prejudice any right that a person may have by virtue of s 94(4) to bring civil proceedings for contravention or apprehended contravention of an enforcement undertaking or an enforcement order: s 94(9).

246. Statutory restrictions.   No relevant person may, without the consent of the Competition Commission[1], or as the case may be, Secretary of State[2]:

(1)   complete any outstanding matters in connection with any arrangements which have resulted in the enterprises concerned ceasing to be distinct enterprises[3];

(2)   make any further arrangements in consequence of that result (other than arrangements which reverse that result)[4]; or

(3)   transfer the ownership or control of any enterprises to which the reference relates[5].

Nor may any relevant person, without the consent of the Commission or Secretary of State (as the case may be), assist in any of the activities listed above[6]. No relevant person may, without the consent of the Commission or Secretary of State (as the case may be) directly or indirectly acquire during the relevant period an interest in shares in a company if any enterprise to which the reference relates is carried on by or under the control of that company[7].

The obligation to comply with these provisions is a duty owed to any person who may be affected by a contravention of the enactment concerned[8]. Any breach of the duty which causes such a person to sustain loss or damage is actionable by him[9]. In any such proceedings it is a defence for that person to show that he took all reasonable steps and exercised all due diligence to avoid contravening the enactment concerned[10].

Compliance with the provisions is also enforceable by civil proceedings brought by the Office of Fair Trading (the 'OFT')[11], the Commission or the Secretary of State as the case may be for an injunction or for interdict or for any other appropriate relief or remedy[12].

1   As to the Competition Commission see PARAS 9–12.
2   As to the Secretary of State see PARA 5.
3   See the Enterprise Act 2002 s 77(2)(a) (see PARA 221), Sch 7 para 7(2)(a) (see PARA 230). As to the meaning of 'enterprise' see PARA 173 note 2.
4   See the Enterprise Act 2002 s 77(2)(b) (see PARA 221), Sch 7 para 7(2)(a) (see PARA 230).
5   See the Enterprise Act 2002 s 77(2)(c) (see PARA 221), Sch 7 para 7(2)(a) (see PARA 230).
6   See the Enterprise Act 2002 s 77(3) (see PARA 221), Sch 7 para 7(3) (see PARA 230).
7   See the Enterprise Act 2002 s 78(2) (see PARA 222), Sch 7 para 8(2) (see PARA 230).
8   Enterprise Act 2002 s 95(1).
9   Enterprise Act 2002 s 95(2).
10 Enterprise Act 2002 s 95(3).

11 As to the OFT see PARAS 6–8.
12 Ie compliance with the Enterprise Act 2002 s 77(2), (3) or s 78(2) is enforceable by civil
     proceedings brought by the OFT or the Commission for an injunction or for an interdict or for
     any other appropriate relief or remedy: s 95(4). Compliance with Sch 7 para 7(2), (3) or Sch 7
     para 8(2) is enforceable by civil proceedings brought by the OFT or the Secretary of State for an
     injunction or for interdict or for any other appropriate relief or remedy: s 95(5).
     Section 95(4), (5) does not prejudice any right that a person may have by virtue of s 95(2) to
     bring civil proceedings for contravention or apprehended contravention of s 77(2), (3) or s 78(2)
     or Sch 7 para 7(2), (3) or Sch 7 para 8(2): s 95(6).

(v) Merger Notices

247.   Merger notices. Any person authorised by regulations[1] may give notice
to the Office of Fair Trading (the 'OFT')[2] of proposed arrangements which might
result in the creation of a relevant merger situation[3]. Such a notice is referred to
as a 'merger notice' and it must be in the prescribed form and state that the
existence of the proposal has been made public[4].

Certain references to the Competition Commission are not permitted if the
period for considering the merger notice has expired without a reference being
made in relation to those arrangements[5].

A merger notice may be withdrawn by or on behalf of the person who gave
the notice by a notice in writing sent to the OFT[6].

1 Ie any person carrying on an enterprise to which the notified arrangements relate: Enterprise
    Act 2002 (Merger Prenotification) Regulations 2003, SI 2003/1369, reg 3. As to the meaning of
    'enterprise' see PARA 173 note 2. 'Notified arrangements' means arrangements of which notice is
    given under the Enterprise Act 2002 s 96(1) or arrangements not differing from them in any
    material respect: s 96(6).
2 As to the OFT see PARAS 6–8.
3 Enterprise Act 2002 s 96(1). As to the meaning of 'relevant merger situation' see PARA 173. A
    merger notice given under s 96(1) is treated as having been received by the OFT on the day on
    which it is in fact received by the OFT: Enterprise Act 2002 (Merger Prenotification)
    Regulations 2003, SI 2003/1369, reg 5. However, where it is received by the OFT on any day
    which is not a working day or after 5.00 pm on any working day, it is treated as having been
    received on the next working day, and the Interpretation Act 1978 s 7 does not apply: Enterprise
    Act 2002 (Merger Prenotification) Regulations 2003, SI 2003/1369, reg 5.
4 Enterprise Act 2002 s 96(2).
5 See PARA 250. As to the period for considering merger notices see PARA 248.
6 Enterprise Act 2002 (Merger Prenotification) Regulations 2003, SI 2003/1369, reg 7. An
    authorisation to act on behalf of another person must be given to the OFT in writing and an
    authorisation to act on behalf of a company must be signed by a director or other officer of that
    company: see reg 14(1), (2). A person who has given an authorisation may revoke it by a notice
    in writing given to the OFT and, where that person is a company, the notice must be signed by
    a director or other officer of that company: reg 14(3).

248.   Period for considering merger notices. The period for considering a
merger notice[1] is generally the period of 20 days beginning with the first day
after the notice has been received by the Office of Fair Trading (the 'OFT')[2] and
any fee[3] to the OFT in respect of the notice has been paid[4]. However, extensions
are possible in the following circumstances.

Where no intervention notice[5] is in force in relation to the matter concerned,
the OFT may by notice to the person who gave the merger notice extend by a
further ten days the period for considering the merger notice[6]. Where an
intervention notice is in force in relation to the matter concerned and there has
been no such extension, the OFT may by notice to the person who gave the
merger notice extend by a further 20 days the period for considering the merger
notice[7]. Where an intervention notice is in force in relation to the matter

concerned and there has been an extension[8], the OFT may by notice to the person who gave the merger notice extend the period for considering the merger notice by a further number of days which, including any extension already made[9], does not exceed 20 days[10].

The OFT may by notice to the person who gave the merger notice extend the period for considering a merger notice if the OFT considers that the person has failed to provide[11] information requested of him in that notice[12]. This extension is for the period until the person concerned provides the information to the satisfaction of the OFT or, if earlier, the cancellation by the OFT of the extension[13].

The OFT may by notice to the person who gave the merger notice extend the period for considering a merger notice if the OFT or the Secretary of State is seeking certain undertakings[14]. This extension is for the period beginning with the receipt of the notice and ending with the earliest of the following events: (1) the giving of the undertakings concerned; (2) the expiry of the period of ten days beginning with the first day after the receipt by the OFT of a notice from the person from whom the undertakings are being sought stating that he does not intend to give the undertakings; or (3) the cancellation by the OFT of the extension[15].

The Secretary of State may by notice to the person who gave the merger notice extend the period for considering a merger notice if he decides to delay a decision[16] as to whether to make a reference to the Competition Commission[17]. The OFT may by notice to the person who gave the merger notice extend the period for considering a merger notice if the European Commission is considering a request made, in relation to the matter concerned, by the United Kingdom (whether alone or with others) (but is not yet proceeding with the matter in pursuance of such a request)[18].

Where the period for considering a merger notice is extended or further extended as described above[19], the period as extended or (as the case may be) further extended is calculated by taking the period being extended and adding to it the period of the extension (whether or not those periods overlap in time)[20].

1   As to the meaning of 'merger notice' see PARA 247.
2   As to the OFT see PARAS 6–8.
3   Ie any fee payable by virtue of the Enterprise Act 2002 s 121 (see PARA 272). For the time at which fees are to be treated as paid see the Enterprise Act 2002 (Merger Prenotification) Regulations 2003, SI 2003/1369, reg 13.
4   Enterprise Act 2002 s 97(1). In determining any period which is expressed in the enactment concerned as a period of days or number of days no account is to be taken of Saturday, Sunday, Good Friday, Christmas Day and any day which is a bank holiday in England and Wales: s 98(3).
5   As to the meaning of 'intervention notice' see PARA 189 note 11.
6   Enterprise Act 2002 s 97(2). A notice under s 97(2) must be given, before the end of the period for considering the merger notice, to the person who gave the merger notice: s 98(1). Any reference in Pt 3 (apart from in ss 97(1), 99(1)) to the period for considering a merger notice is, if that period is extended by virtue of any one or more of s 97(2), (3), (4) (5), (7), (9), (11) in relation to a particular case, to be construed in relation to that case as a reference to that period as so extended; but only one extension is possible under s 97(2), (3) or s 97(4): s 98(4).
7   Enterprise Act 2002 s 97(3). A notice under s 97(3) must be given, before the end of the period for considering the merger notice, to the person who gave the merger notice: s 98(1). See note 6.
8   Ie under the Enterprise Act 2002 s 97(2).
9   See note 8.
10 Enterprise Act 2002 s 97(4). A notice under s 97(4) must be given, before the end of the period for considering the merger notice, to the person who gave the merger notice: s 98(1). See note 6.
11 Ie within the period stated in a notice under the Enterprise Act 2002 s 99(2) and in the authorised or required manner (see PARA 249).

12 Enterprise Act 2002 s 97(5). A notice under s 97(5) must be given, before the end of the period for considering the merger notice, to the person who gave the merger notice: s 98(1). A notice under s 97(5) must also be given within five days of the end of the period within which the information is to be provided and which is stated in the notice under s 99(2) (see PARA 249), and must also inform the person who gave the merger notice of: (1) the OFT's opinion as mentioned in s 97(5); and (2) the OFT's intention to extend the period for considering a merger notice: s 98(2).

13 Enterprise Act 2002 s 97(6). In these circumstances, the OFT must inform the person who gave the merger notice, or a person acting on his behalf: (1) of the fact that it is satisfied as to the provision of the information requested by it or (as the case may be) of its decision to cancel the extension; and (2) of the time at which it is to be treated as so satisfied or (as the case may be) of the time at which the cancellation is to be treated as having effect: Enterprise Act 2002 (Merger Prenotification) Regulations 2003, SI 2003/1369, reg 9.

14 Enterprise Act 2002 s 97(7). This applies where the OFT is seeking undertakings under the Enterprise Act 2002 s 73 (see PARA 217) or (as the case may be) the Secretary of State is seeking undertakings under Sch 7 para 3 (see PARA 229): s 97(7). A notice under s 97(7) must be given, before the end of the period for considering the merger notice, to the person who gave the merger notice: s 98(1). As to the Secretary of State see PARA 5. A notice given to the person who gave the merger notice, or a person acting on his behalf, under s 97(7) is to be treated as having been received by that person on the day on which it is in fact received by that person; except that where it is received by that person on any day which is not a working day or after 5.00 pm on any working day, it is to be treated as having been received on the next working day, and the Interpretation Act 1978 s 7 does not apply: Enterprise Act 2002 (Merger Prenotification) Regulations 2003, SI 2003/1369, reg 12.

15 Enterprise Act 2002 s 97(8). In these circumstances, the OFT must inform the person who gave the merger notice, or a person acting on his behalf of any decision by it to cancel the extension, and of the time at which such a cancellation is to be treated as having effect: Enterprise Act 2002 (Merger Prenotification) Regulations 2003, SI 2003/1369, reg 10. A notice given to the OFT under the Enterprise Act 2002 s 97(8) is to be treated as having been received by it on the day on which it is in fact received by the OFT; except that where it is received by the OFT on any day which is not a working day or after 5.00 pm on any working day, it is to be treated as having been received on the next working day, and the Interpretation Act 1978 s 7 does not apply: Enterprise Act 2002 (Merger Prenotification) Regulations 2003, SI 2003/1369, reg 11.

16 Ie under the Enterprise Act 2002 Sch 7 para 3(6) (see PARA 229).

17 Enterprise Act 2002 s 97(9). This refers to a reference by the Secretary of State to the Commission under s 45 (see PARA 193). As to the Competition Commission see PARAS 9–12. An extension under s 97(9) is for the period of the delay: s 97(10). A notice under s 97(9) must be given, before the end of the period for considering the merger notice, to the person who gave the merger notice: s 98(1).

18 Enterprise Act 2002 s 97(11) (amended by SI 2004/1079). This refers to a request made under art 22(1) of EC Council Regulation 139/2004 (OJ L24, 29.1.2004, p 1) (the 'EC Merger Regulation') (see PARA 74). A notice under the Enterprise Act 2002 s 97(11) must be given, before the end of the period for considering the merger notice, to the person who gave the merger notice: s 98(1). The OFT must, in connection with any notice given by it under the Enterprise Act 2002 s 97(11), by notice inform the person who gave the merger notice of the completion by the European Commission of its consideration of the request of the United Kingdom: s 97(13). As to the meaning of 'United Kingdom' see PARA 401 note 1. An extension under s 97(11) is for the period beginning with the receipt of the notice under s 97(11) and ending with the receipt of a notice under s 97(13): s 97(12). A notice given to the person who gave the merger notice, or a person acting on his behalf, under s 97(11) or s 97(13) is to be treated as having been received by that person on the day on which it is in fact received by that person; except that where it is received by that person on any day which is not a working day or after 5.00 pm on any working day, it is to be treated as having been received on the next working day, and the Interpretation Act 1978 s 7 does not apply: Enterprise Act 2002 (Merger Prenotification) Regulations 2003, SI 2003/1369, reg 12.

19 Ie by virtue of the Enterprise Act 2002 s 97 (see the text and notes 1–18).

20 Enterprise Act 2002 s 98(5). This applies where: (1) the period for considering a merger notice is further extended; (2) the further extension and at least one previous extension is made under one or more of s 97(5), (7), (9), (11); and (3) the same days or fractions of days are included in or comprise the further extension and are included in or comprise at least one such previous extension: s 98(6). In calculating the period of the further extension, any days or fractions of days of the kind mentioned in head (3) are to be disregarded: s 98(7).

249. Functions of the Office of Fair Trading and Secretary of State. The Office of Fair Trading (the 'OFT')[1] must, so far as practicable and when the period for considering any merger notice[2] begins, take such action as the OFT considers appropriate to bring:

(1)   the existence of the proposal;

(2)   the fact that the merger notice has been given; and

(3)   the date on which the period for considering the notice may expire,

to the attention of those whom the OFT considers would be affected if the arrangements were carried into effect[3].

The OFT may by notice to the person who gave the merger notice request him to provide the OFT with such information as the OFT or (as the case may be) the Secretary of State[4] may require for the purpose of carrying out its or (as the case may be) his functions in relation to the merger notice[5].

The OFT may, at any time before the end of the period for considering any merger notice, reject the notice[6] if:

(a)   the OFT suspects that any information given in respect of the notified arrangements[7] (whether in the merger notice or otherwise) by the person who gave the notice or any connected person is in any material respect false or misleading[8];

(b)   the OFT suspects that it is not proposed to carry the notified arrangements into effect[9];

(c)   any prescribed information is not given in the merger notice or any information requested by notice[10] is not provided as required[11]; or

(d)   the OFT considers that the notified arrangements are, or if carried into effect would result in, a concentration with a Community dimension[12].

The Secretary of State may, for the purposes of determining the effect of giving a merger notice and the action which may be or is to be taken by any person in connection with such a notice, by order modify the relevant statutory provisions[13].

1   As to the OFT see PARAS 6–8.
2   As to the meaning of 'merger notice' see PARA 247. As to the period for considering merger notices see PARA 248.
3   Enterprise Act 2002 s 99(1).
4   As to the Secretary of State see PARA 5.
5   Enterprise Act 2002 s 99(2). See the Enterprise Act 2002 (Merger Prenotification) Regulations 2003, SI 2003/1369, reg 9; and PARA 248. A notice under s 99(2) must state: (1) the information required; (2) the period within which the information is to be provided; and (3) the possible consequences of not providing the information within the stated period and in the authorised or required manner: s 99(3). The notice must be given, before the end of the period for considering the merger notice, to the person who gave the merger notice: s 99(4).

Any information which:
(a)   is, or ought to be, known to the person who gave the merger notice or any connected person; and
(b)   is material to the notified arrangements,
or any information requested by the OFT under s 99(2) must be provided or disclosed in writing: Enterprise Act 2002 (Merger Prenotification) Regulations 2003, SI 2003/1369, reg 8(1). Any information provided or disclosed to the OFT under this regulation is to be treated as having been so provided or disclosed on the day on which it is in fact received by the OFT (reg 8(2)); except that where information provided or disclosed to the OFT is received by the OFT on any day which is not a working day or after 5.00 pm on any working day, it is to be treated as having been provided or disclosed to the OFT on the next working day (reg 8(3)). The Interpretation Act 1978 s 7 does not apply in these circumstances: Enterprise Act 2002 (Merger Prenotification) Regulations 2003, SI 2003/1369, reg 8(4). Any information requested by the OFT under the Enterprise Act 2002 is to be treated as provided to the satisfaction of the OFT, for the purposes of s 97(6), on the day on which the OFT informs the person who gave the

merger notice, or a person acting on his behalf, of the fact that it is satisfied as to the provision of the information requested by it: Enterprise Act 2002 (Merger Prenotification) Regulations 2003, SI 2003/1369, reg 8(5).

6 A rejection of a merger notice under the Enterprise Act 2002 s 99(5) must be given in writing and such a notice is to be treated as having been rejected at the time when the rejection is sent to the person who gave the merger notice or a person acting on his behalf: Enterprise Act 2002 (Merger Prenotification) Regulations 2003, SI 2003/1369, reg 6.

7 As to the meaning of 'notified arrangements' see PARA 247 note 1.

8 Enterprise Act 2002 s 99(5)(a). For these purposes, 'connected person', in relation to the person who gave a merger notice, means (1) any person who, for the purposes of s 127, is associated with him; or (2) any subsidiary of the person who gave the merger notice or of any person so associated with him: s 99(6).

9 Enterprise Act 2002 s 99(5)(b).

10 Ie a notice under the Enterprise Act 2002 s 99(2).

11 Enterprise Act 2002 s 99(5)(c).

12 Enterprise Act 2002 s 99(5)(d). This refers to a Community dimension within the meaning of the EC Council Regulation 139/2004 (OJ L24, 29.1.2004, p 1) (the 'EC Merger Regulation') (see PARA 74).

13 Enterprise Act 2002 s 102. The provisions which may be modified are ss 97–101 (see PARAS 248, 250–251).

250. Exceptions to protection given by merger notices. Certain references to the Competition Commission[1] are not permitted if the period for considering the merger notice[2] has expired without a reference being made in relation to those arrangements[3]. However, this does not prevent references being made to the Commission if certain conditions are met[4]. A reference may still be made to the Commission if:

(1) before the end of the period for considering the merger notice, the Office of Fair Trading (the 'OFT') rejects the notice[5];

(2) before the end of that period, any of the enterprises to which the notified arrangements relate cease to be distinct from each other[6];

(3) any information (whether prescribed information or not) that (a) is, or ought to be, known to the person who gave the merger notice or any connected person; and (b) is material to the notified arrangements, is not disclosed to the OFT by such time before the end of that period as may be specified in regulations[7];

(4) at any time after the merger notice is given but before the enterprises to which the notified arrangements relate cease to be distinct from each other, any of those enterprises ceases to be distinct from any enterprise other than an enterprise to which those arrangements relate[8];

(5) the six months beginning with the end of the period for considering the merger notice expires without the enterprises to which the notified arrangements relate ceasing to be distinct from each other[9];

(6) the merger notice is withdrawn[10]; or

(7) any information given in respect of the notified arrangements (whether in the merger notice or otherwise) by the person who gave the notice or any connected person is in any material respect false or misleading[11].

Where (a) two or more transactions which have occurred (or, if any arrangements are carried into effect, will occur) may be treated for the purposes of a reference[12] to the Commission as having occurred simultaneously on a particular date; and (b) the statutory prohibition[13] does not prevent such a reference in relation to the last of those transactions, then a reference is not prevented in relation to any of those transactions which actually occurred less than six months before (i) that date; or (ii) the actual occurrence of another of those transactions in relation to which such a reference may be made[14].

1   As to the Competition Commission see PARAS 9–12.
2   As to the meaning of 'merger notice' see PARA 247. As to the period for considering merger notices see PARA 248.
3   See the Enterprise Act 2002 s 96(3). No reference may be made under the Enterprise Act 2002 s 22, s 33 or s 45 in relation to:
       (1)   arrangements of which notice is given under s 96(1) or arrangements which do not differ from them in any material respect; or
       (2)   the creation of any relevant merger situation which is, or may be, created in consequence of carrying such arrangements into effect,
     if the period for considering the merger notice has expired without a reference being made under that section in relation to those arrangements: s 96(3).
4   See the Enterprise Act 2002 ss 96(4), 100.
5   Enterprise Act 2002 s 100(1)(a). This refers to rejection under s 99(5) (see PARA 249). As to the OFT see PARAS 6–8.
6   Enterprise Act 2002 s 100(1)(b). As to the meaning of 'enterprise' see PARA 173 note 2. As to the meaning of 'notified arrangements' see PARA 247 note 1. References to the enterprises to which the notified arrangements relate are references to those enterprises that would have ceased to be distinct from one another if the arrangements mentioned in the merger notice concerned had been carried into effect at the time when the notice was given: s 100(5).
7   Enterprise Act 2002 s 100(1)(c). The time specified for the purpose of s 100(1)(c) is five working days: Enterprise Act 2002 (Merger Prenotification) Regulations 2003, SI 2003/1369, reg 4.
8   Enterprise Act 2002 s 100(1)(d).
9   Enterprise Act 2002 s 100(1)(e).
10   Enterprise Act 2002 s 100(1)(f).
11   Enterprise Act 2002 s 100(1)(g).
12   Ie a reference under the Enterprise Act 2002 s 22, s 33 or s 45 (see PARAS 172, 182, 193).
13   Ie the Enterprise Act 2002 s 96(3) (see note 3).
14   Enterprise Act 2002 s 100(2), (3). In determining for these purposes the time at which any transaction actually occurred, no account is to be taken of any option or other conditional right until the option is exercised or the condition is satisfied: s 100(4).

251. Regulations. The Secretary of State[1] has power to make regulations relating to merger notices[2]. The regulations may, in particular, make provision relating to: (1) references to periods of time[3]; (2) the manner in which merger notices are authorised or required to be rejected or withdrawn[4]; (3) the time at which notices are to be treated as received[5]; (4) the provision of information[6]; and (5) the circumstances in which a person may be treated as acting on behalf of a person authorised to give a merger notice[7].

1   As to the Secretary of State see PARA 5.
2   Ie he has power to make regulations for the purposes of the Enterprise Act 2002 ss 96–100 (see PARA 247 et seq): s 101(1). In exercise of this power the Enterprise Act 2002 (Merger Prenotification) Regulations 2003, SI 2003/1369, have been made. As to the meaning of 'merger notice' see PARA 247.
3   See the Enterprise Act 2002 s 101(2)(a), (g).
4   See the Enterprise Act 2002 s 101(2)(b).
5   See the Enterprise Act 2002 s 101(2)(c).
6   See the Enterprise Act 2002 s 101(2)(d), (e), (f).
7   See the Enterprise Act 2002 s 101(2)(h).

(vi) General Duties in relation to References

252. Duty of expedition. In deciding whether to make a reference to the Competition Commission[1] in relation to a completed merger[2] or an anticipated merger[3] the Office of Fair Trading (the 'OFT')[4] must have regard, with a view to the prevention or removal of uncertainty, to the need for making a decision as soon as reasonably practicable[5]. The Secretary of State[6] has a corresponding duty of expedition in deciding whether to make a reference[7] to the Commission[8].

1   As to the Competition Commission see PARAS 9–12.

2   Ie under the Enterprise Act 2002 s 22 (see PARA 172).
3   Ie under the Enterprise Act 2002 s 33 (see PARA 182).
4   As to the OFT see PARAS 6–8.
5   Enterprise Act 2002 s 103(1).
6   As to the Secretary of State see PARA 5.
7   Ie under the Enterprise Act 2002 s 45 (see PARA 193) or s 62 (see PARA 208).
8   See the Enterprise Act 2002 s 103(2).

253.   Duty to consult. Where the relevant authority (whether it is the Office of Fair Trading, the Competition Commission or the Secretary of State)[1] is proposing to make a relevant decision[2] in a way which the relevant authority considers is likely to be adverse to the interests of a relevant party[3], then the relevant authority must, so far as practicable, consult that party about what is proposed before making that decision[4]. In consulting the party concerned, the relevant authority must, so far as practicable, give the reasons of the relevant authority for the proposed decision[5]. In considering what is practicable for these purposes the relevant authority must, in particular, have regard to: (1) any restrictions imposed by any timetable for making the decision; and (2) any need to keep what is proposed, or the reasons for it, confidential[6].

1   As to the OFT see PARAS 6–8. As to the Competition Commission see PARAS 9–12. As to the Secretary of State see PARA 5.
2   In the case of the OFT, 'relevant decision' means any decision by the OFT (1) as to whether to make a reference under the Enterprise Act 2002 s 22 (see PARA 172) or s 33 (see PARA 182) or to accept undertakings under s 73 (see PARA 217) instead of making such a reference; or (2) to vary under s 37 (see PARA 185) such a reference: s 104(6)(a). In the case of the Commission, 'relevant decision' means any decision on the questions mentioned in ss 35(1), (3), 36(1), (2), 47 or s 63 (see PARAS 184, 195, 209): s 104(6)(b). In the case of the Secretary of State, 'relevant decision' means any decision by the Secretary of State (a) as to whether to make a reference under s 45 (see PARA 193) or s 62 (see PARA 208); or (b) to vary under s 49 or (as the case may be) s 64 such a reference: s 104(6)(c).
3   Enterprise Act 2002 s 104(1). 'Relevant party' means any person who appears to the relevant authority to control enterprises which are the subject of the reference or possible reference concerned: s 104(6).
4   Enterprise Act 2002 s 104(2). This duty of consultation does not apply in relation to the making of any decision so far as particular provision is made elsewhere by virtue of Pt 3 (ss 22–130) for consultation before the making of that decision: s 104(5). As to the requirement to consult the public in relation to media mergers see PARA 269.
5   Enterprise Act 2002 s 104(3).
6   Enterprise Act 2002 s 104(4).

(vii) Information and Publicity Requirements

254.   General information duties of the Office of Fair Trading and the Commission. Where the Office of Fair Trading (the 'OFT')[1] decides to investigate a matter so as to enable it to decide whether to make a reference to the Competition Commission[2], or so as to make a report to the Secretary of State[3], it must, so far as practicable, take such action as it considers appropriate to bring information about the investigation to the attention of those whom it considers might be affected by the creation of the relevant merger situation[4] concerned or (as the case may be) the special merger situation concerned[5]. Similarly, where the Office of Communications ('OFCOM') decides to investigate a matter so as to make a report to the Secretary of State[6], it must, so far as practicable, take such action as it considers appropriate to bring information about the investigation to the attention of those who it considers might be affected by the creation of the relevant merger situation concerned or (as the case may be) the special merger situation concerned[7]. However there is no such requirement for the OFT or OFCOM to do so in relation to arrangements which might result in the creation of a relevant merger situation if a merger notice has been given[8] in relation to those arrangements[9].

The OFT must give the Commission or OFCOM such information in its possession as the Commission or (as the case may be) OFCOM may reasonably require to enable the Commission or OFCOM to carry out its functions under Part 3 of the Enterprise Act 2002[10]. The OFT must also give any other assistance to the Commission or OFCOM which it may reasonably require for the purpose of assisting it in carrying out its functions under Part 3 of the Act and which it is within the power of the OFT to give[11]. OFCOM is under a corresponding duty to give the Commission or the OFT such information and assistance as may reasonably be required[12].

The OFT must give the Commission or OFCOM any information in its possession which has not been requested by the Commission or (as the case may be) OFCOM but which, in the opinion of the OFT, would be appropriate to give to them for the purpose of assisting them in carrying out their functions under Part 3 of the Act[13]. OFCOM is under a corresponding duty to give the Commission or the OFT such information in its possession too[14].

The OFT, OFCOM and the Commission must give the Secretary of State such information in their possession as the Secretary of State may by direction reasonably require to enable him to carry out his functions under Part 3 of the Act, and they must also give him any other assistance which he may by direction reasonably require for the purpose of assisting him in carrying out those functions and which it is within the power of the OFT, OFCOM or (as the case may be) the Commission to give[15]. The OFT and OFCOM must give the Secretary of State any information in their possession which has not been requested by the Secretary of State but which, in the opinion of the OFT or (as the case may be) OFCOM, would be appropriate to give to the Secretary of State for the purpose of assisting him in carrying out his functions under Part 3 of the Act[16].

The Commission, the Secretary of State, OFCOM and the OFT must have regard to any information provided to them as described above[17].

1   As to the OFT see PARAS 6–8.
2   Ie under the Enterprise Act 2002 s 22 (see PARA 172) or s 33 (see PARA 182). As to the Competition Commission see PARAS 9–12.
3   Ie under the Enterprise Act 2002 s 44 (see PARA 191) or s 61 (see PARA 206). As to the Secretary of State see PARA 5.
4   As to the meaning of 'relevant merger situation' see PARA 173.
5   Enterprise Act 2002 s 105(1). As to the meaning of 'special merger situation' see PARA 204.
6   Ie under the Enterprise Act 2002 s 44A (see PARA 192) or s 61A (see PARA 207).
7   Enterprise Act 2002 s 105(1A) (added by the Communications Act 2003 s 382).
8   Ie under the Enterprise Act 2002 s 96 (see PARA 247). As to the meaning of 'merger notice' see PARA 247.
9   Enterprise Act 2002 s 105(2) (amended by the Communications Act 2003 s 382).
10 Enterprise Act 2002 s 105(3)(a) (amended by the Communications Act 2003 s 382).
11 Enterprise Act 2002 s 105(3)(b) (amended by the Communications Act 2003 s 382).
12 See the Enterprise Act 2002 s 105(3A) (added by the Communications Act 2003 s 382).
13 Enterprise Act 2002 s 105(4) (amended by the Communications Act 2003 s 382).
14 See the Enterprise Act 2002 s 105(4A) (added by the Communications Act 2003 s 382).
15 Enterprise Act 2002 s 105(5) (amended by the Communications Act 2003 s 382). Any such direction must be given in writing, and may be varied or revoked by a subsequent direction: Enterprise Act 2002 s 105(8).
16 Enterprise Act 2002 s 105(6) (amended by the Communications Act 2003 s 382).
17 See the Enterprise Act 2002 s 105(7) (amended by the Communications Act 2003 s 382), Enterprise Act 2002 s 105(7A) (amended by the Communications Act 2003 s 382).

255. Advice and information about references. The Office of Fair Trading (the 'OFT')[1] must prepare and publish general advice and information about the making of references[2] by it, which may at any time be revised and republished[3]. The Competition Commission[4] must prepare and publish general advice and information about the consideration by it of such references and the way in which relevant customer benefits may affect the taking of enforcement action in relation to such references[5]. This advice and information may at any time be revised and republished[6].

Advice and information published by the OFT or the Commission must be prepared with a view to explaining the relevant provisions of Part 3 of the Enterprise Act 2002[7] to persons who are likely to be affected by them, and with a view to indicating how the OFT or (as the case may be) the Commission expects such provisions to operate[8]. The advice or information may include advice or information about the factors which the OFT or (as the case may be) the Commission may take into account in considering whether, and if so how, to exercise a function conferred by Part 3 of the Act[9].

In preparing the advice and information, the OFT and the Commission are each under a duty to consult the other, as well as such other persons they consider appropriate[10]. It must then be published in such manner as the OFT or (as the case may be) the Commission considers appropriate[11].

1 As to the OFT see PARAS 6–8.
2 Ie under the Enterprise Act 2002 s 22 (see PARA 172) or s 33 (see PARA 182).
3 Enterprise Act 2002 s 106(1), (2). Advice and information published by the OFT by virtue of s 106(1) must, in particular, include advice and information about the circumstances in which the duties of the OFT under ss 22, 33 do not apply as a result of EC Council Regulation 139/2004 (OJ L24, 29.1.2004, p 1) (the 'EC Merger Regulation') or anything done under or in accordance with them: Enterprise Act 2002 s 122(2).
  As to advice and information prepared and published by the Secretary of State in connection with media mergers see s 106A; and PARA 270.
4 As to the Competition Commission see PARAS 9–12.
5 Enterprise Act 2002 s 106(3).
6 Enterprise Act 2002 s 106(4).
7 Ie the Enterprise Act 2002 Pt 3 (ss 22–130).
8 Enterprise Act 2002 s 106(5).
9 Enterprise Act 2002 s 106(6). Advice and information published by virtue of s 106(1) or s 106(3) must include such advice and information about the effect of Community law, and anything done under or in accordance with it, on the provisions of Pt 3 as the OFT or (as the case may be) the Commission considers appropriate: s 122(1).
10 Enterprise Act 2002 s 106(8), (9).
11 Enterprise Act 2002 s 106(7).

256. General advisory functions of OFCOM. The Office of Communications ('OFCOM')[1] may, in connection with any case on which it is required to give a report to the Secretary of State[2], give such advice as it considers appropriate to the Secretary of State in relation to (1) any report made in such a case by the Competition Commission[3]; and (2) the taking by the Secretary of State of enforcement action[4]. OFCOM may, if requested to do so by the Secretary of State, give such other advice as it considers appropriate to the Secretary of State in connection with any case on which it is required to give a report[5].

1 As to OFCOM see PARA 19.
2 Ie by virtue of the Enterprise Act 2002 s 44A (see PARA 192) or s 61A (see PARA 207). As to the Secretary of State see PARA 5.
3 Ie under the Enterprise Act 2002 s 50 (see PARA 198) or s 65 (see PARA 211). As to the Competition Commission see PARAS 9–12. OFCOM must publish any advice given by it under s 106B but advice given by it in relation to a report of the Commission under s 50 or s 65 or

related enforcement action must not be published before the report itself is published: s 106B(3) (s 106B added by the Communications Act 2003 s 384).

4   Enterprise Act 2002 s 106B(1) (as added: see note 3). As to enforcement action under the Enterprise Act 2002 Sch 7 see PARAS 228–231.

5   Enterprise Act 2002 s 106B(2) (as added: see note 3).

257. Further publicity requirements. The Office of Fair Trading (the 'OFT')[1] is under a duty to publish (1) specified references made by it[2]; (2) any variations of such references[3]; (3) information relating to decisions to bring cases to the attention of the Secretary of State[4]; (4) certain enforcement undertakings accepted by it[5]; (5) certain enforcement orders[6]; (6) any variation, release or revocation of such an undertaking or order[7]; and (7) certain decisions it has made[8].

The Competition Commission[9] is under a duty to publish: (a) certain cancellations it has made[10]; (b) certain extensions of time periods it has made[11]; (c) certain enforcement orders it has made[12]; (d) certain enforcement undertakings it has accepted[13]; (e) any variation, release or revocation of such orders or undertakings[14]; and (f) certain decisions it has made[15];

The Secretary of State[16] is under a duty to publish: (i) any intervention notice or special intervention notice given by him[17]; (ii) reports of the OFT which have been received by him[18]; (iii) reports of OFCOM which have been received by him[19]; (iv) certain references made by him to the OFT or any decision made by him not to make such a reference[20]; (iv) any variation made by him of such references[21]; (v) reports of the Commission which have been received by him[22]; (vi) notices given by him[23]; (vii) certain enforcement undertakings accepted by him and any variation or release of such an undertaking[24]; and (viii) certain decisions made by him[25]. The Secretary of State must publish his reasons for certain decisions that he makes[26]. He is also under a duty to publish certain reports within specified time limits[27].

Where any person is under a duty[28] to publish the result of any action taken by that person or any decision made by that person, the person concerned must also publish that person's reasons for the action concerned or (as the case may be) the decision concerned[29]. However, such reasons need not, if it is not reasonably practicable to do so, be published at the same time as the result of the action concerned or (as the case may be) as the decision concerned[30].

1   As to the OFT see PARAS 6–8.
2   Ie any reference made by it under the Enterprise Act 2002 s 22 (see PARA 172) or s 33 (see PARA 182) or any decision made by it not to make such a reference (other than a decision made by virtue of s 33(2)(b)): s 107(1)(a).
3   Ie any variation made by it under the Enterprise Act 2002 s 37 of a reference under s 22 or s 33: s 107(1)(b).
4   Ie such information as it considers appropriate about any decision made by it under the Enterprise Act 2002 s 57(1) to bring a case to the attention of the Secretary of State: s 107(1)(c). As to the Secretary of State see PARA 5.
5   Ie any enforcement undertaking accepted by it under the Enterprise Act 2002 s 71 (see PARA 215): s 107(1)(d).
6   Ie any enforcement order made by it under the Enterprise Act 2002 s 72 or s 76 or Sch 7 para 2 (see PARAS 216, 220, 228): s 107(1)(e).
7   Enterprise Act 2002 s 107(1)(f).
8   Ie any decision made by it as mentioned in the Enterprise Act 2002 s 76(6)(b) (s 107(1)(g)) and any decision made by it to dispense with the requirements of Sch 10 (see s 107(1)(h)).
9   As to the Competition Commission see PARAS 9–12.

10 Ie (1) any cancellation by it under the Enterprise Act 2002 s 37(1) (see PARA 185) of a reference under s 33 (s 107(2)(a)); (2) any cancellation by it under s 48(1) or s 53(1) (see PARAS 196, 199) of a reference under s 45 or any cancellation by it under s 64(1) (see PARA 210) of a reference under s 62 (s 107(2)(g)).

11 Ie (1) any extension by it under the Enterprise Act 2002 s 39 of the period within which a report under s 38 is to be prepared and published (see PARAS 186–187) (s 107(2)(c)); (2) any extension by it under s 51 of the period within which a report under s 50 is to be prepared and published (see PARA 198) (s 107(2)(i)); (3) any extension by it under s 51 as applied by s 65(3) of the period within which a report under s 65 is to be prepared and published (see PARA 211) (s 107(2)(k)).

12 Ie any enforcement order made by it under the Enterprise Act 2002 s 76 or s 81 (see PARAS 220, 224): s 107(2)(o).

13 Ie any enforcement undertaking accepted by it under the Enterprise Act 2002 s 80 (see PARA 223): s 107(2)(p).

14 Ie any variation, release or revocation of any enforcement order made by it under the Enterprise Act 2002 s 76 or s 81 or any enforcement undertaking accepted by it under s 80: s 107(2)(o), (p), (q).

15 Ie (1) any decision made by the Commission under the Enterprise Act 2002 s 37(2) to treat a reference made under s 22 (see PARA 172) or s 33 (see PARA 182) as if it had been made under s 33 or (as the case may be) s 22 (s 107(2)(b)); (2) any decision made by the Commission to cancel an extension of the time period as mentioned in s 39(8)(b) (see PARA 187) (s 107(2)(d)); (3) any decision made by the Commission under s 41(2) neither to accept an undertaking under s 82 nor to make an order under s 84 (see PARA 226) (s 107(2)(e)); (4) any decision made by the Commission that there has been a material change of circumstances as mentioned in s 41(3) (see PARA 188) or there is another special reason as mentioned in s 41(3) (s 107(2)(f)); (5) any decision made by the Commission under s 49(1) to treat (a) a reference made under s 45(2) or s 45(3) as if it had been made under s 45(4) or (as the case may be) s 45(5) (see PARA 193); or (b) a reference made under s 45(4) or s 45(5) as if it had been made under s 45(2) or (as the case may be) s 45(3) (s 107(2)(h)); (6) any decision made by the Commission under s 51(8)(b) (see PARA 198) to cancel an extension of the period within which a report under s 50 (see PARA 198) is to be prepared and published (s 107(2)(j)); (7) any decision made by the Commission under s 51(8)(b) as applied by s 65(3) to cancel an extension of the period within which a report under s 65 is to be prepared and published (see PARA 211) (s 107(2)(l)); (8) any decision made by the Commission under s 64(2) to treat a reference made under s 62(2) or s 62(3) as if it had been made under s 62(3) or (as the case may be) s 62(2) (see PARA 208) (s 107(2)(m)); (9) any decision made by the Commission as mentioned in s 76(6)(b) (see PARA 220) (s 107(2)(n)); (10) any decision made by it to dispense with the requirements of Sch 10 (see PARA 241) (s 107(2)(r)).

16 As to the Secretary of State see PARA 5.

17 Enterprise Act 2002 s 107(3)(a). As to the meaning of 'intervention notice' see PARA 189 note 11. As to the meaning of 'special intervention notice 'see PARA 204.

18 Ie any report of the OFT under the Enterprise Act 2002 s 44 (see PARA 191) or s 61 (see PARA 206): s 107(3)(b).

19 Ie any report under the Enterprise Act 2002 s 44A (see PARA 192) or s 61A (see PARA 207): s 107(3)(ba) (added by the Communications Act 2003 Sch 16 para 18(1), (2)).

20 Ie any reference under the Enterprise Act 2002 s 45 (see PARA 193) or s 62 (see PARA 208): s 107(3)(c).

21 Ie any variation made by him under the Enterprise Act 2002 s 49 of a reference under s 45 or under s 64 of a reference under s 62 (see PARA 208): s 107(3)(d).

22 Ie any report of the Commission under the Enterprise Act 2002 s 50 (see PARA 198) or s 65 (see PARA 211): s 107(3)(e).

23 Ie any notice given by him under the Enterprise Act 2002 s 56(1) (see PARA 202): s 107(3)(g).

24 Ie any enforcement undertaking accepted by him under the Enterprise Act 2002 Sch 7 para 1 (see PARA 228) and any variation of release of such an undertaking: s 107(3)(h), (i).

25 Ie (1) any decision made by the Secretary of State neither to accept an undertaking under the Enterprise Act 2002 Sch 7 para 9 nor to make an order under Sch 7 para 11 (see PARA 231) (s 107(3)(f)); (2) any decision made by him as mentioned in Sch 7 para 6(6)(b) (see PARA 229) (s 107(3)(j)); and (3) any decision made by him to dispense with the requirements of Sch 10 (see PARA 241) (s 107(3)(k)). Where the Secretary of State has decided under s 55(2) or s 66(6) to accept an undertaking under Sch 7 para 9 or to make an order under Sch 7 para 11, he must (after the acceptance of the undertaking or (as the case may be) the making of the order) lay details of his decision and his reasons for it, and the Commission's report under s 50 or (as the case may be) s 65, before each House of Parliament: ss 107(11), 118(5).

26 Ie he must publish the reasons for (1) any decision made by him under the Enterprise Act 2002 s 54(2) or s 66(2) (see PARAS 200, 212) (s 107(7)(a)); or (2) any decision to make an order under s 58(3) or vary or revoke such an order (see PARA 203) (s 107(7)(b)). If it is not reasonably practicable to publish the reasons at the same time as the publication of the decision or (as the case may be) the making of the order or variation or revocation, then such reasons may be published after the publication of the decision concerned (in the case of s 107(7)(a)) and after the making of the order or of the variation or revocation (in the case of s 107(7)(b)): s 107(8).

27 The Secretary of State must publish the report of the OFT under the Enterprise Act 2002 s 44, and any report of OFCOM under s 44A, in relation to a matter no later than publication of his decision as to whether to make a reference under s 45 in relation to that matter: s 107(9)(a) (amended by the Communications Act 2003 Sch 16 para 18). He must publish the report of the Commission under the Enterprise Act 2002 s 50 in relation to a matter no later than publication of his decision under s 54(2) in relation to that matter: s 107(9)(b). He must publish the report of the OFT under s 61, and any report of OFCOM under s 61A, in relation to a matter no later than publication of his decision as to whether to make a reference under s 62 in relation to that matter: s 107(10)(a) (amended by the Communications Act 2003 Sch 16 para 18). He must publish the report of the Commission under s 65 in relation to a matter no later than publication of his decision under s 66(2) in relation to that matter: Enterprise Act 2002 s 107(10)(b).

28 Ie by virtue of the Enterprise Act 2002 s 107(1), (2) or s 107(3).

29 Enterprise Act 2002 s 107(4). Section 107(4), (5) does not apply in relation to any information published under s 107(1)(c) (see note 4): s 107(6).

30 Enterprise Act 2002 s 107(5). See note 27.

258. Defamation. For the purposes of the law relating to defamation[1], absolute privilege attaches to any advice, guidance, notice or direction given, or decision or report made, by the Office of Fair Trading (the 'OFT')[2], the Office of Communications ('OFCOM')[3], the Competition Commission[4] or the Secretary of State[5] in the exercise of any of their functions under Part 3[6] of the Enterprise Act 2002[7].

1 See LIBEL AND SLANDER.
2 As to the OFT see PARAS 6–8.
3 As to OFCOM see PARA 19.
4 As to the Competition Commission see PARAS 9–12.
5 As to the Secretary of State see PARA 5.
6 Ie the Enterprise Act 2002 Pt 3 (ss 22–130).
7 Enterprise Act 2002 s 108.

(viii) Investigation Powers

259. Attendance of witnesses and production of documents. The Competition Commission[1] may, for the purpose of any investigation on a reference made to it under Part 3 of the Enterprise Act 2002[2], give notice to any person requiring him to attend at a time and place specified in the notice, and to give evidence to the Commission or a person nominated by the Commission for the purpose[3]. The Commission may, for the purpose of any investigation on a reference made to it under Part 3 of the Act, give notice to any person requiring him (1) to produce any documents which are specified or described in the notice, or fall within a category of document which is specified or described in the notice; and which are in that person's custody or under his control; and (2) to produce them at a time and place so specified and to a person so specified[4]. The Commission may, for the purpose of any investigation on a reference made to it under Part 3 of the Act, give notice to any person who carries on any business requiring him to supply to the Commission such estimates, forecasts, returns or other information as may be specified or described in the notice, and to supply them at a time and place, and in a form and manner, so specified and to a person so specified[5]. The Commission or any person nominated by it for the purpose may, for the purpose of any investigation on a reference made to it under Part 3 of the Act, take evidence on oath, and for that purpose may administer oaths[6].

However, no person is required (a) to give any evidence or produce any documents which he could not be compelled to give or produce in civil proceedings before the court[7]; (b) to supply any information which he could not be compelled to supply in evidence in such proceedings[8]; or (c) to go more than 10 miles from his place of residence unless his necessary travelling expenses are paid or offered to him[9].

1   As to the Competition Commission see PARAS 9–12.
2   Ie the Enterprise Act 2002 Pt 3 (ss 22–130).
3   Enterprise Act 2002 s 109(1). A notice under s 109 must include information about the possible consequences of not complying with the notice: s 109(4).
4   Enterprise Act 2002 s 109(2). The person to whom any document is produced in accordance with a notice under s 109 may, for the purpose of any investigation on a reference made to the Commission under Pt 3, copy the document so produced: s 109(6). Any reference in s 109 to the production of a document includes a reference to the production of a legible and intelligible copy of information recorded otherwise than in legible form: s 109(9).
5   Enterprise Act 2002 s 109(3).
6   Enterprise Act 2002 s 109(5).
7   Enterprise Act 2002 s 109(7)(a). 'Court' means, in relation to England and Wales or Northern Ireland, the High Court: s 109(10).
8   Enterprise Act 2002 s 109(7)(b).
9   Enterprise Act 2002 s 109(8).

260. Enforcement of investigation powers; penalties. Where the Competition Commission[1] considers that a person has, without reasonable excuse, failed to comply with any requirement of a notice requiring the attendance of witnesses or the production of documents[2], it may impose a penalty[3]. Where the Commission considers that a person has intentionally obstructed or delayed another person in the exercise of his powers to take copies of documents produced[4], it may impose a penalty[5]. However, no penalty may be imposed if more than four weeks have passed since the publication of the report of the Commission on the reference concerned[6].

A person commits an offence if he intentionally alters, suppresses or destroys any document which he has been required to produce by a notice from the Commission[7].

In deciding whether and, if so, how to proceed[8], the Commission must have regard to the statement of policy which was most recently published[9] at the time when the failure concerned or (as the case may be) the obstruction or delay concerned occurred[10].

1   As to the Competition Commission see PARAS 9–12.
2   Ie a notice under the Enterprise Act 2002 s 109 (see PARA 259).
3   Enterprise Act 2002 s 110(1). A penalty imposed under s 110(1) is of such amount as the Commission considers appropriate: s 111(1). The amount may be a fixed amount, an amount calculated by reference to a daily rate or a combination of a fixed amount and an amount calculated by reference to a daily rate: s 111(2). No penalty imposed under s 110(1) may: (1) in the case of a fixed amount, exceed £20,000; (2) in the case of an amount calculated by reference to a daily rate, exceed £5,000; and (3) in the case of a fixed amount and an amount calculated by reference to a daily rate, exceed £20,000 and such £5,000 per day: s 111(4); Competition Commission (Penalties) Order 2003, SI 2003/1371, art 2. See also the Competition Commission (Water Industry) Penalties Order 2007, SI 2007/461. An order under the Enterprise Act 2002 s 111(4) may not specify (in the case of a fixed amount), an amount exceeding £30,000: s 111(7)(a). An order under s 111(4) may not specify (in the case of an amount calculated by reference to a daily rate) an amount per day exceeding £15,000: s 111(7)(b). An order under s 111(4) may not specify (in the case of a fixed amount and an amount calculated by reference to a daily rate), a fixed amount exceeding £30,000 and an amount per day exceeding £15,000:

s 111(7)(c). Before making an order under s 111(4) the Secretary of State must consult the Commission and such other persons as he considers appropriate: s 111(8). In imposing a penalty by reference to a daily rate (a) no account is to be taken of any days before the service of the notice under s 112 (see PARA 261) on the person concerned; and (b) unless the Commission determines an earlier date (whether before or after the penalty is imposed), the amount payable ceases to accumulate at the beginning of (i) the day on which the requirement of the notice concerned under s 109 is satisfied or (as the case may be) the obstruction or delay is removed; or (ii) if earlier, the day on which the report of the Commission on the reference concerned is published (or, in the case of a report under s 50 or s 65, given) or, if no such report is published (or given) within the period permitted for that purpose by Pt 3 (ss 22–130), the latest day on which the report may be published (or given) within the permitted period: s 111(5).

The Commission may proceed (whether at the same time or at different times) under s 110(1) and s 39(4) (see PARA 187) or (as the case may be) s 51(4) (see PARA 198) (including that enactment as applied by s 65(3)) in relation to the same failure: s 110(2). The Commission may not proceed against a person under s 110(1) in relation to an act which constitutes an offence under s 110(5) if that person has been found guilty of that offence: s 110(8).

4   Ie in exercise of his powers under the Enterprise Act 2002 s 109(6) (see PARA 259).
5   Enterprise Act 2002 s 110(3). A penalty imposed under s 110(3) is of such amount as the Commission considers appropriate: s 111(1). This is a fixed amount: s 111(3). No such penalty imposed under s 110(3) may exceed £20,000: s 111(6); Competition Commission (Penalties) Order 2003, SI 2003/1371, art 2. See also the Competition Commission (Water Industry) Penalties Order 2007, SI 2007/461. An order under the Enterprise Act 2002 s 111(6) may not specify (in the case of a fixed amount), an amount exceeding £30,000: s 111(7)(a). An order under s 111(6) may not specify (in the case of an amount calculated by reference to a daily rate) an amount per day exceeding £15,000: s 111(7)(b). An order under s 111(6) may not specify (in the case of a fixed amount and an amount calculated by reference to a daily rate), a fixed amount exceeding £30,000 and an amount per day exceeding £15,000: s 111(7)(c). Before making an order under s 111(6) the Secretary of State must consult the Commission and such other persons as he considers appropriate: s 111(8)
6   Enterprise Act 2002 s 110(4). But s 110(4) does not apply in relation to any variation or substitution of the penalty which is permitted by virtue of Pt 3 (ss 22–130): s 110(4).
7   Enterprise Act 2002 s 110(5). A person does not commit an offence under s 110(5) in relation to any act which constitutes a failure to comply with a notice under s 109 if the Commission has proceeded against that person under s 110(1) (see the text and note 3) in relation to that failure: s 110(6). A person who commits an offence under s 110(5) is liable on summary conviction, to a fine not exceeding the statutory maximum; and on conviction on indictment, to imprisonment for a term not exceeding two years or to a fine or to both: s 110(7). The Commission may not proceed against a person under s 110(1) in relation to an act which constitutes an offence under s 110(5) if that person has been found guilty of that offence: s 110(8). The reference in s 110 to the production of a document includes a reference to the production of a legible and intelligible copy of information recorded otherwise than in legible form; and the reference to suppressing a document includes a reference to destroying the means of reproducing information recorded otherwise than in legible form: s 110(10).
8   Ie under the Enterprise Act 2002 s 110(1) or s 110(3) (see notes 3, 5) or s 39(4) (see PARA 187) or s 51(4) (see PARA 198) (including that enactment as applied by s 65(3)).
9   Ie under the Enterprise Act 2002 s 116 (see PARA 265).
10 Enterprise Act 2002 s 110(9).

261. Procedural requirements in relation to penalties. As soon as practicable after imposing a penalty[1], the Competition Commission[2] must give notice of the penalty[3], stating:

(1)   that the Commission has imposed a penalty on the person concerned[4];

(2)   whether the penalty is of a fixed amount, of an amount calculated by reference to a daily rate or of both a fixed amount and an amount calculated by reference to a daily rate[5];

(3)   the amount or amounts concerned and, in the case of an amount calculated by reference to a daily rate, the day on which the amount first starts to accumulate and the day or days on which it might cease to accumulate[6];

(4)   the failure or (as the case may be) the obstruction or delay which the Commission considers gave it the power to impose the penalty[7];

(5)   any other facts which the Commission considers justify the imposition of a penalty and the amount or amounts of the penalty[8];

(6)   the manner in which, and place at which, the penalty is required to be paid to the Commission[9];

(7)   the date or dates, no earlier than the end of the relevant period beginning with the date of service of the notice on the person concerned, by which the penalty or (as the case may be) different portions of it are required to be paid[10];

(8)   that the penalty or (as the case may be) different portions of it may be paid earlier than the date or dates by which it or they are required to be paid[11]; and

(9)   that the person concerned has the right to apply for a different payment date[12] or to appeal[13] and the main details of those rights[14].

Such a notice is given by serving a copy of it on the person on whom the penalty was imposed and by publishing it[15].

The person against whom the penalty was imposed may, within 14 days of the date of service on him of such a notice, apply to the Commission for it to specify a different date or (as the case may be) different dates by which the penalty or (as the case may be) different portions of it are to be paid[16].

1   Ie a penalty under the Enterprise Act 2002 s 110(1) or s 110(3) (see PARA 260).
2   As to the Competition Commission see PARAS 9–12.
3   Enterprise Act 2002 s 112(1).
4   Enterprise Act 2002 s 112(2)(a).
5   Enterprise Act 2002 s 112(2)(b).
6   Enterprise Act 2002 s 112(2)(c).
7   Enterprise Act 2002 s 112(2)(d).
8   Enterprise Act 2002 s 112(2)(e).
9   Enterprise Act 2002 s 112(2)(f).
10 Enterprise Act 2002 s 112(2)(g). In s 112 'relevant period' means the period of 28 days mentioned in s 114(3) (see PARA 263) or, if another period is specified by the Secretary of State under that subsection, that period: s 112(5).
11 Enterprise Act 2002 s 112(2)(h).
12 Ie under the Enterprise Act 2002 s 112(3).
13 Ie under the Enterprise Act 2002 s 114 (see PARA 263).
14 Enterprise Act 2002 s 112(2)(i).
15 Enterprise Act 2002 s 112(4).
16 Enterprise Act 2002 s 112(3). Where an application has been made under s 112(3), the penalty is not required to be paid until the application has been determined, withdrawn or otherwise dealt with: s 113(2).

262.   Payments and interest by instalments.   If the whole or any portion of a penalty[1] is not paid by the date by which it is required to be paid, the unpaid balance from time to time carries interest at the prescribed rate[2]. If a portion of a penalty has not been paid by the date required for it, the Competition Commission[3] may, where it considers it appropriate to do so, require so much of the penalty as has not already been paid (and is capable of being paid immediately) to be paid immediately[4].

Sums received by the Commission in or towards the payment of a penalty, or interest on a penalty, are paid into the Consolidated Fund[5].

1   As to penalties see PARAS 260–261.
2   Enterprise Act 2002 s 113(1). The prescribed rate is the rate for the time being specified in the Judgments Act 1838 s 17: Enterprise Act 2002 s 113(1). As to payments where an application has been made under s 112(3) see s 113(2); and PARA 261.

3   As to the Competition Commission see PARAS 9–12.
4   Enterprise Act 2002 s 113(3).
5   Enterprise Act 2002 s 113(4).

263.   Appeals in relation to penalties.   If a person on whom a penalty is imposed[1] is aggrieved by:

(1)   the imposition or nature of the penalty;

(2)   the amount or amounts of the penalty; or

(3)   the date by which the penalty is required to be paid or (as the case may be) the different dates by which portions of the penalty are required to be paid,

then the person aggrieved may apply to the Competition Appeal Tribunal[2].

If a copy of the penalty notice[3] was served on the person on whom the penalty was imposed, the application to the Competition Appeal Tribunal must be made within the period of 28 days starting with the day on which the copy was served on the person concerned, or within such other period as the Secretary of State may by order specify[4]. If the application relates to a decision of the Competition Commission[5] on an application by the person on whom the penalty was imposed to alter the payment date[6], the application to the Competition Appeal Tribunal must be made within the period of 28 days starting with the day on which the person concerned is notified of the decision, or within such other period as the Secretary of State may by order specify[7].

The Competition Appeal Tribunal may, if it considers it appropriate to do so:

(a)   quash the penalty[8];

(b)   substitute a penalty of a different nature or of such lesser amount or amounts as the Competition Appeal Tribunal considers appropriate[9]; or

(c)   in a case where an application has been made contesting the penalty payment date, substitute for the date or dates imposed by the Commission an alternative date or dates[10];

Where an application has been made to the Competition Appeal Tribunal, the penalty is not required to be paid until the application has been determined, withdrawn or otherwise dealt with[11]. The Commission may agree to reduce the amount or amounts of the penalty in settlement of the application[12]. Where the Competition Appeal Tribunal substitutes a penalty of a different nature or of a lesser amount or amounts it may require the payment of interest on the substituted penalty at such rate or rates, and from such date or dates, as it considers appropriate[13]. Where the Competition Appeal Tribunal specifies as a date by which the penalty, or a portion of the penalty, is to be paid a date before the determination of the application to the Competition Appeal Tribunal, it may require the payment of interest on the penalty, or portion, from that date at such rate as it considers appropriate[14].

An appeal lies to the Court of Appeal on a point of law arising from a decision of the Tribunal or from a decision of the Tribunal as to the amount or amounts of a penalty[15].

1   Ie under the Enterprise Act 2002 s 110(1) or s 110(3) (see PARA 260).
2   Enterprise Act 2002 s 114(1), (2). As to persons aggrieved see ADMINISTRATIVE LAW vol 1(1) (2001 Reissue) PARA 66. As to the Competition Appeal Tribunal see PARAS 13–17.
3   Ie the notice under the Enterprise Act 2002 s 112(1) (see PARA 261).
4   Enterprise Act 2002 s 114(3). As to the Secretary of State see PARA 5.
5   As to the Competition Commission see PARAS 9–12.
6   Ie an application under the Enterprise Act 2002 s 112(3) (see PARA 261).
7   Enterprise Act 2002 s 114(4).
8   Enterprise Act 2002 s 114(5)(a).

9   Enterprise Act 2002 s 114(5)(b). The Competition Appeal Tribunal may not substitute a penalty
    of a different nature under s 114(5)(b) unless it considers that the person on whom the penalty
    is imposed will, or is likely to, pay less under the substituted penalty than he would have paid
    under the original penalty: s 114(6).
10 Enterprise Act 2002 s 114(5)(c).
11 Enterprise Act 2002 s 114(7)(a).
12 Enterprise Act 2002 s 114(7)(b).
13 Enterprise Act 2002 s 114(8).
14 Enterprise Act 2002 s 114(9).
15 Enterprise Act 2002 s 114(10), (12). An appeal to the Court of Appeal may be brought by a
    party to the proceedings before the Tribunal, and it requires the permission of the Tribunal or
    the Court of Appeal: s 114(11).

264. Recovery of penalties. Where a penalty[1] or any portion of such a penalty
has not been paid by the date on which it is required to be paid and:

(1)   no application to the Competition Appeal Tribunal relating to the
      penalty has been made[2] during the period within which such an
      application may be made; or

(2)   any such application which has been made has been determined,
      withdrawn or otherwise dealt with,

the Competition Commission[3] may recover from the person on whom the
penalty was imposed any of the penalty and any interest which has not been
paid[4].

1   Ie a penalty imposed under the Enterprise Act 2002 s 110(1) or s 110(3) (see PARA 260).
2   Ie under the Enterprise Act 2002 s 114 (see PARA 263). As to the Competition Appeal Tribunal
    see PARAS 13–17.
3   As to the Competition Commission see PARAS 9–12.
4   Enterprise Act 2002 s 115. Such penalty and interest may be recovered as a civil debt due to the
    Commission: see s 115.

265. Statement of policy. The Competition Commission[1] must prepare and
publish a statement of policy in relation to the enforcement of notices[2] requiring
the attendance of witnesses or the production of documents[3]. The statement
must, in particular, include a statement about the considerations relevant to the
determination of the nature and amount of any penalty imposed[4].

The Commission may revise its statement of policy and, where it does so, it is
under a duty to publish the revised statement[5]. The Commission must consult
such persons as it considers appropriate when preparing or revising its statement
of policy[6].

1   As to the Competition Commission see PARAS 9–12.
2   Ie notices under the Enterprise Act 2002 s 109 (see PARA 259).
3   Enterprise Act 2002 s 116(1).
4   Enterprise Act 2002 s 116(2). This refers to penalties imposed under s 110(1) or s 110(3) (see
    PARA 260).
5   Enterprise Act 2002 s 116(3).
6   Enterprise Act 2002 s 116(4).

266. Offence of supplying false or misleading information. A person commits
an offence if:

(1)   he supplies any information to the Office of Fair Trading (the 'OFT')[1],
      the Office of Communications ('OFCOM')[2], the Competition
      Commission[3] or the Secretary of State[4] in connection with any of their
      functions under Part 3 of the Enterprise Act 2002[5];

(2)   the information is false or misleading in a material respect[6]; and

(3)   he knows that it is false or misleading in a material respect or is reckless as to whether it is false or misleading in a material respect[7].

A person commits an offence if he:

(a)   supplies any information to another person which he knows to be false or misleading in a material respect; or

(b)   recklessly supplies any information to another person which is false or misleading in a material respect;

knowing that the information is to be used for the purpose of supplying information to the OFT, OFCOM, the Commission or the Secretary of State in connection with any of their functions under Part 3 of the Enterprise Act 2002[8].

1   As to the OFT see PARAS 6–8.
2   As to OFCOM see PARA 19.
3   As to the Competition Commission see PARAS 9–12.
4   As to the Secretary of State see PARA 5.
5   Enterprise Act 2002 s 117(1)(a) (amended by the Communications Act 2003 Sch 16 para 20(1), (2)). See note 8. As to the Enterprise Act 2002 Pt 3 (ss 22–130) see PARA 172 et seq.
6   Enterprise Act 2002 s 117(1)(b). See note 8.
7   Enterprise Act 2002 s 117(1)(c). See note 8.
8   Enterprise Act 2002 s 117(2) (amended by the Communications Act 2003 Sch 16 para 20(1), (3)). A person who commits an offence under the Enterprise Act 2002 s 117(1) or s 117(2) is liable on summary conviction, to a fine not exceeding the statutory maximum; and on conviction on indictment, to imprisonment for a term not exceeding two years or to a fine or to both: s 117(3). As to the statutory maximum see PARA 140 note 9.

(ix) Media Mergers

267.   General functions of OFCOM in relation to media mergers.   The Office of Communications ('OFCOM') has the function of obtaining, compiling and keeping under review information about matters relating to the carrying out of its functions under Part 3 of the Enterprise Act 2002[1]. That function is to be carried out with a view to (among other things) ensuring that OFCOM has sufficient information to take informed decisions and to carry out its other functions effectively[2]. In carrying out that function OFCOM may carry out, commission or support (financially or otherwise) research[3].

1   Enterprise Act 2002 s 119A(1) (s 119A added by the Communications Act 2003 s 385). As to the Enterprise Act 2002 Pt 3 (ss 22–130) see PARA 172 et seq. The Communications Act 2003 s 3 (general duties of OFCOM) does not apply in relation to functions of OFCOM under the Enterprise Act 2002 Pt 3: s 119A(4) (as so added).
2   Enterprise Act 2002 s 119A(2) (as added: see note 1).
3   Enterprise Act 2002 s 119A(3) (as added: see note 1).

268.   Monitoring role of the Office of Fair Trading.   The Office of Fair Trading (the 'OFT')[1] has the function of obtaining, compiling and keeping under review information about matters which may be relevant to the Secretary of State[2] in deciding whether to give a special intervention notice[3] mentioning specified national security considerations[4]. That function is to be carried out with a view to (among other things) ensuring that the Secretary of State is aware of cases where, in the opinion of the OFT, he might wish to consider giving such a notice[5].

1   As to the OFT see PARAS 6–8.
2   As to the Secretary of State see PARA 5.
3   As to the meaning of 'special intervention notice' see PARA 204.
4   Enterprise Act 2002 s 119B(1) (s 119B added by the Communications Act 2003 s 386). The text refers to the considerations mentioned in the Enterprise Act 2002 s 58(2A)–(2C) (see PARA 203).

That function does not extend to obtaining, compiling or keeping under review information with a view to carrying out a detailed analysis in each case of the operation in relation to that case of the consideration specified in s 58(2A)–(2C): s 119B(3) (as so added).

5   Enterprise Act 2002 s 119B(2) (as added: see note 4).

269.   Public consultation in relation to media mergers.   Where the Competition Commission[1]:

(1)   is preparing (a) a report[2] on a reference which specifies a media public interest consideration; or (b) a report[3] on a reference which specifies certain national security considerations[4]; and

(2)   is not under a duty to disregard the consideration concerned,

then it must have regard (among other things) to the need to consult the public so far as they might be affected by the creation of the relevant merger situation[5] or special merger situation[6] concerned and so far as such consultation is practicable[7]. Any such consultation may be undertaken by the Commission by consulting such representative sample of the public or section of the public concerned as the Commission considers appropriate[8].

1   As to the Competition Commission see PARAS 9–12.
2   Ie under the Enterprise Act 2002 s 50 (see PARA 198).
3   Ie under the Enterprise Act 2002 s 65 (see PARA 211).
4   Ie a consideration specified in the Enterprise Act 2002 s 58(2A)–(2C) (see PARA 203).
5   As to the meaning of 'relevant merger situation' see PARA 173.
6   As to the meaning of 'special merger situation' see PARA 204.
7   Enterprise Act 2002 s 104A(1), (2) (s 104A added by the Communications Act 2003 s 381).
8   Enterprise Act 2002 s 104A(3) (as added: see note 7).

270.   Advice and information in relation to media mergers.   The Secretary of State may prepare and publish general advice and information about certain national security considerations[1]. Such advice or information is to be prepared with a view to: (1) explaining the specified national security considerations to persons who are likely to be affected by them; and (2) indicating how the Secretary of State expects Part 3 of the Enterprise Act 2002[2] to operate in relation to such considerations[3]. Any such advice or information must be published in such manner as the Secretary of State considers appropriate[4]. In preparing it, the Secretary of State must consult the Office of Fair Trading (the 'OFT'), the Office of Communications (OFCOM), the Competition Commission and such other persons as he considers appropriate[5]. The Secretary of State may at any time publish revised, or new, advice or information[6].

1   Enterprise Act 2002 s 106A(1) (s 106A added by the Communications Act 2003 s 383). The text refers to the considerations specified in the Enterprise Act 2002 s 58(2A)–(2C) (see PARA 203). As to the Secretary of State see PARA 5.
2   Ie the Enterprise Act 2002 Pt 3 (ss 22–130): see PARA 172 et seq.
3   Enterprise Act 2002 s 106A(3) (as added: see note 1).
4   Enterprise Act 2002 s 106A(4) (as added: see note 1).
5   Enterprise Act 2002 s 106A(5) (as added: see note 1). As to the OFT see PARAS 6–8. As to OFCOM see PARA 19. As to the Competition Commission see PARAS 9–12.
6   Enterprise Act 2002 s 106A(2) (as added: see note 1).

(x)   Review of Decisions

271.   Review of decisions under Part 3 of the Enterprise Act 2002.   Any person aggrieved by a decision of the Office of Fair Trading (the 'OFT')[1], the Office of Communications (OFCOM)[2], the Secretary of State[3] or the Competition Commission[4] under Part 3 of the Enterprise Act 2002[5] in connection with a reference or possible reference in relation to a relevant merger situation[6] or a special merger situation[7] may apply to the Competition Appeal Tribunal for a review of that decision[8]. Except in so far as a direction to the contrary is given by the Competition Appeal Tribunal, the effect of the decision is not suspended by reason of the making of the application[9].

In determining such an application the Competition Appeal Tribunal must apply the same principles as would be applied by a court on an application for judicial review[10]. The Competition Appeal Tribunal may dismiss the application or quash the whole or part of the decision to which it relates[11]. Where it quashes the whole or part of that decision, it may refer the matter back to the original decision maker with a direction to reconsider and make a new decision in accordance with the ruling of the Competition Appeal Tribunal[12].

An appeal lies on any point of law arising from a decision of the Competition Appeal Tribunal to the Court of Appeal[13].

1   For this purpose 'decision' does not include a decision to impose a penalty under the Enterprise Act 2002 s 110(1) or s 110(3) (see PARA 260), but it includes a failure to take a decision permitted or required by Pt 3 (ss 22–130) in connection with a reference or possible reference: s 120(2). As to the OFT see PARAS 6–8. As to persons aggrieved see ADMINISTRATIVE LAW vol 1(1) (2001 Reissue) PARA 66.
2   As to OFCOM see PARA 19.
3   As to the Secretary of State see PARA 5.
4   As to the Competition Commission see PARAS 9–12.
5   Ie the Enterprise Act 2002 Pt 3 (ss 22–130).
6   As to the meaning of 'relevant merger situation' see PARA 173.
7   As to the meaning of 'special merger situation' see PARA 204.
8   Enterprise Act 2002 s 120(1) (amended by the Communications Act 2003 Sch 16 para 22). As to the Competition Appeal Tribunal see PARAS 13–17.
9   Enterprise Act 2002 s 120(3).
10 Enterprise Act 2002 s 120(4). As to judicial review see ADMINISTRATIVE LAW vol 1(1) (2001 Reissue) PARA 58 et seq.
11 Enterprise Act 2002 s 120(5)(a).
12 Enterprise Act 2002 s 120(5)(b).
13 Enterprise Act 2002 s 120(6), (8). An appeal requires the permission of the Tribunal or the Court of Appeal: s 120(7).

(xi) Fees, Orders and Regulations

272. Fees. The Secretary of State[1] may by order require the payment to him or the Office of Fair Trading (the 'OFT')[2] of such fees as may be prescribed by the order in connection with the exercise by the Secretary of State, the OFT, the Office of Communications (OFCOM)[3] and the Competition Commission[4] of certain statutory functions[5]. Such an order may, in particular, provide for fees to be payable in respect of a merger notice[6] or on the occurrence of any event specified in the order[7]. Such events may include:

(1)   the decision by the OFT in relation to a possible reference in relation to a completed or anticipated merger[8] that it is or may be the case that a relevant merger situation has been created or (as the case may be) that arrangements are in progress or in contemplation which, if carried into effect, will result in the creation of a relevant merger situation[9];

(2)   the decision by the Secretary of State in relation to a possible reference in relation to a completed or anticipated merger[10] that it is or may be the case that a relevant merger situation has been created or (as the case may be) that arrangements are in progress or in contemplation which, if carried into effect, will result in the creation of a relevant merger situation[11];

(3)   the decision by the Secretary of State in relation to a possible reference[12] that: (a) it is or may be the case that a special merger situation has been created or (as the case may be) that arrangements are in progress or in contemplation which, if carried into effect, will result in the creation of a special merger situation; and (b) one or more than one consideration mentioned in the special intervention notice is relevant to a consideration of the special merger situation concerned[13]; and

(4)   the decision by the OFT in relation to a possible reference under the Water Industry Act 1991[14] that it is or may be the case that arrangements are in progress which, if carried into effect, will result in a merger of any two or more water enterprises or that such a merger has taken place otherwise than as a result of the carrying into effect of certain specified arrangements[15].

An order may, in particular, contain provision (i) for ascertaining the persons by whom fees are payable; (ii) specifying whether any fee is payable to the Secretary of State or the OFT; (iii) for the amount of any fee to be calculated by reference to matters which may include the value of the turnover of the enterprises concerned; (iv) as to the time when any fee is to be paid; and (v) for the repayment by the Secretary of State or the OFT of the whole or part of any fee in specified circumstances[16].

In determining the amount of any fees to be prescribed by an order, the Secretary of State may take into account all costs incurred by him and by the OFT in respect of the exercise by him, the OFT, OFCOM and the Commission of their respective functions[17].

Fees paid to the Secretary of State or the OFT are paid into the Consolidated Fund[18].

1   As to the Secretary of State see PARA 5.
2   As to the OFT see PARAS 6–8.
3   As to OFCOM see PARA 19.
4   As to the Competition Commission see PARAS 9–12.

5   Ie their functions under or by virtue of the Enterprise Act 2002 Pt 3 (ss 22–130) and the Water Industry Act 1991 ss 32–34, Sch 4ZA: see the Enterprise Act 2002 s 121(1) (amended by the Communications Act 2003 Sch 16 para 23(1), (2)). In exercise of his power under the Enterprise Act 2002 s 121 the Secretary of State has made the Enterprise Act 2002 (Merger Fees and Determination of Turnover) Order 2003, SI 2003/1370 (amended by SI 2004/3204; SI 2005/3558).

6   As to the meaning of 'merger notice' see PARA 247. As to the fee payable in respect of the giving of a merger notice see the Enterprise Act 2002 (Merger Fees and Determination of Turnover) Order 2003, SI 2003/1370, arts 3, 4, 5.

7   Enterprise Act 2002 s 121(2) (amended by the Communications Act 2003 Sch 16 para 23(1), (3)).

8   Ie a reference by the OFT under the Enterprise Act 2002 s 22 (see PARA 172) or s 33 (see PARA 182).

9   Enterprise Act 2002 s 121(3)(a). As to the meaning of 'relevant merger situation' see PARA 173. As to the fee payable in this situation see the Enterprise Act 2002 (Merger Fees and Determination of Turnover) Order 2003, SI 2003/1370, arts 3, 4, 5.

10 Ie a reference by the Secretary of State under the Enterprise Act 2002 s 45 (see PARA 193).

11 Enterprise Act 2002 s 121(3)(b). As to the fee payable in this situation see the Enterprise Act 2002 (Merger Fees and Determination of Turnover) Order 2003, SI 2003/1370, arts 3, 4, 5.

12 Ie a reference by the Secretary of State under the Enterprise Act 2002 s 62 (see PARA 208).

13 Enterprise Act 2002 s 121(3)(c). As to the meaning of 'special merger situation' see PARA 204.

14 Ie a reference under the Water Industry Act 1991 s 32 (see WATER AND WATERWAYS vol 100 (2009) PARAS 150–151).

15 Enterprise Act 2002 s 121(3)(d). The text refers to arrangements that have been the subject of a reference by virtue of the Water Industry Act 1991 s 32(a) (see WATER AND WATERWAYS vol 100 (2009) PARA 150). See the Enterprise Act 2002 (Merger Fees and Determination of Turnover) Order 2003, SI 2003/1370, arts 3, 5.

16 Enterprise Act 2002 s 121(4)(a)–(e) (s 121(4) amended by the Communications Act 2003 Sch 16 para 23(1), (4)). See the Enterprise Act 2002 (Merger Fees and Determination of Turnover) Order 2003, SI 2003/1370, arts 6–10. The turnover of an enterprise is to be determined in accordance with such provisions as may be specified in an order made under the Enterprise Act 2002 s 121: s 121(5). This may include provision: (1) as to the amounts which are, or which are not, to be treated as comprising an enterprise's turnover; (2) as to the date or dates by reference to which an enterprise's turnover is to be determined; (3) restricting the turnover to be taken into consideration to turnover which has a connection of a particular description with the United Kingdom: s 121(6). An order may, in particular, in connection with provisions of the kind mentioned in s 121(5) make provision enabling the Secretary of State or the OFT to determine matters of a description specified in the order (including any of the matters mentioned in s 121(6) (see heads (1)–(3))): s 121(7). See the Enterprise Act 2002 (Merger Fees and Determination of Turnover) Order 2003, SI 2003/1370, art 11.

17 Enterprise Act 2002 s 121(8) (amended by the Communications Act 2003 Sch 16 para 23(1), (5)). The functions referred to in the text are those under or by virtue of the Enterprise Act 2002 Pt 3 and the Water Industry Act 1991 ss 32–34, Sch 4ZA (see note 5).

18 Enterprise Act 2002 s 121(9).

273. Orders and regulations in relation to mergers. Any power of the Secretary of State[1] to make an order or regulations under Part 3 of the Enterprise Act 2002[2] is exercisable by statutory instrument[3]. The power may be exercised so as to make different provision for different cases or different purposes and includes power to make such incidental, supplementary, consequential, transitory, transitional or saving provision as the Secretary of State considers appropriate[4]. The Secretary of State may also modify enactments[5].

1 As to the Secretary of State see PARA 5.
2 Ie under the Enterprise Act 2002 Pt 3 (ss 22–130).
3 Enterprise Act 2002 s 124(1). For drafting provisions see s 124(5)–(10).
4 Enterprise Act 2002 s 124(2).
5 See the Enterprise Act 2002 s 124(3), (4) (amended by the Communications Act 2003 Sch 16 para 24).

(xii) Offences by Bodies Corporate

274. Offences by bodies corporate. Where an offence under Part 3 of the Enterprise Act 2002[1] committed by a body corporate is proved to have been committed with the consent or connivance of, or to be attributable to any neglect on the part of (1) a director, manager, secretary or other similar officer of the body corporate; or (2) a person purporting to act in such a capacity, he as well as the body corporate commits the offence and is liable to be proceeded against and punished accordingly[2].

1 Ie the Enterprise Act 2002 Pt 3 (ss 22–130).
2 Enterprise Act 2002 s 125(1). Where the affairs of a body corporate are managed by its members, s 125(1) applies in relation to the acts and defaults of a member in connection with his functions of management as if he were a director of the body corporate: s 125(2). See further CORPORATIONS. As to offences by Scottish partnerships see s 125(3), (4).

(xiii) Service of Documents

275. Service of documents. Any document required or authorised by virtue of Part 3 of the Enterprise Act 2002[1] to be served on any person may be served:

(1)	by delivering it to him or by leaving it at his proper address or by sending it by post to him at that address[2];
(2)	if the person is a body corporate other than a limited liability partnership, by serving it in accordance with head (1) on the secretary of the body[3];
(3)	if the person is a limited liability partnership, by serving it in accordance with head (1) on a member of the partnership[4]; or
(4)	if the person is a partnership, by serving it in accordance with head (1) on a partner or a person having the control or management of the partnership business[5].

For these purposes[6], the proper address of any person on whom a document is to be served is his last known address, except that (a) in the case of service on a body corporate (other than a limited liability partnership) or its secretary, it is the address of the registered or principal office of the body[7]; (b) in the case of service on a limited liability partnership or a member of the partnership, it is the address of the registered or principal office of the partnership[8]; (c) in the case of service on a partnership or a partner or a person having the control or management of a partnership business, it is the address of the principal office of the partnership[9]. If a person to be served under Part 3 of the Act with any document by another has specified to that other an address within the United Kingdom other than his proper address[10] as the one at which he or someone on his behalf will accept documents of the same description as that document, then in relation to that document, that address is to be treated as his proper address[11].

Any notice in writing or other document required or authorised by virtue of Part 3 of the Act to be served on any person may be served on that person by transmitting the text of the notice or other document to him by means of an electronic communications network or by other means but while in electronic form provided the text is received by that person in legible form and is capable of being used for subsequent reference[12].

The provisions described above do not apply to any document if rules of court make provision about its service[13].

1	Ie the Enterprise Act 2002 Pt 3 (ss 22–130).
2	Enterprise Act 2002 s 126(1)(a).
3	Enterprise Act 2002 s 126(1)(b). References to serving include references to similar expressions (such as giving or sending): see s 126(8).
	As to bodies corporate see COMPANIES; CORPORATIONS. As to limited liability partnerships see PARTNERSHIP vol 79 (2008) PARA 234 et seq.
4	Enterprise Act 2002 s 126(1)(c).
5	Enterprise Act 2002 s 126(1)(d). As to partnerships see generally PARTNERSHIP.
6	Ie for the purposes of the Enterprise Act 2002 s 126 and the Interpretation Act 1978 s 7 in its application to the Enterprise Act 2002 s 126.
7	Enterprise Act 2002 s 126(2)(a). The principal office of a company constituted under the law of a country or territory outside the United Kingdom or of a partnership carrying on business outside the United Kingdom is its principal office within the United Kingdom: s 126(3). As to the meaning of 'United Kingdom' see PARA 401 note 1.
8	Enterprise Act 2002 s 126(2)(b).
9	Enterprise Act 2002 s 126(2)(c).
10	Ie as determined under the Enterprise Act 2002 s 126(2) (see heads (a)–(c) in the text).
11	Enterprise Act 2002 s 126(4), (5). This address is then treated as his proper address for the purposes of s 126 and the Interpretation Act 1978 s 7 in its application to the Enterprise Act 2002 s 126, instead of that determined under s 126(2): s 126(5).
12	Enterprise Act 2002 s 126(6) (amended by the Communications Act 2003 Sch 17 para 174(1), (2)).
13	Enterprise Act 2002 s 126(7).

(3) MARKET INVESTIGATIONS

(i) Market Investigation References

A. MAKING OF REFERENCES

276. Power of the Office of Fair Trading to make a market investigation reference. The Office of Fair Trading (the 'OFT')[1] may make a reference to the Competition Commission[2] if the OFT has reasonable grounds for suspecting that any feature, or combination of features, of a market in the United Kingdom for goods or services prevents, restricts or distorts competition in connection with the supply or acquisition of any goods or services in the United Kingdom or a part of the United Kingdom[3]. For these purposes, any reference to a feature of a market in the United Kingdom for goods or services is a reference to: (1) the structure of the market concerned or any aspect of that structure[4]; (2) any conduct (whether or not in the market concerned) of one or more than one person who supplies or acquires goods or services in the market concerned[5]; or (3) any conduct relating to the market concerned of customers of any person who supplies or acquires goods or services[6].

No market investigation reference may be made by the OFT if a market investigation reference has been made by the appropriate Minister in relation to the same matter but has not been finally determined[7].

1 As to the OFT see PARAS 6–8.
2 As to the Competition Commission see PARAS 9–12.
3 Enterprise Act 2002 s 131(1). As to the duty to consult see PARA 309. As to the requirement to publish information see PARA 311. A reference under s 131 or s 132 (see PARA 277) is referred to as a 'market investigation reference': s 131(6). 'Market in the United Kingdom' includes (1) so far as it operates in the United Kingdom or a part of the United Kingdom, any market which operates there and in another country or territory or in a part of another country or territory; and (2) any market which operates only in a part of the United Kingdom: s 131(6). References to a 'market for goods or services' include references to a market for goods and services: s 131(6). 'Goods' includes buildings and other structures, and also includes ships, aircraft and hovercraft: s 183(1). 'Supply', in relation to the supply of goods, includes supply by way of sale, lease, hire or hire-purchase, and, in relation to buildings or other structures, includes the construction of them by a person for another person: s 183(1). As to the meaning of 'United Kingdom' see PARA 401 note 1.
4 Enterprise Act 2002 s 131(2)(a).
5 Enterprise Act 2002 s 131(2)(b). 'Conduct' includes any failure to act (whether or not intentional) and any other unintentional conduct: s 131(3).
6 Enterprise Act 2002 s 131(2)(c).
7 Enterprise Act 2002 s 131(4)(b). As to market investigation references by the Secretary of State see s 132; and PARA 277. References in Pt 4 (ss 131–184) to a market investigation reference being finally determined are construed in accordance with s 183(3)–(6): s 131(5). No reference may be made under s 131 if the making of the reference is prevented by s 156(1) (see PARA 298): s 131(4)(a).

   For the purposes of Part 4, a market investigation reference is finally determined if (see s 183(3)):
   (1) where no intervention notice under s 139(1) (see PARA 283) has been given in relation to it: (a) the period permitted by s 137 for preparing and publishing a report under s 136 (see PARA 281) has expired and no such report has been prepared and published; (b) such a report has been prepared and published within the period permitted by s 137 and contains the decision that there is no adverse effect on competition; (c) the Commission has decided under s 138(2) (see PARA 282) neither to accept undertakings under s 159 (see PARA 301) nor to make an order under s 161 (see PARA 303); or (d) the Commission has accepted an undertaking under s 159 or made an order under s 161;
   (2) where an intervention notice under s 139(1) (see PARA 283) has been given in relation to it: (a) the period permitted by s 144 (see PARA 288) for the preparation of the report

of the Commission under s 142 (see PARA 286) and for action to be taken in relation to it under s 143(1), (3) (see PARA 287) has expired while the intervention notice is still in force and no such report has been so prepared or no such action has been taken; (b) the Commission has terminated under s 145(1) its investigation (see PARA 289) and the reference is finally determined under head (1) above (disregarding the fact that the notice was given); (c) the report of the Commission has been prepared under s 142 (see PARA 286) and published under s 143(1) (see PARA 287) within the period permitted by s 144 (see PARA 288); (d) the intervention notice was revoked and the reference is finally determined under head (1) above (disregarding the fact that the notice was given); (e) the Secretary of State has failed to make and publish a decision under s 146(2) within the period permitted by s 146(3) (see PARA 290) and the reference is finally determined under head (1) above (disregarding the fact that the notice was given); (f) the Secretary of State has decided under s 146(2) (see PARA 290) that no eligible public interest consideration is relevant and the reference is finally determined under head (1) above (disregarding the fact that the notice was given); (g) the Secretary of State has decided under s 146(2) that a public interest consideration is relevant but has decided under s 147(2) (see PARA 291) neither to accept an undertaking under s 159 (see PARA 301) nor to make an order under s 161 (see PARA 303); or (h) the Secretary of State has decided under s 146(2) (see PARA 290) that a public interest consideration is relevant and has accepted an undertaking under s 159 (see PARA 301) or made an order under s 161 (see PARA 303).

For the purposes of Pt 4 the time when a market investigation reference is finally determined is: (i) in a case falling within head (1)(a) or head (2)(a) above, the expiry of the time concerned; (ii) in a case falling within head (1)(b) or head (2)(c), the publication of the report; (iii) in a case falling within head (1)(d) or head (2)(h), the acceptance of the undertaking concerned or (as the case may be) the making of the order concerned; and (iv) in any other case, the making of the decision or last decision concerned or the taking of the action concerned: s 183(4). The references in s 183(4) to heads (1)(a), (b) and (d) include those enactments as applied by head (2)(b), (d), (e) or (f): s 183(5). In head (iii) the reference to the acceptance of the undertaking concerned or the making of the order concerned, in a case where the enforcement action concerned involves the acceptance of a group of undertakings, the making of a group of orders or the acceptance and making of a group of undertakings and orders, is to be treated as a reference to the acceptance or making of the last undertaking or order in the group; but undertakings or orders which vary, supersede or revoke earlier undertakings or orders are to be disregarded for the purposes of heads (1)(d) and (2)(h) and (iii): s 183(6). 'Action' includes omission; and references to the taking of action include references to refraining from action: s 183(1).

277.   Ministerial power to make market investigation references.   The appropriate Minister[1] may make a market investigation reference to the Competition Commission[2] if he has reasonable grounds for suspecting that any feature[3], or combination of features, of a market in the United Kingdom for goods or services[4] prevents, restricts or distorts competition in connection with the supply[5] or acquisition of any goods or services in the United Kingdom or a part of the United Kingdom[6]. Such a reference may be made where, in relation to any goods or services, the appropriate Minister is not satisfied with a decision of the Office of Fair Trading (the 'OFT') not to make a reference under its power to do so[7]. The appropriate Minister may also make such a reference where, in relation to any goods or services, he has brought information to the attention of the OFT which he considers to be relevant to the question of whether the OFT should make a reference, but he is not satisfied that the OFT will decide, within such period as the appropriate Minister considers to be reasonable, whether to make such a reference[8].

1   'Appropriate Minister' means (1) the Secretary of State; or (2) the Secretary of State and one or more than one other Minister of the Crown acting jointly: Enterprise Act 2002 s 132(5). As to the Secretary of State see PARA 5. 'Minister of the Crown' means the holder of an office in Her Majesty's Government in the United Kingdom and includes the Treasury: s 183(1).

2   As to the Competition Commission see PARAS 9–12. As to the meaning of 'market investigation reference' see PARA 276 note 3.

3   As to the meaning of 'feature of a market' see PARA 276.
4   As to the meanings of 'market for goods or services', 'market in the United Kingdom' and 'goods' see PARA 276 note 3. As to the meaning of 'United Kingdom' see PARA 401 note 1.
5   As to the meaning of 'supply' see PARA 276 note 3.
6   Enterprise Act 2002 s 132(3). As to the duty to consult see PARA 309. As to the requirement to publish information see PARA 311. No reference may be made under s 132 if the making of the reference is prevented by s 156(1) (see PARA 298): s 132(4).
7   Enterprise Act 2002 s 132(1). As to the OFT see PARAS 6–8. As to the power of the OFT to make market investigation reference see s 131; and PARA 276.
8   Enterprise Act 2002 s 132(2).

278.   Contents of references. A market investigation reference[1] must, in particular, specify (1) the enactment[2] under which it is made[3]; (2) the date on which it is made[4]; and (3) the description of goods or services to which the feature or combination of features concerned relates[5]. A market investigation reference may be framed so as to require the Competition Commission[6] to confine its investigation into the effects of features of markets in the United Kingdom for goods or services[7] of a description specified in the reference to the effects of features of such of those markets as exist in connection with: (a) a supply, of a description specified in the reference, of the goods or services concerned; or (b) an acquisition, of a description specified in the reference, of the goods or services concerned[8].

1   As to the meaning of 'market investigation reference' see PARA 276 note 3.
2   'Enactment' includes an Act of the Scottish Parliament, Northern Ireland legislation and an enactment comprised in subordinate legislation, and includes an enactment whenever passed or made: Enterprise Act 2002 s 183(1).
3   Enterprise Act 2002 s 133(1)(a).
4   Enterprise Act 2002 s 133(1)(b).
5   Enterprise Act 2002 s 133(1)(c). As to the meaning of 'feature of a market' see PARA 276. As to the meaning of 'goods' see PARA 276 note 3.
6   As to the Competition Commission see PARAS 9–12.
7   As to the meanings of 'market for goods or services' and 'market in the United Kingdom' see PARA 276 note 3. As to the meaning of 'United Kingdom' see PARA 401 note 1.
8   Enterprise Act 2002 s 133(2)(a), (b). A description of the kind mentioned in s 133(2)(a) or s 133(2)(b) may, in particular, be by reference to: (1) the place where the goods or services are supplied or acquired; or (2) the persons by or to whom they are supplied or by or from whom they are acquired: s 133(3).

B.   DETERMINATION OF REFERENCES

279.   Questions to be decided. On a market investigation reference[1], the Competition Commission[2] must decide whether any feature, or combination of features[3], of each relevant market[4] prevents, restricts or distorts competition in connection with the supply or acquisition of any goods or services in the United Kingdom or a part of the United Kingdom[5].

In relation to a market investigation reference, there is an adverse effect on competition if any feature, or combination of features, of a relevant market prevents, restricts or distorts competition in connection with the supply or acquisition of any goods or services in the United Kingdom or a part of the United Kingdom[6]. If the Commission decides on a market investigation reference that there is an adverse effect on competition, then it must decide the following additional questions:

(1)   whether action should be taken by it[7] for the purpose of remedying, mitigating or preventing the adverse effect on competition concerned or

any detrimental effect on customers[8] so far as it has resulted from, or may be expected to result from, the adverse effect on competition[9];

(2)   whether it should recommend the taking of action by others for the purpose of remedying, mitigating or preventing the adverse effect on competition concerned or any detrimental effect on customers so far as it has resulted from, or may be expected to result from, the adverse effect on competition[10]; and

(3)   in either case, if action should be taken, what action should be taken and what is to be remedied, mitigated or prevented[11].

In deciding these questions, the Commission must, in particular, have regard to the need to achieve as comprehensive a solution as is reasonable and practicable to the adverse effect on competition and any detrimental effects on customers so far as resulting from the adverse effect on competition[12]. It may also have regard to the effect of any action on any relevant customer benefits of the feature or features of the market concerned[13].

1   As to the meaning of 'market investigation reference' see PARA 276 note 3.
2   As to the Competition Commission see PARAS 9–12.
3   As to the meaning of 'feature of a market' see PARA 276.
4   In the Enterprise Act 2002 s 134(1), (2), 'relevant market' means:
    (1)   in the case of s 134(2) so far as it applies in connection with a possible reference, a market in the United Kingdom: (a) for goods or services of a description to be specified in the reference; and (b) which would not be excluded from investigation by virtue of s 133(2) (see s 134(3)(a)); and
    (2)   in any other case, a market in the United Kingdom: (a) for goods or services of a description specified in the reference concerned; and (b) which is not excluded from investigation by virtue of s 133(2) (see s 134(3)(b)).
    As to the meanings of 'market in the United Kingdom' and 'goods' see PARA 276 note 3. As to the meaning of 'United Kingdom' see PARA 401 note 1.
5   Enterprise Act 2002 s 134(1). As to the duty to consult see PARA 309.
6   Enterprise Act 2002 s 134(2).
7   Ie under the Enterprise Act 2002 s 138 (see PARA 282).
8   For the purposes of the Enterprise Act 2002 Pt 4 (ss 131–184) in relation to a market investigation reference, there is a detrimental effect on customers if there is a detrimental effect on customers or future customers in the form of: (1) higher prices, lower quality or less choice of goods or services in any market in the United Kingdom (whether or not the market to which the feature or features concerned relate); or (2) less innovation in relation to such goods or services: s 134(5).
9   Enterprise Act 2002 s 134(4)(a).
10   Enterprise Act 2002 s 134(4)(b).
11   Enterprise Act 2002 s 134(4)(c).
12   Enterprise Act 2002 s 134(6).
13   Enterprise Act 2002 s 134(7). For the purposes of Pt 4 a benefit is a relevant customer benefit of a feature or features of a market if:
    (1)   it is a benefit to customers or future customers in the form of: (a) lower prices, higher quality or greater choice of goods or services in any market in the United Kingdom (whether or not the market to which the feature or features concerned relate); or (b) greater innovation in relation to such goods or services (s 134(8)(a)); and
    (2)   the Commission, the Secretary of State or (as the case may be) the Office of Fair Trading believes that: (a) the benefit has accrued as a result (whether wholly or partly) of the feature or features concerned or may be expected to accrue within a reasonable period as a result (whether wholly or partly) of that feature or those features; and (b) the benefit was, or is, unlikely to accrue without the feature or features concerned (s 134(8)(b)).
    As to the Secretary of State see PARA 5. As to the OFT see PARAS 6–8.

280.   Variation of references. The Office of Fair Trading (the 'OFT')[1] or (as the case may be) the appropriate Minister[2] may at any time vary a market investigation reference[3] made by it or (as the case may be) him[4], having previously consulted the Competition Commission[5] before doing so[6].

Although market investigation references may be varied, no variation is capable of altering the period permitted within which certain reports of the Commission are to be prepared and published[7].

1   As to the OFT see PARAS 6–8.
2   As to the meaning of 'appropriate Minister' see PARA 277 note 1.
3   As to the meaning of 'market investigation reference' see PARA 276 note 3.
4   Enterprise Act 2002 s 135(1).
5   As to the Competition Commission see PARAS 9–12.
6   Enterprise Act 2002 s 135(2). There is no requirement to consult the Commission if it is the Commission which has requested the variation concerned: s 135(3). As to the duty to consult see PARA 309. As to the requirement to publish information see PARA 311.
7   No variation under the Enterprise Act 2002 s 135 is capable of altering the period permitted by s 137 within which the report of the Commission under s 136 (see PARA 281) is to be prepared and published or (as the case may be) the period permitted by s 144 within which the report of the Commission under s 142 (see PARA 286) is to be prepared and published or given: s 135(4). Any duty to publish which is imposed on a person by Pt 4 (ss 131–184), unless the context otherwise requires, is to be construed as a duty on that person to publish in such manner as that person considers appropriate for the purpose of bringing the matter concerned to the attention of those likely to be affected by it: s 183(7).

281.   Investigations and reports.   The Competition Commission[1] must prepare and publish a report on a market investigation reference[2] within the period of two years beginning with the date of the reference[3]. That period may be altered, subject to restrictions[4].

The Commission is under a duty to carry out such investigations as it considers appropriate for the purposes of preparing the report[5]. The report itself must, in particular, contain:

(1)   the decisions of the Commission on the questions which it is required to answer[6];

(2)   its reasons for its decisions[7]; and

(3)   such information as the Commission considers appropriate for facilitating a proper understanding of those questions and of its reasons for its decisions[8].

Where the market investigation reference was made by the Office of Fair Trading (the 'OFT')[9], the Commission must give the report to the OFT at the same time as publishing it[10]. Where the market investigation reference was made by the appropriate Minister, the Commission must give it to the appropriate Minister with a copy to the OFT[11]. Where a market investigation reference has been made by the OFT or the appropriate Minister[12] in circumstances in which a reference could have been made by a relevant sectoral regulator[13], the Commission must, at the same time as the report is published, give a copy of it to the relevant sectoral regulator concerned[14]. Where a reference has been made by a relevant sectoral regulator[15] the Commission must, at the same time as the report is published, give a copy of it to the OFT[16].

1   As to the Competition Commission see PARAS 9–12.
2   As to the meaning of 'market investigation reference' see PARA 276 note 3.
3   Enterprise Act 2002 ss 136(1), 137(1). This period is extended by 20 days where the Secretary of State revokes an intervention notice which has been given under s 139(1) or where the Commission terminates its investigation under s 145(1): see ss 137(2), 151; and PARAS 284, 289. References in Pt 4 (ss 131–184) to the date of a market investigation reference are to be construed as references to the date specified in the reference as the date on which it is made: s 137(7).

4   The Secretary of State may by order amend the Enterprise Act 2002 s 137(1) so as to alter the period of two years mentioned in that subsection or any period for the time being mentioned in that subsection in substitution for that period: s 137(3). However, no alteration may be made which results in the period for the time being mentioned in s 137(1) exceeding two years: s 137(4). Such an order does not affect any period of time within which the Commission is under a duty to prepare and publish its report under s 136 in relation to a market investigation reference if the Commission is already under that duty in relation to that reference when the order is made: s 137(5). Before making an order to alter the time period the Secretary of State must consult the Commission and such other persons as he considers appropriate: s 137(6). As to the Secretary of State see PARA 5.
5   Enterprise Act 2002 s 136(3).
6   Enterprise Act 2002 s 136(2)(a). As to the questions it is required to answer see s 134; and PARA 279.
7   Enterprise Act 2002 s 136(2)(b).
8   Enterprise Act 2002 s 136(2)(c).
9   As to the OFT see PARAS 6–8.
10   Enterprise Act 2002 s 136(4)(a).
11   Enterprise Act 2002 s 136(4)(b). As to the meaning of 'appropriate Minister' see PARA 277 note 1.
12   Ie by the OFT under the Enterprise Act 2002 s 131 (see PARA 276) or by the appropriate Minister under s 132 (see PARA 277).
13   Ie under the Enterprise Act 2002 s 131 as it has effect by virtue of a relevant sectoral enactment: s 136(5). 'Relevant sectoral regulator' means the Gas and Electricity Markets Authority, the Water Services Regulation Authority, the Office of Rail Regulation, the Civil Aviation Authority, the Office of Communications, or the Northern Ireland Authority for Utility Regulation: s 136(8) (amended by Communications Act 2003 s 406(7), Sch 17 para 174(1), (4), Sch 19(1); the Water Act 2003 s 101(1), Sch 7 Pt 2 para 36(1), (2); the Railways and Transport Safety Act 2003 s 16(5), Sch 2 Pt 2 para 19(u); and SI 2006/3336). 'Relevant sectoral enactment' means: (1) in relation to the Gas and Electricity Markets Authority, the Gas Act 1986 s 36A or (as the case may be) the Electricity Act 1989 s 43; (2) in relation to the Water Services Regulation Authority, the Water Industry Act 1991 s 31; (3) in relation to the Office of Rail Regulation, the Railways Act 1993 s 67; (4) in relation to the Civil Aviation Authority, the Transport Act 2000 s 86; (5) in relation to the Office of Communications, the Communications Act 2003 ss 370, 371; (6) in relation to the Northern Ireland Authority for Utility Regulation, the Electricity (Northern Ireland) Order 1992, SI 1992/231, art 46, the Gas (Northern Ireland) Order 1996, SI 1996/276, art 23, or the Water and Sewerage Services (Northern Ireland) Order 2006, SI 2006/1946, art 29: Enterprise Act 2002 s 136(7) (amended by the Communications Act 2003 s 406(1), (7), Sch 17 para 174(1), (4), Sch 19(1); the Water Act 2003 s 101(1), Sch 7 Pt 2 para 36(1), (2); Railways and Transport Safety Act 2003 s 16(5), Sch 2 Pt 2 para 19(u); and SI 2006/3336). The Secretary of State may by order modify the Enterprise Act 2002 s 136(7) or s 136(8): s 136(9).
14   Enterprise Act 2002 s 136(5).
15   Ie under the Enterprise Act 2002 s 131 as it has effect by virtue of a relevant sectoral enactment: s 136(6).
16   Enterprise Act 2002 s 136(6).

282.   Duty to remedy adverse effects. Where a report of the Competition Commission[1] has been prepared and published within the permitted time period[2] and contains the decision that there is one or more than one adverse effect on competition[3], then in relation to each adverse effect it must take such permitted action[4] as it considers to be reasonable and practicable to:

(1)   remedy, mitigate or prevent the adverse effect on competition concerned[5]; and

(2)   remedy, mitigate or prevent any detrimental effects on customers[6] so far as they have resulted from, or may be expected to result from, the adverse effect on competition[7].

The decisions to take such action must be consistent with its decisions as included in its report[8] unless there has been a material change of circumstances since the preparation of the report or the Commission otherwise has a special reason for deciding differently[9]. In making the decision to take appropriate action, the Commission must, in particular, have regard to the need to achieve as comprehensive a solution as is reasonable and practicable to the adverse effect on competition concerned and any detrimental effects on customers so far as resulting from the adverse effect on competition[10]. The Commission may also have regard to the effect of any action on any relevant customer benefits of the feature or features of the market concerned[11]. The Commission must take no action to remedy, mitigate or prevent any detrimental effect on customers so far as it may be expected to result from the adverse effect on competition concerned if: (a) no detrimental effect on customers has resulted from the adverse effect on competition; and (b) the adverse effect on competition is not being remedied, mitigated or prevented[12].

1 As to the Competition Commission see PARAS 9–12.
2 Ie where the report has been prepared under the Enterprise Act 2002 s 136 within the period permitted by s 137 (see PARA 281). As to the requirement to publish information see PARA 311.
3 Enterprise Act 2002 s 138(1). As to the meaning of 'adverse effect on competition' see PARA 279.
4 Ie such action under the Enterprise Act 2002 s 159 (see PARA 301) or s 161 (see PARA 303).
5 Enterprise Act 2002 s 138(2)(a).
6 As to the meaning of 'detrimental effect on customers' see PARA 279 note 8.
7 Enterprise Act 2002 s 138(2)(b).
8 Ie the decisions included in the report by virtue of the Enterprise Act 2002 s 134(4) (see PARA 279).
9 Enterprise Act 2002 s 138(3). As to the requirement to publish information see PARA 311.
10 Enterprise Act 2002 s 138(4).
11 Enterprise Act 2002 s 138(5). As to the meaning of 'feature of a market' see PARA 276. As to the meaning of 'relevant customer benefit' see PARA 279 note 13.
12 Enterprise Act 2002 s 138(6).

(ii) Public Interest Cases

A. INTERVENTION NOTICES

283. Public interest intervention by the Secretary of State. The Secretary of State[1] may give an intervention notice[2] to the Competition Commission[3] or the Office of Fair Trading (the 'OFT')[4] in the following circumstances[5].

He may give an intervention notice to the Commission[6] if:

(1) a market investigation reference[7] has been made to the Competition Commission[8];
(2) no more than four months has passed since the date of the reference[9];
(3) the reference is not finally determined[10]; and
(4) the Secretary of State believes that it is or may be the case that one or more than one public interest consideration is relevant to the case[11].

The Secretary of State may give an intervention notice to the Office of Fair Trading[12] if:

(a) the OFT is considering whether to accept an undertaking[13] instead of making a market investigation reference[14], or is considering whether to accept an undertaking varying or superseding any such undertaking[15];
(b) the OFT has published a notice[16]; and
(c) the Secretary of State believes that it is or may be the case that one or more than one public interest consideration is relevant to the case[17].

Where the Secretary of State has given an intervention notice mentioning a public interest consideration which, at that time, is not finalised, he must, as soon as practicable, take such action as is within his power to ensure that it is finalised[18].

1   As to the Secretary of State see PARA 5.
2   'Intervention notice' means a notice under the Enterprise Act 2002 s 139(1) or s 139(2): s 139(3).
3   As to the Competition Commission see PARAS 9–12.
4   As to the OFT see PARAS 6–8.
5   As to intervention notices given to the Competition Commission see PARAS 284–292. As to intervention notices given to the OFT see PARA 293.
6   No more than one intervention notice may be given under the Enterprise Act 2002 s 139(1) in relation to the same market investigation reference: s 139(4). Where an intervention notice under s 139(1) comes into force in relation to a market investigation reference, s 134(1), (4), (6), (7) (see PARA 279), ss 136(1)–(6), 137(1)–(6) (see PARA 281) and s 138 (see PARA 282) cease to apply in relation to that reference: s 151(1)
7   As to the meaning of 'market investigation reference' see PARA 276 note 3.
8   Enterprise Act 2002 s 139(1)(a).
9   Enterprise Act 2002 s 139(1)(b).
10 Enterprise Act 2002 s 139(1)(c).
11 Enterprise Act 2002 s 139(1)(d). A 'public interest consideration' is a consideration which, at the time of the giving of the intervention notice concerned, is specified in s 153 (see PARA 295) or is not so specified but, in the opinion of the Secretary of State, ought to be so specified: s 139(5). See note 6.
12 No more than one intervention notice may be given under the Enterprise Act 2002 s 139(2) in relation to the same proposed undertaking or in relation to proposed undertakings which do not differ from each other in any material respect: s 139(4).
13 Ie an undertaking under the Enterprise Act 2002 s 154 (see PARA 296).
14 Ie a reference under the Enterprise Act 2002 s 131 (see PARA 276).
15 Enterprise Act 2002 s 139(2)(a).
16 Enterprise Act 2002 s 139(2)(b). The text refers to a notice under s 155(1) or s 155(4) (see PARA 297).
17 Enterprise Act 2002 s 139(2)(c).
18 Enterprise Act 2002 s 139(6). A public interest consideration is finalised if: (1) it is specified in s 153 otherwise than by virtue of an order under s 153(3); or (2) it is specified in s 153 by virtue of an order under s 153(3) and the order providing for it to be so specified has been laid before, and approved by, Parliament in accordance with s 181(6) and within the period mentioned in that subsection: s 139(7).

B. INTERVENTION NOTICES GIVEN TO THE COMPETITION COMMISSION

284.   Notices given to the Competition Commission. An intervention notice given by the Secretary of State to the Competition Commission[1] must state:

(1)   the market investigation reference concerned[2];
(2)   the date of the market investigation reference concerned[3];
(3)   the public interest consideration or considerations which are, or may be, relevant to the case[4]; and
(4)   where any public interest consideration concerned is not finalised, the proposed timetable for finalising it[5].

Where the Secretary of State believes that it is or may be the case that two or more public interest considerations are relevant to the case, he may decide not to mention in the intervention notice such of those considerations as he considers appropriate[6].

The Secretary of State may at any time revoke an intervention notice which has been given to the Commission and which is in force[7]. An intervention notice comes into force when it is given and ceases to be in force when the matter to which it relates is finally determined[8].

1   Ie an intervention notice given under the Enterprise Act 2002 s 139(1) (see PARA 283). As to the meaning of 'intervention notice' see PARA 283 note 2. As to the Secretary of State see PARA 5. As to the Competition Commission see PARAS 9–12.

2   Enterprise Act 2002 s 140(1)(a). As to the meaning of 'market investigation reference' see PARA 276 note 3.

3   Enterprise Act 2002 s 140(1)(b).

4   Enterprise Act 2002 s 140(1)(c). As to the meaning of 'public interest consideration' see PARA 283 note 11. As to public interest considerations being finalised see PARA 283 note 18.

5   Enterprise Act 2002 s 140(1)(d).

6   Enterprise Act 2002 s 140(2).

7   Enterprise Act 2002 s 140(3). Where the Secretary of State revokes an intervention notice which has been given under s 139(1), the Commission must instead proceed under ss 134, 136–138 (see PARAS 279–282): s 151(2). In this case the period within which the Commission is under a duty to prepare and publish its report under s 136 is extended by an additional period of 20 days: s 151(3) (see PARA 281).

8   Enterprise Act 2002 s 140(4). For these purposes a matter to which an intervention notice under s 139(1) relates is finally determined if:

   (1)   the period permitted by s 144 (see PARA 288) for the preparation of the report of the Commission under s 142 (see PARA 286) and for action to be taken in relation to it under s 143(1) or s 143(3) has expired and no such report has been so prepared or no such action has been taken (s 140(5)(a));

   (2)   the Commission decides under s 145(1) (see PARA 289) to terminate its investigation (s 140(5)(b));

   (3)   the report of the Commission has been prepared under s 142 and published under s 143(1) within the period permitted by s 144 (s 140(5)(c));

   (4)   the Secretary of State fails to make and publish a decision under s 146(2) within the period required by s 146(3) (see PARA 290) (s 140(5)(d));

   (5)   the Secretary of State decides under s 146(2) that no eligible public interest consideration is relevant (s 140(5)(e));

   (6)   the Secretary of State decides under s 147(2) neither to accept an undertaking under s 159 nor to make an order under s 161 (see PARA 303) (s 140(5)(f));

   (7)   the Secretary of State accepts an undertaking under s 159 or makes an order under s 161 (see PARA 303) (s 140(5)(g)); or

   (8)   the Secretary of State decides to revoke the intervention notice concerned (s 140(5)(h)).

   In the case falling within head (1) or (4) above, the matter is finally determined at the expiry of the period concerned: s 140(6)(a). In a case falling within head (2), (5), (6) or (8), the matter is finally determined on the making of the decision concerned: s 140(6)(b). In a case falling within head (3), the matter is finally determined on the publication of the report concerned: s 140(6)(c). In a case falling within head (7), the matter is finally determined on the acceptance of the undertaking concerned or (as the case may be) the making of the order concerned: s 140(6)(d). Note that this reference to the acceptance of the undertaking concerned or the making of the order concerned is (in a case where the enforcement action under s 147(2) involves the acceptance of a group of undertakings, the making of a group of orders or the acceptance and making of a group of undertakings and orders) to be treated as a reference to the acceptance or making of the last undertaking or order in the group; but undertakings or orders which vary, supersede or revoke earlier undertakings or orders are to be disregarded for the purposes of s 140(5)(g), (6)(d): s 140(7).

285.   Questions to be decided by the Competition Commission.   Where an intervention notice has been given by the Secretary of State to the Competition Commission[1] and is in force in relation to a market investigation reference[2], then the Commission must decide on the following issues[3].

The Commission must decide whether any feature, or combination of features, of each relevant market[4] prevents, restricts or distorts competition in connection with the supply or acquisition of any goods[5] or services in the United Kingdom or a part of the United Kingdom[6]. If the Commission has decided that there is an adverse effect on competition[7], it must decide the following additional questions:

   (1)   whether action should be taken by the Secretary of State[8] for the purpose of remedying, mitigating or preventing the adverse effect on

competition concerned or any detrimental effect on customers so far as it has resulted from, or may be expected to result from, the adverse effect on competition[9];

(2) whether the Commission should recommend the taking of other action by the Secretary of State or action by persons other than itself and the Secretary of State for the purpose of remedying, mitigating or preventing the adverse effect on competition concerned or any detrimental effect on customers so far as it has resulted from, or may be expected to result from, the adverse effect on competition[10]; and

(3) in either case, if action should be taken, what action should be taken and what is to be remedied, mitigated or prevented[11].

If the Commission has decided that there is an adverse effect on competition, it must also decide separately the following questions[12]:

(a) whether action should be taken by it[13] for the purpose of remedying, mitigating or preventing the adverse effect on competition concerned or any detrimental effect on customers so far as it has resulted from, or may be expected to result from, the adverse effect on competition[14];

(b) whether the Commission should recommend the taking of action by other persons for the purpose of remedying, mitigating or preventing the adverse effect on competition concerned or any detrimental effect on customers so far as it has resulted from, or may be expected to result from, the adverse effect on competition[15]; and

(c) in either case, if action should be taken, what action should be taken and what is to be remedied, mitigated or prevented[16].

In deciding these questions[17], the Commission must, in particular, have regard to the need to achieve as comprehensive a solution as is reasonable and practicable to the adverse effect on competition concerned and any detrimental effects on customers so far as resulting from the adverse effect on competition[18]. The Commission may, in particular, have regard to the effect of any action on any relevant customer benefits of the feature or features of the market concerned[19].

1 Ie an intervention notice given under the Enterprise Act 2002 s 139(1) (see PARA 283). As to the meaning of 'intervention notice' see PARA 283 note 2. As to the Secretary of State see PARA 5. As to the Competition Commission see PARAS 9–12.

2 As to the meaning of 'market investigation reference' see PARA 276 note 3.

3 Enterprise Act 2002 s 141(1). As to the making of decisions under s 141 see PARA 11 note 13. As to the duty to consult see PARA 309.

4 As to the meaning of 'relevant market' see PARA 279 note 4. As to the meaning of 'feature of a market' see PARA 276.

5 As to the meanings of 'supply' and 'goods' see PARA 276 note 3.

6 Enterprise Act 2002 s 141(2). As to the meaning of 'United Kingdom' see PARA 401 note 1.

7 As to the meaning of 'adverse effect on competition' see PARA 279.

8 Ie under the Enterprise Act 2002 s 147 (see PARA 291).

9 Enterprise Act 2002 s 141(3)(a). As to the meaning of 'detrimental effect on customers' see PARA 279 note 8.

10 Enterprise Act 2002 s 141(3)(b).

11 Enterprise Act 2002 s 141(3)(c).

12 This is on the assumption that it is proceeding as mentioned in the Enterprise Act 2002 s 148(1) (see PARA 292).

13 Ie under the Enterprise Act 2002 s 138 (see PARA 282).

14 Enterprise Act 2002 s 141(4)(a).

15 Enterprise Act 2002 s 141(4)(b).

16 Enterprise Act 2002 s 141(4)(c).

17 Ie the questions mentioned in the Enterprise Act 2002 s 141(3), (4) (see heads (1)–(3) and heads (a)–(c) in the text).

18 Enterprise Act 2002 s 141(5).
19 Enterprise Act 2002 s 141(6).

286. Investigations and reports by the Competition Commission. Where an intervention notice has been given by the Secretary of State to the Competition Commission[1] and is in force in relation to a market investigation reference[2], the Commission must prepare a report on the reference and take the relevant action in relation to it[3] within the permitted period[4]. The report must, in particular, contain: (1) the decisions of the Commission on the questions which it is required to answer[5]; (2) its reasons for its decisions[6]; and (3) such information as the Commission considers appropriate for facilitating a proper understanding of those questions and of its reasons for its decisions[7].

The Commission must carry out such investigations as it considers appropriate for the purposes of preparing the report[8].

Where the Secretary of State is under a duty to publish the report, he may exclude a matter from the report if he considers that publication of the matter would be inappropriate[9]. The Commission must advise the Secretary of State as to the matters (if any) which it considers should be so excluded[10].

1 Ie an intervention notice given under the Enterprise Act 2002 s 139(1) (see PARA 283). As to the meaning of 'intervention notice' see PARA 283 note 2. As to the Secretary of State see PARA 5. As to the Competition Commission see PARAS 9–12.
2 As to the meaning of 'market investigation reference' see PARA 276 note 3.
3 Ie action under the Enterprise Act 2002 s 143(1) or s 143(3) (see PARA 287).
4 Enterprise Act 2002 s 142(1). The text refers to the period permitted by s 144 (see PARA 288).
5 Enterprise Act 2002 s 142(2)(a). As to the questions it is required by virtue of s 141 to answer see PARA E111. Where, on a market investigation reference, a member of a group constituted in connection with the reference in pursuance of the Competition Act 1998 Sch 7 para 15 (see PARA 11) disagrees with any decisions contained in the report of the Commission as the decisions of the Commission, the report must, if the member so wishes, include a statement of his disagreement and of his reasons for disagreeing: s 178(1), (2).
6 Enterprise Act 2002 s 142(2)(b).
7 Enterprise Act 2002 s 142(2)(c).
8 Enterprise Act 2002 s 142(3).
9 As to the publication of reports see PARA 287. As to the requirement to publish information see PARA 311. References in ss 136(4)–(6), 143(2), (5)–(7), 148(3)–(5), 172(10) to the giving or laying of a report of the Commission are to be construed as references to the giving or laying of the report as published: s 177(5). Where the Secretary of State is under a duty to publish a report of the Commission under s 142, he may exclude a matter from the report if he considers that publication of the matter would be inappropriate: s 177(1), (2). In deciding what is inappropriate, the Secretary of State must have regard to the considerations mentioned in s 244 (see PARA 334): s 177(3).
10 Enterprise Act 2002 s 177(4).

287. Publication of reports by the Competition Commission. Where an intervention notice has been given by the Secretary of State to the Competition Commission[1] and is in force in relation to a market investigation reference[2], the Commission must publish the report that it is required to prepare[3] if it contains:

(1) the decision of the Commission that there is no adverse effect on competition[4]; or

(2) the decisions of the Commission that there is one or more than one adverse effect on competition but that no action should be taken by it[5].

In the case of a market investigation reference by the Office of Fair Trading (the 'OFT')[6], the Commission must, at the same time as the report is published, give it to the OFT[7]. In the case of a market investigation reference by the appropriate Minister[8], the Commission must give it to the appropriate Minister and give a copy of it to the OFT[9].

Where the report[10] contains the decisions of the Commission that there is one or more than one adverse effect on competition and that action should be taken by it[11], the Commission must give the report to the Secretary of State[12]. The Secretary of State must then publish this report[13].

Where a market investigation reference has been made by the OFT or by the appropriate Minister[14] in circumstances in which a reference could have been made by a relevant sectoral regulator[15] the relevant authority[16] must, at the same time as the report is published[17], give a copy of it to the relevant sectoral regulator concerned[18]. Where a reference has been made by a relevant sectoral regulator[19] the relevant authority must, at the same time as the report is published, give a copy of it to the OFT[20].

1   Ie an intervention notice given under the Enterprise Act 2002 s 139(1) (see PARA 283). As to the meaning of 'intervention notice' see PARA 283 note 2. As to the Secretary of State see PARA 5. As to the Competition Commission see PARAS 9–12.
2   As to the meaning of 'market investigation reference' see PARA 276 note 3.
3   Ie the report it is required to prepare under the Enterprise Act 2002 s 142 (see PARA 286).
4   Enterprise Act 2002 s 143(1)(a). As to the meaning of 'adverse effect on competition' see PARA 279.
5   Enterprise Act 2002 s 143(1)(b). The text refers to the situation where the Commission decides on the question whether action should be taken by it under s 138 for the purpose of remedying, mitigating or preventing the adverse effect on competition concerned or any detrimental effect on customers so far as it has resulted from, or may be expected to result from, the adverse effect on competition (see s 141(4)(a)) and in relation to each adverse effect on competition, that no action should be taken by it: see s 143(1)(b).
6   Ie a reference under the Enterprise Act 2002 s 131 (see PARA 276). As to the OFT see PARAS 6–8.
7   Enterprise Act 2002 s 143(2)(a).
8   Ie a reference under the Enterprise Act 2002 s 132 (see PARA 277). As to the meaning of 'appropriate Minister' see PARA 277 note 1.
9   Enterprise Act 2002 s 143(2)(b).
10 See note 3.
11 The text refers to the situation where the Commission decides on the question whether action should be taken by it under the Enterprise Act 2002 s 138 for the purpose of remedying, mitigating or preventing the adverse effect on competition concerned or any detrimental effect on customers so far as it has resulted from, or may be expected to result from, the adverse effect on competition (see s 141(4)(a)) and in relation to at least one such adverse effect on competition, that action should be taken by it: see s 143(3).
12 Enterprise Act 2002 s 143(3).
13 The Secretary of State must publish, no later than publication of his decision under the Enterprise Act 2002 s 146(2) (see PARA 290) in relation to the case, a report of the Commission given to him under s 143(3) and not required to be published by virtue of s 148(2) (see PARA 292): s 143(4). The Secretary of State must, at the same time as the Commission's report given to him under s 143(3) is published under s 143(4), give a copy of it: (1) in the case of a reference under s 131, to the OFT; and (2) in the case of a reference under s 132, to any other Minister of the Crown who made the reference and to the OFT: s 143(5).
14 Ie by the OFT under the Enterprise Act 2002 s 131 (see PARA 276) or by the appropriate Minister under s 132 (see PARA 277).
15 Ie under the Enterprise Act 2002 s 131 as it has effect by virtue of a relevant sectoral enactment: s 143(6). As to the meanings of 'relevant sectoral regulator' and 'relevant sectoral enactment' see PARA 281 note 13.
16 For these purposes, 'relevant authority' means: (1) in the case of a report published under the Enterprise Act 2002 s 143(1), the Commission; and (2) in the case of a report published under the Enterprise Act 2002 s 143(4), the Secretary of State: s 143(8).
17 Ie under the Enterprise Act 2002 s 143(1) or s 143(4).
18 Enterprise Act 2002 s 143(6).
19 Ie under the Enterprise Act 2002 s 131 as it has effect by virtue of a relevant sectoral enactment: s 143(7).
20 Enterprise Act 2002 s 143(7).

288. Time limits for investigations and reports. The Competition Commission[1] must prepare its report[2] and publish it[3] or (as the case may be) give it to the Secretary of State[4] within the period of two years beginning with the date of the reference[5]. That period may be altered, subject to restrictions[6].

1 As to the Competition Commission see PARAS 9–12.
2 Ie under the Enterprise Act 2002 s 142 (see PARA 286).
3 Ie under the Enterprise Act 2002 s 143(1) (see PARA 287).
4 Ie under the Enterprise Act 2002 s 143(3) (see PARA 287). As to the Secretary of State see PARA 5.
5 Enterprise Act 2002 s 144(1).
6 The Secretary of State may by order amend the Enterprise Act 2002 s 144(1) so as to alter the period of two years mentioned in that subsection or any period for the time being mentioned in that subsection in substitution for that period: s 144(2). However, no alteration may be made which results in the period for the time being mentioned in s 144(1) exceeding two years: s 144(3). An order under s 144(2) does not affect any period of time within which, in relation to a market investigation reference, the Commission is under a duty to prepare its report under s 142 and take action in relation to it under s 143(1) or s 143(3) if the Commission is already under that duty in relation to that reference when the order is made: s 144(4). Before making an order under s 144(2) the Secretary of State must consult the Commission and such other persons as he considers appropriate: s 144(5).

289. Restrictions where public interest considerations not finalised. The Competition Commission[1] must terminate its investigation[2] if:

(1) the intervention notice[3] concerned mentions a public interest consideration[4] which was not finalised on the giving of that notice or public interest considerations which, at that time, were not finalised[5];

(2) no other public interest consideration is mentioned in the notice[6];

(3) at least 24 weeks have elapsed since the giving of the notice[7]; and

(4) the public interest consideration mentioned in the notice has not been finalised within that period of 24 weeks or (as the case may be) none of the public interest considerations mentioned in the notice has been finalised within that period of 24 weeks[8].

Where the intervention notice concerned mentions a public interest consideration which is not finalised on the giving of the notice, the Commission must not give its report to the Secretary of State[9] unless the period of 24 weeks beginning with the giving of the intervention notice concerned has expired or the public interest consideration concerned has been finalised[10].

In reporting on the questions to be decided by it[11], the Commission must disregard:

(a) any public interest consideration which has not been finalised before the giving of the report[12]; and

(b) any public interest consideration which was not finalised on the giving of the intervention notice concerned and has not been finalised within the period of 24 weeks beginning with the giving of the notice concerned[13].

However, these provisions[14] are without prejudice to the power of the Commission to carry out investigations in relation to any public interest consideration to which it might be able to have regard in its report[15].

1 As to the Competition Commission see PARAS 9–12.
2 Ie its investigation under the Enterprise Act 2002 s 142 for the purposes of preparing a report under s 142 (see PARA 286).
     Where the Commission terminates its investigation under s 145(1), it must proceed under ss 134, 136–138 (see PARAS 279–282): s 151(4). Where the Commission is proceeding in this way, the period within which the Commission must prepare and publish its report under s 136

is extended by an additional period of 20 days: s 151(5). In determining this period of 20 days no account is taken of (1) Saturday, Sunday, Good Friday and Christmas Day; and (2) any day which is a bank holiday in England and Wales: s 151(6).

3   As to the meaning of 'intervention notice' see PARA 283 note 2.
4   As to the meaning of 'public interest consideration' see PARA 283 note 11.
5   Enterprise Act 2002 s 145(1)(a). As to public interest considerations being finalised see PARA 283 note 18.
6   Enterprise Act 2002 s 145(1)(b).
7   Enterprise Act 2002 s 145(1)(c).
8   Enterprise Act 2002 s 145(1)(d). As to the requirement to publish information see PARA 311.
9   Ie under the Enterprise Act 2002 s 142 (see PARA 286) in accordance with s 143(3) (see PARA 287).
10 Enterprise Act 2002 s 145(2).
11 Ie the questions mentioned in the Enterprise Act 2002 s 141(3) (see PARA 285 heads (1)–(3)).
12 Enterprise Act 2002 s 145(3).
13 Enterprise Act 2002 s 145(4).
14 Ie the Enterprise Act 2002 s 145(1)–(4) (see the text and notes 1–13).
15 Enterprise Act 2002 s 145(5).

290.   Decision of the Secretary of State.   Where the Secretary of State[1] has received a report of the Competition Commission[2] which:

(1)   has been prepared in relation to an intervention notice[3];
(2)   contains the decisions that there is one or more than one adverse effect on competition[4] and, on the question[5] whether action should be taken by the Commission[6] for the purpose of remedying, mitigating or preventing the adverse effect on competition concerned or any detrimental effect on customers[7] so far as it has resulted from, or may be expected to result from, the adverse effect on competition, and in relation to at least one such adverse effect, that action should be taken by it[8]; and
(3)   has been given to the Secretary of State in the required manner[9],

then he must decide whether any eligible public interest considerations[10] are relevant to any action[11] which the Commission should take for the purpose of remedying, mitigating or preventing any adverse effect on competition concerned or any detrimental effect on customers so far as it has resulted or may be expected to result from any adverse effect on competition[12].

The Secretary of State must make and publish his decision within the period of 90 days beginning with the receipt of the report of the Commission[13].

1   As to the Secretary of State see PARA 5.
2   As to the Competition Commission see PARAS 9–12.
3   Enterprise Act 2002 s 146(1)(a). The text refers to a report which is prepared under s 142 (see PARA 286). As to the meaning of 'intervention notice' see PARA 283 note 2.
4   As to the meaning of 'adverse effect on competition' see PARA 279.
5   Ie the question in the Enterprise Act 2002 s 141(4)(a) (see PARA 285).
6   Ie under the Enterprise Act 2002 s 138 (see PARA 282).
7   As to the meaning of 'detrimental effect on customers' see PARA 279 note 8.
8   Enterprise Act 2002 ss 141(4)(a), 146(1)(b).
9   Enterprise Act 2002 s 146(1)(c). The text refers to the requirements of s 143(3) (see PARA 287).
10 The Enterprise Act 2002 s 146(2) applies both to the situation where there is only one eligible public interest consideration and to the situation where there is more than one eligible public interest consideration. 'Eligible public interest consideration' means a public interest consideration which (1) was mentioned in the intervention notice concerned; and (2) was not disregarded by the Commission for the purposes of its report under the Enterprise Act 2002 s 142: s 146(4). As to the meaning of 'public interest consideration' see PARA 283 note 11.
11 Ie any action which is mentioned in the report by virtue of the Enterprise Act 2002 s 141(4)(a), (c) (see PARA 285).
12 Enterprise Act 2002 s 146(1), (2). As to the requirement to publish information see PARA 311.
13 Enterprise Act 2002 s 146(3).

291. Remedial action by the Secretary of State. Where the Secretary of State has decided[1] that an eligible public interest consideration[2] is relevant[3] and has published his decision within the requisite period[4], then he may, in relation to any adverse effect on competition[5] identified in the report concerned, take such action[6] as he considers to be: (1) reasonable and practicable to remedy, mitigate or prevent the adverse effect on competition concerned, or to remedy, mitigate or prevent any detrimental effect on customers[7] so far as it has resulted from, or may be expected to result from, the adverse effect on competition[8]; and (2) appropriate in the light of the eligible public interest consideration concerned[9].

In making the decision as to what action to take, the Secretary of State must, in particular, have regard to: (a) the need to achieve as comprehensive a solution as is reasonable and practicable to the adverse effect on competition concerned and any detrimental effects on customers so far as resulting from the adverse effect on competition[10]; and (b) the report of the Competition Commission[11]. In having regard to the Commission's report, the Secretary of State must not challenge the decision of the Commission contained in the report that there is one or more than one adverse effect on competition[12]. In making the decision as to what action to take, the Secretary of State may, in particular, have regard to the effect of any action on any relevant customer benefits of the feature or features of the market concerned[13].

The Secretary of State may take no action to remedy, mitigate or prevent any detrimental effect on customers so far as it may be expected to result from the adverse effect on competition concerned if no detrimental effect on customers has resulted from the adverse effect on competition, and the adverse effect on competition is not being remedied, mitigated or prevented[14].

1   Ie under the Enterprise Act 2002 s 146(2) within the period required by s 146(3) (see PARA 290). As to the Secretary of State see PARA 5.
2   The Enterprise Act 2002 s 147 applies both to the situation where there is only one eligible public interest consideration and to the situation where there is more than one eligible public interest consideration. As to the meaning of 'eligible public interest consideration' see PARA 290 note 10; definition applied by s 147(7). As to the meaning of 'public interest consideration' see PARA 283 note 11.
3   Ie as mentioned in the Enterprise Act 2002 s 146(2) (see PARA 290).
4   Enterprise Act 2002 s 147(1). As to the requisite period see s 146(3); and PARA 290.
5   As to the meaning of 'adverse effect on competition' see PARA 279.
6   Ie such action under the Enterprise Act 2002 s 159 (see PARA 301) or s 161 (see PARA 303).
7   As to the meaning of 'detrimental effect on customers' see PARA 279 note 8.
8   Enterprise Act 2002 s 147(2)(a). As to the requirement to publish information see PARA 311.
9   Enterprise Act 2002 s 147(2)(b). See note 2.
10 Enterprise Act 2002 s 147(3)(a).
11 Enterprise Act 2002 s 147(3)(b). The text refers to the report prepared under s 142 (see PARA 286). As to the Competition Commission see PARAS 9–12.
12 Enterprise Act 2002 s 147(4).
13 Enterprise Act 2002 s 147(5). As to the meaning of 'feature of a market' see PARA 276. As to the meaning of 'relevant customer benefit' see PARA 279 note 13.
14 Enterprise Act 2002 s 147(6).

292. Reversion of the matter to the Competition Commission. If the Secretary of State[1] fails, within the requisite period[2], to make and publish his decision[3] as to whether any eligible public interest consideration[4] is relevant or if he decides that no eligible public interest consideration is relevant, then the Competition Commission[5] must proceed[6] to remedy, mitigate or prevent the adverse effect on competition as if the report had been prepared[7] and published[8] in response to the market investigation reference[9].

Where the Commission intends to proceed in a way which is not consistent with its previous decisions as included in its report[10], it must not so proceed without the consent of the Secretary of State[11]. The Secretary of State may not withhold his consent to this unless he believes that the proposed alternative way of proceeding will operate against the public interest[12]. A proposed alternative way of proceeding will operate against the public interest only if any eligible public interest consideration or considerations outweigh the considerations which have led the Commission to propose proceeding in that way[13]. In deciding whether to withhold his consent, the Secretary of State must accept the Commission's view of what (if the only relevant consideration were how to remedy, mitigate or prevent the adverse effect on competition concerned or any detrimental effect on customers so far as resulting from the adverse effect on competition) would be the most appropriate way to proceed[14].

1   As to the Secretary of State see PARA 5.
2   Ie within the period required by the Enterprise Act 2002 s 146(3) (see PARA 290).
3   Ie his decision under the Enterprise Act 2002 s 146(2) (see PARA 290).
4   As to the meaning of 'eligible public interest consideration' see PARA 290 note 10; definition applied by the Enterprise Act 2002 s 148(11).
5   As to the Competition Commission see PARAS 9–12.
6   Ie under the Enterprise Act 2002 s 138 (see PARA 282).
7   Ie prepared under the Enterprise Act 2002 s 136 (see PARA 281).
8   Ie within the period permitted by the Enterprise Act 2002 s 137 (see PARA 281).
9   Enterprise Act 2002 s 148(1). As to the meaning of 'market investigation reference' see PARA 276 note 3.
     The Commission must publish the report which has been prepared by it under s 142 (if still unpublished) (see PARA 286) as soon as it becomes able to proceed by virtue of s 148(1): s 148(2). At the same time as its report is published under s 148(2), the Commission must, in the case of a reference under s 131 (see PARA 276), give a copy of it to the Office of Fair Trading (the 'OFT'), and in the case of a reference under s 132 (see PARA 277), give a copy of it to any Minister of the Crown who made the reference (other than the Secretary of State) and to the OFT: s 148(3). As to the OFT see PARAS 6–8.
     Where a reference has been made by the OFT under s 131 or by the appropriate Minister under s 132 in circumstances in which a reference could have been made by a relevant sectoral regulator under s 131 as it has effect by virtue of a relevant sectoral enactment, the Commission must, at the same time as its report is published under s 148(2), give a copy of it to the relevant sectoral regulator concerned: s 148(4). As to the meaning of 'appropriate Minister' see PARA 277 note 1. As to the meanings of 'relevant sectoral regulator' and 'relevant sectoral enactment' see PARA 281 note 13. Where a reference has been made by a relevant sectoral regulator under s 131 as it has effect by virtue of a relevant sectoral enactment, the Commission must, at the same time as its report is published under s 148(2), give a copy of it to the OFT: s 148(5).
     In relation to proceedings by virtue of s 148(1), the reference in s 138(3) to decisions of the Commission included in its report by virtue of s 134(4) is to be construed as a reference to decisions which were included in the report of the Commission by virtue of s 141(4): s 148(6).
10 Ie by virtue of the Enterprise Act 2002 s 141(4) (see PARA 285).
11 Enterprise Act 2002 s 148(7).
12 Enterprise Act 2002 s 148(8).
13 Enterprise Act 2002 s 148(9).
14 Enterprise Act 2002 s 148(10).

C. INTERVENTION NOTICES GIVEN TO THE OFFICE OF FAIR TRADING

293.   Notices given to the Office of Fair Trading.   An intervention notice given by the Secretary of State to the Office of Fair Trading (the 'OFT')[1] must state:

(1)   the proposed undertaking which may be accepted by the OFT[2];

(2)   the notice of the proposed undertaking[3];

(3)   the public interest consideration or considerations which are, or may be, relevant to the case[4]; and

(4)   where any public interest consideration concerned is not finalised, the proposed timetable for finalising it[5].

Where the Secretary of State believes that it is or may be the case that two or more public interest considerations are relevant to the case, he may decide not to mention in the intervention notice such of those considerations as he considers appropriate[6].

The Secretary of State may at any time revoke an intervention notice which has been given to the OFT and which is in force[7]. An intervention notice comes into force when it is given and ceases to be in force on the occurrence of any of the following events[8]:

(a)   the acceptance by the OFT with the consent of the Secretary of State of an undertaking which is the same as the proposed undertaking mentioned in the intervention notice[9] or which does not differ from it in any material respect[10];

(b)   the decision of the OFT to proceed neither with the proposed undertaking mentioned in the intervention notice[11] nor a proposed undertaking which does not differ from it in any material respect[12]; or

(c)   the decision of the Secretary of State to revoke the intervention notice concerned[13].

1   Ie an intervention notice given under the Enterprise Act 2002 s 139(2) (see PARA 283). As to the meaning of 'intervention notice' see PARA 283 note 2. As to the Secretary of State see PARA 5. As to the OFT see PARAS 6–8. As to the requirement to publish information see PARA 311.

2   Enterprise Act 2002 s 149(1)(a).

3   Enterprise Act 2002 s 149(1)(b). The text refers to the notice under s 155(1) or s 155(4) (see PARA 297).

4   Enterprise Act 2002 s 149(1)(c). As to the meaning of 'public interest consideration' see PARA 283 note 11.

5   Enterprise Act 2002 s 149(1)(d). As to public interest considerations being finalised see PARA 283 note 18.

6   Enterprise Act 2002 s 149(2).

7   Enterprise Act 2002 s 149(3).

8   Enterprise Act 2002 s 149(4).

9   Ie by virtue of the Enterprise Act 2002 s 149(1)(a) (see head (1) in the text).

10   Enterprise Act 2002 s 149(5)(a).

11   See note 9.

12   Enterprise Act 2002 s 149(5)(b).

13   Enterprise Act 2002 s 149(5)(c).

294.   Power of veto of the Secretary of State.   Where an intervention notice has been given by the Secretary of State to the Office of Fair Trading (the 'OFT')[1] and it is in force, the OFT may not, without the consent of the Secretary of State, accept the proposed undertaking concerned or a proposed undertaking which does not differ from it in any material respect[2]. The Secretary of State must withhold his consent if he believes that it is or may be the case that the proposed undertaking will, if accepted, operate against the public interest[3]. A proposed undertaking will, if accepted, operate against the public interest only if any public interest consideration which is mentioned in the intervention notice concerned and has been finalised, or any public interest considerations which are so mentioned and have been finalised, outweigh the considerations which have led the OFT to propose accepting the undertaking[4]. In making his decision as to whether or not to withhold consent, the Secretary of State must accept the OFT's view of what undertakings, if the only relevant consideration were how to remedy, mitigate or prevent the adverse effect on competition[5] concerned or any detrimental effect on customers[6] so far as resulting from the adverse effect on competition, would be most appropriate[7].

Where a public interest consideration which is mentioned in the intervention notice concerned is not finalised on the giving of the notice, the Secretary of State may not make his decision as to whether to give his consent before: (1) the end of the period of 24 weeks beginning with the giving of the intervention notice; or (2) if earlier, the date on which the public interest consideration concerned has been finalised[8].

Subject to the provisions described above[9], the Secretary of State may not withhold his consent to the OFT accepting the undertaking[10].

1 Ie an intervention notice given under the Enterprise Act 2002 s 139(2) (see PARA 283). As to the meaning of 'intervention notice' see PARA 283 note 2. As to the Secretary of State see PARA 5. As to the OFT see PARAS 6–8.
2 Enterprise Act 2002 s 150(1).
3 Enterprise Act 2002 s 150(2).
4 Enterprise Act 2002 s 150(3). As to public interest considerations being finalised see PARA 283 note 18.
5 As to the meaning of 'adverse effect on competition' see PARA 279.
6 As to the meaning of 'detrimental effect on customers' see PARA 279 note 8.
7 Enterprise Act 2002 s 150(4).
8 Enterprise Act 2002 s 150(5).
9 Ie the Enterprise Act 2002 s 150(2)–(5): see the text and notes 3–8.
10 Enterprise Act 2002 s 150(6).

D. NATIONAL SECURITY

295. Duties of the Office of Fair Trading and the Competition Commission in relation to national security. The Office of Fair Trading (the 'OFT')[1] must, in considering whether to make a market investigation reference[2], bring to the attention of the Secretary of State[3] any case which it believes raises any consideration of national security[4] unless it believes that the Secretary of State would consider any such consideration immaterial in the context of the particular case[5].

The Competition Commission[6] must, in investigating any market investigation reference made to it[7] within the previous four months, bring to the attention of the Secretary of State any case which it believes raises any national security consideration[8] unless it believes that the Secretary of State would consider any such consideration immaterial in the context of the particular case[9].

1 As to the OFT see PARAS 6–8.
2 Ie under the Enterprise Act 2002 s 131 (see PARA 276). As to the meaning of 'market investigation reference' see PARA 276 note 3.
3 As to the Secretary of State see PARA 5.
4 Enterprise Act 2002 s 153(1). 'National security' includes public security; and 'public security' has the same meaning as in art 21(4) of EC Council Reg 139/2004 (OJ L24, 29.1.2004, p 1) on the control of concentrations between undertakings (the EC Merger Regulation): Enterprise Act 2002 s 153(2) (amended by SI 2004/1079). The Secretary of State may by order modify the Enterprise Act 2002 s 153 for the purpose of specifying a new consideration or removing or amending any consideration which is for the time being specified: s 153(3). Such an order may apply in relation to cases under consideration by the OFT, by the Secretary of State, by the appropriate Minister (other than the Secretary of State acting alone) or by the Competition Commission before the making of the order as well as cases under consideration on or after the making of the order: s 153(4). The OFT and the Commission must bring to the attention of the Secretary of State any representations about exercising his power under s 153(3) which have been made to the OFT or (as the case may be) the Commission: s 152(3). As to the meaning of 'appropriate Minister' see PARA 277 note 1.
5 Enterprise Act 2002 s 152(1). As to the requirement to publish information see PARA 311.

6   As to the Competition Commission see PARAS 9–12.
7   Ie under the Enterprise Act 2002 s 131 (see PARA 276) or s 132 (see PARA 277).
8   See note 4.
9   Enterprise Act 2002 s 152(2). As to the requirement to publish information see PARA 311.

(iii) Enforcement

A. UNDERTAKINGS AND ORDERS

296. Undertakings in lieu of market investigation references. If the Office of Fair Trading (the 'OFT')[1] considers that it has the power to make a market investigation reference[2] and otherwise intends to make such a reference[3], the OFT may, instead of making such a reference and for the purpose of remedying, mitigating or preventing:

(1)   any adverse effect on competition[4] concerned; or
(2)   any detrimental effect on customers[5] so far as it has resulted from, or may be expected to result from, the adverse effect on competition,

accept, from such persons as it considers appropriate, undertakings to take such action[6] as it considers appropriate[7].

In proceeding under the above provisions[8], the OFT must, in particular, have regard to the need to achieve as comprehensive a solution as is reasonable and practicable to the adverse effect on competition concerned and any detrimental effects on customers so far as resulting from the adverse effect on competition[9]. In so proceeding, the OFT may, in particular, have regard to the effect of any action on any relevant customer benefits[10] of the feature or features of the market[11] concerned[12].

The OFT must take no action under the above provisions[13] to remedy, mitigate or prevent any detrimental effect on customers so far as it may be expected to result from the adverse effect on competition concerned if:

(a)   no detrimental effect on customers has resulted from the adverse effect on competition; and
(b)   the adverse effect on competition is not being remedied, mitigated or prevented[14].

An undertaking under these provisions comes into force when accepted[15]. It may be varied or superseded by another undertaking[16] and may be released by the OFT[17]. The OFT must, as soon as reasonably practicable, consider any representations received by it in relation to varying or releasing such an undertaking[18].

The provisions set out above are subject to the Secretary of State's power to veto the acceptance of an undertaking[19] and also to procedural requirements[20].

1   As to the OFT see PARAS 6–8.
2   Ie a reference under the Enterprise Act 2002 s 131: see PARA 276. As to the meaning of 'market investigation reference' see PARA 276 note 3.
3   Enterprise Act 2002 s 154(1). As to the duty to consult see PARA 309.
4   As to the meaning of 'adverse effect on competition' see PARA 279.
5   As to the meaning of 'detrimental effect on customers' see PARA 279 note 8.
6   As to the meaning of 'action' and 'taking of action' see PARA 184 note 9.
7   Enterprise Act 2002 s 154(2). The provision which may be contained in such an undertaking is not limited to the provision which is permitted by Sch 8 (paras 1–23) (provision that may be contained in certain enforcement orders: see PARA 232 et seq): s 164(1).
8   Ie under the Enterprise Act 2002 s 154(2): see the text and notes 4–7.
9   Enterprise Act 2002 s 154(3).
10   As to the meaning of 'relevant customer benefit' see PARA 279 note 13.
11   As to the meaning of 'feature of a market' see PARA 276.

12 Enterprise Act 2002 s 154(4).
13 See note 8.
14 Enterprise Act 2002 s 154(5).
15 Enterprise Act 2002 s 154(6)(a).
16 Enterprise Act 2002 s 154(6)(b).
17 Enterprise Act 2002 s 154(6)(c). Schedule 10 paras 6–8 (but not Sch 10 para 9) (procedural requirements before terminating undertakings: see PARA 241) apply in relation to the proposed release of undertakings under s 154 (other than in connection with accepting an undertaking under s 154 which varies or supersedes an undertaking under that provision) as they apply in relation to the proposed release of undertakings under s 73 (see PARA 217): s 155(10).
18 Enterprise Act 2002 s 154(7).
19 Ie the Enterprise Act 2002 s 154 is subject to s 150 (see PARA 294): s 154(8). As to the Secretary of State see PARA 5.
20 Ie the Enterprise Act 2002 s 154 is subject to s 155 (see note 17; and PARA 297): s 154(8).

297.   Procedural requirements in relation to undertakings in lieu of market investigation references. Before accepting an undertaking in lieu of a market investigation reference[1], other than an undertaking which varies such an undertaking[2] but not in any material respect, the Office of Fair Trading (the 'OFT')[3] must publish notice of the proposed undertaking[4] and must consider any representations made in accordance with the notice and not withdrawn[5]. Such a notice must state:

(1)   that the OFT proposes to accept the undertaking[6];
(2)   the purpose and effect of the undertaking[7];
(3)   the situation that the undertaking is seeking to deal with[8];
(4)   any other facts which the OFT considers justify the acceptance of the undertaking[9];
(5)   a means of gaining access to an accurate version of the proposed undertaking at all reasonable times[10]; and
(6)   the period[11] within which representations may be made in relation to the proposed undertaking[12].

The matters to be included in such a notice by virtue of heads (1) to (6) above must, in particular, include:

(a)   the terms of the market investigation reference[13] which the OFT considers that it has power to make and which it otherwise intends to make[14]; and
(b)   the adverse effect on competition[15], and any detrimental effect on customers[16] so far as resulting from the adverse effect on competition, which the OFT has identified[17].

The OFT must not accept the undertaking with modifications unless it publishes notice of the proposed modifications[18] and considers any representations made in accordance with the notice and not withdrawn[19]. Such a notice must state:

(i)   the proposed modifications[20];
(ii)   the reasons for them[21]; and
(iii)   the period[22] within which representations may be made in relation to the proposed modifications[23].

If, after publishing notice as described above[24] the OFT decides not to accept the undertaking concerned and not to proceed[25] it must publish notice of that decision[26].

As soon as practicable after accepting an undertaking to which the above provisions apply, the OFT must serve a copy of the undertaking on any person by whom it is given[27] and must publish the undertaking[28].

1 Ie an undertaking under the Enterprise Act 2002 s 154: see PARA 296. As to the meaning of 'market investigation reference' see PARA 276 note 3.
2 As to the variation of undertakings under the Enterprise Act 2002 s 154 see PARA 296 text and note 16.
3 As to the OFT see PARAS 6–8.
4 Enterprise Act 2002 s 155(1)(a). As to the meaning of 'publish' see PARA 186 note 2; and as to the meaning of 'notice' see PARA 314 note 6.
5 Enterprise Act 2002 s 155(1)(b).
6 Enterprise Act 2002 s 155(2)(a).
7 Enterprise Act 2002 s 155(2)(b).
8 Enterprise Act 2002 s 155(2)(c).
9 Enterprise Act 2002 s 155(2)(d).
10 Enterprise Act 2002 s 155(2)(e).
11 The period referred to in head (6) in the text must not be less than 15 days starting with the date of publication of the notice: Enterprise Act 2002 s 155(2)(f).
12 Enterprise Act 2002 s 155(2)(f).
13 Ie the reference under the Enterprise Act 2002 s 131: see PARA 276.
14 Enterprise Act 2002 s 155(3)(a).
15 As to the meaning of 'adverse effect on competition' see PARA 279.
16 As to the meaning of 'detrimental effect on customers' see PARA 279 note 8.
17 Enterprise Act 2002 s 155(3)(b).
18 Enterprise Act 2002 s 155(4)(a). The requirements of s 155(4) (and those of s 155(1)) do not apply if the OFT (1) has already published notice under s 155(1) but not s 155(4) in relation to the proposed undertaking; and (2) considers that the modifications which are now being proposed are not material in any respect: s 155(8). Nor do those requirements apply if the OFT (a) has already published notice under s 155(1) and (4) in relation to the matter concerned; and (b) considers that the further modifications which are now being proposed do not differ in any material respect from the modifications in relation to which notice was last given under s 155(4): s 155(9).
19 Enterprise Act 2002 s 155(4)(b); and see note 18.
20 Enterprise Act 2002 s 155(5)(a).
21 Enterprise Act 2002 s 155(5)(b).
22 The period referred to in head (iii) in the text must be not less than seven days starting with the date of the publication of the notice under the Enterprise Act 2002 s 155(4): s 155(5)(c).
23 Enterprise Act 2002 s 155(5)(c).
24 Ie under the Enterprise Act 2002 s 155(1) (see the text and notes 1–5) or s 155(4) (see the text and notes 18–19).
25 Ie not to proceed by virtue of the Enterprise Act 2002 s 155(8) or (9): see note 18.
26 Enterprise Act 2002 s 155(6).
27 Enterprise Act 2002 s 155(7)(a).
28 Enterprise Act 2002 s 155(7)(b).

298. Effect of undertakings in lieu of market investigation references. No market investigation reference[1] must be made by the Office of Fair Trading (the 'OFT')[2] or the appropriate Minister[3] in relation to any feature, or combination of features, of a market[4] in the United Kingdom[5] for goods or services[6] if:

(1) the OFT has accepted an undertaking or group of undertakings in lieu of a market investigation reference[7] within the previous 12 months[8]; and

(2) the goods[9] or services to which the undertaking or group of undertakings relates are of the same description as the goods or services to which the feature, or combination of features, relates[10].

The above provisions do not, however, prevent the making of a market investigation reference if:

(a) the OFT considers that any undertaking concerned has been breached and has given notice[11] of that fact to the person responsible for giving the undertaking[12]; or

(b) the person responsible for giving any undertaking concerned supplied, in connection with the matter, information to the OFT which was false or misleading in a material respect[13].

1 As to the meaning of 'market investigation reference' see PARA 276 note 3; and as to market investigation references see PARA 276 et seq.
2 As to the OFT see PARAS 6–8.
3 As to the meaning of 'appropriate Minister' see PARA 277 note 1.
4 As to the meaning of 'feature of a market' see PARA 276.
5 As to the meaning of 'United Kingdom' see PARA 401 note 1.
6 As to the meaning of 'market for goods or services' see PARA 276 note 3.
7 Ie an undertaking or group of undertakings under the Enterprise Act 2002 s 154: see PARA 296.
8 Enterprise Act 2002 s 156(1)(a).
9 As to the meaning of 'goods' see PARA 276 note 3.
10 Enterprise Act 2002 s 156(1)(b).
11 As to the meaning of 'notice' see PARA 314 note 6.
12 Enterprise Act 2002 s 156(2)(a).
13 Enterprise Act 2002 s 156(2)(b).

299. Interim undertakings. The relevant authority[1] may, for the purpose of preventing pre-emptive action[2], accept, from such persons as the relevant authority considers appropriate, undertakings to take such action[3] as the relevant authority considers appropriate[4] where:

(1)   a market investigation reference[5] has been made[6];

(2)   a report has been published[7] within the permitted period[8] or, as the case may be, a report prepared[9] and given to the Secretary of State[10] within the permitted period[11] has been published[12]; and

(3)   the market investigation reference concerned is not finally determined[13].

Such an undertaking[14]:

(a)   comes into force when accepted[15];

(b)   may be varied or superseded by another undertaking[16]; and

(c)   may be released by the relevant authority[17];

and the relevant authority must, as soon as reasonably practicable, consider any representations received by the relevant authority in relation to varying or releasing such an undertaking[18].

If it has not previously ceased to be in force, an undertaking under these provisions ceases to be in force when the market investigation reference is finally determined[19].

1 For these purposes and the purposes of the Enterprise Act 2002 s 158 (see PARA 300), the 'relevant authority' means (1) where an intervention notice is in force in relation to the market investigation reference, the Secretary of State; (2) in any other case, the Competition Commission: ss 157(6), 273. As to the meaning of 'intervention notice' see PARA 283 note 2; as to the meaning of 'market investigation reference' see PARA 276 note 3; as to the Secretary of State see PARA 5; and as to the Competition Commission see PARAS 9–12. As to the requirement to publish information see PARA 311.
2 For these purposes and the purposes of the Enterprise Act 2002 s 158 (see PARA 300), 'pre-emptive action' means action which might impede the taking of any action under s 138(2) (see PARA 282) or (as the case may be) s 147(2) (see PARA 291) in relation to the market investigation reference concerned: s 157(6). See also note 3.
3 As to the meaning of 'action' and 'taking of action' see PARA 184 note 9.
4 Enterprise Act 2002 s 157(2).
5 As to market investigation references see PARA 276 et seq.
6 Enterprise Act 2002 s 157(1)(a).
7 Ie under the Enterprise Act 2002 s 136: see PARA 281. As to the meaning of 'publish' see PARA 280 note 7.
8 Ie the period permitted by the Enterprise Act 2002 s 137: see PARA 281.
9 Ie under the Enterprise Act 2002 s 142: see PARA 286.
10 Ie under the Enterprise Act 2002 s 143(3): see PARA 287.

11 Ie the period permitted by the Enterprise Act 2002 s 144: see PARA 288.
12 Enterprise Act 2002 s 157(1)(b).
13 Enterprise Act 2002 s 157(1)(c). As to when a market investigation reference is finally
   determined see s 183(3)–(6); and PARA 276. As to the requirement to publish information see
   PARA 311.
14 Ie an undertaking under the Enterprise Act 2002 s 157. The provision which may be contained
   in such an undertaking is not limited to the provision which is permitted by Sch 8 (paras 1–23)
   (provision that may be contained in certain enforcement orders: see PARA 232 et seq): s 164(1).
15 Enterprise Act 2002 s 157(3)(a).
16 Enterprise Act 2002 s 157(3)(b).
17 Enterprise Act 2002 s 157(3)(c).
18 Enterprise Act 2002 s 157(5).
19 Enterprise Act 2002 s 157(4).

300. Interim orders. The following provisions[1] apply where:
   (1) a market investigation reference[2] has been made[3];
   (2) a report has been published[4] within the permitted period[5] or, as the case
       may be, a report prepared[6] and given to the Secretary of State[7] within
       the permitted period[8] has been published[9]; and
   (3) the market investigation reference concerned is not finally determined[10].
The relevant authority[11] may by order[12], for the purpose of preventing
pre-emptive action[13]:
   (a) prohibit or restrict the doing of things which the relevant authority
       considers would constitute pre-emptive action[14];
   (b) impose on any person concerned obligations as to the carrying on of any
       activities or the safeguarding of any assets[15];
   (c) provide for the carrying on of any activities or the safeguarding of any
       assets either by the appointment of a person to conduct or supervise the
       conduct of any activities (on such terms and with such powers as may
       be specified or described in the order) or in any other manner[16];
   (d) do anything which may be done by virtue of the specified[17] statutory
       provision[18].
Such an order[19]:
   (i) comes into force at such time as is determined by or under the order[20];
       and
   (ii) may be varied or revoked by another order[21];
and the relevant authority must, as soon as reasonably practicable, consider any
representations received by the relevant authority in relation to varying or
revoking such an order[22].
   If it has not previously ceased to be in force, an order under these provisions
ceases to be in force when the market investigation reference is finally
determined[23].

1 Ie the Enterprise Act 2002 s 158(2): see the text and notes 11–18.
2 As to the meaning of 'market investigation reference' see PARA 276 note 3
3 Enterprise Act 2002 s 158(1)(a). As to the making of market investigation references see PARA
   276 et seq.
4 Ie under the Enterprise Act 2002 s 136: see PARA 281. As to the meaning of 'publish' see PARA
   280 note 7. As to the requirement to publish information see PARA 311.
5 Ie the period permitted by the Enterprise Act 2002 s 137: see PARA 281.
6 Ie under the Enterprise Act 2002 s 142: see PARA 286.
7 Ie under the Enterprise Act 2002 s 143(3): see PARA 287. As to the Secretary of State see PARA 5.
8 Ie the period permitted by the Enterprise Act 2002 s 144: see PARA 288.
9 Enterprise Act 2002 s 158(1)(b).
10 Enterprise Act 2002 s 158(1)(c). As to when a market investigation reference is finally
   determined see s 183(3)–(6); and PARA 276.
11 As to the meaning of 'relevant authority' see PARA 299 note 1.

12 If the order is made by the Secretary of State, it is subject to annulment in pursuance of a resolution of either House of Parliament: s 181(4). As to the making of orders under Pt 4 (ss 131–184) see further PARA 318.

13 As to the meaning of 'pre-emptive action' see PARA 299 note 2.

14 Enterprise Act 2002 s 158(2)(a).

15 Enterprise Act 2002 s 158(2)(b).

16 Enterprise Act 2002 s 158(2)(c).

17 Ie by virtue of the Enterprise Act 2002 Sch 8 para 19. An order may (1) require any person to supply information to the relevant authority; (2) where the Office of Fair Trading (the 'OFT') is not the relevant authority, require any person to supply information to the OFT; (3) provide for the publication, by the person who has received information by virtue of head (1) or head (2) above, of that information: Sch 8 para 19. As to the OFT see PARAS 6–8.

18 Enterprise Act 2002 s 158(2)(d); and see note 17.

19 Ie an order under the Enterprise Act 2002 s 158. The following enactments in Pt 3 (ss 22–130) (see PARA 172 et seq) apply in relation to orders under s 158 as they apply in relation to enforcement orders under Pt 3: (1) s 86(1)–(5) (enforcement orders; general provisions: see PARA 232); and (2) s 87 (power of directions conferred by enforcement order: see PARA 240): see s 164(2).

20 Enterprise Act 2002 s 158(3)(a).

21 Enterprise Act 2002 s 158(3)(b).

22 Enterprise Act 2002 s 158(5).

23 Enterprise Act 2002 s 158(4). As to when a market investigation reference is finally determined see s 183(3)–(6); and PARA 276.

301. Final undertakings. The Competition Commission[1] may, in accordance with its duty to remedy adverse effects on competition[2], accept, from such persons as it considers appropriate, undertakings to take action[3] specified or described in the undertakings[4]. Such an undertaking may be varied or superseded by another such undertaking[5].

The Secretary of State[6] may, in accordance with his power to take remedial action[7], accept, from such persons as he considers appropriate, undertakings to take action specified or described in the undertakings[8]; and such an undertaking may also be varied or superseded by another such undertaking[9].

An undertaking under the above provisions comes into force when accepted[10].

An undertaking accepted by the Commission[11] may be released by the Commission and an undertaking accepted by the Secretary of State[12] may be released by the Secretary of State[13]. The Commission or, as the case may be, the Secretary of State must, as soon as reasonably practicable, consider any representations received by it or by him in relation to varying or releasing such an undertaking[14].

1 As to the Competition Commission see PARAS 9–12.

2 Ie in accordance with the Enterprise Act 2002 s 138: see PARA 282.

3 As to the meaning of 'action' and 'taking action' see PARA 276 note 7.

4 Enterprise Act 2002 s 159(1). As to the requirement to publish information see PARA 311.

5 Enterprise Act 2002 s 159(4).

6 As to the Secretary of State see PARA 5.

7 Ie in accordance with the Enterprise Act 2002 s 147: see PARA 291.

8 Enterprise Act 2002 s 159(2).

9 Enterprise Act 2002 s 159(4). As to the requirement to publish information see PARA 311.

10 Enterprise Act 2002 s 159(3). The provision which may be contained in such an undertaking is not limited to the provision which is permitted by Sch 8 (paras 1–23) (provision that may be contained in certain enforcement orders: see PARA 232 et seq): s 164(1). Schedule 10 (procedural requirements for certain undertakings and orders: see PARA 241), other than Sch 10 para 9, applies in relation to undertakings under s 159 as it applies in relation to undertakings under s 82 (see PARA 225): s 165.

11 Ie an undertaking under the Enterprise Act 2002 s 159(1): see the text and notes 1–4.

12 Ie an undertaking under the Enterprise Act 2002 s 159(2): see the text and notes 6–8.

13 Enterprise Act 2002 s 159(5).
14 Enterprise Act 2002 s 159(6).

302.   Order-making power where final undertakings not fulfilled. The relevant authority[1] may, for any of the statutory purposes[2], make an order[3] under the following provisions[4] where that authority considers that:

(1)   a final undertaking accepted by the relevant authority[5] has not been, is not being or will not be fulfilled[6]; or

(2)   in relation to such an undertaking accepted by the relevant authority, information which was false or misleading in a material respect was given to the relevant authority or to the Office of Fair Trading (the 'OFT')[7] by the person giving the undertaking before the relevant authority decided to accept the undertaking[8].

Such an order may contain anything permitted by Schedule 8 to the Enterprise Act 2002[9] and such supplementary, consequential or incidental provision as the relevant authority considers appropriate[10]. The order, or any explanatory material accompanying the order, must state:

(a)   the actions[11] that the persons or description of persons to whom the order is addressed must do or, as the case may be, refrain from doing[12];

(b)   the date on which the order comes into force[13];

(c)   the possible consequences of not complying with the order[14]; and

(d)   the provision of Part 4 of the Enterprise Act 2002[15] under which a review can be sought in relation to the order[16].

Such an order:

(i)   comes into force at such time as is determined by or under the order[17];

(ii)   may contain provision which is different from the provision contained in the undertaking concerned[18]; and

(iii)   may be varied or revoked by another order[19];

but no order must be varied or revoked under these provisions unless the Office of Fair Trading (the 'OFT')[20] advises that such a variation or revocation is appropriate by reason of a change of circumstances[21].

1   For these purposes, 'relevant authority' means (1) in the case of an undertaking accepted under the Enterprise Act 2002 s 159 (see PARA 301) by the Competition Commission, the Commission; and (2) in the case of an undertaking accepted under s 159 by the Secretary of State, the Secretary of State: s 160(7). As to the Commission see PARAS 9–12; and as to the Secretary of State see PARA 5.

2   Ie for any of the purposes mentioned in the Enterprise Act 2002 s 138(2) (see PARA 282) or (as the case may be) s 147(2) (see PARA 291): s 160(2).

3   If the order is made by the Secretary of State, it is subject to annulment in pursuance of a resolution of either House of Parliament: s 181(4). As to the making of orders under Pt 4 (ss 131–184) see further PARA 318.

4   Enterprise Act 2002 s 160(2). Section 138(3)–(6) (see PARA 282) or (as the case may be) s 147(3)–(6) (see PARA 291) applies for the purposes of s 160(2) above as it applies for the purposes of s 138 or s 147: s 160(3).

5   Ie an undertaking accepted under the Enterprise Act 2002 s 159: see PARA 301.

6   See the Enterprise Act 2002 s 160(1)(a).

7   As to the OFT see PARAS 6–8.

8   Enterprise Act 2002 s 160(1)(b).

9   Ie anything permitted by the Enterprise Act 2002 Sch 8 (paras 1–23) (provision that may be contained in certain enforcement orders): see PARA 232 et seq.

10 Enterprise Act 2002 s 160(4). The following enactments in Pt 3 (ss 22–130) (see PARA 172 et seq) apply in relation to orders under s 160 as they apply in relation to enforcement orders under Pt 3: (1) s 86(1)–(5) (enforcement orders; general provisions: see PARA 232); and (2) s 87 (power of directions conferred by enforcement order: see PARA 240): see s 164(2).

Schedule 10 (procedural requirements for certain undertakings and orders: see PARA 241), other than Sch 10 para 9, applies in relation to orders under s 160 as it applies in relation to orders under s 83 (see PARA 225) or s 84 (see PARA 226): s 165.

11 As to the meanings of 'action' and 'taking action' see PARA 276 note 7.
12 Enterprise Act 2002 s 164(3)(a).
13 Enterprise Act 2002 s 164(3)(b).
14 Enterprise Act 2002 s 164(3)(c).
15 Ie the provision of the Enterprise Act 2002 Pt 4 (ss 131–184): see PARAS 276 et seq, 303 et seq.
16 Enterprise Act 2002 s 164(3)(d). As to the review of decisions under Pt 4 see s 179; and PARA 316.
17 Enterprise Act 2002 s 160(5)(a).
18 Enterprise Act 2002 s 160(5)(b).
19 Enterprise Act 2002 s 160(5)(c).
20 As to the OFT see PARAS 6–8.
21 Enterprise Act 2002 s 160(6).

303. Final orders. The Competition Commission[1] may, in accordance with its duty to remedy adverse effects on competition[2], make an order under these provisions[3]. The Secretary of State[4] may also, in accordance with his power to take remedial action[5], make an order[6] under these provisions[7].

Such an order may contain anything permitted by Schedule 8 to the Enterprise Act 2002[8] and such supplementary, consequential or incidental provision as the person making it considers appropriate[9]. The order, or any explanatory material accompanying the order, must state:

(1)   the actions[10] that the persons or description of persons to whom the order is addressed must do or, as the case may be, refrain from doing[11];
(2)   the date on which the order comes into force[12];
(3)   the possible consequences of not complying with the order[13]; and
(4)   the provision of Part 4 of the Enterprise Act 2002[14] under which a review can be sought in relation to the order[15].

Such an order comes into force at such time as is determined by or under the order[16] and may be varied or revoked by another order[17]; but no order must be varied or revoked under these provisions unless the Office of Fair Trading (the 'OFT')[18] advises that such a variation or revocation is appropriate by reason of a change of circumstances[19].

1 As to the Competition Commission see PARAS 9–12.
2 Ie in accordance with the Enterprise Act 2002 s 138: see PARA 282.
3 Enterprise Act 2002 s 161(1). As to the requirement to publish information see PARA 311.
4 As to the Secretary of State see PARA 5.
5 Ie in accordance with the Enterprise Act 2002 s 147: see PARA 291.
6 If the order is made by the Secretary of State, it is subject to annulment in pursuance of a resolution of either House of Parliament: s 181(4). As to the making of orders under Pt 4 (ss 131–184) see further PARA 318.
7 Enterprise Act 2002 s 161(2). As to the requirement to publish information see PARA 311.
8 Ie anything permitted by the Enterprise Act 2002 Sch 8 (paras 1–23) (provision that may be contained in certain enforcement orders): see PARA 232 et seq.
9 Enterprise Act 2002 s 161(3). The following enactments in Pt 3 (ss 22–130) (see PARA 172 et seq) apply in relation to orders under s 161 as they apply in relation to enforcement orders under Pt 3: (1) s 86(1)–(5) (enforcement orders; general provisions: see PARA 232); and (2) s 87 (power of directions conferred by enforcement order: see PARA 240): see s 164(2).
        Schedule 10 (procedural requirements for certain undertakings and orders: see PARA 241), other than Sch 10 para 9, applies in relation to orders under s 161 as it applies in relation to orders under s 83 (see PARA 225) or s 84 (see PARA 226): s 165.
10 As to the meanings of 'action' and 'taking action' see PARA 276 note 7.
11 Enterprise Act 2002 s 164(3)(a).
12 Enterprise Act 2002 s 164(3)(b).
13 Enterprise Act 2002 s 164(3)(c).
14 Ie the provision of the Enterprise Act 2002 Pt 4 (ss 131–184): see PARAS 276 et seq, 304 et seq.

15 Enterprise Act 2002 s 164(3)(d). As to the review of decisions under Pt 4 see s 179; and PARA
     316.
16 Enterprise Act 2002 s 161(4)(a).
17 Enterprise Act 2002 s 161(4)(b).
18 As to the OFT see PARAS 6–8.
19 Enterprise Act 2002 s 161(5).

B. ENFORCEMENT FUNCTIONS OF THE OFFICE OF FAIR TRADING

304.   Duty of the Office of Fair Trading to monitor enforcement undertakings and orders. The Office of Fair Trading (the 'OFT')[1] must keep under review the carrying out of any enforcement undertaking[2] or any enforcement order[3]. The OFT must, in particular, from time to time consider:

(1)   whether an enforcement undertaking or enforcement order has been or is being complied with[4];

(2)   whether, by reason of any change of circumstances, an enforcement undertaking is no longer appropriate and either one or more of the parties to it can be released from it or it needs to be varied or to be superseded by a new enforcement undertaking[5]; and

(3)   whether, by reason of any change of circumstances, an enforcement order is no longer appropriate and needs to be varied or revoked[6].

The OFT must give the Competition Commission[7] or, as the case may be, the Secretary of State[8] such advice as it considers appropriate in relation to:

(a)   any possible variation or release by the Commission or by the Secretary of State of an enforcement undertaking accepted by it or by him[9];

(b)   any possible new enforcement undertaking to be accepted by the Commission or by the Secretary of State so as to supersede another enforcement undertaking given to the Commission or to the Secretary of State[10];

(c)   any possible variation or revocation by the Commission or by the Secretary of State of an enforcement order made by the Commission or by the Secretary of State[11];

(d)   any possible enforcement undertaking to be accepted by the Commission or by the Secretary of State instead of an enforcement order or any possible enforcement order to be made by the Commission or by the Secretary of State instead of an enforcement undertaking[12]; or

(e)   the enforcement[13] of any enforcement undertaking or enforcement order[14].

The OFT must take such action[15] as it considers appropriate in relation to:

(i)   any possible variation or release by it of an undertaking in lieu of a market investigation reference accepted[16] by it[17];

(ii)   any possible new undertaking such as is mentioned in head (i) above to be accepted by it[18] so as to supersede another such undertaking given[19] to it[20];

(iii) the enforcement by it[21] of any enforcement undertaking or enforcement order[22].

The OFT must keep under review the effectiveness of enforcement undertakings accepted under Part 4 of the Enterprise Act 2002[23] and enforcement orders made under that Part[24]; and it must, whenever requested to do so by the Secretary of State and otherwise from time to time, prepare a report of its findings[25]. The OFT must give any report so prepared by it to the Commission[26]. It must also give a copy of the report to the Secretary of State[27] and must publish the report[28].

1 As to the OFT see PARAS 6–8.
2 In the Enterprise Act 2002 Pt 4 (ss 131–184) (see PARA 276 et seq; the text and notes 3–28; and PARA 305 et seq), 'enforcement undertaking' means an undertaking accepted under s 154 (see PARA 296), s 157 (see PARA 299) or s 159 (see PARA 301): s 162(8).
3 Enterprise Act 2002 s 162(1). In Pt 4, 'enforcement order' means an order made under s 158 (see PARA 300), s 160 (see PARA 302) or s 161 (see PARA 303): s 162(8).
4 Enterprise Act 2002 s 162(2)(a).
5 Enterprise Act 2002 s 162(2)(b).
6 Enterprise Act 2002 s 162(2)(c).
7 As to the Competition Commission see PARAS 9–12.
8 As to the Secretary of State see PARA 5.
9 Enterprise Act 2002 s 162(3)(a).
10 Enterprise Act 2002 s 162(3)(b).
11 Enterprise Act 2002 s 162(3)(c).
12 Enterprise Act 2002 s 162(3)(d).
13 Ie by virtue of the Enterprise Act 2002 s 167(6)–(8): see PARA 307.
14 Enterprise Act 2002 s 162(3)(e).
15 As to the meanings of 'action' and 'taking action' see PARA 276 note 7.
16 Ie an undertaking accepted by it under the Enterprise Act 2002 s 154: see PARA 296.
17 See the Enterprise Act 2002 s 162(4)(a).
18 Ie under the Enterprise Act 2002 s 154: see PARA 296.
19 See note 18.
20 See the Enterprise Act 2002 s 162(4)(b).
21 Ie by virtue of the Enterprise Act 2002 s 167(6): see PARA 307.
22 Enterprise Act 2002 s 162(4)(c).
23 Ie under the Enterprise Act 2002 Pt 4: see PARA 276 et seq; the text and notes 1–22; and PARA 305 et seq.
24 Enterprise Act 2002 s 162(5).
25 Enterprise Act 2002 s 162(6).
26 Enterprise Act 2002 s 162(7)(a).
27 Enterprise Act 2002 s 162(7)(b).
28 Enterprise Act 2002 s 162(7)(c). As to the meaning of 'publish' see PARA 280 note 7.

305. Further role of the Office of Fair Trading in relation to undertakings and orders. Where the Competition Commission[1] or the Secretary of State[2] (the 'relevant authority') is considering whether to accept interim[3] or final[4] undertakings, as the case may be[5], the relevant authority may:

(1) require the Office of Fair Trading (the 'OFT')[6] to consult with such persons as the relevant authority considers appropriate with a view to discovering whether they will offer undertakings which the relevant authority would be prepared[7] to accept[8];

(2) require the OFT to report to the relevant authority on the outcome of the OFT's consultations within such period as the relevant authority may require[9].

A report under head (2) above must, in particular, contain advice from the OFT as to whether any undertakings offered should be accepted[10] by the relevant authority[11].

The powers conferred on the relevant authority by the above provisions are without prejudice to the power of the relevant authority to consult the persons concerned itself[12].

If asked by the relevant authority for advice in relation to the taking of enforcement action[13], whether or not by way of undertakings, in a particular case, the OFT must give such advice as it considers appropriate[14].

1 As to the Competition Commission see PARAS 9–12.
2 As to the Secretary of State see PARA 5.
3 Ie undertakings under the Enterprise Act 2002 s 157: see PARA 299.
4 Ie undertakings under the Enterprise Act 2002 s 159: see PARA 301.

5 See the Enterprise Act 2002 s 163(1).
6 As to the OFT see PARAS 6–8.
7 Ie prepared to accept under the Enterprise Act 2002 s 157 or, as the case may be, s 159.
8 Enterprise Act 2002 s 163(2).
9 Enterprise Act 2002 s 163(3).
10 Ie under the Enterprise Act 2002 s 157 or, as the case may be, s 159.
11 Enterprise Act 2002 s 163(4).
12 Enterprise Act 2002 s 163(5).
13 As to the meanings of 'action' and 'taking action' see PARA 276 note 7.
14 Enterprise Act 2002 s 163(6).

C. GENERAL PROVISIONS

306. Register of enforcement undertakings and orders. The Office of Fair Trading (the 'OFT')[1] must compile and maintain a register for the purposes of Part 4[2] of the Enterprise Act 2002[3]. The register must be kept in such form as the OFT considers appropriate[4].

The OFT must ensure that the following matters are entered in the register:

(1) the provisions of any enforcement undertaking[5] accepted by virtue of Part 4 of the 2002 Act, whether by the OFT, the Competition Commission[6], the Secretary of State[7] or a relevant sectoral regulator[8];

(2) the provisions of any enforcement order[9] made by virtue of that Part, whether by the Commission, the Secretary of State or a relevant sectoral regulator[10]; and

(3) the details of any variation, release or revocation of such an undertaking or order[11];

but that duty does not extend to anything of which the OFT is unaware[12].

The Commission, the Secretary of State and any relevant sectoral regulator must inform the OFT of any matters which are to be included in the register by virtue of heads (1) to (3) above and which relate to enforcement undertakings accepted by them or enforcement orders made by them[13].

The OFT must ensure that the contents of the register are available to the public:

(a) during, as a minimum, such hours as may be specified in an order made by the Secretary of State[14]; and

(b) subject to such reasonable fees, if any, as the OFT may determine[15].

If requested by any person to do so and subject to such reasonable fees, if any, as the OFT may determine, the OFT must supply the person concerned with a copy, certified to be true, of the register or of an extract from it[16].

1 As to the OFT see PARAS 6–8.
2 Ie the Enterprise Act 2002 Pt 4 (ss 131–184): see PARA 276 et seq; the text and notes 3–16; and PARA 307 et seq.
3 Enterprise Act 2002 s 166(1).
4 Enterprise Act 2002 s 166(2).
5 As to the meaning of 'enforcement undertaking' see PARA 304 note 2.
6 As to the Competition Commission see PARAS 9–12.
7 As to the Secretary of State see PARA 5.
8 Enterprise Act 2002 s 166(3)(a). As to the meaning of 'relevant sectoral regulator' see PARA 281 note 13.
9 As to the meaning of 'enforcement order' see PARA 304 note 3.
10 Enterprise Act 2002 s 166(3)(b).
11 Enterprise Act 2002 s 166(3)(c).
12 Enterprise Act 2002 s 166(4).
13 Enterprise Act 2002 s 166(5).
14 Enterprise Act 2002 s 166(6)(a). The OFT must ensure that the contents of the register are available to the public (as a minimum) between the hours of 10.00 am and 4.00 pm on any

working day: OFT Registers of Undertakings and Orders (Available Hours) Order 2003, SI 2003/1373, art 3. 'Working day' means any day which is not Saturday, Sunday, Good Friday, Christmas Day, a bank holiday in England and Wales or any other day on which the office of the OFT at which the register is available to the public is closed for business: art 2. As to the making of orders by the Secretary of State under the Enterprise Act 2002 Pt 4 see s 181; and PARA 318.

15　Enterprise Act 2002 s 166(6)(b).
16　Enterprise Act 2002 s 166(7).

307.　Rights to enforce enforcement undertakings and orders.　The following provisions apply to any enforcement undertaking[1] or enforcement order[2].

Any person to whom such an undertaking or order relates has a duty to comply with it[3]. The duty is owed to any person who may be affected by a contravention of the undertaking or, as the case may be, of the order[4]; and any breach of the duty which causes such a person to sustain loss or damage is actionable by him[5]. In any proceedings brought under the above provision[6] against a person to whom an enforcement undertaking or enforcement order relates it is, however, a defence for that person to show that he took all reasonable steps and exercised all due diligence to avoid contravening the undertaking or, as the case may be, the order[7].

Compliance with an enforcement undertaking or an enforcement order is also enforceable by civil proceedings brought by the Office of Fair Trading (the 'OFT')[8] for an injunction or for any other appropriate relief or remedy[9]. Compliance with an interim[10] or final undertaking[11] accepted[12], or with an enforcement order[13], is also enforceable by civil proceedings brought by the relevant authority[14] for an injunction or for any other appropriate relief or remedy[15]. These provisions[16] do not, however, prejudice any right that a person may have[17] to bring civil proceedings for contravention or apprehended contravention of an enforcement undertaking or an enforcement order[18].

1　As to the meaning of 'enforcement undertaking' see PARA 304 note 2.
2　Enterprise Act 2002 s 167(1). As to the meaning of 'enforcement order' see PARA 304 note 3.
3　Enterprise Act 2002 s 167(2).
4　Enterprise Act 2002 s 167(3).
5　Enterprise Act 2002 s 167(4).
6　Ie under the Enterprise Act 2002 s 167(4); see the text and note 5.
7　Enterprise Act 2002 s 167(5).
8　As to the OFT see PARAS 6–8.
9　Enterprise Act 2002 s 167(6).
10　Ie an undertaking accepted under the Enterprise Act 2002 s 157: see PARA 299.
11　Ie an undertaking accepted under the Enterprise Act 2002 s 159: see PARA 301.
12　See notes 10–11.
13　Ie an order under the Enterprise Act 2002 s 158 (see PARA 300), s 160 (see PARA 302) or s 161 (see PARA 303): s 167(7).
14　For these purposes, 'relevant authority' means (1) in the case of an undertaking accepted by the Competition Commission or an order made by the Commission, the Commission; and (2) in the case of an undertaking accepted by the Secretary of State or an order made by the Secretary of State, the Secretary of State: Enterprise Act 2002 s 167(8). As to the Competition Commission see PARAS 9–12; and as to the Secretary of State see PARA 5.
15　Enterprise Act 2002 s 167(7).
16　Ie the Enterprise Act 2002 s 167(6)–(8): see the text and notes 8–15.
17　Ie by virtue of the Enterprise Act 2002 s 167(4): see the text and note 5.
18　Enterprise Act 2002 s 167(9).

(iv)　Regulated Markets

308.　Regulated markets.　Where the Competition Commission[1] or the Secretary of State[2] is considering for the purposes of market investigations[3] whether relevant action would be reasonable and practicable for the purpose of remedying, mitigating or preventing an adverse effect on competition[4] or any detrimental effect on customers[5] so far as resulting from such an effect[6], then the Commission or (as the case may be) the Secretary of State, in deciding whether such action would be reasonable and practicable, must have regard to the relevant statutory functions[7] of the sectoral regulator[8] concerned[9].

A relevant action is:

(1) modifying conditions in force under Part 4 of the Airports Act 1986[10];

(2) modifying the conditions of a licence granted under the Gas Act 1986[11];

(3) modifying the conditions of a licence granted under the Electricity Act 1989[12];

(4) modifying networking arrangements[13];

(5) modifying the conditions of a company's appointment under the Water Industry Act 1991[14];

(6) modifying the conditions of a licence granted under the Water Industry Act 1991[15] or modifying the terms and conditions of an agreement under that Act[16];

(7) modifying the conditions of a licence or infrastructure agreement granted in Northern Ireland[17];

(8) modifying the conditions of a licence granted under the Railways Act 1993[18];

(9) modifying an access agreement or a franchise agreement under the Railways Act 1993[19];

(10) modifying conditions in force in relation to airports in Northern Ireland[20];

(11) modifying the conditions of a gas licence granted in Northern Ireland[21];

(12) modifying the conditions of a licence granted under the Postal Services Act 2000[22];

(13) modifying the conditions of a licence granted in respect of air traffic services under the Transport Act 2000[23];

(14) modifying the conditions of a company's appointment[24] in relation to water and sewerage services in Northern Ireland[25].

Provision has been made for functions under the Enterprise Act 2002 Part 4 to be exercisable by various sectoral regulators[26].

1   As to the Competition Commission see PARAS 9–12.
2   As to the Secretary of State see PARA 5.
3   Ie for the purposes of the Enterprise Act 2002 Pt 4 (ss 131–184) (see PARA 276 et seq).
4   As to the meaning of 'adverse effect on competition' see PARA 279.
5   As to the meaning of 'detrimental effect on customers' see PARA 279 note 8.
6   Enterprise Act 2002 s 168(1).
7   'Relevant statutory functions' means: (1) in relation to conditions in force under the Airports Act 1986 Pt 4 other than any conditions imposed or modified in pursuance of s 40(3) or (4), the duties of the Civil Aviation Authority under s 39(2), (3) (see AIR LAW vol 2 (2008) PARA 230); (2) in relation to any licence granted under the Gas Act 1986 ss 7, 7A, the objectives and duties of the Gas and Electricity Markets Authority under ss 4AA, 4AB(2) (see FUEL AND ENERGY vol 19(2) (2007 Reissue) PARA 789); (3) in relation to any licence granted under the Electricity Act 1989 s 6, the objectives and duties of the Gas and Electricity Markets Authority under ss 3A, 3B(2) (see FUEL AND ENERGY vol 19(2) (2007 Reissue) PARA 1041); (4) in relation to any networking arrangements (within the meaning given by the Communications Act 2003 s 290), the duty of the Office of Communications under s 3(1) to secure the matters mentioned in s 3(2)(c) (see TELECOMMUNICATIONS AND BROADCASTING vol 45(1) (2005 Reissue) PARA 16); (5) in relation to a company's appointment under the Water Industry Act 1991 Pt 2 Ch 1, the duties of the Water Services Regulation Authority under s 2 (see WATER AND WATERWAYS vol 100 (2009) PARA 130); (6) in relation to a licence granted under the Water Industry Act 1991

Pt 2 Ch 1A or an agreement under s 66D, the duties of the Authority under s 2 or under s 2 and s 66D (as the case may be) (see WATER AND WATERWAYS vol 100 (2009) PARAS 130, 341); (7) in relation to any licence granted under the Electricity (Northern Ireland) Order 1992, SI 1992/231 (NI 1), art 10, the duty of the Director General of Electricity Supply for Northern Ireland under art 6; (8) in relation to any licence granted under the Railways Act 1993 s 8, or access agreement within the meaning of s 83(1) the duties of the Office of Rail Regulation under s 4 (see RAILWAYS, INLAND WATERWAYS AND CROSS-COUNTRY PIPELINES vol 39(1A) (Reissue) PARA 33); (9) in relation to a SNRP issued pursuant to the Railways Infrastructure (Access, Management and Licensing of Railway Undertakings) Regulations (Northern Ireland) 2005, SR 2005/537, where none of the conditions of the SNRP relate to consumer protection, the duties of the Department for Regional Development under reg 36; (10) in relation to any franchise agreement (within the meaning given by the Railways Act 1993 s 23(3)), the duties of the Secretary of State, the Scottish Ministers and the National Assembly for Wales under s 4 (see RAILWAYS, INLAND WATERWAYS AND CROSS-COUNTRY PIPELINES vol 39(1A) (Reissue) PARA 33); (11) in relation to conditions in force under the Airports (Northern Ireland) Order 1994, SI 1994/426 (NI 1), Pt 4 other than any conditions imposed or modified in pursuance of art 40(3) or (4), the duties of the Civil Aviation Authority under art 30(2), (3); (12) in relation to any licence granted under the Gas (Northern Ireland) Order 1996, SI 1996/275 (NI 2), art 8, the duties of the Director General of Gas for Northern Ireland under art 5; (13) in relation to any licence granted under the Postal Services Act 2000 s 11, the duties of the Postal Services Commission under ss 3, 5 (see POST OFFICE vol 36(2) (Reissue) PARA 24); (14) in relation to any licence granted under the Transport Act 2000 s 5, the duties of the Civil Aviation Authority under s 87 (see AIR LAW vol 2 (2008) PARA 172); and (15) in relation to a company's appointment under the Water and Sewerage Services (Northern Ireland) Order 2006, SI 2006/3336, Pt III Ch I, the duties of the Northern Ireland Authority for Utility Regulation under art 6: Enterprise Act 2002 s 168(4) (amended by the Communications Act 2003 s 406(1), (7), Sch 17 para 174(1), (5), Sch 19(1), the Water Act 2003 s 101(1), Sch 7 para 36(1), (3)(a), Sch 8 para 55(1), (2)(b), the Railways and Transport Safety Act 2003 s 16(5), Sch 2 para 19(u), the Railways Act 2005 s 59(1), (6), Sch 12 para 18(1), (2), Sch 13 Pt 1, the Railways Infrastructure (Access, Management and Licensing of Railway Undertakings) Regulations (Northern Ireland) 2005, SR 2005/537, reg 1(1) and the Water and Sewerage Services (Northern Ireland) Order 2006, SI 2006/3336 (NI 21), art 308(1), Sch 12 para 46(4)).

The Secretary of State may by order modify the Enterprise Act 2002 s 168(3), (4), (5), (6) or (7): s 168(8). At the date at which this volume states the law no such order had been made.

8 For this purpose, 'sectoral regulator' means the Civil Aviation Authority, the Northern Ireland Authority for Utility Regulation, the Water Services Regulation Authority, the Gas and Electricity Markets Authority, the Office of Communications, the Postal Services Commission, the Office of Rail Regulation, the Secretary of State, the Scottish Ministers or the National Assembly for Wales: Enterprise Act 2002 s 168(5) (amended by the Communications Act 2003 s 406(1), (7), Sch 17 para 174(1), (5)(c), Sch 19(1), the Water Act 2003 s 101(1), Sch 7 Pt 2 para 36(1), (3)(b), the Railways and Transport Safety Act 2003 s 16(5), Sch 2 Pt 2 para 19(u), the Railways Act 2005 s 59(1), (6), Sch 12 paras 18(1), (3), Sch 13 Pt 1, SI 2006/3336). See note 7. As to the sectoral regulators see PARA 18 et seq.

9 Enterprise Act 2002 s 168(2). Where the Commission or the Secretary of State is considering for the purposes of the Enterprise Act 2002 whether modifying the conditions of a licence granted under the Gas Act 1986 s 7 or s 7A (see FUEL AND ENERGY vol 19(2) (2007 Reissue) PARAS 805, 806) or the Electricity Act 1989 s 6 (see FUEL AND ENERGY vol 19(2) (2007 Reissue) PARA 1065) would be reasonable and practicable for the purpose of remedying, mitigating or preventing an adverse effect on competition or any detrimental effect on customers so far as resulting from such an effect, then the Commission or (as the case may be) the Secretary of State may, in deciding whether modifying the conditions of such a licence would be reasonable and practicable, have regard to those matters to which the Gas and Electricity Markets Authority may have regard by virtue of the Gas Act 1986 s 4AA(4) or (as the case may be) the Electricity Act 1989 s 3A(4) (see FUEL AND ENERGY vol 19(2) (2007 Reissue) PARAS 789, 1041): Enterprise Act 2002 s 168(6), (7). See note 7.

10 Ie conditions in force under the Airports Act 1986 Pt 4 (ss 36–56) other than any conditions imposed or modified in pursuance of s 40(3) or (4) (see AIR LAW vol 2 (2008) PARA 228 et seq).

11 Ie granted under the Gas Act 1986 s 7 or s 7A (see FUEL AND ENERGY vol 19(2) (2007 Reissue) PARAS 805, 806).

12 Ie granted under the Electricity Act 1989 s 6 (see FUEL AND ENERGY vol 19(2) (2007 Reissue) PARA 1065).

13 Ie within the meaning given by the Communications Act 2003 s 290 (see TELECOMMUNICATIONS AND BROADCASTING vol 45(1) (2005 Reissue) PARA 279).

14 Ie under the Water Industry Act 1991 Pt 2 Ch 1 (ss 6–17) (see WATER AND WATERWAYS vol 100 (2009) PARA 137 et seq).

15 Ie under the Water Industry Act 1991 Pt 2 Ch 1A (ss 17A–17R) (see WATER AND WATERWAYS vol 100 (2009) PARA 152).

16 Ie under the Water Industry Act 1991 s 66D (see WATER AND WATERWAYS vol 100 (2009) PARA 341).

17 Ie under the Electricity (Northern Ireland) Order 1992, SI 1992/231 (NI 1), art 10 or an SNRP issued pursuant to the Railways Infrastructure (Access, Management and Licensing of Railway Undertakings) Regulations (Northern Ireland) 2005, SR 2005/537.

18 Ie under the Railways Act 1993 s 8 (see RAILWAYS, INLAND WATERWAYS AND CROSS-COUNTRY PIPELINES vol 39(1A) (Reissue) PARA 83).

19 Ie within the meanings given by the Railways Act 1993 ss 23(3), 83(1) (see RAILWAYS, INLAND WATERWAYS AND CROSS-COUNTRY PIPELINES vol 39(1A) (Reissue) PARAS 102, 130).

20 Ie under the Airports (Northern Ireland) Order 1994, SI 1994/426 (NI 1) Pt 4 other than any conditions imposed or modified in pursuance of art 40(3) or (4).

21 Ie under the Gas (Northern Ireland) Order 1996, SI 1996/275 (NI 2), art 8.

22 Ie under the Postal Services Act 2000 s 11 (see POST OFFICE vol 36(2) (Reissue) PARA 80).

23 Ie under the Transport Act 2000 s 5 (see AIR LAW vol 2 (2008) PARA 141).

24 Ie under the Water and Sewerage Services (Northern Ireland) Order 2006, SI 2006/3336 (NI 21), Pt III Ch I.

25 Enterprise Act 2002 s 168(3) (amended by the Communications Act 2003 s 406(1), (7), Sch 17 para 174(1), (5), Sch 19(1), the Water Act 2003 s 101(1), Sch 8 para 55(1), (2), the Railways Infrastructure (Access, Management and Licensing of Railway Undertakings) Regulations (Northern Ireland) 2005, SR 2005/537, reg 45, Sch 5 para 4(a), the Water and Sewerage Services (Northern Ireland) Order 2006, SI 2006/3336 (NI 21), art 308(1), Sch 12 para 46(3)). See note 7.

26 See the Enterprise Act 2002 s 168(9), Sch 9.

(v) Consultation, Information and Publicity

309. Duties of relevant authorities to consult. Where the relevant authority[1] is proposing to make a relevant decision[2] in a way which the relevant authority considers is likely to have a substantial impact on the interests of any person, the relevant authority must, so far as practicable[3], consult that person about what is proposed before making that decision[4]. In consulting the person concerned, the relevant authority must, so far as practicable, give the reasons of the relevant authority for the proposed decision[5].

1 'Relevant authority' means the Office of Fair Trading (the 'OFT'), the appropriate Minister or the Competition Commission: Enterprise Act 2002 s 169(6). As to the meaning of 'appropriate Minister' see PARA 277 note 1. As to the OFT see PARAS 6–8; and as to the Competition Commission see PARAS 9–12.

2 'Relevant decision' means: (1) in the case of the OFT, any decision by the OFT as to whether to make a reference under the Enterprise Act 2002 s 131 (see PARA 276) or accept undertakings under s 154 (see PARA 296) instead of making such a reference, or to vary under s 135 (see PARA 280) such a reference; (2) in the case of the appropriate Minister, any decision by the appropriate Minister as to whether to make a reference under s 132 (see PARA 277), or to vary under s 135 such a reference; and (3) in the case of the Commission, any decision on the questions mentioned in s 134 (see PARA 279) or s 141 (see PARA 285): s 169(6).

3 In considering what is practicable for these purposes, the relevant authority must, in particular, have regard to: (1) any restrictions imposed by any timetable for making the decision; and (2) any need to keep what is proposed, or the reasons for it, confidential: Enterprise Act 2002 s 169(4).

4 Enterprise Act 2002 s 169(1), (2). The duty under s 169 does not apply in relation to the making of any decision so far as particular provision is made elsewhere by virtue of Pt 4 (ss 131–184) for consultation before the making of that decision: s 169(5).

5 Enterprise Act 2002 s 169(3).

310. General information duties. The Office of Fair Trading (the 'OFT')[1] is required to give the Competition Commission[2] such information in its possession as the Commission may reasonably require to enable the Commission to carry out its functions in relation to market investigations[3]. The OFT must also give the Commission any other assistance which the Commission may reasonably require for the purpose of assisting it in carrying out these functions and which it is within the power of the OFT to give[4]. The OFT must give the Commission any information in its possession which has not been requested by the Commission but which, in the opinion of the OFT, would be appropriate to give to the Commission for the purpose of assisting it in carrying out these functions[5].

Similarly, the OFT and the Commission must give the Secretary of State[6] or the appropriate Minister[7] so far as he is not the Secretary of State acting alone: (1) such information in their possession as the Secretary of State or (as the case may be) the appropriate Minister concerned may by direction reasonably require to enable him to carry out his functions in relation to market investigations[8]; and (2) any other assistance which the Secretary of State or (as the case may be) the appropriate Minister concerned may by direction reasonably require for the purpose of assisting him in carrying out these functions and which it is within the power of the OFT or (as the case may be) the Commission to give[9]. The OFT is also required to give the Secretary of State or the appropriate Minister so far as he is not the Secretary of State acting alone any information in its possession which has not been requested by the Secretary of State or (as the case may be) the appropriate Minister concerned but which, in the opinion of the OFT, would be appropriate to give to the Secretary of State or (as the case may be) the appropriate Minister concerned for the purpose of assisting him in carrying out these functions[10].

The Commission and the Secretary of State or (as the case may be) the appropriate Minister concerned must have regard to any such information given to it or him[11].

1   As to the OFT see PARAS 6–8.
2   As to the Competition Commission see PARAS 9–12.
3   Enterprise Act 2002 s 170(1)(a). The Commission's functions in relation to market investigations are those under Pt 4 (ss 131–184) (see PARA 276 et seq).
4   Enterprise Act 2002 s 170(1)(b).
5   Enterprise Act 2002 s 170(2).
6   As to the Secretary of State see PARA 5.
7   As to the meaning of 'appropriate Minister' see PARA 277 note 1.
8   Ie under the Enterprise Act 2002 Pt 4 (see PARA 276 et seq).
9   Enterprise Act 2002 s 170(3). As to the requirement to publish information see PARA 311. Any direction given under s 170(3) must be in writing, and may be varied or revoked by a subsequent direction: s 170(6).
10 Enterprise Act 2002 s 170(4).
11 Enterprise Act 2002 s 170(5).

311.   Advice and information.   The Office of Fair Trading (the 'OFT')[1] is required to prepare and publish general advice and information about the making of market investigation references[2]. The OFT may at any time publish revised, or new, advice or information[3].

The Competition Commission[4] is required to prepare and publish general advice and information about the consideration by it of market investigation references and the way in which relevant customer benefits[5] may affect the taking of enforcement action in relation to such references[6]. The Commission may at any time publish revised, or new, advice or information[7].

Any such advice and information published must be prepared with a view to explaining relevant provisions of Part 4 of the Enterprise Act 2002[8] to persons who are likely to be affected by them, and indicating how the OFT or (as the case may be) the Commission expects such provisions to operate⁹. Advice and information published must include such advice and information about the effect of Community law¹⁰, and anything done under or in accordance with it, on the provisions relating to market investigation references as the OFT or (as the case may be) the Commission considers appropriate¹¹.

Published advice or information may include advice or information about the factors which the OFT or (as the case may be) the Commission may take into account in considering whether, and if so how, to exercise a function relating to market investigation references¹².

Any advice or information published by the OFT or the Commission must be published in such manner as the OFT or (as the case may be) the Commission considers appropriate¹³.

1 As to the OFT see PARAS 6–8.
2 Enterprise Act 2002 s 171(1). As to the meaning of 'market investigation reference' see PARA 276 note 3. Market investigation references are made by the OFT under s 131 (see PARA 276). In preparing any advice or information under this section, the OFT must consult the Competition Commission and such other persons as it considers appropriate: s 171(9).
    See the OFT publication '*Market investigation references–Guidance about the making of references under Part 4 of the Enterprise Act*' (March 2006).
3 Enterprise Act 2002 s 171(2).
4 As to the Competition Commission see PARAS 9–12.
5 As to the meaning of 'relevant customer benefit' see PARA 180.
6 Enterprise Act 2002 s 171(3). In preparing any advice or information, the Commission must consult the OFT and such other persons as it considers appropriate: s 171(10).
    See the Competition Commission publication CC3 '*Market Investigation References: Competition Commission Guidelines*' (June 2003).
7 Enterprise Act 2002 s 171(4).
8 Ie the Enterprise Act 2002 Pt 4 (ss 131–184) (see PARA 276 et seq).
9 Enterprise Act 2002 s 171(5).
10 'Community law' means: (1) all the rights, powers, liabilities, obligations and restrictions from time to time created or arising by or under the Community Treaties; and (2) all the remedies and procedures from time to time provided for by or under the Community Treaties: Enterprise Act 2002 s 171(11). As to the Community Treaties see STATUTES vol 44(1) (Reissue) PARA 1383. As to Community law see PARA 24 et seq.
11 Enterprise Act 2002 s 171(6).
12 Enterprise Act 2002 s 171(7).
13 Enterprise Act 2002 s 171(8).

312. Advice and information. The Office of Fair Trading (the 'OFT')¹ is required to publish: (1) any market investigation reference²; (2) any variation of a market investigation reference made by it³; (3) any decision not to proceed with a proposed undertaking mentioned in an intervention notice⁴; and (4) such information as it considers appropriate about any decision made by it⁵ to bring a case to the attention of the Secretary of State in the interests of national security⁶.

The Competition Commission⁷ is required to publish: (a) any decision made by it⁸ neither to accept an undertaking⁹ nor to make an final order¹⁰; (b) any decision made by it that there has been a material change of circumstances¹¹ or there is another special reason¹²; (c) any termination of an investigation by it on the grounds that a public interest consideration is not finalised¹³; (d) such information as it considers appropriate about any decision made by it on the grounds of national security¹⁴ to bring a case to the attention of the Secretary of State; (e) any enforcement undertaking accepted by it¹⁵; (f) any enforcement order made by it¹⁶; and (g) any variation, release or revocation of such an undertaking or order¹⁷.

The Secretary of State[18] is required to publish: (i) any market investigation reference made by him[19]; (ii) any variation of a market investigation reference made by him[20]; (iii) any intervention notice given by him; (iv) any decision made by him to revoke such a notice; (v) any decision made by him[21] neither to accept an undertaking[22] nor to make an order[23]; (vi) any enforcement undertaking accepted by him[24]; (vii) any variation or release of such an undertaking; and (viii) any direction given by him[25] in connection with the exercise by him of his functions to make a reference[26] to the Commission[27].

The appropriate Minister[28] (other than the Secretary of State acting alone) is required to publish: (A) any market investigation reference made by him[29]; (B) any variation of a market investigation reference made by him[30]; and (C) any direction for the provision of information given by him[31] in connection with the exercise by him of his functions to make a reference[32] to the Commission[33].

Where any of the above persons is under an obligation to publish the result of any action taken by that person or any decision made by that person, the person concerned must also publish that person's reasons for the action concerned or (as the case may be) the decision concerned[34].

The Secretary of State must also publish his reasons for any decision made by him as to the relevance of a public interest consideration[35] or any decision to make an order specifying considerations of national security[36] or to vary or revoke such an order[37].

Where the Secretary of State has decided[38] to accept an undertaking[39] or to make an order[40], after the acceptance of the undertaking or (as the case may be) the making of the order, he must lay details of his decision and his reasons for it, and the Commission's report[41], before each House of Parliament[42].

1   As to the OFT see PARAS 6–8.
2   Ie an reference made by the OFT under the Enterprise Act 2002 s 131 (see PARA 276).
3   Ie under the Enterprise Act 2002 s 135 (see PARA 280).
4   Ie a decision of a kind mentioned in the Enterprise Act 2002 s 149(5)(b) (see PARA 293).
5   Ie under the Enterprise Act 2002 s 152(1) (see PARA 295).
6   Enterprise Act 2002 s 172(1). As to the Secretary of State see PARA 5.
7   As to the Competition Commission see PARAS 9–12.
8   Ie under the Enterprise Act 2002 s 138(2) (see PARA 282).
9   Ie under the Enterprise Act 2002 s 159 (see PARA 301).
10 Ie under the Enterprise Act 2002 s 161 (see PARA 303).
11 Ie as mentioned in the Enterprise Act 2002 s 138(3) (see PARA 282).
12 Ie as mentioned in the Enterprise Act 2002 s 138 (see PARA 282).
13 Ie under the Enterprise Act 2002 s 145(1) (see PARA 289).
14 Ie under the Enterprise Act 2002 s 152(2) (see PARA 295).
15 Ie under the Enterprise Act 2002 s 157 (see PARA 299).
16 Ie under the Enterprise Act 2002 s 158 (see PARA 300).

17 Enterprise Act 2002 s 172(2).
18 As to the Secretary of State see PARA 5.
19 Ie under the Enterprise Act 2002 s 132 (see PARA 277).
20 Ie under the Enterprise Act 2002 s 135 (see PARA 280).
21 Ie under the Enterprise Act 2002 s 147(2) (see PARA 291).
22 Ie under the Enterprise Act 2002 s 159 (see PARA 301).
23 Ie under the Enterprise Act 2002 s 161 (see PARA 303).
24 Ie under the Enterprise Act 2002 s 157 (see PARA 299).
25 Ie under the Enterprise Act 2002 s 170(3) (see PARA 310).
26 Ie under the Enterprise Act 2002 s 132(3) (see PARA 277).

27 Enterprise Act 2002 s 172(3).
28 As to the meaning of 'appropriate Minister' see PARA 277 note 1.
29 Ie under the Enterprise Act 2002 s 132 (see PARA 277).
30 Ie under the Enterprise Act 2002 s 135 (see PARA 280).
31 Ie under the Enterprise Act 2002 s 170(3) (see PARA 310).

32 Ie under the Enterprise Act 2002 s 132(3) (see PARA 277).
33 Enterprise Act 2002 s 172(4).
34 Enterprise Act 2002 s 172(5). Such reasons need not, if it is not reasonably practicable to do so,
    be published at the same time as the result of the action concerned or (as the case may be) as the
    decision concerned: s 172(6). The provisions of s 172(5), (6) do not apply in relation to any case
    falling within head (4) or head (d) in the text: s 172(7).
35 Ie under the Enterprise Act 2002 s 146(2) (see PARA 290).
36 Ie under the Enterprise Act 2002 s 153(3) (see PARA 295).
37 Enterprise Act 2002 s 172(8). Such reasons may be published after the publication of the
    decision concerned, or the making of the order or of the variation or revocation, if it is not
    reasonably practicable to publish them at the same time as the publication of the decision or (as
    the case may be) the making of the order or variation or revocation: s 172(9).
38 Ie under the Enterprise Act 2002 s 147(2) (see PARA 291).
39 Ie under the Enterprise Act 2002 s 159 (see PARA 301).
40 Ie under the Enterprise Act 2002 s 161 (see PARA 303).
41 Ie under the Enterprise Act 2002 s 142 (see PARA 286).
42 Enterprise Act 2002 s 172(10).

313.   Defamation.   For the purposes of the law relating to defamation[1],
absolute privilege attaches to any advice, guidance, notice or direction given, or
decision or report made, by the Office of Fair Trading (the 'OFT')[2], by the
Secretary of State[3], by the appropriate Minister[4] (other than the Secretary of
State acting alone) or by the Competition Commission[5] in the exercise of any of
their functions relating to market investigations[6].

1 As to the law relating to defamation see LIBEL AND SLANDER vol 28 (Reissue) PARA 1 et seq.
2 As to the OFT see PARAS 6–8.
3 As to the Secretary of State see PARA 5.
4 As to the meaning of 'appropriate Minister' see PARA 277 note 1.
5 As to the Competition Commission see PARAS 9–12.
6 Enterprise Act 2002 s 173. Functions relating to market investigations are those under Pt 4
   (ss 131–184) (see PARA 276 et seq).

(vi) Investigation Powers

314.   Investigation powers of the Office of Fair Trading.   The Office of Fair
Trading (the 'OFT')[1] may exercise any of the following investigation powers for
the purpose of assisting it in deciding whether to make a market investigation
reference[2] or to accept undertakings[3] instead of making such a reference[4].
However, the OFT must not exercise any of the following powers for the purpose
of assisting it as mentioned above unless it already believes that it has power to
make such a reference[5].

In exercise of its investigation powers, the OFT may give notice[6] to any
person requiring him to attend at a time and place specified in the notice and to
give evidence to the OFT or a person nominated by the OFT for the purpose[7].
The OFT may also give notice to any person requiring him to produce at a time
and place so specified and to a person so specified any documents which are
specified or described in the notice, or fall within a category of document which
is specified or described in the notice and are in that person's custody or under
his control[8]. The OFT may give notice to any person who carries on any
business[9] requiring him to supply at a time and place, and in a form and manner,
so specified and to a person so specified such estimates, forecasts, returns or
other information as may be specified or described in the notice[10].

The person to whom any document is produced in accordance with a notice
may copy the document so produced, for the purpose of assisting the OFT in

deciding whether to make a market investigation reference or to accept undertakings instead of making such a reference[11].

No person is required: (1) to give any evidence or produce any documents which he could not be compelled to give or produce in civil proceedings before the High Court; or (2) to supply any information which he could not be compelled to supply in evidence in such proceedings[12]. In addition, no person may be required, in compliance with a notice under the above provisions, to go more than 10 miles from his place of residence unless his necessary travelling expenses are paid or offered to him[13].

A person commits an offence if he, intentionally and without reasonable excuse, fails to comply with any requirement of such a notice or if he intentionally and without reasonable excuse alters, suppresses or destroys any document which he has been required to produce by such a notice[14]. A person also commits an offence if he intentionally obstructs or delays the OFT in the exercise of its investigation powers[15] or any person empowered to copy documents[16].

1   As to the OFT see PARAS 6–8.
2   Ie a reference under the Enterprise Act 2002 s 131 (see PARA 276).
3   Ie under the Enterprise Act 2002 s 154 (see PARA 296).
4   Enterprise Act 2002 s 174(1).
5   Enterprise Act 2002 s 174(2).
6   A notice under the Enterprise Act 2002 s 174 must include information about the possible consequences of not complying with the notice: s 174(6). 'Notice' means notice in writing: s 183(1).
7   Enterprise Act 2002 s 174(3).
8   Enterprise Act 2002 s 174(4). Any reference in s 174 to the production of a document includes a reference to the production of a legible and intelligible copy of information recorded otherwise than in legible form: s 174(10).
9   'Business' includes a professional practice and includes any other undertaking which is carried on for gain or reward or which is an undertaking in the course of which goods or services are supplied otherwise than free of charge: s 183(1). As to the meaning of 'goods' see PARA 276 note 3.
10 Enterprise Act 2002 s 174(5).
11 Enterprise Act 2002 s 174(7).
12 Enterprise Act 2002 s 174(8), (11). See CIVIL PROCEDURE vol 11 (2009) PARA 749 et seq.
13 Enterprise Act 2002 s 174(9).
14 Enterprise Act 2002 s 175(1), (2). A person who commits an offence under s 175(1) or (2) is liable: (1) on summary conviction, to a fine not exceeding the statutory maximum; (2) on conviction on indictment, to imprisonment for a term not exceeding two years or to a fine or to both: s 175(3). As to the statutory maximum see PARA 140 note 9.
15 Ie under the Enterprise Act 2002 s 174 (see the text and notes 1–13).
16 Enterprise Act 2002 s 175(4). A person who commits such an offence is liable: (1) on summary conviction, to a fine not exceeding the statutory maximum; (2) on conviction on indictment, to a fine: s 175(5).

315.   Investigation powers of the Competition Commission. The Competition Commission[1] has the same investigation powers in relation to market investigations[2] as it has in relation to mergers[3].

1   As to the Competition Commission see PARAS 9–12.
2   Ie for the purposes of the Enterprise Act 2002 Pt 4 (ss 131–184) (see PARA 276 et seq).
3   Enterprise Act 2002 s 176(1). The provisions relating to mergers are set out in Pt 3 (ss 22–130) (see PARA 172 et seq). As to the Commission's investigation powers see s 109 (attendance of witnesses and production of documents) (see PARA 259); s 110 (enforcement of powers under s 109; general) (see PARA 260); s 111 (penalties) (see PARA 260); s 112 (penalties: main procedural requirements) (see PARA 261); s 113 (payments and interest by instalments) (see PARA 262); s 114 (appeals in relation to penalties) (see PARA 263); s 115 (recovery of penalties) (see

PARA 264); and s 116 (statement of policy) (see PARA 265). As to the modification of s 110 see s 176(2); and as to the modification of s 111(5)(b)(ii) see s 176(3).

(vii) General Provisions

316.   Review of decisions.   Any person aggrieved by a decision[1] of the Office of Fair Trading (the 'OFT')[2], the appropriate Minister[3], the Secretary of State[4] or the Competition Commission[5] in connection with a market investigation reference[6] or possible reference may apply to the Competition Appeal Tribunal[7] for a review of that decision[8]. Except in so far as a direction to the contrary is given by the Competition Appeal Tribunal, the effect of the decision is not suspended by reason of the making of the application[9].

In determining such an application the Competition Appeal Tribunal is required to apply the same principles as would be applied by a court on an application for judicial review[10].

The Competition Appeal Tribunal may dismiss the application or quash the whole or part of the decision to which it relates[11]. Where it quashes the whole or part of the decision, the Tribunal may refer the matter back to the original decision maker with a direction to reconsider and make a new decision in accordance with the ruling of the Competition Appeal Tribunal[12].

An appeal lies on any point of law arising from a decision of the Competition Appeal Tribunal to the Court of Appeal[13]. Permission to appeal must be granted by the Tribunal or the Court of Appeal[14].

1 For this purpose, 'decision': (1) does not include a decision to impose a penalty under the Enterprise Act 2002 s 110(1) or (3) as applied by s 176 (see PARA 315); but (2) includes a failure to take a decision permitted or required by Pt 4 (ss 131–184) in connection with a market investigation reference or possible reference (see PARA 276 et seq): s 179(2).
2 As to the OFT see PARAS 6–8.
3 As to the meaning of 'appropriate Minister' see PARA 277 note 1.
4 As to the Secretary of State see PARA 5.
5 As to the Competition Commission see PARAS 9–12.
6 Ie a reference under the Enterprise Act 2002 Pt 4 (see PARA 276 et seq).
7 As to the Competition Appeal Tribunal see PARAS 13–17.
8 Enterprise Act 2002 s 179(1).
9 Enterprise Act 2002 s 179(3).
10 Enterprise Act 2002 s 179(4). As to judicial review see ADMINISTRATIVE LAW vol 1(1) (2001 Reissue) PARA 58 et seq.
11 Enterprise Act 2002 s 179(5)(a).
12 Enterprise Act 2002 s 179(5)(b).
13 Enterprise Act 2002 s 179(6), (8).
14 Enterprise Act 2002 s 179(7).

317.   Offences in relation to market investigations.   A person commits an offence if:
(1)   he supplies any information to the Office of Fair Trading (the 'OFT')[1], the Competition Commission[2], the Secretary of State[3] or the appropriate Minister[4] (so far as he is not the Secretary of State acting alone) in connection with any of their functions under Part 4 of the Enterprise Act 2002[5];
(2)   the information is false or misleading in a material respect; and
(3)   he knows that it is false or misleading in a material respect or is reckless as to whether it is false or misleading in a material respect[6].

A person also commits an offence if he: (a) supplies any information to another person which he knows to be false or misleading in a material respect; or (b) recklessly supplies any information to another person which is false or misleading in a material respect, knowing that the information is to be used for the purpose of supplying information to the OFT, the Commission, the Secretary of State or the appropriate Minister in connection with any of their functions under Part 4 of the Act[7].

Where an offence under Part 4 of the Enterprise Act 2002 committed by a body corporate is proved to have been committed with the consent or connivance of, or to be attributable to any neglect on the part of a director, manager, secretary or other similar officer of the body corporate or a person purporting to act in such a capacity, he as well as the body corporate commits the offence and is liable to be proceeded against and punished accordingly[8].

1   As to the OFT see PARAS 6–8.
2   As to the Competition Commission see PARAS 9–12.
3   As to the Secretary of State see PARA 5.
4   As to the meaning of 'appropriate Minister' see PARA 277 note 1.
5   Ie the Enterprise Act 2002 Pt 4 (ss 131–184) see PARA 276 et seq.
6   Enterprise Act 2002 s 117(1); applied by s 180(1), (2) (amended by the Communications Act 2003 s 289(1), Sch 16 para 26). A person who commits such an offence is liable on summary conviction, to a fine not exceeding the statutory maximum; and on conviction on indictment, to imprisonment for a term not exceeding two years or to a fine or to both: ss 117(3), s 180(1). As to the statutory maximum see PARA 140 note 9.
7   Enterprise Act 2002 s 117(2); applied by s 180(1). See note 6.
8   Enterprise Act 2002 s 125(1); applied by s 180(1). Where the affairs of a body corporate are managed by its members, s 125(1) applies in relation to the acts and defaults of a member in connection with his functions of management as if he were a director of the body corporate: s 125(2). See further CORPORATIONS. As to offences by Scottish partnerships see s 125(3), (4).

318.   Orders and service of documents. Any power of the Secretary of State[1] to make an order under Part 4 of the Enterprise Act 2002[2] is exercisable by statutory instrument[3]. Any power of the Secretary of State to make an order under Part 4 may be exercised so as to make different provision for different cases or different purposes and includes power to make such incidental, supplementary, consequential, transitory, transitional or saving provision as the Secretary of State considers appropriate[4].

Certain orders made by the Secretary of State[5] are subject to annulment in pursuance of a resolution of either House of Parliament[6], and others[7] require a draft to be laid before and approved by a resolution of, each House of Parliament[8].

An order made by the Secretary of State in relation to national security[9] must be laid before Parliament after being made and ceases to have effect unless approved, within the period of 28 days beginning with the day on which it is made, by a resolution of each House of Parliament[10]. If an order made by the Secretary of State ceases to have effect, any modification made by it of an enactment is repealed (and the previous enactment revived) but without prejudice to the validity of anything done in connection with that modification before the order ceased to have effect and without prejudice to the making of a new order[11]. If an order made by the Secretary of State in relation to national security would otherwise be treated for the purposes of the standing orders of either House of Parliament as a hybrid instrument, it must proceed in that House as if it were not such an instrument[12].

The requirements relating to service of documents in relation to mergers[13] also apply in relation to market investigations[14].

1   As to the Secretary of State see PARA 5.
2   Ie the Enterprise Act 2002 Pt 4 (ss 131–184) (see PARA 276 et seq).

3 Enterprise Act 2002 s 181(1). References to an order made under Pt 4 include references to an order made under s 111(4) or (6) (see PARA 260) or s 114(3)(b) or (4)(b) (see PARA 263) as applied by s 176 (see PARA 315) and an order made under s 128(6) as applied by s 183(2): s 181(10). The provisions of s 127(1)(b), (4)–(6) (see PARA 176) and s 128 (see PARA 172 note 5) apply for the purposes of Pt 4 as they apply for the purposes of Pt 3 (ss 22–130) (see PARA 172 et seq): s 183(2).

4 Enterprise Act 2002 s 181(2). The power of the Secretary of State under s 136(9) (see PARA 281), s 137(3) (see PARA 281), s 144(2) (see PARA 288), s 153(3) (see PARA 295) or s 168(8) (see PARA 308) as extended by s 181(2) may be exercised by modifying any enactment comprised in or made under the Enterprise Act 2002, or any other enactment: s 181(3).

5 Ie orders made under the Enterprise Act 2002 s 137(3) (see PARA 281), s 144(2) (see PARA 288), s 158 (see PARA 300), s 160 (see PARA 302) or s 161 (see PARA 303), or under s 111(4) or (6) (see PARA 260) or s 114(3)(b) or (4)(b) (see PARA 263) as applied by s 176 (see PARA 315).

6 Enterprise Act 2002 s 181(4).

7 Ie the Enterprise Act 2002 s 136(9) (see PARA 281) or s 168(8) (see PARA 308), or s 128(6) (see PARA 172) as applied by s 183(2) (see note 3).

8 Enterprise Act 2002 s 181(5).

9 Ie under the Enterprise Act 2002 s 153(3) (see PARA 295).

10 Enterprise Act 2002 s 181(6). In calculating the period of 28 days mentioned in s 181(6), no account is to be taken of any time during which Parliament is dissolved or prorogued or during which both Houses are adjourned for more than four days: s 181(7).

11 Enterprise Act 2002 s 181(8).

12 Enterprise Act 2002 s 181(9). As to hybrid instruments see PARLIAMENT vol 34 (Reissue) PARA 946.

13 Ie the Enterprise Act 2002 s 126 (see PARA 275).

14 Enterprise Act 2002 s 182. The provisions relating to market investigations are contained in Pt 4 (ss 131–184) (see PARA 276 et seq).

(4) CARTEL OFFENCE

(i) In general

319. Meaning of cartel offence. An individual is guilty of an offence[1] if he dishonestly agrees with one or more other persons to make or implement, or to cause to be made or implemented, arrangements of the following kind relating to at least two undertakings[2] (A and B)[3]. The arrangements must be ones which, if operating as the parties to the agreement intend, would:

(1) directly or indirectly fix a price for the supply[4] by A in the United Kingdom[5] (otherwise than to B) of a product or service[6];

(2) limit or prevent supply by A in the United Kingdom of a product or service[7];

(3) limit or prevent production[8] by A in the United Kingdom of a product[9];

(4) divide between A and B the supply in the United Kingdom of a product or service to a customer or customers[10];

(5) divide between A and B customers for the supply in the United Kingdom of a product or service[11]; or

(6) be bid-rigging arrangements[12].

Unless head (4), head (5) or head (6) above applies, the arrangements must also be ones which, if operating as the parties to the agreement intend, would:

(a) directly or indirectly fix a price for the supply[13] by B in the United Kingdom (otherwise than to A) of a product or service[14];

(b) limit or prevent supply by B in the United Kingdom of a product or service[15]; or

(c) limit or prevent production[16] by B in the United Kingdom of a product[17].

The essence of the cartel offence is the personal responsibility of an individual in arrangements that have been part of the national and international commercial framework for many years[18].

1   A person guilty of such an offence is liable on conviction on indictment, to imprisonment for a term not exceeding five years or to a fine, or to both; on summary conviction, to imprisonment for a term not exceeding six months or to a fine not exceeding the statutory maximum, or to both: Enterprise Act 2002 s 190(1). As to the statutory maximum see PARA 140 note 9. The following factors are relevant to any sentence passed pursuant to ss 188, 190: (1) the gravity and nature of the offence; (2) the duration of the offence; (3) the degree of culpability of the defendant in implementing the cartel agreement; (4) his degree of culpability in enforcing that agreement; and (5) whether the defendant's conduct was contrary to guidelines laid down in a company compliance manual. The court may regard the following mitigating factors as suggesting leniency: (a) any co-operation the defendant may have provided in respect of the inquiry; (b) whether the defendant was compelled to participate in the cartel under duress; (c) whether the offence was a first offence; and (d) any personal circumstances of the defendant: *R v Whittle* [2008] EWCA Crim 2560 at [34], (2008) Times, 27 November, [2008] All ER (D) 133 (Nov). These factors are not, however, to be regarded as exhaustive: *R v Whittle* [2008] EWCA Crim 2560 at [35], (2008) Times, 27 November, [2008] All ER (D) 133 (Nov).

     As to prosecutions see s 190(2)–(4); and PARA 320; and as to investigations of cartel offences see PARA 321 et seq. *R v Whittle* [2008] EWCA Crim 2560, (2008) Times, 27 November, [2008] All ER (D) 133 (Nov) was the first prosecution to be brought under these provisions. The defendants were employed by a specialist manufacturer of marine hose and ancillary equipment. They were charged under the Enterprise Act 2002 s 188 with dishonestly agreeing to implement bid-rigging arrangements (see head (6) in the text). The cartel had consisted of all the principal manufacturers of marine hose. The defendants, who had no previous convictions, were arrested in the United States of America for breaching anti-competition laws. They made full and detailed admissions, volunteered full confessions and indicated to the authorities that, if prosecuted, they would plead guilty to a United Kingdom cartel offence. Each defendant entered into a formal plea agreement with the United States authorities in terms that, provided the defendant was sentenced in the United Kingdom to not less than the terms of imprisonment stated in the agreement, he would not be expected to return to the United States to serve any period in custody there. The defendants entered guilty pleas and returned to the United Kingdom where they pleaded guilty to a cartel offence, pursuant to s 188. The sentences imposed were of longer duration than those provided for in the agreements with the United States authorities and the defendants appealed. On appeal, shorter sentences were substituted; but the Court of Appeal, while making reference to the factors referred to in heads (1)–(5) and (a)–(c) above, emphasised that it was not offering general guidance on sentencing levels in cases of this nature: see *R v Whittle* [2008] EWCA Crim 2560 at [13], [33], (2008) Times, 27 November, [2008] All ER (D) 133 (Nov).

2   For these purposes, 'undertaking' has the same meaning as in the Competition Act 1998 Pt 1 (ss 1–60): Enterprise Act 2002 s 188(7).

3   Enterprise Act 2002 s 188(1).

4   In the Enterprise Act 2002 s 188(2)(a)–(d), (3) (see heads (1)–(4), (a)–(c) in the text), references to supply or production are to supply or production in the appropriate circumstances (as to which see s 189; and notes 6, 7, 9, 10, 14, 15, 17): s 188(4).

5   As to the meaning of 'United Kingdom' see PARA 401 note 1.

6   Enterprise Act 2002 s 188(2)(a). For s 188(2)(a), the appropriate circumstances are that A's supply of the product or service would be at a level in the supply chain at which the product or service would at the same time be supplied by B in the United Kingdom: s 189(1).

7   Enterprise Act 2002 s 188(2)(b). For s 188(2)(b), the appropriate circumstances are that A's supply of the product or service would be at a level in the supply chain (1) at which the product or service would at the same time be supplied by B in the United Kingdom; or (2) at which supply by B in the United Kingdom of the product or service would be limited or prevented by the arrangements: s 189(2). See also note 4.

8   See note 4.

9   Enterprise Act 2002 s 188(2)(c). For s 188(2)(c), the appropriate circumstances are that A's production of the product would be at a level in the production chain (1) at which the product would at the same time be produced by B in the United Kingdom; or (2) at which production by B in the United Kingdom of the product would be limited or prevented by the arrangements: s 189(3).

10 Enterprise Act 2002 s 188(2)(d). For s 188(2)(d), the appropriate circumstances are that A's
   supply of the product or service would be at the same level in the supply chain as B's: s 189(4).
   See also note 4.
11 Enterprise Act 2002 s 188(2)(e).
12 Enterprise Act 2002 s 188(2)(f). 'Bid-rigging arrangements' are arrangements under which, in
   response to a request for bids for the supply of a product or service in the United Kingdom, or
   for the production of a product in the United Kingdom (1) A but not B may make a bid; or (2)
   A and B may each make a bid but, in one case or both, only a bid arrived at in accordance with
   the arrangements (s 188(5)); but arrangements are not bid-rigging arrangements if, under them,
   the person requesting bids would be informed of them at or before the time when a bid is made
   (s 188(6)). See *R v Whittle* [2008] EWCA Crim 2560 at [7], (2008) Times, 27 November, [2008]
   All ER (D) 133 (Nov).
13 See note 4.
14 Enterprise Act 2002 s 188(3)(a). For s 188(3)(a), the appropriate circumstances are that B's
   supply of the product or service would be at a level in the supply chain at which the product or
   service would at the same time be supplied by A in the United Kingdom: s 189(5).
15 Enterprise Act 2002 s 188(3)(b). For s 188(3)(b), the appropriate circumstances are that B's
   supply of the product or service would be at a level in the supply chain (1) at which the product
   or service would at the same time be supplied by A in the United Kingdom; or (2) at which
   supply by A in the United Kingdom of the product or service would be limited or prevented by
   the arrangements: s 189(6). See also note 4.
16 See note 4.
17 Enterprise Act 2002 s 188(3)(c). For s 188(3)(c), the appropriate circumstances are that B's
   production of the product would be at a level in the production chain (1) at which the product
   would at the same time be produced by A in the United Kingdom; or (2) at which production by
   A in the United Kingdom of the product would be limited or prevented by the arrangements:
   s 189(7).
18 *R v Whittle* [2008] EWCA Crim 2560 at [2], (2008) Times, 27 November, [2008] All ER (D)
   133 (Nov).

320. Prosecution of cartel offences. In England and Wales and Northern
Ireland, proceedings for a cartel offence[1] may be instituted only by the Director
of the Serious Fraud Office[2] or by or with the consent of the Office of Fair
Trading (the 'OFT')[3]. No proceedings may be brought for such an offence in
respect of an agreement outside the United Kingdom[4], unless it has been
implemented in whole or in part in the United Kingdom[5].

Where, for the purpose of the investigation or prosecution of cartel offences,
the OFT gives a person written notice under this provision, no proceedings for a
cartel offence that falls within a description specified in the notice may be
brought against that person in England and Wales or Northern Ireland except in
circumstances specified in the notice[6].

1 Ie an offence under the Enterprise Act 2002 s 188: see PARA 319.
2 Enterprise Act 2002 s 190(2)(a). As to the Director of the Serious Fraud Office see CRIMINAL
  LAW, EVIDENCE AND PROCEDURE vol 11(3) (2006 Reissue) PARA 1067.
3 Enterprise Act 2002 s 190(2)(a). As to the OFT see PARAS 6–8.
4 As to the meaning of 'United Kingdom' see PARA 401 note 1.
5 Enterprise Act 2002 s 190(3).
6 Enterprise Act 2002 s 190(4).

(ii) Criminal Investigations by the Office of Fair Trading

321. Investigation of cartel offence. The Office of Fair Trading (the 'OFT')[1]
may conduct an investigation if there are reasonable grounds for suspecting that
a cartel offence[2] has been committed[3]. The investigatory powers[4] of the OFT are
exercisable, but only for the purposes of an investigation under the above
provision[5], in any case where it appears to the OFT that there is good reason to
exercise them for the purpose of investigating the affairs, or any aspect of the
affairs, of any person (the 'person under investigation')[6].

1   As to the OFT see PARAS 6–8.
2   Ie an offence under the Enterprise Act 2002 s 188: see PARA 319.
3   Enterprise Act 2002 s 192(1).
4   Ie the OFT's powers under the Enterprise Act 2002 ss 193, 194: see PARA 322.
5   Ie an investigation under the Enterprise Act 2002 s 192(1): see the text and notes 1–3.
6   Enterprise Act 2002 s 192(2).

322.   Powers of investigation. The Office of Fair Trading (the 'OFT')[1] may by notice in writing[2]:

(1)   require the person under investigation[3], or any other person who it has reason to believe has relevant information, to answer questions, or otherwise provide information, with respect to any matter relevant to the investigation at a specified place and either at a specified time or forthwith[4];

(2)   require the person under investigation, or any other person, to produce, at a specified place and either at a specified time or forthwith, specified documents[5], or documents of a specified description, which appear to the OFT to relate to any matter relevant to the investigation[6].

If any such documents as are mentioned in head (2) above are produced, the OFT may:

(a)   take copies or extracts from them[7];

(b)   require the person producing them to provide an explanation of any of them[8];

and if any such documents are not produced, the OFT may require the person who was required to produce them to state, to the best of his knowledge and belief, where they are[9].

On an application made by the OFT to the High Court[10] in accordance with rules of court[11], a judge may issue a warrant[12] if he is satisfied that there are reasonable grounds for believing that there are on any premises documents which the OFT has power under the above provisions to require to be produced for the purposes of an investigation[13] and that:

(i)   a person has failed to comply with a requirement under those provisions to produce the documents[14];

(ii)   it is not practicable to serve a notice under those provisions in relation to them[15]; or

(iii)   the service of such a notice in relation to them might seriously prejudice the investigation[16].

Such a warrant must authorise a named officer of the OFT, and any other officers of the OFT whom the OFT has authorised in writing to accompany the named officer:

(A)   to enter the premises, using such force as is reasonably necessary for the purpose[17];

(B)   to search the premises and either take possession of any documents appearing to be of the relevant kind[18], or take, in relation to any documents appearing to be of the relevant kind, any other steps which may appear to be necessary for preserving them or preventing interference with them[19];

(C)   to require any person to provide an explanation of any document appearing to be of the relevant kind or to state, to the best of his knowledge and belief, where it may be found[20];

(D)   to require any information which is stored in any electronic form and is accessible from the premises and which the named officer considers relates to any matter relevant to the investigation, to be produced in a form in which it can be taken away, and in which it is visible and legible or from which it can readily be produced in a visible and legible form[21].

Such a warrant may authorise persons specified in the warrant to accompany the named officer who is executing it[22].

The warrant must:

(aa) state the address or other identification of the premises to be subject to the warrant;

(bb) state the names of the named officer[23] and of any other officers or other persons who may accompany him in executing the warrant;

(cc) set out the action which the warrant authorises the persons executing it to take[24];

(dd) give the date on which the warrant is issued; and

(ee) state that the named officer has given the required[25] undertaking[26].

It must also state the name and judicial title of the person making it, bear the date on which it is given or made, and be sealed by the court[27]. Upon the issue of a warrant the court will provide to the OFT the sealed warrant and the notice of the powers to search premises and the rights of occupiers[28], and a copy of the sealed warrant and the notice for service on the occupier or person in charge of the premises subject to the warrant[29].

A named officer attending premises to execute a warrant must, if the premises are occupied, produce the warrant and notice immediately upon arrival at the premises to the occupier or any other person entitled to grant access to the premises, explaining the authority under which entry is sought[30]. As soon as possible after his arrival at the premises, he must personally serve a copy of the warrant and notice on the occupier or person appearing to him to be in charge of the premises[31], but he is not required to serve the warrant and notice personally if he reasonably believes this would frustrate the object of the search or endanger officers or other people[32]. If the occupier is not present, the named officer must leave copies of the warrant and notice of the powers to search premises and of the rights of occupiers in a prominent place on the premises or appropriate part of the premises, recording the name of the named officer in charge of the search and the date and time of the search, unless the named officer reasonably believes recording or disclosing his name might put him in danger[33]. The named officer must also comply with any order which the court may make for service of any other documents relating to the application[34]. Unless the court otherwise orders, the initial production of a warrant and entry to premises under the authority of the warrant must take place at a reasonable hour, unless this might frustrate the purpose of the search[35]; but once persons named in the warrant have entered premises under the authority of a warrant, they may, whilst the warrant remains in force, either remain on the premises or re-enter the premises to continue executing the warrant[36]. If the persons executing a warrant propose to remove any items from the premises pursuant to the warrant they must, unless it is impracticable, make a list of all the items to be removed, supply a copy of the list to the occupier or person appearing to be in charge of the premises and give that person a reasonable opportunity to check the list before removing any of the items[37].

The warrant will expire one month after the date on which it is issued[38]. Intentional obstruction of a person exercising his powers under such a warrant is an offence[39].

The occupier or person in charge of premises in relation to which a warrant has been issued may apply[40] to vary or discharge the warrant[41]. Such an application to stop a warrant from being executed must be made immediately upon the warrant being served[42]. A person applying to vary or discharge a warrant must first inform the named officer that he is making the application[43].

The OFT may authorise any competent person who is not an officer of the OFT to exercise on its behalf all or any of the powers conferred[44] by the statutory provisions set out above[45]. No such authority may be granted except for the purpose of investigating the affairs, or any aspect of the affairs, of a person specified in the authority[46]. No person is bound to comply with any requirement imposed by a person exercising powers by virtue of any authority so granted unless he has, if required to do so, produced evidence of his authority[47].

1   As to the OFT see PARAS 6–8.

2   A notice under the Enterprise Act 2002 s 193(1) or (2) (see heads (1), (2) in the text) must indicate (1) the subject matter and purpose of the investigation; and (2) the nature of the offences created by s 201 (see PARA 325): s 193(5). As to the meaning of 'writing' see PARA 354 note 20.

3   For the purposes of the Enterprise Act 2002 ss 192–201 (see PARA 321; the text and notes 1–2, 4–10; and PARAS 323–325), 'person under investigation' has the meaning given in s 192(2) (see PARA 321): s 202.

4   Enterprise Act 2002 s 193(1). Non-compliance without reasonable excuse is an offence, as is making a false statement in this connection: see PARA 325.

5   For the purposes of the Enterprise Act 2002 ss 192–201, 'documents' includes information recorded in any form and, in relation to information recorded otherwise than in a form in which it is visible and legible, references to its production include references to producing it in a form in which it is visible and legible or from which it can readily be produced in a visible and legible form: s 202.

6   Enterprise Act 2002 s 193(2). Non-compliance without reasonable excuse is an offence, as is the deliberate falsification, concealment, destruction or disposal of relevant documents: see PARA 325.

7   Enterprise Act 2002 s 193(3)(a).

8   Enterprise Act 2002 s 193(3)(b). Non-compliance without reasonable excuse is an offence, as is making a false statement in this connection: see PARA 325.

9   Enterprise Act 2002 s 193(4). Non-compliance without reasonable excuse is an offence, as is making a false statement in this connection: see PARA 325.

10 In Scotland, the application is made by the procurator fiscal to the sheriff: see the Enterprise Act 2002 s 194(1).

11 An application by the OFT for a warrant under the Enterprise Act 2002 must be made to a High Court judge using the Part 8 procedure as modified by *Practice Direction—Application for a Warrant under the Enterprise Act 2002*: paras 1.1(6), 2.1. The application must be made to a judge of the Chancery Division at the Royal Courts of Justice: para 2.2. The application is made without notice and the claim form may be issued without naming a defendant: para 2.3. CPR 8.1(3), 8.3, 8.4, 8.5(2)–(6), 8.6(1), 8.7 and 8.8 do not apply: *Practice Direction—Application for a Warrant under the Enterprise Act 2002* para 2.3. As to the Part 8 procedure see CIVIL PROCEDURE vol 11 (2009) PARA 127 et seq.

The court will not serve any claim form, warrant, or other document filed or issued in such an application except in accordance with an order of the judge hearing the application: *Practice Direction—Application for a Warrant under the Enterprise Act 2002* para 3.1. CPR 5.4(2), 5.4B and 5.4C (see CIVIL PROCEDURE vol 11 (2009) PARA 82) do not apply, and *Practice Direction—Application for a Warrant under the Enterprise Act 2002* paras 3.3, 3.4 have effect in their place: para 3.2. When a claim form is issued the court file will be marked 'Not for disclosure' and, unless a High Court judge grants permission, the court records relating to the application (including the claim form and documents filed in support and any warrant or order that is issued) will not be made available by the court for any person to inspect or copy, either before or after the hearing of the application: para 3.3. An application for permission under para 3.3 must be made on notice to the OFT in accordance with CPR Pt 23 (see CIVIL PROCEDURE vol 11 (2009) PARA 303 et seq): *Practice Direction—Application for a Warrant under the Enterprise Act 2002* para 3.4. As to the contents of the claim form, affidavit and documents in support see paras 4.1–4.6; and as to listing see para 5. An application for a warrant will be heard and determined in private, unless the judge hearing it directs otherwise: para 6.1.

12 The court will not issue a warrant unless there has been filed a written undertaking, signed by the named officer, to comply with *Practice Direction—Application for a Warrant under the Enterprise Act 2002* para 8.1 (see the text and notes 30–32): para 6.2. In Scotland, a warrant is issued by the sheriff: see the Enterprise Act 2002 s 194(1).

13 Enterprise Act 2002 s 194(1)(a).

14 Enterprise Act 2002 s 194(1)(b)(i).

15 Enterprise Act 2002 s 194(1)(b)(ii).

16 Enterprise Act 2002 s 194(1)(b)(iii).

17 Enterprise Act 2002 s 194(2)(a).

18 Documents are of the relevant kind if they are of a kind in respect of which the application under the Enterprise Act 2002 s 194(1) was granted: s 194(3).

19 Enterprise Act 2002 s 194(2)(b). The Criminal Justice and Police Act 2001 s 50 (additional powers of seizure from premises: see CRIMINAL LAW, EVIDENCE AND PROCEDURE vol 11(2) (2006 Reissue) PARA 890) applies to powers of seizure conferred by the Enterprise Act 2002 s 194(2): Criminal Justice and Police Act 2001 Sch 1 para 73B (added by the Enterprise Act 2002 s 194(5)). See also the Criminal Justice and Police Act 2001 s 59, which makes provision about applications relating to property seized in the exercise of the powers conferred by (among other provisions) the Enterprise Act 2002 194(2); and CRIMINAL LAW, EVIDENCE AND PROCEDURE vol 11(2) (2006 Reissue) PARA 898.

20 Enterprise Act 2002 s 194(2)(c).

21 Enterprise Act 2002 s 194(2)(d).

22 Enterprise Act 2002 s 194(4).

23 'Officer' means an officer of the OFT; and 'named officer' means the person identified in a warrant as the principal officer or person in charge of executing that warrant: *Practice Direction—Application for a Warrant under the Enterprise Act 2002* para 1.1(3), (4). See, however, the text and notes 44–47.

24 Ie under the Enterprise Act 2002 s 194: see the text and notes 10–22.

25 Ie the undertaking required by *Practice Direction—Application for a Warrant under the Enterprise Act 2002* para 6.2: see note 12.

26 *Practice Direction—Application for a Warrant under the Enterprise Act 2002* para 7.1.

27 See *Practice Direction—Application for a Warrant under the Enterprise Act 2002* para 7.2, applying CPR 40.2 (as to which see CIVIL PROCEDURE vol 12 (2009) PARA 1137).

28 *Practice Direction—Application for a Warrant under the Enterprise Act 2002* paras 1.1(5), 7.3.(1).

29 *Practice Direction—Application for a Warrant under the Enterprise Act 2002* para 7.3(2).

30 *Practice Direction—Application for a Warrant under the Enterprise Act 2002* para 8.1(a).

31 *Practice Direction—Application for a Warrant under the Enterprise Act 2002* para 8.1(b).

32 *Practice Direction—Application for a Warrant under the Enterprise Act 2002* para 8.1.

33 *Practice Direction—Application for a Warrant under the Enterprise Act 2002* para 8.2.

34 *Practice Direction—Application for a Warrant under the Enterprise Act 2002* para 8.3.

35 *Practice Direction—Application for a Warrant under the Enterprise Act 2002* para 8.4(1).

36 *Practice Direction—Application for a Warrant under the Enterprise Act 2002* para 8.4(2).

37 *Practice Direction—Application for a Warrant under the Enterprise Act 2002* para 8.5.

38 *Practice Direction—Application for a Warrant under the Enterprise Act 2002* para 10.

39 See PARA 325.

40 The application should be made to the judge who issued the warrant, or, if he is not available, to another judge of the Chancery Division: *Practice Direction—Application for a Warrant under the Enterprise Act 2002* para 9.4.

41 *Practice Direction—Application for a Warrant under the Enterprise Act 2002* para 9.1.

42 *Practice Direction—Application for a Warrant under the Enterprise Act 2002* para 9.2.

43 *Practice Direction—Application for a Warrant under the Enterprise Act 2002* para 9.3.

44 Ie the powers conferred by the Enterprise Act 2002 s 193 or s 194: see the text and notes 1–22.

45 Enterprise Act 2002 s 195(1).

46 Enterprise Act 2002 s 195(2).

47 Enterprise Act 2002 s 195(3).

323.   Privileged information and use of statements. A person may not be required under the investigatory powers set out in the previous paragraph[1] to disclose any information or produce any document[2] which he would be entitled to refuse to disclose or produce on grounds of legal professional privilege[3] in proceedings in the High Court, except that a lawyer may be required to provide the name and address of his client[4]. Nor may a person be required[5] to disclose any information or produce any document in respect of which he owes an obligation of confidence by virtue of carrying on any banking business unless:

(1)   the person to whom the obligation of confidence is owed consents to the disclosure or production; or

(2)   the Office of Fair Trading (the 'OFT')[6] has authorised the making of the requirement[7].

A statement by a person in response to a requirement imposed by virtue of the OFT's investigatory powers[8] may only be used in evidence against him:

(a)   on a prosecution for an offence[9] in connection with making a false or misleading statement[10]; or

(b)   on a prosecution for some other offence where in giving evidence he makes a statement inconsistent with it[11].

The statement may not, however, be used against that person by virtue of head (b) above unless evidence relating to it is adduced, or a question relating to it is asked, by or on behalf of that person in the proceedings arising out of the prosecution[12].

A statement made by a person in response to a requirement imposed by virtue of any of certain statutory powers of investigation by the OFT under the Competition Act 1998[13] may not be used in evidence against him on a prosecution for a cartel offence[14] unless, in the proceedings, in giving evidence, he makes a statement inconsistent with it and evidence relating to it is adduced, or a question relating to it is asked, by him or on his behalf[15].

1   Ie under the Enterprise Act 2002 s 193 or s 194: see PARA 322.
2   As to the meaning of 'documents' see PARA 322 note 5.
3   As to legal professional privilege see LEGAL PROFESSIONS vol 65 (2008) PARAS 507, 511.
4   Enterprise Act 2002 s 196(1). Section 196(1) is modified in its application to Scotland: see s 196(3).
5   See note 1.
6   As to the OFT see PARAS 6–8.
7   Enterprise Act 2002 s 196(2).
8   Ie imposed by virtue of the Enterprise Act 2002 s 193 or s 194: see PARA 322.
9   Ie an offence under the Enterprise Act 2002 s 201(2): see PARA 325.
10   Enterprise Act 2002 s 197(1)(a).
11   Enterprise Act 2002 s 197(1)(b).
12   Enterprise Act 2002 s 197(2).
13   Ie by virtue of any of the Competition Act 1998 ss 26–28: see PARAS 129–131.
14   Ie an offence under the Enterprise Act 2002 s 188: see PARA 319.
15   Competition Act 1998 s 30A (added by the Enterprise Act 2002 s 198).

324.   Surveillance powers and authorisation of action in respect of property. The chairman of the Office of Fair Trading (the 'OFT')[1] has power to grant authorisations for the carrying out of intrusive surveillance under the Regulation of Investigatory Powers Act 2000[2], but only if he believes that the authorisation is necessary for the purpose of preventing or detecting a cartel offence[3] and that the authorised surveillance is proportionate to what is sought to be achieved by carrying it out[4]. The chairman of the OFT must not grant an authorisation for the carrying out of intrusive surveillance except on an application made by an officer of the OFT[5]. If the chairman is absent and the case is urgent, the application may be made to and considered by an officer of the OFT designated by it for the statutory purposes as a person entitled so to act in an urgent case[6]. Except in urgent cases, the authorisation does not have effect until it has been approved by an ordinary Surveillance Commissioner[7]. An ordinary Surveillance Commissioner may quash an authorisation at any time if he is not satisfied that the statutory grounds for making it are satisfied[8]. The Chairman of the OFT may appeal to the Chief Surveillance Commissioner against such a decision[9]. These provisions are discussed in more detail elsewhere in this work[10].

The chairman of the OFT also has power to authorise interference with property or with wireless telegraphy where he believes that such action is necessary for the purpose of preventing or detecting a cartel offence and that the taking of the action is proportionate to what the action seeks to achieve[11]. This power is also discussed in more detail elsewhere in this work[12].

1   As to the OFT see PARAS 6–8.
2   See the Regulation of Investigatory Powers Act 2000 s 32(1), (6)(n) (s 32(6)(n) added by the Enterprise Act 2002 s 199(1), (2)(b)); and POLICE vol 36(1) (2007 Reissue) PARA 497. As to the meaning of 'intrusive surveillance' see POLICE vol 36(1) (2007 Reissue) PARA 489.
3   Ie an offence under the Enterprise Act 2002 s 188: see PARA 319.
4   See the Regulation of Investigatory Powers Act 2000 s 32(2), (3), (3A) (s 32(3A) added by the Enterprise Act 2002 s 199(1), (2)(a)); and POLICE vol 36(1) (2007 Reissue) PARA 497.
5   See the Regulation of Investigatory Powers Act 2000 s 33(4A) (added by the Enterprise Act 2002 s 199(1), (3)); and POLICE vol 36(1) (2007 Reissue) PARA 499.
6   See the Regulation of Investigatory Powers Act 2000 s 34(1)–(3), (4)(m) (amended for these purposes by the Enterprise Act 2002 s 199(1), (5)); and POLICE vol 36(1) (2007 Reissue) PARA 500.
7   See the Regulation of Investigatory Powers Act 2000 s 36 (amended for these purposes by the Enterprise Act 2002 s 199(1), (7)); and POLICE vol 36(1) (2007 Reissue) PARA 502.
8   See the Regulation of Investigatory Powers Act 2000 s 37 (amended for these purposes by the Enterprise Act 2002 s 199(1), (8)); and POLICE vol 36(1) (2007 Reissue) PARA 503.
9   See the Regulation of Investigatory Powers Act 2000 s 38 (amended for these purposes by the Enterprise Act 2002 s 199(1), (9)); and POLICE vol 36(1) (2007 Reissue) PARA 504.
10 See POLICE vol 36(1) (2007 Reissue) PARA 489 et seq.
11 See the Police Act 1997 s 93 (amended for these purposes by the Enterprise Act 2002 s 200(2), (2)); and POLICE vol 36(1) (2007 Reissue) PARA 483.
12 See POLICE vol 36(1) (2007 Reissue) PARA 483 et seq.

325.   Offences in relation to investigation of cartel offences.   Any person who without reasonable excuse fails to comply with a requirement imposed on him under the statutory powers of investigation[1] conferred on the Office of Fair Trading (the 'OFT')[2] is guilty of an offence[3], as is a person who, in purported compliance with such a requirement, makes a statement which he knows to be false or misleading in a material particular[4] or recklessly makes a statement which is false or misleading in a material particular[5].

Where any person:

(1)   knows or suspects that an investigation by the Serious Fraud Office[6] or the OFT into a cartel offence[7] is being or is likely to be carried out; and

(2)   falsifies, conceals, destroys or otherwise disposes of, or causes or permits the falsification, concealment, destruction or disposal of documents[8] which he knows or suspects are or would be relevant to such an investigation,

he is guilty of an offence unless he proves that he had no intention of concealing the facts disclosed by the documents from the persons carrying out such an investigation[9].

A person who intentionally obstructs a person in the exercise of his powers under a warrant issued under the statutory powers of investigation[10] is also guilty of an offence[11].

1   Ie under the Enterprise Act 2002 s 193 or s 194: see PARA 322.

2 As to the OFT see PARAS 6–8.
3 See the Enterprise Act 2002 s 201(1). A person guilty of such an offence is liable on summary conviction to imprisonment for a term not exceeding six months or to a fine not exceeding level 5 on the standard scale, or to both: s 201(1). As to the standard scale see PARA 16 note 18.
4 Enterprise Act 2002 s 201(2)(a). A person guilty of an offence under s 201(2) is liable (1) on conviction on indictment, to imprisonment for a term not exceeding two years or to a fine, or to both; and (2) on summary conviction, to imprisonment for a term not exceeding six months or to a fine not exceeding the statutory maximum, or to both: s 201(3). As to the statutory maximum see PARA 140 note 9.
5 Enterprise Act 2002 s 201(2)(b). As to the penalty for such an offence see note 4.
6 As to the Serious Fraud Office see CRIMINAL LAW, EVIDENCE AND PROCEDURE vol 11(3) (2006 Reissue) PARA 1067 et seq.
7 Ie an offence under the Enterprise Act 2002 s 188: see PARA 319.
8 As to the meaning of 'documents' see PARA 322 note 5.
9 Enterprise Act 2002 s 201(4). A person guilty of an offence under s 201(4) is liable (1) on conviction on indictment, to imprisonment for a term not exceeding five years or to a fine, or to both; and (2) on summary conviction, to imprisonment for a term not exceeding six months or to a fine not exceeding the statutory maximum, or to both: s 201(5).
10 Ie a warrant issued under the Enterprise Act 2002 s 194: see PARA 322.
11 Enterprise Act 2002 s 201(6). A person guilty of such an offence is liable (1) on conviction on indictment, to imprisonment for a term not exceeding two years or to a fine, or to both; and (2) on summary conviction, to a fine not exceeding the statutory maximum: s 201(6).

(5) INFORMATION

(i) Restrictions on Disclosure

326. General restriction on disclosure of specified information. The following provisions apply to specified information[1] which relates to:

(1)   the affairs of an individual;
(2)   any business of an undertaking[2].

Such information must not be disclosed during the lifetime of the individual[3], or while the undertaking continues in existence[4], unless the disclosure is permitted under Part 9[5] of the Enterprise Act 2002[6]. This does not, however, prevent the disclosure of any information if the information has on an earlier occasion been disclosed to the public in circumstances which do not contravene:

(a)   the above restriction[7];
(b)   any other enactment or rule of law prohibiting or restricting the disclosure of the information[8].

Nothing in Part 9 of the 2002 Act authorises a disclosure of information which contravenes the Data Protection Act 1998[9] and nothing in that Part affects the Competition Appeal Tribunal[10]. Nor, with one exception[11], do the provisions of that Part affect any power or duty to disclose information which exists apart from those provisions[12].

1   As to the meaning of 'specified information' see PARA 327.
2   Enterprise Act 2002 s 237(1).
3   Enterprise Act 2002 s 237(2)(a).
4   Enterprise Act 2002 s 237(2)(b).
5   Ie under the Enterprise Act 2002 Pt 9 (ss 237–247): see the text and notes 1–4, 6–12; and PARA 327 et seq.
6   Enterprise Act 2002 s 237(2). A person who discloses information in contravention of s 237(2) is guilty of an offence: see PARA 335.
7   Ie the Enterprise Act 2002 s 237(2): see the text and notes 3–6.
8   Enterprise Act 2002 s 237(3).
9   Enterprise Act 2002 s 237(4). As to the Data Protection Act 1998 see CONFIDENCE AND DATA PROTECTION vol 8(1) (2003 Reissue) PARA 503 et seq.
10   Enterprise Act 2002 s 237(5). As to the Competition Appeal Tribunal see PARAS 13–17.

11 Ie with the exception of the Enterprise Act 2002 s 244: see PARA 334.
12 See the Enterprise Act 2002 s 237(6). As to the construction of s 237(6) see *Dumfries and Galloway Council v Dunion, Scottish Information Comr* [2008] CSIH 12, 2008 SC 327, 2008 Scot (D) 8/2.

327. Specified information. The following provisions apply for the purposes of Part 9[1] of the Enterprise Act 2002[2].

Information is specified information if it comes to a public authority[3] in connection with the exercise of any function it has under or by virtue of:

(1)   Part 1[4], Part 3[5], Part 4[6], Part 6[7], Part 7[8] or Part 8[9] of that Act;
(2)   an enactment[10] specified in Schedule 14 to that Act[11];
(3)   such subordinate legislation as the Secretary of State may by order[12] specify for these purposes[13];

and it is immaterial whether information comes to a public authority before or after 7 November 2002[14].

1   Ie the Enterprise Act 2002 Pt 9 (ss 237–247): see PARA 326; the text and notes 2–14; and PARA 328 et seq.
2   Enterprise Act 2002 s 238(8).
3   'Public authority' (except in the expression 'overseas public authority') (see PARA 333) must be construed in accordance with the Human Rights Act 1998 s 6: Enterprise Act 2002 s 238(3). For those purposes, 'public authority' includes (1) a court or tribunal; and (2) any person certain of whose functions are functions of a public nature, but does not include either House of Parliament or a person exercising functions in connection with proceedings in Parliament: Human Rights Act 1998 s 6(3). At the date at which this volume states the law, 'Parliament' in s 6(3) does not include the House of Lords in its judicial capacity: s 6(4) (repealed by the Constitutional Reform Act 2005 Sch 9 Pt I para 66(4) as from 1 October 2009; as from that date, the jurisdiction of the House of Lords to hear appeals will be transferred to the new Supreme Court established under Pt 3 (ss 23–60)). In relation to a particular act, a person is not a public authority by virtue only of the Human Rights Act 1998 s 6(3)(b) (see head (2) above) if the nature of the act is private: s 6(5). See further CONSTITUTIONAL LAW AND HUMAN RIGHTS.
4   Ie the Enterprise Act 2002 Pt 1 (ss 1–11): see PARA 6 et seq.
5   Ie the Enterprise Act 2002 Pt 3 (ss 22–130): see PARA 172 et seq.
6   Ie the Enterprise Act 2002 Pt 4 (ss 131–184): see PARA 276 et seq.
7   Ie the Enterprise Act 2002 Pt 6 (ss 188–202): see PARA 319 et seq.
8   Ie the Enterprise Act 2002 Pt 7 (ss 203–209): see PARAS 8, 151, 171, 232 et seq.
9   Ie the Enterprise Act 2002 Pt 8 (ss 210–236): see PARA 339 et seq.
10 In head (2) in the text, the reference to an enactment includes a reference to an enactment contained in (1) an Act of the Scottish Parliament; (2) Northern Ireland legislation; (3) subordinate legislation: Enterprise Act 2002 s 238(4). For the purposes of Pt 9, 'subordinate legislation' has the same meaning as in the Interpretation Act 1978 s 21(1) (ie Orders in Council, orders, rules, regulations, schemes, warrants, byelaws and other instruments made or to be made under any Act) and includes an instrument made under (a) an Act of the Scottish Parliament; (b) Northern Ireland legislation: Enterprise Act 2002 s 246.
11 The enactments so specified are: (1) the Fair Trading Act 1973 Pts I, III–VII (all repealed), Pt VIII (repealed except for s 93B) and Pt XI (ss 118–123) (pyramid selling and similar trading schemes: see SALE OF GOODS AND SUPPLY OF SERVICES vol 41 (2005 Reissue) PARA 853 et seq); (2) the Trade Descriptions Act 1968 (see SALE OF GOODS AND SUPPLY OF SERVICES vol 41 (2005 Reissue) PARA 471 et seq); (3) the Hallmarking Act 1973 (see SALE OF GOODS AND SUPPLY OF SERVICES vol 41 (2005 Reissue) PARA 765); (4) the Prices Act 1974 (see SALE OF GOODS AND SUPPLY OF SERVICES vol 41 (2005 Reissue) PARA 681 et seq); (5) the Consumer Credit Act 1974 (see CONSUMER CREDIT vol 9(1) (Reissue) PARA 78 et seq; SALE OF GOODS AND SUPPLY OF SERVICES vol 41 (2005 Reissue) PARAS 763, 768 et seq); (6) the Customs and Excise Management Act 1979 (see CUSTOMS AND EXCISE); (7) the Estate Agents Act 1979 (see AGENCY vol 1 (2008) PARA 239 et seq); (8) the Competition Act 1980 (see PARAS 3, 10, 115; and SALE OF GOODS AND SUPPLY OF SERVICES vol 41 (2005 Reissue) PARA 405); (9) the Video Recordings Act 1984 (see LICENSING AND GAMBLING vol 67 (2008) PARA 276 et seq); (10) the Consumer Protection Act 1987 (see SALE OF GOODS AND SUPPLY OF SERVICES vol 41 (2005 Reissue) PARA 518 et seq) and the corresponding Northern Ireland legislation; (11) the Copyright, Designs and Patents Act 1988 (see COPYRIGHT, DESIGN RIGHT AND RELATED RIGHTS; PATENTS AND REGISTERED DESIGNS); (12) the Property Misdescriptions Act 1991 (see SALE OF GOODS AND

SUPPLY OF SERVICES vol 41 (2005 Reissue) PARA 791 et seq); (13) the Timeshare Act 1992 (see SALE OF GOODS AND SUPPLY OF SERVICES vol 41 (2005 Reissue) PARA 868 et seq); (14) the Clean Air Act 1993 (see PROTECTION OF ENVIRONMENT AND PUBLIC HEALTH vol 38 (2006 Reissue) PARAS 190 et seq, 413–444); (15) the Value Added Tax Act 1994 (see VALUE ADDED TAX); (16) the Trade Marks Act 1994 (see TRADE MARKS AND TRADE NAMES); (17) the Competition Act 1998 (see PARA 115 et seq); (18) the Financial Services and Markets Act 2000 Pt X Ch III (ss 159–164), Pt XVIII Ch II (ss 302–310) (competition scrutiny: see FINANCIAL SERVICES AND INSTITUTIONS vol 48 (2008) PARA 38 et seq, FINANCIAL SERVICES AND INSTITUTIONS vol 49 (2008) PARA 730 et seq); (19) an order made under the Financial Services and Markets Act 2000 s 95 (competition scrutiny: see FINANCIAL SERVICES AND INSTITUTIONS vol 48 (2008) PARA 432); (20) the Fireworks Act 2003 (see EXPLOSIVES); (21) the Compensation Act 2006 (see LEGAL PROFESSIONS vol 65 (2008) PARA 553 et seq; and DAMAGES; NEGLIGENCE); and (22) the Consumers, Estate Agents and Redress Act 2007 (see SALE OF GOODS AND SUPPLY OF SERVICES vol 41 (2005 Reissue) PARA 444; and AGENCY): Enterprise Act 2002 Sch 14 (amended by the Fireworks Act 2003 s 12(3); the Consumers, Estate Agents and Redress Act 2007 s 29(1); and by SI 2003/1400; SI 2003/2580; SI 2007/2977; SI 2008/1277).

The Secretary of State may by order amend the Enterprise Act 2002 Sch 14: s 238(5). The power to make such an order includes power to add, vary or remove a reference to any provision of (a) an Act of the Scottish Parliament; (b) Northern Ireland legislation: s 238(6). An order under s 238 must be made by statutory instrument subject to annulment in pursuance of a resolution of either House of Parliament: s 238(7). In the exercise of this power, the Secretary of State has made the amending orders cited above. As to the Secretary of State see PARA 5.

12 As to the making of such an order see the Enterprise Act 2002 s 238(7), cited in note 11.

13 Enterprise Act 2002 s 238(1). As to the subordinate legislation specified for the purposes of s 238(1)(c) (see head (3) in the text) see the Enterprise Act 2002 (Part 9 Restrictions on Disclosure of Information) (Amendment and Specification) Order 2003, SI 2003/1400, Sch 3 (amended by SI 2005/1803; SI 2007/1846; SI 2008/1277; SI 2008/1816); the Enterprise Act 2002 (Part 9 Restrictions on Disclosure of Information) (Specification) Order 2004, SI 2004/693, Sch 1 (amended by SI 2004/3201; SI 2006/3418; SI 2008/37; SI 2008/1597; SI 2008/2164); the Enterprise Act 2002 (Part 9 Restrictions on Disclosure of Information) (Amendment and Specification) Order 2007, SI 2007/2977, art 3.

14 Enterprise Act 2002 s 238(2). 7 November 2002 is the date of the passing of the Enterprise Act 2002, which received royal assent on that date.

(ii) Permitted Disclosure

328. Disclosure with consent. Part 9 of the Enterprise Act 2002[1] does not prohibit the disclosure by a public authority[2] of information held by it to any other person if it obtains each required consent[3].

If the information was obtained by the authority from a person who had the information lawfully and the authority knows the identity of that person, the consent of that person is required[4].

If the information relates to the affairs of an individual, the consent of the individual is required[5].

If the information relates to the business of an undertaking, the consent of the person for the time being carrying on the business is required[6]; and for these purposes consent may be given:

(1)   in the case of a company, by a director, secretary or other officer of the company;

(2)   in the case of a partnership, by a partner;

(3)   in the case of an unincorporated body or association, by a person concerned in the management or control of the body or association[7].

1   Ie the Enterprise Act 2002 Pt 9 (ss 237–247): see PARAS 326–327; the text and notes 2–7; and PARA 329 et seq.
2   As to the meaning of 'public authority' see PARA 327 note 3.
3   Enterprise Act 2002 s 239(1).
4   Enterprise Act 2002 s 239(2).
5   Enterprise Act 2002 s 239(3).

6   Enterprise Act 2002 s 239(4).
7   Enterprise Act 2002 s 239(5).

329.   Disclosure for the purposes of Community obligations. Part 9 of the Enterprise Act 2002[1] does not prohibit the disclosure of information held by a public authority[2] to another person if the disclosure is required for the purpose of a Community obligation[3].

1   Ie the Enterprise Act 2002 Pt 9 (ss 237–247): see PARAS 326–328, 330 et seq.
2   As to the meaning of 'public authority' see PARA 327 note 3.
3   Enterprise Act 2002 s 240.

330.   Disclosure to facilitate the exercise of statutory functions. A public authority[1] which holds information to which the general restriction on disclosure applies[2] may disclose that information for the purpose of facilitating[3] the exercise by the authority of any function it has under or by virtue of the Enterprise Act 2002 or any other enactment[3]. If information is disclosed under the above provision[4] so that it is not made available to the public, it must not be further disclosed by a person to whom it is so disclosed other than with the agreement of the public authority for the purpose mentioned in that provision[5].

A public authority which holds information to which the general restriction on disclosure applies[6] may also disclose that information to any other person for the purpose of facilitating the exercise by that person of any function he has under or by virtue of:

(1)   the Enterprise Act 2002;
(2)   an enactment specified in Schedule 15 to that Act[7];
(3)   such subordinate legislation as the Secretary of State may by order[8] specify for these purposes[9].

Information disclosed under heads (1) to (3) above must not be used by the person to whom it is disclosed for any purpose other than a purpose relating to a function mentioned in those heads[10].

1   As to the meaning of 'public authority' see PARA 327 note 3.
2   Ie information to which the Enterprise Act 2002 s 237 applies: see PARA 326.
3   Enterprise Act 2002 s 241(1). In s 241(1) the reference to an enactment includes a reference to an enactment contained in (1) an Act of the Scottish Parliament; (2) Northern Ireland legislation; (3) subordinate legislation: s 241(5). As to the meaning of 'subordinate legislation' see PARA 327 note 10.
     It has been held in Scotland that 'function', construed in the context of s 241(1), connotes an act or activity susceptible of being facilitated by disclosure of information and does not connote an act or activity consisting of the disclosure of information: see *Dumfries and Galloway Council v Dunion, Scottish Information Comr* [2008] CSIH 12, 2008 SC 327, 2008 Scot (D) 8/2.
4   Ie under the Enterprise Act 2002 s 241(1): see the text and notes 1–3.
5   Enterprise Act 2002 s 241(2).
6   See note 2.
7   The enactments so specified are: (1) the Gun Barrel Proof Act 1868 (see CRIMINAL LAW, EVIDENCE AND PROCEDURE vol 11(1) (2006 Reissue) PARAS 129, 355, CRIMINAL LAW, EVIDENCE AND PROCEDURE vol 11(2) (2006 Reissue) PARA 667; TRADE MARKS AND TRADE NAMES vol 48 (2007 Reissue) PARA 487); (2) the Gun Barrel Proof Act 1950 (largely repealed); (3) the Trade Descriptions Act 1968 (see SALE OF GOODS AND SUPPLY OF SERVICES vol 41 (2005 Reissue) PARA 471 et seq); (4) the Unsolicited Goods and Services Act 1971 (see SALE OF GOODS AND SUPPLY OF SERVICES vol 41 (2005 Reissue) PARA 657 et seq) and the corresponding Northern Ireland provisions; (5) the Fair Trading Act 1973 (largely repealed; as to regulation of pyramid selling and similar trading schemes under that Act see SALE OF GOODS AND SUPPLY OF SERVICES vol 41 (2005 Reissue) PARA 853 et seq); (6) the Hallmarking Act 1973 (see SALE OF GOODS AND SUPPLY OF SERVICES vol 41 (2005 Reissue) PARA 765); (7) the Prices Act 1974 (see SALE OF GOODS AND SUPPLY OF SERVICES vol 41 (2005 Reissue) PARA 681 et seq); (8) the relevant statutory provisions

within the meaning of the Health and Safety at Work etc Act 1974 Pt I (ss 1–54) (see HEALTH
AND SAFETY AT WORK) and the corresponding Northern Ireland provisions; (9) the Consumer
Credit Act 1974 (see CONSUMER CREDIT vol 9(1) (Reissue) PARA 78 et seq; SALE OF GOODS AND
SUPPLY OF SERVICES vol 41 (2005 Reissue) PARAS 763, 768 et seq); (10) the Gun Barrel Proof
Act 1978 (see CRIMINAL LAW, EVIDENCE AND PROCEDURE vol 11(1) (2006 Reissue) PARAS 129,
355, CRIMINAL LAW, EVIDENCE AND PROCEDURE vol 11(2) (2006 Reissue) PARA 667; TRADE
MARKS AND TRADE NAMES vol 48 (2007 Reissue) PARA 487); (11) the Estate Agents Act 1979
(see AGENCY vol 1 (2008) PARA 239 et seq); (12) the Competition Act 1980 (see PARAS 3, 10,
115; and SALE OF GOODS AND SUPPLY OF SERVICES vol 41 (2005 Reissue) PARA 405); (13) the
National Audit Act 1983 (see CONSTITUTIONAL LAW AND HUMAN RIGHTS); (14) the
Telecommunications Act 1984 (largely repealed); (15) the Video Recordings Act 1984 (see
LICENSING AND GAMBLING vol 67 (2008) PARA 276 et seq); (16) the Weights and Measures
Act 1985 (see WEIGHTS AND MEASURES) and Northern Ireland weights and measures legislation;
(17) the Airports Act 1986 (see AIR LAW) and Northern Ireland airports legislation; (18) the Gas
Act 1986 (see FUEL AND ENERGY); (19) the Insolvency Act 1986 (see BANKRUPTCY AND
INDIVIDUAL INSOLVENCY; COMPANY AND PARTNERSHIP INSOLVENCY) and Northern Ireland
insolvency legislation; (20) the Company Directors Disqualification Act 1986 (see COMPANIES)
and similar Northern Ireland legislation; (21) the Financial Services Act 1986 (repealed: see now
the Financial Services and Markets Act 2000; and FINANCIAL SERVICES AND INSTITUTIONS); (22)
the Consumer Protection Act 1987 (see SALE OF GOODS AND SUPPLY OF SERVICES vol 41 (2005
Reissue) PARA 518 et seq) and the corresponding Northern Ireland legislation; (23) the Banking
Act 1987 (repealed); (24) the Education Reform Act 1988 (see EDUCATION); (25) the Copyright,
Designs and Patents Act 1988 (see COPYRIGHT, DESIGN RIGHT AND RELATED RIGHTS; PATENTS
AND REGISTERED DESIGNS); (26) the Education (Unrecognised Degrees) (Northern Ireland)
Order 1988, SI 1988/1989; (27) the Water Act 1989 (largely repealed); (28) the Electricity
Act 1989 (see FUEL AND ENERGY) and Northern Ireland electricity legislation; (29) the
Companies Act 1989 (see COMPANIES) and the corresponding Northern Ireland legislation; (30)
the Courts and Legal Services Act 1990 (see COURTS; LEGAL PROFESSIONS); (31) the
Broadcasting Act 1990 (see TELECOMMUNICATIONS AND BROADCASTING); (32) the Property
Misdescriptions Act 1991 (see SALE OF GOODS AND SUPPLY OF SERVICES vol 41 (2005 Reissue)
PARA 791 et seq); (33) the Water Industry Act 1991 (see WATER AND WATERWAYS); (34) the
Water Resources Act 1991 (see WATER AND WATERWAYS); (35) the Statutory Water Companies
Act 1991 (see WATER AND WATERWAYS); (36) the Land Drainage Act 1991 (see WATER AND
WATERWAYS); (37) the Water Consolidation (Consequential Provisions) Act 1991 (see WATER
AND WATERWAYS); (38) the Timeshare Act 1992 (see SALE OF GOODS AND SUPPLY OF SERVICES
vol 41 (2005 Reissue) PARA 868 et seq); (39) the Clean Air Act 1993 (see PROTECTION OF
ENVIRONMENT AND PUBLIC HEALTH vol 38 (2006 Reissue) PARAS 190 et seq, 413–444); (40) the
Railways Act 1993 (see RAILWAYS, INLAND WATERWAYS AND CROSS-COUNTRY PIPELINES); (41)
the Coal Industry Act 1994 (see MINES, MINERALS AND QUARRIES); (42) the Trade Marks
Act 1994 (see TRADE MARKS AND TRADE NAMES); (43) the Gas Act 1995 (see FUEL AND
ENERGY) and the corresponding Northern Ireland legislation; (44) the Broadcasting Act 1996
(see TELECOMMUNICATIONS AND BROADCASTING); (45) the Competition Act 1998 (see PARA
115 et seq); (46) the Financial Services and Markets Act 2000 (see FINANCIAL SERVICES AND
INSTITUTIONS); (47) the Government Resources and Accounts Act 2000 (see CONSTITUTIONAL
LAW AND HUMAN RIGHTS); (48) the Postal Services Act 2000 (see POST OFFICE); (49) the Utilities
Act 2000 (see FUEL AND ENERGY); (50) the Transport Act 2000 (see AIR LAW; RAILWAYS,
INLAND WATERWAYS AND CROSS-COUNTRY PIPELINES; ROAD TRAFFIC); (51) the
Communications Act 2003 (see TELECOMMUNICATIONS AND BROADCASTING); (52) the
Fireworks Act 2003 (see EXPLOSIVES); (53) the Water Act 2003 (see WATER AND WATERWAYS)
and certain Northern Ireland water and sewerage legislation; (54) the Railways Act 2005 (see
RAILWAYS, INLAND WATERWAYS AND CROSS-COUNTRY PIPELINES); (55) the Gambling Act 2005
(see LICENSING AND GAMBLING); (56) the Compensation Act 2006 (see LEGAL PROFESSIONS
vol 65 (2008) PARA 553 et seq; and DAMAGES; NEGLIGENCE); (57) the Wireless Telegraphy
Act 2006 (see TELECOMMUNICATIONS AND BROADCASTING); (58) the Consumers, Estate Agents
and Redress Act 2007 (see SALE OF GOODS AND SUPPLY OF SERVICES vol 41 (2005 Reissue) PARA
444; and AGENCY); and (59) the Companies Acts (as defined in the Companies Act 2006 s 2)
(see COMPANIES): Enterprise Act 2002 Sch 15 (amended by the Communications Act 2003
Sch 17 para 174(1), (7); the Fireworks Act 2003 s 12(3); the Water Act 2003 Sch 7 Pt 2
para 36(1), (4); the Railways Act 2005 Sch 12 para 18(1), (4); the Consumers, Estate Agents and
Redress Act 2007 s 29(2); and by SI 2003/1400; SI 2006/2909; SI 2006/3336; SI 2007/2194;
SI 2007/2977).

The Secretary of State may by order amend the Enterprise Act 2002 Sch 15: s 241(6). The
power to make such an order includes power to add, vary or remove a reference to any

provision of (a) an Act of the Scottish Parliament; (b) Northern Ireland legislation: s 241(7). An order under s 214 must be made by statutory instrument subject to annulment in pursuance of a resolution of either House of Parliament: s 241(8). In the exercise of this power, the Secretary of State has made the amending orders cited above. As to the Secretary of State see PARA 5.

8 As to the making of the order see s 241(8), cited in note 7.

9 Enterprise Act 2002 s 241(3). As to the subordinate legislation specified for the purposes of s 241(3)(c) (see head (3) in the text) see the Enterprise Act 2002 (Part 9 Restrictions on Disclosure of Information) (Amendment and Specification) Order 2003, SI 2003/1400, Sch 4 (amended by SI 2005/1803; SI 2006/599; SI 2006/1057; SI 2007/1846; SI 2008/1277; SI 2008/1816); the Enterprise Act 2002 (Part 9 Restrictions on Disclosure of Information) (Specification) Order 2004, SI 2004/693, Sch 1 (amended by SI 2004/3201; SI 2006/3418; SI 2008/37; SI 2008/1597; SI 2008/2164).

10 Enterprise Act 2002 s 241(4). A person commits an offence if he uses information so disclosed to him for an unauthorised purpose: see PARA 335.

331. Disclosure for the purposes of civil proceedings. A public authority[1] which holds prescribed information[2] to which the general restriction on disclosure applies[3] may disclose that information to any person:

(1) for the purposes of, or in connection with, prescribed civil proceedings[4], including prospective proceedings, in the United Kingdom[5] or elsewhere; or

(2) for the purposes of obtaining legal advice in relation to such proceedings; or

(3) otherwise for the purposes of establishing, enforcing or defending legal rights that are or may be the subject of such proceedings[6].

Certain information may not, however, be so disclosed[7].

Information disclosed under these provisions must not be used by the person to whom it is disclosed for any purpose other than those specified in heads (1) to (3) above[8].

1 As to the meaning of 'public authority' see PARA 327 note 3.

2 For these purposes, 'prescribed' means prescribed by order of the Secretary of State: Enterprise Act 2002 s 241A(3) (s 241A added by the Companies Act 2006 s 1281). An order under the Enterprise Act 2002 s 241A: (1) may prescribe information, or civil proceedings, for the purposes of s 241A by reference to such factors as appear to the Secretary of State to be appropriate; (2) may prescribe for those purposes all information, or civil proceedings, or all information or civil proceedings not falling within one or more specified exceptions; (3) must be made by statutory instrument subject to annulment in pursuance of a resolution of either House of Parliament: s 241A(4) (as so added). As to the Secretary of State see PARA 5.

In the exercise of these powers the Secretary of State has made the Enterprise Act 2002 (Disclosure of Information for Civil Proceedings etc) Order 2007, SI 2007/2193, which came into force on 1 October 2007: art 1(1). The prescribed information is all specified information to which the Enterprise Act 2002 s 237 applies (see PARA 326) (other than the categories of information set out in s 241A(2): see note 7) with the exception of (a) information which comes to the Office of Fair Trading (the 'OFT') in connection with the exercise of its functions under: (i) s 5(1) (acquisition of information etc: see PARA 7) with a view to exercising its functions under s 6 (provision of information etc to the public: see PARA 7), s 7 (provision of information and advice to ministers etc: see PARA 7), or s 8 (promoting good consumer practice: see PARA 7); (ii) s 11 (super-complaints to OFT: see PARA 8); (iii) s 92 (duty of OFT to monitor orders and undertakings relating to mergers: see PARA 243); (iv) s 162 (duty of OFT to monitor orders and undertakings relating to market investigations: see PARA 304); (v) Pt 6 (ss 188–202) (cartel offence: see PARA 319 et seq); (vi) Sch 24 paras 14–18 (monopoly references, enforcement undertakings and orders); (b) information which comes to a regulator in connection with the exercise of its functions under s 11 (super-complaints to OFT) as applied by s 205 (super-complaints to regulators other than OFT: see PARA 8); and (c) information which comes to Her Majesty's Revenue and Customs in connection with the exercise of their functions under the Customs and Excise Management Act 1979 and the Value Added Tax Act 1994 (see CUSTOMS AND EXCISE; VALUE ADDED TAX): Enterprise Act 2002 (Disclosure of Information for Civil Proceedings etc) Order 2007, SI 2007/2193, arts 1(2), 2. As to the meaning of 'specified information' see PARA 327; and as to the OFT see PARAS 6–8.

3   Ie information to which the Enterprise Act 2002 s 237 applies: see PARA 326.
4   The following civil proceedings are prescribed for these purposes: (1) proceedings relating to or
     arising out of a legal right or obligation of a consumer; (2) proceedings relating to or arising out
     of the infringement of an intellectual property right; (3) proceedings relating to or arising out of
     passing off or the misuse of a trade secret: Enterprise Act 2002 (Disclosure of Information for
     Civil Proceedings etc) Order 2007, SI 2007/2193, art 3(1). In head (1) above, a 'consumer' is an
     individual who (a) is acting outside his trade, business or profession; or (b) is acting with a view
     to carrying on a business but not in the course of a business carried on by him: art 3(2). In head
     (2) above, an 'intellectual property right' includes a patent, copyright, and analogous or related
     right, database right, registered or unregistered design right, registered trade mark, topography
     right, supplementary protection certificate, plant variety right, protected designation of origin or
     a protected geographical indication: art 3(3).
5   As to the meaning of 'United Kingdom' see PARA 401 note 1.
6   Enterprise Act 2002 s 241A(1) (as added: see note 2).
7   The Enterprise Act 2002 s 241A(1) (see the text and notes 1–6) does not apply to (1)
     information which comes to a public authority in connection with an investigation under the
     Fair Trading Act 1973 Pt IV, Pt V or Pt VI (all repealed) or under the Competition Act 1980 s 11
     (see PARA 10); (2) competition information within the meaning of the Financial Services and
     Markets Act 2000 s 351 (see FINANCIAL SERVICES AND INSTITUTIONS vol 48 (2008) PARA 479);
     (3) information which comes to a public authority in connection with an investigation under the
     Enterprise Act 2002 Pt 3 (ss 22–130) (see PARA 172 et seq) or Pt 4 (ss 131–184) (see PARA 276
     et seq) or s 174 (see PARA 314); (4) information which comes to a public authority in connection
     with an investigation under the Competition Act 1998 (see PARA 115 et seq): Enterprise
     Act 2002 s 241A(2) (as added: see note 2).
8   Enterprise Act 2002 s 241A(5) (as added: see note 2). A person commits an offence if he uses
     information so disclosed to him for an unauthorised purpose: see PARA 335.

332.   Disclosure for the purposes of criminal proceedings. A public authority[1]
which holds information to which the general restriction on disclosure applies[2]
may disclose that information to any person:

    (1)   in connection with the investigation of any criminal offence in any part
            of the United Kingdom[3];

    (2)   for the purposes of any criminal proceedings there;

    (3)   for the purpose of any decision whether to start or bring to an end such
            an investigation or proceedings[4].

A public authority must not, however, make a disclosure under these provisions
unless it is satisfied that the making of the disclosure is proportionate to what is
sought to be achieved by it[5].

Information so disclosed must not be used by the person to whom it is
disclosed for any purpose other than that for which it is disclosed[6].

1   As to the meaning of 'public authority' see PARA 327 note 3.
2   Ie information to which the Enterprise Act 2002 s 237 applies: see PARA 326.
3   As to the meaning of 'United Kingdom' see PARA 401 note 1.
4   Enterprise Act 2002 s 242(1).
5   Enterprise Act 2002 s 242(3).
6   Enterprise Act 2002 s 242(2). A person commits an offence if he uses information so disclosed
     to him for an unauthorised purpose: see PARA 335.

333.   Overseas disclosures. A public authority[1] which holds information to
which the general restriction on disclosure applies[2] (the 'discloser') may disclose
that information to an overseas public authority[3] for the following purpose[4],
namely the purpose of facilitating the exercise by the overseas public authority of
any function which it has relating to:

    (1)   carrying out investigations in connection with the enforcement of any
            relevant legislation[5] by means of civil proceedings[6];

    (2)   bringing civil proceedings for the enforcement of such legislation or the
            conduct of such proceedings[7];

(3)　　the investigation of crime[8];

(4)　　bringing criminal proceedings or the conduct of such proceedings[9];

(5)　　deciding whether to start or bring to an end such investigations or proceedings[10].

Certain information may not, however, be so disclosed[11].

The Secretary of State[12] may direct that a disclosure permitted by these provisions must not be made if he thinks that in connection with any matter in respect of which the disclosure could be made it is more appropriate:

(a)　　if any investigation is to be carried out, that it is carried out by an authority in the United Kingdom or in another specified country or territory[13];

(b)　　if any proceedings are to be brought, that they are brought in a court in the United Kingdom or in another specified country or territory[14];

and he must take such steps as he thinks are appropriate to bring such a direction to the attention of persons likely to be affected by it[15].

In deciding whether to disclose information under these provisions a public authority must have regard in particular to the following considerations:

(i)　　whether the matter in respect of which the disclosure is sought is sufficiently serious to justify making the disclosure[16];

(ii)　　whether the law of the country or territory to whose authority the disclosure would be made provides appropriate protection[17] against self-incrimination in criminal proceedings[18];

(iii)　　whether the law of that country or territory provides appropriate protection in relation to the storage and disclosure of personal data[19];

(iv)　　whether there are arrangements in place for the provision of mutual assistance as between the United Kingdom and that country or territory in relation to the disclosure of information of the kind to which the general restriction on disclosure[20] applies[21].

The Secretary of State may by order[22] modify the list of considerations in heads (i) to (iv) above[23]. He may also, by order, add to those considerations[24] or remove any of those considerations[25].

Information disclosed under these provisions:

(A)　　may be disclosed subject to the condition that it must not be further disclosed without the agreement of the discloser[26]; and

(B)　　must not otherwise be used by the overseas public authority to which it is disclosed for any purpose other than that for which it is first disclosed[27].

1　　As to the meaning of 'public authority' see PARA 327 note 3.

2　　Ie information to which the Enterprise Act 2002 s 237 applies: see PARA 326.

3　　An 'overseas public authority' is a person or body in any country or territory outside the United Kingdom which appears to the discloser to exercise functions of a public nature in relation to any of the matters mentioned in the Enterprise Act 2002 s 243(2)(a)–(e) (see heads (1)–(5) in the text): s 243(11). As to the meaning of 'United Kingdom' see PARA 401 note 1.

4　　Enterprise Act 2002 s 243(1).

5　　'Relevant legislation' is (1) the Enterprise Act 2002, any enactment specified in Sch 14 (see PARA 327 note 11) and such subordinate legislation as is specified by order for the purposes of s 238(1) (see PARA 327 note 13); (2) any enactment or subordinate legislation specified in an order under s 211(2) (see PARA 340); (3) any enactment or subordinate legislation specified in an order under s 212(3) (see PARA 341); (4) legislation in any country or territory outside the United Kingdom which appears to the discloser to make provision corresponding to the Enterprise Act 2002 or to any such enactment or subordinate legislation: s 243(12). As to the meaning of 'subordinate legislation' see PARA 327 note 10.

6　　Enterprise Act 2002 s 243(2)(a).

7　　Enterprise Act 2002 s 243(2)(b).

8   Enterprise Act 2002 s 243(2)(c).
9   Enterprise Act 2002 s 243(2)(d).
10   Enterprise Act 2002 s 243(2)(e).
11   The Enterprise Act 2002 s 243(1) (see the text and notes 1–4) does not apply to any of the following: (1) information which is held by a person who is designated by virtue of s 213(4) (see PARA 342) as a designated enforcer for the purposes of Pt 8 (ss 210–236) (see PARA 339 et seq); (2) information which comes to a public authority in connection with an investigation under the Fair Trading Act 1973 Pt IV, Pt V or Pt VI (all repealed) or under the Competition Act 1980 s 11 (see PARA 10); (3) competition information within the meaning of the Financial Services and Markets Act 2000 s 351 (see FINANCIAL SERVICES AND INSTITUTIONS vol 48 (2008) PARA 479); (4) information which comes to a public authority in connection with an investigation under the Enterprise Act 2002 Pt 3 (ss 22–130) (see PARA 172 et seq) or Pt 4 (ss 131–184) (see PARA 276 et seq) or s 174 (see PARA 314): Enterprise Act 2002 s 243(3).
12   As to the Secretary of State see PARA 5.
13   Enterprise Act 2002 s 243(4)(a). A person who discloses information in contravention of such a direction is guilty of an offence: see PARA 335.
14   Enterprise Act 2002 s 243(4)(b); and see note 13.
15   Enterprise Act 2002 s 243(5).
16   Enterprise Act 2002 s 243(6)(a).
17   Protection is appropriate if it provides protection in relation to the matter in question which corresponds to that so provided in any part of the United Kingdom: Enterprise Act 2002 s 243(7).
18   Enterprise Act 2002 s 243(6)(b).
19   Enterprise Act 2002 s 243(6)(c).
20   See note 2.
21   Enterprise Act 2002 s 243(6)(d).
22   An order under the Enterprise Act 2002 s 243(8) must be made by statutory instrument subject to annulment in pursuance of a resolution of either House of Parliament: s 243(9). At the date at which this volume states the law, no such order had been made.
23   Enterprise Act 2002 s 243(8)(a); and see note 22.
24   Enterprise Act 2002 s 243(8)(b); and see note 22.
25   Enterprise Act 2002 s 243(8)(c); and see note 22.
26   Enterprise Act 2002 s 243(10)(a).
27   Enterprise Act 2002 s 243(10)(b). A person commits an offence if he uses information so disclosed to him for an unauthorised purpose: see PARA 335.

334. Considerations relevant to disclosure. A public authority[1] must have regard to the following considerations before disclosing any specified[2] information[3].

The first consideration is the need to exclude from disclosure, so far as practicable, any information whose disclosure the authority thinks is contrary to the public interest[4].

The second consideration is the need to exclude from disclosure, so far as practicable:

(1)   commercial information whose disclosure the authority thinks might significantly harm the legitimate business interests of the undertaking to which it relates[5]; or

(2)   information relating to the private affairs of an individual whose disclosure the authority thinks might significantly harm the individual's interests[6].

The third consideration is the extent to which the disclosure of the information mentioned in head (1) or head (2) above is necessary for the purpose for which the authority is permitted to make the disclosure[7].

Additional considerations apply in the case of overseas disclosures[8].

1   As to the meaning of 'public authority' see PARA 327 note 3.
2   Ie specified information within the meaning of the Enterprise Act 2002 s 238(1): see PARA 327.
3   Enterprise Act 2002 s 244(1).
4   Enterprise Act 2002 s 244(2).

5 Enterprise Act 2002 s 244(3)(a).
6 Enterprise Act 2002 s 244(3)(b).
7 Enterprise Act 2002 s 244(4).
8 See PARA 333.

(iii) Offences

335. Offences in relation to disclosure. A person commits an offence[1] if he:

(1) discloses information to which the general restriction on disclosure applies[2] in contravention[3] of that restriction[4];

(2) discloses information in contravention of a direction with regard to overseas disclosure given[5] by the Secretary of State[6];

(3) uses information disclosed to him under Part 9 of the Enterprise Act 2002[7] for a purpose which is not permitted under that Part[8].

1 A person who commits an offence under the Enterprise Act 2002 s 245 (see heads (1)–(3) in the text) is liable (1) on summary conviction to imprisonment for a term not exceeding three months or to a fine not exceeding the statutory maximum, or to both; (2) on conviction on indictment to imprisonment for a term not exceeding two years or to a fine, or to both: s 245(4). As to the statutory maximum see PARA 140 note 9.
2 Ie information to which the Enterprise Act 2002 s 237 applies: see PARA 326.
3 Ie in contravention of the Enterprise Act 2002 s 237(2): see PARA 326.
4 Enterprise Act 2002 s 245(1). As to the penalty for such an offence see note 1.
5 Ie a direction given under the Enterprise Act 2002 s 243(4): see PARA 333.
6 See the Enterprise Act 2002 s 245(2). As to the penalty for such an offence see note 1. As to the Secretary of State see PARA 5.
7 Ie under the Enterprise Act 2002 Pt 9 (ss 237–247): see PARA 326 et seq.
8 Enterprise Act 2002 s 245(3). As to the penalty for such an offence see note 1.

5. FAIR TRADING

(1) INTRODUCTION

336. Consumer protection; in general. In addition to its role as the competition authority[1], the Office of Fair Trading (the 'OFT') is the United Kingdom's consumer authority. The OFT has the function of promoting good practice in the carrying out of activities which may affect the economic interests of consumers in the United Kingdom[2]. In carrying out that function, the OFT may approve consumer codes[3]. The OFT also manages Consumer Direct, a telephone helpline and online service providing impartial advice and information to consumers[4].

The OFT has a number of enforcement duties and a range of enforcement powers derived from consumer protection legislation, notably: the Consumer Credit Act 1974[5]; the Estate Agents Act 1979[6]; the Unfair Terms in Consumer Contracts Regulations 1999[7]; the Consumer Protection (Distance Selling) Regulations 2000[8]; the Consumer Protection from Unfair Trading Regulations 2008[9]; the Business Protection from Misleading Marketing Regulations 2008[10]; and Part 8 of the Enterprise Act 2002[11].

Sector regulators have been put in place to ensure the protection of consumers in relation to utilities[12].

1   As to the OFT's general functions see PARA 7. As to the OFT see PARAS 6–8.
2   See the Enterprise Act 2002 s 8(1); and PARA 7. As to the meaning of 'United Kingdom' see PARA 401 note 1.
3   See the Enterprise Act 2002 s 8(2); and PARA 7.
4   See OFT *Statement of Consumer Protection Enforcement Principles* (December 2008) (OFT964).
5   See CONSUMER CREDIT vol 9(1) (Reissue) PARA 78 et seq.
6   See PARA 338.
7   Ie the Unfair Terms in Consumer Contracts Regulations 1999, SI 1999/2083. See SALE OF GOODS AND SUPPLY OF SERVICES vol 41 (2005 Reissue) PARA 452 et seq.
8   Ie the Consumer Protection (Distance Selling) Regulations 2000, SI 2000/2334. See SALE OF GOODS AND SUPPLY OF SERVICES vol 41 (2005 Reissue) PARA 673 et seq.
9   Ie the Consumer Protection from Unfair Trading Regulations 2008, SI 2008/1277. See generally SALE OF GOODS AND SUPPLY OF SERVICES.
10   Ie the Business Protection from Misleading Marketing Regulations 2008, SI 2008/1276. See SALE OF GOODS AND SUPPLY OF SERVICES vol 41 (2005 Reissue) PARA 731 et seq.
11   See PARA 339 et seq.
12   See PARA 18 et seq.

337. Codes of practice. As an important alternative to powers of legal enforcement as a means of diminishing unfair conduct, the Office of Fair Trading (the 'OFT')[1] may make arrangements for approving consumer codes[2] and may, in accordance with the arrangements, give its approval to or withdraw its approval from any consumer code[3].

1   As to the OFT see PARAS 6–8.

2   'Consumer code' means a code of practice or other document (however described) intended, with a view to safeguarding or promoting the interests of consumers, to regulate by any means the conduct of persons engaged in the supply of goods or services to consumers (or the conduct of their employees or representatives): Enterprise Act 2002 s 8(6).

3   Enterprise Act 2002 s 8(2). See also PARA 7. See the OFT's *Consumer Codes Approval Scheme – Core criteria and guidance* (March 2008) (OFT390).

338. Control of estate agents. Powers have been given to the Office of Fair Trading (the 'OFT')[1] under the Estate Agents Act 1979 to prohibit unfit persons from engaging in estate agency work[2]. It is the duty of the OFT generally to superintend the working and enforcement of the Act and, where necessary or expedient, itself to take steps to enforce it[3].

1 As to the OFT see PARAS 6–8.
2 See the Estate Agents Act 1979 s 3; and AGENCY vol 1 (2008) PARA 267.
3 See the Estate Agents Act 1979 s 25; and AGENCY vol 1 (2008) PARA 278.

(2) ENFORCEMENT OF CONSUMER LEGISLATION UNDER THE ENTERPRISE ACT 2002

(i) In general

339. Consumers. In relation to the enforcement of certain consumer legislation under the Enterprise Act 2002[1], references to consumers are to be construed as follows[2].

In relation to a domestic infringement[3] a consumer is an individual in respect of whom the following conditions are satisfied[4]:

(1)   the first condition is that: (a) goods[5] are or are sought to be supplied to the individual (whether by way of sale or otherwise) in the course of a business[6] carried on by the person supplying or seeking to supply them; or (b) services[7] are or are sought to be supplied to the individual in the course of a business carried on by the person supplying or seeking to supply them[8];

(2)   the second condition is that: (a) the individual receives or seeks to receive the goods or services otherwise than in the course of a business carried on by him; or (b) the individual receives or seeks to receive the goods or services with a view to carrying on a business but not in the course of a business carried on by him[9].

In relation to a Community infringement[10] a consumer is a person who is a consumer for the purposes of the Injunctions Directive[11], and the listed Directive[12] or the listed Regulation[13] concerned[14].

1 Ie in the Enterprise Act 2002 Pt 8 (ss 210–236). The Enterprise Act 2002 Pt 8 binds the Crown; but the powers conferred by ss 227A–227D (see PARAS 355–357) are not exercisable in relation to premises occupied by the Crown: s 236 (substituted by SI 2006/3363). The Enterprise Act 2002 Pt 8 is specified for the purposes of the Regulatory Enforcement and Sanctions Act 2008 Pt 1 (ss 1–21): see s 4(2), Sch 3. See further LOCAL GOVERNMENT.
2 Enterprise Act 2002 s 210(1).
3 As to domestic infringements see PARA 340.
4 Enterprise Act 2002 s 210(2).
5 'Goods' include buildings and other structures and ships, aircraft and hovercraft: Enterprise Act 2002 s 232(1), (2). The supply of goods includes: (1) supply by way of sale, lease, hire or hire purchase; (2) in relation to buildings and other structures, construction of them by one person for another: s 232(3). Goods or services which are supplied wholly or partly outside the United Kingdom must be taken to be supplied to or for a person in the United Kingdom if they are supplied in accordance with arrangements falling within s 232(5): s 232(4). Arrangements fall within s 232(5) if they are made by any means and: (a) at the time the arrangements are made the person seeking the supply is in the United Kingdom; or (b) at the time the goods or services are supplied (or ought to be supplied in accordance with the arrangements) the person responsible under the arrangements for effecting the supply is in or has a place of business in the United Kingdom: s 232(5). As to the meaning of 'United Kingdom' see PARA 401 note 1.

    Where a reference is made in Pt 8 to a person supplying or seeking to supply goods under a hire-purchase agreement, a credit-sale agreement or a conditional sale agreement, the reference includes a reference to a person who conducts any antecedent negotiations relating to the agreement: s 233(1), (2). 'Hire-purchase agreement', 'credit-sale agreement', 'conditional sale agreement' and 'antecedent negotiations' are to be construed in accordance with the Consumer Credit Act 1974 s 189 (see CONSUMER CREDIT vol 9(1) (Reissue) PARAS 93, 95, 177): Enterprise Act 2002 s 233(3).

6   A business includes: (1) professional practice; (2) any other undertaking carried on for gain or reward; (3) any undertaking in the course of which goods or services are supplied otherwise than free of charge: Enterprise Act 2002 s 210(8). For the purposes of a domestic infringement it is immaterial whether a person supplying goods or services has a place of business in the United Kingdom: s 210(5).

7   The supply of services does not include the provision of services under a contract of service or of apprenticeship whether it is express or implied and (if it is express) whether it is oral or in writing: Enterprise Act 2002 s 234(1), (2). The supply of services includes: (1) performing for gain or reward any activity other than the supply of goods; (2) rendering services to order; (3) the provision of services by making them available to potential users: s 234(3). The supply of services includes making arrangements for the use of computer software or for granting access to data stored in any form which is not readily accessible: s 234(4). The supply of services includes making arrangements by means of a relevant agreement (within the meaning of the Telecommunications Act 1984 Sch 2 para 29 (see TELECOMMUNICATIONS AND BROADCASTING vol 45(1) (2005 Reissue) PARA 155)) for sharing the use of telecommunications apparatus: Enterprise Act 2002 s 234(5) (amended by the Communications Act 2003 Sch 17 para 174(1), (6)).

The supply of services also includes permitting or making arrangements to permit the use of land in such circumstances as the Secretary of State specifies by order: Enterprise Act 2002 s 234(6). The power to make such an order must be exercised by statutory instrument, a draft of which must have been laid before Parliament and approved by a resolution of each House: s 234(7), (8). In exercise of this power, the Enterprise Act 2002 (Supply of Services) Order 2003, SI 2003/1594, has been made. As to the Secretary of State see PARA 5.

8   Enterprise Act 2002 s 210(3).

9   Enterprise Act 2002 s 210(4).

10 As to Community infringements see PARA 341.

11 The Injunctions Directive is EC Directive 98/27 of the European Parliament and of the Council on injunctions for the protection of consumers' interests (OJ L166, 11.6.98, p 51): Enterprise Act 2002 s 235.

12 A Directive is a listed Directive if it is a Directive of the Council of the European Communities or of the European Parliament and of the Council, and if it is specified in the Enterprise Act 2002 Sch 13 or to the extent that any of its provisions is so specified: s 210(7). The following Directives have been specified in the Enterprise Act 2002 Sch 13 Pt 1 (amended by SI 2004/2095; SI 2006/3363; SI 2008/1277): EEC Council Directive 85/577 to protect the consumer in respect of contracts negotiated away from business premises (OJ L372, 31.12.85, p 31); EEC Council Directive 87/102 for the approximation of the laws, regulations and administrative provisions of the Member States concerning consumer credit (OJ L42, 12.2.87, p 48); EEC Council Directive 90/314 on package travel, package holidays and package tours (OJ L158, 23.6.90, p 59); EEC Council Directive 93/13 on unfair terms in consumer contracts (OJ L95, 21.4.93, p 29); EC Directive 97/7 of the European Parliament and of the Council on the protection of consumers in respect of distance contracts (OJ L144, 4.6.97, p 19); EC Directive 98/6 of the European Parliament and of the Council on consumer protection in the indication of the prices of products offered to consumers (OJ L80, 18.3.98, p 27); EC Directive 1999/44 of the European Parliament and of the Council on certain aspects of the sale of consumer goods and associated guarantees (OJ L171, 7.7.99, p 12); EC Directive 2000/31 of the European Parliament and of the Council on certain legal aspects of information society services, in particular electronic commerce, in the Internal Market ('Directive on electronic commerce') (OJ L178, 17.7.2000, p 1); EC Directive 2002/65 of the European Parliament and of the Council concerning the distance marketing of consumer financial services and amending EEC Council Directive 90/619 and EC Directives 97/7 and 98/27 (OJ L271, 9.10.2002, p 16); EC Regulation 261/2004 of the European Parliament and of the Council establishing common rules on compensation and assistance to air passengers in the event of denied boarding and of cancellation or long delay of flights (OJ L46, 17.2.2004, p 1); EC Directive 2005/29 of the European Parliament and of the Council concerning unfair business-to-consumer commercial practices in the internal market (OJ L149, 11.6.2005, p 22); EC Directive 2008/122 of the European Parliament and of the Council on the protection of consumers in respect of certain aspects of timeshare, long-term holiday product, resale and exchange contracts (OJ L33, 3.2.2009, p 10).

The following provisions of Directives have been specified in the Enterprise Act 2002 Sch 13 Pt 2 (amended by SI 2005/2759; SI 2008/1277): EEC Council Directive 89/552 on the co-ordination of certain provisions laid down by law, regulation or administrative action in Member States concerning the pursuit of television broadcasting activities (OJ L298, 17.10.89, p 23) arts 10–21; EC Directive 2001/83 of the European Parliament and of the Council on the Community Code relating to medicinal products for human use (OJ L311, 28.11.2001, p 67) arts 86–100 as read with EC Directive 2004/24 of the European Parliament and of the Council amending, as regards traditional herbal medicinal products, the code (OJ L136, 30.4.2004, p 85), and EC Directive 2004/27 of the European Parliament and of the Council also amending the code (OJ L136, 30.4.2004, p 34).

The Secretary of State may by order modify the Enterprise Act 2002 Sch 13: s 210(9). An order under this provision must be made by statutory instrument subject to annulment in pursuance of a resolution of either House of Parliament: s 210(10). In exercise of this power the Enterprise Act 2002 (Part 8 Community Infringements Specified UK Laws) Order 2003, SI 2003/1374, has been made.

13 A Regulation is a listed Regulation if it is a Regulation of the Council of the European Communities or of the European Parliament and of the Council, and if it is specified in the Enterprise Act 2002 Sch 13 or to the extent that any of its provisions is so specified (see note 12): s 210(7A) (added by SI 2006/3363).

14 Enterprise Act 2002 s 210(6).

340. Domestic infringements. A domestic infringement is an act or omission which: (1) is done or made by a person in the course of a business; (2) harms the collective interests of consumers[1] in the United Kingdom[2]; and (3) is of a description specified by the Secretary of State by order[3] which consists of any of the following[4]:

(a) a contravention of an enactment[5] which imposes a duty, prohibition or restriction enforceable by criminal proceedings[6];

(b) an act done or omission made in breach of contract[7];

(c) an act done or omission made in breach of a non-contractual duty owed to a person by virtue of an enactment or rule of law and enforceable by civil proceedings[8];

(d) an act or omission in respect of which an enactment provides for a remedy or sanction enforceable by civil proceedings[9];

(e) an act done or omission made by a person supplying or seeking to supply goods or services as a result of which an agreement or security relating to the supply is void or unenforceable to any extent[10];

(f) an act or omission by which a person supplying or seeking to supply goods or services purports or attempts to exercise a right or remedy relating to the supply in circumstances where the exercise of the right or remedy is restricted or excluded under or by virtue of an enactment[11];

(g) an act or omission by which a person supplying or seeking to supply goods or services purports or attempts to avoid (to any extent) liability relating to the supply in circumstances where such avoidance is restricted or prevented under an enactment[12].

An order may provide that any description of an act or omission falling within heads (a) to (g) is not a domestic infringement[13].

For these purposes it is immaterial: (i) whether or not any duty, prohibition or restriction exists in relation to consumers as such; (ii) whether or not any remedy or sanction is provided for the benefit of consumers as such; (iii) whether or not any proceedings have been brought in relation to the act or omission; (iv) whether or not any person has been convicted of an offence in respect of the contravention mentioned in head (a) above; (v) whether or not there is a waiver in respect of the breach of contract mentioned in head (b) above[14].

1 As to the meaning of 'consumers' see PARA 339.

2   It has been held in Scotland that harm to the collective interests of consumers for these purposes
     will normally be inferred from the existence of a number of individual breaches of contract or
     other relevant defaults on the part of a trader, but it has to be possible to conclude that
     something more exists than an accumulation of individual breaches; the extra element is harm to
     the public generally, in their capacity as consumers, or more precisely to the section of the public
     who are likely to buy or consider buying the trader's goods: see *Office of Fair Trading v MB
     Designs (Scotland) Ltd, Martin Black and Paul Bradley Bett* [2005] CSOH 85 at [31],
     2005 SCLR 894 at [31]. As to the meaning of 'United Kingdom' see PARA 401 note 1.
3   As to the Secretary of State see PARA 5. The power to make an order under the Enterprise
     Act 2002 s 211 must be exercised by statutory instrument but no such order may be made unless
     a draft of it has been laid before Parliament and approved by a resolution of each House:
     s 211(6), (7). In exercise of this power the Enterprise Act 2002 (Part 8 Community
     Infringements Specified UK Laws) Order 2003, SI 2003/1374, has been made.
4   Enterprise Act 2002 s 211(1).
5   References to an enactment include references to subordinate legislation (within the meaning of
     the Interpretation Act 1978 (see STATUTES vol 44(1) (Reissue) PARA 1381)): Enterprise Act 2002
     s 211(5).
6   Enterprise Act 2002 s 211(2)(a).
7   Enterprise Act 2002 s 211(2)(b). As to evidence in proceedings under Pt 8 (ss 210–236) that
     such an act or omission has occurred see s 228; and PARA 353.
8   Enterprise Act 2002 s 211(2)(c). As to evidence in proceedings under Pt 8 that such an act or
     omission has occurred see s 228; and PARA 353.
9   Enterprise Act 2002 s 211(2)(d). As to evidence in proceedings under Pt 8 that such an act or
     omission has occurred see s 228; and PARA 353.
10   Enterprise Act 2002 s 211(2)(e).
11   Enterprise Act 2002 s 211(2)(f).
12   Enterprise Act 2002 s 211(2)(g).
13   Enterprise Act 2002 s 211(3).
14   Enterprise Act 2002 s 211(4).

341.   Community infringements. A Community infringement is an act or
omission which harms the collective interests of consumers[1] and which:

(1)   contravenes a listed Directive[2] as given effect by the laws, regulations or
       administrative provisions of an EEA state[3];
(2)   contravenes such laws, regulations or administrative provisions which
       provide additional permitted protections[4];
(3)   contravenes a listed Regulation[5]; or
(4)   contravenes any laws, regulations or administrative provisions of an
       EEA state which give effect to a listed Regulation[6].

The Secretary of State may by order[7] specify for these purposes the law in the
United Kingdom[8] which:

(a)   gives effect to the listed Directives;
(b)   provides additional permitted protections; or
(c)   gives effect to a listed Regulation[9].

1   As to the meaning of 'consumers' see PARA 339.
2   For these purposes, references to a listed Directive must be construed in accordance with the
     Enterprise Act 2002 s 210 (see PARA 339 note 12): s 212(4).
3   Enterprise Act 2002 s 212(1)(a) (amended by SI 2006/3363). As to evidence in proceedings
     under the Enterprise Act 2002 Pt 8 (ss 210–236) that such an act or omission has occurred see
     s 228; and PARA 353. 'EEA state', in relation to any time, means (1) a state which at that time is
     a member state of the European Community; or (2) any other state which at that time is a party
     to the EEA agreement: Interpretation Act 1978 Sch 1 (definition added by the Legislative and
     Regulatory Reform Act 2006 s 26(1); applied by the Enterprise Act 2002 s 212(5) (substituted
     by SI 2007/528)). 'EEA agreement' means the agreement on the European Economic Area signed
     at Oporto on 2 May 1992, together with the Protocol adjusting that agreement signed at
     Brussels on 17 March 1993, as modified or supplemented from time to time: Interpretation
     Act 1978 Sch 1 (definition as so added and applied).
4   Enterprise Act 2002 s 212(1)(b). As to evidence in proceedings under Pt 8 that such an act or
     omission has occurred see s 228; and PARA 353. The laws, regulations or administrative

provisions of an EEA state which give effect to a listed Directive provide additional permitted protections if (1) they provide protection for consumers which is in addition to the minimum protection required by the Directive concerned; and (2) such additional protection is permitted by that Directive: Enterprise Act 2002 s 212(2).

5   Enterprise Act 2002 s 212(1)(c) (added by SI 2006/3363). As to evidence in proceedings under the Enterprise Act 2002 Pt 8 that such an act or omission has occurred see s 228; and PARA 353. For these purposes, references to a listed Regulation must be construed in accordance with the Enterprise Act 2002 s 210 (see PARA 339 note 13): s 212(4) (amended by SI 2006/3363).

6   Enterprise Act 2002 s 212(1)(d) (added by SI 2006/3363). As to evidence in proceedings under the Enterprise Act 2002 Pt 8 that such an act or omission has occurred see s 228; and PARA 353.

7   As to the Secretary of State see PARA 5. An order under the Enterprise Act 2002 s 212 must be made by statutory instrument subject to annulment in pursuance of a resolution of either House of Parliament: s 212(6). See also note 9.

8   As to the meaning of 'United Kingdom' see PARA 401 note 1.

9   Enterprise Act 2002 s 212(3) (amended by SI 2006/3363). In the exercise of this power the following orders have been made: (1) the Enterprise Act 2002 (Part 8 Community Infringements Specified UK Laws) Order 2003, SI 2003/1374; (2) the Enterprise Act 2002 (Part 8 Community Infringements Specified UK Laws) (Amendment) Order 2005, SI 2005/2418; and (3) the Enterprise Act 2002 (Part 8 Community Infringements Specified UK Laws) Order 2006, SI 2006/3372.

342.   Enforcers. Each of the following is a general enforcer[1]:

(1)   the Office of Fair Trading (the 'OFT')[2];

(2)   every local weights and measures authority in Great Britain[3];

(3)   the Department of Enterprise, Trade and Investment in Northern Ireland[4].

A designated enforcer[5] is any person or body (whether or not incorporated) which the Secretary of State[6] thinks has as one of its purposes the protection of the collective interests of consumers[7] and designates[8] by order[9]. If requested to do so by a designated enforcer which is designated in respect of one or more Community infringements[10] the Secretary of State must notify the Commission of the European Communities of its name and purpose and of the Community infringements in respect of which it is designated[11]. The Secretary of State must also notify the Commission:

(a)   of the fact that a person or body in respect of which he has given such notice[12] ceases to be a designated enforcer;

(b)   of any change in the name or purpose of a designated enforcer in respect of which he has given such notice;

(c)   of any change to the Community infringements in respect of which a designated enforcer is designated[13].

A Community enforcer is a qualified entity for the purposes of the Injunctions Directive[14] (i) which is for the time being specified in the list published[15] in the Official Journal of the European Communities; but (ii) which is not a general enforcer, a designated enforcer or a CPC enforcer[16]. Each of the following, being bodies or persons designated by the Secretary of State under the relevant provision[17] of the CPC Regulation[18], is a CPC enforcer[19]:

(A)   the OFT;

(B)   the Civil Aviation Authority[20];

(C)   the Financial Services Authority[21];

(D)   the Secretary of State for Health;

(E)   the Department of Health, Social Services and Public Safety in Northern Ireland;

(F)   the Office of Communications[22];

(G)   the Department of Enterprise, Trade and Investment in Northern Ireland;

(H)   every local weights and measures authority in Great Britain;
(I)   the Independent Committee for the Supervision of Standards of the
      Telephone Information Services[23].

1   References in the Enterprise Act 2002 Pt 8 (ss 210–236) to a general enforcer, a designated
    enforcer (see the text and notes 5–9) or a CPC enforcer (see the text and notes 17–23) are to be
    read, in the case of a person or body which is more than one kind of enforcer, as references to
    that person or body acting in its capacity as a general enforcer, designated enforcer or (as the
    case may be) CPC enforcer: s 235B (added by SI 2006/3363).
2   As to the OFT see PARAS 6–8.
3   As to local weights and measures authorities see WEIGHTS AND MEASURES vol 50 (2005 Reissue)
    PARA 20. As to the meaning of 'Great Britain' see PARA 395 note 2.
4   Enterprise Act 2002 s 213(1).
5   As to dual enforcers see note 1.
6   As to the Secretary of State see PARA 5.
7   As to the meaning of 'consumers' see PARA 339.
8   The Secretary of State may designate a public body only if he is satisfied that it is independent:
    Enterprise Act 2002 s 213(3). The designation of a body by virtue of s 213(3) is conclusive
    evidence for the purposes of any question arising under Pt 8 that the body is a public body:
    s 213(8).
        The Secretary of State may designate a person or body which is not a public body only if the
    person or body (as the case may be) satisfies such criteria as the Secretary of State specifies by
    order: s 213(4). An order under s 213 may make different provision for different purposes
    (s 213(7)) and must be made by statutory instrument subject to annulment in pursuance of a
    resolution of either House of Parliament (s 213(9)). As to the specified criteria see the Enterprise
    Act 2002 (Part 8 Designated Enforcers: Criteria for Designation, Designation of Public Bodies as
    Designated Enforcers and Transitional Provisions) Order 2003, SI 2003/1399, arts 3, 4.
9   Enterprise Act 2002 s 213(2). An order under s 213 may designate an enforcer in respect of (1)
    all infringements; (2) infringements of such descriptions as are specified in the order: s 213(6).
    See also note 8. The following public bodies are designated under s 213(2) as designated
    enforcers in respect of all infringements: the Civil Aviation Authority (see note 20); the Director
    General of Electricity Supply for Northern Ireland; the Director General of Gas for Northern
    Ireland; the Office of Communications (see note 22); the Water Services Regulation Authority
    (see WATER AND WATERWAYS vol 100 (2009) PARA 109 et seq); the Gas and Electricity Markets
    Authority ('GEMA') (see FUEL AND ENERGY vol 19(1) (2007 Reissue) PARA 708); the
    Information Commissioner (see CONFIDENCE AND DATA PROTECTION vol 8(1) (2003 Reissue)
    PARA 518); and the Office of Rail Regulation (see RAILWAYS, INLAND WATERWAYS AND
    CROSS-COUNTRY PIPELINES vol 39(1A) (Reissue) PARA 49 et seq): Enterprise Act 2002 (Part 8
    Designated Enforcers: Criteria for Designation, Designation of Public Bodies as Designated
    Enforcers and Transitional Provisions) Order 2003, SI 2003/1399, art 5, Schedule (amended by
    SI 2003/3182, art 3, SI 2006/522; and by virtue of the Railways and Transport Safety Act 2003
    Sch 3 para 4). The Financial Services Authority (see note 21) is also designated as a designated
    enforcer in respect of all infringements (Enterprise Act 2002 (Part 8) (Designation of the
    Financial Services Authority as a Designated Enforcer) Order 2004, SI 2004/935, art 2) as is the
    Consumers' Association (Enterprise Act 2002 (Part 8) (Designation of the Consumers'
    Association) Order 2005, SI 2005/917, art 2). As to the Consumers' Association see SALE OF
    GOODS AND SUPPLY OF SERVICES vol 41 (2005 Reissue) PARA 445.
10 As to the meaning of 'Community infringements' see PARA 341.
11 Enterprise Act 2002 s 213(10).
12 Ie notice under the Enterprise Act 2002 s 213(10): see the text and notes 10–11.
13 Enterprise Act 2002 s 213(11).
14 As to the meaning of 'Injunctions Directive' see PARA 339 note 11.
15 Ie in pursuance of EC Directive 98/27 of the European Parliament and of the Council on
    injunctions for the protection of consumers' interests (OJ L166, 11.6.98, p 51) art 4.3.
16 Enterprise Act 2002 s 213(5) (amended by SI 2006/3363).
17 Ie under EC Regulation 2006/2004 of the European Parliament and of the Council on
    co-operation between national authorities responsible for the enforcement of consumer
    protection laws (OJ L364, 9.12.2004, p 1) art 4(1) or 4(2). See also note 18.
18 The CPC Regulation is EC Regulation 2006/2004 of the European Parliament and of the
    Council on co-operation between national authorities responsible for the enforcement of
    consumer protection laws (OJ L364, 9.12.2004, p 1) as amended by the Unfair Commercial
    Practices Directive; and the Unfair Commercial Practices Directive is EC Directive 2005/29 of

the European Parliament and of the Council concerning unfair business-to-consumer commercial practices in the internal market (OJ L149, 11.6.2005, p 22): Enterprise Act 2002 s 235A (added by SI 2006/3363).

19 As to dual enforcers see note 1.
20 As to the Civil Aviation Authority see AIR LAW vol 2 (2008) PARA 50 et seq.
21 As to the Financial Services Authority see FINANCIAL SERVICES AND INSTITUTIONS vol 48 (2008) PARA 4 et seq.
22 As to the Office of Communications ('OFCOM') see TELECOMMUNICATIONS AND BROADCASTING vol 45(1) (2005 Reissue) PARA 2 et seq.
23 Enterprise Act 2002 s 213(5A) (added by SI 2006/3363). As to the Independent Committee for the Supervision of Standards of the Telephone Information Services ('ICTIS') see TELECOMMUNICATIONS AND BROADCASTING vol 45(1) (2005 Reissue) PARA 51.

343. Advice and information to be published by the Office of Fair Trading. As soon as reasonably practicable after 7 November 2002[1] the Office of Fair Trading (the 'OFT')[2] was to prepare and publish advice and information with a view to:

(1) explaining the provisions of Part 8 of the Enterprise Act 2002[3] to persons who are likely to be affected by them; and

(2) indicating how the OFT expects such provisions to operate[4].

Advice or information published in pursuance of head (2) above may include advice or information about the factors which the OFT may take into account in considering how to exercise the functions conferred on it by Part 8 of that Act[5].

The OFT may at any time publish revised or new advice or information[6].

Advice or information published by the OFT under these provisions is to be published in such form and in such manner as it considers appropriate[7].

In preparing advice or information under these provisions the OFT must consult such persons as it thinks are representative of persons affected by Part 8 of the Enterprise Act 2002[8]. If any proposed advice or information relates to a matter in respect of which another general or CPC enforcer[9] or a designated enforcer[10] may act the persons to be consulted must include that enforcer[11].

The first advice and guidance prepared under these provisions was published in June 2003[12].

1 Ie the date of the passing of the Enterprise Act 2002. The Enterprise Act 2002 received royal assent on 7 November 2002.
2 As to the OFT see PARAS 6–8.
3 Ie the Enterprise Act 2002 Pt 8 (ss 210–236): see PARAS 339 et seq, 344 et seq.
4 Enterprise Act 2002 s 229(1). See the OFT's *Enforcement of Consumer Protection Legislation — Guidance on Part 8 of the Enterprise Act 2002* (June 2003) OFT512.
5 Enterprise Act 2002 s 229(3).
6 Enterprise Act 2002 s 229(2).
7 Enterprise Act 2002 s 229(4).
8 Enterprise Act 2002 s 229(5).
9 As to the meanings of 'general enforcer' and 'CPC enforcer' see PARA 342.
10 As to the meaning of 'designated enforcer' see PARA 342.
11 Enterprise Act 2002 s 229(6) (amended by SI 2006/3363).
12 See note 4.

(ii) Enforcement Procedure

344. Consultation. An enforcer[1] must not make an application for an enforcement order[2] unless he has engaged in appropriate consultation[3] with the person against whom the enforcement order would be made, and with the Office of Fair Trading (the 'OFT')[4] if it is not the enforcer[5]. This requirement does not, however, apply if the OFT thinks that an application for an enforcement order should be made without delay[6]; and it ceases to apply:

(1)   for the purposes of an application for an enforcement order at the end of the period of 14 days beginning with the day after the person against whom the enforcement order would be made receives a request for consultation from the enforcer[7];

(2)   for the purposes of an application for an interim enforcement order at the end of the period of seven days beginning with the day after the person against whom the interim enforcement order would be made receives a request for consultation from the enforcer[8].

The Secretary of State may by order[9] make rules in relation to consultation under these provisions[10]. Rules have been so made in respect of the making and receipt of an enforcer's initial request for consultation to the person concerned[11].

1   As to enforcers see PARA 342.
2   For these purposes, except in the Enterprise Act 2002 s 214(4) (see heads (1), (2) in the text), references to an enforcement order include references to an interim enforcement order: s 214(7). As to applications for an enforcement order see PARA 345; as to enforcement orders see PARA 346; and as to interim enforcement orders see PARA 347.
3   Appropriate consultation is consultation for the purpose of: (1) achieving the cessation of the infringement in a case where an infringement is occurring; (2) ensuring that there will be no repetition of the infringement in a case where the infringement has occurred; (3) ensuring that there will be no repetition of the infringement in a case where the cessation of the infringement is achieved under head (1) above; (4) ensuring that the infringement does not take place in the case of a Community infringement which the enforcer believes is likely to take place: Enterprise Act 2002 s 214(2). As to domestic infringements see PARA 340; and as to Community infringements see PARA 341.
4   As to the OFT's general functions see PARA 7. As to the OFT see PARAS 6–8.
5   Enterprise Act 2002 s 214(1).
6   Enterprise Act 2002 s 214(3).
7   Enterprise Act 2002 s 214(4)(a).
8   Enterprise Act 2002 s 214(4)(b).
9   As to the Secretary of State see PARA 5. The power to make an order under the Enterprise Act 2002 s 214 must be made by statutory instrument subject to annulment in pursuance of a resolution of either House of Parliament: s 214(6).
10   Enterprise Act 2002 s 214(5). In the exercise of this power, the Enterprise Act 2002 (Part 8 Request for Consultation) Order 2003, SI 2003/1375, which lays down rules in respect of the making and receipt of an enforcer's initial request for consultation to the person concerned, has been made.
11   See note 10.

345. Applications. An application for an enforcement order[1] must name the person the enforcer[2] thinks:

(1)   has engaged or is engaging in conduct which constitutes a domestic or a Community infringement[3]; or

(2)   is likely to engage in conduct which constitutes a Community infringement[4].

A general enforcer[5] may make an application for an enforcement order in respect of any infringement[6]; a designated enforcer[7] may make an application for an enforcement order in respect of an infringement to which his designation relates[8]; a Community enforcer[9] may make an application for an enforcement order in respect of a Community infringement[10]; and a CPC enforcer[11] may make an application for an enforcement order in respect of a Community infringement[12].

If the Office of Fair Trading (the 'OFT')[13] believes that an enforcer other than the OFT intends to apply for an enforcement order, then in such a case the OFT may direct that if an application in respect of a particular infringement is to be made it must be made:

(a)   only by the OFT; or

(b)   only by such other enforcer as the OFT directs[14];

but these provisions[15] do not prevent an application for an enforcement order being made by a Community enforcer[16]. If the OFT directs that only it may make an application, that does not prevent the OFT or any enforcer from accepting an undertaking[17] or prevent the OFT from taking such other steps it thinks appropriate (apart from making an application) for the purpose of securing that the infringement is not committed, continued or repeated[18]. The OFT may vary or withdraw a direction so given[19] and must take such steps as it thinks appropriate to bring a direction (or a variation or withdrawal of a direction) to the attention of enforcers it thinks may be affected by it[20].

If the person against whom the order is sought carries on business or has a place of business in England and Wales or Northern Ireland, the High Court or a county court has jurisdiction to make an enforcement order[21]. If an application for an enforcement order is made by a Community enforcer, the court may examine whether the purpose of the enforcer[22] justifies its making the application[23]; and if the court thinks that the purpose of the Community enforcer does not justify its making the application the court may refuse the application on that ground alone[24].

An enforcer which is not the OFT must notify the OFT of the result of an application[25] under the above provisions[26].

1   For the purposes of the Enterprise Act 2002 ss 215, 216 (see the text and notes 2–26), references to an enforcement order include references to an interim enforcement order: s 214(7). As to enforcement orders see PARA 346; and as to interim enforcement orders see PARA 347.
2   As to enforcers see PARA 342.
3   As to the meaning of 'domestic infringement' see PARA 340; and as to the meaning of 'Community infringement' see PARA 341.
4   Enterprise Act 2002 s 215(1).
5   As to the meaning of 'general enforcer' see PARA 342; and as to dual enforcers see PARA 342 note 1.
6   Enterprise Act 2002 s 215(2).
7   As to the meaning of 'designated enforcer' see PARA 342; and as to dual enforcers see PARA 342 note 1.
8   Enterprise Act 2002 s 215(3).
9   As to the meaning of 'Community enforcer' see PARA 342.
10 Enterprise Act 2002 s 215(4).
11 As to the meaning of 'CPC enforcer' see PARA 342; and as to dual enforcers see PARA 342 note 1.
12 Enterprise Act 2002 s 215(4A) (added by SI 2006/3363).
13 As to the OFT's general functions see PARA 7. As to the OFT see PARAS 6–8.
14 Enterprise Act 2002 s 216(1), (2).
15 Ie the Enterprise Act 2002 s 216: see the text and notes 13–14, 16–20.
16 Enterprise Act 2002 s 216(6).
17 Ie an undertaking under the Enterprise Act 2002 s 219: see PARA 349.
18 Enterprise Act 2002 s 216(3).
19 Enterprise Act 2002 s 216(4).
20 Enterprise Act 2002 s 216(5).
21 Enterprise Act 2002 s 215(5)(a). If the person against whom the order is sought carries on business or has a place of business in Scotland, the Court of Session or the sheriff has jurisdiction to make an enforcement order: s 215(5)(b).
22 The purpose of a Community enforcer must be construed by reference to the Injunctions Directive: Enterprise Act 2002 s 215(8). As to the meaning of 'Injunctions Directive' see PARA 339 note 11.
23 Enterprise Act 2002 s 215(6).
24 Enterprise Act 2002 s 215(7).
25 Ie an application under the Enterprise Act 2002 s 215: see the text and notes 1–12, 21–26.
26 Enterprise Act 2002 s 215(9).

346. Enforcement orders made, or undertakings accepted by, the court. The following provisions apply:

(1)   if an application for an enforcement order is made[1] and the court[2] finds that the person named in the application has engaged in conduct which constitutes the infringement[3];

(2)   if such an application is made in relation to a Community infringement[4] and the court finds that the person named in the application is likely to engage in conduct which constitutes the infringement[5].

If these provisions apply the court may make an enforcement order against the person[6]. In considering whether to make an enforcement order the court must have regard to whether the person named in the application has (a) given an undertaking[7] in respect of certain specified conduct[8]; (b) has failed to comply with the undertaking[9].

An enforcement order must indicate the nature of the conduct to which the finding under head (1) or head (2) relates, and must direct the person to comply with the requirements set out in heads (i) to (iii) below[10]. A person complies with those requirements if he:

(i)   does not continue or repeat the conduct;

(ii)   does not engage in such conduct in the course of his business or another business;

(iii)   does not consent to or connive in the carrying out of such conduct by a body corporate with which he has[11] a special relationship[12];

but head (i) above does not apply in the case of a finding under head (2) above[13].

An enforcement order may require a person against whom the order is made to publish, in such form and manner and to such extent as the court thinks appropriate for the purpose of eliminating any continuing effects of the infringement, (A) the order; (B) a corrective statement[14].

If the court makes a finding under head (1) or head (2) above it may accept an undertaking by the person either to comply with heads (i) to (iii) above, or to take steps which the court believes will secure that he so complies[15]; and such an undertaking may include a further undertaking by the person to publish, in such form and manner and to such extent as the court thinks appropriate for the purpose of eliminating any continuing effects of the infringement, (*aa*) the terms of the undertaking; (*bb*) a corrective statement[16]. If the court makes a finding under head (1) or head (2) above, and accepts such an undertaking, it must not make an enforcement order in respect of the infringement to which the undertaking relates[17].

An enforcement order made by a court in one part of the United Kingdom[18] has effect in any other part of the United Kingdom as if made by a court in that part[19].

1   Ie an application under the Enterprise Act 2002 s 215: see PARA 345.
2   As to the court with jurisdiction to make an enforcement order see PARA 345.
3   Enterprise Act 2002 s 217(1). As to domestic and Community infringements see PARAS 340, 341. It has been held in Scotland that the conduct of a trader before and after 20 June 2003 (when the Enterprise Act 2002 Pt 8 (ss 210–236) came into force) is relevant to the question of whether an enforcement order ought to be granted and that to that extent Pt 8 is intended to have retrospective effect: see *Office of Fair Trading v MB Designs (Scotland) Ltd, Martin Black and Paul Bradley Bett* [2005] CSOH 85 at [23], 2005 SCLR 894 at [23].
4   As to the meaning of 'Community infringement' see PARA 341.
5   Enterprise Act 2002 s 217(2).
6   Enterprise Act 2002 s 217(3).
7   Ie an undertaking under the Enterprise Act 2002 s 219: see PARA 349.
8   Ie conduct such as is mentioned in the Enterprise Act 2002 s 219(3): see PARA 349.

9 Enterprise Act 2002 s 217(4).
10 Enterprise Act 2002 s 217(5).
11 Ie within the meaning of the Enterprise Act 2002 s 222(3): see PARA 352.
12 Enterprise Act 2002 s 217(6). If an order is made as mentioned in s 222(5) or an undertaking is accepted as mentioned in s 222(6) (see PARA 352), s 217(6) is substituted by s 222(9): see PARA 352 note 8.
13 Enterprise Act 2002 s 217(7).
14 Enterprise Act 2002 s 217(8).
15 Enterprise Act 2002 s 217(9).
16 Enterprise Act 2002 s 217(10).
17 Enterprise Act 2002 s 217(11).
18 As to the meaning of 'United Kingdom' see PARA 401 note 1.
19 Enterprise Act 2002 s 217(12).

347. Interim enforcement orders made or undertakings accepted by the court.
The court[1] may make an interim enforcement order against a person named in the application for the order[2] if it appears to the court:

(1) that it is alleged that the person is engaged in conduct which constitutes a domestic or Community infringement[3] or is likely to engage in conduct which constitutes a Community infringement[4];

(2) that if the application had been an application for an enforcement order[5] it would be likely to be granted[6];

(3) that it is expedient that the conduct is prohibited or prevented, as the case may be, immediately[7]; and

(4) if no notice of the application has been given to the person named in the application, that it is appropriate to make an interim enforcement order without notice[8].

An interim enforcement order must indicate the nature of the alleged conduct, and direct the person to comply with the requirements set out in heads (a) to (c) below[9]. A person complies with those requirements if he:

(a) does not continue or repeat the conduct;

(b) does not engage in such conduct in the course of his business or another business;

(c) does not consent to or connive in the carrying out of such conduct by a body corporate with which he has[10] a special relationship[11];

but head (a) above does not apply in so far as the application is made in respect of an allegation that the person is likely to engage in conduct which constitutes a Community infringement[12].

An application for an interim enforcement order against a person may be made at any time before an application for an enforcement order against the person in respect of the same conduct is determined[13]. An application for an interim enforcement order must refer to all matters which are known to the applicant, and which are material to the question whether or not the application is granted[14]. If an application for an interim enforcement order is made without notice, the application must state why no notice has been given[15].

The court may vary or discharge an interim enforcement order on the application of:

(i) the enforcer[16] who applied for the order;

(ii) the person against whom it is made[17].

An interim enforcement order against a person is discharged on the determination of an application for an enforcement order made against the person in respect of the same conduct[18].

If it appears to the court as mentioned in heads (1) to (3) above the court may, instead of making an interim enforcement order, accept an undertaking from the person named in the application either to comply with heads (a) to (c) above, or to take steps which the court believes will secure that he so complies[19].

An interim enforcement order made by a court in one part of the United Kingdom[20] has effect in any other part of the United Kingdom as if made by a court in that part[21].

1 As to the courts with jurisdiction to make interim enforcement orders see PARA 345.
2 As to applications see PARA 345.
3 As to the meaning of 'domestic infringement' see PARA 340; and as to the meaning of 'Community infringement' see PARA 341.
4 Enterprise Act 2002 s 218(1)(a).
5 As to enforcement orders see PARA 346.
6 Enterprise Act 2002 s 218(1)(b). It has been held in Scotland that 'likely' in the Enterprise Act 2002 s 218(1)(b) means 'more likely than not': see *Office of Fair Trading v MB Designs (Scotland) Ltd, Martin Black and Paul Bradley Bett* [2005] CSOH 85 at [21], 2005 SCLR 894 at [21].
7 Enterprise Act 2002 s 218(1)(c).
8 Enterprise Act 2002 s 218(1)(d).
9 Enterprise Act 2002 s 218(2).
10 Ie within the meaning of the Enterprise Act 2002 s 222(3): see PARA 352.
11 Enterprise Act 2002 s 218(3). If an order is made as mentioned in s 222(5) or an undertaking is accepted as mentioned in s 222(6) (see PARA 352), s 218(3) is substituted by s 222(9): see PARA 352 note 8.
12 Enterprise Act 2002 s 218(4).
13 Enterprise Act 2002 s 218(5).
14 Enterprise Act 2002 s 218(6).
15 Enterprise Act 2002 s 218(7).
16 As to enforcers see PARA 342.
17 Enterprise Act 2002 s 218(8).
18 Enterprise Act 2002 s 218(9).
19 Enterprise Act 2002 s 218(10).
20 As to the meaning of 'United Kingdom' see PARA 401 note 1.
21 Enterprise Act 2002 s 218(11).

348.   Unfair commercial practices: substantiation of claims.   Where an application[1] for an enforcement order[2] or for an interim enforcement order[3] is made in respect of a Community infringement involving a contravention of the Unfair Commercial Practices Directive[4], then for the purposes of considering the application the court[5] may require the person named in the application to provide evidence as to the accuracy of any factual claim made as part of a commercial practice[6] of that person if, taking into account the legitimate interests of that person and any other party to the proceedings, it appears appropriate in the circumstances[7]. If, having been so required to provide evidence as to the accuracy of a factual claim, a person either fails to provide such evidence, or provides evidence as to the accuracy of the factual claim that the court considers inadequate, the court may consider that the factual claim is inaccurate[8].

1 As to applications see PARA 345.
2 As to enforcement orders see PARA 346.
3 As to interim enforcement orders see PARA 347.
4 Ie a contravention of EC Directive 2005/29 of the European Parliament and of the Council concerning unfair business-to-consumer commercial practices in the internal market (OJ L149, 11.6.2005, p 22).
5 As to the courts having jurisdiction to consider the application see PARA 345.
6 For these purposes, 'commercial practice' means any act, omission, course of conduct, representation or commercial communication (including advertising and marketing) by a trader, which is directly connected with the promotion, sale or supply of a product to or from consumers, whether occurring before, during or after a commercial transaction (if any) in

relation to a product: Consumer Protection from Unfair Trading Regulations 2008, SI 2008/1277, reg 2(1) (definition applied by the Enterprise Act 2002 s 218A(4) (s 218A added by SI 2008/1277)).

7   Enterprise Act 2002 s 218A(1), (2) (as added: see note 6).
8   Enterprise Act 2002 s 218A(3) (as added: see note 6).

349.   Undertakings which may be accepted by the enforcer. The following provisions apply if an enforcer[1] has power to make an application[2] for an enforcement order or an interim enforcement order[3].

In such a case the enforcer may accept from a person who the enforcer believes:

(1)   has engaged in conduct which constitutes an infringement[4];
(2)   is engaging in such conduct;
(3)   is likely to engage in conduct which constitutes a Community infringement[5],

an undertaking that the person will comply with the requirements set out in heads (a) to (c) below[6]. A person complies with those requirements if he:

(a)   does not continue or repeat the conduct;
(b)   does not engage in such conduct in the course of his business or another business;
(c)   does not consent to or connive in the carrying out of such conduct by a body corporate with which he has[7] a special relationship[8];

but head (a) above does not apply in the case of an undertaking given by a person in so far as an undertaking may be accepted from him by virtue of head (3) above[9].

A CPC enforcer[10] who has accepted an undertaking under these provisions may either accept a further undertaking from the person concerned to publish the terms of the undertaking[11] or take steps itself to publish the undertaking[12]. In each case the undertaking must be published in such form and manner and to such extent as the CPC enforcer thinks appropriate for the purpose of eliminating any continuing effects of the Community infringement[13].

If an enforcer accepts an undertaking under these provisions it must notify the Office of Fair Trading (the 'OFT')[14] of the terms of the undertaking and of the identity of the person who gave it[15].

1   As to enforcers see PARA 342.
2   Ie an application under the Enterprise Act 2002 s 215: see PARA 345.
3   See the Enterprise Act 2002 s 219(1). As to enforcement orders see PARA 346; and as to interim enforcement orders see PARA 347.
4   As to domestic infringements see PARA 340; and as to Community infringements see PARA 341.
5   As to the meaning of 'community infringement' see PARA 341.
6   See the Enterprise Act 2002 s 219(2), (3).
7   Ie within the meaning of the Enterprise Act 2002 s 222(3): see PARA 352.
8   Enterprise Act 2002 s 219(4). If an undertaking is accepted as mentioned in s 222(7) (see PARA 352), s 219(4) is substituted by s 222(9): see PARA 352 note 8.
9   See the Enterprise Act 2002 s 219(5).
10   As to the meaning of 'CPC enforcer' see PARA 342; and as to dual enforcers see PARA 342 note 1.
11   Enterprise Act 2002 s 219(5A)(a) (s 219(5A), (5B) added by SI 2006/3363).
12   Enterprise Act 2002 s 219(5A)(b) (as added: see note 11).
13   Enterprise Act 2002 s 219(5B) (as added: see note 11).
14   As to the OFT see PARAS 6–8.
15   Enterprise Act 2002 s 219(6).

350.   Further proceedings. The following provisions apply if the court[1] makes an enforcement order[2], makes an interim enforcement order[3] or accepts[4] an undertaking[5]. In such a case the Office of Fair Trading (the 'OFT')[6] has the same right to apply to the court in respect of a failure to comply with the order or undertaking as the enforcer[7] who made the application for the order[8]. An application to the court in respect of a failure to comply with an undertaking may include an application for an enforcement order or for an interim enforcement order[9]. If the court finds that an undertaking is not being complied with it may make an enforcement order or an interim enforcement order, instead of making any other order it has power to make[10].

If an enforcer which is not the OFT makes an application in respect of the failure of a person to comply with an enforcement order, an interim enforcement order or an undertaking[11] the enforcer must notify the OFT of the application and of any order made by the court on the application[12].

1   As to the court having jurisdiction see PARA 345.
2   Ie under the Enterprise Act 2002 s 217: see PARA 346.
3   Ie under the Enterprise Act 2002 s 218: see PARA 347.
4   Ie under the Enterprise Act 2002 s 217 or s 218: see PARAS 346, 347.
5   Enterprise Act 2002 s 220(1).
6   As to the OFT see PARAS 6–8.
7   As to enforcers see PARA 342.
8   Enterprise Act 2002 s 220(2).
9   Enterprise Act 2002 s 220(3). In the case of an application for an enforcement order or for an interim enforcement order as mentioned in s 220(3), ss 214, 216 (see PARAS 344, 345) must be ignored and s 215 (see PARA 345), s 217 (see PARA 346) or s 218 (see PARA 347) (as the case may be) applies subject to the following modifications: (1) s 215(1)(b) must be ignored; (2) s 215(5) must be ignored and the application must be made to the court which accepted the undertaking; (3) s 217(9)–(11) must be ignored; (4) s 218(10) must be ignored: s 220(5).
10 Enterprise Act 2002 s 220(4).
11 Ie an undertaking given under the Enterprise Act 2002 s 217 or s 218: see PARAS 346, 347.
12 Enterprise Act 2002 s 220(6).

351. Proceedings in relation to Community infringements. Every general enforcer[1] and every designated enforcer[2] which is a public body[3] has power to take proceedings in EEA states[4] other than the United Kingdom[5] for the cessation or prohibition of a Community infringement[6].

Every general enforcer, every designated enforcer and every CPC enforcer[7] may co-operate with a Community enforcer[8]:

(1)   for the purpose of bringing proceedings in EEA states other than the United Kingdom for the cessation or prohibition of a Community infringement[9];

(2)   in connection with the exercise by the Community enforcer of its functions under Part 8[10] of the Enterprise Act 2002[11].

1   As to the meaning of 'general enforcer' see PARA 342; and as to dual enforcers see PARA 342 note 1.
2   As to the meaning of 'designated enforcer' see PARA 342; and as to dual enforcers see PARA 342 note 1.
3   The designation of a body by virtue of the Enterprise Act 2002 s 213(3) (see PARA 342) is conclusive evidence for the purposes of any question arising under Pt 8 (ss 210–236) that the body is a public body: s 213(8).
4   An EEA state is a state which is a contracting party to the Agreement on the European Economic Area signed at Oporto on 2 May 1992 as adjusted by the Protocol signed at Brussels on 17 March 1993: Enterprise Act 2002 s 221(5).
5   As to the meaning of 'United Kingdom' see PARA 401 note 1.
6   Enterprise Act 2002 s 221(1), (2). As to the meaning of 'Community infringement' see PARA 341.
7   As to the meaning of 'CPC enforcer' see PARA 342; and as to dual enforcers see PARA 342 note 1.

8   As to the meaning of 'Community enforcer' see PARA 342.
9   Ie for the purpose of bringing proceedings mentioned in the Enterprise Act 2002 s 221(2): see the text and notes 4–6.
10 Ie under the Enterprise Act 2002 Pt 8 (ss 210–236): see PARAS 339 et seq, 352 et seq.
11 Enterprise Act 2002 s 221(3), (4) (s 221(3) amended by SI 2006/3363).

352. Bodies corporate. If the person whose conduct constitutes a domestic infringement[1] or a Community infringement[2] is a body corporate, then if the conduct takes place with the consent or connivance of a person (an 'accessory') who has a special relationship with the body corporate, the consent or connivance is also conduct which constitutes the infringement[3]. For these purposes, a person has a special relationship with a body corporate if he is a controller[4] of the body corporate, or a director, manager, secretary or other similar officer of the body corporate or a person purporting to act in such a capacity[5]. An enforcement order[6] or an interim enforcement order[7] may be made against an accessory in respect of an infringement whether or not such an order is made against the body corporate[8]; and the court[9] may accept an undertaking[10] from an accessory in respect of an infringement whether or not it accepts such an undertaking from the body corporate[11]. An enforcer[12] may also accept an undertaking[13] from an accessory in respect of an infringement whether or not it accepts such an undertaking from the body corporate[14].

If a court makes an enforcement order or an interim enforcement order against a body corporate and:

(1)   at the time the order is made the body corporate is a member of a group of interconnected bodies corporate[15];

(2)   at any time when the order is in force the body corporate becomes a member of a group of interconnected bodies corporate; or

(3)   at any time when the order is in force a group of interconnected bodies corporate of which the body corporate is a member is increased by the addition of one or more further members,

the court may direct that the order is binding upon all of the members of the group as if each of them were the body corporate against which the order is made[16].

1   As to the meaning of 'domestic infringement' see PARA 340.
2   As to the meaning of 'Community infringement' see PARA 341.
3   Enterprise Act 2002 s 222(1), (2).
4   A person is a controller of a body corporate if (1) the directors of the body corporate or of another body corporate which is its controller are accustomed to act in accordance with the person's directions or instructions; or (2) either alone or with an associate or associates he is entitled to exercise or control the exercise of one third or more of the voting power at any general meeting of the body corporate or of another body corporate which is its controller: Enterprise Act 2002 s 222(4). A person is an associate of an individual if (a) he is the spouse or civil partner of the individual; (b) he is a relative of the individual; (c) he is a relative of the individual's spouse or civil partner; (d) he is the spouse or civil partner of a relative of the individual; (e) he is the spouse or civil partner of a relative of the individual's spouse or civil partner; (f) he lives in the same household as the individual otherwise than merely because he or the individual is the other's employer, tenant, lodger or boarder; (g) he is a relative of a person who is an associate of the individual by virtue of head (f) above; (h) he has at some time in the past fallen within any of heads (a)–(g) above: Enterprise Act 2002 s 222(10) (amended by the Civil Partnership Act 2004 Sch 27 para 169). A person is also an associate of (i) an individual with whom he is in partnership; (ii) an individual who is an associate of the individual mentioned in head (i) above; (iii) a body corporate if he is a controller of it or he is an associate of a person who is a controller of the body corporate: Enterprise Act 2002 s 222(11). A body corporate is an associate of another body corporate if (A) the same person is a controller of both; (B) a person is a controller of one and persons who are his associates are controllers of the other; (C) a person is a controller of one and he and persons who are his associates are

controllers of the other; (D) a group of two or more persons is a controller of each company and the groups consist of the same persons; (E) a group of two or more persons is a controller of each company and the groups may be regarded as consisting of the same persons by treating (in one or more cases) a member of either group as replaced by a person of whom he is an associate: s 222(12). A relative is a brother, sister, uncle, aunt, nephew, niece, lineal ancestor or lineal descendant: s 222(13).

5   Enterprise Act 2002 s 222(3).
6   As to enforcement orders see PARA 346.
7   As to interim enforcement orders see PARA 347.
8   Enterprise Act 2002 s 222(5). Section 222(9) applies if (1) an order is made as mentioned in s 222(5); or (2) an undertaking is accepted as mentioned in s 222(6) or (7) (see the text and notes 9–14): s 222(8). In such a case for s 217(6) (see PARA 346), s 218(3) (see PARA 347) or s 219(4) (see PARA 349) (as the case may be) there is substituted the following provision: 'A person complies with this subsection if he (a) does not continue or repeat the conduct; (b) does not in the course of any business carried on by him engage in conduct such as that which constitutes the infringement committed by the body corporate mentioned in s 222(1); (c) does not consent to or connive in the carrying out of such conduct by another body corporate with which he has a special relationship (within the meaning of s 222(3)).': s 222(9).
9   As to the court having jurisdiction see PARA 345.
10   Ie under the Enterprise Act 2002 s 217(9) or s 218(10): see PARAS 346, 347.
11   Enterprise Act 2002 s 222(6). See further s 222(8), (9), cited in note 8.
12   As to enforcers see PARA 342.
13   Ie under the Enterprise Act 2002 s 219: see PARA 349.
14   Enterprise Act 2002 s 222(7). See further s 222(8), (9), cited in note 8.
15   A group of interconnected bodies corporate is a group consisting of two or more bodies corporate all of whom are interconnected with each other: Enterprise Act 2002 s 223(3). Any two bodies corporate are interconnected if one of them is a subsidiary of the other, or if both of them are subsidiaries of the same body corporate: s 223(4). 'Subsidiary' must be construed in accordance with the Companies Act 1985 s 736 (repealed by the Companies Act 2006 Sch 16 and replaced by the Companies Act 2006 s 1159, with effect from 1 October 2009): Enterprise Act 2002 s 223(5).
16   Enterprise Act 2002 s 223(1), (2).

353. Evidence. With the exception of proceedings for an offence of obstructing, or failing to co-operate with, powers of entry[1], proceedings under Part 8 of the Enterprise Act 2002[2] are civil proceedings for the purposes of the provisions of the law of evidence[3] making convictions admissible as evidence in civil proceedings[4].

In proceedings under that Part, any finding by a court in civil proceedings that a specified act or omission[5] has occurred is admissible as evidence that the act or omission occurred[6] and, unless the contrary is proved, is sufficient evidence that the act or omission occurred[7]; but this does not apply to any finding which has been reversed on appeal[8] or which has been varied on appeal so as to negative it[9].

1   Enterprise Act 2002 s 228(4) (added by SI 2006/3363). The offence referred to in the text is an offence under the Enterprise Act 2002 s 227E (see PARAS 355–357): s 228(4) (as so added). ·
2   Ie proceedings under the Enterprise Act 2002 Pt 8 (ss 210–236): see PARAS 339 et seq, 354 et seq.
3   Ie for the purposes of the Civil Evidence Act 1968 s 11 (see CIVIL PROCEDURE vol 12 (2009) PARA 1208) and the corresponding provisions in Scotland and Northern Ireland.
4   Enterprise Act 2002 s 228(1).
5   Ie an act or omission mentioned in the Enterprise Act 2002 s 211(2)(b), (c) or (d) (see PARA 340) or s 212(1) (see PARA 341): s 228(2).
6   Enterprise Act 2002 s 228(2)(a).
7   Enterprise Act 2002 s 228(2)(b).
8   Enterprise Act 2002 s 228(3)(a).
9   Enterprise Act 2002 s 228(3)(b).

(iii) Information

354. Information required by the Office of Fair Trading and other enforcers.
The Office of Fair Trading (the 'OFT')[1] may for any of the purposes mentioned in heads (1) to (4) below give notice to any person requiring the person to provide it with the information specified in the notice[2]. Those purposes are:

(1)   to enable the OFT to exercise or to consider whether to exercise any function it has under Part 8 of the Enterprise Act 2002[3];

(2)   to enable a designated enforcer[4] which is not a public body[5] to consider whether to exercise any function it has under Part 8 of that Act;

(3)   to enable a Community enforcer[6] to consider whether to exercise any function it has under that Part;

(4)   to ascertain whether a person has complied with or is complying with an enforcement order[7], an interim enforcement order[8] or an undertaking given to the court[9] or to an enforcer[10].

Every general enforcer[11] other than the OFT, every designated enforcer which is a public body[12] and every CPC enforcer[13] other than the OFT may, for any of the purposes mentioned in heads (a) and (b) below, give notice to any person requiring the person to provide the enforcer with the information specified in the notice[14]. Those purposes are:

(a)   to enable the enforcer to exercise or to consider whether to exercise any function it has under Part 8 of the Enterprise Act 2002;

(b)   to ascertain whether a person has complied with or is complying with an enforcement order or an interim enforcement order made on the application[15] of the enforcer, or an undertaking given to the court[16] following such an application, or an undertaking given[17] to the enforcer[18].

A notice given under the above provisions[19] must be in writing[20] and must specify the purpose for which the information is required[21]. If the purpose is as mentioned in head (1), head (2), head (3) or head (a) above, the notice must also specify the function concerned[22]. A notice may specify the time within which and manner in which it is to be complied with[23] and may require the production of documents or any description of documents[24]. An enforcer may take copies of any documents produced in compliance with such a requirement[25]. A notice may also specify the form in which information is to be provided[26]. A notice must not, however, require a person to provide any information or produce any document which he would be entitled to refuse to provide or produce in proceedings in the High Court on the grounds of legal professional privilege[27]. A notice may be varied or revoked by a subsequent notice[28].

If a person fails to comply with a notice given under the above provisions[29] the enforcer who gave the notice may make an application to a court with jurisdiction to make an enforcement order[30]; and if it appears to the court that the person to whom the notice was given has failed to comply with the notice the court may make an order[31] which may:

(i)   require the person to whom the notice was given to do anything the court thinks it is reasonable for him to do for any of the purposes mentioned in heads (1) to (4) or heads (a) to (b) above, as the case may be, to ensure that the notice is complied with[32];

(ii)   require the person to meet all the costs or expenses of the application[33].

1   As to the OFT see PARAS 6–8.
2   Enterprise Act 2002 s 224(1).

3 Ie under the Enterprise Act 2002 Pt 8 (ss 210–236): see PARAS 339 et seq, 355 et seq.
4 As to the meaning of 'designated enforcer' see PARA 342; and as to dual enforcers see PARA 342 note 1.
5 Ie a designated enforcer to which the Enterprise Act 2002 s 225 (see the text and notes 11–18) does not apply: s 224(2)(b). The designation of a body by virtue of s 213(3) (see PARA 342) is conclusive evidence for the purposes of any question arising under Pt 8 that the body is a public body: s 213(8).
6 As to the meaning of 'Community enforcer' see PARA 342.
7 As to enforcement orders see PARA 346.
8 As to interim enforcement orders see PARA 347.
9 Ie an undertaking given under the Enterprise Act 2002 s 217(9) (see PARA 346) or s 218(10) (see PARA 347).
10 See the Enterprise Act 2002 s 224(2). An undertaking may be given to an enforcer under the Enterprise Act 2002 s 219: see PARA 349.
11 As to the meaning of 'general enforcer' see PARA 342; and as to dual enforcers see PARA 342 note 1.
12 As to whether a designated enforcer is a public body see note 5.
13 As to the meaning of 'CPC enforcer' see PARA 342; and as to dual enforcers see PARA 342 note 1.
14 Enterprise Act 2002 s 225(1).
15 As to applications see PARA 345.
16 See note 9.
17 Ie an undertaking given under the Enterprise Act 2002 s 219: see PARA 349.
18 Enterprise Act 2002 s 225(2).
19 Ie a notice given under the Enterprise Act 2002 s 224 or s 225: see the text and notes 1–18.
20 'Writing' includes typing, printing, lithography, photography and other modes of representing or reproducing words in a visible form, and expressions referring to writing are construed accordingly: Interpretation Act 1978 Sch 1.
21 Enterprise Act 2002 s 226(1), (2).
22 Enterprise Act 2002 s 226(3).
23 Enterprise Act 2002 s 226(4).
24 Enterprise Act 2002 s 226(5).
25 Enterprise Act 2002 s 226(6).
26 Enterprise Act 2002 s 226(6A) (added by SI 2006/3363).
27 Enterprise Act 2002 s 226(8)(a). As to legal professional privilege see LEGAL PROFESSIONS vol 65 (2008) PARAS 507, 511. Nor must it require a person to provide any information or produce any document which he would be entitled to refuse to refuse to provide or produce in proceedings in the Court of Session on the grounds of confidentiality of communications: s 226(8)(b).
28 Enterprise Act 2002 s 226(7).
29 Se note 19.
30 See the Enterprise Act 2002 s 227(1), (6). As to the courts with jurisdiction to make an enforcement order see PARA 345.
31 Enterprise Act 2002 s 227(2).
32 Enterprise Act 2002 s 227(3).
33 Enterprise Act 2002 s 227(4). If the person is a company or association the court in proceeding under s 227(4) may require any officer of the company or association who is responsible for the failure to meet the costs or expenses (s 227(5)); and for these purposes an officer of a company is a person who is a director, manager, secretary or other similar officer of the company (s 227(6)).

355.   Power to enter premises without warrant. An officer of a CPC enforcer[1] who reasonably suspects:

(1)   that there has been, or is likely to be, a Community infringement[2] may for any purpose relating to the functions of the CPC enforcer under Part 8 of the Enterprise Act 2002[3] enter any premises[4] to investigate whether there has been, or is likely to be, such an infringement[5];

(2)   that there is, or has been, a failure to comply with a relevant enforcement measure[6] may for any purpose relating to the functions of

the CPC enforcer under Part 8 of that Act enter any premises to investigate whether a person is complying with, or has complied with, the relevant enforcement measure[7].

An appropriate notice must be given[8] to the occupier[9] of the premises before an officer of a CPC enforcer enters them under head (1) and head (2) above[10]. An appropriate notice is a notice in writing[11] given by an officer of a CPC enforcer which:

(a) gives at least two working days'[12] notice of entry on the premises;
(b) sets out why the entry is necessary; and
(c) indicates the nature of the offence[13] of obstructing, or failing to co-operate with, powers of entry[14].

The requirement to give an appropriate notice does not, however, apply if such a notice cannot be given despite all reasonably practicable steps having been taken to do so[15]. In that case, the officer entering the premises must produce to any occupier that he finds on the premises a document setting out why the entry is necessary and indicating the nature of the offence referred to in head (c) above[16].

In all cases, the officer entering the premises must produce to any occupier evidence of his identity and, in the case of an authorised officer of a CPC enforcer[17], his authorisation, if asked to do so[18]. An officer of a CPC enforcer who enters premises by virtue of the above provisions may only do so at a reasonable time[19]. He may take with him such persons and equipment as he considers appropriate[20]. If the premises are unoccupied or the occupier is temporarily absent, the officer must take reasonable steps to ensure that when he leaves the premises they are as secure as they were before he entered[21].

The powers exercisable when entry is made under these provisions are discussed below[22].

A person commits an offence if, without reasonable excuse, he intentionally obstructs, or fails to co-operate with, an officer of a CPC enforcer who is exercising or seeking to exercise a power under the above provisions[23].

The powers conferred by the above provisions are not exercisable in relation to premises occupied by the Crown[24].

1   For the purposes of the Enterprise Act 2002 ss 227A–227F (see the text and notes 2–24; and PARAS 356–358), 'officer of a CPC enforcer' means (1) an officer of a local weights and measures authority in Great Britain; or (2) an authorised officer of a CPC enforcer which is not a local weights and measures authority in Great Britain; and 'authorised officer of a CPC enforcer' means an officer of a CPC enforcer who is authorised by that enforcer for the purposes of Pt 8 (ss 210–236): s 227A(9) (ss 227A, 227D, 227E added by SI 2006/3363). As to the meaning of 'CPC enforcer' see PARA 342; and as to dual enforcers see PARA 342 note 1. As to local weights and measures authorities see WEIGHTS AND MEASURES vol 50 (2005 Reissue) PARA 20; and as to the meaning of 'Great Britain' see PARA 395 note 2.
2   As to the meaning of 'Community infringement' see PARA 341.
3   Ie under the Enterprise Act 2002 Pt 8 (ss 210–236): see PARAS 339 et seq, 356 et seq.
4   For the purposes of the Enterprise Act 2002 ss 227A–227F, 'premises' includes vehicles but does not include any premises which are used only as a dwelling: s 227A(9) (as added: see note 1).
5   Enterprise Act 2002 s 227A(1) (as added: see note 1).
6   For the purposes of the Enterprise Act 2002 ss 227A–227F, 'relevant enforcement measure' means (1) an enforcement order made under s 217 (see PARA 346) on the application of the CPC enforcer; (2) an interim enforcement order made under s 218 (see PARA 347) on the application of the CPC enforcer; (3) an undertaking under s 217(9) (see PARA 346) in connection with an application made by the CPC enforcer for an enforcement order under s 217; (4) an undertaking under s 218(10) (see PARA 347) in connection with an application made by the CPC enforcer for an interim enforcement order under s 218; or (5) an undertaking under s 219 (see PARA 349) to the CPC enforcer: s 227A(9) (as added: see note 1).
7   Enterprise Act 2002 s 227A(2) (as added: see note 1).

8   For these purposes, 'give', in relation to the giving of a notice to the occupier of premises, includes delivering or leaving it at the premises or sending it there by post: Enterprise Act 2002 s 227A(8) (as added: see note 1). See also note 9.
9   For the purposes of the Enterprise Act 2002 ss 227A–227F, 'occupier' means any person whom the officer concerned reasonably suspects to be the occupier: s 227A(9) (as added: see note 1).
10 Enterprise Act 2002 s 227A(3) (as added: see note 1).
11 As to the meaning of 'writing' see PARA 354 note 20.
12 For these purposes, 'working day' means a day which is not (1) Saturday or Sunday; or (2) Christmas Day, Good Friday or a day which is a bank holiday under the Banking and Financial Dealings Act 1971 in the part of the United Kingdom in which the premises are situated: Enterprise Act 2002 s 227A(8) (as added: see note 1) As to the meaning of 'United Kingdom' see PARA 401 note 1.
13 Ie the offence created by the Enterprise Act 2002 s 227E: see the text and note 23.
14 Enterprise Act 2002 s 227A(4) (as added: see note 1).
15 Enterprise Act 2002 s 227A(5) (as added: see note 1).
16 Enterprise Act 2002 s 227A(6) (as added: see note 1).
17 See note 1.
18 Enterprise Act 2002 s 227A(7) (as added: see note 1).
19 Enterprise Act 2002 s 227D(1) (as added: see note 1).
20 Enterprise Act 2002 s 227D(2) (as added: see note 1).
21 Enterprise Act 2002 s 227D(3) (as added: see note 1).
22 See PARA 356.
23 Enterprise Act 2002 s 227E(1) (as added: see note 1). A person guilty of such an offence is liable, on summary conviction, to a fine not exceeding level 5 on the standard scale: s 227E(2) (as so added). As to the standard scale see PARA 16 note 18.
24 See PARA 339 note 1.

356.   Powers exercisable on the premises where entry is made without warrant. An officer of a CPC enforcer[1] may, in the exercise of his powers of entry without a warrant[2]:

(1)   observe the carrying on of a business on the premises[3];
(2)   inspect goods[4] or documents[5] on the premises[6];
(3)   require any person on the premises to produce goods or documents[7] within such period as the officer considers to be reasonable[8];
(4)   seize goods or documents to carry out tests on them on the premises or seize, remove and retain them to carry out tests on them elsewhere[9]; or
(5)   seize, remove and retain goods or documents which he reasonably suspects may be required as evidence of a Community infringement[10] or a breach of a relevant enforcement measure[11].

An officer of a CPC enforcer may take copies of, or extracts from, any documents to which he has access by virtue of heads (1) to (5) above[12]. Nothing in these provisions, however, authorises action to be taken in relation to anything which, in proceedings in the High Court, a person would be entitled to refuse to produce on the grounds of legal professional privilege[13].

The powers conferred by the above provisions are not exercisable in relation to premises occupied by the Crown[14].

1   As to the meaning of 'officer of a CPC enforcer' see PARA 355 note 1; as to the meaning of 'CPC enforcer' see PARA 342; and as to dual enforcers see PARA 342 note 1.
2   Ie his powers under the Enterprise Act 2002 s 227A: see PARA 356.
3   Enterprise Act 2002 s 227B(1)(a) (ss 227B, 227E added by SI 2006/3363). As to the meaning of 'premises' see PARA 355 note 4.
4   As to the meaning of 'goods' see PARA 339 note 5.
5   For these purposes, 'document' includes information recorded in any form: Enterprise Act 2002 s 227B(5) (as added: see note 3).
6   Enterprise Act 2002 s 227B(1)(b) (as added: see note 3).

7 The reference in the Enterprise Act 2002 s 227B(1)(c) (see head (3) in the text) to the production of documents is, in the case of a document which contains information recorded otherwise than in legible form, a reference to the production of a copy of the information in legible form: s 227B(6) (as added: see note 3).

8 Enterprise Act 2002 s 227B(1)(c) (as added: see note 3). The power in the Enterprise Act 2002 s 227B(1)(c) to require a person to produce goods or documents includes the power to require him (1) to state, to the best of his knowledge and belief, where the goods or documents are; (2) to give an explanation of the goods or documents; and (3) to secure that any goods or documents produced are authenticated or verified in such manner as the officer considers appropriate: s 227B(2) (as added: see note 3).

A person commits an offence if, without reasonable excuse, he intentionally obstructs, or fails to co-operate with, an officer of a CPC enforcer who is exercising or seeking to exercise a power under s 227B: s 227E(1) (as added: see note 3). A person guilty of such an offence is liable, on summary conviction, to a fine not exceeding level 5 on the standard scale: s 227E(2) (as so added). As to the standard scale see PARA 16 note 18.

9 Enterprise Act 2002 s 227B(1)(d) (as added: see note 3).

10 As to the meaning of 'Community infringement' see PARA 341.

11 Enterprise Act 2002 s 227B(1) (as added: see note 3). As to the meaning of 'relevant enforcement measure' see PARA 355 note 6.

12 Enterprise Act 2002 s 227B(3) (as added: see note 3).

13 Enterprise Act 2002 s 227B(4) (as added: see note 3). As to legal professional privilege see LEGAL PROFESSIONS vol 65 (2008) PARAS 507, 511. Section 227B(4) is modified in relation to Scotland: see s 227B(7) (as so added).

14 See PARA 339 note 1.

357. Power to enter premises with warrant. A justice of the peace[1] may issue a warrant authorising an officer of a CPC enforcer[2] to enter premises[3] for the statutory purposes[4] if the justice of the peace considers that there are reasonable grounds for believing that condition A is met and that either condition B, C or D is met[5]. Condition A is that there are, on the premises, goods[6] or documents to which an officer of a CPC enforcer would be entitled to have access[7] on entry without a warrant[8]. Condition B is that an officer of a CPC enforcer acting under the powers to enter premises without a warrant[9], has been, or would be likely to be, refused admission to the premises or access to the goods or documents[10]. Condition C is that the goods or documents would be likely to be concealed or interfered with[11] if an appropriate notice were given[12] under the power to enter premise without a warrant[13]. Condition D is that there is likely to be nobody at the premises capable of granting admission[14].

A warrant under these provisions authorises the officer of the CPC enforcer:

(1) to enter the premises specified in the warrant, using reasonable force if necessary[15];

(2) to do anything on the premises that an officer of the CPC enforcer would be able to do if he had entered the premises under the power[16] to enter premises without a warrant[17];

(3) to search for goods or documents which he has required a person on the premises to produce where that person has failed to comply with such a requirement[18];

(4) to the extent that it is reasonably necessary to do so, to require any person who is responsible for discharging any of the functions of the business being carried on at the premises under inspection[19] to break open a container and, if that person does not comply with the requirement, or if such a person cannot be identified after all reasonably practicable steps have been taken to identify such a person, to do so himself[20];

(5) to take any other steps which he considers to be reasonably necessary to

preserve, or prevent interference with, goods or documents to which he would be entitled to have access under the powers[21] to enter premises without a warrant[22].

Such a warrant is issued on information on oath given by an officer of a CPC enforcer[23] and ceases to have effect at the end of the period of one month beginning with the day of issue[24]. It must, on request, be produced to the occupier[25] of the premises for inspection[26].

An officer of a CPC enforcer who enters premises by virtue of the above provisions may take with him such persons and equipment as he considers appropriate[27]. If the premises are unoccupied or the occupier is temporarily absent, the officer must take reasonable steps to ensure that when he leaves the premises they are as secure as they were before he entered[28].

A person commits an offence if, without reasonable excuse, he intentionally obstructs, or fails to co-operate with, an officer of a CPC enforcer who is exercising or seeking to exercise a power under the above provisions[29].

The powers conferred by the above provisions are not exercisable in relation to premises occupied by the Crown[30].

1   Ie or in Northern Ireland, a lay magistrate: Enterprise Act 2002 s 227C(11) (ss 227C, 227D, 227E added by SI 2006/3363). In its application to Scotland, the Enterprise Act 2002 s 227C has effect as if the references in s 227C(1) to a justice of the peace included references to a sheriff: s 227C(10)(a) (as so added).
2   As to the meaning of 'officer of a CPC enforcer' see PARA 355 note 1; as to the meaning of 'CPC enforcer' see PARA 342; and as to dual enforcers see PARA 342 note 1.
3   As to the meaning of 'premises' see PARA 355 note 4.
4   Ie for purposes falling within the Enterprise Act 2002 s 227A(1) or (2): see PARA 355.
5   Enterprise Act 2002 s 227C(1) (as added: see note 1).
6   As to the meaning of 'goods' see PARA 339 note 5.
7   Ie under the Enterprise Act 2002 ss 227A, 227B: see PARAS 355, 356.
8   Enterprise Act 2002 s 227C(2) (as added: see note 1).
9   See note 7.
10   Enterprise Act 2002 s 227C(3) (as added: see note 1).
11   For these purposes, any reference to goods or documents being interfered with includes a reference to them being destroyed: Enterprise Act 2002 s 227C(9) (as added: see note 1).
12   Ie an appropriate notice under the Enterprise Act 2002 s 227A: see PARA 355.
13   Enterprise Act 2002 s 227C(4) (as added: see note 1).
14   Enterprise Act 2002 s 227C(5) (as added: see note 1).
15   Enterprise Act 2002 s 227C(6)(a) (as added: see note 1).
16   Ie under the Enterprise Act 2002 s 227A: see PARA 355.
17   Enterprise Act 2002 s 227C(6)(b) (as added: see note 1).
18   Enterprise Act 2002 s 227C(6)(c) (as added: see note 1).
19   Ie any person to whom the Enterprise Act 2002 s 227C(7) applies.
20   Enterprise Act 2002 s 227C(6)(d), (7) (as added: see note 1).
21   See note 7.
22   Enterprise Act 2002 s 227C(6)(e) (as added: see note 1).
23   Enterprise Act 2002 s 227C(8)(a) (as added: see note 1). This provision is modified in relation to Scotland: see s 227C(10)(b) (as so added).
24   Enterprise Act 2002 s 227C(8)(b) (as added: see note 1).
25   As to the meaning of 'occupier' see PARA 355 note 9.
26   Enterprise Act 2002 s 227C(8)(c) (as added: see note 1).
27   Enterprise Act 2002 s 227D(2) (as added: see note 1).
28   Enterprise Act 2002 s 227D(3) (as added: see note 1).
29   Enterprise Act 2002 s 227E(1) (as added: see note 1). A person guilty of such an offence is liable, on summary conviction, to a fine not exceeding level 5 on the standard scale: s 227E(2) (as so added). As to the standard scale see PARA 16 note 18. Additional sanctions may be imposed under the Regulatory Enforcement and Sanctions Act 2008 Pt 3 (ss 36–71): see s 37(2), Sch 6. See further ADMINISTRATIVE LAW.
30   See PARA 339 note 1.

358. Retention of documents and goods seized under powers of entry. No documents seized under the powers of entry set out in the previous paragraphs[1] may be retained for a period of more than three months[2].

No goods[3] seized under those powers of entry[4] may be retained for a period of more than three months unless they are reasonably required in connection with the exercise of any function of a CPC enforcer[5] under Part 8[6] of the Enterprise Act 2002[7]. Where goods are so required they may be retained for as long as they are so required[8].

1   Ie seized under the Enterprise Act 2002 ss 227A–227D: see PARAS 355–357.
2   Enterprise Act 2002 s 227F(1) (s 227F added by SI 2006/3363).
3   As to the meaning of 'goods' see PARA 339 note 5.
4   See note 1.
5   As to the meaning of 'CPC enforcer' see PARA 342; and as to dual enforcers see PARA 342 note 1.
6   Ie under the Enterprise Act 2002 Pt 8 (ss 210–236): see PARAS 339 et seq, 359 et seq.
7   Enterprise Act 2002 s 227F(2) (as added: see note 2).
8   Enterprise Act 2002 s 227F(3) (as added: see note 2).

(iv) Notices to be given to the Office of Fair Trading

359. Notice to the Office of Fair Trading of intended prosecution. If a local weights and measures authority in England and Wales[1] intends to start proceedings for an offence under an enactment or subordinate legislation[2] specified by the Secretary of State by order[3] for these purposes[4], the following provisions apply[5].

The authority must give the Office of Fair Trading (the 'OFT')[6]:
(1)   notice of its intention to start the proceedings;
(2)   a summary of the evidence it intends to lead in respect of the charges[7].
The authority must not start the proceedings until whichever is the earlier of the following:
(a)   the end of the period of 14 days starting with the day on which the authority gives the notice;
(b)   the day on which it is notified by the OFT that the OFT has received the notice and summary given under heads (1) and (2) above[8].
The authority must also notify the OFT of the outcome of the proceedings after they are finally determined[9].

Such proceedings are not, however, invalid by reason only of the failure of the authority to comply with these provisions[10].

1   As to local weights and measures authorities see WEIGHTS AND MEASURES vol 50 (2005 Reissue) PARA 20.
2   For these purposes, 'subordinate legislation' means Orders in Council, orders, rules, regulations, schemes, warrants, byelaws and other instruments made or to be made under any Act: Interpretation Act 1978 s 21(1) (definition applied by the Enterprise Act 2002 s 230(6)).
3   An order under the Enterprise Act 2003 s 230 (see the text and notes 1–2, 4–10) must be made by statutory instrument subject to annulment in pursuance of a resolution of either House of Parliament: s 230(7). As to the Secretary of State see PARA 5; and as to the exercise of this power see note 4.
4   As to the specified enactments and subordinate legislation see the Enterprise Act 2002 (Part 8 Notice to OFT of Intended Prosecution Specified Enactments, Revocation and Transitional Provision) Order 2003, SI 2003/1376, Schedule; the Enterprise Act 2002 (Part 8 Notice to OFT of Intended Prosecution Specified Enactments) Order 2006, SI 2006/3371, art 3.
5   Enterprise Act 2002 s 230(1).
6   As to the OFT see PARAS 6–8.
7   Enterprise Act 2002 s 230(2).
8   Enterprise Act 2002 s 230(3).

9   Enterprise Act 2002 s 230(4).
10 Enterprise Act 2002 s 230(5).

360. Notice to the Office of Fair Trading of convictions and judgments. The following provisions apply if:

(1)   a person is convicted of an offence by or before a court in the United Kingdom[1]; or

(2)   a judgment is given[2] against a person by a court in civil proceedings in the United Kingdom[3].

The court may make arrangements to bring the conviction or judgment to the attention of the Office of Fair Trading (the 'OFT')[4] if it appears to the court:

(a)   having regard to the functions of the OFT under Part 8 of the Enterprise Act 2002[5] or under the Estate Agents Act 1979[6] that it is expedient for the conviction or judgment to be brought to the attention of the OFT; and

(b)   that without such arrangements the conviction or judgment may not be brought to the attention of the OFT[7].

For the purposes of heads (a) and (b) above it is immaterial that the proceedings have been finally disposed of by the court[8].

1   As to the meaning of 'United Kingdom' see PARA 401 note 1.
2   For these purposes, 'judgment' includes an order or decree and references to the giving of the judgment must be construed accordingly: Enterprise Act 2002 s 231(4).
3   Enterprise Act 2002 s 231(1).
4   As to the OFT see PARAS 6–8.
5   Ie the Enterprise Act 2002 Pt 8 (ss 210–236): see PARA 339 et seq.
6   As to the Estate Agents Act 1979 see AGENCY vol 1 (2008) PARA 239 et seq.
7   Enterprise Act 2002 s 231(2).
8   Enterprise Act 2002 s 231(3).

6. MONOPOLIES, COMPETITION AND THE COMMON LAW

361. Meaning and sources of 'monopoly'. It is a monopoly and against the policy of the law for any person or group of persons to secure the sole exercise of any known trade[1] throughout the country[2], unless permitted by Crown prerogative[3] or statute[4].

A monopoly may come into being by Crown grant[5] or by statute[6], by the exercise of intellectual property rights[7], or from the activities of private persons or combinations of private persons[8].

1   An exclusive right granted by a landowner to exercise rights over his land is not a monopoly: *British South Africa Co v De Beers Consolidated Mines Ltd* [1910] 2 Ch 502, CA (revsd without affecting this point sub nom *De Beers Consolidated Mines Ltd v British South Africa Co* [1912] AC 52, HL); see HIGHWAYS, STREETS AND BRIDGES vol 21 (2004 Reissue) PARA 898 (ferry a monopoly); MARKETS, FAIRS AND STREET TRADING vol 29(2) (Reissue) PARA 1005 (holder of a franchise has a monopoly of the market). As to grants of rights over land see EASEMENTS AND PROFITS A PRENDRE vol 16(2) (Reissue) PARA 46 et seq. As to the meaning of 'trade' see PARA 369.

2   *Ipswich Tailors' Case* (1614) 11 Co Rep 53a; *Mitchel v Reynolds* (1711) 1 P Wms 181 at 187; *North-Western Salt Co Ltd v Electrolytic Alkali Co Ltd* [1913] 3 KB 422, CA (revsd on appeal [1914] AC 461, HL, on a point of pleading). Cf *East India Co v Sandys* (1685) Skin 132, 165, 197, 223 at 226, where it was said 'a monopoly is an immoral act, but only against the politic part of our law; which if it happens to be of advantage to the public as this trade is, then it ceases also to be against the politic part of our law and so not within the law of monopolies'. The old offences of badgering, forestalling, regrating and engrossing were abolished by 7 & 8 Vict c 24 (Forestalling, regrating, etc) (1844) s 1 (repealed): see *Mogul Steamship Co v McGregor, Gow & Co* (1889) 23 QBD 598 at 629, CA, per Fry LJ; *North-Western Salt Co Ltd v Electrolytic Alkali Co Ltd* [1913] 3 KB 422 at 444, CA, per Farwell LJ; *A-G of Commonwealth of Australia v Adelaide Steamship Co Ltd* [1913] AC 781 at 793, PC, a case decided on an Australian Act, but containing a number of dicta of general application. Cf MARKETS, FAIRS AND STREET TRADING vol 29(2) (Reissue) PARA 1048 (disturbance of owner's exclusive right).

3   See PARA 362.

4   See PARA 364.

5   See PARA 362.

6   See PARA 364.

7   See eg *British Leyland Motor Corpn Ltd v Armstrong Patents Co Ltd* [1986] AC 577, [1986] 1 All ER 850, HL, where a car manufacturer was able to exercise a monopoly in the supply of spare parts through use of copyright in design drawings; see further COPYRIGHT, DESIGN RIGHT AND RELATED RIGHTS vol 9(2) (2006 Reissue) PARAS 25–27 (copyright in artistic works).

8   See PARA 367 et seq.

362. Grant of monopoly by the Crown. The Crown cannot grant a monopoly without statutory authority[1], except where the Crown has a prerogative of granting an exclusive right to print[2].

1   The earliest authority for this proposition may be derived from Magna Carta 1215. The reissue Magna Carta 1297 (25 Edw 1) (see CONSTITUTIONAL LAW AND HUMAN RIGHTS vol 8(2) (Reissue) PARA 372) employs the phrase 'Nullus liber homo ... disseisetur de libero tenemento vel liberatibus vel liberis consuetudinibus suis' ('no free-man ... shall be disseised of his freehold, or liberties, or free customs'), which was interpreted by Coke (2 Co Inst 47) as covering property in goods as well as other franchises and liberties; cf the argument in *Nightingale v Bridges* (1689) 1 Show 135 at 139; 5 Bac Abr, Monopoly (A); 3 Co Inst 182–183; Com Dig, Trade (D4); *Case of Monopolies* (1602) 11 Co Rep 84b, where a grant by letters patent of the sole right of making playing cards was held void as a monopoly against common law; *North-Western Salt Co Ltd v Electrolytic Alkali Co Ltd* [1913] 3 KB 422 at 445, CA, per Farwell LJ; *A-G of Commonwealth of Australia v Adelaide Steamship Co Ltd* [1913] AC 781, PC. See also *BBC v Johns* [1965] Ch 32 at 79, [1964] 1 All ER 923 at 941, CA, per Diplock LJ. In *East India Co v Sandys* (1685) Skin 132, 165, 197, 223, it was held that a grant to a

company of the sole right of trading to the East Indies was good; but in *Nightingale v Bridges* (1689) 1 Show 135 it was held (although there was no considered judgment) that, although the Crown may give to a corporation the exclusive right to trade and hold territories within prescribed limits, yet a clause prohibiting others to trade within those limits under pain of imprisonment and forfeiture, and authorising the search and seizure of ships and goods, is void. The Crown's right to create such companies and to give them exclusive rights to trade was not disputed, but only the forfeiture clause. In 1694 (Commons Journals, 19 January 1694, pp 64–65) it was resolved 'that all subjects of England have equal right to trade to the East Indies unless prohibited by Act of Parliament': cf *Mitchel v Reynolds* (1711) 1 P Wms 181. In *East India Co v Sandys* (1685) Skin 132, 165, 197, 223 the validity of the grant was based on the Crown's prerogative to control trade with foreigners and to create companies. Cf *Michelborne v Michelborne* (1610) 2 Brownl 296. See CONSTITUTIONAL LAW AND HUMAN RIGHTS vol 8(2) (Reissue) PARA 876 (freedom of trade); CORPORATIONS vol 9(2) (2006 Reissue) PARA 1133 (Crown's grant of a charter by special statute). As to licences to alien enemies to trade see WAR AND ARMED CONFLICT vol 49(1) (2005 Reissue) PARA 576 et seq.

2   As to the prerogative of the Crown to grant exclusive rights to print statutes, rules and orders, the Authorised Version of the Bible, the Book of Common Prayer, charts and ordnance maps, see COPYRIGHT, DESIGN RIGHT AND RELATED RIGHTS vol 9(2) (2006 Reissue) PARA 5, and as to Crown copyright see COPYRIGHT, DESIGN RIGHT AND RELATED RIGHTS vol 9(2) (2006 Reissue) PARAS 144–149. As to the prerogative of the Crown generally see CONSTITUTIONAL LAW AND HUMAN RIGHTS vol 8(2) (Reissue) PARA 367 et seq; and cf *Mounson v Lyster* (1632) W Jo 231; *Earl of Yarmouth v Darrel* (1685) 3 Mod Rep 75; *Stationers' Co v Parker* (1685) Skin 233.

363.   The Statute of Monopolies. By the Statute of Monopolies (1623), all monopolies, licences and letters patent for the sole buying, selling, making, working and using of anything within the realm[1] were declared void[2] with the exception of letters patent thereafter granted for 14 years or under to the first and true inventors of a manner of new manufacture which others at the time of the grant were not using[3].

1   The statute does not extend to foreign trade: *East India Co v Sandys* (1685) Skin 132, 165, 197, 223.

2   Statute of Monopolies (1623) s 1 (partly repealed by the Statute Law (Repeals) Act 1969 s 1, Schedule Pt VII); Warrants and Patents Act (Ireland) 1459 (repealed by the Statute Law (Repeals) Act 1969 Schedule Pt VIII). See *A-G of Commonwealth of Australia v Adelaide Steamship Co Ltd* [1913] AC 781, PC; and CONSTITUTIONAL LAW AND HUMAN RIGHTS vol 8(2) (Reissue) PARA 875 (grants of monopolies by the Crown); PATENTS AND REGISTERED DESIGNS vol 79 (2008) PARA 339 (historical development of the patent system).

3   Statute of Monopolies (1623) s 6 (amended by the Statute Law Revision Act 1888). The term of a patent is now normally 20 years from the date of filing the application: see PATENTS AND REGISTERED DESIGNS vol 79 (2008) PARA 339. Monopolies previously granted by statute were exempted from prohibition (Statute of Monopolies (1623) s 7 (amended by the Statute Law Revision Act 1888)); and the statute did not affect any grants, charters, letters patent, or any customs of any city, borough or town corporate, or any corporation, company or fellowship of any art, trade or occupation (Statute of Monopolies (1623) s 9 (amended by the Statute Law Revision Act 1888)).

364.   Statutory monopolies. There are certain monopolies in existence which have been authorised by statute, for example the provision of postal services[1] and the issue of bank notes in England and Wales by the Bank of England[2]. A number of statutory monopolies in former publicly owned industries have in recent years been abolished[3].

1   See the Postal Services Act 2000 s 6; and POST OFFICE vol 36(2) (Reissue) PARA 78.
2   See the Bank Charter Act 1844 s 11; and FINANCIAL SERVICES AND INSTITUTIONS vol 49 (2008) PARA 796.
3   See eg in relation to electricity, the Electricity Act 1989 ss 65, 66 (see FUEL AND ENERGY vol 19(2) (2007 Reissue) PARA 1034).

365. The modern legislation. Monopolies may arise where a market, either local or national, is controlled by a single person or a combination of persons. Since 1948 there has been a return to statutory supervision of such monopolies[1] and to restrictions on restrictive trade practices generally, and successive statutes have widened the scope of that supervision and those restrictions.

The Monopolies and Restrictive Practices (Inquiry and Control) Act 1948[2] set up a commission, now known as the Competition Commission[3], and empowered it to investigate and report on any industry referred to it in which the supply, processing or export of any goods was subject to monopoly conditions[4], and certain government departments were given powers to make orders where such conditions were found to operate against the public interest[5]. From 1965 the Commission's jurisdiction extended to the supply of services in the United Kingdom[6], and from 1973 statutory monopolies were included in its purview. The relevant provisions on the investigation of 'monopoly situations' are now contained in the Enterprise Act 2002[7].

Since the entry into force of the Competition Act 1998 on 1 March 2000, agreements that prevent, restrict or distort competition[8] and the abuse of a dominant position[9] are prohibited.

1 As to the repeal of earlier statutes dealing with monopolies see PARA 361 note 2. For the changing attitude of the law during the last century to restraint of trade in general see PARAS 386–388. For the present effect of the common law on monopolies see PARA 366.

2 The Monopolies and Restrictive Practices (Inquiry and Control) Act 1948 was repealed and replaced by the Fair Trading Act 1973 which in turn was repealed by the Competition Act 1998 (see PARA 115).

3 As to the Competition Commission see PARAS 12–13.

4 See the Monopolies and Restrictive Practices (Inquiry and Control) Act 1948 ss 1–9, 14, 15, 20 (repealed). No reference could be made of statutory monopolies other than those arising from patents or trade marks: s 2(1) (repealed).

5 See the Monopolies and Restrictive Practices (Inquiry and Control) Act 1948 ss 10–13 (repealed).

6 See the Monopolies and Mergers Act 1965 (repealed).

7 See PARA 276 et seq.

8 See PARAS 116–124.

9 See PARAS 125–128.

366. Subsisting effect of common law on monopolies. Despite the wide scope of the Enterprise Act 2002 and the Competition Act 1998, the common law has not been displaced[1], and it may still be necessary to consider whether an agreement is void as a monopoly or otherwise as being in restraint of trade at common law[2].

1 Thus the High Court could, it seems, still hold an agreement void as creating an unlawful monopoly at common law.

2 See PARA 367. As to restraint of trade in general see PARA 377 et seq.

367. Attempts to control markets. An agreement may be illegal at common law if, by causing the control of a trade or industry to pass into the hands of an individual or of a group of individuals, it creates a monopoly calculated to enhance prices to an unreasonable extent[1].

The agreement must be considered in the light of all surrounding circumstances[2], including agreements made between the parties and third persons[3], possible competition from abroad and the effect on it of tariffs[4], and the benefits accruing to the public from regulated supply, economy of resources and elimination of cut-throat competition[5].

Such an agreement is merely unenforceable; it is not illegal in any criminal sense, nor does it give any cause of action to a third person injured by its operation[6]. Unless the agreement is illegal on the face of it, the issue of illegality must be raised in the particulars of claim[7].

However, it is no monopoly if the control, being lawfully and fairly obtained, is limited to particular persons or places[8] or to a particular kind or make of article for which a substitute is obtainable[9], and an agreement among traders to prevent competition among themselves and even to keep up prices is not necessarily invalid at common law, if it is carried out by provisions reasonably necessary for the purpose and not detrimental to the public[10]. However, such agreements would normally infringe the Competition Act 1998[11], and would also be likely to infringe European competition law in so far as they affect trade between member states[12].

1   *North-Western Salt Co Ltd v Electrolytic Alkali Co Ltd* (1912), as reported in 107 LT 439, CA (revsd [1914] AC 461, HL, on the grounds that the contract was not illegal on the face of it, and that the issue of illegality had not been raised on the pleadings). The judgments of the majority in the Court of Appeal laying down the principle set out in the text were criticised as to their application of the principle to the facts of the case, but the principle itself was not doubted: see per Lord Haldane LC at 469, 471–472. See also *E Underwood & Son Ltd v Barker* [1899] 1 Ch 300, CA; *A-G of Commonwealth of Australia v Adelaide Steamship Co Ltd* [1913] AC 781 at 796, PC; *Palmolive Co (of England) Ltd v Freedman* [1928] Ch 264, CA.

2   *North-Western Salt Co Ltd v Electrolytic Alkali Co Ltd* [1914] AC 461 at 469, HL, per Lord Haldane LC.

3   Such other agreements are relevant for the purpose of ascertaining the object of the restrictions imposed in the agreement under consideration and whether such restrictions are reasonably necessary for the protection of the covenantees' interest: see *North-Western Salt Co Ltd v Electrolytic Alkali Co Ltd* (1912), as reported in 107 LT 439 at 440, CA, per Vaughan Williams LJ (on appeal [1914] AC 461 at 470, HL, per Lord Haldane LC). The dictum that 'no evidence is given in these public policy cases' (*Mogul Steamship Co v McGregor, Gow & Co* [1892] AC 25 at 45, HL, per Lord Bramwell) does not mean that such evidence is not to be admitted (*North-Western Salt Co Ltd v Electrolytic Alkali Co Ltd* at 440). See also *E Underwood & Son Ltd v Barker* [1899] 1 Ch 300 at 306, CA, where Lindley MR said that the contract must be construed with reference to the business of the claimant which it was the object of the parties to protect.

4   *North-Western Salt Co Ltd v Electrolytic Alkali Co Ltd* [1914] AC 461 at 469, HL, per Lord Haldane LC; *A-G of Commonwealth of Australia v Adelaide Steamship Co Ltd* [1913] AC 781 at 796, PC.

5   *North-Western Salt Co Ltd v Electrolytic Alkali Co Ltd* [1914] AC 461 at 469, 471, HL, per Lord Haldane LC, and at 481 per Lord Sumner.

6   *North-Western Salt Co Ltd v Electrolytic Alkali Co Ltd* (1912), as reported in 107 LT 439 at 444, CA, per Farwell LJ; *Mogul Steamship Co v McGregor, Gow & Co* [1892] AC 25, HL; *A-G of Commonwealth of Australia v Adelaide Steamship Co Ltd* [1913] AC 781 at 797, PC. See also the cases on restraint of trade cited in PARA 433 notes 2–3.

7   *North-Western Salt Co Ltd v Electrolytic Alkali Co Ltd* [1914] AC 461, HL; and, as to particulars of claim, see CIVIL PROCEDURE vol 11 (2009) PARA 584 et seq. Although illegality should be pleaded, the court, if the contract concerned is illegal on the face of it, may refuse to enforce it. It appears that if the agreement is not illegal on the face of it the burden of proving the facts rendering it illegal is upon the party alleging illegality: see *North-Western Salt Co Ltd v Electrolytic Alkali Co Ltd* at 480 per Lord Sumner, and *Palmolive Co (of England) Ltd v Freedman* [1928] Ch 264 at 271, CA, per Lord Hanworth MR; but cf *North-Western Salt Co Ltd v Electrolytic Alkali Co Ltd* at 470 per Lord Haldane LC. See also *A-G of Commonwealth of Australia v Adelaide Steamship Co Ltd* [1913] AC 781 at 797, PC.

8   *Freemantle v Silk Throwsters' Co* (1668) 1 Lev 229, where a byelaw of a company binding members not to have over a certain number of spindles per week was held not a monopoly, but a restraint of a monopoly and therefore good; *Mitchel v Reynolds* (1711) 1 P Wms 181 at 187. An agreement by one trader to take a particular class of goods exclusively from another is not in restraint of trade: *Servais Bouchard v Prince's-Hall Restaurant Ltd* (1904) 20 TLR 574, CA; *British Oxygen Co v Liquid Air Ltd* [1925] Ch 383.

9   *Palmolive Co (of England) Ltd v Freedman* [1928] Ch 264, CA, where the agreement by the defendant, a retailer, was not to sell a particular brand of toilet soap manufactured by the claimants 'however acquired' below an agreed price.

10 *Kirkman v Shawcross* (1794) 6 Term Rep 14 (where an agreement by a number of dyers not to receive goods to be dyed except on the terms that they should have a general lien was held legal and to have created a legal agreement between a party and a person sending goods with knowledge of it); *Hearn v Griffin* (1815) 2 Chit 407 (where an agreement between postmasters not to compete was held legal); *Wickens v Evans* (1829) 3 Y & J 318 (where an agreement between traders to parcel out England, not to compete or assist rival traders, and not to purchase certain goods in a certain place at prices higher than certain agreed prices was held legal); *Shrewsbury and Birmingham Rly Co v London and North Western Rly Co* (1851) 17 QB 652 (where an agreement excluding competition was held legal); *Jones v North* (1875) LR 19 Eq 426 (where an agreement between traders to sell goods at a certain price, and that some of them should not tender for a contract at a lower price than one or more of the others, was held legal); *Collins v Locke* (1879) 4 App Cas 674 at 685, PC (where a number of stevedores parcelled out the shipping of a port among themselves by allotting to each the ships consigned to certain named traders, and it was held a reasonable provision that if any of the traders refused to allow the work to be done by the party to whom it was allotted the party securing the work should make good the loss to the party losing it; but a provision which in effect provided that, if a ship was loaded by a person other than the consignee and such person did not choose the stevedore entitled under the agreement, no other party to the agreement should do the work was held to be unreasonable); *Cade v Daly* [1910] 1 IR 306 (where an agreement not to sell below certain prices was held enforceable if reasonably limited (distinguishing *Urmston v Whitelegg Bros* (1890) 63 LT 455, where an agreement not to sell at less than a specified price for ten years, under a penalty, was held unenforceable; and *Mogul Steamship Co v McGregor, Gow & Co* [1892] AC 25, HL)). See also *Keppell v Bailey* (1834) 2 My & K 517 (where it was questioned whether an agreement by lessees of ironworks with a railway company to procure all their limestone from a certain quarry and convey all of it along the railway at an agreed charge was an unreasonable restraint, the case being decided on a different point); *Toby v Major* (1899) 107 LT Jo 489 per Darling J, who queried whether an agreement between German bakers to remove the competition of an English baker by buying him out and restraining him from trading within three miles was against public policy; *North-Western Salt Co Ltd v Electrolytic Alkali Co Ltd* [1913] 3 KB 422, CA (revsd [1914] AC 461, HL); *A-G of Commonwealth of Australia v Adelaide Steamship Co Ltd* [1913] AC 781, PC; *Palmolive Co (of England) Ltd v Freedman* [1928] Ch 264, CA (see note 9). As to bidding agreements at auctions see AUCTION vol 2(3) (Reissue) PARA 246.

11 See PARAS 116–124.

12 Ie the EC Treaty art 81: see PARAS 4, 61 et seq. As to the EC Treaty (ie the Treaty establishing the European Community (Rome, 25 March 1957; TS 1 (1973); Cmnd 5179)) see PARA 24 note 1. The numbering for the EC Treaty used in this title is as revised by the Treaty of Amsterdam: see PARA 24 note 1.

368. Restrictions as to user. Even though the object or effect may be to secure a monopoly, a trader selling goods, other than articles protected by a patent[1], or letting them for hire may, at common law, by the contract of sale or lease prohibit their use with goods supplied by rival traders[2] and attach other conditions calculated to protect himself from such rivals[3]. However, such a prohibition may infringe the Competition Act 1998[4] and may lead to infringement of European competition law[5].

1 As to this exception and its limitations see PATENTS AND REGISTERED DESIGNS vol 79 (2008) PARA 403 et seq (restrictions on contracts).

2 *Mallan v May* (1843) 11 M & W 653 at 668; *Leather Cloth Co v Lorsont* (1869) LR 9 Eq 345; *United Shoe Machinery Co of Canada v Brunet* [1909] AC 330, PC.

3 *Jones v Lees* (1856) 1 H & N 189, where the covenant was by the licensee of a patented improvement for a term not to make or vend the machine without the improvement during the term; *British United Shoe Machinery Co v Somervell Bros* (1906) 95 LT 711, where there was a lease of machines with a condition that they should be used to their full capacity during the term, so far as the number of goods made in the factory would permit. As to the position in relation to goods which were exempted goods under the Resale Prices Act 1976 (repealed) see *National Phonograph Co Ltd v Edison-Bell Consolidated Phonograph Co Ltd* [1908]

1 Ch 335, CA, where there was a sale of phonographs to wholesale dealers on terms that they should not sell to dealers who had not signed a retailer's agreement, or to dealers placed on a 'suspended list', both classes of dealers being bound not to sell at less than current list prices; see also *National Phonograph Co Ltd v Edison-Bell Consolidated Phonograph Co Ltd* at 356 per Lord Alverstone CJ, who said 'I cannot see any objection to a trader in such a trade saying that he will not, if he can help it, allow his machines to be at the disposal of his trade rivals'. If a person has agreed not to sell to a person on a 'suspended list' he does not commit a breach of that agreement if he sells to such a person in ignorance induced by fraud; *National Phonograph Co Ltd v Edison-Bell Consolidated Phonograph Co Ltd* at 368 per Kennedy LJ. See also *Dunlop Pneumatic Tyre Co Ltd v Selfridge & Co Ltd* (1913) 29 TLR 270 (revsd on appeal [1915] AC 847, HL, where the point referred to here was not discussed).

4   See PARA 116 et seq.

5   Ie the EC Treaty arts 81, 82: see PARAS 4, 24 et seq. As to the EC Treaty (ie the Treaty establishing the European Community (Rome, 25 March 1957; TS 1 (1973); Cmnd 5179)) see PARA 24 note 1. The numbering for the EC Treaty used in this title is as revised by the Treaty of Amsterdam: see PARA 24 note 1.

7. TRADE AND FREEDOM TO TRADE

(1) TRADE AND BUSINESS

369. Meaning of 'trade'. 'Trade'[1] in its primary meaning is the exchange of goods for goods or goods for money, and in a secondary meaning it is any business carried on[2] with a view to profit, whether manual or mercantile, as distinguished from the liberal arts or learned professions and from agriculture[3]. However, the word is of very general application[4], and must always be considered in the context in which it is used[5]. As used in various revenue Acts, 'trade' is not limited to buying and selling[6], but may include manufacture[7]. In the expression 'restraint of trade' the word is used in its loosest sense to cover every kind of trade, business, profession or occupation[8].

1 As to the exercise of trade see PARA 372.
2 As to where a trade is carried on see *Crookston Bros v Inland Revenue* 1911 SC 217; and COMPANIES; CORPORATIONS vol 9(2) (2006 Reissue) PARA 1125.
3 The statement in the text summarises the dictionary definitions, but as to the immateriality of 'a view to profit' in the legal conception of the term see PARA 371 note 1. See also *Chartered Mercantile Bank of India, London and China v Wilson* (1877) 3 ExD 108 at 120 per Pollock B; *Grainger & Son v Gough (Surveyor of Taxes)* [1896] AC 325 at 336, HL, per Lord Herschell (a wine merchant exercises his trade 'by making or buying wine and selling it again with a view to profit'), and at 345 per Lord Davey; *Taxation Comrs v Kirk* [1900] AC 588 at 592, PC ('the word 'trade' no doubt primarily means traffic by way of sale or exchange or commercial dealing, but may have a larger meaning so as to include manufactures'); *Palmer v Snow* [1900] 1 Qb 725 at 727, DC ('trade' is buying and selling); *Robinson v Groscourt* (1695) 5 Mod Rep 104 at 108 (music and dancing are not trades, but professions); cf *Wannel v City Chamberlain of London* (1725) 1 Stra 675; *Speak v Powell* (1873) LR 9 Exch 25 at 27 (the occupation of a circus proprietor is not a trade; nor is that of an actor or professional gymnast or theatre proprietor); *Harris v Amery* (1865) LR 1 CP 148 at 154 (banking is not a trade); but cf *Hall v Franklin* (1838) 3 M & W 259 (banking is included in the words 'dealing for profit'); *R v Industrial Disputes Tribunal, ex p East Anglian Trustee Savings Bank* [1954] 2 All ER 730 at 731–732, [1954] 1 WLR 1093 at 1096, DC, per Lord Goddard CJ (ordinarily speaking, banking is a trade); *Frampton v Gillison* [1927] 1 Ch 196, CA (carrying on a sub-post office does not infringe a restrictive covenant against 'trading'); *Pauley v Kenaldo Ltd* [1953] 1 All ER 226, [1953] 1 WLR 187 (cloakroom attendant; arrangement 'by way of trade' for the purposes of legislation replaced by the statutory provisions as to wages councils (now abolished); and cf the following decisions on other similar legislation: *Skinner v Jack Breach Ltd* [1927] 2 KB 220, DC; *R v Minister of Labour, ex p National Trade Defence Association* [1932] 1 KB 1, CA). See also *R v Industrial Disputes Tribunal, ex p Courage & Co Ltd* [1956] 3 All ER 411, [1956] 1 WLR 1062, DC ('section of trade or industry' not confined to a particular undertaking). Statutes enacting that everyone might sell commodities in any city by gross or retail were held not to apply to artificers or manufacturers: *City of London Case* (1610) 8 Co Rep 121b at 128a. The making and using of a decoy pond for ducks which entails labour and expense was treated as trade (*Keeble v Hickeringill* (1706) 11 East 574n), but not the mere chance of capturing or of enjoying the presence of animals ferae naturae which come to a place of their own accord and are not fit for human food, such as rooks (*Hannam v Mockett* (1824) 2 B & C 934); but see *Read v Edwards* (1864) 17 CBNS 245 at 258; *Allen v Flood* [1898] AC 1 at 36, HL, per Cave J; and ANIMALS vol 2 (2008) PARA 710 et seq. For an analysis of different kinds of trade see the arguments of Sawyer A-G in *East India Co v Sandys* (1685) Skin 197 at 198.
4 See eg *National Association of Local Government Officers v Bolton Corpn* [1943] AC 166 at 184–185, [1942] 2 All ER 425 at 432–433, HL, per Lord Wright ('trade or industry').
5 As to the meaning of 'trade or business' in relation to the Agricultural Holdings Act 1986 s 1 see *Rutherford v Maurer* [1962] 1 QB 16, [1961] 2 All ER 775, CA (decided on the previous provision in the Agricultural Holdings Act 1948 s 1 (repealed)); in relation to bankruptcy legislation see BANKRUPTCY AND INDIVIDUAL INSOLVENCY vol 3(2) (2002 Reissue) PARAS 51, 587; in relation to companies legislation see COMPANIES; in relation to income tax see INCOME TAXATION vol 23(1) (Reissue) PARA 105; and in relation to restrictive covenants in conveyances or leases see LANDLORD AND TENANT vol 27(1) (2006 Reissue) PARA 501. As to 'use for trade'

in relation to weights and measures see the Weights and Measures Act 1985 s 7; and WEIGHTS AND MEASURES vol 50 (2005 Reissue) PARA 66. As to trade customs and usages see CUSTOM AND USAGE vol 12(1) (Reissue) PARAS 605, 687 et seq; INSURANCE vol 25 (2003 Reissue) PARAS 232 et seq, 407. For the distinction between trade purposes and domestic purposes in relation to water supply see WATER AND WATERWAYS vol 100 (2009) PARA 334, and for the distinction between commercial waste, industrial waste and household waste, which has replaced the former distinction between trade refuse and domestic refuse see PROTECTION OF ENVIRONMENT AND PUBLIC HEALTH vol 38 (2006 Reissue) PARA 237. Under the Sunday Observance Act 1677 (repealed), the following were held not to be tradesmen: a farmer (*R v Cleworth* (1864) 4 B & S 927; but farming is a business: see *Harris v Amery* (1865) LR 1 CP 148), a barber (*Palmer v Snow* [1900] 1 QB 725, DC; but a barber's business was expressly included in the definition of 'retail trade or business' under the Shops Act 1950 (repealed) s 74(1)), and an estate agent (*Gregory v Fearn* [1953] 2 All ER 559, [1953] 1 WLR 974, CA); cf *Hawkey v Stirling* [1918] 1 KB 63, DC, where an amusements caterer who sold various articles such as rings and darts to enable purchasers to enter into competitions on his premises with these articles was held to be trafficking in goods and a tradesman.

6   See *Chartered Mercantile Bank of India, London and China v Wilson* (1877) 3 ExD 108, where occupation for the purposes of a telegraph company was held to be occupation for the purpose of trade only for the purposes of exemption from the former inhabited house duty; see also at 113 per Kelly CB ('It was not the intention of the legislature to limit the meaning of the word 'trade' to buying and selling; though that is the literal meaning of the word'), and at 115 ('We may reasonably say that it ('trade') was intended to embrace a great variety of different operations though all of a commercial character; something therefore like a warehouse, like a shop, like a counting house'); *Barry (Inspector of Taxes) v Cordy* [1946] 2 All ER 396, CA; *Edinburgh Life Assurance Co v Inland Revenue Solicitor* (1875) 2 R 394, Ct of Sess (distinguished in *Chartered Mercantile Bank of India, London and China v Wilson* (1877) 3 ExD 108 at 115 (a life assurance company is not a trader)). Cf *Citizens Insurance Co of Canada v Parsons, Queen Insurance Co v Parsons* (1881) 7 App Cas 96 at 111–112, PC; *Re Duty on Estate of Incorporated Council of Law Reporting for England and Wales* (1888) 22 QBD 279, DC, where a limited company publishing and selling law reports, but precluded from paying a dividend, apparently carried on a trade within the Customs and Inland Revenue Act 1885 s 11 (repealed); but the word 'business' was there also used. Cf INCOME TAXATION vol 23(1) (Reissue) PARA 105.

7   See *Taxation Comrs v Kirk* [1900] AC 588 at 592, PC. Trade may also include an adventure or concern in the nature of trade: see INCOME TAXATION vol 23(1) (Reissue) PARA 105.

8   For a list of the trades to which the doctrine of restraint of trade has been applied see PARA 432. As to contracts in restraint of trade generally see PARA 377 et seq.

370. Meaning of 'business'. 'Business'[1] is a wider term than 'trade', and not synonymous with it, and means almost anything which is an occupation as distinguished from a pleasure[2]. However, the term must be construed according to its context[3].

1   As to the exercise of business see PARA 372.

2   *Doe d Wetherell v Bird* (1834) 2 Ad & El 161 (the use of premises as a private lunatic asylum is not a trade; cf at 166 per Lord Denman CJ ('Every trade is a business, but every business is not a trade; to answer that description it must be conducted by buying and selling')); *Harris v Amery* (1865) LR 1 CP 148 at 154 per Willes J; *Rolls v Miller* (1884) 27 ChD 71, CA (the carrying on of a charitable home for working girls, boarded without payment, is not a trade, but it is the business of a lodging-house keeper; and cf at 88 per Lindley LJ ('The word ('business') means almost anything which is an occupation as distinguished from a pleasure, anything which is an occupation or duty which requires attention is a business')); *Town Investments Ltd v Department of the Environment* [1978] AC 359, [1977] 1 All ER 813, HL. See also BANKRUPTCY AND INDIVIDUAL INSOLVENCY vol 3(2) (2002 Reissue) PARA 587; COMPANIES vol 7(1) (2004 Reissue) PARA 201; LANDLORD AND TENANT vol 27(1) (2006 Reissue) PARA 501; and cf PARTNERSHIP vol 79 (2008) PARA 6. The business of a solicitor is a 'profession' and not a 'trade or business' within the meaning of a statute which draws a distinction between those terms: see *Stuchbery v General Accident, Fire and Life Assurance Corpn Ltd* [1949] 2 KB 256, [1949] 1 All ER 1026, CA.

3   The pursuit by a person gratuitously of a spare time activity in his own home does not fall within the Landlord and Tenant Act 1954 s 23(2), which defines 'business' as including a trade, profession or employment (*Abernethie v AM and J Kleiman Ltd* [1970] 1 QB 10, [1969]

2 All ER 790, CA); nor does taking in lodgers and making virtually no profit out of it (*Lewis v Weldcrest Ltd* [1978] 3 All ER 1226, [1978] 1 WLR 1107, CA), nor does an activity conducted merely for pleasure and social enjoyment constitute a business for the purpose of what is now the Value Added Tax Act 1994 s 4(1) (*Customs and Excise Comrs v Lord Fisher* [1981] 2 All ER 147).

371. Disregard of profit. Profit, or the intention to make profit, is not an essential part of the legal definition of a trade or business unless the particular context so requires; and payment or profit does not of itself constitute a trade or business[1].

1   *Bramwell v Lacy* (1879) 10 ChD 691; *Rolls v Miller* (1884) 27 ChD 71, CA; *Paddington Burial Board v IRC* (1884) 13 QBD 9, DC. See also *Rael-Brook Ltd v Minister of Housing and Local Government* [1967] 2 QB 65, [1967] 1 All ER 262, DC. For the case of a trade see *Re Duty on Estate of Incorporated Council of Law Reporting for England and Wales* (1888) 22 QBD 279 at 293, DC, per Lord Coleridge CJ ('the definition of the mere word 'trade' does not necessarily mean something by which a profit is made'); but the particular context may import profit: see the cases cited in PARA 369 note 3; see also LANDLORD AND TENANT vol 27(1) (2006 Reissue) PARA 501. Sometimes the words 'gain' or 'profit' are expressly used, as in 57 Geo 3 c 99 (Residence on benefices, etc) (England) (1817) s 3 (repealed). Under the Customs and Inland Revenue Act 1878 s 13 (repealed), occupation for the purposes of a reading-room and library (*London Library v Carter (Surveyor of Taxes)* (1890) 6 TLR 161), or medical institute (*British Institute of Preventive Medicine v Styles* (1895) 11 TLR 432), with no payment of dividends, was held not to be an occupation 'for the purposes of any trade or business ... by which the occupier seeks a profit'. Under the Companies Act 1862 s 4 (repealed), farming and grazing was held to be a 'business that has for its object the acquisition of gain': *Harris v Amery* (1865) LR 1 CP 148. See also the following further decisions under repealed enactments: *Shoyle v Taylor* (1607) Cro Jac 178; *City of London Case* (1610) 8 Co Rep 121b at 128a; *Raynard v Chase* (1756) 1 Burr 2 (sleeping partner: see PARA 372 note 1); *Beach v Turner* (1769) 4 Burr 2450.

372. Exercise of trade or business. The words 'to exercise a trade or business' imply that the trade or business must be habitually or systematically exercised; they do not apply to isolated transactions[1]. Moreover, it is not trading for a person to make articles for his own use or the use of his family or of a family which he serves[2], or to work for his own purposes only[3].

1   *Grainger & Son v Gough (Surveyor of Taxes)* [1896] AC 325 at 343, HL, per Lord Morris (dissenting on the main question in the case from the majority of the court); *Newman v Oughton* [1911] 1 KB 792, DC; *Spiers and Pond Ltd v Green* [1912] 3 KB 576, DC; see BANKRUPTCY AND INDIVIDUAL INSOLVENCY vol 3(2) (2002 Reissue) PARA 125; CONSUMER CREDIT vol 9(1) (Reissue) PARA 56. However, if a person carrying on a particular business does a single isolated preliminary first act in that business, he is carrying it on: see *A-G v Plymouth Corpn* (1909) 100 LT 742 at 744, CA, per Buckley LJ. As to a sleeping partner see *Hobbs v Young* (1691) 2 Salk 610, where a person who directed the trade was held to be exercising it, but not a journeyman; *Raynard v Chase* (1756) 1 Burr 2, where under a penal Act in restraint of trade, which was strictly construed, a partner who shared profit and loss but took no part in the management was held not to be exercising the trade. As to how far a sleeping partner is bound see PARTNERSHIP vol 79 (2008) PARA 45.

2   *Shoyle v Taylor* (1607) Cro Jac 178; *City of London Case* (1610) 8 Co Rep 121b at 128a, 129a ('It is not properly said that one uses a manual occupation when he makes no more than for himself, as he who brews or bakes for his own use'); *Ipswich Taylors' Case* (1614) 11 Co Rep 53a at 54a, where a domestic servant making garments for his master was not exercising a trade within the meaning of a penal enactment in restraint of trade or the byelaw of a corporation of tailors; *Norris v Staps* (1616) Hob 120 at 211 (it is not exercising a trade to do it privately, as a tailor in a house, or the like); *Hobbs v Young* (1691) 2 Salk 610.

3   *Fazakerley v Wiltshire* (1721) 1 Stra 462, where a byelaw regulating porters did not apply to a person carrying his own goods; *A-G v Plymouth Corpn* (1909) 100 LT 742, CA (it is not carrying on the business of a wharfinger to use one's own wharf for loading and unloading materials for one's own works; nor is it 'permitting' such a business to be carried on to lease neighbouring land with leave to the lessee to use the wharf for loading or unloading materials for his own works).

(2) SALE OF GOODWILL

373. Implied sale; form of transfer. The sale of a business implies the sale of its goodwill[1], even though goodwill is not expressly mentioned[2], but an agreement by a partner to retire from a firm is not necessarily equivalent to an agreement to sell the goodwill[3].

A transfer of goodwill can be effected without writing, except in so far as writing may be required by the Law of Property (Miscellaneous Provisions) Act 1989[4] in a transfer involving also the sale of land[5].

1   As to the nature of goodwill generally see PERSONAL PROPERTY vol 35 (Reissue) PARA 1206 et seq. As to goodwill to which a mortgagee is entitled see MORTGAGE vol 32 (2005 Reissue) PARA 398. As to compensation for loss of goodwill on compulsory acquisition see COMPULSORY ACQUISITION OF LAND vol 8(1) (2003 Reissue) PARAS 299, 305; see also *LCC v Tobin* [1959] 1 All ER 649, [1959] 1 WLR 354, CA. As to goodwill in companies' accounts see COMPANIES vol 7(2) (2004 Reissue) PARA 1205. Goodwill is part of fixed capital (see COMPANIES vol 7(2) (2004 Reissue) PARA 1184), and a charge on a company's property or assets includes goodwill (see COMPANIES vol 7(2) (2004 Reissue) PARA 1544).

2   *Shipwright v Clements* (1871) 19 WR 599. It passes with the stock-in-trade or the premises, according to the circumstances of each case: *England v Downs* (1842) 6 Beav 269. As to goodwill in partnership cases generally see PARTNERSHIP vol 79 (2008) PARAS 23, 172, 203, 213–217. As to whether a transfer of a solicitor's business and goodwill carries the right to clients' deeds and papers see LEGAL PROFESSIONS vol 66 (2009) PARA 785.

3   *Gray v Smith* (1889) 43 ChD 208 at 221, CA, per Cotton LJ (distinguishing *Levy v Walker* (1879) 10 ChD 436, CA). However, when a partner assigns his share in a business it is clearly intended that the goodwill is to pass: *Churton v Douglas* (1859) John 174 at 186. As to prohibitions of the sale of goodwill of medical practices in the national health service see HEALTH SERVICES vol 54 (2008) PARA 273 et seq.

4   See the Law of Property (Miscellaneous Provisions) Act 1989 s 2; and LANDLORD AND TENANT vol 27(1) (2006 Reissue) PARA 79 et seq; SALE OF LAND vol 42 (Reissue) PARA 32 et seq.

5   *IRC v G Angus & Co, IRC v Lewis* (1889) 23 QBD 579 at 593, CA, per Lord Esher MR; the proposition was admitted in argument (at 587). An agreement by a partner to assign a share of partnership assets which include an interest in land is within what is now the Law of Property (Miscellaneous Provisions) Act 1989 s 2: *Gray v Smith* (1889) 43 ChD 208, CA.

374. Rights of transferee. A transfer of goodwill confers on the transferee the exclusive right to carry on the business transferred, the exclusive right to represent himself as carrying on such business[1] and, as against the transferor, the exclusive right to use the name under which the business has been carried on[2], but the name must not be so used as to expose the transferor to a risk of personal liability owing to his being held out as the owner of, or a partner in, the business[3].

1   *Walker v Mottram* (1881) 19 ChD 355 at 363, CA. The transferee may also restrain any other person from untruly representing that he carries on, or is the successor to, such business: *Rickerby v Reay* (1903) 20 RPC 380.

2   *Banks v Gibson* (1865) 34 Beav 566 at 569 per Romilly MR; *Levy v Walker* (1879) 10 ChD 436 at 448, CA; *Thynne v Shove* (1890) 45 ChD 577; *Re David and Matthews* [1899] 1 Ch 378 at 384; *Burchell v Wilde* [1900] 1 Ch 551 at 558, CA, per Byrne J; *Mrs Pomeroy Ltd v Scalé* (1906) 22 TLR 795 (subsequent proceedings 23 TLR 170); *RJ Reuter & Co Ltd v Mulhens* (1953) 70 RPC 102 at 121 (affd [1954] Ch 50, [1953] 2 All ER 1160, CA) (involuntary transfer of enemy-owned goodwill). An agreement to retire from a firm, with no express assignment of the goodwill, does not, however, give the remaining partner the right to use the name of the retiring partner (*Gray v Smith* (1889) 43 ChD 208, CA; see also *Hall v Barrows* (1863) 4 De GJ & Sm 150; *Leather Cloth Co v American Leather Cloth Co* (1865) 11 HL Cas 523; *Scott v Rowland* (1872) 26 LT 391), but it is otherwise where the goodwill is divided between partners (*Burchell v Wilde* [1900] 1 Ch 551, CA). See PARTNERSHIP vol 79 (2008) PARAS 172, 213 et seq. As to trade names and trade marks generally see TRADE MARKS AND TRADE NAMES.

3   *Chappell v Griffith* (1885) 53 LT 459; *Chatteris v Isaacson* (1887) 57 LT 177; *Thynne v Shove* (1890) 45 ChD 577; *Jennings v Jennings* [1898] 1 Ch 378 at 388; *Burchell v Wilde* [1900]

1 Ch 551, CA; *Townsend v Jarman* [1900] 2 Ch 698 at 705; *RJ Reuter & Co Ltd v Mulhens* (1953) 70 RPC 102 at 121 per Danckwerts J (affd [1954] Ch 50, [1953] 2 All ER 1160, CA) (involuntary transfer of enemy-owned goodwill). As to the right to use a partnership name see PARTNERSHIP vol 79 (2008) PARAS 172, 215 et seq. Whether the name is a real or fancy name is material in deciding whether such a risk is caused: *Chatteris v Isaacson* (1887) 57 LT 177; *Gray v Smith* (1889) 43 ChD 208, CA; *Thynne v Shove* (1890) 45 ChD 577 at 582. See also *Churton v Douglas* (1859) John 174 at 190. Where the vendor has carried on the business in a name not his own and sold the goodwill with the exclusive right to use that name, he may not afterwards trade under that name in competition with the purchaser; and there may be cases in which the name is so identified with the business that the vendor may not use it even in the absence of express words granting the rights in it to the purchaser: *Mrs Pomeroy Ltd v Scalé* (1906) 23 TLR 170.

375. Position of vendor. In the absence of an express restrictive covenant, no covenant by the vendor of the goodwill of a business not to set up a competing business will be implied, and he may set up a competing business[1], unless he is estopped by conduct amounting to fraud which has encouraged others to involve themselves in the business sold, or to pay him money, in the confidence that he will not trade again either at all or within a limited area[2]. He may advertise himself as having been a partner in, or the founder of or a manager or employee in, the old business[3]; but he may not represent himself to be a successor to, or as carrying on a continuation of, the old business[4], or use the trade marks of the old business[5].

Similarly, a person who has sold the goodwill[6] may not solicit privately any person who was a customer of the business prior to the sale[7], although he may advertise publicly and deal with such persons as come to him unsolicited[8], or, apparently, with such persons as, having been solicited, at first resist such solicitation but subsequently come to him without further solicitation because of dissatisfaction with the old firm[9].

1 *Trego v Hunt* [1896] AC 7, HL. See also *Shackle v Baker* (1808) 14 Ves 468 at 469; *Cruttwell v Lye* (1810) 17 Ves 335 at 346; *Bozon v Farlow* (1816) 1 Mer 459 at 474; *Harrison v Gardner* (1817) 2 Madd 198 at 219; *Kennedy v Lee* (1817) 3 Mer 441 at 455 (see Collyer's Law of Partnership (2nd Edn) 102–103); *Cook v Collingridge* (1825) 27 Beav 456; *Re Thomas, ex p Thomas* (1841) 2 Mont D & De G 294 (on appeal (1842) 3 Mont D & De G 40); *Morris v Moss* (1855) 25 LJCh 194; *Davies v Hodgson* (1858) 25 Beav 177; *Churton v Douglas* (1859) John 174 at 187; *Mellersh v Keen* (1859) 27 Beav 236; *Smith v Everett* (1859) 27 Beav 446 at 452; *Mellersh v Keen (No 2)* (1860) 28 Beav 453; *Hall v Barrows* (1863) 4 De GJ & Sm 150 at 159; *Johnson v Helleley* (1864) 2 De GJ & Sm 446, where the form of advertisement settled by the court on the sale of a partnership business emphasised the right of the partners to carry on a similar business; *Hudson v Osborne* (1869) 39 LJCh 79 at 82; *Reynolds v Bullock* (1878) 47 LJCh 773; *Steuart v Gladstone* (1879) 10 ChD 626 at 662, CA, per Bramwell LJ; *Leggott v Barrett* (1880) 15 ChD 306, CA; *Mogford v Courtenay* (1881) 45 LT 303; *Taylor v Neate* (1888) 39 ChD 538 at 542; *Page v Ratliffe* (1897) 76 LT 63, CA; *Jennings v Jennings* [1898] 1 Ch 378 at 382; *Re David and Matthews* [1899] 1 Ch 378; *Curl Bros Ltd v Webster* [1904] 1 Ch 685. However, where partners have agreed to dissolve and sell the goodwill one partner may not, pending the sale, carry on the partnership business on his own account to the prejudice of the partnership property: *Turner v Major* (1862) 3 Giff 442. As to the rights of partners to the goodwill generally see PARTNERSHIP vol 79 (2008) PARAS 172, 213–217.

2 *Shackle v Baker* (1808) 14 Ves 468; *Cruttwell v Lye* (1810) 17 Ves 335 at 341 per Lord Eldon LC; *Harrison v Gardener* (1817) 2 Madd 198.

3 *Trego v Hunt* [1896] AC 7, HL. See also *Hudson v Osborne* (1869) 39 LJCh 79 at 82; *Hookham v Pottage* (1872) 8 Ch App 91. It is, of course, otherwise if he has agreed to the contrary, as in *Wolmershausen v O'Connor* (1877) 36 LT 921.

4 *Trego v Hunt* [1896] AC 7 at 21, HL. See also *Shackle v Baker* (1808) 14 Ves 468; *Cruttwell v Lye* (1810) 17 Ves 335 RC 342; *Harrison v Gardner* (1817) 2 Madd 198; *Rodgers v Nowill* (1853) 3 De GM & G 614; *Churton v Douglas* (1859) John 174 at 193; *Hudson v Osborne* (1869) 39 LJCh 79; *Leggott v Barrett* (1880) 15 ChD 306 at 315, CA; *Mogford v Courtenay* (1881) 45 LT 303; *Vernon v Hallam* (1886) 34 ChD 748 at 752; *Curl Bros Ltd v Webster*

[1904] 1 Ch 685; *May v May* (1914) 31 RPC 325, DC. This prohibition applies to a bankrupt whose business has been sold by his trustee: *Hudson v Osborne* (1869) 39 LJCh 79; see BANKRUPTCY AND INDIVIDUAL INSOLVENCY vol 3(2) (2002 Reissue) PARA 424.

5   *Hudson v Osborne* (1869) 39 LJCh 79. Registered trade marks are assignable and transmissible with or without the goodwill of a business: see the Trade Marks Act 1994 s 24(1); and TRADE MARKS AND TRADE NAMES vol 48 (2007 Reissue) PARA 129.

6   This applies also to a partner where by the terms of his agreement the goodwill belongs to the other partner: see the text and note 7; and PARTNERSHIP vol 79 (2008) PARA 213.

7   *Trego v Hunt* [1896] AC 7, HL (overruling *Pearson v Pearson* (1884) 27 ChD 145, CA; *Vernon v Hallam* (1886) 34 ChD 748, and *Collier v Chadwick* (1886) cited in 34 ChD at 751–752, CA, and approving *Labouchere v Dawson* (1872) LR 13 Eq 322, and *Ginesi v Cooper & Co* (1880) 14 ChD 596, except in so far as the injunction in that case prevented the defendant from issuing public advertisements or dealing with old customers at all). See also *Leggott v Barrett* (1880) 15 ChD 306, CA; *Walker v Mottram* (1881) 19 ChD 355, CA (disapproving *Ginesi v Cooper & Co* (1880) 14 ChD 596, in so far as it prohibited dealing with old customers); *Mogford v Courtenay* (1881) 45 LT 303; *West London Syndicate v IRC* [1898] 2 QB 507 at 523, CA, per Rigby LJ; *Jennings v Jennings* [1898] 1 Ch 378 at 382; *Gillingham v Beddow* [1900] 2 Ch 242; *Gargan v Ruttle* [1931] IR 152. Quaere whether the vendor of goodwill may solicit potential customers of the business prior to the sale, on which point there is no authority. An express provision authorising the vendor to set up a similar business may be such as to allow him to solicit old customers, however, and to this extent *Pearson v Pearson* (1884) 27 ChD 145, CA, is not overruled by *Trego v Hunt* [1896] AC 7, HL: see *Jennings v Jennings* [1898] 1 Ch 378 at 385; *Re David and Matthews* [1899] 1 Ch 378; *Gillingham v Beddow* [1900] 2 Ch 242 at 244. The prohibition extends to executors carrying out a contract for the sale of a business entered into by the testator (*Boorne v Wicker* [1927] 1 Ch 667), but it does not extend to a bankrupt whose business has been sold by his trustee (*Walker v Mottram* (1881) 19 ChD 355, CA), or to the original owner of property assigned to a trustee for the benefit of creditors (*Green & Sons (Northampton) Ltd v Morris* [1914] 1 Ch 562), even if the debtor covenants to aid to the utmost of his power the realisation of the property (*Farey v Cooper* [1927] 2 KB 384, CA), apparently because the sale or assignment is involuntary in such cases (see *Jennings v Jennings* [1898] 1 Ch 378 at 383, 389–390; and BANKRUPTCY AND INDIVIDUAL INSOLVENCY vol 3(2) (2002 Reissue) PARA 424). If the trustee of the bankrupt has actively helped to deprive the purchaser of the benefit of his contract by assisting the bankrupt to start again in trade, it may be a question whether the purchaser is, as against the trustee, bound to carry out his contract: see *Cruttwell v Lye* (1810) 17 Ves 335 at 347 per Lord Eldon LC. A partner expelled from a partnership is, apparently, in the same position as a bankrupt or other involuntary vendor: *Dawson v Beeson* (1882) 22 ChD 504, CA; see PARTNERSHIP vol 79 (2008) PARA 213.

8   *Labouchere v Dawson* (1872) LR 13 Eq 322; *Leggott v Barrett* (1880) 15 ChD 306, CA; *Trego v Hunt* [1896] AC 7 at 12–13, HL, per Lord Herschell, and at 23 per Lord Macnaghten.

9   *Leggott v Barrett* (1880) 15 ChD 306 at 316, CA, per Cotton LJ. Apparently, damages may be given for such first solicitation, although there will be no injunction against the subsequent dealing, and, apparently, he may not solicit such persons who have come unsolicited if they remain customers of the old firm: *Leggott v Barrett*; *Curl Bros Ltd v Webster* [1904] 1 Ch 685.

376. Goodwill apart from premises. An agreement to sell goodwill unconnected with any premises is probably too uncertain to be enforced by specific performance[1], but specific performance will be decreed of an agreement to sell a goodwill mainly or entirely annexed to premises which are sold with it[2].

1   *Bozon v Farlow* (1816) 1 Mer 459 (specific performance of an agreement to purchase an attorney's business refused); *Baxter v Conolly* (1820) 1 Jac & W 576 at 580 per Lord Eldon LC; *Coslake v Till* (1826) 1 Russ 376; *May v Thomson* (1882) 20 ChD 705, CA, where Jessel MR, during the argument, at 715, doubted whether an agreement to sell a medical practice could be specifically enforced, although specific performance was refused on the ground that there was no concluded agreement; *Thornbury v Bevill* (1842) 1 Y & C Ch Cas 554, where it was doubted whether specific performance could be decreed of an agreement by one solicitor to permit another to use his name, although such an agreement is not illegal. But in *Cooper v Hood* (1858) 26 Beav 293 at 299, Romilly MR was of opinion that a contract for sale of 'goodwill etc' might not be too uncertain for specific performance, although specific performance was refused on the ground of other uncertainties, and in *Beswick v Beswick* [1968] AC 58, [1967] 2 All ER 1197, HL, specific performance was ordered in favour of the personal representative of the vendor of a contract for the sale of goodwill without business premises: see SPECIFIC

PERFORMANCE vol 44(1) (Reissue) PARA 844 et seq. In relation to goodwill and a solicitor's business see also *Arundell v Bell* (1883) 52 LJCh 537, CA; and LEGAL PROFESSIONS vol 66 (2009) PARA 785. As to prohibitions on the sale of goodwill of medical practices in the national health service see HEALTH SERVICES vol 54 (2008) PARA 273 et seq.

2 *Dakin v Cope* (1827) 2 Russ 170; *Darbey v Whitaker* (1857) 4 Drew 134 at 139. See also *IRC v G Angus & Co, IRC v Lewis* (1889) 23 QBD 579 at 593, CA, per Lord Esher MR.

(3) RESTRAINT OF TRADE

(i) Introduction

377. Freedom of trade. It is a general principle of the common law that a man is entitled to exercise any lawful trade or calling as and where he wills[1], and the law has always regarded jealously any interference with trade, even at the risk of interference with freedom of contract[2], as it is public policy[3] to oppose all restraints upon liberty of individual action which are injurious to the interests of the state[4]. The principle is not confined to restraint of trade in the ordinary meaning of the word 'trade'[5]. Moreover, it extends to contracts restricting the way in which a tradesman carries on his business on a piece of land[6], and to restraints imposed by the rules or practices of professional or other bodies controlling particular activities[7].

In upholding freedom to trade, public authorities should not distinguish between lawful trades[8].

1 See PARA 378 et seq; and CONSTITUTIONAL LAW AND HUMAN RIGHTS vol 8(2) (Reissue) PARA 876.

2 *Mitchel v Reynolds* (1711) 1 P Wms 181 at 187; *Homer v Ashford and Ainsworth* (1825) 3 Bing 322 at 326 per Best CJ; *R v Batt* (1834) 6 C & P 329; *Hilton v Eckersley* (1855) 6 E & B 47 (affd (1856) 6 E & B 66 at 75, Ex Ch; approved in *Quinn v Leathem* [1901] AC 495 at 525, HL, per Lord Brampton); *R v Druitt, Lawrence and Adamson* (1867) 10 Cox CC 592 at 600; *Nordenfelt v Maxim Nordenfelt Guns and Ammunition Co Ltd* [1894] AC 535 at 552, HL, per Lord Watson; *Trego v Hunt* [1896] AC 7 at 24, HL, per Lord Macnaghten; *E Underwood & Son Ltd v Barker* [1899] 1 Ch 300 at 308, CA, per Rigby LJ; *Quinn v Leathem* [1901] AC 495 at 534, HL, per Lord Lindley; *Mason v Provident Clothing and Supply Co Ltd* [1913] AC 724 at 738, HL, per Lord Shaw of Dunfermline; *A-G of Commonwealth of Australia v Adelaide Steamship Co Ltd* [1913] AC 781 at 793, PC; *Herbert Morris Ltd v Saxelby* [1916] 1 AC 688 at 699, HL, per Lord Atkinson; *McEllistrim v Ballymacelligott Co-operative Agricultural and Dairy Society Ltd* [1919] AC 548 at 571, HL, per Lord Finlay; cf *Mogul Steamship Co v McGregor, Gow & Co* [1892] AC 25 at 36, HL, per Lord Halsbury LC. See also *Hughes v Architects' Registration Council of the United Kingdom* [1957] 2 QB 550 at 563, [1957] 2 All ER 436 at 443, DC, per Devlin J.

3 See *Nagle v Feilden* [1966] 2 QB 633, [1966] 1 All ER 689, CA (practice of the Jockey Club to refuse to grant training licences to women). As to public policy generally see *Richardson v Mellish* (1824) 2 Bing 229; *Egerton v Earl Brownlow* (1853) 4 HL Cas 1; *Fender v St John-Mildmay* [1938] AC 1 at 38, [1937] 3 All ER 402 at 424, HL, per Lord Wright; *Giles v Thompson* [1993] 3 All ER 321, CA, per Steyn LJ at 333–336 (affd [1994] 1 AC 142, [1993] 3 All ER 321, HL). It is not against public policy as being in restraint of trade for a divorce petitioner, with a view to protecting the respondent's honour, to bind a co-respondent by agreement not to come for a period of years within a certain area, although it is conceivable that in some cases a covenant having apparently no reference to trade may be a colourable device in restraint of trade: *Upton v Henderson* (1912) 106 LT 839. As to agreements contrary to public policy generally see CONTRACT vol 9(1) (Reissue) PARA 841 et seq. Political policy must be distinguished: see CONTRACT vol 9(1) (Reissue) PARA 842.

4 *Horner v Graves* (1831) 7 Bing 735 at 743; *Wallis v Day* (1837) 2 M & W 273; *Whittaker v Howe* (1841) 3 Beav 383 (questioned, but not on this point, in *Tallis v Tallis* (1853) 1 E & B 391); *Leather Cloth Co v Lorsont* (1869) LR 9 Eq 345; *Nordenfelt v Maxim Nordenfelt Guns and Ammunition Co Ltd* [1894] AC 535 at 552, HL; *Tivoli, Manchester, Ltd v Colley* (1904) 20 TLR 437; *Russell v Amalgamated Society of Carpenters and Joiners* [1910] 1 KB 506 at 516, CA (affd [1912] AC 421, HL). See also *AG Spalding & Bros v AW Gamage Ltd and*

Benetfink & Co Ltd (1913) 29 TLR 541. This point was not considered in the Court of Appeal ((1914) 110 LT 530) or in the House of Lords ((1915) 84 LJCh 449). See generally the cases cited in notes 3, 5, and cases on restraint of trade in PARA 381 et seq.

5   See *Hepworth Manufacturing Co Ltd v Ryott* [1920] 1 Ch 1 at 26, CA, per Atkin LJ, where a covenant by a film actor not to use a pseudonym by which he was known while in the plaintiffs' employ was held to be in restraint of trade. See also *Neville v Dominion of Canada News Co Ltd* [1915] 3 KB 556, CA, where a covenant by a newspaper not to comment on the covenantees' business was held to be in restraint of trade; *Eastham v Newcastle United Football Club Ltd* [1964] Ch 413, [1963] 3 All ER 139 (restraints on professional footballers); *Nagle v Feilden* [1966] 2 QB 633, [1966] 1 All ER 689, CA (see note 3); *A Schroeder Music Publishing Co Ltd v Macaulay* [1974] 3 All ER 616, [1974] 1 WLR 1308, HL (song-writer's agreement to provide exclusive services to publishers); *Clifford Davis Management Ltd v WEA Records Ltd* [1975] 1 All ER 237, [1975] 1 WLR 61, CA (song-writers' agreement to assign world-wide copyright for a period of 5 years, extendable to 10); *Greig v Insole* [1978] 3 All ER 449, [1978] 1 WLR 302 (restraints on professional cricketers). The doctrine may apply to an agreement for the acquisition of a franchise: see *Budget Rent a Car International Inc v Mamos Slough Ltd* (1977) 121 Sol Jo 374, CA. As to the ordinary meaning of 'trade' see PARA 369. The early cases on customs and byelaws repeatedly state the general principle: see *Davenant v Hurdis* (1598) Moore KB 576 (referred to in *Case of Monopolies* (1602) 11 Co Rep 84b at 86a); *Case of Monopolies*; *Ipswich Taylors' Case* (1614) 11 Co Rep 53a; *Norris v Staps* (1616) Hob 210 at 211; *Hesketh v Braddock* (1766) 3 Burr 1847; *R v Coopers' Co, Newcastle* (1798) 7 Term Rep 543; *R v Tappenden* (1802) 3 East 186; *Clark v Le Cren* (1829) 9 B & C 52 at 58 per Bayley J. On the same principle 5 Eliz 1 c 4 (Artificers and apprentices) (1562–3) (repealed), which forbade the exercise etc of certain trades without previous apprenticeship, was construed strictly: *R v Turnith* (1669) 1 Mod Rep 26; *Raynard v Chase* (1756) 1 Burr 2 at 6. In *R v Maddox* (1706) 2 Salk 613, that Act was described as 'a hard law'. As to the treatment for tax purposes of the consideration for a restrictive covenant by an office holder or employee see INCOME TAXATION vol 23(1) (Reissue) PARAS 194, 687.

6   *Petrofina (Great Britain) Ltd v Martin* [1966] Ch 146, [1966] 1 All ER 126, CA (solus agreement in gross, restricting the supply of motor fuel to one particular supplier). See also *Esso Petroleum Co Ltd v Harper's Garage (Stourport) Ltd* [1968] AC 269, [1967] 1 All ER 699, HL, where the doctrine was held to apply to covenants in a mortgage. But the doctrine does not apply where a person enters into possession under a lease containing restrictive covenants: *Cleveland Petroleum Co Ltd v Dartstone Ltd* [1969] 1 All ER 201, [1969] 1 WLR 116, CA. As to the treatment of 'land agreements' under the Competition Act 1998 see PARAS 142, 143.

7   See *Eastham v Newcastle United Football Club Ltd* [1964] Ch 413, [1963] 3 All ER 139; *Nagle v Feilden* [1966] 2 QB 633, [1966] 1 All ER 689, CA; *Pharmaceutical Society of Great Britain v Dickson* [1970] AC 403, [1968] 2 All ER 686, HL; *Greig v Insole* [1978] 3 All ER 449, [1978] 1 WLR 302; *Watson v Prager* [1991] 3 All ER 487, [1991] 1 WLR 726, EAT. Restraints may also result from agreements between employers: see *Kores Manufacturing Co Ltd v Kolok Manufacturing Co Ltd* [1959] Ch 108, [1958] 2 All ER 65, CA; and PARA 388 note 1. As to restrictions on the professions and trades which may be carried on by a barrister see LEGAL PROFESSIONS vol 66 (2009) PARA 1033 et seq; as to fellows and members of the Royal College of Physicians see MEDICAL PROFESSIONS vol 30(1) (Reissue) PARA 64.

8   See *R v Coventry City Council, ex p Phoenix Aviation* [1995] 3 All ER 37, DC.

378. Classification of restraints.

Restraints upon the general freedom to trade may be roughly divided into restraints imposed on a person by statute[1], by operation of law[2], by agreement[3] and by the rules or practices of professional or other bodies controlling particular activities[4].

1   See PARAS 379–380.
2   See PARA 381.
3   See PARA 382.
4   See PARA 382.

379. Restraints by statute.

Restraints of trade by statute[1] include all those cases in which certain trades have been absolutely forbidden by Parliament[2], or in which restrictions have been imposed by Parliament on the carrying on of particular trades and professions with a view to the maintenance of a proper standard of competence in, and a proper control over, those engaged in them[3], or with a view to the protection of employees and the public[4] or public order[5], or the public health and safety[6], or for purposes of revenue[7]. The legislature has also interfered to restrict traders from themselves imposing restraints[8], and important provisions in the law of the European Union also must be considered[9].

1   In this title such cases only are dealt with as are not conveniently grouped under other headings, and for particular cases reference should be made to the appropriate titles. As to byelaws in restraint of trade see LOCAL GOVERNMENT vol 69 (2009) PARA 565; and as to such byelaws by corporations see CORPORATIONS vol 9(2) (2006 Reissue) PARA 1196.

2   Eg the slave trade: see CRIMINAL LAW, EVIDENCE AND PROCEDURE vol 11(2) (2006 Reissue) PARAS 824–825.

3   Eg the professions of doctors, dentists, nurses and midwives, opticians, dispensers of hearing aids, chemists and apothecaries (see MEDICAL PROFESSIONS vol 30(1) (Reissue) PARA 1 et seq); and solicitors (see LEGAL PROFESSIONS vol 65 (2008) PARA 600 et seq).

4   See eg the Health and Safety at Work etc Act 1974 (see HEALTH AND SAFETY AT WORK vol 20(1) (Reissue) PARA 502 et seq); the Consumer Credit Act 1974 (see CONSUMER CREDIT; see also PLEDGES AND PAWNS vol 36(1) (2007 Reissue) PARA 41); and the Weights and Measures Act 1985 (see WEIGHTS AND MEASURES vol 50 (2005 Reissue) PARA 1 et seq).

5   Eg intoxicating liquor (see LICENSING AND GAMBLING), and pedlars (see MARKETS, FAIRS AND STREET TRADING vol 29(2) (Reissue) PARA 1117 et seq).

6   Eg the sale of food (see FOOD vol 18(2) (Reissue) PARA 201 et seq), of explosives (see EXPLOSIVES vol 17(2) (Reissue) PARAS 921 et seq, 971 et seq), of firearms (see CRIMINAL LAW, EVIDENCE AND PROCEDURE vol 11(2) (2006 Reissue) PARA 630 et seq), of medicinal products, controlled drugs and of poisons (see MEDICINAL PRODUCTS AND DRUGS vol 30(2) (Reissue) PARAS 237 et seq, 284 et seq); see also the Consumer Protection Act 1987 Pt II (ss 11–19) for wide powers to impose restraints in the interest of consumer safety (see SALE OF GOODS AND SUPPLY OF SERVICES vol 41 (2005 Reissue) PARA 528 et seq).

7   See LICENSING AND GAMBLING; CUSTOMS AND EXCISE vol 12(3) (2007 Reissue) PARA 896 et seq.

8   See PARA 365 et seq.

9   See the EC Treaty arts 81, 82; and PARAS 4, 61 et seq, 68 et seq. As to the EC Treaty (ie the Treaty establishing the European Community (Rome, 25 March 1957; TS 1 (1973); Cmnd 5179)) see PARA 24 note 1. The numbering for the EC Treaty used in this title is as revised by the Treaty of Amsterdam: see PARA 24 note 1.

380. Restraints by statute: reform of law which imposes burdens. A minister of the Crown[1] may by order[2] make any provision which he considers would remove or reduce any burden[3], or the overall burdens, resulting directly or indirectly for any person from any legislation[4]. The provision that may be made includes: (1) provision abolishing, conferring or transferring, or providing for the delegation of, functions of any description; (2) provision creating or abolishing a body or office, and provision made by amending or repealing any enactment[5].

A minister of the Crown may also by order[6] make any provision which he considers would secure that regulatory functions[7] are exercised so as to comply with the principles that: (a) regulatory activities should be carried out in a way which is transparent, accountable, proportionate and consistent; (b) regulatory activities should be targeted only at cases in which action is needed[8]. The provision that may be made includes: (i) provision modifying the way in which a regulatory function is exercised by any person; (ii) provision amending the constitution of a body exercising regulatory functions which is established by or under an enactment; (iii) provision transferring, or providing for the delegation of, the regulatory functions conferred on any person[9], and provision made by amending or repealing any enactment[10].

A minister may not make such provision[11], other than provision which merely restates an enactment[12], unless he considers that the following conditions, where relevant, are satisfied in relation to that provision:

(A)   the policy objective intended to be secured by the provision could not be satisfactorily secured by non-legislative means;

(B)   the effect of the provision is proportionate to the policy objective;

(C)   the provision, taken as a whole, strikes a fair balance between the public interest and the interests of any person adversely affected by it;

(D)   the provision does not remove any necessary protection;

(E)   the provision does not prevent any person from continuing to exercise any right or freedom which that person might reasonably expect to continue to exercise;

(F)   the provision is not of constitutional significance[13].

1   As to the meaning of 'Minister of the Crown' see the Ministers of the Crown Act 1975 (see CONSTITUTIONAL LAW AND HUMAN RIGHTS); definition applied by the Legislative and Regulatory Reform Act 2006 s 32(1).

2   Such an order must be made by statutory instrument in accordance with the Legislative and Regulatory Reform Act 2006 Pt 1 (ss 1–20): ss 1(10), 12(1). It may contain such consequential, supplementary, incidental or transitional provision (including provision made by amending or repealing any enactment or other provision) as the minister making it considers appropriate: s 1(8). An order may bind the Crown: s 1(9). A minister may not make such an order unless: (1) he has consulted in accordance with s 13; (2) following that consultation, he has laid a draft order and explanatory document before Parliament in accordance with s 14; and (3) the order is made, as determined under s 15, in accordance with: (a) the negative resolution procedure (see s 16); (b) the affirmative resolution procedure (see s 17); or (c) the super-affirmative resolution procedure (see s 18): s 12(2).

3   'Burden' means any of the following: (1) a financial cost; (2) an administrative inconvenience; (3) an obstacle to efficiency, productivity or profitability; or (4) a sanction, criminal or otherwise, which affects the carrying on of any lawful activity: Legislative and Regulatory Reform Act 2006 s 1(3). A financial cost or administrative inconvenience may result from the form of any legislation (for example, where the legislation is hard to understand): s 1(5). Provision may not be made in relation to any burden which affects only a minister of the Crown or government department, unless it affects the minister or department in the exercise of a regulatory function: s 1(4). As to the meaning of 'regulatory function' see note 7.

4   Legislative and Regulatory Reform Act 2006 s 1(1), (2). 'Legislation' means any of the following or a provision of any of the following: (1) a public general Act or local Act, whenever passed; (2) a Measure or Act of the National Assembly for Wales; or (3) any Order in Council, order, rules, regulations, scheme, warrant, byelaw or other subordinate instrument made at any time under an Act referred to in head (1), or a Measure or Act of the National Assembly for Wales, but does not include any instrument which is, or is made under, Northern Ireland legislation: Legislative and Regulatory Reform Act 2006 s 1(6) (amended by SI 2007/1388).

5   Legislative and Regulatory Reform Act 2006 s 1(7). As to subordinate legislation see s 4 (amended by SI 2007/1388). An order under the Legislative and Regulatory Reform Act 2006 Pt 1 may not make provision to impose, abolish or vary any tax (see the Legislative and Regulatory Reform Act 2006 s 5); nor must it create or significantly affect criminal penalties (see s 6) or allow forcible entry (see s 7). An order may not make provision amending or repealing any provision of the Legislative and Regulatory Reform Act 2006 Pt 1 or the Human Rights Act 1998: Legislative and Regulatory Reform Act 2006 s 8. An order under Pt 1 may not, except by virtue of s 1(8) (see note 2) or s 2(7) (see note 6), make provision which would be within the legislative competence of the Scottish Parliament if it were contained in an Act of that Parliament (Legislative and Regulatory Reform Act 2006 s 9), make provision to amend or repeal any Northern Ireland legislation (s 10), or, except with the agreement of the National Assembly for Wales, make provision which would be within the legislative competence of the Assembly (see s 11 (substituted by SI 2007/1388)).

6   Such an order must be made in accordance with the Legislative and Regulatory Reform Act 2006 Pt 1; may bind the Crown; and may contain such consequential, supplementary, incidental or transitional provision (including provision made by amending or repealing any enactment or other provision) as the minister making it considers appropriate: s 2(7)–(9).

7   'Regulatory function' means: (1) a function under any enactment of imposing requirements, restrictions or conditions, or setting standards or giving guidance, in relation to any activity; or (2) a function which relates to the securing of compliance with, or the enforcement of, requirements, restrictions, conditions, standards or guidance which under or by virtue of any enactment relate to any activity: Legislative and Regulatory Reform Act 2006 s 32(2). In heads (1) and (2) the references to a function include a function exercisable by or on behalf of the Crown but do not include any function exercisable by any body of, or any person holding office

in, the Church of England, or any function of conducting criminal or civil proceedings: s 32(3). References to an activity include providing goods and services and employing or offering employment to any person: s 32(4). As to the exercise of regulatory functions see ss 21–24 (s 24 amended by SI 2007/1388).

8   Legislative and Regulatory Reform Act 2006 s 2(1)–(3). The provision that may be made does not include provision conferring any new regulatory function or abolishing any regulatory function: s 2(6). The following order has been made under this provision: see the Legislative Reform (Health and Safety Executive) Order 2008, SI 2008/960; and HEALTH AND SAFETY AT WORK vol 20(1) (Reissue) PARA 570.

9   The provision referred to in head (iii) in the text includes provision: (1) to create a new body to which, or a new office to the holder of which, regulatory functions are transferred; (2) to abolish a body from which, or office from the holder of which, regulatory functions are transferred: Legislative and Regulatory Reform Act 2006 s 2(5).

10 Legislative and Regulatory Reform Act 2006 s 2(4). As to the making of orders under Pt 1 see note 5.

11 Ie under the Legislative and Regulatory Reform Act 2006 s 1(1) or s 2(1).

12 To 'restate' an enactment means to replace it with alterations only of form or arrangement (and for these purposes to remove an ambiguity is to make an alteration other than one of form or arrangement): Legislative and Regulatory Reform Act 2006 s 3(5). A minister may not make provision which merely restates an enactment unless he considers that the provision made would make the law more accessible or more easily understood: s 3(3), (4).

13 Legislative and Regulatory Reform Act 2006 s 3(1), (2).

381.   Restraints by operation of law.   Restraints may be imposed on a person by operation of law when one trader is given confidential information by another; apart from any contract, he is not entitled to use the information for the purposes of trade by way of competition with the other trader[1].

1   *Saltman Engineering Co Ltd v Campbell Engineering Co Ltd* [1963] 3 All ER 413n, CA; *Peter Pan Manufacturing Corpn v Corsets Silhouette Ltd* [1963] 3 All ER 402, [1964] 1 WLR 96. See also PARAS 409–410; EQUITY vol 16(2) (Reissue) PARA 855; and CIVIL PROCEDURE vol 11 (2009) PARA 331 et seq. The relief which may be obtained for a breach of the obligation of confidence includes an injunction, an account of profits or damages, and delivery up or destruction of offending goods: *Peter Pan Manufacturing Corpn v Corsets Silhouette Ltd*. As to the scope of an inquiry as to damages see *National Broach and Machine Co v Churchill Gear Machines Ltd* [1965] 2 All ER 961, [1965] 1 WLR 1199, CA; affd sub nom *Churchill Gear Machines Ltd v National Broach and Machine Co* [1966] 3 All ER 923n, [1967] 1 WLR 384, HL. See *Seager v Copydex Ltd* [1967] 2 All ER 415, [1967] 1 WLR 923, CA, where damages were awarded for the use of an unpatented invention disclosed during abortive negotiations; see further *Seager v Copydex Ltd (No 2)* [1969] 2 All ER 718, [1969] 1 WLR 809, CA; *Dowson and Mason Ltd v Potter* [1986] 2 All ER 418, [1986] 1 WLR 1419, CA.

382.   Restraints by agreement and by professional or other bodies.   Restraints may be imposed by agreement or by the rules or practices of professional or other bodies controlling particular activities[1]. A person may be restrained from carrying on his trade by reason of an agreement voluntarily entered into by him with that object[2]. In such a case the general principle of freedom of trade[3] must be applied with due regard to the principles that public policy requires for persons of full age and understanding the utmost freedom to contract[4], and that it is public policy to allow a trader to dispose of his business to a successor by whom it may be efficiently carried on[5], and to afford to an employer an unrestricted choice of able assistants and the opportunity to instruct them in his trade and its secrets without fear of their becoming his competitors[6].

1   Restraint by custom, when not abolished by statute, is now obsolete: see CUSTOM AND USAGE vol 12(1) (Reissue) PARA 646. The law of involuntary restraint by Crown grants is now governed by statute (see PATENTS AND REGISTERED DESIGNS vol 79 (2008) PARA 302 et seq), as is in practically all cases the law of restraint by byelaw, and the distinction between general and partial voluntary restraints has disappeared: see PARA 387. As to trade combinations see the cases cited in PARA 432 note 75.

2 Apart from agreement a retiring partner or the vendor of a business is at liberty to start a competing business: see PARA 375; and PARTNERSHIP vol 79 (2008) PARAS 172, 213 et seq. See *WWF-World Wide Fund for Nature (formerly World Wildlife Fund) v World Wrestling Federation Entertainment Inc* [2002] EWCA Civ 196, [2002] FSR 530 (agreement concluded as part of dispute settlement presumed to be sound unless proved otherwise by defendant).

3 See PARA 377.

4 *Printing and Numerical Registering Co v Sampson* (1875) LR 19 Eq 462; *Middleton v Brown* (1878) 47 LJCh 411, CA; *Rousillon v Rousillon* (1880) 14 ChD 351 at 365; *Badische Anilin und Soda Fabrik v Schott, Segner & Co* [1892] 3 Ch 447 at 452; *Continental Tyre and Rubber (Great Britain) Co Ltd v Heath* (1913) 29 TLR 308 at 310; *A-G of Commonwealth of Australia v Adelaide Steamship Co Ltd* [1913] AC 781, PC; *Herbert Morris Ltd v Saxelby* [1916] 1 AC 688 at 697, HL, per Lord Atkinson; *Attwood v Lamont* [1920] 3 KB 571 at 577, CA, per Lord Sterndale MR; *Esso Petroleum Co Ltd v Harper's Garage (Stourport) Ltd* [1968] AC 269 at 304–305, [1967] 1 All ER 699 at 711–712, HL, per Lord Morris of Borth-y-Gest. See also *Texaco Ltd v Mulberry Filling Station Ltd* [1972] 1 All ER 513, [1972] 1 WLR 814.

5 *Nordenfelt v Maxim Nordenfelt Guns and Ammunition Co Ltd* [1894] AC 535 at 552, HL, per Lord Watson; *Mason v Provident Clothing and Supply Co Ltd* [1913] AC 724 at 738, HL, per Lord Shaw of Dunfermline. Cf *E Underwood & Son Ltd v Barker* [1899] 1 Ch 300 at 310, CA, per Vaughan Williams LJ in his dissenting judgment. See also *Broad v Jollyfe* (1620) Cro Jac 596; *Anon* (1641) March 77; *Prugnell v Gosse* (1648) Aleyn 67; *Mitchel v Reynolds* (1711) 1 P Wms 181 at 187; *Homer v Ashford and Ainsworth* (1825) 3 Bing 322; *Horner v Graves* (1831) 7 Bing 735 at 742; *Mallan v May* (1843) 11 M & W 653; *Leather Cloth Co v Lorsont* (1869) LR 9 Eq 345; *Vernon v Hallam* (1886) 34 ChD 748; *Connors Bros Ltd v Connors* [1940] 4 All ER 179 at 190–191, PC. A trade or business may be sold even though it depends upon the personal character of the man who carries it on: see PARA 414.

6 *Homer v Ashford and Ainsworth* (1825) 3 Bing 322 at 326; *Mallan v May* (1843) 11 M & W 653 at 666 per Parke B; *Mumford v Gething* (1859) 7 CBNS 305 at 319 per Erle CJ; *Fitch v Dewes* [1921] 2 AC 158 at 162–167, HL, per Lord Birkenhead LC. Note, however, that it is not lawful to impose a covenant against competition simpliciter: this is legitimate only to the extent that the covenantee has an interest meriting protection; see PARA 389.

383. Restraints of trade contrary to public policy. A restraint of trade will be contrary to public policy unless the person imposing the restraint has a legitimate interest meriting protection[1], the restraint is reasonable as between the parties[2] and the restraint is reasonable in the public interest[3].

Contracts in restraint of trade are prima facie void. The onus of proof is on the party supporting the contract to show that the restraint goes no further than is reasonably necessary to protect a legitimate interest of the covenantee meriting protection[4]. If this onus is discharged, the onus of showing that the restraint is nevertheless injurious to the public is on the party attacking the contract[5]. Contracts in restraint of trade are unenforceable, but not unlawful or illegal[6]. A third party cannot bring an action for damages against the parties to an agreement in unreasonable restraint of trade[7]. However, a declaration may be obtainable[8], as may an interim or final injunction[9]. An action may lie in respect of agreements that infringe the Chapter I prohibition in the Competition Act 1998[10] or the competition provisions in the EC Treaty[11].

In order to be valid, a contract in restraint of trade must, apart from satisfying the test of reasonableness between the parties and in the public interest, also satisfy the following conditions: (1) it must be founded on good consideration[12]; and (2) it must not be too vague[13].

1 See PARA 389.
2 See PARA 390 et seq.
3 See PARA 412.
4 *Mason v Provident Clothing and Supply Co Ltd* [1913] AC 724 at 733, HL, per Lord Haldane LC; *Herbert Morris Ltd v Saxelby* [1916] 1 AC 688 at 700, HL, per Lord Atkinson, and at 707 per Lord Parker of Waddington; *Attwood v Lamont* [1920] 3 KB 571 at 587, CA, per Younger LJ; *Hepworth Manufacturing Co Ltd v Ryott* [1920] 1 Ch 1 at 26, CA, per Atkin LJ; *Putsman v Taylor* [1927] 1 KB 637 at 645, DC, per Talbot J (on appeal

(1927] 1 KB 741, CA); *Gilford Motor Co Ltd v Home* [1933] Ch 935 at 946, CA, per Foxwell J, and at 966 per Romer LJ; *Triplex Safety Glass Co v Scorah* [1938] Ch 211 at 215, [1937] 4 All ER 693 at 697 per Farwell J; *Routh v Jones* [1947] 1 All ER 758 at 763, CA, where Lord Greene MB preferred the dicta of Lord Parker of Waddington and of Younger LJ, referred to in this note, to that of Lord Birkenhead LC in *Fitch v Dewes* [1921] 2 AC 158 at 162, HL. The proposition is inconsistent with earlier authority: see *Eastes v Russ* [1914] 1 Ch 468 at 475, CA, per Cozens-Hardy MR; *Fitch v Dewes* at 162; see also the text and note 5. As to illegality of contract generally see CONTRACT vol 9(1) (Reissue) PARA 836 et seq.

5   *Herbert Morris Ltd v Saxelby* [1916] 1 AC 688 at 700, 708, HL. The distinction is probably of little practical significance: 'The reason for the distinction may be obscure, but it will seldom arise since once the agreement is before the court it is open to the scrutiny of the court in all its surrounding circumstances as a question of law': *Esso Petroleum Co Ltd v Harper's Garage (Stourport) Ltd* [1968] AC 269 at 319, [1967] 1 All ER 699 at 721, HL, per Lord Hodson. See also *Texaco Ltd v Mulberry Filling Station Ltd* [1972] 1 All ER 513, [1972] 1 WLR 814.

6   *Mogul Steamship Co Ltd v McGregor, Gow & Co* [1892] AC 25, HL; *Esso Petroleum Co Ltd v Harper's Garage (Stourport) Ltd* [1968] AC 269, [1967] 1 All ER 699, HL; *Brekkes Ltd v Cattel* [1972] Ch 105, [1971] 1 All ER 1031; cf *Cooke v Football Association* [1972] CLY 516; *R v General Medical Council, ex p Colman* [1990] 1 All ER 489 at 508, CA, per Ralph Gibson LJ ('An unreasonable restraint of trade is not itself an illegal provision. It is unenforceable because contrary to public policy'); *Boddington v Lawton* [1994] ICR 478.

7   *Mogul Steamship Co v McGregor, Gow and Co* [1892] AC 25, HL.

8   *Eastham v Newcastle United Football Club Ltd* [1964] Ch 413, [1963] 3 All ER 139; *Dickson v Pharmaceutical Society of Great Britain* [1967] Ch 708, [1967] 2 All ER 558, CA; affd sub nom *Pharmaceutical Society of Great Britain v Dickson* [1970] AC 403, [1968] 2 All ER 686, HL; *Blackler v New Zealand Rugby Football League Inc* [1968] NZLR 547, NZ CA; *Greig v Insole* [1978] 3 All ER 449, [1978] 1 WLR 302; *McInnes v Onslow Fane* [1978] 3 All ER 211, [1978] 1 WLR 1520; *Hughes v Western Australian Cricket Association Inc* (1986) 69 ALR 660, Aust Fed Ct.

9   *Nagle v Feilden* [1966] 2 QB 633, [1966] 1 All ER 689, CA; *Newport Association Football Club Ltd v Football Association of Wales Ltd* [1995] 2 All ER 87.

10   Ie in the Competition Act 1998. See PARA 116 et seq.

11   Ie the EC Treaty art 81: see PARAS 4, 61 et seq. As to the EC Treaty (ie the Treaty establishing the European Community (Rome, 25 March 1957; TS 1 (1973); Cmnd 5179)) see PARA 24 note 1. The numbering for the EC Treaty used in this title is as revised by the Treaty of Amsterdam: see PARA 24 note 1.

12   See PARAS 413–416.

13   See PARA 423.

384.   Judicial notice of restraint of trade.   As a general rule, the point that a contract is unenforceable as being in restraint of trade is not one that the court is entitled to take of its own initiative unless it is raised on the pleadings[1]. However, a contract in restraint of trade may on the face of it be so unreasonable as between the parties, or so detrimental to the public, that if the court has before it evidence of all the surrounding circumstances it may on its own initiative refuse to enforce it, even though the matter is not pleaded[2].

1   *Petrofina (Great Britain) Ltd v Martin* [1966] Ch 146 at 180, [1966] 1 All ER 126 at 137, CA, per Diplock LJ; *Panayiotou v Sony Music Entertainment (UK) Ltd* [1994] EMLR 233.

2   *North-Western Salt Co Ltd v Electrolytic Alkali Co Ltd* [1914] AC 461 at 476, HL, per Lord Moulton, and at 478 per Lord Parker of Waddingon. As to judicial notice of illegality generally see CIVIL PROCEDURE vol 11 (2009) PARA 782.

385.   Domestic and European Union competition law.   Restraints subject to the restraint of trade doctrine may attract the application of the domestic competition law of the United Kingdom[1] and the competition rules in the EC Treaty[2].

1   In particular the Chapter I prohibition in the Competition Act 1998: see PARA 116 et seq.

2   In particular the EC Treaty art 81: see PARAS 4, 61 et seq. As to the EC Treaty (ie the Treaty establishing the European Community (Rome, 25 March 1957; TS 1 (1973); Cmnd 5179)) see PARA 24 note 1. The numbering for the EC Treaty used in this title is as revised by the Treaty of Amsterdam: see PARA 24 note 1.

(ii) Scope of the Restraint of Trade Doctrine

386. Development of the principle relating to restraint by agreement. Decisions on public policy are subject to change and development with the change and development of trade and the means of communication and the evolution of economic thought[1]. However, while the general principle once applicable to agreements in restraint of trade has been considerably modified by later decisions, the old cases have not been rendered obsolete on such questions as consideration[2], measurement of distance[3], severability[4], parties[5] and reasonableness of restraint generally[6].

In the earliest times it would probably have been held that all contracts in restraint of trade, whether general or partial, were void, but the severity of this principle was gradually relaxed[7], and it became the rule that a partial restraint might be good if reasonable[8], although a general restraint was of necessity void[9].

A restraint was regarded as general if it was unlimited as to space, that is, apparently, if it extended over the whole of the United Kingdom[10] or substantially so[11] (the extension of such restraint to foreign countries being immaterial[12]), even though limited as to time[13]. It was not, however, so regarded if, although unlimited as to space, it was limited as to the persons with whom the covenantor might deal[14], or as to the manner in which or the name under which the trade might be carried on[15], or, it appears, as to the capacity in which the covenantor might engage in the trade[16]. The mere fact that it was unlimited as to time did not constitute it a general restraint[17].

1   *Archer v Marsh* (1837) 6 Ad & El 959; *Davies v Davies* (1887) 36 ChD 359 at 396, CA, per Fry LJ; *Badische Anilin und Soda Fabrik v Schott, Segner & Co* [1892] 3 Ch 447 at 452; *Nordenfelt v Maxim Nordenfelt Guns and Ammunition Co Ltd* [1894] AC 535 at 553, HL, per Lord Watson; *Dubowski & Sons v Goldstein* [1896] 1 QB 478, CA; *North-Western Salt Co Ltd v Electrolytic Alkali Co Ltd* (1912) as reported in 107 LT 439 at 445, CA, per Farwell LJ; *Herbert Morris Ltd v Saxelby* [1916] 1 AC 688 at 716, HL, per Lord Shaw of Dunfermline; *Bull v Pitney-Bowes Ltd* [1966] 3 All ER 384 at 388, [1967] 1 WLR 273 at 276. As to public policy see PARA 377 note 3; and CONTRACT vol 9(1) (Reissue) PARA 841 et seq.
2   See PARAS 413–416.
3   See PARA 402.
4   See PARAS 433–434.
5   See PARAS 417–419.
6   See PARA 390 et seq.
7   *Dier's Case* (1414) YB 2 Hen 5, fo 5, pl 26; *Colgate v Bacheler* (1602) Cro Eliz 872; *Broad v Jollyfe* (1620) Cro Jac 596; *Prugnell v Gosse* (1648) Aleyn 67; *Nordenfelt v Maxim Nordenfelt Guns and Ammunition Co Ltd* [1894] AC 535 at 541, 556, 564, HL (affg sub nom *Maxim Nordenfelt Guns and Ammunition Co v Nordenfelt* [1893] 1 Ch 630 at 647, CA); *Continental Tyre and Rubber (Great Britain) Co Ltd v Heath* (1913) 29 TLR 308 at 309; *A-G of Commonwealth of Australia v Adelaide Steamship Co Ltd* [1913] AC 781, PC.
8   *Rogers v Parrey* (1613) 2 Bulst 136; *Mitchel v Reynolds* (1711) 1 P Wms 181. The proposition will be found stated in practically all the cases on the subject.
9   *Dier's Case* (1414) YB 2 Hen 5, fo 5, pl 26 (where, however, there was fraud and compulsion: see *Broad v Jollyfe* (1620) Cro Jac 596; *Mitchel v Reynolds* (1711) 1 P Wms 181); *Colgate v Bacheler* (1602) Cro Eliz 872; *Ipswich Taylors' Case* (1614) 11 Co Rep 53a; *Anon* (1641) March 77; *Mitchel v Reynolds*; *Chesman v Nainby* (1727) 1 Bro Parl Cas 234, HL; *Gunmakers Co v Fell* (1742) Willes 384 at 388; *Davis v Mason* (1793) 5 Term Rep 118; *Shackle v Baker* (1808) 14 Ves 468; *Morris v Colman* (1812) 18 Ves 437 at 438 per Lord Eldon LC; *Harrison v Gardner* (1817) 2 Madd 198; *Bryson v Whitehead* (1822) 1 Sim & St 74 at 77 (trade

secret: see PARA 409); *Homer v Ashford and Ainsworth* (1825) 3 Bing 322; *Wickens v Evans* (1829) 3 Y & J 318; *Hutton v Parker* (1839) 7 Dowl 739; *Exeter Co of Taylors v Clarke* (1684) 2 Show 345.

10 *Mitchel v Reynolds* (1711) 1 P Wms 181 at 182, where in describing a general restraint the words used were 'not to exercise a trade throughout the kingdom'. The law was not clear as to this, and in *Horner v Graves* (1831) 7 Bing 735, those words were said to be rather an instance than a limit of the application of the rule: see the cases cited in note 11.

11 In *Price v Green* (1847) 16 M & W 346, Ex Ch, 'London and 600 miles' (ie England, Wales, and nineteen-twentieths of Scotland) was treated as general (London being held severable: see PARAS 433–434). In *Jones v Lees* (1856) 1 H & N 189, 'England' was treated as general. In *Harms v Parsons* (1862) 32 Beav 328, a restraint covering England but not Scotland was treated as partial. In *Leather Cloth Co v Lorsont* (1869) LR 9 Eq 345 at 351, Great Britain was referred to as the test; cf *Ward v Byrne* (1839) 5 M & W 548. In *Rousillon v Rousillon* (1880) 14 ChD 351 at 366, a restraint unlimited as to space was discussed on the basis that it extended to England and Wales; and in *Maxim Nordenfelt Guns and Ammunition Co v Nordenfelt* [1893] 1 Ch 630 at 648, CA, Lindley LJ, and at 651 Bowen LJ, speak of England; although in [1894] AC 535 at 550, HL, Lord Herschell LC, and at 574, Lord Macnaghten, seem to refer to the United Kingdom.

12 In *Nordenfelt v Maxim Nordenfelt Guns and Ammunition Co Ltd* [1894] AC 535 at 550, HL, Lord Herschell said that the courts in laying down the rule had reference only to the United Kingdom and would not have considered it against public policy to restrain a person who had sold his business from setting up a rival business in another country. Cf *Leather Cloth Co v Lorsont* (1869) LR 9 Eq 345 at 351. As to restraints extending beyond the United Kingdom see PARA 401.

13 *Dier's Case* (1414) YB 2 Hen 5, fo 5, pl 26; *Hunlocke v Blacklowe* (1670) 2 Saund 156; *Colmer v Clark* (1734) 7 Mod Rep 230; *M'Allen v Churchill* (1826) 11 Moore CP 483; *Ward v Byrne* (1839) 5 M & W 548; *Hinde v Gray* (1840) 1 Man & G 195; *Proctor v Sargent* (1840) 2 Man & G 20 at 33; *Davies v Davies* (1887) 36 ChD 359, CA; *Nordenfelt v Maxim Nordenfelt Guns and Ammunition Co Ltd* [1894] AC 535 at 543, 553, HL; but see, contra, *Badische Anilin und Soda Fabrik v Schott, Segner & Co* [1892] 3 Ch 447 at 450 per Chitty J; *Davies v Davies* at 382 per Cotton LJ, and at 391 per Bowen LJ.

14 *Hunlocke v Blacklowe* (1670) 2 Saund 156; *Mitchel v Reynolds* (1711) 1 P Wms 181 at 185; *Gale v Reed* (1806) 8 East 80; *Nicholls v Stretton* (1843) 7 Beav 42 (subsequent proceedings (1847) 10 QB 346 at 350); *Rannie v Irvine* (1844) 7 Man & G 969; *May v O'Neill* (1875) 44 LJCh 660; *Collins v Locke* (1879) 4 App Cas 674, PC; *Baines v Geary* (1887) 35 ChD 154; *Mills v Dunham* [1891] 1 Ch 576, CA.

15 *Jones v Lees* (1856) 1 H & N 189. See also *Maxim Nordenfelt Guns and Ammunition Co v Nordenfelt* [1893] 1 Ch 630 at 654, 657, CA, per Bowen LJ. Compare the distinction between rules in restraint of trade and rules (now obsolete) regulating trade. As to a restriction as to name see *Vernon v Hallam* (1886) 34 ChD 748 (covenant not to carry on the business of a manufacturer anywhere for five years under a particular name is not a general restraint or void); *Wolmershausen v O'Connor* (1877) 36 LT 921 (covenant not to hold out as formerly connected in trade with another is not in general restraint or void).

16 *Wallis v Day* (1837) 2 M & W 273, where a covenant by the vendor of a carrier's business, in consideration of weekly payments, never to trade as a carrier except as the servant of the covenantee was held good.

17 *Clerke v Comer* (1734) Lee temp Hard 53; *Hitchcock v Coker* (1837) 6 Ad & El 438, Ex Ch; *Archer v Marsh* (1837) 6 Ad & El 959; *Elves v Crofts* (1850) 10 CB 241; *Tallis v Tallis* (1853) 1 E & B 391; *Catt v Tourle* (1869) 4 Ch App 654; *Davies v Davies* (1887) 36 ChD 359 at 390, CA, per Bowen LJ.

387. Repudiation of distinction between general and partial restraint. The doctrine that there was an essential distinction between a general and a partial restraint of trade was in time repudiated[1], and the rule now is clear that restraints, whether general or partial, may be good if they are reasonable[2]. Any restriction upon freedom of contract to which the restraint of trade doctrine applies must be shown to be reasonably necessary for the purpose of freedom of trade[3].

1 In *Nordenfelt v Maxim Nordenfelt Guns and Ammunition Co Ltd* [1894] AC 535, HL, a doubt was expressed (see at 557 per Lord Ashbourne, and at 562 per Lord Macnaghten) whether it

had ever existed at any time. A similar doubt had been expressed in *Rousillon v Rousillon* (1880) 14 ChD 351 at 366–369; cf *Horner v Graves* (1831) 7 Bing 735; *Whittaker v Howe* (1841) 3 Beav 383, where a restraint extending over Great Britain was held good; *Jones v Lees* (1856) 1 H & N 189, where a covenant by a licensee of a patent, with no limit of space, was held good; *Harms v Parsons* (1862) as reported in 32 LJ Ch 247, where Romilly MR quoted *Whittaker v Howe*, without disapproval; *Leather Cloth Co v Lorsont* (1869) LR 9 Eq 345, where a restraint extending over Europe was held good, but the decision apparently was to be explained as a case of a trade secret (cf *Allsopp v Wheatcroft* (1872) LR 15 Eq 59 at 64 per Wickens V-C); *Harvey v Corpe* (1885) 79 LT Jo 246, where a restraint covering Europe was held reasonable in the case of an army meat contractor; *Davies v Davies* (1887) 36 ChD 359 at 398, CA, per Fry LJ. The contrary view was expressed in *Mallan v May* (1843) 11 M & W 653; *Nicholls v Stretton* (1847) 10 QB 346 at 353 per Patteson J; *Tallis v Tallis* (1853) 1 E & B 391; cf *Vernon v Hallam* (1886) 34 ChD 748 at 751, citing *Homer v Ashford and Ainsworth* (1825) 3 Bing 322 at 326 per Best J; *Davies v Davies* (1887) 36 ChD 359 at 382, 385–386, 398; *Nordenfelt v Maxim Nordenfelt Guns and Ammunition Co Ltd* [1894] AC 535 at 546, HL, per Lord Herschell LC. For dicta on the question since *Nordenfelt v Maxim Nordenfelt Guns and Ammunition Co Ltd* see *E Underwood & Son Ltd v Barker* [1899] 1 Ch 300, CA; *Dowden and Pook Ltd v Pook* [1904] 1 KB 45 at 51, CA; *Beetham v Fraser* (1904) 21 TLR 8, DC; *Russell v Amalgamated Society of Carpenters and Joiners* [1910] 1 KB 506 at 520, CA (affd [1912] AC 421, HL); *North-Western Salt Co Ltd v Electrolytic Alkali Co Ltd* (1912) as reported in 107 LT 439 at 445, CA, per Farwell LJ; *Continental Tyre and Rubber (Great Britain) Co Ltd v Heath* (1913) 29 TLR 308; *A-G of Commonwealth of Australia v Adelaide Steamship Co Ltd* [1913] AC 781, PC.

2   The restraint must be reasonable in the interests of the public, the covenantee and the covenantor. For separate consideration of these aspects of reasonableness see PARAS 389, 412. For the general principle see *Nordenfelt v Maxim Nordenfelt Guns and Ammunition Co Ltd* [1894] AC 535 at 548, HL, per Lord Herschell LC; *Dubowski & Sons v Goldstein* [1896] 1 QB 478 at 484, CA; *Trego v Hunt* [1896] AC 7 at 27, HL; *Stride v Martin* (1897) 77 LT 600, DC; *William Robinson & Co Ltd v Heuer* [1898] 2 Ch 451 at 455, CA; *Haynes v Doman* [1899] 2 Ch 13 at 17, CA; *Hood and Moore's Stores Ltd v Jones* (1899) 81 LT 169; *E Underwood & Son Ltd v Barker* [1899] 1 Ch 300 at 304, CA; *Marshalls Ltd v Leek* (1900) 17 TLR 26; *Dowden and Pook Ltd v Pook* [1904] 1 KB 45 at 52–53, 55, CA; *Tivoli, Manchester, Ltd v Colley* (1904) 20 TLR 437; *Lamson Pneumatic Tube Co v Phillips* (1904) 91 LT 363, CA; *Beetham v Fraser* (1904) 21 TLR 8, DC; *Hooper and Ashby v Willis* (1906) 94 LT 624, CA; *Mouchel v Cubitt & Co* (1907) 24 RPC 194; *Lewis and Lewis v Durnford* (1907) 24 TLR 64; *White, Tomkins and Courage v Wilson* (1907) 23 TLR 469; *United Shoe Machinery Co of Canada v Brunet* [1909] AC 330, PC, explaining and distinguishing *Nordenfelt v Maxim Nordenfelt Guns and Ammunition Co Ltd* [1894] AC 535, HL; *Bromley v Smith* [1909] 2 KB 235; *Sir WC Leng & Co Ltd v Andrews* [1909] 1 Ch 763 at 766, CA; *Russell v Amalgamated Society of Carpenters and Joiners* [1910] 1 KB 506 at 521, CA (affd [1912] AC 421, HL); *North-Western Salt Co Ltd v Electrolytic Alkali Co Ltd* (1912) as reported in 107 LT 439 at 445, CA, per Farwell LJ; *Continental Tyre and Rubber (Great Britain) Co Ltd v Heath* (1913) 29 TLR 308; *A-G of Commonwealth of Australia v Adelaide Steamship Co Ltd* [1913] AC 781, PC; *Mason v Provident Clothing and Supply Co Ltd* [1913] AC 724 at 733, HL; *Herbert Morris Ltd v Saxelby* [1916] 1 AC 688 at 700, 707, HL; *Attwood v Lamont* [1920] 3 KB 571 at 584, CA; *Connors Bros Ltd v Connors* [1940] 4 All ER 179, PC; and the cases cited in PARA 390 note 1.

3   *Printing and Numerical Registering Co v Sampson* (1875) LR 19 Eq 462 at 465 per Jessel MR; *Rousillon v Rousillon* (1880) 14 ChD 351 at 365. A restraint reasonably necessary for the protection of the covenantee must prevail unless some specific ground of public policy can be clearly established against it: *E Underwood & Son Ltd v Barker* [1899] 1 Ch 300, CA. As to what may constitute such ground of public policy see *Russell v Amalgamated Society of Carpenters and Joiners* [1912] AC 421, HL, where the area from which employers, not parties to the agreement, could obtain workmen was unreasonably restricted. For an instance of an unlawful monopoly see *North-Western Salt Co Ltd v Electrolytic Alkali Co Ltd* (1912) as reported in 107 LT 439, CA; revsd [1914] AC 461, HL, on a point of pleading; see also PARA 361.

388.   Agreements subject to the restraint of trade doctrine. The restraint of trade doctrine is capable of application to agreements made:

    (1)   between vendors and purchasers of businesses;

    (2)   between partners;

(3)   between employers and employees[1];

(4)   between independent traders or groups of traders with a view to eliminating or reducing competition, regulating output and the like;

(5)   between employers with a view to united action in relation to those whom they employ; and

(6)   between employees with a view to united action in relation to their employers[2].

However, this is not an exhaustive list of the scope of application of the doctrine: the categories of agreements in restraint of trade are not closed[3]. It may be that contracts of a kind that have gained a general commercial acceptance are not subject to the restraint of trade doctrine[4], whereas the fact that there is inequality of bargaining power between the parties to an agreement may be a factor in determining whether the doctrine is applicable[5], as may the fact that a covenantee has a conflict of interest which may be detrimental to the position of the covenantor[6]. A professional or other body which controls particular activities may be found to be acting in restraint of trade in certain circumstances[7]. However, where a body invested with statutory powers exercises those powers lawfully and not unreasonably, its decisions cannot be challenged under the restraint of trade doctrine[8].

There is a public policy in favour of the settlement of disputes in litigation; in consequence of this, the court will not allow a genuine and proper compromise of earlier litigation alleging restraint of trade itself to be challenged as being in restraint of trade[9].

1   With regard to these first three classes of agreements, although occasional distinctions are to be noted (the law taking a stricter view of the third class: see PARA 390 et seq), the same general rules apply, and there is no sufficient reason for treating them as distinct categories. The principles applying as between a vendor and purchaser of a business are also applicable to the sale of stocks or shares in a company by a vendor who enters into restrictive covenants with the purchaser (see *Connors Bros Ltd v Connors* [1940] 4 All ER 179 at 191, PC), and those applying as between employer and employee are applicable to an agreement between two employers where each agrees not to employ persons previously employed by the other (*Kores Manufacturing Co Ltd v Kolok Manufacturing Co Ltd* [1959] Ch 108, [1958] 2 All ER 65, CA; see also *Eastham v Newcastle United Football Club Ltd* [1964] Ch 413, [1963] 3 All ER 139). As to restraints as between employers and employees see also EMPLOYMENT vol 39 (2009) PARAS 19–20. As to restraints imposed by vendors and lessors of land and houses see LANDLORD AND TENANT vol 27(1) (2006 Reissue) PARAS 513–521, 526–529; SALE OF LAND vol 42 (Reissue) PARAS 331–335. The doctrine of restraint of trade is not confined to restraints on persons but applies also to restraints on the use of land, including restraints imposed by covenants in mortgages: *Esso Petroleum Co Ltd v Harper's Garage (Stourport) Ltd* [1968] AC 269, [1967] 1 All ER 699, HL. Restrictions on the user of a particular house or piece of land imposed on a lease or sale do not, however, normally fall within the doctrine in so far as they do not restrict a pre-existing freedom of the lessee or purchaser to trade there (*Esso Petroleum Co Ltd v Harper's Garage (Stourport) Ltd*; see also *Cleveland Petroleum Co Ltd v Dartstone Ltd* [1969] 1 All ER 201, [1969] 1 WLR 116, CA (where a solus agreement in a lease was held to be valid)), but the decisions on the subject are relevant on the questions of the meaning of 'trade' and the acts which constitute breach of covenant (see *Taff Vale Rly Co (Directors etc) v Macnabb* (1873) LR 6 HL 169 (agreement on lease of a dock); *Gloucester City Council v Williams* (1990) 88 LGR 853, CA; *Robinson v Golden Chips (Wholesale) Ltd* [1971] NZLR 257, NZ CA; *Quadramain Pty Ltd v Sevastapol Investments Pty Ltd* (1976) 8 ALR 555, Aust HC). The court will strike down a 'sham' transaction, however: *Amoco Australia Pty Ltd v Rocca Bros Motor Engineering Co Pty Ltd* [1975] AC 561, [1975] 1 All ER 968, PC. As to the treatment of 'land agreements' under the Competition Act 1998 see PARAS 142, 143.

2   As to these last two classes of agreements see EMPLOYMENT vol 40 (2009) PARA 846 et seq.

3   See *Petrofina (Great Britain) Ltd v Martin* [1966] Ch 146 at 169, [1966] 1 All ER 126 at 131, CA, per Lord Denning MR; *Esso Petroleum Co Ltd v Harper's Garage (Stourport) Ltd* [1968] AC 269 at 337, [1967] 1 All ER 699 at 732, HL, per Lord Wilberforce.

4 See *Esso Petroleum Co Ltd v Harper's Garage (Stourport) Ltd* [1968] AC 269 at 332–333, [1967] 1 All ER 699 at 729–730, HL, per Lord Wilberforce, and at 328 and 727 per Lord Pearce.

5 See *A Schroeder Music Publishing Co Ltd v Macaulay* [1974] 3 All ER 616, [1974] 1 WLR 1308, HL. However, it is not a prerequisite that any such element be present: *Panayiotou v Sony Music Entertainment (UK) Ltd* [1994] EMLR 233.

6 *Watson v Prager* [1991] 3 All ER 487 at 505–506, [1991] 1 WLR 726 at 747.

7 See PARA 377 note 7.

8 *R v General Medical Council, ex p Colman* [1990] 1 All ER 489 at 508–509, CA, per Ralph Gibson LJ, and at 510 per Lord Donaldson of Lymington MR.

9 *Panayiotou v Sony Music Entertainment (UK) Ltd* [1994] EMLR 233, following *Binder v Alachouzos* [1972] 2 QB 151, [1972] 2 All ER 189, CA, and *Colchester Borough Council v Smith* [1992] Ch 421, [1992] 2 All ER 561, CA.

(iii) Legitimate Interests of a Covenantee that Merit Protection

389.   Restraint must be to protect a legitimate interest. A restraint of trade will be contrary to public policy unless it is imposed to protect a legitimate interest of the covenantee; there cannot be a restraint of trade in gross[1]. The restraint must be, for example, for the protection of a business in which the covenantee is interested. Thus, a purchaser of a business is entitled to protect himself against competition per se on the part of the vendor[2]. However, a company controlling, controlled by or interested in another company, or in which another company has an interest, cannot impose on an employee an area of restraint which is wider than is necessary for the protection of its own business in an attempt to protect the business of such other company[3]. In an agreement for the sale of a business the reasonableness of a vendor's restrictive covenant is to be judged by the extent and circumstances of the business sold and not by those of any business of the purchaser of which, after transfer, the business sold is to form a part[4].

An employer is not entitled to protect himself against competition per se on the part of an employee after the employment has ceased[5].

Where the true skills and art of a job lie in the make-up of the person performing it, such as his personality, temperament and ability to get on with people, there is no proprietary right which an employer can claim to protect for himself as part of his business[6].

1 *Mitchel v Reynolds* (1711) 1 P Wms 181 at 190, where it was said that 'It would be unreasonable to fix a certain loss on one side without any benefit to the other'; *Horner v Graves* (1831) 7 Bing 735 at 743; *Townsend v Jarman* [1900] 2 Ch 698 at 702 per Farwell J; *Henry Leetham & Sons Ltd v Johnstone-White* [1907] 1 Ch 322 at 326, CA; *British Reinforced Concrete Engineering Co Ltd v Schelff* [1921] 2 Ch 563; *Vancouver Malt and Sake Brewing Co Ltd v Vancouver Breweries Ltd* [1934] AC 181, PC. The covenantee must be interested in the business at the date of entering into the agreement: *Great Western and Metropolitan Dairies Ltd v Gibbs* (1918) 34 TLR 344. Apparently a covenant may be valid even though entered into by an employee as part of the consideration for his release from his contract of service: *Spink (Bournemouth) Ltd v Spink* [1936] Ch 544, [1936] 1 All ER 597. It appears that a mere sentimental interest on the part of the covenantee will not justify a restraint, and the only suggestion in the cases that this is possible is in *Kimberley v Jennings* (1836) 6 Sim 340 at 351 per Shadwell V-C; but see *Upton v Henderson* (1912) 106 LT 839; and PARA 377 note 3. As to what may constitute an interest in a business see *Everton v Longmore* (1899) 15 TLR 356, CA, where a body of the nature of a friendly society was held entitled to enforce a covenant by a doctor; *Ballachulish Slate Quarries Ltd v Grant* (1903) 5 F 1105, Ct of Sess, where a quarry company engaging a doctor to attend its employees with liberty to take other practice was held entitled to enforce a covenant against his practising in the district on the termination of his employment; cf *Mineral Water Bottle Exchange and Trade Protection Society v Booth* (1887) 36 ChD 465 at 469, CA. For examples of other interests which have been recognised see *Eastham v Newcastle United Football Club Ltd* [1964] Ch 413, [1963] 3 All ER 139; *Greig v*

Insole [1978] 3 All ER 449, [1978] 1 WLR 302; *Dawnay, Day & Co Ltd v De Braconier
d'Alphen* [1998] ICR 1068, [1997] IRLR 442, CA.

2   *Herbert Morris Ltd v Saxelby* [1916] 1 AC 688 at 709, HL, per Lord Parker of Waddington;
Attwood v Lamont [1920] 3 KB 571 at 589, CA, per Younger LJ. The restraint must be
confined to the area within which competition will in all probability enure to the injury of the
purchaser: *Herbert Morris Ltd v Saxelby* at 709 per Lord Parker of Waddington. See also
Nordenfelt v Maxim Nordenfelt Guns and Ammunition Co Ltd [1894] AC 535 at 548, HL, per
Lord Herschell LC; *Southland Frozen Meat and Produce Export Co Ltd v Nelson Bros Ltd*
[1898] AC 442, PC (agreement on purchase of the output of a business for a limited period).
The same principles apply where a retiring partner sells his share: *Williams v Williams* (1818) 2
Swan 253; see PARTNERSHIP vol 79 (2008) PARA 213 et seq.

3   *Henry Leetham & Sons Ltd v Johnstone-White* [1907] 1 Ch 322, CA; see also *Continental Tyre
and Rubber (Great Britain) Co Ltd v Heath* (1913) 29 TLR 308 at 310. But see *Stenhouse
Australia Ltd v Phillips* [1974] AC 391, [1974] 1 All ER 117, PC, where a company's business
was to some extent transacted for it by subsidiaries as its agencies or instrumentalities and a
covenant which protected the business so transacted was held reasonable. See also *Beckett
Investment Management Group Ltd v Hall* [2007] EWCA Civ 613, [2007] ICR 1539 (company
and subsidiaries viewed as one concern directed by company so that covenant not defeated by
fact company's business transacted by subsidiaries).

4   *British Reinforced Concrete Engineering Co Ltd v Schelff* [1921] 2 Ch 563, not following
Smedley's Ltd v Smedley [1921] 2 Ch 580n. See also *Goldsoll v Goldman* [1915] 1 Ch 292, CA;
Vancouver Malt and Sake Brewing Co Ltd v Vancouver Breweries Ltd [1934] AC 181, PC.

5   *Herbert Morris Ltd v Saxelby* [1916] 1 AC 688, HL, applied in *Kores Manufacturing Co Ltd v
Kolok Manufacturing Co Ltd* [1959] Ch 108, [1958] 2 All ER 65, CA, where an agreement
between two employers by which each agreed not to employ persons employed by the other
within the previous five years was held invalid. An employer has no legitimate interest in
preventing an employee, after leaving his service, from entering the service of a competitor
merely on the ground that he is a competitor: *Attwood v Lamont* [1920] 3 KB 571 at 589, CA,
per Younger LJ; *Kores Manufacturing Co Ltd v Kolok Manufacturing Co Ltd* at 126 and at 74
per Jenkins LJ, followed in *Kerchiss v Colora Printing Inks Ltd* [1960] RPC 235, where the
particular agreement was held valid. See also *Sir WC Leng & Co Ltd v Andrews* [1909]
1 Ch 763, CA; *Ropeways Ltd v Hoyle* (1919) 88 LJCh 446; *Bowler v Lovegrove* [1921]
1 Ch 642 at 650 per PO Lawrence J; and see *Vandervell Products Ltd v McLeod* [1957] RPC
185, CA; *Eastham v Newcastle United Football Club Ltd* [1964] Ch 413 at 431, [1963]
3 All ER 139 at 148; *Commercial Plastics Ltd v Vincent* [1965] 1 QB 623, [1964] 3 All ER
546, CA; *Gledhow Autoparts Ltd v Delaney* [1965] 3 All ER 288, [1965] 1 WLR 1366, CA,
where a restraint on dealing with all garages in the area, not merely those called on by the
salesman during his employment, was held unreasonable; *Sadler v Imperial Life Assurance Co
of Canada Ltd* [1988] IRLR 388 (proviso purporting to remove entitlement to post-termination
commission if employee continued to work in insurance industry was held unreasonable); *Office
Angels Ltd v Rainer-Thomas and O'Connor* [1991] IRLR 214, CA; *Wincanton Ltd v Cranny*
[2000] IRLR 716, CA.

6   *Cantor Fitzgerald (UK) Ltd v Wallace* [1992] IRLR 215.

(iv) Reasonableness between the Parties

A. IN GENERAL

390.   Function of the court. It is for the court to decide, as a matter of law,
whether a contract in restraint of trade is reasonable[1]. This entails a
consideration of the reasonableness of the restraints between the parties[2] and in
the public interest[3]. Any disputed questions as to the nature of the business, as to
what is customary in it, as to the number and situation of its customers, as to any
particular dangers requiring precautions and the like are questions of fact, and
all these matters are relevant to the question of reasonableness[4].

1   *Mitchel v Reynolds* (1711) 1 P Wms 181 at 195; *Chesman v Nainby* (1727) 2 Stra 739 (affd 1
Bro Parl Cas 234, HL); *Davis v Mason* (1793) 5 Term Rep 118; *Horner v Graves* (1831) 7 Bing
735; *Proctor v Sargent* (1840) 2 Man & G 20; *Mallan v May* (1843) 11 M & W 653; *Tallis v
Tallis* (1853) 1 E & B 391; *Dowden and Pook Ltd v Pook* [1904] 1 KB 45, CA; *Lamson*

Pneumatic Tube Co v Phillips (1904) 91 LT 363 at 368, CA; *Sir WC Leng & Co Ltd v Andrews* [1909] 1 Ch 763 at 770, CA, per Fletcher Moulton LJ, and at 772 per Farwell LJ; *Russell v Amalgamated Society of Carpenters and Joiners* [1910] 1 KB 506 at 522, CA (affd, but without reference to this point, [1912] AC 421, HL); *North-Western Salt Co Ltd v Electrolytic Alkali Co Ltd* (1912) as reported in 107 LT 439 at 445, CA, per Farwell LJ. As to the admissibility of evidence of contracts between the covenantee and other persons see *North-Western Salt Co Ltd v Electrolytic Alkali Co Ltd* at 440; *A-G of Commonwealth of Australia v Adelaide Steamship Co Ltd* [1913] AC 781 at 797, PC; *Mason v Provident Clothing and Supply Co Ltd* [1913] AC 724, HL; *Herbert Morris Ltd v Saxelby* [1916] 1 AC 688 at 707, HL, per Lord Parker of Waddington. A court must first determine the extent of any restraint before it can form a view as to whether the restraint is valid: *Società Esplosivi Industriali SpA v Ordnance Technologies (UK) Ltd (formerly SEI (UK) Ltd)* [2004] EWHC 48 (Ch), [2004] 1 All ER (Comm) 619.

2   As to reasonableness between the parties regarding the character of the business to be protected, the extent of area of operation of the covenant, its duration, customers and name and confidential matters see PARAS 391–411.

3   As to reasonableness in the public interest see PARA 412.

4   *Mumford v Gething* (1859) 7 CBNS 305; *Haynes v Doman* [1899] 2 Ch 13 at 24, CA; *Dowden and Pook Ltd v Pook* [1904] 1 KB 45 at 52, 54, CA; *Lamson Pneumatic Tube Co v Phillips* (1904) 91 LT 363, CA; *Mason v Provident Clothing and Supply Co Ltd* [1913] AC 724, HL. It is also a question of fact whether a business alleged to be carried on by the covenantor is his business (*Clark v Howard* (1860) 2 F & F 125), but whether there has been a breach is a question of law (*Kemp v Sober* (1851) 1 Sim NS 517 (affd (1852) 19 LTOS 308); *Turner v Evans* (1852) 2 De GM & G 740; *Wickenden v Webster* (1856) 6 E & B 387). It has been said that the number of inhabitants in the area of restriction is irrelevant: *Mallan v May* (1843) 11 M & W 653 at 667 per Parke B; but cf *Hitchcock v Coker* (1837) 6 Ad & El 438 at 454, Ex Ch, per Tindal CJ; *Proctor v Sargent* (1840) as reported in 10 LJCP 34 at 36 per Maule J and Tindal CJ, and at 39 per Bosanquet J, referring, however, to proceedings on demurrer and the impossibility of the court taking judicial notice of the population of a district without evidence.

391.   Test to be applied. In estimating the reasonableness of an agreement in restraint of trade, extravagant possibilities should not be taken into account[1]. Evidence as to the mode in which the agreement has been carried out may not be relevant to the question of its construction[2], nor is evidence that the covenantee or other persons think it reasonably necessary[3]. That it is unusual is evidence to show that it is unreasonable[4], and, conversely, that it is customary is evidence that it is reasonable[5].

1   *Rannie v Irvine* (1844) 7 Man & G 969, where it was held that if the restraint is on trading as a baker with a limited number of customers, it is not necessary to consider the possibility of one of them going to a village where the covenantor is the only baker; *Nordenfelt v Maxim Nordenfelt Guns and Ammunition Co Ltd* [1894] AC 535 at 574, HL, per Lord Macnaghten; *E Underwood & Son Ltd v Barker* [1899] 1 Ch 300 at 306, CA, per Lindley MR; *Haynes v Doman* [1899] 2 Ch 13 at 26, CA, per Lindley MR, where it was held that if the covenant is intended to prevent an employee from betraying business methods, it is not necessary to consider the possibility of his leaving his employment so soon as to have acquired no knowledge of those methods. See also *Commercial Plastics Ltd v Vincent* [1965] 1 QB 623, [1964] 3 All ER 546, CA; *Home Counties Dairies Ltd v Skilton* [1970] 1 All ER 1227, [1970] 1 WLR 526, CA. As to construction of the contract generally see PARA 420 et seq.

2   *Elves v Crofts* (1850) 10 CB 241; *Jacoby v Whitmore* (1883) 49 LT 335 at 337, CA, per Brett MR; *Perls v Saalfeld* [1892] 2 Ch 149 at 151, 153, CA; *Russell v Amalgamated Society of Carpenters and Joiners* [1910] 1 KB 506 at 522, CA (affd, but without reference to this point, [1912] AC 421, HL); *Lovell and Christmas Ltd v Wall* (1911) 27 TLR 236, CA.

3   *Haynes v Doman* [1899] 2 Ch 13 at 24, CA; *Sir WC Leng & Co Ltd v Andrews* [1909] 1 Ch 763 at 772, CA; *Eastham v Newcastle United Football Club Ltd* [1964] Ch 413 at 438, [1963] 3 All ER 139 at 150.

4   *Sir WC Leng & Co Ltd v Andrews* [1909] 1 Ch 763 at 767, 770, CA, where the restraint imposed on a newspaper reporter from ever being connected with any other newspaper within 20 miles (and where no instance was proved of a similar restriction in the trade) was held unreasonable. For cases where the covenant was held unreasonable in itself and the covenantor was a minor at the date of the agreement see *Pearks Ltd v Cullen* (1912) 28 TLR 371; *Mason v Provident Clothing and Supply Co Ltd* [1913] AC 724 at 732, HL.

5   *Catt v Tourle* (1869) 4 Ch App 654 at 659; *Cornwall v Hawkins* (1872) 41 LJCh 435 at 436;
    Sir WC Leng & Co Ltd v Andrews [1909] 1 Ch 763 at 770, CA, per Fletcher Moulton LJ.

392.   Time for determining reasonableness.   If a covenant was reasonable
when made, subsequent events do not affect its validity[1]. The court ascertains
what was the intention of the parties from the whole agreement and the
circumstances at the time at which it was entered into[2].

1   *Elves v Crofts* (1850) 10 CB 241; *Jacoby v Whitmore* (1883) 49 LT 335 at 337–338, CA;
    Townsend v Jarman [1900] 2 Ch 698 at 703; *Dowden and Pook Ltd v Pook* [1904] 1 KB 45 at
    55, CA, per Cozens-Hardy LJ; *Lamson Pneumatic Tube Co v Phillips* (1904) 91 LT 363 at
    367, CA, per Vaughan Williams LJ; *Bridge v Deacons* [1984] AC 705 at 718, sub nom *Deacons
    v Bridge* [1984] 2 All ER 19 at 25, PC; *Clarke v Newland* [1991] 1 All ER 397, CA, per Neill LJ
    at 402. Cf *Keppell v Bailey* (1834) 2 My & K 517 at 530; *Kimberley v Jennings* (1836) 6 Sim
    340 at 350; *Jones v Lees* (1856) 1 H & N 189. But in *Shell UK Ltd v Lostock Garage Ltd*
    [1977] 1 All ER 481, [1976] 1 WLR 1187, CA, the court declined to enforce a valid solus
    agreement in circumstances in which it had become unfair and prejudicial to the covenantor. See
    also *Passmore v Moreland* [1999] 3 All ER 1005, [1999] 1 CMLR 1129, CA, in which the
    Court of Appeal held that an agreement may be void at one time under the EC Treaty art 81 but
    become valid where circumstances change and vice versa; the court, at 519–520, commented on
    the judgment in *Shell UK Ltd v Lostock Garage Ltd*. As to the EC Treaty (ie the Treaty
    establishing the European Community (Rome, 25 March 1957; TS 1 (1973); Cmnd 5179)) see
    PARA 24 note 1. The numbering for the EC Treaty used in this title is as revised by the Treaty of
    Amsterdam: see PARA 24 note 1.

2   *Keppell v Bailey* (1834) 2 My & K 517 at 530; *Kimberley v Jennings* (1836) 6 Sim 340 at 350;
    Mumford v Gething (1859) 7 CBNS 305; *Clarkson v Edge* (1863) 33 Beav 227; *Taff Vale
    Rly Co (Directors etc) v Macnabb* (1873) LR 6 HL 169 at 179 per Lord Colonsay; *Palmer v
    Mallet* (1887) 36 ChD 411, CA, where the words 'set up or carry on the profession or business
    of a surgeon' in the recital of a bond were construed in the light of words 'as assistant of any
    other person' in the defeasance clause; but, apparently, apart from this, acting as assistant to a
    surgeon is 'carrying on the profession' (see PARA 428). But an absolute covenant in a bond will
    not be qualified by a recital, in the absence of an application to rectify: see *Bird v Lake* (1863)
    1 Hem & M 338 at 341 per Page Wood V-C ('Covenants of this kind are sometimes held to be
    restricted by the recitals in the deed, but I never knew of a case in which such a covenant was
    enlarged by the recital'); *Mills v Dunham* [1891] 1 Ch 576, CA; *Perls v Saalfeld* [1892]
    2 Ch 149 at 154, CA; *Moenich v Fenestre* (1892) 61 LJCh 737 at 740, CA, per Lindley LJ;
    Rogers v Maddocks [1892] 3 Ch 346 at 354, 356, CA; *Badische Anilin und Soda Fabrik v
    Schott, Segner & Co* [1892] 3 Ch 447 at 452; *Dubowski & Sons v Goldstein* [1896] 1 QB
    478, CA; *Hood and Moore's Stores Ltd v Jones* (1899) 81 LT 169; *E Underwood & Son Ltd v
    Barker* [1899] 1 Ch 300, CA; *Marshalls Ltd v Leek* (1900) 17 TLR 26; *Henry Leetham &
    Sons Ltd v Johnstone-White* [1907] 1 Ch 322, CA, where a contract with the agent for a
    number of interdependent companies was construed as a separate contract with the company in
    whose service the covenantor acted; and, apparently, would have been a separate contract with
    any company to whose service he might have been transferred; *Cavendish v Tarry* (1908) 52 Sol
    Jo 726; *Coleborne v Kearns* (1912) 46 ILT 305, CA, where the words 'leave employment' were
    held not to cover dismissal; c f *Cave v Horsell* [1912] 3 KB 533, CA (meaning of 'adjoining'). See
    also *Hadsley v Dayer-Smith* [1914] AC 979 at 983, HL, per Lord Shaw of Dunfermline;
    Gledhow Autoparts Ltd v Delaney [1965] 3 All ER 288, [1965] 1 WLR 1366, CA; *Home
    Counties Dairies Ltd v Skilton* [1970] 1 All ER 1227, [1970] 1 WLR 526, CA; *Marion
    White Ltd v Francis* [1972] 3 All ER 857, [1972] 1 WLR 1423, CA. Other agreements existing
    between the covenantor and other persons may be considered with reference to the question of
    reasonableness and public interest: *North-Western Salt Co Ltd v Electrolytic Alkali Co Ltd*
    [1913] 3 KB 422, CA; revsd on other grounds [1914] AC 461, HL.

393.   Consideration of agreement as a whole.   It is the covenant in restraint of
trade as a whole which must be considered, not the particular breach complained
of, and the court will not decide on the reasonableness of the covenantor's
conduct in each particular case as it arises[1]. Where, however, the covenant
includes trades or places or persons, and in respect of some of them it is

reasonable while in respect of others it is not, the part which is reasonable, if it can be severed from the rest, will be enforced in the event of a breach of that part[2].

1 _Davies v Davies_ (1887) 36 ChD 359 at 387, CA, per Cotton LJ; _Baker v Hedgecock_ (1888) 39 ChD 520. In _Tallis v Tallis_ (1853) 1 E & B 391 at 412, Lord Campbell CJ said 'We have limited our judgment to the parts of the contract to which these breaches relate, because, if these are valid, the invalidity of other parts of the contract is immaterial'; but this, apparently, must be taken in relation to the rules as to severability: see PARAS 433–434.

2 _Chesman v Nainby_ (1727) 1 Bro Parl Cas 234, HL; _Mallan v May_ (1843) 11 M & W 653; _Price v Green_ (1847) 16 M & W 346, Ex Ch; _Baines v Geary_ (1887) 35 ChD 154; _Hooper and Ashby v Willis_ (1905) 21 TLR 691 at 692 per Kekewich J (affd (1906) 22 TLR 451, CA); _Lievre v Mayonnet_ (1913) 2 LJCCR 4. As to severability see PARAS 433–434.

394.   Difference between employment and sale of business. The court takes a stricter and less favourable view of covenants entered into between employer and employee than it does of similar covenants between vendor and purchaser[1], or in partnership agreements, and accordingly a restraint may be unreasonable as between employer and employee which would be reasonable as between the vendor and purchaser of a business[2].

1 _Ronbar Enterprises Ltd v Green_ [1954] 2 All ER 266 at 270, [1954] 1 WLR 815 at 820, CA, per Jenkins LJ (partnership agreement). This statement was made in reference to possible differences in the law as to severance: see PARAS 433–434. For a borderline case where the relationship between the parties was held analogous to that of employer and employee see _Jenkins v Reid_ [1948] 1 All ER 471 (medical practice; plaintiff not a party to deed of partnership between her husband and defendant); for borderline cases where the relationship between the parties was considered to be analogous to a vendor and purchaser relationship see _Prontaprint plc v London Litho Ltd_ [1987] FSR 315 (franchise agreement); _Allied Dunbar (Frank Weisinger) Ltd v Weisinger_ [1988] IRLR 60 (covenant between former self-employed sales associate and company); _Systems Reliability Holdings plc v Smith_ [1990] IRLR 377 (covenant between employer and employee on latter's purchase of shares in employer); _Kall-Kwik Printing (UK) Ltd v Rush_ [1996] FSR 114 (franchise agreement); _Alliance Paper Group plc v Prestwich_ [1996] IRLR 25 (sale of shares by vendor who then entered into a contract of services with the purchasing company).

2 _Nordenfelt v Maxim Nordenfelt Guns and Ammunition Co Ltd_ [1894] AC 535 at 566, HL, per Lord Macnaghten; _E Underwood & Son Ltd v Barker_ [1899] 1 Ch 300 at 305, CA, and see at 310 per Vaughan Williams LJ (dissenting, but not on this point); _Mason v Provident Clothing and Supply Co Ltd_ [1913] AC 724 at 738, HL, per Lord Shaw of Dunfermline; _Herbert Morris Ltd v Saxelby_ [1916] 1 AC 688 at 701, HL, per Lord Atkinson, and at 709 per Lord Parker of Waddington; _Great Western and Metropolitan Dairies Ltd v Gibbs_ (1918) 34 TLR 344; _Attwood v Lamont_ [1920] 3 KB 571, CA. Cf _North-Western Salt Co v Electrolytic Alkali Co Ltd_ [1914] AC 461 at 470, HL, per Lord Haldane LC; _English Hop Growers Ltd v Dering_ [1928] 2 KB 174 at 180, CA, per Scrutton LJ; _M & S Drapers (a firm) v Reynolds_ [1956] 3 All ER 814 at 820–821, [1957] 1 WLR 9 at 18–19, CA, per Denning LJ; see also _Allied Dunbar (Frank Weisinger) Ltd v Weisinger_ [1988] IRLR 60 at 63–64; _Systems Reliability Holdings plc v Smith_ [1990] IRLR 377 at 382.

395.   Commercial agents. In agreements between a principal and a commercial agent[1] to which the Commercial Agents (Council Directive) Regulations 1993 apply[2] a restraint of trade clause is valid only if and to the extent that:

(1)   it is concluded in writing; and

(2)   it relates to the geographical area of the group of customers and the geographical area entrusted to the commercial agent and to the kind of goods covered by his agency under the contract[3].

A restraint of trade clause in these circumstances is valid for not more than two years after termination of the agency contract[4].

1   'Commercial agent' means a self-employed intermediary who has continuing authority to
    negotiate the sale or purchase of goods on behalf of another person (the 'principal'), or to
    negotiate and conclude a sale or purchase of goods on behalf of and in the name of that
    principal: Commercial Agents (Council Directive) Regulations 1993, SI 1993/3053, reg 2(1).
    Certain positions with similar characteristics to those set out in that definition are specifically
    excluded from it: see reg 2(1)(i)–(iii).
2   The regulations apply in relation to the activities of commercial agents in Great Britain, except
    where the parties have agreed that the agency contract is governed by the law of another
    member state of the European Union: see the Commercial Agents (Council Directive)
    Regulations 1993, SI 1993/3053, reg 1(2)–(3) (reg 1(3) substituted by SI 1998/2868). 'Great
    Britain' means England, Scotland and Wales: Union with Scotland Act 1706, preamble art I;
    Interpretation Act 1978 s 22(1), Sch 2 para 5(a).
3   Commercial Agents (Council Directive) Regulations 1993, SI 1993/3053, reg 20(1).
4   Commercial Agents (Council Directive) Regulations 1993, SI 1993/3053, reg 20(2).

B.   CHARACTER OF THE BUSINESS TO BE PROTECTED

396.   The business from which the covenantor is restrained.   A restraint
otherwise unobjectionable may be unreasonably wide if it restrains the
covenantor from carrying on any business whatsoever[1], or a business different in
character from that carried on by the covenantee[2], or a business of a like
character to that carried on by the covenantee but subsequently set up in a
different place[3], or a business which, although carried on by the covenantee, is
not the business in which the covenantor was employed[4], or a business not
carried on by the covenantee in a place to which the restraint purports to
extend[5]. The reasonableness of the restraint is to be judged with reference to the
extent of the business sold and not with reference to the business of the
purchaser[6].

1   *Baker v Hedgecock* (1888) 39 ChD 520; *Perls v Saalfeld* [1892] 2 Ch 149, CA, where a
    covenant by a clerk to an oil importer and agent not to take a situation or establish himself
    within 15 miles of London for three years without the consent of the covenantee, such consent
    not to be withheld if it were proved to the covenantee's satisfaction that the situation or business
    was not in respect of the class of goods sold by the covenantee, was held void. As to provisos
    against withholding consent see PARA 421 note 3; *Woods v Thorburn* (1897) 41 Sol Jo 756 ('any
    other business': too wide); *Ehrman v Bartholomew* [1898] 1 Ch 671 ('any other business': too
    wide); cf *Reeve v Marsh* (1906) 23 TLR 24 at 25 per Parker J; *Morris & Co v Ryle* (1910) 103
    LT 545, CA, where a restraint on a hop merchant's salesman from any dealing in any goods
    whatever with persons whom he had dealt with during his employment was held unreasonable;
    JA Mont (UK) Ltd v Mills [1993] IRLR 172, CA ('another company in the tissue industry': too
    wide); *Wincanton Ltd v Cranny* [2000] IRLR 716, CA (restraint prohibiting involvement in any
    capacity in any business of whatever kind which was wholly or partly in competition with any
    business carried on by the company was held too wide to be enforceable).
2   *Rogers v Maddocks* [1892] 3 Ch 346 at 355, CA, per Lindley LJ, where it was held that the
    selling of an article wholesale and retail did not constitute two distinct businesses, but one
    business carried on in different ways, and although a salesman has during his employment only
    dealt with wholesale agents, a covenant to restrain him from both wholesale and retail trade
    may be reasonable; *Bromley v Smith* [1909] 2 KB 235, where a covenant by a baker's employee
    not to carry on the business of a restaurant keeper was held unreasonable although the
    covenantee, at the time of the covenant, contemplated the keeping of a restaurant, but it was
    suggested, at 241 per Channell J, that if the covenantor's engagement had been for the
    contemplated as well as for the existing business, the restraint might have been reasonable;
    Goldsoll v Goldman [1915] 1 Ch 292, CA, where a covenant entered into on the sale of a
    business dealing in imitation jewellery not to be concerned in the business of dealing in real or
    imitation jewellery was held too wide; *Routh v Jones* [1947] 1 All ER 758, CA, where covenants
    by a doctor's assistant not to practise or cause or assist any other person to practise in any
    department of medicine, surgery or midwifery and not to accept or give any professional
    appointment were both held to be unreasonably wide (followed in *Jenkins v Reid* [1948]
    1 All ER 471 and in *Lyne-Pirkis v Jones* [1969] 3 All ER 738, [1969] 1 WLR 1293, CA, where
    a covenant by a partner in a general medical practice was held to preclude practice as a

consultant and was therefore too wide; see *Peyton v Mindham* [1971] 3 All ER 1215, [1972] 1 WLR 8). See *British Reinforced Concrete Engineering Co Ltd v Schelff* [1921] 2 Ch 563; *Wyatt v Kreglinger and Fernau* [1933] 1 KB 793, CA; cf *Beetham v Fraser* (1904) 21 TLR 8, DC.

3   *Davies, Turner & Co v Lowen* (1891) 64 LT 655, where a covenant as to any business similar to the business 'now or hereafter to be carried on' by the covenantee was held unreasonable, but severable; *Dubowski & Sons v Goldstein* [1896] 1 QB 478, CA; *Beetham v Fraser* (1904) 21 TLR 8, DC, where it was admitted that a restraint from competition with the business of the covenantee at any addresses in the future was void; cf *Chesman v Nainby* (1727) 1 Bro Parl Cas 234, HL, where the restraint was within half a mile (1) of the covenantee's house, or (2) of any house to which he should remove; and the validity of head (2) was not expressly decided upon, but its presence did not invalidate the whole; *Berlitz School of Languages v Duchêne* (1903) 6 F 181, Ct of Sess. The restraint must cover only such businesses as are carried on by the covenantee at the time of the agreement, and the covenant will not be saved by the covenantee subsequently acquiring businesses within the restraint: *Great Western and Metropolitan Dairies Ltd v Gibbs* (1918) 34 TLR 344.

4   *Henry Leetham & Sons Ltd v Johnstone-White* [1907] 1 Ch 322 at 327, CA, per Farwell LJ. But in *Stewart v Stewart* (1899) 1 F 1158, Ct of Sess, it was held in Scotland that a restraint from carrying on a business by a person not employed in it was good.

5   *Davies, Turner & Co v Lowen* (1891) 64 LT 655 (carrier's clerk; time, 12 months; area, London, Birmingham, Liverpool and New York, and within 50 miles of each; Birmingham held void, as covenantees had no business there, but severable); *Continental Tyre and Rubber (Great Britain) Co Ltd v Heath* (1913) 29 TLR 308 at 310 (traveller for tyre company; time, one year; area, United Kingdom, Germany, France; Germany and France void for the like reason, but severable); *SV Nevanas & Co Ltd v Walker and Foreman* [1914] 1 Ch 413 (manager of company importing meat in Australian trade; covenant covering American trade also; void); *Goldsoll v Goldman* [1915] 1 Ch 292, CA (sale of business in imitation jewellery carried on in London; area, London, United Kingdom, Isle of Man, France, the United States, Russia, Spain etc; void but severable); *Spence v Mercantile Bank of India Ltd* (1921) 37 TLR 390 (on appeal 37 TLR 745, CA) (covenant by clerk of bank doing business in certain but not all eastern countries not to enter service of any eastern bank; void); *Greer v Sketchley Ltd* [1979] FSR 197, CA (covenant by director of dry cleaning business carried on in certain parts only of England and Wales; area, United Kingdom; too wide).

6   *British Reinforced Concrete Engineering Co Ltd v Schelff* [1921] 2 Ch 563 (sale of small business in road reinforcements to purchasers carrying on large similar business; area, United Kingdom; void).

397. Change of locality.

A business, although of the same character, is a different business if it is subsequently set up in a wholly different locality[1], but not if the business is merely removed to another place in the same neighbourhood[2].

1   *Dubowski & Sons v Goldstein* [1896] 1 QB 478, CA; *Doe d Calvert v Reid* (1830) 10 B & C 849. As to the position in relation to covenants in brewers leases see LANDLORD AND TENANT vol 27(1) (2006 Reissue) PARA 546 et seq.

2   *Jacoby v Whitmore* (1883) 49 LT 335, CA. In *Marshall and Murray Ltd v Jones* (1913) 29 TLR 351, the restraint was specifically limited to customers served by and from a named dairy, and it was held that this could not be taken to refer to the same business set up in a different place.

398. Status and occupation of covenantor.

The position of the covenantor in the business may be a matter for consideration, as the danger of competition in the case, for instance, of a manager may be greater than in the case of a clerk[1]. Regard must also be had to the nature of the occupation for which the covenantor is employed[2].

1   Cf *Lamson Pneumatic Tube Co v Phillips* (1904) 91 LT 363 at 368, CA, per Romer LJ; *Pearks Ltd v Cullen* (1912) 28 TLR 371; *M & S Drapers (a firm) v Reynolds* [1956] 3 All ER 814 at 817, [1957] 1 WLR 9 at 13, CA, per Hodson LJ.

2   'A man whose business is a corn miller's business, and who requires to protect that, cannot, if he has also a furniture business, require the covenantee, who enters into his service as an employee in the corn business, to enter into covenants restricting him from entering into competition with

him in the furniture business also': *Henry Leetham & Sons Ltd v Johnstone-White* [1907] 1 Ch 322 at 327, CA, per Farwell LJ. See also *Ehrman v Bartholomew* [1898] 1 Ch 671; *Great Western and Metropolitan Dairies Ltd v Gibbs* (1918) 34 TLR 344; *Ropeways Ltd v Hoyle* (1919) 88 LJCh 446; *Vincents of Reading v Fogden* (1932) 48 TLR 613; cf *Ronbar Enterprises Ltd v Green* [1954] 2 All ER 266 at 269, [1954] 1 WLR 815 at 819, CA, where a covenant in a partnership agreement was held not to be too wide merely because it extended to salaried employment, or employment at a wage, in a similar or competing business.

C. EXTENT OF AREA OF OPERATION

399.   Reasonableness as to area.   The reasonableness of an area of restraint depends upon the nature of the business to be protected[1] and the manner in which it is carried on. Where it is a business carried on by a small number of people, with customers widely distributed, a very large area will be allowed[2], and a wider restraint may be reasonable in a business carried on by agents or correspondence[3] than in one necessitating constant attendance in person[4].

The restraint may be reasonable even if its area is apparently greater than the area of the business of the covenantee[5].

A sales representative may reasonably be restrained from representing a rival firm over the same ground[6].

1   In a credit betting business an area restraint, as distinct from a covenant against solicitation of customers, may be inappropriate: see *SW Strange Ltd v Mann* [1965] 1 All ER 1069, [1965] 1 WLR 629. It must always depend on the particular circumstances whether an area restriction between an employer and employee can be supported, i e the nature of the employer's business and the nature of the employment and all the other circumstances of the particular case: see *T Lucas & Co Ltd v Mitchell* [1972] 2 All ER 1035, [1972] 1 WLR 938; revsd on other grounds [1974] Ch 129, [1972] 3 All ER 689, CA. As to co-operative trading see *Bellshill and Mossend Co-operative Society Ltd v Dalziel Co-operative Society Ltd* [1960] AC 832, [1960] 1 All ER 673, HL, where an arbitration award restricting a co-operative society from trading in a particular area was held not binding (disapproving *Birtley and District Co-operative Society Ltd v Windy Nook and District Industrial Co-operative Society (No 2)* [1960] 2 QB 1, [1959] 1 All ER 623).

2   *Tallis v Tallis* (1853) 1 E & B 391 (publisher; London and 150 miles reasonable); *Harms v Parsons* (1862) 32 Beav 328 (horsehair manufacturers; 200 miles reasonable); *Harvey v Corpe* (1885) 79 LT Jo 246 (army meat contractors; restraint over Europe reasonable); *Moenich v Fenestre* (1892) 67 LT 602, CA (agent and commission merchant; United Kingdom reasonable); *Lamson Pneumatic Tube Co v Phillips* (1904) 91 LT 363, CA (eastern hemisphere reasonable where a new invention to be used in large shops); but in *Dowden and Pook Ltd v Pook* [1904] 1 KB 45, CA, a world-wide restraint was held unreasonable in view of the limited nature of the covenantees' business; and in *Stuart and Simpson v Halstead* (1911) 55 Sol Jo 598, the United Kingdom was held too wide in the case of an advertising agent; *Caribonum Co Ltd v Le Couch* (1913) 109 LT 385 (on appeal 109 LT 587, CA); *SV Nevanas & Co Ltd v Walker and Foreman* [1914] 1 Ch 413 (meat importer; United Kingdom; too wide); *Goldsoll v Goldman* [1915] 1 Ch 292, CA (dealer in imitation jewellery; United States and many European countries; too wide); *Spence v Mercantile Bank of India Ltd* (1921) 37 TLR 390 (on appeal 37 TLR 745, CA) (covenant by clerk of bank doing business in certain eastern countries not to enter service of any eastern bank; too wide); *Wyatt v Kreglinger and Fernau* [1933] 1 KB 793, CA ('the wool trade'; no limit in time or space; too wide); *Vancouver Malt and Sake Brewing Co Ltd v Vancouver Breweries Ltd* [1934] AC 181, PC (world-wide restriction; too wide); *Connors Bros Ltd v Connors* [1940] 4 All ER 179, PC (whole of Canada; reasonable; unnecessary to prove sales in every part); *Vandervell Products Ltd v McLeod* [1957] RPC 185 at 190–191, CA (engineering foreman; two years; no limit of space; too wide); *Commercial Plastics Ltd v Vincent* [1965] 1 QB 623, [1964] 3 All ER 546, CA (plastics technician; one year; no limit of space; too wide). Cf *Littlewoods Organisation Ltd v Harris* [1978] 1 All ER 1026, [1977] 1 WLR 1472, CA (covenant construed as extending only to United Kingdom). See also *Putsman v Taylor* [1927] 1 KB 637, DC (on appeal [1927] 1 KB 741, CA); *Spencer v Marchington* [1988] IRLR 392 (employment agency; two years; within 25 miles of Banbury; too wide); *Office Angels Ltd v Rainer-Thomas and O'Connor* [1991] IRLR 214, CA (employment agency; six months; within 1.2 square miles, including most of the City of London; too wide); *Marley Tile Co Ltd v*

Johnson [1982] IRLR 75, CA ('not to compete in any area in which [the covenantor] was active'; too wide); *JA* Mont (*UK*) *Ltd v Mills* [1993] IRLR 172, CA (no area limit; too wide); and see the cases cited in note 6 and PARA 401 note 2.

3   Eg a solicitor (*Bunn v Guy* (1803) 1 Smith KB 1 (150 miles round London reasonable); *Galsworthy v Strutt* (1848) 1 Exch 659 (50 miles from Ely Place reasonable); *Austen v Boys* (1858) 2 De G & J 626 (100 miles, but question of area not in issue); *Howard v Woodward* (1864) 10 Jur NS 1123 (50 miles reasonable); *Nordenfelt v Maxim Nordenfelt Guns and Ammunition Co Ltd* [1894] AC 535 at 573, HL, per Lord Macnaghten, approving *Whittaker v Howe* (1841) 3 Beav 383 (solicitor; England and Scotland reasonable); but in *Woodbridge & Sons v Bellamy* [1911] 1 Ch 326 at 327, CA, Cozens-Hardy MR doubted the reasonableness of restraining a solicitor's clerk from doing business for any client within an area, as opposed to carrying on business within the area (see PARA 431)); or an accountant (*Isitt and Jenks v Ganson* (1899) 43 Sol Jo 744 (England reasonable)); or a stockbroker (*Lyddon v Thomas* (1901) 17 TLR 450 (50 miles reasonable)). See further the list of trades, professions etc set out in PARA 432.

4   Eg a doctor (*Davis v Mason* (1793) 5 Term Rep 118 (10 miles reasonable); *Hayward v Young* (1818) 2 Chit 407 (20 miles reasonable); *Hastings v Whitley* (1848) 2 Exch 611 (10 miles reasonable); *Sainter v Ferguson* (1849) 7 CB 716 (7 miles reasonable); *Giles v Hart* (1859) 1 LT 154 (5 miles reasonable); *Everton v Longmore* (1899) 15 TLR 356, CA (5 miles reasonable); *Whitehill v Bradford* [1952] Ch 236, [1952] 1 All ER 115, CA (10 miles reasonable); cf *Lyne Pirkis v Jones* [1969] 3 All ER 738, [1969] 1 WLR 1293, CA (see note 5)); or a dentist (*Horner v Graves* (1831) 7 Bing 735 (100 miles unreasonable); *Mallan v May* (1843) 11 M & W 653 (London (then containing 1,500,000 inhabitants) reasonable; but any of the towns in England or Scotland where covenantees might have been practising during term of service unreasonable)); or a schoolmaster (*Smith v Hawthorn* (1897) 76 LT 716 (9 miles reasonable)); or a canvasser in a local area (*Mason v Provident Clothing and Supply Co Ltd* [1913] AC 724, HL (25 miles of London, or of any place where he was employed by the covenantees, unreasonable)); or a laboratory assistant (*Eastes v Russ* [1914] 1 Ch 468, CA (London; 10 miles of laboratory; no time limit; unreasonable)); or a cashier (*Great Western and Metropolitan Dairies Ltd v Gibbs* (1918) 34 TLR 344 (20 miles unreasonable)); or a manager (*Empire Meat Co Ltd v Patrick* [1939] 2 All ER 85, CA (butcher's shop; 5 miles unreasonable)). See the list of trades, professions etc set out in PARA 432.

5   *Tallis v Tallis* (1853) 1 E & B 391 at 411 per Lord Campbell CJ; cf *Gale v Reed* (1806) 8 East 80; *Whittaker v Howe* (1841) 3 Beav 383; *Harms v Parsons* (1862) 32 Beav 328. See also *Lyne-Pirkis v Jones* [1969] 3 All ER 738, [1969] 1 WLR 1293, CA, where in relation to a general medical practice in which substantially all the patients were within a 5 mile radius, a restraint of 10 miles was held void on other grounds. On the other hand, a comparatively small area may cover large towns unconnected with the place where the business is carried on, and so be unreasonable: see eg *D Bates & Co v Dale* [1937] 3 All ER 650 at 654 (accountant, 15 years; 15 miles from Leek Town Hall; void).

6   *Mumford v Gething* (1859) 7 CBNS 305; *Parsons v Cotterill* (1887) 56 LT 839 (traveller to wine and spirit merchant; 50 miles of Burton-on-Trent; no limit of time; held reasonable, the covenantee's business extending over the whole area); *Cussen v O'Connor* (1893) 32 LR Ir 330 (traveller restrained from travelling in any county in which he had travelled for covenantee); cf *Chafer Ltd v Lilley* [1947] LJR 231 (traveller in Wisbech district; restraint throughout United Kingdom; too wide). See also *Gledhow Autoparts Ltd v Delaney* [1965] 3 All ER 288, [1965] 1 WLR 1366, CA (restraint on dealing with all garages in area, not merely those called upon, too wide).

400.   Residence.   A restraint against residing in a neighbourhood, apart from actually carrying on business there, may be a necessary measure of protection[1].

1   *Atkyns v Kinnier* (1850) 4 Exch 776 (surgeon); cf *Rawlinson v Clarke* (1845) 14 M & W 187 (surgeon; the validity of the covenant against residing was not in issue). In *Dendy v Henderson* (1855) 11 Exch 194 at 199 per Alderson B, the point was raised but not decided. Cf *Wilkinson v Wilkinson* (1871) LR 12 Eq 604, where a condition in a will requiring a legatee to reside elsewhere than at the place where her husband had to live was held void; *Edmundson v Render* [1905] 2 Ch 320 at 323 per Buckley J; *Denny's Trustee v Denny and Warr* [1919] 1 KB 583; and WILLS vol 50 (2005 Reissue) PARA 436.

401.   Restraint extending outside the United Kingdom.   A restraint extending beyond the United Kingdom[1], and even over the whole world, may be reasonable if the covenantee's business is such as to require so extensive a protection[2]. It is uncertain whether a restraint unlimited in terms or expressly extending beyond the United Kingdom, and reasonable if only applied to the United Kingdom, is to be considered void because such extension is unreasonable[3].

1 'United Kingdom' means Great Britain and Northern Ireland: Interpretation Act 1978 s 5, Sch 1. As to the meaning of 'Great Britain' see PARA 395 note 2. Neither the Isle of Man nor the Channel Islands are within the United Kingdom. See further CONSTITUTIONAL LAW AND HUMAN RIGHTS vol 8(2) (Reissue) PARA 3.

2 *Nordenfelt v Maxim Nordenfelt Guns and Ammunition Co Ltd* [1894] AC 535, HL (manufacture of guns and ammunition with a limited number of customers all over the world); see at 550 per Lord Herschell LC, and at 554 per Lord Watson. Since *Nordenfelt v Maxim Nordenfelt Guns and Ammunition Co Ltd*, the view of the law expressed in *Allsopp v Wheatcroft* (1872) LR 15 Eq 59 at 64 per Wickens V-C, that 'a covenant not to carry on a lawful trade, unlimited as to space, is on the face of it void', must no longer be regarded as the true view; and *Ward v Byrne* (1839) 5 M & W 548 is overruled so far as it is an authority for that proposition. As to the development of the law generally see PARA 386 et seq. For restraints beyond the United Kingdom see also *E Underwood & Son Ltd v Barker* [1899] 1 Ch 300, CA, which decided that a hay and straw merchant with business in the United Kingdom, France, Belgium, and Canada may, apparently, restrain an employee from engaging in the business in those countries; but if the extension beyond the United Kingdom is unreasonable, the covenant is severable; *Lamson Pneumatic Tube Co v Phillips* (1904) 91 LT 363, CA; *Continental Tyre and Rubber (Great Britain) Co Ltd v Heath* (1913) 29 TLR 308 (rubber tyre company; restraint as to United Kingdom held good; extensions to France and Germany severable). For instances of world-wide restraints held good see *Rousillon v Rousillon* (1880) 14 ChD 351; *Badische Anilin und Soda Fabrik v Schott, Segner & Co* [1892] 3 Ch 447; *Ropeways Ltd v Hoyle* (1919) 88 LJCh 446 (obiter); *Scully (UK) Ltd v Lee* [1998] IRLR 259, CA. For a restraint as to Europe held to be good see *Leather Cloth Co v Lorsont* (1869) LR 9 Eq 345.

3 *Leather Cloth Co v Lorsont* (1869) LR 9 Eq 345 at 351 per James V-C ('If the covenant is good as to Great Britain, we need not concern ourselves with its extension to France and Germany'); *Maxim Nordenfelt Guns and Ammunition Co v Nordenfelt* [1893] 1 Ch 630 at 651, CA, per Lindley LJ (it is not contrary to public policy to give effect to a covenant entered into for the purpose of preventing a man from assisting foreigners with an English trader who has bought his business) (affd [1894] AC 535 at 550, HL, per Lord Herschell, and at 574 per Lord Macnaghten; see PARA 386 note 11); *E Underwood & Son Ltd v Barker* [1899] 1 Ch 300 at 307, CA, per Lindley MB ('If the restraint is unreasonable as to the foreign countries named, which I do not think it is, still the agreement as to them is clearly severable from that part of it which relates to this country'); cf at 308 per Rigby LJ. In *Dowden and Pook Ltd v Pook* [1904] 1 KB 45, CA, a covenant unlimited as to space was treated as covering the whole world, and therefore unreasonably wide (applied in *Commercial Plastics Ltd v Vincent* [1965] 1 QB 623, [1964] 3 All ER 546, CA, where the court declined to sever the restriction); cf *Littlewoods Organisation Ltd v Harris* [1978] 1 All ER 1026, [1977] 1 WLR 1472, CA, where the restraint was construed as limited to the United Kingdom. In *Lamson Pneumatic Tube Co v Phillips* (1904) 91 LT 363, CA, where the manager of a business having by its nature few and scattered customers covenanted not to be engaged in a similar business in the eastern hemisphere, the Court of Appeal (Cozens-Hardy LJ dissenting) treated the question as open, however, and, as the covenant was held to be reasonable to its fullest extent, no decision was necessary; cf at 367 per Vaughan Williams LJ. The decision in *Vancouver Malt and Sake Brewing Co Ltd v Vancouver Breweries Ltd* [1934] AC 181, PC, where a world-wide restraint was held unreasonable and void, does not decide this point since it appears that the restraint would have been unreasonable even if confined to Canada. The point is in most cases an academic one since the restraint is usually severable: see *Goldsoll v Goldman* [1915] 1 Ch 292, CA, where a restraint unreasonable as to foreign countries and reasonable as to the United Kingdom and the Isle of Man was held severable and enforceable as to the latter part.

402. Measurement of distance. In measuring distance, unless the contract[1] contains words to the contrary[2], the measurement is to be made not by the nearest accessible way, but in a straight line on a map, disregarding actual inequalities of the surface[3].

When the distance between houses is in question, the measurement should be between the nearest points of each, not between the doors[4].

If by the contract the distance is to be measured by the usual streets or ways of approach, it must be measured by any usual public way, not necessarily by that which is most frequented[5].

1   As to the measurement of distances for the purposes of statutes see the Interpretation Act 1978 s 8; and STATUTES vol 44(1) (Reissue) PARA 1387.

2   See e g *Atkyns v Kinnier* (1850) 4 Exch 776 (2½ miles 'measuring by the usual streets or ways of approach'); *Smith v Hancock* [1894] 2 Ch 377, CA ('measured by the nearest cart road').

3   *Mouflet v Cole* (1872) LR 8 Exch 32, Ex Ch, following *Leigh v Hind* (1829) 9 B & C 774 at 779 per Parke J, and *Duignan v Walker* (1859) John 446, and disapproving *Woods v Dennett* (1817) 2 Stark 89, and the view of the majority of the court in *Leigh v Hind*. Cf *Robertson v Buchanan* (1904) 73 LJCh 408, CA ('as the crow flies').

4   *Mouflet v Cole* (1872) LR 8 Exch 32, Ex Ch.

5   *Atkyns v Kinnier* (1850) 4 Exch 776; cf *Hares v Curtin* [1913] 2 KB 328, DC.

D. DURATION OF RESTRAINT

403. Restraint as to time in general. The length of the period of restraint is an important matter for consideration[1], but the absence of a limit will not make a restraint void if it is otherwise reasonable[2], for it is reasonable that a restraint imposed, in respect of the limit as to time, for the protection of a business should be wide enough to protect that business in the hands not only of the covenantee, but also of his legatee, representative or assignee, and with this object the restraint may be co-extensive with the lifetime of the covenantor[3], and is not affected by the fact that the original covenantee has ceased to carry on business[4] or is dead[5].

1   *Proctor v Sargent* (1840) 2 Man & G 20; *Sir WC Leng & Co Ltd v Andrews* [1909] 1 Ch 763 at 771, CA, per Fletcher Moulton LJ, and at 774 per Farwell LJ; *Eastes v Russ* [1914] 1 Ch 468, CA (assistant in pathological laboratory; 10 miles; no time limit; bad); *Wyatt v Kreglinger and Fernau* [1933] 1 KB 793, CA (manager; wool trade; no time limit; bad); *Pellow v Ivey* (1933) 49 TLR 422 (hairdresser and tobacconist; within the borough; no time limit; bad); *M & S Drapers (a firm) v Reynolds* [1956] 3 All ER 814, [1957] 1 WLR 9, CA (collector salesman; five years; bad); *Petrofina (Great Britain) Ltd v Martin* [1966] Ch 146, [1966] 1 All ER 126, CA (tie to one supplier of petrol; 12 years; bad); *Esso Petroleum Co Ltd v Harper's Garage (Stourport) Ltd* [1968] AC 269, [1967] 1 All ER 699, HL (tie of under five years reasonable; tie of 21 years unreasonable); *Alec Lobb (Garages) Ltd v Total Oil GB Ltd* [1985] 1 All ER 303, [1985] 1 WLR 173, CA (21 year underlease with exclusive purchasing term as to petrol; break clauses after seven and 14 years; reasonable); see *Dayer-Smith v Hadsley* (1913) 108 LT 897, CA (affd sub nom *Hadsley v Dayer-Smith* [1914] AC 979, HL); *Scully (UK) Ltd v Lee* [1998] IRLR 259, CA (non-solicitation covenant in contract of employment for two years after termination of employment unreasonable); cf *Joseph Evans & Co Ltd v Heathcote* [1918] 1 KB 418, CA (agreement to control prices; no time limit or power of withdrawal; bad).

2   *Chesman v Nainby* (1727) 1 Bro Parl Cas 234, HL (linen-draper; half mile; no time limit; good); *Colmer v Clark* (1734) 7 Mod Rep 230 (tally-man; within City and Westminster; seven years; good); *Hayward v Young* (1818) 2 Chit 407 (surgeon; 20 miles; no time limit; good); *Hitchcock v Coker* (1837) 6 Ad & El 438, Ex Ch (druggist; 3 miles; no time limit; good); *Archer v Marsh* (1837) 6 Ad & El 959 (carrier; not to compete; no time limit; good); *Mallan v May* (1843) 11 M & W 653 (dentist; London; no time limit; good); *Nicholls v Stretton* (1847) 10 QB 346 (solicitor; not to act for clients of covenantee; no time limit; good); *Elves v Crofts* (1850) 10 CB 241 (butcher; 5 miles; no time limit; good); *Giles v Hart* (1859) 1 LT 154 (surgeon; 5 miles; no time limit; good); *Catt v Tourle* (1869) 4 Ch App 654 (publican; tied house covenant on conveyance of land; no time limit; good); *Jacoby v Whitmore* (1883) 49 LT 335, CA (oil and colour man; no time limit; good); *Davies v Davies* (1887) 36 ChD 359 at 390, CA, per Bowen LJ; *Hood and Moore's Stores Ltd v Jones* (1899) 81 LT 169 (corn dealer; 2 miles; no time limit; good); *Haynes v Doman* [1899] 2 Ch 13 at 18, CA, per Stirling J, and at 23 per Lindley LJ; *Fitch v Dewes* [1921] 2 AC 158, HL (solicitor's managing clerk; 7 miles; no time limit; good). Sometimes the time limit is 'so long as the covenantee carries on business', or similar words; and cf *Short Horn Dairy Co v Hall* (1887) 83 LT Jo 45, where the carrying on of

a company's business by a receiver and manager in a debenture holder's action was held not to be carrying on business within the meaning of the covenant; see EMPLOYMENT vol 39 (2009) PARAS 19–20.

3   *Hitchcock v Coker* (1837) 6 Ad & El 438 at 454, Ex Ch; *Haynes v Doman* [1899] 2 Ch 13 at 18, CA, per Stirling J; cf *Chesman v Nainby* (1727) 1 Bro Parl Cas 234, HL; *Bunn v Guy* (1803) 1 Smith KB 1; *Hayward v Young* (1818) 2 Chit 407; *Williams v Williams* (1818) 2 Swan 253; *Bryson v Whitehead* (1822) 1 Sim & St 74; *Wickens v Evans* (1829) 3 Y & J 318; *Archer v Marsh* (1837) 6 Ad & El 959; *Price v Green* (1847) 16 M & W 346, Ex Ch (covenant enforced by executor of covenantee); *Pemberton v Vaughan* (1847) 10 QB 87; *Atkyns v Kinnier* (1850) 4 Exch 776; *Avery v Langford* (1854) Kay 663; *Benwell v Inns* (1857) 24 Beav 307; *Gravely v Barnard* (1874) LR 18 Eq 518; *Jacoby v Whitmore* (1883) 49 LT 335, CA; *Smith v Hawthorn* (1897) 76 LT 716; *Baines v Geary* (1887) 35 ChD 154 (assigns mentioned); *Hood and Moore's Stores Ltd v Jones* (1899) 81 LT 169; but see *Berlitz School of Languages v Duchêne* (1903) 6 F 181, Ct of Sess; and EMPLOYMENT vol 39 (2009) PARAS 19–20. If the restriction as to space is considered to be reasonable, it is seldom in a case where the sale of a goodwill is concerned that the restriction can be held to be unreasonable because there is no limit as to time; *Connors Bros Ltd v Connors* [1940] 4 All ER 179 at 195, PC.

4   *Elves v Crofts* (1850) 10 CB 241, where the business had ceased to be carried on either by the covenantee or by any assign, the plaintiff being the original covenantee; *Jacoby v Whitmore* (1883) 49 LT 335, CA; *Automobile Carnage Builders Ltd v Sayers* (1909) 101 LT 419, where the benefit of a restrictive covenant with partners who assigned to a company was held to pass to the assignee; *Townsend v Jarman* [1900] 2 Ch 698 at 703.

5   *Hastings v Whitley* (1848) 2 Exch 611 (action by executors of covenantee on covenant not to carry on business as a surgeon at a particular place at any time); *Smith v Hawthorn* (1897) 76 LT 716.

404.   Contracts of employment. The doctrine of restraint of trade has normally no application to restrictions which operate during the period of employment, but where the restrictions may have the effect of sterilising rather than absorbing a person's capacity for work the contracts may be subject to examination[1]. With that qualification, an employer may secure the whole time of his employee during the period of service[2], which may last for the employee's lifetime[3]. However, a restraint, although it is reasonable if applied during the period of service, may be unreasonably wide if applied after the termination of that period, and where a covenantor during the period left his service without having been dismissed, the restraint was only enforced by injunction for the residue of the period[4].

1   *Esso Petroleum Co Ltd v Harper's Garage (Stourport) Ltd* [1968] AC 269 at 328–329, [1967] 1 All ER 699 at 726–727, HL, per Lord Pearce (citing *Young v Timmins* (1831) 1 Cr & J 331), and at 336 and 732 per Lord Wilberforce; *A Schroeder Music Publishing Co Ltd v Macaulay* [1974] 3 All ER 616, [1974] 1 WLR 1308, HL. The observation of Branson J in *Warner Bros Pictures Inc v Nelson* [1937] 1 KB 209 at 214, [1936] 3 All ER 160 at 163 ('Where … the covenants are all concerned with what is to happen whilst the defendant is employed by the plaintiffs and not thereafter, there is no room for the application of the doctrine of restraint of trade') is too widely stated.

2   *William Robinson & Co Ltd v Heuer* [1898] 2 Ch 451 at 455, CA, per Lindley MR, and at 458 per Chitty LJ. Cf the covenants in *Homer v Ashford and Ainsworth* (1825) 3 Bing 322 (not to work for any other person during term of service); *King v Hansell* (1860) 5 H & N 106 (commission agent during term of service not to engage in same trade within 10 miles); *Allsopp v Wheatcroft* (1872) LR 15 Eq 59 (during the term of service not to engage in the sale of any other articles or goods whatsoever); *Welstead v Hadley* (1904) 21 TLR 165, CA; *Tivoli, Manchester, Ltd v Colley* (1904) 20 TLR 437; *Hartley v Cummings* (1847) 5 CB 247, where an agreement to serve the employer and his partners for seven years, and not during the term to serve anybody else or join any workmen's union without consent; to give instruction gratis if required; the employer to make minimum weekly payments, and if necessary provide work to keep the wage up to the minimum, with power, in case of the employee's illness or misconduct or the employers' discontinuance of business, to employ any other person and to cease to pay wages, was held no restraint of trade; *Pilkington v Scott* (1846) 15 M & W 657, where an agreement to serve for seven years at certain wages when and so long as the employee should be

employed, and not to work for any other person during the term, with liberty to the employers to employ any other person in case of illness and an option to dismiss at one month's notice was held mutual, reasonable and made on good consideration; it was also held that there was an undertaking to employ for the seven years; but see *A Schroeder Music Publishing Co Ltd v Macaulay* [1974] 3 All ER 616, [1974] 1 WLR 1308, HL, where a song-writer's undertaking to provide exclusive services and to assign copyrights to the publishers who were under no obligation to publish was held in restraint of trade and invalid; *Clifford Davis Management Ltd v WEA Records Ltd* [1975] 1 All ER 237, [1975] 1 WLR 61, CA; and cf *Phillips v Stevens* (1899) 15 TLR 325, DC; *Warner Bros Pictures Inc v Nelson* [1937] 1 KB 209, [1936] 3 All ER 160; *Gaumont-British Picture Corpn Ltd v Alexander* [1936] 2 All ER 1686; cf *Wyatt v Kreglinger and Fernau* [1933] 1 KB 793, CA (ex-employee on pension; agreement held in restraint of trade) (followed in *Bull v Pitney-Bowes Ltd* [1966] 3 All ER 384, [1967] 1 WLR 273). See also *Eastham v Newcastle United Football Club Ltd* [1964] Ch 413, [1963] 3 All ER 139; *Greig v Insole* [1978] 3 All ER 449, [1978] 1 WLR 302. As to the enforcing by injunction of express and implied negative covenants in contracts of service see CIVIL PROCEDURE vol 11 (2009) PARA 448 et seq. As to proceedings for procuring breach of contracts of service see TORT vol 45(2) (Reissue) PARAS 688–692.

3   *Wallis v Day* (1837) 2 M & W 273; *Warner Bros Pictures Inc v Nelson* [1937] 1 KB 209, [1936] 3 All ER 160. Cf *WH Milsted & Son Ltd v Hamp and Ross and Glendinning Ltd* [1927] WN 233, where such a contract of service terminable only by notice given by the employer was held bad by Eve J, as being 'wholly one-sided'; and see the cases cited in note 2; and EMPLOYMENT vol 39 (2009) PARA 20. An injunction will not be granted to enforce a covenant applicable during the period of the covenantor's engagement if the granting of the injunction would be equivalent to enforcing specifically an agreement for personal service: *William Robinson & Co Ltd v Heuer* [1898] 2 Ch 451 at 455–456, CA; *Ehrman v Bartholomew* [1898] 1 Ch 671 at 674; *Rely-a-Bell Burglar and Fire Alarm Co Ltd v Eisler* [1926] Ch 609; *Warner Bros Pictures Inc v Nelson* [1937] 1 KB 209, [1936] 3 All ER 160; see CIVIL PROCEDURE vol 11 (2009) PARA 448 et seq.

4   *William Robinson & Co Ltd v Heuer* [1898] 2 Ch 451, CA; *Rely-a-Bell Burglar and Fire Alarm Co Ltd v Eisler* [1926] Ch 609. Cf *Ehrman v Bartholomew* [1898] 1 Ch 671.

405.   Transfer of Undertakings (Protection of Employment) Regulations 2006. A restrictive covenant in an employee's contract of employment which is to come into force on the termination of his employment is capable of transfer under the Transfer of Undertakings (Protection of Employment) Regulations 2006[1] and as such is enforceable by the purchaser of the employer's business[2].

1   See the Transfer of Undertakings (Protection of Employment) Regulations 2006, SI 2006/246, reg 4; and EMPLOYMENT vol 39 (2009) PARA 114. The regulations implement EC Council Directive 2001/23 (OJ L82, 22.3.2001, p 16) on the approximation of the law relating to business transfers.

2   *Morris Angel & Son Ltd v Hollande* [1993] 3 All ER 569, [1993] ICR 71, CA.

406.   Term of lease. Where a covenant in restraint of trade accompanies an assignment of the term of a lease, it is not limited to the length of the term[1] unless it is expressly so provided[2].

1   *Elves v Crofts* (1850) 10 CB 241.
2   Eg as in *Mitchel v Reynolds* (1711) 1 P Wms 181, where the restraint was limited to the term (five years) of the lease assigned; *Hinde v Gray* (1840) 1 Man & G 195, where the restraint was limited to the term of the lease, but was held void because it was unlimited as to space; *Rannie v Irvine* (1844) 7 Man & G 969.

E. CUSTOMERS AND NAME

407.   Restraint as to customers. A restraint may be reasonable because it is limited to dealings with particular persons, for instance the persons who were customers of a business during the period of the covenantor's service[1], or a particular trade rival[2].

However, the fact that a restraint relates to the covenantor's customers before his service with the covenantee began may be a factor weighing against the validity of the restriction[3].

In the absence of an express covenant, the general law does not afford protection to an employer against a former employee soliciting the employer's customers[4].

1 *Nicholls v Stretton* (1847) 10 QB 346, where a restraint on a solicitor's clerk against acting for (1) persons who had been clients during the term of service, and (2) persons who might thereafter become clients, was held as to the first restraint reasonable, and as to the second severable; *Baines v Geary* (1887) 35 ChD 154, where a restraint on a milk carrier against serving 'any of the customers served by or belonging at any time' to the covenantee, was held divisible into (a) customers during the term of service, (b) customers at any other time, and (a) was held reasonable, and (b) severable; but as to severability see PARAS 433–434. This distinction as to customers appears to be still valid in spite of the dicta in *Dubowski & Sons v Goldstein* [1896] 1 QB 478 at 482, CA, per Lord Esher MR, and at 485 per Rigby LJ. These were not followed by Neville J in *Konski v Peet* [1915] 1 Ch 530, or by Lawrence J in *East Essex Farmers Ltd v Holder* [1926] WN 230. See also *Gilford Motor Co Ltd v Horne* [1933] Ch 935, CA (applied in *GW Plowman & Son Ltd v Ash* [1964] 2 All ER 10, [1964] 1 WLR 568, CA); *Home Counties Dairies Ltd v Skilton* [1970] 1 All ER 1227, [1970] 1 WLR 526, CA. The fact that a particular customer has indicated an unwillingness to continue doing business with the covenantee is not a reason for refusing relief: *John Michael Design plc v Cooke* [1987] 2 All ER 332 at 334, [1987] ICR 445 at 448, CA. A restraint may be unreasonable if the restraint, although limited as to persons, covers all business whatever (*Morris & Co v Ryle* (1910) 26 TLR 678, CA), or if it covers customers outside the area of the covenantor's employment (*Spafax (1965) Ltd v Dommett* (1972) 116 Sol Jo 711, CA, where a salesman for West Cornwall, whose employer's business was countrywide, was restrained from dealing with anyone who was a customer of the employer at the date of termination of his employment, and the restraint was held to be too wide; *Financial Collection Agencies (UK) Ltd v Batey* (1973) 117 Sol Jo 416, CA). A restraint against soliciting potential customers of the employer would be unreasonable: *Business Seating (Renovations) Ltd v Broad* [1989] ICR 729 at 734 per Millett J. A restraint against soliciting persons who become customers after the termination of the contract of employment is unreasonable: *Austin Knight (UK) v Hinds* [1994] FSR 52; *Aramark plc v Somerville* 1995 SLT 749.

2 *Howard v Danner* (1901) 17 TLR 548, where a covenant by a restaurant waiter not during the year to enter the service of a specified rival restaurant was held good. See also *Littlewoods Organisation Ltd v Harris* [1978] 1 All ER 1026, [1977] 1 WLR 1472, CA.

3 See *M & S Drapers (a firm) v Reynolds* [1956] 3 All ER 814 at 816, [1957] 1 WLR 9 at 13, CA, per Hodson LJ, and at 818–819 and 17–18 per Morris LJ, where a large proportion of customers covered by a covenant entered into by a collector salesman for credit drapers had formed a connection with the defendant salesman before he entered the plaintiffs' service.

4 *Wallace Bogan & Co v Cove* [1997] IRLR 453, CA.

408. Restraint as to name. A person may be restrained from carrying on business anywhere under a particular name[1] or in a particular capacity[2] or from representing himself, even truthfully, to have been connected in trade with the covenantee[3] provided the restraint is reasonable[4].

1 *Vernon v Hallam* (1886) 34 ChD 748. As to the application of this principle to companies see COMPANIES vol 7(1) (2004 Reissue) PARA 355 et seq; see also PARTNERSHIP vol 79 (2008) PARAS 27, 172, 213.

2 *Wallis v Day* (1837) 2 M & W 273, where the covenantor was never to trade on his own account, but only as assistant to the covenantee for weekly payments.

3 *Wolmershausen v O'Connor* (1877) 36 LT 921, where a covenant by a retiring partner not to carry on business within 10 miles of O, and not, by publication, advertisement, circular, or otherwise, to hold himself out as formerly connected with the covenantee was held reasonable, and a breach to describe himself as 'late of O and formerly of M,' at which places the partners had carried on, and the covenantee continued to carry on business.

4 *Hepworth Manufacturing Co Ltd v Ryott* [1920] 1 Ch 1, CA, where a covenant by a film actor not to use his stage name, after the determination of his contract, for any purpose whatever was held unreasonable.

F. CONFIDENTIAL MATTERS

409.   Sale of trade secret. A contract not to divulge a trade secret may be reasonable even though unlimited as to space or time, and a restraint imposed in order to give effect to such a contract would apparently be treated in the same way, but in no case has an absolutely unlimited restriction been under consideration[1].

1   *Bryson v Whitehead* (1822) 1 Sim & St 74, where in settling the terms of a deed to give effect to an agreement to sell a dyer's business with a trade secret, Leach V-C directed a covenant, unlimited as to space, to restrain the use of the secret for 20 years, i e a general covenant when general covenants were regarded as of necessity void (see PARA 386); *Leather Cloth Co v Lorsont* (1869) LR 9 Eq 345 at 354 per James V-C; *Allsopp v Wheatcroft* (1872) LR 15 Eq 59 at 64 per Wickens V-C, commenting on *Leather Cloth Co v Lorsont*; *Hagg v Darley* (1878) 47 LJCh 567, where there was no limit of space, but a limit of time for 14 years; *Davies v Davies* (1887) 36 ChD 359 at 384, CA, per Cotton LJ, commenting on *Leather Cloth Co v Lorsont*; see also *Herbert Morris Ltd v Saxelby* [1916] 1 AC 688 at 710, HL, per Lord Parker of Waddington; cf *Haynes v Doman* [1899] 2 Ch 13, CA; *Caribonum Co Ltd v Le Couch* (1913) 109 LT 385 (on appeal 109 LT 587, CA).

410.   Confidential information and statutory exemption. The obligation not to disclose confidential information or to act in breach of confidence imposed by the general law[1] is not invalidated by the doctrine of restraint of trade. In addition an employer may be entitled to enforce a restrictive covenant taken for his protection against an ex-employee where, from the nature of the business or of the employment, the ex-employee has special opportunities of becoming acquainted with the customers and of acquiring confidential information such as trade secrets[2]. There is an implied term imposed on the employee after the termination of his employment not to disclose information of a sufficiently high degree of confidentiality as to amount to a trade secret; this term does not, however, extend to all information which is confidential only in the sense that an unauthorised disclosure to a third party while the employment subsisted would be a clear breach of the duty of good faith[3].

Where there are contracts or orders for the production of defence materials, the disclosure of technical information in breach of a restrictive covenant is permitted by statute to a covenantor authorised by certain authorities from whom the covenantee is entitled to receive compensation[4].

1   See EQUITY vol 16(2) (Reissue) PARA 855. Information which is merely know-how will not be protected: see *Amways Corpn v Eurway International Ltd* [1974] RPC 82; *Faccenda Chicken Ltd v Fowler* [1987] Ch 117, [1986] 1 All ER 617, CA; *Lancashire Fires Ltd v SA Lyons & Co Ltd* [1997] IRLR 113, [1996] FSR 629, CA. Information which is in the public domain is not confidential: *Brooks v Olyslager OMS (UK) Ltd* [1998] IRLR 590, CA. As to the prevention of the disclosure of confidential information generally see CIVIL PROCEDURE vol 11 (2009) PARAS 475–476; *Amber Size and Chemical Co Ltd v Menzel* [1913] 2 Ch 239; *O Mustad & Son v S Allcock & Co Ltd and Dosen* (1928) [1963] 3 All ER 416, [1964] 1 WLR 109n, HL. See also COPYRIGHT, DESIGN RIGHT AND RELATED RIGHTS vol 9(2) (2006 Reissue) PARA 13. As to implied terms in contracts of service not to divulge information see EMPLOYMENT vol 39 (2009) PARA 90. As to disclosure generally see CIVIL PROCEDURE vol 11 (2009) PARA 538 et seq.
2   *Mineral Water Bottle Exchange and Trade Protection Society v Booth* (1887) 36 ChD 465 at 471, CA; *Badische Anilin und Soda Fabrik v Schott, Segner & Co* [1892] 3 Ch 447 at 453; *William Robinson & Co Ltd v Heuer* [1898] 2 Ch 451 at 455, CA (confidential clerk); *E Underwood & Son Ltd v Barker* [1899] 1 Ch 300 at 307, CA (distinguishing *Ward v Byrne* (1839) 5 M & W 548); *Haynes v Doman* [1899] 2 Ch 13 at 17–18, CA (traveller); *Barr v Craven* (1903) 20 TLR 51, CA (insurance agent); *White, Tomkins and Courage v Wilson* (1907) 23 TLR 469; *Lewis and Lewis v Durnford* (1907) 24 TLR 64 (solicitor's clerk); *Bromley v Smith* [1909] 2 KB 235 at 240 (milk seller); *Continental Tyre and Rubber (Great Britain) Co Ltd v Heath* (1913) 29 TLR 308. Cf *Proctor v Sargent* (1840) 2 Man & G 20 (milk seller); *Cornwall v Hawkins* (1872) 41 LJCh 435 (milk seller); *Middleton v Brown* (1878) 47

LJCh 411, CA (vendor of oil by men in the street); *Forster & Sons Ltd v Suggett* (1918) 35 TLR 87 (engineer); *Fitch v Dewes* [1921] 2 AC 158, HL (solicitor's managing clerk); *Putsman v Taylor* [1927] 1 KB 637, DC (on appeal [1927] 1 KB 741, CA) (tailor's cutter and manager); *Kerchiss v Colora Printing Inks Ltd* [1960] RPC 235 (lath manufacturer); *Scorer v Seymour-Johns* [1966] 3 All ER 347, [1966] 1 WLR 1419, CA (estate agent's branch manager and negotiator); *Littlewoods Organisation Ltd v Harris* [1978] 1 All ER 1026, [1977] 1 WLR 1472, CA (director of mail order business); *Thomas v Farr plc* [2007] EWCA Civ 118, [2007] ICR 932 (director of insurance broker).

Persons in other employments have been held not to be in a similar confidential position: *Sir WC Leng & Co Ltd v Andrews* [1909] 1 Ch 763, CA (reporters); *Pearks Ltd v Cullen* (1912) 28 TLR 371 (shop assistants); *Mason v Provident Clothing and Supply Co Ltd* [1913] AC 724, HL (canvassers); *Herbert Morris Ltd v Saxelby* [1916] 1 AC 688, HL (engineers); *Bowler v Lovegrove* [1921] 1 Ch 642 (clerks to estate agents); *Vincents of Reading v Fogden* (1932) 48 TLR 613 (car salesmen). See also *Eastes v Russ* [1914] 1 Ch 468, CA; *Spence v Mercantile Bank of India Ltd* (1921) 37 TLR 390 (on appeal 37 TLR 745, CA). As to the appropriateness of taking a restrictive covenant see *Printers and Finishers Ltd v Holloway* [1964] 3 All ER 731, [1965] 1 WLR 1; *Littlewoods Organisation Ltd v Harris* [1978] 1 All ER 1026, [1977] 1 WLR 1472, CA; *Lawrence David Ltd v Ashton* [1991] 1 All ER 385 at 394, CA, doubting *Thomas Marshall (Exports) Ltd v Guinle* [1979] Ch 227, [1978] 3 All ER 193.

3 *Faccenda Chicken Ltd v Fowler* [1987] Ch 117, [1986] 1 All ER 617, CA; see also *Balston Ltd v Headline Filters Ltd* [1987] FSR 330; *Lock International plc v Beswick* [1989] 3 All ER 373, [1989] 1 WLR 1268; *Lansing Linde Ltd v Kerr* [1991] 1 All ER 418, [1991] 1 WLR 251, CA; *TSB Bank plc v Connell* 1997 SLT 1254; *FSS Travel and Leisure Systems Ltd v Johnson* [1998] IRLR 382, CA; *AT Poeton (Gloucester Plating) Ltd v Horton* [2000] ICR 1208, CA. Quaere whether it is possible to restrict by an express covenant confidential information not covered by the term implied by law: see *Faccenda Chicken Ltd v Fowler* [1987] Ch 117 at 137, [1986] 1 All ER 617 at 626, CA, per Neill LJ; *Balston Ltd v Headline Filters Ltd* [1987] FSR 330 at 347–348; *Systems Reliability Holdings plc v Smith* [1990] IRLR 377.

4 See the Defence Contracts Act 1958 ss 2–6; and WAR AND ARMED CONFLICT vol 49(1) (2005 Reissue) PARAS 588–589.

411. Knowledge and skill acquired during employment.

411. Knowledge and skill acquired during employment. Apart from the protection of trade secrets or confidential information[1], an employer is not entitled to restrain an employee from making use, after the employment has ceased, of any knowledge or skill gained during the period of employment[2], but a covenant reasonably necessary to protect an employer against the betrayal of trade secrets or confidential information is not void merely because it unavoidably protects the employer against competition[3].

1 See PARA 410.

2 *Herbert Morris Ltd v Saxelby* [1916] 1 AC 688 at 710, HL, per Lord Parker of Waddington. See also *Sir WC Leng & Co Ltd v Andrews* [1909] 1 Ch 763, CA; *Attwood v Lamont* [1920] 3 KB 571 at 589, CA, per Younger LJ; *Triplex Safety Glass Co Ltd v Scorah* [1938] Ch 211 at 215, [1937] 4 All ER 693 at 697; *Kores Manufacturing Co Ltd v Kolok Manufacturing Co Ltd* [1959] Ch 108, [1958] 2 All ER 65, CA, where an agreement between employers in which no distinction was made between employees possessed of secrets etc and those not so possessed was held void. See also *Vandervell Products Ltd v McLeod* [1957] RPC 185, CA; *Commercial Plastics Ltd v Vincent* [1965] 1 QB 623, [1964] 3 All ER 546, CA; and note 3.

3 *Haynes v Doman* [1899] 2 Ch 13 at 23, CA, per Lord Lindley MR; *Herbert Morris Ltd v Saxelby* [1916] 1 AC 688 at 710, HL, per Lord Parker of Waddington; *Attwood v Lamont* [1920] 3 KB 571 at 597, CA, per Younger LJ; *Spence v Mercantile Bank of India Ltd* (1921) 37 TLR 390 at 394 per Greer LJ. See also *Forster & Sons Ltd v Suggett* (1918) 35 TLR 87, where the covenant by a works engineer of glass works was not to divulge trade secrets during the period of employment and thereafter, and not to carry on or be interested in any similar business in the United Kingdom for a period of five years. Cf *Vandervell Products Ltd v McLeod* [1957] RPC 185, CA, where a covenant by an engineering foreman not to take service with a 'competitor' was held not restricted to a competitor in the line of business involving the trade secrets and was therefore too wide; *Commercial Plastics Ltd v Vincent* [1965] 1 QB 623, [1964] 3 All ER 546, CA.

(v) Reasonableness in the Public Interest

412.   The interests of the public, the covenantee and the covenantor. A covenant in restraint of trade must be reasonable with reference to the interest of the public[1]. Many agreements or practices which might be detrimental to the public interest may be investigated under the provisions of domestic or European Union competition law[2].

1   *Nordenfelt v Maxim Nordenfelt Guns and Ammunition Co Ltd* [1894] AC 535 at 565, HL, per Lord Macnaghten; *Mason v Provident Clothing and Supply Co Ltd* [1913] AC 724 at 733, HL, per Lord Haldane LC; *Herbert Morris Ltd v Saxelby* [1916] 1 AC 688 at 707, HL, per Lord Parker of Waddington. See also *Texaco Ltd v Mulberry Filling Station Ltd* [1972] 1 All ER 513, [1972] 1 WLR 814. The effect of a covenant upon the public interest is a separate matter from its effect upon the interests of the parties and must be considered separately: *Horwood v Millar's Timber and Trading Co Ltd* [1917] 1 KB 305 at 318, CA, per Scrutton LJ; *Herbert Morris Ltd v Saxelby* [1916] 1 AC 688 at 708, HL, per Lord Parker of Waddington; but cf *Esso Petroleum Co Ltd v Harper's Garage (Stourport) Ltd* [1968] AC 269 at 324, [1967] 1 All ER 699 at 724, HL, per Lord Pearce. Except in the case of monopoly (see PARA 361 et seq), a restraint reasonably necessary for the covenantee will very seldom be unreasonable with reference to the public interest: see *Nordenfelt v Maxim Nordenfelt Guns and Ammunition Co Ltd* [1894] AC 535, HL; *A-G of Commonwealth of Australia v Adelaide Steamship Co Ltd* [1913] AC 781 at 795–796, PC; *Tool Metal Manufacturing Co Ltd v Tungsten Electric Co Ltd* [1955] 2 All ER 657 at 662, 686–688, [1955] 1 WLR 761 at 767, 800, HL; but cf *McEllistrim v Ballymacelligott Co-operative Agricultural and Dairy Society Ltd* [1919] AC 548 at 562, HL, per Lord Birkenhead LC. Where a restrictive agreement is entered into which is no wider than is reasonably necessary for the covenantee's protection in his business, it is difficult to imagine circumstances which will render such an agreement injurious to the public interest; apart from contracts induced by fraud, duress or undue influence or impeachable on any other recognised ground of invalidity, a restriction which is reasonably necessary for the protection of a man's business cannot be held invalid on grounds of public policy unless some specific ground can be clearly established: see *E Underwood & Son Ltd v Barker* [1899] 1 Ch 300 at 305, CA, per Lindley MR, suggesting that some pernicious monopoly may afford such ground. But since, in relation to many agreements containing restrictions, there may be wider issues affecting the interests of the public than those which relate merely to the interests of the parties, it is important that the vitality of the requirement stated in the text should continue to be recognised: see *Esso Petroleum Co Ltd v Harper's Garage (Stourport) Ltd* [1968] AC 269 at 341, [1967] 1 All ER 699 at 735, HL, per Lord Wilberforce.
2   As to domestic competition law see PARAS 3, 115 et seq; and as to EU competition law see PARA 24 et seq.

(vi) Consideration

413.   Necessity for valuable consideration. There must be a valuable and legal consideration for an agreement in restraint of trade[1], even if the covenant is by deed[2]. The consideration may be shown either on the face of the agreement or by extrinsic evidence[3], or may be reasonably inferred from the agreement[4].

1   *Mitchel v Reynolds* (1711) 1 P Wms 181; *Colmer v Clark* (1734) 7 Mod Rep 230; *Gunmakers Co v Fell* (1742) Willes 384 at 388. See also *Re Tovey, ex p Lyne* (1841) 5 Jur 1088.
2   *Mitchel v Reynolds* (1711) 1 P Wms 181 at 192; *Davis v Mason* (1793) 5 Term Rep 118; *Homer v Ashford and Ainsworth* (1825) 3 Bing 322; *Mallan v May* (1843) 11 M & W 653 at 665 per Parke B; *Gravely v Barnard* (1874) LR 18 Eq 518. Cf *Bunn v Guy* (1803) 1 Smith KB 1 at 11. However, it is to be noted that this point has not really been considered in any case decided under more modern conditions, and for an argument against the proposition that consideration would now be required for a deed see Matthews and Adler's Law relating to Covenants in Restraint of Trade (1907 Edn) p 69 et seq. Cf CONTRACT vol 9(1) (Reissue) PARA 621; DEEDS AND OTHER INSTRUMENTS vol 13 (2007 Reissue) PARA 57. As to covenants by deed generally see DEEDS AND OTHER INSTRUMENTS vol 13 (2007 Reissue) PARA 1 et seq; EQUITY vol 16(2) (Reissue) PARA 906.

3   *Mitchel v Reynolds* (1711) 1 P Wms 181; *Homer v Ashford and Ainsworth* (1825) 3 Bing 322;
    Hitchcock v Coker (1837) 6 Ad & El 438, Ex Ch; *Hutton v Parker* (1839) 7 Dowl 739;
    Mumford v Gething (1859) 7 CBNS 305; *Cooper v Southgate* (1894) 10 R 552, DC.
4   *Gravely v Barnard* (1874) LR 18 Eq 518.

414. Legality of consideration. That the consideration for an agreement in
restraint of trade must be legal is obvious[1]. There is no illegality in the sale of a
business which depends on the personal character of the person who carries it
on, even though the vendor is induced by a mere pecuniary consideration to
recommend the purchaser to the clients[2].

1   *Hitchcock v Coker* (1837) 6 Ad & El 438, Ex Ch.
2   *Bunn v Guy* (1803) 1 Smith KB 1 (solicitor's business); *Candler v Candler* (1821) Jac 225 at 231
    per Lord Eldon LC; *Gilfillan v Henderson* (1833) 2 Cl & Fin 1, HL; *Whittaker v Howe* (1841)
    3 Beav 383 at 389, 393; *Thornbury v Bevill* (1842) 1 Y & C Ch Cas 554. As to public policy
    generally see PARA 377 note 3; and CONTRACT vol 9(1) (Reissue) PARA 841 et seq.

415. Sufficiency of consideration. A consideration is sufficient if it has some
value and is not merely illusory[1]. Mere employment at will is a sufficient
consideration[2]; so is the continuation of an existing employment at will[3]. If the
covenantor is already in the employment of the covenantee at the date of the
covenant, it will depend upon the particular circumstances of the case whether
the covenant was really a part of the contract of service[4], and even if it was not,
there appears to be sufficient consideration in the fact that if the employee
refused to sign the covenant the employer might take the first opportunity of
legally determining the service[5].

When once it is established that there is a consideration of some value, the
court will not inquire into its adequacy[6]. However, the quantum of the
consideration may be relevant when determining the reasonableness of the
agreement[7], and the one-sidedness of an agreement may be a ground for striking
it down[8].

1   *Austen v Boys* (1858) 2 De G & J 626 at 637 per Lord Chelmsford LC (affg (1857) 24 Beav
    598); *Benwell v Inns* (1857) 24 Beav 307, where, on an agreement to employ for one month and
    thereafter at one month's notice at such wages as might from time to time be agreed upon, it was
    held that there was sufficient consideration; *Hood and Moore's Stores Ltd v Jones* (1899) 81 LT
    169, where it was held that commission in addition to wages is consideration, as is the mere
    continuation of a pre-existing engagement. In the case of a waiter who receives tips, 4 shillings
    a week was not merely a colourable consideration: *Howard v Danner* (1901) 17 TLR 548.
    Employment at one or two weeks' notice is sufficient consideration, even in the case of a
    covenantor who is a minor: *Cornwall v Hawkins* (1872) 41 LJCh 435; *Fellows v Wood* (1888)
    59 LT 513; *Evans v Ware* [1892] 3 Ch 502 at 504.
2   *Davis v Mason* (1793) 5 Term Rep 118; *Sainter v Ferguson* (1849) 7 CB 716 at 726 per
    Wilde CJ; *Gravely v Barnard* (1874) LR 18 Eq 518; *Cooper v Southgate* (1894) 10 R 552 at
    553, DC, per Wright J.
3   *Gravely v Barnard* (1874) LR 18 Eq 518; cf *Hitchcock v Coker* (1837) 6 Ad & El 438, Ex Ch,
    where the covenantor entered into the covenant after he had entered the service of the
    covenantee.
4   See *Mumford v Gething* (1859) 7 CBNS 305, where the covenantor orally agreed to serve as a
    traveller, it being understood that the agreement was to be reduced to writing; having served for
    three or four weeks the covenantor then sighted the covenant, and it was held that until then the
    employment was only inchoate, and that if he had refused to sign the plaintiff could have
    refused to employ him; *Woodbridge & Sons v Bellamy* [1911] 1 Ch 326 at 332, CA, per Eve J,
    where an employer engaged an employee on 4 April, telling him to begin work on 17 April, and
    the covenant signed on 16 April was held to be part of the contract of service (the judgment was
    reversed in the Court of Appeal, but on another point). Cf EMPLOYMENT vol 39 (2009) PARA
    20.
5   *Woodbridge & Sons v Bellamy* [1911] 1 Ch 326 at 332–333, CA, per Eve J; but see *Coleborne
    v Kearns* (1912) 46 ILT 305 at 306, CA, per Holmes LJ. See also *Spink (Bournemouth) Ltd v*

Spink [1936] Ch 544 at 548, [1936] 1 All ER 597 at 600, where Luxmoore J expresses, obiter, the view that the release by an employer of an employee from a contract of service may be good consideration for a covenant then entered into by the employee. A contract by which a party is promised a pension so long as he does not enter a trade is as much in restraint of trade as one where a party contracts directly not to enter the trade: *Wyatt v Kreglinger and Fernau* [1933] 1 KB 793, CA, followed in *Bull v Pitney-Bones Ltd* [1966] 3 All ER 384, [1967] 1 WLR 273.

6   *Hitchcock v Coker* (1837) 6 Ad & El 438, Ex Ch, overruling on this point the previous cases in which the adequacy or fairness of the consideration had been regarded as matters to be taken into account, namely *Mitchel v Reynolds* (1711) 1 P Wms 181; *Davis v Mason* (1793) 5 Term Rep 118; *Gale v Reed* (1806) 8 East 80 at 86; *Homer v Ashford and Ainsworth* (1825) 3 Bing 322 at 327; *Horner v Graves* (1831) 7 Bing 735; *Young v Timmins* (1831) 1 Cr & J 331; and *Keppell v Bailey* (1834) 2 My & K 517 at 520. For the present rule see *Archer v Marsh* (1837) 6 Ad & El 959; *Leighton v Wales* (1838) 3 M & W 545; *Pilkington v Scott* (1846) 15 M & W 657; *Sainter v Ferguson* (1849) 7 CB 716 at 727 per Coltman J; *Tallis v Tallis* (1853) 1 E & B 391; *Gravely v Barnard* (1874) LR 18 Eq 518 at 522; *Middleton v Brown* (1878) 47 LJCh 411, CA; *Collins v Locke* (1879) 4 App Cas 674 at 686, PC; *Rousillon v Rousillon* (1880) 14 ChD 351 at 359, 363; *Davies v Davies* (1887) 36 ChD 359, CA; *Evans v Ware* [1892] 3 Ch 502; *Howard v Danner* (1901) 17 TLR 548; *Tivoli, Manchester, Ltd v Colley* (1904) 20 TLR 437; and cf *Price v Green* (1847) 16 M & W 346, Ex Ch; *Herbert Morris Ltd v Saxelby* [1916] 1 AC 688 at 707, HL, per Lord Parker of Waddington; *Attwood v Lamont* [1920] 3 KB 571 at 589, CA, per Younger LJ; *M & S Drapers (a firm) v Reynolds* [1956] 3 All ER 814, [1957] 1 WLR 9, CA. See also CONTRACT vol 9(1) (Reissue) PARA 736; and cf SPECIFIC PERFORMANCE vol 44(1) (Reissue) PARA 868.

7   *Nordenfelt v Maxim Nordenfelt Guns and Ammunition Co Ltd* [1894] AC 535 at 565, HL; *Amoco Australia Pty Ltd v Rocca Bros Motor Engineering Co Pty Ltd* [1975] AC 561 at 579, [1975] 1 All ER 968 at 978, PC; *Alec Lobb (Garages) Ltd v Total Oil GB Ltd* [1985] 1 All ER 303 at 309–310, [1985] 1 WLR 173 at 179, CA, per Dillon LJ, at 315 and 185 per Dunn LJ and at 319 and 191 per Waller LJ.

8   *A Schroeder Music Publishing Co Ltd v Macaulay* [1974] 3 All ER 616, [1974] 1 WLR 1308, HL; *Clifford Davis Management Ltd v WEA Records Ltd* [1975] 1 All ER 237, [1975] 1 WLR 61, CA.

416.   Partnership.

A partnership determinable at any time on one month's notice is a sufficient consideration for an agreement in restraint of trade[1]. Where a restraint is imposed on a retiring partner, the consideration is the whole of the partnership agreement[2].

1   *Leighton v Wales* (1838) 3 M & W 545.
2   *Austen v Boys* (1858) 2 De G & J 626 at 637 per Lord Chelmsford LC. As to when a partner will be restrained see PARTNERSHIP vol 79 (2008) PARAS 166 et seq, 213–215.

(vii) Parties and Assignees

417.   General principles.

The ordinary rules of contract apply to all questions as to parties to an agreement in restraint of trade[1], and it is necessary to notice here only restraints in contracts with minors, and assignment and devolution on death[2].

1   See CONTRACT vol 9(1) (Reissue) PARAS 604, 1079 et seq. A receiver and manager of a business has authority to enter into agreements with the employees containing covenants in restraint of trade: *Howard v Danner* (1901) 17 TLR 548; and see RECEIVERS vol 39(2) (Reissue) PARA 490.
2   See PARA 418 et seq.

418.   Minors.

A fair and reasonable restrictive covenant in a contract of service or apprenticeship entered into by a minor will be enforced against him after he comes of age[1], and the presence of a penalty or liquidated damages clause does not invalidate the whole agreement[2], but the burden lies on the covenantee to show that the contract as a whole is for the minor's benefit, and that the covenant is only what is usual in such cases[3].

A reasonably limited covenant is binding on a minor even though it contains restrictions which are void, if those restrictions can be severed[4] from the valid part of the covenant[5].

1   *Fellows v Wood* (1888) 59 LT 513, DC (dairyman; covenant by minor not to serve persons who were customers during term of service; time, two years; held for benefit of minor); *Evans v Ware* [1892] 3 Ch 502 (dairyman; covenant by minor not to compete; 5 miles; two years; held for minor's benefit); *Gadd v Thompson* [1911] 1 KB 304, DC (covenant by architect's apprentice; 10 miles; ten years; held reasonable) (following *Bromley v Smith* [1909] 2 KB 235 at 242); Cf *Leslie v Fitzpatrick* (1877) 3 QBD 229. If after coming of age a minor continues for a substantial time in the service of an employer under a contract void because it is not for his benefit, a new contract on the same terms will, apparently, be inferred, and its reasonableness will be decided by the rules applicable to an adult: *Hooper and Ashby v Willis* (1905) 21 TLR 691 per Kekewich J (affd (1906) 22 TLR 451, CA, but not on this point, as the restraint was held unreasonable irrespective of minority); cf *Cornwall v Hawkins* (1872) 41 LJCh 435; *Brown v Harper* (1893) 68 LT 488; see EMPLOYMENT vol 39 (2009) PARA 16. As to minors' contracts being binding if beneficial as a whole see *Roberts v Gray* [1913] 1 KB 520, CA; and BANKRUPTCY AND INDIVIDUAL INSOLVENCY vol 3(2) (2002 Reissue) PARA 12. Cf *Hooper and Ashby v Willis* (1905) 21 TLR 691, where it was held that a contract containing a restrictive covenant signed by an employee who was a minor but not by the employer, is not apparently a contract for the minor's benefit. As to the ages of minority and majority see generally CHILDREN AND YOUNG PERSONS vol 5(3) (2008 Reissue) PARAS 1–3.
    An injunction will not be granted to restrain a breach of a contract of apprenticeship during the apprenticeship (see CIVIL PROCEDURE vol 11 (2009) PARA 461), although an apprentice may be held liable to pay the premium as the price of necessaries (see *Walter v Everard* [1891] 2 QB 369, CA). It is not certain whether an injunction would be granted, during minority, to restrain a breach of a restrictive covenant in a contract of service: see *De Francesco v Barnum* (1890) 45 ChD 430; and *Gadd v Thompson* [1911] 1 KB 304 at 308, where Phillimore J said that the price of instruction of an apprentice who was a minor need not necessarily be money, but may consist in part of a restrictive covenant. In *Morrison Fleet & Co Ltd v Fletcher* (1900) 17 TLR 95, an injunction was granted by Sir Francis Jeune restraining a covenantor while apparently still under age, although the contract contained a liquidated damages clause. In *Richards v Whitham* (1892) 66 LT 695, CA, it was suggested that in the absence of a covenant by an articled clerk who was a minor, a person who had entered into a bond for securing that the clerk should not practise within a certain area and was sued on the bond might have a remedy over by injunction against the clerk. As to minors' contracts of apprenticeship see EMPLOYMENT vol 39 (2009) PARA 9.

2   *Morrison Fleet & Co Ltd v Fletcher* (1900) 17 TLR 95. Cf *Hayne v Burchell* (1890) 35 Sol Jo 88, CA, where such a clause was present in a minor's covenant but, there being no breach, the question was not raised.

3   *Sir WC Leng & Co Ltd v Andrews* [1909] 1 Ch 763 at 769, CA, per Cozens-Hardy MR, but the covenant was there held unreasonable even for an adult; cf *Leslie v Fitzpatrick* (1877) 3 QBD 229 at 232. In *Capes v Hutton* (1826) 2 Russ 357, an injunction was refused where in articles of clerkship to a solicitor, entered into by a minor, the minor covenanted not to practise within 12 miles, and his father covenanted that on coming of age he should enter into a bond to that effect, and, no bond having been executed, the covenantor broke the covenant after coming of age. But apparently the case was decided on the ground that the remedy, if any, lay against the father.

4   As to severability see PARAS 433–434.

5   *Bromley v Smith* [1909] 2 KB 235 at 242, explaining *Corn v Matthews* [1893] 1 QB 310 at 314, CA. If a stipulation in an apprenticeship deed makes the whole contract unfair to the minor, the whole contract is void, but 'the whole contract' means the whole contract so far as it was operative: *Bromley v Smith* at 243 per Channell J; cf *Gadd v Thompson* [1911] 1 KB 304, DC.

419.   Representatives and assignees. A covenant imposed for the protection of a business and its goodwill[1] is for the benefit of the business, and not merely of the individual covenantee. The benefit of it passes, therefore, to the representatives or assignees of the covenantee, whether they are expressly mentioned or not[2]. It forms part of the goodwill which passes on an assignment of the business[3], and it passes to the assignee of part of the business of the original covenantee[4].

However, on the construction of the covenant a different intention may appear; for instance, a covenant not to trade so as directly or indirectly to affect continuing partners is personal to those partners[5].

1   As to goodwill see PERSONAL PROPERTY vol 35 (Reissue) PARA 1206. See also PARTNERSHIP vol 79 (2008) PARA 213 et seq.
2   See PARA 403; and cf *Martin v Brunsden* (1894) 98 LT Jo 237, DC; *Hood and Moore's Stores Ltd v Jones* (1899) 81 LT 169 (plaintiffs the assignees of the covenantee); *Chafer Ltd v Lilley* [1947] LJR 231; *Marshall and Murray Ltd v Jones* (1913) 29 TLR 351, where, however, the restraint was as to customers served by and from a specified dairy, and it was held not to apply to customers of the same business transferred to another place; *Wessex Dairies Ltd v Smith* [1935] 2 KB 80, CA (plaintiffs sued as equitable assignees). As to tied house covenants in brewers' leases see LANDLORD AND TENANT vol 27(1) (2006 Reissue) PARA 546. See generally CONTRACT vol 9(1) (Reissue) PARAS 757–758; EXECUTORS AND ADMINISTRATORS vol 17(2) (Reissue) PARAS 335 et seq, 454 et seq.
3   *Jacoby v Whitmore* (1883) 49 LT 335 at 337, CA; *Showell v Winkup* (1889) 60 LT 389; *Batho v Tunks* [1892] WN 101; *John Bros Abergarw Brewery Co v Holmes* [1900] 1 Ch 188; *Townsend v Jarman* [1900] 2 Ch 698 at 703; *Welstead v Hadley* (1904) 21 TLR 165, CA; *Automobile Carriage Builders Ltd v Sayers* (1909) 101 LT 419. See also *Smith v Hawthorn* (1897) 76 LT 716. As to the sale of partnership goodwill generally see PARTNERSHIP vol 79 (2008) PARA 213 et seq.
4   *Benwell v Inns* (1857) 24 Beav 307; *Baines v Geary* (1887) 35 ChD 154 at 159.
5   *Davies v Davies* (1887) 36 ChD 359 at 388, 394, CA, where the covenant in question was in addition to a covenant intended to protect the goodwill (distinguishing *Jacoby v Whitmore* (1883) 49 LT 335, CA). For an instance of a covenant not to 'affect' a business being held bad see *Reeve v Marsh* (1906) 23 TLR 24. As to the burden of a restrictive covenant see *Bird v Lake* (1863) 1 Hem & M 111, 338. Cf *Cooke v Colcraft* (1773) 2 Wm Bl 856, where a personal representative was held not to be bound by the testator's covenant. It is submitted that, in principle, the burden of a covenant does not pass to the assignee of the covenantor, although there appears to be no reported case on the subject: see PARTNERSHIP vol 79 (2008) PARA 213 et seq. As to tied house covenants see LANDLORD AND TENANT vol 27(1) (2006 Reissue) PARA 546.

(viii)   Form, Construction and Certainty

A. IN GENERAL

420.   Application of ordinary rules. In construing a contract which is in restraint of trade the ordinary rules applicable to contracts must be applied[1]. No special formalities are required.

1   *Mills v Dunham* [1891] 1 Ch 576, CA; *Dubowski & Sons v Goldstein* [1896] 1 QB 478, CA; *Hood and Moore's Stores Ltd v Jones* (1899) 81 LT 169; *Haynes v Doman* [1899] 2 Ch 13, CA. As to the rules relating to the construction of contracts see DEEDS AND OTHER INSTRUMENTS vol 13 (2007 Reissue) PARA 164 et seq.

421.   Construction by context. The contract must first be construed without reference to legality or illegality[1]. Where a clause is ambiguous, the maxim 'ut res magis valeat quam pereat' will apply[2], and words which are general and might impose an unreasonable restraint have frequently, by reference to the context and the circumstances, been construed as having a limited meaning[3], but only where there is a real ambiguity[4].

1   *Konski v Peet* [1915] 1 Ch 530 at 538 per Neville J; *Clarke v Newland* [1991] 1 All ER 397 at 402, CA, per Neill LJ.

2 *Mills v Dunham* [1891] 1 Ch 576, CA; *Perls v Saalfeld* [1892] 2 Ch 149, CA; *Cattermoul v Jared* (1909) 53 Sol Jo 244. As to this maxim of construction (that it may be made operative rather than null) see DEEDS AND OTHER INSTRUMENTS vol 13 (2007 Reissue) PARA 177.

3 *Gale v Reed* (1806) 8 East 80, where a covenant against dealing with any persons except public bodies and to employ the covenantee exclusively to make all articles ordered by or for the covenantor's friends was held not to include persons whom the covenantor introduced but the covenantee refused to supply; *Avery v Langford* (1854) Kay 663, where it was held that the words 'any trading establishment' were limited to trade likely to interfere with that of the covenantee; *King v Hansell* (1860) 5 H & N 106, where a covenant general in terms as to time was construed as being limited to the term of the covenantor's service; *Rousillon v Rousillon* (1880) 14 ChD 351, where 'the champagne trade' was construed to mean the importing and exporting of wines from Champagne and not necessarily to include also the making of wine in Champagne; *Hayne v Burchell* (1890) 35 Sol Jo 88, CA, where 'client' was construed as client during term of articles, 'business' was construed as business of a solicitor and 'being a client' construed as being a person habitually employing the solicitor; *Mills v Dunham* [1891] 1 Ch 576, CA, where 'transact business' was held to refer to business similar to that of the covenantee; *Moenich v Fenestre* (1892) 67 LT 602, CA, where 'any trade or business' was held to mean any trade or business of a commission merchant and 'at any time previously' was held to refer only to the term at the covenantor's employment; *Dubowski & Sons v Goldstein* [1896] 1 QB 478, CA, where 'the said business' was construed as the business then carried on at a certain place; *Haynes v Doman* [1899] 2 Ch 13, CA, where a covenant not to engage in the plaintiff's business with a limited class of people mentioned in the agreement was held reasonable; *Hood and Moore's Stores Ltd v Jones* (1899) 81 LT 169, where 'business' was held to mean business of the same nature as that in which the covenantor was employed; *Barr v Craven* (1903) 89 LT 574, CA, where 'the business' was construed as the business of the agency in the locality worked by the covenantor, an insurance agent; *Reeve v Marsh* (1906) 23 TLR 24, where a covenant not to affect or interfere with or prejudice a business was held not to prohibit the setting up of a rival business; *Lewis and Lewis v Durnford* (1907) 24 TLR 64, where a covenant not to act as a solicitor for any person who is or has within the previous five years been a client of the covenantees was held to refer to clients at the time of termination of the service or within five years before; *Mouchel v Cubitt & Co* (1907) 24 RPC 194, where 'at any time' was held to be limited to the period of a licence (see also *Bescol (Electric) Ltd v Merlin Mouldings Ltd* (1952) 69 RPC 297; and PATENTS AND REGISTERED DESIGNS vol 79 (2008) PARA 511); *Cattermoul v Jared* (1909) 53 Sol Jo 244, where 'house' was construed as public house; *Gaumont-British Picture Corpn Ltd v Alexander* [1936] 2 All ER 1686, where a clause general in terms was held to be limited to the period of service; *CW Plowman & Son Ltd v Ash* [1964] 2 All ER 10, [1964] 1 WLR 568, CA (covenant confined to non-solicitation in respect of goods which were the subject of the defendant's employment); *Home Counties Dairies Ltd v Skilton* [1970] 1 All ER 1227, [1970] 1 WLR 526, CA (covenant confined to employment of a milk roundsman by dairymen); *Littlewoods Organisation Ltd v Harris* [1978] 1 All ER 1026, [1977] 1 WLR 1472, CA, where a covenant not to enter into a contract of service with a rival organisation carrying on various businesses in many countries was construed as limited to the organisation's mail order business carried on in the United Kingdom; *Business Seating (Renovations) Ltd v Broad* [1989] ICR 729; *Clarke v Newland* [1991] 1 All ER 397, CA. See also *Putsman v Taylor* [1927] 1 KB 637 at 647, DC, per Talbot J (on appeal [1927] 1 KB 741, CA); and cf *Kimberley v Jennings* (1836) 6 Sim 340; *Southland Frozen Meat and Produce Export Co Ltd v Nelson Bros Ltd* [1898] AC 442, PC. As to the extent to which a proviso against the covenantee's unreasonably withholding consent will validate an otherwise over-wide restriction see *Chafer Ltd v Lilley* [1947] LJR 231; and cf *Perls v Saalfeld* [1892] 2 Ch 149, CA; *Kerchiss v Colora Printing Inks Ltd* [1960] RPC 235.

4 *Konski v Peet Ltd* [1915] 1 Ch 530 at 538 per Neville J, where the court refused to construe a covenant against soliciting customers generally as a covenant against soliciting customers during the covenantor's employment. See also *Mumford v Gething* (1859) 7 CBNS 305, where the court refused to limit a restraint in general terms to the term of the covenantor's service; *Baker v Hedgecock* (1888) 39 ChD 520, where the court declined to put a limited meaning on 'any business whatsoever'; *Ehrman v Bartholomew* [1898] 1 Ch 671, where prohibition against acting in any other business during the period of employment, namely ten years, was held bad; *Marshalls Ltd v Leek* (1900) 17 TLR 26, where the court refused to limit a restraint in general terms to the period of the covenantor's service; *Continental Tyre and Rubber (Great Britain) Co Ltd v Heath* (1913) 29 TLR 308 at 310, where a restraint as to sale of india-rubber goods was held not too wide for tyre manufacturers; *SV Nevanas & Co Ltd v Walker and Foreman* [1914] 1 Ch 413, where the court refused to construe a restraint from importing meat in general terms as a restraint from importing meat from Australia, the trade to be protected;

Eastes v Russ [1914] 1 Ch 468, CA, where the court refused to limit a general restraint from engaging in similar work to the period of covenantor's service; *Vandervell Products Ltd v McLeod* [1957] RPC 185, CA, where the court declined to construe 'competitors', as limited to competitors in the line of business covered by trade secrets. See also *Commercial Plastics Ltd v Vincent* [1965] 1 QB 623, [1964] 3 All ER 546, CA; and c f *Mason v Provident Clothing and Supply Co Ltd* [1913] AC 724 at 742, HL, per Lord Shaw of Dunfermline; *JA Mont (UK) Ltd v Mills* [1993] IRLR 172, CA.

422. Ordinary meaning of words. Words must be construed in their ordinary business meaning[1]. The ordinary rules for the construction of contracts[2] apply in determining, for instance, whether a covenant in restraint of trade is joint or joint and several[3], whether a minor is or is not bound[4], whether oral evidence may be admitted to prove that a term has a secondary meaning[5], whether the contract may be rescinded or rectified[6], or whether the agreement is harsh and unconscionable[7].

1   *William Cory & Son Ltd v Harrison* [1906] AC 274, HL. As to the meaning of 'London' see *Sutcliffe and Bingham Ltd v Holwill* (1912) 134 LT Jo 156; *Provident Clothing and Supply Co Ltd v Mason* [1913] 1 KB 65 at 75, CA, per Buckley LJ (revsd sub nom *Mason v Provident Clothing and Supply Co Ltd* [1913] AC 724, HL, but apparently without affecting this point); and DEEDS AND OTHER INSTRUMENTS vol 13 (2007 Reissue) PARA 164 et seq.
2   As to the construction of contracts generally see DEEDS AND OTHER INSTRUMENTS vol 13 (2007 Reissue) PARA 164 et seq.
3   *Palmer v Mallet* (1887) 36 ChD 411, CA; and see CONTRACT vol 9(1) (Reissue) PARA 1083.
4   See PARA 418; BANKRUPTCY AND INDIVIDUAL INSOLVENCY vol 3(2) (2002 Reissue) PARA 12; and EMPLOYMENT vol 39 (2009) PARA 16.
5   *Lovell and Christmas Ltd v Wall* (1911) 104 LT 85, CA; and see PARA 391 text and notes 2–3; and DEEDS AND OTHER INSTRUMENTS vol 13 (2007 Reissue) PARA 185 et seq.
6   *Lovell and Christmas Ltd v Wall* (1911) 104 LT 85, CA. See MISREPRESENTATION AND FRAUD vol 31 (2003 Reissue) PARA 814 et seq; MISTAKE vol 32 (2005 Reissue) PARA 55 et seq.
7   *Middleton v Brown* (1878) 47 LJCh 411, CA; c f *Kimberley v Jennings* (1836) 6 Sim 340; *Croft v Haw* (1836) 5 LJCh 305. Mere inadequacy of consideration is, however, no objection: see PARA 415. As to oppressiveness of contract see further SPECIFIC PERFORMANCE vol 44(1) (Reissue) PARA 863 et seq.

423. Certainty. The agreement in restraint of trade must not be too vague[1], and the parties cannot leave it to the court to frame their agreement to meet a particular breach[2].

1   *Catt v Tourle* (1869) 4 Ch App 654, where a tied house covenant in a brewer's lease was not void for uncertainty; *Stride v Martin* (1897) 77 LT 600, DC, where a covenant was taken on the sale of a milk business and it was held that 'in the neighbourhood' meant in the immediate neighbourhood, where there could be competition, and the covenant was not too vague; *Marshalls Ltd v Leek* (1900) 17 TLR 26, where the covenant was not to enter into business competition either for himself or as manager or assistant, and it was held not too vague; *Barr v Craven* (1903) 89 LT 574, CA, where a covenant by an insurance agent 'not to interfere directly or indirectly with any of the business' was held limited to business in a particular locality, and the injunction was limited to procuring transfers from the covenantees to a rival society of policies which were in the agent's books during his employment; *Connors Bros Ltd v Connors* [1940] 4 All ER 179 at 189, PC, where 'directly or indirectly engaged in the sardine business' was held not too vague; *Beetham v Fraser* (1904) 21 TLR 8, DC, where a covenant not to enter into any business arrangement in competition that would in any way interfere with the business of the covenantee was held too vague (although apparently similar words may be operative in modifying a covenant otherwise too wide: *Leather Cloth Co v Lorsont* (1869) LR 9 Eq 345 at 355); *Reeve v Marsh* (1906) 23 TLR 24, where a covenant not to 'interfere with, prejudice or in any manner affect' a business was regarded as too vague, although the case was decided on the ground that it did not forbid the setting up of a rival business; *Coleborne v Kearns* (1912) 46 ILT 305, CA, where the words 'should we leave your employment' were considered too vague; and c f *Maxim Nordenfelt Guns and Ammunition Co v Nordenfelt* (1892) as reported in 67 LT 469 at 471, where a covenant to give the exclusive benefit of all new inventions and improvements and to communicate all such innovations was held not too vague; *Mason v*

Provident Clothing and Supply Co Ltd [1913] AC 724, HL; see CONTRACT vol 9(1) (Reissue) PARA 672; DEEDS AND OTHER INSTRUMENTS vol 13 (2007 Reissue) PARAS 208–209, 214–216.

2   A covenant to retire from a trade 'so far as the law allows' is void: *Davies v Davies* (1887) 36 ChD 359, CA; see CONTRACT vol 9(1) (Reissue) PARA 672.

424.   Covenants in restraint not 'usual covenants'.   Covenants in restraint of trade in a lease of premises in a trading locality are not 'usual covenants'[1], and a covenant on the sale of a business restricting the vendor from carrying on a like business is not mere common form, and a demand for such a covenant amounts to a reopening of negotiations[2].

1   *Propert v Parker* (1832) 3 My & K 280; see LANDLORD AND TENANT vol 27(1) (2006 Reissue) PARA 83.
2   *Bristol, Cardiff and Swansea Aerated Bread Co v Maggs* (1890) 44 ChD 616.

425.   Waiver and release.   It is no breach of a covenant in restraint of trade if the act complained of is done with the assent and for the benefit of the assignee[1].

A consent given on one occasion to the covenantor's engaging in the trade is not a release of the covenant for the future[2].

1   *Rawlinson v Clarke* (1845) 14 M & W 187. See also *Maythorn v Palmer* (1864) 11 LT 261.
2   *Showell v Winkup* (1889) 60 LT 389, where a covenant by a brewer's traveller, limited as to area and time, was not released by an agreement by the covenantees that the covenantor should be employed by a company to which they sold their business. As to waiver and release generally see CONTRACT vol 9(1) (Reissue) PARAS 1025–1029 (waiver), 1052–1054 (release).

B.   PARTICULAR CASES

426.   Meaning of 'similar business'.   In deciding whether a person is engaged in a business similar to another business, the test is whether his business is so like the other as seriously to compete with it[1].

1   *Drew v Guy* [1894] 3 Ch 25, CA, where in relation to a covenant in a lease, the supply of chops, steaks etc was held to be similar to the supply of hot meals and alcoholic drinks; *Castelli v Middleton* (1901) 17 TLR 373, where the covenant not to compete was given by the vendor of a business of manufacturing annatto (a vegetable colouring matter) and food preservatives, who then engaged in a business mainly concerned in manufacturing dairy utensils, but also to a limited extent in selling by retail annatto and food preservatives, chiefly bought wholesale from the covenantee, and was held to be engaged in a competing business; *Automobile Carnage Builders Ltd v Sayers* (1909) 101 LT 419. See *Provident Clothing and Supply Co Ltd v Mason* [1913] 1 KB 65 at 70–71, CA, per Vaughan Williams LJ (revsd, but not on this point, sub nom *Mason v Provident Clothing and Supply Co Ltd* [1913] AC 724, HL); and *Vandervell Products Ltd v McLeod* [1957] RPC 185, CA (meaning of 'competitors').

427.   Directors, managers and creditors as persons carrying on or interested in a business.   A person who is a director of a company carrying on a business carries on or is engaged, concerned or interested in that business[1].

A person who is engaged as an assistant or manager at a fixed salary not depending on profits or gross returns is not 'directly or indirectly interested' in the business[2] since an 'interest' means a proprietary or pecuniary interest[3], although it does not include a person who is merely a creditor of a person who carries on the business[4]; nor is such an assistant or manager thereby 'exercising or carrying on' a business[5], but he is 'engaged' or 'concerned' in it[6].

1   *Castelli v Middleton* (1901) 17 TLR 373. As to the meaning of 'carry on business' see generally PARAS 370–372.
2   *Gophir Diamond Co v Wood* [1902] 1 Ch 950, applying *Smith v Hancock* [1894] 2 Ch 377, CA. Cf *Newling v Dobell* (1868) 38 LJCh 111 at 112 per Malins V-C.

3   *Smith v Hancock* [1894] 2 Ch 377 at 386, 390, CA; *Gophir Diamond Co v Wood* [1902]
    1 Ch 950. Cf *George Hill & Co v Hill* (1886) 35 WR 137, where it was held that 'interested'
    means entitled to profits, and 'concerned' means having something to do with it. See also *Batts
    Combe Quarry Ltd v Ford* [1943] Ch 51, [1942] 2 All ER 639, CA; and note 4.

4   *William Cory & Son Ltd v Harrison* [1906] AC 274, HL. Cf *Bird v Lake* (1863) 1 Hem & M
    111, 338; *Smith v Hancock* [1894] 2 Ch 377, CA (see earlier proceedings [1894] 1 Ch 209 at
    217 per Kekewich J); *Southland Frozen Meat and Produce Export Co Ltd v Nelson Bros Ltd*
    [1898] AC 442 at 446, PC. However, a person who lends money on the terms of receiving as
    interest a share of the profits of a business is 'directly or indirectly engaged' in that business
    (*Cooper v Page* (1876) 34 LT 90), and a person who provides the capital free of charge 'assists
    in carrying on' or is 'concerned with' the business (*Batts Combe Quarry Ltd v Ford* [1943]
    Ch 51, [1942] 2 All ER 639, CA, where 'employed' was held to cover negotiating for initial
    equipment).

5   *Clark v Watkins* (1863) 11 WR 319, where a chemist's assistant covenanted not to carry on the
    business 'in his own name or for his own benefit or in the name or names or for the benefit of
    any person or persons in D', and it was held no breach to act as an employee and to take orders
    within the area for persons carrying on business outside the area; *Allen v Taylor* (1870) 18 WR
    888 (on appeal 19 WR 35 at 36 per Lord Hatherley LC), where on the sale of the business of a
    rag merchant the covenant was not to 'exercise or carry on the trade ... either in his own name
    or that of any other person'; *Graham v Lewis* (1888) 22 QBD 1, CA, where it was held that a
    solicitor's clerk did not 'carry on business' in the City of London for the purpose of jurisdiction
    of the former Mayor's Court. As to the meaning of 'carry on business' in relation to bankruptcy
    see BANKRUPTCY AND INDIVIDUAL INSOLVENCY vol 3(2) (2002 Reissue) PARA 125.

6   *Rolfe v Rolfe* (1846) 15 Sim 88 at 90, where on the dissolution of a tailor's partnership the
    covenant was not to engage in tailoring, either alone or with any other person, and it was held
    to be a breach to act as foreman to a tailor; *Newling v Dobell* (1868) 19 LT 408, where on the
    sale of a tailor's business the covenant was not to carry on or be concerned or interested in a
    tailoring business, and it was held to be a breach when the covenantor took employment as a
    journeyman with a nephew; *Jones v Heavens* (1877) 4 ChD 636, where the covenant was not to
    carry on or be concerned in carrying on the business of a saddler, or to sell goods in any way
    connected with that trade, and it was held to be a breach to act as a journeyman; *Baxter v Lewis*
    (1886) 30 Sol Jo 705, 754, where a covenant, given on the sale of a tobacconist's business, not
    to carry on or be concerned directly or indirectly with such a business was held breached when
    the covenantor first became manager for a company, and then a shopman, there being a strong
    suspicion of bad faith; *George Hill & Co v Hill* (1886) 35 WR 137, where on the sale of a
    butcher's business a covenant not to 'engage in or be in any way concerned or interested in' any
    similar business was held to be breached by employment in the business; *Watts v Smith* (1890)
    62 LT 453, where a covenant by a draper's assistant not to engage in a similar business was
    breached by becoming an assistant at a salary; *Cade v Calfe* (1906) 22 TLR 243, where a
    covenant not to be 'directly or indirectly engaged, concerned or interested' was held breached by
    entering into the service of another; *Cavendish v Tarry* (1908) 52 Sol Jo 726, where a covenant
    not to be 'concerned or interested' was broken by becoming a weekly servant; *Pearks Ltd v
    Cullen* (1912) 28 TLR 371, where a covenant not to be engaged in business was held broken by
    being employed as an assistant; but the whole covenant was held bad. However, in
    Ramoneur Co Ltd v Brixey (1911) 104 LT 809, DC, a covenant by a chimney sweep not to
    undertake any work or orders of any kind except for the covenantees, or to carry on or be
    concerned in the business either by himself or in conjunction with any person, was held not to
    apply to employment as a servant. Cf *Dales v Weaber* (1870) 18 WR 993, where 'with the
    assistance of any other person' was held to mean as assistant of any other person where the
    covenantor had set up a business in the area of restraint, and then sold that business to another
    person and became his manager. In *Lievre v Mayonnet* (1913) 2 LJCCR 4 it was held that 'not
    to teach or give instructions nor advertise himself as a teacher of any language' did not mean set
    up for himself only; to enter the service of another was a breach.

428. Person practising as solicitor or surgeon. A solicitor acting as managing
clerk at a fixed salary to another solicitor is not practising as a solicitor[1],
although a person acting as assistant to a surgeon may be carrying on the
profession of a surgeon[2].

1   *Way v Bishop* [1928] Ch 647, CA, distinguishing *Palmer v Mallet* (1887) 36 ChD 411, CA, and
    criticising *Robertson v Willmott* (1909) 25 TLR 681. See further PARA 432 note 67.

2 *Palmer v Mallet* (1887) 36 ChD 411, CA, distinguishing *Allen v Taylor* (1871) 19 WR 556. See further PARA 432 note 27.

429.   Business carried on by husband or wife. A man does not carry on and is not interested in a business which is carried on in good faith by, and belongs to, his wife[1], nor is a woman interested or concerned in a business by marrying a man who carries it on and assisting him in it[2].

1 *Smith v Hancock* [1894] 2 Ch 377, CA (even though he helps her by writing a circular inviting 'old friends' to be customers, and by introducing her to dealers, and in other ways). Apparently, he is not 'interested' by merely taking a friendly interest in forwarding a business set up by a stranger (see *Smith v Hancock* at 391 per AL Smith LJ); but apparently, it is not unreasonable to require a covenantor 'not to induce or assist any other person to commence the business' (*Lyddon v Thomas* (1901) 17 TLR 450, where such a covenant, inter alia, was held reasonable).
2 *Loe v Lardner* (1856) 4 WR 597 (licensed house).

430.   Business falling within particular description. Where the question is whether the covenantor is carrying on a certain specified trade or business, the words describing the trade or business must be taken in their ordinary business meaning subject to the general rules applicable as to the admission of evidence of a secondary meaning[1].

Although the subject matter may be the same, the business of a merchant or dealer is distinct from that of a manufacturer[2] and the business of a stockbroker from that of a stockdealer[3], but the selling of goods wholesale is not a business distinct from the selling of the same goods retail[4].

1 *May v O'Neill* (1875) 44 LJCh 660, where it was held that the business of a solicitor includes practice in every court in which a solicitor may appear, including a court in which he has to enter his name specially on a roll before practising; *McFarlane v Hilton* [1899] 1 Ch 884, where a covenant not to publish a sporting paper was not broken by publication of a paper recording amateur sports, but with no racing intelligence or betting odds. As to the meaning of a covenant by a retiring partner not to attend as a dentist any patients of the remaining partners see *Harris v Mansbridge* (1900) 17 TLR 21. See also *Bowler v Lovegrove* [1921] 1 Ch 642, where it was held that the defendant by carrying on the business of an estate agent committed no breach of a covenant not to carry on the business of auctioneers and estate agents. As to the sale of liquor see LANDLORD AND TENANT vol 27(1) (2006 Reissue) PARA 505. As to the general rules for the admission of evidence of a secondary meaning see DEEDS AND OTHER INSTRUMENTS vol 13 (2007 Reissue) PARA 198 et seq.
2 *Josselyn v Parson* (1872) LR 7 Exch 127, where a covenant not to travel for any porter, ale or spirit merchant was held not to be breached by travelling for a brewer, for a merchant is one who buys and sells, not one who sells his own manufactures; *Lovell and Christmas Ltd v Wall* (1911) 104 LT 85, CA, deciding that 'provision merchant' includes a margarine dealer, but not a margarine manufacturer, even though he sells his products within the area of restraint. See also *Automobile Carriage Builders Ltd v Sayers* (1909) 101 LT 419, where a covenant with motor carriage builders not to carry on or be engaged in any business 'similar to or including the business' of the covenantees was held to be broken by selling motor carriages, although the covenantor contended that he did not manufacture, but he had held himself out as a manufacturer; but cf *Harms v Parsons* (1862) 32 Beav 328, where a covenant not to carry on the trade of a horsehair manufacturer was held to cover buying and selling manufactured horsehair; *Castelli v Middleton* (1901) 17 TLR 373; and PARA 369 note 3.
3 The proposition was admitted without argument in *Lyddon v Thomas* (1901) 17 TLR 450.
4 *Rogers v Maddocks* [1892] 3 Ch 346, CA.

431.   Carrying on business within prohibited area. A solicitor does not carry on business in an area by writing from outside the area to persons, and on behalf of persons, within it[1], although he carries on business or practises within an area if he appears regularly at courts in the area[2]. Nor does he 'take away clients' from another solicitor if he acts for persons who have been clients of the other but have left him[3].

A doctor who attends a few patients at their own request within the area of restraint, but has no residence or premises there, does not 'set up in practice' there, but he does 'practise' there[4], and it seems that a trader who applies for orders or supplies goods within an area carries on business there, even though he has no premises there[5].

An estate agent who advertises houses within the area of restraint and puts up his boards on them carries on the business of an estate agent within the area[6].

A person does not carry on, and is not interested or concerned in, a business within an area by merely acting, outside the area, for a person carrying on business within it[7]; but a newspaper is published within an area, if substantial numbers are distributed from an office in that area, even though the chief place of printing and publishing is outside the area[8].

1   *Woodbridge & Sons v Bellamy* [1911] 1 Ch 326 at 336, CA, per Cozens-Hardy MR; see further at 338 per Fletcher Moulton LJ ('carry on business' refers to that which a solicitor does at his place of business), distinguishing *Edmundson v Render* [1905] 2 Ch 320, where the covenant was not to do within the area any work or act usually done by solicitors, and where it was held by Buckley J a breach for the covenantor, instructed outside the area, to send a solicitor's letter to a person within the area; a demand made, or advice given, by letter is an act done at the address of the addressee, and the post office is the agent of the sender. See also *Edmundson v Render* (1904) 90 LT 814, where the covenant was the same as above, but different breaches were alleged and where it was held by Kekewich J as follows: to obtain probate of the will of a person who died within the area is apparently a breach; to correspond with a witness within the area for the purpose of obtaining probate of a will of a person who died without the area is apparently not a breach; to advertise the letting of a farm within the area in a paper published outside, but circulating within, the area, is not a breach; to take proceedings in a county court within the area, although without attending there either in person or by a clerk, is a breach, for the district judge is the agent of the claimant's solicitor for the purpose; to attend at the execution of a will within the area is a breach unless, apparently, done as a friendly act without fee; but it is no breach to prepare a will for a person within the area on instructions received outside the area, and to send it for execution within the area. Cf *Freeman v Fox* (1911) 55 Sol Jo 650, where a covenant not to practise or act as a solicitor was held not to be broken by doing one act of a solicitor and writing several letters to persons within the area.
2   *Llewellyn v Simpson* (1891) 91 LT Jo 9.
3   *Hayne v Burchell* (1890) 35 Sol Jo 88, CA. Where solicitors in partnership agree that on dissolution neither is to do business with 'original clients' of the other, 'original clients' comprise those who were clients of either before the partnership and those who during the partnership were by arrangement particularly the clients of either: *Badham v Williams* (1900) 83 LT 141.
4   *Robertson v Buchanan* (1904) 73 LJCh 408, CA. However, apparently, it would be 'setting up in practice' to drive regularly round the area (*Robertson v Buchanan* at 410 per Vaughan Williams LJ), or to attend a large number of patients at their invitation (at 411 per Stirling LJ). In *Rogers v Drury* (1887) 57 LJCh 504, a doctor who had covenanted not to practise or reside in the area or otherwise directly or indirectly to enter into competition with the purchaser of his practice was held to have committed a breach by attending patients who summoned him and stated that in no event would they have called in the purchaser; but a dentist retiring from partnership who covenants not to attend any patients of the other partners may attend such persons as during the partnership were particularly his patients (*Harris v Mansbridge* (1900) 17 TLR 21), and, apparently, a dentist who by his articles of partnership is on dissolution in certain circumstances expressly entitled to practise may attend patients of the old firm, but it is uncertain whether he may solicit such patients (*Clifford v Philhips* (1907) 51 Sol Jo 748). Cf PARTNERSHIP vol 79 (2008) PARA 213 et seq.
5   *Turner v Evans* (1852) 2 De GM & G 740, where on the sale of a wine merchant's business the vendor covenanted never 'by himself, his partner or agent, or otherwise howsoever, either directly or indirectly' to 'set up, embark in, or carry on' the business; *Brampton v Beddoes* (1863) 13 CBNS 538, where a covenant given on the sale of a drapery business not to carry on or assist in carrying on such a business was held breached by supplying customers within the area from a place beyond it. Apparently a stockbroker who has covenanted not to carry on business within an area may start an office outside the area and deal with clients within it, but not tout for clients within the area: *Lyddon v Thomas* (1901) 17 TLR 450 per Farwell J.
6   *Hadsley v Dayer-Smith* [1914] AC 979 at 984, HL, per Lord Shaw of Dunfermline.

7   *Fairbrother v England* (1891) 40 WR 220, where in respect of a covenant given on the dissolution of an auctioneers' and estate agents' partnership not to carry on 'directly or indirectly on his own account or as agent or assistant of or in partnership with, any other person', or to be 'interested or concerned', it was no breach to advertise outside the area houses within the area on behalf of a person carrying on business within the area.

8   *McFarlane v Hulton* [1899] 1 Ch 884.

432.   Instances of covenants affecting particular trades, businesses and professions.   Restrictive covenants have been considered by the courts in relation, inter alia, to the following trades, businesses and professions: accountant[1], actor[2], advertising agency[3], agent and commercial traveller[4], architect and surveyor[5], auctioneer and estate agent[6], author[7], baker[8], bank manager and clerk[9], barrister practising in place where the professions of barrister and solicitor are fused[10], bill-poster[11], bookmaker[12], boxer[13], brass-founder[14], brewer[15], butcher[16], car salesman[17], carrier[18], cashier[19], cheesemonger[20], chemist[21], chimney-sweep[22], dairyman and milk seller[23], dancer[24], debt collector[25], dentist[26], doctor and surgeon[27], draper and hosier[28], dry cleaner[29], dyer[30], employment agency[31], financial services[32], film actor[33], fishmonger[34], garage proprietor[35], glass maker[36], glove maker[37], greengrocer and fruiterer[38], grocer[39], hairdresser[40], insurance company[41], jeweller[42], laboratory assistant[43], mail order business[44], manufacturer[45], merchant and dealer[46], milliner[47], motor coach proprietor[48], music hall artiste[49], newspaper proprietor, reporter or employee[50], newspaper seller[51], oil and colourman[52], opera singer[53], optician[54], patent agent[55], patentee[56], perfumer[57], petrol filling station owner[58], photographer[59], publican[60], publisher[61], restaurant keeper[62], retail dealer[63], rope maker[64], saddler[65], schoolmaster and teacher[66], solicitor[67], song writer[68], stage coach proprietor[69], stevedore[70], stockbroker[71], tailor[72], tally-man[73], tobacconist[74], trade protection society or association[75], undertaker[76] and waiter[77].

1   *Brown v Harper* (1893) 68 LT 488 (clients during the term of service; no time limit; covenantor a minor; good); *Isitt and Jenks v Ganson* (1899) 107 LT Jo 423 (England; seven years; good); cf *D Bates & Co v Dale* [1937] 3 All ER 650 (15 miles; 15 years; bad).

2   *Lumley v Wagner* (1852) 1 De GM & G 604; and see LICENSING AND GAMBLING vol 67 (2008) PARA 237.

3   *Rex Stewart Jeffries Parker Ginsberg Ltd v Parker* [1988] IRLR 483, CA.

4   *Homer v Ashford and Ainsworth* (1825) 3 Bing 322 (stated towns; 14 years; question of consideration); *Kimberley v Jennings* (1836) 6 Sim 340 (restraint during term of service); *Mumford v Gething* (1859) 7 CBNS 305 (travelling for rival over same ground; no time limit; good); *King v Hansell* (1860) 5 H & N 106 (term of service); *Josselyn v Parson* (1872) LR 7 Exch 127 (25 miles; 12 months; question of breach only); *Allsopp v Wheatcroft* (1872) LR 15 Eq 59 (no limit of space; two years; bad); *Middleton v Brown* (1878) 47 LJCh 411, CA (8 miles; 12 months; good); *Rousillon v Rousillon* (1880) 14 ChD 351 (see note 46); *Parsons v Cotterill* (1887) 56 LT 839 (see note 46); *Showell v Winkup* (1889) 60 LT 389 (20 miles; two years; good); *Mills v Dunham* [1891] 1 Ch 576, CA (customers during term of service; good); *Moenich v Fenestre* (1892) 67 LT 602, CA (competing business in United Kingdom; five years; good); *Perls v Saalfeld* [1892] 2 Ch 149, CA (15 miles; three years; bad as applying to all businesses whatever); *Rogers v Maddocks* [1892] 3 Ch 346, CA (100 miles; two years; good, but part severable); *Badische Anilin und Soda Fabrik v Schott, Segner & Co* [1892] 3 Ch 447 (no limit of space; three years; good); *General Accident Assurance Corpn v Noel* [1902] 1 KB 377 (50 miles; one year; good; question of election between damages and injunction); *Barr v Craven* (1903) 89 LT 574, CA (district in which agent had acted; no time limit; good); *Henry Leetham & Sons Ltd v Johnstone-White* [1907] 1 Ch 322, CA (United Kingdom and Ireland; five years; bad; question as to restraint in gross; see PARA 389); *Morris & Co v Ryle* (1910) 103 LT 545, CA (sale of any goods whatever to, or any dealings with, persons whom covenantor called on during term of service; five years; bad); *Stuart and Simpson v Halstead* (1911) 55 Sol Jo 598 (United Kingdom; no time limit; bad); *Sutcliffe and Bingham Ltd v Holwill* (1912) 134 LT Jo 156 (districts in which covenantor travelled for covenantees; 12 months; good; meaning of 'London'); *Coleborne*

v Kearns (1912) 46 ILT 305, CA (meaning of 'leave employment'); *Mason v Provident Clothing and Supply Co Ltd* [1913] AC 724, HL (25 miles of London where the covenantees carry on business; three years; bad); *Continental Tyre and Rubber (Great Britain) Co Ltd v Heath* (1913) 29 TLR 308 (United Kingdom, Germany or France; one year; 'india-rubber goods whether wholesale or retail'; good as to United Kingdom; Germany and France severable); *Chafer Ltd v Lilley* [1947] LJR 231 (business in Wisbech district; throughout United Kingdom; area too wide); *M & S Drapers (a firm) v Reynolds* [1956] 3 All ER 814, [1957] 1 WLR 9, CA (five years; bad); *GW Plowman & Son Ltd v Ash* [1964] 2 All ER 10, [1964] 1 WLR 568, CA (customers during term of service; two years; good; it was not an objection that the covenant might cover persons who had ceased to be customers before end of period of service); *Gledhow Autoparts Ltd v Delaney* [1965] 3 All ER 288, [1965] 1 WLR 1366, CA (area restraint; three years; the restraint covered many garages which never became customers of the employer and on which the traveller might never have called; bad); *T Lucas & Co Ltd v Mitchell* [1972] 2 All ER 1035, [1972] 1 WLR 938 (area restraint; bad since the covenant against soliciting or supplying to customers would have adequately protected the employer's trade connection) (revsd [1974] Ch 129, [1972] 3 All ER 689, CA, on the ground that the area restraint was severable); *Spafax (1965) Ltd v Dommett* (1972) 116 Sol Jo 711, CA (see PARA 407 note 1); cf *Cussen v O'Connor* (1893) 32 LR Ir 330 (similar business in counties travelled by covenantor for covenantee; 12 years, or two years from determination of engagement; good, but injunction limited to two years from determination of engagement).

5   *Robertson v Willmott* (1909) 25 TLR 681 (10 miles; five years; good; question of breach only); *Gadd v Thompson* [1911] 1 KB 304, DC (10 miles; ten years; covenantor a minor; good).

6   *Fairbrother v England* (1891) 40 WR 220 (2 miles; three years; apparently good, but no breach); *Hadsley v Dayer-Smith* [1914] AC 979, HL (1 mile; ten years; apparently good; question of breach); *Bowler v Lovegrove* [1921] 1 Ch 642 (1 year; district of employment; bad but no breach); *Scorer v Seymour-Johns* [1966] 3 All ER 347, [1966] 1 WLR 1419, CA (5 miles; three years; good); *Calvert, Hunt and Barden v Elton* (1974) 233 Estates Gazette 391 (3 miles; three years; good).

7   *Morris v Colman* (1812) 18 Ves 437 (covenant in partnership articles not to write for any but covenantee's theatre; good); and see PRESS, PRINTING AND PUBLISHING vol 36(2) (Reissue) PARA 401.

8   *Mitchel v Reynolds* (1711) 1 P Wms 181 (particular parish; five years (term of lease); good); *Rannie v Irvine* (1844) 7 Man & G 969 (1 mile; term of lease; good; also, customers then dealing at the premises; same time; good); *Clark v Howard* (1860) 2 F & F 125 (limit as to any new baking business in certain town; no time limit; good; question of breach only); *Toby v Major* (1899) 43 Sol Jo 778 (3 miles; no time limit; apparently bad); *Bromley v Smith* [1909] 2 KB 235 (10 miles; three years; good).

9   *London and Yorkshire Bank Ltd v Pritt* (1887) 56 LJCh 987 (5 miles; 12 months; good); *National Provincial Bank of England v Marshall* (1888) 40 ChD 112, CA (2 miles; two years; good); *Spence v Mercantile Bank of India Ltd* (1921) 37 TLR 390 (on appeal 37 TLR 745, CA) ('no eastern bank'; no time limit; bad).

10 *Home v Douglas* (1912) Times, 15 November.

11 *General Billposting Co Ltd v Atkinson* [1909] AC 118, HL (50 miles; two years; apparently good, but the question discussed related to the determination of whole contract by wrongful dismissal; see PARA 436).

12 *SW Strange Ltd v Mann* [1965] 1 All ER 1069, [1965] 1 WLR 629 (manager of credit betting business; Cheltenham and any place within 12 miles; three years; area restriction inappropriate in the particular circumstances).

13 *Watson v Prager* [1991] 3 All ER 487, [1991] 1 WLR 726.

14 *Young v Timmins* (1831) 1 Cr & J 331 (question of consideration).

15 *Hinde v Gray* (1840) 1 Man & G 195 (no limit of space; ten years; bad); *Allsopp v Wheatcroft* (1872) LR 15 Eq 59; *Showell v Winkup* (1889) 60 LT 389; *Rogers v Maddocks* [1892] 3 Ch 346, CA; *Vancouver Malt and Sake Brewing Co Ltd v Vancouver Breweries Ltd* [1934] AC 181, PC (world-wide; 15 years; bad; restraint in gross).

16 *Elves v Crofts* (1850) 10 CB 241 (5 miles; no time limit; good); *George Hill & Co v Hill* (1886) 35 WR 137 (10 miles; so long as covenantee should carry on the business; good; question of breach only); *Cooper v Southgate* (1894) 10 R 552, DC (1 mile; no time limit; apparently good, but question of consideration only); *Empire Meat Co Ltd v Patrick* [1939] 2 All ER 85, CA (5 miles; five years; some area agreement justifiable but distance too great).

17 *Vincents of Reading v Fogden* (1932) 48 TLR 613 (15 miles; three years; bad).

18 *Archer v Marsh* (1837) 6 Ad & El 959 (not to compete; no time limit; good, but question of consideration only); *Wallis v Day* (1837) 2 M & W 273 (unlimited as to space and time, but limited as to capacity in which covenantor might trade; good); *Davies, Turner & Co v Lowen*

(1891) 64 LT 655 (London and other places, and within 50 miles of each; good as to London, bad as to place where covenantee had no business; bad also as to 'business to be hereafter carried on'); *Macfarlane v Dumbarton Steamboat Co* (1899) 36 SLR 771 (United Kingdom; ten years; bad; canvassing customers of business sold; injunction granted).

19 *Great Western and Metropolitan Dairies Ltd v Gibbs* (1918) 34 TLR 344 (20 miles; one year; assist in any capacity; bad; also description of business too wide).

20 *Woods v Dennett* (1817) 2 Stark 89 (1 mile; no time limit; good, but question of measurement only) (overruled by *Mouflet v Cole* (1872) LR 8 Exch 32, Ex Ch); *Harrison v Gardner* (1817) 2 Madd 198 (injunction granted on ground of fraud; no written agreement).

21 *Hitchcock v Coker* (1837) 6 Ad & El 438, Ex Ch (3 miles; no time limit; good); *Clark v Watkins* (1863) 11 WR 319 (7 miles; so long as covenantee had any interest in the business; good, but question of breach only); *Marshalls Ltd v Leek* (1900) 17 TLR 26 (not to enter into competition; no time limit; good).

22 *Ramoneur Co Ltd v Brixey* (1911) 104 LT 809, DC (3 miles; no time limit; question of breach only).

23 *Proctor v Sargent* (1840) 2 Man & G 20 (5 miles; two years; good); *Benwell v Inns* (1857) 24 Beav 307 (3 miles; two years; good); *Cornwall v Hawkins* (1872) 41 LJCh 435 (2 miles; two years; covenantor a minor; good); *Baines v Geary* (1887) 35 ChD 154 (customers during term of service; no time limit; good); *Short Horn Dairy Co Ltd v Hall* (1887) 83 LT Jo 45 (question of breach); *Fellows v Wood* (1888) 59 LT 513 (customers during term of service; two years; covenantor a minor; good); *Evans v Ware* [1892] 3 Ch 502 (5 miles; two years; covenantor a minor; good); *Batho v Tunks* [1892] WN 101 (customers during term of service; no time limit; good); *Dubowski & Sons v Goldstein* [1896] 1 QB 478, CA (customers during term of service; no time limit; good; doubtful as to customers at any time); *Stride v Martin* (1897) 77 LT 600, DC (particular neighbourhoods; no time limit; good); *Merriott v Martin* (1899) 43 Sol Jo 717 (Southampton; one year; good); *Morrison Fleet & Co Ltd v Fletcher* (1900) 17 TLR 95 (2 miles; no time limit; covenantor a minor; good); *Marshall and Murray Ltd v Jones* (1913) 29 TLR 351 (question of breach; 'customers served by and from' a particular dairy); *Express Dairy Co v Jackson* (1929) 99 LJKB 181 (two years not unreasonable); *Home Counties Dairies Ltd v Skilton* [1970] 1 All ER 1227, [1970] 1 WLR 526, CA (customers served during last six months of employment; one year; good); *Dairy Crest Ltd v Pigott* [1989] ICR 92, CA (two years; court to decide upon the appropriate evidence whether in particular circumstances restraint unreasonable; interlocutory injunction granted to covenantee).

24 *De Francesco v Barnum* (1889) 43 ChD 165 (question of proceedings against apprentice during term of apprenticeship): see LICENSING AND GAMBLING vol 67 (2008) PARA 237.

25 *Financial Collection Agencies (UK) Ltd v Batey* (1973) 117 Sol Jo 416, CA (debt collector employed in Birmingham office; six months; clients of employer during period of employment; area of restriction Birmingham, Glasgow, Leeds, Liverpool, Manchester; area too wide and covenant too uncertain; bad).

26 *Horner v Graves* (1831) 7 Bing 735 (100 miles; no time limit; bad); *Mallan v May* (1843) 11 M & W 653 (London, or any place in England or Scotland where covenantees might have been practising during term of service; no time limit; good as to London; bad as to the rest); *Harris v Mansbridge* (1900) 17 TLR 21 (question of breach); *Clifford v Phillips* (1907) 51 Sol Jo 748 (question of breach).

27 *Davis v Mason* (1793) 5 Term Rep 118 (10 miles; 14 years; good); *Hayward v Young* (1818) 2 Chit 407 (20 miles; no time limit; good); *Davies v Penton* (1827) 6 B & C 216 (5 miles; no time limit; good); *Rawlinson v Clarke* (1845) 14 M & W 187 (3 miles; no time limit; good; question of breach); *Hastings v Whitley* (1848) 2 Exch 611 (10 miles; no time limit; good); *Sainter v Ferguson* (1849) 7 CB 716 (7 miles; no time limit; good); *Atkyns v Kinnier* (1850) 4 Exch 776 (2½ miles; no time limit; good); *Giles v Hart* (1859) 1 LT 154 (5 miles; no time limit; good); *Carnes v Nesbitt* (1862) 7 H & N 778 (5 miles; no time limit; good; question of damages or injunction); *Fox v Scard* (1863) 33 Beav 327 (12 miles; life of covenantee and ten years; good; question of damages or injunction); *Gravely v Barnard* (1874) LR 18 Eq 518 (10 miles; so long as covenantee or assignee should practise; good); *Palmer v Mallet* (1887) 36 ChD 411, CA (10 miles; no time limit; good); *Rogers v Drury* (1887) 57 LJCh 504 (question of breach only); *Everton v Longmore* (1899) 15 TLR 356, CA (5 miles; three years; good); *Ballachulish Slate Quarries Ltd v Grant* (1903) 5 F 1105, Ct of Sess (the district in which the covenantor had been employed; no time limit; good); *Robertson v Buchanan* (1904) 73 LJCh 408, CA (2 miles; ten years; good; question of breach only); *Routh v Jones* [1947] 1 All ER 758, CA (10 miles; five years; not excessive, but void because forbidden employments too wide); *Jenkins v Reid* [1948] 1 All ER 471 (5 miles; life; too wide); *Whitehill v Bradford* [1952] Ch 236, [1952] 1 All ER 115, CA (10 miles; 21 year period; not excessive; principles not affected by the national health service); *Kerr v Morris* [1987] Ch 90, [1986] 3 All ER 217, CA (2 miles; two years: interlocutory

injunction granted); *Clarke v Newland* [1991] 1 All ER 397, CA (not to practise 'in the practice area'; three years; enforceable). But see *Macfarlane v Kent* [1965] 2 All ER 376 at 381, [1965] 1 WLR 1019 at 1024, where it was questioned whether a covenant not to practise within a prescribed area could ever be reasonable where it was designed to protect the goodwill of a medical practice which could not be sold and had no significant number of paying patients. A covenant not to attend patients who were patients of the partnership would be sufficient to protect goodwill. See also *Lyne-Pirkis v Jones* [1969] 3 All ER 738, [1969] 1 WLR 1293, CA, where in relation to a general practitioner partnership in which substantially all the patients were within a 5-mile radius but the restraint was of a 10-mile radius, it was held that the area might be reasonable, but the restraint void because the forbidden employment was too wide (distinguished in *Clarke v Newland* [1991] 1 All ER 397, CA); *Peyton v Mindham* [1971] 3 All ER 1215, [1972] 1 WLR 8. As to the prohibition of the sale of the goodwill of medical practices in the national health service see HEALTH SERVICES vol 54 (2008) PARA 273 et seq.

28 *Broad v Jollyfe* (1620) Cro Jac 596; *Chesman v Nainby* (1727) 1 Bro Parl Cas 234, HL (half a mile at covenantee's house; no time limit; good; but half a mile of any house to which covenantee might move apparently bad); *Brampton v Beddoes* (1863) 13 CBNS 538 (2 miles; no time limit; good; question of breach only); *Watts v Smith* (1890) 62 LT 453 (half a mile; six months; good; question of breach only); *Bailey v Skinner and Fleming, Reid & Co* (1898) 42 Sol Jo 780 (covenant in lease; carrying on part of a business not a breach).

29 *Greer v Sketchley Ltd* [1979] IRLR 445, [1979] FSR 197, CA (director of business which extended only to part of England and Wales; United Kingdom; 12 months; bad).

30 *Dier's Case* (1414) YB 2 Hen 5, fo 5, pl 26; *Bryson v Whitehead* (1822) 1 Sim & St 74 (no limit of space; 20 years; trade secret; good).

31 *Spencer v Marchington* [1988] IRLR 392; *Office Angels Ltd v Rainer-Thomas and O'Connor* [1991] IRLR 214, CA.

32 *Allied Dunbar (Frank Weisinger) Ltd v Weisinger* [1988] IRLR 60. See also *Beckett Investment Management Group Ltd v Hall* [2007] EWCA Civ 613, [2007] IRLR 793; *Arbuthnot Fund Managers Ltd v Rawlings* [2003] EWCA Civ 518, [2003] All ER (D) 181 (Mar); *Lapthorne v Eurofi Ltd* [2001] EWCA Civ 993, [2001] All ER (D) 209 (Jun).

33 *Hepworth Manufacturing Co Ltd v Ryott* [1920] 1 Ch 1, CA (covenant to act under pseudonym and not on leaving employment to use pseudonym for any purpose whatever; bad). See also LICENSING AND GAMBLING vol 67 (2008) PARA 237.

34 *Woods v Thornburn* (1897) 41 Sol Jo 756 (3 miles; no time limit; bad, as applying to 'any other business').

35 *Spink (Bournemouth) Ltd v Spink* [1936] Ch 544, [1936] 1 All ER 597 (10 miles; five years; good).

36 *Pilkington v Scott* (1846) 15 M & W 657 (question of consideration in contract of employment); *Hartley v Cummings* (1847) 5 CB 247 (question of mutuality in contract of employment); *Phillips v Stevens* (1899) 15 TLR 325, DC (question of mutuality in contract of employment).

37 *Daggett v Ryman* (1868) 17 LT 486 (particular place or neighbourhood; no time limit; question of enforcement).

38 *Cavendish v Tarry* (1908) 52 Sol Jo 726 (20 miles; 20 years; good).

39 *Smith v Hancock* [1894] 2 Ch 377, CA (5 miles; ten years; question of breach only); *Pearks Ltd v Cullen* (1912) 28 TLR 371 (shop assistant and occasional canvasser; not to 'establish, carry on, or be engaged in or interested in a business of a similar character' to that of covenantees; 2 miles of any shop of covenantees at which he had been employed within 12 months; two years; bad).

40 *Pellow v Ivey* (1933) 49 TLR 422 (within particular borough; no time limit; bad); *Marion White Ltd v Francis* [1972] 3 All ER 857, [1972] 1 WLR 1423, CA (12 months; half a mile; good).

41 *General Accident Assurance Corpn v Noel* [1902] 1 KB 377; *Barr v Craven* (1903) 89 LT 574, CA; see note 4.

42 *Goldsoll v Goldman* [1915] 1 Ch 292, CA (business in imitation jewellery; restraints as to real and imitation jewellery, United Kingdom, France, United States etc; good, when limited to imitation jewellery and to area in which business carried on).

43 *Eastes v Russ* [1914] 1 Ch 468, CA (10 miles; no time limit; bad).

44 *Littlewoods Organisation Ltd v Harris* [1978] 1 All ER 1026, [1977] 1 WLR 1472, CA (director in charge of company's mail order business; not to enter employment of rival company or its subsidiaries; 12 months; covenant construed as applying only to rival company's mail order business carried on in United Kingdom; good).

45 *Jones v Lees* (1856) 1 H & N 189 (covenant as to use of patent with machine; good); *Harms v Parsons* (1862) 32 Beav 328 (200 miles; no time limit; good); *Clarkson v Edge* (1863) 33 Beav

227 (20 miles; no time limit; good); *Maythorn v Palmer* (1864) 11 LT 261 (question of breach only); *Leather Cloth Co v Lorsont* (1869) LR 9 Eq 345 (Europe; no time limit; good); *Hagg v Darley* (1878) 47 LJCh 567 (no limit of space; 14 years; trade secret; good); *Vernon v Hallam* (1886) 34 ChD 748 (covenant not to trade in particular name; good); *Davies v Davies* (1887) 36 ChD 359, CA (restraint so far as the law allows; bad); *Mills v Dunham* [1891] 1 Ch 576, CA (customers during term of service; good); *Badische Anilin und Soda Fabrik v Schott, Segner & Co* [1892] 3 Ch 447; *Nordenfelt v Maxim Nordenfelt Guns and Ammunition Co Ltd* [1894] AC 535, HL (whole world; 25 years; good); *William Robinson & Co Ltd v Heuer* [1898] 2 Ch 451, CA (question of covenant applicable during term of service: see PARA 404); *Haynes v Doman* [1899] 2 Ch 13, CA (25 miles; no time limit; good); *Elliman Sons & Co v Carrington & Son Ltd* [1901] 2 Ch 275 (sale of goods; restraint against selling below certain prices; good); *Castelli v Middleton* (1901) 17 TLR 373 (no limit of space or time; good, but decision was as to breach only); *Dowden and Pook Ltd v Pook* [1904] 1 KB 45, CA (no limit airspace; five years; bad); *Lamson Pneumatic Tube Co v Phillips* (1904) 91 LT 363, CA (eastern hemisphere; five years; good); *White, Tomkins and Courage v Wilson* (1907) 23 TLR 469 (no limit of space, but limit to special business; five years; good); *Automobile Carriage Builders Ltd v Sayers* (1909) 101 LT 419 (20 miles; ten years from date of engagement; good); *United Shoe Machinery Co of Canada v Brunet* [1909] AC 330, PC (conditions attached to lease of machines; good); *Caribonum Co Ltd v Le Couch* (1913) 109 LT 385 (on appeal 109 LT 587, CA) (trade secret); *Gilford Motor Co Ltd v Horne* [1933] Ch 935, CA (customers or those in habit of dealing during term of service; good); *Tool Metal Manufacturing Co Ltd v Tungsten Electric Co Ltd* [1955] 2 All ER 657, [1955] 1 WLR 761, HL (condition imposing penalties on licensee of patent upon manufacture of more than certain quantities of patented article, payable even after expiration of patent; good).

46 *Hardy v Martin* (1783) 1 Bro CC 419n (brandy merchant; London and 5 miles; 19 years; limit as to quantity sold; good, but question was penalty or damages; see PARA 438 note 1); *Ward v Byrne* (1839) 5 M & W 548 (coal merchant; no limit of space; nine months; bad; but limited as to customers; two years; apparently good); *Turner v Evans* (1852) 2 De GM & G 740 (wine merchant; Carnarvon, Anglesey and Merioneth; no time limit; good, but question of breach only); *Avery v Langford* (1854) Kay 663 (general merchant; large part of Cornwall; no time limit; good); *Mumford v Gething* (1859) 7 CBNS 305 (lace merchants: see note 4); *King v Hansell* (1860) 5 H & N 106 (wine and spirit merchants); *Bishop v Kitchin* (1868) 38 LJQB 20 (hop merchant); *Allen v Taylor* (1870) 39 LJCh 627 (rag merchant; 10 miles; five years; good; question of breach only); *Josselyn v Parson* (1872) LR 7 Exch 127 (ale and spirit merchant: see note 4); *Rousillon v Rousillon* (1880) 14 ChD 351 (wine merchant; no limit of space; two-year limit as a traveller, ten-year limit as to establishing himself in the trade; good); *Webb v Clark* (1884) 78 LT Jo 96 (provision dealer; 1 mile; no time limit; good); *Harvey v Corpe* (1885) 79 LT Jo 246 (see PARA 399 note 2); *Parsons v Cotterill* (1887) 56 LT 839 (wine merchant; 50 miles; no time limit; good); *Perls v Saafield* [1892] 2 Ch 149, CA (oil merchant: see note 4); *Moenich v Fenestre* (1892) 67 LT 602, CA (commission merchant: see note 4); *Ehrman v Bartholomew* [1898] 1 Ch 671 (wine merchant; 'any other business' during term of service; ten years; covenantor left service at end of seven months in breach of contract; bad); *E Underwood & Son Ltd v Barker* [1899] 1 Ch 300, CA (hay and straw merchant; United Kingdom, France, Belgium, Holland and Canada; 12 months; good); *Hood and Moore's Stores Ltd v Jones* (1899) 81 LT 169 (hay and corn merchants; 2 miles; no time limit; good); *Townsend v Jarman* [1900] 2 Ch 698 (seed and corn merchant; 40 miles; 21 years; question of covenant in gross: see PARA 389); *Delius v Müller* (1901) 45 Sol Jo 737 (wool merchant; 50 miles; ten years; good); *Gophir Diamond Co v Wood* [1902] 1 Ch 950 (jeweller; 20 miles; three years; no dispute as to validity; question of breach); *Servais Bouchard v Prince's Hall Restaurant Ltd* (1904) 20 TLR 574, CA (contract to take wine exclusively from one firm; good); *Hooper and Ashby v Willis* (1906) 22 TLR 451, CA (builders' merchant; 30 miles from either of two places; 14 years; bad); *Cade v Calfe* (1906) 22 TLR 243 (coal merchant; 3 miles; two years; good, but question of breach); *Reeve v Marsh* (1906) 23 TLR 24 (coal and corn merchant; no limit of space; two years; 'directly or indirectly interfere with prejudice or in any manner affect' business of covenantee; held not to prohibit setting up rival business; questionable whether too vague); *William Cory & Son Ltd v Harrison* [1906] AC 274, HL (coal merchant; Great Britain and Isle of Man; no limit of time; validity of covenant not questioned; question of breach); *Henry Leetham & Sons Ltd v Johnstone-White* [1907] 1 Ch 322, CA (hay and corn dealer; see note 4); *Morris & Co v Ryle* (1910) 26 TLR 678, CA (hop merchant: see note 4); *Lovell and Christmas Ltd v Wall* (1911) 104 LT 85, CA (provision merchant; London, Liverpool and Manchester; no time limit; good, but question of breach only); *British Reinforced Concrete Engineering Co Ltd v Schelff* [1921] 2 Ch 563 (road material dealers; duration of war and three years thereafter; United Kingdom; be concerned in or act as servant of any one concerned in; bad because (1) area too wide; (2)

servant clause unreasonable; (3) protection extended beyond business sold); *East Essex Farmers Ltd v Holder* [1926] WN 230 (corn seed, and coal merchants; (a) 25 miles; ten years; bad; (b) soliciting customers who might become such after employment; bad).

47 *Shackle v Baker* (1808) 14 Ves 468 (no writing; interlocutory injunction refused).

48 *Foley v Classique Coaches Ltd* [1934] 2 KB 1, CA (covenant on sale of land to buy all petrol used for business carried on such land from covenantees; good). See also note 69.

49 *Tivoli, Manchester, Ltd v Colley* (1904) 20 TLR 437 (20 miles; term of engagement and six months afterwards; good); *London Music Hall Ltd v Austin* (1908) Times, 16 December (engagement for different weeks over a long period; agreement not to perform at halls in given area within eight months prior to completion of engagement held to refer to each separate week); and see LICENSING AND GAMBLING vol 67 (2008) PARA 237.

50 *McFarlane v Hilton* [1899] 1 Ch 884 (question of breach only); *Sir WC Leng & Co Ltd v Andrews* [1909] 1 Ch 763, CA (20 miles; no time limit; covenantee a minor; bad); *Ronbar Enterprises Ltd v Green* [1954] 2 All ER 266, [1954] 1 WLR 815, CA (unlimited in area; not too wide if restricted to apply to competing businesses; application to similar businesses severed).

51 *Cooke v Colcraft* (1773) 2 Wm Bl 856 (question of burden of covenant passing to executors).

52 *Jacoby v Whitmore* (1883) 49 LT 335, CA (1 mile; no time limit; good).

53 *Lumley v Wagner* (1852) 1 De GM & G 604; and see LICENSING AND GAMBLING vol 67 (2008) PARA 237.

54 *Dales v Weaber* (1870) 18 WR 993 (5 miles; no time limit; good; question of breach only).

55 *Lake v Harrison* (1897) 13 TLR 568 (4 miles; two years; good; question of breach).

56 *Jones v Lees* (1856) 1 H & N 189; *Printing and Numerical Registering Co v Sampson* (1875) LR 19 Eq 462 (covenant to assign future patent rights; good); *Mouchel v Cubitt & Co* (1907) 24 RPC 194 (covenant by licensee not to execute work in competition with the patent during term of licence; good); *Bescol (Electric) Ltd v Merlin Mouldings Ltd* (1952) 69 RPC 297 (undertaking not to manufacture 'in future', held limited to duration of patent; good); *Tool Metal Manufacturing Co Ltd v Tungsten Electric Co Ltd* [1955] 2 All ER 657, [1955] 1 WLR 761, HL (condition imposing penalties on licensee upon manufacture of more than certain quantities of patented article, payable even after expiration of patent; good); see also PATENTS AND REGISTERED DESIGNS vol 79 (2008) PARAS 403, 511.

57 *Price v Green* (1847) 16 M & W 346, Ex Ch (London and Westminster; no time limit; good; but 600 miles bad).

58 *Petrofina (Great Britain) Ltd v Martin* [1966] Ch 146, [1966] 1 All ER 126, CA (solus agreement in gross, restricting covenantor to single supplier of petrol for minimum of 12 years; some restrictions also with regard to lubricating oils; covenantor bound to keep station open at all reasonable hours and required, on a sale of the station, to procure the purchaser to assume the obligations of the agreement; bad); *Esso Petroleum Co Ltd v Harper's Garage (Stourport) Ltd* [1968] AC 269, [1967] 1 All ER 699, HL (tie of four years and five months, good; tie of 21 years, bad; doctrine of restraint of trade not excluded by reason of covenants being contained in mortgage). But see *Cleveland Petroleum Co Ltd v Dartstone Ltd* [1969] 1 All ER 201, [1969] 1 WLR 116, CA, where the doctrine of restraint of trade was held not to apply to restrictions in a lease under which the covenantor entered into possession. Cf *Alec Lobb (Garages) Ltd v Total Oil GB Ltd* [1985] 1 All ER 303, [1985] 1 WLR 173, CA (lease and lease-back).

59 *Stewart v Stewart* (1899) 1 F 1158, Ct of Sess (20 miles; no time limit; good, but question of covenant by a person not employed in the business to be protected: see PARA 389).

60 *M'Allen v Churchill* (1826) 11 Moore CP 483 (no limit of space; five years; apparently bad); *Loe v Lardner* (1856) 4 WR 597 (1 mile; no time limit; question of breach only); *Mouflet v Cole* (1872) LR 8 Exch 32, Ex Ch (half a mile; no time limit; good, but question of measurement only, overruling *Leigh v Hind* (1829) 9 B & C 774); *Clegg v Hands* (1890) 44 ChD 503, CA (tied house covenant); *Cattermoul v Jared* (1909) 53 Sol Jo 244 (question of construction).

61 *Tallis v Tallis* (1853) 1 E & B 391 (London, Middlesex, Surrey, 150 miles from General Post Office; Edinburgh, Dublin, and 50 miles from each; any place in Great Britain or Ireland where covenantee or his successors might carry on business or have carried on business within the past six months; no time limit; good as to London and 150 miles and other places where covenantee carried on business); *Welstead v Hadley* (1904) 21 TLR 165, CA (London and 20 miles; ten years; good).

62 *Bird v Lake* (1863) 1 Hem & M 111, 338 (1 mile; no time limit; good, but question of breach only); *Drew v Guy* [1894] 3 Ch 25, CA (meaning of 'similar business').

63 *Pemberton v Vaughan* (1847) 10 QB 87 (maker and seller of ginger beer; 1 mile; no time limit; good); *Middleton v Brown* (1878) 47 LJCh 411, CA (oil vendor in street; 8 miles; 12 months; good).

64 *Gale v Reed* (1806) 8 East 80 (question of consideration in contract for exclusive employment).
65 *Jones v Heavens* (1877) 4 ChD 636 (10 miles; no time limit; good, but question of breach only).
66 *Smith v Hawthorn* (1897) 76 LT 716 (9 miles; 12 years; good); *Berlitz School of Languages v Duchêne* (1903) 6 F 181, Ct of Sess (any town where covenantor employed, or where there is a branch of covenantee's business, or within 10 miles; two years; not certain whether good); *Lievre v Mayonnet* (1913) 2 LJCCR 4 (10 miles of Bradford and at certain other places; five years; uncertain whether too wide, but severable).
67 *Bunn v Guy* (1803) 1 Smith KB 1 (150 miles; no time limit; good); *Capes v Hutton* (1826) 2 Russ 357 (question of minority; covenant by father of articled clerk); *Whittaker v Howe* (1841) 3 Beav 383 (Great Britain; 20 years; good); *Nicholls v Stretton* (1847) 10 QB 346 (clients during term of service; no time limit; good, and severable); *Galsworthy v Strutt* (1848) 1 Exch 659 (seven years; 50 miles; good; decision as to liquidated damages or penalty); *Dendy v Henderson* (1855) 11 Exch 194 (21 years; 21 miles; good); *Duignan v Walker* (1859) John 446 (7 miles; no time limit; good; question of measurement); *Howard v Woodward* (1864) 10 Jur NS 1123 (50 miles; no time limit; good); *May v O'Neill* (1875) 44 LJCh 660 (London, Middlesex and Essex; no time limit; good; also, clients of covenantee during term of service; no limit of space or time; good); *Hayne v Burchell* (1890) 35 Sol Jo 88, CA (not to take away or transact business for clients of covenantee; life of covenantee; apparently good, but no breach); *Llewellyn v Simpson* (1891) 91 LT Jo 9 (question of breach only); *Richards v Whitham* (1892) 66 LT 695, CA (question of enforcement of covenant by articled clerk, a minor, and remedy of covenantor who has undertaken liability on account of minor); *Badham v Williams* (1900) 83 LT 141 (question of breach only); *Edmundson v Render* [1905] 2 Ch 320 (15 miles; no time limit; good); *Lewis and Lewis v Durnford* (1907) 24 TLR 64; *Woodbridge & Sons v Bellamy* [1911] 1 Ch 326, CA; *Freeman v Fox* (1911) 55 Sol Jo 650 (question of breach); *Fitch v Dewes* [1921] 2 AC 158, HL (7 miles; no time limit; good); *Way v Bishop* [1928] Ch 647, CA (5 miles; ten years; validity of restraint not questioned; question of breach); *Dickson v Jones* [1939] 3 All ER 182 (15 miles; life; too wide); *Bridge v Deacons (a firm)* [1984] AC 705, sub nom *Deacons (a firm) v Bridge* [1984] 2 All ER 19, PC (Hong Kong; not for 5 years to act as a solicitor for a client of the firm within 3 years of the covenantor leaving the firm; good), in this case the Privy Council specifically disagreed with the view of the Court of Appeal in *Oswald Hickson, Collier & Co v Carter-Ruck* [1984] AC 720n, [1984] 2 All ER 15, CA, that a clause in a solicitor's partnership deed preventing one of the partners from acting for a client in the future would be contrary to public policy; see also *Edwards v Worboys* [1984] AC 724n, [1984] 2 WLR 850n, CA (not to practise within 5 miles of the firm, not to act for anyone resident within 5 miles of the firm, not to act for any client of the firm within five years of the covenantor leaving the firm: interlocutory injunctions to enforce covenants granted); *Briggs v Oates* [1991] 1 All ER 407 (salaried partner; termination of agreement a breach of contract; restraint of trade clause therefore not binding; further, 5 miles, five year clause in employment contract where employee wrongfully dismissed 'grossly unreasonable'). An English barrister practising in a colony or dependency where the functions of barristers and solicitors are fused may be restrained from practice: *Home v Douglas* (1912) Times, 15 November.
68 *A Schroeder Music Publishing Co Ltd v Macaulay* [1974] 3 All ER 616, [1974] 1 WLR 1308, HL, where there was an agreement in the publishers' standard form for a song writer's exclusive services for a period of five years automatically extended to ten years if royalties in the initial period exceeded a certain sum. The song writer was obliged to assign world copyright in all his musical compositions during the term, but there was no obligation on the publishers to publish so that the song writer might receive almost no remuneration; the song writer had no right to terminate the agreement. It was held that the restrictions required justification and were bad. See also *Clifford Davis Management Ltd v WEA Records Ltd* [1975] 1 All ER 237, [1975] 1 WLR 61, CA; *Zang Tumb Tuum Records Ltd v Johnson* [1993] EMLR 61, (1989) Independent, 2 August, CA; *Panayiotou v Sony Music Entertainment (UK) Ltd* [1994] EMLR 233.
69 *Williams v Williams* (1818) 2 Swan 253 (any coach between Reading and London; no time limit; good); *Leighton v Wales* (1838) 3 M & W 545 (not to compete; so long as covenantee carried on the business; good, but question of consideration only).
70 *Collins v Locke* (1879) 4 App Cas 674, PC (agreement to prevent competition: see PARA 367 note 10).
71 *Lyddon v Thomas* (1901) 17 TLR 450 (50 miles; 20 years; good).
72 *Hunlocke v Blacklowe* (1670) 2 Saund 156; *Rolfe v Rolfe* (1846) 15 Sim 88 (20 miles; no time limit; good); *Newling v Dobell* (1868) 38 LJCh 111 (5 miles to east and 2 miles to west of High Holborn; three years; good); *Davey v Shannon* (1879) 4 ExD 81 (5 miles; no time limit; question of fraud); *Nicoll v Beere* (1885) 53 LT 659 (10 miles; three years; good); *Baker v Hedgecock* (1888) 39 ChD 520 (1 mile; two years; covenant bad as restraining from all

business); *Beetham v Fraser* (1904) 21 TLR 8 ('not to enter into any business arrangement in competition with or that would in any way interfere with' business of covenantee; bad as too wide and too vague); *Attwood v Lamont* [1920] 3 KB 571, CA (10 miles; no time limit; bad); *Putsman v Taylor* [1927] 1 KB 741, CA (covenants for five years (1) not to set up as tailor; (2) not to enter employment of trade rival; (3) not to be employed by any tailor in certain districts; good).

73 *Colmer v Clark* (1734) 7 Mod Rep 230 (within 'Westminster and bills of mortality' (ie the metropolitan area before 1855); seven years; good).

74 *Baxter v Lewis* (1886) 30 Sol Jo 705, 754 (5 miles; no time limit; good); *Pellow v Ivey* (1933) 49 TLR 422 (within the borough; no time limit; bad).

75 See *Ware and De Freville Ltd v Motor Trade Association* [1921] 3 KB 40, CA; *Auto-Mart (London) Ltd v Chilton* (1927) 43 TLR 463; *Hardie and Lane Ltd v Chilton* [1928] 2 KB 306, CA; *R v Denyer* [1926] 2 KB 258, CCA; *Thorne v Motor Trade Association* [1937] AC 797, [1937] 3 All ER 157, HL; *Berg v Sadler and Moore* [1937] 2 KB 158, [1937] 1 All ER 637, CA; *British Motor Trade Association v Salvadori* [1949] Ch 556, [1949] 1 All ER 208.

76 *Martin v Brunsden* (1894) 98 LTJo 237, DC (1 mile; ten years; good); *Dottridge Bros Ltd v Crook* (1907) 23 TLR 644 (10 miles; no time limit; good); *Dawson v Taylor* (1959) 110 L Jo 121 (within boroughs of Warwick and Leamington; five years; good).

77 *Howard v Danner* (1901) 17 TLR 548 (service of rival restaurant; less than one year; good; question of consideration only).

(ix) Severability

433. Severance of unenforceable part. A contract in unreasonable restraint of trade is unenforceable; it is not illegal in any criminal sense, nor does it give a cause of action to any third person injured by its operation[1]. Its presence does not necessarily vitiate the whole contract[2], and parts of an agreement in restraint of trade may be severable and effect may be given to that part which is reasonable[3], whether the severance is in respect of subject matter[4], or of space[5], or of time[6], or of persons with whom there may be dealings[7].

Severance will be more readily allowed of a restraint between vendor and purchaser than of one between employer and employee[8].

1 See PARA 383 note 6.
2 *Baines v Geary* (1887) 35 ChD 154 at 158; *Re Prudential Assurance Co's Trust Deed, Horne v Prudential Assurance Co Ltd* [1934] Ch 338, where the inclusion of a covenant in restraint of trade was held not to invalidate the pension scheme as a whole. Cf *M'Allen v Churchill* (1826) 11 Moore CP 483; *Dendy v Henderson* (1855) 11 Exch 194 at 201 per Martin B; *Marshall v NM Financial Management Ltd* [1997] 1 WLR 1527, [1997] ICR 1065, CA.
3 As to the general principle see *Winchcombe v Pigot* (1614) 2 Bulst 246, sub nom *Pigot's Case* (1614) 11 Co Rep 26b at 27a; *Wallis v Day* (1837) 2 M & W 273, where it was held that if a party makes several contracts, one of which is illegal, he is nevertheless liable to perform the others; and CONTRACT vol 9(1) (Reissue) PARA 877. As to severing in the case of byelaws see CORPORATIONS vol 9(2) (2006 Reissue) PARA 1195; LOCAL GOVERNMENT vol 69 (2009) PARA 560. As to reasonableness generally see PARA 390 et seq.
4 *Mumford v Gething* (1859) 7 CBNS 305; *Davies v Davies* (1887) 36 ChD 359 at 372 per Kekewich J (revsd by the Court of Appeal, but not so as to affect the general proposition that covenants may be severed in a proper case); *Parsons v Cotterill* (1887) 56 LT 839, where the restraint was as to the business of a wine and spirit merchant, or any branch of it, and apparently it was considered that the sale of beer, if included, may be severable; *Baker v Hedgecock* (1888) 39 ChD 520, where Chitty J refused to sever (see PARA 434 note 1); *Rogers v Maddocks* [1892] 3 Ch 346, CA, where a restraint as to selling ale, beer etc was held severable from a restraint from selling aerated waters; *Moenich v Fenestre* (1892) 67 LT 602 at 604, CA, per Stirling J, where it was apparently considered that goods with which the covenantor dealt might be severed from goods with which he had ceased to deal; *Maxim Nordenfelt Guns and Ammunition Co v Nordenfelt* [1893] 1 Ch 630, CA, where a restraint as to the business of a manufacturer of guns etc was held severable from a restraint against any business competing with that for the time being carried on by the covenantees (cf on appeal sub nom *Nordenfelt v Maxim Nordenfelt Guns and Ammunition Co Ltd* [1894] AC 535 at 560, HL, per Lord Macnaghten); *William Robinson & Co Ltd v Heuer* [1898] 2 Ch 451, CA, where a

restraint as to any business similar to that of the covenantee was held severable from a restraint as to any business whatever and from a power to extend the term of the restraint; *Haynes v Doman* [1899] 2 Ch 13 at 24, CA, where it was held, in considering a restraint as to the same kind of business as the covenantee's, that any part of the restraint which was unreasonable would be severed; *Beetham v Fraser* (1904) 21 TLR 8, DC, where the court refused to sever (see PARA 434 note 2); *Hooper and Ashby v Willis* (1905) 21 TLR 691 (affd (1906) 22 TLR 451, CA), where a restraint as to the business of a builders' merchant was held severable from a restraint against manufacturing or dealing in cement and other materials manufactured by the covenantees during the term of service or any other business of a like nature to the business carried on or which might be carried on during the term, but an area of 30 miles was unreasonable and could not be severed; *Bromley v Smith* [1909] 2 KB 235, where a restraint as to the business of a baker was held severable from a restraint against carrying on business as a confectioner or carrying on other business; *Continental Tyre and Rubber (Great Britain) Co Ltd v Heath* (1913) 29 TLR 308, where a restraint as to 'india-rubber goods whether wholesale or retail' imposed on a rubber tyre company salesman was held not severable but as to the area of restraint, the United Kingdom was held severable from Germany and France; *SV Nevanas & Co Ltd v Walker and Foreman* [1914] 1 Ch 413, where the covenant was not to carry on the business of importer of meat or any other trade or business similar to any trade or business carried on by the covenantees and the restraint not to carry on a business of importer of meat was held severable; *Goldsoll v Goldman* [1915] 1 Ch 292, CA, where the restraint was as to real or imitation jewellery and the restraint as to imitation jewellery was held severable, as was the restraint as to the United Kingdom, which could be severed from a restraint from selling in other parts of the world; *British Reinforced Concrete Engineering Co Ltd v Schelff* [1921] 2 Ch 563, where the covenant by the vendor of the business of selling certain products was not to carry on or be concerned as an employee in any business for the manufacture or sale of any products, and it was held that the manufacture clause was severable but that the employment clause was not severable because this was the main purport of the covenant; *Putsman v Taylor* [1927] 1 KB 637, DC (on appeal [1927] 1 KB 741, CA, where the question of severance was not considered), where a covenant by a tailors' manager and cutter employed at A was not to set up as a tailor nor to be employed in any capacity by any tailor in A, B or C, and it was held that the restraint not to be so employed at A was severable (cf *Sir WC Leng & Co Ltd v Andrews* [1909] 1 Ch 763 at 766, CA, where the court refused to treat the covenant as severable); *Atwood v Lamont* [1920] 3 KB 571, CA, where a covenant by an assistant to a draper, tailor and general outfitter not to be concerned in the trade or business of, among other things, a tailor, dressmaker, general draper or outfitter within 10 miles was held not severable; *Ronbar Enterprises Ltd v Green* [1954] 2 All ER 266, [1954] 1 WLR 815, CA, where a restraint unlimited in area was held severable so as to apply to competing business only, and not to similar businesses; *T Lucas & Co Ltd v Mitchell* [1974] Ch 129, [1972] 3 All ER 689, CA, where a restraint on dealing in goods and on soliciting and supplying was held severable. Cf also *Horwood v Millar's Timber and Trading Co Ltd* [1917] 1 KB 305, CA. See also I Smith LC (13th Edn) 486–489.

5   *Chesman v Nainby* (1727) 1 Bro Parl Cas 234, HL, where a restraint not to trade within half a mile of the covenantee's house was severable from the provision 'or any house he might remove to'; *Mallan v May* (1843) 11 M & W 653, where the restraint on a dentist's assistant not to practise in London was severable from the restraint against practising in any of the towns or places in England or Scotland where the covenantees might have been practising during the period of service; *Rannie v Irvine* (1844) 7 Man & G 969 (see PARA 391 note 1); *Price v Green* (1847) 16 M & W 346, Ex Ch, where on the sale of a share of a partnership in a perfumer's business a restraint as to London and Westminster was severed from the words '600 miles therefrom' and it was said that there is no distinction in this respect between a covenant and a bond; *Tallis v Tallis* (1853) 1 E & B 391, where a restraint as to London and 150 miles was held reasonable and as to Edinburgh and Dublin held severable, if unreasonable; *Dendy v Henderson* (1855) 11 Exch 194 at 201 per Martin B; *Leather Cloth Co v Lorsont* (1869) LR 9 Eq 345 at 351 per James V-C; *Baker v Hedgecock* (1888) 39 ChD 520, where Chitty J refused to sever (see PARA 434 note 1); *Davies, Turner & Co v Lowen* (1891) 64 LT 655, where a restraint as to a town in which the covenantees had no business was held severable, as was a restraint as to business 'hereafter to be carried on'; *E Underwood & Son Ltd v Barker* [1899] 1 Ch 300, CA, where the restraint related to the business of a hay and straw merchant in the United Kingdom and certain foreign countries and the view was that the agreement as to the foreign countries would be severable if unreasonable but that in this instance such a provision was not unreasonable (see PARA 401 notes 2–3); *Beetham v Fraser* (1904) 21 TLR 8, DC, where the court refused to sever (see PARA 434 note 2); *Hooper and Ashby v Willis* (1905) 21 TLR 691 (affd (1906) 22 TLR 451, CA) (see note 4; and PARA 434 note 1); *Continental Tyre and Rubber*

(*Great Britain*) *Co Ltd v Heath* (1913) 29 TLR 308 (see note 4); *Lievre v Mayonnet* (1913) 2 LJCCR 4, where the restraint was as to Bradford and 10 miles, and also as to certain other places, and Bradford was held severable; *Caribonum Co Ltd v Le Couch* (1913) 109 LT 385 (on appeal 109 LT 587, CA); *Mason v Provident Clothing and Supply Co Ltd* [1913] AC 724, HL, where the court refused to enforce such part as it might consider reasonable of a restriction on carrying on business within 25 miles of London; *Goldsoll v Goldman* [1915] 1 Ch 292, CA (see note 4); *Attwood v Lamont* [1920] 3 KB 571, CA (see note 4); *Ronbar Enterprises Ltd v Green* [1954] 2 All ER 266, [1954] 1 WLR 815, CA (see note 4); *Scorer v Seymour-Johns* [1966] 3 All ER 347, [1966] 1 WLR 1419, CA, where a covenant by an estate agent's clerk and negotiator not to carry on or work in similar business within 5 miles of the branch office which he managed or the head office was held severable as to the head office.

6   *Baker v Hedgecock* (1888) 39 ChD 520, where Chitty J refused to sever (see PARA 434 note 1); *Lewis and Lewis v Durnford* (1907) 24 TLR 64, where a restraint on a solicitor's clerk not to solicit 'any person who for the time being is or who has within five years previously been a client' of the covenantees or not to act for 'any person who is or has within the previous five years been a client' of the covenantees was held to refer to the date of termination of service and was therefore reasonable but, had it been unreasonable, it would have been severable; *Caribonum Co Ltd v Le Couch* (1913) 109 LT 385 (on appeal 109 LT 587, CA); *Rex Stewart Jeffries Parker Ginsberg Ltd v Parker* [1988] IRLR 483, CA (covenant not to solicit anyone who 'is or has been during your period of employment a customer of the company': words 'is or' severed as they could apply to new customers of the company after the employee's employment terminated).

7   *Rannie v Irvine* (1844) 7 Man & G 969 (see PARA 391 note 1); *Nicholls v Stretton* (1847) 10 QB 346, where a restraint on a solicitor's clerk as to clients of the covenantee before or during the term of service was held severable from a restraint as to clients who became so afterwards (cf earlier proceedings for an injunction in equity on the same covenant (1843) 7 Beav 42: see PARA 407 note 1); *Leather Cloth Co v Lorsont* (1869) LR 9 Eq 345 at 351 per James V-C; *Baines v Geary* (1887) 35 ChD 154, where a restraint imposed on a milk carrier as to customers belonging at any time to the covenantee was held good as to those who were customers during the term of service (see PARA 407 note 1); *Mills v Dunham* [1891] 1 Ch 576 at 581, CA, per Chitty J, where a covenant not to call on or solicit orders from or deal with customers was apparently severable; *Clements v London and North Western Rly Co* [1894] 2 QB 482, CA; *Dubowski & Sons v Goldstein* [1896] 1 QB 478 at 483, CA, where the restraint as to (1) customers during the term of service, and (2) customers afterwards, was held severable if (2) was unreasonable but it was questionable if it was unreasonable (see PARA 407 note 1); *Lewis and Lewis v Durnford* (1907) 24 TLR 64 (see note 6); *Rex Stewart Jeffries Parker Ginsberg Ltd v Parker* [1988] IRLR 483, CA (see note 6) (covenant not to solicit customers of the company 'or associated companies': words 'or associated companies' severed).

8   See *Ronbar Enterprises Ltd v Green* [1954] 2 All ER 266 at 270, [1954] 1 WLR 815 at 820, CA, per Jenkins LJ, applying *Goldsoll v Goldman* [1915] 1 Ch 292, CA, and distinguishing *Attwood v Lamont* [1920] 3 KB 571, CA, on this point. Cf *Putsman v Taylor* [1927] 1 KB 637 at 641, DC; and note 4.

434.   Conditions for severance.   An agreement may be severed if:

(1)   the severed parts are independent of one another and are substantially equivalent to a number of separate covenants[1];

(2)   the severance can be effected without affecting the meaning of the part remaining[2], and

(3)   the excess to be severed is not a part of the main purport and substance of the agreement[3].

On a similar principle, where a covenant is so worded as to cover cases which may possibly arise but to which it cannot reasonably be applied, the unreasonable and hypothetical cases may be treated as severable and the covenant will not be void as a whole[4].

1   *Price v Green* (1847) 16 M & W 346, Ex Ch; *Baker v Hedgecock* (1888) 39 ChD 520, where the restraint was as to 'any business whatsoever' and the court refused to hold this good in so far as it referred to the business of a tailor; *Woods v Thornburn* (1897) 41 Sol Jo 756, where a restraint as to 'any other business' was held not severable and too wide; *Hooper and Ashby v Willis* (1905) 21 TLR 691 (affd (1906) 22 TLR 451, CA); *Mason v Provident Clothing and Supply Co Ltd* [1913] AC 724 at 745, HL, per Lord Moulton; *SV Nevanas & Co Ltd v Walker*

and Foreman [1914] 1 Ch 413; *Goldsoll v Goldman* [1915] 1 Ch 292, CA; *Horwood v Millar's Timber and Trading Co Ltd* [1917] 1 KB 305, CA; *Attwood v Lamont* [1920] 3 KB 571, CA; *Putsman v Taylor* [1927] 1 KB 637, DC (on appeal [1927] 1 KB 741, CA, where the question of severance was not considered); *Ronbar Enterprises Ltd v Green* [1954] 2 All ER 266, [1954] 1 WLR 815, CA; *Amoco Australia Pty Ltd v Rocca Bros Motor Engineering Co Pty Ltd* [1975] AC 561, [1975] 1 All ER 968, PC, where severance was not permitted of covenants in restraint of trade which formed the very essence of a lease; *Sadler v Imperial Life Assurance Co of Canada Ltd* [1988] IRLR 388 at 391–392. See also *Continental Tyre and Rubber (Great Britain) Co Ltd v Heath* (1913) 29 TLR 308 at 310 per Scrutton J (approving *Baker v Hedgecock* (1888) 39 ChD 520). Cf *Alec Lobb (Garages) Ltd v Total Oil GB Ltd* [1985] 1 All ER 303, [1985] 1 WLR 173, CA.

2   *Perls v Saalfeld* [1892] 2 Ch 149 at 157, CA, where a covenant by a clerk to an oil importer etc not to accept a situation or establish himself within 15 miles for three years without permission not to be withheld if the covenantee was satisfied that the situation was not in a competing business was held unreasonable; *Haynes v Doman* [1899] 2 Ch 13 at 25, CA, where Lindley MR said 'I am not considering restrictions so worded as to be partly good and partly bad, and in which the good parts are dependent on the bad. Such restrictions are void in toto, the bad parts infecting and destroying the whole'; *Beetham v Fraser* (1904) 21 TLR 8, DC, where Lord Alverstone CJ said: 'We cannot break up covenants of this sort unless, after severance, an enforceable contract remains'; *SV Nevanas & Co Ltd v Walker and Foreman* [1914] 1 Ch 413 at 422 per Sargant J; *Attwood v Lamont* [1920] 3 KB 571 at 577, CA, per Lord Sterndale MR; *British Reinforced Concrete Engineering Co Ltd v Schelff* [1921] 2 Ch 563; *Putsman v Taylor* [1927] 1 KB 637, DC (on appeal [1927] 1 KB 741, CA, where the question of severance was not considered); *Sadler v Imperial Life Assurance Co of Canada Ltd* [1988] IRLR 388. Cf *Card v Hope* (1824) 2 B & C 661 at 672. However, it is not the law that severance is always permissible where it can effectively be accomplished by the use of a blue pencil, and this test is a misleading one: *Attwood v Lamont* [1920] 3 KB 571 at 578, CA, per Lord Sterndale MR, and at 593 per Younger LJ.

3   *Mason v Provident Clothing and Supply Co Ltd* [1913] AC 724 at 745, HL, per Lord Moulton; *Horwood v Millar's Timber and Trading Co Ltd* [1917] 1 KB 305, CA; *Attwood v Lamont* [1920] 3 KB 571 at 594, CA, per Younger LJ; *British Reinforced Concrete Engineering Co Ltd v Schelff* [1921] 2 Ch 563. See also *Amoco Australia Pty Ltd v Rocca Bros Motor Engineering Co Pty Ltd* [1975] AC 561, [1975] 1 All ER 968, PC; *Bennett v Bennett* [1952] 1 KB 249 at 254, [1952] 1 All ER 413 at 417, CA; *Goodinson v Goodinson* [1954] 2 QB 118 at 123–124, [1954] 2 All ER 255 at 258, CA; *Sadler v Imperial Life Assurance Co of Canada Ltd* [1988] IRLR 388; *Alec Lobb (Garages) Ltd v Total Oil GB Ltd* [1985] 1 All ER 303 at 311, [1985] 1 WLR 173 at 181, CA, per Dillon LJ, at 315–316 and 186 per Dunn LJ, and at 320 and 191 per Waller LJ; *Inntrepreneur Estates Ltd v Mason* [1993] 2 CMLR 293; and *Inntrepreneur Estates (GL) Ltd v Boyes* (1993) 68 P & CR 77, [1993] 2 EGLR 112, CA (case concerning unenforceability of agreements infringing the EC Treaty art 85(1) (now 81(1): see generally PARA 61 et seq)). It is submitted that Lord Moulton's observation as reported in *Mason v Provident Clothing and Supply Co Ltd* [1913] AC 724 at 745, HL, that the excess severed must be of trivial importance or merely technical does not correctly state the law. See also *SV Nevanas & Co Ltd v Walker and Foreman* [1914] 1 Ch 413 at 423 per Sargant J; *Goldsoll v Goldman* [1915] 1 Ch 292, CA; *British Reinforced Concrete Engineering Co Ltd v Schelff* [1921] 2 Ch 563; *Putsman v Taylor* [1927] 1 KB 637, DC (on appeal [1927] 1 KB 741, CA); *T Lucas & Co Ltd v Mitchell* [1974] Ch 129, [1972] 3 All ER 689, CA.

4   *Haynes v Doman* [1899] 2 Ch 13 at 24–25, CA, per Lindley MR; c f *Mitchel v Reynolds* (1711) 1 P Wms 181 at 197; *Rannie v Irvine* (1844) 7 Man & G 969 at 976; *Taff Vale Rly Co (Directors etc) v Macnabb* (1873) LR 6 HL 169 at 178–179 per Lord Colonsay; *Rousillon v Rousillon* (1880) 14 ChD 351 at 366; *Nordenfelt v Maxim Nordenfelt Guns and Ammunition Co Ltd* [1894] AC 535 at 574, HL; see PARA 391 note 1.

(x) Remedies for Breach

435. Election between alternative remedies. In a proper case a valid covenant in restraint of trade may be enforced by injunction notwithstanding that it provides for the payment of a sum by way of liquidated damages[1]. However, the covenantee cannot obtain both the sum by way of liquidated damages and an injunction, but must elect between the two[2] with the exception that he should be able to obtain damages for past breaches even though he requires an injunction in relation to future ones. Election may be made in the statement of case, and is not affected by the fact that both remedies have been claimed[3].

1   *Fox v Scard* (1863) 33 Beav 327; *William Robinson & Co Ltd v Heuer* [1898] 2 Ch 451 at 458, CA, per Chitty J. In *Jones v Heavens* (1877) 4 ChD 636, the contrary proposition was argued, but the point was ignored in the judgment. Where a company is set up as a cloak to enable the covenantor to carry out a breach of covenant, the company may be restrained by injunction as well as the covenantor: *Gilford Motor Co Ltd v Horne* [1933] Ch 935, CA. See further CIVIL PROCEDURE vol 11 (2009) PARA 428. For instances of enforcement of injunctions by committal see *Middleton v Brown* (1878) 47 LJCh 411, CA; *Dottridge Bros Ltd v Crook* (1907) 23 TLR 644. As to the enforcement of injunctions generally see CIVIL PROCEDURE vol 12 (2009) PARA 1249. The court has, apparently, a discretion to limit the extent of the injunction: cf *Cussen v O'Connor* (1893) 32 LR Ir 330. The injunction should, it seems specify so far as possible the precise nature of the acts prohibited: *Provident Clothing and Supply Co Ltd v Mason* [1913] 1 KB 65 at 77, CA; revsd without affecting this point sub nom *Mason v Provident Clothing and Supply Co Ltd* [1913] AC 724, HL.

2   *Sainter v Ferguson* (1894) 1 Mac & G 286; *Coles v Sims* (1854) 5 De GM & G 1; *Carnes v Nesbitt* (1862) 7 H & N 778; *Fox v Scard* (1863) 33 Beav 327; *Howard v Woodward* (1864) 10 Jur NS 1123; *Young v Chalkley* (1867) 16 LT 286; *National Provincial Bank of England v Marshall* (1888) 40 ChD 112, CA; *General Accident Assurance Corpn v Noel* [1902] 1 KB 377; cf *French v Macale* (1842) 2 Dr & War 269 at 276; *Robb v Green* [1895] 2 QB 315, CA; *Lewis and Lewis v Durnford* (1907) 24 TLR 64. As to the common law principle of election see generally ESTOPPEL vol 16(2) (Reissue) PARA 962.

3   *Lewis and Lewis v Durnford* (1907) 24 TLR 64. Cf *Cargill v Bower* (1878) 10 ChD 502 at 508; and see generally CIVIL PROCEDURE. In *Sainter v Ferguson* (1849) 1 Mac & G 286, the covenantee had recovered judgment for the liquidated damages and costs at law, and proved for the costs only in bankruptcy, and it was held that he had elected, although, apparently, the court might on a proper application have made an order so limited as to keep his right alive. Cf *Fox v Scard* (1863) 33 Beav 327, where it was held that if a claimant recovered only nominal damages at law in a case where a court of equity had sent him to law to try his right, he did not lose his right to an injunction; it would be otherwise if he obtained substantial damages. Occasionally the court has refused costs to a defendant who has successfully established that his covenant is in restraint of trade: *Allsopp v Wheatcroft* (1872) LR 15 Eq 59; *Ehrman v Bartholomew* [1898] 1 Ch 671 at 674; *Lamson Pneumatic Tube Co v Phillips* (1904) 91 LT 363, CA, where, however, as the judgment was reversed in the Court of Appeal, no question as to those costs arose in that court.

436.   Mutuality of performance of covenants.

A restrictive covenant will not be enforced by injunction, nor will damages be awarded for its breach[1], if the stipulations of the covenantee and covenantor are mutually dependent, unless the covenantee has performed and is willing and able to perform in future his part of the contract of which the covenant forms a part[2]. However, such a covenant will be enforced even though the agreement contains other covenants which cannot be specifically enforced, if those other covenants are capable of being separated[3].

Where an employer repudiates a contract of employment, and the employee accepts the repudiation, any restrictive covenant in the contract of employment is thereby terminated, so that the question of its reasonableness does not arise[4].

1   *Measures Bros Ltd v Measures* [1910] 2 Ch 248 at 262, CA, per Kennedy LJ. Cf CIVIL PROCEDURE vol 11 (2009) PARA 467.

2   *General Billposting Co Ltd v Atkinson* [1909] AC 118, HL; *Measures Bros Ltd v Measures* [1910] 2 Ch 248 at 262, CA, where it was held that a compulsory winding-up order operates as a wrongful dismissal of a covenantor, releasing him from his covenant: see COMPANY AND PARTNERSHIP INSOLVENCY vol 7(3) (2004 Reissue) PARA 490; but cf *Welstead v Hadley* (1904) 21 TLR 165, CA, where the appointment of a receiver for debenture holders and dismissal by him of the managing director does not release the director from a covenant not to trade. However, if an employee is paid a week's salary in lieu of notice and dismissed, that is not a wrongful dismissal releasing him from a restrictive covenant: *W Dennis & Sons Ltd v Tunnard Bros and Moore* (1911) 56 Sol Jo 162. As to the question whether stipulations are dependent or independent see CONTRACT vol 9(1) (Reissue) PARA 967; DEEDS AND OTHER INSTRUMENTS

vol 13 (2007 Reissue) PARA 266 et seq. As to the effect of the claimant's conduct on the right to an injunction see CIVIL PROCEDURE vol 11 (2009) PARA 467.

3   *Whittaker v Howe* (1841) 3 Beav 383 at 395; *Rolfe v Rolfe* (1846) 15 Sim 88, where A, a retiring partner in a tailor's business, covenanted with B not to trade within certain limits, and B covenanted to employ A so long as B continued in the business; an injunction was granted against A, although B's covenant could not have been specifically enforced; *Daggett v Ryman* (1868) 17 LT 486; cf *Kemble v Kean* (1829) 6 Sim 333 at 335 per Shadwell V-C. As to the enforcement of positive and negative covenants, and the cases in which negative covenants will be implied, see CIVIL PROCEDURE vol 11 (2009) PARA 448 et seq.

4   *Rock Refrigeration Ltd v Jones* [1997] 1 All ER 1, [1997] ICR 938, CA, overruling *D v M* [1996] IRLR 192.

437. Affirmation and acquiescence. It is not possible to challenge a contract as being in restraint of trade after it has been affirmed[1] at common law; nor where there has been acquiescence[2] in equity[3].

1   As to affirmation see CONTRACT vol 9(1) (Reissue) PARAS 1010–1011.
2   As to acquiescence see EQUITY vol 16(2) (Reissue) PARA 909.
3   *Panayiotou v Sony Entertainment (UK) Ltd* [1994] EMLR 233.

438. Liquidated sum. Where liquidated damages are fixed by the agreement, the covenantee is entitled to the agreed sum, unless the sum is in reality a penalty and not liquidated damages[1], but it seems clear that he cannot recover the agreed sum more than once[2].

1   *Shackle v Baker* (1808) 14 Ves 468; *Davies v Penton* (1827) 6 B & C 216; *Leighton v Wales* (1838) 3 M & W 545; *Boys v Ancell* (1839) 7 Scott 364; *Horner v Flintoff* (1842) 9 M & W 678; *Price v Green* (1847) 16 M & W 346, Ex Ch; *Galsworthy v Strutt* (1848) 1 Exch 659; *Atkyns v Kinnier* (1850) 4 Exch 776; *Marshalls Ltd v Leek* (1900) 17 TLR 26. Cf *Astley v Weldon* (1801) 2 Bos & P 346 at 352 per Lord Eldon CJ (disapproving *Hardy v Martin* (1783) 1 Bro CC 419n); *Pemberton v Vaughan* (1847) 10 QB 87; *National Provincial Bank of England v Marshall* (1888) 40 ChD 112 at 116, CA, per Cotton LJ. In *Mitchel v Reynolds* (1711) 1 P Wms 181 at 187, 194, it was said that the enforcement of a contract in lawful restraint of trade by a penalty was lawful, but the penalty was in fact treated as liquidated damages. A sum may be recovered as liquidated damages although described as a penalty: *Sainter v Ferguson* (1849) 7 CB 716; see generally DAMAGES vol 12(1) (Reissue) PARAS 1065–1067; *Upton v Henderson* (1912) 106 LT 839; *Webster v Bosanquet* [1912] AC 394, PC.
2   Cf *Galsworthy v Strutt* (1848) 1 Exch 659 at 663 per Parke B.

439. Effect of offer to pay liquidated sum. A covenantor cannot, by offering to pay the penalty or liquidated damages agreed, in general release himself from his covenant[1], but it is a question of construction in each case whether or not the fixed sum is intended to be the price of liberty to do the act complained of[2].

1   *French v Macale* (1842) 2 Dr & War 269.
2   *Roper v Bartholomew* (1823) 12 Price 797; *French v Macale* (1842) 2 Dr & War 269. See DEEDS AND OTHER INSTRUMENTS vol 13 (2007 Reissue) PARA 272; CIVIL PROCEDURE vol 11 (2009) PARA 450.

440. Interim injunctions. An interim injunction to enforce a contractual obligation in restraint of trade may be granted in appropriate circumstances; there is no rule placing such obligations in a special category for this purpose[1]. However, where the enforceability of a restrictive covenant in an employment contract is in issue in interim proceedings, the court may determine that a speedy trial would be appropriate[2].

1   *Dairy Crest Ltd v Pigott* [1989] ICR 92, CA; *Lawrence David Ltd v Ashton* [1991] 1 All ER 385, CA, not following dicta in *Fellowes & Son v Fisher* [1976] QB 122, [1975] 2 All ER 829, CA; *Office Overload Ltd v Gunn* [1977] FSR 39, CA.
2   *Lawrence David Ltd v Ashton* [1991] 1 All ER 385, CA.

(xi) Conflict of Laws

441–500.   Conflict of laws. The rules which govern contracts in restraint of trade are as applicable to foreigners trading in England as to English traders; and if a contract is void as against the public policy of England it will not be enforced in an English court even though made in a country where no objection could be raised to it[1].

The court may grant relief where the restriction on the covenantor is outside the territory[2].

1   *Rousillon v Rousillon* (1880) 14 ChD 351 at 369. See CONFLICT OF LAWS vol 8(3) (Reissue) PARAS 31, 358.
2   *Blackler v New Zealand Rugby Football League Inc* [1968] NZLR 547, NZ CA.

COMPULSORY ACQUISITION OF LAND

1. POWERS TO ACQUIRE LAND

(1) NATURE OF COMPULSORY PURCHASE

501.   Compulsory purchase and requisitioning. Where land or an interest in land is purchased or taken under statutory powers[1] without the agreement of the owner[2] it is said to have been compulsorily acquired[3], but where there is statutory power to take mere possession of the land without the acquisition of any estate or interest in it apart from the possession, it is said to have been requisitioned. Statutes giving requisitioning powers are usually named so as to indicate the limitation of the power given[4].

1   See e g the Lands Clauses Consolidation Act 1845 s 18; the Compulsory Purchase Act 1965 s 5; and PARA 616. See also the Acquisition of Land Act 1981 s 2; and PARA 557.
2   Even where there is power to acquire land compulsorily the acquisition may be effected by agreement. As to when an acquisition amounts to one by agreement, and when it amounts to compulsory purchase, see PARA 550.
3   Where, however, there is a purchase of the whole or any part of any statutory undertaking under any enactment in that behalf prescribing the terms on which the purchase is to be effected, the provisions of the Land Compensation Act 1961 as to compulsory acquisitions of land are excluded (s 36(1)); and it has been held that transfers of industries to public ownership did not amount to a compulsory purchase or sale (*John Hudson & Co Ltd v Kirkness (Inspector of Taxes)* [1954] 1 All ER 29, [1954] 1 WLR 40, CA; affd sub nom *Kirkness (Inspector of Taxes) v John Hudson & Co Ltd* [1955] AC 696, [1955] 2 All ER 345, HL). For the purposes of the Land Compensation Act 1961, 'statutory undertaking' means an undertaking established under any enactment: s 36(2). 'Enactment' includes an enactment in any local or private Act of Parliament and an order, rule, regulation, byelaw or scheme made under an Act of Parliament (s 39(1)); and references in the Land Compensation Act 1961 to any enactment are to be construed as references to that enactment as amended by or under any other enactment (s 39(9)).
    As to the exclusion of statutory undertakers' land from compulsory purchase under the Acquisition of Land Act 1981 see s 16; and PARA 564.
4   See e g the Requisitioned Land and War Works Act 1945; and the Requisitioned Land and War Works Act 1948. Such powers of requisitioning are usually for the defence of the realm: see WAR AND ARMED CONFLICT vol 49(1) (2005 Reissue) PARAS 508–532.

502.   Nature of power of compulsory acquisition. A statutory power to acquire or take land compulsorily is usually a power to take the whole land and the interests in it, but a statute may specifically authorise the purchase of a stratum of the land[1] or the creation of an easement[2] or some statutory right over the land[3].

Where a power is given to purchase or otherwise acquire land or a right over it, provision is invariably made for the payment of compensation or purchase money for the interests in the land purchased or made subject to the right[4]. Persons without such interests in the land, for example persons entitled to the benefit of a right of way or other easement over the acquired land or to the benefit of a restrictive covenant with respect to the land or to the benefit of maintaining statutory works on it, will receive no compensation or purchase money and will continue to enjoy their rights after the acquisition until the acquiring authority does some act in pursuance of the statutory purchase adversely affecting the right of way, easement, covenant or statutory right, whereupon a right to compensation may arise[5].

Whether the statutory purpose giving rise to the acquisition may be effected notwithstanding the possibility of injury to the rights of other persons will depend upon the construction of the statutory power[6]; and the persons entitled to a right of way, easement, covenant or statutory right will have no remedy for any injury they suffer unless provision is made for compensation for that injury[7]. Any compensation provided for is given in lieu of the right of action those persons would have had but for the statutory authorisation[8], although there is also a statutory right to compensation for injury by statutory works which would not have given rise to any cause of action[9].

Some statutes anticipate that injury to such rights is inevitable, and give special power to extinguish rights of way over the acquired land[10] and deal with the rights of statutory undertakers with apparatus on and rights over the land[11].

The principal subject of this title is the general law and procedure concerning powers of compulsory acquisition of land or of an existing interest in land, and the compensation or purchase money payable by reason of the exercise of those powers. Powers of acquisition specific to the subjects of particular classes of legislation are considered in detail in the titles of this work appropriate to those subjects[12].

1   See PARAS 532–534.
2   See eg the Civil Aviation Act 1982 s 44 (see AIR LAW vol 2 (2008) PARA 191 et seq); and the Highways Act 1980 s 250 (see HIGHWAYS, STREETS AND BRIDGES vol 21 (2004 Reissue) PARA 85). Without specific authorisation, easements may be acquired by agreement only: see PARA 533.
3   See eg the Highways Act 1980 s 250; and HIGHWAYS, STREETS AND BRIDGES vol 21 (2004 Reissue) PARA 85.
4   See PARA 715 et seq.
5   See PARA 877 et seq.
6   See PARA 859.
7   See *Caledonian Rly Co v Walker's Trustees* (1882) 7 App Cas 259 at 293, HL; and PARA 859.
8   See PARA 879.
9   See the Land Compensation Act 1973 Pt I (ss 1–19); and PARA 883 et seq.
10 See eg the Town and Country Planning Act 1990 ss 247, 248, 271–273 (see HIGHWAYS, STREETS AND BRIDGES vol 21 (2004 Reissue) PARAS 71, 72, 83, 97, 214; TOWN AND COUNTRY PLANNING vol 46(3) (Reissue) PARAS 1019–1022); and the Acquisition of Land Act 1981 s 32 (see HIGHWAYS, STREETS AND BRIDGES vol 21 (2004 Reissue) PARA 806). See also PARA 858.
11 See PARA 858.

12 Many of these powers apply the general provisions discussed in this title: see eg the Electricity Act 1989 s 10(1), Sch 3; and FUEL AND ENERGY vol 19(2) (2007 Reissue) PARA 1281 et seq.

(2) THE EMPOWERING ENACTMENTS

503.   The legislation.   Up to the middle of the nineteenth century the power to acquire land was usually given by local or private Act, identifying the particular land to be acquired and providing for the procedure for the acquisition, for compensation and for conveyance[1], but the Lands Clauses Consolidation Act 1845[2] was enacted to provide a uniform acquisition procedure which would be incorporated in the special Act[3] which authorised the specific acquisition[4].

Later it became necessary for local authorities and other public bodies to have a continuous general power to acquire land in the discharge of their functions, so various public general Acts were passed giving general acquisition powers, some of which allowed an acquiring authority to purchase any land for its purposes without any further authorisation[5], but most of which provided that the powers of compulsory acquisition could only be exercised with regard to specific land by a provisional order which usually had to be confirmed by Parliament[6]. Modern statutes authorising compulsory acquisition normally require a compulsory purchase order (as opposed to a provisional order), to be confirmed by a government department[7]; and confirmation by Parliament is required only in the case of the acquisition of special land[8]. A uniform compulsory purchase order procedure was provided by the Acquisition of Land (Authorisation Procedure) Act 1946, which incorporated many of the provisions of the Lands Clauses Consolidation Act 1845 now re-enacted in the Compulsory Purchase Act 1965[9]. The Acquisition of Land (Authorisation Procedure) Act 1946 has been applied by many modern Acts authorising compulsory acquisition and has been consolidated in the Acquisition of Land Act 1981[10].

1   As to powers under local Acts see PARA 504.
2   See PARA 509 et seq. Many of the provisions of the Lands Clauses Consolidation Act 1845 were incorporated in the Acquisition of Land (Authorisation Procedure) Act 1946 s 1, Sch 2 (repealed) but are now re-enacted in the Compulsory Purchase Act 1965: see PARA 513. See also the text and note 8.
3   As to the meaning of 'special Act' see PARA 509.
4   Ie unless the Lands Clauses Consolidation Act 1845, or its provisions, were specifically excluded or varied.
5   See PARA 524.
6   This was known as the 'provisional order procedure'. See further PARA 506.
7   The public general Act confers the power of compulsory purchase for particular purposes. The acquiring authority, acting under the public general power, submits a compulsory purchase order to the confirming authority for confirmation. The confirming authority can confirm, refuse or vary the order. Most compulsory acquisitions now occur under the procedure which is, in most cases, governed by the Acquisition of Land Act 1981: see PARA 556 et seq.
8   See note 2; and PARAS 569, 572 et seq.
9   See PARAS 509 et seq, 556 et seq.
10 See PARA 556 note 1.

504. Acquisition under local Act. Where a power to acquire land compulsorily is necessary for the carrying out of some undertaking, and there are no available powers under existing statutes, it will be necessary to promote a local or private Bill. The procedure is regulated by parliamentary standing orders, under which, when power is sought to acquire land compulsorily, the promoters of the Bill must give notice by public advertisement and by personal service on the persons likely to be affected, and must deposit plans with books of reference showing the land proposed to be acquired and the names of the owners, lessees and occupiers of the land[1].

When passed, the Act, which will be classed as a local and personal Act[2] in the statute book, authorises the compulsory acquisition of such of the land so shown as is required for the purposes of the undertaking[3]. Among local and personal Acts a few instances will be found in which land not specifically described has been authorised to be acquired from time to time as required[4].

1   As to the procedure on the promotion of private Bills see PARLIAMENT vol 34 (Reissue) PARA 847.
2   As to local and personal Acts see STATUTES vol 44(1) (Reissue) PARAS 1213–1214.
3   As to the incorporation of the Lands Clauses Acts or the Compulsory Purchase Act 1965 see PARAS 509, 513. As to the time for the exercise of the powers see PARA 617.
4   See e g the Metropolitan Paving Act 1817 ss 80–96 (repealed), under which land could be taken as occasion required for the purpose of widening and improving London streets. This means of compulsory acquisition is now rarely used because of the procedures contained in the Transport and Works Act 1992: see PARA 507.

505. Acquisition under public general Act. Some public general Acts authorise the acquisition of specific land where the land is required for a special purpose[1] and the body or person authorised may proceed directly to acquire the land in accordance with the provisions of the Act. Other public general Acts have given a general power to take limited quantities of land for particular purposes without the land being specified in the Act, in which case the land is only identified when the purchase is negotiated or a notice to treat is given[2].

It is, however, now customary for public general Acts to give power to take land for particular purposes[3] without specifying the land but to provide for a further authorisation procedure after the land required for the particular purpose has been decided upon. The authorisation may be by provisional order[4] or by compulsory purchase order[5].

1 See eg the Land Registry (New Buildings) Act 1900 (repealed); and the Public Works (Festival of Britain) Act 1949 (repealed). See also the Roosevelt Memorial Act 1946, which provided for the compulsory extinguishment of private rights over Grosvenor Square and its maintenance as a public garden.

2 See eg the Admiralty (Signal Stations) Act 1815 (repealed); the Customs Consolidation Act 1853 ss 33–345 (repealed); and the Coastguard Act 1925 s 1(3) (repealed). Under those Acts, the acquiring authority could compulsorily acquire land without any further authorisation.

3 Ie to establish the principle that land may be compulsorily acquired for such purposes. See eg the power to acquire land under the Crossrail Act 2008 ss 6, 7; and RAILWAYS, INLAND WATERWAYS AND CROSS-COUNTRY PIPELINES vol 39(1A) (Reissue) PARA 325.

4 See PARA 506.

5 See PARA 556.

506. Provisional order authorisation. Where a statute confers power in general terms on authorities or undertakers, or classes of authorities or undertakers, to take land for specified purposes without specifying the land to be taken and requiring specific authority by provisional order to take any specified land, the acquiring authority or undertakers must, by means of advertisements and notices served on owners, lessees and occupiers of the land in question, give notice of the intention to petition the authority having power to make the order. This authority is usually a government department. The petition must contain full particulars and supporting evidence showing that the provisions of the particular empowering Act have been complied with.

The authority empowered to make the order must then consider the petition and may be required to direct the holding of a public local inquiry to hear objections to the making of the order[1]. If the authority is then satisfied that power to take the land should be given, a provisional order is made and a Bill submitted to Parliament to confirm the order, which does not have effect until so confirmed.

If a petition is presented against a Bill to confirm an order whilst the Bill is pending in either House of Parliament, the petitioner may appear before the select committee to which the Bill is referred and oppose the order as in the case of a private Bill[2].

This procedure has been almost totally replaced by the procedures for the making of compulsory purchase orders[3] and the procedures set out in the Transport and Works Act 1992[4]. In practice it therefore now applies to very few compulsory acquisitions.

1 The actual procedure depends on the particular Act under which the provisional order is made, and slight variations exist. Eg under the Military Lands Act 1892 s 2(7)(b), a public local inquiry must be held unless the petition is dismissed (see ARMED FORCES vol 2(2) (Reissue) PARAS 120–122); whereas under the Light Railways Act 1896 s 7(3) (repealed subject to transitional provisions), there was no requirement of a public local inquiry to consider objections.

2 See eg the Military Lands Act 1892 s 2(10); and ARMED FORCES vol 2(2) (Reissue) PARA 121. The procedure in Parliament on provisional orders and private Bills is provided by the standing orders of each House: see PARLIAMENT vol 34 (Reissue) PARA 845 et seq.

3 See PARA 556 et seq.

4 See PARA 507.

507. Compulsory acquisition under the Transport and Works Act 1992.
Under the Transport and Works Act 1992, a new procedure was introduced for authorising the construction of works such as tramways and railways and associated compulsory acquisition of land. The Secretary of State[1] may make works orders by statutory instrument authorising the construction of railways, tramways, inland waterways and associated infrastructure[2]. The works order may provide for the compulsory acquisition of land and the creation and extinguishment of rights over land[3].

An application for a works order is made to the Secretary of State after the requirements for advertising the application have been complied with[4]. If objections are validly made and not withdrawn by the local authority for the area or by an owner, lessee or occupier[5], the Secretary of State must hold a public inquiry or a hearing[6]. The Secretary of State has power to approve a works order with or without modifications[7] and any person aggrieved[8] may challenge the Secretary of State's decision in the High Court[9].

A works order will be subject to special parliamentary procedure[10] where a compulsory purchase order would be subject to such a procedure under the Acquisition of Land Act 1981[11].

1   In any enactment, 'Secretary of State' means one of Her Majesty's principal Secretaries of State: see the Interpretation Act 1978 s 5, Sch 1. The office of Secretary of State is a unified office, and in law each Secretary of State is capable of performing the functions of all or any of them: see CONSTITUTIONAL LAW AND HUMAN RIGHTS vol 8(2) (Reissue) PARA 355.

      All functions of a Minister of the Crown under the Transport and Works Act 1992 ss 1, 3, so far as they are exercisable in relation to Wales, are now exercisable by the Welsh Ministers, having been transferred to the National Assembly for Wales (except where any such order would have effect both in Wales and England): see the National Assembly for Wales (Transfer of Functions) Order 1999, SI 1999/672, art 2, Sch 1; and the Government of Wales Act 2006 s 162(1), Sch 11 para 30. So far as the order-making functions of the Secretary of State under the Transport and Works Act 1992 ss 1, 3 are exercisable in relation to Wales, they are exercisable only with the agreement of the National Assembly of Wales: see the National Assembly for Wales (Transfer of Functions) Order 1999, SI 1999/672, art 5, Sch 2. The order-making powers conferred by the Transport and Works Act 1992 s 2 have not been transferred to the Welsh Ministers: National Assembly for Wales (Transfer of Functions) Order 1999, SI 1999/672, art 2, Sch 1. As to the Welsh Assembly Government and the Welsh Ministers see CONSTITUTIONAL LAW AND HUMAN RIGHTS.

2   See the Transport and Works Act 1992 ss 1–3; and RAILWAYS, INLAND WATERWAYS AND CROSS-COUNTRY PIPELINES vol 39(1A) (Reissue) PARA 302 et seq. See also the Transport and Works Act 1992 (Commencement No 3 and Transitional Provisions) Order 1992, SI 1992/2784.

3   See the Transport and Works Act 1992 s 5, Sch 1; and RAILWAYS, INLAND WATERWAYS AND CROSS-COUNTRY PIPELINES vol 39(1A) (Reissue) PARAS 303, 523. All functions of a Minister of the Crown under the Transport and Works Act 1992 ss 5, 11–13, 22, so far as they are exercisable in relation to Wales, are exercisable by the Welsh Ministers, having been transferred to the National Assembly for Wales by the National Assembly for Wales (Transfer of Functions) Order 1999, SI 1999/672, art 2, Sch 1.

4   See the Transport and Works Act 1992 s 6; the Transport and Works Act 1992 (Applications and Objections Procedure) Rules 2006, SI 2006/1466; and RAILWAYS, INLAND WATERWAYS AND CROSS-COUNTRY PIPELINES vol 39(1A) (Reissue) PARAS 307, 525. The rule-making powers conferred by the Transport and Works Act 1992 s 6(2)–(6) have not been transferred to the Welsh Ministers, but are exercisable in relation to Wales only with their agreement: see the National Assembly for Wales (Transfer of Functions) Order 1999, SI 1999/672, arts 2, 5, Schs 1, 2.

5   As to objections see the Transport and Works Act 1992 s 10; and RAILWAYS, INLAND WATERWAYS AND CROSS-COUNTRY PIPELINES vol 39(1A) (Reissue) PARAS 311, 528. The rule-making powers conferred by the Transport and Works Act 1992 s 10 have not been transferred to the Welsh Ministers, but are exercisable in relation to Wales only with their agreement: see the National Assembly for Wales (Transfer of Functions) Order 1999, SI 1999/672, arts 2, 5, Schs 1, 2.

6 See the Transport and Works Act 1992 s 11; and RAILWAYS, INLAND WATERWAYS AND CROSS-COUNTRY PIPELINES vol 39(1A) (Reissue) PARAS 312, 529. Rules as to the conduct of the inquiry or hearing are contained in the Transport and Works (Inquiries Procedure) Rules 2004, SI 2004/2018, made under the Tribunals and Inquiries Act 1992 s 9: see RAILWAYS, INLAND WATERWAYS AND CROSS-COUNTRY PIPELINES vol 39(1A) (Reissue) PARAS 312, 529.

7 See the Transport and Works Act 1992 s 13; and RAILWAYS, INLAND WATERWAYS AND CROSS-COUNTRY PIPELINES vol 39(1A) (Reissue) PARAS 314, 531.

8 As to the meaning of 'person aggrieved' see ADMINISTRATIVE LAW vol 1(1) (2001 Reissue) PARA 66. See also PARA 612 note 1.

9 See the Transport and Works Act 1992 s 22; and RAILWAYS, INLAND WATERWAYS AND CROSS-COUNTRY PIPELINES vol 39(1A) (Reissue) PARAS 318, 535.

10 As to special parliamentary procedure see PARA 605.

11 Transport and Works Act 1992 s 12(1). See the Acquisition of Land Act 1981 ss 17, 18, 19, 28, Sch 3; and PARAS 603–604, 606 et seq. Orders made by the Welsh Ministers under the Transport and Works Act 1992 are subject to special parliamentary procedure to such extent as is provided for by the references under the Acquisition of Land Act 1981 ss 12–18, Sch 3 para 5: see the National Assembly for Wales (Transfer of Functions) Order 1999, SI 1999/672, art 2, Sch 1.

508. Compulsory acquisition under the Planning Act 2008. The system of development consent for nationally significant infrastructure projects[1], which was introduced by the Planning Act 2008[2], takes the form of development consent orders which may give developers certain powers for the purpose of facilitating the project[3]. These may include the power to acquire land compulsorily where there is a compelling case in the public interest[4]. The Planning Act 2008 applies the procedure for compulsory purchase in Part 1 of the Compulsory Purchase Act 1965[5] to the compulsory acquisition of land under development consent orders as if the order were a compulsory purchase order under the Acquisition of Land Act 1981[6].

1 See PARAS 535–544; and TOWN AND COUNTRY PLANNING. As to the meaning of 'nationally significant infrastructure project' see PARA 535 note 3.
2 At the date at which this volume states the law the Planning Act 2008 was not fully in force.
3 See PARA 535 et seq; and TOWN AND COUNTRY PLANNING.
4 See the Planning Act 2008 s 122 (not yet in force); and PARA 535.
5 The Compulsory Purchase Act 1965 Pt 1 (ss 1–32) has effect with the omission of s 4 (time limit for exercise of compulsory purchase powers) (see PARAS 550, 617), s 10 (compensation for injurious affection) (see PARA 718), and Sch 3 para 3(3) (provision as to giving of bonds) (see PARAS 639, 641): see the Planning Act 2008 s 125 (not yet in force); and PARA 536. As to the application of the Compulsory Purchase Act 1965 see PARA 513.
6 See the Planning Act 2008 s 125(2) (not yet in force).

(3) INCORPORATION OF ACTS IN EMPOWERING ENACTMENTS

(i) Incorporation of Lands Clauses Acts in Empowering Enactments

509. Incorporation of Lands Clauses Acts in local Acts as special Act. Before the Lands Clauses Acts 1845 to 1895[1], empowering or special Acts authorising works of a public nature provided their own mode of acquisition, compensation and completion of purchase of land. Parliament then deemed it expedient, in the Lands Clauses Consolidation Act 1845, to comprise in one general Act the various provisions usually found in statutes relative to the acquisition of land required for works of a public nature and the compensation to be made, so as to avoid the necessity of repeating these provisions in each empowering Act, and so as to ensure greater uniformity in the provisions themselves[2].

The Lands Clauses Acts apply to every undertaking of a public nature[3] authorised by any Act passed after 8 May 1845[4] which empowers the purchase or taking of lands for that undertaking[5], and they are incorporated with that empowering Act, whether expressly mentioned or not[6], and all their clauses and provisions apply to the undertaking, so far as they are applicable[7], unless they are expressly varied or excepted by that Act[8]. Where an Act passed before 8 May 1845 authorises an undertaking, and that Act is varied by a subsequent Act which provides for the taking of other lands for the same undertaking, the Lands Clauses Acts apply to the whole undertaking[9] so far as applicable[10].

The Lands Clauses Acts, as well as the clauses and provisions of every other Act which is incorporated with the empowering enactment, are to be construed together[11] as forming one Act called the 'special Act'[12].

1   Ie the Lands Clauses Consolidation Act 1845 and the Lands Clauses Consolidation Acts Amendment Act 1860, and any Acts for the time being in force amending those Acts: Interpretation Act 1978 s 5, Sch 1. See STATUTES vol 44(1) (Reissue) PARA 1229. The Lands Clauses Consolidation Act 1845 was extensively amended by the Compulsory Purchase Act 1965 s 39(4), Sch 8.

2   See the Lands Clauses Consolidation Act 1845 preamble; and *Metropolitan District Rly Co v Sharpe* (1880) 5 App Cas 425 at 440, HL. The provisions of the Lands Clauses Consolidation Act 1845 as to compensation and the assessment of it are affected by the Land Compensation Act 1961, and the jurisdiction for assessment was transferred to the Lands Tribunal by the Lands Tribunal Act 1949, with minor exceptions. The Lands Tribunal was abolished on 1 June 2009 and its functions were transferred to the Upper Tribunal: see PARA 720.

3   They do not apply to matters sanctioned by private estate Acts: *Wale v Westminster Palace Hotel Co* (1860) 8 CBNS 276; *Re Sion College, ex p London Corpn* (1887) 57 LT 743, CA. The Lands Clauses Consolidation Act 1845 does not apply to the acquisition of land under the Crossrail Act 2008 s 6(1): see Sch 6 Pt 2 para 1; and RAILWAYS, INLAND WATERWAYS AND CROSS-COUNTRY PIPELINES vol 39(1A) (Reissue) PARA 325.

4   Ie the date of the passing of the Lands Clauses Consolidation Act 1845.

5   Lands Clauses Consolidation Act 1845 s 1.

6   It is, however, usual to incorporate the Lands Clauses Acts in express terms. For an example of the application of those Acts see the Coast Protection Act 1949 s 27(3). For an example of a power of incorporation by subordinate instrument see the Harbours Act 1964 ss 14(3), 16(6); and PORTS AND HARBOURS vol 36(1) (2007 Reissue) PARAS 629, 646. The Lands Clauses Acts may be partially incorporated. As to the interpretation of such a provision in an empowering enactment see *R v London Corpn* (1867) LR 2 QB 292; *Ferrar v London Sewers Comrs* (1869) LR 4 Exch 227, Ex Ch, distinguishing *Broadbent v Imperial Gas Co* (1857) 7 De GM & G 436 at 447–448 (affd without this point being taken sub nom *Imperial Gas Light and Coke Co v Broadbent* (1859) 7 HL Cas 600); *Dungey v London Corpn* (1869) 38 LJCP 298. The Lands Clauses Consolidation Act 1845 s 5, which formerly gave guidance on such interpretation, was repealed by the Statute Law (Repeals) Act 1993 s 1(1), Sch 1 Pt XIV. For an example of the partial application of the Lands Clauses Acts see the Compulsory Purchase Act 1965 s 37(3), applying the Lands Clauses Consolidation Act 1845 ss 127–132 (sale of superfluous land) in relation to land acquired in pursuance of a compulsory purchase order under the Pipe-lines Act 1962 s 11. See further PARA 380 et seq; and RAILWAYS, INLAND WATERWAYS AND CROSS-COUNTRY PIPELINES vol 39(1A) (Reissue) PARA 595 et seq.

7   See *Re Cherry's Settled Estates* (1862) 31 LJCh 351; *Re Westminster Estate of the Parish of St Sepulchre, ex p Vicar of St Sepulchre* (1864) 4 De GJ & Sm 232; *Re Spitalfields Schools and Comrs of Woods and Forests* (1870) LR 10 Eq 671; *Re Wood's Estate, ex p Works and Buildings Comrs* (1886) 31 ChD 607 at 617–618, CA; *Re Mills' Estate, ex p Works and Public Buildings Comrs* (1886) 34 ChD 24, CA.

8   Lands Clauses Consolidation Act 1845 s 1; *Central Control Board (Liquor Traffic) v Cannon Brewery Co Ltd* [1919] AC 744, HL. The Lands Clauses Acts are no longer incorporated in relation to compulsory purchases in accordance with the procedure provided by the Acquisition of Land Act 1981, but the Compulsory Purchase Act 1965 Pt I (ss 1–32), re-enacting the Lands Clauses Acts in relation to compulsory purchase orders, applies instead: see PARA 15 et seq. For examples of the exclusion of the Lands Clauses Acts see the Channel Tunnel Act 1987 s 37(6); the Cardiff Bay Barrage Act 1993 s 4(5); and the Croydon Tramlink Act 1994 s 5(3).

9   *Lancashire and Yorkshire Rly Co v Evans* (1851) 15 Beav 322; *Re London and Birmingham Rly Co's Act 1833, Re London and North Western Rly Co's Act 1846, ex p Eton College* (1850) 20 LJCh 1.

10 Eg the Lands Clauses Consolidation Act 1845 s 16 (subscription of capital: see PARA 615) may not be applicable to the extension of a previously authorised undertaking: *Weld v South Western Rly Co* (1862) 32 Beav 340; *R v Great Western Rly Co* (1852) 1 E & B 253.

11 See PARA 510.

12 See the Lands Clauses Consolidation Act 1845 ss 1, 2.

510. Construction together of special Act and Lands Clauses Acts. When incorporated the special Act[1] and the Lands Clauses Acts[2] are construed together as forming one Act[3].

In construing the special Act and the provisions of the Lands Clauses Acts together, questions have arisen as to the extent to which the former has varied the latter. The general rule of construction when two Acts are to be construed as one is that every part of each of them must be construed as if it had been contained in the one Act unless there is some manifest discrepancy making it necessary to hold that the later Act has to some extent modified something found in the earlier Act[4]. The Lands Clauses Acts are to be followed unless the special Act by express words or necessary intendment varies or excepts them[5]. A variation showing that a provision is inapplicable will have the same effect as an express variation[6].

Where the special Act makes provisions as to a particular subject matter which differ from the corresponding provisions in the Lands Clauses Acts, but do not cover the whole of those provisions in the Lands Clauses Acts, the provisions not covered will apply[7].

Difficulties of construction have also arisen owing to words used in special Acts to include clauses differing from the statutory headings[8]. In such cases effect must be given to the words of the special Act[9], but slight variations may not be material[10]. The effect to be given to these introductory headings in construing the sections ranged under them is not governed by any general rule. They may be referred to in order to determine the sense of any doubtful expression in a section[11].

1 As to the meaning of 'special Act' see PARA 509.

2 As to the Lands Clauses Acts see PARA 509 note 1.

3 Lands Clauses Consolidation Act 1845 s 1.

4 *Canada Southern Rly Co v International Bridge Co* (1883) 8 App Cas 723 at 727, PC; *Hart v Hudson Bros Ltd* [1928] 2 KB 629, DC; *Phillips v Parnaby* [1934] 2 KB 299, DC; and see further STATUTES vol 44(1) (Reissue) PARA 1485.

5 *R v London Corpn* (1867) LR 2 QB 292 at 295 per Blackburn J (in delivering the judgment of the court); *Weld v South Western Rly Co* (1863) 32 Beav 340. For applications of the rule see *Ex p Rayner* (1878) 3 QBD 446; *Metropolitan District Rly Co v Sharpe* (1880) 5 App Cas 425, HL.

6 *Metropolitan District Rly Co v Sharpe* (1880) 5 App Cas 425 at 441, HL, per Lord Blackburn.

7 *Re Westminster Estate of the Parish of St Sepulchre, ex p Vicar of St Sepulchre* (1864) 4 De GJ & Sm 232; *R v St Luke's, Chelsea* (1871) LR 7 QB 148, Ex Ch; and see the cases cited in PARA 879 notes 2–3.

8 As to the incorporation or exclusion of clauses contained in the Lands Clauses Acts see PARA 509.

9 *Broadbent v Imperial Gas Co* (1857) 7 De GM & G 436 at 447 per Lord Cranworth; *Kirby v Harrogate School Board* [1896] 1 Ch 437 at 448, CA.

10 *R v London Corpn* (1867) LR 2 QB 292.

11 *Hammersmith and City Rly Co v Brand* (1869) LR 4 HL 171 at 203 per Lord Chelmsford; *Eastern Counties and London and Blackwall Rly Cos v Marriage* (1860) 9 HL Cas 32; and cf *Bryan v Child* (1850) 5 Exch 368; *Latham v Lafone* (1867) LR 2 Exch 115 at 123; *Lang v Kerr, Anderson & Co* (1878) 3 App Cas 529 at 536, HL; *Union Steamship Co of New Zealand v Melbourne Harbour Trust Comrs* (1884) 9 App Cas 365, PC, decided under other statutes.

511.   Construction of definitions in Lands Clauses Acts. In construing the Lands Clauses Acts[1] certain words have defined meanings. 'Prescribed' means prescribed or provided for in the special Act[2], and the sentence in which that word occurs is construed as if, instead of the word 'prescribed', the expression 'prescribed for that purpose in the special Act' had been used[3]. The 'works' or the 'undertaking' means the works or undertaking, of whatever nature, authorised by the special Act to be executed, and is not confined to the execution of works and undertakings of a purely physical nature[4]; and the 'promoters of the undertaking' means the parties, whether a company, undertakers, commissioners, trustees, corporations or private persons, empowered by the special Act to execute those works or undertakings[5]. Those parties are referred to below as the 'undertakers'.

Certain other words and expressions have meanings assigned to them which apply both in the Land Clauses Acts and in the special Act, unless there is something either in the subject or context repugnant to such construction[6]. 'Lands' extends to messuages, lands, tenements and hereditaments of any tenure[7]. As used in several sections it includes incorporeal hereditaments, but in others it does not[8]; it may include an option to purchase land but will not include such an option unless otherwise provided[9]. The definition does not, however, apply so as to permit the compulsory acquisition of part only of the land by taking a stratum or part only of the interest in the land, or by requiring a lease, easement or right over the land unless specially provided, or the acquiring or taking of an interest against the land[10].

In provisions where notice is required to be given to the owner of any land, or where the authority or consent of any such owner is required to some act, 'owner' means any person or corporation who would be entitled under the Lands Clauses Acts or the special Act to sell and convey the land to the undertakers[11].

Provision is also made for the construction of expressions relating to number, gender and time[12].

1   As to the Lands Clauses Acts see PARA 509 note 1.
2   As to the meaning of 'special Act' see PARA 509.
3   Lands Clauses Consolidation Act 1845 s 2.
4   Lands Clauses Consolidation Act 1845 s 2; and see *Central Control Board (Liquor Traffic) v Cannon Brewery Co Ltd* [1919] AC 744, HL, where the expression was held to include the control of the liquor traffic.
5   Lands Clauses Consolidation Act 1845 s 2.
6   Lands Clauses Consolidation Act 1845 s 3. For examples of repugnancy see *Clark v London School Board* (1874) 9 Ch App 120; *Worsley v South Devon Rly Co* (1851) 16 QB 539.
7   Lands Clauses Consolidation Act 1845 s 3. 'Lease' includes an agreement for a lease: s 3.
8   *Great Western Rly Co v Swindon and Cheltenham Rly Co* (1884) 9 App Cas 787 at 800 et seq, HL, per Lord Watson, and at 808 per Lord Bramwell; *R v Cambrian Rly Co* (1871) LR 6 QB 422 at 427 per Cockburn CJ, and at 431 per Blackburn J, which was overruled on another point in *Hopkins v Great Northern Rly Co* (1877) 2 QBD 224, CA; *Hill v Midland Rly Co* (1882) 21 ChD 143; *Pinchin v London and Blackwall Rly Co* (1854) 5 De GM & G 851, 24 LJCh 417; *Re Brewer* (1875) 1 ChD 409, CA.
9   *Oppenheimer v Minister of Transport* [1942] 1 KB 242, [1941] 3 All ER 485, where an option to purchase land was held to be 'lands or an interest therein' within the meaning of the Lands Clauses Consolidation Act 1845 s 49 (repealed).
10 See PARAS 532–534.
11 Lands Clauses Consolidation Act 1845 s 3.
12 Words importing the singular number only include the plural number and words importing the plural number only include the singular number; words importing the masculine gender only include females; and 'month' means a calendar month: Lands Clauses Consolidation Act 1845 s 3.

512.　Access to special Act.　All persons interested in the special Act[1] must be able to have access to it[2]. For this purpose a company[3] must, at all times after the expiration of six months from the passing of the special Act, keep a Queen's printers' copy of it in its principal office of business; and where the undertaking is such that the works[4] are not confined to one town or place, as in the case of a railway or canal, it must also, within those six months, deposit another such copy of the special Act in the office of each of the clerks of the county councils of the several counties into which the works extend[5]. Failure on the part of the company to keep or deposit the copies of the Act renders it liable to a fine[6].

The clerks of the councils are required to receive, and they and the company must retain, these copies, and permit all persons interested to inspect the Act at all reasonable hours, and make copies of or extracts from it, on payment for every inspection, and a further sum for every hour during which the inspection continues after the first hour[7]. It is an offence to fail to comply with these provisions[8].

1　As to the meaning of 'special Act' see PARA 509.
2　See the Lands Clauses Consolidation Act 1845 ss 150, 151; and the text and notes 3–8. These sections are not generally incorporated where the power to acquire is derived from a public general Act, and they are not re-enacted in the Compulsory Purchase Act 1965 in relation to compulsory purchase orders, which may be otherwise inspected: see PARA 559.
3　The expression 'company' is used in the Lands Clauses Consolidation Act 1845 ss 150, 151, and not 'the promoters of the undertaking', as in other sections: see PARA 511.
4　As to the meaning of 'works' see PARA 511.
5　Lands Clauses Consolidation Act 1845 s 150; Courts Act 1971 s 56(1), Sch 8 Pt I para 1(2).
6　If the offence is tried on indictment there is no specific limit to the fine: see the Criminal Law Act 1977 s 32(1). If it is tried summarily, the penalty is a fine not exceeding level 2 on the standard scale: Lands Clauses Consolidation Act 1845 s 151; Criminal Justice Act 1982 ss 38, 46. Appeal for any party aggrieved by any determination or adjudication with respect to any penalty or forfeiture under the Lands Clauses Acts or under the special Act lies to the Crown Court: Lands Clauses Consolidation Act 1845 s 146 (amended by the Courts Act 1971 s 56(2), Sch 9 Pt I).
7　Lands Clauses Consolidation Act 1845 s 150; Local Government Act 1972 s 228(5).
8　The offence is punishable on summary conviction by a penalty not exceeding level 1 on the standard scale: Local Government Act 1972 s 228(7) (amended by virtue of the Criminal Justice Act 1982 ss 38, 46).

(ii)　Application of Compulsory Purchase Act 1965 to Acquisitions Authorised by Compulsory Purchase Orders

513.　Application of Compulsory Purchase Act 1965.　Part I of the Compulsory Purchase Act 1965[1], which re-enacts various provisions of the Lands Clauses Acts[2], applies to any compulsory purchase to which the provisions of Part II of the Acquisition of Land Act 1981[3] apply or to which Schedule 1 to that Act applies, that is, authorisations of purchase by a compulsory purchase order under the 1981 Act[4].

1　Ie the Compulsory Purchase Act 1965 Pt I (ss 1–32): see PARA 549 et seq.
2　As to the Lands Clauses Acts see PARA 509 note 1.
3　Ie the Acquisition of Land Act 1981 Pt II (ss 10–15): see PARA 558 et seq.
4　Compulsory Purchase Act 1965 s 1(1) (substituted by the Acquisition of Land Act 1981 s 34, Sch 4 para 14(1), (2)). Subject to exceptions and modifications, the Compulsory Purchase Act 1965 Pt I is also applied by s 37 to compulsory purchase orders under the Pipe-lines Act 1962 s 11 (see RAILWAYS, INLAND WATERWAYS AND CROSS-COUNTRY PIPELINES vol 39(1A) (Reissue) PARA 595 et seq) made after 1 January 1966: see the Compulsory Purchase Act 1965 s 37(1), (4) (s 37(1) amended by the Acquisition of Land Act 1981 s 34(1), Sch 4 para 14(7)). For those purposes, the Compulsory Purchase Act 1965 s 11(1), (2) (see PARAS 639, 645), s 30 (see PARA 618) and s 31 (see PARA 668) do not apply: s 37(2).

As to the application of the Compulsory Purchase Act 1965 see also the Channel Tunnel Act 1987 s 37(4), (5); and the Crossrail Act 2008 Sch 6 Pt 2 paras 2, 3 (see RAILWAYS, INLAND WATERWAYS AND CROSS-COUNTRY PIPELINES vol 39(1A) (Reissue) PARA 325). As to the application of the Compulsory Purchase Act 1965 to development consent orders made in connection with nationally significant infrastructure projects see the Planning Act 2008 (not yet fully in force); and PARAS 508, 535–544.

514.   Construction of Compulsory Purchase Act 1965 with empowering enactment as special Act.   In construing Part I of the Compulsory Purchase Act 1965[1], the enactment under which the purchase is authorised and the compulsory purchase order[2] are to be deemed to be the special Act[3].

1   Ie the Compulsory Purchase Act 1965 Pt I (ss 1–32): see PARA 549 et seq.
2   For these purposes, 'compulsory purchase order' has the same meaning as in the Acquisition of Land Act 1981 (see PARA 557 note 1): Compulsory Purchase Act 1965 s 1(1)(b) (substituted by the Acquisition of Land Act 1981 s 34(1), Sch 4 para 14(1), (2)).
3   Compulsory Purchase Act 1965 s 1(2) (amended by the Acquisition of Land Act 1981 s 34(3), Sch 6 Pt I). For the purposes of the Compulsory Purchase Act 1965 Pt I as applied by s 37 (see PARA 513 note 4), the 'special Act' means the Pipe-lines Act 1962 together with the compulsory purchase order under s 11: Compulsory Purchase Act 1965 s 37(1). See further RAILWAYS, INLAND WATERWAYS AND CROSS-COUNTRY PIPELINES vol 39(1A) (Reissue) PARA 595 et seq. Compare the meaning of 'special Act' in PARA 509. As to the effect of the construction of the Acquisition of Land Act 1981 and the empowering enactment see PARA 510. No provision is made for access to the special Act, but the compulsory purchase order may be inspected: see PARA 571.

(iii)   Incorporation of Railways Clauses Consolidation Act 1845

515.   Incorporation in local Acts and compulsory purchase orders of provisions excluding minerals.   A local Act may incorporate the provisions of the Railways Clauses Consolidation Act 1845 giving power to exclude minerals from the purchase of land[1] and restricting the working of minerals[2]. Otherwise minerals must be purchased as included in the land to be acquired[3].

In the case also of acquisitions of land authorised by a compulsory purchase order to which the Acquisition of Land Act 1981 applies[4] there is express power to incorporate in the order the provisions of the 1845 Act referred to above[5]. Otherwise minerals must be purchased as included in the land to be acquired[6].

1   Ie the Railways Clauses Consolidation Act 1845 s 77: see MINES, MINERALS AND QUARRIES vol 31 (2003 Reissue) PARA 144.
2   Ie the Railways Clauses Consolidation Act 1845 ss 78–85: see MINES, MINERALS AND QUARRIES vol 31 (2003 Reissue) PARAS 144, 162 et seq.
3   See PARA 534.
4   See PARA 556.
5   See the Acquisition of Land Act 1981 s 3, Sch 2 paras 1–5; and MINES, MINERALS AND QUARRIES vol 31 (2003 Reissue) PARA 137 et seq.
6   See PARA 534.

(iv)   Application of Land Compensation Act 1961

516.   Application of Land Compensation Act 1961 where land is authorised to be acquired compulsorily.   Where by or under any statute, whether passed before or after 22 June 1961[1], land[2] is authorised to be acquired compulsorily, any question of disputed compensation is to be referred to the Upper Tribunal[3] and is to be determined by it in accordance with the provisions of the Land Compensation Act 1961[4] which provide, inter alia, rules for the assessment of compensation[5] and the matters to be taken into account[6].

1 Ie the date the Land Compensation Act 1961 was passed.
2 For these purposes, 'land' means any corporeal hereditament, including a building, and includes any interest or right in or over land and any right to water; and 'building' includes any structure or erection and any part of a building as so defined, but does not include plant or machinery comprised in a building: Land Compensation Act 1961 s 39(1).
3 As to references to the Upper Tribunal see the Land Compensation Act 1961 ss 2–4; and PARAS 716–717, 724 et seq. As to the Upper Tribunal see PARA 720; and ADMINISTRATIVE LAW.
4 Land Compensation Act 1961 s 1.
5 See the Land Compensation Act 1961 ss 5–22; and PARA 754 et seq.
6 See the Land Compensation Act 1961 ss 31–39; and PARAS 636, 721, 762 et seq. See also *Taylor v North West Water Ltd* [1995] RVR 83, Lands Tribunal.

517. Application to the Crown. The Land Compensation Act 1961 applies in relation to the acquisition of interests in land[1], whether compulsorily or by agreement, by government departments, being authorities possessing compulsory purchase powers[2], as it applies in relation to the acquisition of interests in land by such authorities which are not government departments[3].

1 As to the meaning of 'land' see PARA 516 note 2.
2 As to the meaning of 'authority possessing compulsory purchase powers' see PARA 763 note 6.
3 Land Compensation Act 1961 s 33.

518. Special provision in relation to ecclesiastical property in England. Where ecclesiastical property[1] in England is vested in the incumbent of a benefice which is vacant it is treated for the purposes of the Land Compensation Act 1961 as being vested in the Diocesan Board of Finance for the diocese in which the land is situated[2].

1 For these purposes, 'ecclesiastical property' means land belonging to any ecclesiastical benefice of the Church of England, or being or forming part of a church subject to the jurisdiction of a bishop of any diocese of the Church of England or the site of such a church, or being or forming part of a burial ground subject to such jurisdiction: Land Compensation Act 1961 s 34(2) (amended by the Church of England (Miscellaneous Provisions) Measure 2006 s 14, Sch 5 para 8(b)). As to the meaning of 'land' see PARA 516 note 2.
2 Land Compensation Act 1961 s 34(1) (amended by the Church of England (Miscellaneous Provisions) Measure 2006 Sch 5 para 8(a)). See ECCLESIASTICAL LAW.

(4) ACQUIRING AUTHORITIES

519. Acquisition by royal prerogative or by government department. The right to take land or affect injuriously some or all of the rights of ownership in land, whether by the taking of those rights or their curtailment, was originally a prerogative right enjoyed by the sovereign power in the state[1], but even in time of war and where land is required only temporarily the executive prefers to act under statutory authority[2].

In normal times Ministers or government departments requiring land are given statutory power to purchase it which is similar to the powers given to local authorities and other public bodies[3].

1 The sovereign power of Parliament is unrestricted, and there is no need to rely on any doctrine of state necessity: see CONSTITUTIONAL LAW AND HUMAN RIGHTS vol 8(2) (Reissue) PARA 17.
2 This is normally so even in times of national emergency: see eg statutes conferring powers to requisition, such as under the Emergency Powers (Defence) Act 1940 (repealed). Such powers may be wider and more comprehensive than the prerogative powers: see eg *A-G v De Keyser's Royal Hotel Ltd* [1920] AC 508, HL. In exceptional cases the old prerogative power is still exercised, subject however to compensation: see *Burmah Oil Co (Burma Trading) Ltd v Lord Advocate* [1965] AC 75, [1964] 2 All ER 348, HL.
3 See PARA 572 et seq.

520.   Acquisition by public bodies requiring land for statutory purposes.
Where a person or statutory body is given statutory power to carry out works or
to give effect to some other statutory purpose, and the ownership of land is
necessary for that purpose, the person or body, if he or it has no or insufficient
land for the purpose, will require power to purchase or otherwise acquire land
by agreement or, in default of agreement, compulsorily[1], unless power is given to
do works on the land without acquiring it by purchase or otherwise[2].

The need for land is usually for immediate requirements for the statutory
purpose, and statutory power is given accordingly[3], but in some cases power has
been given to acquire land in advance of requirements[4].

The purposes for which powers of acquisition are given may be specifically
defined by statute[5] as, for example, in private Acts authorising a railway project.
In public general Acts, however, it is normal for those purposes to be defined in
general terms[6], leaving it to a compulsory purchase order to define the particular
project[7].

1   As to statutory powers to acquire land see PARA 521 et seq. As to the right to purchase money or
    compensation see PARAS 616, 715 et seq.
2   As to such powers and the right to compensation see PARA 521.
3   As to the time for the exercise of statutory powers see PARAS 617, 852.
4   As to such powers see PARA 526 note 1.
5   As to the purposes of a compulsory acquisition see PARA 526.
6   See eg the Town and Country Planning Act 1990 s 226; and TOWN AND COUNTRY PLANNING
    vol 46(2) (Reissue) PARA 934 et seq.
7   See PARA 503.

521.   Power to purchase or power to take for use.   Where a statute gives a
power to purchase land it is implicit that the acquiring authority is to pay the
purchase price, even if not expressly stated. The statute will define the
acquisition procedure[1] and the matters to be taken into account in assessing the
purchase price[2]. The same applies if the statute gives power to purchase a right in
or over land without any necessity to purchase the land itself[3]. Where, however,
a statute gives power merely to take over the use of land, purchase money will
not be payable[4], and whether or not compensation is payable is a question of
statutory construction[5]. Persons with no right to purchase money or
compensation for an interest on a compulsory purchase may have a right to
payments for disturbance when displaced from land[6], or voluntary payments
may be made[7].

Where a statute merely gives power to execute works in or over land,
purchase money is not payable; but in such cases the statute may make provision
for a right to compensation for the injurious affection of the land. If the statute
does not do so, no right to compensation will arise[8]. Even if there is provision for
the vesting of the works themselves, on completion, in the authority empowered
to do the works, this is merely a statutory transfer of the right to use the land for
the purposes of the works, so long as those purposes exist, and is not a purchase
of the land[9]. There is no need to purchase land for the execution of works where
the statute gives sufficient power to execute the works without purchasing the
land[10].

A statute may give powers to execute works on a highway in which there is
already sufficient property vested in the authority to justify the use of the
highway for the works, and so no purchase of the land will be necessary[11].

The statutory transfer of an undertaking is not a compulsory acquisition of
land, even though the land owned by the undertaking is also transferred[12].

1　Ie a notice to treat, inviting claims to the purchase money or compensation: see PARA 616 et seq.
2　See PARA 753 et seq.
3　See PARA 532 et seq.
4　Eg upon requisitioning. Thus there is no ownership enabling the requisitioning authority to grant a tenancy: see *Southgate Borough Council v Watson* [1944] KB 541, [1944] 1 All ER 603, CA; *Minister of Agriculture and Fisheries v Matthews* [1950] 1 KB 148, [1949] 2 All ER 724.
5　See *Rockingham Sisters of Charity v R* [1922] 2 AC 315 at 322, PC. Nevertheless, an intention to take away a subject's property without compensation must be clear: see *Central Control Board (Liquor Traffic) v Cannon Brewery Co Ltd* [1919] AC 744, HL. For an example see the Opencast Coal Act 1958 s 4 (compulsory rights orders); and MINES, MINERALS AND QUARRIES vol 31 (2003 Reissue) PARA 422.
6　See the Land Compensation Act 1973 ss 37, 38; and PARAS 838–839.
7　See the Land Compensation Act 1973 s 37(5); and PARA 838.
8　See PARAS 859, 877 et seq. Similarly, if the works cause injury to land on which they are not executed there will be no right to compensation unless such a right is provided: see PARAS 859, 877 et seq. See also note 9.
9　For an example of a power to execute works over the land without involving the acquisition of land see local authorities' former powers under the Public Health Act 1936 s 15(1)(b) (repealed) to construct a public sewer in, on or over any land. 'Land' included buildings (Interpretation Act 1889 s 3 (repealed: see now the Interpretation Act 1978 s 5, Sch 1); *Hutton v Esher UDC* [1974] Ch 167, [1973] 2 All ER 1123, CA), so the power included power, where necessary, to demolish buildings: *Hutton v Esher UDC*. Although, when completed, the public sewer itself (ie not merely the materials of which it was made but also the space it occupied: *Taylor v Oldham Corpn* (1876) 4 ChD 395 at 411) would vest in the local authority under the Public Health Act 1936 s 20 (repealed), no purchase of land was involved but only the right of any person who had sustained damage through the exercise of the power to full compensation from the local authority.
10　See *Roderick v Aston Local Board* (1877) 5 ChD 328, CA; *London and North Western Rly Co v Westminster Corpn* [1904] 1 Ch 759, CA.
11　See *London and North Western Rly Co v Westminster Corpn* [1904] 1 Ch 759 at 765–766, CA, in relation to the former vesting of the subsoil of London streets sufficient for the construction of public conveniences under the Public Health (London) Act 1936 s 113(2) (repealed). See also *Escott v Newport Corpn* [1904] 2 KB 369, where there was power to erect poles in a street and so interfere with the subsoil, and it was held that there was no need to purchase land for the purpose but only a right to compensation for any injury caused.
12　See the Land Compensation Act 1961 s 36(1); and PARA 501. See also *John Hudson & Co Ltd v Kirkness (Inspector of Taxes)* [1954] 1 All ER 29, [1954] 1 WLR 40, CA; affd sub nom *Kirkness (Inspector of Taxes) v John Hudson & Co Ltd* [1955] AC 696, [1955] 2 All ER 345, HL.

522.　Power to require information. A statutory power to require information applies to information about land[1] in relation to which an acquiring authority[2] is entitled to exercise a power of compulsory purchase[3]. The acquiring authority may serve a notice on: (1) the occupier of the land; (2) any person who has an interest in the land either as freeholder, mortgagee or lessee; (3) any person who directly or indirectly receives rent for the land; (4) any person who, in pursuance of an agreement between himself and a person interested in the land, is authorised to manage the land or to arrange for the letting of it[4], requiring him to give to the authority in writing (a) the name and address of any person he believes to be an owner, lessee, tenant (whatever the tenancy period) or occupier of the land; and (b) the name and address of any person he believes to have an interest in the land[5].

The notice (which must be in writing[6]) must specify the period within which the information must be given to the acquiring authority (being a period of not less than 14 days beginning with the day on which the notice is served)[7]. The notice must also specify or describe the land, the compulsory purchase power, and the enactment which confers the power[8].

A person commits an offence if he fails without reasonable excuse to comply with such a notice[9]. A person commits an offence if, in response to a notice served on him under these provisions he gives information which is false in a material particular, and when he does so, he knows or ought reasonably to know that the information is false[10]. If either such offence is committed by a body corporate and is proved to have been committed with the consent or connivance of, or to be attributable to any neglect on the part of a director, manager, secretary or other similar officer of the body corporate, or by a person purporting to act in any such capacity, he, as well as the body corporate, is guilty of that offence and liable to be proceeded against accordingly[11].

1   'Land' includes (1) messuages, tenements and hereditaments; and (2) in relation to compulsory purchase under any enactment, includes anything falling within any definition of the expression in that enactment: Acquisition of Land Act 1981 s 7(1).

2   'Acquiring authority', in relation to a compulsory purchase, means the Minister, local authority or other person who may be authorised to purchase the land compulsorily: Acquisition of Land Act 1981 s 7(1).

   'Local authority' means: (1) a billing authority or a precepting authority as defined in the Local Government Finance Act 1992 s 69 (see LOCAL GOVERNMENT vol 29(1) (Reissue) PARA 524; RATING AND COUNCIL TAX vol 39(1B) (Reissue) PARAS 5, 229); (2) the London Fire and Emergency Planning Authority (see FIRE SERVICES vol 18(2) (Reissue) PARA 17); (3) a fire and rescue authority in Wales constituted by a scheme under the Fire and Rescue Services Act 2004 s 2 or a scheme to which s 4 applies (see FIRE SERVICES); (4) a levying body within the meaning of the Local Government Finance Act 1988 s 74 (see LOCAL GOVERNMENT vol 29(1) (Reissue) PARA 530) or a body as regards which s 75 applies (see LOCAL GOVERNMENT vol 29(1) (Reissue) PARA 530); (5) any joint board or joint committee if all the constituent authorities are such authorities as are described in heads (1)–(4) above; and (6) the Honourable Society of the Inner Temple or the Honourable Society of the Middle Temple: Acquisition of Land Act 1981 s 7(1) (definition substituted by the Local Government Finance (Repeals, Savings and Consequential Amendments) Order 1990, SI 1990/776, art 8, Sch 3 para 23; and amended by the Local Government Finance Act 1992 s 117(1), Sch 13 para 52; the Police and Magistrates' Courts Act 1994 s 93, Sch 9 Pt I; the Greater London Authority Act 1999 s 328(8), Sch 29 para 34; and the Fire and Rescue Services Act 2004 s 53(1), Sch 1 para 53(1), (2)).

3   Acquisition of Land Act 1981 s 5A(1) (ss 5A, 5B added by the Planning and Compulsory Purchase Act 2004 s 105).

4   Acquisition of Land Act 1981 s 5A(4) (as added: see note 3).

5   Acquisition of Land Act 1981 s 5A(2) (as added: see note 3). This power is exercisable for the purpose of enabling the acquiring authority to acquire the land: s 5A(3) (as so added).

6   Acquisition of Land Act 1981 s 5A(7) (as added: see note 3).

7   Acquisition of Land Act 1981 s 5A(5) (as added: see note 3).

8   Acquisition of Land Act 1981 s 5A(6) (as added: see note 3).

9   Acquisition of Land Act 1981 s 5B(1) (as added: see note 3). A person guilty of an offence under s 5B is liable on summary conviction to a fine not exceeding level 5 on the standard scale: s 5B(5) (as so added). 'Standard scale' means the standard scale of maximum fines for summary offences as set out in the Criminal Justice Act 1982 s 37: see the Interpretation Act 1978 s 5, Sch 1 (definition added by the Criminal Justice Act 1988 s 170(1), Sch 15 PARA 58); and CRIMINAL LAW, EVIDENCE AND PROCEDURE vol 11(4) (2006 Reissue) PARA 1676; MAGISTRATES vol 29(2) (Reissue) PARA 804. At the date at which this volume states the law, the standard scale is as follows: level 1, £200; level 2, £500; level 3, £1,000; level 4, £2,500; level 5, £5,000: Criminal Justice Act 1982 s 37(2) (substituted by the Criminal Justice Act 1991 s 17(1)). As to the determination of the amount of the fine actually imposed, as distinct from the level on the standard scale which it may not exceed, see the Criminal Justice Act 2003 s 164; and MAGISTRATES vol 29(2) (Reissue) PARA 807.

10 Acquisition of Land Act 1981 s 5B(2) (as added: see note 3). As to the penalty for this offence see note 9.

11 Acquisition of Land Act 1981 s 5B(3) (as added: see note 3). As to the meaning of 'director' for these purposes see the Town and Country Planning Act 1990 s 331(2); and TOWN AND COUNTRY PLANNING vol 46(1) (Reissue) PARA 55.

(5) LAND SUBJECT TO ACQUISITION

(i) In general

523.　Specification of land. The land which may be acquired may be unspecified in the empowering enactment or special Act[1] except as to general area[2], it may be specified in it by plans or sections[3] or it may await specification by a compulsory purchase order authorising the acquisition of defined land for the purposes of the empowering enactment[4].

1　As to the meaning of 'special Act' see PARAS 509, 514.
2　See PARA 524.
3　See PARA 525.
4　See PARAS 514, 558.

524.　Land unspecified in special Act. Many special Acts[1] give compulsory powers of purchase over a large area, but provide that only so much of that land may be taken as is actually required[2]. Such a power does not extend to inalienable lands unless it is extended by special provision or necessary implication[3]. In any case the power will be limited to acquisition for the authorised purposes[4].

1　As to the meaning of 'special Act' see PARAS 509, 514.

2　See eg the Coastguard Act 1925 s 1(2).

3　*R v Minister of Health, ex p Villiers* [1936] 2 KB 29 at 44, [1936] 1 All ER 817 at 823, DC; but see now PARA 530. As to the exclusion and protection of certain land see PARA 529 et seq.
4　See PARA 526.

525.　Land specifically described in special Act. Special Acts[1] commonly authorise land to be taken by providing that, for the purposes of the Act, the undertakers may enter upon, take, and use the land delineated and described in the deposited plans and books of reference or any of them[2].

The plans and books of reference are only binding to the extent to which they are incorporated and referred to in the special Act, and only for the purpose in regard to which that Act refers to them[3]. Representations on the plans as to the position, extent or nature of the works proposed to be constructed are not binding on the undertakers unless the representations are incorporated in the Act, even though the effect of the representations may have prevented the landowner from opposing the Bill when before Parliament[4]. In the same way, notices given before the promotion of the Bill as to the extent of land proposed to be taken will not prevent the undertakers from taking a greater quantity if the Act in fact authorises it[5]. Conversely, undertakers cannot execute works shown on the deposited plans unless power to do so is expressly given in the special Act[6].

Before the undertakers can take land under a clause in the above form it must appear that the land in question is delineated on the plans[7]. Land within the limits of deviation is considered to be delineated, even though all the outside boundaries are not shown[8]. Land partly within and partly outside these limits may be held not to be delineated if only some of its boundaries are shown. In disputes of this nature the question turns upon whether, upon looking at the plans, the landowner can reasonably be deemed to have had notice that his land might be required, and the answer in each particular case will depend upon the size and nature of the particular close of land and the extent to which the boundaries are indicated[9]. Land outside the limits of deviation may, of course, be taken if properly delineated and required[10].

1 As to the meaning of 'special Act' see PARAS 509, 514.

2 Provision for the correction of errors and omissions in deposited plans and books of reference is commonly made in a special Act or enactments incorporated with it. A provision of this nature usually requires notice to be given to the owners, occupiers or lessees affected, a certificate of two justices that the error or omission arose from a mistake and the deposit of the certificate or copy of it with the appropriate officer of the local authority: see eg the Railways Clauses Consolidation Act 1845 s 7 (repealed).

3 *North British Rly Co v Tod* (1846) 12 Cl & Fin 722, HL; *Beardmer v London and North Western Rly Co* (1849) 1 Mac & G 112 at 114 per Lord Cottenham; *Taff Vale Rly Co v Cardiff Rly Co* [1917] 1 Ch 299, CA.

4 See the cases cited in note 3; and *Breynton v London and North Western Rly Co* (1846) 10 Beav 238; *R v Caledonian Rly Co* (1850) 16 QB 19; *Ware v Regent's Canal Co* (1858) 3 De G & J 212; *A-G v Great Eastern Rly Co* (1872) 7 Ch App 475; affd (1873) LR 6 HL 367.

5 *Re Huddersfield Corpn and Jacomb* (1874) 10 Ch App 92. The accidental omission of the names of persons interested in land from the book of reference will not prevent the land from being taken: *Kemp v West End of London and Crystal Palace Rly Co* (1855) 1 K & J 681.

6 *A-G v Great Northern Rly Co* (1850) 4 De G & Sm 75 (further proceedings 15 Jur 387); *R v Wycombe Rly Co* (1867) LR 2 QB 310 at 319 per Cockburn CJ.

7 *Dowling v Pontypool, Caerleon and Newport Rly Co* (1874) LR 18 Eq 714.

8 *Wrigley v Lancashire and Yorkshire Rly Co* (1863) 9 Jur NS 710; *Dowling v Pontypool, Caerleon and Newport Rly Co* (1874) LR 18 Eq 714. The purpose for which limits of deviation are introduced into plans is to allow a certain latitude in the construction of the centre line of the works authorised, and they are not intended in themselves to define the area within which land may be taken: see *Finck v London and South-Western Rly Co* (1890) 44 ChD 330 at 347, 351, 353, CA; *Doe d Payne v Bristol and Exeter Rly Co* (1840) 6 M & W 320; *Cardiff Rly Co v Taff Vale Rly Co* [1905] 2 Ch 289.

9 See the cases cited in note 8; and *Protheroe v Tottenham and Forest Gate Rly Co* [1891] 3 Ch 278, CA; *Coats v Caledonian Rly Co* (1904) 6 F 1042, Ct of Sess.

10 *Crawford v Chester and Holyhead Rly Co* (1847) 11 Jur 917; *Finck v London and South-Western Rly Co* (1890) 44 ChD 330, CA.

526. Land only for purposes authorised.

The Act which confers the power of taking land must be considered in order to ascertain the purposes for which the land may be taken[1]. These purposes may include the execution of works, in which case land may be taken for all the works, of whatsoever nature, authorised to be executed[2].

All undertakers, whether local authorities or companies formed for trade, can take land only for those purposes for which the legislature has invested them with the power; if they attempt to take it for any collateral object, the court will restrain them by injunction[3]; and they may not take land and at the same time agree not to use it for the statutory purposes[4].

If there is any doubt as to the powers to take land, the Act will be construed in favour of the landowner[5], but in the case of local authorities carrying out public improvements, the interest of the public as well as of the landowner will be considered in construing a doubtful provision[6].

If the purposes for which the land is required are legitimate, the undertakers are the persons to determine which portion of the land is required[7]. In coming to a determination they must act honestly and in good faith with a view to using the land for the authorised purpose, and not for any sinister or collateral purposes[8]. It is immaterial that the works might be carried out in another way which might cause less inconvenience[9], and the fact that under their statutory powers the undertakers could have taken other land instead of the land taken, which would have been less harmful to the claimant, cannot be used to found an action for damages for negligence[10].

Undertakers of particular classes of undertaking have been authorised to purchase land for what are called extraordinary purposes, which seem to be purposes for which it was not foreseen, at the time of the passing of the special Act, that land would, of necessity, be required[11]. Land for these purposes can only be acquired by agreement, and the quantity of the land as well as the purposes for which it may be purchased are generally specified in the special Act[12].

Undertakers may sell the land so acquired and purchase other land for the same purposes, and, so long as the amount held does not exceed the prescribed[13] quantity, they may deal with the land as an ordinary proprietor may do[14]. Land acquired for extraordinary purposes is not subject to the provisions relating to superfluous land[15].

1   *Simpson v South Staffordshire Waterworks Co* (1865) 34 LJCh 380 at 387 per Lord Westbury. See also *Palmer v Minister of Housing and Local Government and Romford Corpn* (1952) 3 P & CR 165, CA (claim that acquisition was in advance of requirements where there was no such power). There is no power to acquire land in advance of requirements unless specially authorised by statute; for examples of such authority see the Housing Act 1985 s 17(4); the Local Government Act 1972 s 120(2). As to acquisitions for collateral objects see the text and notes 3–4.

2   See the definitions of 'undertaking' and 'works' in the Lands Clauses Consolidation Act 1845 s 2 (see PARA 511); and the Compulsory Purchase Act 1965 s 1(4) (see PARA 549 note 3). Thus, in the case of a railway, these would ordinarily include not only the line itself but also stations, warehouses, offices, yards and other conveniences (*Cother v Midland Rly Co* (1848) 5 Ry & Can Cas 187 at 193–194 per Lord Cottenham; *Sadd v Maldon, Witham and Braintree Rly Co* (1851) 6 Exch 143; cf *Boland v Canadian National Rly Co* [1927] AC 198, PC, where a subway was held not to be a part of a railway undertaking); and in the case of a dock there would be included quays, wharves and warehouses (*London Association of Shipowners and Brokers v London and India Docks Joint Committee* [1892] 3 Ch 242 at 249–250, CA, per Lindley LJ); but in the case of a tramway, where land was authorised to be acquired only for the construction of buildings 'necessary for the working of the tramway', it was held that dwellings and a recreation ground for the use of the company's inspectors were not included (*West India Electric Co Ltd v Kingston Corpn* [1914] AC 986, PC).

3   See *Meravale Builders Ltd v Secretary of State for the Environment* (1978) 36 P & CR 87 (land acquired for housing; authority not entitled to build road other than for access). See also *Galloway v London Corpn* (1886) LR 1 HL 34 at 43 per Lord Cranworth; *Marquess of Clanricarde v Congested Districts Board for Ireland* (1914) 79 JP 481, HL; *Sydney Municipal Council v Campbell* [1925] AC 338, PC; and see other cases cited in note 5. Thus, a railway company having the ordinary powers of constructing a railway was restrained from taking land in order to obtain materials with which to make an embankment (*Bentinck v Norfolk Estuary Co* (1857) 26 LJCh 404; *Eversfield v Mid-Sussex Rly Co* (1858) 3 De G & J 286; *Lund v Midland Rly Co* (1865) 34 LJCh 276), or in order to carry out an agreement with a landowner (*Vane v Cockermouth, Keswick and Penrith Rly Co* (1865) 13 WR 1015; *Lord Carington v Wycombe Rly Co* (1868) 3 Ch App 377 at 381, 385). The undertakers may take land in order to make accommodation works for adjoining owners and occupiers, where such works are required to be made: see the Railways Clauses Consolidation Act 1845 s 68; and *Wilkinson v Hull etc Rly and Dock Co* (1882) 20 ChD 323, CA; *Lord Beauchamp v Great Western Rly Co* (1868) 3 Ch App 745; and cf *Dodd v Salisbury and Yeovil Rly Co* (1859) 1 Giff 158. When a field is authorised to be taken by a water company in order to make a tunnel, and only part is required, the company cannot take the whole field and use the remainder for sinking wells and erecting pumping machinery: *Simpson v South Staffordshire Waterworks Co* (1865) 34 LJCh 380; *Cardiff Corpn v Cardiff Waterworks Co* (1859) 5 Jur NS 953. See also *Simpsons Motor Sales (London) Ltd v Hendon Corpn* [1964] AC 1088, [1963] 2 All ER 484, HL (where the purposes of use became vague, but no determination to use outside authorised purposes); *Capital Investments Ltd v Wednesfield UDC* [1965] Ch 774, [1964] 1 All ER 655 (change of intention, but within the authorised powers). Local authorities authorised to take land to widen a street cannot under that power take land merely to alter the level of the street (*Lynch v London Sewers Comrs* (1886) 32 ChD 72, CA), and they cannot take it for purposes of resale unless power is given to them by the special Act (*Gard v London Sewers Comrs* (1885) 28 ChD

486, CA); see also *JL Denman & Co Ltd v Westminster Corpn, JC Cording & Co Ltd v Westminster Corpn* [1906] 1 Ch 464; *Fernley v Limehouse Board of Works* (1899) 68 LJCh 344.

4 *Ayr Harbour Trustees v Oswald* (1883) 8 App Cas 623, HL; *Re Heywood's Conveyance, Cheshire Lines Committee v Liverpool Corpn* [1938] 2 All ER 230.

5 *Webb v Manchester and Leeds Rly Co* (1839) 4 My & Cr 116 at 120 per Lord Cottenham; *Lee v Milner* (1837) 2 Y & C Ex 611; *Gray v Liverpool and Bury Rly Co* (1846) 9 Beav 391; *Re London and Birmingham Rly Co's Act 1833, Re London and North Western Rly Co's Act 1846, ex p Eton College* (1850) 20 LJCh 1; *Simpson v South Staffordshire Waterworks Co* (1865) 34 LJCh 380; *Cardiff Corpn v Cardiff Waterworks Co* (1859) 5 Jur NS 953; and see *Gildart v Gladstone* (1809) 11 East 675 at 685; *Scales v Pickering* (1828) 4 Bing 448. However, the court will not allow persons to avail themselves of omissions in the powers given to the undertakers in order to make exorbitant claims: *Bell v Hull and Selby Rly Co* (1840) 1 Ry & Can Cas 616.

6 *Galloway v London Corpn* (1866) LR 1 HL 34; *Quinton v Bristol Corpn* (1874) LR 17 Eq 524; *Rolls v London School Board* (1884) 27 ChD 639 at 642; *North London Rly Co v Metropolitan Board of Works* (1859) 28 LJCh 909; *Batson v London School Board* (1903) 67 JP 457.

7 *Stockton and Darlington Rly Co v Brown* (1860) 9 HL Cas 246; *Webb v Manchester and Leeds Rly Co* (1839) 4 My & Cr 116.

8 See the cases cited in note 7; and *Flower v London, Brighton and South Coast Rly Co* (1865) 34 LJCh 540; *Kemp v South Eastern Rly Co* (1872) 7 Ch App 364; *Errington v Metropolitan District Rly Co* (1882) 19 ChD 559, CA; *Marquess of Clanricarde v Congested Districts Board for Ireland* (1914) 79 JP 481, HL; *Sydney Municipal Council v Campbell* [1925] AC 338, PC. As to the evidence necessary see the cases cited above. If the purpose is apparently legitimate, the burden of proving the contrary will lie upon the landowner: *Marquess of Clanricarde v Congested Districts Board for Ireland*. The same principles are applicable when undertakers are authorised to interfere with lands, e g in laying sewers or water mains: *Earl of Derby v Bury Improvement Comrs* (1869) LR 4 Exch 222 at 225, Ex Ch, per Willes J; *Lewis v Weston-super-Mare Local Board* (1888) 40 ChD 55.

9 See the cases cited in note 7; and *London, Brighton and South Coast Rly Co v Truman* (1885) 11 App Cas 45, HL; *R v Pease* (1832) 4 B & Ad 30; *Lamb v North London Rly Co* (1869) 4 Ch App 522.

10 See *Tutin v Northallerton RDC* (1947) 91 Sol Jo 383, when the principle enunciated by Lord Atkinson in *Lagan Navigation Co v Lambeg Bleaching, Dyeing and Finishing Co Ltd* [1927] AC 226 at 243, HL, that if statutory powers might as well be exercised in a manner hurtful or innocuous to third parties, the person exercising them would be negligent if he chose the former, both being available, was held inapplicable to the taking of land under statutory powers.

11 See *Hooper v Bourne* (1877) 3 QBD 258 at 272, CA, per Bramwell LJ; affd (1880) 5 App Cas 1, HL.

12 See the Markets and Fairs Clauses Act 1847 s 9; the Harbours, Docks, and Piers Clauses Act 1847 s 20. As to the purchase of such land see the Lands Clauses Consolidation Act 1845 s 12. It may be land included within the limits of deviation: *Hooper v Bourne* (1877) 3 QBD 258, CA; affd (1880) 5 App Cas 1, HL. As to the meaning of 'special Act' see PARAS 509, 514.

13 Undertakers may not purchase more than the prescribed quantity of land from any party under a legal disability, or enabled only to sell under powers conferred by the special Act or the Lands Clauses Acts; if they purchase the prescribed quantity of land from such a party and afterwards sell the whole or part of it, that party cannot sell other land to them in lieu of the land sold: see the Land Clauses Consolidation Act 1845 s 14. As to the Lands Clauses Acts see PARA 509 note 1. As to the persons enabled to sell by the Lands Clauses Acts see PARA 553.

14 See the Lands Clauses Consolidation Act 1845 s 13; and *City of Glasgow Union Rly Co v Caledonian Rly Co* (1871) LR 2 Sc & Div 160 at 165, HL, per Lord Westbury. Where the land sold was purchased by the undertakers subject to a restrictive covenant which was ultra vires the undertakers, the covenant did not bind the purchaser to whom the promoters sold the land in question: *Re South Eastern Rly Co and Wiffin's Contract* [1907] 2 Ch 366, as explained in *Stourcliffe Estates Co Ltd v Bournemouth Corpn* [1910] 2 Ch 12, CA.

15 *City of Glasgow Union Rly Co v Caledonian Rly Co* (1871) LR 2 Sc & Div 160, HL; *Hooper v Bourne* (1877) 3 QBD 258, CA. For the provisions relating to superfluous land see PARA 901 et seq.

527.   Land for whole undertaking only; reimbursement and exchange. Land may not be taken where there is no intention, or no ability, to complete the whole undertaking[1]; nor may land be taken for the purpose of going beyond the statutory powers[2].

If the special Act[3] clearly authorises the land to be taken for the actual works only, a local authority or other public body will be restrained from taking more than is actually necessary for the works[4], but where an existing public body is entrusted with the duty of making public improvements, the powers thus entrusted to it for such a purpose will not be subject to a strict and restrictive construction, and more land than might be absolutely necessary to effect the desired improvements may be taken[5].

A power to acquire land to be given in exchange for the land acquired is given in some special Acts[6] to facilitate the acquisition of land such as commons and open spaces when land is required to be given in exchange as a condition of acquisition[7].

1   See *Agar v Regent's Canal Co* (1814) 1 Swan 250n; *Cohen v Wilkinson* (1849) 1 Mac & G 481.
2   *Simpson v South Staffordshire Waterworks Co* (1865) 34 LJCh 380; *Cardiff Corpn v Cardiff Waterworks Co* (1859) 5 Jur NS 953; *Colman v Eastern Counties Rly Co* (1846) 10 Beav 1.
3   As to the meaning of 'special Act' see PARAS 509, 514.
4   *Donaldson v South Shields Corpn* (1899) 68 LJCh 162, CA; *JL Denman & Co Ltd v Westminster Corpn, JC Cording & Co Ltd v Westminster Corpn* [1906] 1 Ch 464; *Fernley v Limehouse Board of Works* (1899) 68 LJCh 344. See also *Rolls v London School Board* (1884) 27 ChD 639.
5   *Galloway v London Corpn* (1866) LR 1 HL 34; *Quinton v Bristol Corpn* (1874) LR 17 Eq 524.
6   See eg the Highways Act 1980 s 239(5); and HIGHWAYS, STREETS AND BRIDGES vol 21 (2004 Reissue) PARA 77.
7   See PARAS 531, 604, 609.

528.   Compulsory purchase orders comprising ancient monuments. The Secretary of State[1] may compulsorily acquire ancient monuments[2] for the purposes of securing their preservation[3].

1   As to the Secretary of State see PARA 507 note 1. All functions of a Minister of the Crown under the Ancient Monuments and Archaeological Areas Act 1979, except the Treasury function under s 50, so far as they are exercisable in relation to Wales, have been transferred to the Welsh Ministers: see the National Assembly for Wales (Transfer of Functions) Order 1999, SI 1999/672, art 2, Sch 1; Government of Wales Act 2006 s 162(1), Sch 11 para 30.
2   As to the meaning of 'ancient monument' see the Ancient Monuments and Archaeological Areas Act 1979 s 61(12); and OPEN SPACES AND ANCIENT MONUMENTS vol 34 (Reissue) PARA 372.
3   See the Ancient Monuments and Archaeological Areas Act 1979 s 10; and OPEN SPACES AND ANCIENT MONUMENTS vol 34 (Reissue) PARA 373. The Acquisition of Land Act 1981 applies to any such compulsory acquisition: see the Ancient Monuments and Archaeological Areas Act 1979 s 10(2) (amended by the Acquisition of Land Act 1981 s 34, Sch 4 para 1, Sch 6 Pt I).

(ii) Exclusion and Protection of Certain Land

529.   In general. Some Acts expressly exempt from compulsory acquisition land such as parks, gardens or land of local authorities or other bodies; the enactment may be one giving only a general power of compulsory acquisition[1] or one providing for land otherwise to be specified for acquisition in a compulsory purchase order[2].

Further protection is given generally in the process of acquisition by the right afforded to an owner, part only of whose property is required, to insist upon the whole property being taken[3].

1   See eg the restrictions imposed on the compulsory acquisition of land for allotments in the Land Settlement (Facilities) Act 1919 s 16; and AGRICULTURAL LAND vol 1 (2008) PARA 546.

2   As to the making and confirmation of compulsory purchase orders see PARA 557 et seq.
3   See PARAS 621–630.

530.   Inalienable land.   Where the power to acquire compulsorily was only a general power, there was formerly no power to acquire compulsorily land made inalienable by statute; only if express power was given to acquire that land could it be so acquired[1]. Now, however, except in so far as any express provision of any such enactment restricts the exercise of the power, any power conferred by or under the Acquisition of Land Act 1981, the Acquisition of Land (Authorisation Procedure) Act 1946 or any enactment passed before the commencement of the 1946 Act[2] to purchase land[3] compulsorily is exercisable notwithstanding any other enactment providing that the land is to be inalienable[4].

Some protection from acquisition is provided both for land which is inalienable, and for certain other categories of land, by the statutory provisions relating to special parliamentary procedure[5].

1   Cf *R v Minister of Health, ex p Villiers* [1936] 2 KB 29 at 44–45, [1936] 1 All ER 817 at 823–824, DC.

2   The Acquisition of Land (Authorisation Procedure) Act 1946 (repealed) came into force on 18 April 1946.

3   As to the meaning of 'land' for these purposes see PARA 522 note 1. As to the meaning of 'compulsory purchase' see PARA 557 note 1.

4   Acquisition of Land Act 1981 s 9. This gives general power to take inalienable land under Acts passed before 1946 but not under Acts passed after then unless deemed to have been passed before the Acquisition of Land (Authorisation Procedure) Act 1946 (repealed). For example, the New Towns Act 1981 is deemed to have been passed before the commencement of the Acquisition of Land Act 1981 for these purposes: see the New Towns Act 1981 s 72(2) (amended by the Acquisition of Land Act 1981 s 34(1), Sch 4 para 33); and TOWN AND COUNTRY PLANNING vol 46(3) (Reissue) PARAS 1333–1334.

5   See PARA 603 et seq.

531.   Commons, open spaces, local authority land etc.   Where commons are specified for acquisition in the empowering enactment they may be acquired under the terms of that Act, but where there is only a general authority to acquire land under the Lands Clauses Acts[1] or any Act incorporating those Acts, acquisition will be invalid unless made by any government department or made with the consent of the Secretary of State[2]. Where commons[3], open spaces[4] or fuel or field garden allotments[5] are authorised to be purchased by a compulsory purchase order to which the Acquisition of Land Act 1981 applies[6] the order is subject to special parliamentary procedure[7] unless the Secretary of State is satisfied:

(1)   that there has been or will be given in exchange for such land[8] other land, not being less in area and being equally advantageous to the persons, if any, entitled to rights of common or other rights, and to the public, and that the land given in exchange has been or will be vested in the persons in whom the land purchased was vested, and subject to the like rights, trusts and incidents as attach to the land purchased[9]; or

(2)   that the land is being purchased in order to secure its preservation or improve its management[10]; or

(3)   that the land does not exceed 250 square yards in extent or is required for the widening or drainage of an existing highway or partly for the widening and partly for the drainage of such a highway and that the

giving in exchange of other land is unnecessary, whether in the interests of the persons, if any, entitled to rights of common or other rights or in the interests of the public[11],

and certifies accordingly[12].

Land belonging to local authorities, statutory undertakers or the National Trust and held inalienably which is included in such a compulsory purchase order may also be entitled to the protection of special parliamentary procedure[13].

These provisions are modified in their application to compulsory rights orders under the Opencast Coal Act 1958[14] and do not apply in relation to the compulsory purchase of a right to store gas in an underground gas storage[15] or of any right[16] as respects wells, boreholes and shafts in a storage area or protective area[17].

1   As to the Lands Clauses Acts see PARA 509 note 1.
2   See the Commons Act 1899 s 22(1), Sch 1; and COMMONS vol 6 (2003 Reissue) PARA 498. As to the Secretary of State see PARA 507 note 1. All functions of a Minister of the Crown under the Commons Act 1899, so far as they are exercisable in relation to Wales, are now exercisable by the Welsh Ministers: see the National Assembly for Wales (Transfer of Functions) Order 1999, SI 1999/672, art 2, Sch 1; and Government of Wales Act 2006 s 162(1), Sch 11 para 30. As to the Welsh Assembly Government and the Welsh Ministers see CONSTITUTIONAL LAW AND HUMAN RIGHTS.
3   'Common' includes any land subject to be inclosed under the Inclosure Acts 1845 to 1882, and any town or village green: Acquisition of Land Act 1981 s 19(4). As to the Inclosure Acts 1845 to 1882 see COMMONS.
4   'Open space' means any land laid out as a public garden, or used for the purposes of public recreation, or land being a disused burial ground: Acquisition of Land Act 1981 s 19(4).
5   'Fuel or field garden allotment' means any allotment set out as a fuel allotment, or a field garden allotment, under an Inclosure Act: Acquisition of Land Act 1981 s 19(4). See further AGRICULTURAL LAND vol 1 (2008) PARA 511 et seq.
6   See PARA 557 et seq. As to the meaning of 'compulsory purchase order' see PARA 557 note 1.
7   As to special parliamentary procedure see PARA 605.
8   As to the meaning of 'land' for these purposes see PARA 522 note 1.
9   Acquisition of Land Act 1981 s 19(1)(a). No additional compensation is payable under the Land Compensation Act 1961 s 5 r 2 (see PARA 754) or the Compulsory Purchase Act 1965 s 7 (see PARA 810) where the acquiring authority had offered to the holders of rights of common land of a suitable size and character contiguous to the common: *Lay v Norfolk County Council* [1997] RVR 9n, Lands Tribunal.
10 Acquisition of Land Act 1981 s 19(1)(aa) (added by the Planning and Compensation Act 1991 s 70, Sch 15 para 12(1)(a)).
11 Acquisition of Land Act 1981 s 19(1)(b).
12 Acquisition of Land Act 1981 s 19(1). All functions of a Minister of the Crown under the Acquisition of Land Act 1981, except s 8(4) (see PARA 564 note 5), so far as they are exercisable in relation to Wales, have been transferred to the Welsh Ministers; and orders made or confirmed by them are subject to special parliamentary procedure as provided for in s 18 (see PARA 603), Sch 3 para 5 (see PARA 608): see the National Assembly for Wales (Transfer of Functions) Order 1999, SI 1999/672, art 2, Sch 1; and the Government of Wales Act 2006 s 162(1), Sch 11 para 30. Subject to the Acquisition of Land Act 1981 s 24 (court's powers to quash certificate: see PARA 614), the certificate becomes operative on the date on which notice of giving it is first published in accordance with the statutory provisions: s 26(2). As to publication of notice of intention to give the certificate and the right to make objections see PARA 604. Power to acquire compulsorily land to be given in exchange is conferred by some Acts: see eg the Highways Act 1980 s 239(5); and HIGHWAYS, STREETS AND BRIDGES vol 21 (2004 Reissue) PARA 77. The court has jurisdiction to hear a challenge on substantive as well as purely procedural grounds to a certificate under the Acquisition of Land Act 1981 s 19 that equally advantageous land is being provided: *Greenwich London Borough Council v Secretary of State for the Environment and Secretary of State for Transport, Yates v Secretary of State for the Environment and Secretary of State for Transport* [1994] JPL 607. As to the acquisition of new rights over commons etc see PARA 609.
13 See PARAS 603, 608.
14 See the Acquisition of Land Act 1981 s 29(7); and PARA 610.

15   Ie a right under the Gas Act 1965 s 12(1): see FUEL AND ENERGY vol 19(2) (2007 Reissue) PARA 998.

16   Ie any right under the Gas Act 1965 s 13(2) or s 13(3): see FUEL AND ENERGY vol 19(2) (2007 Reissue) PARA 999.

17   See the Acquisition of Land Act 1981 s 30; and PARA 611.

(iii) Power to Acquire Leases, Strata or Easements Only

532.   Existing interests, easements and rights. Where powers are given by statute to acquire land compulsorily, the whole interest must be acquired notwithstanding the definition of 'land' in the empowering enactment as including easements or rights over land, unless special provision is made, and there is no power to require and acquire an easement, right or lease only[1]. So also, unless special provision is made, the whole land must be acquired, and there is no power to require and acquire only a stratum or section of the land[2].

Where there are interests against the land acquired[3], such as a right of way or some other easement or a restrictive covenant enjoyed by the owner of other land, the acquiring authority has no obligation or power, in the absence of express power, to acquire those rights compulsorily[4] and, if the authority interferes with the rights, the owners who have the benefit of the rights are not entitled to a notice to treat for the acquisition of the land to be taken, but are entitled only to compensation for the injury[5].

If the land acquired has attached to it the benefit of a right of way or other easement with respect to other land, that benefit will pass to the acquiring authority on the conveyance of the land acquired[6].

A local authority[7] may by means of a compulsory purchase order acquire such new rights over land[8] as may be specified in the order[9]. New rights over land may also be acquired by certain other authorities and undertakers[10].

1   See PARA 533; and *Sovmots Investments Ltd v Secretary of State for the Environment, Brompton Securities Ltd v Secretary of State for the Environment* [1977] QB 411, [1976] 3 All ER 720, CA (revsd on other grounds [1979] AC 144, [1977] 2 All ER 385, HL).

2   See PARA 534. Unless entry is required, leases for more than a year need not be purchased but may be allowed to expire or to become interests of less than a year: see PARA 698. If entered upon and by mistake omitted to be purchased they may be dealt with as explained in PARA 648. Interests for a year or less may be allowed to expire or be terminated by notice to quit or notice requiring possession: see PARA 699.

3   See *Thicknesse v Lancaster Canal Co* (1838) 4 M & W 472.

4   See eg the National Parks and Access to the Countryside Act 1949 ss 103(6), 114(1); and OPEN SPACES AND ANCIENT MONUMENTS vol 34 (Reissue) PARA 204.

5   *Macey v Metropolitan Board of Works* (1864) 33 LJCh 377; *Clark v London School Board* (1874) 9 Ch App 120; *Duke of Bedford v Dawson* (1875) LR 20 Eq 353; *Badham v Marris* (1881) 52 LJCh 237n; *Swainston v Finn and Metropolitan Board of Works* (1883) 52 LJCh 235; *Bush v Trowbridge Waterworks Co* (1875) LR 19 Eq 291 (affd 10 Ch App 459); *London School Board v Smith* [1895] WN 37; *Thicknesse v Lancaster Canal Co* (1838) 4 M & W 472. See further PARAS 878–879. The owner of such a right is not entitled to notice of a compulsory purchase order: see PARA 560 note 3. Instead of providing for compensation for injury to a right of way, some statutes provide for its extinguishment subject to compensation: see PARA 858.

6   See PARA 658.

7   For these purposes, 'local authority' means a county council, a county borough council, a district council, a London borough council, the Common Council of the City of London, the Council of the Isles of Scilly, a police authority established under the Police Act 1996 s 3, the Metropolitan Police Authority, a joint authority established by the Local Government Act 1985 Pt IV (ss 23–42), an authority established for an area in England by an order under the Local Government and Public Involvement in Health Act 2007 s 207 (joint waste authorities), and the London Fire and Emergency Planning Authority: Local Government (Miscellaneous Provisions) Act 1976 s 44(1) (definition substituted by the Local Government Act 1985 s 84, Sch 14 para 53(b); amended by s 102(2), Sch 17; the Education Reform Act 1988 s 237(2), Sch 13 Pt I; the

Police and Magistrates' Courts Act 1994 s 43, Sch 4 para 18; the Police Act 1996 s 103, Sch 7 para 1(2)(k); the Police Act 1997 s 88, Sch 6 para 13; the Greater London Authority Act 1999 ss 325, 328, 423, Sch 27 para 41, Sch 29 Pt I para 24(a), Sch 34 Pt VIII; the Criminal Justice and Police Act 2001 ss 128(1), 137, Sch 6 Pt 2 para 35, Sch 7 Pt 5(1); the Local Government and Public Involvement in Health Act 2007 s 209(2), Sch 13 Pt 2 para 33(a); and SI 1996/3071). The Broads Authority is treated as a local authority for these purposes: see the Local Government (Miscellaneous Provisions) Act 1976 s 44(1A) (added by the Norfolk and Suffolk Broads Act 1988 s 21, Sch 6 para 15). As to areas and authorities in England and Wales see LOCAL GOVERNMENT vol 69 (2009) PARA 22 et seq; and as to administrative areas and authorities in London see LONDON GOVERNMENT vol 29(2) (Reissue) PARA 29 et seq. As to joint authorities see LOCAL GOVERNMENT vol 69 (2009) PARA 47 et seq. As to police authorities see POLICE vol 36(1) (2007 Reissue) PARA 139 et seq. As to the Metropolitan Police Authority see LONDON GOVERNMENT vol 29(2) (Reissue) PARA 216; POLICE vol 36(1) (2007 Reissue) PARA 147 et seq. As to the London Fire and Emergency Planning Authority see FIRE SERVICES vol 18(2) (Reissue) PARA 17; LONDON GOVERNMENT vol 29(2) (Reissue) PARA 217. As to the Broads Authority see OPEN SPACES AND ANCIENT MONUMENTS vol 34 (Reissue) PARA 130.

8 As to the meaning of 'land' see PARA 28 note 3.
9 See the Local Government (Miscellaneous Provisions) Act 1976 s 13; the Acquisition of Land Act 1981 s 28(b); and LOCAL GOVERNMENT vol 69 (2009) PARA 511.
10 See the Acquisition of Land Act 1981 s 28, Sch 3; and PARA 606 et seq.

533. Whole interest in land to be purchased unless power to create and purchase lease, easements or rights only. There is no power to create and take an interest in land, such as a lease, without acquiring the freehold or other interests unless specific power to do so is given in the special Act[1]; nor is there power to create and purchase an easement without purchasing the land unless special provision is made[2] or in either case the owner agrees[3].

1 *Great Western Rly Co v Swindon and Cheltenham Rly Co* (1884) 9 App Cas 787 at 798, 800–801, HL, per Lord Watson. For examples of such a specific power see the Small Holdings and Allotments Act 1908 s 39 (see AGRICULTURAL LAND vol 1 (2008) PARA 535 et seq). As to the meaning of 'special Act' see PARAS 509, 514.
2 *Hill v Midland Rly Co* (1882) 21 ChD 143 at 147; *Great Western Rly Co v Swindon and Cheltenham Rly Co* (1884) 9 App Cas 787 at 802, HL; *Ramsden v Manchester, South Junction and Altrincham Rly Co* (1848) 1 Exch 723; *Sparrow v Oxford, Worcester and Wolverhampton Rly Co* (1852) 2 De GM & G 94 at 108 per Lord Cranworth; and see *Falkner v Somerset and Dorset Rly Co* (1873) LR 16 Eq 458. For examples of powers to acquire easements or rights over land by creating them see the National Parks and Access to the Countryside Act 1949 ss 103(6), 114(1) (see OPEN SPACES AND ANCIENT MONUMENTS vol 34 (Reissue) PARA 204); and the Highways Act 1980 s 250 (see HIGHWAYS, STREETS AND BRIDGES vol 21 (2004 Reissue) PARAS 85, 97).
3 *Pinchin v London and Blackwall Rly Co* (1854) 5 De GM & G 851 at 862, 24 LJCh 417 at 420 per Lord Cranworth LC; *Re Metropolitan District Rly Co and Cosh* (1880) 13 ChD 607 at 616, CA, per Jessel MR; *Re London School Board and Foster* (1903) 87 LT 700, CA.

534. Whole land to be purchased unless power to acquire or exclude strata. The acquiring authority[1] cannot acquire compulsorily a stratum of land or appropriate and use the subsoil, as for the purpose of making a tunnel, but must acquire the entire land[2] unless there is specific power to acquire a stratum or easement or right through the land or the owner agrees[3]. Thus the minerals must also be purchased unless there is power to exclude them from purchase[4].

1 As to the meaning of 'acquiring authority' see PARA 522 note 2.
2 *Errington v Metropolitan District Rly Co* (1882) 19 ChD 559, CA; *Great Western Rly Co v Swindon and Cheltenham Rly Co* (1884) 9 App Cas 787 at 800, HL; *Farmer v Waterloo and City Rly Co* [1895] 1 Ch 527; *Ramsden v Manchester, South Junction and Altrincham Rly Co* (1848) 1 Exch 723; *Goodson v Richardson* (1874) 9 Ch App 221. Power to appropriate and use subsoil is equivalent to power to take it: *Metropolitan Rly Co v Fowler* [1893] AC 416 at 426, HL, per Lord Watson.
3 *Great Western Rly Co v Swindon and Cheltenham Rly Co* (1884) 9 App Cas 787 at 801, HL. See also the cases cited in PARA 533 note 3.

4   In the case of acquisitions authorised by compulsory purchase orders to which the Acquisition
    of Land Act 1981 applies (see PARA 556), power is given to incorporate with the compulsory
    purchase order the Acquisition of Land Act 1981 Sch 2 Pt II (para 2) (which re-enacts the
    Railway Clauses Consolidation Act 1845 s 77 (exclusion of minerals from the purchase of the
    land)), or the Acquisition of Land Act 1981 Sch 2 Pts II, III (paras 2–9) (which together re-enact
    the Railways Clauses Consolidation Act 1845 ss 78–85 (restricting the working of minerals)):
    see the Acquisition of Land Act 1981 s 3, Sch 2 para 1 (amended by the Coal Industry Act 1994
    s 67(1), Sch 9 para 27(3) as from the restructuring date appointed under ss 7(1), 68(2)). See
    further MINES, MINERALS AND QUARRIES.

(6) NATIONALLY SIGNIFICANT INFRASTRUCTURE PROJECTS

535.   Compulsory acquisition as part of development consent. As from a day
to be appointed the following provisions have effect[1].

Where development[2] is or forms part of a nationally significant infrastructure
project[3] then development consent under the Planning Act 2008 (as opposed to
planning consent) is required[4]. An order granting development consent may
impose requirements in connection with the development for which consent is
granted[5]. An order granting development consent may, in particular, include
provision authorising the compulsory acquisition of land[6]; but it may only do so
if the decision-maker[7] is satisfied that:

(1)   the land (a) is required for the development to which the development
      consent relates; (b) is required to facilitate or is incidental to that
      development; or (c) is replacement land which is to be given in exchange
      for the order land[8]; and

(2)   there is a compelling case in the public interest for the land to be
      acquired compulsorily[9].

An order granting development consent may include provision authorising the
compulsory acquisition of land only if the decision-maker is satisfied that one of
the following conditions is met[10]. The conditions are: (i) that the application for
the order included a request for compulsory acquisition of the land to be
authorised; (ii) that all persons with an interest in the land consent to the
inclusion of the provision; and (iii) that the prescribed procedure has been
followed in relation to the land[11].

1   At the date at which this volume states the law the Planning Act 2008 was not fully in force.
2   As to the meaning of 'development' see the Town and Country Planning Act 1990 (and TOWN
    AND COUNTRY PLANNING vol 46(1) (Reissue) PARA 217); definition applied by the Planning
    Act 2008 s 32 (not yet in force). As to development for which development consent may be
    granted see s 115 (not yet in force).
3   'Nationally significant infrastructure project' means a project which consists of any of the
    following: (1) the construction or extension of a generating station; (2) the installation of an
    electric line above ground; (3) development relating to underground gas storage facilities; (4) the
    construction or alteration of an LNG facility; (5) the construction or alteration of a gas
    reception facility; (6) the construction of a pipe-line by a gas transporter; (7) the construction of
    a pipe-line other than by a gas transporter; (8) highway-related development; (9) airport-related
    development; (10) the construction or alteration of harbour facilities; (11) the construction or
    alteration of a railway; (12) the construction or alteration of a rail freight interchange; (13) the
    construction or alteration of a dam or reservoir; (14) development relating to the transfer of
    water resources; (15) the construction or alteration of a waste water treatment plant; (16) the
    construction or alteration of a hazardous waste facility: Planning Act 2008 s 14(1) (not yet in
    force). See further TOWN AND COUNTRY PLANNING.
4   Planning Act 2008 s 31 (not yet in force). Consent under the Planning Act 2008 is referred to as
    'development consent': see s 31 (not yet in force), s 235. A body called the Infrastructure
    Planning Commission (see ss 1–4 (not yet in force)) determines applications for development

consent for nationally significant infrastructure projects and, in doing so, takes into consideration the national policy statements made by the Government (see ss 5–13). See further TOWN AND COUNTRY PLANNING.

5   Planning Act 2008 s 120(1) (not yet in force). As to what the requirements may include see s 120(2)–(9) (not yet in force).

6   The Secretary of State may issue guidance about the making of an order granting development consent which includes provision authorising the compulsory acquisition of land; Planning Act 2008 s 124(1) (not yet in force). If a Panel or the Council of the Infrastructure Planning Commission proposes to make such an order, it must have regard to any such guidance: s 124(2) (not yet in force). As to the Secretary of State see PARA 507 note 1.

7   'Decision-maker' in relation to an application for an order granting development consent means (1) the Panel that has the function of deciding the application; or (2) where the Council or the Secretary of State has the function of deciding the application, means the Council or (as the case may be) the Secretary of State: s 103(2) (not yet in force), s 235.

8   Planning Act 2008 s 122(1), (2) (not yet in force). See ss 131, 132 (not yet in force); and TOWN AND COUNTRY PLANNING.

9   Planning Act 2008 s 122(1), (3) (not yet in force).

10 Planning Act 2008 s 123(1) (not yet in force).

11 Planning Act 2008 s 123(2), (3), (4) (not yet in force).

536.   Application of compulsory acquisition legislation.   As from a day to be appointed the following provisions have effect[1].

Where an order granting development consent[2] includes provision authorising the compulsory acquisition of land Part 1 of the Compulsory Purchase Act 1965[3] applies to the compulsory acquisition of land under the order as it applies to a compulsory purchase to which Part 2 of the Acquisition of Land Act 1981[4] applies as if the order were a compulsory purchase order under that Act[5].

1   At the date at which this volume states the law the Planning Act 2008 was not fully in force.

2   As to the meaning of 'development consent' see PARA 535 note 4.

3   Ie the Compulsory Purchase Act 1965 Pt 1 (ss 1–32). Part 1 of the Compulsory Purchase Act 1965 has effect, for these purposes, with the omission of s 4 (time limit for exercise of compulsory purchase powers: see PARAS 550, 617), s 10 (compensation for injurious affection: see PARA 718) and Sch 3 para 3(3) (giving of bonds: see PARA 641).

4   Ie the Acquisition of Land Act 1981 Pt 2 (ss 10–15): see PARA 557 et seq.

5   Planning Act 2008 s 125(1), (2) (not yet in force). Note that this is subject to any contrary provision made by the order granting development consent: s 125(6) (not yet in force).

537.   Compensation for compulsory acquisition.   As from a day to be appointed the following provisions have effect[1].

Where an order granting development consent[2] includes provision authorising the compulsory acquisition of land[3], the order may not include provision the effect of which is to modify the application of a compensation provision[4], except to the extent necessary to apply the provision to the compulsory acquisition of land authorised by the order[5]. Nor may the order include provision the effect of which is to exclude the application of a compensation provision[6].

1   At the date at which this volume states the law the Planning Act 2008 was not fully in force.

2   As to the meaning of 'development consent' see PARA 535 note 4.

3   Planning Act 2008 s 126(1) (not yet in force).

4   A compensation provision is a provision of or made under an Act which relates to compensation for the compulsory acquisition of land: Planning Act 2008 s 126(4) (not yet in force). As to claims for compensation in respect of compulsory acquisition see PARA 715 et seq. As to the amount of compensation and the date at which it is assessed see PARA 753 et seq. As to compensation for severance see PARA 810 et seq.

5   Planning Act 2008 s 125(2) (not yet in force).

6   Planning Act 2008 s 125(3) (not yet in force).

538.   Compensation in cases where there is no right to claim in nuisance.   As from a day to be appointed the following provisions have effect[1].

If[2] there is a defence of statutory authority in civil or criminal proceedings for nuisance[3] in respect of any authorised works[4], then a person by whom or on whose behalf any authorised works are carried out must pay compensation to any person whose land is injuriously affected by the carrying out of the works[5]. Certain provisions of the Compulsory Purchase Act 1965[6] and the Land Compensation Act 1973[7] apply in these circumstances. A dispute as to whether compensation is payable, or as to the amount of the compensation, must be referred to the Upper Tribunal[8].

1   At the date at which this volume states the law the Planning Act 2008 was not fully in force.
2   Ie by virtue of the Planning Act 2008 s 158 (not yet in force) or an order granting development consent: s 152(1) (not yet in force). As to the meaning of 'development consent' see PARA 535 note 4.
3   As to nuisance see generally NUISANCE.
4   'Authorised works' are (1) development for which consent is granted by an order granting development consent; (2) anything else authorised by an order granting development consent: Planning Act 2008 s 152(2) (not yet in force).
5   Planning Act 2008 s 152(3) (not yet in force).
6   The Compulsory Purchase Act 1965 s 10(2) (limitation on compensation: see PARA 718) applies to the Planning Act 2008 s 152(3) as it applies to the Compulsory Purchase Act 1965 s 10: Planning Act 2008 s 152(5) (not yet in force). Any rule or principle applied to the construction of the Compulsory Purchase Act 1965 s 10 must be applied to the construction of the Planning Act 2008 s 152(3) (with any necessary modifications): s 152(6) (not yet in force).
7   The Land Compensation Act 1973 Pt 1 (ss 1–19) (compensation for depreciation of land value by physical factors caused by use of public works) (see PARA 884 et seq) applies in relation to authorised works as if (1) references in that Part to any public works were to any authorised works; (2) references in that Part to the responsible authority were to the person for whose benefit the order granting development consent has effect for the time being; and (3) s 1(6) (see PARA 884) and s 17 (see PARA 894) were omitted: Planning Act 2008 s 152(7) (not yet in force).
8   Planning Act 2008 s 152(4) (not yet in force) (amended by SI 2009/1307). An order granting development consent may not include provision the effect of which is to remove or modify the application of the Planning Act 2008 s 152(1)–(7): see s 152(8) (not yet in force). As to the Upper Tribunal see PARA 720; and ADMINISTRATIVE LAW.

539. Statutory undertakers' land. As from a day to be appointed the following provisions have effect[1].

An order granting development consent[2] may only include provision authorising the compulsory acquisition of statutory undertakers'[3] land if certain conditions are met[4]. The conditions apply in relation to land if:

(1)   the land has been acquired by statutory undertakers for the purposes of their undertaking[5];

(2)   a representation has been made about an application for an order granting development consent before the completion of the examination of the application, and the representation has not been withdrawn[6]; and

(3)   as a result of the representation the decision-maker[7] is satisfied that: (a) the land is used for the purposes of carrying on the statutory undertakers' undertaking; or (b) an interest in the land is held for those purposes[8].

The conditions are as follows. An order granting development consent may include provision authorising the compulsory acquisition of statutory undertakers' land only to the extent that the Secretary of State[9] is satisfied that the nature and situation of the land are such that it can be purchased and not replaced without serious detriment to the carrying on of the undertaking, or if purchased it can be replaced by other land belonging to, or available for acquisition by, the undertakers without serious detriment to the carrying on of the undertaking[10]. The Secretary of State must issue a certificate to that effect[11].

An order granting development consent may include provision authorising the compulsory acquisition of a right over statutory undertakers' land by the creation of a new right over land only to the extent that the Secretary of State is satisfied that the nature and situation of the land are such that the right can be purchased without serious detriment to the carrying on of the undertaking, or any detriment to the carrying on of the undertaking, in consequence of the acquisition of the right, can be made good by the undertakers by the use of other land belonging to or available for acquisition by them[12]. The Secretary of State must issue a certificate to that effect[13].

If the Secretary of State issues such a certificate[14] he must publish in one or more local newspapers circulating in the locality in which the statutory undertakers' land is situated a notice in the prescribed form that the certificate has been given[15]. In a case where a Panel or the Council of the Infrastructure Planning Commission[16] is the decision-maker, the Secretary of State must notify the Commission that the certificate has been given[17].

Where the development to which the order granting development consent relates is development relating to underground gas storage facilities then the provisions described above may not apply[18].

1   At the date at which this volume states the law the Planning Act 2008 was not fully in force.
2   Such orders may be subject to special parliamentary procedure: see PARA 540. As to the meaning of 'development consent' see PARA 535 note 4.
3   As to the meaning of 'statutory undertakers' see PARA 561 note 8; definition applied by the Planning Act 2008 s 127(8) (not yet in force). The term also includes the undertakers (1) which are deemed to be statutory undertakers for the purposes of that Act, by virtue of another enactment; (2) which are statutory undertakers for the purposes of the Acquisition of Land Act 1981 s 16(1), (2) (see PARA 564): Planning Act 2008 s 127(8) (not yet in force). In the application of s 127 to a statutory undertaker which is a health service body (as defined in the National Health Service and Community Care Act 1990 s 60(7): see HEALTH SERVICES vol 54 (2008) PARA 75 et seq), references to land acquired or available for acquisition by the statutory undertakers are to be construed as references to land acquired or available for acquisition by the Secretary of State for use or occupation by the body: Planning Act 2008 s 127(9) (not yet in force).
4   See the text and notes 5–18.
5   Planning Act 2008 s 127(1)(a) (not yet in force).
6   Planning Act 2008 s 127(1)(b) (not yet in force).
7   As to the meaning of 'decision-maker' see PARA 535 note 7.
8   Planning Act 2008 s 127(1)(c) (not yet in force).
9   As to the Secretary of State see PARA 507 note 1.
10 Planning Act 2008 s 127(2)(a), (3) (not yet in force). The provisions of s 127(2), (3) do not apply in a case within s 127(5) (see the text and notes 12–13): see s 127(4) (not yet in force).
11 Planning Act 2008 s 127(2)(b) (not yet in force). See note 10.
12 Planning Act 2008 s 127(5)(a), (6) (not yet in force). See note 10.
13 Planning Act 2008 s 127(5)(b) (not yet in force). See note 10.
14 Ie under the Planning Act 2008 s 127(2) or s 127(5) (not yet in force).
15 Planning Act 2008 s 127(7)(a) (not yet in force).
16 See the Planning Act 2008; and TOWN AND COUNTRY PLANNING.
17 Planning Act 2008 s 127(7)(b) (not yet in force).
18 Where the development to which the order granting development consent relates is development relating to underground gas storage facilities (see the Planning Act 2008 s 14; and PARA 535 note 3) and the order authorises the compulsory acquisition of:
    (1)   the right to store gas in underground storage facilities; or
    (2)   the right to stop up a well, borehole or shaft, or prevent its use by another person; or
    (3)   a right of way over land,
    by the creation of a new right within head (1), (2) or (3), then the Planning Act 2008 has effect in relation to the compulsory acquisition of the right with the omission of ss 127–132: see s 133 (not yet in force).

540. Development consent orders comprising land of local authorities, statutory undertakers and the National Trust. As from a day to be appointed the following provisions have effect[1].

Where land:

(1)   is the property of a local authority[2]; or

(2)   has been acquired by statutory undertakers[3] (other than a local authority) for the purposes of their undertaking[4]; or

(3)   belongs to, and is held inalienably by, the National Trust[5],

then an order granting development consent[6] is subject to special parliamentary procedure[7] (to the extent that the order authorises the compulsory acquisition of such land[8]) if a representation has been made by the local authority or the statutory undertakers or the National Trust (as the case may be) about the application for the order granting development consent before the completion of the examination of the application, and the representation has not been withdrawn[9].

Where the development to which the order granting development consent relates is development relating to underground gas storage facilities then the provisions described above may not apply[10].

1   At the date at which this volume states the law the Planning Act 2008 was not fully in force.
2   Planning Act 2008 s 128(1)(a) (not yet in force). As to the meaning of 'local authority' see PARA 522 note 2; definition applied by the Planning Act 2008 s 128(5) (not yet in force).
3   As to the meaning of 'statutory undertakers' see PARA 561 note 8; definition applied by the Planning Act 2008 s 128(5) (not yet in force). The term also includes the undertakers (1) which are deemed to be statutory undertakers for the purposes of the Acquisition of Land Act 1981, by virtue of another enactment; (2) which are statutory undertakers for the purposes of s 16(1), (2): Planning Act 2008 s 128(5) (not yet in force). In the application of s 128 to a statutory undertaker which is a health service body (see the National Health Service and Community Care Act 1990 s 60(7); and HEALTH SERVICES vol 54 (2008) PARA 75 et seq), the reference to land acquired by statutory undertakers is to be construed as a reference to land acquired by the Secretary of State for use or occupation by the body: Planning Act 2008 s 128(6) (not yet in force). As to the Secretary of State see PARA 507 note 1.
4   Planning Act 2008 s 128(1)(b) (not yet in force).
5   Planning Act 2008 s 130(1) (not yet in force). 'Held inalienably', in relation to land belonging to the National Trust, means that the land is inalienable under the National Trust Act 1907 s 21 or the National Trust Act 1939 s 8: Planning Act 2008 s 130(4) (not yet in force). 'National Trust' means the National Trust for Places of Historic Interest or Natural Beauty incorporated by the National Trust Act 1907: Planning Act 2008 s 130(5) (not yet in force).
6   As to the meaning of 'development consent' see PARA 535 note 4.
7   As to special parliamentary procedure see PARA 605. As to special parliamentary procedure for certain compulsory purchase orders see PARA 603 et seq.
8   Planning Act 2008 ss 128(2), 130(2) (not yet in force). Except in relation to the National Trust, these provisions (ie s 128(2)) do not apply to the compulsory acquisition of land if the person acquiring the land is any of the following: (1) a local authority; (2) a National Park authority; (3) an urban development corporation; (4) a Welsh planning board; (5) statutory undertakers; (6) a Minister of the Crown: ss 128(4), 129(1) (not yet in force). As to the meaning of 'local authority' for these purposes see PARA 603 note 11; definition applied by s 129(2) (not yet in force). As to the meaning of 'statutory undertakers' for these purposes see PARA 561 note 8; definition applied by s 129(2) (not yet in force). The term also includes the authorities, bodies and undertakers which are deemed to be statutory undertakers for the purposes of the Acquisition of Land Act 1981, by virtue of another enactment, or which are statutory undertakers for the purposes of s 17(3) (see PARA 603): Planning Act 2008 s 129(2) (not yet in force). 'Welsh planning board' means a board constituted under the Town and Country Planning Act 1990 s 2(1B): see TOWN AND COUNTRY PLANNING vol 46(1) (Reissue) PARA 30.
9   Planning Act 2008 ss 128(3), 130(3) (not yet in force).
10 Where the development to which the order granting development consent relates is development relating to underground gas storage facilities (see the Planning Act 2008 s 14; and PARA 535 note 3) and the order authorises the compulsory acquisition of:
      (1)   the right to store gas in underground storage facilities; or

(2)   the right to stop up a well, borehole or shaft, or prevent its use by another person; or

(3)   a right of way over land,

by the creation of a new right within head (1), (2) or (3), then the Planning Act 2008 has effect in relation to the compulsory acquisition of the right with the omission of ss 127–132: see s 133 (not yet in force).

541.   Development consent orders comprising commons, open spaces and allotments.   As from a day to be appointed the following provisions have effect[1].

An order granting development consent[2] is subject to special parliamentary procedure[3], to the extent that the order authorises the compulsory acquisition of land forming part of a common, open space or fuel or field garden allotment[4], unless the Secretary of State[5] issues a certificate[6] stating he is satisfied that:

(1)   replacement land[7] has been or will be given in exchange for the order land[8], and the replacement land has been or will be vested in the prospective seller[9] and subject to the same rights, trusts and incidents as attach to the order land[10]; or

(2)   the order land does not exceed 200 square metres in extent or is required for the widening or drainage of an existing highway or partly for the widening and partly for the drainage of such a highway, and the giving in exchange of other land is unnecessary, whether in the interests of the persons, if any, entitled to rights of common or other rights or in the interests of the public[11].

If the Secretary of State proposes to issue a certificate he must give notice[12] of the proposal or direct the person who applied for the order granting development consent to do so, and must also give any persons interested in the proposal an opportunity to make representations about the proposal[13]. He may cause a public local inquiry to be held in relation to the proposal[14]. He may issue the certificate only after considering any representations made about the proposal, and (if an inquiry has been held), the report of the person who held the inquiry[15]. Where a certificate is issued, the Secretary of State must publish in one or more local newspapers circulating in the locality in which the order land is situated a notice in the prescribed form that the certificate has been given, or direct the person who applied for the order granting development consent to do so[16]. Where a Panel or the Council of the Infrastructure Planning Commission[17] is the decision-maker[18], the Secretary of State must notify the Commission that the certificate has been given, or direct the person who applied for the order granting development consent to do so[19].

If an order granting development consent authorises the compulsory acquisition of land forming part of a common, open space or fuel or field garden allotment, it may include provision for vesting replacement land given in exchange[20] in the prospective seller[21] and may also contain provision for discharging the order land from all rights, trusts and incidents to which it is subject[22].

Where the development to which the order granting development consent relates is development relating to underground gas storage facilities[23] and the order authorises the compulsory acquisition of the right to store gas in underground storage facilities[24], then the provisions described above do not apply[25].

1   At the date at which this volume states the law the Planning Act 2008 was not fully in force.

2   As to the meaning of 'development consent' see PARA 535 note 4.

3   As to special parliamentary procedure see PARA 605. As to special parliamentary procedure for certain compulsory purchase orders see PARA 603 et seq.

4 Planning Act 2008 s 131(1) (not yet in force). As to the meaning of 'common' see PARA 531 note 3; as to the meaning of 'fuel or field garden allotment' see PARA 531 note 5; and as to the meaning of 'open space' see PARA 531 note 4; definitions applied by the Planning Act 2008 s 131(12) (not yet in force). Section 131 does not apply in a case to which s 132 (see PARA 542) applies: s 131(2) (not yet in force).
5 As to the Secretary of State see PARA 507 note 1.
6 Planning Act 2008 s 131(3)(b) (not yet in force).
7 'Replacement land' means land which is not less in area than the order land and which is no less advantageous to the persons, if any, entitled to rights of common or other rights, and to the public: Planning Act 2008 s 131(12) (not yet in force).
8 'Order land' means the land authorised to be compulsorily acquired: Planning Act 2008 s 131(12) (not yet in force).
9 'Prospective seller' means the person or persons in whom the order land is vested: Planning Act 2008 s 131(12) (not yet in force).
10 Planning Act 2008 s 131(3)(a), (4) (not yet in force).
11 Planning Act 2008 s 131(3)(a), (5) (not yet in force).
12 The notice must be given in such form and manner as the Secretary of State may direct: Planning Act 2008 s 131(9) (not yet in force).
13 Planning Act 2008 s 131(6) (not yet in force).
14 Planning Act 2008 s 131(7) (not yet in force).
15 Planning Act 2008 s 131(8) (not yet in force).
16 Planning Act 2008 s 131(10)(a) (not yet in force).
17 See the Planning Act 2008; and TOWN AND COUNTRY PLANNING.
18 As to the meaning of 'decision-maker' see PARA 535 note 7.
19 Planning Act 2008 s 131(10)(b) (not yet in force).
20 See the Planning Act 2008 s 131(4); and head (1) in the text.
21 Ie subject to the rights, trusts and incidents mentioned in the Planning Act 2008 s 131(4) (see head (1) in the text): s 131(11)(a) (not yet in force).
22 Planning Act 2008 s 131(11)(b) (not yet in force). See note 21.
23 See the Planning Act 2008 s 14; and PARA 535 note 3.
24 Planning Act 2008 s 133(1), (2) (not yet in force).
25 Planning Act 2008 s 133(3) (not yet in force).

542. Acquisition of new rights over commons, open spaces and allotments.
As from a day to be appointed the following provisions have effect[1].

An order granting development consent[2] is subject to special parliamentary procedure[3], to the extent that the order authorises the compulsory acquisition of a right over land forming part of a common, open space or fuel or field garden allotment[4] by the creation of a new right over land, unless the Secretary of State[5] issues a certificate[6] stating that he is satisfied that:

(1)   the order land[7], when burdened with the order right[8], will be no less advantageous than it was before to: (a) the persons in whom it is vested; (b) other persons, if any, entitled to rights of common or other rights; and (c) the public[9]; or

(2)   replacement land[10] has been or will be given in exchange for the order right, and the replacement land has been or will be vested in the persons in whom the order land is vested and subject to the same rights, trusts and incidents as attach to the order land (ignoring the order granting development consent)[11]; or

(3)   the order land does not exceed 200 square metres in extent or the order right is required in connection with the widening or drainage of an existing highway or in connection partly with the widening and partly with the drainage of such a highway, and the giving of other land in exchange for the order right is unnecessary, whether in the interests of the persons, if any, entitled to rights of common or other rights or in the interests of the public[12].

If the Secretary of State proposes to issue a certificate he must give notice[13] of the proposal or direct the person who applied for the order granting development consent to do so, and must also give any persons interested in the proposal an opportunity to make representations about the proposal[14]. He may also cause a public local inquiry to be held in relation to the proposal[15]. He may issue the certificate only after considering any representations made about the proposal, and (if an inquiry has been held), the report of the person who held the inquiry[16]. Where a certificate is issued, the Secretary of State must publish in one or more local newspapers circulating in the locality in which the order land is situated a notice in the prescribed form that the certificate has been given, or direct the person who applied for the order granting development consent to do so[17]. Where a Panel or the Council of the Infrastructure Planning Commission[18] is the decision-maker[19], the Secretary of State must notify the Commission that the certificate has been given, or direct the person who applied for the order granting development consent to do so[20].

If an order granting development consent authorises the compulsory acquisition of a right over land forming part of a common, open space or fuel or field garden allotment, by the creation of a new right over land, it may include provision for vesting replacement land given in exchange[21] in the persons in whom the order land is vested[22], and may also contain provision for discharging the order land from all rights, trusts and incidents to which it has previously been subject so far as their continuance would be inconsistent with the exercise of the order right[23].

Where the development to which the order granting development consent relates is development relating to underground gas storage facilities then the provisions described above may not apply[24].

1 At the date at which this volume states the law the Planning Act 2008 was not fully in force.
2 As to the meaning of 'development consent' see PARA 535 note 4.
3 As to special parliamentary procedure see PARA 605. As to special parliamentary procedure for certain compulsory purchase orders see PARA 603 et seq. See in particular PARA 609.
4 Planning Act 2008 s 132(1) (not yet in force). As to the meaning of 'common' see PARA 531 note 3; as to the meaning of 'fuel or field garden allotment' see PARA 531 note 5; and as to the meaning of 'open space' see PARA 531 note 4; definitions applied by the Planning Act 2008 s 132(12) (not yet in force). Section 131 (see PARA 541) does not apply in a case to which s 132 applies: s 131(2) (not yet in force).
5 As to the Secretary of State see PARA 507 note 1.
6 Planning Act 2008 s 132(2)(b) (not yet in force).
7 'Order land' means the land to which the Planning Act 2008 s 132 applies over which the order right is to be exercisable: s 132(12) (not yet in force).
8 'Order right' means the right authorised to be compulsorily acquired: Planning Act 2008 s 132(12) (not yet in force).
9 Planning Act 2008 s 132(2)(a), (3) (not yet in force).
10 'Replacement land' means land which will be adequate to compensate the following persons for the disadvantages which result from the compulsory acquisition of the order right: (1) the persons in whom the order land is vested; (2) the persons, if any, entitled to rights of common or other rights over the order land; and (3) the public: Planning Act 2008 s 132(12) (not yet in force).
11 Planning Act 2008 s 132(2)(a), (4) (not yet in force).
12 Planning Act 2008 s 132(2)(a), (5) (not yet in force).
13 The notice must be given in such form and manner as the Secretary of State may direct: Planning Act 2008 s 132(9) (not yet in force).
14 Planning Act 2008 s 132(6) (not yet in force).
15 Planning Act 2008 s 132(7) (not yet in force).
16 Planning Act 2008 s 132(8) (not yet in force).
17 Planning Act 2008 s 132(10)(a) (not yet in force).
18 See the Planning Act 2008; and TOWN AND COUNTRY PLANNING.

19 As to the meaning of 'decision-maker' see PARA 535 note 7.
20 Planning Act 2008 s 132(10)(b) (not yet in force).
21 See the Planning Act 2008 s 132(4); and head (2) in the text.
22 Ie subject to the rights, trusts and incidents mentioned in the Planning Act 2008 s 132(4) (see head (2) in the text): s 132(11)(a) (not yet in force).
23 Planning Act 2008 s 132(11)(b) (not yet in force).
24 Where the development to which the order granting development consent relates is development relating to underground gas storage facilities (see the Planning Act 2008 s 14; and PARA 535 note 3) and the order authorises the compulsory acquisition of:
    (1)   the right to store gas in underground storage facilities; or
    (2)   the right to stop up a well, borehole or shaft, or prevent its use by another person; or
    (3)   a right of way over land,
    by the creation of a new right within head (1), (2) or (3), then the Planning Act 2008 has effect in relation to the compulsory acquisition of the right with the omission of ss 127–132: see s 133 (not yet in force).

543.   Notice of authorisation of compulsory acquisition.   As from a day to be appointed the following provisions have effect[1].

Where an order is made granting development consent[2], and the order includes provision authorising the compulsory acquisition of land[3], then after the order has been made, the prospective purchaser[4] must serve a compulsory acquisition notice[5] and a copy of the order on the required persons[6] and also affix a compulsory acquisition[7] notice to a conspicuous object or objects on or near the order land[8]. The prospective purchaser must also publish a compulsory acquisition notice in one or more local newspapers circulating in the locality in which the order land is situated[9].

1 At the date at which this volume states the law the Planning Act 2008 was not fully in force.
2 As to the meaning of 'development consent' see PARA 535 note 4.
3 Planning Act 2008 s 134(1) (not yet in force).
4 'Prospective purchaser' means:
    (1)   in a case where the order granting development consent authorises the compulsory acquisition of a right over land by the creation of a new right, the person for whose benefit the order authorises the creation of the right (Planning Act 2008 s 134(2)(a) (not yet in force));
    (2)   in any other case where the order granting development consent authorises the compulsory acquisition of land, the person authorised by the order to compulsorily acquire the land (s 134(2)(b) (not yet in force)).
5 A compulsory acquisition notice is a notice in the prescribed form: (1) describing the order land; (2) in a case where the order granting development consent authorises the compulsory acquisition of a right over land by the creation of a new right, describing the right; (3) stating that the order granting development consent includes provision authorising the compulsory acquisition of a right over the land by the creation of a right over it or (as the case may be) the compulsory acquisition of the land; and (4) stating that a person aggrieved by the order may challenge the order only in accordance with the Planning Act 2008 s 118: s 134(7) (not yet in force). See also note 7.
6 Ie on any person who, if the order granting development consent were a compulsory purchase order, would be a qualifying person for the purposes of the Acquisition of Land Act 1981 s 12(1) (see PARA 560) (notice to owners, lessees and occupiers): Planning Act 2008 s 134(3)(a), (4) (not yet in force).
7 A compulsory acquisition notice which is affixed under the Planning Act 2008 s 134(3)(b) must also name a place where a copy of the order granting development consent may be inspected at all reasonable hours: s 134(8) (not yet in force).
8 Planning Act 2008 s 134(3)(b) (not yet in force). 'Order land' means: (1) in a case where the order granting development consent authorises the compulsory acquisition of a right over land by the creation of a new right, the land over which the right is to be exercisable; (2) in any other case where the order granting development consent authorises the compulsory acquisition of land, the land authorised to be compulsorily acquired: s 134(2).
    A compulsory acquisition notice which is affixed under s 134(3)(b) must: (1) be addressed to persons occupying or having an interest in the order land; and (2) so far as practicable, be kept

in place by the prospective purchaser until the end of the period of six weeks beginning with the
date on which the order is published: s 134(5) (not yet in force).

9   Planning Act 2008 s 134(6) (not yet in force).

544.   Crown land. As from a day to be appointed the following provisions
have effect[1].

An order granting development consent[2] may include provision authorising
the compulsory acquisition of an interest in Crown land only if (1) it is an
interest which is for the time being held otherwise than by or on behalf of the
Crown[3]; and (2) the appropriate Crown authority consents to the acquisition[4].
An order granting development consent may include any other provision
applying in relation to Crown land, or rights benefiting the Crown[5], only if the
appropriate Crown authority consents to the inclusion of the provision[6].

1   At the date at which this volume states the law the Planning Act 2008 was not fully in force.
2   As to the meaning of 'development consent' see PARA 535 note 4.
3   Planning Act 2008 s 135(1)(a) (not yet in force). For these purposes 'the Crown' includes: (1) the
     Duchy of Lancaster; (2) the Duchy of Cornwall; (3) the Speaker of the House of Lords; (4) the
     Speaker of the House of Commons; (5) the Corporate Officer of the House of Lords; (6) the
     Corporate Officer of the House of Commons: s 135(4) (not yet in force).
4   Planning Act 2008 s 135(1)(b) (not yet in force).
5   The reference to rights benefiting the Crown does not include rights which benefit the general
     public: Planning Act 2008 s 135(3) (not yet in force).
6   Planning Act 2008 s 135(2) (not yet in force).

2. RIGHTS OF OWNERS ETC TO REQUIRE PURCHASE OF INTERESTS

(1) INTERESTS AFFECTED BY PLANNING DECISIONS OR ORDERS

545. In general. Where, as a result of certain planning decisions[1], land is incapable of reasonably beneficial use[2], the owner of the land or a person entitled to an interest in the land may serve a purchase notice requiring the relevant council[3] of the area in which the land is situated to purchase his interest in that land[4]. The council on which the purchase notice was served must serve a response notice stating either:

(1)   that it is willing to comply with the purchase notice, or that another local authority or specified statutory undertakers has or have agreed to comply with it in the council's place[5]; or

(2)   that the council is not willing to comply and has not found any other local authority or statutory undertakers willing to comply, and that the council has sent a copy of the purchase notice and of the response notice to the Secretary of State[6].

Where a response notice has been served in accordance with head (1) above, the council or, as the case may be, the other local authority or statutory undertakers specified in it is or are deemed to be authorised to acquire the interest of the owner compulsorily[7] and to have served a notice to treat[8] in respect of it on the date of service of the response notice[9]. Where head (2) above applies, the Secretary of State must consider whether to confirm the purchase notice[10] or to take other action[11] in respect of it[12]. Where the land has a restricted use[13] he need not confirm the purchase notice[14]. Where he confirms the purchase notice, the council on which it was served, or another local authority or statutory undertakers substituted for that council by the Secretary of State[15], is or are deemed to be authorised to acquire the interest of the owner compulsorily and to have served a notice to treat in respect of it on such day as the Secretary of State may direct[16].

Special statutory provision is made with regard to agricultural units[17] and listed buildings[18].

All these provisions are considered in detail elsewhere in this work[19].

1   Ie the decisions mentioned in the Town and Country Planning Act 1990 s 137(1): see TOWN AND COUNTRY PLANNING vol 46(2) (Reissue) PARA 966.
2   As to the meaning of 'reasonably beneficial use' see TOWN AND COUNTRY PLANNING vol 46(2) (Reissue) PARA 968.
3   Ie the council of the district, Welsh county, county borough or London borough: Town and Country Planning Act 1990 s 137(2) (amended by the Local Government (Wales) Act 1994 s 20(4), Sch 6 para 24(3)).
4   See the Town and Country Planning Act 1990 s 137(1), (2); and TOWN AND COUNTRY PLANNING vol 46(2) (Reissue) PARA 966.
5   See the Town and Country Planning Act 1990 s 139(1)(a), (b); and TOWN AND COUNTRY PLANNING vol 46(2) (Reissue) PARA 970.
6   See the Town and Country Planning Act 1990 s 139(1)(c); and TOWN AND COUNTRY PLANNING vol 46(2) (Reissue) PARA 970. As to the Secretary of State see PARA 507 note 1. The functions of a Minister of the Crown under the Town and Country Planning Act 1990 s 139, so far as they are exercisable in relation to Wales, are now exercisable by the Welsh Ministers: see the National Assembly for Wales (Transfer of Functions) Order 1999, SI 1999/672, art 2, Sch 1; and the Government of Wales Act 2006 s 162(1), Sch 11 para 30. As to the Welsh Assembly Government and the Welsh Ministers see CONSTITUTIONAL LAW AND HUMAN RIGHTS.

7   Ie in accordance with the Town and Country Planning Act 1990 Pt IX (ss 226–246) (see TOWN AND COUNTRY PLANNING) or, in the case of statutory undertakers, in accordance with any statutory provision, however expressed, under which they have power, or may be authorised, to purchase land compulsorily for the purposes of their undertaking: s 148(1).

8   As to the service of notices to treat see PARAS 616–620; and TOWN AND COUNTRY PLANNING vol 46(2) (Reissue) PARA 933.

9   See the Town and Country Planning Act 1990 s 139(3); and TOWN AND COUNTRY PLANNING vol 46(2) (Reissue) PARA 970. A notice to treat which is deemed to have been so served may not be withdrawn under the Land Compensation Act 1961 s 31 (see PARA 636): Town and Country Planning Act 1990 s 139(5).

10   As to confirmation of the purchase notice see TOWN AND COUNTRY PLANNING vol 46(2) (Reissue) PARAS 971–972.

11   As to the action which he may take see TOWN AND COUNTRY PLANNING vol 46(2) (Reissue) PARA 972.

12   Town and Country Planning Act 1990 s 140(1). The functions of a Minister of the Crown under s 140, so far as exercisable in relation to Wales, are now exercisable by the Welsh Ministers: see the National Assembly for Wales (Transfer of Functions) Order 1999, SI 1999/672, art 2, Sch 1; and the Government of Wales Act 2006 s 162(1), Sch 11 para 30. As to the Welsh Assembly Government and the Welsh Ministers see CONSTITUTIONAL LAW AND HUMAN RIGHTS.

13   As to the meaning of 'restricted use' see TOWN AND COUNTRY PLANNING vol 46(2) (Reissue) PARA 973.

14   See the Town and Country Planning Act 1990 s 142(1), (3); and TOWN AND COUNTRY PLANNING vol 46(2) (Reissue) PARA 972.

15   Ie by virtue of a modification to the purchase notice made by virtue of the Town and Country Planning Act 1990 s 141(4): see TOWN AND COUNTRY PLANNING vol 46(2) (Reissue) PARA 972.

16   See TOWN AND COUNTRY PLANNING vol 46(2) (Reissue) PARA 974.

17   See TOWN AND COUNTRY PLANNING vol 46(2) (Reissue) PARAS 975–976.

18   See TOWN AND COUNTRY PLANNING vol 46(3) (Reissue) PARA 1072.

19   See TOWN AND COUNTRY PLANNING.

546.   Compensation.   Where compensation is payable in respect of expenditure incurred in carrying out any works on land[1], any compensation payable in respect of the acquisition of an interest in the land in pursuance of a purchase notice[2] must be reduced by an amount equal to the value of those works[3].

Where the Secretary of State directs[4] that, if an application for it is made, planning permission[5] must be granted for the development[6] of any land[7], and it is shown that the permitted development value[8] of the interest in that land in respect of which the purchase notice was served is less than its value calculated on the assumption that planning permission would be granted for development consisting of (1) specified rebuilding operations or the maintenance, improvement or alteration of a building[9] subject to the statutory condition[10] relating thereto[11]; and (2) the use as two or more separate dwelling houses of any building which at a material date was used as a single dwelling house[12], the local planning authority[13], on a claim made to it, must pay the person entitled to that interest compensation of an amount equal to the difference[14].

1   Ie by virtue of the Town and Country Planning Act 1990 s 107 (which provides for compensation for revocation or modification of planning permissions): see TOWN AND COUNTRY PLANNING vol 46(2) (Reissue) PARA 914.

2   As to purchase notices see PARA 545; and TOWN AND COUNTRY PLANNING vol 46(2) (Reissue) PARA 966 et seq.

3   See the Town and Country Planning Act 1990 s 144(1); and TOWN AND COUNTRY PLANNING vol 46(2) (Reissue) PARA 977.

4   Ie under the Town and Country Planning Act 1990 s 141(3): see TOWN AND COUNTRY PLANNING vol 46(2) (Reissue) PARA 972. As to the Secretary of State see PARA 507 note 1. The functions of a Minister of the Crown under the Town and Country Planning Act 1990 s 141, so far as they are exercisable in relation to Wales, are now exercisable by the Welsh Ministers: see the National Assembly for Wales (Transfer of Functions) Order 1999, SI 1999/672, art 2, Sch 1;

and the Government of Wales Act 2006 s 162(1), Sch 11 para 30. As to the Welsh Assembly Government and the Welsh Ministers see CONSTITUTIONAL LAW AND HUMAN RIGHTS.

5   'Planning permission' means permission under the Town and Country Planning Act 1990 Pt III (ss 55–106B) (see TOWN AND COUNTRY PLANNING): s 336(1) (definition amended by the Planning and Compensation Act 1991 ss 32, 84(6), Sch 7 paras 8, 52(1), (2)(g), Sch 19 Pt I).

6   As to the meaning of 'development' see TOWN AND COUNTRY PLANNING vol 46(1) (Reissue) PARA 217.

7   See the Town and Country Planning Act 1990 s 144(2)(a).

8   For these purposes, 'permitted development value', in relation to an interest in land in respect of which a direction is given under the Town and Country Planning Act 1990 s 141(3), means the value of that interest calculated with regard to that direction but on the assumption that no planning permission would be granted otherwise than in accordance with that direction: s 144(6).

9   Ie development of a class specified in the Town and Country Planning Act 1990 s 107(4), Sch 3 para 1: see TOWN AND COUNTRY PLANNING vol 46(2) (Reissue) PARA 914. See also PARA 765 note 5.

10   Ie subject to the condition set out in the Town and Country Planning Act 1990 s 111(5), Sch 10: see TOWN AND COUNTRY PLANNING vol 46(2) (Reissue) PARA 918.

11   Town and Country Planning Act 1990 s 144(2)(b), (6) (amended by the Planning and Compensation Act 1991 s 31(4), Sch 6 paras 8, 19).

12   Ie development of a class specified in the Town and Country Planning Act 1990 Sch 3 para 2: see TOWN AND COUNTRY PLANNING vol 46(2) (Reissue) PARA 920. See also PARA 765 note 8.

13   As to local planning authorities see TOWN AND COUNTRY PLANNING vol 46(1) (Reissue) PARA 28 et seq.

14   Town and Country Planning Act 1990 s 144(2), (6) (as amended: see note 11). See further (and for similar provisions with regard to listed buildings) TOWN AND COUNTRY PLANNING vol 46(2) (Reissue) PARA 977.

(2) INTERESTS AFFECTED BY PLANNING BLIGHT

547. In general. Land to which specified statutory provisions apply[1] and which is identified as being affected by the planning proposals of public authorities is referred to as 'blighted land'[2]. A person with a qualifying interest[3] in blighted land who has made reasonable endeavours to sell that interest but has been unable to do so except at a price substantially lower than that for which it might reasonably have been expected to sell if no part of the relevant hereditament or agricultural unit[4] were, or were likely to be, comprised in blighted land, may serve a blight notice[5] on the appropriate authority[6] requiring it to purchase that interest to the extent specified in, and otherwise in accordance with, the relevant[7] statutory provisions[8].

The appropriate authority may serve a counter-notice objecting to the blight notice[9], in which case the claimant may require the objection to be referred to the Upper Tribunal (the 'Tribunal')[10].

Where a counter-notice has been served, and either (1) no counter-notice objecting to it is served; or (2) where such a counter-notice has been served, the objection is withdrawn or is not upheld on a reference to the Tribunal, the appropriate authority is deemed to be authorised to acquire the claimant's interest compulsorily and to have served a notice to treat[11] in respect of it on the specified date[12]. Where the counter-notice specifies that the authority is willing to acquire part only of a hereditament or affected area[13], and the claimant accepts this proposal, or where on a reference to the Tribunal the Tribunal makes a declaration[14] in respect of that part of the hereditament or affected area, then the appropriate authority is deemed to be authorised to acquire compulsorily the claimant's interest in the specified part of the hereditament or affected area, but not in any other part, and to have served a notice to treat in respect of it on the specified date[15].

A blight notice may be withdrawn in certain circumstances[16].

Special statutory provision is made with regard to partially affected agricultural units[17] and the powers of personal representatives, mortgagees and partnerships[18].

All these provisions are considered in detail elsewhere in this work[19].

1   Ie land to which the Town and Country Planning Act 1990 Sch 13 applies: see TOWN AND COUNTRY PLANNING vol 46(2) (Reissue) PARA 978 et seq.

2   See the Town and Country Planning Act 1990 s 149(1).

3   As to the meaning of 'qualifying interest' see the Town and Country Planning Act 1990 s 149(2); and TOWN AND COUNTRY PLANNING vol 46(2) (Reissue) PARA 987.

4   As to the meanings of 'hereditament' and 'agricultural unit' see the Town and Country Planning Act 1990 s 171(1); and TOWN AND COUNTRY PLANNING vol 46(2) (Reissue) PARAS 987, 993.

5   As to blight notices see TOWN AND COUNTRY PLANNING vol 46(2) (Reissue) PARA 990.

6   As to the meaning of 'appropriate authority' see TOWN AND COUNTRY PLANNING vol 46(2) (Reissue) PARA 990.

7   Ie the Town and Country Planning Act 1990 Pt VI Ch II (ss 149–171): see TOWN AND COUNTRY PLANNING.

8   See the Town and Country Planning Act 1990 s 150(1); and TOWN AND COUNTRY PLANNING vol 46(2) (Reissue) PARA 992.

9   See TOWN AND COUNTRY PLANNING vol 46(2) (Reissue) PARA 993.

10 As to the Upper Tribunal see PARA 720; and ADMINISTRATIVE LAW.

11 As to the service of notices to treat see PARAS 616–620. See also TOWN AND COUNTRY PLANNING vol 46(2) (Reissue) PARA 933.

12 See the Town and Country Planning Act 1990 s 154(1), (2); and TOWN AND COUNTRY PLANNING vol 46(2) (Reissue) PARA 997. For the specified date see s 154(3); and TOWN AND COUNTRY PLANNING vol 46(2) (Reissue) PARA 997.

13 'Affected area', in relation to an agricultural unit, means so much of that unit as consists of blighted land on the date of service of a blight notice in respect of it: see the Town and Country Planning Act 1990 s 171(1), (5).

14 Ie in accordance with the Town and Country Planning Act 1990 s 153(6): see TOWN AND COUNTRY PLANNING vol 46(2) (Reissue) PARA 996.

15 See the Town and Country Planning Act 1990 s 154(4), (5); and TOWN AND COUNTRY PLANNING vol 46(2) (Reissue) PARA 997.

16 See the Town and Country Planning Act 1990 s 156; and TOWN AND COUNTRY PLANNING vol 46(2) (Reissue) PARA 999.

17 See TOWN AND COUNTRY PLANNING vol 46(2) (Reissue) PARA 1000 et seq.

18 See TOWN AND COUNTRY PLANNING vol 46(2) (Reissue) PARAS 1003–1006.

19 See TOWN AND COUNTRY PLANNING.

548.   Compensation.   If, where an interest in land is acquired in pursuance of a blight notice[1], there is a compulsory purchase order in force containing a direction for minimum compensation[2], the compensation payable must be assessed in accordance with that direction and as if the notice to treat deemed to have been served[3] had been served in pursuance of the compulsory purchase order[4]. If there is a compulsory purchase order in force under the statutory provisions relating to the acquisition of land for clearance[5], the compensation payable must be assessed in accordance with the Housing Act 1985 and as if the notice to treat deemed to have been served had been served in respect of that compulsory purchase order[6].

Compensation payable on the acquisition of an interest in the unaffected area of an agricultural unit[7], or so much of the affected area[8] as is not specified in a counter-notice, where one has been served[9], must be assessed on the normal[10] statutory assumptions[11].

1   As to blight notices see PARA 547; and TOWN AND COUNTRY PLANNING vol 46(2) (Reissue) PARA 990.

2   Ie an order under the Acquisition of Land Act 1981 s 1 (see PARA 556) as applied by the Planning (Listed Buildings and Conservation Areas) Act 1990 s 47 and containing a direction under s 50: see TOWN AND COUNTRY PLANNING vol 46(3) (Reissue) PARA 1159.

3   Ie under the Town and Country Planning Act 1990 s 154: see PARA 547; and TOWN AND COUNTRY PLANNING vol 46(2) (Reissue) PARA 997. As to the service of notices to treat see PARAS 616–620; and TOWN AND COUNTRY PLANNING vol 46(2) (Reissue) PARA 933.

4   See the Town and Country Planning Act 1990 s 157(1); and TOWN AND COUNTRY PLANNING vol 46(2) (Reissue) PARA 1008.

5   Ie under the Housing Act 1985 s 290: see HOUSING vol 22 (2006 Reissue) PARA 425 et seq.

6   See the Town and Country Planning Act 1990 s 157(2); and TOWN AND COUNTRY PLANNING vol 46(2) (Reissue) PARA 1008.

7   As to the meaning of 'agricultural unit' see the Town and Country Planning Act 1990 s 171(1); and TOWN AND COUNTRY PLANNING vol 46(2) (Reissue) PARAS 987, 993.

8   As to the meaning of 'affected area' see PARA 547 note 13.

9   Ie served on the grounds specified in the Town and Country Planning Act 1990 s 151(4)(c): see TOWN AND COUNTRY PLANNING vol 46(2) (Reissue) PARA 993.

10 Ie the assumptions mentioned in the Land Compensation Act 1973 s 5(2)–(4): see PARA 896.

11 Town and Country Planning Act 1990 s 157(3); and see TOWN AND COUNTRY PLANNING vol 46(2) (Reissue) PARA 1008.

3. STEPS IN THE ACQUISITION OF LAND

(1) SURVEY BEFORE ACQUISITION

549. Power to enter land to survey. For the purpose merely of surveying and taking levels of any of the land[1] subject to compulsory purchase[2], of probing or boring to ascertain the nature of the soil and of setting out the line of the works[3], the undertakers[4] or the acquiring authority[5], after giving not less than three nor more than 14 days' notice[6] to the owners[7] or occupiers of that land, may enter[8] on that land; but the undertakers or the authority must make compensation for any damage thereby occasioned to the owners or occupiers of the land, and any question of disputed compensation[9] must be referred to the Upper Tribunal[10].

1   'Land' includes anything falling within any definition of that expression in the enactment under which the purchase is authorised: Compulsory Purchase Act 1965 s 1(3). See also PARA 511 text to note 7.
2   'Subject to compulsory purchase', in relation to land, means land the compulsory purchase of which is authorised by the compulsory purchase order: Compulsory Purchase Act 1965 s 1(3).
3   'Works' means the works, of whatever nature, authorised to be executed by the special Act: Compulsory Purchase Act 1965 s 1(4). See also PARA 511 text to note 4. As to the meaning of 'special Act' see PARAS 509, 514. Where, however, the Compulsory Purchase Act 1965 Pt I (ss 1–32) applies by virtue of the Town and Country Planning Act 1990 Pt IX (ss 226–246) (see TOWN AND COUNTRY PLANNING) or of the Planning (Listed Buildings and Conservation Areas) Act 1990 s 52 (see TOWN AND COUNTRY PLANNING vol 46(3) (Reissue) PARA 1161), references therein to the execution of works are to be construed in accordance with the Town and Country Planning Act 1990 s 245(4) or, as the case may be, the Planning (Listed Buildings and Conservation Areas) Act 1990 s 52(2) (see TOWN AND COUNTRY PLANNING vol 46(3) (Reissue) PARA 1161): Compulsory Purchase Act 1965 s 1(4) (amended by the Planning (Consequential Provisions) Act 1990 s 4, Sch 2 para 13(1)).
4   As to the meaning of 'undertakers' see PARA 511.
5   'Acquiring authority' means the person authorised by the compulsory purchase order to purchase the land: Compulsory Purchase Act 1965 s 1(3) (definition amended by the Acquisition of Land Act 1981 s 34(3), Sch 6 Pt I).
6   As to when an inspection will be granted if no notice is given see *Fooks v Wilts, Somerset and Weymouth Rly Co* (1846) 5 Hare 199.
7   Where any notice is to be given to the owner of any land, or where any act is authorised or required to be done with the consent of any such owner, the word 'owner', unless the context otherwise requires, means any person having power to sell and convey the land to the acquiring authority: Compulsory Purchase Act 1965 s 1(6); and see PARA 511 text to note 11.
8   This does not, however, amount to entry in order to determine the date of valuation or the date from which to calculate interest on compensation: *Courage Ltd v Kingswood District Council* (1978) 35 P & CR 436, Lands Tribunal.
9   Compensation payable under the Compulsory Purchase Act 1965 s 11(3) carries interest at the rate for the time being prescribed under the Land Compensation Act 1961 s 32 (see PARA 641 note 6) for the withdrawal of the notice to treat: see the Planning and Compensation Act 1991 s 80(1), Sch 18 Pt I. Payments on account may be made of such compensation or interest (see s 80(2)), recoverable where it is subsequently agreed or determined that there was no liability to pay the compensation or interest or that the payment on account was excessive (see s 80(3)).
The Compulsory Purchase Act 1965 s 11 is modified in relation to the compulsory acquisition of rights by, inter alia:
(1)   a local authority (see the Local Government (Miscellaneous Provisions) Act 1976 s 13(3)(b), Sch 1 para 9; and LOCAL GOVERNMENT vol 69 (2009) PARA 511);
(2)   urban development corporations (see the Local Government, Planning and Land Act 1980 s 144, Sch 28 para 23(4); and TOWN AND COUNTRY PLANNING vol 46(1) (Reissue) PARA 180);
(3)   highway authorities (see the Highways Act 1980 s 250(5)(a), Sch 19 para 9; and HIGHWAYS, STREETS AND BRIDGES vol 21 (2004 Reissue) PARAS 49 et seq, 85);
(4)   gas transporters (see the Gas Act 1986 s 9(3), Sch 3 para 10; and FUEL AND ENERGY vol 19(2) (2007 Reissue) PARA 841);

(5)   housing action trusts (see the Housing Act 1988 s 78(2), Sch 10 para 23(2); and HOUSING vol 22 (2006 Reissue) PARA 340);

(6)   licence holders under the Electricity Act 1989 (see s 10(1), Sch 3 para 11; and FUEL AND ENERGY vol 19(2) (2007 Reissue) PARA 1284);

(7)   the Environment Agency (see the Water Resources Act 1991 s 154(5), Sch 18 para 6; the Environment Act 1995 (Consequential Amendments) Regulations 1996, SI 1996/593, reg 2, Sch 1; and WATER AND WATERWAYS vol 101 (2009) PARA 453);

(8)   water and sewerage undertakers (see the Water Industry Act 1991 s 155(5), Sch 9 para 6; and WATER AND WATERWAYS vol 101 (2009) PARA 453);

(9)   regional development agencies (see the Regional Development Agencies Act 1998 s 20, Sch 5 para 5(2); and TRADE, INDUSTRY AND INDUSTRIAL RELATIONS vol 47 (2001 Reissue) PARA 901); and

(10)   universal service providers (see the Postal Services Act 2000 s 95, Sch 5 para 10; and POST OFFICE).

10 Lands Clauses Consolidation Act 1845 s 84 proviso (where that Act applies: see PARA 509); Compulsory Purchase Act 1965 s 11(3) (amended by SI 2009/1307) (where that Act applies: see PARA 513). As to the Upper Tribunal see PARA 720; and ADMINISTRATIVE LAW. Wider powers of entry for survey are given by some empowering enactments: see eg the Housing Act 1985 s 260 (see HOUSING vol 22 (2006 Reissue) PARA 442); the Local Government (Miscellaneous Provisions) Act 1976 s 15 (see LOCAL GOVERNMENT vol 69 (2009) PARA 532); and the Town and Country Planning Act 1990 ss 324(6), 325 (see TOWN AND COUNTRY PLANNING vol 46(1) (Reissue) PARAS 57–58).

(2) PURCHASE BY AGREEMENT

550.   Purchase with or without service of notice to treat. Undertakers[1] or an acquiring authority[2] empowered to purchase land compulsorily need not exercise such compulsory powers of acquisition but may acquire it by agreement[3].

The undertakers or acquiring authority may agree with any of the owners[4] of the land subject to compulsory purchase[5], and with all parties having any estate or interest in any of the land or who are enabled[6] to sell and convey or release any of that land, for the absolute purchase, for a consideration in money or money's worth, of any of that land and of all estates and interests in it[7]. An agreement to purchase is not affected by the time limit imposed on the exercise of the power of compulsory purchase[8].

The agreement may be effected without the service of a notice to treat or after the service of a notice to treat and without using compulsory powers of reference following such notice[9]; but the land will nonetheless be acquired under the empowering enactment or special Act and the provisions of that Act, and any Act incorporated by it or applicable to it, will apply to the purchase except so far as they are inconsistent with a purchase by agreement[10].

Undertakers or an acquiring authority may, in the agreement, enter into restrictive covenants affecting the land purchased, but not so as to impose any fetter on the exercise of the statutory powers entrusted to them by Parliament[11], and any covenants which impose such a fetter are void[12]. Normally, the power to purchase compulsorily does not enable a compulsory acquisition of a stratum of land as a limited interest only in the land, or an easement over it, without acquiring it[13], but the undertakers or acquiring authority may acquire such a stratum or an interest or easement where the owner is willing to sell it, provided those rights are sufficient for the purposes contemplated by the special Act[14].

1   As to the meaning of 'undertakers' see PARA 511.
2   As to the meaning of 'acquiring authority' see PARA 549 note 5.

3   Provision as to acquisition by agreement may be made in the special Act (as to the meaning of which see PARAS 509, 514). The power to acquire by agreement is given by the Lands

Clauses Consolidation Act 1845 s 6 (where that Act is incorporated: see PARA 509); or by the Compulsory Purchase Act 1965 s 3 (where that Act applies: see PARA 513). See the text and notes 4–14.

4   As to the meaning of 'owner' see PARA 549 note 7. See also PARA 511 text to note 11.

5   As to the meaning of 'land' see PARA 549 note 1. See also PARA 511 text to note 7. As to the meaning of 'subject to compulsory purchase' see PARA 549 note 2.

6   Ie by the special Act or by the Lands Clauses Consolidation Act 1845 s 6, or the Compulsory Purchase Act 1965 s 2, Sch 1, as the case may be, or, where the Compulsory Purchase Act 1965 applies, by any other enactment (see s 3): see PARA 553.

7   Lands Clauses Consolidation Act 1845 s 6 (referring, however, only to consideration in money and not to consideration in money's worth); Compulsory Purchase Act 1965 s 3 (amended by the Planning and Compensation Act 1991 s 70, Sch 15 para 3).

8   As to the time limit imposed in the case of compulsory purchase see the Lands Clauses Consolidation Act 1845 s 123; and the Compulsory Purchase Act 1965 s 4 (amended by the Housing Act 1974 s 116; and by the Housing (Consequential Provisions) Act 1985 s 3, Sch 1 Pt I); and see *Webb v Direct London and Portsmouth Rly Co* (1851) 9 Hare 129 at 140; *Worsley v South Devon Rly Co* (1851) 16 QB 539 at 545; *Rangeley v Midland Rly Co* (1868) 3 Ch App 306; *Kemp v South Eastern Rly Co* (1872) 7 Ch App 364.

9   As to service of a notice to treat see PARA 618. Such service is not the exercise of compulsory powers, but a condition precedent to their exercise, and it may be followed by an agreement or by the enforcement of compulsory powers: *Re Uxbridge and Rickmansworth Rly Co* (1890) 43 ChD 536, CA. See also PARAS 616 note 5, 631–637.

10 *Hooper v Bourne* (1877) 3 QBD 258 at 273, CA (affd (1880) 5 App Cas 1, HL); *Kirby v Harrogate School Board* [1896] 1 Ch 437, CA. Where, however, an authority which has power to purchase land compulsorily on authorisation by a compulsory purchase order purchases land by agreement before being authorised to acquire it compulsorily, this will not be a purchase under a compulsory purchase power and only those provisions of the Compulsory Purchase Act 1965 relating to purchase by agreement will apply; thus, inter alia, s 10, which gives a right to compensation for injurious works apart from compensation for land purchased (see PARA 878), will not apply: see eg the Small Holdings and Allotments Act 1908 s 38; and AGRICULTURAL LAND vol 1 (2008) PARAS 524–525. There will accordingly be no power to do works to the injury of rights of way or to infringe restrictive covenants unless the statutory purpose would inevitably lead to that injury: see PARA 859. Where such power is required the authority should seek authorisation of the purchase by a compulsory purchase order.
    In many cases powers to cause such injury are not required and purchase by agreement without authorisation to purchase compulsorily takes place; but, with the right to have such authorisation, the purchase price is not likely to be other than the compulsory purchase price and accordingly various statutory provisions as to the assessment of the compulsory purchase price are applied also to the purchase price on such an agreement: see PARAS 796, 849. Other powers are similarly applied: see PARA 772.

11 *Stourcliffe Estates Co Ltd v Bournemouth Corpn* [1910] 2 Ch 12, CA, where it was held that the undertakers could enter into a restrictive covenant which merely precluded them from exercising a subsidiary power, the exercise of which was not imperative for the purposes for which the land was acquired, but permissive only. The undertakers can grant an easement, provided it is not inconsistent with the purposes for which the land was acquired: *South Eastern Rly Co v Associated Portland Cement Manufacturers (1900) Ltd* [1910] 1 Ch 12, CA.

12 *Ayr Harbour Trustees v Oswald* (1883) 8 App Cas 623, HL; *Re Heywood's Conveyance, Cheshire Lines Committee v Liverpool Corpn* [1938] 2 All ER 230.

13 See PARA 534.

14 *Great Western Rly Co v Swindon and Cheltenham Extension Rly Co* (1884) 9 App Cas 787 at 801, HL; and see PARA 534.

551.   Consideration for the sale.   The consideration for the sale must be in money or money's worth[1]. Consideration may no longer comprise an annual rentcharge payable by the acquiring authority[2].

A person selling by agreement to an authority possessing compulsory purchase powers may apply for a certificate of appropriate alternative development[3].

1   See the Lands Clauses Consolidation Act 1845 s 6; the Compulsory Purchase Act 1965 s 3; and PARA 550.

2   See the Rentcharges Act 1977 ss 2, 17(2), Sch 2. The Lands Clauses Consolidation Act 1845 s 11 (amended by the Administration of Justice Act 1965 s 34, Sch 2; and extended by the Lands

Clauses Consolidation Acts Amendment Act 1860 s 2 to all cases of sale and purchase or compensation under the Lands Clauses Consolidation Act 1845 where the parties interested in the sale, or entitled to the compensation, are under any disability or incapacity) which provides for the recovery of such rentcharges, is thus of little practical effect.

3 See the Land Compensation Act 1961 ss 17, 22(2)(c); and PARA 772.

552. Application of general law to agreements. Agreements for the purchase of land by undertakers or an acquiring authority[1] are governed by the general law, as, for example, in regard to formalities[2], the time for completion[3], specific performance[4], and interest[5]. If the agreement provides that the price is to be fixed by reference to an arbitrator, the provisions of the Lands Clauses Acts[6] applicable to arbitrations, as, for example, those dealing with costs, will not apply to the reference[7] unless it is expressly so agreed.

1 See PARAS 550–551.

2 See e g *Crampton v Varna Rly Co* (1872) 7 Ch App 562. As to the formalities required see the Law of Property (Miscellaneous Provisions) Act 1989 s 2; and SALE OF LAND vol 42 (Reissue) PARA 29.

3 See *Baker v Metropolitan Rly Co* (1862) 31 Beav 504. As to the time for exercising an option to purchase see *Rangeley v Midland Rly Co* (1868) 3 Ch App 306; *Kemp v South Eastern Rly Co* (1872) 7 Ch App 364; and see *Tiverton and North Devon Rly Co v Loosemore* (1884) 9 App Cas 480, HL.

4 *Wilson v West Hartlepool Harbour and Rly Co* (1865) 34 LJCh 241; *Inge v Birmingham, Wolverhampton and Stour Valley Rly Co* (1853) 3 De GM & G 658; *Regent's Canal Co v Ware* (1857) 23 Beav 575; *Gunston v East Gloucestershire Rly Co* (1868) 18 LT 8; *Ingram v Midland Rly Co* (1860) 3 LT 533; *Tillett v Charing Cross Bridge Co* (1859) 28 LJCh 863.

5 *Catling v Great Northern Rly Co* (1869) 18 WR 121, CA; *Rhys v Dare Valley Rly Co* (1874) LR 19 Eq 93; *Re Pigott and Great Western Rly Co* (1881) 18 ChD 146; *Leggott v Metropolitan Rly Co* (1870) 5 Ch App 716; *Fletcher v Lancashire and Yorkshire Rly Co* [1902] 1 Ch 901; *Re Richard and Great Western Rly Co* [1905] 1 KB 68, CA; *Re Duke of Northumberland and Tynemouth Corpn* [1909] 2 KB 374.

6 As to the Lands Clauses Acts see PARA 509 note 1.

7 *Catling v Great Northern Rly Co* (1869) 18 WR 121, CA; *Doulton v Metropolitan Board of Works* (1870) LR 5 QB 333; *Wombwell v Barnsley Corpn* (1877) 36 LT 708; *Bygrave v Metropolitan Board of Works* (1886) 32 ChD 147, CA; and see *Re Lindsay's Settlement* [1941] Ch 170, [1941] 1 All ER 104 (abandonment of arbitration under the Lands Clauses Acts by agreement).

553. Persons entitled to sell, including persons under disability. All persons who are seised, possessed of or entitled to any land[1], or any estate or interest in any of the land, which the undertakers[2] or acquiring authority[3] may agree to purchase, are authorised to sell and convey or release it to that authority, and to enter into all necessary agreements for that purpose[4]. This power applies, in particular, to corporations, tenants in tail or for life, trustees for charitable or other purposes[5] and persons for the time being entitled to the receipt of the rent and profits of any such land in possession or subject to any lease for years or for any less interest[6].

The powers so conferred on any person, other than a lessee for a term of years or for any less interest, may be exercised not only on behalf of himself and his successors, but also for and on behalf of every person entitled in reversion, remainder or expectancy after him, or in defeasance of his estate[7]. Trustees for a beneficiary under any disability may exercise those powers on behalf of that beneficiary to the same extent that the beneficiary could have exercised those powers if he had not been under any disability[8].

Any power of releasing land from any rent, charge or incumbrance, or of agreeing to the apportionment of any such rent, charge or incumbrance, may lawfully be exercised by any person enabled under the above provisions to sell and convey or release land to the undertakers or the acquiring authority[9].

In most cases in which persons under disability are beneficially interested, the legal estate in land should be able to be conveyed on acquisition of it by agreement either by trustees[10] or under the Settled Land Act 1925 (if an existing settlement[11]), or by personal representatives[12]. In such cases there will be power to give a receipt for the purchase money without its being paid into court; but if it is payable to trustees of land or Settled Land Act trustees it must be paid to two or more trustees or a trust corporation[13].

Nothing in the above provisions or in the special Act[14] enables a local authority to sell, without the prior consent of the Secretary of State, any land which it could not otherwise have sold without that consent, except where the undertakers are, or the acquiring authority is, authorised to purchase the land compulsorily[15]. In other cases the exercise of powers to sell is, by statute, subject to the obtaining of consent[16] and, if the necessary consent is not obtained, title in respect of persons under a disability will have to be made on payment into court[17].

If the sale purports to be carried out under the Lands Clauses Acts or the Compulsory Purchase Act 1965, its validity must be determined according to their provisions independently of other powers[18].

1   As to the meaning of 'land' see PARA 549 note 1. See also PARA 511 text to note 7.
2   As to the meaning of 'undertakers' see PARA 511.
3   As to the meaning of 'acquiring authority' see PARA 92 note 5.
4   Lands Clauses Consolidation Act 1845 s 7; Compulsory Purchase Act 1965 s 2, Sch 1 para 2(1). Lessees are thereby released from their covenants against assignment and for subsequent breaches of covenants which they are prevented from performing: *Slipper v Tottenham and Hampstead Junction Rly Co* (1867) LR 4 Eq 112; *Baily v De Crespigny* (1869) LR 4 QB 180; *Harding v Metropolitan Rly Co* (1872) 7 Ch App 154 at 159; and see *Mills v East London Union* (1872) LR 8 CP 79; *Wadham v Marlow* (1784) 8 East 315n.
5   Where notice to treat is served both on the trustees and on the beneficiary, but the purchase money is fixed as between the acquiring authority and the beneficiary by a reference to arbitration in which the trustees take no part, the authority cannot require the sale to be completed as a sale by the trustees, but it must be completed as a sale by the beneficiary: see *Re Pigott and Great Western Rly Co* (1881) 18 ChD 146. See also *Peters v Lewes and East Grinstead Rly Co* (1881) 18 ChD 429, CA; *Lippincott v Smyth* (1860) 29 LJCh 520; *Hall v London, Chatham and Dover Rly Co* (1866) 14 LT 351.
6   Lands Clauses Consolidation Act 1845 s 7 (amended by the Compulsory Purchase Act 1965 s 39(4), Sch 8 Pt II); Compulsory Purchase Act 1965 Sch 1 para 2(2). As to receivers appointed by the court see *Tink v Rundle* (1847) 10 Beav 318.
7   Lands Clauses Consolidation Act 1845 s 7 (as amended: see note 6); Compulsory Purchase Act 1965 Sch 1 para 2(3). These provisions have effect subject to the Law of Property Act 1925 s 42(7), which provides that if, on a compulsory purchase, title could have been made without payment into court, title must be made in that way unless the purchaser otherwise elects: see the Compulsory Purchase Act 1965 Sch 1 paras 1(1), 2(3). As to payment into court see PARA 555. If the reversion is in the Crown, the Crown's consent is necessary: *Re Cuckfield Burial Board* (1854) 24 LJCh 585.
8   See the Lands Clauses Consolidation Act 1845 s 7 (as amended (see note 6); further amended by the Mental Treatment Act 1930 ss 20(5), 22(3); and by virtue of the Mental Health Act 1983 s 148, Sch 5 para 29); Compulsory Purchase Act 1965 Sch 1 para 2(4). These provisions have effect as if references to disabilities did not include references to minors, married women or persons suffering from mental disorder: see the Law of Property (Amendment) Act 1924 s 9, Sch 9; the Compulsory Purchase Act 1965 Sch 1 para 1(2)(a). They also do not have effect in relation to a person who lacks capacity (within the meaning of the Mental Capacity Act 2005) for the purposes of the Compulsory Purchase Act 1965 if (1) there is a donee of an enduring power of attorney or lasting power of attorney (within the meaning of the Mental Capacity Act 2005: see MENTAL HEALTH vol 30(2) (Reissue) PARA 648), or a deputy appointed for the person by the Court of Protection; and (2) the donee or deputy has power in relation to the

person for the purposes of the Compulsory Purchase Act 1965: Sch 1 para 2(1)(b) (substituted by the Mental Capacity Act 2005 Sch 6 para 12).

Married women are in any case no longer subject to any legal disability in English law; and although the capacity of a married woman to contract is governed by the law of her domicile (see *Guepratte v Young* (1851) 4 De G & Sm 217), such incapacity, in relation to a contract where both parties are in England, may be invoked only if the other party was aware of it, or negligent in not being aware of it, at the time of the conclusion of the contract: see the Contracts (Applicable Law) Act 1990 ss 1, 2; the Rome Convention (ie the Convention on the Law Applicable to Contractual Obligations (Rome, 19 June 1980)) art 11; and CONFLICT OF LAWS.

9   Lands Clauses Consolidation Act 1845 s 8 (amended by the Compulsory Purchase Act 1965 s 39(4), Sch 8 Pt II); Compulsory Purchase Act 1965 Sch 1 para 3(b). See further the Lands Clauses Consolidation Act 1845 ss 108–121; the Compulsory Purchase Act 1965 ss 14–20; and PARAS 698–714.

10   As to the overreaching powers upon conveyances of legal estates in land by trustees see the Law of Property Act 1925 s 2; and REAL PROPERTY vol 39(2) (Reissue) PARAS 247–252. As to trusts of land see REAL PROPERTY vol 39(2) (Reissue) PARA 64 et seq.

11   With limited exceptions, it has not been possible to create a new settlement under the Settled Land Act 1925 since the coming into force of the Trusts of Land and Appointment of Trustees Act 1996 on 1 January 1997; and an existing settlement will cease permanently to be a settlement for the purposes of the Settled Land Act 1925 when there is no relevant property which is, or is deemed to be, subject to the settlement: see the Trusts of Land and Appointment of Trustees Act 1996 s 2; and REAL PROPERTY vol 39(2) (Reissue) PARA 65; SETTLEMENTS vol 42 (Reissue) PARAS 606, 675 et seq.

12   See the Administration of Estates Act 1925 ss 2, 39 (s 2 amended by the Law of Property (Miscellaneous Provisions) Act 1994 ss 16(1), 21(2), Sch 2); and EXECUTORS AND ADMINISTRATORS vol 17(2) (Reissue) PARA 438.

13   Law of Property Act 1925 s 27(2) (substituted by the Law of Property (Amendment) Act 1926 s 7, Schedule; and amended by the Trusts of Land and Appointment of Trustees Act 1996 s 25(1), Sch 3 para 4(8)(b)); Settled Land Act 1925 s 94(1); Trustee Act 1925 s 14 (amended by the Law of Property (Amendment) Act 1926 Schedule; the Trusts of Land and Appointment of Trustees Act 1996 Sch 3 para 3(3); and the Trustee Act 2000 s 40(1), Sch 2 Pt II para 19). In these cases there will be no need for payment into court: see note 7.

14   As to the meaning of 'special Act' see PARAS 509, 514.

15   Lands Clauses Consolidation Act 1845 s 15; Compulsory Purchase Act 1965 s 38(2); Secretary of State for the Environment Order 1970, SI 1970/1681; Secretary of State for the Environment, Transport and the Regions Order 1997, SI 1997/2971; Secretary of State for the Environment, Food and Rural Affairs Order 2001, SI 2001/2568. As to the application of the Compulsory Purchase Act 1965 Pt I (ss 1–32) to sales by agreement under certain enactments see further the Compulsory Purchase Act 1965 s 38(3), (4). As to consent to sales see the Local Government Act 1972 ss 123(2), 128; and the Town and Country Planning Act 1959 s 26 which, however, is excluded by the Local Government Act 1972 s 128(3); and see LOCAL GOVERNMENT vol 69 (2009) PARA 529. As to the Secretary of State see PARA 507 note 1.

16   See eg the Universities and College Estates Act 1925 s 2(2) (repealed except in relation to Winchester and Eton by the Universities and College Estates Act 1964 s 2, Sch 1 para 1).

17   See *Re Great Western Railway (New Railways) Act 1905, ex p Great Western Rly Co* (1909) 74 JP 21, CA.

18   *Peters v Lewes and East Grinstead Rly Co* (1881) 18 ChD 429, CA.

554.   Assessment of consideration where persons under disability. When the land[1] is to be purchased or taken from any person under any disability[2] or incapacity, who has no power to sell or convey it except under the special Act[3], the Lands Clauses Acts[4], or the Compulsory Purchase Act 1965, the purchase money or compensation to be paid, and also the compensation for any permanent damage or injury to any land held by that person[5], must not be less than an amount determined by the valuation of two able practical surveyors[6], except where the amount has been determined[7] under compulsory powers[8].

1   As to the meaning of 'land' see PARA 549 note 1. See also PARA 511 text to note 7.
2   As to the meaning of 'disability' for these purposes see PARA 553 note 8.
3   As to the meaning of 'special Act' see PARAS 509, 514.
4   As to the Lands Clauses Acts see PARA 509 note 1.

5   *Stone v Yeovil Corpn* (1876) 2 CPD 99, CA.
6   Lands Clauses Consolidation Act 1845 s 9; Lands Clauses Consolidation Acts Amendment
    Act 1860 s 4; Compulsory Purchase Act 1965 Sch 1 paras 4(1), (5), 5(1). The valuation is to be
    by two able practical surveyors, one appointed by each party, and, in default of agreement
    between the surveyors, by a third surveyor nominated by two justices on the application of
    either party; and a certificate of the correctness of his valuation must be annexed by the surveyor
    to the valuation: Lands Clauses Consolidation Act 1845 s 9; Compulsory Purchase Act 1965
    Sch 1 paras 4(1), (2), (3), (5), 5(1). A certificate of value of the land being sold may be obtained
    by any person selling the land from the Upper Tribunal on written application to the registrar
    with such information as he may require: Land Compensation Act 1961 s 35 (amended by
    SI 2009/1307); Lands Tribunal Rules 1996, SI 1996/1022, r 40. As to the Upper Tribunal see
    PARA 720; and ADMINISTRATIVE LAW.
        As to the necessity for such a certificate in proceedings to enforce the sale see *Wycombe
    Rly Co v Donnington Hospital* (1866) 1 Ch App 268; *Bridgend Gas and Water Co v Dunraven*
    (1885) 31 ChD 219. A party cannot appoint himself as surveyor: *Peters v Lewes and East
    Grinstead Rly Co* (1881) 18 ChD 429 at 438, CA. Cf the statutory provisions respecting sales
    under the Settled Land Act 1925: see s 39; and SETTLEMENTS vol 42 (Reissue) PARA 827 et seq.
    As to settlements see PARA 553 note 11.
7   Ie where the amount has been determined by the Upper Tribunal or by the valuation of a
    surveyor selected from the members of the Upper Tribunal who are members or fellows of the
    Royal Institution of Chartered Surveyors, in the case of absent or untraced owners: Compulsory
    Purchase Act 1965 s 5(3), Sch 1 paras 4(1), (4), 5(1), Sch 2 para 1(1)(b) (amended by
    SI 2009/1307).
8   Lands Clauses Consolidation Act 1845 s 9; Lands Clauses Consolidation Acts Amendment
    Act 1860 s 4; Compulsory Purchase Act 1965 Sch 1 paras 4(1), (4), 5(1).

555.   Payment into court where persons under disability.   When the land[1] is
purchased from persons under disability[2] who are enabled to sell and convey
only under the special Act[3], the Lands Clauses Acts[4] or the Compulsory Purchase
Act 1965[5], the purchase money or compensation must in general be paid into
court for the benefit of the persons interested in the manner provided in those
Acts[6].

1   As to the meaning of 'land' see PARA 549 note 1. See also PARA 511 text to note 7.
2   As to the meaning of 'disability' for these purposes see PARA 553 note 8.
3   As to the meaning of 'special Act' see PARAS 509, 514.
4   As to the Lands Clauses Acts see PARA 509 note 1.
5   See PARA 553.
6   Lands Clauses Consolidation Act 1845 s 9; Compulsory Purchase Act 1965 s 2, Sch 1
    para 6(1), (2). References to payment into court are references to payment into the Supreme
    Court: s 25(1). The Lands Clauses Consolidation Act 1845 s 9 refers to deposit in the Bank of
    England, but it is thought that this should now be construed as a reference to payment into the
    Supreme Court. As from 1 October 2009, the reference to the Supreme Court in the
    Compulsory Purchase Act 1965 s 25 is replaced by a reference to the Senior Courts by the
    Constitutional Reform Act 2005 s 59(5), Sch 11 para 4(1), (3). As to acquisitions where there is
    power to acquire under a compulsory purchase order see PARAS 667–669. See further PARA 661.
    As to payment in and the application of the money see the Lands Clauses Consolidation
    Act 1845 ss 69–80; the Compulsory Purchase Act 1965 Sch 1 para 6; and PARAS 667–669.

(3) COMPULSORY PURCHASE ORDERS

(i) In general

556.   Application and incorporation of Acquisition of Land Act 1981.   In
respect of most compulsory acquisitions, the procedures for the making and
confirmation of compulsory purchase orders contained in the Acquisition of
Land Act 1981 are applied[1]. Since 1946, the procedure now contained in the
Acquisition of Land Act 1981 and previously enacted in the Acquisition of Land
(Authorisation Procedure) Act 1946 has been incorporated in a host of

enactments[2] conferring powers of compulsory acquisition on Ministers of the Crown, local authorities[3] and a variety of public bodies including statutory undertakers[4].

The Acquisition of Land Act 1981 prescribes a standard procedure for use where land is to be acquired compulsorily by public authorities, but its procedures only apply where this is specifically required[5]. The provisions of the Act apply to compulsory acquisitions under most, but not all[6], public general Acts in force at the time of its commencement[7] and also to compulsory acquisitions under the enabling Acts specified in the Acquisition of Land Act 1981[8]. Most, but not all, Acts authorising compulsory acquisition passed since the commencement of the 1981 Act have incorporated the procedures in that Act and the procedures therein contained now apply to most compulsory acquisitions by public authorities[9]. The procedures in the 1981 Act do not apply to Acts in which the 1981 Act is not specifically incorporated[10] and under certain empowering enactments, the procedures in the 1981 Act have been incorporated in a varied form[11].

1   The procedure for the making and confirmation of compulsory purchase orders under various Acts conferring powers of compulsory acquisition differed in many respects until the Acquisition of Land (Authorisation Procedure) Act 1946 (repealed) provided a uniform procedure for the making of compulsory purchase orders for the acquisition of land by local authorities under powers conferred by public enactments (with limited exceptions) in force immediately before the passing of that Act. It not only repealed most of the previous provisions in those enactments relating to compulsory purchase orders but also substituted authorisation by compulsory purchase order for authorisation by provisional order in other Acts: see the Acquisition of Land (Authorisation Procedure) Act 1946 s 10(3), Sch 6 (repealed). The Acquisition of Land (Authorisation Procedure) Act 1946 could also be applied to acquisitions by a local authority under a local Act similarly in force where the local Act conferred a power to authorise compulsory acquisition: see the Acquisition of Land (Authorisation Procedure) Act 1946 s 7 (repealed).
2   See e g the Ancient Monuments and Archaeological Areas Act 1979 s 10 (see OPEN SPACES AND ANCIENT MONUMENTS vol 34 (Reissue) PARA 373); the Electricity Act 1989 s 10(1), Sch 3 para 5 (see FUEL AND ENERGY vol 19(2) (2007 Reissue) PARAS 1282, 1284); and the Water Industry Act 1991 s 155(4) (see WATER AND WATERWAYS vol 101 (2009) PARA 453).
3   As to the meaning of 'local authority' see PARA 522 note 2.
4   As to the meaning of 'statutory undertaker' see PARA 561 note 8.
5   See the Acquisition of Land Act 1981 s 1(1). The Acquisition of Land Act 1981 may apply by virtue of any other enactment, whether or not passed or made before that Act (s 1(1)(a)); and 'enactment' includes any statutory instrument (s 1(3)). Apart from the Acts set out in s 1(2) (see note 8), the specific statutory provision applying the Acquisition of Land Act 1981 will normally be found in the enabling Act: see the examples cited in note 2.
    The Acquisition of Land Act 1981 does not extend to Northern Ireland: see s 35(1), (3).
6   See e g the Pipe-lines Act 1962 ss 11–14 (see RAILWAYS, INLAND WATERWAYS AND CROSS-COUNTRY PIPELINES vol 39(1A) (Reissue) PARA 595 et seq); the Forestry Act 1967 s 40 (see FORESTRY vol 19(1) (2007 Reissue) PARA 44 et seq); and the New Towns Act 1981 ss 10–16 (see TOWN AND COUNTRY PLANNING vol 46(3) (Reissue) PARA 1333 et seq).
7   Acquisition of Land Act 1981 s 1(1), Sch 5 para 5. The commencement date was 30 January 1982: s 35(2).
8   See the Acquisition of Land Act 1981 s 1(1)(b). The enactments specified are: the Metropolitan Police Act 1886 s 2; the Military Lands Act 1892 s 1(3); the Small Holdings and Allotments Act 1908 ss 25(1), 39(1); the Development and Road Improvement Funds Act 1909 s 5(1) (repealed) as it applied to acquisition by local authorities (as defined in the Acquisition of Land Act 1981 s 7(1) (see PARA 522 note 2)) or by the Secretary of State; and the Education Act 1996 s 530(1): see the Acquisition of Land Act 1981 s 1(2) (amended by the Water Act 1989 s 190(3), Sch 27 Pt I; the Education Act 1996 s 582(1), Sch 37 para 50; and the Statute Law (Repeals) Act 2004). As from a day to be appointed, the Metropolitan Police Act 1886 s 2 is repealed by the Greater London Authority Act 1999 s 423, Sch 34 Pt VII. At the date at which this volume states the law, no such day had been appointed. As to the Secretary of State see PARA 507 note 1.

9　See eg the Gas Act 1986 s 9(3), Sch 3 para 4; the Electricity Act 1989 s 10(1), Sch 3 para 5; and FUEL AND ENERGY vol 19(2) (2007 Reissue) PARAS 841, 1284.

10　See eg the New Towns Act 1981 s 10(1), Sch 4 Pt I (paras 1–6) (where alternative but similar procedures are provided for); and TOWN AND COUNTRY PLANNING vol 46(3) (Reissue) PARAS 1333, 1337.

11　See eg the Airports Act 1986 s 59(1) (see AIR LAW vol 2 (2008) PARA 189); the Housing Act 1988 s 78(1), Sch 10 Pt I (paras 1, 3) (see HOUSING vol 22 (2006 Reissue) PARA 340); the Town and Country Planning Act 1990 ss 226, 228, 245 (see TOWN AND COUNTRY PLANNING vol 46(2) (Reissue) PARAS 936, 941, 944); the Water Industry Act 1991 ss 155(4), 188, Sch 14 and the Water Resources Act 1991 ss 154(4), 182, Sch 23 (see WATER AND WATERWAYS vol 101 (2009) PARAS 453, 492).

(ii) Purchases by Authorities other than Ministers of the Crown

A. MAKING OF COMPULSORY PURCHASE ORDER

557. Making of compulsory purchase order. A compulsory purchase order[1] authorising a compulsory purchase by an authority other than a Minister of the Crown[2] must be made by that authority (the 'acquiring authority')[3] and submitted to and confirmed by the authority having power under the empowering enactment to authorise the purchase (the 'confirming authority')[4] in accordance with the relevant statutory provisions[5]. Part II of the Acquisition of Land Act 1981[6] applies to any such compulsory acquisition made under Acts incorporating that Act[7].

1　Ie an order authorising a compulsory purchase: see the Acquisition of Land Act 1981 ss 2(1), 7(1). 'Compulsory purchase' means a compulsory purchase of land, being a compulsory purchase to which the Acquisition of Land Act 1981 applies by virtue of any enactment, whether or not passed or made before the Acquisition of Land Act 1981 was passed, or a compulsory purchase under a specified enactment (see PARA 556 note 8): s 1(1). As to the meaning of 'land' see PARA 522 note 1.

2　All functions of a Minister of the Crown under the Acquisition of Land Act 1981, except s 8(4) (see PARA 564), so far as they are exercisable in relation to Wales, have been transferred to the Welsh Ministers; and orders made or confirmed by them are subject to special parliamentary procedure as provided for in s 18 (see PARA 603), Sch 3 para 5 (see PARA 608): see the National Assembly for Wales (Transfer of Functions) Order 1999, SI 1999/672, art 2, Sch 1; and the Government of Wales Act 2006 s 162(1), Sch 11 para 30. As to the Welsh Assembly Government and the Welsh Ministers see CONSTITUTIONAL LAW AND HUMAN RIGHTS.

3　As to the meaning of 'acquiring authority' see PARA 522 note 2.

4　'Confirming authority', in relation to a compulsory purchase, means, where the acquiring authority is not a Minister, the Minister having power to authorise the acquiring authority to purchase the land compulsorily: Acquisition of Land Act 1981 s 7(1). All functions of a Minister of the Crown under the Acquisition of Land Act 1981, except s 8(4) (see PARA 564), so far as they are exercisable in relation to Wales, have been transferred to the Welsh Ministers; and orders made or confirmed by them are subject to special parliamentary procedure as provided for in s 18 (see PARA 603), Sch 3 para 5 (see PARA 608): see the National Assembly for Wales (Transfer of Functions) Order 1999, SI 1999/672, art 2, Sch 1; and the Government of Wales Act 2006 s 162(1), Sch 11 para 30. As to the Welsh Assembly Government and the Welsh Ministers see CONSTITUTIONAL LAW AND HUMAN RIGHTS.

5　Acquisition of Land Act 1981 s 2(2). See PARA 558 et seq.

6　Ie the Acquisition of Land Act 1981 Pt II (ss 10–15): see PARA 558 et seq.

7　See the Acquisition of Land Act 1981 ss 1, 10(1); and PARA 556. Part II is also applied, subject to modifications, to compulsory rights orders in respect of opencast coal operations made under the Opencast Coal Act 1958 s 4 (see MINES, MINERALS AND QUARRIES vol 31 (2003 Reissue) PARA 422), subject to the provisions of the Acquisition of Land Act 1981 s 29: see the Opencast Coal Act 1958 s 4(4A) (added by the Acquisition of Land Act 1981 s 34(1), Sch 4 para 11(1), (2)). See further PARA 610. Land occupied for opencast coal purposes is protected from compulsory acquisition by the Opencast Coal Act 1958 s 38: see further MINES, MINERALS AND QUARRIES vol 31 (2003 Reissue) PARA 407.

558.   Form of compulsory purchase order.   The compulsory purchase order[1] must be made by the acquiring authority[2] in the prescribed form[3] and must describe the land[4] to which it applies by reference to a map[5]. A schedule attached to the order must describe in detail the land to be acquired[6]. The purpose for which the order is made must be specified in it[7].

1   As to the meanings of 'compulsory purchase' and 'compulsory purchase order' see PARA 557 note 1.
2   As to the meaning of 'acquiring authority' see PARA 522 note 2.
3   Acquisition of Land Act 1981 s 10(2). Guidance is issued as to the formalities to be complied with in sealing and identifying the documents required to be contained in an order: see *Office of the Deputy Prime Minister Circular 06/2004: Compulsory Purchase and the Crichel Down Rules* (31 October 2004). A compulsory purchase order will be valid notwithstanding that it is sealed on a date subsequent to the date on the order as long as there is no deliberate attempt to cause a landowner to act to his detriment: *Burke v Secretary of State for the Environment* (1992) 26 HLR 10, CA.
     Anything which, by the Acquisition of Land Act 1981 Pt II (ss 10–15) (see PARA 559 et seq), by Pt III (ss 16–22) (see PARAS 564, 603 et seq), by s 2(3), Sch 1 (see PARA 572 et seq), or by s 28, Sch 3 (see PARA 606 et seq), is required or authorised to be prescribed must be prescribed by regulations made by the Secretary of State by statutory instrument: s 7(2). As to the Secretary of State see PARA 507 note 1. The regulation-making function provided for in s 7(2) has been transferred to the Welsh Ministers but only so far as it is exercisable in relation to such orders as fall to be made or confirmed by them: see the National Assembly for Wales (Transfer of Functions) Order 1999, SI 1999/672, art 2, Sch 1; and the Government of Wales Act 2006 s 162(1), Sch 11 para 30. As to the Welsh Assembly Government and the Welsh Ministers see CONSTITUTIONAL LAW AND HUMAN RIGHTS.
     In exercise of the power so conferred, the Compulsory Purchase of Land (Prescribed Forms) (Ministers) Regulations 2004, SI 2004/2595, and the Compulsory Purchase of Land (Prescribed Forms) (National Assembly for Wales) Regulations 2004, SI 2004/2732, have been made for England and Wales respectively.
     For the purposes of the Acquisition of Land Act 1981 s 10, the prescribed form of compulsory purchase order (other than a clearance compulsory purchase order) is set out in the Compulsory Purchase of Land (Prescribed Forms) (Ministers) Regulations 2004, SI 2004/2595, Schedule, Form 1 (see reg 3(a)(i)), and the Compulsory Purchase of Land (Prescribed Forms) (National Assembly for Wales) Regulations 2004, SI 2004/2732, Schedule, Form 1 (see reg 3(1)(a)). If the order provides for the vesting of land given in exchange pursuant to the Acquisition of Land Act 1981 s 19 or Sch 3 para 6 (commons, open spaces etc: see PARAS 604, 609), the form of the order must follow the prescribed form as set out in the Compulsory Purchase of Land (Prescribed Forms) (Ministers) Regulations 2004, SI 2004/2595, Schedule, Form 2 (see reg 3(a)(ii)); or the Compulsory Purchase of Land (Prescribed Forms) (National Assembly for Wales) Regulations 2004, SI 2004/2732, Schedule, Form 2 (see reg 3(1)(b)). If it does not so provide, but provides for discharging the land purchased from rights, trusts and incidents pursuant to the Acquisition of Land Act 1981 s 19 or Sch 3 para 6, the order must be as set out in the Compulsory Purchase of Land (Prescribed Forms) (Ministers) Regulations 2004, SI 2004/2595, Schedule, Form 3 (see reg 3(a)(iii)); or the Compulsory Purchase of Land (Prescribed Forms) (National Assembly for Wales) Regulations 2004, SI 2004/2732, Schedule, Form 3 (see reg 3(1)(c)).
     The form of a clearance compulsory purchase order must be as set out in the Compulsory Purchase of Land (Prescribed Forms) (Ministers) Regulations 2004, SI 2004/2595, Schedule, Form 4 (see reg 3(b)(i)) or the Compulsory Purchase of Land (Prescribed Forms) (National Assembly for Wales) Regulations 2004, SI 2004/2732, Schedule, Form 4 (see reg 3(2)(a)). If the order provides for the vesting of land given in exchange pursuant to the Acquisition of Land Act 1981 s 19 or Sch 3 para 6 (commons, open spaces etc) the form of order must be as set out in the Compulsory Purchase of Land (Prescribed Forms) (Ministers) Regulations 2004, SI 2004/2595, Schedule, Form 5 (see reg 3(b)(ii)) or the Compulsory Purchase of Land (Prescribed Forms) (National Assembly for Wales) Regulations 2004, SI 2004/2732, Schedule, Form 5 (reg 3(2)(b)). If it does not so provide but provides for discharging the land purchased from rights, trusts and incidents pursuant to the Acquisition of Land Act 1981 s 19 or Sch 3 para 6, the order must be as set out in the Compulsory Purchase of Land (Prescribed Forms) (Ministers) Regulations 2004, SI 2004/2595, Schedule, Form 6 (see reg 3(b)(iii)) or the Compulsory Purchase of Land (Prescribed Forms) (National Assembly for Wales) Regulations 2004, SI 2004/2732, Schedule, Form 6 (reg 3(2)(c)).

'Clearance compulsory purchase order' means a compulsory purchase order made pursuant to the Housing Act 1985 s 290 (see HOUSING vol 22 (2006 Reissue) PARA 427): Compulsory Purchase of Land (Prescribed Forms) (Ministers) Regulations 2004, SI 2004/2595, reg 2; Compulsory Purchase of Land (Prescribed Forms) (National Assembly for Wales) Regulations 2004, SI 2004/2732, reg 2.

For the relevant form of compulsory rights order under the Opencast Coal Act 1958 s 4 see the Opencast Coal (Compulsory Rights, Drainage and Rights of Way) (Forms) Regulations 1994, SI 1994/3097, reg 3(a)(ii), Schedule, Form 2. See further PARA 557 note 7.

4 As to the meaning of 'land' see PARA 522 note 1. In relation to compulsory purchase under any enactment, 'land' includes anything falling within any definition of the expression in that enactment and within the definition set out in PARA 522 note 1, but it does not include rights against the land (see *Grimley v Minister of Housing and Local Government* [1971] 2 QB 96, [1971] 2 All ER 431) unless special statutory provision is made (see PARA 532). Whether or not incorporeal hereditaments fall within the definition of 'land' will be determined by construction of the empowering enactment.

5 Acquisition of Land Act 1981 s 10(2). The map should be of a sufficient scale to allow the extent of the acquisition to be clearly identified. For further guidance on the making of compulsory purchase orders see *Office of the Deputy Prime Minister Circular 06/2004: Compulsory Purchase and the Crichel Down Rules* (31 October 2004); and for the order map (or maps) see Appendix V.

6 The schedule has five columns: (1) the number of the plot (if more than one) from the map; (2) the extent, description and situation of the land in such detail as to allow the land to be identified; (3) the names of the owners or reputed owners; (4) the names of the lessees or reputed lessees; and (5) the names of the occupiers: see the Compulsory Purchase of Land (Prescribed Forms) (Ministers) Regulations 2004, SI 2004/2595, Schedule, Forms 1–6; Compulsory Purchase of Land (Prescribed Forms) (National Assembly for Wales) Regulations 2004, SI 2004/2732, Schedule, Forms 1–6.

7 See Compulsory Purchase of Land (Prescribed Forms) (Ministers) Regulations 2004, SI 2004/2595, Schedule, Forms 1–6; Compulsory Purchase of Land (Prescribed Forms) (National Assembly for Wales) Regulations 2004, SI 2004/2732, Schedule, Forms 1–6. As to the purpose of the compulsory purchase order see PARA 526.

559. Advertisement of compulsory purchase order. Before submitting the order to the confirming authority[1], the acquiring authority[2] must place a copy of the order and of the accompanying map[3] at a place, such as the acquiring authority's offices, in the locality in which the land[4] comprised in the order is situated, so that interested persons may inspect them[5].

The acquiring authority must then, in two successive weeks, publish in one or more local newspapers circulating in the locality in which that land is situated a notice in the prescribed form[6] stating that the order has been made and is about to be submitted for confirmation, describing the land and stating the purpose for which it is required, naming the place where a copy of the order and map may be inspected, and specifying the time (not being less than 21 days from the first publication of the notice) within which, and the manner in which, objections to the order may be made[7].

In addition, the acquiring authority must affix a notice in the prescribed form to a conspicuous object or objects on or near the land comprised in the order[8].

1 As to the meaning of 'confirming authority' see PARA 557 note 4.
2 As to the meaning of 'acquiring authority' see PARA 522 note 2.
3 As to the map see PARA 558 note 5.
4 As to the meaning of 'land' see PARA 522 note 1.
5 See the Acquisition of Land Act 1981 ss 10(3), 11(2)(c).

6 For the prescribed form of newspaper notice see the Compulsory Purchase of Land (Prescribed Forms) (Ministers) Regulations 2004, SI 2004/2595, reg 3(c), Schedule, Form 7; Compulsory Purchase of Land (Prescribed Forms) (National Assembly for Wales) Regulations 2004, SI 2004/2732, reg 3(3), Schedule, Form 7. In the case of compulsory rights orders under the Opencast Coal Act 1958 s 4 (see MINES, MINERALS AND QUARRIES vol 31 (2003 Reissue) PARA

422), the relevant form of notice is contained in the Opencast Coal (Compulsory Rights, Drainage and Rights of Way) (Forms) Regulations 1994, SI 1994/3097, reg 3(a)(iii), Schedule, Form 3. See further PARA 557 note 6.

7   Acquisition of Land Act 1981 ss 10(3), 11(1), (2). As to objections see PARA 563 et seq.

8   Acquisition of Land Act 1981 s 11(3) (s 11(3), (4) added by the Planning and Compulsory Purchase Act 2004 s 100(1), (4), (8)). This notice must be addressed to persons occupying or having an interest in the land, and must (1) state that the order has been made and is about to be submitted for confirmation; (2) describe the land and state the purpose for which the land is required; (3) name a place within the locality where a copy of the order and map may be inspected; and (4) specify the time (not being less than 21 days from the day when the notice is first affixed) within which, and the manner in which, objections to the order can be made: Acquisition of Land Act 1981 s 11(4) (as so added).

560. Notice of order to qualifying persons.

560.   Notice of order to qualifying persons. The acquiring authority[1] must serve[2] on every qualifying person[3], a notice in the prescribed form[4] stating the effect of the order and that it is about to be submitted for confirmation and specifying the time (not being less than 21 days from the service of the notice) within which and the manner in which objections to the order may be made[5]. In the case of ecclesiastical property[6], notice must also be served on the Diocesan Board of Finance for the diocese in which the land is situated.[7]

Acquiring authorities are also required to serve a copy of their statement of reasons for making the order on the persons mentioned above, and, in so far as practicable, such a statement should also be served on any applicant for planning permission in respect of the land[8].

1   As to the meaning of 'acquiring authority' see PARA 522 note 2.
2   As to the mode of service see PARA 561.
3   A person is a qualifying person, in relation to land comprised in an order, if: (1) he is an owner, lessee, tenant (whatever the tenancy period) or occupier of the land; or (2) he is either (a) a person to whom the acquiring authority would, if proceeding under the Compulsory Purchase Act 1965 s 5(1) (see PARA 616), be required to give a notice to treat; or (b) a person the acquiring authority thinks is likely to be entitled to make a relevant claim if the order is confirmed and the compulsory purchase takes place, so far as he is known to the acquiring authority after making diligent inquiry: Acquisition of Land Act 1981 s 12(2), (2A)(a), (b) (s 12(2), (2A), (2B) added by the Planning and Compulsory Purchase Act 2004 s 100(1), (5), (8)). A relevant claim is a claim for compensation under the Compulsory Purchase Act 1965 s 10 (compensation for injurious affection: see PARAS 718, 878): Planning and Compulsory Purchase Act 2004 s 12(2B) (as so added).
    In relation to any land, 'owner' means a person, other than a mortgagee not in possession, who is for the time being entitled to dispose of the fee simple of the land, whether in possession or in reversion, and includes also: (i) a person holding or entitled to the rents and profits of the land under a lease or agreement the unexpired term of which exceeds three years; and (ii) a person who would have power to sell and convey or release the land to the acquiring authority if a compulsory purchase order were operative: Acquisition of Land Act 1981 s 7(1) (definition amended by the Planning and Compensation Act 1991 s 70, Sch 15 Pt I para 9). A person with an easement of support over land comprised in the order is not an owner of land entitled to service, even if the empowering enactment defines 'land' as easements and rights over land: *Grimley v Minister of Housing and Local Government* [1971] 2 QB 96, [1971] 2 All ER 341. See further PARAS 532–533. As to easements generally see EASEMENTS AND PROFITS A PRENDRE.
    To assist in identifying the persons entitled to service of notice, local authorities have a general power to require the occupier or other person having an interest in the land to state the name and address of the owner, mortgagee or lessee: see the Local Government (Miscellaneous Provisions) Act 1976 s 16; and LOCAL GOVERNMENT vol 69 (2009) PARA 533.
4   For the prescribed form see the Compulsory Purchase of Land (Prescribed Forms) (Ministers) Regulations 2004, SI 2004/2595, reg 3(d), Schedule, Forms 8 and 9; Compulsory Purchase of Land (Prescribed Forms) (National Assembly for Wales) Regulations 2004, SI 2004/2732, reg 3(4), Schedule, Forms 8 and 9.
    Where a compulsory purchase order is made under the Planning (Listed Buildings and Conservation Areas) Act 1990 s 47 (compulsory acquisition of listed buildings in need of repair: see TOWN AND COUNTRY PLANNING vol 46(3) (Reissue) PARAS 1154–1155, 1157), the

following information must be included in the form: (1) in all such cases, an additional paragraph stating that any person having an interest in the listed building which it is proposed to acquire compulsorily may apply to the magistrates' court for an order staying further proceedings within 28 days after service of the notice, and an additional paragraph stating that the position with respect to the order is subject to any action taken under the Planning (Listed Buildings and Conservation Areas) Act 1990, which also provides for appeals against decisions of the court; (2) in any case where the notice is required by s 50(3) (minimum compensation in the case of a building deliberately left derelict: see TOWN AND COUNTRY PLANNING vol 46(3) (Reissue) PARA 1159) to include a statement that the authority or Minister has included a direction for minimum compensation, an additional paragraph stating that such a direction has been included, explaining the meaning of this and drawing attention to the right under s 50 to apply to a magistrates' court, within 28 days after service of the notice, for an order that such a direction is not to be included: see the Compulsory Purchase of Land (Prescribed Forms) (Ministers) Regulations 2004, SI 2004/2595, reg 4; Compulsory Purchase of Land (Prescribed Forms) (National Assembly for Wales) Regulations 2004, SI 2004/2732, reg 4.

In the case of compulsory rights orders under the Opencast Coal Act 1958 s 4 (see MINES, MINERALS AND QUARRIES vol 31 (2003 Reissue) PARA 422): (a) the provisions of the Acquisition of Land Act 1981 s 12 are substituted by s 29(4) (see PARA 610); and (b) the relevant form of notice is contained in the Opencast Coal (Compulsory Rights, Drainage and Rights of Way) (Forms) Regulations 1994, SI 1994/3097, reg 3(a)(iv), Schedule, Form 4. See also PARA 557 note 7.

5   Acquisition of Land Act 1981 ss 10(3), 12(1). As to objections see PARA 563 et seq.
6   'Ecclesiastical property' means land belonging to any ecclesiastical benefice of the Church of England, or being or forming part of a church subject to the jurisdiction of the bishop of any diocese of the Church of England or the site of such a church, or being or forming part of a burial ground subject to such jurisdiction (see ECCLESIASTICAL LAW): Acquisition of Land Act 1981 s 12(3) (amended by the Planning and Compensation Act 1991 s 70, Sch 15 para 27; and the Church of England (Miscellaneous Provisions) Measure 2006 s 14, Sch 5 para 24(1)).
7   Acquisition of Land Act 1981 s 12(3) (amended by the Church of England (Miscellaneous Provisions) Measure 2006 Sch 5 para 24(1)).
8   *Office of the Deputy Prime Minister Circular 06/2004: Compulsory Purchase and the Crichel Down Rules* (31 October 2004) para 35. As to the contents of such a statement of reasons see also Appendix R.

561. Service of notices. Any notice or other document required or authorised to be served in relation to the making and confirmation of the compulsory purchase order[1] may be served on any person either by delivering it to him or by leaving it at his proper address[2] or by post, but the document will not be duly served by post unless it is sent by registered letter or by the recorded delivery service[3]. Any such document required or authorised to be served upon an incorporated company or body will be duly served if it is served upon the secretary or clerk of the company or body[4].

Service of the notice on the occupier of the land may not be good service on the owner of the land even if the occupier of the land is the owner's agent[5].

If the authority with jurisdiction to make the order in connection with which the document is to be served is satisfied that reasonable inquiry has been made and that it is not practicable to ascertain the name or address of an owner[6], lessee, tenant or occupier of land[7] on whom any such document is to be served, the document may be served by addressing it to him by the description of 'owner', 'lessee', 'tenant' or 'occupier' of the land (describing it) to which it relates, and by delivering it to some person on the land or, if there is no person on the land to whom it may be delivered, by leaving it or a copy of it on or near the land[8].

1   Ie authorised or required to be served under the Acquisition of Land Act 1981.
2   For this purpose, and for the purposes of the Interpretation Act 1978 s 7 (service by post: see STATUTES vol 44(1) (Reissue) PARA 1388), the proper address of the secretary or clerk of any incorporated company or body is that of its registered or principal office, and the proper address of any other person is his last known address, except where the person to be served has

furnished an address for service, in which case his proper address for these purposes is the address furnished: Acquisition of Land Act 1981 s 6(3). Service by post will be deemed to be effected by properly addressing, prepaying and posting a letter containing the document and, unless the contrary is proved, will be deemed to have been effected at the time at which the letter would be delivered in the ordinary course of post: see the Interpretation Act 1978 s 7.

3   Acquisition of Land Act 1981 s 6(1). Any reference in any legislation or legal document to 'Registered Post' or 'the Registered Service' is to be taken to be a reference to 'Special Delivery', as it is the same service in all material respects: see the Royal Mail Group Ltd's Successor Postal Services Company Inland Letter Post Scheme 2001, Schedule 2; and POST OFFICE vol 36(2) (Reissue) PARAS 116–119.

4   Acquisition of Land Act 1981 s 6(2).

5   *Shepherd v Norwich Corpn* (1885) 30 ChD 553.

6   As to the meaning of 'owner' see PARA 560 note 3.

7   As to the meaning of 'land' see PARA 522 note 1.

8   Acquisition of Land Act 1981 s 6(4) (amended by the Planning and Compensation Act 1991 s 70, Sch 15 para 8; and the Planning and Compulsory Purchase Act 2004 s 100(1), (2), (8)). The Acquisition of Land Act 1981 s 6(4) does not apply to notices served under s 5A: s 5A(8) (added by the Planning and Compulsory Purchase Act 2004 s 105); see PARA 522.

This provision does not, however, have effect in relation to an owner, lessee, tenant or occupier being a local authority, statutory undertakers or the National Trust: Acquisition of Land Act 1981 s 6(4) proviso (amended by the Planning and Compulsory Purchase Act 2004 s 100(1), (2), (8)). 'National Trust' means the National Trust for Places of Historic Interest or Natural Beauty incorporated by the National Trust Act 1907 (see OPEN SPACES AND ANCIENT MONUMENTS vol 34 (Reissue) PARA 103 et seq): Acquisition of Land Act 1981 s 7(1). As to the meaning of 'local authority' see PARA 522 note 2.

Unless the context otherwise requires, 'statutory undertakers' means:

(1)   any person authorised by any enactment to construct, work or carry on: (a) any railway, light railway, tramway, road transport, water transport, canal or inland navigation undertaking; or (b) any dock, harbour, pier or lighthouse undertaking; or (c) any undertaking for the supply of hydraulic power; or

(2)   the Civil Aviation Authority or a person who holds a licence under the Transport Act 2000 Pt 1 Ch 1 (to the extent that the person is carrying out activities authorised by the licence) (see AIR LAW vol 2 (2008) PARA 50 et seq); or

(3)   a universal service provider in connection with the provision of a universal postal service,

and for these purposes, 'enactment' means any Act or any order or scheme made under or confirmed by an Act: Acquisition of Land Act 1981 s 8(1) (amended by the Telecommunications Act 1984 s 109(6), Sch 7 Pt I; the Airports Act 1986 s 83(5), Sch 6 Pt I; the Gas Act 1986 s 67(3), (4), Sch 8 para 17, Sch 9 Pt I; the Electricity Act 1989 s 112(4), Sch 18; the Water Act 1989 s 190(1), Sch 25 para 65; the Postal Services Act 2000 (Consequential Modifications No 1) Order 2001, SI 2001/1149, art 3(1), Schedule 1 para 54(1), (2), 2(b); and the Transport Act 2000 (Consequential Amendments) Order 2001, SI 2001/4050, art 2, Schedule Pt II para 5(a)(i)). The following are deemed to be statutory undertakers, and their undertakings statutory undertakings, for this purpose:

(i)   a gas transporter (see the Gas Act 1995 s 16(1), Sch 4 para 2(1)(xxxi), (11)(d); and FUEL AND ENERGY vol 19(2) (2007 Reissue) PARA 835 et seq);

(ii)   a relevant airport operator within the meaning of the Airports Act 1986 (see s 58, Sch 2 para 1(1); and AIR LAW vol 2 (2008) PARA 189);

(iii)   the Environment Agency, every water undertaker and every sewerage undertaker (see the Water Act 1989 Sch 25 para 1(1), (2)(xxvii); the Environment Act 1995 (Consequential Amendments) Regulations 1996, SI 1996/593, reg 2, Sch 1; and PROTECTION OF ENVIRONMENT AND PUBLIC HEALTH vol 38 (2006 Reissue) PARA 614 et seq; WATER AND WATERWAYS vol 100 (2009) PARAS 137, 318 et seq);

(iv)   the holder of a licence under the Electricity Act 1989 s 6 who is entitled to exercise any power of compulsory acquisition conferred by s 10, Sch 3 (see s 112(1), Sch 16 para 2(2)(g), (9); and FUEL AND ENERGY vol 19(2) (2007 Reissue) PARA 1281 et seq).

The undertaking of a person who holds a licence under the Transport Act 2000 Pt 1 Ch I (see head (2) above) is considered to be a statutory undertaking for the purposes of the Acquisition of Land Act 1981 only to the extent that it is the person's undertaking as a licence holder (s 8(1ZA) (added by the Transport Act 2000 (Consequential Amendments) Order 2001, SI 2001/4050, art 2, Schedule Pt II para 5(a)(ii))); and the undertaking of a universal service provider (see head (3) above) is taken to be his statutory undertaking for the purposes of the Acquisition of Land Act 1981 only so far as relating to the provision of a universal postal service and references to his undertaking are to be construed accordingly (s 8(1A) (added by the Postal Services Act 2000 (Consequential Modifications No 1) Order 2001, SI 2001/1149, art 3(1), Sch 1 para 54(1), (2)(b))).

562.   Submission of order for confirmation.   When the making of a compulsory purchase order[1] has been advertised and the necessary notices have been served on the owners, lessees, tenants and occupiers[2], the order must be submitted to the confirming authority[3].

1   As to the meaning of 'compulsory purchase order' see PARA 557 note 1.
2   See PARAS 559–561.
3   See the Acquisition of Land Act 1981 s 10(3). As to the meaning of 'confirming authority' see PARA 557 note 4. The empowering enactment may impose a time limit for the submission of the order for confirmation: see eg the Housing Act 1985 s 17(4); and HOUSING vol 22 (2006 Reissue) PARA 235.

563.   Right of objection to compulsory purchase order.   Objections to a compulsory purchase order[1] may be made in the manner and in the time provided in the notices[2] and must be made to the confirming authority[3]. They must be made in writing and the grounds of objection should be stated, for the confirming authority may require an objector to state the grounds in writing and may disregard the objection if it is satisfied that the objection relates exclusively to matters which can be dealt with by the tribunal by which the compensation is to be assessed[4].

1   As to the meaning of 'compulsory purchase order' see PARA 557 note 1.
2   See PARAS 560–561. Objections to the inclusion of operational land of statutory undertakers may be made and the land may be excluded from the order: see PARA 564.
3   Objections may be made by owners, lessees, tenants and occupiers served with a notice of the order (see PARAS 560–561) and other persons, but the objections of other persons may for certain purposes be disregarded (see PARA 565). As to the meaning of 'confirming authority' see PARA 557 note 4.
4   See the Acquisition of Land Act 1981 s 13(4); and PARA 565.

564.   Representations by statutory undertakers as alternative to objections. Where the land[1] comprised in a compulsory purchase order[2] includes land which has been acquired by statutory undertakers[3] for the purposes of their undertaking, they may make representations, within the time within which objections to the order can be made[4], to the appropriate minister[5]. If that minister is satisfied that any of the land is used for the purposes of carrying on the undertaking, or that an interest in any of the land is held for those purposes[6], and provided that the representation made to him is not withdrawn[7], the order must not be confirmed, or made, so as to authorise the compulsory purchase of any land in respect of which that minister is so satisfied, except land in respect of which he certifies[8] that he is satisfied that its nature and situation are such that: (1) it can be purchased and not replaced without serious detriment to the carrying on of the undertaking[9]; or (2) if purchased it can be replaced by other land belonging to, or available for acquisition by, the undertakers without such serious detriment[10].

In the case of acquisitions of land of statutory undertakers under the Town and Country Planning Act 1990[11], the Planning (Listed Buildings and Conservation Areas) Act 1990[12], certain provisions of the Local Government, Planning and Land Act 1980[13], or the Welsh Development Agency Act 1975[14], the order may be confirmed or made without the appropriate certificate[15] provided that it has been confirmed (or made) by the appropriate minister jointly with the minister or ministers who would normally make the order[16].

1   As to the meaning of 'land' see PARA 522 note 1. In relation to the compulsory purchase of a
    right under the Gas Act 1965 s 12(1), s 13(2) or s 13(3) (see FUEL AND ENERGY vol 19(2) (2007
    Reissue) PARAS 998–999), references to the land for these purposes include references to any
    land held with the stratum of land constituting the underground gas storage: see the Acquisition
    of Land Act 1981 s 30(1); and PARA 611.
2   As to the meaning of 'compulsory purchase order' see PARA 557 note 1.
3   For these purposes, 'statutory undertakers' includes:
    (1)   a health service body, as defined in the National Health Service and Community Care
          Act 1990 s 60(7);
    (2)   a National Health Service Trust established under the National Health Service Act 2006
          s 25 or the National Health Service (Wales) Act 2006 s 29;
    (3)   an NHS foundation trust;
    (4)   a Primary Care Trust established under the National Health Service Act 2006 s 18; and
    (5)   a Local Health Board established under the National Health Service (Wales) Act 2006
          s 11;
    but in relation to a health service body, as so defined, any reference in the Acquisition of Land
    Act 1981 s 16(1), (2) to land acquired or available for acquisition by the statutory undertakers
    is to be construed as a reference to land acquired or available for acquisition by the Secretary of
    State for use or occupation by that body: s 16(3) (added by the National Health Service and
    Community Care Act 1990 s 60, Sch 8 para 8(1); and amended by the National Health Service
    Reform and Health Care Professional Act 2002 ss 6(2), 37(2), Sch 5 para 25, Sch 9 Pt 1; the
    National Health Service (Consequential Provisions) Act 2006 s 2, Sch 1 paras 59, 60; and
    SI 2000/90). As to the bodies mentioned above see further HEALTH SERVICES. As to the meaning
    of 'statutory undertakers' generally see PARA 561 note 8.
4   As to the time within which objections may be made see the Acquisition of Land Act 1981
    ss 11(2), (d), 12(1)(c); and PARAS 559–560.
5   See the Acquisition of Land Act 1981 s 16(1). 'Appropriate minister' means: (1) in the
    Acquisition of Land Act 1981 in relation to any statutory undertakers, the Secretary of State
    (s 8(3)); or (2) the appropriate minister as prescribed in the empowering enactment (see e g the
    Gas Act 1995 s 16(1), Sch 4 para 2(11)(d); the Electricity Act 1989 s 112(1), Sch 16 para
    3(2)(h); and the Water Act 1989 s 190(1), Sch 25 para 1(9), (10)(ix)). If a question arises as to
    which minister is the appropriate minister, the question is to be determined by the Treasury:
    Acquisition of Land Act 1981 s 8(4). As to the Treasury see CONSTITUTIONAL LAW AND HUMAN
    RIGHTS vol 8(2) (Reissue) PARAS 512–517. As to the Secretary of State see PARA 507 note 1. The
    functions of the Secretary of State as the 'appropriate minister' under the Acquisition of Land
    Act 1981, except s 8(4), are now exercisable by the Welsh Ministers but only so far as they
    relate to water and sewerage undertakers (treated as statutory undertakers for these purposes by
    virtue of the Water Act 1989 Sch 25) except under the Acquisition of Land Act 1981 s 16 where
    those functions are also transferred in relation to the bodies and trusts referred to in s 16(3) (see
    note 3): see the National Assembly for Wales (Transfer of Functions) Order 1999, SI 1999/672,
    art 2, Sch 1; and the Government of Wales Act 2006 s 162(1), Sch 11 para 30. As to the Welsh
    Assembly Government and the Welsh Ministers see CONSTITUTIONAL LAW AND HUMAN
    RIGHTS.
6   Acquisition of Land Act 1981 s 16(1)(a), (b). This provision does not protect land acquired by
    statutory undertakers other than for the purposes of their undertaking.
7   Acquisition of Land Act 1981 s 16(1) (amended by the Planning and Compensation Act 1991
    s 70, Sch 15 para 10(1)).
8   As soon as may be after the giving of a certificate under the Acquisition of Land Act 1981 Pt III
    (ss 16–22), the acquiring authority must publish in one or more local newspapers circulating in
    the locality in which the land comprised in the order is situated a notice in the prescribed form
    stating that the certificate has been given: s 22. For the prescribed form see the Compulsory
    Purchase of Land (Prescribed Forms) (Ministers) Regulations 2004, SI 2004/2595, reg 3(f),
    Schedule, Form 12; and the Compulsory Purchase of Land (Prescribed Forms) (National
    Assembly for Wales) Regulations 2004, SI 2004/2732, reg 3(6), Schedule, Form 12.
       In the case of compulsory rights orders under the Opencast Coal Act 1958 s 4 (see MINES,
    MINERALS AND QUARRIES vol 31 (2003 Reissue) PARA 422), the relevant form of notice is
    contained in the Opencast Coal (Compulsory Rights, Drainage and Rights of Way) (Forms)
    Regulations 1994, SI 1994/3097, reg 3(a)(v), Schedule, Form 5. See further PARA 557 note 7.
    Subject to the Acquisition of Land Act 1981 s 24 (court's power to quash certificate: see PARA
    614), the certificate becomes operative on the date on which the notice is first published: s 26(2).
9   Acquisition of Land Act 1981 s 16(2)(a).
10 Acquisition of Land Act 1981 s 16(2)(b).

11 See TOWN AND COUNTRY PLANNING; HIGHWAYS, STREETS AND BRIDGES. These functions of the Secretary of State, so far as they are exercisable in relation to Wales, are exercisable by the Welsh Ministers: see the National Assembly for Wales (Transfer of Functions) Order 1999, SI 1999/672, art 2, Sch 1; and the Government of Wales Act 2006 s 162(1), Sch 11 para 30.

12 See TOWN AND COUNTRY PLANNING. These functions of the Secretary of State, so far as they are exercisable in relation to Wales, are exercisable by the Welsh Ministers: see the National Assembly for Wales (Transfer of Functions) Order 1999, SI 1999/672, art 2, Sch 1; and the Government of Wales Act 2006 s 162(1), Sch 11 para 30.

13 Ie under the Local Government, Planning and Land Act 1980 s 142 or s 143 (acquisition by urban development corporation: see TOWN AND COUNTRY PLANNING vol 46(3) (Reissue) PARAS 1455–1457). These functions of the Secretary of State, so far as they are exercisable in relation to Wales, are exercisable by the Welsh Ministers: see the National Assembly for Wales (Transfer of Functions) Order 1999, SI 1999/672, art 2, Sch 1; and the Government of Wales Act 2006 s 162(1), Sch 11 para 30.

14 Ie by virtue of the Welsh Development Agency Act 1975 s 21A, Sch 4: see TRADE, INDUSTRY AND INDUSTRIAL RELATIONS vol 47 (2001 Reissue) PARA 856 et seq.

15 See the Acquisition of Land Act 1981 s 31(1) (substituted by the Planning and Compensation Act 1991 s 4, Sch 2 para 53(2); and amended by the Government of Wales Act 1998 ss 128, 135(3), 152, Sch 14 para 19, Sch 18 Pt V), and the Acquisition of Land Act 1981 s 31(2) (substituted by the Planning and Compensation Act 1991 s 70, Sch 15 Pt I para 10(2)), disapplying the Acquisition of Land Act 1981 s 16(2).

16 Acquisition of Land Act 1981 s 31(2) (as substituted: see note 15). Where, in accordance with this provision, a compulsory acquisition is effected under a compulsory purchase order confirmed or made without the appropriate minister's certificate, the Town and Country Planning Act 1990 ss 280–282 (measure of compensation) apply in accordance with s 281(1)(c) (see TOWN AND COUNTRY PLANNING vol 46(3) (Reissue) PARAS 1028–1030): Acquisition of Land Act 1981 s 31(4) (amended by the Planning and Compensation Act 1991 Sch 2 para 53(2)).

B. CONFIRMATION OF COMPULSORY PURCHASE ORDER

565. Confirmation of order where no objections are outstanding or objections are disregarded. The confirming authority[1] may confirm a compulsory purchase order[2] with or without modifications if it is satisfied that the notice requirements[3] have been complied with and that either (1) no relevant objection[4] is made; or (2) every relevant objection made is either withdrawn or disregarded[5].

The confirming authority may require every person who makes a relevant objection to state the grounds of the objection in writing[6]. If the confirming authority is satisfied that an objection relates exclusively to matters which can be dealt with by the tribunal by whom the compensation is to be assessed it may disregard the objection[7].

1 As to the meaning of 'confirming authority' see PARA 557 note 4.

2 As to the meaning of 'compulsory purchase order' see PARA 557 note 1.

3 The notice requirements are the requirements under the Acquisition of Land Act 1981 ss 11, 12 (see PARAS 559, 560) to publish, affix and serve notices in connection with the compulsory purchase order: s 13(5) (s 13 substituted by the Planning and Compulsory Purchase Act 2004 s 100(1), (6), (8)).

4 A relevant objection is an objection by a person who is a qualifying person for the purposes of the Acquisition of Land Act 1981 s 12(2) (see PARA 560), but if such a person qualifies only by virtue of s 12(2A)(b) (see PARA 560) and the confirming authority thinks that he is not likely to be entitled to make a relevant claim his objection is not a relevant objection: s 13(6) (as substituted: see note 3).

5 Acquisition of Land Act 1981 s 13(1), (2) (as substituted: see note 3). 'Disregarded' means disregarded under s 13(4) (see the text and note 7) or under any other power to disregard a relevant objection contained in the enactment providing for the compulsory purchase: s 13(7) (as so substituted).

   If confirmation of the order would necessarily infringe some legal principle, the confirming authority must refuse to confirm it: see *London and Westcliff Properties Ltd v Minister of*

Housing and Local Government [1961] 1 All ER 610, [1961] 1 WLR 519. The confirming authority is entitled to refuse to confirm an order where the acquiring authority has failed to convince it of the need for the order: see *R v Secretary of State for the Environment, ex p Melton Borough Council* (1986) 52 P & CR 318. In *Procter & Gamble v Secretary of State for the Environment* [1992] 1 EGLR 265, CA, it was confirmed that a compulsory purchase order made for one purpose cannot lawfully be confirmed for another or additional purpose. In *Glasgow City District Council v Secretary of State for Scotland* [1990] 2 EGLR 18, a decision by the confirming authority not to confirm an order with a modification excluding a parcel of land from the order, notwithstanding that the inspector had found that the development was possible with the modification, was upheld.

If confirmation is refused there is no bar to the making of a fresh order with respect to the same land: see *Land Realisation Co Ltd v Postmaster-General* [1950] Ch 435, [1950] 1 All ER 1062.

6   Acquisition of Land Act 1981 s 13(3) (as substituted: see note 3).
7   Acquisition of Land Act 1981 s 13(4) (as substituted: see note 3).
     An objection may be disregarded in the case of a compulsory purchase order of land for development and other planning purposes under the Town and Country Planning Act 1990 s 226 or s 228, if, in the opinion of the confirming authority or the First Secretary of State, the objection amounts in substance to an objection to the provisions of the development plan defining the proposed use of that land and other land: see s 245(1); and TOWN AND COUNTRY PLANNING vol 46(2) (Reissue) PARA 944. As to the transfer of functions under the Town and Country Planning Act 1990 s 226 or s 228 to the First Secretary of State see the Transfer of Functions (Transport, Local Government and the Regions) Order 2002, SI 2002/2626, art 15. See also *Chesterfield Properties v Secretary of State for the Environment, Transport and the Regions* (1997) 76 P & CR 117 (under the Town and Country Planning Act 1990 s 226, there is no requirement for a precedent fact before the Secretary of State can confirm a compulsory purchase order, so it was not necessary for him to conclude on the balance of probabilities that the development would take place before finding a public interest); *Gala Leisure Ltd v Secretary of State for the Environment, Transport and the Regions* (2000) 82 P & CR 118 (the lawfulness of the decision made by the Secretary of State depends upon a proper consideration of all the circumstances in the case).

566.   Confirmation of order where there are remaining objections. The following provisions apply where a compulsory purchase order[1] has been confirmed and there is a remaining objection (that is a relevant objection is made which is neither withdrawn, nor disregarded)[2]. In such a case the confirming authority[3] may proceed under the written representations procedure[4] (1) if the order is not subject to special parliamentary procedure; (2) in the case of an order concerning land owned by a statutory undertaker, if a certificate has been given permitting the purchase of certain land[5]; and (3) if every person who has made a remaining objection consents in the prescribed manner[6].

If heads (1) to (3) do not apply or if the confirming authority decides not to proceed under the written representations procedure, it must either cause a public local inquiry to be held, or give every person who has made a remaining objection an opportunity of appearing before and being heard by a person appointed by the confirming authority for the purpose[7]. If a person who has made a remaining objection takes the opportunity to appear before a person so appointed, the confirming authority must give the acquiring authority and any other person it thinks appropriate the opportunity to be heard at the same time[8].

The confirming authority may confirm the order with or without modifications if it has considered the objection and either it has followed the written representations procedure or, if an inquiry was held or a person was appointed to hear the person with the remaining objection, it has considered the report of the person who held the inquiry or who was so appointed[9].

Where the confirming authority decides to follow the written representations procedure[10], the confirming authority may make orders as to the costs of the parties to the written representations procedure, and as to which party must pay the costs[11]. The costs incurred by the confirming authority in connection with the written representations procedure must be paid by the acquiring authority, if the confirming authority so directs[12]. The confirming authority may certify the amount of its costs, and any amount so certified and directed to be paid by the acquiring authority is recoverable summarily by the confirming authority as a civil debt[13].

1   As to the meaning of 'compulsory purchase order' see PARA 557 note 1.
2   Acquisition of Land Act 1981 s 13A(1), (7) (ss 13A, 13B added by the Planning and Compulsory Purchase Act 2004 s 100(1), (6), (8)). As to the meaning of 'relevant objection' see PARA 565 note 4. As to the meaning of 'disregarded' see PARA 565 note 5.
3   As to the meaning of 'confirming authority' see PARA 557 note 4.
4   The written representations procedure is such procedure as is prescribed for the purposes of the Acquisition of Land Act 1981 s 13A including provision affording an opportunity to (1) every person who has made a remaining objection; (2) the acquiring authority; and (3) any other person the confirming authority thinks appropriate, to make written representations as to whether the order should be confirmed: s 13A(6) (as added: see note 2). Regulations under s 13A(6) may make provision as to the giving of reasons for decisions taken in cases where the written representations procedure is followed: s 13B(7) (as so added).
       As to the written representations procedure see the Compulsory Purchase of Land (Written Representations Procedure) (Ministers) Regulations 2004, SI 2004/2594; and the Compulsory Purchase of Land (Written Representations Procedure) (National Assembly for Wales) Regulations 2004, SI 2004/2730; and PARA 580 et seq.
5   Ie an order to which the Acquisition of Land Act 1981 s 16 applies: see PARA 564.
6   Acquisition of Land Act 1981 s 13A(2) (as added: see note 2).
7   Acquisition of Land Act 1981 s 13A(3) (as added: see note 2). As to the inquiries procedure see s 5(1); and the Compulsory Purchase (Inquiries Procedure) Rules 2007, SI 2007/3617; and PARA 587 et seq.
8   Acquisition of Land Act 1981 s 13A(4) (as added: see note 2). As to the meaning of 'acquiring authority' see PARA 522 note 2.
9   Acquisition of Land Act 1981 s 13A(5) (as added: see note 2).
10 Acquisition of Land Act 1981 s 13B(1) (as added: see note 2).
11 Acquisition of Land Act 1981 s 13B(2) (as added: see note 2). Such an order may be made a rule of the High Court on the application of any party named in the order: s 13B(3) (as so added).
12 Acquisition of Land Act 1981 s 13B(4) (as added: see note 2).
13 Acquisition of Land Act 1981 s 13B(5) (as added: see note 2). The Housing and Planning Act 1986 s 42(2) (recovery of Minister's costs in connection with inquiries) applies to the written representations procedure as if the procedure is an inquiry specified in s 42(1): Acquisition of Land Act 1981 s 13B(6) (as so added).

567. Confirmation in stages. The confirming authority[1] may confirm an order (with or without modifications) so far as it relates to part of the land comprised in the order (referred to as the 'relevant part') if[2] (1) the confirming authority is satisfied that the order ought to be confirmed so far as it relates to the relevant part but has not for the time being determined whether the order ought to be confirmed so far as it relates to the remaining part[3]; and (2) the confirming authority is satisfied that the notice requirements have been complied with[4].

If there is a remaining objection[5] in respect of the order, the confirming authority may only act as described above after complying with certain statutory provisions[6]. However, it may act without complying with those provisions if it is satisfied that all remaining objections relate solely to the remaining part of the land[7].

If the confirming authority does so act[8] (a) it must give a direction postponing consideration of the order, so far as it relates to the remaining part, until such time as may be specified by or under the direction; (b) the order so far as it relates to each part of the land must be treated as a separate order[9].

1   As to the meaning of 'confirming authority' see PARA 557 note 4.
2   Acquisition of Land Act 1981 s 13C(1) (s 13C added by the Planning and Compulsory Purchase Act 2004 s 100(1), (6), (8)).
3   Acquisition of Land Act 1981 s 13C(2)(a) (as added: see note 2).
4   Acquisition of Land Act 1981 s 13C(2)(b) (as added: see note 2). As to the notice requirements see s 13 (see PARA 565 note 3): s 13C(7) (as so added).
5   As to remaining objections see s 13A (see PARA 566): s 13C(8) (as added: see note 2).
6   Acquisition of Land Act 1981 s 13C(3) (as added: see note 2). The provisions referred to are s 13A(2) or s 13A(3), as the case may be: see PARA 566.
7   Acquisition of Land Act 1981 s 13C(4) (as added: see note 2).
8   Ie the confirming authority acts under the Acquisition of Land Act 1981 s 13C(1): see the text and note 2.
9   Acquisition of Land Act 1981 s 13C(5) (as added: see note 2). It is not necessary for the Secretary of State to specify a date for the making of the final consideration: *R (on the application of Neptune Wharf Ltd) v Secretary of State for Trade and Industry* [2007] EWHC 1036 (Admin), [2007] 3 All ER 676.

568.   Confirming authority's duties as to confirmation. When the Secretary of State as the confirming authority[1] is considering representations made at a public inquiry and the inspector's report[2], he is acting in a quasi-judicial capacity[3], but when a confirming authority comes to make its substantive decision, its function is purely administrative, and the exercise of discretion vested in it to decide whether or not to confirm the order is an administrative act, the merits of which may not be challenged in the courts, although the confirming authority can be called upon to answer for it to Parliament[4]. In coming to its decision, it may have regard to its own views as to general policy and to information acquired in its purely executive capacity[5]. So far as this information relates to general policy[6] or comes from extraneous sources[7], the confirming authority is under no obligation to disclose it, but if it relates to the answering of objections it must be disclosed to an objector to enable him to challenge it, even if the authority receives it after the end of the inquiry[8].

Accordingly, if the confirming authority properly considers objections and the report of the inquiry[9] before coming to its decision, and has acted in good faith and has fairly listened to both sides and followed the general principles of natural justice, its decision may not be questioned[10]. Its decision may be contrary to the recommendations of the person holding the inquiry or the person appointed to hear objections. However, where the confirming authority has not observed the procedural rules regarding the reopening of the inquiry[11], the order may be quashed[12].

1   As to the meaning of 'confirming authority' see PARA 557 note 4. As to the Secretary of State see PARA 507 note 1.
2   As to public inquiries see PARA 587 et seq. As to the inspector's report see PARA 598.
3   See eg *B Johnson & Co (Builders) Ltd v Minister of Health* [1947] 2 All ER 395, CA; *Bushell v Secretary of State for the Environment* [1981] AC 75, [1980] 2 All ER 608, HL.
4   See eg *Bushell v Secretary of State for the Environment* [1981] AC 75, [1980] 2 All ER 608, HL; *Franklin v Minister of Town and Country Planning* [1948] AC 87, [1947] 2 All ER 289, HL; *B Johnson & Co (Builders) Ltd v Minister of Health* [1947] 2 All ER 395 at 399, CA, per Lord Greene MR.
5   See *Price v Minister of Health* [1947] 1 All ER 47; *Summers v Minister of Health* [1947] 1 All ER 184; *B Johnson & Co (Builders) Ltd v Minister of Health* [1947] 2 All ER 395 at 401, CA.
6   *B Johnson & Co (Builders) Ltd v Minister of Health* [1947] 2 All ER 395, CA; *Re City of Plymouth (City Centre) Declaratory Order 1946, Robinson v Minister of Town and Country Planning* [1947] KB 702, [1947] 1 All ER 851, CA; *Darlassis v Minister of Education* (1954) 118 JP 452. Cf *Franklin v Minister of Town and Country Planning* [1948] AC 87, [1947] 2 All ER 289, HL.

7   *Price v Minister of Health* [1947] 1 All ER 47 (letters received by minister before public inquiry not shown to objectors, nor in evidence at public inquiry); *Summers v Minister of Health* [1947] 1 All ER 184; *B Johnson & Co (Builders) Ltd v Minister of Health* [1947] 2 All ER 395 at 404, CA.

8   *Stafford v Minister of Health* [1946] KB 621; *Errington v Minister of Health* [1935] 1 KB 249, CA. See also *Hamilton v Roxburghshire County Council* 1970 SC 248.

9   Like other departmental documents, the inspector's report is privileged from disclosure: *Local Government Board v Arlidge* [1915] AC 120, HL; *William Denby & Sons Ltd v Minister of Health* [1936] 1 KB 337; *Darlassis v Minister of Education* (1954) 118 JP 452.

10 *Board of Education v Rice* [1911] AC 179 at 182, HL; *Local Government Board v Arlidge* [1915] AC 120, HL; *Stafford v Minister of Health* [1946] KB 621. If the decision letter of the Secretary of State is in agreement with the inspector's report and recommendation, there is no obligation on the Secretary of State to mention all the material considerations in the inspector's report: see *London Welsh Association Ltd v Secretary of State for the Environment* [1980] 2 EGLR 17, CA. As to the rules of natural justice see ADMINISTRATIVE LAW vol 1(1) (2001 Reissue) PARA 95 et seq.

11 See the Compulsory Purchase (Inquiries Procedure) Rules 2007, SI 2007/3617, r 16; and PARA 596.

12 *Meravale Builders Ltd v Secretary of State for the Environment* (1978) 36 P & CR 87.

569. Land not originally included in the order.

The order as confirmed by the confirming authority[1] does not, unless all persons interested consent, authorise the acquiring authority[2] to purchase compulsorily any land[3] which the order would not have authorised that authority to purchase compulsorily if it had been confirmed without modification[4].

1   As to the meaning of 'confirming authority' see PARA 557 note 4.
2   As to the meaning of 'acquiring authority' see PARA 522 note 2.
3   As to the meaning of 'land' see PARA 522 note 1.
4   Acquisition of Land Act 1981 s 14. As to confirmation of the order where no objections are outstanding or the objects are disregarded see PARA 565. As to confirmation of the order where there are remaining objections see PARA 566.

570. Confirmation by the acquiring authority.

The power to confirm an order may be exercised by the acquiring authority[1] (instead of the confirming authority[2]) if the confirming authority has notified the acquiring authority to that effect, and the notice has not been revoked[3]. The confirming authority may give such notice if it is satisfied that the notice requirements[4] have been complied with, that no objection[5] has been made in relation to the proposed confirmation or that all objections have been withdrawn, and that the order is capable of being confirmed without modification[6].

The power to confirm an order does not include any power to confirm the order with modifications, or to confirm only a part of the order[7]. The acquiring authority must notify the confirming authority as soon as reasonably practicable after it has determined whether or not to confirm the order[8]. An order confirmed by the acquiring authority is to have the same effect as if it were confirmed by the confirming authority[9].

1   As to the meaning of 'acquiring authority' see PARA 522 note 2.
2   As to the meaning of 'confirming authority' see PARA 557 note 4.
3   Acquisition of Land Act 1981 s 14A(1) (s 14A added by the Planning and Compulsory Purchase Act 2004 s 102(1), (2)). This provision does not apply to an order in respect of land falling within the Acquisition of Land Act 1981 s 16(1) or Sch 3 para 3(1), or forming part of a common, open space or fuel or field garden allotment for the purposes of s 19: s 14A(2) (as so added).
4   As to the notice requirements see s 13 (see PARA 565 note 3): s 14A(11) (as added: see note 3). Notices must be in writing: s 14A(10) (as so added).

5   An 'objection' is an objection made by any person (whether or not a person mentioned in the
     Acquisition of Land Act 1981 s 12(2) (see PARA 560), including an objection which is
     disregarded: s 14A(4) (as added: see note 3). As to the meaning of 'disregarded' see PARA 565
     note 5.
6   Acquisition of Land Act 1981 s 14A(3) (as added: see note 3). The confirming authority may
     revoke a notice given by it, but a notice may not be revoked if the determination has already
     been made and notified by the acquiring authority: s 14A(7), (8) (as so added).
7   Acquisition of Land Act 1981 s 14A(5) (as added: see note 3).
8   Acquisition of Land Act 1981 s 14A(6) (as added: see note 3).
9   Acquisition of Land Act 1981 s 14A(9) (as added: see note 3).

571.   Notices after confirmation of order.   After the order has been confirmed,
the acquiring authority[1] must (1) serve a confirmation notice[2] and a copy of the
order as confirmed on each person on whom a notice was required to be served[3];
and (2) affix a confirmation notice to a conspicuous object or objects on or near
the land comprised in the order[4]. The acquiring authority must also publish a
confirmation notice in one or more local newspapers circulating in the locality in
which the land comprised in the order is situated[5].

1   As to the meaning of 'acquiring authority' see PARA 522 note 2.
2   A 'confirmation notice' is a notice (1) describing the land; (2) stating that the order has been
     confirmed; (3) except in the case of a notice under head (1) in the text naming a place where a
     copy of the order as confirmed and of the map referred to there may be inspected at all
     reasonable hours; (4) that a person aggrieved by the order may apply to the High Court (see the
     Acquisition of Land Act 1981 s 23; and PARA 612): s 15(4) (s 15 substituted by the Planning and
     Compulsory Purchase Act 2004 s 100(7)). A confirmation notice must be in the prescribed form:
     Acquisition of Land Act 1981 s 15(5) (as so substituted). For the prescribed form see the
     Compulsory Purchase of Land (Prescribed Forms) (Ministers) Regulations 2004, SI 2004/2595,
     reg 3(3), Schedule Forms 10, 11; and the Compulsory Purchase of Land (Prescribed Forms)
     (National Assembly for Wales) Regulations 2004, SI 2004/2732, reg 3(5), Schedule Forms 10,
     11.
        In the case of compulsory rights orders under the Opencast Coal Act 1958 s 4 (see MINES,
     MINERALS AND QUARRIES vol 31 (2003 Reissue) PARA 422), the relevant form of notice is
     contained in the Opencast Coal (Compulsory Rights, Drainage and Rights of Way) (Forms)
     Regulations 1994, SI 1994/3097, reg 3(a)(iii), Schedule, Form 3. See further PARA 557 note 7.
3   Ie under the Acquisition of Land Act 1981 s 12: see PARA 560.
4   Acquisition of Land Act 1981 s 15(1) (as substituted: see note 2). The notice under head (2) in
     the text must be addressed to persons occupying or having an interest in the land, so far as
     practicable, and be kept in place by the acquiring authority until the expiry of a period of six
     weeks beginning with the date when the order becomes operative: s 15(2) (as so substituted).
     Such notices must include a statement as to the effect of any direction given under s 13C(5)(a)
     (see PARA 567): s 13C(6) (substituted by the Planning and Compulsory Purchase Act 2004
     s 100(6)).
5   Acquisition of Land Act 1981 s 15(3) (as substituted: see note 2).

(iii) Compulsory Purchase Orders made by Ministers

A. MAKING OF COMPULSORY PURCHASE ORDER IN DRAFT

572.   Making of compulsory purchase orders by ministers.   A compulsory
purchase order[1] authorising a compulsory purchase by a minister under the
Acquisition of Land Act 1981, so that the minister is both the acquiring[2] and the
confirming authority[3], must be made in accordance with special statutory[4]
procedures[5]. The order must be prepared in draft in such form as the minister
may determine[6], but must describe the land[7] to which it applies by reference to a
map[8].

It has been held that there is sufficient judicial control of the whole process to make the Secretary of State's powers[9] not incompatible with the rights guaranteed by the Human Rights Act 1998[10].

1   As to the meaning of 'compulsory purchase order' see PARA 557 note 1.
2   As to the meaning of 'acquiring authority' see PARA 522 note 2.
3   As to the meaning of 'confirming authority' see PARA 557 note 4.
4   Ie in accordance with the Acquisition of Land Act 1981 Sch 1: s 2(3), Sch 1 para 1(1).
5   Acquisition of Land Act 1981 Sch 1 para 1(1).
6   Acquisition of Land Act 1981 Sch 1 para 1(2), (3). All functions of a Minister of the Crown under the Acquisition of Land Act 1981, except s 8(4) (see PARA 564), so far as they are exercisable in relation to Wales, are now exercisable by the Welsh Ministers: see the National Assembly for Wales (Transfer of Functions) Order 1999, SI 1999/672, art 2, Sch 1; and the Government of Wales Act 2006 s 162(1), Sch 11 para 30. As to the Welsh Assembly Government and the Welsh Ministers see CONSTITUTIONAL LAW AND HUMAN RIGHTS.
7   As to the meaning of 'land' see PARA 522 note 2.
8   Acquisition of Land Act 1981 Sch 1 para 1(2).
9   Ie his powers under the Acquisition of Land Act 1981 s 2(3) and Sch 1 para 4 (as to which see PARA 575). As to the Secretary of State see PARA 507 note 1.
10 See *Secretary of State for the Environment, Transport and the Regions v Legal and General Assurance Society Ltd, R (on the application of Alconbury Developments Ltd) v Secretary of State for the Environment, Transport and the Regions* [2001] UKHL 23, [2003] 2 AC 295, [2001] 2 All ER 929; and PARA 575. In particular, these powers are not incompatible with the Convention for the Protection of Human Rights and Fundamental Freedoms (Rome, 4 November 1950; TS 1 (1973); Cmnd 5179) art 6(1) (right to a fair trial). As to the right to a fair trial generally see CONSTITUTIONAL LAW AND HUMAN RIGHTS vol 8(2) (Reissue) PARA 134 et seq. As to the Convention generally see CONSTITUTIONAL LAW AND HUMAN RIGHTS vol 8(2) (Reissue) PARA 122 et seq.

573.   Advertisement of compulsory purchase order. As soon as may be after the draft of the order[1] has been prepared, and before making the order, the Minister must publish a notice in the prescribed form[2], in two successive weeks, in one or more local newspapers circulating in the locality in which the land[3] comprised in the draft order is situated[4]. The notice must:

(1)   state that the order has been prepared in draft and is about to be made;
(2)   describe the land and state the purpose for which the land is required;
(3)   name a place within the locality where a copy of the draft order and of the map referred to in it may be inspected; and
(4)   specify the time, not being less than 21 days from the first publication of the notice, within which, and the manner in which, objections to the draft order can be made[5].

In addition, the Minister must affix a notice in the prescribed form to a conspicuous object or objects on or near the land comprised in the draft order[6].

The Minister must serve on every qualifying person[7] a notice in the prescribed form[8] stating the effect of the draft order and that it is about to be made, and specifying the time, not being less than 21 days from service of the notice, within which, and the manner in which, objections to the draft order can be made[9]. Where any such notice is required to be served on an owner of land and the land is ecclesiastical property, a like notice must be served on the Diocesan Board of Finance for the diocese in which the land is situated[10].

1   As to the draft order see PARA 572.
2   For the prescribed form see the Compulsory Purchase of Land (Prescribed Forms) (Ministers) Regulations 2004, SI 2004/2595, reg 3(c), Schedule, Form 7; and the Compulsory Purchase of Land (Prescribed Forms) (National Assembly for Wales) Regulations 2004, SI 2004/2595, reg 3(3), Schedule, Form 7. The Minister may make such modifications of the form of the notice as appear to him to be requisite: see the Acquisition of Land Act 1981 Sch 1 para 1(5). All functions of a Minister of the Crown under the Acquisition of Land Act 1981, except s 8(4) (see

PARA 564), so far as they are exercisable in relation to Wales, are now exercisable by the Welsh Ministers: see the National Assembly for Wales (Transfer of Functions) Order 1999, SI 1999/672, art 2, Sch 1; and the Government of Wales Act 2006 s 162(1), Sch 11 para 30. As to the Welsh Assembly Government and the Welsh Ministers see CONSTITUTIONAL LAW AND HUMAN RIGHTS.

3   As to the meaning of 'land' see PARA 522 note 1.
4   Acquisition of Land Act 1981 Sch 1 paras 1(4), 2(1).
5   Acquisition of Land Act 1981 Sch 1 para 2(2).
6   Acquisition of Land Act 1981 Sch 1 para 2(3) (Sch 1 paras 2(3), (4) added by the Planning and Compulsory Purchase Act 2004 s 101(1), (2), (6)). This notice must be addressed to persons occupying or having an interest in the land, and must set out each of the matters mentioned in heads (1)–(4) in the text (but reading the reference there to first publication of the notice as a reference to the day when the notice is first affixed): Acquisition of Land Act 1981 Sch 1 para 2(4) (as so added).
7   A person is a qualifying person, in relation to land comprised in a draft order, if (1) he is an owner, lessee, tenant (whatever the tenancy period) or occupier of any such land; or (2) he is (a) a person to whom the Minister would, if proceeding under the Compulsory Purchase Act 1965 s 5(1), be required to give a notice to treat; or (b) a person the Minister thinks is likely to be entitled to make a relevant claim if the order is made and the compulsory purchase takes place, so far as he is known to the Minister after making diligent inquiry: Acquisition of Land Act 1981 Sch 1 para 3(2), (2A) (added by the Planning and Compulsory Purchase Act 2004 s 101(1), (3), (6)). A relevant claim is a claim for compensation under the Compulsory Purchase Act 1965 s 10 (compensation for injurious affection) (see PARAS 718, 878): Acquisition of Land Act 1981 Sch 1 para 3(2B) (as so added).
8   For the prescribed form see the Compulsory Purchase of Land (Prescribed Forms) (Ministers) Regulations 2004, SI 2004/2595, reg 3(3), Schedule Forms 8, 9; and the Compulsory Purchase of Land (Prescribed Forms) (National Assembly for Wales) Regulations 2004, SI 2004/2732, reg 3(5), Schedule Forms 8, 9. Where the order is made under the Planning (Listed Buildings and Conservation Areas) Act 1990 s 47 (compulsory acquisition of listed buildings in need of repair: see TOWN AND COUNTRY PLANNING vol 46(3) (Reissue) PARAS 1154–1155, 1157), additional information must be included in the notice: see the Compulsory Purchase of Land Regulations 1994, SI 1994/2145, reg 4; and PARA 560 note 4. The Minister may make such modifications in the form of the notice as appear to him to be requisite: see the Acquisition of Land Act 1981 Sch 1 para 1(5).
9   Acquisition of Land Act 1981 Sch 1 para 3(1). As to the service of notices see PARA 561.
10 Acquisition of Land Act 1981 Sch 1 para 3(3) (amended by the Church of England (Miscellaneous Provisions) Measure 2006 s 14, Sch 5 para 24(2)). For these purposes, 'ecclesiastical property' means land belonging to any ecclesiastical benefice of the Church of England, or being or forming part of a church subject to the jurisdiction of the bishop of any diocese of the Church of England or the site of such a church, or being or forming part of a burial ground subject to such jurisdiction: Acquisition of Land Act 1981 Sch 1 para 3(3) (as so amended); and see ECCLESIASTICAL LAW.

574.   Right of objection and representations by statutory undertakers.

Objections to a compulsory purchase order[1] may be made in the manner and in the time provided in the notices[2] and must be made in the specified manner[3]. The Minister may require an objector to state the grounds in writing and may disregard the objection if he is satisfied that the objection relates exclusively to matters which can be dealt with by the tribunal by which the compensation is to be assessed[4].

Statutory undertakers[5] may make representations to the Minister if their land[6] is included in the land comprised in a compulsory purchase order[7].

1   As to the meaning of 'compulsory purchase order' see PARA 557 note 1.
2   See PARA 573.
3   See PARA 573.
4   See the Acquisition of Land Act 1981 Sch 1 para 4; and PARA 575. All functions of a Minister of the Crown under the Acquisition of Land Act 1981, except s 8(4) (see PARA 564), so far as they are exercisable in relation to Wales, are now exercisable by the Welsh Ministers: see the National Assembly for Wales (Transfer of Functions) Order 1999, SI 1999/672, art 2, Sch 1; and

the Government of Wales Act 2006 s 162(1), Sch 11 para 30. As to the Welsh Assembly
Government and the Welsh Ministers see CONSTITUTIONAL LAW AND HUMAN RIGHTS.

5   As to the meaning of 'statutory undertakers' see PARA 561 note 8. For the extended meaning of
'statutory undertakers' for these purposes see PARA 564 note 3.

6   Ie land which has been acquired for the purposes of their undertaking: see the Acquisition of
Land Act 1981 s 16(1); and PARA 564. As to the meaning of 'land' see PARA 522 note 1.

7   See PARA 564.

B. MAKING OF FINAL ORDER

**575.   Making of order where no objections are outstanding or objections are
disregarded.** The Minister[1] may make a compulsory purchase order[2] with or
without modifications if he is satisfied that the notice requirements[3] have been
complied with, and that either (1) no relevant objection[4] is made; or (2) every
relevant objection made is either withdrawn or disregarded[5].

The appropriate authority[6] may require every person who makes a relevant
objection to state the grounds of the objection in writing[7]. If the appropriate
authority is satisfied that an objection relates exclusively to matters which can be
dealt with by the tribunal by whom the compensation is to be assessed it may
disregard the objection[8].

1   All functions of a Minister of the Crown under the Acquisition of Land Act 1981, except s 8(4)
(see PARA 564), so far as they are exercisable in relation to Wales, are now exercisable by the
Welsh Ministers: see the National Assembly for Wales (Transfer of Functions) Order 1999,
SI 1999/672, art 2, Sch 1; and the Government of Wales Act 2006 s 162(1), Sch 11 para 30. As
to the Welsh Assembly Government and the Welsh Ministers see CONSTITUTIONAL LAW AND
HUMAN RIGHTS.
       When acting in this way, the Minister is not himself an independent and impartial tribunal
for the purposes of the Convention for the Protection of Human Rights and Fundamental
Freedoms (Rome, 4 November 1950; TS 1 (1973); Cmnd 5179) art 6(1) (right to a fair trial),
which applies because planning decisions are determinative of an applicant's civil rights and the
Human Rights Act 1998 s 6(1) requires a public authority to act in a way which is not
inconsistent with the rights guaranteed therein. However, there is sufficient judicial control of
the whole process to make these powers not incompatible with the Convention right, as required
by the Human Rights Act 1998 s 6(1), because the legality of the decision taken and the
procedures followed in making such a decision are open to judicial review: *Secretary of State for
the Environment, Transport and the Regions v Legal and General Assurance Society Ltd, R (on
the application of Alconbury Developments Ltd) v Secretary of State for the Environment,
Transport and the Regions* [2001] UKHL 23, [2003] 2 AC 295, [2001] 2 All ER 929.
Furthermore, the nature of any decision taken by the Secretary of State may be reviewed by any
independent and impartial tribunal with the jurisdiction (such as a hearing before a
quasi-judicial inspector who is obliged to give reasons), and this provides an additional
safeguard where the High Court's power of review may be limited: *Secretary of State for the
Environment, Transport and the Regions v Legal and General Assurance Society Ltd, R (on the
application of Alconbury Developments Ltd) v Secretary of State for the Environment,
Transport and the Regions.* At the same time, where the decision is 'administrative' (ie with
regard to policy and its application to particular facts, or concerning expediency), it would be
profoundly undemocratic for the courts to re-determine its merits: *Secretary of State for the
Environment, Transport and the Regions v Legal and General Assurance Society Ltd, R (on the
application of Alconbury Developments Ltd) v Secretary of State for the Environment,
Transport and the Regions.* As to the right to a fair trial generally see CONSTITUTIONAL LAW
AND HUMAN RIGHTS vol 8(2) (Reissue) PARA 134 et seq. As to the Convention generally see
CONSTITUTIONAL LAW AND HUMAN RIGHTS vol 8(2) (Reissue) PARA 122 et seq. As to judicial
review see ADMINISTRATIVE LAW vol 1(1) (2001 Reissue) PARA 58 et seq.

2   As to the meaning of 'compulsory purchase order' see PARA 557 note 1.

3   The notice requirements are the requirements under the Acquisition of Land Act 1981 Sch 1
paras 2 and 3 (see PARA 573) to publish, affix and serve notices in connection with the
compulsory purchase order: Sch 1 para 4(5) (Sch 1 para 4 substituted by the Planning and
Compulsory Purchase Act 2004 s 101(1), (4)).

4   A relevant objection is an objection by a person who is a qualifying person for the purposes of the Acquisition of Land Act 1981 Sch 1 para 3(2) (see PARA 573 note 7), but if such a person qualifies only by virtue of Sch 1 para 3(2A)(b) and the Minister thinks that he is not likely to be entitled to make a relevant claim his objection is not a relevant objection: Sch 1 para 4(6) (as substituted: see note 3).

5   Acquisition of Land Act 1981 Sch 1 para 4(1), (2) (as substituted: see note 3). 'Disregarded' means disregarded under Sch 1 para 4(4) (see the text and note 8) or under any other power to disregard a relevant objection contained in the enactment providing for the compulsory purchase: Sch 1 para 4(7) (as substituted: see note 3).

6   The appropriate authority is: (1) in the case of an order proposed to be made in the exercise of highway land acquisition powers, the Minister and the planning Minister acting jointly; (2) in any other case, the Minister: Acquisition of Land Act 1981 Sch 1 para 4(8), (9) (as substituted: see note 3). The planning Minister is the Secretary of State for the time being having general responsibility in planning matters: Sch 1 para 4(10) (as so substituted). As to the Secretary of State see PARA 507 note 1.

7   Acquisition of Land Act 1981 Sch 1 para 4(3) (as substituted: see note 3).

8   Acquisition of Land Act 1981 Sch 1 para 4(4) (as substituted: see note 3).

576. Making of order where there are remaining objections. The following provisions apply where a compulsory purchase order[1] is to be made and there is a remaining objection (that is a relevant objection is made which is neither withdrawn, nor disregarded)[2]. In such a case the appropriate authority[3] may proceed under the written representations procedure[4] (1) if the order is not subject to special parliamentary procedure; (2) in the case of an order concerning land owned by a statutory undertaker, if a certificate has been given permitting the purchase of certain land[5]; and (3) if every person who has made a remaining objection consents in the prescribed manner[6].

If heads (1) to (3) do not apply or if the appropriate authority decides not to proceed under them, it must either cause a public local inquiry to be held, or must give every person who has made a remaining objection an opportunity of appearing before and being heard by a person appointed by the appropriate authority for the purpose[7]. If a person who has made a remaining objection takes the opportunity to appear before a person appointed for the purpose, the appropriate authority must give any other person it thinks appropriate the opportunity to be heard at the same time[8].

The Minister may make the order with or without modifications if the appropriate authority has considered the objection, and either (a) the appropriate authority has followed the written representations procedure; or (b) if an inquiry was held or a person was appointed[9], the appropriate authority has considered the report of the person who held the inquiry or who was so appointed[10].

1   As to the meaning of 'compulsory purchase order' see PARA 557 note 1.

2   Acquisition of Land Act 1981 Sch 1 para 4A(1) (Sch 1 para 4A added by the Planning and Compulsory Purchase Act 2004 s 101(1), (4), (6)).

3   As to the meaning of 'appropriate authority' see PARA 575 note 6; definition applied by the Acquisition of Land Act 1981 Sch 1 para 4A(9) (as added: see note 2).

4   The written representations procedure is such procedure as is prescribed for the purposes of the Acquisition of Land Act 1981 Sch 1 para 4A including provision affording an opportunity to every person who has made a remaining objection, and any other person the appropriate authority thinks appropriate, to make written representations as to whether the order should be made: Sch 1 para 4A(7) (as added: see note 2). Such regulations may make provision as to the giving of reasons for decisions taken in cases where the written representations procedure is followed: Sch 1 para 4A(8) (as so added). As to the written representations procedure see the Compulsory Purchase of Land (Written Representations Procedure) (Ministers) Regulations 2004, SI 2004/2594; and the Compulsory Purchase of Land (Written Representations Procedure) (National Assembly for Wales) Regulations 2004, SI 2004/2730; and PARA 580 et seq.

5   Ie an order to which the Acquisition of Land Act 1981 s 16 applies: see PARA 564.
6   Acquisition of Land Act 1981 Sch 1 para 4A(2) (as added: see note 2).
7   Acquisition of Land Act 1981 Sch 1 para 4A(3) (as added: see note 2). As to the inquiries procedure see the Compulsory Purchase (Inquiries Procedure) Rules 2007, SI 2007/3617; and PARA 587 et seq.
8   Acquisition of Land Act 1981 Sch 1 para 4A(4) (as added: see note 2).
9   Ie in a case which falls within the Acquisition of Land Act 1981 Sch 1 para 4A(3), a person was appointed to hear the objection: see the text and note 7.
10 Acquisition of Land Act 1981 Sch 1 para 4A(5), (6) (as added: see note 2). All functions of a Minister of the Crown under the Acquisition of Land Act 1981, except s 8(4) (see PARA 564), so far as they are exercisable in relation to Wales, are now exercisable by the Welsh Ministers: see the National Assembly for Wales (Transfer of Functions) Order 1999, SI 1999/672, art 2, Sch 1; and the Government of Wales Act 2006 s 162(1), Sch 11 para 30. As to the Welsh Assembly Government and the Welsh Ministers see CONSTITUTIONAL LAW AND HUMAN RIGHTS.

577.   Confirmation in stages.   The Minister[1] may make an order (with or without modifications) so far as it relates to part of the land comprised in the draft order (referred to as the 'relevant part') if[2] (1) the Minister or, if there is a remaining objection in respect of the order, the appropriate authority is satisfied that the order ought to be made so far as it relates to the relevant part but has not for the time being determined whether the order ought to be made so far as it relates to the remaining part[3]; and (2) the Minister is satisfied that the notice requirements have been complied with[4].

If there is a remaining objection[5] in respect of the order, the Minister may only act as described above after the appropriate authority has complied with certain statutory provisions[6]. However, he may act without the appropriate authority having complied with those provisions if he is satisfied that all remaining objections relate solely to the remaining part of the land[7].

If the Minister does so act[8] (a) he must give a direction postponing consideration of the order, so far as it relates to the remaining part, until such time as may be specified by or under the direction; (b) the order so far as it relates to each part of the land must be treated as a separate order[9].

1   All functions of a Minister of the Crown under the Acquisition of Land Act 1981, except s 8(4) (see PARA 564), so far as they are exercisable in relation to Wales, are now exercisable by the Welsh Ministers: see the National Assembly for Wales (Transfer of Functions) Order 1999, SI 1999/672, art 2, Sch 1; and the Government of Wales Act 2006 s 162(1), Sch 11 para 30. As to the Welsh Assembly Government and the Welsh Ministers see CONSTITUTIONAL LAW AND HUMAN RIGHTS.
2   Acquisition of Land Act 1981 Sch 1 para 4B(1) (Sch 1 para 4B added by the Planning and Compulsory Purchase Act 2004 s 101(1), (4), (6)).
3   Acquisition of Land Act 1981 Sch 1 para 4B(2)(a) (as added: see note 2).
4   Acquisition of Land Act 1981 Sch 1 para 4B(2)(b) (as added: see note 2). As to the notice requirements see PARA 573.
5   As to remaining objections see PARA 576.
6   Acquisition of Land Act 1981 Sch 1 para 4B(3) (as added: see note 2). The provisions referred to in the text are Sch 1 para 4A(2) or Sch 1 para 4A(3) as the case may be: see PARA 576.
7   Acquisition of Land Act 1981 Sch 1 para 4B(4) (as added: see note 2).
8   Ie under the Acquisition of Land Act 1981 Sch 1 para 4B(1): see the text and note 2.
9   Acquisition of Land Act 1981 Sch 1 para 4B(5) (as added: see note 2).

578.   Land not originally included in draft order.   The order, as made by the Minister[1], does not, unless all persons interested consent, authorise the Minister to purchase compulsorily any land[2] which the draft order would not have authorised the Minister to purchase compulsorily if it had been made without modification[3].

1   All functions of a Minister of the Crown under the Acquisition of Land Act 1981, except s 8(4) (see PARA 564), so far as they are exercisable in relation to Wales, are now exercisable by the Welsh Ministers: see the National Assembly for Wales (Transfer of Functions) Order 1999, SI 1999/672, art 2, Sch 1; and the Government of Wales Act 2006 s 162(1), Sch 11 para 30. As to the Welsh Assembly Government and the Welsh Ministers see CONSTITUTIONAL LAW AND HUMAN RIGHTS.
2   As to the meaning of 'land' see PARA 522 note 1.
3   Acquisition of Land Act 1981 Sch 1 para 5. As to the making of an order where there are no objections outstanding or objections are disregarded see PARA 575. As to the confirmation of an order where there are remaining objections see PARA 576.

579.   Notices after making of order.   After the order has been made, the Minister[1] must (1) serve a making notice[2], and a copy of the order as made, on each person on whom a notice was required to be served[3]; and (2) affix a making notice to a conspicuous object or objects on or near the land comprised in the order[4]. The Minister must also publish a making notice in one or more local newspapers circulating in the locality in which the land comprised in the order is situated[5].

1   All functions of a Minister of the Crown under the Acquisition of Land Act 1981, except s 8(4) (see PARA 564), so far as they are exercisable in relation to Wales, are now exercisable by the Welsh Ministers: see the National Assembly for Wales (Transfer of Functions) Order 1999, SI 1999/672, art 2, Sch 1; and the Government of Wales Act 2006 s 162(1), Sch 11 para 30. As to the Welsh Assembly Government and the Welsh Ministers see CONSTITUTIONAL LAW AND HUMAN RIGHTS.
2   A making notice is a notice in the prescribed form: (1) describing the land; (2) stating that the order has been made; (3) (except in the case of a notice under head (1) in the text) naming a place where a copy of the order as made and of the map referred to there may be inspected at all reasonable hours; (4) that a person aggrieved by the order may apply to the High Court as mentioned in the Acquisition of Land Act 1981 s 23 (see PARA 612): Sch 1 para 6(4), (5) (Sch 1 para 6 substituted by the Planning and Compulsory Purchase Act 2004 s 101(1), (5), (6)). The notice must also include a statement as to the effect of the direction postponing consideration of the order under the Acquisition of Land Act 1981 Sch 1 para 4B(5) (see PARA 577): Sch 1 para 4B(6) (added by the Planning and Compulsory Purchase Act 2004 s 101(1), (4), (6)). For the prescribed form see the Compulsory Purchase of Land (Prescribed Forms) (Ministers) Regulations 2004, SI 2004/2595, reg 3(e), Schedule, Form 10; and the Compulsory Purchase of Land (Prescribed Forms) (National Assembly for Wales) Regulations 2004, SI 2004/2732, reg 3(5), Schedule, Form 10.
3   Ie under the Acquisition of Land Act 1981 Sch 1 para 3: see PARA 573.
4   Acquisition of Land Act 1981 Sch 1 para 6(1) (as substituted: see note 2). The notice under head (2) in the text must be addressed to persons occupying or having an interest in the land, and so far as practicable, be kept in place by the acquiring authority until the expiry of a period of six weeks beginning with the date when the order becomes operative: Sch 1 para 6(2) (as so substituted). As to the meaning of 'land' see PARA 522 note 1.
5   Acquisition of Land Act 1981 Sch 1 para 6(3) (as substituted: see note 2).

(iv) Written Representations Procedure

580.   Introduction.   If there are objections to the compulsory purchase of land in England and Wales, the written representations procedure may be used as an alternative to holding an inquiry or hearing, provided that all those objectors whose objections have not been disregarded or withdrawn consent in the prescribed manner[1]. The Compulsory Purchase of Land (Written Representations Procedure) (Ministers) Regulations 2004[2] apply only where the confirming authority[3] or acquiring authority[4] is a Minister of the Crown[5], and the procedure the regulations set out may only be used for compulsory purchase orders in England and Wales that are subject to the Acquisition of Land Act 1981 and are not subject to special parliamentary procedure[6]. The Compulsory Purchase of

Land (Written Representations Procedure) (National Assembly for Wales) Regulations 2004[7], make comparable provision and apply where the Welsh Ministers are the confirming or acquiring authority in relation to the compulsory acquisition of land in Wales where the Acquisition of Land Act 1981 applies[8].

1   See the Acquisition of Land Act 1981 ss 13, 13A, 13B (see PARA 565 et seq), Sch 1 paras 4, 4A, 4B (see PARA 575 et seq).
2   Ie the Compulsory Purchase of Land (Written Representations Procedure) (Ministers) Regulations 2004, SI 2004/2594: see PARA 581 et seq.
3   As to the meaning of 'confirming authority' see PARA 557 note 4.
4   As to the meaning of 'acquiring authority' see PARA 522 note 2.
5   Compulsory Purchase of Land (Written Representations Procedure) (Ministers) Regulations 2004, SI 2004/2594, reg 1.
6   As to special parliamentary procedure see PARA 605.
7   Ie the Compulsory Purchase of Land (Written Representations Procedure) (National Assembly for Wales) Regulations 2004, SI 2004/2730: see PARA 581 et seq.
8   Compulsory Purchase of Land (Written Representations Procedure) (National Assembly for Wales) Regulations 2004, SI 2004/2730, reg 1. Pursuant to the establishment of the Welsh Assembly Government under the Government of Wales Act 2006, the Welsh Ministers now perform those statutory functions that had previously been exercised by the National Assembly for Wales: see s 162(1), Sch 11 para 30. As to the Welsh Assembly Government and the Welsh Ministers see CONSTITUTIONAL LAW AND HUMAN RIGHTS.

581.   Consent to follow written representations procedure.   Where the authorising authority[1] wishes to follow the written representations procedure and the statutory requirements[2] are satisfied, it must send to each remaining objector[3] a consent form[4]. A remaining objector who wishes to consent to the written representations procedure must complete the consent form and return it to the address specified in the consent form by such means as will ensure that it is received at that address not later than the date specified in the consent form[5].

Provision is made in relation to Wales for the manner in which a remaining objector may consent to the use of the written representations procedure by the Welsh Ministers[6].

1   Ie the confirming authority or an appropriate authority: Compulsory Purchase of Land (Written Representations Procedure) (Ministers) Regulations 2004, SI 2004/2594, reg 2. As to the meaning of 'confirming authority' see PARA 557 note 4.
2   Ie the requirements of the Acquisition of Land Act 1981 s 13A(2)(a) and, if applicable, of s 13A(2)(b) are satisfied (see PARA 566), or the requirements of Sch 1 para 4A(2)(a) and, if applicable, Sch 1 para 4A(2)(b) are satisfied (see PARA 576).
3   For these purposes, 'remaining objector' means a person who has a remaining objection within the meaning of the Acquisition of Land Act 1981 s 13A (see PARA 566) or, as the case may be, Sch 1 para 4A (see PARA 576): Compulsory Purchase of Land (Written Representations Procedure) (Ministers) Regulations 2004, SI 2004/2594, reg 2.
4   Compulsory Purchase of Land (Written Representations Procedure) (Ministers) Regulations 2004, SI 2004/2594, reg 3(1).
5   Compulsory Purchase of Land (Written Representations Procedure) (Ministers) Regulations 2004, SI 2004/2594, reg 3(2).
6   See the Compulsory Purchase of Land (Written Representations Procedure) (National Assembly for Wales) Regulations 2004, SI 2004/2730, reg 3; and PARA 580.

582.   Notification of decision to follow the written representations procedure.
Where the authorising authority[1] decides to follow the written representations procedure, it must inform each remaining objector[2] and the acquiring authority[3], if not the authorising authority, in writing of:
   (1)   the starting date[4];
   (2)   the reference number allocated to the issue[5];

(3)   the address to which written communications to the authorising authority are to be sent[6]; and

(4)   the title or description of every statement then in the possession of the authorising authority which it intends to consider in determining the issue[7].

Comparable provision is made in relation to Wales[8].

1   As to the meaning of 'authorising authority' see PARA 581 note 1.
2   As to the meaning of 'remaining objector' see PARA 581 note 3.
3   As to the meaning of 'acquiring authority' see PARA 522 note 2.
4   Compulsory Purchase of Land (Written Representations Procedure) (Ministers) Regulations 2004, SI 2004/2594, reg 4(a). 'Starting date' means the date of which notice is given in accordance with reg 4(a): see reg 2.
5   Compulsory Purchase of Land (Written Representations Procedure) (Ministers) Regulations 2004, SI 2004/2594, reg 4(b). 'Issue' means the submission seeking confirmation of a compulsory purchase order pursuant to the Acquisition of Land Act 1981 s 2(2) or the issue whether or not to make a compulsory purchase order prepared in draft under Sch 1 pursuant to s 2(3): Compulsory Purchase of Land (Written Representations Procedure) (Ministers) Regulations 2004, SI 2004/2594, reg 2.
6   Compulsory Purchase of Land (Written Representations Procedure) (Ministers) Regulations 2004, SI 2004/2594, reg 4(c).
7   Compulsory Purchase of Land (Written Representations Procedure) (Ministers) Regulations 2004, SI 2004/2594, reg 4(d). 'Statement' includes a photograph, map or plan, but excludes any oral statement: reg 2.
8   See the Compulsory Purchase of Land (Written Representations Procedure) (National Assembly for Wales) Regulations 2004, SI 2004/2730, reg 4; and PARA 580.

583. Representations. Any initial statement[1] provided by the acquiring authority[2], when it served notice[3] to a person who, for the purposes of the written representations procedure, is a remaining objector[4] is treated as part of the acquiring authority's representations[5]. If an acquiring authority which is not the authorising authority[6] has not previously supplied the authorising authority with a copy of the initial statement, it must do so within five working days of the starting date[7], or such longer period as the authorising authority may in the particular case allow[8]. The authorising authority may disregard any initial statement (other than one previously supplied) that is not supplied within that period[9].

The remaining objection[10] of a remaining objector is treated for the purposes of the written representations procedure as part of his representations; and, if it has not previously supplied the acquiring authority with a copy of the objection, the authorising authority (if not the acquiring authority) must send a copy of the objection to the acquiring authority not later than five working days after the starting date[11].

If the acquiring authority wishes to make further representations in support of the issue[12], it may do so provided that such representations are received by the authorising authority not later than 14 working days after the starting date, or such longer period as the authorising authority may in the particular case allow[13]. If the acquiring authority wishes to treat its initial statement as its only representations in relation to the issue, it must notify the authorising authority and each remaining objector accordingly[14]. The authorising authority may disregard further representations[15] if they are received by the authorising authority after the relevant period[16]. The authorising authority must send as soon as practicable to each remaining objector a copy of further representations made by the acquiring authority or notification that no such representations are to be taken into account[17].

A remaining objector may make further representations[18] or notify the authorising authority and the acquiring authority that he does not wish to make further representations[19]. The authorising authority (if not the acquiring authority) must send as soon as practicable to the acquiring authority a copy of any further representations made by a remaining objector or notification that no such representations are to be taken into account[20]. The acquiring authority may make representations to the authorising authority in relation to a remaining objector's further representations which must be received by the authorising authority not later than ten working days after the authorising authority sends a copy of the representations, or such longer period as the authorising authority may in the particular case allow[21]. The authorising authority must send as soon as practicable to each remaining objector any representations made by the acquiring authority or notification that no such representations are to be taken into account[22]. The authorising authority may request the acquiring authority and each remaining objector to provide the authorising authority with additional copies of representations within such reasonable time scale as the authorising authority may specify[23].

Comparable provision is made in relation to Wales for the manner in which representations may be made and considered[24].

1 As to the meaning of 'statement' see PARA 582 note 7.
2 As to the meaning of 'acquiring authority' see PARA 522 note 2.
3 Ie under the Acquisition of Land Act 1981 s 12(1) (see PARA 560) or Sch 1 para 3(1) (see PARA 573).
4 As to the meaning of 'remaining objector' see PARA 581 note 3.
5 Compulsory Purchase of Land (Written Representations Procedure) (Ministers) Regulations 2004, SI 2004/2594, reg 5(1). 'Representations' means written representations, statements and supporting documents: reg 2.
6 As to the meaning of 'authorising authority' see PARA 581 note 1.
7 As to the meaning of 'starting date' see PARA 582 note 4. 'Working day' means any day other than a Saturday, Sunday, Christmas Day, Good Friday or a day which is a bank holiday under the Banking and Financial Dealings Act 1971: Compulsory Purchase of Land (Written Representations Procedure) (Ministers) Regulations 2004, SI 2004/2594, reg 2.
8 Compulsory Purchase of Land (Written Representations Procedure) (Ministers) Regulations 2004, SI 2004/2594, reg 5(2).
9 Compulsory Purchase of Land (Written Representations Procedure) (Ministers) Regulations 2004, SI 2004/2594, reg 5(2).
10 As to the meaning of 'remaining objection' see PARAS 566, 576.
11 Compulsory Purchase of Land (Written Representations Procedure) (Ministers) Regulations 2004, SI 2004/2594, reg 5(3).
12 As to the meaning of 'issue' see PARA 582 note 5.
13 Compulsory Purchase of Land (Written Representations Procedure) (Ministers) Regulations 2004, SI 2004/2594, reg 5(4)(a).
14 Compulsory Purchase of Land (Written Representations Procedure) (Ministers) Regulations 2004, SI 2004/2594, reg 5(4)(b).
15 Ie made under the Compulsory Purchase of Land (Written Representations Procedure) (Ministers) Regulations 2004, SI 2004/2594, reg 5(4).
16 Compulsory Purchase of Land (Written Representations Procedure) (Ministers) Regulations 2004, SI 2004/2594, reg 5(5).
17 Compulsory Purchase of Land (Written Representations Procedure) (Ministers) Regulations 2004, SI 2004/2594, reg 5(6).
18 Such representations must be received by the authorising authority not later than 15 working days after the authorising authority sends a copy of further representations or notification under the Compulsory Purchase of Land (Written Representations Procedure) (Ministers) Regulations 2004, SI 2004/2594, reg 5(6) (see the text and note 17), or such longer period as the authorising authority may in the particular case allow: reg 5(7)(a). The authorising authority may disregard representations made under reg 5(7) received by the authorising authority after the relevant period: reg 5(8).

19 Compulsory Purchase of Land (Written Representations Procedure) (Ministers) Regulations 2004, SI 2004/2594, reg 5(7)(b).
20 Compulsory Purchase of Land (Written Representations Procedure) (Ministers) Regulations 2004, SI 2004/2594, reg 5(9).
21 Compulsory Purchase of Land (Written Representations Procedure) (Ministers) Regulations 2004, SI 2004/2594, reg 5(10). The authorising authority may disregard representations made under reg 5(10) if they are received by the authorising authority after the relevant period: reg 5(11).
22 Compulsory Purchase of Land (Written Representations Procedure) (Ministers) Regulations 2004, SI 2004/2594, reg 5(12).
23 Compulsory Purchase of Land (Written Representations Procedure) (Ministers) Regulations 2004, SI 2004/2594, reg 5(13).
24 See the Compulsory Purchase of Land (Written Representations Procedure) (National Assembly for Wales) Regulations 2004, SI 2004/2730, regs 5, 7; and PARA 580.

584. Third party representations. The authorising authority[1] may permit third party representations[2] to be made by any person who is not an acquiring authority[3] or remaining objector[4] to be received by the authorising authority not later than 14 working days after the starting date[5], or such longer period as the authorising authority may in the particular case allow[6]. The authorising authority may disregard any such third party representations if they are received by the authorising authority after the relevant period[7].

The authorising authority must send as soon as practicable to each remaining objector and the acquiring authority, if not the authorising authority, a copy of any such third party representations, or notification that no such representations are to be taken into account[8]. The acquiring authority may make representations to the authorising authority in relation to any third party representations to be received not later than ten working days after the authorising authority sends a copy of the third party representations to the acquiring authority, or such longer period as the authorising authority may in the particular case allow[9]. The authorising authority may disregard these representations[10] if they are received by the authorising authority after the relevant period[11].

The authorising authority may request any person making third party representations or the acquiring authority to provide the authorising authority with additional copies of representations within such reasonable time scale as the authorising authority may specify[12].

Comparable provision is made in relation to Wales for the manner in which third party representations may be made and considered[13].

1 As to the meaning of 'authorising authority' see PARA 581 note 1.
2 Ie representations made under the Compulsory Purchase of Land (Written Representations Procedure) (Ministers) Regulations 2004, SI 2004/2594, reg 6(1). As to the meaning of 'representations' see PARA 583 note 5.
3 As to the meaning of 'acquiring authority' see PARA 522 note 2.
4 As to the meaning of 'remaining objector' see PARA 581 note 3.
5 As to the meaning of 'starting date' see PARA 582 note 4.
6 Compulsory Purchase of Land (Written Representations Procedure) (Ministers) Regulations 2004, SI 2004/2594, reg 6(1).
7 Compulsory Purchase of Land (Written Representations Procedure) (Ministers) Regulations 2004, SI 2004/2594, reg 6(2).
8 Compulsory Purchase of Land (Written Representations Procedure) (Ministers) Regulations 2004, SI 2004/2594, reg 6(3).
9 Compulsory Purchase of Land (Written Representations Procedure) (Ministers) Regulations 2004, SI 2004/2594, reg 6(4).
10 Ie representations made under the Compulsory Purchase of Land (Written Representations Procedure) (Ministers) Regulations 2004, SI 2004/2594, reg 6(4).
11 Compulsory Purchase of Land (Written Representations Procedure) (Ministers) Regulations 2004, SI 2004/2594, reg 6(5).

12 Compulsory Purchase of Land (Written Representations Procedure) (Ministers) Regulations 2004, SI 2004/2594, reg 6(6).
13 See the Compulsory Purchase of Land (Written Representations Procedure) (National Assembly for Wales) Regulations 2004, SI 2004/2730, regs 6, 7; and PARA 580.

585. Inspections. The authorising authority[1] may appoint an inspector to consider the statements[2] and representations[3], and to undertake a site inspection, if appropriate and to report in writing to the authorising authority with a recommendation in respect of the issue[4]. The inspector may, at any time, make:

(1) an unaccompanied inspection without giving prior notice to the acquiring authority[5] or the remaining objectors[6]; or

(2) an inspection in the company of a representative of the acquiring authority and each remaining objector[7],

of land which is the subject of the compulsory purchase order and of the surrounding area[8]. In the case of an accompanied inspection, the authorising authority must send notification of the date and time of the inspection to the acquiring authority if it is not the authorising authority and the remaining objectors not later than five working days before that date[9]. The inspector is not bound to defer an inspection at the time appointed[10]. If a request for an accompanied inspection is made by the acquiring authority or a remaining objector and is received by the authorising authority not later than ten working days after the starting date, the authorising authority must arrange for such an inspection to take place[11].

Comparable provision is made in relation to Wales for the manner in which inspectors are appointed and inspections may be made[12].

1 As to the meaning of 'authorising authority' see PARA 581 note 1.
2 Ie the statements under the Compulsory Purchase of Land (Written Representations Procedure) (Ministers) Regulations 2004, SI 2004/2594, reg 4(d): see PARA 582. As to the meaning of 'statement' see PARA 582 note 7.
3 Ie the representations provided in accordance with the Compulsory Purchase of Land (Written Representations Procedure) (Ministers) Regulations 2004, SI 2004/2594, regs 5, 6: see PARAS 583, 584. As to the meaning of 'representations' see PARA 583 note 5.
4 Compulsory Purchase of Land (Written Representations Procedure) (Ministers) Regulations 2004, SI 2004/2594, reg 7. As to the meaning of 'issue' see PARA 582 note 5.
5 As to the meaning of 'acquiring authority' see PARA 522 note 2.
6 Compulsory Purchase of Land (Written Representations Procedure) (Ministers) Regulations 2004, SI 2004/2594, reg 8(1)(a). As to the meaning of 'remaining objector' see PARA 581 note 3.
7 Compulsory Purchase of Land (Written Representations Procedure) (Ministers) Regulations 2004, SI 2004/2594, reg 8(1)(b).
8 Compulsory Purchase of Land (Written Representations Procedure) (Ministers) Regulations 2004, SI 2004/2594, reg 8(1).
9 Compulsory Purchase of Land (Written Representations Procedure) (Ministers) Regulations 2004, SI 2004/2594, reg 8(2).
10 Compulsory Purchase of Land (Written Representations Procedure) (Ministers) Regulations 2004, SI 2004/2594, reg 8(3).
11 Compulsory Purchase of Land (Written Representations Procedure) (Ministers) Regulations 2004, SI 2004/2594, reg 8(4).
12 See the Compulsory Purchase of Land (Written Representations Procedure) (National Assembly for Wales) Regulations 2004, SI 2004/2730, regs 7, 8; and PARA 580.

586. Decision. Where the authorising authority[1] considers that it has sufficient material to make a decision on the issue[2], it may do so notwithstanding that (1) the acquiring authority[3] or a remaining objector[4] gave notice that it or he wished to make further representations[5]; and (2) no further representations have been provided within the specified period[6]. However, a decision may not be made unless the authorising authority has given to the acquiring authority and to each remaining objector notice of its intention to make a decision, and at least ten working days have elapsed since that notice was given[7].

The authorising authority must send written notice of its decision and of the reasons for it to the acquiring authority, each remaining objector and any other person permitted to make third party representations[8]. Where an inspector was appointed[9], the acquiring authority, each remaining objector and any other person permitted to make third party representations may apply to the authorising authority in writing for a copy of the inspector's report[10]. Where the authorising authority receives such an application it must send a copy of the report to the applicant not later than ten working days after receipt of the application[11].

The acquiring authority, each remaining objector and any other person permitted to make third party representations may apply to the authorising authority in writing for the opportunity to inspect any document appended to the inspector's report or otherwise taken into account by the authorising authority in reaching its decision[12]. Such an application must be made before the expiry of six weeks beginning with the date of first publication of the confirmation notice[13] or, as the case may be, the making notice[14]. The authorising authority must, as soon as reasonably practicable after receiving such an application, make arrangements for enabling the inspection to take place; but it is not required to make available for inspection any document that has previously been supplied to the person by whom the application is made[15].

Comparable provision is made in relation to Wales for the manner in which the Welsh Ministers may make and give notification of their decision[16].

1   As to the meaning of 'authorising authority' see PARA 581 note 1.
2   As to the meaning of 'issue' see PARA 582 note 5.
3   As to the meaning of 'acquiring authority' see PARA 522 note 2.
4   As to the meaning of 'remaining objector' see PARA 581 note 3.
5   Compulsory Purchase of Land (Written Representations Procedure) (Ministers) Regulations 2004, SI 2004/2594, reg 9(1)(a). As to the meaning of 'representations' see PARA 583 note 5.
6   Compulsory Purchase of Land (Written Representations Procedure) (Ministers) Regulations 2004, SI 2004/2594, reg 9(1)(b). The specified period is the period specified in reg 5 or reg 6 or such longer period as has been allowed in the particular case: see reg 9(1)(b).
7   Compulsory Purchase of Land (Written Representations Procedure) (Ministers) Regulations 2004, SI 2004/2594, reg 9(2).
8   Compulsory Purchase of Land (Written Representations Procedure) (Ministers) Regulations 2004, SI 2004/2594, reg 10(1). As to third party representations see reg 6; and PARA 584.
9   Ie under the Compulsory Purchase of Land (Written Representations Procedure) (Ministers) Regulations 2004, SI 2004/2594, reg 7: see PARA 585.
10 Compulsory Purchase of Land (Written Representations Procedure) (Ministers) Regulations 2004, SI 2004/2594, reg 10(2). The application must be made within 28 days of the date of the notice being sent: see reg 10(2).
11 Compulsory Purchase of Land (Written Representations Procedure) (Ministers) Regulations 2004, SI 2004/2594, reg 10(3).
12 Compulsory Purchase of Land (Written Representations Procedure) (Ministers) Regulations 2004, SI 2004/2594, reg 10(4).
13 Ie pursuant to the Acquisition of Land Act 1981 s 15(3): see PARA 571. As to the meaning of 'confirmation notice' see PARA 571 note 2.
14 Compulsory Purchase of Land (Written Representations Procedure) (Ministers) Regulations 2004, SI 2004/2594, reg 10(5). The reference in the text to a making notice is to a notice made pursuant to the Acquisition of Land Act 1981 Sch 1 para 6(3): see PARA 579. As to the meaning of 'making notice' see PARA 579 note 2.

15 Compulsory Purchase of Land (Written Representations Procedure) (Ministers) Regulations 2004, SI 2004/2594, reg 10(6).
16 See the Compulsory Purchase of Land (Written Representations Procedure) (National Assembly for Wales) Regulations 2004, SI 2004/2730, regs 10, 11, 12; and PARA 580.

(v) Inquiries Procedure

587. Introduction. The Compulsory Purchase (Inquiries Procedure) Rules 2007[1] prescribe the procedure to be followed in connection with public local inquiries relating to the authorisation of compulsory purchase orders. They relate to orders where a Minister is either the confirming authority[2] in the case of a non-ministerial order[3] or, in the case of inquiries relating to a compulsory purchase order made in draft by a United Kingdom government Minister, the appropriate authority[4].

The Compulsory Purchase (Inquiries Procedure) Rules 2007 replace the Compulsory Purchase by Non-Ministerial Acquiring Authorities (Inquiries Procedure) Rules 1990[5] and the Compulsory Purchase by Ministers (Inquiries Procedure) Rules 1994[6] in relation to England, but those otherwise revoked rules still apply where the Welsh Ministers are the authorising authority[7].

1 See the Compulsory Purchase (Inquiries Procedure) Rules 2007, SI 2007/3617; and PARA 588 et seq.
2 As to the meaning of 'confirming authority' see PARA 557 note 4.
3 Ie where a confirming authority causes a public local inquiry to be held pursuant to the Acquisition of Land Act 1981 s 13A(3)(a) (compulsory purchase by local or other authority; remaining objections) (see PARA 566): Compulsory Purchase (Inquiries Procedure) Rules 2007, SI 2007/3617, r 1.
4 Ie where an appropriate authority causes a public local inquiry to be held pursuant to the Acquisition of Land Act 1981 Sch 1 para 4A(3)(a) (compulsory purchase by Minister—remaining objections) (see PARA 576): Compulsory Purchase (Inquiries Procedure) Rules 2007, SI 2007/3617, r 1. As to the appropriate authority see PARA 575 note 6.
5 Ie the Compulsory Purchase by Non-Ministerial Acquiring Authorities (Inquiries Procedure) Rules 1990, SI 1990/512.
6 Compulsory Purchase by Ministers (Inquiries Procedure) Rules 1994, SI 1994/3264.
7 Compulsory Purchase (Inquiries Procedure) Rules 2007, SI 2007/3617, r 22. As to the meaning of 'authorising authority' see PARA 588 note 1. The Compulsory Purchase by Non-Ministerial Acquiring Authorities (Inquiries Procedure) Rules 1990, SI 1990/512, apply in relation to compulsory purchase orders which have been made by non-ministerial acquiring authorities and submitted for confirmation under the Acquisition of Land Act 1981 Pt 2 (ss 10–15): see PARA 566 et seq. The Compulsory Purchase by Ministers (Inquiries Procedure) Rules 1994, SI 1994/3264, apply in relation to compulsory purchase orders which have been published in draft under the Acquisition of Land Act 1981 Sch 1 (see PARA 576 et seq). As to the Welsh Assembly Government and the Welsh Ministers see CONSTITUTIONAL LAW AND HUMAN RIGHTS.

588. Preliminary action to be taken by the authorising authority. The authorising authority[1] must give written notice of its intention to cause an inquiry to be held[2]. In the case of an inquiry which relates to a ministerial order[3], notice must be given to each remaining objector[4] by a date which is not later than five weeks after the expiry of the time within which objections to the draft order may be made[5]. In the case of an inquiry which relates to a non-ministerial order[6], notice must be given to the acquiring authority[7] and to each remaining objector by a date which is not later than five weeks after whichever is the later of (1) the expiry of the time within which objections to the order may be made; or (2) the submission of the order to the authorising authority for confirmation[8].

At the same time as notice is given, the authorising authority must also give written notice to the acquiring authority (where that authority is not the authorising authority) of the substance of each objection made by a remaining objector, and, so far as practicable, the substance of any other objections[9].

Comparable provision is made where the Welsh Ministers are the authorising authority[10].

1 'Authorising authority' means the confirming authority where the Acquisition of Land Act 1981 s 13A(3)(a) (see PARA 566) applies or the appropriate authority where Sch 1 para 4A(3)(a) (see PARA 576) applies: Compulsory Purchase (Inquiries Procedure) Rules 2007, SI 2007/3617, r 2. As to the meaning of 'confirming authority' see PARA 557 note 4.

2 Compulsory Purchase (Inquiries Procedure) Rules 2007, SI 2007/3617, r 3(1). 'Inquiry' means a public local inquiry in relation to which the Compulsory Purchase (Inquiries Procedure) Rules 2007, SI 2007/3617, apply: r 2. As to sending notices by post see r 21.

3 'Ministerial order' means a compulsory purchase order prepared in draft in accordance with the Acquisition of Land Act 1981 Sch 1 (see PARA 572 et seq): Compulsory Purchase (Inquiries Procedure) Rules 2007, SI 2007/3617, r 2.

4 'Remaining objector' means a person who has a remaining objection within the meaning of the Acquisition of Land Act 1981 s 13A (see PARA 566) or, as the case may be, Sch 1 para 4A(1) (see PARA 576): Compulsory Purchase (Inquiries Procedure) Rules 2007, SI 2007/3617, r 2.

5 Compulsory Purchase (Inquiries Procedure) Rules 2007, SI 2007/3617, r 3(2). The authorising authority may at any time in any particular case allow further time for the taking of any step which is to be taken by virtue of the rules: see r 20.

6 'Non-ministerial order' means a compulsory purchase order made and submitted for confirmation in accordance with the Acquisition of Land Act 1981 Pt 2 (see PARA 557 et seq): Compulsory Purchase (Inquiries Procedure) Rules 2007, SI 2007/3617, r 2.

7 As to the meaning of 'acquiring authority' see PARA 522 note 2.

8 Compulsory Purchase (Inquiries Procedure) Rules 2007, SI 2007/3617, r 3(3).

9 Compulsory Purchase (Inquiries Procedure) Rules 2007, SI 2007/3617, r 3(4).

10 See the Compulsory Purchase by Non-Ministerial Acquiring Authorities (Inquiries Procedure) Rules 1990, SI 1990/512, rr 4, 5; and the Compulsory Purchase by Ministers (Inquiries Procedure) Rules 1994, SI 1994/3264, r 4; and PARA 587.

589.   Pre-inquiry meetings. If it appears to the authorising authority[1] to be desirable, the authorising authority may cause a pre-inquiry meeting to be held and, where it does so the authorising authority must give notice of its intention to hold one[2]. The pre-inquiry meeting (or, where there is to be more than one, the first pre-inquiry meeting) must be held not later than 16 weeks after the relevant date[3]. The authorising authority must advertise notice of its intention to cause a pre-inquiry meeting to be held in one or more local newspapers circulating in the locality in which the land is situated not later than three weeks after the relevant date[4].

The acquiring authority[5] must, not later than eight weeks after the relevant date, send its outline statement[6] to each remaining objector[7] and, in the case of a non-ministerial order[8], to the authorising authority[9]. The authorising authority may by notice in writing require any remaining objector, and any other person who has notified it of his intention or wish to appear at the inquiry, to send, within eight weeks of the date of such notice, an outline statement to the authorising authority and to any other person specified in the notice including, in the case of a non-ministerial order, the acquiring authority[10].

The authorising authority must give not less than three weeks' written notice of the meeting to each remaining objector, and any other person whose presence at the meeting seems to it to be desirable, and (in the case of a non-ministerial order) the acquiring authority[11]. The authorising authority must also give notice of the date, time and place of the pre-inquiry meeting by either or both fixing a notice on or near the land[12] and publishing a notice in one or more newspapers circulating in the locality in which the land is situated[13].

An inspector presides at a pre-inquiry meeting[14] and determines the matters to be discussed and the procedure to be followed[15]. In particular he may require any person present at the meeting who, in his opinion, is behaving in a disruptive manner to leave, and he may refuse to permit that person to return or to attend any further pre-inquiry meetings relating to the same inquiry or he may permit that person to return or to attend any further pre-inquiry meetings relating to the same inquiry only on such conditions as he may specify[16].

Where a pre-inquiry meeting has been held[17], the inspector may hold another meeting and must arrange for such notice to be given of that other meeting as appears to him to be necessary[18]. Where no pre-inquiry meeting is held, the inspector may hold a pre-inquiry meeting if he thinks it desirable, and must arrange for not less than three weeks' written notice of the meeting to be given to (1) the authorising authority (2) the acquiring authority (in the case of a non-ministerial order); (3) each remaining objector; (4) any other person known at the date of the notice to be entitled to appear at the inquiry; and (5) any other person whose presence at the meeting appears to him to be desirable[19].

Comparable provision is made where the Welsh Ministers are the authorising authority[20].

1 As to the meaning of 'authorising authority' see PARA 588 note 1.
2 Compulsory Purchase (Inquiries Procedure) Rules 2007, SI 2007/3617, r 4. 'Pre-inquiry meeting' means a meeting held before an inquiry to consider what may be done with a view to securing that the inquiry is conducted efficiently and expeditiously; and where two or more such meetings are held references to the conclusion of a pre-inquiry meeting are references to the conclusion of the final meeting: r 2.
3 Compulsory Purchase (Inquiries Procedure) Rules 2007, SI 2007/3617, r 4. 'Relevant date' means the date of the authorising authority's notice under r 3(2) or r 3(3) (see PARA 588): r 4.
4 Compulsory Purchase (Inquiries Procedure) Rules 2007, SI 2007/3617, r 5(1).
5 As to the meaning of 'acquiring authority' see PARA 522 note 2.
6 'Outline statement', means a written statement of the principal submissions which a person proposes to put forward at an inquiry: Compulsory Purchase (Inquiries Procedure) Rules 2007, SI 2007/3617, r 2.
7 As to the meaning of 'remaining objector' see PARA 588 note 4.
8 As to the meaning of 'non-ministerial order' see PARA 588 note 6.
9 Compulsory Purchase (Inquiries Procedure) Rules 2007, SI 2007/3617, r 5(2).
10 Compulsory Purchase (Inquiries Procedure) Rules 2007, SI 2007/3617, r 5(3).
11 Compulsory Purchase (Inquiries Procedure) Rules 2007, SI 2007/3617, r 5(4).
12 Ie fixing a notice to a conspicuous object or place on or near the land, or where the land extends for more than 5 km, at intervals of not more than 5 km, and also in at least one place in the locality in which the land is situated where public notices are usually posted: Compulsory Purchase (Inquiries Procedure) Rules 2007, SI 2007/3617, r 5(5)(a).
13 Compulsory Purchase (Inquiries Procedure) Rules 2007, SI 2007/3617, r 5(5)(b).
14 Compulsory Purchase (Inquiries Procedure) Rules 2007, SI 2007/3617, r 6(1). 'Inspector' means a person appointed by the authorising authority to hold an inquiry or a re-opened inquiry: r 2.
15 Compulsory Purchase (Inquiries Procedure) Rules 2007, SI 2007/3617, r 6(4).
16 Compulsory Purchase (Inquiries Procedure) Rules 2007, SI 2007/3617, r 6(4).
17 Ie under the Compulsory Purchase (Inquiries Procedure) Rules 2007, SI 2007/3617, r 4.
18 Compulsory Purchase (Inquiries Procedure) Rules 2007, SI 2007/3617, r 6(2).
19 Compulsory Purchase (Inquiries Procedure) Rules 2007, SI 2007/3617, r 6(3).
20 See the Compulsory Purchase by Non-Ministerial Acquiring Authorities (Inquiries Procedure) Rules 1990, SI 1990/512, rr 6, 8; and the Compulsory Purchase by Ministers (Inquiries Procedure) Rules 1994, SI 1994/3264, rr 5, 7, 8; and PARA 587.

590. Statements of case. A statement of case is a written statement comprising (1) full particulars of the case which a person proposes to put forward at the inquiry (including where that person is the acquiring authority[1] the reasons for making the order); and (2) copies of, or relevant extracts from, any documents referred to in such statements and a list of any documents to which that person intends to refer or which he intends to put in evidence[2].

The acquiring authority must send a statement of case to each remaining objector[3] and, in the case of a non-ministerial order[4], to the authorising authority[5]. Where a pre-inquiry meeting[6] is held, it must be sent not later than four weeks after the conclusion of that meeting, and in any other case, it must be sent not later than six weeks after the relevant date[7]. Unless every document, or the relevant part of every document, which the acquiring authority intends to refer to or put in evidence at the inquiry has been copied to each remaining objector, the acquiring authority must send to each remaining objector a notice naming each place where a copy of those documents may be inspected free of charge at all reasonable hours until the date of commencement of the inquiry[8].

The authorising authority[9] may by notice in writing require any remaining objector and any other person who has notified the authority of an intention to appear at the inquiry to send a statement of case to the authorising authority and to any other person specified in the notice (including, in the case of a non-ministerial order, the acquiring authority) within six weeks from the date of the notice[10]. The authorising authority must supply a copy of the acquiring authority's statement of case to any person who is not a remaining objector but who has thus been required to send a statement of case[11].

The authorising authority or an inspector[12] may require any person who has sent a statement of case to provide such further information about the matters contained in it as the authorising authority or inspector may specify[13].

The acquiring authority must afford to any person who so requests a reasonable opportunity to inspect, and where practicable take copies of any statement or document which has been sent to it under the rules described above[14].

Comparable provision is made where the Welsh Ministers are the authorising authority[15].

1 As to the meaning of 'acquiring authority' see PARA 522 note 2.
2 Compulsory Purchase (Inquiries Procedure) Rules 2007, SI 2007/3617, r 2.
3 As to the meaning of 'remaining objector' see PARA 588 note 4.
4 As to the meaning of 'non-ministerial order' see PARA 588 note 6.
5 Compulsory Purchase (Inquiries Procedure) Rules 2007, SI 2007/3617, r 7(1).
6 As to the meaning of 'pre-inquiry meeting' see PARA 589 note 2.
7 Compulsory Purchase (Inquiries Procedure) Rules 2007, SI 2007/3617, r 7(1).
8 Compulsory Purchase (Inquiries Procedure) Rules 2007, SI 2007/3617, r 7(2). Each place so named must be as close as reasonably possible to the land: r 7(2).
9 As to the meaning of 'authorising authority' see PARA 588 note 1.
10 Compulsory Purchase (Inquiries Procedure) Rules 2007, SI 2007/3617, r 7(3).
11 Compulsory Purchase (Inquiries Procedure) Rules 2007, SI 2007/3617, r 7(4).
12 As to the inspector see PARA 589 note 14.
13 Compulsory Purchase (Inquiries Procedure) Rules 2007, SI 2007/3617, r 7(5).
14 Compulsory Purchase (Inquiries Procedure) Rules 2007, SI 2007/3617, r 7(6). The acquiring authority must specify in the statement sent in accordance with r 7(1) the time and place at which the opportunity will be afforded: r 7(6).
15 See the Compulsory Purchase by Non-Ministerial Acquiring Authorities (Inquiries Procedure) Rules 1990, SI 1990/512, r 7; and the Compulsory Purchase by Ministers (Inquiries Procedure) Rules 1994, SI 1994/3264, r 6; and PARA 587.

591. Inquiry timetable. Where a pre-inquiry meeting is held[1] the inspector[2] must, and in any other case may, arrange a timetable for the proceedings at, or at part of, an inquiry and may at any time vary the timetable[3]. Any changes to the timetable must be notified to every person entitled to appear at the inquiry[4]. The inspector may specify in the timetable the date by which any statement of evidence and summary of evidence is to be sent to him[5].

Where a timetable has been arranged, the inspector must no later than four weeks before the start of the inquiry send to every person entitled to appear at the inquiry a copy of the timetable for the proceedings[6].

Comparable provision is made where the Welsh Ministers are the authorising authority[7].

1 Ie pursuant to the Compulsory Purchase (Inquiries Procedure) Rules 2007, SI 2007/3617, r 4 or r 6: see PARA 589. As to the meaning of 'pre-inquiry meeting' see PARA 589 note 2.
2 As to the inspector see PARA 589 note 14.
3 Compulsory Purchase (Inquiries Procedure) Rules 2007, SI 2007/3617, r 8(1) (which is subject to the provisions of r 10(1)(b): see PARA 593).
4 Compulsory Purchase (Inquiries Procedure) Rules 2007, SI 2007/3617, r 8(1).
5 Compulsory Purchase (Inquiries Procedure) Rules 2007, SI 2007/3617, r 8(2). As to statements of evidence see PARA 590. As to the summary of evidence see r 15(1); and PARA 595.
6 Compulsory Purchase (Inquiries Procedure) Rules 2007, SI 2007/3617, r 8(3).
7 See the Compulsory Purchase by Non-Ministerial Acquiring Authorities (Inquiries Procedure) Rules 1990, SI 1990/512, r 9; and the Compulsory Purchase by Ministers (Inquiries Procedure) Rules 1994, SI 1994/3264, r 8; and PARA 587.

592. Notice of appointment of assessor. An assessor is a person appointed by the authorising authority[1] to sit with an inspector[2] at an inquiry (or re-opened inquiry) to advise the inspector on such matters arising as the authorising authority may specify[3]. Where the authorising authority appoints an assessor, it must give written notice of the name of the assessor and of the matters on which he is to advise the inspector to: (1) every remaining objector[4]; (2) any other person who has sent an outline statement or a statement of case[5]; and (3) in the case of a non-ministerial order[6], the acquiring authority[7].

Comparable provision is made where the Welsh Ministers are the authorising authority[8].

1 As to the meaning of 'authorising authority' see PARA 588 note 1.
2 As to the inspector see PARA 589 note 14.
3 Compulsory Purchase (Inquiries Procedure) Rules 2007, SI 2007/3617, r 2.
4 Compulsory Purchase (Inquiries Procedure) Rules 2007, SI 2007/3617, r 9(a). As to the meaning of 'remaining objector' see PARA 588 note 4.
5 Compulsory Purchase (Inquiries Procedure) Rules 2007, SI 2007/3617, r 9(b). As to the meaning of 'outline statement' see PARA 589 note 6. As to statements of case see PARA 590.
6 As to the meaning of 'non-ministerial order' see PARA 588 note 6.
7 Compulsory Purchase (Inquiries Procedure) Rules 2007, SI 2007/3617, r 9(c). As to the meaning of 'acquiring authority' see PARA 522 note 2.
8 See the Compulsory Purchase by Non-Ministerial Acquiring Authorities (Inquiries Procedure) Rules 1990, SI 1990/512, r 10; and the Compulsory Purchase by Ministers (Inquiries Procedure) Rules 1994, SI 1994/3264, r 9; and PARA 587.

593. Date and notification of inquiry. Where there is no pre-inquiry meeting[1], the date fixed by the authorising authority[2] for the holding of an inquiry must be no later than 22 weeks after the relevant date[3]. Where a pre-inquiry meeting (or where there is more than one, the final pre-inquiry meeting) is held, the date for the holding of the inquiry must be not later than eight weeks after the conclusion of that meeting[4]. Where the authorising authority is satisfied that in all the circumstances of the case it is impracticable to hold the inquiry within the periods mentioned above, the date for the inquiry must be fixed at the earliest practicable date after the end of that period[5].

Unless the authorising authority agrees a lesser period of notice with the acquiring authority[6] (where it is not that authority) and with each remaining objector[7], the authorising authority must give not less than six weeks' written notice of the date, time and place fixed by it for the holding of an inquiry to every remaining objector and to every person who has sent an outline statement or a statement of case[8].

The authorising authority may vary the date fixed for the holding of an inquiry[9], and it may also vary the time or place for the holding of an inquiry and must give such notice of the variation as appears to it to be reasonable[10]. Where it is satisfied that it is reasonable to do so and having regard to the nature of the compulsory purchase order or the draft order, the authorising authority may direct that the inquiry is to be held partly in one place and partly in another place[11].

In relation to a ministerial order[12] the acquiring authority must, not later than two weeks before the date fixed for the holding of the inquiry, display a notice of the inquiry[13] and publish notice of the inquiry in one or more newspapers circulating in the locality in which the land is situated[14]. In relation to a non-ministerial order[15], the acquiring authority must, not later than two weeks before the date fixed for the holding of the inquiry, display a notice of the inquiry[16] unless the authorising authority directs otherwise[17]. The acquiring authority must also, if the authorising authority so directs, publish notice of the inquiry in one or more newspapers circulating in the locality in which the land is situated[18].

A notice so displayed or published[19] must contain a clear statement indicating the date, time and place of the inquiry, and of the powers under which the order has been made, together with a description of the land sufficient to identify its approximate location without reference to the map referred to in the order[20].

Comparable provision is made where the Welsh Ministers are the authorising authority[21].

1 As to the meaning of 'pre-inquiry meeting' see PARA 589 note 2.
2 As to the meaning of 'authorising authority' see PARA 588 note 1.
3 Compulsory Purchase (Inquiries Procedure) Rules 2007, SI 2007/3617, r 10(1)(a). As to the meaning of 'relevant date' see PARA 589 note 3.
4 Compulsory Purchase (Inquiries Procedure) Rules 2007, SI 2007/3617, r 10(1)(b).
5 Compulsory Purchase (Inquiries Procedure) Rules 2007, SI 2007/3617, r 10(1)(c).
6 As to the meaning of 'acquiring authority' see PARA 522 note 2.
7 As to the meaning of 'remaining objector' see PARA 588 note 4.
8 Compulsory Purchase (Inquiries Procedure) Rules 2007, SI 2007/3617, r 10(2). As to the meaning of 'outline statement' see PARA 589 note 6. As to statements of case see PARA 590.
9 It may vary the date whether or not the date as varied complies with the requirements of the Compulsory Purchase (Inquiries Procedure) Rules 2007, SI 2007/3617, r 10(1): see r 10(3). Rule 10(2) applies in relation to the varied date as it applied in relation to the date originally fixed: see r 10(3).
10 Compulsory Purchase (Inquiries Procedure) Rules 2007, SI 2007/3617, r 10(4).
11 Compulsory Purchase (Inquiries Procedure) Rules 2007, SI 2007/3617, r 10(5).
12 As to the meaning of 'ministerial order' see PARA 588 note 3.
13 Ie display a notice (1) by attaching it to the land or to a conspicuous object or place on or near the land; and, where the land extends for more than 5 km, at intervals of not more than 5 km; and (2) in at least one place in the locality in which the land is situated where public notices are usually posted: Compulsory Purchase (Inquiries Procedure) Rules 2007, SI 2007/3617, r 11(1)(a).
14 Compulsory Purchase (Inquiries Procedure) Rules 2007, SI 2007/3617, r 11(1)(b).
15 As to the meaning of 'non-ministerial order' see PARA 588 note 6.
16 Ie in accordance with the requirements of the Compulsory Purchase (Inquiries Procedure) Rules 2007, SI 2007/3617, r 11(1)(a): see note 13.
17 Compulsory Purchase (Inquiries Procedure) Rules 2007, SI 2007/3617, r 11(2)(a).
18 Ie in accordance with the requirements of the Compulsory Purchase (Inquiries Procedure) Rules 2007, SI 2007/3617, r 11(1)(b): see r 11(2)(b).

19 Ie pursuant to the Compulsory Purchase (Inquiries Procedure) Rules 2007, SI 2007/3617, r 11(1) or r 11(2).
20 Compulsory Purchase (Inquiries Procedure) Rules 2007, SI 2007/3617, r 11(3).
21 See the Compulsory Purchase by Non-Ministerial Acquiring Authorities (Inquiries Procedure) Rules 1990, SI 1990/512, r 11; and the Compulsory Purchase by Ministers (Inquiries Procedure) Rules 1994, SI 1994/3264, r 10; and PARA 587.

594. Persons entitled to appear at the inquiry. Every remaining objector[1] and any other person who has sent an outline statement[2] or a statement of case[3] is entitled to appear at the inquiry[4]. In relation to a non-ministerial order[5], the acquiring authority[6] is also entitled to appear at the inquiry[7]. The inspector[8] may permit any other person to appear at the inquiry, and such permission must not be unreasonably withheld[9].

Any person entitled or permitted to appear may do so on his own behalf or be represented by counsel, solicitor or any other person[10]. An inspector may allow one or more persons to appear on behalf of some or all of any persons having a similar interest in the matter under inquiry[11].

In relation to a ministerial order[12] the acquiring authority may be represented at the inquiry by counsel or solicitor or by an officer of its department or other person authorised by the acquiring authority to represent it[13]. The acquiring authority must make a representative available at the inquiry to give evidence in elucidation of the statement of case, and such representative is subject to cross-examination to the same extent as any other witness[14]. However, the representative of the acquiring authority is not required to answer any question which in the opinion of the inspector is directed to the merits of government policy[15].

Where a government department (other than the department of a Minister who is the acquiring authority) has made a statement or representation in writing in support of the compulsory purchase order or the draft order and the acquiring authority has included that statement in its statement of case, a representative of the department concerned must be made available to attend the inquiry[16]. Such a representative must state the reasons for the view expressed by his department and give evidence, and he is subject to cross-examination to the same extent as any other witness[17]. However, a representative of a government department is not required to answer any question which in the opinion of the inspector is directed to the merits of government policy[18].

Comparable provision is made where the Welsh Ministers are the authorising authority[19].

1 As to the meaning of 'remaining objector' see PARA 588 note 4.
2 As to the meaning of 'outline statement' see PARA 589 note 6.
3 As to statements of case see PARA 590.
4 Compulsory Purchase (Inquiries Procedure) Rules 2007, SI 2007/3617, r 14(1).
5 As to the meaning of 'non-ministerial order' see PARA 588 note 6.
6 As to the meaning of 'acquiring authority' see PARA 522 note 2.
7 Compulsory Purchase (Inquiries Procedure) Rules 2007, SI 2007/3617, r 14(2).
8 As to the inspector see PARA 589 note 14.
9 Compulsory Purchase (Inquiries Procedure) Rules 2007, SI 2007/3617, r 14(3).
10 Compulsory Purchase (Inquiries Procedure) Rules 2007, SI 2007/3617, r 14(4).
11 Compulsory Purchase (Inquiries Procedure) Rules 2007, SI 2007/3617, r 14(5).
12 As to the meaning of 'ministerial order' see PARA 588 note 3.
13 Compulsory Purchase (Inquiries Procedure) Rules 2007, SI 2007/3617, r 12(1)(a).
14 Compulsory Purchase (Inquiries Procedure) Rules 2007, SI 2007/3617, r 12(1)(b).
15 Compulsory Purchase (Inquiries Procedure) Rules 2007, SI 2007/3617, r 12(2).
16 Compulsory Purchase (Inquiries Procedure) Rules 2007, SI 2007/3617, r 13(1).
17 Compulsory Purchase (Inquiries Procedure) Rules 2007, SI 2007/3617, r 13(2).

18 Compulsory Purchase (Inquiries Procedure) Rules 2007, SI 2007/3617, r 13(3).
19 See the Compulsory Purchase by Non-Ministerial Acquiring Authorities (Inquiries Procedure)
    Rules 1990, SI 1990/512, rr 12, 13; and the Compulsory Purchase by Ministers (Inquiries
    Procedure) Rules 1994, SI 1994/3264, rr 11, 12, 13; and PARA 587. Any reference in the
    Compulsory Purchase by Non-Ministerial Acquiring Authorities (Inquiries Procedure)
    Rules 1990, SI 1990/512, or the Compulsory Purchase by Ministers (Inquiries Procedure)
    Rules 1994, SI 1994/3264, to government policy has effect as if it included a reference to policy
    adopted or formulated by the Welsh Ministers: see the National Assembly for Wales (Transfer of
    Functions) Order 2000, SI 2000/253, art 6(1), (2), Sch 4.

595.   Evidence at the inquiry.   A person entitled to appear at an inquiry[1] to give, or to call another person to give, evidence at the inquiry by reading a statement of that evidence must send to the inspector[2] and (in the case of non-ministerial orders[3]) to the acquiring authority[4], a copy of that statement and (where the statement contains more than 1,500 words), a written summary of it together with any relevant supporting documents[5].

Where the acquiring authority sends a copy of a statement of evidence or a summary to the inspector, it must at the same time send a copy to every remaining objector[6] and any other person who has sent an outline statement or a statement of case[7].

The statement and the summary (if any) must be sent to the inspector and to the acquiring authority not later than three weeks before the date fixed for the commencement of the inquiry, or alternatively by the date specified in the timetable[8]. Only the summary (if there is one) is read at the inquiry unless the inspector permits or requires otherwise[9].

The acquiring authority must afford to any person who so requests a reasonable opportunity to inspect and, where practicable and on payment of a reasonable charge, take copies of any such document sent to or by it[10].

Comparable provision is made where the Welsh Ministers are the authorising authority[11].

1   See PARA 594.
2   As to the inspector see PARA 589 note 14.
3   As to the meaning of 'non-ministerial order' see PARA 588 note 6.
4   As to the meaning of 'acquiring authority' see PARA 522 note 2.
5   Compulsory Purchase (Inquiries Procedure) Rules 2007, SI 2007/3617, r 15(1). No written
    summary is required where the statement contains not more than 1,500 words: r 15(2). The
    Local Government Act 1972 s 250(2), (3) (giving evidence on inquiries: see LOCAL
    GOVERNMENT vol 69 (2009) PARA 105) applies to a public local inquiry held in pursuance of the
    Acquisition of Land Act 1981: s 5(2).
6   As to the meaning of 'remaining objector' see PARA 588 note 4.
7   Compulsory Purchase (Inquiries Procedure) Rules 2007, SI 2007/3617, r 15(6). As to the
    meaning of 'outline statement' see PARA 589 note 6. As to statements of case see PARA 590.
8   Compulsory Purchase (Inquiries Procedure) Rules 2007, SI 2007/3617, r 15(3). As to the
    timetable see PARA 591.
9   Compulsory Purchase (Inquiries Procedure) Rules 2007, SI 2007/3617, r 15(4)
10 Compulsory Purchase (Inquiries Procedure) Rules 2007, SI 2007/3617, r 15(5).
11 See the Compulsory Purchase by Non-Ministerial Acquiring Authorities (Inquiries Procedure)
    Rules 1990, SI 1990/512, r 14; and the Compulsory Purchase by Ministers (Inquiries Procedure)
    Rules 1994, SI 1994/3264, r 14; and PARA 587.

596.   Procedure at the inquiry.   Except as otherwise provided by the rules of procedure[1], the inspector[2] determines the procedure at the inquiry[3]. Unless in any particular case the inspector, with the consent of the acquiring authority[4], otherwise determines, the acquiring authority begins and has the right of final reply[5]. The other persons entitled or permitted to appear are heard in such order as the inspector may determine[6].

A person entitled to appear at the inquiry[7] is entitled to call evidence, and the acquiring authority and the remaining objectors[8] are entitled to cross-examine persons giving evidence, but the calling of evidence and the cross-examination of persons is otherwise at the inspector's discretion[9]. The inspector may refuse to permit the giving or production of evidence, the cross-examination of persons giving evidence, or the presentation of any other matter which he considers to be irrelevant or repetitious[10]. Where he refuses to permit the giving of oral evidence, the person wishing to give the evidence may submit to him in writing any evidence or other matters before the close of the inquiry[11].

Where a person gives evidence at an inquiry by reading a summary of his statement of evidence[12], the statement is (unless he notifies the inspector that he wishes to rely on the contents of that summary only[13]) treated as tendered in evidence; and the person whose evidence the statement contains is then subject to cross-examination on it to the same extent as if it were evidence he had given orally[14].

The inspector may direct the acquiring authority to provide facilities so that any person appearing at the inquiry may be afforded a reasonable opportunity to inspect, and where practicable and on payment of a reasonable charge, take copies of, any documents open to public inspection[15].

The inspector may require any person appearing or present at the inquiry who, in his opinion, is behaving in a disruptive manner to leave and may refuse to permit that person to return, or may permit him to return only on such conditions as he may specify; but any such person may submit to him in writing any evidence or other matters before the close of the inquiry[16].

The inspector may allow any person to alter or add to a statement of case[17] so far as may be necessary for the purposes of the inquiry[18]. However, he must (if necessary by adjourning the inquiry) give every remaining objector and any other person who has sent an outline statement[19] or a statement of case an adequate opportunity of considering any new matter of fact or document introduced by the acquiring authority[20].

The inspector may proceed with an inquiry in the absence of any person entitled to appear at it[21]. He may also take into account any written representation or evidence or any other document received by him from any person before an inquiry opens or during the inquiry, provided that he discloses it at the inquiry[22].

The inspector may from time to time adjourn the inquiry and, if the date, time and place of the resumed inquiry are announced at the inquiry before the adjournment, no further notice is required[23].

Comparable provision is made where the Welsh Ministers are the authorising authority[24].

1   Ie as provided by the Compulsory Purchase (Inquiries Procedure) Rules 2007, SI 2007/3617: see PARA 587 et seq.
2   As to the inspector see PARA 589 note 14.
3   Compulsory Purchase (Inquiries Procedure) Rules 2007, SI 2007/3617, r 16(1).
4   As to the meaning of 'acquiring authority' see PARA 522 note 2.
5   Compulsory Purchase (Inquiries Procedure) Rules 2007, SI 2007/3617, r 16(2).
6   Compulsory Purchase (Inquiries Procedure) Rules 2007, SI 2007/3617, r 16(2).
7   Ie by virtue of the Compulsory Purchase (Inquiries Procedure) Rules 2007, SI 2007/3617, r 14(1) or r 14(2): see PARA 594.
8   As to the meaning of 'remaining objector' see PARA 588 note 4.
9   Compulsory Purchase (Inquiries Procedure) Rules 2007, SI 2007/3617, r 16(3) (which is subject to r 16(2), (4), (5), (7)).

10 Compulsory Purchase (Inquiries Procedure) Rules 2007, SI 2007/3617, r 16(4). The inspector has a wide discretion as to what evidence is considered relevant and the court will only intervene in exceptional circumstances. For an example of when the court will intervene see *R v Secretary of State for the Environment, ex p Royal Borough of Kensington and Chelsea* [1987] JPL 567.
11 Compulsory Purchase (Inquiries Procedure) Rules 2007, SI 2007/3617, r 16(4).
12 As to the statement of evidence see PARA 595.
13 As to the summary see PARA 595.
14 Compulsory Purchase (Inquiries Procedure) Rules 2007, SI 2007/3617, r 16(5).
15 Compulsory Purchase (Inquiries Procedure) Rules 2007, SI 2007/3617, r 16(6).
16 Compulsory Purchase (Inquiries Procedure) Rules 2007, SI 2007/3617, r 16(7).
17 As to statements of case see PARA 590.
18 Compulsory Purchase (Inquiries Procedure) Rules 2007, SI 2007/3617, r 16(8).
19 As to the meaning of 'outline statement' see PARA 589 note 6.
20 Compulsory Purchase (Inquiries Procedure) Rules 2007, SI 2007/3617, r 16(8).
21 Compulsory Purchase (Inquiries Procedure) Rules 2007, SI 2007/3617, r 16(9). As to appearance at the inquiry see PARA 594.
22 Compulsory Purchase (Inquiries Procedure) Rules 2007, SI 2007/3617, r 16(10).
23 Compulsory Purchase (Inquiries Procedure) Rules 2007, SI 2007/3617, r 16(11). As to the circumstances in which the inspector would be obliged to adjourn the inquiry see *Orakpo v London Borough of Wandsworth and Secretary of State for the Environment* (1990) 24 HLR 370, CA. For considerations to be taken into account when an objector seeks an adjournment see *Ostreicher v Secretary of State for the Environment* [1978] 3 All ER 82, [1978] 1 WLR 810, CA.
24 See the Compulsory Purchase by Non-Ministerial Acquiring Authorities (Inquiries Procedure) Rules 1990, SI 1990/512, r 15; and the Compulsory Purchase by Ministers (Inquiries Procedure) Rules 1994, SI 1994/3264, r 15; and PARA 587.

597. Site inspections. The inspector[1] may make an unaccompanied inspection of the land before or during the inquiry without giving notice of his intention to the persons entitled to appear at the inquiry[2].

The inspector may, during the inquiry or after its close, inspect the land in the company of a representative of the acquiring authority[3] and any remaining objector[4]. He must make such an inspection if so requested by either the acquiring authority or by any remaining objector before or during the inquiry[5]. Where he intends to make such an inspection[6] he must announce during the inquiry the date and time at which he proposes to make it[7].

Comparable provision is made where the Welsh Ministers are the authorising authority[8].

1 As to the inspector see PARA 589 note 14.
2 Compulsory Purchase (Inquiries Procedure) Rules 2007, SI 2007/3617, r 17(1). As to the persons entitled to appear at the inquiry see PARA 594.
3 As to the meaning of 'acquiring authority' see PARA 522 note 2.
4 Compulsory Purchase (Inquiries Procedure) Rules 2007, SI 2007/3617, r 17(2). As to the meaning of 'remaining objector' see PARA 588 note 4. He is not bound to defer an inspection where any person mentioned r 17(2) is not present at the time appointed: r 17(4).
5 Compulsory Purchase (Inquiries Procedure) Rules 2007, SI 2007/3617, r 17(2). See note 4.
6 Ie an inspection of the kind described in the Compulsory Purchase (Inquiries Procedure) Rules 2007, SI 2007/3617, r 17(2).
7 Compulsory Purchase (Inquiries Procedure) Rules 2007, SI 2007/3617, r 17(3).
8 See the Compulsory Purchase by Non-Ministerial Acquiring Authorities (Inquiries Procedure) Rules 1990, SI 1990/512, r 16; and the Compulsory Purchase by Ministers (Inquiries Procedure) Rules 1994, SI 1994/3264, r 16; and PARA 587.

598. Procedure after the inquiry. After the close of the inquiry, the inspector[1] must make a report in writing to the authorising authority[2] which includes his conclusions and recommendations, or (as the case may be) his reasons for not making any recommendations[3]. Where an assessor has been appointed[4], he may, after the close of the inquiry, make a report in writing to the inspector in respect of the matters on which he was appointed to advise[5]. Where the assessor makes such a report, the inspector must append it to his own report and state in his own report whether and to what extent he agrees or disagrees with the assessor's report and, where he disagrees with the assessor, his reasons for that disagreement[6].

If, after the close of the inquiry, the authorising authority (1) differs from the inspector on any matter of fact mentioned in, or appearing to it to be material to, a conclusion reached by the inspector; or (2) takes into consideration any new evidence or new matter of fact, other than a matter of government policy[7], and is for that reason disposed to disagree with a recommendation made by the inspector, the authorising authority must not come to a decision which is at variance with that recommendation without first notifying the persons who appeared at the inquiry of its disagreement and the reasons for it[8]. The authorising authority must give every person who was notified in this way an opportunity of making written representations to it within three weeks of the date of the notification, or (if it has taken into consideration any new evidence or new matter of fact, other than a matter of government policy) of asking within that period for the re-opening of the inquiry[9].

The authorising authority may, as it thinks fit, cause an inquiry to be re-opened to afford an opportunity for persons to be heard on such matters relating to the order as it may specify[10]. It is obliged to cause the inquiry to be re-opened if asked by the acquiring authority[11] (in relation to a non-ministerial order[12]) or by a remaining objector[13] in the circumstances and within the prescribed period[14]. Where an inquiry is re-opened (whether by the same or a different inspector) the authorising authority must send to those persons who appeared at the inquiry a written statement of the specified matters[15], and the appropriate notice must be given of the date for the re-opened inquiry[16].

Comparable provision is made where the Welsh Ministers are the authorising authority[17].

1　As to the inspector see PARA 589 note 14.
2　As to the meaning of 'authorising authority' see PARA 588 note 1.
3　Compulsory Purchase (Inquiries Procedure) Rules 2007, SI 2007/3617, r 18(1). See also *Bushell v Secretary of State for the Environment* [1981] AC 75, [1980] 2 All ER 608, HL (a highways inquiry case), for comments on the purpose of the public inquiry procedure and the inspector's report. The report should contain a summary of the main evidence and arguments presented to the inspector along with findings of fact which led to his conclusions: see *Hope v Secretary of State for Environment* (1975) 31 P & CR 120. See also *Bolton Metropolitan Borough Council v Secretary of State for the Environment and Greater Manchester Waste Disposal Authority* (1990) 61 P & CR 343, CA.
4　As to the assessor see PARA 592.
5　Compulsory Purchase (Inquiries Procedure) Rules 2007, SI 2007/3617, r 18(2).
6　Compulsory Purchase (Inquiries Procedure) Rules 2007, SI 2007/3617, r 18(3).
7　See PARA 594.
8　Compulsory Purchase (Inquiries Procedure) Rules 2007, SI 2007/3617, r 18(4). As to appearance at the inquiry see PARA 594.
9　Compulsory Purchase (Inquiries Procedure) Rules 2007, SI 2007/3617, r 18(5).
10　Compulsory Purchase (Inquiries Procedure) Rules 2007, SI 2007/3617, r 18(6).
11　As to the meaning of 'acquiring authority' see PARA 522 note 2.
12　As to the meaning of 'non-ministerial order' see PARA 588 note 6.
13　As to the meaning of 'remaining objector' see PARA 588 note 4.
14　Compulsory Purchase (Inquiries Procedure) Rules 2007, SI 2007/3617, r 18(6). The prescribed period referred to is the period mentioned in r 18(5): see the text and note 9.
15　Compulsory Purchase (Inquiries Procedure) Rules 2007, SI 2007/3617, r 18(6)(a).
16　Ie the Compulsory Purchase (Inquiries Procedure) Rules 2007, SI 2007/3617, r 10(2)–(5) (see PARA 593) applies as if references to an inquiry were references to a re-opened inquiry, and four

weeks' written notice must be given of the date, time and place fixed for the holding of the re-opened inquiry to every remaining objector and every person who sent an outline statement or a statement of case: rr 10(2), 18(6)(b).

17 See the Compulsory Purchase by Non-Ministerial Acquiring Authorities (Inquiries Procedure) Rules 1990, SI 1990/512, r 17; and the Compulsory Purchase by Ministers (Inquiries Procedure) Rules 1994, SI 1994/3264, r 17; and PARA 587.

599.   Notice of the decision.   The authorising authority[1] must give notice of its decision and the reasons for it in writing to:

(1)   in the case of a non-ministerial order, the acquiring authority[2];

(2)   each remaining objector[3];

(3)   any person entitled to appear at the inquiry who did appear at it[4]; and

(4)   any other person who, having appeared at the inquiry, asked to be notified of the decision[5].

Where a copy of the inspector's report[6] is not sent with the notice of the decision, the notice must be accompanied by a copy of his conclusions and of any recommendations made by him; and if a person entitled to be notified of the decision has not received a copy of that report, he must be supplied with a copy of it on written application made to the authorising authority within four weeks of the date of the decision[7].

Comparable provision is made where the Welsh Ministers are the authorising authority[8].

1   As to the meaning of 'authorising authority' see PARA 588 note 1.
2   Compulsory Purchase (Inquiries Procedure) Rules 2007, SI 2007/3617, r 19(1)(a). As to the meaning of 'non-ministerial order' see PARA 588 note 6. As to the meaning of 'acquiring authority' see PARA 522 note 2.
3   Compulsory Purchase (Inquiries Procedure) Rules 2007, SI 2007/3617, r 19(1)(b). As to the meaning of 'remaining objector' see PARA 588 note 4.
4   Compulsory Purchase (Inquiries Procedure) Rules 2007, SI 2007/3617, r 19(1)(c). As to appearance at the inquiry see PARA 594.
5   Compulsory Purchase (Inquiries Procedure) Rules 2007, SI 2007/3617, r 19(1)(d).
6   'Report' includes any assessor's report appended to the inspector's report but does not include any other documents so appended; but any person who has received a copy of the report may apply in writing to the authorising authority within six weeks of the publication of the notice of confirmation of the order pursuant to the Acquisition of Land Act 1981 s 15 (see PARA 571), or making of the order pursuant to Sch 1 para 6 (see PARA 579), as the case may be, for an opportunity to inspect such documents and the authorising authority must afford him that opportunity: Compulsory Purchase (Inquiries Procedure) Rules 2007, SI 2007/3617, r 19(3).
7   Compulsory Purchase (Inquiries Procedure) Rules 2007, SI 2007/3617, r 19(2).
8   See the Compulsory Purchase by Non-Ministerial Acquiring Authorities (Inquiries Procedure) Rules 1990, SI 1990/512, r 18; and the Compulsory Purchase by Ministers (Inquiries Procedure) Rules 1994, SI 1994/3264, r 18; and PARA 587.

600.   Costs of the inquiry.   The Secretary of State may order the expenses of the inquiry to be paid by such local authority or party to the inquiry as he may direct, and may recover the amounts certified by him as payable, summarily as a civil debt[1]. He may also provide as between parties for the payment of their costs, and any party named in the order may have the order made a rule of the High Court and enforce payment accordingly[2]. It seems, however, to be the usual practice to refrain from making any order for costs as between the parties[3], save that an award of costs will normally be made to a successful objector whose land is excluded[4]. There is no rule of practice, such as commonly applies in courts of law, that the costs should follow the event.

1   Local Government Act 1972 s 250(4) (amended by the Housing and Planning Act 1986 s 49(2), Sch 12 Pt III); applied by the Acquisition of Land Act 1981 s 5(3). As to the Secretary of State

see PARA 507 note 1. The Local Government Act 1972 s 250 has effect as if references to the Secretary of State included reference to the National Assembly for Wales (now the Welsh Ministers): National Assembly for Wales (Transfer of Functions) Order 1999, SI 1999/672, art 2 Sch 1. As to the Welsh Ministers see CONSTITUTIONAL LAW AND HUMAN RIGHTS.

2   Local Government Act 1972 s 250(5) (as applied: see note 1).

3   See, however, *Re Wood's Application* (1952) 3 P & CR 238, DC.

4   See Department of the Environment Circular 8/93 *Award of costs incurred in planning and other (including compulsory purchase order) proceedings* Annex 6 paras 1–7. Costs will not be awarded in favour of an unsuccessful objector. Costs may be awarded against a party who has acted unreasonably, vexatiously or frivolously or who has necessitated a postponement or adjournment.

601. Hearings before persons appointed to hear objections. Where no public local inquiry is to be held but objections are to be heard by a person appointed by the confirming authority[1] or the Minister[2] to hear objections[3], the provisions of the procedural rules applicable to public local inquiries[4] do not apply; but such a formal hearing must be distinguished from purely informal discussions which sometimes take place when objectors do not insist on an inquiry or hearing[5].

1   As to the meaning of 'confirming authority' see PARA 557 note 4.

2   See PARA 576 note 10.

3   See the Acquisition of Land Act 1981 s 13A(3) (see PARA 566) and Sch 1 para 4A(3) (see PARA 576).

4   Ie the Compulsory Purchase (Inquiries Procedure) Rules 2007, SI 2007/3617: see PARA 587 et seq.

5   Cf *Ealing Borough Council v Minister of Housing and Local Government* [1952] Ch 856, [1952] 2 All ER 639, where a hearing was required under what is now the Town and Country Planning Act 1990 s 140(3), (4) (see TOWN AND COUNTRY PLANNING vol 46(2) (Reissue) PARA 971), and the discussions which in fact took place did not satisfy the statutory requirements.

(vi) Date of Operation of Compulsory Purchase Order

602. In general. Unless it is subject to special parliamentary procedure[1], a compulsory purchase order[2] becomes operative on the date on which the notice of confirmation, or, in the case of an order made by a Minister, the making, of the order is first published[3] unless an application to the High Court has been made questioning the validity of the order and the order is suspended or quashed[4].

A compulsory rights order under the Opencast Coal Act 1958[5] becomes operative either on the date mentioned above or such later date, not being more than one year after confirmation of the order, as may be determined by the Secretary of State and specified in the order as confirmed[6].

1   As to special parliamentary procedure see PARA 605.

2   As to the meaning of 'compulsory purchase order' see PARA 557 note 1.

3   Acquisition of Land Act 1981 s 26(1). The publication must be in accordance with the Act (see PARAS 571, 579): s 26(1).

4   See the Acquisition of Land Act 1981 s 24; and PARA 614.

5   Ie under the Opencast Coal Act 1958 s 4: see MINES, MINERALS AND QUARRIES vol 31 (2003 Reissue) PARA 422.

6   See the Acquisition of Land Act 1981 s 29(9); and PARA 610. As to the Secretary of State see PARA 507 note 1.

(vii) Confirmation by Special Parliamentary Procedure

603. Compulsory purchase orders comprising land of local authorities, statutory undertakers and the National Trust. In so far as a compulsory purchase order[1] authorises the compulsory purchase of land[2] which:

(1)   is the property of a local authority[3]; or

(2)   has been acquired by statutory undertakers[4] (not being local authorities) for the purposes of their undertaking[5]; or

(3)   belongs to, and is held inalienably[6] by, the National Trust[7],

the order will be subject to special parliamentary procedure[8] if an objection to the order has been made by the local authority, the statutory undertakers or the National Trust and that objection has not been withdrawn[9].

In order that the land may be protected by the requirement of special parliamentary procedure it must be land within the particular description at the time when objections may be duly made[10].

Except in relation to National Trust land these provisions do not, however, apply to the compulsory acquisition of an interest in land where the person acquiring the land is a specified local authority[11], a national park authority[12], an urban development corporation, a Welsh planning board[13], any specified statutory undertakers[14] or a Minister[15].

1   As to the meanings of 'compulsory purchase order' and 'compulsory purchase' see PARA 557 note 1.

2   As to the meaning of 'land' see PARA 522 note 1. In relation to the compulsory purchase of a right under the Gas Act 1965 s 12(1), s 13(2) or s 13(3) (see FUEL AND ENERGY vol 19(2) (2007 Reissue) PARAS 998–999), references to the land include references to any land held with the stratum of land constituting the underground gas storage: see the Acquisition of Land Act 1981 s 30; and PARA 611.

3   Acquisition of Land Act 1981 s 17(1)(a). As to the meaning of 'local authority' see PARA 522 note 2.

4   The Acquisition of Land Act 1981 s 16(3) (extended meaning of 'statutory undertakers': see PARA 564 note 3) applies for these purposes as it applies in relation to s 16(1), (2) (see PARA 564): s 17(2A) (added by the National Health Service and Community Care Act 1990 s 60, Sch 8 para 8(2)). As to the meaning of 'statutory undertakers' generally see PARA 561 note 8.

5   Acquisition of Land Act 1981 s 17(1)(b).

6   'Held inalienably' means that the land is inalienable under the National Trust Act 1907 s 21 or the National Trust Act 1939 s 8 (see OPEN SPACES AND ANCIENT MONUMENTS vol 34 (Reissue) PARA 111): Acquisition of Land Act 1981 s 18(3).

7   Acquisition of Land Act 1981 s 18(1). As to the meaning of 'National Trust' see PARA 561 note 8.

8   As to special parliamentary procedure see PARA 605. As to the application of special parliamentary procedure to development consent orders for nationally significant infrastructure projects see PARA 540.

9   Acquisition of Land Act 1981 ss 17(2), 18(2).

10   An objection made by a local authority within the due time but before it acquired the ownership of the land is not an objection duly made for this purpose: *Middlesex County Council v Minister of Housing and Local Government* [1953] 1 QB 12, [1952] 2 All ER 709, CA.

11   The local authorities specified for these purposes are:

(1)   in relation to England, the council of a county or district, the Broads Authority, the council of a London borough, the Common Council of the City of London, the London Fire and Emergency Planning Authority, a police authority established under the Police Act 1996 s 3, and a joint authority established by the Local Government Act 1985 Pt IV (ss 23–42) or an authority established for an area in England by an order under the Local Government and Public Involvement in Health Act 2007 s 207 (joint waste authorities); and

(2)   in relation to Wales, the council of a county or county borough or a police authority established under the Police Act 1996 s 3,

and this definition applies to the Isles of Scilly as if the Council of those Isles were the council of a county: Acquisition of Land Act 1981 s 17(4) (definition amended by the Local Government Act 1985 ss 84, 102(2), Sch 14 para 60, Sch 17; the Education Reform Act 1988 s 237(2), Sch 13 Pt I; the Norfolk and Suffolk Broads Act 1988 s 21, Sch 6 para 22; the Police and Magistrates' Courts Act 1994 s 43, Sch 4 para 55; the Local Government (Wales) Act 1994 s 66(6), Sch 16 para 64(1); the Police Act 1996 s 103, Sch 7 para 1(1), (2)(q); the Police Act 1997 s 134(1), Sch 9 para 43; the Greater London Authority Act 1999 s 328(8), Sch 29 Pt I para 34; the Criminal Justice and Police Act 2001 ss 128(1), 137, Sch 6 Pt 3 para 65, Sch 7

Pt 5(1); and the Local Government and Public Involvement in Health Act 2007 s 209(2), Sch 13 Pt 2 para 37). As to areas and authorities in England and Wales see LOCAL GOVERNMENT vol 69 (2009) PARA 22 et seq; and as to administrative areas and authorities in London see LONDON GOVERNMENT vol 29(2) (Reissue) PARA 29 et seq. As to the Broads Authority see OPEN SPACES AND ANCIENT MONUMENTS vol 34 (Reissue) PARA 130. As to the London Fire and Emergency Planning Authority see FIRE SERVICES vol 18(2) (Reissue) PARA 17; LONDON GOVERNMENT vol 29(2) (Reissue) PARA 217. As to police authorities see POLICE vol 36(1) (2007 Reissue) PARA 139 et seq. As to joint authorities see LOCAL GOVERNMENT 69 (2009) PARA 47 et seq.

12 As to national park authorities see OPEN SPACES AND ANCIENT MONUMENTS vol 34 (Reissue) PARA 157 et seq.

13 'Welsh planning board' means a board constituted under the Town and Country Planning Act 1990 s 2(1B) (see TOWN AND COUNTRY PLANNING vol 46(1) (Reissue) PARA 30): Acquisition of Land Act 1981 s 17(4) (definition added by the Local Government (Wales) Act 1994 s 20(4), Sch 6 para 17(1); and amended by the Environment Act 1995 s 120, Sch 24).

14 For these purposes, 'statutory undertakers' includes: (1) a National Health Service trust established under the National Health Service and Community Care Act 1990 Pt I (ss 1–26); (2) an NHS foundation trust; (3) the Schools Funding Council for Wales; (4) a Primary Care Trust established under the National Health Service Act 1977 s 16A; and (5) any authority, body or undertakers specified in an order made by the Secretary of State: Acquisition of Land Act 1981 s 17(4) (definition amended by the National Health Service and Community Care Act 1990 s 66(1), Sch 9 para 23; the Education Act 1993 s 11; the Coal Industry Act 1994 s 67(1), (8), Sch 9 para 27(1), Sch 11 Pt II; the Education Act 1996 s 582(1), Sch 37 para 51; the School Standards and Framework Act 1998 s 140(3), Sch 31; the Health and Social Care (Community Health and Standards) Act 2003 Sch 4 para 49; and SI 2000/90). See HEALTH SERVICES. As to the Secretary of State see PARA 507 note 1. The reference to 'statutory undertakers' has been modified so as to include a reference to a regional development agency: see the Regional Development Agencies Act 1998 s 20, Sch 5 Pt I para 2. As to regional development agencies see TRADE, INDUSTRY AND INDUSTRIAL RELATIONS vol 47 (2001 Reissue) PARA 896. An order of the Secretary of State under head (4) must be made by statutory instrument subject to annulment in pursuance of a resolution of either House of Parliament: Acquisition of Land Act 1981 s 17(5). At the date at which this volume states the law, no such order had been made, but it is submitted that the Community Land (Statutory Undertakers) Order 1976, SI 1976/18, has effect as if made under these provisions.

15 Acquisition of Land Act 1981 s 17(3) (amended by the Planning and Compensation Act 1991 s 70, Sch 15 para 11; the Local Government (Wales) Act 1994 s 20(4), Sch 6 para 17(1); the Environment Act 1995 ss 78, 120(3), Sch 10 para 21(1), Sch 24; the Government of Wales Act 1998 ss 128, 152, Sch 14 para 17, Sch 18 Pt V; and SI 2005/3226).

All functions of a Minister of the Crown under the Acquisition of Land Act 1981, except for s 8(4) (see PARA 564), so far as they are exercisable in relation to Wales, are now exercisable by the Welsh Ministers: see the National Assembly for Wales (Transfer of Functions) Order 1999, SI 1999/672, art 2, Sch 1; and the Government of Wales Act 2006 s 162(1), Sch 11 para 30. As to the Welsh Assembly Government and the Welsh Ministers see CONSTITUTIONAL LAW AND HUMAN RIGHTS.

The Acquisition of Land Act 1981 s 17 does not apply in relation to compulsory rights orders under the Opencast Coal Act 1958 s 4 (see MINES, MINERALS AND QUARRIES vol 31 (2003 Reissue) PARA 422): see the Acquisition of Land Act 1981 s 29(6A); and PARA 610.

604. Compulsory purchase orders comprising commons, open spaces and allotments. In so far as a compulsory purchase order[1] authorises the purchase of any land[2] forming part of a common[3], open space[4] or fuel or field garden allotment[5], the order is subject to special parliamentary procedure[6] except where excluded by a certificate of the Secretary of State[7]. Where it is proposed to give such a certificate, the Secretary of State must direct the acquiring authority[8] to give public notice of his intention to do so[9]. After affording opportunity to all persons interested to make representations and objections, and after causing a public local inquiry[10] to be held in any case where it appears to him to be expedient to do so, having regard to any representations or objections made, the Secretary of State may give the certificate after considering any such representations and objections and, if an inquiry has been held, the report of the person who held it[11].

Except where the Secretary of State has given a certificate that the land is being purchased to secure its preservation or improve its management[12], a compulsory purchase order may provide for vesting land given in exchange[13] in the persons in whom the land purchased was vested, and subject to the like rights, trusts and incidents as attach to the land purchased[14] and discharging the land purchased from all rights, trusts and incidents to which it was previously subject[15].

These provisions are modified in their application to compulsory rights orders under the Opencast Coal Act 1958[16] and do not apply in relation to the compulsory purchase of a right to store gas in an underground gas storage[17] or of any right[18] as respects wells, boreholes and shafts in a storage area or protective area[19].

1   As to the meaning of 'compulsory purchase order' see PARA 557 note 1.
2   As to the meaning of 'land' see PARA 522 note 1.
3   As to the meaning of 'common' see PARA 531 note 3.
4   As to the meaning of 'open space' see PARA 531 note 4.
5   As to the meaning of 'fuel or field garden allotment' see PARA 531 note 5.
6   As to special parliamentary procedure see PARA 605. As to the application of special parliamentary procedure to development consent orders for nationally significant infrastructure projects see PARA 540.
7   See the Acquisition of Land Act 1981 s 19(1); and PARA 531. As to the Secretary of State see PARA 507 note 1. All functions of a Minister of the Crown under the Acquisition of Land Act 1981, except s 8(4) (see PARA 564), so far as they are exercisable in relation to Wales, are now exercisable by the Welsh Ministers: see the National Assembly for Wales (Transfer of Functions) Order 1999, SI 1999/672, art 2, Sch 1; and the Government of Wales Act 2006 s 162(1), Sch 11 para 30. As to the Welsh Assembly Government and the Welsh Ministers see CONSTITUTIONAL LAW AND HUMAN RIGHTS. Orders made or confirmed by the Welsh Ministers are subject to special parliamentary procedure as provided for in s 18 (see PARA 603), Sch 3 para 5 (see PARA 608): National Assembly for Wales (Transfer of Functions) Order 1999, SI 1999/672, art 2, Sch 1.
8   As to the meaning of 'acquiring authority' see PARA 522 note 2.
9   Acquisition of Land Act 1981 s 19(2) (amended by the Planning and Compensation Act 1991 s 70, Sch 15 para 12(1)(b)). Notice must be given in such form and manner as the Secretary of State may direct: Acquisition of Land Act 1981 s 19(2A) (added by the Planning and Compensation Act 1991 Sch 15 para 12(1)(c)). See the Compulsory Purchase of Land (Prescribed Forms) (Ministers) Regulations 2004, SI 2004/2595, reg 3, Schedule, Form 12; and the Compulsory Purchase of Land (Prescribed Forms) (National Assembly for Wales) Regulations 2004, SI 2004/2732, reg 3, Schedule, Form 12.
10 As to the procedure applicable to a public local inquiry see PARA 587 et seq.
11 Acquisition of Land Act 1981 s 19(2) (as amended: see note 9). As to notice of the giving of the certificate see s 22; and PARA 564 note 8. Subject to the Acquisition of Land Act 1981 s 24 (court's power to quash certificate: see PARA 614), the certificate becomes operative on the date on which notice of the giving of it is first so published: s 26(2).
12 Ie a certificate in accordance with the Acquisition of Land Act 1981 s 19(1)(aa): see PARA 531.
13 Ie as mentioned in the Acquisition of Land Act 1981 s 19(1): see PARA 531.
14 Ie subject to the rights, trust and incidents mentioned in the Acquisition of Land Act 1981 s 19(1): see PARA 531.
15 Acquisition of Land Act 1981 s 19(3) (amended by the Planning and Compensation Act 1991 Sch 15 para 12(1)(d)). As to the acquisition of new rights over such land see PARA 609.
16 See the Acquisition of Land Act 1981 s 29(7); and PARA 610.
17 Ie under the Gas Act 1965 s 12(1): see FUEL AND ENERGY vol 19(2) (2007 Reissue) PARA 998.
18 Ie any right under the Gas Act 1965 s 13(2) or s 13(3): see FUEL AND ENERGY vol 19(2) (2007 Reissue) PARA 999.
19 See the Acquisition of Land Act 1981 s 30(2); and PARA 611.

605. Special parliamentary procedure. Where special parliamentary procedure applies to a compulsory purchase order[1], its effect is[2] that the order is of no effect until it has been laid before Parliament by the appropriate Minister and has been brought into operation in accordance with the statutory provisions[3].

No order may be so laid before Parliament until the requirements of the empowering enactment preliminary to the making or confirmation of the order have been complied with, and a notice of the intention to lay the order before Parliament has been published in the London Gazette[4]. A short period is allowed for the presentation of petitions by way of general objection or for amendment to the order, and a further short period is allowed in which the order may be annulled by resolution of either House of Parliament, or referred to a joint committee of both Houses for the consideration of any petition[5]. If the joint committee's report is that the order should not be approved, or if amendments are made which are unacceptable to the minister concerned, authorisation of the acquisition requires the introduction and passing of a special type of confirming Bill[6]. In other cases an Act of Parliament is not needed[7], but amendments may have to be accepted. Thus where this procedure is made applicable, a compulsory purchase order is subject to a measure of parliamentary control, in some ways resembling the procedure by provisional order but less cumbersome in practice[8]. Except in the few cases where a confirming Act is passed, a compulsory purchase order made under this procedure will be open to question in the court on the same limited grounds as would have been available if it had not been laid before Parliament[9].

1   See PARAS 603–604. As to the meaning of 'compulsory purchase order' see PARA 557 note 1. In the case of land falling within two or more of the categories specified in the Acquisition of Land Act 1981 ss 17–19 (see PARAS 531, 603–604) or s 28, Sch 3 paras 4–6 (see PARAS 608–609), a compulsory purchase order will be subject to special parliamentary procedure if required to be subject to it by any of those provisions: s 21, Sch 3 para 8.
2   Special parliamentary procedure applies where, by any Act passed after 20 December 1945, power to make or confirm orders is conferred on any authority with the requirement that the order be subject to special parliamentary procedure: Statutory Orders (Special Procedure) Act 1945 s 1(1). See PARLIAMENT vol 34 (Reissue) PARA 914.
3   Statutory Orders (Special Procedure) Act 1945 s 1(2). See further PARLIAMENT vol 34 (Reissue) PARAS 914, 925.
4   See the Statutory Orders (Special Procedure) Act 1945 s 2(1); and PARLIAMENT vol 34 (Reissue) PARAS 915–916.
5   See the Statutory Orders (Special Procedure) Act 1945 ss 3–5; and PARLIAMENT vol 34 (Reissue) PARA 917 et seq.
6   See the Statutory Orders (Special Procedure) Act 1945 s 6(2) proviso, (3)–(5); and PARLIAMENT vol 34 (Reissue) PARA 926.
7   See the Statutory Orders (Special Procedure) Act 1945 ss 4(3), 6(1), (2); and PARLIAMENT vol 34 (Reissue) PARA 925.
8   As to the provisional order procedure see PARA 506.
9   See the Acquisition of Land Act 1981 ss 23, 26(1), 27; and PARAS 612–614.

(viii) Special Procedures relating to the Acquisition of Rights over Land

606. Acquisition of rights over land by the creation of new rights. Specific statutory authority is generally required for the compulsory acquisition of rights over land by the creation of new rights. The Acquisition of Land Act 1981 provides a uniform code for such acquisitions as authorised by the Acts specified therein[1] and has effect with the modifications necessary to make it apply to the compulsory acquisition of a right[2] as it applies to the compulsory acquisition of land[3] so that references to land are to be read as referring to, or as including references to, the right acquired or to be acquired, or to land over which the right is, or is to be, exercisable, according to the requirements of the particular context[4]. Those provisions do not, however, apply to a compulsory purchase of a right to store gas in an underground gas storage[5] or of any right[6] as respects wells, boreholes and shafts in a storage area or protective area[7].

1   See the Acquisition of Land Act 1981 s 28, Sch 3; and PARA 607 et seq. Schedule 3 applies to the compulsory acquisition of rights over land by the creation of new rights by virtue of: (1) the Welsh Development Agency Act 1975 s 21A (see TRADE, INDUSTRY AND INDUSTRIAL RELATIONS vol 47 (2001 Reissue) PARA 856 et seq); (2) the Local Government (Miscellaneous Provisions) Act 1976 s 13(1) (see LOCAL GOVERNMENT vol 69 (2009) PARA 511); (3) the Local Government, Planning and Land Act 1980 s 142(4) (see TOWN AND COUNTRY PLANNING vol 46(3) (Reissue) PARA 1455); (4) the Highways Act 1980 s 250 (see HIGHWAYS, STREETS AND BRIDGES vol 21 (2004 Reissue) PARA 85); (5) the Gas Act 1986 s 9(3), Sch 3 para 1 (see FUEL AND ENERGY vol 19(2) (2007 Reissue) PARA 841); (6) the Electricity Act 1989 s 10(1), Sch 3 para 1 (see FUEL AND ENERGY vol 19(2) (2007 Reissue) PARA 1283); and (7) the Communications Act 2003 s 118, Sch 4 para 3(3) (see TELECOMMUNICATIONS AND BROADCASTING vol 45(1) (2005 Reissue) PARA 152): Acquisition of Land Act 1981 s 28 (amended by the Gas Act 1986 s 67(1), Sch 7 para 29; the Electricity Act 1989 s 112(1), Sch 16 para 28; the Government of Wales Act 1998 s 128, Sch 14 para 18, Sch 18 Pt IV; and the Communications Act 2003 s 406, Sch 17 para 58, Sch 19).

2   For these purposes, 'right' means a right to which the Acquisition of Land Act 1981 s 28 applies, or any right to which Sch 3 is applied by any Act passed after the Acquisition of Land Act 1981: Sch 3 para 1.

3   As to the meaning of 'land' see PARA 522 note 1.

4   Acquisition of Land Act 1981 Sch 3 para 2(1). Without prejudice to the generality of Sch 3 para 2(1), Sch 3 paras 3–9 (see PARA 607 et seq) applies to the compulsory acquisition of a right in substitution for Pt III (ss 16–22) (see PARAS 531, 564, 603–605): Sch 3 para 2(2).

5   Ie under the Gas Act 1965 s 12(1): see FUEL AND ENERGY vol 19(2) (2007 Reissue) PARA 998.

6   Ie any right under the Gas Act 1965 s 13(2) or s 13(3): see FUEL AND ENERGY vol 19(2) (2007 Reissue) PARA 999.

7   See the Acquisition of Land Act 1981 s 30(3); and PARA 611.

607. Acquisition of new rights over statutory undertakers' land. The following provisions apply where: (1) the land[1] over which a right[2] is to be acquired by virtue of a compulsory purchase order[3] includes land which has been acquired by statutory undertakers[4] for the purposes of their undertaking; and (2) on a representation made to the appropriate Minister[5] before the expiration of the time within which objections can be made[6], he is satisfied that any of that land is used for the purposes of the carrying on of their undertaking, or that an interest in any of that land is held for those purposes[7]. If the representation is not withdrawn, the compulsory purchase order must not be confirmed or made so as to authorise the compulsory purchase of a right over any such land as to which that minister is so satisfied, except land as to which he is satisfied, and so certifies that its nature and situation are such: (a) that the right can be purchased without serious detriment to the carrying on of the undertaking; or (b) that any detriment to the carrying on of the undertaking, in consequence of the acquisition of the right, can be made good by the undertakers by the use of other land belonging to or available for acquisition by them[8]. As soon as may be after he has given such a certificate, the acquiring authority[9] must publish in one or more local newspapers circulating in the locality in which the land comprised in the order is situated a notice in the prescribed form[10] stating that the certificate has been given[11]. Subject to the court's power to quash the certificate[12], it becomes operative on the date on which such notice is first published[13].

In the case of acquisitions of land of statutory undertakers under the Town and Country Planning Act 1990[14], the Planning (Listed Buildings and Conservation Areas) Act 1990[15], certain provisions of the Local Government, Planning and Land Act 1980[16], or the Welsh Development Agency Act 1975[17], the order may be confirmed or made without the appropriate certificate[18] provided that it has been confirmed (or made) by the appropriate Minister jointly with the Minister or Ministers who would normally make the order[19].

1   As to the meaning of 'land' see PARA 522 note 1. See also PARA 606 text to note 4.
2   As to the meaning of 'right' see PARA 606 note 2.
3   As to the meaning of 'compulsory purchase order' see PARA 557 note 1.
4   As to the meaning of 'statutory undertakers' see PARA 561 note 8.
5   As to the meaning of 'appropriate Minister' see PARA 564 note 5.
6   As to the making of objections see PARA 563.
7   Acquisition of Land Act 1981 Sch 3 para 3(1). As to the acquisitions to which Sch 3 applies see PARA 606.
8   Acquisition of Land Act 1981 Sch 3 para 3(1), (2) (Sch 3 para 3(1) amended by the Planning and Compensation Act 1991 s 70, Sch 15 para 10(1)).
9   As to the meaning of 'acquiring authority' see PARA 522 note 2.
10   For the prescribed form of notice stating that the certificate has been given see the Compulsory Purchase of Land (Prescribed Forms) (Ministers) Regulations 2004, SI 2004/2595, reg 3, Schedule, Form 12; and the Compulsory Purchase of Land (Prescribed Forms) (National Assembly for Wales) Regulations 2004, SI 2004/2732, reg 3, Schedule, Form 12.
11   Acquisition of Land Act 1981 Sch 3 para 9.
12   Ie under the Acquisition of Land Act 1981 s 24: see PARA 614.
13   Acquisition of Land Act 1981 s 26(2).
14   See the Town and Country Planning Act 1990 ss 226, 228, 244, 245(1) (see TOWN AND COUNTRY PLANNING vol 46(2) (Reissue) PARA 941 et seq), and s 254 (see HIGHWAYS, STREETS AND BRIDGES vol 21 (2004 Reissue) PARAS 87–88).
15   See the Planning (Listed Buildings and Conservation Areas) Act 1990 s 47; and TOWN AND COUNTRY PLANNING vol 46(3) (Reissue) PARAS 1154–1155, 1157.
16   Ie under the Local Government, Planning and Land Act 1980 s 142 or s 143 (acquisition by urban development corporation): see TOWN AND COUNTRY PLANNING vol 46(3) (Reissue) PARAS 1455–1457.
17   Ie by virtue of the Welsh Development Agency Act 1975 s 21A, Sch 4: see TRADE, INDUSTRY AND INDUSTRIAL RELATIONS vol 47 (2001 Reissue) PARA 856 et seq.
18   See the Acquisition of Land Act 1981 s 31(1) (substituted by the Planning and Compensation Act 1991 s 4, Sch 2 para 53(2); and amended by the Government of Wales Act 1998 ss 128, 135(3), 152, Sch 14 para 19, Sch 18 Pt V), and the Acquisition of Land Act 1981 s 31(2) (substituted by the Planning and Compensation Act 1991 s 70, Sch 15 Pt I para 10(2)), disapplying the Acquisition of Land Act 1981 s 16(2) and Sch 3 para 3(2).
19   Acquisition of Land Act 1981 s 31(2) (as substituted: see note 18). Where, in accordance with this provision, a compulsory acquisition is effected under a compulsory purchase order confirmed or made without the appropriate Minister's certificate, the Town and Country Planning Act 1990 ss 280–282 (measure of compensation) apply in accordance with s 281(1)(c) (see TOWN AND COUNTRY PLANNING vol 46(3) (Reissue) PARAS 1028–1030): Acquisition of Land Act 1981 s 31(4) (amended by the Planning and Compensation Act 1991 Sch 2 para 53(2)).
     All functions of a Minister of the Crown under the Acquisition of Land Act 1981, except s 8(4) (see PARA 564), so far as they are exercisable in relation to Wales, are now exercisable by the Welsh Ministers: see the National Assembly for Wales (Transfer of Functions) Order 1999, SI 1999/672, art 2, Sch 1; and the Government of Wales Act 2006 s 162(1), Sch 11 para 30. As to the Welsh Assembly Government and the Welsh Ministers see CONSTITUTIONAL LAW AND HUMAN RIGHTS.

608.   Acquisition of new rights where order subject to special parliamentary procedure.   In so far as a compulsory purchase order[1] authorises the compulsory purchase of rights[2] over land[3] which:

(1)   is the property of a local authority[4]; or
(2)   has been acquired by statutory undertakers[5] (not being local authorities) for the purposes of their undertaking[6]; or
(3)   belongs to, and is held inalienably[7] by, the National Trust[8],

the order will be subject to special parliamentary procedure[9] if an objection to the order has been made by the local authority, the statutory undertakers or the National Trust and that objection has not been withdrawn[10].

Except in relation to National Trust land these provisions do not, however, apply to the compulsory acquisition of an interest in land where the person acquiring the land is a specified local authority[11], an urban development corporation, a national park authority, a Welsh planning board, any specified statutory undertakers[12] or a Minister[13].

1   As to the meaning of 'compulsory purchase order' see PARA 557 note 1.
2   As to the meaning of 'right' see PARA 606 note 2.
3   As to the meaning of 'land' see PARA 522 note 1. See also PARA 606 text to note 4.
4   Acquisition of Land Act 1981 Sch 3 para 4(1)(a). As to the meaning of 'local authority' see PARA 522 note 2.
5   As to the meaning of 'statutory undertakers' see PARA 561 note 8.
6   Acquisition of Land Act 1981 Sch 3 para 4(1)(b).
7   'Held inalienably' means that the land is inalienable under the National Trust Act 1907 s 21 or the National Trust Act 1939 s 8 (see OPEN SPACES AND ANCIENT MONUMENTS vol 34 (Reissue) PARA 111): Acquisition of Land Act 1981 Sch 3 para 5(3).
8   Acquisition of Land Act 1981 Sch 3 para 5(1). As to the meaning of 'National Trust' see PARA 561 note 8.
9   As to special parliamentary procedure see PARA 605. All functions of a Minister of the Crown under the Acquisition of Land Act 1981, except for s 8(4) (see PARA 564), so far as they are exercisable in relation to Wales, are now exercisable by the Welsh Ministers: see the National Assembly for Wales (Transfer of Functions) Order 1999, SI 1999/672, art 2, Sch 1; and the Government of Wales Act 2006 s 162(1), Sch 11 para 30. Orders made or confirmed by the Welsh Ministers are subject to special parliamentary procedure as provided for in the Acquisition of Land Act 1981 s 18 (see PARA 603), Sch 3 para 5: National Assembly for Wales (Transfer of Functions) Order 1999, SI 1999/672, art 2, Sch 1. As to the Welsh Assembly Government and the Welsh Ministers see CONSTITUTIONAL LAW AND HUMAN RIGHTS.
10 Acquisition of Land Act 1981 Sch 3 paras 4(2), 5(2).
11 For these purposes, 'local authority' means: (1) in relation to England, the council of a county or district, the council of a London borough, and the Common Council of the City of London; and (2) in relation to Wales, the council of a county or county borough; and this definition applies to the Isles of Scilly as if the Council of those Isles were the council of a county: Acquisition of Land Act 1981 Sch 3 para 4(4) (definition amended by virtue of the Local Government Act 1985 s 1; and the Local Government (Wales) Act 1994 s 66(6), Sch 16 para 64(2)). The Acquisition of Land Act 1981 Sch 3 para 4 refers to the Greater London Council, but this was abolished in 1986: see LOCAL GOVERNMENT vol 69 (2009) PARAS 17, 35; LONDON GOVERNMENT vol 29(2) (Reissue) PARA 33. As to areas and authorities in England and Wales see LOCAL GOVERNMENT vol 69 (2009) PARA 22 et seq. As to administrative areas and authorities in London see LONDON GOVERNMENT vol 29(2) (Reissue) PARA 29 et seq.
12 For these purposes, 'statutory undertakers' has the same meaning as it has for the purposes of the Acquisition of Land Act 1981 s 17(3) (see PARA 603 note 14): Sch 3 para 4(4). That definition may be amended by virtue of s 17(5): see PARA 603 note 14.
13 Acquisition of Land Act 1981 Sch 3 para 4(3) (amended by the Planning and Compensation Act 1991 s 70, Sch 15 para 11; the Local Government (Wales) Act 1994 s 20(4), Sch 6 para 17(2); the Environment Act 1995 ss 78, 120(3), Sch 10 para 21(2), Sch 24; the Government of Wales Act 1998 ss 128, 152, Sch 14 Pt II paras 16, 20, Sch 18 Pt V; and SI 2005/3226). 'Welsh planning board' means a board constituted under the Town and Country Planning Act 1990 s 2(1B) (see TOWN AND COUNTRY PLANNING vol 46(1) (Reissue) PARA 30): Acquisition of Land Act 1981 Sch 3 para 4(4) (definition added by the Local Government (Wales) Act 1994 Sch 6 para 17(2); and amended by the Environment Act 1995 s 120, Sch 24). As to national park authorities see OPEN SPACES AND ANCIENT MONUMENTS vol 34 (Reissue) PARA 157 et seq.

609. Acquisition of new rights over commons, open spaces and allotments. In so far as a compulsory purchase order[1] authorises the acquisition of a right[2] over land[3] forming part of a common[4], open space[5] or fuel or field garden allotment[6], it is subject to special parliamentary procedure unless the Secretary of State is satisfied[7]:

(1)   that the land, when burdened with that right, will be no less

advantageous to those persons in whom it is vested and other persons, if any, entitled to rights of common and other rights, and to the public, than it was before[8];

(2)   that the right is being acquired in order to secure the preservation or improve the management of the land[9];

(3)   that there has been or will be given in exchange for the right additional land which will be adequate as respects the persons in whom there is vested the land over which the right is to be acquired, the persons, if any, entitled to rights of common or other rights over that land, and the public, to compensate them for the disadvantages which result from the acquisition of the right, and that the additional land has been or will be vested in the persons in whom there is vested the land over which the right is to be acquired, and subject to the like rights, trusts and incidents as attach to that land apart from the compulsory purchase order[10]; or

(4)   that the land affected by the right to be acquired does not exceed 250 square yards in extent, and that the giving of other land in exchange for the right is unnecessary, whether in the interests of the persons, if any, entitled to rights of common or other rights or in the interests of the public[11],

and certifies accordingly[12].

Where it is proposed to give a certificate under these provisions, the Secretary of State must direct the acquiring authority[13] to give public notice of his intention to do so[14]. After affording opportunity to all persons interested to make representations and objections, and after causing a public local inquiry[15] to be held in any case where it appears to him to be expedient to do so, having regard to any representations or objections so made, the Secretary of State may give the certificate after considering any representations and objections made and, if an inquiry has been held, the report of the person who held the inquiry[16].

A compulsory purchase order may provide for vesting land given in exchange as mentioned in head (3) above in the persons, and subject to the rights, there mentioned, and, except where the Secretary of State has given his certificate under head (2) above, for discharging the land over which any right is to be acquired from all rights, trusts and incidents to which it has previously been subject so far as their continuance would be inconsistent with the exercise of that right[17].

1   As to the meaning of 'compulsory purchase order' see PARA 557 note 1. As to the acquisition of new rights over commons, open spaces and allotments as a result of development consent orders under the Planning Act 2008 see PARA 542.
2   As to the meaning of 'right' see PARA 606 note 2.
3   As to the meaning of 'land' see PARA 522 note 1. See also PARA 606 text to note 4.
4   For these purposes, 'common' includes any land subject to be inclosed under the Inclosure Acts 1845 to 1882, and any town or village green: Acquisition of Land Act 1981 Sch 3 para 6(5). As to the Inclosure Acts 1845 to 1882 see COMMONS.
5   For these purposes, 'open space' means any land laid out as a public garden, or used for the purpose of public recreation, or land being a disused burial ground: Acquisition of Land Act 1981 Sch 3 para 6(5).
6   For these purposes, 'fuel or field garden allotment' means any allotment set out as fuel allotment, or a field garden allotment, under an Inclosure Act: Acquisition of Land Act 1981 Sch 3 para 6(5).
7   As to special parliamentary procedure see PARA 605. As to the Secretary of State see PARA 507 note 1. All functions of a Minister of the Crown under the Acquisition of Land Act 1981, except for s 8(4) (see PARA 564), so far as they are exercisable in relation to Wales, are now exercisable by the Welsh Ministers: see the National Assembly for Wales (Transfer of Functions) Order 1999, SI 1999/672, art 2, Sch 1; and the Government of Wales Act 2006 s 162(1), Sch 11

para 30. Orders made or confirmed by the Welsh Ministers are subject to special parliamentary procedure as provided for in s 18 (see PARA 603), Sch 3 para 5 (see PARA 608): National Assembly for Wales (Transfer of Functions) Order 1999, SI 1999/672, art 2, Sch 1. As to the Welsh Assembly Government and the Welsh Ministers see CONSTITUTIONAL LAW AND HUMAN RIGHTS.

8   Acquisition of Land Act 1981 Sch 3 para 6(1)(a).
9   Acquisition of Land Act 1981 Sch 3 para 6(1)(aa) (added by the Planning and Compensation Act 1991 s 70, Sch 15 para 12(2)(a)).
10   Acquisition of Land Act 1981 Sch 3 para 6(1)(b).
11   Acquisition of Land Act 1981 Sch 3 para 6(1)(c). In the case of a compulsory purchase order under the Highways Act 1980, this provision has effect as if after the word 'extent' there were inserted the words 'or the right is required in connection with the widening or drainage of an existing highway or in connection partly with the widening and partly with the drainage of such a highway': Acquisition of Land Act 1981 Sch 3 para 6(2).
12   Acquisition of Land Act 1981 Sch 3 para 6(1). As soon as may be after the giving of the certificate, the acquiring authority must publish in one or more local newspapers circulating in the locality in which the land comprised in the order is situated a notice in the prescribed form stating that the certificate has been given: Sch 3 para 9. For the prescribed form of notice see the Compulsory Purchase of Land (Prescribed Forms) (Ministers) Regulations 2004, SI 2004/2595, reg 3(f), Schedule, Form 12; and the Compulsory Purchase of Land (Prescribed Forms) (National Assembly for Wales) Regulations 2004, SI 2004/2732, reg 3(6), Schedule, Form 12.
13   As to the meaning of 'acquiring authority' see PARA 522 note 2.
14   Acquisition of Land Act 1981 Sch 3 para 6(3) (amended by the Planning and Compensation Act 1991 Sch 15 para 12(2)(b)). The notice must be given in such form and manner as the Secretary of State may direct: Acquisition of Land Act 1981 Sch 3 para 6(3A) (added by the Planning and Compensation Act 1991 Sch 15 para 12(2)(c)).

15   As to the procedure for the holding of the inquiry see the Acquisition of Land Act 1981 s 5; the Compulsory Purchase (Inquiries Procedure) Rules 2007, SI 2007/3617; and PARA 587 et seq.
16   Acquisition of Land Act 1981 Sch 3 para 6(3). Subject to s 24 (court's power to quash certificate: see PARA 614), the certificate becomes operative on the date on which notice of the giving of it is first published in accordance with the Acquisition of Land Act 1981: s 26(2).
17   Acquisition of Land Act 1981 Sch 3 para 6(4) (amended by the Planning and Compensation Act 1991 Sch 15 para 12(2)(d)).

610. Compulsory rights orders under the Opencast Coal Act 1958. In its application to compulsory rights orders by the Opencast Coal Act 1958[1] the Acquisition of Land Act 1981 has effect subject to general[2] and specific[3] modifications[4].

1   Ie by the Opencast Coal Act 1958 s 4: see MINES, MINERALS AND QUARRIES vol 31 (2003 Reissue) PARA 422. Functions of a Minister of the Crown under the Opencast Coal Act 1958, with certain reservations, so far as they are exercisable in relation to Wales, were transferred to the National Assembly for Wales (see the National Assembly for Wales (Transfer of Functions) Order 1999, SI 1999/672, art 2, Sch 1) and are now exercisable by the Welsh Ministers (see the Government of Wales Act 2006 s 162(1), Sch 11 para 30). As to the Welsh Assembly Government and the Welsh Ministers see CONSTITUTIONAL LAW AND HUMAN RIGHTS.

2   The general modifications are that the Acquisition of Land Act 1981 Pts II–IV (ss 10–27) (see PARAS 557 et seq, 612 et seq) apply as if in those provisions: (1) any reference to a compulsory purchase order were a reference to a compulsory rights order; (2) any reference to the acquiring authority were a reference to the Coal Authority and any reference to the confirming authority were a reference to the Secretary of State; and (3) any reference to authorising the compulsory purchase of land were a reference to operating so as to confer on the Coal Authority temporary rights of occupation and use of land: s 29(1), (2) (s 29(2) amended by the Coal Industry Act 1987 s 1(2), Sch 1 para 40; and by the Coal Industry Act 1994 s 67(1), (8), Sch 9 para 27(2), Sch 11 Pt II). As to the meaning of 'compulsory purchase order' see PARA 557 note 1. As to the meaning of 'confirming authority' see PARA 557 note 4; and as to the meaning of 'land' see PARA 522 note 1. As to the Coal Authority see MINES, MINERALS AND QUARRIES vol 31 (2003 Reissue) PARA 52 et seq. As to the Secretary of State see PARA 507 note 1. All functions of a Minister of the Crown under the Acquisition of Land Act 1981, except s 8(4) (see PARA 564), so far as they are exercisable in relation to Wales, are now exercisable by the Welsh Ministers: see the National Assembly for Wales (Transfer of Functions) Order 1999, SI 1999/672, art 2,

Sch 1; and the Government of Wales Act 2006 s 162(1), Sch 11 para 30. As to the Welsh Assembly Government and the Welsh Ministers see CONSTITUTIONAL LAW AND HUMAN RIGHTS.

3   The specific modifications are as follows:
(1)   the Acquisition of Land Act 1981 Pt II has effect as if for s 12 (see PARA 560) there were substituted the provisions set out in s 29(4) (see s 29(1), (4));
(2)   s 13 (see PARA 565) applies as if for the reference to a qualifying person for the purposes of s 12(2) there were substituted a reference to any person who, in relation to the order, is a person directly concerned (s 29(5) (amended by the Planning and Compulsory Purchase Act 2004 s 118(2), Sch 7 para 12));
(3)   except where the Secretary of State is proceeding concurrently with respect to an application for opencast planning permission and a compulsory rights order, he may disregard an objection to such an order if he is satisfied that it relates to the question whether opencast planning permission should be granted or should have been granted and either: (a) it relates exclusively to that question; or (b) in so far as it relates to other matters, they consist entirely of matters which can be dealt with in the assessment of compensation, but this is without prejudice to the operation of the Acquisition of Land Act 1981 s 13 (s 29(6) (amended by the Housing and Planning Act 1986 s 39(3), Sch 8 para 18));
(4)   the Acquisition of Land Act 1981 Pt III is to apply as if s 17 (see PARA 603) were omitted (s 29(6A) (added by the Coal Industry Act 1994 s 67(1), (8), Sch 9 para 27(2)));
(5)   in the Acquisition of Land Act 1981 s 19 (see PARAS 531, 604): (a) any reference to giving other land in exchange is to be construed as a reference to making other land available during the period for which the compulsory rights order is to have effect; (b) the provisions of s 19 as to the vesting of land, and as to its being subject to the like rights, trusts and incidents as the land purchased, apply with the necessary modifications; and (c) s 19(3)(b) does not apply (s 29(7));
(6)   s 23 (see PARA 612) applies as if in s 23(1) for the first reference to the Acquisition of Land Act 1981 there were substituted a reference to the Opencast Coal Act 1958 and in the Acquisition of Land Act 1981 s 23(3)(a) the reference to the Acquisition of Land Act 1981 included a reference to the Opencast Coal Act 1958 (Acquisition of Land Act 1981 s 29(8));
(7)   the date on which the compulsory rights order becomes operative is to be that mentioned in s 26(1) (see PARA 602) or such later date, not being more than one year after confirmation of the order, as may be determined by the Secretary of State and specified in the order as confirmed (s 29(9)); and
(8)   in the application of the Acquisition of Land Act 1981 to compulsory rights orders, 'prescribed' means prescribed by regulations under the Opencast Coal Act 1958 (Acquisition of Land Act 1981 s 29(10)).
For these purposes, 'opencast planning permission' and 'persons directly concerned' have the same meanings as in the Opencast Coal Act 1958 (see MINES, MINERALS AND QUARRIES vol 31 (2003 Reissue) PARAS 407, 422): Acquisition of Land Act 1981 s 29(11) (substituted by the Housing and Planning Act 1986 s 39(3), Sch 8 Pt II para 18).
4   Acquisition of Land Act 1981 s 29(1). Any modifications of particular provisions of the Acquisition of Land Act 1981 which are specified in s 29(4)–(11) (see note 3) have effect, in relation to those provisions, in addition to the general modifications mentioned in s 29(2) (see note 2): s 29(3).

611.   Acquisition of rights in connection with the underground storage of gas.
In relation to the compulsory purchase of a right to store gas in an underground gas storage[1] or of any right as respects wells, boreholes and shafts in a storage area or protective area[2], the Acquisition of Land Act 1981, the enactments incorporated with it and the Compulsory Purchase Act 1965 have effect as if:
(1)   references, whatever the terms used, to the land[3] comprised in the compulsory purchase order[4] were construed, where the context so requires, as references to the stratum of land constituting the underground gas storage or, as the case may be, the land comprising the well, borehole or shaft; and

(2)   references to the obtaining or taking possession of the land so
      comprised were construed as references to the exercise of the right[5].
In relation to the compulsory purchase of a right to store gas in an
underground gas storage the Acquisition of Land Act 1981 has effect subject to
specified[6] modifications[7].

1   Ie under the Gas Act 1965 s 12(1): see FUEL AND ENERGY vol 19(2) (2007 Reissue) PARA 998.
2   Ie any right under the Gas Act 1965 s 13(2) or s 13(3): see FUEL AND ENERGY vol 19(2) (2007
    Reissue) PARA 999.
3   As to the meaning of 'land' see PARA 522 note 1.
4   As to the meaning of 'compulsory purchase order' see PARA 557 note 1.
5   Acquisition of Land Act 1981 s 30(1).
6   In relation to the compulsory purchase of such a right, the Acquisition of Land Act 1981 has
    effect as if in ss 16–18 (see PARAS 564, 603) references to the land comprised in the compulsory
    purchase order included references to any land held with the stratum of land constituting the
    underground gas storage and as if s 19 (see PARAS 531, 604) were omitted: s 30(2).
7   Acquisition of Land Act 1981 s 30(2). Section 28 and Sch 3 (see PARA 607 et seq) do not apply
    to a compulsory purchase to which s 30 applies: s 30(3).

(ix) Validity of Orders and Certificates

612.   Grounds for application to the High Court. If any person aggrieved[1] by:
(1)   a compulsory purchase order[2] desires to question its validity, or the
      validity of any provision contained in it, on the ground that the
      authorisation of a compulsory purchase granted by it is not empowered
      to be granted under the Acquisition of Land Act 1981 or the
      empowering enactment[3]; or
(2)   a compulsory purchase order[4] or a certificate[5] desires to question its
      validity on the ground that any relevant requirement[6] has not been
      complied with in relation to the order or certificate[7],
he may make an application to the High Court[8].
The application must be made within six weeks: (a) from the date on which
notice of the confirmation or making of the order is first published[9]; or (b) from
the date on which notice of the giving of the certificate is first published[10]; or (c)
in the case of a compulsory purchase order subject to special parliamentary
procedure[11] which is not excluded[12] from this provision, from the date on which
the order becomes operative[13].
Subject to this power to apply to the High Court, a compulsory purchase
order or certificate may not be questioned in any legal proceedings whatsoever[14],
either before or after it has been made, confirmed or given[15] and not even in a
case of fraud or bad faith[16] or where the complainant has been given no
opportunity of knowing of his right to apply to the High Court[17].

1   'Person aggrieved' means a person who has a particular grievance of his own beyond some
    inconvenience suffered by him in common with the rest of the public: see eg *R v Manchester
    Legal Aid Committee, ex p R A Brand & Co Ltd* [1952] 2 QB 413 at 431–432, [1952] 1 All ER
    480 at 491, DC, citing *R v Nicholson* [1899] 2 QB 455 at 470, CA. It must be a legal grievance:
    see *Re Sidebotham, ex p Sidebotham* (1880) 14 ChD 458 at 465, CA. In *Martin v Bearsden and
    Milngavie District Council* 1987 SLT 300, Lord Clyde drew a distinction between those who
    might fairly be described as having a close interest in the outcome and those who have no such
    interest. Owners, lessees and occupiers of the land to be purchased who are entitled to be served
    with the notice of the making of the order would come within the definition, although in *George
    v Secretary of State for the Environment* (1979) 38 P & CR 609, CA, it was held that a wife
    who had acquired a house jointly with her husband was not entitled to challenge a compulsory
    purchase order made in respect of the house where only the husband had been served with
    notice of the making of the order, since she had not been substantially prejudiced by the failure
    to serve her; sed quaere.

It may be that other persons not required to be served with notice of the making of the order would now be held to come within the definition of 'person aggrieved' despite the narrow view taken by earlier authorities: see e g *Buxton v Minister of Housing and Local Government* [1961] 1 QB 278, [1960] 3 All ER 408, in which it was held that a 'person aggrieved' was limited to a person whose legal rights had been infringed. Although there is no recent authority as to the meaning of 'persons aggrieved' under the Acquisition of Land Act 1981, the same phrase in relation to applications to quash planning permissions has been given a far wider meaning than simply those persons whose legal rights have been affected. In *Turner v Secretary of State for the Environment* (1973) 28 P & CR 123, a case under what is now the Town and Country Planning Act 1990 s 288 (see TOWN AND COUNTRY PLANNING vol 46(1) (Reissue) PARA 47), Ackner J declined to follow *Buxton v Minister of Housing and Local Government* and held that any person who, in the ordinary sense of the word, is aggrieved by the decision and certainly any person who has attended and made representations at the inquiry, should have rights to challenge the decision in the courts. It is submitted that in the absence of further authority as to the meaning of 'person aggrieved' under the Acquisition of Land Act 1981, the scope of the phrase will remain uncertain. See further ADMINISTRATIVE LAW vol 1(1) (2001 Reissue) PARA 66.

2   As to the meaning of 'compulsory purchase order' see PARA 557 note 1.
3   Acquisition of Land Act 1981 s 23(1). The empowering enactment referred to is any such enactment as is mentioned in s 1(1) (see PARA 556): s 23(1).
4   Acquisition of Land Act 1981 s 23(2)(a).
5   Ie a certificate under the Acquisition of Land Act 1981 Pt III (ss 16–22) (see PARAS 531, 564, 603–604) or s 28, Sch 3 (see PARA 606 et seq): s 23(2)(b).
6   'Relevant requirement' means any requirement of: (1) the Acquisition of Land Act 1981 or of any regulation under s 7(2) (see PARA 558); or (2) the Tribunals and Inquiries Act 1992 (see e g s 10 (duty to give reasons); and ADMINISTRATIVE LAW vol 1(1) (2001 Reissue) PARA 112) or of any rules made, or having effect as if made, under that Act (see e g the Compulsory Purchase (Inquiries Procedure) Rules 2007, SI 2007/3617; and PARA 587 et seq): Acquisition of Land Act 1981 s 23(3) (amended by the Tribunals and Inquiries Act 1992 s 18(1), Sch 3 para 14).
7   Acquisition of Land Act 1981 s 23(2).
8   Acquisition of Land Act 1981 s 23(1), (2). See *Walker v Secretary of State for Communities and Local Government; R (on the application of Walker) v Blackburn and Darwen Borough Council* [2008] EWHC 62 (Admin), [2008] All ER (D) 156 (Jan); *Maley v Secretary of State for Communities and Local Government* [2008] EWHC 2652 (Admin), [2008] All ER (D) 98 (Aug). As to the mode of application see PARA 613.
9   Acquisition of Land Act 1981 s 23(4)(b). For the purposes of s 23(4)(b), 'six weeks' means 42 days from the day following the date on which the notice of completion or making of the order was first published, and the corresponding date rule does not apply: *Okolo v Secretary of State for the Environment* [1997] 4 All ER 242, CA. The High Court has no jurisdiction to hear an application made prior to publication of the notice, and the time limit prescribed by the Acquisition of Land Act 1981 s 23(4)(b) constitutes a six-week window, which begins only with the date on which the notice of confirmation is first published: *Enterprise Inns plc v Secretary of State for the Environment, Transport and the Regions* (2000) 81 P & CR 236. Publication must be in accordance with the Acquisition of Land Act 1981 (see PARAS 565, 571): s 23(4)(b).
10 Acquisition of Land Act 1981 s 23(4)(c). Publication must be in accordance with the Acquisition of Land Act 1981 (see PARAS 565, 571): s 23(4)(c).
11 Ie an order to which the Statutory Orders (Special Procedure) Act 1945 applies: see PARA 605.
12 The Acquisition of Land Act 1981 Pt IV (ss 23–27) does not apply to an order which is confirmed by Act of Parliament under the Statutory Orders (Special Procedure) Act 1945 s 6 (see PARLIAMENT vol 34 (Reissue) PARAS 925–926): see the Acquisition of Land Act 1981 s 27.
13 Acquisition of Land Act 1981 s 23(4)(a). The date referred to is the date on which the order becomes operative under the Statutory Orders (Special Procedure) Act 1945 (see PARLIAMENT vol 34 (Reissue) PARA 912 et seq): Acquisition of Land Act 1981 s 23(4)(a). Section 23 is modified in its application to compulsory rights orders under the Opencast Coal Act 1958: see the Acquisition of Land Act 1981 s 29(8); and PARA 610.
14 See *R v Secretary of State for the Environment, ex p Ostler* [1977] QB 122, [1976] 3 All ER 90, CA. See also *Tutin v Northallerton RDC* (1947) 91 Sol Jo 383, CA, where an application to the High Court for a declaration after the expiration of the six weeks' time limit was refused as being in effect an attempt to extend the time.
15 Acquisition of Land Act 1981 s 25.
16 See *R v Secretary of State for the Environment, ex p Ostler* [1977] QB 122, [1976] 3 All ER 90, CA.

17 See *Uttoxeter UDC v Clarke* [1952] 1 All ER 1318; *Woollett v Minister of Agriculture and Fisheries* [1955] 1 QB 103, [1954] 3 All ER 529, CA.

613. Mode of application. Application to the High Court to question the validity of a compulsory purchase order or Minister's certificate is made to a single judge of the Queen's Bench Division[1] using the procedure for claims under Part 8 of the Civil Procedure Rules[2]. The claim form must be filed at the Administrative Court[3] and must state that Part 8 applies and state the question which the claimant wants the court to decide or the remedy which the claimant is seeking and the legal basis for the claim to that remedy[4]. Where the application relates to a compulsory purchase order made by an authority other than the appropriate Minister or government department, the claim form must be served on the authority that made the order[5].

1 *Practice Direction—Alternative Procedure for Claims* PD 8 paras 22.1, 22.2.
2 *Practice Direction—Alternative Procedure for Claims* PD 8 paras 9.1, 9.4. As to the procedure under CPR Pt 8 see CIVIL PROCEDURE vol 11 (2009) PARA 127 et seq.
3 *Practice Direction—Alternative Procedure for Claims* PD 8 para 22.3.
4 See CPR 8.2; and CIVIL PROCEDURE vol 11 (2009) PARA 128. The ground of the application relied upon is important. The Acquisition of Land Act 1981 s 24(2)(b) (see PARA 614) provides that the court may only quash a compulsory purchase order or any provision contained therein, or any certificate, because of a failure to comply with any requirement of the legislation, if the interests of the applicant have been substantially prejudiced, whereas where the ground is that the order is outside the powers of the Acquisition of Land Act 1981 or the empowering enactment, no such substantial prejudice need be shown. As to 'substantial prejudice' see PARA 614 note 8. The courts have, at times, had difficulty in defining under which ground an order is challengeable (see *Gordondale Investments Ltd v Secretary of State for the Environment* (1971) 23 P & CR 334 at 342, CA, per Megaw LJ); but it would appear that a failure to comply with a procedural requirement (see the Acquisition of Land Act 1981 s 23(2); and PARA 612) may also mean that the order thus made is not within the powers of the Act (see *Fairmount Investments Ltd v Secretary of State for the Environment* [1976] 2 All ER 865, [1976] 1 WLR 1255, HL, per Lord Russell).
5 *Practice Direction—Alternative Procedure for Claims* PD 8 para 22.4.

614. Court's powers. Upon an application challenging the validity of a compulsory purchase order or certificate[1] the court may, by interim order[2], suspend the operation of the compulsory purchase order or any provision contained in it, or the operation of the certificate, either generally or in so far as it affects any property of the applicant, until the final determination of the proceedings[3].

In the case of an application on the ground that an order is not empowered to be granted[4], the court, if satisfied on that ground[5], may quash the order or any provision in it, or the certificate, either generally or in so far as it affects any property of the applicant[6]. In the case of an application on the grounds of failure to comply with any relevant requirement[7], the court may similarly quash the order or any provision in it, or the certificate, if satisfied that the applicant's interests have been substantially prejudiced[8].

In considering whether to quash an order, the court may take into consideration matters occurring between the making of the order and its confirmation[9] but must limit itself to matters available to the confirming authority[10].

1 Ie an application under the Acquisition of Land Act 1981 s 23: see PARA 612. As to the meaning of 'compulsory purchase order' see PARA 557 note 1.
2 As to orders for interim remedies see CPR Pt 25; and CIVIL PROCEDURE vol 11 (2009) PARA 315.
3 Acquisition of Land Act 1981 s 24(1). Where the proper procedure for the order has not been followed, the court may prefer to quash the order rather than suspend it until the omission has

been rectified: *Richardson v Minister of Housing and Local Government* (1956) 8 P & CR 29. As to the right of appeal against a Minister's certificate see PARA 612.

4 Ie under the Acquisition of Land Act 1981 or any such enactment as is mentioned in s 1(1) (see PARA 556): s 24(2)(a).

5 Ie if satisfied that the order is, in purpose or object, ultra vires the statute under which the authority authorising it purports to act or is ultra vires the authorising authority. This will be so where any of the following are present: (1) there was no statutory basis for the order; (2) the confirming authority has made a decision which no reasonable confirming authority properly directed in the law could have made; (3) the confirming authority has taken into account an immaterial consideration or has failed to take into account a material consideration; and/or (4) confirmation of the order involved a breach of the rules of natural justice: see *Ashbridge Investments Ltd v Minister of Housing and Local Government* [1965] 3 All ER 371 at 374, [1965] 1 WLR 1320 at 1325, CA, per Lord Denning MR.

6 Acquisition of Land Act 1981 s 24(2)(a).

7 As to the meaning of 'relevant requirement' see PARA 612 note 6.

8 Acquisition of Land Act 1981 s 24(2)(b). 'Substantial prejudice' has been held to mean the loss of a chance of being better off in relation to the proposed order; and the applicant does not have to show that the decision would have been different if the requirement had been complied with: see *Hibernian Property Co Ltd v Secretary of State for the Environment* (1973) 27 P & CR 197. See also *Wilson v Secretary of State for the Environment* [1974] 1 All ER 428, [1973] 1 WLR 1083; *George v Secretary of State for the Environment* (1979) 38 P & CR 609, CA; *Martin v Bearsden and Milngavie District Council* 1987 SLT 300; *Greenwich London Borough Council v Secretary of State for the Environment and Spar Environments Ltd* [1981] JPL 809. See also *Save Britain's Heritage v Secretary of State for the Environment* [1991] 2 All ER 10, sub nom *Save Britain's Heritage v Number 1 Poultry Ltd* [1991] 1 WLR 153, HL ('substantial prejudice' caused where the reasons for the decision were so poorly expressed as to raise a real doubt as to whether the decision had been made within the powers of the relevant Act). Failure to serve notices on a person entitled to receive them, whereby, through lack of knowledge of the proposed order, he is deprived of the opportunity of objecting and of being heard at an inquiry, substantially prejudices his interests (*Brown v Ministry of Housing and Local Government* [1953] 2 All ER 1385 at 1387), unless he in fact knew of the proposed order (*Grimley v Minister of Housing and Local Government* [1971] 2 QB 96, [1971] 2 All ER 431). The onus of proof of substantial prejudice is on the applicant: see *Save Britain's Heritage v Secretary of State for the Environment* above at 24–25 and 167–168 per Lord Bridge; *Gordondale Investments Ltd v Secretary of State for the Environment* (1971) 23 P & CR 334 at 340, CA, per Lord Denning MR. As to persons entitled to receive notices see PARA 560. As to prejudice of the applicant's interests see PARA 568.

9 See *London and Westcliff Properties Ltd v Minister of Housing and Local Government* [1961] 1 All ER 610, [1961] 1 WLR 519.

10 See *Ashbridge Investments Ltd v Minister of Housing and Local Government* [1965] 3 All ER 371, [1965] 1 WLR 1320, CA.

(4) CONDITIONS PRECEDENT TO EXERCISE OF COMPULSORY POWERS

(i) Subscription of Capital

615. Subscription of capital under binding contract to pay. Under the Lands Clauses Acts[1], where an undertaking is intended to be carried into effect by means of capital to be subscribed by the undertakers[2], the whole of the capital or estimated sum for defraying the expenses of the undertaking must be subscribed under a binding contract for payment before any of the powers in relation to the compulsory taking[3] can be put into force[4]. When the Lands Clauses Acts are not incorporated and the special Act[5] makes no provision in that behalf, the undertakers are not required to show a sufficiency of funds[6]; but if the undertaking cannot be completed, and the undertakers have made a mistake as to the sum necessary to complete it, an injunction may be granted to restrain further proceedings by them[7].

1   As to the Lands Clauses Acts see PARA 509 note 1.
2   As to the meaning of 'undertakers' see PARA 511.
3   For this purpose the service of notice to treat is not an exercise of compulsory powers: see *Guest v Poole and Bournemouth Rly Co* (1870) LR 5 CP 553; *Re Uxbridge and Rickmansworth Rly Co* (1890) 43 ChD 536, CA; and see *Goodwin Foster Brown Ltd v Derby Corpn* [1934] 2 KB 23. As to taking possession of an easement see *Great Western Rly Co v Swindon and Cheltenham Rly Co* (1884) 9 App Cas 787, HL.
4   Lands Clauses Consolidation Act 1845 s 16. As to evidence of subscription by a certificate of two justices see s 17; and see *Ystalyfera Iron Co v Neath and Brecon Rly Co* (1873) LR 17 Eq 142. The restriction does not apply to additional works by an existing company: see *R v Great Western Rly Co* (1852) 1 E & B 253; *Weld v South Western Rly Co* (1863) 32 Beav 340. Any exercise of powers contrary to this requirement is ultra vires: *R v Ambergate, Nottingham, and Boston, and Eastern Junction Rly Co* (1853) 1 E & B 372. As to the validity of companies' acts and the power of directors to bind a company see COMPANIES vol 7(1) (2004 Reissue) PARAS 430–432.
5   As to the meaning of 'special Act' see PARAS 509, 514.
6   *Salmon v Randall* (1838) 3 My & Cr 439.
7   *Agar v Regent's Canal Co* (1814) 1 Swan 250n; *King's Lynn Corpn v Pemberton* (1818) 1 Swan 244 at 250; *Blakemore v Glamorganshire Canal Navigation* (1832) 1 My & K 154 at 164; *Lee v Milner* (1837) 2 Y & C Ex 611 at 619; *Gray v Liverpool and Bury Rly Co* (1846) 9 Beav 391 at 394, 400; *Cohen v Wilkinson* (1849) 1 Mac & G 481. See also CIVIL PROCEDURE vol 11 (2009) PARA 331 et seq.

(ii) Notice to Treat

616. Notice to treat to precede exercise of compulsory powers. If the undertakers[1] or the acquiring authority[2] need to use their compulsory powers[3] to purchase any of the land subject to compulsory purchase[4], they must give a notice (a 'notice to treat')[5] to all persons interested in[6], or having power to sell and convey or release[7], the land so far as known to them after making diligent inquiry[8]. A notice to treat ceases to have effect at the end of the period of three years beginning with the date on which it is served unless:

(1)   the compensation has been agreed or awarded or has been either paid or paid into court[9];
(2)   a general vesting declaration has been executed[10];
(3)   the acquiring authority has entered on and taken possession of the land specified in the notice[11]; or
(4)   the question of compensation has been referred to the Upper Tribunal[12].

The time limit may be extended by agreement with the acquiring authority[13]. Where a notice to treat ceases to have effect[14], the acquiring authority must immediately give notice of that fact to the person on whom the notice to treat was served and any other person who, since it was served, could have made an agreement[15] to have the time limit extended[16]. The acquiring authority is liable to pay compensation to any person entitled to a notice to treat for any loss or expenses occasioned to him by the giving of the notice and its ceasing to have effect[17]. In default of agreement, the amount of any such compensation is to be determined by the Upper Tribunal[18].

A notice to treat may bear a date different from that on which it is served[19]. There is no specified form of notice[20] but every notice to treat must:

(a)   give particulars of the land to which it relates;
(b)   demand particulars of the recipient's estate and interest in the land, and of the claim he makes in respect of the land; and
(c)   state that the undertakers or the acquiring authority are willing to treat

for the purchase of the land and as to the compensation to be made for the damage which may be sustained by reason of the execution of the works[21].

If the appropriate person is prevented from treating because he is absent from the United Kingdom, or if he cannot be found after diligent inquiry has been made, the compensation or purchase money, including compensation for severance or other injurious affection, must be determined by the valuation of a surveyor and the money paid into court[22].

1   As to the meaning of 'undertakers' see PARA 511.
2   As to the meaning of 'acquiring authority' see PARA 549 note 5.
3   As to the power to purchase by agreement without using such powers see PARA 550.
4   As to the meaning of 'land' see PARA 549 note 1. See also PARA 511 text to note 7. As to the meaning of 'subject to compulsory purchase' see PARA 549 note 2.
5   Although there is some authority for saying that, at least in some circumstances, the service of a notice to treat is not an exercise of compulsory powers, but is a condition precedent to their exercise (see *Guest v Poole and Bournemouth Rly Co* (1870) LR 5 CP 553; *Re Uxbridge and Rickmansworth Rly Co* (1890) 43 ChD 536, CA; *Goodwin Foster Brown Ltd v Derby Corpn* [1934] 2 KB 23), it is clear that the service of a notice within the prescribed time establishes the right to set in motion the machinery to complete a compulsory purchase (*Tiverton and North Devon Rly Co v Loosemore* (1884) 9 App Cas 480 at 484, HL; and see PARA 617 note 3). See also *Grice v Dudley Corpn* [1958] Ch 329 at 338, [1957] 2 All ER 673 at 678 per Upjohn J.
6   As to such persons see PARA 619.
7   As to such persons see PARA 553.
8   Lands Clauses Consolidation Act 1845 s 18 (where that Act is incorporated: see PARA 509); Compulsory Purchase Act 1965 s 5(1) (where that Act applies: see PARA 513). There is, however, no requirement to serve a notice to treat where the authority seeks to acquire commonable rights and has followed the procedure for their acquisition laid down in Sch 4 (see COMMONS): see *Mid Glamorgan County Council v Ogwr Borough Council* (1994) 68 P & CR 1, CA; on appeal sub nom *Lewis v Mid Glamorgan County Council* [1995] 1 All ER 760, [1995] 1 WLR 313, HL.
9   Compulsory Purchase Act 1965 s 5(2A)(a) (s 5(2A)–(2E) added by the Planning and Compensation Act 1991 s 67). As to payment into court see PARAS 555, 640.
10 Compulsory Purchase Act 1965 s 5(2A)(b) (as added: see note 9). See the Compulsory Purchase (Vesting Declarations) Act 1981 s 4: see PARA 687.
11 Compulsory Purchase Act 1965 s 5(2A)(c) (as added: see note 9).
12 Compulsory Purchase Act 1965 s 5(2A)(d) (as added (see note 9); amended by SI 2009/1307).
13 See the Compulsory Purchase Act 1965 s 5(2B) (as added: see note 9). In the case of such agreement, the notice to treat ceases to have effect at the end of the period as extended unless (1) any of the events referred to in heads (1)–(4) in the text have then taken place; or (2) the parties have agreed to a further extension of the period, in which case this provision applies again at the end of the period as further extended, and so on: s 5(2B) (as so added).
14 Ie by virtue of the Compulsory Purchase Act 1965 s 5(2A) or s 5(2B): see the text and notes 9–13.
15 Ie under the Compulsory Purchase Act 1965 s 5(2B): see the text and note 13.
16 Compulsory Purchase Act 1965 s 5(2C)(a) (as added: see note 9). Payments on account of such compensation may be made, which may be recoverable if it is later agreed or determined that the person making the payments is not liable to pay compensation, or that the amount paid was excessive: Planning and Compensation Act 1991 s 80(2), (3), Sch 18 Pt II.
17 Compulsory Purchase Act 1965 s 5(2C)(b) (as added: see note 9).
18 Compulsory Purchase Act 1965 s 5(2D) (as added (see note 9); amended by SI 2009/1307). Compensation so payable to any person carries interest at the rate prescribed under the Land Compensation Act 1961 s 32 (see PARA 641) from the date on which he was entitled to be given notice under the Compulsory Purchase Act 1965 s 5(2C) until payment: s 5(2E) (as added: see note 9). Payments on account of such interest may be made, which may be recoverable if it is later agreed or determined that the person making the payments is not liable to pay compensation, or that the amount paid was excessive: Planning and Compensation Act 1991 s 80(2), (3), Sch 18 Pt II.
19 *Cohen v Haringey London Borough Council* (1980) 42 P & CR 6, CA.
20 *Coats v Caledonian Rly Co* (1904) 6 F 1042, Ct of Sess; *Renton v North British Rly Co* (1845) 8 D 247, Ct of Sess.

21　Lands Clauses Consolidation Act 1845 s 18; Compulsory Purchase Act 1965 s 5(2)(a)–(c). See also *Lewis v Hackney London Borough Council* [1990] 2 EGLR 15, CA. As to the meaning of 'works' see PARA 549 note 3. See also PARA 511 text to note 4.
22　See PARA 718. As to service of the notice to treat on the land in such a case see PARA 618. 'United Kingdom' means Great Britain and Northern Ireland: Interpretation Act 1978 s 5, Sch 1. 'Great Britain' means England, Scotland and Wales: Union with Scotland Act 1706, preamble art I; Interpretation Act 1978 s 22(1), Sch 2 para 5(a). Neither the Isle of Man nor the Channel Islands are within the United Kingdom. See further CONSTITUTIONAL LAW AND HUMAN RIGHTS vol 8(2) (Reissue) PARA 3.

617. Time for service of notice to treat. The time within which a notice to treat must be served may be prescribed by the empowering enactment or special Act[1]. If the Lands Clauses Acts are incorporated[2] the powers for the compulsory purchase or taking of land may not be exercised after (1) the expiration of the prescribed period; and (2) if no period is prescribed, the expiration of three years from the passing of the special Act[3].

If the special Act also limits the period of execution of the works and a notice to treat has been given within the prescribed time, but no further step has been taken by the acquiring authority or the owners, and the period for completion of the works has expired, neither of the parties can claim the benefit of the notice unless the delay can be explained[4].

The period for exercising compulsory powers may be extended by a subsequent Act which may validate notices previously given[5].

In the case of a compulsory purchase authorised by a compulsory purchase order to which the Compulsory Purchase Act 1965 applies[6], the enactment under which the purchase is empowered and the compulsory purchase order are deemed to be the special Act[7] and the time limit for service of the notice to treat is three years from the date when the order became operative[8].

1　As to the meaning of 'special Act' see PARAS 509, 514.
2　As to the Lands Clauses Acts see PARA 509 note 1.
3　Lands Clauses Consolidation Act 1845 s 123. For the purpose of the right to exercise compulsory powers it is sufficient if a notice to treat is served within the prescribed time: see *Marquis of Salisbury v Great Northern Rly Co* (1852) 17 QB 840; *Tiverton and North Devon Rly Co v Loosemore* (1884) 9 App Cas 480 at 493, HL. In calculating the period, the day on which the special Act was passed is excluded: see *Goldsmiths' Co v West Metropolitan Rly Co* [1904] 1 KB 1, CA. Where periods are prescribed for taking land for specific purposes, but none for other purposes, the three years' limit will apply to those other purposes: *Seymour v London and South Western Rly Co* (1859) 5 Jur NS 753. If the Lands Clauses Consolidation Act 1845 s 123 is not incorporated and no time is limited by the special Act, a notice to treat may be served so long as power to do so is required for the purposes of the Act: see *Salmon v Randall* (1838) 3 My & Cr 439; *Thicknesse v Lancaster Canal Co* (1838) 4 M & W 472.
4　*Tiverton and North Devon Rly Co v Loosemore* (1884) 9 App Cas 480 at 493, HL; *R v Birmingham and Oxford Junction Rly Co* (1851) 15 QB 634, Ex Ch; *Sparrow v Oxford, Worcester and Wolverhampton Rly Co* (1851) 9 Hare 436 (on appeal (1852) 2 De GM & G 94); and cf *Brocklebank v Whitehaven Junction Rly Co* (1847) 5 Ry & Can Cas 373; *Wood v North Staffordshire Rly Co* (1849) 3 De G & Sm 368. As to enforcing rights after the period fixed for the completion of the works see *Richmond v North London Rly Co* (1868) 3 Ch App 679. Works may be completed after that date if it is not necessary to rely upon statutory powers: see *Great Western Rly Co v Midland Rly Co* [1908] 2 Ch 644, CA; affd sub nom *Midland Rly Co v Great Western Rly Co* [1909] AC 445, HL.
5　*Ystalyfera Iron Co v Neath and Brecon Rly Co* (1873) LR 17 Eq 142; *Bentley v Rotherham and Kimberworth Local Board of Health* (1876) 4 ChD 588; and see *Williams v South Wales Rly Co* (1849) 3 De G & Sm 354; *Dun River Navigation Co v North Midland Rly Co* (1838) 1 Ry & Can Cas 135.
6　As to such orders see PARA 513.
7　See PARA 514.
8　Compulsory Purchase Act 1965 s 4. The date of operation of such an order is the date on which notice of the making or confirmation of the order is published, unless another date is stipulated

in the order: see the Acquisition of Land Act 1981 s 26(1); and PARA 602. No account is to be taken of any period during which an authority is prevented from serving notice to treat by virtue of the Housing Act 1985 s 305 (building subject to compulsory purchase order under s 290 becoming listed after the making of the order; no service of notice to treat without the Secretary of State's consent to demolition: see HOUSING vol 22 (2006 Reissue) PARA 436): s 305(7).

The Compulsory Purchase Act 1965 s 4 does not apply to an acquisition of land under the Crossrail Act 2008 s 6(1): see Sch 6 Pt 2 para 3; and RAILWAYS, INLAND WATERWAYS AND CROSS-COUNTRY PIPELINES vol 39(1A) (Reissue) PARA 325.

618. Mode of service of notice to treat. In order that both parties may be bound, a notice to treat must be served in accordance with the statutory requirements[1].

If a notice to treat is not served on the proper person within the prescribed period, it may not be adopted by him by service of a counter-notice[2]; but if the counter-notice is acted upon the parties may be estopped from setting up the invalidity of the notice to treat[3]. Service on the occupier is not sufficient unless it can be shown that the owner could not be found, and if the notice relates to land in the occupation of more than one tenant, the notice for the owner must be served on each occupier, and must show that it is for the owner, service on an agent being insufficient[4].

1   *Shepherd v Norwich Corpn* (1885) 30 ChD 553 at 573; *R v Great Northern Rly Co* (1876) 2 QBD 151 at 154–155; *Fagan v Knowsley Metropolitan Borough* (1985) 50 P & CR 363, CA. The provisions of the Acquisition of Land Act 1981 s 6 (see PARA 561) apply to the service of notices to treat under the Compulsory Purchase Act 1965: s 30 (substituted by the Acquisition of Land Act 1981 s 34(1), Sch 4 para 14(4)). See also the Lands Clauses Consolidation Act 1845 ss 19, 20.

2   *Treadwell v London and South Western Rly Co* (1884) 54 LJCh 565, 51 LT 894. A counter-notice is one which, in relevant circumstances, may be served by the owner requiring all land to be taken where notice to take part only is given: see PARA 625. As to service on the undertakers under the Lands Clauses Consolidation Act 1845 see s 134. As to the meaning of 'undertakers' see PARA 511.

3   *Pinchin v London and Blackwall Rly Co* (1854) 1 K & J 34; on appeal 5 De GM & G 851, 24 LJCh 417.

4   *Shepherd v Norwich Corpn* (1885) 30 ChD 553 at 570. See also *Fagan v Knowsley Metropolitan Borough* (1985) 50 P & CR 363, CA (notice served on brother as agent of owner living in Australia).

619. Persons entitled to be served with notice to treat. The persons entitled to be served with a notice to treat are all those who are interested in the land[1] or who have power to sell and convey or release it[2]. The freehold owner is entitled to be served, as is a person entitled under an enforceable contract of sale[3] or a person entitled to an option to purchase[4], but not a person entitled to a mere right of pre-emption[5].

Where any ecclesiastical property is vested in the incumbent of a benefice which is vacant, it is treated as being vested in the Diocesan Board of Finance for the diocese in which the land is situated, and any notice to treat is served, or is deemed to have been served, accordingly[6].

Lessees must be served, including those who are holding under agreements equivalent to a lease in equity[7], but tenants with an interest from year to year or less are not entitled to a notice[8]. Mining lessees who have a right to sink pits in the surface of the land to be acquired are also entitled to a notice[9]. Mortgagees, including equitable mortgagees, must be served[10]. Licensees are not entitled to a notice to treat[11] unless there is special power to purchase such rights[12].

Where the owner of an interest in land creates an interest after the service on him of a notice to treat, that interest is not entitled to a notice to treat and compensation, and some interests, although entitled to a notice to treat, may be disregarded by the Upper Tribunal[13].

There is no power compulsorily to take less than the whole interest in the land and create and require a leasehold interest or to create and acquire an easement over the land unless there is a special power to acquire such a right[14]. If, however, there is such a power and the works cannot be executed before the easement is acquired, the owner of the land must be served with a notice to treat in respect of the easement[15]. So also, where there is a special power to acquire compulsorily a stratum only of the land, the owner of the land is entitled to a notice to treat[16].

Persons who have existing rights against the land to be acquired, such as rights of way or other easements or the benefit of restrictive covenants, are not entitled to a notice to treat because there is no power to acquire those rights unless special provision is made, but only a power injuriously to affect them[17]. If a power were given to acquire those rights, the right to a notice to treat would depend on the terms of the power[18].

1 See PARA 616; and the text and notes 2–18.
2 See PARA 553.
3 *Hillingdon Estates Co v Stonefield Estates Ltd* [1952] Ch 627, [1952] 1 All ER 853.
4 *Oppenheimer v Minister of Transport* [1942] 1 KB 242, [1941] 3 All ER 485.
5 *Clout v Metropolitan and District Rlys Joint Committee* (1883) 48 LT 257. This includes a person who has acquired rights as a squatter: *Perry v Clissold* [1907] AC 73, PC. As to the effect of a notice to treat in respect of land subject to a lease see PARA 633.
6 Church of England (Miscellaneous Provisions) Measure 1978 s 8(1) (amended by the Church of England (Miscellaneous Provisions) Measure 2006 s 11). For these purposes, 'ecclesiastical property' means land being or forming part of a church subject to the jurisdiction of a bishop of any diocese (other than the diocese of Sodor and Man) or the site of such a church, or being or forming part of a burial ground subject to such jurisdiction; and 'land' includes anything falling within any definition of that expression in the enactment under which the purchase is authorised: Church of England (Miscellaneous Provisions) Measure 1978 s 8(2). See further ECCLESIASTICAL LAW.
7 *Re King's Leasehold Estates, ex p East of London Rly Co* (1873) LR 16 Eq 521; *Sweetman v Metropolitan Rly Co* (1864) 1 Hem & M 543; *Birmingham and District Land Co v London and North Western Rly Co* (1888) 40 ChD 268, CA.
8 See PARAS 699, 702. This includes a person who has acquired rights as a squatter: *Perry v Clissold* [1907] AC 73, PC.
9 *Re Masters and Great Western Rly Co* [1901] 2 KB 84, CA.
10 *Rogers v Kingston-upon-Hull Dock Co* (1864) 34 LJCh 165; *Martin v London, Chatham and Dover Rly Co* (1866) 1 Ch App 501 at 505; *Cooke v LCC* [1911] 1 Ch 604 at 609; *University Life Assurance Society v Metropolitan Rly Co* [1866] WN 167; *London and India Dock Co v North London Rly Co* (1903) Times, 6 February. As to special powers for acquisition of mortgagees' interests see further PARA 712.
11 See *Frank Warr & Co Ltd v LCC* [1904] 1 KB 713, CA (licence to use theatre premises for business of supplying refreshments), following *Municipal Freehold Land Co v Metropolitan and District Rlys Joint Committee* (1883) Cab & El 184 (licence to use boardroom and desk at certain times); *Bird v Great Eastern Rly Co* (1865) 19 CBNS 268 (licence to shoot over land); but the owner of the land may be liable for damages for breach of contract (see *Walton Harvey Ltd v Walker and Homfrays Ltd* [1931] 1 Ch 274, CA), and must claim for disturbance in respect of it: see PARA 814.
12 See note 18.
13 See PARA 632. As to the Upper Tribunal see PARA 720; and ADMINISTRATIVE LAW.
14 See PARA 533 note 2. As to easements generally see EASEMENTS AND PROFITS A PRENDRE.
15 See *Ramsden v Manchester, South Junction and Altrincham Rly Co* (1848) 1 Exch 723; and PARA 533 note 2. If the power to execute the works can be exercised without first acquiring a right or easement over the land, then the notice prescribed by the special Act will be sufficient and no notice to treat need be served, even if land is subsequently vested in the acquiring

authority by virtue of the works executed: see *West Midlands Joint Electricity Authority v Pitt* [1932] 2 KB 1, CA; *Thornton v Nutter* (1867) 31 JP 419; *Roderick v Aston Local Board* (1877) 5 ChD 328, CA; *North London Rly Co v Metropolitan Board of Works* (1859) 28 LJCh 909; *Hughes v Metropolitan Board of Works* (1861) 4 LT 318. The execution of works such as the erection of posts is merely a power to affect the land injuriously: see *Escott v Newport Corpn* [1904] 2 KB 369. As to the meaning of 'special Act' see PARAS 509, 514.

16 See *Farmer v Waterloo and City Rly Co* [1895] 1 Ch 527; and PARA 534 note 2.
17 See PARA 532.
18 For a power to acquire rights over and against the land see eg the National Parks and Access to the Countryside Act 1949 ss 103(6), 114(1); and OPEN SPACES AND ANCIENT MONUMENTS vol 34 (Reissue) PARA 204.

620. Service of further notice to treat. The acquiring authority may serve the same person with more than one notice to treat in respect of different areas of land. Thus, if the land specified in one notice is not sufficient for the purposes of its undertaking, it may serve another for the purchase of additional land[1], or, having purchased the surface under a power to purchase the surface and omit the minerals, it may serve a further notice in respect of the minerals[2]. If a notice to treat has been validly withdrawn, the authority may serve another in respect of the same or part of the same property, so long as the time for compulsory purchase remains unexpired[3]. Similarly, if the land required is mortgaged and only the mortgagor has been served with notice, the authority may subsequently serve a notice to treat on the mortgagee, although it may have entered into possession of the land as against the mortgagor[4].

1 *Simpson v Lancaster and Carlisle Rly Co* (1847) 15 Sim 580; *Stamps v Birmingham and Stour Valley Rly Co* (1848) 2 Ph 673; and see *Williams v South Wales Rly Co* (1849) 3 De G & Sm 354.
2 *Errington v Metropolitan District Rly Co* (1882) 19 ChD 559, CA. As to the exclusion of minerals see PARAS 515, 534.
3 *Ashton Vale Iron Co Ltd v Bristol Corpn* [1901] 1 Ch 591, CA.
4 *Cooke v LCC* [1911] 1 Ch 604. See PARA 711.

(iii) Owner's Rights where Notice to Treat is for Part Only of Land

621. Restriction on taking part only of property. When the notice to treat[1] relates to part only of any agricultural land, house or other building or factory, and the party served is able and willing to sell and convey the whole of his interest in it, then, in cases where the appropriate statutory provision applies, he may require the undertakers to purchase and take the whole, and he cannot be required at any time to sell and convey a part only[2].

If a notice to treat will sever land and leave less than half an acre in the owner's hands he may, in certain circumstances, require that to be purchased[3]; and if a notice to treat requires land to be taken so as to intersect the owner's land and he requires communications to be made, the undertakers may in certain circumstances require him to sell the two pieces[4].

It is a common provision in special Acts to authorise the undertakers expressly to take specified parts only of houses, buildings or manufactories[5].

1 See PARA 616 et seq.
2 See PARAS 622, 625, 628.
3 See PARA 629.
4 See PARA 630.
5 Eg to take the forecourts of houses in order to widen a street: see the clause construed by the court in *Genders v LCC* [1915] 1 Ch 1, CA. As to the meaning of 'special Act' see PARAS 509, 514.

622. Counter-notice where notice to treat is for part of agricultural land.
Where an acquiring authority[1] serves notice to treat, or is deemed to have served
a notice to treat[2], in respect of any agricultural land[3] on a person, whether in
occupation or not, who has a greater interest in the land than as tenant for a year
or from year to year[4], and that person has such an interest in other agricultural
land[5] comprised in the same agricultural unit[6] as that to which the notice relates,
the person on whom the notice is served (the 'claimant') may, within the period
of two months beginning with the date of the service or deemed service of the
notice to treat, serve on the acquiring authority a counter-notice (1) claiming that
the other land is not reasonably capable of being farmed[7], either by itself or in
conjunction with other relevant land[8], as a separate agricultural unit[9]; and (2)
requiring the acquiring authority to purchase his interest in the whole of the
other land[10]. Where he serves a counter-notice, the claimant must also, within
the same two months' period, serve a copy of it on any other person who has an
interest in the land to which the requirement in the counter-notice relates,
although failure to do so will not invalidate the counter-notice[11].

This power is without prejudice to the power of an owner of agricultural land
who would otherwise be left with less than half an acre to insist[12] on the whole
being taken, or the power of the acquiring authority to require the owner to sell
to it land[13] of less than half an acre which the owner would otherwise be left
with after severance[14].

These provisions[15] apply in relation to the acquisition of interests in land,
whether compulsorily or by agreement, by government departments which are
authorities possessing compulsory purchase powers[16] as they apply in relation to
the acquisition of interests in land by such authorities which are not government
departments[17].

1   In relation to an interest in land, 'acquiring authority' means the person or body of persons by
    whom the interest is, or is proposed to be, acquired: Land Compensation Act 1961 s 39(1)
    (definition applied by the Land Compensation Act 1973 s 87(1)).
2   Ie a notice to treat deemed to have been served by virtue of any of the provisions of the
    Compulsory Purchase (Vesting Declarations) Act 1981 Pt III (ss 7–9) (see PARAS 689, 693–694):
    see the Land Compensation Act 1973 s 53(5) (amended by the Land Compensation (Scotland)
    Act 1973 s 81(1), Sch 2 Pt I; the Compulsory Purchase (Vesting Declarations) Act 1981 s 16(1),
    Sch 3; and the Planning (Consequential Provisions) Act 1990 s 4, Sch 1 Pt I).
3   'Agricultural land' means land used for agriculture which is so used for the purposes of a trade
    or business, or which is designated by the Secretary of State for the purposes of the Agriculture
    Act 1947 s 109(1), and includes any land so designated as land which in the opinion of the
    Secretary of State ought to be brought into use for agriculture: s 109(1) (definition applied by
    the Land Compensation Act 1973 s 87(1) (amended by the Land Compensation (Scotland)
    Act 1973 Sch 2 Pt I)). Such designations must not extend to land used as pleasure grounds,
    private gardens or allotment gardens, or to land kept or preserved mainly or exclusively for the
    purposes of sport or recreation, except where the Secretary of State is satisfied that its use for
    agriculture would not be inconsistent with its use for those purposes and it is so stated in the
    designation: Agriculture Act 1947 s 109(1) proviso (definition as so applied). 'Agriculture'
    includes horticulture, fruit and seed growing, dairy farming, livestock keeping and breeding, the
    use of land as grazing, meadow or osier land, market gardens and nursery grounds, and the use
    of land for woodlands where that use is ancillary to the farming of land for other agricultural
    purposes; and 'agricultural' is to be construed accordingly: s 109(3) (definition as so applied).
        Note that functions which were exercised by the Minister of Agriculture, Fisheries and Food
    have been transferred to the Secretary of State (see PARA 507 note 1): see the Ministry of
    Agriculture, Fisheries and Food (Dissolution) Order 2002, SI 2002/794. Functions of a Minister
    of the Crown under the Agriculture Act 1947 are, so far as exercisable in relation to Wales, now
    exercised by the Welsh Ministers: see the National Assembly for Wales (Transfer of Functions)
    Order 1999, SI 1999/672, art 2, Sch 1; and the Government of Wales Act 2006 s 162(1), Sch 11
    para 30. As to the Welsh Assembly Government and the Welsh Ministers see CONSTITUTIONAL
    LAW AND HUMAN RIGHTS.

4　As to the right of a tenant for a year, or from year to year, to serve a counter-notice when served with a notice of entry on part of his holding see the Land Compensation Act 1973 ss 55, 56(1); and PARAS 703–705.

5　Where an acquiring authority has served a notice to treat in respect of any of the other agricultural land, or such a notice is deemed to have been served by virtue of the Town and Country Planning Act 1990 ss 137–144 (see TOWN AND COUNTRY PLANNING vol 46(2) (Reissue) PARA 966 et seq) then unless and until that notice to treat is withdrawn, the provisions of the Land Compensation Act 1973 s 53 and s 54 (effect of counter-notice: see PARA 623) have effect as if that land did not form part of that other agricultural land: s 53(4) (amended by the Planning (Consequential Provisions) Act 1990 Sch 2 para 29(9)).

6　'Agricultural unit' means land which is occupied as a unit for agricultural purposes, including any dwellinghouse or other building occupied by the same person for the purpose of farming the land: Town and Country Planning Act 1990 s 171(1) (definition applied by the Land Compensation Act 1973 s 87(1) (amended by the Planning (Consequential Provisions) Act 1990 Sch 2 para 29(1))).

7　For these purposes, references to the farming of land include references to the carrying on in relation to the land of any agricultural activities: Land Compensation Act 1973 s 87(1).

8　'Other relevant land' means (1) land comprised in the same agricultural unit as the land to which the notice to treat or deemed notice to treat relates, being land in which the claimant does not have an interest greater than as tenant for a year or from year to year (Land Compensation Act 1973 s 53(3)(a), (5)); and (2) land comprised in any other agricultural unit occupied by him on the date of the service of the notice to treat or deemed notice to treat, being land in respect of which he is then entitled to a greater interest than as tenant for a year or from year to year (s 53(3)(b), (5)). Where the acquiring authority has served such a notice to treat in respect of the other relevant land, or such a notice is deemed to have been served by virtue of the Town and Country Planning Act 1990 ss 137–144 (see TOWN AND COUNTRY PLANNING vol 46(2) (Reissue) PARA 966 et seq), then unless and until that notice is withdrawn, the provisions of the Land Compensation Act 1973 ss 53, 54 have effect as if that land did not constitute other relevant land: s 53(4) (as amended: see note 5).

9　Land Compensation Act 1973 s 53(1)(a).

10　Land Compensation Act 1973 s 53(1)(b).

11　Land Compensation Act 1973 s 53(2).

12　Ie under the Lands Clauses Consolidation Act 1845 s 93; or the Compulsory Purchase Act 1965 s 8(2): see PARA 629.

13　Ie under the Lands Clauses Consolidation Act 1845 s 94; or the Compulsory Purchase Act 1965 s 8(3): see PARA 630.

14　Land Compensation Act 1973 s 53(6) (amended by the Land Compensation (Scotland) Act 1977 Sch 2 Pt I).

15　Ie the Land Compensation Act 1973 Pt IV (ss 44–64): see PARA 623 et seq.

16　As to the meaning of 'authority possessing compulsory purchase powers' see PARA 763 note 6 (definition applied by the Land Compensation Act 1973 s 87(1)).

17　Land Compensation Act 1973 s 84(2).

623.　Effect of counter-notice as to agricultural land compelling purchase of other land outside compulsory purchase powers. If the acquiring authority[1] does not, within the two months' period beginning with the date of service of a counter-notice[2], agree in writing to accept the counter-notice as valid, the claimant[3] or the authority may, within two months after the end of that period, refer it to the Upper Tribunal (the 'Tribunal'); and on that reference the Tribunal must determine whether the claim in the counter-notice is justified and declare the counter-notice valid or invalid in accordance with that determination[4].

Where a counter-notice is accepted as, or declared to be, valid, the acquiring authority is deemed (1) to be authorised to acquire compulsorily, under the enactment by virtue of which it is empowered to acquire the land in respect of which the notice to treat was served or deemed to be served, the claimant's interest in the land to which the requirement in the counter-notice relates[5]; and (2) to have served a notice to treat in respect of that land on the date on which the first-mentioned notice to treat was served[6]. There is no power to withdraw that notice to treat deemed to have been served[7].

A claimant may withdraw a counter-notice at any time before the compensation payable in respect of a compulsory acquisition in pursuance of the counter-notice has been determined by the Tribunal, or at any time before the end of six weeks beginning with the date on which the compensation is so determined; and where a counter-notice is so withdrawn any notice to treat deemed to have been served in consequence of it is to be deemed to have been withdrawn[8].

The compensation payable in respect of the acquisition of an interest in land in pursuance of a notice to treat deemed to have been served by virtue of these provisions must be assessed on the basis of certain statutory assumptions[9].

1   As to the meaning of 'acquiring authority' see PARA 622 note 1.
2   Ie under the Land Compensation Act 1973 s 53(1): see PARA 622.
3   As to the meaning of 'claimant' see PARA 622.
4   Land Compensation Act 1973 s 54(1) (amended by SI 2009/1307). As to the Upper Tribunal see PARA 720; and ADMINISTRATIVE LAW.
5   Land Compensation Act 1973 s 54(2)(a).
6   Land Compensation Act 1973 s 54(2)(b).
7   See the Land Compensation Act 1973 s 54(4), which excludes the power conferred by the Land Compensation Act 1961 s 31 (see PARA 636) but which is expressed to be without prejudice to the Land Compensation Act 1973 s 54(3) (deemed withdrawal: see the text and note 8).
8   Land Compensation Act 1973 s 54(3) (amended by SI 2009/1307).
9   Land Compensation Act 1973 s 54(5). The assumptions referred to are those mentioned in s 5(2), (3), (4): see PARA 896.

624.   Effect of counter-notice as to agricultural land where lessee's interest only in land outside compulsory purchase powers compelled to be taken.   Where there is power to purchase land compulsorily, there is normally no power to require a leasehold interest only in the land to be acquired unless there is special provision to the contrary[1]. Where, however, an acquiring authority[2] is compelled to purchase an interest in other land by a counter-notice[3], the authority may find itself with the lessee's interest in the other land but without the lessor's interest. Where, therefore, the authority becomes, or will become, entitled[4] to a lease of any land, but not to the lessor's interest, the authority may offer to surrender the lease to the lessor on such terms as it considers reasonable[5].

The question of what terms are reasonable may be referred to the Upper Tribunal (the 'Tribunal') by the authority or the lessor and if, at the expiration of three months after the date of the offer to surrender the lease, the authority and the lessor have not agreed on that question, and that question has not been referred to the Tribunal by the lessor, it must be so referred by the authority[6]. If the question is referred to the Tribunal, the lessor is deemed to have accepted the surrender of the lease at the expiration of one month after the date of the Tribunal's determination or on such other date as the Tribunal may direct, and to have agreed with the authority on the terms of the surrender which the Tribunal has held to be reasonable[7].

Where the lessor refuses to accept any sum payable to him by virtue of the Tribunal's decision or refuses or fails to make out his title to the acquiring authority's satisfaction, that authority may pay into court any sum so payable to the lessor[8]. Where an acquiring authority which becomes so entitled to the lease of any land is a body incorporated by or under any enactment, the authority's corporate powers will, if they would not otherwise do so, include power to farm that land[9].

1   See PARA 533.
2   As to the meaning of 'acquiring authority' see PARA 622 note 1.

3   See PARA 622.
4   Ie by virtue of the Land Compensation Act 1973 s 54: see the text and notes 5–9; and PARA 623.
5   Land Compensation Act 1973 s 54(6)(a). For this purpose, any terms as to surrender contained in the lease must be disregarded: s 54(6).
6   Land Compensation Act 1973 s 54(6)(b) (amended by SI 2009/1307). As to the Upper Tribunal see PARA 720; and ADMINISTRATIVE LAW.
7   Land Compensation Act 1973 s 54(6)(c).
8   Land Compensation Act 1973 s 54(7). The provisions of the Compulsory Purchase Act 1965 s 9(2), (5) (deposit of compensation in cases of refusal to convey etc: see PARAS 661, 664) apply, with the necessary modifications, to the sum deposited: Land Compensation Act 1973 s 54(7). As to payment into court under the Compulsory Purchase Act 1965 see PARA 555 note 6.
9   Land Compensation Act 1973 s 54(8). As to references to farming land see PARA 622 note 7.

625.   Counter-notice where notice to treat under the Lands Clauses Acts relates to part of premises. No party[1] may at any time be required to sell or convey to the undertakers[2] a part only of any house[3] or other building[4] or manufactory[5] if he is willing and able to sell and convey the whole of it[6]. It follows that if a notice to treat is served which relates to part only of a house or other building or manufactory, the party from whom the acquisition is to be made may, if he is willing and able to sell and convey the whole, by counter-notice require the undertakers to take the whole of the premises. No particular form of notice is required provided it is made clear what the undertakers are required to take[7].

The owner cannot require a different or larger part to be taken; what has to be offered is the whole[8]; but the insertion in the special Act[9], at the owner's instance, of provisions for the protection of his property will not prevent him from exercising his right to require the whole to be taken[10].

The owner may signify his desire that the undertakers should take the whole of the premises at any time before they have begun to put their compulsory powers into motion[11], provided he has not by his conduct estopped himself from doing so, as, for example, by agreeing to the price to be paid for the part[12]. The submission of a claim for a part, and uncompleted negotiations as to the compensation to be paid for the part, will not estop him from claiming that they should take the whole[13]. Where the special Act makes particular provisions relating to the acquisition of parts of premises, the owner may be required to serve notice in a particular form and within a particular time.

1   Ie no party able to sell and convey the whole of the property: see *Governors of St Thomas's Hospital v Charing Cross Rly Co* (1861) 1 John & H 400; *Lord Grosvenor v Hampstead Junction Rly Co* (1857) 26 LJCh 731. A lessee of a house may require the undertakers to purchase his interest in the whole house independently of the lessor's rights: *Pulling v London, Chatham and Dover Rly Co* (1864) 33 LJCh 505. Similarly, if a person has a leasehold interest in a house and part of a garden, and a freehold interest in the remaining part, the undertakers, if required to take the whole, cannot insist on taking either part: *MacGregor v Metropolitan Rly Co* (1866) 14 LT 354; *Richards v Swansea Improvement and Tramways Co* (1878) 9 ChD 425, CA; *Siegenberg v Metropolitan District Rly Co* (1883) 49 LT 554. If a lessor sells part and a lessee the whole of his land, the undertakers may remain liable on the covenants as to the parts not acquired from the lessor: *Piggott v Middlesex County Council* [1909] 1 Ch 134.
2   As to the meaning of 'undertakers' see PARA 511.
3   As to the meaning of 'house' see PARA 626.
4   Ie something in the nature of a house: see *Regent's Canal and Dock Co v LCC* [1912] 1 Ch 583; and PARA 626.
5   As to the meaning of 'manufactory' see PARA 626.
6   Lands Clauses Consolidation Act 1845 s 92 (where that Act is incorporated: see PARA 509). As to the modified provision where the Compulsory Purchase Act 1965 applies see PARA 628.
7   *Gardner v Charing Cross Rly Co* (1861) 2 John & H 248; *Spackman v Great Western Rly Co* (1855) 1 Jur NS 790; *Pollard v Middlesex County Council* (1906) 95 LT 870; *Richards v Swansea Improvement and Tramways Co* (1878) 9 ChD 425, CA; *Binney v Hammersmith and City Rly Co* (1863) 8 LT 161.

8 *Pulling v London, Chatham and Dover Rly Co* (1864) 33 LJCh 505; *Thompson v Tottenham and Forest Gate Rly Co* (1892) 67 LT 416.
9 As to the meaning of 'special Act' see PARAS 509, 514.
10 See *Sparrow v Oxford, Worcester and Wolverhampton Rly Co* (1852) 2 De GM & G 94; *Governors of St Thomas's Hospital v Charing Cross Rly Co* (1861) 1 John & H 400. If the whole is taken the undertakers are released from the restrictive provision: *Governors of St Thomas's Hospital v Charing Cross Rly Co* at 401.
11 Service of the notice to treat is not by itself an exercise of compulsory powers: *Goodwin Foster Brown Ltd v Derby Corpn* [1934] 2 KB 23; and see PARA 616 note 5.
12 *Gardner v Charing Cross Rly Co* (1861) 2 John & H 248; *Barker v North Staffordshire Rly Co* (1848) 5 Ry & Can Cas 401, 2 De G & Sm 55; *Pollard v Middlesex County Council* (1906) 95 LT 870.
13 *Lavers v LCC* (1905) 93 LT 233; *Pollard v Middlesex County Council* (1906) 95 LT 870.

626. Meanings of 'house', 'building' and 'manufactory'. By a 'house' or 'building' is meant more than the mere fabric. 'House' includes the house, garden and curtilage; in fact all that would pass on the conveyance of a house[1]. It also means more than a dwelling house or residence, and includes a shop, or an inn[2], or a building built for one purpose, such as a hospital[3]. 'Building' includes separate buildings in one ambit used for a common purpose[4]. Conversely, one building used as two dwelling houses, as in the case of semi-detached houses, is treated as two separate houses[5]. Unfinished houses are also considered to be houses[6].

In determining whether premises are a manufactory, regard must be had to the main use to which they are put[7]. If the main business is manufacturing, the undertakers may be required to take the whole of the premises, even though part may be used for other purposes[8], or may be temporarily let to another occupier[9]. If a manufactory is partly worked by water power, and undertakers desire to take the water and the arrangements for storing and conveying the power, they may be required to take the whole manufactory[10]. Where, however, the main business carried on upon premises is not manufacture, it is immaterial that some manufacture should be carried on incidentally to it and in such a case the undertakers may take the whole of the part used for manufacture without being required to take the other parts[11]. Similarly, they may take the part not used as the manufactory without taking the part so used[12].

The date of service of the notice to treat fixes the time when the premises are to be considered in order to determine whether the land proposed to be purchased or taken is part of a house, building, or manufactory[13]. Changes made after that date are immaterial[14]. If made in good faith, changes of use or occupation may be made at any time before the service of the notice[15].

1 *Grosvenor v Hampstead Junction Rly Co* (1857) 26 LJCh 731; *Cole v West London and Crystal Palace Rly Co* (1859) 28 LJCh 767; *Marson v London, Chatham and Dover Rly Co* (1868) LR 6 Eq 101 (further proceedings (1869) LR 7 Eq 546); *Governors of St Thomas's Hospital v Charing Cross Rly Co* (1861) 1 John & H 400; *Richards v Swansea Improvement and Tramways Co* (1878) 9 ChD 425, CA. Thus, it would include a shrubbery and the various orchards and gardens connected with a house (*Hewson v South Western Rly Co* (1860) 8 WR 467; *King v Wycombe Rly Co* (1860) 29 LJCh 462; *Salter v Metropolitan District Rly Co* (1870) LR 9 Eq 432), and might include a paddock behind a house and accessible only from the garden (*Barnes v Southsea Rly Co* (1884) 27 ChD 536; *Low v Staines Reservoir Joint Committee* (1900) 64 JP 212, CA); and also the courtyard to a house (*Caledonian Rly Co v Turcan* [1898] AC 256, HL). It does not, however, include all land which the owner of the house may possess and enjoy along with the house, such as fields used for grazing (*Pulling v London, Chatham and Dover Rly Co* (1864) 33 LJCh 505; *Steele v Midland Rly Co* (1866) 1 Ch App 275; *Fergusson v London, Brighton and South Coast Rly Co* (1863) 11 WR 1088), or gardens and stables on the opposite side of the road, purchased subsequently to the purchase of the house (*Kerford v Seacombe, Hoylake and Deeside Rly Co* (1888) 57 LJCh 270; and see

Chambers v London, Chatham and Dover Rly Co (1863) 11 WR 479), or a private road leading to a mansion house (*Allhusen v Ealing and South Harrow Rly Co* (1898) 78 LT 285 at 286). Similarly, if a cottage stands in a nursery garden, the garden will not be deemed to be part of the house: *Falkner v Somerset and Dorset Rly Co* (1873) LR 16 Eq 458.

2   *Richards v Swansea Improvement and Tramways Co* (1878) 9 ChD 425 at 431, CA.
3   *Governors of St Thomas's Hospital v Charing Cross Rly Co* (1861) 1 John & H 400.
4   See eg *Richards v Swansea Improvement and Tramways Co* (1878) 9 ChD 425, CA; *Siegenberg v Metropolitan District Rly Co* (1883) 49 LT 554; *Greswolde-Williams v Newcastle-upon-Tyne Corpn* (1927) 92 JP 13 (building let out in offices). A church is a 'house or building' (and can be assumed to be a building) and includes adjacent halls and outbuildings: *London Transport Executive v Congregational Union of England and Wales (Inc)* (1978) 37 P & CR 155.
5   *Harvie v South Devon Rly Co* (1874) 32 LT 1, CA.
6   *Alexander v Crystal Palace Rly Co* (1862) 30 Beav 556.
7   *Richards v Swansea Improvement and Tramways Co* (1878) 9 ChD 425 at 434–436, CA.
8   Eg for a rubbish heap (*Sparrow v Oxford, Worcester and Wolverhampton Rly Co* (1852) 2 De GM & G 94), or warehouses (*Spackman v Great Western Rly Co* (1855) 1 Jur NS 790).
9   *Brook v Manchester, Sheffield and Lincolnshire Rly Co* [1895] 2 Ch 571.
10   *Furniss v Midland Rly Co* (1868) LR 6 Eq 473.
11   *Benington & Sons v Metropolitan Board of Works* (1886) 54 LT 837, where blending and packing tea was the principal business, and the making of packing cases an incidental part.
12   *Reddin v Metropolitan Board of Works* (1862) 4 De GF & J 532.
13   *Richards v Swansea Improvement and Tramways Co* (1878) 9 ChD 425, CA.
14   *Chambers v London, Chatham and Dover Rly Co* (1863) 11 WR 479; *Littler v Rhyl Improvement Comrs* [1878] WN 219.
15   *Richards v Swansea Improvement and Tramways Co* (1878) 9 ChD 425, CA.

627.   Effect of counter-notice under the Lands Clauses Acts.   The effect under the Lands Clauses Acts[1] of the counter-notice when validly given is to enable the undertakers either to purchase the whole or to withdraw their notice to treat[2]. If the notice to treat is withdrawn, the subsequent withdrawal of the counter-notice does not revive the original notice to treat[3]; the parties are relegated to the same position as they were in before the notice to treat was served, and if they so desire the undertakers can serve a fresh notice as to the same premises or as to a different part of them[4]. If, however, the owner withdraws his counter-notice before the undertakers have signified their desire either to take the whole or to withdraw the notice to treat, the original notice to treat stands[5]. No formal notice to take, or of their intention to take, the whole is required to be given by the undertakers on receiving a counter-notice, provided they signified their intention in such a way as to bind themselves[6]. The appointment of an arbitrator does not prevent them from withdrawing their notice to treat[7].

An owner who has served a valid counter-notice may obtain an injunction to restrain the undertakers from taking part only[8], or a declaration that they cannot purchase or take part[9], or, if they have entered, a declaration that they must take the whole[10]. In such a case, the deposit to be made on entry before the purchase is completed must be the value of the whole premises[11].

When the counter-notice is given in a case where it is not valid, the undertakers may disregard it and proceed with the notice to treat[12], and they will not be bound by the counter-notice, even though it may have been accepted by their solicitors[13]. A valid counter-notice given upon service of an invalid notice to treat, and acted upon, may estop the parties from setting up the invalidity[14].

1   As to the Lands Clauses Acts see PARA 509 note 1.
2   *King v Wycombe Rly Co* (1860) 29 LJCh 462; *R v London and South Western Rly Co* (1848) 12 QB 775; *R v London and Greenwich Rly Co* (1842) 3 QB 166; *Wild v Woolwich Borough Council* [1910] 1 Ch 35, CA. As to withdrawal of notices to treat see generally PARA 636.
3   *Ex p Quicke* (1865) 12 LT 580.
4   *Ashton Vale Iron Co Ltd v Bristol Corpn* [1901] 1 Ch 591, CA.

5   *Pinchin v London and Blackwall Rly Co* (1854) 1 K & J 34; on appeal 5 De GM & G 851, 24 LJCh 417.
6   *Schwinge v London and Blackwall Rly Co* (1855) 24 LJCh 405.
7   *Grierson v Cheshire Lines Committee* (1874) LR 19 Eq 83; *Ashton Vale Iron Co Ltd v Bristol Corpn* [1901] 1 Ch 591 at 601, CA.
8   *Barnes v Southsea Rly Co* (1884) 27 ChD 536; *Lavers v LCC* (1905) 93 LT 233; *Marson v London, Chatham and Dover Rly Co* (1869) LR 7 Eq 546.
9   *Richards v Swansea Improvement and Tramways Co* (1878) 9 ChD 425, CA.
10 *King v Wycombe Rly Co* (1860) 29 LJCh 462; *Sparrow v Oxford, Worcester and Wolverhampton Rly Co* (1852) 2 De GM & G 94.
11 *Giles v London, Chatham and Dover Rly Co* (1861) 30 LJCh 603; *Underwood v Bedford and Cambridge Rly Co* (1861) 7 Jur NS 941; *Gardner v Charing Cross Rly Co* (1861) 2 John & H 248. As to entry see PARA 638.
12 *Harvie v South Devon Rly Co* (1874) 32 LT 1, CA; *Loosemore v Tiverton and North Devon Rly Co* (1882) 22 ChD 25 at 35, 50, CA; on appeal sub nom *Tiverton and North Devon Rly Co v Loosemore* (1884) 9 App Cas 480 at 484, HL.
13 *Treadwell v London and South Western Rly Co* (1884) 54 LJCh 565, 51 LT 894.
14 *Pinchin v London and Blackwall Rly Co* (1854) 5 De GM & G 851, 24 LJCh 417.

628.   Counter-notice where notice to treat under the Compulsory Purchase Act 1965 relates to part of premises.   Where the authorisation of the compulsory purchase is by a compulsory purchase order to which the Compulsory Purchase Act 1965 applies[1], no person is required to sell a part only of any house, building or manufactory[2], or of a park[3] or garden[4] belonging to a house, if he is willing and able to sell the whole of those premises, unless the Upper Tribunal (the 'Tribunal') determines that:

(1)   in the case of a house, building or manufactory, the part proposed to be acquired can be taken without material detriment to the house, building or manufactory; or

(2)   in the case of a park or garden, the part proposed to be acquired can be taken without seriously affecting the amenity[5] or convenience of the house[6].

If the Tribunal so determines, it must award compensation in respect of any loss due to the severance of the part proposed to be acquired, in addition to its value; and thereupon the party interested is required to sell to the acquiring authority[7] that part of the premises[8].

In determining whether or not there is material detriment as mentioned in head (1) above, or whether or not amenity or convenience is seriously affected as mentioned in head (2) above, the Tribunal may consider all the circumstances and the mode and manner in which the property is to be taken[9] and must take into account not only the effect of the severance but also the use to be made of the part proposed to be acquired and, in a case where the part is proposed to be acquired for works or other purposes extending to other land, the effect of the whole of the works and the use to be made of the other land[10].

1   As to such orders see PARA 513.
2   As to the meanings of 'house', 'building' and 'manufactory' see PARA 626.
3   A 'park' need not be large, and land may be a park although it is let for grazing: see *Re Ripon (Highfield) Housing Confirmation Order 1938, White and Collins v Minister of Health* [1939] 2 KB 838, [1939] 3 All ER 548, CA.
4   The 'root idea' of a garden is that it is 'a substantially homogenous area, substantially devoted to the growth of fruits, flowers and vegetables': see *Bomford v Osborne (Inspector of Taxes)* [1942] AC 14 at 40, [1941] 2 All ER 426 at 442, HL, per Lord Wright. Where there is a cultivated garden which is separated from an adjoining piece of rough pasture, the rough pasture cannot be regarded as part of the garden: *Methuen-Campbell v Walters* [1979] QB 525, [1979] 1 All ER 606, CA; and see *McAlpine v Secretary of State for the Environment* (1994) 159 LG Rev 429, (1994) Times, 6 December.

5   As to the meaning of 'amenity' see *Re Ellis and Ruislip-Northwood UDC* [1920] 1 KB 343 at 370, CA, per Scrutton LJ; and TOWN AND COUNTRY PLANNING vol 46(1) (Reissue) PARA 158.

6   Compulsory Purchase Act 1965 s 8(1) (amended by SI 2009/1307). See *Ravenseft Properties Ltd v London Borough of Hillingdon* (1968) 20 P & CR 483, Lands Tribunal; *McMillan v Strathclyde Regional Council* [1983] 1 EGLR 188, Lands Tribunal for Scotland. Apart from the provision as to part of a park or garden and the Upper Tribunal's power to determine that the part can be taken without material detriment to the whole, the Compulsory Purchase Act 1965 s 8(1) is in the same terms as the Lands Clauses Consolidation Act 1845 s 92, and, subject to the above differences, the judicial decisions on the latter would appear to apply to the former: see PARAS 625–627. As to the Upper Tribunal see PARA 720; and ADMINISTRATIVE LAW.

7   As to the meaning of 'acquiring authority' for these purposes see PARA 549 note 5.

8   Compulsory Purchase Act 1965 s 8(1) (amended by SI 2009/1307). Notice of an application for a determination by the Tribunal must be served on an acquiring authority prior to the authority entering the property: *Glasshouse Properties Ltd v Secretary of State for Transport* (1993) 66 P & CR 285, Lands Tribunal. It seems that the compensation must be awarded on the same principles as compensation for severance etc where no counter-notice has been served: see PARA 810 et seq. The Compulsory Purchase Act 1965 s 8(1) is modified or substituted in relation to the compulsory acquisition of rights by, inter alia:

    (1)   a local authority (see the Local Government (Miscellaneous Provisions) Act 1976 s 13(3)(b), Sch 1 para 7; and LOCAL GOVERNMENT vol 69 (2009) PARA 511);

    (2)   urban development corporations (see the Local Government, Planning and Land Act 1980 s 144, Sch 28 para 23(2); and TOWN AND COUNTRY PLANNING vol 46(1) (Reissue) PARA 180);

    (3)   highway authorities (see the Highways Act 1980 s 250(5)(a), Sch 19 para 7; and HIGHWAYS, STREETS AND BRIDGES vol 21 (2004 Reissue) PARAS 49 et seq, 85);

    (4)   gas transporters (see the Gas Act 1986 s 9(3), Sch 3 para 8; and FUEL AND ENERGY vol 19(2) (2007 Reissue) PARA 841);

    (5)   housing action trusts (see the Housing Act 1988 s 78(2), Sch 10 para 22; and HOUSING vol 22 (2006 Reissue) PARA 340);

    (6)   licence holders under the Electricity Act 1989 (see s 10(1), Sch 3 para 9; and FUEL AND ENERGY vol 19(2) (2007 Reissue) PARA 1284);

    (7)   the Environment Agency (see the Water Resources Act 1991 s 154(5), Sch 18 para 4; the Environment Act 1995 (Consequential Amendments) Regulations 1996, SI 1996/593, reg 2, Sch 1; and WATER AND WATERWAYS vol 101 (2009) PARA 453);

    (8)   water and sewerage undertakers (see the Water Industry Act 1991 s 155(5), Sch 9 para 4; and WATER AND WATERWAYS vol 101 (2009) PARA 453);

    (9)   regional development agencies (see the Regional Development Agencies Act 1998 s 20, Sch 5 para 4; and TRADE, INDUSTRY AND INDUSTRIAL RELATIONS vol 47 (2001 Reissue) PARA 901); and

    (10)   universal service providers (see the Postal Services Act 2000 s 95, Sch 5 para 8; and POST OFFICE).

    In considering, for the purposes of heads (3)–(4), (6)–(8), (10) above, the extent of any material detriment to a house, building or manufactory or any extent to which the amenity or convenience of a house is affected, the Upper Tribunal must have regard not only to the right which is to be acquired over the land, but also to any adjoining or adjacent land belonging to the same owner and subject to compulsory purchase: see the Compulsory Purchase Act 1965 s 8 (amended by SI 2009/1307).

9   *Re Gonty and Manchester, Sheffield and Lincolnshire Rly Co's Arbitration* [1896] 2 QB 439, CA (decided on a similar decision in a local Act), where the taking of the land would have been materially detrimental by depriving the landowner of access to his remaining land but for the fact that the railway company had given an undertaking not to take his land in such a way as to deprive the landowner of access and to provide a permanent right of way equivalent to the original access; see also *Caledonian Rly Co v Turcan* [1898] AC 256, HL. A special Act may empower the tribunal, if the part proposed to be taken is not severable without material detriment to the whole, to determine whether or not any other part less than the whole is severable without material detriment, and may empower the undertakers to take that other part without being obliged to purchase the whole if it is so severable. As to the meaning of 'special Act' see PARAS 509, 514.

10   Land Compensation Act 1973 s 58(1) (amended by the Compulsory Purchase (Vesting Declarations) Act 1981 s 16(3), Sch 5; the Planning (Consequential Provisions) Act 1990 s 4, Sch 2 para 29(10); and SI 2009/1307). The Land Compensation Act 1973 s 58(1) is applied with the necessary modifications to any determination under the Compulsory Purchase Act 1965 s 8(1) as substituted as mentioned in note 8 heads (3)–(4), (7)–(8): see the Land

Compensation Act 1973 s 58(2)(a) (amended by the Highways Act 1980 s 343(2), Sch 24 para 23; the Gas Act 1986 s 67(1), Sch 7 para 14(2); the Water Act 1989 s 190(1), Sch 25 para 44(2); and the Water Consolidation (Consequential Provisions) Act 1991 s 2(1), Sch 1 para 23). The Land Compensation Act 1973 s 58(1) is also applied with necessary modifications to any determination under any provision corresponding to or substituted for the Compulsory Purchase Act 1965 s 8(1), contained in, or in an instrument made under, any other enactment passed after the Land Compensation Act 1973: see s 58(2)(b).

629. Intersected land not in a town or built upon. Where any land[1] which is not situated in a town or built upon[2] is cut through and divided by the authorised works so as to leave, either on both sides or on one side of the works[3], less than half an acre of land, the owner of that small piece of land may require the undertakers[4] or acquiring authority[5] to purchase it[6] along with the land subject to compulsory purchase[7], unless the owner has other adjoining land to which it can be joined, so as to be conveniently occupied with it, in which case, if so required by the owner, the undertakers or authority must at their own expense join the piece of land so left to the adjoining land by removing the fences and levelling the sites and by soiling it in a satisfactory and workmanlike manner[8].

1   As to the meaning of 'land' see PARA 549 note 1. See also PARA 511 text and note 7.

2   'Town' is used in its popular sense, and 'built upon' means continuously built upon, as in a town: *Lord Carington v Wycombe Rly Co* (1868) 3 Ch App 377; *Directors etc of the London and South Western Rly Co v Blackmore* (1870) LR 4 HL 610; *R v Cottle* (1851) 16 QB 412 at 421–422; *Elliott v South Devon Rly Co* (1848) 2 Exch 725. A market garden with a cottage on it is not land built upon: *Falkner v Somerset and Dorset Rly Co* (1873) LR 16 Eq 458.

3   As to the meaning of 'works' see PARA 549 note 3. See also PARA 511.

4   As to the meaning of 'undertakers' see PARA 511.

5   As to the meaning of 'acquiring authority' for these purposes see PARA 549 note 5.

6   As to including this land in a reference as to the purchase price see *Re North Staffordshire Rly Co and Wood* (1848) 2 Exch 244.

7   Lands Clauses Consolidation Act 1845 s 93; Compulsory Purchase Act 1965 s 8(2).

8   Lands Clauses Consolidation Act 1845 s 93 (which uses the phrase 'sufficient and workmanlike manner'); Compulsory Purchase Act 1965 s 8(2) proviso.

     Note that s 8 is completely substituted by the provisions mentioned in PARA 628 note 8 heads (2), (5), so that the provisions set out in the text and notes 1–7 above do not apply in relation to the acquisition of rights by urban development corporations and housing action trusts.

630. Intersected land requiring expensive communications. Where any land[1], whether in a town or not, and whether built upon or not[2], is cut through and divided by the authorised works so as to leave, either on both sides or on one side of the works[3], a quantity of land which is less than half an acre, or of less value than the expense of making a bridge, culvert, or such other communication between the divided land as the undertakers[4] or acquiring authority[5] can be compelled to make under the provisions of the special and incorporated Acts[6], and the owner of the divided lands has no other land adjoining the small piece of land, and he requires the undertakers or the acquiring authority to make the communication, they may require the owner to sell to them the small piece of land[7]. Any dispute as to the value of the piece of land or as to what would be the expense of making the communication must be determined by the Upper Tribunal, and either party to proceedings for determining the compensation to be paid for the land may require the Upper Tribunal to make its determination in those proceedings[8].

1   As to the meaning of 'land' see PARA 549 note 1. See also PARA 511 text to note 7.

2   As to the meanings of 'town' and 'built upon' see PARA 629 note 2. See also *Eastern Counties and London and Blackwall Rly Cos v Marriage* (1860) 9 HL Cas 32.
3   As to the meaning of 'works' see PARA 549 note 3. See also PARA 511.
4   As to the meaning of 'undertakers' see PARA 511.
5   As to the meaning of 'acquiring authority' see PARA 549 note 5.
6   Eg under the Railways Clauses Consolidation Act 1845 s 68: see *Falls v Belfast and Ballymena Rly Co* (1849) 12 ILR 233, Ex Ch. The Compulsory Purchase Act 1965 s 8(3) simply uses the phrase '... less value than the expense of making the communication between the divided land'. As to the meaning of 'special Act' see PARAS 509, 514.
7   Lands Clauses Consolidation Act 1845 s 94; Compulsory Purchase Act 1965 s 8(3).
8   Lands Clauses Consolidation Act 1845 s 94; Compulsory Purchase Act 1965 s 8(3) (amended by SI 2009/1307). As to costs in the proceedings see *Cobb v Mid Wales Rly Co* (1866) LR 1 QB 342; and PARA 746. As to the Upper Tribunal see PARA 720; and ADMINISTRATIVE LAW.

    Note that the Compulsory Purchase Act 1965 s 8 is completely substituted by the provisions mentioned in PARA 628 note 8 heads (2), (5), so that the provisions set out in the text and notes 1–7 above do not apply in relation to the acquisition of rights by urban development corporations and housing action trusts.

(iv) Effect of Notice to Treat

631. Relation of parties as vendor and purchaser after notice to treat. In the nineteenth century, the courts characterised the effect of serving a notice to treat as establishing a relation analogous in some respects to that of vendor and purchaser, a relation which binds the owner of the land to give up the land subject to compensation, and which binds the undertakers or acquiring authority to take the land, although no contract of sale exists until the price is ascertained, and the land remains the property of the landowner[1].

The current view modifies this to the extent that the notice to treat is seen as no more than notification of an intention to take the land from the owner, which does not bring the parties into a contractual relationship and does not prohibit the owner from disposing of his interest[2]. Unless the notice to treat is withdrawn, either party has the right to have the price ascertained and the purchase completed in the manner provided by the Lands Clauses Acts[3] or the Compulsory Purchase Act 1965 or any Acts modifying those Acts[4].

When the price has been ascertained, the elements of a complete agreement between the parties exist, and, except so far as excluded by the special Act[5], the parties' rights and duties are the same as those arising out of an ordinary contract for the sale of land[6], including the right to have the contract enforced by specific performance[7], and the owner's interest then, but not before, becomes an interest in personalty[8]. When the price has been fixed, the agreement so constituted is registrable as an estate contract in the land charges register[9], and may be protected by the registration of a notice[10].

1   *Fotherby v Metropolitan Rly Co* (1866) LR 2 CP 188 at 193; *Haynes v Haynes* (1861) 1 Drew & Sm 426 at 450; *Adams v London and Blackwall Rly Co* (1850) 2 Mac & G 118; *Tiverton and North Devon Rly Co v Loosemore* (1884) 9 App Cas 480 at 493, 503, 511, HL; *Mercer v Liverpool, St Helen's and South Lancashire Rly Co* [1903] 1 KB 652 at 661, CA, per Stirling LJ (approved [1904] AC 461 at 463, 465, HL); *Cardiff Corpn v Cook* [1923] 2 Ch 115; and see *Edinburgh and District Water Trustees v Clippens Oil Co* (1902) 87 LT 275, HL; *Wild v Woolwich Borough Council* [1910] 1 Ch 35, CA.
2   *Guest v Poole and Bournemouth Rly Co* (1870) LR 5 CP 553 at 557 per Willes J; *Hillingdon Estates Co v Stonefield Estates Ltd* [1952] Ch 627, [1952] 1 All ER 853; *Birmingham Corpn v West Midland Baptist (Trust) Association (Inc)* [1970] AC 874 at 892, 903, 909, [1969] 3 All ER 172 at 175, 184, 188, HL. See also PARA 616.
3   As to the Lands Clauses Acts see PARA 509 note 1.
4   *Fotherby v Metropolitan Rly Co* (1866) LR 2 CP 188; *Tiverton and North Devon Rly Co v Loosemore* (1884) 9 App Cas 480 at 493, HL; and see *R v Hungerford Market Co* (1832) 4 B

& Ad 327; *Birch v St Marylebone Vestry* (1869) 20 LT 697. As to the right of withdrawal see PARA 636. As to the assessment of compensation see PARAS 715 et seq, 753 et seq.
5 As to the meaning of 'special Act' see PARAS 509, 514.
6 See the cases cited in note 1. Where negotiations are still 'subject to contract', the agreement as to price will not be binding on the parties: *Munton v GLC* [1976] 2 All ER 815, [1976] 1 WLR 649, CA.
7 *Harding v Metropolitan Rly Co* (1872) 7 Ch App 154. The agreement, together with the right of enforcement, is subject to a right of withdrawal: see PARA 636. See also the cases cited in PARA 651 note 5.
8 *Haynes v Haynes* (1861) 1 Drew & Sm 426 at 451 et seq. As to the doctrine of conversion see EQUITY vol 16(2) (Reissue) PARA 701 et seq.
9 Land Charges Act 1972 s 2(4), Class C(iv). As to the effect of failure to register see LAND CHARGES vol 26 (2004 Reissue) PARA 693.
10 See the Land Registration Act 2002 s 32; and LAND REGISTRATION vol 26 (2004 Reissue) PARA 995.

632. Effect of notice to treat on owner's rights and duties. The owner of an interest in land at the date of the notice to treat continues as owner until there is a contract of sale[1]. He may continue to deal with his interest as he likes and may sell, convey or otherwise deal with it[2], and it is for him, and not the undertakers or acquiring authority, to insure the premises[3].

The owner may not, however, increase the burden of compensation payable by the undertakers or acquiring authority either by the creation of a new interest in the land taken or the land held with it[4] or by effecting improvements to the land so as to alter the quality of the subject matter[5]. There would therefore be no obligation to serve a notice to treat in respect of any such new interest[6]. This restriction on the person served with a notice to treat relates to the creation of an interest and, as a person served with that notice can sell or convey it or otherwise deal with it, there is nothing to prevent the owner of a freehold interest determining or acquiring any leasehold interest or the owner of a leasehold interest acquiring the freehold[7].

Additional provision to similar effect is made by statute in certain cases. Where there is an acquisition under a compulsory purchase order to which the Acquisition of Land Act 1981 applies[8], the Upper Tribunal (the 'Tribunal')[9] may not take into account any interest in land[10], or any enhancement of the value of any interest in land, by reason of any building erected, work done or improvement or alteration made, whether on the land purchased or on any other land with which the claimant is, or was at the time of the erection, doing or making of the building, works, improvement or alteration, directly or indirectly concerned, if the Tribunal is satisfied that the creation of the interest[11], the erection of the building, the doing of the work, the making of the improvement or the alteration, as the case may be, was not reasonably necessary and was undertaken with a view to obtaining compensation or increased compensation[12].

1 See PARA 631.
2 *Mercer v Liverpool, St Helen's and South Lancashire Rly Co* [1904] AC 461, HL; *Dawson v Great Northern and City Rly Co* [1905] 1 KB 260 at 268–269, CA; *Sewell v Harrow and Uxbridge Rly Co* (1902) 19 TLR 130 (on appeal (1903) 20 TLR 21, CA); *Carnochan v Norwich and Spalding Rly Co* (1858) 26 Beav 169; *Cardiff Corpn v Cook* [1923] 2 Ch 115; and cf *Metropolitan Rly Co v Woodhouse* (1865) 34 LJCh 297.
3 See *Birmingham Corpn v West Midland Baptist (Trust) Association (Inc)* [1970] AC 874 at 899, 908, 911, [1969] 3 All ER 172 at 180, 187, 190, HL, overruling *Phoenix Assurance Co v Spooner* [1905] 2 KB 753. See also *Matthey v Curling* [1922] 2 AC 180, HL; *Re King, Robinson v Gray* [1963] Ch 459, [1963] 1 All ER 781, CA.
4 As to such land and the right to compensation for severance or other injurious affection in respect of it see *Mercer v Liverpool, St Helen's and South Lancashire Rly Co* [1904] AC 461, HL; and PARA 810.

5   *Mercer v Liverpool, St Helen's and South Lancashire Rly Co* [1904] AC 461 at 465, HL, per Lord Lindley; *Cardiff Corpn v Cook* [1923] 2 Ch 115; *Re Marylebone (Stingo Lane) Improvement Act, ex p Edwards* (1871) LR 12 Eq 389; and see *Johnson v Edgware, Highgate and London Rly Co* (1866) 35 Beav 480, 14 LT 45; *Wilkins v Birmingham Corpn* (1883) 25 ChD 78. As to weekly tenants let in after the notice to treat having no right to compensation see *Re Marylebone (Stingo Lane) Improvement Act, ex p Edwards.* If such an interest is created, the compensation payable in respect of the interest out of which it is created is deemed to include the value of the new interest (see *Mercer v Liverpool, St Helen's and South Lancashire Rly Co* above), and where the undertakers or acquiring authority as owners use their power of taking possession (see PARAS 639, 645) with respect to the new interest there would be eviction by title paramount (see *Cuthbertson v Irving* (1859) 4 H & N 742; affd (1860) 6 H & N 135) and the lessee would have no claim on his lessor (see *Manchester, Sheffield and Lincolnshire Rly Co v Anderson* [1898] 2 Ch 394, CA) unless the lessor had failed to disclose the existence of the compulsory purchase order and the notice to treat when creating the interest (see *Walton Harvey Ltd v Walker and Homfrays Ltd* [1931] 1 Ch 274, CA). The principle that the owner may not deal with his property so as to increase the undertakers' or acquiring authority's burden after service of a notice to treat applies equally to dealings with undertakings liable to compulsory acquisition in accordance with an Act of Parliament: see *Chocolate Express Omnibus Co v London Passenger Transport Board* (1934) 152 LT 63, CA.

6   Otherwise, if the owner so created an interest after the time for exercising the compulsory powers had expired, the undertakers or acquiring authority would be saddled with the interest with no power to acquire it compulsorily.

7   It was not unusual for undertakers or an acquiring authority to induce the landlord to terminate a tenancy (see PARA 698), or for a mortgagor to redeem the equity of redemption or to purchase the mortgagee's interest (see PARA 711). As to an ineffective surrender see *Zick v London United Tramways Ltd* [1908] 2 KB 126, CA; and as to the use of covenants by the lessor to obtain possession see PARA 633. As to the effect of the termination of a tenancy on the valuation of an interest see PARA 804.

8   As to such orders see the Acquisition of Land Act 1981 ss 1, 2; and PARAS 556–557.

9   As to the Upper Tribunal see PARA 720; and ADMINISTRATIVE LAW.

10 As to the meaning of 'land' see PARA 522 note 1.

11 This would not be apt to effect an interest created after a notice to treat and excluded under the above provisions. There is no restriction on the termination of an interest or on its assignment.

12 Acquisition of Land Act 1981 s 4(1), (2) (amended by SI 2009/1307).
    The Acquisition of Land Act 1981 s 4 is applied by, inter alia, the Water Industry Act 1991 s 167, Sch 11 para 6; and by the Water Resources Act 1991 s 168, Sch 19 para 6: see WATER AND WATERWAYS vol 101 (2009) PARA 459. The increase in the acquiring authority's burden in respect of compensation which is so prohibited must arise from the alteration of the land or the creation of a new interest, and does not apply to the termination of an interest: see *Birmingham Corpn v West Midland Baptist (Trust) Association (Inc)* [1970] AC 874 at 893, 904, [1969] 3 All ER 172 at 175, 184, HL; *R v Kennedy* [1893] 1 QB 533; and the cases cited in note 5. See, however, *Banham v London Borough of Hackney* (1970) 22 P & CR 922, Lands Tribunal, where the Tribunal found it necessary to consider whether the termination of an interest increased the burden.

633.   Effect of notice to treat on other interests.   The service of a notice to treat on the owner of the interest in the land does not frustrate an enforceable contract of sale, and the purchaser is also entitled to a notice to treat[1]. A person entitled to an interest in land under a building agreement is not affected but is entitled to a notice to treat[2]. The liability of a lessee under covenants in the lease is not affected by the service of a notice to treat for his interest[3]. The lessor is entitled to the benefit of the covenants until the conveyance of his interest, and is entitled to recover damages for breaches of covenant by the lessee occurring before the conveyance of the lessor's interest, although he is not so entitled afterwards[4].

If a lease contains a proviso that if any part of the land leased is compulsorily acquired the lessor may re-enter and repossess it, the service of a notice to treat brings the proviso into operation[5], but where the lease contains a proviso enabling the lessor to re-enter for the purpose of building, the lessor cannot take advantage of the proviso to enhance the value of his interest[6].

1 *Hillingdon Estates Co v Stonefield Estates Ltd* [1952] Ch 627, [1952] 1 All ER 853. See also *Johnson & Co (Barbados) Ltd v NSR Ltd* [1997] AC 400, [1996] 3 WLR 583, PC (the issuing of a notice under Barbados law did not prevent the vendor from giving vacant possession in accordance with an agreed contract of sale for the land, and it was to be presumed, in the absence of specific provision to the contrary, that the purchaser had agreed to take the normal risks incidental to land ownership as from the date of the contract, including the risk of interference with ownership rights by the Crown or by statutory authorities).

2 *Birmingham and District Land Co v London and North Western Rly Co* (1888) 40 ChD 268, CA; *Re Furness and Willesden UDC* (1905) 70 JP 25.

3 *Mills v East London Union* (1872) LR 8 CP 79; *Harding v Metropolitan Rly Co* (1872) 7 Ch App 154; *Matthey v Curling* [1922] 2 AC 180, HL. The lessee remains liable after the assignment of his interest (but is entitled on that assignment to the usual covenants for indemnity) unless the tenancy is a new tenancy to which the Landlord and Tenant (Covenants) Act 1995 s 5 (tenant released from covenants on assignment of tenancy) applies, ie a new tenancy granted on or after 1 January 1996 otherwise than in pursuance of an agreement entered into, or a court order made, before that date: see ss 1(1), (3), 31(1); and the Landlord and Tenant (Covenants) Act 1995 (Commencement) Order 1995, SI 1995/2963.

4 *Re King, Robinson v Gray* [1963] Ch 459 at 488, 497, [1963] 1 All ER 781 at 792–793, 798, CA.

5 *Re Morgan and London and North Western Rly Co* [1896] 2 QB 469; *Re Athlone Rifle Range* [1902] 1 IR 433.

6 *Johnson v Edgware, Highgate and London Rly Co* (1866) 35 Beav 480, 14 LT 45.

634. Right to assessment of compensation. A person served with a notice to treat has the right to have the price ascertained and the purchase completed in accordance with statute[1].

The notice to treat confers the right to have the compensation ascertained in respect of all the land mentioned in it, and all the subsequent proceedings must have relation to the whole of the land to which the notice to treat refers[2]. Without the consent of the other, neither party can have the value of part only of the land assessed[3]. Each person on whom a notice to treat is served is entitled to have the compensation as regards his own particular interest assessed separately[4].

The right to the compensation to be assessed may be assigned and dealt with as property[5], but the sum which may be due is not a debt which can be attached by garnishee order until the conveyance has in fact been executed[6].

1 See PARA 631.

2 *Stone v Commercial Rly Co* (1839) 4 My & Cr 122; *Ecclesiastical Comrs v London Sewers Comrs* (1880) 14 ChD 305; *Ex p Bailey* (1852) Bail Ct Cas 66.

3 *Thompson v Tottenham and Forest Gate Rly Co* (1892) 67 LT 416.

4 See *Abrahams v London Corpn* (1868) LR 6 Eq 625.

5 *Dawson v Great Northern and City Rly Co* [1905] 1 KB 260 at 271, CA.

6 *Richardson v Elmit* (1876) 2 CPD 9; *Howell v Metropolitan District Rly Co* (1881) 19 ChD 508.

635. Time of valuation. The value of the land must be assessed at the prices current at the time of entry, agreement or assessment, whichever is the earliest; what is to be valued is the land and the interests in it at that time[1], subject to the rule that interests created or works beyond the necessities of continued enjoyment by the owner after service of the notice to treat, which add to the undertakers' or acquiring authority's burdens[2], must be disregarded; and interests created or works executed for the purpose of increasing compensation must be disregarded where the Acquisition of Land Act 1981 applies[3].

1 *Birmingham Corpn v West Midland Baptist (Trust) Association (Inc)* [1970] AC 874 at 899, 907, 911, [1969] 3 All ER 172 at 180, 187, 190, HL; applied in *Munton v GLC* [1976] 2 All ER 815, [1976] 1 WLR 649, CA. In a case where possession of land has been taken in

separate parcels at different dates, the date for assessment of compensation is the date of the first taking of possession: *Chilton v Telford Development Corpn* [1987] 3 All ER 992, [1987] 1 WLR 872, CA. Where there is an appeal, compensation is assessed according to the market value at the date of the original hearing: *Hoveringham Gravels Ltd v Chiltern District Council* (1978) 39 P & CR 414, Lands Tribunal; *Washington Development Corpn v Bamlings (Washington) Ltd* (1984) 52 P & CR 267, [1985] 1 EGLR 16, CA (possession of land taken piecemeal).

2   *Birmingham Corpn v West Midland Baptist (Trust) Association (Inc)* [1970] AC 874 at 899, 904–905, 910, [1969] 3 All ER 172 at 180, 184–185, 189, HL.

3   See *Birmingham Corpn v West Midland Baptist (Trust) Association (Inc)* [1970] AC 874, [1969] 3 All ER 172, HL; and PARA 632.

636.   Withdrawal of notice to treat.   A notice to treat can always be withdrawn with the consent of both parties[1]. The right to withdraw, arising when the party served with the notice is entitled to require the undertakers to take more land than they desire and does so require[2], amounts to withdrawal by consent[3].

Where the person served with a notice to treat[4] has delivered to the acquiring authority[5] a notice in writing of the amount claimed by him containing the necessary particulars of the nature of his interest and the details of the amount claimed in time so as to enable the authority to make a proper offer[6], the authority may, at any time within six weeks after delivery of the notice of claim for compensation, withdraw any notice to treat served on the claimant or on any other person interested in the land authorised to be acquired[7]. The authority is, however, then liable to pay compensation to the claimant or other person for any loss[8] or expenses occasioned to him by the giving and withdrawal of the notice[9].

If the claimant fails to deliver a proper notice of claim[10], the acquiring authority may withdraw any notice to treat which has been served on him, or on any other person interested in the land authorised to be acquired, at any time after the decision of the Upper Tribunal (the 'Tribunal') on his claim but not later than six weeks after the final determination of the claim by the Tribunal[11], unless the authority has entered into possession of the land by virtue of the notice to treat[12]. The person served with the notice to treat will be entitled to compensation for any loss or expense incurred before the time when, in the Tribunal's opinion, a proper notice of claim should have been delivered[13]. So long as the authority is entitled to withdraw a notice to treat under this power, it cannot be compelled to take the land to which the notice relates or to pay any compensation awarded in respect of the taking[14].

Power to withdraw a notice to treat may also be given by the special Act[15].

The above powers to withdraw a notice to treat may be excluded[16].

1   *Haynes v Haynes* (1861) 1 Drew & Sm 426 at 456; *Tiverton and North Devon Rly Co v Loosemore* (1884) 9 App Cas 480 at 506, 516, HL; *Tawney v Lynn and Ely Rly Co* (1847) 16 LJCh 282. The consent may be implied from the conduct of the parties.

2   Eg to take a whole house, when part only is required: see PARA 625.

3   *Wild v Woolwich Borough Council* [1910] 1 Ch 35, CA. See also PARA 637.

4   In relation to a compulsory acquisition in pursuance of a notice to treat, the 'notice to treat' means the notice to treat in pursuance of which the relevant interest is acquired: Land Compensation Act 1961 s 39(2). 'Relevant interest' means the interest acquired in pursuance of that notice: s 39(2). References in the Land Compensation Act 1961 to a notice to treat include references to a notice to treat which, under any enactment, is deemed to have been served, and references to the service of such a notice and to the date of service are to be construed accordingly: s 39(8). As to the meaning of 'enactment' see PARA 501 note 3. Any reference in s 39(2) to a notice to treat is to be construed, in relation to (1) the vesting of land in an urban development corporation, as a reference to a notice under the Local Government, Planning and Land Act 1980 s 141 (see TOWN AND COUNTRY PLANNING vol 46(3) (Reissue) PARA 1454) (s 141(5), Sch 27 paras 9, 13); (2) the vesting of land in a housing action trust, as a reference to

an order under the Housing Act 1988 s 76 (see HOUSING vol 22 (2006 Reissue) PARA 339) (s 76(6), Sch 9 paras 6, 10); (3) the vesting of land in the Urban Regeneration Agency, as a reference to an order under the Leasehold Reform, Housing and Urban Development Act 1993 s 161(1) (prospectively repealed) (see TRADE, INDUSTRY AND INDUSTRIAL RELATIONS vol 47 (2001 Reissue) PARA 851) (s 161(4), Sch 19 paras 1, 5 (prospectively repealed by the Housing and Regeneration Act 2008 ss 56, 321(1), Sch 8 para 63, Sch 16)). References in the Land Compensation Act 1961 to the date of service of a notice to treat are to be treated for those purposes as references to the date on which the relevant order comes into force (see the Local Government, Planning and Land Act 1980 Sch 27 para 10; the Housing Act 1988 Sch 9 para 7; and the Leasehold Reform, Housing and Urban Development Act 1993 Sch 19 para 2).

5   As to the meaning of 'acquiring authority' see PARA 622 note 1.
6   Ie a notice under the Land Compensation Act 1961 s 4(1)(b), (2): see PARA 716.
7   Land Compensation Act 1961 s 31(1). As to the meaning of 'land' see PARA 516 note 2. The notice may be withdrawn even after possession has been taken and an adequate payment made: *R v Northumbrian Water Ltd, ex p Able UK Ltd* [1995] TLR 683, sub nom *R v Northumberland Water Ltd, ex p Able UK Ltd* [1996] RVR 146. In such an event the advance payment is returnable: *R v Northumbrian Water Ltd, ex p Able UK Ltd.*
8   As to such loss see *Duke of Grafton v Secretary of State for Air* (1956) 6 P & CR 374, CA (surveyor's fees); *LCC v Montague Burton Ltd* [1934] 1 KB 360, DC (ground rent and interest on money borrowed).
9   Land Compensation Act 1961 s 31(3). Compensation payable under s 31(3) carries interest at the rate for the time being prescribed under s 32 (see PARA 641) from the date of the withdrawal of the notice to treat: Planning and Compensation Act 1991 s 80(1), Sch 18 Pt I. Payments on account may be made of such compensation or interest (s 80(2)) and may be recoverable where it is subsequently agreed or determined that there was no liability to pay the compensation or interest or that the payment on account was excessive (s 80(3)). In default of agreement the amount of the compensation must be determined by the Upper Tribunal: Land Compensation Act 1961 s 31(4) (amended by SI 2009/1307). The Upper Tribunal has jurisdiction to consider a disputed compensation claim even where the requirements of the Land Compensation Act 1961 s 31 have not been met, if the parties have agreed that the acquiring authority can withdraw its notice to treat on condition that the landowner is to be compensated for proven losses: *Williams v Blaenau Gwent Borough Council* (1994) 67 P & CR 393, Lands Tribunal. However, the cause of action arises when the notice to treat is withdrawn and the Limitation Act 1980 s 9 (see LIMITATION PERIODS vol 68 (2008) PARA 1005) applies: *Williams v Blaenau Gwent Borough Council (No 2)* [1999] 2 EGLR 195, Lands Tribunal (applying *Hillingdon London Borough Council v ARC Ltd* [1999] Ch 139, (1997) 75 P & CR 346, CA: see PARA 645). The Lands Tribunal was abolished on 1 June 2009 and its functions were transferred to the Upper Tribunal: see PARA 720.
10 See the text to note 6.
11 The claim is not to be deemed to be finally determined so long as the time for requiring the Upper Tribunal to state a case with respect to it, or for appealing from any decision on the points raised by a case so stated, has not expired: Land Compensation Act 1961 s 31(6) (amended by SI 2009/1307). As to the Upper Tribunal see PARA 720; and ADMINISTRATIVE LAW.
12 Land Compensation Act 1961 s 31(2) (amended by SI 2009/1307).
13 Land Compensation Act 1961 s 31(3) (amended by SI 2009/1307). As to the compensation see the text and note 9; and see *Methodist Church Trustees v North Tyneside Metropolitan Borough Council* (1979) 38 P & CR 665.
14 Land Compensation Act 1961 s 31(5).
15 See eg the Small Holdings and Allotments Act 1908 s 39(8); and AGRICULTURAL LAND vol 1 (2008) PARA 549; and see *R v Woods and Forests Comrs, ex p Budge* (1850) 15 QB 761 at 774. As to the meaning of 'special Act' see PARAS 509, 514.
16 Land Compensation Act 1961 s 40(2)(a). For provisions excluding the power, mostly in relation to notices deemed to have been served, see the Agriculture Act 1967 s 49(7)(ii) (see AGRICULTURAL LAND vol 1 (2008) PARA 666); the Forestry Act 1967 s 22(5) (see FORESTRY vol 19(1) (2007 Reissue) PARA 145); the Town and Country Planning Act 1990 ss 139(5), 143(8), 146(6), 167 (see TOWN AND COUNTRY PLANNING vol 46(2) (Reissue) PARAS 970, 974, 976, 997). See also the Land Compensation Act 1973 s 54(4) (see PARA 623) and the Compulsory Purchase (Vesting Declarations) Act 1981 s 7(3) (see PARA 689).

637.   Effect of failure to take subsequent steps after notice to treat. A party who, by laches or misconduct, delays the completion of the quasi-contract to purchase may thereby deprive himself of the right to enforce the notice to treat[1].

Similarly, the conduct of the parties may amount to a waiver of their rights under the notice, as, for example, if after some delay the acquiring authority informs the owner of the land of its intention to abandon the undertaking[2]. The implied acceptance of an invalid notice as valid, by proceeding as if it were valid, may prevent the parties from contesting its validity at a later stage[3].

1   *Grice v Dudley Corpn* [1958] Ch 329, [1957] 2 All ER 673. A railway undertaker might do so
     by delaying to complete until the time for executing the authorised works had expired: *Tiverton
     and North Devon Rly Co v Loosemore* (1884) 9 App Cas 480 at 496, HL; *Richmond v North
     London Rly Co* (1868) LR 5 Eq 352 (affd 3 Ch App 679 at 680 per Lord Cairns LC). A special
     power was given by the Town and Country Planning Act 1959 s 14 (repealed) to take steps to
     acquire land under long-standing notices to treat given before 6 August 1947 without affecting
     the question as to the validity of the notice to treat.
         As to lapse of a notice to treat under the Compulsory Purchase Act 1965 s 5(2A) see PARA
     616.
2   *Hedges v Metropolitan Rly Co* (1860) 28 Beav 109; *Stretton v Great Western and Brentford
     Rly Co* (1870) 5 Ch App 751. Thus, in a claim by the undertakers to ascertain the validity of a
     notice to treat, the landowner is entitled to raise the defence that the undertakers have
     improperly depreciated the value of the property: *London Corpn v Horner* (1914) 111 LT
     512, CA.
3   *Lynch v London Sewers Comrs* (1886) 32 ChD 72, CA; *R v South Holland Drainage
     Committee Men* (1838) 8 Ad & El 429; *Pinchin v London and Blackwall Rly Co* (1854) 5 De
     GM & G 851, 24 LJCh 417.

(5) ENTRY BEFORE COMPLETION

(i) Entry with Owner's Consent or after Payment of Compensation

638.   Necessity for consent or payment.   Except with the consent of the owners and occupiers[1], the undertakers[2] or acquiring authority[3] may not enter upon any of the land subject to compulsory purchase[4] until the compensation payable for the respective interests in the land has been agreed or awarded and has been paid to the persons having those interests or paid into court[5]. The undertakers or acquiring authority may, however, enter and use the land without having paid the compensation upon making certain payments into court by way of security and giving bonds[6]. Furthermore, some special Acts[7], and the Compulsory Purchase Act 1965 in its application to acquisitions authorised by a compulsory purchase order[8], provide for entry after service of a notice to treat without such payment into court[9].

If the undertakers are authorised by the special Act to enter upon land for the purpose of acquiring an interest in it, such as the appropriation and use of the subsoil in order to make a tunnel, they can only make the entry on such of the above conditions as apply to the particular authorisation[10]. Where the special Act enables the acquiring authority to compel the creation of an easement, an entry on land for the purpose of creating those easements is subject to the above limitations and conditions[11]. Some special Acts authorise the entry on land in order to acquire certain rights and to do certain work, as, for example, to lay pipes[12] without purchasing land or any easement over it, in which case the undertakers can enter without complying with the above conditions[13].

1   Once given, the consent cannot be withdrawn: see *Knapp v London, Chatham and Dover
     Rly Co* (1863) 2 H & C 212; and PARA 644 note 4. For a temporary purpose the occupier's
     consent may be sufficient: *Standish v Liverpool Corpn* (1852) 1 Drew 1.
2   As to the meaning of 'undertakers' see PARA 511.
3   As to the meaning of 'acquiring authority' for these purposes see PARA 549 note 5.
4   Where the Lands Clauses Consolidation Act 1845 is incorporated (see PARA 509), the land is
     that which the undertakers are empowered to take and which is required to be permanently

used; and under certain Acts land may be required for temporary purposes: see e g the Railways Clauses Consolidation Act 1845 ss 30–44; and RAILWAYS, INLAND WATERWAYS AND CROSS-COUNTRY PIPELINES. Where the Compulsory Purchase Act 1965 applies (see PARA 513), the land is the land the compulsory purchase of which is authorised by the compulsory purchase order: see PARA 549 note 2. As to the meaning of 'land' see PARA 549 note 1. See also PARA 511 text to note 7.

5   Lands Clauses Consolidation Act 1845 s 84 (amended by the Administration of Justice Act 1965 s 17(1), Sch 1); Compulsory Purchase Act 1965 s 11(4). As to payment into court see PARAS 555 note 6, 640. Section 11 is modified in relation to the compulsory acquisition of rights by, inter alia:

    (1)   a local authority (see the Local Government (Miscellaneous Provisions) Act 1976 s 13(3)(b), Sch 1 para 9; and LOCAL GOVERNMENT vol 69 (2009) PARA 511);

    (2)   urban development corporations (see the Local Government, Planning and Land Act 1980 s 144, Sch 28 para 23(4); and TOWN AND COUNTRY PLANNING vol 46(1) (Reissue) PARA 180);

    (3)   highway authorities (see the Highways Act 1980 s 250(5)(a), Sch 19 para 9; and HIGHWAYS, STREETS AND BRIDGES vol 21 (2004 Reissue) PARAS 49 et seq, 85);

    (4)   gas transporters (see the Gas Act 1986 s 9(3), Sch 3 para 10; and FUEL AND ENERGY vol 19(2) (2007 Reissue) PARA 841);

    (5)   housing action trusts (see the Housing Act 1988 s 78(2), Sch 10 para 23(2); and HOUSING vol 22 (2006 Reissue) PARA 340);

    (6)   licence holders under the Electricity Act 1989 (see s 10(1), Sch 3 para 11; and FUEL AND ENERGY vol 19(2) (2007 Reissue) PARA 1284);

    (7)   the Environment Agency (see the Water Resources Act 1991 s 154(5), Sch 18 para 6; the Environment Act 1995 (Consequential Amendments) Regulations 1996, SI 1996/593, reg 2, Sch 1; and WATER AND WATERWAYS vol 101 (2009) PARA 453);

    (8)   water and sewerage undertakers (see the Water Industry Act 1991 s 155(5), Sch 9 para 6; and WATER AND WATERWAYS vol 101 (2009) PARA 453);

    (9)   regional development agencies (see the Regional Development Agencies Act 1998 s 20, Sch 5 para 5(2); and TRADE, INDUSTRY AND INDUSTRIAL RELATIONS vol 47 (2001 Reissue) PARA 901); and

    (10)   universal service providers (see the Postal Services Act 2000 s 95, Sch 5 para 10; and POST OFFICE).

6   See PARAS 640–641.

7   As to the meaning of 'special Act' see PARAS 509, 514.

8   As to compulsory purchase orders see PARA 556 et seq.

9   See PARA 645. A notice to treat is not rendered invalid by reason of its being served after the authority has taken possession of the land: *Cohen v Haringey London Borough Council* (1980) 42 P & CR 6, CA.

10   *Farmer v Waterloo and City Rly Co* [1895] 1 Ch 527, applying *Metropolitan Rly Co v Fowler* [1893] AC 416 at 423, HL; and see *Spencer v Metropolitan Board of Works* (1882) 22 ChD 142, CA.

11   *Hill v Midland Rly Co* (1882) 21 ChD 143, as explained in *Great Western Rly Co v Swindon and Cheltenham Rly Co* (1884) 9 App Cas 787 at 802, 811, HL. See also *Midland Rly Co v Great Western Rly Co* [1909] AC 445, HL. The interference with an easement over the land taken is not an entry on land for the purposes of requiring the conditions for entry before completion to apply as respects the person entitled to the easement: *Clark v London School Board* (1874) 9 Ch App 120 at 124; *Bush v Trowbridge Waterworks Co* (1875) 10 Ch App 459; and see PARA 532.

12   See e g the Water Industry Act 1991 ss 158, 159; and WATER AND WATERWAYS vol 101 (2009) PARAS 462–463.

13   *Roderick v Aston Local Board* (1877) 5 ChD 328, CA; *North London Rly Co v Metropolitan Board of Works* (1859) 28 LJCh 909.

(ii) Entry without Consent or Payment, on Payment into Court or Bond

639. Entry on payment into court; bond securing purchase money. When the undertakers[1] or acquiring authority[2] desire[3] to enter upon and use, without consent, any of the land[4] which they require to purchase before an agreement has been come to or award made for the purchase money or compensation to be paid by them in respect of that land, they may do so, without having first paid or deposited the purchase money or compensation, on the terms of (1) paying into the Supreme Court[5] by way of security either the amount of purchase money or compensation claimed by any party interested or entitled to sell and convey the land (the 'owner')[6] who does not consent to that entry or such a sum as is determined by an able practical surveyor[7] to be the value of that land, or of the interest in it which that party is entitled or able to sell and convey; and (2) delivering a bond with sureties[8] for a sum equal to the sum so deposited[9].

The value of the land to be so determined includes the damage by severance or other injurious affection so far as it can be estimated, as well as the value of the land itself [10]. The surveyor should properly examine the premises so as to form a fair judgment[11]; if he does so in good faith, the fact that the sum is inadequate, or that he valued without sufficient knowledge of the relevant facts, does not entitle the owner to an injunction restraining the undertakers or acquiring authority from taking possession of the land pending a proper valuation[12]. When the undertakers or authority are authorised to purchase a right in land the surveyor determines only the value of that right, and not of the whole land[13]. If there is a dispute as to the title, but both claimants are known, the amount must be settled by the appropriate procedure before the land can be vested in the undertakers[14].

1 As to the meaning of 'undertakers' see PARA 511.
2 As to the meaning of 'acquiring authority' for these purposes see PARA 549 note 5.
3 The power of entry after deposit and bond does not appear to be confined to cases of urgent necessity: see *Loosemore v Tiverton and North Devon Rly Co* (1882) 22 ChD 25 at 39, 46, CA; on appeal sub nom *Tiverton and North Devon Rly Co v Loosemore* (1884) 9 App Cas 480, HL.
4 As to the meaning of 'land' see PARA 549 note 1. See also PARA 511 text to note 7.
5 As to payment into court see PARAS 555 note 6, 640. As from 1 October 2009, the reference to the Supreme Court is replaced by a reference to the Senior Courts: see the Lands Clauses Consolidation Act 1845 s 85 (prospectively amended by the Constitutional Reform Act 2005 s 59(5), Sch 11 para 9).
6 As to such persons see PARA 553.
7 Where the Lands Clauses Consolidation Act 1845 is incorporated (see PARA 509), the surveyor must be appointed by two justices of the peace acting together: s 85. So also where the Compulsory Purchase Act 1965 applies (see PARA 513), the surveyor must be appointed by two justices of the peace, acting together: s 11(2), Sch 3 para 2(2). Notice of an application to appoint a surveyor need not be given to the owner of the land: see *Bridges v Wilts, Somerset and Weymouth Rly Co* (1847) 16 LJCh 335; *Langham v Great Northern Rly Co* (1848) 1 De G & Sm 486 at 499.
8 As to bonds see PARA 641.
9 Lands Clauses Consolidation Act 1845 s 85 (amended by the Administration of Justice Act 1965 s 17(1), Sch 1); Compulsory Purchase Act 1965 s 25(1), Sch 3 paras 1, 2(1), 3(1). Where the undertakers or acquiring authority are required to take the whole of the premises after serving a notice to treat for part of them, the deposit must be the value of the whole: *Giles v London Chatham and Dover Rly Co* (1861) 30 LJCh 603; *Underwood v Bedford and Cambridge Rly Co* (1861) 7 Jur NS 941; *Gardner v Charing Cross Rly Co* (1861) 2 John & H 248. Where one notice to treat is served in respect of several parcels of land, the undertakers or authority must deposit the value of the whole before entering some only of the parcels: *Barker v North Staffordshire Rly Co* (1848) 5 Ry & Can Cas 401, 2 De G & Sm 55; *Ford v Plymouth, Devonport and South Western Junction Rly Co* [1887] WN 201.
10 *Field v Carnarvon and Llanberis Rly Co* (1867) LR 5 Eq 190.
11 *Cotter v Metropolitan Rly Co* (1864) 4 New Rep 454, 12 WR 1021. See also *Barker v North Staffordshire Rly Co* (1848) 5 Ry & Can Cas 401, 2 De G & Sm 55; *Stamps v Birmingham, Wolverhampton and Stour Valley Rly Co* (1848) 7 Hare 251 at 256 (on appeal on other grounds 2 Ph 673).
12 *River Roden Co Ltd v Barking Town UDC* (1902) 18 TLR 608, CA.
13 *Hill v Midland Rly Co* (1882) 21 ChD 143; and see *Lambert v Dublin, Wicklow and Wexford Rly Co* (1890) 25 LR Ir 163. See also *Loosemore v Tiverton and North Devon Rly Co* (1882)

22 ChD 25 at 42–43, CA (on appeal sub nom *Tiverton and North Devon Rly Co v Loosemore* (1884) 9 App Cas 480, HL); *Ex p Neath and Brecon Rly Co* (1876) 2 ChD 201 (minerals excluded).

14   *Ex p London and South Western Rly Co* (1869) 38 LJCh 527; *Re Lowestoft Manor and Great Eastern Rly Co, ex p Reeve* (1883) 24 ChD 253, CA.

640.   Payment into court. The deposit is made by paying the money into the Supreme Court[1]. One or more accounts must be opened and kept in the Accountant General's name at such bank or banks as may be designated by the Lord Chancellor with Treasury concurrence[2]. Lodgments of money are made directly to the bank to the credit of the Accountant General's account[3]. Where the money lodged directly with the bank has been received and credited to the Accountant General's account, the bank must certify on the lodgment direction[4] that funds have been lodged and must send it to the Court Funds Office[5]. The deposit is for the benefit of the persons interested and is subject to the control and disposition of the High Court[6].

1   Lands Clauses Consolidation Act 1845 s 85 (amended by the Administration of Justice Act 1965 s 17(1), Sch 1) (where that Act is incorporated: see PARA 509); Compulsory Purchase Act 1965 s 25(1). As from 1 October 2009, the reference to the Supreme Court is replaced by a reference to the Senior Courts: see the Lands Clauses Consolidation Act 1845 s 85 (prospectively amended by the Constitutional Reform Act 2005 s 59(5), Sch 11 para 9); and the Compulsory Purchase Act 1965 s 25(1) (prospectively amended by the Constitutional Reform Act 2005 Sch 11 para 4).

2   Administration of Justice Act 1982 s 38(2). As to the Treasury see CONSTITUTIONAL LAW AND HUMAN RIGHTS vol 8(2) (Reissue) PARAS 512–517.

3   Court Funds Rules 1987, SI 1987/821, r 16(5) (amended by SI 1999/1021; SI 2003/375).

4   Ie the lodgment direction issued under the Court Funds Rules 1987, SI 1987/821, r 14: see r 18.

5   Court Funds Rules 1987, SI 1987/821, r 18.

6   See PARA 642. As to the payment of costs see *Re London, Brighton and South Coast Rly Co, ex p Flower* (1866) 1 Ch App 599; *Ex p Morris* (1871) LR 12 Eq 418; *Charlton v Rolleston* (1884) 28 ChD 237, CA.

641.   Bond. In addition to making the deposit[1], the undertakers[2] or acquiring authority[3] must give or tender to the owner a bond under their common or official seal if they are a corporation, or if not, then under the hands and seals of them or any two of them, with two sufficient sureties[4], in a penal sum equal to the sum to be deposited, conditioned for payment to the owner, or for payment into the Supreme Court[5], of all the purchase money or compensation which may be agreed or awarded, together with interest on it[6], from the time of entering on the land[7] until the purchase money or compensation is paid to that party or into court[8].

1   See PARA 640.

2   As to the meaning of 'undertakers' see PARA 511.

3   As to the meaning of 'acquiring authority' see PARA 549 note 5.

4   Where the parties do not agree as to the sureties they must be approved by two justices: Lands Clauses Consolidation Act 1845 s 85; Compulsory Purchase Act 1965 s 11(2), Sch 3 para 3(3). As to the procedure see *Bridges v Wilts, Somerset and Weymouth Rly Co* (1847) 16 LJCh 335. As to the undertakers' solicitors acting as sureties see *Langham v Great Northern Rly Co* (1848) 1 De G & Sm 486. In special Acts it is often provided that the bond shall be sufficient without the addition of any sureties. As to the meaning of 'special Act' see PARAS 509, 514.

    The Compulsory Purchase Act 1965 Sch 3 para 3 does not apply to acquisitions of land under the Crossrail Act 2008 s 6(1): see Sch 6 Pt 2 para 3; and RAILWAYS, INLAND WATERWAYS AND CROSS-COUNTRY PIPELINES vol 39(1A) (Reissue) PARA 325.

5   As from 1 October 2009, the reference to the Supreme Court is replaced by a reference to the Senior Courts: see the Lands Clauses Consolidation Act 1845 s 85 (prospectively amended by

the Constitutional Reform Act 2005 s 59(5), Sch 11 para 9); and the Compulsory Purchase Act 1965 s 25(1) (prospectively amended by the Constitutional Reform Act 2005 Sch 11 para 4).

6 The rate of interest is that prescribed by regulations under the Land Compensation Act 1961 s 32. With effect from 31 December 1995, the Acquisition of Land (Rate of Interest after Entry) Regulations 1995, SI 1995/2262, prescribe a rate of 0.5% below the standard rate: reg 2(1). For these purposes, the standard rate is: (1) the base rate quoted by the reference banks and effective on the reference day most recently preceding the day on which entry onto the land has been made or, where that day is a reference day, such reference day; and (2) the base rate quoted by the reference banks and effective on each subsequent reference day preceding payment of compensation: regs 1, 2(2). If different base rates are quoted by different banks and effective on a reference day, the rate which, when the base rate quoted by each reference bank is ranked in a descending sequence of seven, is fourth in the sequence is to be used to obtain the standard rate: reg 2(3). If more than one base rate is quoted by a reference bank and effective on a reference day, the last quoted rate is to be treated as the base rate quoted by that reference bank and effective on that day: reg 2(4). The reference banks, in relation to any reference day, are the seven largest persons who: (a) have permission under the Financial Services and Markets Act 2000 Pt 4 to accept deposits; (b) are incorporated in the United Kingdom and carrying on there a regulated activity of accepting deposits; and (c) quote a base rate in sterling effective as mentioned in the Acquisition of Land (Rate of Interest after Entry) Regulations 1995, SI 1995/2262, reg 2(2)–(4) (see above) (reg 2(5)(a) (substituted by SI 2001/3649)); and the size of a person is determined by reference to his total consolidated gross assets (together with any subsidiary) denominated in sterling, as shown in his audited end-year accounts last published before the relevant reference day: Acquisition of Land (Rate of Interest after Entry) Regulations 1995, SI 1995/2262, reg 2(5)(b), (6) (amended by SI 2001/3649). The reference days are 31 March, 30 June, 30 September and 31 December or, if any such day is not a business day, the next business day: Acquisition of Land (Rate of Interest after Entry) Regulations 1995, SI 1995/2262, reg 2(7). As to the meaning of 'United Kingdom' see PARA 100 note 21.

Payments on account may be made of any interest payable on any such bond, which are recoverable if the payments are subsequently agreed or determined not to be due, or shown to be excessive: see the Planning and Compensation Act 1991 s 80(2), (3).

7 As to the meaning of 'land' see PARA 549 note 1. See also PARA 511 text to note 7.

8 Lands Clauses Consolidation Act 1845 s 85 (amended by the Administration of Justice Act 1965 s 17(1), Sch 1); Compulsory Purchase Act 1965 ss 11(2), 25(1), Sch 3 para 3(1)–(3). As to variations and additions in the form of the bond see *Hosking v Phillips* (1848) 3 Exch 168; *Poynder v Great Northern Rly Co* (1847) 2 Ph 330; *Langham v Great Northern Rly Co* (1848) 1 De G & Sm 486; *Cotter v Metropolitan Rly Co* (1864) 4 New Rep 454, 12 WR 1021; *Willey v South Eastern Rly Co* (1849) 1 Mac & G 58.

642. Application of money paid in until performance of bond. The money paid into court[1] must remain there by way of security to the parties whose land has been entered upon, for the performance of the condition of the bond given by the undertakers or the acquiring authority[2]. If dealt with under the Administration of Justice Act 1982[3], the money must be accumulated and, upon the condition of the bond being fully performed, the Chancery Division of the High Court may, on the application by summons[4] of the undertakers[5] or the acquiring authority[6], order the money or the proceeds of the securities in which it has been invested together with the accumulation of it to be paid to the undertakers or the authority[7]. If the condition has not been fully performed, the court may order the money to be applied in such manner as it thinks fit for the benefit of the parties for whose security it was paid[8].

In order that the money should be repaid, it is not necessary that all questions between the parties should be settled, as, for example, the payment of costs[9]. It is enough that the condition of the bond has been performed, either by payment to the person to whom the bond was given[10] or, in case of refusal by him, into court[11]. If the purchase is abandoned with the consent of the owner of the land, the undertakers or acquiring authority will be entitled to repayment of the money[12]. If the condition of the bond is not performed, the owner of the land will be entitled, on an application by him to the court, to have the money paid out to him[13]. If the price has been fixed by agreement or otherwise, he may also bring a claim for specific performance[14], or he may enforce his lien on the land as an ordinary vendor, in which case the money in court will be paid in respect of the purchase price[15]. If the price fixed is larger than the sum in court, and there is delay in completion, the owner of the land is entitled to have the amount of the deposit increased until it is equal to the price[16].

1   See PARA 640.
2   Lands Clauses Consolidation Act 1845 s 86 (substituted by the Administration of Justice Act 1965 s 17(1), Sch 1); Compulsory Purchase Act 1965 s 11(2), Sch 3 para 4(1).
3   Ie under the Administration of Justice Act 1982 s 38: see CIVIL PROCEDURE vol 12 (2009) PARA 1548.
4   See the Supreme Court Act 1981 s 61(1), (3), Sch 1 para 1; CPR Pt 8 (claim forms); and *Practice Direction—Miscellaneous Provisions about Payments into Court* PD37. See also *Re Neath and Brecon Rly Co* (1874) 9 Ch App 263; *Martin v London, Chatham and Dover Rly Co* (1866) 1 Ch App 501. As from 1 October 2009, the Supreme Court Act 1981 is renamed 'the Senior Courts Act 1981' by the Constitutional Reform Act 2005 Sch 11 para 1.
5   As to the meaning of 'undertakers' see PARA 511.
6   As to the meaning of 'acquiring authority' see PARA 549 note 5.
7   Lands Clauses Consolidation Act 1845 s 86 (as substituted (see note 2); amended by the Administration of Justice Act 1982 s 46(2)(a)); Compulsory Purchase Act 1965 s 25(1), Sch 3 para 4(2), (3); Interpretation Act 1978 s 17(2)(a). As to costs see PARA 666.
8   Lands Clauses Consolidation Act 1845 s 86 (as substituted: see note 2); Compulsory Purchase Act 1965 Sch 3 para 4(4).
9   *Re London and South Western Railway Extension Act, ex p Stevens* (1848) 2 Ph 772; *Ex p Great Northern Rly Co* (1848) 16 Sim 169 (further proceedings 5 Ry & Can Cas 269); *Re Wimbledon and Dorking Railway Act 1857, ex p Wimbledon and Dorking Rly Co* (1863) 9 LT 703.
10 *Ex p Midland Rly Co* [1904] 1 Ch 61, CA.
11 *Ex p Midland Rly Co* [1904] 1 Ch 61, CA; *Re Fooks* (1849) 2 Mac & G 357. For an example where it had not been performed see *Ex p London and South Western Rly Co* (1869) 38 LJCh 527. As to the evidence necessary to show that the condition has been performed see *Re London and North Western Rly Co* (1872) 26 LT 687; *Ex p Midland Rly Co* (1894) 38 Sol Jo 289.
12 *Ex p Birmingham, Wolverhampton and Dudley Rly Co* (1863) 1 Hem & M 772; and cf *Royal Bank of Canada v R* [1913] AC 283, PC.
13 *Re Mutlow's Estate* (1878) 10 ChD 131.
14 *Earl of Jersey v Briton Ferry Floating Dock Co* (1869) LR 7 Eq 409 at 413.
15 *Walker v Ware, Hadham and Buntingford Rly Co* (1865) LR 1 Eq 195; *Betty v London, Chatham and Dover Rly Co* [1867] WN 169; *Wing v Tottenham and Hampstead Junction Rly Co* (1868) 3 Ch App 740.
16 *Ashford v London, Chatham and Dover Rly Co* (1866) 14 LT 787; *Ex p London, Tilbury and Southend Rly Co* (1853) 1 WR 533.

643.   Time and mode of entry.   Entry, upon making a deposit and giving a bond, is a right consequent upon service of a notice to treat[1]. If a notice to treat is served within the time limited for the exercise of the powers of compulsory purchase, entry may be made after the expiration of that period, at any rate up to the limit of the time, if any, prescribed for the construction of the works[2]. The undertakers or acquiring authority may exercise the power to enter before completion of the purchase, even though there is no urgent necessity for immediate entry[3]. The power to enter includes the power to use the land[4]. If the undertakers or acquiring authority purport to enter under this power, but are in fact acting ultra vires, the entry will not assist their title, and will render them liable in damages[5].

1   *Tiverton and North Devon Rly Co v Loosemore* (1884) 9 App Cas 480 at 488, 495, 503, HL; *Doe d Armitstead v North Staffordshire Rly Co* (1851) 16 QB 526 at 536; *Great Western Rly Co v Swindon and Cheltenham Rly Co* (1884) 9 App Cas 787 at 805, 810, HL. If an

agreement for purchase has been made without a notice to treat, leaving the price to be ascertained as stipulated, the power of entry may be exercised: see *Ramsden v Manchester, South Junction and Altrincham Rly Co* (1848) 1 Exch 723; *Tiverton and North Devon Rly Co v Loosemore* above at 502–503. Although service of the notice to treat used to be characterised as creating a relationship between the parties analogous to that of vendor and purchaser, that analogy is now treated with caution: see PARA 631. As to service of the notice to treat see PARAS 617–618. As to giving a bond see PARA 641.

2   *Marquis of Salisbury v Great Northern Rly Co* (1852) 17 QB 840; *Tiverton and North Devon Rly Co v Loosemore* (1884) 9 App Cas 480 at 488, 495, 503, HL; *Doe d Armitstead v North Staffordshire Rly Co* (1851) 16 QB 526 at 536.
3   *Loosemore v Tiverton and North Devon Rly Co* (1882) 22 ChD 25 at 39, 46, CA; on appeal sub nom *Tiverton and North Devon Rly Co v Loosemore* (1884) 9 App Cas 480, HL, commenting on *Field v Carnarvon and Llanberis Rly Co* (1867) LR 5 Eq 190.
4   See the cases cited in note 2.
5   *Batson v London School Board* (1903) 67 JP 457.

644.   Unauthorised entry.   If the undertakers or acquiring authority enter without complying with any of the conditions to be observed prior to entry, they may be sued in trespass for damages[1], or for possession[2], and an injunction may be granted to restrain them from remaining in possession or using the land until they have complied with the necessary conditions[3]. These proceedings will not lie, however, at the instance of a person who has consented to the entry but who subsequently desires to withdraw his consent[4], which may be presumed from that person's conduct[5]. They will lie at the instance of any person having a legal or equitable interest in the land[6], unless by a mistake, in good faith, there has been an omission to purchase his interest, in which case the undertakers or acquiring authority may remain in possession for a certain time to enable them to purchase the interest[7].

If the undertakers[8] or acquiring authority[9] or any of their contractors wilfully[10] enter on and take possession of any of the land subject to compulsory purchase[11] in contravention of the conditions to be observed before entry[12], the undertakers or authority are subject to a penalty payable to the person in possession of that land[13] with additional penalties for each day on which they so remain in possession after any such sum has been adjudged to be forfeited[14]. These penalties are recoverable in addition to the amount of any damage done to the land by reason of the entry and taking possession[15]. Distress may be levied for the recovery of the penalties[16].

1   *Ramsden v Manchester, South Junction and Altrincham Rly Co* (1848) 1 Exch 723. As to entry in order to secure the public safety see *Tower v Eastern Counties Rly Co* (1843) 3 Ry & Can Cas 374.
2   *Stretton v Great Western and Brentford Rly Co* (1870) 5 Ch App 751; *Marquis of Salisbury v Great Northern Rly Co* (1858) 5 CBNS 174.
3   *Ranken v East and West India Docks and Birmingham Junction Rly Co* (1849) 12 Beav 298; *Perks v Wycombe Rly Co* (1862) 10 WR 788; *Cardwell v Midland Rly Co* (1904) 21 TLR 22, CA; and see *Goodson v Richardson* (1874) 9 Ch App 221; *Marriott v East Grinstead Gas and Water Co* [1909] 1 Ch 70; *Deere v Guest* (1836) 1 My & Cr 516; *Poynder v Great Northern Rly Co* (1847) 2 Ph 330; *Willey v South Eastern Rly Co* (1849) 1 Mac & G 58; *Lind v Isle of Wight Ferry Co* (1862) 1 New Rep 13; *Wood v Charing Cross Rly Co* (1863) 33 Beav 290; *Armstrong v Waterford and Limerick Rly Co* (1846) 10 I Eq R 60.
4   *Doe d Hudson v Leeds and Bradford Rly Co* (1851) 16 QB 796; *Knapp v London, Chatham and Dover Rly Co* (1863) 2 H & C 212; and see *Langford v Brighton, Lewes and Hastings Rly Co* (1845) 4 Ry & Can Cas 69.
5   *Greenhalgh v Manchester and Birmingham Rly Co* (1838) 3 My & Cr 784; and see *Marquis of Salisbury v Great Northern Rly Co* (1858) 5 CBNS 174.
6   *Martin v London, Chatham and Dover Rly Co* (1866) 1 Ch App 501; *Rogers v Kingston-upon-Hull Dock Co* (1864) 34 LJCh 165; *Birmingham and District Land Co v London and North Western Rly Co* (1888) 40 ChD 268, CA; and cf *Cooke v LCC* [1911]

1   Ch 604, where it was held that the promoters could serve a notice to treat on mortgagees and proceed against them in the ordinary way, even though they had entered into possession of the land as against the mortgagor.

7   See PARA 648.

8   As to the meaning of 'undertakers' see PARA 511.

9   As to the meaning of 'acquiring authority' see PARA 549 note 5.

10   Entry is not wilful if made under a mistaken idea that the conditions had been complied with (*Steele v Midland Rly Co* (1869) 21 LT 387; *Hutchinson v Manchester, Bury and Rossendale Rly Co* (1846) 15 M & W 314); and no penalty is incurred under these provisions if compensation has been paid in good faith and without collusion to any person whom the undertakers or acquiring authority reasonably believed to be entitled to it, or if it has been paid into court for the benefit of a person entitled to the land, or paid into court by way of security, even if that person was not in fact legally entitled to it (Lands Clauses Consolidation Act 1845 s 89 proviso; Compulsory Purchase Act 1965 s 12(6)).

11   As to the meaning of 'land' see PARA 549 note 1. See also PARA 511 text to note 7. As to the meaning of 'subject to compulsory purchase' see PARA 549 note 2.

12   As to these conditions see PARA 639. As to the exclusion of those conditions and the substitution of alternative powers of entry see PARA 645.

13   Lands Clauses Consolidation Act 1845 s 89; Compulsory Purchase Act 1965 s 12(1). Penalties for wrongful entry are recoverable before a magistrates' court summarily as a civil debt: Lands Clauses Consolidation Act 1845 s 89; Compulsory Purchase Act 1965 s 12(2). Appeal lies from a magistrates' court to the Crown Court: Lands Clauses Consolidation Act 1845 s 146; Compulsory Purchase Act 1965 s 12(3) (both amended by the Courts Act 1971 s 56(2), Sch 9 Pt I).

14   Lands Clauses Consolidation Act 1845 s 89; Compulsory Purchase Act 1965 s 12(4). Penalties for wrongfully continuing in possession are recoverable in the High Court and in any such proceedings the magistrates' court's decision is not conclusive as to the undertakers' or acquiring authority's right of entry: Lands Clauses Consolidation Act 1845 s 89 (amended by the Administration of Justice Act 1965 s 34, Sch 2), Lands Clauses Consolidation Act 1845 ss 90, 136 (s 136 amended by the Summary Jurisdiction Act 1884 s 4, Schedule); Compulsory Purchase Act 1965 s 12(5). See also note 13.

15   Lands Clauses Consolidation Act 1845 s 89; Compulsory Purchase Act 1965 s 12(1). Section 12 is modified in order to correspond to the modifications made to s 11 in relation to the compulsory acquisition of rights by, inter alia:

    (1)   a local authority (see the Local Government (Miscellaneous Provisions) Act 1976 s 13(3)(b), Sch 1 para 9; and LOCAL GOVERNMENT vol 69 (2009) PARA 511);

    (2)   urban development corporations (see the Local Government, Planning and Land Act 1980 s 144, Sch 28 para 23(4); and TOWN AND COUNTRY PLANNING vol 46(1) (Reissue) PARA 180);

    (3)   highway authorities (see the Highways Act 1980 s 250(5)(a), Sch 19 para 9; and HIGHWAYS, STREETS AND BRIDGES vol 21 (2004 Reissue) PARAS 49 et seq, 85);

    (4)   gas transporters (see the Gas Act 1986 s 9(3), Sch 3 para 10; and FUEL AND ENERGY vol 19(2) (2007 Reissue) PARA 841);

    (5)   housing action trusts (see the Housing Act 1988 s 78(2), Sch 10 para 23(2); and HOUSING vol 22 (2006 Reissue) PARA 340);

    (6)   licence holders under the Electricity Act 1989 (see s 10(1), Sch 3 para 11; and FUEL AND ENERGY vol 19(2) (2007 Reissue) PARA 1284);

    (7)   the Environment Agency (see the Water Resources Act 1991 s 154(5), Sch 18 para 6; the Environment Act 1995 (Consequential Amendments) Regulations 1996, SI 1996/593, reg 2, Sch 1; and WATER AND WATERWAYS vol 101 (2009) PARA 453);

    (8)   water and sewerage undertakers (see the Water Industry Act 1991 s 155(5), Sch 9 para 6; and WATER AND WATERWAYS vol 101 (2009) PARA 453;

    (9)   regional development agencies (see the Regional Development Agencies Act 1998 s 20, Sch 5 para 5(2); and TRADE, INDUSTRY AND INDUSTRIAL RELATIONS vol 47 (2001 Reissue) PARA 901); and

    (10)   universal service providers (see the Postal Services Act 2000 s 95, Sch 5 para 10; and POST OFFICE).

16   No distress levied under the Compulsory Purchase Act 1965 is to be deemed unlawful, nor is the person making the distress to be deemed a trespasser on account of any defect or want of form in the warrant of distress or other proceedings relating to the distress; and the person making the distress is not to be deemed a trespasser ab initio on account of any irregularity afterwards committed by him so, however, that any person aggrieved by any defect or irregularity may recover full satisfaction for the special damage in civil proceedings: Compulsory Purchase

Act 1965 s 29(1) (prospectively repealed by the Tribunals, Courts and Enforcement 2007
ss 62(3), 146, Sch 13 paras 27, 29, Sch 23 Pt 3). At the date at which this volume states the law
no day had been appointed for the repeal of this provision to take effect. The corresponding
provisions of the Lands Clauses Consolidation Act 1845 (ie ss 138, 141) have already been
repealed (see the Statute Law (Repeals) Act 1993).

(iii) Entry without Consent, Payment, Payment into Court or Bond

645.   Entry on notice after notice to treat.   If, where the power to acquire land
is under a compulsory purchase order to which the Compulsory Purchase
Act 1965 applies[1], the acquiring authority[2] has served notice to treat[3] in respect
of any of the land[4] and has served on the owner[5], lessee and occupier of that land
not less than 14 days' notice[6], the authority may enter[7] on and take possession of
that land or such part of it as is specified in the notice[8]. Any compensation
agreed or awarded for the land carries interest at the prescribed rate[9] from the
time of entry until the compensation is paid or is paid into court[10]. Payments on
account may be made of such compensation or interest so payable[11] which may
be recoverable where it is subsequently agreed or determined that there was no
liability to pay the compensation or interest or that the payment on account was
excessive[12].

1   See PARA 513.
2   As to the meaning of 'acquiring authority' see PARA 549 note 5.
3   As to the persons entitled to a notice to treat see PARA 619. A tenant from year to year is not
    entitled to a notice to treat (see PARA 702), but may be given one, and his right to compensation
    will arise on entry: see *R v Stone* (1866) LR 1 QB 529; and PARA 701 note 2. However, his
    compensation will be derived from the Compulsory Purchase Act 1965 s 20 (see PARAS
    699–700, 702): see *R v Kennedy* [1893] 1 QB 533; *Newham London Borough Council v
    Benjamin* [1968] 1 All ER 1195, [1968] 1 WLR 694, CA.
4   As to the meaning of 'land' see PARA 549 note 1.
5   As to the meaning of 'owner' see PARA 549 note 7.
6   Where the notice is required to be served on an owner of land which is ecclesiastical property as
    defined in the Acquisition of Land Act 1981 s 12(3) (see PARA 560), a similar notice must be
    served on the Diocesan Board of Finance for the diocese in which the land is situated:
    Compulsory Purchase Act 1965 s 11(1) (amended by the Acquisition of Land Act 1981 s 34(1),
    Sch 4 para 14(1), (3); and the Church of England (Miscellaneous Provisions) Measure 2006
    s 14, Sch 5 para 12(1)).
7   As to unauthorised entry or entry on the wrong land see PARA 644. As to the position where
    land is taken by stages following a single notice of entry see *Chilton v Telford Development
    Corpn* [1987] 3 All ER 992, [1987] 1 WLR 872, CA.
8   Compulsory Purchase Act 1965 s 11(1). As to the modification of s 11 in relation to the
    compulsory acquisition of rights by, inter alia, local authorities, urban development
    corporations, highway authorities, gas transporters, housing action trusts, licence holders under
    the Electricity Act 1989, the Environment Agency, water and sewerage undertakers, regional
    development agencies and universal service providers see PARA 638 note 5. The Compulsory
    Acquisition Act 1965 s 11(1) is modified in relation to acquisitions under the Crossrail Act 2008
    s 6(1): see Sch 6 Pt 2 para 3; and RAILWAYS, INLAND WATERWAYS AND CROSS-COUNTRY
    PIPELINES vol 39(1A) (Reissue) PARA 325.
9   Ie under the Land Compensation Act 1961 s 32: see PARA 641.
10 Compulsory Purchase Act 1965 s 11(1). An immediate right to compensation arises at the date
    of entry and, in the absence of any agreement, is enforceable only at the suit of the claimant
    before the Upper Tribunal, which is a court of law for the purposes of the Limitation Act 1980
    s 38, and whose exercise in quantification is, in reality, an 'action to recover' a sum of money,
    subject to the limitation period laid down in s 9 (see LIMITATION PERIODS vol 68 (2008) PARA
    1005): *Hillingdon London Borough Council v ARC Ltd* [1999] Ch 139, (1997) 75 P & CR
    346, CA. As to payment into court see PARA 640. As to the Upper Tribunal: see PARA 720; and
    ADMINISTRATIVE LAW.
11 Planning and Compensation Act 1991 s 80(2), Sch 18 Pt II.
12 Planning and Compensation Act 1991 s 80(3).

(iv) Enforcement of Right to Enter

646. Entry peaceably or on warrant for possession. If the undertakers[1] or acquiring authority[2] are authorised[3] to enter upon and take possession of land[4] required for the purposes of the undertaking, and the owner or occupier of any of that land or any other person refuses to give up possession, or hinders the undertakers or the authority from entering upon or taking possession of that land, the undertakers or the authority may enter peaceably[5] or issue their warrant to the sheriff or enforcement officer[6] to deliver possession of the land to the person appointed in the warrant to receive it[7]. On receipt of the warrant, the person to whom it is issued must deliver possession of the land accordingly[8].

Nothing in the Protection from Eviction Act 1977 affects the operation of these provisions[9].

1   As to the meaning of 'undertakers' see PARA 511.
2   As to the meaning of 'acquiring authority' see PARA 549 note 5.

3   Ie under the Lands Clauses Acts or the Compulsory Purchase Act 1965, or under the special Act or any Act incorporated therewith: see the Lands Clauses Consolidation Act 1845 s 91; and the Compulsory Purchase Act 1965 s 13(1). As to the meaning of 'special Act' see PARAS 509, 514. As to the Lands Clauses Acts see PARA 509 note 1.

4   As to the meaning of 'land' see PARA 549 note 1. See also PARA 511 text to note 7.

5   The issue of a warrant is not necessary unless entry is actually resisted: *Loosemore v Tiverton and North Devon Rly Co* (1882) 22 ChD 25 at 41, CA; on appeal sub nom *Tiverton and North Devon Rly Co v Loosemore* (1884) 9 App Cas 480, HL.

6   'Sheriff' includes an under sheriff or legally competent deputy, and means the sheriff for the area where the land or any part of it is situated: Lands Clauses Consolidation Act 1845 s 3; Compulsory Purchase Act 1965 s 13(6).

7   Lands Clauses Consolidation Act 1845 s 91(1) (amended by the Tribunals, Courts and Enforcement Act 2007 s 139) (where the Lands Clauses Consolidation Act 1845 is incorporated: see PARA 509); Compulsory Purchase Act 1965 s 13(1) (amended by the Tribunals, Courts and Enforcement Act 2007 s 139) (where the Compulsory Purchase Act 1965 applies: see PARA 513).

8   Lands Clauses Consolidation Act 1845 s 91(1) (as amended: see note 7); Compulsory Purchase Act 1965 s 13(2) (as amended: see note 7). If, by virtue of the Courts Act 2003 Sch 7 para 3A, the warrant is issued to two or more persons collectively, the duty to deliver possession of lands applies to the person to whom the warrant is allocated in accordance with the approved arrangements mentioned in that Schedule: Lands Clauses Consolidation Act 1845 s 91(2) (added by the Tribunals, Courts and Enforcement Act 2007 s 139); Compulsory Purchase Act 1965 s 13(2A) (added by the Tribunals, Courts and Enforcement Act 2007 s 139).

     The Compulsory Purchase Act 1965 s 13(2) is modified in order to correspond to the modifications made to s 11 in relation to the compulsory acquisition of rights by, inter alia:

    (1)   a local authority (see the Local Government (Miscellaneous Provisions) Act 1976 s 13(3)(b), Sch 1 para 9; and LOCAL GOVERNMENT vol 69 (2009) PARA 511);

    (2)   urban development corporations (see the Local Government, Planning and Land Act 1980 s 144, Sch 28 para 23(4); and TOWN AND COUNTRY PLANNING vol 46(1) (Reissue) PARA 180);

    (3)   highway authorities (see the Highways Act 1980 s 250(5)(a), Sch 19 para 9; and HIGHWAYS, STREETS AND BRIDGES vol 21 (2004 Reissue) PARAS 49 et seq, 85);

    (4)   gas transporters (see the Gas Act 1986 s 9(3), Sch 3 para 10; and FUEL AND ENERGY vol 19(2) (2007 Reissue) PARA 841);

    (5)   housing action trusts (see the Housing Act 1988 s 78(2), Sch 10 para 23(2); and HOUSING vol 22 (2006 Reissue) PARA 340);

    (6)   licence holders under the Electricity Act 1989 (see s 10(1), Sch 3 para 11; and FUEL AND ENERGY vol 19(2) (2007 Reissue) PARA 1284);

    (7)   the Environment Agency (see the Water Resources Act 1991 s 154(5), Sch 18 para 6; the Environment Act 1995 (Consequential Amendments) Regulations 1996, SI 1996/593, reg 2, Sch 1; and WATER AND WATERWAYS vol 101 (2009) PARA 453);

    (8)   water and sewerage undertakers (see the Water Industry Act 1991 s 155(5), Sch 9 para 6; and WATER AND WATERWAYS vol 101 (2009) PARA 453);

(9) regional development agencies (see the Regional Development Agencies Act 1998 s 20, Sch 5 para 5(2); and TRADE, INDUSTRY AND INDUSTRIAL RELATIONS vol 47 (2001 Reissue) PARA 901); and

(10) universal service providers (see the Postal Services Act 2000 s 95, Sch 5 para 10; and POST OFFICE).

9 Protection from Eviction Act 1977 s 9(4)(e). See further CRIMINAL LAW, EVIDENCE AND PROCEDURE vol 11(1) (2006 Reissue) PARAS 608–609; LANDLORD AND TENANT vol 27(1) (2006 Reissue) PARAS 214–215, 653.

647. Costs of warrant for possession. The costs accruing by reason of the issue and execution of the warrant[1], to be settled by the person executing the warrant must be paid by the person refusing to give possession, and the amount of those costs must be deducted and retained by the undertakers[2] or acquiring authority from the compensation, if any, payable by them to that person[3].

If no compensation is so payable, or if the compensation is less than the costs, then the costs or the excess beyond the compensation, if not paid on demand, must be levied by distress[4], and upon application to any justice of the peace for that purpose he must issue his warrant accordingly[5]. If the compensation has been paid into court, the costs may be ordered to be paid out of the fund in court[6].

1 Ie the warrant for delivery of possession: see PARA 646.
2 As to the meaning of 'undertakers' see PARA 511.
3 Lands Clauses Consolidation Act 1845 s 91; Compulsory Purchase Act 1965 s 13(3) (both amended by the Tribunals, Courts and Enforcement Act 2007 s 139). As to the meaning of 'acquiring authority' see PARA 549 note 5.
4 As to distress see PARA 644 note 16. As from a day to be appointed the reference to distress is repealed and in its place is inserted a reference to recovery under the procedure in the Tribunals, Courts and Enforcement Act 2007 Sch 12 (taking control of goods) (not yet in force): see the Lands Clauses Consolidation Act 1845 s 91(1) (prospectively amended by the Tribunals, Courts and Enforcement Act 2007 Sch 13 para 7); Compulsory Purchase Act 1965 s 13(4) (prospectively amended by the Tribunals, Courts and Enforcement Act 2007 Sch 13 paras 27, 28). At the date at which this volume states the law no such day had been appointed.
5 Lands Clauses Consolidation Act 1845 s 91; Compulsory Purchase Act 1965 s 13(4). Any surplus arising from the sale under the distress, after satisfying the amount due and the expenses of the distress and sale, must be returned on demand to the person whose goods and chattels have been distrained: s 13(5). This provision is prospectively repealed by the Tribunals, Courts and Enforcement Act 2007 Sch 13 paras 27, 28, Sch 23 Pt 3 as from a day to be appointed. At the date at which this volume states the law no such day had been appointed. The corresponding provision of the Lands Clauses Consolidation Act 1845 (ie s 138) is already repealed: see PARA 644 note 16.
6 *Re Schmarr* [1902] 1 Ch 326 at 331, CA; *Re Turner's Estate and Metropolitan Railway Act 1860* (1861) 5 LT 524. As to payment into court see PARAS 555 note 6, 640.

(6) INTERESTS OMITTED BY MISTAKE FROM PURCHASE OR COMPENSATION

648. Acquiring authority's right to remain in possession. If, at any time after the undertakers[1] have entered upon any land which under the Lands Clauses Acts[2] or the special Act[3] or incorporated Acts they were authorised to purchase, which is permanently required for the purposes of the special Act, or after an acquiring authority[4] has entered upon any of the land subject to compulsory purchase[5], it appears that they have through mistake or inadvertence[6] failed or omitted duly to purchase or to pay compensation for any estate, right or interest in, or charge affecting, that land, then, whether the period allowed for the purchase of the land[7] has expired or not, the undertakers or the acquiring authority are entitled to remain in the undisturbed possession of the land, provided they purchase or pay compensation in the required time and manner[8]. Thus, if after the purchase and taking of land from an ostensible owner the undertakers or the acquiring authority become aware of the existence of a mortgage which they do not dispute, the mortgagee cannot eject them until the time has expired in which they may make compensation[9], nor can an owner do so if by reason of a mistake in the book of reference[10] they have taken more land than was shown by the measurements in that book[11].

If the undertakers or the authority dispute the existence of the right or interest, however, a claim for possession may be brought against them by the claimant in order to establish his right, but in such a case execution will be postponed for the same period[12].

1 As to the meaning of 'undertakers' see PARA 511.
2 As to the Lands Clauses Acts see PARA 509 note 1.
3 As to the meaning of 'special Act' see PARAS 509, 514.
4 As to the meaning of 'acquiring authority' see PARA 549 note 5.
5 As to the meaning of 'land' see PARA 549 note 1. See also PARA 511 text to note 7. As to the meaning of 'subject to compulsory purchase' see PARA 549 note 2.

6 The provision does not apply in the case of mere neglect, and, if the undertakers or the acquiring authority are aware of the existence of the right or interest, previous mistakes or ignorance will not bring them within the provision and they may be liable to actions for possession or in trespass and be restrained by injunction: see *Martin v London Chatham and Dover Rly Co* (1866) 1 Ch App 501; *Stretton v Great Western and Brentford Rly Co* (1870) 5 Ch App 751; *Thomas v Barry Dock and Rlys Co* (1889) 5 TLR 360; *Cardwell v Midland Rly Co* (1904) 21 TLR 22, CA; and see *Cooke v LCC* [1911] 1 Ch 604. As to the principles on which the courts act in granting injunctions in these cases see *Wood v Charing Cross Rly Co* (1863) 33 Beav 290; *Garrett v Banstead and Epsom Downs Rly Co* (1864) 13 WR 878; *Munro v Wivenhoe and Brightlingsea Rly Co* (1865) 13 WR 880; *Webster v South Eastern Rly Co* (1851) 1 Sim NS 272; *Lind v Isle of Wight Ferry Co* (1862) 1 New Rep 13.
7 Ie the period specified in the Compulsory Purchase Act 1965 s 4: see PARA 617.
8 Lands Clauses Consolidation Act 1845 s 124 (where that Act is incorporated: see PARA 509); Compulsory Purchase Act 1965 s 22(1), (2) (where that Act applies: see PARA 513). See *Union Railways (North) Ltd v Kent County Council* [2009] EWCA Civ 363, [2009] RVR 146, [2009] All ER (D) 56 (May) (right of owner of interest in land to initiate proceedings).
   The Compulsory Purchase Act 1965 s 22 is modified in relation to the compulsory acquisition of rights by, inter alia:
   (1) a local authority (see the Local Government (Miscellaneous Provisions) Act 1976 s 13(3)(b), Sch 1 para 11; and LOCAL GOVERNMENT vol 69 (2009) PARA 511);
   (2) urban development corporations (see the Local Government, Planning and Land Act 1980 s 144, Sch 28 para 23(6); and TOWN AND COUNTRY PLANNING vol 46(1) (Reissue) PARA 180);
   (3) highway authorities (see the Highways Act 1980 s 250(5)(a), Sch 19 para 11; and HIGHWAYS, STREETS AND BRIDGES vol 21 (2004 Reissue) PARAS 49 et seq, 85);
   (4) gas transporters (see the Gas Act 1986 s 9(3), Sch 3 para 12; and FUEL AND ENERGY vol 19(2) (2007 Reissue) PARA 841);
   (5) housing action trusts (see the Housing Act 1988 s 78(2), Sch 10 para 23(4); and HOUSING vol 22 (2006 Reissue) PARA 340);
   (6) licence holders under the Electricity Act 1989 (see s 10(1), Sch 3 para 13; and FUEL AND ENERGY vol 19(2) (2007 Reissue) PARA 1284);
   (7) the Environment Agency (see the Water Resources Act 1991 s 154(5), Sch 18 para 8; the Environment Act 1995 (Consequential Amendments) Regulations 1996, SI 1996/593, reg 2, Sch 1; and WATER AND WATERWAYS vol 101 (2009) PARA 453);
   (8) water and sewerage undertakers (see the Water Industry Act 1991 s 155(5), Sch 9 para 8; and WATER AND WATERWAYS vol 101 (2009) PARA 453);
   (9) regional development agencies (see the Regional Development Agencies Act 1998 s 20, Sch 5 para 5(4); and TRADE, INDUSTRY AND INDUSTRIAL RELATIONS vol 47 (2001 Reissue) PARA 901); and
   (10) universal service providers (see the Postal Services Act 2000 s 95, Sch 5 para 12; and POST OFFICE).

The Compulsory Purchase Act 1965 s 22(2) is also modified in relation to the acquisition of land under the Crossrail Act 2008 s 6(1): see Sch 6 Pt 2 para 3; and RAILWAYS, INLAND WATERWAYS AND CROSS-COUNTRY PIPELINES vol 39(1A) (Reissue) PARA 325.

9 *Jolly v Wimbledon and Dorking Rly Co* (1861) 31 LJQB 95, Ex Ch.

10 The undertakers may have power under their special Act or an enactment incorporated with it to correct mistakes or omissions in deposited plans or books of reference: see PARA 525 note 2.

11 *Hyde v Manchester Corpn* (1852) 5 De G & Sm 249; *Kemp v West End of London and Crystal Palace Rly Co* (1855) 1 K & J 681. Cf *Omagh Urban Council v Henderson* [1907] 2 IR 310.

12 *Marquis of Salisbury v Great Northern Rly Co* (1858) 5 CBNS 174; *Doe d Hyde v Manchester Corpn* (1852) 12 CB 474.

649.   Possession on purchase or payment of compensation. The condition entitling the undertakers[1] or the acquiring authority[2] to remain in possession of the land[3] is that within six months after notice of the estate, right, interest or charge, in cases where they do not dispute the claim, or in cases of dispute then within six months after the claim has been finally established by law in favour of the claimant[4], they must purchase or pay compensation for the estate, right, interest in, or charge affecting the land[5] which they have failed or omitted to purchase or pay compensation for[6]. They must also, within that time, pay to any person who may establish a right to it full compensation for the mesne profits[7] or interest which would have accrued to those persons during the interval between the undertakers' or authority's entry on the land and the time of the payment of the purchase money or compensation, so far as the mesne profits or interest may be recoverable in any proceedings[8].

1   As to the meaning of 'undertakers' see PARA 511.
2   As to the meaning of 'acquiring authority' see PARA 549 note 5.
3   Ie in the circumstances set out in PARA 648.
4   Lands Clauses Consolidation Act 1845 s 124 (where that Act is incorporated: see PARA 509); Compulsory Purchase Act 1965 s 22(3) (where that Act applies: see PARA 513). Thus, if a claim for possession is brought, and application is made for a new trial, the matter is not finally determined until the new trial is refused: *Hyde v Manchester Corpn* (1852) 5 De G & Sm 249. For a case on a dispute as to minerals decided after many years see *Caledonian Rly Co v Davidson* [1903] AC 22, HL.
5   As to the meaning of 'land' see PARA 549 note 1. See also PARA 511 text to note 7.
6   Lands Clauses Consolidation Act 1845 s 124; Compulsory Purchase Act 1965 s 22(1)(a).
7   'Mesne profits' means the mesne profits or interest which would have accrued to the persons concerned during the interval between the entry of the acquiring authority and the time when the compensation is paid, so far as such mesne profits or interest may be recoverable in any proceedings: Compulsory Purchase Act 1965 s 22(5); and see the Lands Clauses Consolidation Act 1845 s 124.
8   Lands Clauses Consolidation Act 1845 s 124; Compulsory Purchase Act 1965 s 22(1)(b), (5). As to the modification of s 22 in relation to the compulsory acquisition of rights by, inter alia, a local authority, urban development corporations, highway authorities, gas transporters, housing action trusts, licence holders under the Electricity Act 1989, the Environment Agency, water and sewerage undertakers, regional development agencies and universal service providers see PARA 648 note 8.

650.   Ascertainment of compensation. The purchase money or compensation must be agreed on, or awarded and paid, whether to the claimants or into court, in the same manner as, according to the provisions of the Lands Clauses Acts[1] or the Compulsory Purchase Act 1965[2], it would have been agreed on or awarded and paid if the undertakers[3] or the acquiring authority[4] had purchased the estate, right, interest or charge before entering upon the land[5], or as near thereto as circumstances will admit[6]. In assessing the compensation the value of the land and of any estate or interest in it, or of any mesne profits[7] of the land, is to be taken to be the value when the undertakers or the acquiring authority entered on the land, and without regard to any improvements or works made in or upon the land by the undertakers or the acquiring authority, and as though the works had not been constructed[8].

1   As to the Lands Clauses Acts see PARA 509 note 1.
2   As to the agreement, award and payment of compensation see PARAS 715 et seq, 753 et seq.
3   As to the meaning of 'undertakers' see PARA 511.
4   As to the meaning of 'acquiring authority' see PARA 549 note 5.
5   As to the meaning of 'land' see PARA 549 note 1. See also PARA 511 text to note 7.
6   Lands Clauses Consolidation Act 1845 s 124 (where that Act is incorporated: see PARA 509); Compulsory Purchase Act 1965 s 22(1) (where that Act applies: see PARA 513). As to payment into court see PARAS 555 note 6, 640.
7   As to the meaning of 'mesne profits' see PARA 649 note 7.
8   Lands Clauses Consolidation Act 1845 s 125; Compulsory Purchase Act 1965 s 22(4). As to the modification of s 22 in relation to the compulsory acquisition of rights by, inter alia, a local authority, urban development corporations, highway authorities, gas transporters, housing action trusts, licence holders under the Electricity Act 1989, the Environment Agency, water and sewerage undertakers, regional development agencies and universal service providers see PARA 648 note 8. As to the measure of damages when the promoters have entered with notice of the interest see *Stretton v Great Western and Brentford Rly Co* (1870) 5 Ch App 751.

(7) COMPLETION OF PURCHASE

(i) Right to Completion and Specific Performance

651. Right to completion and specific performance after notice to treat or entry and ascertainment of price. When notice to treat has been served or land has been entered upon under an empowering enactment with which the Lands Clauses Acts are incorporated[1] or under a compulsory purchase order to which the Compulsory Purchase Act 1965[2] applies[3], and the price or compensation has been ascertained either by agreement or assessment, the relation of vendor and purchaser is established between the parties in the same way as under a formal agreement, subject to the purchaser's right to withdraw the notice to treat after determination of the amount of compensation where the vendor has failed to serve a proper notice of claim[4]. All the ordinary rules apply, unless the special Act contains provisions to the contrary[5].

Either the vendor[6] or the undertakers or acquiring authority[7] can accordingly enforce the contract by specific performance, but the owner must show that he has a good title to the land, and specific performance will therefore only be granted subject to his title being investigated and proved[8]. He must also be prepared to execute a conveyance, and it will be a defence to an action for the price that the conveyance has not been executed by him[9]. When there is no question as to title, he can compel the undertakers or authority to take a conveyance[10] or accept an assignment of a lease with all proper covenants[11], even though they may have already paid the purchase money. After a good title is shown and possession is offered, they will be liable to pay interest on the purchase money[12], if there is nothing in the Act under which the land was acquired to indicate a contrary intention[13].

1   As to the Lands Clauses Acts and their incorporation see PARA 509.
2   As to the application of the Compulsory Purchase Act 1965 in place of the Lands Clauses Acts see PARA 513.
3   As to notices to treat see the Lands Clauses Consolidation Act 1845 s 18; the Compulsory Purchase Act 1965 s 5(1); and PARA 616. As to the form of the notice see PARA 616; and as to service of the notice see PARAS 617–618.

As to entry on land with or without consent see the Lands Clauses Consolidation Act 1845 ss 84, 85; the Compulsory Purchase Act 1965 s 11, Sch 3; and PARA 638 et seq.

4 See the Lands Compensation Act 1961 s 31; the Land Compensation Act 1973 s 54(4); and PARA 636.

5 *Regent's Canal Co v Ware* (1857) 23 Beav 575; *Mason v Stokes Bay Rly and Pier Co* (1862) 32 LJCh 110; cf *London Corpn v Horner* (1914) 111 LT 512, CA; and see PARA 631 et seq. Cf *John Hudson & Co Ltd v Kirkness (Inspector of Taxes)* [1954] 1 All ER 29, [1954] 1 WLR 40, CA, distinguishing between the compulsory vesting of property by a statute with fixed compensation provided and compulsory acquisition taking place under the authority of a statute. As to the meaning of 'special Act' see PARAS 509, 514.

6 *Adams v London and Blackwall Rly Co* (1850) 2 Mac & G 118.

7 See note 5.

8 *Gunston v East Gloucestershire Rly Co* (1868) 18 LT 8. See further SPECIFIC PERFORMANCE vol 44(1) (Reissue) PARA 838.

9 *East London Union v Metropolitan Rly Co* (1869) LR 4 Exch 309, following the general principle in *Laird v Pim* (1841) 7 M & W 474.

10 *Re Cary-Elwes' Contract* [1906] 2 Ch 143.

11 *Harding v Metropolitan Rly Co* (1872) 7 Ch App 154.

12 *Re Pigott and Great Western Rly Co* (1881) 18 ChD 146.

13 *Inglewood Pulp and Paper Co v New Brunswick Electric Power Commission* [1928] AC 492, PC. Where entry has been made before completion interest is payable from the date of entry: see PARA 639 et seq. Where compensation is assessed by the Upper Tribunal before entry interest may be payable from the date of the award: see PARA 745. As to the Upper Tribunal see PARA 720; and ADMINISTRATIVE LAW. As to the right to interest where an advance payment has been made see PARA 657.

(ii) Advance Payment of Compensation

652. Making of advance payment of compensation. Where an acquiring authority[1] has taken possession of any land[2], the person entitled to the compensation (the 'claimant') may request[3] the authority to make an advance payment on account of any compensation payable by it for the compulsory acquisition of any interest in that land[4], whereupon the authority must make an advance payment[5] equal to 90 per cent of (1) the agreed amount of the compensation[6]; or (2) if no agreement has been reached, an amount equal to the compensation as estimated by the authority[7].

Any such advance payment must be made not later than three months after the date on which the request is made, or, if those three months end before the authority takes possession of the land[8], on the date on which it takes possession[9].

1 As to the meaning of 'acquiring authority' for these purposes see PARA 622 note 1.

2 Where, instead of taking possession of land, an acquiring authority serves a notice in respect of the land allowing tenants to continue in possession under the Housing Act 1985 s 583, this provision has effect as if it had taken possession of the land on the date on which that notice was served: Land Compensation Act 1973 s 52(11) (amended by the Housing (Consequential Provisions) Act 1985 s 4, Sch 2 para 24(6)). Where the authority has acquired a right over land, the reference in the text to taking possession of the land must be read as a reference to first entering the land for the purpose of exercising that right: Land Compensation Act 1973 s 52(12).

3 The request must be in writing, giving particulars of the claimant's interest in the land so far as not already given pursuant to a notice to treat, and must be accompanied or supplemented by such other particulars as the acquiring authority may reasonably require to enable it to estimate the amount of the compensation in respect of which the advance payment is to be made: Land Compensation Act 1973 s 52(2). As to the notice to treat see PARA 616 et seq.

4 This provision applies, with the necessary modifications, to compensation for the compulsory acquisition of a right over land as it does to compensation for the compulsory acquisition of an interest in land: Land Compensation Act 1973 s 52(12). As to the right to accrued interest where an advance payment is made see PARA 657.

5 Land Compensation Act 1973 s 52(1), (2). If the acquiring authority has taken possession of part of the land specified in a notice of entry, or in respect of which a payment into court has

been made, the compensation mentioned in s 52(1) is the compensation payable for the compulsory acquisition of the interest in the whole of the land: s 52(1A) (s 52(1A), (1B) added by the Planning and Compulsory Purchase Act 2004 s 104(1), (2)). Notice of entry and payment into court must be construed in accordance with the Land Compensation Act 1961 s 5A (see PARA 755): Land Compensation Act 1973 s 52(1B) (as so added). See *Hall v Sandwell Metropolitan Borough Council (No 2)* [2008] RVR 350, Lands Tribunal.

6   Land Compensation Act 1973 s 52(3)(a). If the land is subject to a mortgage ss 52ZA, 52ZB apply (see PARA 653 et seq): s 52(6) (substituted by the Planning and Compulsory Purchase Act 2004 s 104(1), (2)).

7   Land Compensation Act 1973 s 52(3)(b).

8   See note 2.

9   Land Compensation Act 1973 s 52(4). Section 52(4) applies to a payment which may be or is made under s 52ZA (see PARA 653) or s 52ZB (see PARA 654) as it applies to a payment which may be or is made under s 52: s 52ZC(4) (added by the Planning and Compulsory Purchase Act 2004 s 104(1), (3)). If the compensation is in respect of an interest which is settled land for the purposes of the Settled Land Act 1925, the advance must be made to the persons entitled to give a discharge for capital money and will be treated as capital money arising under that Act: Land Compensation Act 1973 s 52(7).

653.   Land subject to mortgage within the 90 per cent threshold. The following provisions apply if (1) an acquiring authority[1] takes possession of land; (2) a request is made[2] for an advance payment; and (3) the land is subject to a mortgage the principal[3] of which does not exceed 90 per cent of the relevant amount[4].

The advance payment made to the claimant must be reduced by the amount the acquiring authority thinks will be required by it to secure the release of the interest of the mortgagee (or all the mortgagees if there is more than one)[5]. The acquiring authority must pay to the mortgagee the amount the acquiring authority thinks will be required by it to secure the release of the mortgagee's interest, if the claimant so requests, and the mortgagee consents to the making of the payment[6]. If there is more than one mortgagee each mortgagee must be paid individually[7], but payment must not be made to a mortgagee before the interest of each mortgagee whose interest has priority to his interest is released[8]. The amount of the advance payment made to the claimant[9] and the amount of the payments made to mortgagees[10] must not in aggregate exceed 90 per cent of the relevant amount[11].

If the acquiring authority estimated the compensation and it appears to the acquiring authority that its estimate was too low and it revises the estimate, and a request is made by the claimant[12], then the provisions described above[13] must be re-applied on the basis of the revised estimate[14].

1   As to the meaning of 'acquiring authority' for these purposes see PARA 622 note 1.

2   Ie in accordance with the Land Compensation Act 1973 s 52(2): see PARA 652.

3   If the land is subject to more than one mortgage, 'principal' refers to the aggregate of the principals of all of the mortgagees: Land Compensation Act 1973 s 52ZC(6) (ss 52ZA–52ZC added by the Planning and Compulsory Act 2004 s 104(3)).

4   Land Compensation Act 1973 s 52ZA(1) (as added: see note 3). The 'relevant amount' is the amount of the compensation agreed or estimated as mentioned in s 52(3) (see PARA 652): s 52ZC(5) (as so added). The claimant must provide the acquiring authority with such information as it may require to enable it to give effect to s 52ZA: s 52ZC(2) (as so added). As to the meaning of 'claimant' for these purposes see PARA 652. The claimant in relation to settled land for the purposes of the Settled Land Act 1925 is the person entitled to give a discharge for capital money: s 52ZC(11) (as so added).

5   Land Compensation Act 1973 s 52ZA(2) (as added: see note 3).

6   Land Compensation Act 1973 s 52ZA(3) (as added: see note 3). Such a request must be made in writing and must be accompanied by the written consent of the mortgagee: s 52ZC(3) (as so added).

7   Ie the Land Compensation Act 1973 s 52ZA(3) applies to each mortgagee individually: see the
    text to note 6.
8   Land Compensation Act 1973 s 52ZA(4) (as added: see note 3).
9   Ie under the Land Compensation Act 1973 s 52.
10 Ie under the Land Compensation Act 1973 s 52ZA.
11 Land Compensation Act 1973 s 52ZA(5) (as added: see note 3).
12 Ie in accordance with the Land Compensation Act 1973 s 52(2).
13 Ie the Land Compensation Act 1973 s 52ZA(2)–(5): see the text and notes 1–11.
14 Land Compensation Act 1973 s 52ZA(6), (7) (as added: see note 3).

654.   Land subject to mortgage exceeding the 90 per cent threshold.   If an acquiring authority[1] takes possession of land, a request is made[2] for an advance payment, and the land is subject to a mortgage the principal[3] of which exceeds 90 per cent of the relevant amount[4], then no advance payment is to be made to the claimant[5]. But the acquiring authority must pay to the mortgagee the lesser of 90 per cent of the value of the land[6] or the principal of the mortgagee's mortgage, if the claimant so requests, and the mortgagee consents to the making of the payment[7].

If there is more than one mortgagee, payment must not be made to a mortgagee until the interest of each mortgagee whose interest has priority to his interest is released[8]. The total payments must not in any event exceed 90 per cent of the value of the land[9].

If the acquiring authority estimated the compensation, it appears to the acquiring authority that its estimate was too low and it revises the estimate, a request for an advance payment[10] would have been successful if the revised estimate had been used instead of the estimate, and a request is made by the claimant[11], then the relevant statutory provisions[12] must be applied on the basis of the revised estimate[13].

If the acquiring authority estimated the value of the land, it appears to the acquiring authority that its estimate was too low and it revises the estimate, and a request is made by the claimant in writing, any balance found to be due to a mortgagee on the basis of the revised estimate is payable in accordance with the provisions[14] described above[15].

1   As to the meaning of 'acquiring authority' for these purposes see PARA 622 note 1.
2   Ie in accordance with the Land Compensation Act 1973 s 52(2): see PARA 652.
3   As to the meaning of 'principal' see PARA 653 note 3.
4   As to the meaning of 'relevant amount' see PARA 653 note 4.
5   Land Compensation Act 1973 s 52ZB(1), (2) (ss 52ZB, 52ZC added by the Planning and
    Compulsory Act 2004 s 104(3)). The claimant must provide the acquiring authority with such
    information as it may require to enable it to give effect to s 52ZB: see s 52ZC(2) (as so added).
    As to the meaning of 'claimant' for these purposes see PARA 652. The claimant in relation to
    settled land for the purposes of the Settled Land Act 1925 is the person entitled to give a
    discharge for capital money: s 52ZC(11) (as so added).
6   The 'value of the land' is the value agreed by the claimant and the acquiring authority, or (failing
    such agreement), estimated by the acquiring authority: Land Compensation Act 1973 s 52ZB(5)
    (as added: see note 5). The value of the land is to be calculated in accordance with the Land
    Compensation Act 1961 s 5 r 2 (see PARA 754) whether or not compensation is or is likely to be
    assessed in due course in accordance with s 5 r 5: Land Compensation Act 1973 s 52ZB(6) (as
    so added).
7   Land Compensation Act 1973 s 52ZB(3), (4) (as added: see note 5). Such a request must be
    made in writing and must be accompanied by the written consent of the mortgagee: s 52ZC(3)
    (as so added).
8   Land Compensation Act 1973 s 52ZB(7) (as added: see note 5).
9   Land Compensation Act 1973 s 52ZB(8) (as added: see note 5).
10 Ie the condition in the Land Compensation Act 1973 s 52ZA: see PARA 653.
11 Ie in accordance with the Land Compensation Act 1973 s 52(2): see PARA 652.
12 Ie the Land Compensation Act 1973 s 52ZA(2)–(5): see PARA 653.

13 Land Compensation Act 1973 s 52ZB(9), (10) (as added: see note 5).
14 Ie the Land Compensation Act 1973 s 52ZB.
15 Land Compensation Act 1973 s 52ZB(11) (as added: see note 5).

655.   Supplementary provisions relating to mortgaged land.   An advance
payment to a mortgagee[1] must be (1) applied by the mortgagee in or towards the
discharge of the principal, interest and costs and any other money due under the
mortgage[2]; (2) taken to be a payment on account of compensation and treated[3]
as if it were an advance payment[4]; (3) taken, with effect from the date of the
payment, to reduce by the amount of the payment the amount in respect of
which interest accrues[5]; (4) taken into account for the purposes of determining
any payments (or payments into court) which may be made[6].

If the amount, or aggregate amount, of payments[7] on the basis of the
acquiring authority's[8] estimate of the compensation exceeds the compensation as
finally determined or agreed, the excess must be repaid by the claimant[9].

In certain circumstances payments to mortgagees are prohibited[10].

1   Ie under the Land Compensation Act 1973 s 52ZA (see PARA 653) or s 52ZB (see PARA 654).
2   Land Compensation Act 1973 s 52ZC(7)(a) (s 52ZC added by the Planning and Compulsory
    Purchase Act 2004 s 104(1), (3)).
3   Ie for the purposes of the Land Compensation Act 1973 s 52(10): see PARA 656.
4   Land Compensation Act 1973 s 52ZC(7)(b) (as added: see note 2). This refers to being treated
    as an advance payment under s 52: see PARA 652.
5   Land Compensation Act 1973 s 52ZC(7)(c) (as added: see note 2). This refers to interest which
    accrues for the purposes of the Compulsory Purchase Act 1965 s 11(1), Sch 3 and the Lands
    Clauses Consolidation Act 1845 s 85: see PARA 639.
6   Land Compensation Act 1973 s 52ZC(7)(d) (as added: see note 2). This refers to payments into
    court for the purposes of the Compulsory Purchase Act 1965 ss 14–16: see PARAS 712–714.
7   Ie the amount or aggregate amount of payments under (1) the Land Compensation Act 1973
    s 52 (see PARA 652) and s 52ZA (see PARA 653); or (2) s 52ZB (see PARA 654).
8   As to the meaning of 'acquiring authority' for these purposes see PARA 622 note 1.
9   Land Compensation Act 1973 s 52ZC(8) (as added: see note 2). As to the meaning of 'claimant'
    for these purposes see PARA 652.
10 No payment must be made to a mortgagee if:
    (1)   the compulsory acquisition is only of a right over land (Land Compensation Act 1973
          s 52ZC(9)(b) (as added: see note 2)); or
    (2)   payment has been made under the Compulsory Purchase Act 1965 s 14(2) (see PARA
          712) (Land Compensation Act 1973 s 52ZC(9)(a), (10)(a) (as so added));
    (3)   a notice under the Compulsory Purchase Act 1965 s 14(3) (see PARA 712) has been
          given (Land Compensation Act 1973 s 52ZC(10)(b) (as so added));
    (4)   there is an agreement under the Compulsory Purchase Act 1965 s 15(1) or 16(1) (see
          PARAS 713–714) or the matter has been referred to the Upper Tribunal under s 15 or
          s 16 (Land Compensation Act 1973 s 52ZC(10)(c) (as so added; further amended by
          SI 2009/1307)).
    As to the Upper Tribunal see PARA 720; and ADMINISTRATIVE LAW.

656.   Effect of advance payment of compensation.   Before an acquiring
authority[1] makes an advance payment on account of compensation in respect of
any interest in land[2], it must deposit with the council of the district or London
borough or Welsh county or county borough in which the land is situated
particulars of the payment to be made, the compensation and the interest in land
to which it relates[3]. Any particulars so deposited are a local land charge and the
council with whom any such particulars are deposited is treated[4] as the
originating authority as respects the charge thereby constituted[5]. Where a local
land charge is registered in the appropriate local land charges register[6] and the
advance payment to which the charge relates is made to the claimant[7], then if he
afterwards disposes of the interest in the land to, or creates an interest in the land

in favour of, a person other than the acquiring authority, the amount of the advance payment, together with any accrued interest paid[8], must be set off against any sum payable by the authority to that other person in respect of the compulsory acquisition of the interest disposed of or the compulsory acquisition or release of the interest created[9].

Where, at any time after an advance payment has been made on the basis of the acquiring authority's estimate of the compensation, it appears to the acquiring authority that its estimate was too low, it must, if a request in that behalf is duly made[10], pay to the claimant the balance of the amount of the advance payment calculated as at that time[11]. Where the amount, or aggregate amount, of any payment made on the basis of the authority's estimate of the compensation exceeds the compensation as finally determined or agreed, the excess must be repaid; and if after any payment has been made to any person it is discovered that he was not entitled to it, the amount of the payment is recoverable by the acquiring authority[12].

Where an advance payment has been made under these provisions on account of any compensation, the statutory provisions relating to refusal to convey on tender of compensation[13] have effect as if references to the compensation were references to the unpaid balance of the compensation[14].

1   As to the meaning of 'acquiring authority' for these purposes see PARA 622 note 1.
2   Ie an advance payment under the Land Compensation Act 1973 s 52: see PARA 652.
3   Land Compensation Act 1973 s 52(8) (amended by the Local Land Charges Act 1975 s 17(2), Sch 1; and the Local Government (Wales) Act 1994 s 66(6), Sch 16 para 40(3)). The provisions of s 52(8)–(9) (see the text and notes below) apply to a payment which may be or is made under s 52ZA (see PARA 653) or s 52ZB (see PARA 654) as they apply to a payment which may be or is made under s 52: s 52ZC(4) (added by the Planning and Compulsory Purchase Act 2004 s 104(1), (3)).
4   Ie for the purposes of the Local Land Charges Act 1975: see LAND CHARGES.
5   Land Compensation Act 1973 s 52(8A) (added by the Local Land Charges Act 1975 s 17(2)).
6   Ie pursuant to the Land Compensation Act 1973 s 52(8A): see the text and note 5.
7   As to the meaning of 'claimant' for these purposes see PARA 652.
8   Ie under the Land Compensation Act 1973 s 52A: see PARA 657.
9   Land Compensation Act 1973 s 52(9) (amended by the Local Land Charges Act 1975 s 17(2); and the Planning and Compensation Act 1991 s 70, Sch 15 para 24).
10 Ie in accordance with the Land Compensation Act 1973 s 52(2): see PARA 652.
11 Land Compensation Act 1973 s 52(4A) (added by the Planning and Compensation Act 1991 s 63(1)).
12 Land Compensation Act 1973 s 52(5) (substituted by the Planning and Compensation Act 1991 s 63(1)).
13 Ie the Lands Clauses Consolidation Act 1845 s 76; and the Compulsory Purchase Act 1965 s 9: see PARAS 661, 663, 664.
14 Land Compensation Act 1973 s 52(10) (amended by the Planning and Compensation Act 1991 s 84(6), Sch 19 Pt III). A payment made to a mortgagee under the Land Compensation Act 1973 s 52ZA (see PARA 653) or s 52ZB (see PARA 654) must be taken to be a payment on account of compensation and treated for the purposes of s 52(10) as if it were an advance payment under s 52: s 52ZC(7)(b) (as added: see note 3).

657. Right to interest where advance payment made. Where the compensation to be paid by the acquiring authority[1] for the compulsory acquisition of any interest in land would otherwise carry interest[2], then, if the authority makes an advance payment[3] to any person on account of the compensation, it must at the same time make a payment to that person of accrued interest[4], for the period beginning with the date of entry, on the amount of the compensation agreed or estimated (the 'total amount')[5]. If the authority makes an increased payment[6] to any person on account of the compensation, it must at the same time make a payment to him of accrued interest, for the period beginning with the date of entry, on the amount by reference to which that payment was calculated, less the amount by reference to which the preceding payment[7] was calculated[8].

If, on an anniversary of the date on which the authority made an advance payment[9] to any person on account of the compensation, the amount of the accrued interest on the unpaid balance[10] or the aggregate amount of the accrued interest on any unpaid balances[11] exceeds £1,000[12], the authority must make a payment to the claimant[13] of the amount or aggregate amount[14]. On paying the outstanding compensation, the acquiring authority must pay the amount of the accrued interest on the unpaid balance or the aggregate amount of the accrued interest on any unpaid balances[15].

Where the amount, or aggregate amount, of any advance payment made on the basis of the acquiring authority's estimate of the compensation is greater than the compensation as finally determined or agreed and, accordingly, the interest paid is excessive, the excess must be repaid[16]. If, after any interest on any amount has been paid to any person under these provisions, it is discovered that he was not entitled to the amount, the interest is recoverable by the acquiring authority[17].

1   As to the meaning of 'acquiring authority' for these purposes see PARA 622 note 1.
2   Ie under the Compulsory Purchase Act 1965 s 11(1) (see PARA 645) or any bond under s 11(2), Sch 3 or the Lands Clauses Consolidation Act 1845 s 85 (see PARA 639 et seq): Land Compensation Act 1973 s 52A(1) (s 52A added by the Planning and Compensation Act 1991 s 63(2)). Where any payment has been made under the Land Compensation Act 1973 s 52(1) on account of any compensation (see PARA 652), the acquiring authority is not required to pay interest under the Compulsory Purchase Act 1965 s 11(1) or under any such bond: Land Compensation Act 1973 s 52A(9) (as so added).
3   Ie under the Land Compensation Act 1973 s 52(1): see PARA 652.
4   For these purposes, interest accrues: (1) at the rate prescribed under the Land Compensation Act 1961 s 32 (see PARA 641); or (2) in the case of a bond under the Lands Clauses Consolidation Act 1845 s 85, at the rate specified in that provision: Land Compensation Act 1973 s 52A(8)(a) (as added: see note 2). Any losses occasioned by unavoidable delay in the payment of the balance of monies owed as compensation cannot be redressed by the payment of interest, which is fixed at the Treasury rate as prescribed by s 52A(8)(a) and does not itself carry any element of compensation with it: *Mallick v Liverpool City Council* (1999) 79 P & CR 1, [1999] 2 EGLR 7, CA. The Lands Clauses Consolidation Act 1845 s 85 specifies a rate of interest of 5%; but the Land Compensation Act 1961 s 32 specifically states that the prescribed rate is to replace that rate of 5%; the effect of head (2) above is therefore unclear, but it appears that for this purpose only the rate of interest of 5% is to be applied.
5   Land Compensation Act 1973 s 52A(1), (2)(a) (s 52A as added (see note 2); s 52A(2) substituted by the Planning and Compulsory Purchase Act 2004 s 104(1), (3)). For these purposes, the amount by reference to which a payment under s 52(1) or (4A) was calculated is the amount referred to in s 52(3)(a) or s 52(3)(b) for the purposes of that calculation (see PARA 652): s 52A(8)(b) (as so added).
6   Ie a payment under the Land Compensation Act 1973 s 52(4A): see PARA 656.
7   Ie under the Land Compensation Act 1973 s 52(1) (see PARA 652) or s 52(4A) (see PARA 656).
8   Land Compensation Act 1973 s 52A(3) (as added: see note 2).
9   Ie under the Land Compensation Act 1973 s 52(1): see PARA 652.
10 Ie under the Land Compensation Act 1973 s 52A(2): s 52A(5)(a) (as added: see note 2). The difference between the paid amount and the total amount is an unpaid balance for these purposes: s 52A(2)(b) (as added and substituted: see notes 2, 5). The paid amount is (1) the amount of the payment under the Land Compensation Act 1973 s 52(1) (see PARA 652); or (2) if the land is subject to a mortgage, the aggregate of that amount and the amount of any payment made under s 52ZA(3) (see PARA 653): s 52A(2A) (added by the Planning and Compulsory Purchase Act 2004 s 104(1), (3)).
      For the purposes of the Land Compensation Act 1973 s 52A(5), (6), interest accrues on any unpaid balance for the period beginning with (a) the making of the payment under s 52(1) (see

PARA 652) or, as the case may be, s 52(4A) (see PARA 656); or (b) if any payment has already been made in respect of that balance under s 52A(5), the date of the preceding payment thereunder: s 52A(7) (as added: see note 2).

11 Where the authority makes a payment under the Land Compensation Act 1973 s 52(4A) on account of the compensation, the difference between (1) the amount of the payment; and (2) the amount by reference to which it was calculated less the amount by reference to which the preceding payment under s 52(1) or s 52(4A) was calculated, is an unpaid balance for these purposes: s 52A(4) (as added: see note 2).

12 The Secretary of State may from time to time by order substitute another sum for the sum so specified; and the power to make such orders is exercisable by statutory instrument subject to annulment in pursuance of a resolution of either House of Parliament: Land Compensation Act 1973 s 52A(12) (as added: see note 2). At the date at which this volume states the law, no such order had been made. As to the Secretary of State see PARA 507 note 1. These functions of the Secretary of State, so far as they are exercisable in relation to Wales, are now exercisable by the Welsh Ministers: see the National Assembly for Wales (Transfer of Functions) Order 1999, SI 1999/672, art 2, Sch 1; and the Government of Wales Act 2006 s 162(1), Sch 11 para 30. As to the Welsh Assembly Government and the Welsh Ministers see CONSTITUTIONAL LAW AND HUMAN RIGHTS.

13 As to the meaning of 'claimant' for these purposes see PARA 652.

14 Land Compensation Act 1973 s 52A(5) (as added: see note 2).

15 Land Compensation Act 1973 s 52A(6) (as added: see note 2).

16 Land Compensation Act 1973 s 52A(10) (as added: see note 2).

17 Land Compensation Act 1973 s 52A(11) (as added: see note 2).

(iii) Conveyance or Transfer

658. Form and execution of conveyance or transfer. Certain forms of conveyance are provided by the Lands Clauses Acts[1] and the Compulsory Purchase Act 1965 for acquisitions authorised by compulsory purchase order[2], but in practice these are seldom used and the conveyance is usually made in accordance with forms similar to those used on ordinary conveyances on sale[3].

If the compensation payable includes payment in respect of disturbance, the compensation for disturbance is part of the consideration for the sale, and the aggregate of that compensation and of all other compensation (including compensation for severance or other injurious affection payable) is the figure to be inserted in the conveyance or transfer on which stamp duty at the rate appropriate to the purchase money payable on a conveyance on sale is to be paid[4]. The instrument by which the transfer is effected must be produced to the Commissioners of Inland Revenue by the acquiring authority within 30 days of its execution[5], together with such other documents as are required[6].

Where the sale is by agreement[7], it seems that the same covenants for title should be given as in the case of an ordinary sale[8]; but where there is a compulsory purchase it seems that the undertakers or acquiring authority can only require a conveyance in the statutory form[9] or a form similar to it[10], and the statutory form includes no covenants for title, nor does its wording incorporate the covenants implied by statute[11]. If title is not made out to the undertakers' or authority's satisfaction, they can dispense with the conveyance and execute a deed poll vesting the land in themselves after making deposit[12].

1 As to the Lands Clauses Acts see PARA 509 note 1.

2 See the Lands Clauses Consolidation Act 1845 s 81 (amended by the Compulsory Purchase Act 1965 s 39(4), Sch 8 Pt II); the Lands Clauses Consolidation Act 1845 Schs (A), (B) (where that Act is incorporated: see PARA 509); and the Compulsory Purchase Act 1965 s 23(6), Sch 5 (where that Act applies: see PARA 513). A conveyance made in the prescribed form, or as near to it as the circumstances admit, is effectual to vest the land conveyed by it in the undertakers or the acquiring authority and operates to bar and destroy all estates, rights, titles, remainders, reversions, limitations, trusts and interests relating to the land which have been purchased or compensated for by the consideration mentioned in the conveyance: Lands

Clauses Consolidation Act 1845 s 81 (as so amended); Compulsory Purchase Act 1965 s 23(6). As to purchase by vesting declaration for speedy acquisition see PARA 686 et seq. As to the meaning of 'acquiring authority' for these purposes see PARA 549 note 5. As to the meaning of 'undertakers' see PARA 511. As to the meaning of 'land' see PARA 549 note 1. See also PARA 511 text to note 7.

3   As to vesting declarations as alternative steps see PARA 686 et seq.

4   *IRC v Glasgow and South Western Rly Co* (1887) 12 App Cas 315, HL; *Horn v Sunderland Corpn* [1941] 2 KB 26 at 34, [1941] 1 All ER 480 at 485–486, CA.

5   Finance Act 1931 s 28(1).

6   See the Finance Act 1931 s 28(1). The documents referred to are those required in order to comply with the provisions of s 28(1), Sch 2: see further STAMP DUTIES AND STAMP DUTY RESERVE TAX vol 44(1) (Reissue) PARA 1026.

7   See PARA 550.

8   As to the implied covenants for title see the Law of Property (Miscellaneous Provisions) Act 1994 Pt I (ss 1–13); and REAL PROPERTY.

9   See the Lands Clauses Consolidation Act 1845 Schs (A), (B); the Compulsory Purchase Act 1965 Sch 5.

10   See the Lands Clauses Consolidation Act 1845 s 81 (as amended: see note 2); the Compulsory Purchase Act 1965 s 23(6).

11   The forms contained in the Lands Clauses Consolidation Act 1845 Schs (A), (B) and the Compulsory Purchase Act 1965 Sch 5 contain no wording which would have resulted in the implication of a covenant by virtue of the Law of Property Act 1925 s 76 (repealed); and the Law of Property (Miscellaneous Provisions) Act 1994 s 9 (modifications of statutory forms) is thus of no application.

12   See PARA 663.

659.   Costs of conveyance.   Under the Lands Clauses Acts[1] or, in the case of an acquisition authorised by a compulsory purchase order, under the Compulsory Purchase Act 1965[2], the costs of all conveyances of land purchased under the special Act[3] and the Acts incorporated in it, or of the land subject to compulsory purchase[4], must be borne by the undertakers[5] or by the acquiring authority[6], whether the sale is voluntary or compulsory[7]. These costs include all charges and expenses incurred on the vendor's as well as on the purchaser's part:

(1)   of all conveyances and assurances of the land, and of any outstanding terms of interest in it;

(2)   of deducing, evidencing and verifying the title to the land, terms or interests; and

(3)   of making out and furnishing such abstracts and attested copies as the undertakers or authority may require,

and all other reasonable expenses incident to the investigation, deduction and verification of the title[8]. Where the sale takes place under an agreement, the provision as to costs may be varied by the agreement[9].

If, in order formally to complete a title otherwise good, the undertakers or authority require letters of administration to be taken out, or some act to be done which would not otherwise have been necessary, they must pay the costs occasioned by it[10]. The costs of any necessary application to the court to appoint a person to convey are also payable by the undertakers or authority[11], as are the costs of conveyancing counsel when required[12]. The costs of the conveyance do not include costs of preliminary negotiations, or the costs of apportioning ground rents when part of leasehold property is taken[13], or costs of collateral agreements[14].

The undertakers or acquiring authority are not entitled to refuse to take a conveyance merely to save expense[15].

1   As to the Lands Clauses Acts see PARA 509 note 1.

2   As to the acquisitions to which the Compulsory Purchase Act 1965 applies see PARA 513.

3   As to the meaning of 'special Act' see PARAS 509, 514.

4   As to the meaning of 'land' see PARA 549 note 1. See also PARA 511 text to note 7. As to the meaning of 'subject to compulsory purchase' see PARA 549 note 2.

5   As to the meaning of 'undertakers' see PARA 511.

6   As to the meaning of 'acquiring authority' see PARA 549 note 5.

7   Lands Clauses Consolidation Act 1845 s 82 (where that Act is incorporated: see PARA 509); Compulsory Purchase Act 1965 s 23(1) (where that Act applies: see PARA 513); *Re Burdekin* [1895] 2 Ch 136, CA. As to purchase by agreement see PARA 550 et seq.

8   Lands Clauses Consolidation Act 1845 s 82; Compulsory Purchase Act 1965 s 23(2). For examples under other Acts see *Re London and Greenwich Rly Co, ex p Addey's Charity Feoffees* (1843) 12 LJCh 513; *Re Strachan's Estate and Metropolitan Improvement Acts* (1851) 9 Hare 185. In certain circumstances, legal costs incurred before the notice to treat can be recovered: see *Prasad v Wolverhampton Borough Council* [1983] Ch 333, [1983] 2 All ER 140, CA.

9   See *Re London and South Western Railway Act 1855, ex p Phillips* (1862) 32 LJCh 102; *Re Middlesex County Light Railways Order 1903* [1908] WN 167.

10   *Re Liverpool Improvement Act* (1868) LR 5 Eq 282 (overruling *Re South Wales Rly Co* (1851) 14 Beav 418); *Re Thames Tunnel (Rotherhithe and Ratcliff) Act 1900* [1908] 1 Ch 493, CA; and see *Re South City Market Co, ex p Keatley* (1890) 25 LR Ir 263; *Re Bear Island Defence Works and Doyle* [1903] 1 IR 164, CA. Costs of taking out probate to the estate of a deceased person who had agreed to sell a leasehold interest have been held not to be payable by the undertakers: *Re Elementary Education Acts 1870 and 1873* [1909] 1 Ch 55, CA. If the undertakers or acquiring authority pay the money into court by reason of the failure of an owner under a disability to make a good title, they will be required to pay similar costs on application to the court for payment out: see the Lands Clauses Consolidation Act 1845 s 80; the Compulsory Purchase Act 1965 s 26(1)(c), (2), (3); and PARA 680 note 3. As to the costs of registering title see *Re Belfast and Northern Counties Rly Co, ex p Gilmore* [1895] 1 IR 297.

11   *Re Lowry's Will* (1872) LR 15 Eq 78; *Re Nash's Estate* (1855) 4 WR 111; *Re Eastern Counties and Tilbury Junction Rly Co, ex p Cave* (1855) 26 LTOS 176. However, they will not be obliged to pay costs incurred in respect of such part of the application as fails: see *Re Jacobs, Baldwin v Pescott* [1908] 2 Ch 691.

12   *Re Spooner's Estate* (1854) 1 K & J 220. As to solicitors' costs see generally LEGAL PROFESSIONS vol 66 (2009) PARA 931 et seq.

13   *Re Hampstead Junction Rly Co, ex p Buck* (1863) 1 Hem & M 519: see PARA 707.

14   Eg an agreement to carry the vendor's goods at a fixed price: *Re Lietch and Kewney (Solicitors)* (1867) 15 WR 1055.

15   *Re Cary-Elwes' Contract* [1906] 2 Ch 143.

660.   Taxation and recovery of costs of conveyance. When the undertakers[1] or the acquiring authority[2] and the party entitled to costs cannot agree as to the amount, the costs must be taxed by a costs judge[3] on an order of the court obtained by either of the parties[4], although such an order cannot be obtained by the undertakers after the costs have been paid[5].

The expense of taxation is borne by the undertakers or the acquiring authority unless upon the taxation one-sixth of the amount of the costs is disallowed, in which case the costs of the taxation are borne by the party whose costs have been taxed, and the amount must be ascertained by the master and deducted by him accordingly in his certificate of taxation[6].

The undertakers or the acquiring authority must pay the sum certified by the master to be due in respect of the costs to the party entitled to them, and in default the sum may be recovered in the same way as any other costs payable under an order of the Senior Courts[7]. The master's taxation of these costs is open to review by the court[8].

1   As to the meaning of 'undertakers' see PARA 511.

2   As to the meaning of 'acquiring authority' see PARA 549 note 5.

3   Ie one of the Supreme Court taxing masters: see CPR 43.2(1)(b). As from 1 October 2009, the references to the Supreme Court are repealed and replaced with references to the Senior Courts: see the Compulsory Purchase Act 1965 s 23(3), (4) (prospectively amended by the Constitutional Reform Act 2005 s 59(5), Sch 11 Pt 2 para 4).

4   Lands Clauses Consolidation Act 1845 s 83 (amended by the Administration of Justice Act 1965 s 34, Sch 2) (where the Lands Clauses Consolidation Act 1845 is incorporated: see PARA 509); Compulsory Purchase Act 1965 s 23(3) (where that Act applies: see PARA 513). See further CIVIL PROCEDURE vol 12 (2009) PARA 1729 et seq. Where there is an agreement as to costs which includes matters not within the ambit of the above provisions, the order should not be made under the Lands Clauses Consolidation Act 1845 s 83: see *Middlesex County Light Railways Order 1903* [1908] WN 167. See also *Re North Eastern Railway Company Act 1901, Re Lands Clauses Consolidation Acts 1845, 1860, 1869, Holden v North Eastern Rly Co* (1904) 48 Sol Jo 526.

5   *Re South Eastern Rly Co, ex p Somerville* (1883) 23 ChD 167. Costs agreed to be paid on the abandonment of an inquisition are not taxable under this provision: *Marquis of Drogheda v Great Southern and Western Rly Co* (1847) 12 I Eq R 103.

6   Lands Clauses Consolidation Act 1845 s 83; Compulsory Purchase Act 1965 s 23(5).

7   Lands Clauses Consolidation Act 1845 s 83 (as amended: see note 4); Compulsory Purchase Act 1965 s 23(4). See note 3.

8   See *Re West Ferry Road, Poplar, London, Re Padwick's Estate* [1955] 2 All ER 638, [1955] 1 WLR 751, CA; see also *Owen v London and North Western Rly Co* (1867) LR 3 QB 54 at 60–61; *Sandback Charity Trustees v North Staffordshire Rly Co* (1877) 3 QBD 1 at 5, CA, per Brett LJ.

(iv) Deed Poll on Owner's Refusal to take Compensation etc or Absence

661.   Payment into court; owner's refusal to take compensation, make title or convey.   If the owner of any of the land[1] purchased by the undertakers[2] or the acquiring authority[3], or of any interest in the land so purchased, on tender of the purchase money or compensation either agreed or awarded to be paid in respect of the land or interest (1) refuses to accept it[4]; or (2) neglects or fails to make out a title to their satisfaction; or (3) refuses to convey or release the land as directed, the undertakers or authority may pay the purchase money or compensation[5] into court[6]. The compensation so paid into court must be placed to the credit of the parties interested in the land and the undertakers or acquiring authority must, so far as they can, give those parties' descriptions[7].

1   As to the meaning of 'land' see PARA 549 note 1. See also PARA 511 text to note 7.

2   As to the meaning of 'undertakers' see PARA 511.

3   As to the meaning of 'acquiring authority' see PARA 549 note 5.

4   If by reason of any disability the parties are unable to accept the purchase money this is not a refusal, even if other parties might complete for them: *Re Leeds Grammar School* [1901] 1 Ch 228. Other provision is made for such parties: see PARA 667.

5   If an advance payment of compensation has been made under the Land Compensation Act 1973 s 52(1) (see PARA 652), the reference here to compensation must be read as if it were a reference to the balance of the compensation remaining unpaid: see s 52(10)(a); and PARA 656.

6   Lands Clauses Consolidation Act 1845 s 76 (amended by the Administration of Justice Act 1965 s 17, Sch 1; the Compulsory Purchase Act 1965 s 39(4), Sch 8 Pt III; and prospectively amended by the Constitutional Reform Act 2005 s 59(5), Sch 11 Pt 2 para 9) (where the Lands Clauses Consolidation Act 1845 is incorporated: see PARA 509); Compulsory Purchase Act 1965 s 9(1) (where that Act applies: see PARA 513). Similar provision is made for cases where an owner is abroad or cannot be found: see PARA 662. As to payment into court see PARAS 555 note 6, 640.

7   Compulsory Purchase Act 1965 s 9(2).

662.   Payment into court in owner's absence.   Where the owner of the land[1] is absent from the United Kingdom[2], or cannot after diligent inquiry be found, and the undertakers[3] or the acquiring authority[4] have had the compensation assessed by a surveyor[5], they may pay into court the compensation so determined to the credit of the parties interested in the land, giving their descriptions so far as they are in a position to do so[6].

1   As to the meaning of 'land' see PARA 549 note 1. See also PARA 511 text to note 7.

2   As to the meaning of 'United Kingdom' see PARA 616 note 22.
3   As to the meaning of 'undertakers' see PARA 511.
4   As to the meaning of 'acquiring authority' see PARA 549 note 5.
5   See PARAS 616, 718.
6   See the Lands Clauses Consolidation Act 1845 s 76 (amended by the Administration of Justice Act 1965 s 17, Sch 1; and the Compulsory Purchase Act 1965 s 39(4), Sch 8 Pt III) (where the Lands Clauses Consolidation Act 1845 is incorporated: see PARA 509); the Compulsory Purchase Act 1965 s 5(3), Sch 2 para 2(1) (where that Act applies: see PARA 513). As to payment into court see PARAS 555 note 6, 640.

663.   Execution of deed poll.   After the payment of the purchase money or compensation into court[1], the undertakers[2] or the acquiring authority[3] may, if they think fit, execute a deed poll, under their common seal or by an officer duly appointed for that purpose[4] if they are a corporation, or if the undertakers are not a corporation under the hands of the undertakers or any two of them[5], containing a description of the land in respect of which the payment into court has been made[6] and declaring the circumstances under which and the names of the parties to whose credit the payment in has been made[7]. The deed poll must be stamped with the stamp duty which would have been payable upon a conveyance to the undertakers or acquiring authority of the land described in it[8]. Thereupon, all the estate and interest in the land of the parties for whose use, and in respect of which, the purchase money or compensation has been paid into court will vest absolutely in the undertakers or the authority, and as against those parties they will be entitled to immediate possession of the land[9]. The procedure confers no rights as against third parties, and is not applicable to cases where the person purporting to sell has no title at all to the land[10]. In order that an estate or interest may vest, the person who fails to make out a good title must have some title, and the failure to make out a title must arise from an independent estate or interest outstanding in a third party; the effect of this procedure is to vest in the undertakers or authority the estate and interest of the person so failing, and no more[11]. Thus, if the person whose interest has been agreed to be acquired proves to have only an inchoate possessory title, the undertakers or authority acquire this interest only, and the real owner will not afterwards be barred from asserting his rights[12].

The undertakers or acquiring authority, therefore, before adopting the above procedure of vesting the property by means of a deed poll, ought to give the owner an opportunity of making a good title[13]. If they have entered into an agreement with any person for the purchase of land, and that person fails to make out a good title, he cannot compel them to adopt this procedure; but if they do not, they cannot remain in possession under the agreement[14].

1   See PARAS 661–662.
2   As to the meaning of 'undertakers' see PARA 511.
3   As to the meaning of 'acquiring authority' see PARA 549 note 5.
4   Ie in accordance with the Law of Property Act 1925 s 74(4): see CORPORATIONS vol 9(2) (2006 Reissue) PARA 1267.

5   Any rule of law which required a seal for the valid execution of an instrument as a deed by an individual has, except in relation to a corporation sole, been abolished: Law of Property (Miscellaneous Provisions) Act 1989 s 1(1)(b), (10). These provisions have effect as to signing, sealing or delivery of an instrument by an individual in place of any provision of the Lands Clauses Consolidation Act 1845 as to signing, sealing or delivery; and the requirement in s 77 that, where the undertakers are not a corporation, the deed poll is to be executed under seal is accordingly of no effect in relation to deeds executed on or after 31 July 1990: see the Law of Property Act 1989 s 1(7); and the Law of Property (Miscellaneous Provisions) Act 1989 (Commencement) Order 1990, SI 1990/1175. See further DEEDS AND OTHER INSTRUMENTS vol 13 (2007 Reissue) PARA 32.

6   See PARAS 661–662.

7   Lands Clauses Consolidation Act 1845 s 77 (amended by the Administration of Justice Act 1965 s 17(1), Sch 1; and the Compulsory Purchase Act 1965 s 39(4), Sch 8 Pt II) (where the Lands Clauses Consolidation Act 1845 is incorporated: see PARA 509); Compulsory Purchase Act 1965 ss 9(3), 28(1) (where that Act applies: see PARA 513). The Lands Clauses Consolidation Act 1845 s 77 is amended in relation to Northern Ireland by SI 2005/1452. As to absent owners see the Compulsory Purchase Act 1965 s 5(3), Sch 2 para 2(2). The provisions of the Compulsory Purchase Act 1965 as to the execution of deeds poll have effect subject to the Law of Property Act 1925 s 7(4) (under which any such power of disposing of a legal estate exercisable by a person who is not the estate owner is, when practicable, to be exercised in the name and on behalf of the estate owner: see REAL PROPERTY vol 39(2) (Reissue) PARA 246): Compulsory Purchase Act 1965 s 28(3).

8   Lands Clauses Consolidation Act 1845 s 77 (as amended: see note 7); Compulsory Purchase Act 1965 s 28(2). As to the requirements to be complied with as to the production of the instrument effecting the conveyance see PARA 658.

9   Lands Clauses Consolidation Act 1845 s 77 (as amended: see note 7); Compulsory Purchase Act 1965 s 9(4). The intention and effect of the Lands Clauses Consolidation Act 1845 s 77 is to vest in the authority whatever estates and interests in the land the party being compensated had at the time immediately before the deed poll so that if such a party acted contrary to the rights so conferred then, for the purposes of the Limitation Act 1980 s 15, Sch 1 para 8(1), time would start to run from the date of the execution of the deed poll because that is when causes of action based on the rights thereby created start to accrue: *Rhondda Cynon Taff Borough Council v Watkins* [2003] EWCA Civ 129, [2003] 1 WLR 1864, [2003] 2 P & CR 271. As to absent owners see the Compulsory Purchase Act 1965 s 5(3), Sch 2 para 2(3).

Section 9(4) and Sch 2 para 2(3) are modified in relation to the compulsory acquisition of rights by, inter alia:

(1)   a local authority (see the Local Government (Miscellaneous Provisions) Act 1976 s 13(3)(b), Sch 1 para 8; and LOCAL GOVERNMENT vol 69 (2009) PARA 511);

(2)   urban development corporations (see the Local Government, Planning and Land Act 1980 s 144, Sch 28 para 23(3); and TOWN AND COUNTRY PLANNING vol 46(1) (Reissue) PARA 180);

(3)   highway authorities (see the Highways Act 1980 s 250(5)(a), Sch 19 para 8; and HIGHWAYS, STREETS AND BRIDGES vol 21 (2004 Reissue) PARAS 49 et seq, 85);

(4)   gas transporters (see the Gas Act 1986 s 9(3), Sch 3 para 9; and FUEL AND ENERGY vol 19(2) (2007 Reissue) PARA 841);

(5)   housing action trusts (see the Housing Act 1988 s 78(2), Sch 10 para 23(1); and HOUSING vol 22 (2006 Reissue) PARA 340);

(6)   licence holders under the Electricity Act 1989 (see s 10(1), Sch 3 para 10; and FUEL AND ENERGY vol 19(2) (2007 Reissue) PARA 1284);

(7)   the Environment Agency (see the Water Resources Act 1991 s 154(5), Sch 18 para 5; the Environment Act 1995 (Consequential Amendments) Regulations 1996, SI 1996/593, reg 2, Sch 1; and WATER AND WATERWAYS vol 101 (2009) PARA 453);

(8)   water and sewerage undertakers (see the Water Industry Act 1991 s 155(5), Sch 9 para 5; and WATER AND WATERWAYS vol 101 (2009) PARA 453);

(9)   regional development agencies (see the Regional Development Agencies Act 1998 s 20, Sch 5 para 5(1); and TRADE, INDUSTRY AND INDUSTRIAL RELATIONS vol 47 (2001 Reissue) PARA 901); and

(10) universal service providers (see the Postal Services Act 2000 s 95, Sch 5 para 9(2); and POST OFFICE).

10   *Wells v Chelmsford Local Board of Health* (1880) 15 ChD 108.

11   *Douglass v London and North Western Rly Co* (1857) 3 K & J 173.

12   *Ex p Winder* (1877) 6 ChD 696; *Gedye v Works and Public Buildings Comrs* [1891] 2 Ch 630, CA; *Wells v Chelmsford Local Board of Health* (1880) 15 ChD 108. See also *Re Harris, ex p LCC* [1901] 1 Ch 931; and *Ex p Burdett Coutts* [1927] 2 Ch 98.

13   *Doe d Hutchinson v Manchester, Bury and Rossendale Rly Co* (1845) 15 LJ Ex 208.

14   *Douglass v London and North Western Rly Co* (1857) 3 K & J 173.

664.   Application for payment out.   On the application of any person[1] claiming all or any part of the money paid into court[2], or claiming all or any part of the land[3] in respect of which it was paid into court, or any interest in it, the Chancery Division of the High Court may order its distribution according to the claimants' respective estates, titles or interests; and if, before the money is distributed, it is placed in an investment account or otherwise invested[4], the court may likewise order payment of the dividends of it, and may make such other order as it thinks fit[5]. The applicant states his intention to seek a court order by means of an application notice[6].

Thus, a legal or equitable mortgagee may apply for payment out to him of the amount due on his mortgage and of arrears of interest up to six years[7]. Persons may also apply who are entitled in respect of trade claims or loss of profits[8], or who have established their title by other proceedings[9]. If the undertakers pay off any of these interests, they may themselves apply for payment out[10].

1   As to such persons see the text and notes 7–10; and PARA 665.
2   As to payment into court see PARAS 555 note 6, 640.
3   As to the meaning of 'land' see PARA 549 note 1. See also PARA 511 text to note 7.
4   Ie under the Administration of Justice Act 1982 s 38: see CIVIL PROCEDURE vol 12 (2009) PARA 1548.
5   Lands Clauses Consolidation Act 1845 s 78 (amended by the Administration of Justice Act 1965 ss 17(1), 34, Schs 1, 2; and the Administration of Justice Act 1982 s 46(2)(a)(iii)) (where the Lands Clauses Consolidation Act 1845 is incorporated: see PARA 509); Compulsory Purchase Act 1965 s 9(5) (where that Act applies: see PARA 513); Interpretation Act 1978 s 17(2)(a); and see *Practice Direction—Miscellaneous Provisions about Payments into Court* PD37. As to absent owners see the Compulsory Purchase Act 1965 s 5(3), Sch 2 para 3(1).
6   *Practice Direction—Miscellaneous Provisions about Payments into Court* PD37 para 2. An application for the court's permission to take the money out of court is made under CPR Pt 23: *Practice Direction—Miscellaneous Provisions about Payments into Court* PD37 para 2.2.
7   *Re Marriage, ex p London, Tilbury and Southend Rly Co and Eastern Counties and London and Blackwall Rly Co* (1861) 9 WR 843; *Re Stead's Mortgaged Estates* (1876) 2 ChD 713; *Pile v Pile, ex p Lambton* (1876) 3 ChD 36, CA. See further LIMITATION PERIODS.
8   *Cooper v Metropolitan Board of Works* (1883) 25 ChD 472, CA.
9   *Galliers v Metropolitan Rly Co* (1871) LR 11 Eq 410.
10 *Re Marriage, ex p London, Tilbury and Southend Rly Co and Eastern Counties and London and Blackwall Rly Co* (1861) 9 WR 843; *Cooper v Metropolitan Board of Works* (1883) 25 ChD 472 at 480, CA.

665.   Court's powers as to distribution of money.   The court uses its own machinery to determine the interest of the party applying, and also to apportion the amount due to him[1]. Thus, if the money paid in represents the value of more land or of a greater interest in land than that to which the claimant can make title, the court will order an inquiry as to the extent of his interest, and will order an amount equivalent to it to be paid to him, the balance being either retained in court or paid out to the undertakers[2].

If various persons having interests in the land apply, the court will also determine their respective rights[3]. When there are rival claims in respect of the money in court, the rival claimants may be brought before the court by permission being granted to the applicant to serve them, except in the case of the Crown, which cannot be so brought before the court[4]. The matter in dispute may, however, be settled by other proceedings[5], and the court may direct the application to stand over until it is so settled[6].

If any question arises respecting the title to the land in respect of which the money has been paid into court[7], the persons respectively in possession of the land as being the owners, or in receipt of the rents of the land as being entitled to them at the time the land was purchased or taken, are deemed to have been lawfully entitled to the land until the contrary is shown to the court's satisfaction; and, unless the contrary is so shown, the persons so in possession, and all persons claiming under them or consistently with their possession, are deemed to be entitled to the money so paid in, and to the interest or dividends of it or of the securities purchased with it, and the same must be paid and applied accordingly[8]. Thus, persons who have merely possessory titles[9], or titles which would have ripened into possessory titles but for the undertakers' action[10], are entitled to the deposited money or to the dividends. The court will not, however, order the corpus of the fund to be paid out until the possessory title would have ripened[11]. Similarly, where part of an owner's land is taken, the court, on being satisfied that he has a title which can be supported, will order the money or the dividends to be paid to him without further proof or argument because his title to the remainder of the land ought not to be jeopardised[12]. Persons in possession of closed burial grounds are similarly entitled to the fund in court[13].

A person who has gone into possession for a lesser interest than the fee simple, such as a lessee, and is in possession under that interest at the date of the payment in, cannot claim the whole of the money in court as the value of the land although the reversioner is unknown, as he is not in possession as owner, but is only entitled to so much as represents the value of the interest in respect of which he is in possession[14].

1   *Brandon v Brandon* (1864) 2 Drew & Sm 305.

2   *Re Alston's Estate* (1856) 5 WR 189, where it was admitted that a small part of the land originally claimed, and in respect of which the money was paid in, did not belong to the claimant; *Re Perks' Estate* (1853) 1 Sm & G 545; *Re North London Rly Co, ex p Cooper* (1865) 34 LJCh 373; *Re North London Rly Co, ex p Hayne* (1865) 12 LT 200.

3   *Re Marriage, ex p London, Tilbury and Southend Rly Co and Eastern Counties and London and Blackwall Rly Co* (1861) 9 WR 843; *Re Stead's Mortgaged Estates* (1876) 2 ChD 713; *Re County of London (Devons Road, Poplar) Housing Confirmation Order 1945* [1956] 1 All ER 818, [1956] 1 WLR 499.

4   *Re Lowestoft Manor and Great Eastern Rly Co, ex p Reeve* (1883) 24 ChD 253 at 256, CA.

5   *Bogg v Midland Rly Co* (1867) LR 4 Eq 310; *Cooper v Metropolitan Board of Works* (1883) 25 ChD 472, CA; *Pile v Pile, ex p Lambton* (1876) 3 ChD 36, CA; *Galliers v Metropolitan Rly Co* (1871) LR 11 Eq 410; *Birmingham and District Land Co v London and North Western Rly Co* (1888) 40 ChD 268, CA.

6   *Re Lowestoft Manor and Great Eastern Rly Co, ex p Reeve* (1883) 24 ChD 253, CA; and see *Re St Pancras Burial Ground* (1866) LR 3 Eq 173; *Ex p Freemen and Stallingers of Sunderland* (1852) 1 Drew 184.

7   See PARAS 661–662.

8   Lands Clauses Consolidation Act 1845 s 79 (amended by the Administration of Justice Act 1965 s 17(1), Sch 1) (where the Lands Clauses Consolidation Act 1845 is incorporated: see PARA 509); Compulsory Purchase Act 1965 s 25(3) (where that Act applies: see PARA 513).

9   *Re Cook's Estate* (1863) 8 LT 759; *Re Alston's Estate* (1856) 5 WR 189; *Ex p Webster* [1866] WN 246. Cf *Perry v Clissold* [1907] AC 73, PC.

10 *Re Evans* (1873) 42 LJCh 357; *Ex p Winder* (1877) 6 ChD 696; *Re Metropolitan Street Improvement Act 1877, ex p Chamberlain* (1880) 14 ChD 323; *Re Harris, ex p LCC* [1901] 1 Ch 931; *Re Harris, Hansler v Harris* [1909] WN 181; and cf *Re Greenough, Re Hollinsworth* (1871) 19 WR 580. Where the payment into court was not made in pursuance of the provisions of the Lands Clauses Acts, the court, in *Ex p Burdett Coutts* [1927] 2 Ch 98, directed the money to be paid out to the person with whom the contract had been made, as his title had not been proved to be defective. As to the Lands Clauses Acts see PARA 509 note 1.

11 *Re Harris, ex p LCC* [1901] 1 Ch 931.

12 *Re Sterry's Estate* (1855) 3 WR 561; *Re St Pancras Burial Ground* (1866) LR 3 Eq 173; and see *Ex p Freemen and Stallingers of Sunderland* (1852) 1 Drew 184 at 189.

13 *Re St Pancras Burial Ground* (1866) LR 3 Eq 173; and see *Campbell v Liverpool Corpn* (1870) LR 9 Eq 579.

14 *Gedye v Works and Public Buildings Comrs* [1891] 2 Ch 630, CA; *Re Harris, ex p LCC* [1901] 1 Ch 931; *Ex p Burdett Coutts* [1927] 2 Ch 98.

666.   Court's power to award costs.   Where the Lands Clauses Acts[1] are incorporated in the special Act[2] or the Compulsory Purchase Act 1965 applies[3], the court has power, in all cases of money paid into court as purchase money or compensation under those Acts[4], to order the undertakers[5] or acquiring authority[6] to pay the costs[7] of or incurred in consequence of the purchase of the land[8], and the cost of investing the money in court or of reinvesting it in other land[9], except where the money has been so paid or deposited by reason of the wilful refusal of any person entitled to it to accept or receive it or to convey or release the land in respect of which the money was payable, or by reason of the wilful neglect of any person to make out a good title to the land[10]. In these excepted cases, and in all cases of money paid into court under Acts not incorporating the Lands Clauses Acts, the costs of and incidental to all proceedings in the civil division of the Court of Appeal, the High Court and any county court, are in the discretion of the court or judge unless there are express statutory provisions or rules of court to the contrary[11].

By wilful refusal or wilful neglect is meant a refusal or neglect without any reason[12], or with only a frivolous reason, or by imposing an improper condition such as the prior payment of costs[13]. If the vendor has a substantial reason, whether invalid or not, the refusal or neglect is not considered wilful[14]. A refusal is not wilful because the service of the notice to treat is considered invalid on substantial, though wrong, grounds[15], or because the vendor is legally advised that the undertakers or acquiring authority have no power to take the land[16], or because he has not paid off incumbrances which exceed the price to be paid for the land or procured the holders to join in the conveyance[17]; but a refusal is wilful where, after the compulsory purchase order has been confirmed, the vendor is legally advised that the order may be bad[18].

1 As to the Lands Clauses Acts see PARA 509 note 1.
2 This is subject to any variation in the special Act of the provisions in the Lands Clauses Acts, as to which see *Re St Katherine's Dock Co* (1866) 14 WR 978. As to the meaning of 'special Act' see PARAS 509, 514.
3 As to the application of the Compulsory Purchase Act 1965 see PARA 513.
4 See PARAS 661–662.
5 As to the meaning of 'undertakers' see PARA 511.
6 As to the meaning of 'acquiring authority' see PARA 549 note 5.
7 For these purposes, references to costs include references to all reasonable charges and expenses incidental to the matters mentioned in the Compulsory Purchase Act 1965 s 26 (see the text and notes 1–6 above, 8–10 below) and to the cost of (1) obtaining the proper orders for any of the purposes set out therein; (2) obtaining the orders for the payment of dividends out of the compensation; (3) obtaining the orders for the payment out of court of the principal amount of the compensation, or of any securities in which it is invested; and (4) all proceedings relating to such orders, except such as are occasioned by litigation between adverse claimants: s 26(3).
8 As to the meaning of 'land' see PARA 549 note 1. See also PARA 511 text to note 7.
9 See the Lands Clauses Consolidation Act 1845 s 80 (amended by the Administration of Justice Act 1965 s 17(1), Sch 1) (where the Lands Clauses Consolidation Act 1845 is incorporated: see PARA 509); and the Compulsory Purchase Act 1965 s 26(2) (where that Act applies: see PARA 513). This also applies to money paid in respect of persons unknown, as they are not excepted cases. The costs of not more than one application for reinvestment may be allowed unless it appears to the High Court that it is for the benefit of the parties interested in the compensation that it should be invested in the purchase of land in different sums and at different times: s 26(4).
10 Lands Clauses Consolidation Act 1845 s 80 (amended by the Administration of Justice Act 1965 Sch 1); Compulsory Purchase Act 1965 s 26(1). As from 1 October 2009, the Lands Clauses Consolidation Act 1845 s 80 is amended to refer to the 'Senior Courts' instead of the 'Supreme Court': see s 80 (prospectively amended by the Constitutional Reform Act 2005 s 59(5), Sch 11 para 9).
An incumbrancer who has an honest claim and has to apply for payment out of court of his money will not be deprived of costs merely because his mortgagor had not conducted the proceedings in such a way as would entitle the mortgagor to costs: *Dublin Corpn v Carroll* (1915) 49 ILT 60, CA.

11 See the Supreme Court Act 1981 s 51(1) (substituted by the Courts and Legal Services Act 1990 s 4(1)); and *Re Schmarr* [1902] 1 Ch 326, CA; *Re Fisher* [1894] 1 Ch 450, CA; *Dublin Corpn v Carroll* (1915) 49 ILT 60, CA. As from a day to be appointed the Supreme Court Act 1981 is renamed as 'the Senior Courts Act 1981' by the Constitutional Reform Act 2005 Sch 11 para 1. At the date at which this volume states the law no such day had been appointed.
12 See *Re Dublin Corpn, ex p Dowling* (1881) 7 LR Ir 173.
13 *Re Turner's Estate and Metropolitan Railway Act 1860* (1861) 5 LT 524.
14 *Re Windsor, Staines and South Western Railway Act* (1850) 12 Beav 522; *Ex p Birkbeck Freehold Land Society* (1883) 24 ChD 119; *Re Leeds Grammar School* [1901] 1 Ch 228.
15 *Re East India Docks and Birmingham Junction Railway Act, ex p Bradshaw* (1848) 16 Sim 174; *Ex p Railstone* (1851) 15 Jur 1028; *Re Metropolitan District Rly Co, ex p Lawson* (1869) 17 WR 186.
16 *Re Ryde Comrs, ex p Dashwood* (1856) 26 LJCh 299; *Re St Luke's Vestry Middlesex and London School Board* [1889] WN 102.
17 *Re Crystal Palace Rly Co, Re Divers* (1855) 1 Jur NS 995; *Re Nash, Re London Tilbury and Southend Railway Act 1852* (1855) 25 LJCh 20, sub nom *Re Nash, Re Lands Clauses Consolidation Act 1945* 1 Jur NS 1082.
18 *Re Jones and Cardiganshire County Council* (1913) 57 Sol Jo 374.

(v) Deed Poll where Persons under Disability etc

667. Payment of purchase money into court or to trustees for persons under disability. Where any interest in land is purchased or taken from a person under disability who is not entitled to sell or convey except under the provisions of the special Act[1], the Lands Clauses Acts[2] or the Compulsory Purchase Act 1965, the purchase money or compensation, if it amounts to £200 or more, must be paid into the Senior Courts[3]. If it exceeds £20 but does not exceed £200, the purchase money or compensation may be paid into court or to two trustees[4], and if it does not exceed £20 it must be paid to the person entitled[5]. These provisions are limited in their application because the power to sell and convey land of a person under disability has been otherwise extended[6]. Where the undertakers have compulsory powers and title can be made under a subsisting contract, whether by virtue of a notice to treat or otherwise, without payment into court, title is to be made in that way unless, to avoid expense or delay or for any special reason, the undertakers consider it expedient that the money should be paid into court[7].

1 As to the Lands Clauses Acts see PARA 509 note 1.
2 As to the meaning of 'special Act' see PARAS 509, 514.
3 See PARA 668 et seq. As from 1 October 2009, references to the Supreme Court will be replaced with references to 'the Senior Courts' as a result of the amendments made by Constitutional Reform Act 2005.
4 See PARA 684.
5 See PARA 685.
6 See PARA 553.
7 Law of Property Act 1925 s 42(7). Apart from this provision, the undertakers could not insist on the sale being carried out under other statutory powers to save themselves expense: see *Re Pigott and Great Western Rly Co* (1881) 18 ChD 146; *Re Lady Bentinck and London and North Western Rly Co* (1895) 12 TLR 100; *Re Leeds Grammar School* [1901] 1 Ch 228.

668. Payment in respect of ecclesiastical, university or college land. Where the land[1] acquired under the authority of a compulsory purchase order to which the Compulsory Purchase Act 1965 applies[2] is ecclesiastical property[3], any sums agreed or awarded for the purchase of the land, or to be paid by way of compensation for damage sustained by reason of severance or injury affecting it, are not to be paid as otherwise directed by that Act[4] but must be paid to the Diocesan Board of Finance for the diocese in which the land is situated and must be applied for the purposes for which the proceeds of a sale by agreement of the land would be applicable under any enactment or measure authorising such a sale or disposing of the proceeds of such a sale[5].

Where the land acquired belongs to the Universities of Oxford, Cambridge or Durham or any of their colleges[6], and the purchase money or compensation would otherwise be required to be paid, or has been paid, into court or to trustees, the money or compensation may instead be paid to the university or college[7].

1   As to the meaning of 'land' see PARA 549 note 1.
2   See PARA 513.
3   Ie ecclesiastical property as defined in the Acquisition of Land Act 1981 s 12(3): see PARA 560 note 6.
4   As to the payment of purchase money and compensation see PARA 638 et seq.
5   Compulsory Purchase Act 1965 s 31 (amended by the Acquisition of Land Act 1981 s 34(1), Sch 4 para 14(5); the Planning and Compensation Act 1991 Sch 15 para 19; and the Church of England (Miscellaneous Provisions) Measure 2006 s 14, Sch 5 para 12). The Compulsory Purchase Act 1965 s 31 does not apply in relation to a compulsory purchase order under the Pipe-lines Act 1962 s 11 (see RAILWAYS, INLAND WATERWAYS AND CROSS-COUNTRY PIPELINES vol 39(1A) (Reissue) PARA 595 et seq): Compulsory Purchase Act 1965 s 37(2).
6   Ie a university or college to which the Universities and College Estates Act 1925 applies, other than Eton or Winchester: see s 1.
7   Universities and College Estates Act 1925 s 28(1), (2) (amended by virtue of the Universities and College Estates Act 1964 ss 2, 3, Sch 1 para 12(1)).

669.   Payment into court of £200 or over.   When any land[1] or any interest in it is purchased or taken from a person under disability who is not entitled to sell or convey it except under the provisions of the special Act[2], the Lands Clauses Acts[3] or the Compulsory Purchase Act 1965[4], the purchase price or compensation payable in respect of the land or interest, or in respect of any permanent damage to any such land, must be paid into the Senior Courts[5] if it amounts to or exceeds £200[6].

All sums of money exceeding £200 payable by the undertakers[7] or the acquiring authority[8] in respect of the taking, using or interfering with any land under a contract or agreement with any person who is not entitled to dispose of the land absolutely for his own benefit must be paid into court[9] and any such contracting party may not retain for his own use: (1) any part of any sums agreed or contracted to be paid for or in respect of the taking, using or interfering with any of the land; or (2) any part of any sums agreed or contracted to be paid in lieu of bridges, tunnels or other accommodation works[10]. All such money is deemed to be contracted to be paid for and on account of the several parties interested in the land, whether in possession or in remainder, reversion or expectancy[11].

Furthermore, if, in order to obtain possession, the undertakers or the acquiring authority have been compelled to pay the money to or on behalf of a person under disability, that person may be required to pay it into court[12].

If necessary, the undertakers or the authority will be compelled by mandatory order to pay the money into court[13]; but as the requirement of the payment is for the safe custody of the money and is not necessary in order to perfect the title of the undertakers or the authority, the court may sanction the application of the money to some proper purpose without the payment in[14].

1   As to the meaning of 'land' see PARA 549 note 1. See also PARA 511 text to note 7.
2   As to the meaning of 'special Act' see PARAS 509, 514.
3   Ie under the Lands Clauses Consolidation Act 1845 s 7 (where that Act is incorporated: see PARA 509): see PARA 553. As to the classes of person referred to see *Kelland v Fulford* (1877) 6

    ChD 491; *Newton v Metropolitan Rly Co* (1861) 8 Jur NS 738; *Re Chelsea Waterworks Co* (1887) 56 LJCh 640. As to the Lands Clauses Acts see PARA 509 note 1.

4 Ie the Compulsory Purchase Act 1965 s 2, Sch 1 paras 1–3 (where that Act applies: see PARA 513): see PARAS 553–554. See also note 5.

5 As from a day to be appointed the references in the Lands Clauses Consolidation Act 1845 ss 69, 73 to the Supreme Court are repealed and replaced with references to the Senior Courts: see ss 69, 73 (both prospectively amended by the Constitutional Reform Act 2005 s 59(5), Sch 11 para 9).

6 See the Lands Clauses Consolidation Act 1845 s 69 (amended by the Administration of Justice Act 1965 s 17(1), Sch 1; and the Compulsory Purchase Act 1965 Sch 8 Pt II); and the Compulsory Purchase Act 1965 Sch 1 para 6(1), (2). This is subject to the provisions of Sch 1: see the text and notes 7–11; and PARAS 553–554, 670 et seq. As to payment into court see PARAS 555 note 6, 640. These provisions are limited in their application because the power to sell and convey land of a person under disability has been otherwise extended: see PARA 553. As to when money paid in will pass under a conveyance of his property by the party entitled see *Ex p Ballinrobe and Claremorris Light Rly Co and Kenny* [1913] 1 IR 519.

7 As to the meaning of 'undertakers' see PARA 511.

8 As to the meaning of 'acquiring authority' see PARA 549 note 5.

9 If the sum exceeds £20 but is less than £200, it may be paid to two trustees, instead of into court: see PARA 684.

10 Lands Clauses Consolidation Act 1845 s 73 (amended by the Administration of Justice Act 1965 Sch 1); Compulsory Purchase Act 1965 Sch 1 para 9(1), as read with the enactments cited in note 6.

11 Lands Clauses Consolidation Act 1845 s 73 (as amended: see note 10); Compulsory Purchase Act 1965 Sch 1 para 9(2). This provision does not otherwise affect contracts by persons under a disability under the Lands Clauses Consolidation Act 1845 s 7 or the Compulsory Purchase Act 1965 Sch 1 paras 1–3: see *Taylor v Directors etc of Chichester and Midhurst Rly Co* (1870) LR 4 HL 628. As to payment under contract to a tenant for life for not opposing a bill see *Pole v Pole* (1865) 2 Drew & Sm 420.

12 *London and North Western Rly Co v Lancaster Corpn* (1851) 15 Beav 22. Alternatively other provision for safety may be made by the court: see the text to note 14.

13 *Barnett v Great Eastern Rly Co* (1868) 18 LT 408; *Williams v Llanelly Rly Co* (1868) 19 LT 310.

14 *Re London, Brighton and South Coast Rly Co, ex p Earl of Abergavenny* (1856) 4 WR 315; *Re Milnes (a Person of Unsound Mind)* (1875) 1 ChD 28, CA.

670. Execution of deed poll. When the compensation agreed or awarded in respect of the land purchased or taken has been paid into court[1], the owner of the land[2], when required so to do by the undertakers[3] or acquiring authority[4], must duly convey the land or interest to them or as they direct[5]. In default of doing so, or if he fails to make a good title to the land to their satisfaction, they may execute a deed poll containing a description of the land and reciting its acquisition by them, the names of the parties from whom it was purchased, the amount of the compensation paid into court, and the default[6].

On execution of the deed poll, all the estate and interest in the land belonging to, or capable of being sold and conveyed by, any person as between whom and the undertakers or authority the compensation was agreed or awarded and paid into court, will vest absolutely in the undertakers or authority; and as against all such persons, and all parties on behalf of whom they are enabled to sell and convey[7], the undertakers or authority will be entitled to immediate possession of the land[8].

1 See PARA 669.

2 In this context, 'owner' includes all parties who are enabled to sell or convey the land by the Lands Clauses Consolidation Act 1845 (see s 75) or by the Compulsory Purchase Act 1965 s 2, Sch 1 (see Sch 1 para 10(1)). As to the meaning of 'land' see PARA 549 note 1. See also PARA 511 text to note 7.

3 As to the meaning of 'undertakers' see PARA 511.

4 As to the meaning of 'acquiring authority' see PARA 549 note 5.

5   Lands Clauses Consolidation Act 1845 s 75 (amended by the Administration of Justice Act 1965 s 17(1), Sch 1) (where the Lands Clauses Consolidation Act 1845 is incorporated: see PARA 509); Compulsory Purchase Act 1965 Sch 1 para 10(1) (where that Act applies: see PARA 513). These provisions are limited in their application because the power to sell and convey land of a person under disability has been otherwise extended: see PARA 553. As to the sealing, stamping and execution of deeds poll see PARA 663. The undertakers or authority may not execute a deed poll instead of a conveyance merely to save themselves expense: *Re Cary-Elwes' Contract* [1906] 2 Ch 143.

6   Lands Clauses Consolidation Act 1845 s 75 (as amended: see note 5); Compulsory Purchase Act 1965 Sch 1 para 10(2). The Lands Clauses Consolidation Act 1845 s 75 is amended in relation to Northern Ireland by SI 2005/1452.

7   See PARA 669.

8   Lands Clauses Consolidation Act 1845 s 75; Compulsory Purchase Act 1965 Sch 1 para 10(3). Schedule 1 para 10(3) is modified in relation to the compulsory acquisition of rights by, inter alia:

   (1)   a local authority (see the Local Government (Miscellaneous Provisions) Act 1976 s 13(3)(b), Sch 1 para 8; and LOCAL GOVERNMENT vol 69 (2009) PARA 511);

   (2)   urban development corporations (see the Local Government, Planning and Land Act 1980 s 144, Sch 28 para 23(3); and TOWN AND COUNTRY PLANNING vol 46(1) (Reissue) PARA 180);

   (3)   highway authorities (see the Highways Act 1980 s 250(5)(a), Sch 19 para 8; and HIGHWAYS, STREETS AND BRIDGES vol 21 (2004 Reissue) PARAS 49 et seq, 85);

   (4)   gas transporters (see the Gas Act 1986 s 9(3), Sch 3 para 9; and FUEL AND ENERGY vol 19(2) (2007 Reissue) PARA 841);

   (5)   housing action trusts (see the Housing Act 1988 s 78(2), Sch 10 para 23(1); and HOUSING vol 22 (2006 Reissue) PARA 340);

   (6)   licence holders under the Electricity Act 1989 (see s 10(1), Sch 3 para 10; and FUEL AND ENERGY vol 19(2) (2007 Reissue) PARA 1284);

   (7)   the Environment Agency (see the Water Resources Act 1991 s 154(5), Sch 18 para 5; the Environment Act 1995 (Consequential Amendments) Regulations 1996, SI 1996/593, reg 2, Sch 1; and WATER AND WATERWAYS vol 101 (2009) PARA 453);

   (8)   water and sewerage undertakers (see the Water Industry Act 1991 s 155(5), Sch 9 para 5; and WATER AND WATERWAYS vol 101 (2009) PARA 453);

   (9)   regional development agencies (see the Regional Development Agencies Act 1998 s 20, Sch 5 para 5(1); and TRADE, INDUSTRY AND INDUSTRIAL RELATIONS vol 47 (2001 Reissue) PARA 901); and

   (10) universal service providers (see the Postal Services Act 2000 s 95, Sch 5 para 9(2); and POST OFFICE).

671.   Investment of money paid in and disposal of income. Until the money paid in is applied, it will be placed in an investment account or otherwise invested under the Administration of Justice Act 1982[1]. If the money paid in is so dealt with, the annual proceeds of it must be paid to the person who would for the time being have been entitled to the rents and profits of the land in respect of which the compensation was paid[2]. The interim investment and payment of the proceeds or income may be made on an order of the Chancery Division of the High Court made on the application[3] of the party who would have been entitled to the rents and profits of the land in respect of which the money has been paid in[4]. If there is more than one sum of money in court in respect of two or more pieces of land to the rents and profits of which one person would have been entitled, the application of all the sums may be dealt with as one[5].

1   Lands Clauses Consolidation Act 1845 s 70 (amended by the Statute Law Revision Act 1892; the Administration of Justice Act 1965 s 17(1), Sch 1; and the Administration of Justice Act 1982 s 46(2)(a)(iii)); Compulsory Purchase Act 1965 s 25(1); Interpretation Act 1978 s 17(2)(a). The money is invested under the Administration of Justice Act 1982 s 38: see CIVIL PROCEDURE vol 12 (2009) PARA 1548. These provisions are limited in their application because the power to sell and convey land of a person under disability has been otherwise extended: see PARA 553.

2   Lands Clauses Consolidation Act 1845 s 70 (as amended: see note 1); Compulsory Purchase Act 1965 s 2, Sch 1 para 6(3). As to the meaning of 'land' see PARA 549 note 1. See also PARA

511 text to note 7. The proceeds or income may be ordered to be paid to the person who was tenant for life of the land taken, even though the conveyance has not been executed, provided the undertakers or acquiring authority have taken possession (*Re Wrey* (1865) 13 WR 543; *Ex p Cofield* (1847) 11 Jur 1071; *Re Hungerford* (1855) 1 K & J 413). They may be ordered to be paid to trustees, whether private (see *Re Clinton* (1860) 6 Jur NS 601; *Re Coulson's Settlement* (1867) 17 LT 27; *Re Pryor's Settlement Trusts* (1876) 35 LT 202; *Re Foy's Trusts* (1875) 23 WR 744; *Re Metropolitan Rly Co and Maire* [1876] WN 245; *Re Goe's Estate* (1854) 3 WR 119), or charitable (see *Re Collins' Charity* (1851) 20 LJCh 168), and to persons entitled to the fees, if any, of disused burial grounds (*Ex p Rector of Liverpool* (1870) LR 11 Eq 15; *Ex p Rector of St Martin's, Birmingham* (1870) LR 11 Eq 23; *Re St Pancras Burial Ground* (1866) LR 3 Eq 173). Where there are successive interests the order may direct that the dividends be paid to the person entitled for the time being, as in the case of rectors and vicars (*Re Rector etc of St Benet's* (1865) 12 LT 762; *A-G v Brandreth* (1842) 1 Y & C Ch Cas 200; *Re East Lincolnshire Rly Co's Acts, ex p Archbishop of Canterbury* (1848) 5 Ry & Can Cas 699), or to a man for his life and then to his wife (*Re How's Trusts* (1850) 15 Jur 266; *Re Lowndes' Trust* (1851) 20 LJCh 422; *Re Brent's Trusts* (1860) 8 WR 270). If the order is not made in this form, a fresh order may be necessary: *Re Jolliffe's Estate* (1870) LR 9 Eq 668. The dividends unpaid at the date of the death of any person entitled to the rents and profits will be apportioned and paid to his personal representatives: see the Court Funds Rules 1987, SI 1987/821, r 43.

3   See *Practice Direction—Miscellaneous Provisions about Payments into Court* PD37 para 3.
4   Lands Clauses Consolidation Act 1845 s 70 (as amended (see note 1); and further amended by the Administration of Justice Act 1965 s 34, Sch 2); Compulsory Purchase Act 1965 Sch 1 para 6(3), (4). As to costs see PARAS 672–673.
5   See PARA 675 text and note 7.

672.   Costs of investment. Pending the permanent application of the money paid into court[1], the undertakers[2] or acquiring authority[3] may be ordered to pay the costs of investing the money[4], even if a contract for the purchase of land as a permanent investment has been entered into[5]. The order does not affect the liability of the undertakers or authority to pay the costs of a subsequent permanent investment[6]. The court also has power to order them to pay the costs of more than one interim investment, as, for example, of an investment on mortgage when under a previous order the money has been invested in consols[7]. Such an investment on mortgage may, however, be treated as a permanent investment[8].

1   See PARA 671. As to payment into court see PARAS 555 note 6, 640.
2   As to the meaning of 'undertakers' see PARA 511.
3   As to the meaning of 'acquiring authority' see PARA 549 note 5.
4   See the Lands Clauses Consolidation Act 1845 s 80; the Compulsory Purchase Act 1965 s 26(2)(b); and PARA 666. These provisions are limited in their application because the power to sell and convey land of a person under disability has been otherwise extended: see PARA 553.
5   *Re Liverpool etc Rly Co* (1853) 17 Beav 392.
6   *Re Dodd's Estate* (1871) 19 WR 741; *Re Wilkinson's Estate* (1868) 18 LT 17; *Re Gaselee* [1901] 1 Ch 923 at 928.
7   *Re Blyth's Trusts* (1873) LR 16 Eq 468 at 469 per Lord Selborne LC; *Re Hereford, Hay and Brecon Rly Co* (1864) 13 WR 134; *Re Nepton's Charity* (1906) 22 TLR 442; *Re Sewart's Estate* (1874) LR 18 Eq 278; *Re Smith's Estate* (1870) LR 9 Eq 178; *Reading v Hamilton* (1862) 5 LT 628. Before *Re Blyth's Trusts* above, the practice was unsettled. See *Re Lomax* (1864) 34 Beav 294; *Re Flemon's Trusts* (1870) LR 10 Eq 612. For a case of reinvestment in stock see *Re Brown* (1890) 63 LT 131, CA.
8   *Re Gedling Rectory* (1885) 53 LT 244.

673.   Costs on payment of income. The undertakers[1] or acquiring authority[2] are liable to pay the costs of obtaining orders for the payment of dividends on the money paid into court[3]; however, if two applications are made when one would have sufficed, they will only be required to pay the costs of one[4].

1   As to the meaning of 'undertakers' see PARA 511.
2   As to the meaning of 'acquiring authority' see PARA 549 note 5.

3   See the Lands Clauses Consolidation Act 1845 s 80; the Compulsory Purchase Act 1965
     s 26(3)(b); and PARA 666. See also PARA 669. As to payment into court see PARAS 555 note 6,
     640. These provisions are limited in their application because the power to sell and convey land
     of a person under disability has been otherwise extended: see PARA 553.

4   Eg if a second order for payment of dividends is required because the first was not drawn so as
     to cover persons successively entitled, the court may exercise its discretion to order the
     undertakers or authority to pay the costs: *Re Pryor's Settlement Trusts* (1876) 35 LT 202; *Re
     Andenshaw School* (1863) 1 New Rep 255; *Re Goe's Estate* (1854) 3 WR 119; *Re Bazett's
     Trustees* (1850) 16 LTOS 279; *Ex p Ecclesiastical Comrs* (1870) 39 LJCh 623; *Re Grand
     Junction Railway Acts, ex p Hordern* (1848) 2 De G & Sm 263; *Re Metropolitan Rly Co and
     Maire* [1876] WN 245; *Re Ryder* (1887) 37 ChD 595. As to payment of dividends in case of
     resettlement see *Re Pick's Settlement* (1862) 31 LJCh 495; *Re Shakespeare Walk School* (1879)
     12 ChD 178. Where there are several funds in court belonging to the same trust, and only one
     application is necessary, the costs of one only will be allowed: *Re Wilts, Somerset and
     Weymouth Rly Co, Re South Devon Rly Co, Re Cornwall Rly Co, ex p Lord Broke* (1863) 11
     WR 505; *Re Pattison's Devised Estates, Re Pattison's Settled Estates* (1876) 4 ChD 207; *Re
     Gore Langton's Estates* (1875) 10 Ch App 328; and cf *Re Midland Great Western Rly Co*
     (1881) 9 LR Ir 16. The various undertakers may be ordered to bear the costs in equal shares: *Ex
     p Sunbury-on-Thames UDC, ex p Staines Reservoirs Joint Committee* (1922) 86 JP Jo 153. For
     other examples see *Re Spooner's Estate* (1854) 1 K & J 220; *Re London and North Western
     Railway Co's Act 1846 and Rugby and Stamford Railway Act 1846, Re Baroness Braye's Settled
     Estates* (1863) 11 WR 333; *Re Long's Trust* (1864) 33 LJCh 620; *Re Nicholls's Trust Estates*
     (1866) 35 LJCh 516.

674.   Application of purchase money or compensation.   The purchase money
or compensation paid into court[1] must remain there until applied on an order of
the High Court[2] to one or more of the following purposes:

(1)   in the discharge of any debt or incumbrance affecting the land or
       affecting other land settled with it on the same or the like trusts or
       purposes[3]; or

(2)   in the purchase of other land to be conveyed, limited and settled upon
       like trusts and purposes and in the same manner as the land stood
       settled in respect of which the purchase money or compensation was
       paid[4]; or

(3)   if the money or compensation was paid in respect of any buildings taken
       or injured by the proximity of the works[5], in removing or replacing the
       buildings or substituting other buildings in such manner as the High
       Court may direct[6]; or

(4)   in payment to any party becoming absolutely entitled to the purchase
       money or compensation[7].

1   See the Lands Clauses Consolidation Act 1845 s 69; the Compulsory Purchase Act 1965 Sch 1
     para 6(1), (2); and PARA 669. These provisions are limited in their application because the
     power to sell and convey land of a person under disability has been otherwise extended: see
     PARA 553.

2   As to applications for such orders see PARA 675.

3   Lands Clauses Consolidation Act 1845 s 69 (amended by the Administration of Justice Act 1965
     s 17(1), Sch 1; and the Compulsory Purchase Act 1965 s 39(4), Sch 8 Pt II) (where the Lands
     Clauses Consolidation Act 1845 is incorporated: see PARA 509); Compulsory Purchase Act 1965
     Sch 1 para 6(2)(a) (where that Act applies: see PARA 513). As to the meaning of 'land' see PARA
     549 note 1. See also PARA 511 text to note 7. Note that it is no longer possible to create a new
     settlement under the Settled Land Act 1925: see PARA 553 note 11.
         A corporation may be allowed to apply the money to pay off mortgages on other corporate
     land or tolls, or to pay off bonds the interest on which was payable out of the common fund,
     which was mainly made up of the rents and profits of land: *Re Derby Municipal Estates* (1876)
     3 ChD 289; *Re Eastern Counties Rly Co, ex p Cambridge Corpn* (1848) 5 Ry & Can Cas 204;
     and see *Re Public Fortification Acts, ex p Hythe Corpn* (1840) 4 Y & C Ex 55; *Re Dublin,
     Wicklow and Wexford Rly Co, ex p Tottenham* (1884) 13 LR Ir 479; *Re Dublin, Wicklow and
     Wexford Rly Co, ex p Richards* (1890) 25 LR Ir 175.

The order may sanction the application of the money to purchasing the surrender of beneficial leaseholds (*Re Manchester, Sheffield and Lincolnshire Rly Co, ex p Sheffield Corpn* (1855) 21 Beav 162, 25 LJCh 587; *Ex p Bishop of London* (1860) 2 De GF & J 14; *Ex p London Corpn* (1868) LR 5 Eq 418; *Re Marquis of Townshend's Estates and Lynn and Fakenham Railway Act 1876* [1882] WN 7); in paying off rent to prevent re-entry on leasehold premises (*Re London-Street, Greenwich and London, Chatham and Dover Railway (Further Powers) Act 1881* (1887) 57 LT 673); in redeeming quit rents and rentcharges (*Re Public Works Comrs, ex p Studdert* (1856) 6 I Ch R 53; *Re Comrs of Church Temporalities, Ireland, ex p Lord Leconfield* (1874) IR 8 Eq 559; *Re Dublin, Wicklow and Wexford Rly Co, ex p Tottenham* (1884) 13 LR Ir 479); in reinstating structures to prevent a sale under a building Act (*Re Davis' Estate and Crystal Palace and West Railway Act, ex p Davis* (1858) 3 De G & J 144); or in paying off expenses under the Inclosure Acts (*Re Oxford, Worcester etc Rly Co, ex p Lockwood* (1851) 14 Beav 158; *Ex p Queen's College, Cambridge* (1849) 14 Beav 159n; *Vernon v Earl Manvers* (1862) 32 LJCh 244). It may not, however, be applied in paying off charges payable by the person in possession, and not charged on the inheritance: *Re Louth and East Coast Rly Co, ex p Rector of Grimoldby* (1876) 2 ChD 225; *Re Hull Railway and Dock Act, ex p Rector of Kirksmeaton* (1882) 20 ChD 203; *Re Public Works Comrs, ex p Studdert* (1856) 6 I Ch R 53; and cf *Ex p LCC, ex p Vicar of Christ Church, East Greenwich* [1896] 1 Ch 520.

4   Lands Clauses Consolidation Act 1845 s 69; Compulsory Purchase Act 1965 Sch 1 para 6(2)(b). See *Kelland v Fulford* (1877) 6 ChD 491 at 494 per Jessel MR; *Ex p Vicar of Castle Bytham, ex p Midland Rly Co* [1895] 1 Ch 348; and cf *Re Eastern Counties Rly Co, ex p Vicar of Sawston* (1858) 27 LJCh 755; *Re Browne and Oxford and Bletchley Junction and Buckinghamshire Railway Acts* (1852) 6 Ry & Can Cas 733; *Re Cheshunt College* (1855) 3 WR 638; *Dixon v Jackson* (1856) 25 LJCh 588; *Re Buckingham* (1876) 2 ChD 690, CA; *Re Taylor's Estate* (1871) 40 LJCh 454 (land in Isle of Man). In the absence of special circumstances, the purchase money for freehold land will not be allowed to be laid out in the purchase of leaseholds (*Re Lancashire and Yorkshire Rly Co, ex p Macaulay* (1854) 23 LJCh 815; *Ex p Master, Fellows and Scholars of Trinity College, Cambridge* (1868) 18 LT 849; *Re Rehoboth Chapel* (1874) 44 LJCh 375; *Re Cann's Estate, Re Norfolk Railway Co's Acts* (1850) 19 LJCh 376) or in equities of redemption (*Re Cheltenham and Great Western Rly Co, ex p Craven* (1848) 17 LJCh 215; *Ex p Portadown, Dungannon and Omagh Junction Rly Co* (1876) 10 IR Eq 368); but the purchase money for leaseholds may be laid out in buying freeholds (*Re Brasher's Trust* (1858) 6 WR 406; *Re Parker's Estate* (1872) LR 13 Eq 495; and cf *Re Coyte's Estate, Re Liverpool Docks Acts* (1851) 1 Sim NS 202). The erection of permanent buildings has been authorised where it was for the benefit of the estate or trust, on the ground that this was equivalent to a purchase: see *Re London and North Western Railway Act 1861, ex p Liverpool Corpn* (1866) 1 Ch App 596; *Re Leigh's Estate* (1871) 6 Ch App 887; *Drake v Trefusis* (1875) 10 Ch App 364. Money paid for part of a glebe has been allowed to be laid out in building a new rectory (*Re Incumbent of Whitfield* (1861) 1 John & H 610; *Ex p Rector of Bradfield St Claire* (1875) 32 LT 248; *Ex p Rector of Hartington* (1875) 23 WR 484; *Ex p Rector of Claypole* (1873) LR 16 Eq 574; *Ex p Vicar of St Botolph, Aldgate* [1894] 3 Ch 544); in drainage works on the glebe (*Re Vicar of Queen Camel, Re Great Western Railway Act and Wilts, Somerset and Weymouth Amendment Act 1846* (1863) 8 LT 233); and in repairing a church porch (*Ex p Parson etc of St Alphage* (1886) 55 LT 314).

When a small sum remains after such a purchase, the court may authorise it to be paid out to trustees to be applied on permanent improvements (*Re Kinsey* (1863) 1 New Rep 303; *Ex p Barrett* (1850) 19 LJCh 415); and if the balance remaining is less than £20 it may be paid out to the parties entitled to the rents and profits for their own use and benefit (see PARA 685). As to money paid in respect of leases and reversions see PARA 682. The Settled Land Act 1925 provides that where the money is liable to be laid out in the purchase of land to be made subject to a settlement, it may be invested or applied as capital money arising under the Settled Land Act 1925 on the like terms, if any, respecting costs and other things, as nearly as circumstances admit, and, notwithstanding anything in that Act according to the same procedure, as if the modes of investment or application authorised under that Act were authorised under the Lands Clauses Consolidation Act 1845 or the Compulsory Purchase Act 1965, as the case may be: see the Settled Land Act 1925 s 76; and SETTLEMENTS vol 42 (Reissue) PARA 797. Note that it is no longer possible to create a new settlement under the Settled Land Act 1925: see PARA 553 note 11.

5   As to the meaning of 'works' see PARA 549 note 3. See also PARA 511 text to note 4.

6   Lands Clauses Consolidation Act 1845 s 69; Compulsory Purchase Act 1965 Sch 1 para 6(2)(c). Thus money paid for land taken by a railway undertaking has been authorised to be laid out in removing and altering farm buildings rendered unsafe or unsuitable by reason of the

construction of the railway (*Re Johnson's Settlements* (1869) LR 8 Eq 348), and in building new ones (*Re Oxford, Worcester and Wolverhampton Rly Co, ex p Milward* (1859) 29 LJCh 245; *Re Kent Coast Rly Co, ex p Dean and Chapter of Canterbury* (1862) 7 LT 240, 10 WR 505; *Re Buckinghamshire Rly Co, ex p Churchwardens and Overseers of Bicester* (1848) 5 Ry & Can Cas 205). Money paid for almshouses may be laid out in building others (*Re Southampton and Dorchester Railway Act, ex p Thorner's Charity* (1848) 12 LTOS 266; and see *Re St Thomas's Hospital* (1863) 11 WR 1018).

7   Lands Clauses Consolidation Act 1845 s 69; Compulsory Purchase Act 1965 Sch 1 para 6(2)(d). Thus it may be paid to a person who comes of age if he is then entitled to it for his own use (*Kelland v Fulford* (1877) 6 ChD 491 at 495; *Re Hall's Estate* (1870) LR 9 Eq 179; *Re Cant's Estate* (1859) 4 De G & J 503), or to a tenant in tail but not as a person absolutely entitled until he has executed a disentailing deed (*Re Broadwood's Settled Estates* (1875) 1 ChD 438; *Re Reynolds* (1876) 3 ChD 61, CA), unless the sum is trifling (*Re Watson* (1864) 4 New Rep 528; *Stead v Harper* [1896] WN 46).

     Statutory bodies with or without powers of sale of land may be entitled to have the money paid out to them (*Re Chelsea Waterworks Co* (1887) 56 LJCh 640; *Re Brumby and Frodingham UDC* (1904) 69 JP 96; *Ex p King's College, Cambridge* [1891] 1 Ch 677; *Ex p Watford UDC* (1914) 78 JP Jo 160) if they have obtained any necessary consents (*Ex p Great Western Railway (New Railways) Act 1905, ex p Great Western Rly Co* (1909) 74 JP 21, CA). Trustees with power of sale may be authorised to receive payment out (*Re Gooch's Estate* (1876) 3 ChD 742; *Re Hobson's Trusts* (1878) 7 ChD 708, CA; *Re St Luke's, Middlesex, Vestry* [1880] WN 58; *Re Thomas's Settlement* (1882) 30 WR 244; *Re London, Brighton and South Coast Rly Co, ex p Bowman* [1888] WN 179; *Re Smith, ex p London and North Western Rly Co and Midland Rly Co* (1888) 40 ChD 386, CA; *Re Morgan, Smith v May* [1900] 2 Ch 474); and so may the trustees of a charity (*Re Faversham Charities* (1862) 5 LT 787; *Ex p Haberdashers' Co* (1886) 55 LT 758; *Re Clergy Orphan Corpn* [1894] 3 Ch 145, CA; *Re Sheffield Corpn and Trustees of St William's Roman Catholic Chapel and Schools, Sheffield* [1903] 1 Ch 208; *Re Islington Borough Council* (1907) 97 LT 78; *Re Wesleyan Methodist Chapel, South Street, Wandsworth* [1909] 1 Ch 454; but cf *Re Bristol Free Grammar School Estates* (1878) 47 LJCh 317; *Re Bishop Monk's Horfield Trust* (1881) 29 WR 462; *Re Rector and Churchwardens of St Alban's, Wood Street* (1891) 66 LT 51). The transfer of a fund to another account is equivalent to payment out of court: *Melling v Bird* (1853) 22 LJCh 599.

675. Application to court for disposal of money and payment out. The money paid into court may be applied or paid out on an order of the Chancery Division of the High Court, made at the instance of the party who would have been entitled to the rents and profits of the land in respect of which the money has been paid in[1]. Thus consecutive tenants for life may apply[2], but not a remainderman[3] or an annuitant[4]. In the case of disused burial grounds, the party entitled to the burial fees, if any, would be the proper person to apply[5].

The application is made by application notice[6]. If there is more than one sum of money in court in respect of two or more pieces of land to the rents and profits of which one person would have been entitled, the application of all the sums may be dealt with as one[7].

In cases of discharging incumbrances, or laying out the money in buildings and improvements, the remaindermen and the trustees of the settlement should generally be served, so that they may have an opportunity of objecting[8]. Incumbrancers should generally be served on applications for payment out, but the costs of their appearance, if not necessary, will not be payable by the undertakers or acquiring authority[9]. On applications by a trustee, it seems that the beneficiary need not be served[10], unless his presence is necessary for the purpose of distributing the fund[11]. A person having an ascertained share in the fund may apply for payment out without serving the other persons entitled to shares, but it would be otherwise if the shares had to be ascertained[12].

1   Lands Clauses Consolidation Act 1845 s 70 (amended by the Administration of Justice Act 1965 s 17(1), Sch 1) (where the Lands Clauses Consolidation Act 1845 is incorporated: see PARA 509); Compulsory Purchase Act 1965 Sch 1 para 6(4) (where that Act applies: see PARA 513). As

to payment into court see PARAS 555 note 6, 640. These provisions are limited in their application because the power to sell and convey land of a person under disability has been otherwise extended: see PARA 553.
2 *Re Jolliffe's Estate* (1870) LR 9 Eq 668.
3 *Nash v Nash* (1868) 37 LJCh 927.
4 *Re St Katherine Dock Co* (1828) 2 Y & J 386; and see *Ex p Cofield* (1847) 11 Jur 1071; *Re London and Tilbury Rly Co, Re Pedley's Estate* (1855) 1 Jur NS 654.
5 Eg the rector (*Ex p Rector of Liverpool* (1870) LR 11 Eq 15; *Ex p Rector of St Martin's, Birmingham* (1870) LR 11 Eq 23), or the trustees of the ground (*Re St Pancras Burial Ground* (1866) LR 3 Eq 173; and cf *Champneys v Arrowsmith* (1867) LR 3 CP 107).
6 See *Practice Direction—Miscellaneous Provisions about Payments into Court* PD37 para 3.
7 *Re Manchester, Sheffield and Lincolnshire Rly Co, ex p Sheffield Corpn* (1855) 21 Beav 162, 25 LJCh 587; *Re Lord Arden's Estates* (1875) 10 Ch App 445; *Re Browse's Trusts* (1866) 14 LT 37; *Re Southampton and Dorchester Rly Co, ex p King's College, Cambridge* (1852) 5 De G & Sm 621; *Re Gore Langton's Estates* (1875) 10 Ch App 328.
8 *Re Leigh's Estate* (1871) 6 Ch App 887; *Re Furness Rly Co, Re Romney* (1863) 3 New Rep 287; and see *Re Olive's Estate* (1890) 44 ChD 316; *Re Browne and Oxford and Bletchley Junction and Buckinghamshire Railway Acts* (1852) 6 Ry & Can Cas 733; *Re Cann's Estate, Re Norfolk Railway Co's Acts* (1850) 19 LJCh 376; *Re Piggin, ex p Mansfield Rly Co* [1913] 2 Ch 326. Patrons of a living should also be served: *Ex p Vicar of Castle Bytham, ex p Midland Rly Co* [1895] 1 Ch 348. The costs of an affidavit of service when required will be payable by the undertakers: *Re Halstead United Charities* (1875) LR 20 Eq 48; *Re Artisans' and Labourers' Dwellings Improvement Act 1875, ex p Jones* (1880) 14 ChD 624; *Re Ruck's Trusts* (1895) 13 R 637. As to the costs of persons served see PARA 676. Note that it is no longer possible to create a new settlement under the Settled Land Act 1925: see PARA 553 note 11.
9 *Re Halstead United Charities* (1875) LR 20 Eq 48; *Re Artisans' and Labourers' Dwellings Improvement Act 1875, ex p Jones* (1880) 14 ChD 624; *Re Ruck's Trusts* (1895) 13 R 637; *Ex p Mercers' Co* (1879) 10 ChD 481. Cf *Re Hatfield's Estate (No 2)* (1863) 32 Beav 252; *Re Brooke* (1864) 12 WR 1128; *Re Baroness Braye's Settled Estates* (1863) 32 LJCh 432.
10 *Re East, ex p East* (1853) 2 WR 111; *Re Gooch's Estate* (1876) 3 ChD 742.
11 *Re Long's Trust* (1864) 10 Jur NS 417. As to the appearance of the trustees of a settlement on the application of a person becoming entitled absolutely see *Re Burnell's Estate* (1864) 12 WR 568; *Ex p Metropolitan Rly Co* (1868) 16 WR 996. As to the appearance of the tenant for life on the application of the trustees of the settlement see *Re Piggin, ex p Mansfield Rly Co* [1913] 2 Ch 326. Note that it is no longer possible to create a new settlement under the Settled Land Act 1925: see PARA 553 note 11.
12 *Re Midland Rly Co* (1847) 11 Jur 1095; *Re Clarke's Devisees* (1858) 6 WR 812. As to separate applications by persons having the same interests and employing the same solicitor see *Re Nicholls' Trust Estates* (1866) 35 LJCh 516. As to the costs of application for payment out see PARA 680.

676. Costs of persons served. The undertakers or acquiring authority will only be ordered to pay the costs of service upon persons necessarily served; and if those persons, when served, appear unnecessarily, they will not be entitled to their costs[1].

If the application is simply for the reinvestment of money in land, and there are mortgagees or annuitants whose rights are not otherwise affected, the proper course is to serve them, giving them an intimation that if they appear at the hearing they will probably have to pay their own costs[2].

In the case of settled land, when the money is to be laid out in other land, the remainderman need not be served or appear, and the costs of service upon and of appearance by him will be disallowed[3].

When the money has been deposited in respect of land which is the subject of a claim, the parties to the action should be served, and in a proper case will be allowed their costs of appearance[4].

Similar rules apply on an application for investment[5]. Thus, mortgagees and other incumbrancers should not be served[6] unless they are in occupation[7]. It is proper to serve the undertakers or acquiring authority[8]. The costs occasioned by improper service may be ordered to be paid by the applicant or out of the fund[9], and a similar order may be made where, by reason of default or delay, or the applicant's failure to serve, additional costs have been incurred[10].

1   See CIVIL PROCEDURE vol 12 (2009) PARA 1737 et seq. Undertakers will not be ordered to pay costs of such parts of the summons as may have failed: *Re Jacobs, Baldwin v Pescott* [1908] 2 Ch 691.

2   *Re Gore Langton's Estates* (1875) 10 Ch App 328 at 333; *Re Duggan's Trusts* (1869) LR 8 Eq 697.

3   *Re Yorkshire, Doncaster and Goole Rly Co, Re Dylar's Estate* (1855) 1 Jur NS 975; *Re Browne and Oxford and Bletchley Junction and Buckinghamshire Railway Acts* (1852) 6 Ry & Can Cas 733; *Re Bowes's Estate* (1864) 10 Jur NS 817; *Re Gore Langton's Estates* (1875) 10 Ch App 328. Note that it is no longer possible to create a new settlement under the Settled Land Act 1925: see PARA 553 note 11.

4   *Haynes v Barton* (1866) LR 1 Eq 422; *Picard v Mitchell* (1850) 12 Beav 486; *Re Brandon's Estate* (1862) 2 Drew & Sm 162.

5   *Re Dowling's Trusts* (1876) 45 LJCh 568; *Re Finch's Estate* (1866) 14 WR 472; *Re Leigh's Estate* (1871) 6 Ch App 887.

6   *Re Morris's Settled Estates* (1875) LR 20 Eq 470; *Re Webster's Settled Estates, South Eastern Railway Act and Lands Clauses Consolidation Act* (1854) 2 Sm & G, App vi; *Re Lancashire and Yorkshire Rly Co, ex p Smith* (1849) 6 Ry & Can Cas 150; *Ex p Bishop of London* (1860) 2 De GF & J 14; *Re Thomas's Estate, Re Ely Valley Railway Act 1857 and Lands Clauses Consolidation Act 1845, ex p Cozens* (1864) 12 WR 546; *Re Smith* (1865) 14 WR 218; *Ex p Cofield* (1847) 11 Jur 1071; *Re Ruck's Trusts* (1895) 13 R 637; *Re Osborne's Estate* [1878] WN 179.

7   *Re Hungerford's Trust* (1857) 3 K & J 455; *Re Nash, Re London, Tilbury and Southend Railway Act 1852* (1855) 25 LJCh 20, sub nom *Re Nash, Re Lands Clauses Consolidation Act 1845* 1 Jur NS 1082.

8   *Re Charity of King Edward VI's Almshouses at Saffron Walden* (1868) 37 LJCh 664.

9   *Re Lancashire and Yorkshire Rly Co, Wilson v Foster* (1859) 28 LJCh 410; *Re Incumbent of Whitfield* (1861) 1 John & H 610.

10 *Re Clarke's Estate* (1882) 21 ChD 776; *Re Leigh's Estate* (1871) 6 Ch App 887.

677.   Costs of purchase and of discharging debts etc.   The undertakers[1] or acquiring authority[2] may be ordered to pay the costs of, or incurred in consequence of, the purchase of the land, other than those otherwise provided for, including all reasonable charges and expenses incidental to the purchase, the costs of obtaining the proper orders, and the costs of all proceedings relating to such orders except such as are occasioned by litigation between adverse claimants[3]. They will also be liable to pay the costs for the discharge of any debt or incumbrance affecting the land or other land settled with it on the same or like trusts or purposes[4]. If the money is employed in discharging incumbrances or in the purchase of leaseholds by the reversioner, the practice is to order the undertakers or authority to pay only the costs of having the money paid out, but not of the reinvestment[5].

1   As to the meaning of 'undertakers' see PARA 511.

2   As to the meaning of 'acquiring authority' see PARA 549 note 5.

3   Lands Clauses Consolidation Act 1845 s 80 (amended by the Administration of Justice Act 1965 s 17(1), Sch 1) (where the Lands Clauses Consolidation Act 1845 is incorporated; see PARA 509); Compulsory Purchase Act 1965 s 26(2)(a), (3)(a), (d) (where that Act applies: see PARA 513). See also PARAS 666, 678–681. As to such other costs see PARA 640 note 6 (costs on payment into court on entry without consent), PARA 659 (costs of conveyance), and PARAS 718 note 15, 746 (costs of assessment). These provisions are limited in their application because the power to sell and convey land of a person under disability has been otherwise extended: see PARA 553. As to the meaning of 'land' see PARA 549 note 1. See also PARA 511 text to note 7.

4   See the Lands Clauses Consolidation Act 1845 s 69; the Compulsory Purchase Act 1965 Sch 1 para 6(2)(a); and PARA 669. As to the discharge of debts etc see PARA 674. Note that it is no longer possible to create a new settlement under the Settled Land Act 1925: see PARA 553 note 11.

5   *Re Manchester, Sheffield, and Lincolnshire Rly Co, ex p Sheffield Corpn* (1855) 21 Beav 162, 25 LJCh 587; *Re Sheffield Waterworks Co, ex p Sheffield Town Trustees* (1860) 8 WR 602; *Re Mark's Trusts* [1877] WN 63; *Ex p London Corpn* (1868) LR 5 Eq 418; and cf *Re Eastern Counties Rly Co, ex p Earl of Hardwicke* (1848) 17 LJCh 422; *Re Lancaster and Carlisle Rly Co, ex p Yeates* (1847) 12 Jur 279; *Re Lord Stanley of Alderley's Estate* (1872) LR 14 Eq 227; *Re Dublin, Wicklow and Wexford Rly Co, ex p Richards* (1890) 25 LR Ir 175.

678. Costs on purchase of other land. The undertakers[1] or acquiring authority[2] may be ordered to pay the costs of, or incurred in consequence of, the purchase of the land, other than those otherwise provided for[3]. They will be liable to pay the costs in respect of the purchase of other land to be conveyed, limited and settled upon like trusts and purposes, and in the same manner, as the land in respect of which the compensation was paid stood settled[4]; but the costs of not more than one application for reinvestment in land may be allowed unless it appears to the High Court that it is for the benefit of the parties interested in the compensation that it should be invested in the purchase of land in different sums and at different times[5], and not then if the undertakers or authority can show that the reinvestments are capricious, vexatious or unnecessary[6].

Where the money is invested with other money provided by the applicant, the undertakers or authority will be ordered to pay the whole costs of reinvestment, except so far as they are increased by reason of the purchase money exceeding the money paid in[7]. If there are two or more funds in court, and these are invested together, the undertakers or acquiring authorities are entitled to a contribution from others who are under a similar obligation to pay the costs[8]. The general costs of the application and of the purchase are borne equally, unless there are special circumstances, of which the inequality of the amounts is not necessarily one[9]; but the ad valorem stamp, the surveyor's fee, and, in some cases, the solicitor's charges, have been apportioned rateably[10]. If some of the parties who have paid money into court are not liable to pay costs, the other undertakers or authorities are only liable to pay the proportion they would have been liable to pay if all had been liable[11]. If some of those who have paid in have amalgamated, they will be treated as one for the purposes of costs[12]. If the deposited money belongs to persons who have become absolutely entitled, the undertakers or authority may be ordered to pay the costs of reinvestment[13]; and they may also be ordered to do so where, by reason of the owner's death, the land purchased will be held on trusts differing from those in existence when the land was taken[14].

If the court does not sanction the proposed investment, the undertakers or authority are not required to pay the costs of the abortive application, and may be allowed their costs out of the fund in court[15]; and if the applicant has acted in good faith for the benefit of the estate in making the application, his costs will also be allowed out of the money in court[16]. If the court approves the purchase, but it is not completed owing to the failure to make, or because of the great expense of making, a good title, the undertakers or authority are required to pay the costs[17], but not if the purchase is abandoned on insufficient grounds[18].

The costs which the undertakers or authority are ordinarily required to pay on the purchase of land as a reinvestment are such costs as, in the case of an open contract, would be purchaser's costs[19]. These include the costs of the reference to chambers for all investigation of title, and of the conveyancing counsel to the court when necessary[20]; and the costs of the petitioner's solicitor for investigation of the title and preparing and completing the conveyance[21]. They do not include costs of private counsel, except for consultation on difficult points[22], and they do not include costs ordinarily paid by the vendor even though the contract makes them payable by the purchaser[23]. If, by reason of the applicants being under disability, additional costs are incurred, as where the applicants are trustees of a charity[24] or hold ecclesiastical offices[25], or when the land or fund is subject to a suit[26], the undertakers or authority may be ordered to pay the costs reasonably incurred in consequence[27].

1   As to the meaning of 'undertakers' see PARA 511.
2   As to the meaning of 'acquiring authority' see PARA 549 note 5.
3   See the Lands Clauses Consolidation Act 1845 s 80; the Compulsory Purchase Act 1965 s 26(2)(a), (3)(a), (d); and PARA 677. These provisions are limited in their application because the power to sell and convey land of a person under disability has been otherwise extended: see PARA 553. The liability of the undertakers for costs of reinvestment appears to be the same whether the money is deposited as required by the Lands Clauses Acts or paid in an alternative manner in accordance with the provisions of other enactments (eg under the Universities and College Estates Act 1925 s 28: see PARA 668): see the *Final Report of the Expert Committee on Compensation and Betterment* (Cmd 6386) (1942) para 179. As to the meaning of 'land' see PARA 549 note 1. See also PARA 511 text to note 7.
4   See the Lands Clauses Consolidation Act 1845 s 69; the Compulsory Purchase Act 1965 Sch 1 para 6(2)(b); and PARA 669. As to the purchase of other land see PARA 674. Note that it is no longer possible to create a new settlement under the Settled Land Act 1925: see PARA 553 note 11.
5   Lands Clauses Consolidation Act 1845 s 80 proviso (amended by the Administration of Justice Act 1965 s 17(1), Sch 1) (where the Lands Clauses Consolidation Act 1845 is incorporated: see PARA 509); Compulsory Purchase Act 1965 s 26(4) (where that Act applies: see PARA 513).
6   *Re Brandon's Estate* (1862) 2 Drew & Sm 162 at 166; *Re Trustees of St Bartholomew's Hospital* (1859) 4 Drew 425 at 426; *Ex p Fishmongers' Co* (1862) 1 New Rep 85; *Re Woolley's Trust, Re East and West India Docks and Birmingham Junction Railway Act 1846* (1853) 17 Jur 850; and cf *Re London and Birmingham Rly Co, ex p Provost and Fellows of Eton College* (1842) 3 Ry & Can Cas 271; *Re London and Birmingham Rly Co, ex p Boxmoor Waste Lands Trustees* (1844) 3 Ry & Can Cas 513; *Re St Katherine's Dock Co* (1844) 3 Ry & Can Cas 514; *Re London and Birmingham Rly to Northampton, ex p Bouverie* (1846) 4 Ry & Can Cas 229; *Re Merchant Taylors' Co* (1847) 10 Beav 485; *Jones v Lewis* (1850) 2 Mac & G 163; *Ex p St Katharine's Hospital* (1881) 17 ChD 378, decided under similar provisions in special Acts. As to the meaning of 'special Act' see PARAS 509, 514.
7   *Re Clark* [1906] 1 Ch 615; *Re Metropolitan Rly Co and Gonville and Caius College, Cambridge* (1887) reported in [1906] 1 Ch 619n (stating the principle laid down in *Re Sheffield and Lincolnshire Railway Act, ex p Hodge* (1848) 16 Sim 159; *Re Southampton and Dorchester Rly Co, ex p King's College, Cambridge* (1852) 5 De G & Sm 621; *Re Branmer's Estate* (1849) 14 Jur 236; *Re Loveband's Settled Estates* (1860) 30 LJCh 94). The orders made in *Ex p Perpetual Curate of Bilston* (1889) 37 WR 460 and *Re Bagot's Settled Estates* (1866) 14 WR 471 are not now followed. The rule laid down in *Re Clark* above applies to an application for payment out: see PARA 680.
8   *Ex p Bishop of London* (1860) 2 De GF & J 14; *A-G v Rochester Corpn* (1867) 16 LT 408, 15 WR 765; *Ex p Ecclesiastical Comrs for England* (1865) 11 Jur NS 461; *Re Metropolitan Rly Co and Gonville and Caius College, Cambridge* (1887) reported in [1906] 1 Ch 619n.
9   See the cases cited in note 8. See also *Ex p Governors of Christ's Hospital* (1864) 2 Hem & M 166; *Re Byron's Estate* (1863) 1 De GJ & Sm 358; *Re Merton College* (1864) 1 De GJ & Sm 361; *Ex p Master, Fellows and Scholars of Trinity College, Cambridge* (1868) 18 LT 849; and see *Re Leigh's Estate* (1871) 6 Ch App 887; *Re Manchester and Leeds Rly Co, ex p Gaskell* (1876) 2 ChD 360; *Ex p Governors of Christ's Hospital* (1879) 27 WR 458.
10 *Re Bishopsgate Foundation* [1894] 1 Ch 185; *Ex p Bishop of London* (1860) 2 De GF & J 14; *Ex p London Corpn* (1868) LR 5 Eq 418; and see *Ex p Christchurch* (1861) 9 WR 474; *Ex p Governors of St Bartholomew's Hospital* (1875) LR 20 Eq 369; *A-G v St John's Hospital, Bath* [1893] 3 Ch 151.
11 Thus where there were 17 separate funds in court, and six of the defendants were not liable to pay costs, the remaining 11 were ordered each to pay one-seventeenth of the total costs: *Ex p Ecclesiastical Comrs for England* (1865) 11 Jur NS 461. See also *A-G v Rochester Corpn* (1867) 16 LT 408, 15 WR 765.
12 *Ex p Corpus Christi College, Oxford* (1871) LR 13 Eq 334; *Re Manchester and Leeds Rly Co, ex p Gaskell* (1876) 2 ChD 360; *Re Midland Great Western Rly Co* (1881) 9 LR Ir 16. If a line

is leased, the lessors remain liable (*Re Carlisle and Silloth Rly Co* (1863) 33 Beav 253); if the undertaking is assigned, the assignors become liable (*Ex p Vicar of Sheffield* (1904) 68 JP 313).

13   *Re Jones's Trust Estate* (1870) as reported in 39 LJCh 190; *Re Dodd's Estate* (1871) 19 WR 741; and see *Re De Beauvoir* (1860) 29 LJCh 567 at 570, sub nom *Re Benyon's Trusts* 8 WR 425.

14   *Re De Beauvoir* (1860) 29 LJCh 567, sub nom *Re Benyon's Trusts* 8 WR 425; and cf *Re Parker's Estate* (1872) LR 13 Eq 495; *Re Eastern Counties Rly Co, Re Lands Clauses Consolidation Act 1845, ex p Peyton's Settlement* (1856) 4 WR 380.

15   *Re Hardy's Estate* (1854) 18 Jur 370; *Ex p Stevens* (1851) 15 Jur 243; *Re Macdonald's Trusts of the Will, Re London and Blackwall Rly Co* (1860) 2 LT 168. They must pay the costs of obtaining the particular order that is made, not of that part of the summons which failed: *Re Jacobs, Baldwin v Pescott* [1908] 2 Ch 691.

16   Cf *Re Leigh's Estate* (1871) 6 Ch App 887. See also the Lands Clauses Consolidation Act 1845 s 73; the Compulsory Purchase Act 1965 Sch 1 para 9; and PARA 669.

17   *Re Woolley's Trust, Re East and West India Docks and Birmingham Junction Railway Act 1846* (1853) 17 Jur 850; *Ex p Rector of Holywell* (1865) 2 Drew & Sm 463; *Re Carney's Trusts* (1872) 20 WR 407; *Re North Staffordshire Rly Co, ex p Vaudrey's Trusts* (1861) 3 Giff 224.

18   *Re Lands Clauses Consolidation Act 1845, ex p Copley* (1858) 4 Jur NS 297.

19   *Ex p Governors of Christ's Hospital* (1875) LR 20 Eq 605; *Re Temple Church Lands* (1877) 47 LJCh 160; *Re Eastern Counties Rly Co, ex p Vicar of Sawston* (1858) 27 LJCh 755; *Ex p Thavie's Charity Trustees* [1905] 1 Ch 403; *Re North Staffordshire Rly Co, ex p Incumbent of Alsager* (1854) 2 Eq Rep 327.

20   These may be dispensed with if the amount is small: *Re Blomfield* (1876) 25 WR 37; *Re Lapworth Charity* [1879] WN 37. If the money is invested before the purchase is approved, the undertakers or authority are not required to pay the costs of purchase: *Ex p Bouverie* (1848) 5 Ry & Can Cas 431; *Re Bishop Monk's Horfield Trust* (1881) 29 WR 462.

21   *Re Merchant Taylors' Co* (1885) 30 ChD 28, CA; and see *Re Stewart* (1889) 41 ChD 494.

22   *Re Jones's Settled Estates* (1858) 6 WR 762.

23   See the cases cited in note 19.

24   *Re Governors of Christ's Hospital* (1864) 12 WR 669 (costs of enrolment). Cf *Re St Paul's Schools, Finsbury* (1883) 52 LJCh 454 (costs connected with a new scheme required for other reasons than the taking of the land not included); and cf PARA 681 note 7.

25   *Ex p Vicar of Creech St Michael* (1852) 21 LJCh 677.

26   *Carpmael v Proffitt* (1854) 17 Jur 875.

27   See also *Armitage v Askham* (1855) 1 Jur NS 227; *Re Brandon's Estate* (1862) 2 Drew & Sm 162.

679.   Costs of payment in respect of removing or replacing buildings.   The undertakers[1] or acquiring authority[2] may be ordered to pay the costs of, or in consequence of, the purchase of the land, other than those otherwise provided for[3], and will be liable, if the compensation was paid in respect of any buildings taken or injured by the proximity of the works, for costs in respect of removing or replacing the buildings or substituting other buildings[4]. If the money is applied in erecting buildings, whether in substitution for others or not, this is treated as a payment out, and the undertakers or authority pay only the costs of the application and of the payment out[5]. Thus, the costs of planning and superintending the buildings[6], or of the surveyor's certificate that the works have been completed[7], are not payable, but the costs of a certificate of the sum due will be payable by the undertakers or authority[8].

1   As to the meaning of 'undertakers' see PARA 511.

2   As to the meaning of 'acquiring authority' see PARA 549 note 5.

3   See the Lands Clauses Consolidation Act 1845 s 80; the Compulsory Purchase Act 1965 s 26(2)(a), (3)(a), (d); and PARA 677. These provisions are limited in their application because the power to sell and convey land of a person under disability has been otherwise extended: see PARA 553. As to the meaning of 'land' see PARA 549 note 1. See also PARA 511 note 7.

4   See the Lands Clauses Consolidation Act 1845 s 69; the Compulsory Purchase Act 1965 Sch 1 para 6(2)(c); and PARA 669. As to the removal or replacement of buildings see PARA 674. As to the meaning of 'works' see PARA 549 note 3. See also PARA 511 text to note 4. As to the meaning of 'building' see PARA 626.

5   *Re Incumbent of Whitfield* (1861) 1 John & H 610; *Re Lathropp's Charity* (1866) LR 1 Eq 467 (distinguishing *Re Buckinghamshire Rly Co* (1850) 14 Jur 1065); *Ex p Rector of Claypole* (1873) LR 16 Eq 574; *Ex p Rector of Shipton-under-Wychwood* (1871) 19 WR 549; *Ex p Rector of Gamston* (1876) 1 ChD 477. As to substituted buildings see *Re Southampton and Dorchester Railway Act, ex p Thorner's Charity* (1848) 12 LTOS 266; *Re Chelsea Waterworks Co, ex p Minister and Churchwardens of St John's, Fulham* (1856) 28 LTOS 173; *Re Kent Coast Rly Co, ex p Dean and Chapter of Canterbury* (1862) 7 LT 240, 10 WR 505; *Re St Thomas's Hospital* (1863) 11 WR 1018.

6   *Re Butcher's Co* (1885) 53 LT 491.

7   *Ex p Rector of Shipton-under-Wychwood* (1871) 19 WR 549.

8   *Re Arden* (1894) 70 LT 506, CA.

680. Costs of application for payment out. The undertakers[1] or the acquiring authority[2] are liable to pay costs of obtaining orders for the payment out of court of the principal amount of the purchase money or compensation or of any securities in which it is vested, except such as are occasioned by litigation between adverse claimants[3]. This will include the brokerage on the sale of the securities in which the money has been invested[4]. They will also be required to pay all costs incurred in investigating[5] and making good the claimant's title, such as the costs of a disentailing assurance[6], of a power of attorney[7] and of taking out letters of administration[8], in cases where the taking of the land has rendered these necessary when they would not otherwise have been required. They must also pay the extra costs incurred by the owner dealing in the ordinary way with the money after it has been paid into court[9]. For example, if the land taken was the subject of a settlement, and the tenant for life exercises a power of appointment under the settlement[10], or if a reversioner mortgages his reversionary interest[11], the undertakers or authority must pay the costs of the parties requiring to be served in consequence. If, by reason of the money having been deposited in respect of a lease, part of the corpus has to be sold periodically and paid out, they will also be liable for the costs of those sales[12].

Where the fund in court comprises not only the money paid into court on the compulsory acquisition of the land, but also other money, the undertakers or authority will be ordered to pay the whole costs of the application for payment out of the fund, except in so far as the costs have been increased by reason of the inclusion in the application of the other money[13].

When an application is made for the money to be transferred to another account in court, and the undertakers' or authority's name is omitted from the title to that other account, the transfer is deemed to be equivalent to a payment out, and the undertakers or authority will be ordered to pay the costs of the application and transfer[14], but thereafter their liability ceases[15]. If the transfer is to the credit of an action, all persons having the same interest in the money should be joined in the making of the application, unless there is good reason why they should not be joined, and, if they appear separately without good reason, the undertakers or authority ought not to be ordered to pay their costs[16]. All parties to the claim should be served with the application and the undertakers or authority are liable to pay the costs of service and of the appearance of the parties[17] other than the cost of appearance of parties who, having no objection to the order sought, ought not to appear[18]. The appearance of the trustee of the settlement is usually necessary, and his costs will be allowed[19].

If several persons have interests in the fund, but their interests are not adverse, the undertakers or authority will be required to pay all the costs of determining the respective shares, including the costs of construing a will[20]. Thus, if the money has been deposited in respect of land the subject of a mortgage, they may be ordered to pay the costs of the inquiry as to the amount due to the mortgagee[21].

The undertakers or authority are not required to pay the costs of unsuccessful applications for payment out, and the unsuccessful applicant may be ordered to pay the undertakers' or authority's costs[22]. They are not required to pay the costs of litigation between adverse claimants to the money[23], but if they pay money into court because they know of such adverse claims they will be liable to pay the ordinary costs of investment and of payment out[24]. They will also be required to pay the costs of proving the rightful claimant's title, but not any additional costs caused by the adverse claim[25]. Similarly, if the right to the fund depends on the construction of a will or other document, they will be ordered to pay one set of costs in connection with it[26]. If two adverse claimants mutually agree to apply for payment out, the undertakers or authority will be required to pay the costs incurred in connection with the payment out[27].

1   As to the meaning of 'undertakers' see PARA 511.
2   As to the meaning of 'acquiring authority' see PARA 549 note 5.
3   Lands Clauses Consolidation Act 1845 s 80 (amended by the Administration of Justice Act 1965 s 17(1), Sch 1) (where the Lands Clauses Consolidation Act 1845 is incorporated: see PARA 509); Compulsory Purchase Act 1965 s 26(2)(a), (3)(a), (c), (d) (where that Act applies: see PARA 513). See also *Re Gooch's Estate* (1876) 3 ChD 742; *Re Ellison's Estate* (1856) 25 LJCh 379; *Re Wood Green Gospel Hall Charity, ex p Middlesex County Council* [1909] 1 Ch 263 (costs of application to Charity Commissioners for new scheme). These provisions are limited in their application because the power to sell and convey land of a person under disability has been otherwise extended: see PARA 553. Under special Acts not incorporating the Lands Clauses Acts a different rule applied: see *Re Eastern Counties Rly Co, ex p Earl of Hardwicke* (1848) 17 LJCh 422; *Re Bristol and Exeter Rly Co, ex p Gore-Langton* (1847) 11 Jur 686. As to the allowance of fees for attendance before the Accountant General see *Re Butler's Will, ex p Metropolitan Board of Works* (1912) 106 LT 673. As to the Lands Clauses Acts see PARA 509 note 1. As to the meaning of 'special Act' see PARAS 509, 514.
4   *Re Magdalen College, Oxford* [1901] 2 Ch 786; and see also *Ex p Emmanuel Hospital* (1908) 24 TLR 261.
5   *Re Spooner's Estate* (1854) 1 K & J 220; *Re Singleton's Estate, ex p Fleetwood Rly Co* (1863) 9 Jur NS 941.
6   *Brooking's Devisees v South Devon Rly Co* (1859) 2 Giff 31. Cf *Re Merchant Shipping Act 1854, ex p Allen* (1881) 7 LR Ir 124.
7   *Re Godley* (1847) 10 I Eq R 222; *Re Kearns, ex p Lurgan UDC* [1902] 1 IR 157. Cf *Re Belfast and Northern Counties Rly Co, ex p Gilmore* [1895] 1 IR 297.
8   *Re Lloyd and North London Railway (City Branch) Act 1861* [1896] 2 Ch 397, adopting decisions in *Re Dublin Junction Rlys, ex p Kelly* (1893) 31 LR Ir 137, and in *Re Midland Great Western (Ireland) Rly Co, ex p Rorke* [1894] 1 IR 146, and approved in *Re Griggs, ex p London School Board* [1914] 2 Ch 547, CA. See also *Re Waterford and Limerick Rly Co, ex p Baron Harlech* [1896] 1 IR 507; *Re Kearns, ex p Lurgan UDC* [1902] 1 IR 157; *Re Bear Island Defence Works and Doyle* [1903] 1 IR 164, CA. See PARA 659.
9   *Eden v Thompson* (1864) 2 Hem & M 6 at 8 per Wood V-C; *Re Lye's Estate, Re Berks and Hants Extension Railway Act 1859* (1866) 13 LT 664. Cf *Re Gough's Trusts, ex p Great Western Rly Co* (1883) 24 ChD 569; *Re Jones's Trust Estate* (1870) 39 LJCh 190, 18 WR 312; *Re London-Street, Greenwich and London, Chatham and Dover Railway (Further Powers) Act 1881* (1887) 57 LT 673.
10 *Re Brooshooft's Settlement* (1889) 42 ChD 250; and cf *Re Byrom* (1859) 5 Jur NS 261. Note that it is no longer possible to create a new settlement under the Settled Land Act 1925: see PARA 553 note 11.
11 *Re Olive's Estate* (1890) 44 ChD 316.
12 *Re Long's Estate* (1853) 1 WR 226; *Re Edmunds* (1866) 35 LJCh 538.
13 *Re Lynn and Fakenham Railway (Extension) Act 1880* (1909) 100 LT 432.
14 *Melling v Bird* (1853) 22 LJCh 599.

15 *Fisher v Fisher* (1874) LR 17 Eq 340 at 341; *Prescott v Wood* (1868) 37 LJCh 691; *Nock v Nock* [1879] WN 125. As to costs when the new account is still entitled to the undertakers' or authority's name see *Drake v Greaves* (1886) 33 ChD 609; *Brown v Fenwick* (1866) 35 LJCh 241.

16 *Melling v Bird* (1853) 22 LJCh 599; *Re Picton's Estate* (1855) 3 WR 327.

17 *Eden v Thompson* (1864) 2 Hem & M 6; *Dinning v Henderson* (1848) 2 De G & Sm 485; *Henniker v Chafy* (1860) 28 Beav 621; *Re English's Settlement* (1888) 39 ChD 556.

18 *Sidney v Wilmer (No 2)* (1862) 31 Beav 338; *Eden v Thompson* (1864) 2 Hem & M 6.

19 *Re English's Settlement* (1888) 39 ChD 556; *Re Burnell's Estate* (1864) 12 WR 568.
    On a transfer to the official custodian for charities, there is no need for service on corporations or persons interested and costs of service are not payable by the undertakers or authority: *Re Prebend of St Margaret, Leicester* (1864) 10 LT 221; *Re Rector and Churchwardens of St Alban's, Wood Street* (1891) 66 LT 51. Any funds for the time being vested in the Accountant General and held by him in trust for any charity may, if the Accountant General on an application made in that behalf to him by the Charity Commission or the appropriate authority thinks fit so to direct, be transferred to the Official Custodian for Charities or the appropriate authority, as the case may be: see the Administration of Justice Act 1982 s 41(1) (amended by the Charities Act 2006 s 75(1), Sch 8 para 67; and the Church of England (Miscellaneous Provisions) Measure 2006 s 14, Sch 5 para 25(a)); and CHARITIES vol 5(2) (2001 Reissue) PARA 275.

20 *Askew v Woodhead* (1880) 14 ChD 27 at 36, CA; *Re Gregson's Trusts* (1864) 2 Hem & M 504 (revsd on another point 2 De GJ & Sm 428); *Re Singleton's Estate, ex p Fleetwood Rly Co* (1863) 9 Jur NS 941; *Re Hinks's Estate* (1853) 2 WR 108; *Re Noake's Will* (1880) 28 WR 762; *Ex p Collins* (1850) 19 LJCh 244; and see *Re Williams, ex p Great Southern and Western Rly Co* (1877) 11 IR Eq 497.

21 *Re Bareham* (1881) 17 ChD 329, CA; *Re Olive's Estate* (1890) 44 ChD 316.

22 *Ex p Winder* (1877) 6 ChD 696 at 705; *Re Jacobs, Baldwin v Pescott* [1908] 2 Ch 691.

23 Lands Clauses Consolidation Act 1845 s 80; Compulsory Purchase Act 1965 s 26(3)(d).

24 *Ex p Palmer, Cox and Bellingham* (1849) 13 Jur 781; *Hore v Smith* (1849) 14 Jur 55; *Re North London Rly Co, ex p Cooper* (1865) 34 LJCh 373; *Re Duke of Norfolk's Settled Estates* (1874) 31 LT 79; *Re Courts of Justice Comrs* [1868] WN 124. If the money is paid in at the request of one of the claimants, and the other afterwards withdraws his claim, the undertakers or authority would appear not to be liable: *Re English* (1865) 13 WR 932. If they have treated both claimants as vendors and have paid two sums into court, they may have to pay the costs of both: *Re Butterfield* (1861) 9 WR 805.

25 *Re Spooner's Estate* (1854) 1 K & J 220; *Re Joliffe* (1857) 3 Jur NS 633; *Re North London Rly Co, ex p Cooper* (1865) 34 LJCh 373; *Re Catling's Estate* [1890] WN 75. As to the form of order see *Re Cant's Estate* (1859) 1 De GF & J 153; *Hood v West Ham Corpn, Re West Ham Corpn Act 1902* (1910) 74 JP 179. It is the taxing officer's duty to disallow such of the costs as are, in his opinion, occasioned by litigation between adverse claimants, whether the order follows the decision in *Re Cant's Estate* above and excepts such costs, or is drawn up in accordance with the practice not to except such costs unless the question is raised at the hearing: *Hood v West Ham Corpn, Re West Ham Corpn Act 1902*. Costs of negotiations for the settlement of a dispute affecting the title of the land acquired are costs occasioned by adverse litigation: *Hood v West Ham Corpn, Re West Ham Corpn Act 1902*. Opposition by the Charity Commission to an application for payment out by a corporation claiming to be absolutely entitled on the ground that it had no power to sell without the Commission's consent does not constitute adverse litigation: *Re Clergy Orphan Corpn* [1894] 3 Ch 145 at 147, CA.

26 *Re Mid Kent Railway Act 1856, ex p Styan* (1859) John 387; *Re Tookey's Trust, Re Bucks Rly Co* (1852) 16 Jur 708; *Ex p Yates* (1869) 17 WR 872; *Re Longworth's Estate* (1853) 1 K & J 1.

27 *Re Spooner's Estate* (1854) 1 K & J 220.

681.   Costs of purchasing and taking land. The undertakers[1] or acquiring authority[2] may be ordered to pay the costs of or incurred in consequence of the purchase of the land not otherwise provided for[3], including all reasonable charges and expenses incidental to the purchase, the costs of obtaining the proper orders and the costs of all proceedings relating to those orders except such as are occasioned by litigation between adverse clients[4]. Where, therefore, additional costs are incurred in applications to the court which are rendered necessary by reason of mental disorder[5] or because of the existence of an administration action[6], or, where the vendors are trustees of a charity, in applying to the Charity Commission and obtaining a new scheme[7], the undertakers or authority may be ordered to pay these additional costs.

When the money has been paid into court as security before entry by the undertakers or authority, they may be ordered to pay certain costs connected with the taking of the land, but not costs the payment of which is provided for under other provisions[8], even though these in fact remain unpaid[9]. When part of land subject to leases has been taken, the undertakers or authority have been ordered to pay the costs of apportioning the rents among the various parties and also the costs incurred with regard to settling accommodation works[10]. Similarly, when the undertaking was abandoned after entry subject to compensation to the landowner for disturbance, they have been ordered to pay the costs of ascertaining this compensation[11], but the court has power to make only a general order as to these costs, and cannot order them to be paid out of the money in court[12].

1   As to the meaning of 'undertakers' see PARA 511.
2   As to the meaning of 'acquiring authority' see PARA 549 note 5.
3   See PARA 677 note 3. As to the meaning of 'land' see PARA 549 note 1. See also PARA 511 text to note 7.
4   See the Lands Clauses Consolidation Act 1845 s 80 (amended by the Administration of Justice Act 1965 s 17(1), Sch 1) (where the Lands Clauses Consolidation Act 1845 is incorporated: see PARA 509); the Compulsory Purchase Act 1965 s 26(2)(a), (3)(a), (d) (where that Act applies: see PARA 513). See also PARA 677 text to note 3. These provisions are limited in their application because the power to sell and convey land of a person under disability has been otherwise extended: see PARA 553.
5   *Re Taylor and York and North Midland Rly Co* (1849) 1 Mac & G 210; *Re Walker, ex p Manchester and Leeds Rly Co* (1851) 7 Ry & Can Cas 129; *Re Briscoe* (1864) 2 De GJ & Sm 249.
6   *Haynes v Barton* (1861) 1 Drew & Sm 483; *Haynes v Barton* (1866) LR 1 Eq 422; *Picard v Mitchell* (1850) 12 Beav 486.
7   *Re Wood Green Gospel Hall Charity, ex p Middlesex County Council* [1909] 1 Ch 263. These costs will not be allowed where the formulation of a new scheme was not the direct result of the acquisition of the land: see PARA 678 note 24. As to the Charity Commission see CHARITIES vol 5(2) (2001 Reissue) PARA 486 et seq.
8   See PARA 677 note 3.
9   *Ex p Great Northern Rly Co* (1848) 5 Ry & Can Cas 269; and see *Ex p Morris* (1871) LR 12 Eq 418 (costs of summoning jury, which became unnecessary owing to agreement being reached); *Re Pardoe's Account and Epping Forest Act 1878* [1882] WN 33 (costs of assessing compensation when Lands Clauses Acts provisions as to costs not incorporated). See also *Metropolitan District Rly Co v Sharpe* (1880) 5 App Cas 425, HL (costs provisions of Lands Clauses Acts applied where procedure for assessment of compensation substituted by special Act). As to the Lands Clauses Acts see PARA 509 note 1. As to the meaning of 'special Act' see PARAS 509, 514.
10   *Re London, Brighton and South Coast Rly Co, ex p Flower* (1866) 1 Ch App 599; and see *Re Hampstead Junction Rly Co, ex p Buck* (1863) 1 Hem & M 519.
11   *Charlton v Rolleston* (1884) 28 ChD 237, CA.
12   *Re Neath and Brecon Rly Co* (1874) 9 Ch App 263.

682. Money paid into court in respect of leases or reversions. When the money or compensation paid into court has been paid in respect of any lease or agreement for a lease[1], or any estate in land[2] less than the whole fee simple, or of any reversion dependent on any such lease or estate, the High Court, on the application of any person interested in the money[3], may order it to be laid out, invested, accumulated and paid, in such manner as it may consider will give the persons interested in the money the same benefit as they might lawfully have had from the lease, estate or reversion, or as near to it as may be[4]. Such orders may also be made in respect of money paid for renewable leaseholds[5] or in respect of compensation for leaving minerals unworked so as to afford support when the minerals have been let on lease[6].

The method of distribution depends on the nature of the parties' interests. Thus, if leasehold had been settled in trust for a tenant for life with remainder over, he is entitled to be paid such yearly sum raised out of the income and corpus as will exhaust the fund in the number of years which the lease had to run[7]. Where it transpires that the lease would have terminated during the life of the tenant for life, he is entitled to the whole sum, so that if he has only been paid the income he becomes entitled, at the date when the lease would have terminated, to have the corpus paid to him[8]. If the lease was renewable from time to time so as to be practically perpetual, the tenant for life was only entitled to the income[9]. If a person is entitled to an annuity charged on the leasehold, and the income is not sufficient to pay it, a portion of the corpus will be sold from time to time to make up the deficiency[10].

When the money in court is in respect of reversions dependent on leases, a tenant for life is entitled to no more than the amount of the rent he received as lessor so long as the lease would have continued; so if the land was let at less than the rack rent, or if during the term the property had increased in value, he will only be paid the amount of the rent out of the income, and the balance will be accumulated until the end of the lease[11], after which he will be entitled to the income on the whole sum[12]. In the case of compensation paid for minerals required to be left unworked, which would have been worked out during the life of the tenant for life, and in respect of which he would have received royalties, the sum will be apportioned as rent accruing from day to day to the tenant for life during whose life tenancy the minerals would have been worked out[13]. In cases of property held by corporations not for their own beneficial interest, the court may authorise the whole of the income to be paid out, even where it is in excess of the rent received[14].

1   As to the meaning of 'lease' see PARA 511 note 7. See also *Re King's Leasehold Estates, ex p East of London Rly Co* (1873) LR 16 Eq 521.
2   As to the meaning of 'land' see PARA 549 note 1. See also PARA 511 text to note 7.
3   See *Practice Direction—Miscellaneous Provisions about Payments into Court* PD37 para 3. As to service on the remainderman on applications by tenants for life see *Re Crane's Estate* (1869) LR 7 Eq 322. A tenant who has received notice to quit from the owner is not a party interested in the money: *Ex p Nadin* (1848) 17 LJCh 421.
4   Lands Clauses Consolidation Act 1845 s 74 (amended by the Administration of Justice Act 1965 ss 17(1), 34, Schs 1, 2; and the Compulsory Purchase Act 1965 s 39(4), Sch 8 Pt II) (where the Lands Clauses Consolidation Act 1845 is incorporated: see PARA 509); Compulsory Purchase Act 1965 s 25(2) (where that Act applies: see PARA 513). These provisions are limited in their application because the power to sell and convey land of a person under disability has been otherwise extended: see PARA 553. Cf the corresponding provision in the Settled Land Act 1925 s 79: see SETTLEMENTS vol 42 (Reissue) PARA 807. As to settlements see PARA 553 note 11. An order will not be made for payment out to the lessor of arrears of rent: *Re Dublin Corpn and Baker, ex p Thompson* [1912] 1 IR 498.
5   *Re Wood's Estate* (1870) LR 10 Eq 572.
6   *Re Barrington, Gamlen v Lyon* (1886) 33 ChD 523; *Cardigan v Curzon-Howe* (1898) 14 TLR 550. Cf *Re Robinson's Settlement Trusts* [1891] 3 Ch 129. As to minerals generally see MINES, MINERALS AND QUARRIES.
7   *Askew v Woodhead* (1880) 14 ChD 27, CA (approving *Re Phillips' Trusts* (1868) LR 6 Eq 250); *Re Sewell's Trusts* (1870) 23 LT 835; *Re Hunt's Estate* [1884] WN 181; *Re Walsh's Trust* (1881) 7 LR Ir 554; *Re South City Market Co, ex p Bergin* (1884) 13 LR Ir 245. See also *Re Duke of Leeds and Coal Acts 1938 to 1943, Duke of Leeds v Davenport* [1947] Ch 525, [1947] 2 All ER 200 (approved in *Williams v Sharpe* [1949] Ch 595, [1949] 2 All ER 102, CA); *Re Scholfield's Will Trusts, Scholfield v Scholfield* [1949] Ch 341, [1949] 1 All ER 490 (war damage value payments derived from settled leaseholds invested in purchasing annuities for periods

corresponding to the unexpired leasehold terms). Note that it is no longer possible to create a new settlement under the Settled Land Act 1925: see PARA 553 note 11.

8   *Re Beaufoy's Estate* (1852) 1 Sm & G 20; cf *Phillips v Sarjent* (1848) 7 Hare 33 at 37.
9   *Re Wood's Estate* (1870) LR 10 Eq 572; and see *Re Barber's Settled Estates* (1881) 18 ChD 624. See also *Ex p Precentor of St Paul's* (1855) 1 K & J 538 (lease renewable as payment of fine). Perpetually renewable leases are converted into terms of 2,000 years by the Law of Property Act 1922 ss 145, 190, Sch 15, the fines payable on renewal being converted into additional rent: see LANDLORD AND TENANT vol 27(1) (2006 Reissue) PARA 541.
10 *Re London, Brighton and South Coast Rly Co, ex p Wilkinson* (1849) 3 De G & Sm 633; *Re Treacher's Settlement* (1868) 18 LT 810.
11 *Re Wootton's Estate* (1866) LR 1 Eq 589; *Re Wilkes' Estate* (1880) 16 ChD 597; *Re Mette's Estate* (1868) LR 7 Eq 72; *Cottrell v Cottrell* (1885) 28 ChD 628; *Re Bowyer's Settled Estate* (1892) 36 Sol Jo 347; and cf *Re Duke of Westminster's Settled Estates, Duke of Westminster v Earl of Shaftesbury* [1921] 1 Ch 585. As regards ecclesiastical property see *Re South Western Railway Co's Acts, ex p Rector of Lambeth* (1846) 4 Ry & Can Cas 231; *Ex p Bishop of Winchester* (1852) 10 Hare 137; *Ex p Dean and Chapter of Gloucester* (1850) 19 LJCh 400; *Ex p Dean and Chapter of Christchurch* (1853) 23 LJCh 149; *Re Wimbledon and Croydon Railway Act, ex p Archbishop of Canterbury* (1854) 23 LTOS 219.
12 *Re Wilkes' Estate* (1880) 16 ChD 597.
13 *Cardigan v Curzon-Howe* (1898) 14 TLR 550; *Re Barrington, Gamlen v Lyon* (1886) 33 ChD 523; and cf *Re Robinson's Settlement Trusts* [1891] 3 Ch 129.
14 *Re Dean of Westminster, Re Hampstead Junction Rly Co* (1858) 26 Beav 214; *Ex p Trustees of St Thomas's Church Lands and Temple Church Lands, Bristol* (1870) 23 LT 135; *Re South Western Railway Co's Acts, ex p Rector of Lambeth* (1846) 4 Ry & Can Cas 231.

683.   Discretionary payments to tenants for life and limited owners. The court, and trustees to whom sums of under £200 have been paid instead of payment into court[1], may, if they think fit, allot to any tenant for life or for any other partial or qualified estate, for his own use, a part of the sum paid into court or to the trustees, as compensation for any injury, inconvenience or annoyance which he may have sustained independently of the actual value of the land and of the damage occasioned to the land held with it, by reason of the taking of the land and the execution of the works[2]. A tenant for life is not allowed any capital sum for matters in respect of which he is entitled to the income of the money in court, and the income may be deemed sufficient compensation. Thus he may not be entitled to any capital sum in respect of minerals[3] even though they might be worked out in his lifetime[3]. He may, however, be allowed out of the money in court a sum to cover the costs he may properly have incurred in connection with the purchase or taking of the land, such as the costs of preliminary negotiation[4], of an arbitration as to the price of the land when the award has been less than the amount offered[5], and other similar matters[6].

Costs incurred by a tenant for life in opposing the special Act[7] while passing as a Bill through Parliament are not payable out of the fund in court under the Lands Clauses Acts[8], but the court can authorise the payment of these costs out of the money in court either under its general jurisdiction[9] or under the Settled Land Act 1925[10].

1   See the Lands Clauses Consolidation Act 1845 s 71; the Compulsory Purchase Act 1965 s 2, Sch 1 para 7(1); and PARA 684.
2   Lands Clauses Consolidation Act 1845 s 73 (amended by the Administration of Justice Act 1965 s 17(1), Sch 1) (where the Lands Clauses Consolidation Act 1845 is incorporated: see PARA 509); Compulsory Purchase Act 1965 Sch 1 para 9(3) (where that Act applies: see PARA 513). See also *Taylor v Directors etc of Chichester and Midhurst Rly Co* (1870) LR 4 HL 628 at 643. These provisions are limited in their application because the power to sell and convey land of a person under disability has been otherwise extended: see PARA 553.
    Thus a sum may be allowed to a rector for annoyance caused to him by the construction of a railway in what was part of his glebe (*Re East Lincolnshire Rly Co, ex p Rector of Little*

Steeping (1848) 5 Ry & Can Cas 207; *Re Saunderton Glebe Lands, ex p Rector of Saunderton* [1903] 1 Ch 480; *Re Collis's Estate* (1866) 14 LT 352); or to a tenant for life for money laid out on a road for which the promoters agreed to pay (*Re Duke of Marlborough's Estate Act, ex p Lord Churchill* (1849) 13 Jur 738; on appeal (1850) 15 LTOS 341). As to the present practice relating to land which is ecclesiastical property see PARA 668. As to the meaning of 'land' see PARA 549 note 1. As to the meaning of 'works' see PARA 549 note 3. See also PARA 511 text to notes 4, 7.

3   *Re Robinson's Settlement Trusts* [1891] 3 Ch 129; but see *Cardigan v Curzon-Howe* (1898) 14 TLR 550.
4   *Re Strathmore Estates* (1874) LR 18 Eq 338 at 339; *Re Oldham's Estate* [1871] WN 190.
5   *Re Earl of Berkeley's Will* (1874) 10 Ch App 56; *Re Aubrey's Estates and South Wales Railway Act* (1853) 17 Jur 874; *Ex p Perpetual Curate of Whitworth* (1871) 24 LT 126.
6   *Re Great Yeldham Glebe Lands* (1869) LR 9 Eq 68; *Blackford v Davis* (1869) 4 Ch App 304; *Rees v Metropolitan Board of Works* (1880) 14 ChD 372.
7   As to the meaning of 'special Act' see PARAS 509, 514.
8   *Re Earl of Berkeley's Will* (1874) 10 Ch App 56; *Re Nicoll's Estate* [1878] WN 154. As to the Lands Clauses Acts see PARA 509 note 1.
9   *Re Ormrod's Settled Estate* [1892] 2 Ch 318; *Re LCC, ex p Pennington* (1901) 84 LT 808; and cf *A-G v Brecon Corpn* (1878) 10 ChD 204.
10 See the Settled Land Act 1925 s 92; and SETTLEMENTS vol 42 (Reissue) PARA 825. As to settlements see PARA 553 note 11.

(vi) Payment of Small Sums to Trustees or Persons Entitled instead of into Court

684.   Payment to trustees of sums less than £200.   If the purchase money or compensation exceeds £20 but does not exceed £200, it may, with the approval of the undertakers[1] or acquiring authority[2], be paid into court[3], or be paid to two trustees approved by the undertakers or authority and nominated in writing signed by the person entitled to the rents or profits of the land in respect of which it is paid[4]. Both the compensation paid to the trustees and the income arising from it must be applied by them in accordance with the statutory provisions applying to sums exceeding £200[5] save that it is unnecessary to obtain a High Court order, and until so applied the compensation may be invested in government or real securities[6].

1   As to the meaning of 'undertakers' see PARA 511.
2   As to the meaning of 'acquiring authority' see PARA 549 note 5.
3   As to payment into court see PARAS 555 note 6, 640.
4   Lands Clauses Consolidation Act 1845 s 71 (amended by the Administration of Justice Act 1965 s 17(1), Sch 1; and the Compulsory Purchase Act 1965 s 39(4), Sch 8 Pt II) (where the Lands Clauses Consolidation Act 1845 is incorporated: see PARA 509); Compulsory Purchase Act 1965 Sch 1 para 7(1) (where that Act applies: see PARA 513). These provisions are limited in their application because the power to sell and convey land of a person under disability has been otherwise extended: see PARA 553. As to the application of sums paid into court see PARA 669 et seq. As to the meaning of 'land' see PARA 549 note 1. See also PARA 511 text to note 7.
5   See PARA 669 et seq. As to the trustees' power to make discretionary payments to limited owners see PARA 683.
6   Lands Clauses Consolidation Act 1845 s 71 (as amended: see note 4) (applying s 70: see PARA 671 note 1); Compulsory Purchase Act 1965 Sch 1 para 7(2).

685.   Payment to persons entitled of sums of £20 or less.   If the purchase money or compensation does not exceed £20 it must be paid to the person entitled to the rents and profits of the land[1] in respect of which it is payable, for his own use and benefit[2].

1   As to the meaning of 'land' see PARA 549 note 1. See also PARA 511 text to note 7.
2   Lands Clauses Consolidation Act 1845 s 72 (amended by the Compulsory Purchase Act 1965 s 39(4), Sch 8 Pt II) (where the Lands Clauses Consolidation Act 1845 is incorporated: see PARA

509); Compulsory Purchase Act 1965 Sch 1 para 8 (where that Act applies: see PARA 513). See also *Re Lord Egremont* (1848) 12 Jur 618; *Re London and Birmingham Railway Co's Act, ex p Rector of Loughton* (1849) 5 Ry & Can Cas 591; *Re Hichin's Estate* (1853) 1 WR 505; *Re Bateman's Estate* (1852) 21 LJCh 691; *Ex p Vicar of Sheffield* (1904) 68 JP 313. These provisions are limited in their application because the power to sell and convey land of a person under disability has been otherwise extended: see PARA 553.

(8) VESTING DECLARATIONS AS ALTERNATIVE STEPS

(i) Making and Effect of Vesting Declarations

686. Condition precedent to power to make vesting declaration. Where any Minister or local or other public authority[1] authorised to acquire land[2] by means of a compulsory purchase order[3] desires to make a general vesting declaration[4] with respect to any land which is subject to the compulsory purchase order, that acquiring authority must include in the statutory notice of making or confirmation of the order[5], or in a notice[6] given subsequently and before the service of a notice to treat[7] in respect of that land[8]:

(1)	a prescribed statement[9] of the effect of the statutory provisions[10] relating to the execution and effect of that declaration[11]; and

(2)	a notification to the effect that every person who, if a general vesting declaration were executed in respect of all the land comprised in the order, other than land in respect of which notice to treat has been served, would be entitled to claim compensation in respect of any of the land[12], is invited to give information to the authority by making a declaration in the prescribed form[13] with respect to his name and address and the land in question[14].

A notice complying with these provisions must be registered in the register of local land charges by the proper officer of the local authority for the area in which that land, or any part of that land, is situated[15].

1	Ie a Minister or local or other public authority to whom or to which the provisions of the Compulsory Purchase (Vesting Declarations) Act 1981 apply, and referred to therein as an 'acquiring authority': see ss 1(2), 2(1). The Compulsory Purchase (Vesting Declarations) Act 1981 enables any such authority to vest in himself or itself by a declaration land which he or it is authorised by a compulsory purchase order to acquire: see s 1(1).
	The functions of a Minister of the Crown under the Compulsory Purchase (Vesting Declarations) Act 1981, so far as they are exercisable in relation to Wales, are now exercisable by the Welsh Ministers: see the National Assembly for Wales (Transfer of Functions) Order 1999, SI 1999/672, art 2, Sch 1; and the Government of Wales Act 2006 s 162(1), Sch 11 para 30. As to the Welsh Assembly Government and the Welsh Ministers see CONSTITUTIONAL LAW AND HUMAN RIGHTS.
2	'Land', in relation to compulsory acquisition by an acquiring authority, has the same meaning as in the relevant enactments; and 'relevant enactments', in relation to an acquiring authority, means the enactments under which that authority may acquire or be authorised to acquire land compulsorily and which prescribe a procedure for effecting the compulsory acquisition by that authority by means of a compulsory purchase order: Compulsory Purchase (Vesting Declarations) Act 1981 s 2(1).
3	As to compulsory purchase orders see PARA 556 et seq.
4	'General vesting declaration' means a declaration executed under the Compulsory Purchase (Vesting Declarations) Act 1981 s 4 (see PARA 687): s 2(1). The following orders have the same effect as general vesting declarations, ie any order vesting land in: (1) an urban development corporation under the Local Government, Planning and Land Act 1980 s 141 (see s 141(4); and TOWN AND COUNTRY PLANNING vol 46(3) (Reissue) PARA 1454); (2) a housing action trust under the Housing Act 1988 s 76 (see s 76(5); and HOUSING vol 22 (2006 Reissue) PARA 339); (3) the Urban Regeneration Agency under the Leasehold Reform, Housing and Urban Development Act 1993 s 161(1) (repealed) (see s 161(4) (repealed); and TRADE, INDUSTRY AND INDUSTRIAL RELATIONS vol 47 (2001 Reissue) PARA 851); and (4) regional development agencies

under the Regional Development Agencies Act 1998 s 19(1) (see s 19(6); and TRADE, INDUSTRY AND INDUSTRIAL RELATIONS vol 47 (2001 Reissue) PARA 900). The Compulsory Purchase (Vesting Declarations) Act 1981 is modified in relation to: (a) an order under head (1) (see s 15, Sch 2); (b) an order under head (2) (see the Housing Act 1988 s 76(5), Sch 9 para 12); (c) an order under head (3) (see the Leasehold Reform, Housing and Urban Development Act 1993 s 161(5), Sch 19 paras 6, 7); and (d) an order under head (4) (see the Regional Development Agencies Act 1998 s 19(6), Sch 4 paras 6–9).

5   For these purposes, 'statutory notice of confirmation', in relation to a compulsory purchase order, means the notice of the confirmation of the order which is required to be published or served by the Acquisition of Land Act 1981 s 15 (see PARA 571), or by any other provision of the relevant enactments corresponding thereto; and where the acquiring authority is a minister, for references to the statutory notice of confirmation of the order there are to be substituted references to the notice of the making of the order which is required to be published or served by s 2(3), Sch 1 para 6 (see PARA 579), or any other provision of the relevant enactments corresponding thereto: Compulsory Purchase (Vesting Declarations) Act 1981 s 3(5), (6).

6   Ie a notice to which the requirements of the relevant enactments with respect to the publication and service of a notice of the making or confirmation of a compulsory purchase order apply: Compulsory Purchase (Vesting Declarations) Act 1981 s 3(1)(b), (6).

7   As to the notice to treat see PARA 616 et seq.

8   Compulsory Purchase (Vesting Declarations) Act 1981 s 3(1), (2). These provisions apply except where a notice to treat has actually been served: see s 7(1), (2); and PARA 689. Section 3 is modified in its application to land acquired under the Crossrail Act 2008 s 6(1): see Sch 6 Pt 2 paras 4, 5; and RAILWAYS, INLAND WATERWAYS AND CROSS-COUNTRY PIPELINES vol 39(1A) (Reissue) PARA 325.

9   'Prescribed' means prescribed by regulations made by the Secretary of State by statutory instrument subject to annulment in pursuance of a resolution of either House of Parliament: Compulsory Purchase (Vesting Declarations) Act 1981 s 2(1). For the prescribed form of statement see the Compulsory Purchase of Land (Vesting Declarations) Regulations 1990, SI 1990/497, reg 3(b), Schedule, Form 2 Pt I. As to the Secretary of State see PARA 507 note 1.

10   Ie the effect of the Compulsory Purchase (Vesting Declarations) Act 1981 Pts II, III (ss 3–9).

11   Compulsory Purchase (Vesting Declarations) Act 1981 s 3(1), (3)(a). A notice under s 3 is not an exercise of powers of compulsory purchase under the Compulsory Purchase Act 1965 s 4 (see PARA 617): *Co-operative Insurance Society Ltd v Hastings Borough Council* [1993] 2 EGLR 19; not following *Westminster City Council v Quereshi* [1991] 1 EGLR 256.

12   As to the persons who would be entitled to compensation see PARAS 560, 619, 715.

13   For the prescribed form see the Compulsory Purchase of Land (Vesting Declarations) Regulations 1990, SI 1990/497, reg 3(b), Schedule, Form 2 Pt II.

14   Compulsory Purchase (Vesting Declarations) Act 1981 s 3(1), (3)(b). The Town and Country Planning Act 1990 s 330 (power to acquire information as to interests in land: see TOWN AND COUNTRY PLANNING) has effect as if the Compulsory Purchase (Vesting Declarations) Act 1981 were part of the Town and Country Planning Act 1990: Compulsory Purchase (Vesting Declarations) Act 1981 s 2(3) (amended by the Planning (Consequential Provisions) Act 1990 s 4, Sch 2 para 52(1)).

15   Compulsory Purchase (Vesting Declarations) Act 1981 s 3(4). As to the registration of local land charges see the Local Land Charges Act 1975 s 3(2)(a); and LAND CHARGES.

687.   Form, execution and vesting date of declaration.   The acquiring authority[1] may execute a declaration in the prescribed form[2] in respect of any land[3] which it is authorised to acquire by the compulsory purchase order[4], vesting the land in itself from the end of a specified period which must not be less than 28 days from the date on which the service of the required notices[5] is completed[6]. The first day after the end of that period is the vesting date in relation to such a general vesting declaration[7].

The declaration may not be executed before the compulsory purchase order has come into operation[8]; and may not be executed before the end of the period of two months beginning with the date of the first publication of the notice of the making or confirmation of the compulsory purchase order or the subsequent notice containing the prescribed information[9] or such longer period, if any, as may be specified in that notice[10], except with the written consent of every occupier of any land specified in the declaration[11].

1 As to the meaning of 'acquiring authority' see PARA 686 note 1.
2 For the prescribed form see the Compulsory Purchase of Land (Vesting Declarations) Regulations 1990, SI 1990/497, reg 3(a), Schedule, Form 1.
3 As to the meaning of 'land' see PARA 686 note 2.
4 As to compulsory purchase orders see PARA 556 et seq.
5 Ie the notices required by the Compulsory Purchase (Vesting Declarations) Act 1981 s 6: see PARA 688.
6 Compulsory Purchase (Vesting Declarations) Act 1981 s 4(1). A certificate by the acquiring authority that the service of those notices was completed on a date specified in the certificate is conclusive evidence of the fact so stated: s 4(2).
7 Compulsory Purchase (Vesting Declarations) Act 1981 s 4(3).
8 Compulsory Purchase (Vesting Declarations) Act 1981 s 5(2). As to the date of coming into operation see PARA 602. Section 5(2) applies in particular where the compulsory purchase order is subject to special parliamentary procedure (see PARAS 603–605) and therefore does not come into operation in accordance with the Acquisition of Land Act 1981 s 26(1) (see PARA 602) or any corresponding provision of the relevant enactments: Compulsory Purchase (Vesting Declarations) Act 1981 s 5(2). As to the meaning of 'relevant enactments' see PARA 686 note 2.
  Section 5 is modified in relation to land acquired under the Crossrail Act 2008 s 6(1): see Sch 6 Pt 2 paras 4, 5; and RAILWAYS, INLAND WATERWAYS AND CROSS-COUNTRY PIPELINES vol 39(1A) (Reissue) PARA 325.
9 Ie the notice complying with the Compulsory Purchase (Vesting Declarations) Act 1981 s 3: see PARA 686.
10 Compulsory Purchase (Vesting Declarations) Act 1981 s 5(1).
11 Compulsory Purchase (Vesting Declarations) Act 1981 s 5(1) proviso.

688. Notice before vesting date to owners and occupiers of effect of declaration. As soon as may be after executing a general vesting declaration[1], the acquiring authority[2] must serve[3]:

(1) on every occupier of any of the land[4] specified in the declaration, other than land in which there subsists a minor tenancy[5] or a long tenancy which is about to expire[6]; and

(2) on every other person who has given information to the authority with respect to any of that land in pursuance of the invitation published and served[7],

a notice in the prescribed form[8] specifying the land and stating the effect of the declaration[9].

1 As to the meaning of 'general vesting declaration' see PARA 686 note 4.
2 As to the meaning of 'acquiring authority' see PARA 686 note 1.
3 The Town and Country Planning Act 1990 s 329 (service of notices: see TOWN AND COUNTRY PLANNING vol 46(1) (Reissue) PARA 54) applies as if the Compulsory Purchase (Vesting Declarations) Act 1981 s 6 formed part of the Town and Country Planning Act 1990: Compulsory Purchase (Vesting Declarations) Act 1981 s 6(2) (amended by the Planning (Consequential Provisions) Act 1990 s 4, Sch 2 para 52(2)).
4 As to the meaning of 'land' see PARA 686 note 2.
5 'Minor tenancy' means a tenancy for a year or from year to year or any lesser interest; and 'tenancy' has the same meaning as in the Landlord and Tenant Act 1954 (see s 69(1); and LANDLORD AND TENANT vol 27(1) (2006 Reissue) PARA 455): Compulsory Purchase (Vesting Declarations) Act 1981 s 2(1).
6 Compulsory Purchase (Vesting Declarations) Act 1981 s 6(1)(a). 'Long tenancy which is about to expire', in relation to a general vesting declaration, means a tenancy granted for an interest greater than a minor tenancy, but having on the vesting date a period still to run which is not more than the specified period (ie the period, longer than a year, specified for these purposes in the declaration in relation to the land in which the tenancy subsists): s 2(1), (2). In determining for these purposes what period a tenancy still has to run on the vesting date it must be assumed that: (1) the tenant will exercise any option to renew and will not exercise any option to

terminate the tenancy, then or thereafter available to him; and (2) the landlord will exercise any option to terminate the tenancy then or thereafter available to him: s 2(2). As to the vesting date see PARA 687.

7   Compulsory Purchase (Vesting Declarations) Act 1981 s 6(1)(b). The invitation referred to is that published and served under s 3(1): see PARA 686.

8   For the prescribed form of notice see the Compulsory Purchase of Land (Vesting Declarations) Regulations 1990, SI 1990/497, reg 3(c), Schedule, Form 3.

9   Compulsory Purchase (Vesting Declarations) Act 1981 s 6(1). As to evidence of the service of notices under s 6 see PARA 687 note 6.

689.   Effect of vesting declaration.   On the vesting date[1] the provisions of the Land Compensation Act 1961[2] and of the Compulsory Purchase Act 1965[3] will apply as if, on the date on which the general vesting declaration[4] was executed[5], a notice to treat[6] had been served on every person on whom the acquiring authority[7] could otherwise have served such a notice[8], other than any person entitled to an interest in the land in respect of which a notice to treat had actually been served before the vesting date[9] and other than any person entitled to a minor tenancy[10] or a long tenancy which is about to expire[11].

The power to withdraw a notice to treat[12] is not exercisable in respect of a notice to treat which is so deemed to be served[13].

1   As to the vesting date see PARA 687.
2   Ie as modified by the Acquisition of Land Act 1981 s 4 (see PARA 632): Compulsory Purchase (Vesting Declarations) Act 1981 s 7(1)(a). The Land Compensation Act 1961 relates to claims for compensation (see PARA 715 et seq) and the measure and assessment of compensation (see PARAS 695 note 7, 753 et seq), and provides, inter alia, power to withdraw a notice to treat (see PARA 636); but see the text and notes 12–13.
3   The Compulsory Purchase Act 1965 provides for notices to treat (see PARA 616), objections to taking only part of the land (see PARAS 628, 690), the right of entry (see PARAS 616, 619, 638 et seq, 693, 715), the right to compensation or purchase money and apportionment of rent (see PARA 695), interests omitted by mistake (but the provisions are excluded: see PARA 693 note 4), and completion, inter alia, by deed poll (see PARA 661 et seq).
4   As to the meaning of 'general vesting declaration' see PARA 686 note 4.
5   As to the date on which a declaration may be made see PARA 687.
6   As to the notice to treat see PARA 616 et seq.
7   As to the meaning of 'acquiring authority' see PARA 686 note 1.
8   Ie on every person on whom the acquiring authority could have served a notice to treat under the Compulsory Purchase Act 1965 s 5 (see PARA 616), on the assumption that the authority required to take the whole of the land specified in the declaration and had knowledge of all those persons: Compulsory Purchase (Vesting Declarations) Act 1981 s 7(1), (2).
9   If notice to treat is actually served, the acquisition will continue on the ordinary procedure.
10 As to the meaning of 'minor tenancy' see PARA 688 note 5. As to the effect of the declaration on such tenancies see PARA 694.
11 Compulsory Purchase (Vesting Declarations) Act 1981 s 7(1). As to the meaning of 'long tenancy which is about to expire' see PARA 688 note 6. As to the effect of the declaration on such tenancies see PARA 694.
12 Ie the power conferred by the Land Compensation Act 1961 s 31: see PARA 636.
13 Compulsory Purchase (Vesting Declarations) Act 1981 s 7(3).

(ii) Counter-notice where Declaration comprises Part Only of Property

690.   Counter-notice by person able and willing to sell the whole.   If a general vesting declaration[1] comprises part only of a house, building or factory[2] or of a park[3] or garden[4] belonging to a house, any person who is able to sell the whole of it may, by a notice (a 'notice of objection to severance') served on the acquiring authority[5] within the time allowed[6], require it to purchase his interest in the whole[7]. Where notice of objection to severance is served within the time allowed, then, notwithstanding the provisions for vesting the land in the acquiring authority[8], the interest in respect of which the notice is served will not so vest[9]; and, if the person entitled to the interest is entitled to possession of the land[10], the authority will not be entitled to enter upon or take possession of it[11] until, in either case, the notice has been disposed of [12].

1   As to the meaning of 'general vesting declaration' see PARA 686 note 4.
2   As to the meanings of 'house', 'building' and 'factory' cf PARA 626.
3   As to the meaning of 'park' see PARA 628 note 3.
4   As to the meaning of 'garden' see PARA 628 note 4.
5   As to the meaning of 'acquiring authority' see PARA 686 note 1.
6   Except as provided by the Compulsory Purchase (Vesting Declarations) Act 1981 Sch 1 para 10 (see PARA 692), the notice will not have effect if it is served more than 28 days after the date on which notice under s 6 (see PARA 688) is served on the person given the notice of objection to severance: Sch 1 para 2(2).
7   Compulsory Purchase (Vesting Declarations) Act 1981 Sch 1 paras 1, 2(1). No form of notice of objection to severance has been prescribed. The Compulsory Purchase Act 1965 s 8(1) (which makes other provision for objection to severance of buildings, gardens etc: see PARA 628) does not apply to land in respect of which a general vesting declaration is made: Compulsory Purchase (Vesting Declarations) Act 1981 Sch 1 para 2(3).
8   Ie the provisions of the Compulsory Purchase (Vesting Declarations) Act 1981 s 8: see PARA 693.
9   Compulsory Purchase (Vesting Declarations) Act 1981 Sch 1 para 3(a).
10 As to the meaning of 'land' see PARA 686 note 2.
11 Compulsory Purchase (Vesting Declarations) Act 1981 Sch 1 para 3(b).
12 Compulsory Purchase (Vesting Declarations) Act 1981 Sch 1 para 3. The notice must be disposed of in accordance with the provisions of Sch 1 paras 2–10: see PARA 691 et seq.

691.   Acquiring authority's response to counter-notice. Within three months after a person has served on an acquiring authority[1] a notice of objection to severance[2], the acquiring authority must either:

(1)   serve notice on that person withdrawing the notice to treat deemed to have been served on him[3] in respect of his interest in the land proposed to be severed[4]; or

(2)   serve notice on him that the general vesting declaration[5] is to have effect in relation to his interest in that land as if the whole of that land had been comprised in the declaration, and, if part only of that land was comprised in the compulsory purchase order, in that order[6]; or

(3)   refer the notice of objection to severance to the Upper Tribunal (the 'Tribunal') and notify him that it has been so referred[7].

If the authority does not take any such action within the period allowed, then at the end of that period the authority will be deemed to have withdrawn the deemed notice to treat in accordance with head (1) above[8].

If a deemed notice to treat is so withdrawn in respect of a person's interest[9], or is so deemed to have been withdrawn[10], that interest will not vest in the acquiring authority by virtue of the general vesting declaration[11]; and if that person is entitled to possession of the land, the authority will not be entitled by virtue of the declaration to enter upon or take possession of it[12].

If the authority serves notice on the objector to severance that the general vesting declaration is to have effect as if the whole of the land had been comprised in the declaration[13], the declaration and, where applicable, the compulsory purchase order, will have effect as mentioned in head (2) above, whether or not the acquiring authority could otherwise[14] have been authorised to acquire the interest in question in the whole of the land proposed to be severed[15].

If the authority refers a notice of objection to severance to the Tribunal[16] and on that reference the Tribunal determines that the part of the land proposed to be severed which is comprised in the general vesting declaration can be taken, either, in the case of a house, building or factory[17], without material detriment, or, in the case of a park or garden[18], without seriously affecting the amenity[19] or convenience of the house[20], that notice will be disposed of and the suspension of vesting and right of entry will cease[21]. If, on such a reference, the Tribunal does not make such a determination, it must determine the area of that land[22] which the acquiring authority ought to be required to take[23]. The general vesting declaration will then have effect in relation to the interest in that area of the person who served the notice of objection to severance as if the whole of that area had been comprised in the declaration, whether or not the authority could otherwise have been authorised to acquire that interest in the whole of that area; and where part of the area determined by the Tribunal was not comprised in the compulsory purchase order, the declaration has effect as if the whole of that area had been comprised in the order as well as in the declaration[24].

1   As to the meaning of 'acquiring authority' see PARA 686 note 1.
2   See PARA 690.
3   As to the deemed notice to treat see PARA 689.
4   Compulsory Purchase (Vesting Declarations) Act 1981 Sch 1 para 4(1)(a). Deemed notice to treat cannot be withdrawn after the vesting date (see s 7(3); and PARA 689); but Sch 1 para 4(1)(a) has effect notwithstanding s 7(3): Sch 1 para 4(2). 'Land proposed to be severed' means land in respect of which notice of objection to severance is served: Sch 1 para 1. As to the meaning of 'land' see PARA 686 note 2. As to the effect of a late notice see PARA 692.
5   As to the meaning of 'general vesting declaration' see PARA 686 note 4.
6   Compulsory Purchase (Vesting Declarations) Act 1981 Sch 1 para 4(1)(b). As to compulsory purchase orders see PARA 556 et seq.
7   Compulsory Purchase (Vesting Declarations) Act 1981 Sch 1 para 4(1)(c) (amended by SI 2009/1307). As to the Upper Tribunal see PARA 720; and ADMINISTRATIVE LAW.
8   Compulsory Purchase (Vesting Declarations) Act 1981 Sch 1 para 5.
9   Ie in accordance with the Compulsory Purchase (Vesting Declarations) Act 1981 Sch 1 para 4(1): see head (1) in the text.
10 Ie in accordance with the Compulsory Purchase (Vesting Declarations) Act 1981 Sch 1 para 5: see the text to note 8.
11 Compulsory Purchase (Vesting Declarations) Act 1981 Sch 1 para 6(a).
12 Compulsory Purchase (Vesting Declarations) Act 1981 Sch 1 para 6(b).
13 Ie the authority takes action in accordance with head (2) in the text.
14 Ie apart from the Compulsory Purchase (Vesting Declarations) Act 1981 Sch 1 Pt I (paras 1–10).
15 Compulsory Purchase (Vesting Declarations) Act 1981 Sch 1 para 7.
16 Ie in accordance with head (3) in the text.
17 As to the meanings of 'house', 'building' and 'manufactory' see PARA 626.
18 As to the meaning of 'park' see PARA 628 note 3. As to the meaning of 'garden' see PARA 628 note 4.
19 As to the meaning of 'amenity' see *Re Ellis and Ruislip-Northwood UDC* [1920] 1 KB 343 at 370, CA, per Scrutton LJ; and TOWN AND COUNTRY PLANNING vol 46(1) (Reissue) PARA 158.
20 In making a determination in any of the cases mentioned in the text to notes 16–19, the Tribunal must take into account not only the effect of the severance but also the use to be made of the part proposed to be acquired and, where the part is proposed to be acquired for works or other purposes extending to other land, the effect of the whole of the works and the use to be made of the other land: Compulsory Purchase (Vesting Declarations) Act 1981 Sch 1 para 8(2).
21 Compulsory Purchase (Vesting Declarations) Act 1981 Sch 1 para 8(1) (amended by SI 2009/1307). The Compulsory Purchase (Vesting Declarations) Act 1981 Sch 1 para 3 (see PARA 690) ceases to have effect in relation to the notice: Sch 1 para 8(1).
22 Ie the whole of the land, or a part which includes the part comprised in the general vesting declaration: Compulsory Purchase (Vesting Declarations) Act 1981 Sch 1 para 9(1).
23 Compulsory Purchase (Vesting Declarations) Act 1981 Sch 1 para 9(1).
24 Compulsory Purchase (Vesting Declarations) Act 1981 Sch 1 para 9(1), (2) (amended by SI 2009/1307).

692.   Effect of counter-notice served out of time.   Where a person is entitled to serve a notice of objection to severance[1] and it is proved:

(1)   that he never received the notice required to be served on him[2] or that he received that notice less than 28 days before, or on, or after, the date on which the period specified in the general vesting declaration[3] expired[4]; and

(2)   that a notice of objection to severance served by him was served not more than 28 days after the date on which he first had knowledge of the execution of the general vesting declaration[5],

that notice has effect notwithstanding that it is served after the expiration of the time allowed[6].

1   Ie in accordance with the Compulsory Purchase (Vesting Declarations) Act 1981 Sch 1 para 2(1): see PARA 690. As to the meaning of 'notice of objection to severance' see PARA 690.
2   Ie required by the Compulsory Purchase (Vesting Declarations) Act 1981 s 6: see PARA 688.
3   As to the meaning of 'general vesting declaration' see PARA 686 note 4.
4   Compulsory Purchase (Vesting Declarations) Act 1981 Sch 1 para 10(1)(a).
5   Compulsory Purchase (Vesting Declarations) Act 1981 Sch 1 para 10(1)(b).
6   Compulsory Purchase (Vesting Declarations) Act 1981 Sch 1 para 10(1). As to the time allowed see Sch 1 para 2(2); and PARA 690 note 6. Where, in such circumstances, a person serves a notice of objection to severance after the end of the period specified in the general vesting declaration, then in relation to that notice: (1) the provisions of Sch 1 paras 3, 6 (see PARAS 690–691) do not have effect; (2) the provisions of Sch 1 para 4 (see PARA 691) have effect as if Sch 1 para 4(1)(a) (see PARA 691 head (1)) were omitted; (3) the provisions of Sch 1 para 5 (see PARA 691) have effect so as to refer to sub-paragraph (1)(b) instead of sub-paragraph (1)(a); and (4) the provisions of Sch 1 para 8 (see PARA 691) do not have effect, but without prejudice to the making by the Upper Tribunal of any such determination as is mentioned therein: Sch 1 para 10(2). As to the Upper Tribunal see PARA 720; and ADMINISTRATIVE LAW.

(iii)   Entry onto and Vesting of Land

693.   In general.   On the vesting date[1], the land[2] specified in the general vesting declaration[3], together with the right to enter upon and take possession of it[4], vests in the acquiring authority[5] as if the circumstances in which an authority authorised to purchase land compulsorily has any power to execute a deed poll had arisen in respect of all the land and all interests in it[6] and the acquiring authority had duly exercised that power accordingly on the vesting date[7].

Where, after land has become vested in the acquiring authority, a person retains possession of any document relating to the title to the land, he is deemed to have given to the acquiring authority an acknowledgment in writing of the authority's right to production of that document and to delivery of copies of it, and, except where he retains possession of the document as mortgagee or trustee or otherwise in a fiduciary capacity, an undertaking for its safe custody[8].

1   As to the vesting date see PARA 687.
2   As to the meaning of 'land' see PARA 686 note 2.
3   As to the meaning of 'general vesting declaration' see PARA 686 note 4.
4   The Compulsory Purchase Act 1965 s 11(1) (power to enter upon land after service of notice to treat: see PARA 645) does not apply to land specified in a general vesting declaration: Compulsory Purchase (Vesting Declarations) Act 1981 s 8(3). The power of entry is postponed in the case of land subject to a minor tenancy etc: see PARA 694.
5   This is subject to the special provisions with respect to land subject to a minor tenancy etc: see PARA 694. As to the meaning of 'acquiring authority' see PARA 686 note 1.
6   Ie any power to execute a deed poll under the Compulsory Purchase Act 1965 Pt I (ss 1–32) (see PARA 661 et seq) and whether for vesting land or any interest in land in the acquiring authority or for extinguishing the whole or part of any rent-service, rentcharge, chief or other rent, or other payment or incumbrance: Compulsory Purchase (Vesting Declarations) Act 1981 s 8(1)(a), (2).

7	Compulsory Purchase (Vesting Declarations) Act 1981 s 8(1)(b).
8	Compulsory Purchase (Vesting Declarations) Act 1981 s 14. The Law of Property Act 1925 s 64
	(production and safe custody of documents: see REAL PROPERTY vol 39(2) (Reissue) PARA 243)
	has effect accordingly, and on the basis that the acknowledgment and undertaking did not
	contain any such expression of contrary intention as is mentioned in s 64: Compulsory Purchase
	(Vesting Declarations) Act 1981 s 14.

694. Minor tenancy or long tenancy which is about to expire. Where any land[1] specified in a general vesting declaration[2] is land in which there subsists a minor tenancy[3] or a long tenancy which is about to expire[4], the right of entry[5] is not exercisable with respect to that land unless, after serving a notice to treat in respect of that tenancy[6]: (1) the acquiring authority[7] has served on every occupier of any of the land in which the tenancy subsists a notice stating that at the end of a specified period of not less than 14 days from the date on which the notice is served it intends to enter upon and take possession of the land specified in the notice; and (2) that period has expired[8]. The vesting of the land in the acquiring authority will be subject to the tenancy until that period expires or the tenancy comes to an end, whichever first occurs[9].

1	As to the meaning of 'land' see PARA 686 note 2.
2	As to the meaning of 'general vesting declaration' see PARA 686 note 4.
3	As to the meaning of 'minor tenancy' see PARA 688 note 5.
4	As to the meaning of 'long tenancy which is about to expire' see PARA 688 note 6.
5	Ie the right conferred by the Compulsory Purchase (Vesting Declarations) Act 1981 s 8(1): see
	PARA 693.
6	Such a tenancy will not have been the subject of a deemed notice to treat under the Compulsory
	Purchase (Vesting Declarations) Act 1981 s 7: see PARA 689.
7	As to the meaning of 'acquiring authority' see PARA 686 note 1.
8	Compulsory Purchase (Vesting Declarations) Act 1981 s 9(1), (2).
9	Compulsory Purchase (Vesting Declarations) Act 1981 s 9(3).

(iv) Compensation

695. Liability to pay compensation. Where any of the land[1] specified in a general vesting declaration[2] has become vested in an acquiring authority[3], the authority is liable to pay the same compensation and the same interest on the compensation agreed or awarded as it would have been liable to pay if it had taken possession of the land under the Compulsory Purchase Act 1965[4]; but the time within which a question of disputed compensation, arising out of an acquisition of an interest in land in respect of which a notice to treat is deemed[5] to have been served, may be referred to the Upper Tribunal is six years from the date at which the person claiming compensation, or a person under whom he derives title, first knew, or could reasonably be expected to have known, of the vesting of the interest[6].

Where after the execution of a general vesting declaration a person (the 'claimant') claims compensation in respect of the acquisition by the acquiring authority of an interest in land by virtue of the declaration, and the authority pays compensation in respect of that interest, then if it is shown that: (1) the land or the claimant's interest in it was subject to an incumbrance which was not disclosed in the particulars of his claim; and (2) by reason of that incumbrance, the compensation paid exceeded the compensation to which he was entitled in respect of that interest[7], the authority may recover the amount of the excess from the claimant[8]. Moreover, if after such payment it is subsequently shown that the claimant was not entitled to the interest, either in the whole or in part of the land to which the claim related, the authority may recover from him an amount equal to the compensation paid or to so much of that compensation as, on the proper apportionment of it[9], is attributable to that part of the land[10].

Any person who, in consequence of the vesting of the land in an acquiring authority[11], is relieved from any liability, whether in respect of a rentcharge, rent under a tenancy[12], mortgage interest or any other matter, and makes any payment as in satisfaction or in part satisfaction of that liability, is entitled to recover the sum paid as money had and received to his use by the person to whom it was paid, if he shows that when he made the payment he did not know of the facts which constituted the cause of his being so relieved or of one or more of those facts[13].

1   As to the meaning of 'land' see PARA 686 note 2.
2   As to the meaning of 'general vesting declaration' see PARA 686 note 4.
3   As to the meaning of 'acquiring authority' see PARA 686 note 1.
4   Ie under the Compulsory Purchase Act 1965 s 11(1): see PARA 645.
5   Ie by virtue of the Compulsory Purchase (Vesting Declarations) Act 1981 Pt III (ss 7–9): see PARA 689 et seq.
6   Compulsory Purchase (Vesting Declarations) Act 1981 s 10(1), (3) (amended by SI 2009/1307). The Compulsory Purchase (Vesting Declarations) Act 1981 s 10(3) is to be construed as one with the Limitation Act 1980 Pt I (ss 1–27): Compulsory Purchase (Vesting Declarations) Act 1981 s 10(3). As to construction as one see STATUTES vol 44(1) (Reissue) PARA 1485. The limitation period in s 10(3), being a procedural rather than a jurisdictional provision, is capable of being waived, either expressly or by conduct, so that it would be unconscionable for one of the parties to seek to rely upon the limitation period subsequently: *Co-operative Wholesale Society Ltd v Chester-le-Street District Council* [1998] 3 EGLR 11, CA. See also *RWE Npower plc v Kent County Council* [2006] RVR 103. The Compulsory Purchase Act 1965 s 22 and Sch 2 (absent and untraced owners: see PARA 662 et seq) do not apply to the compensation to be paid for any interest in land in respect of which a notice to treat is deemed to have been served by virtue of the Compulsory Purchase (Vesting Declarations) Act 1981 Pt III: s 10(2). As to the Upper Tribunal see PARA 720; and ADMINISTRATIVE LAW.
7   Any question arising as to the amount of the compensation to which the claimant was entitled in respect of an interest in land is to be referred to and determined by the Upper Tribunal; and the Land Compensation Act 1961 s 2 (public sittings, limitation on number of expert witnesses and other matters: see PARAS 735, 742–744) applies in relation to the determination of the question subject to any necessary modifications: Compulsory Purchase (Vesting Declarations) Act 1981 s 11(4) (amended by SI 2009/1307).
8   Compulsory Purchase (Vesting Declarations) Act 1981 s 11(1), (2). Subject to s 11(4) (see note 7), any amount recoverable by the acquiring authority is recoverable in any court of competent jurisdiction: s 11(5). If the acquiring authority is a local authority as defined in the Town and Country Planning Act 1990 s 336(1) (see TOWN AND COUNTRY PLANNING vol 46(1) (Reissue) PARA 3), any sum so recovered must be applied towards the repayment of any debt incurred in acquiring or redeveloping the land, or if no debt was so incurred must be paid into the account out of which sums incurred in the acquisition of that land were paid: Compulsory Purchase (Vesting Declarations) Act 1981 s 11(6) (amended by the Planning (Consequential Provisions) Act 1990 s 4, Sch 2 para 52(3)).
9   Any question arising as to the apportionment of any compensation paid must be referred to and determined by the Upper Tribunal: Compulsory Purchase (Vesting Declarations) Act 1981 s 11(4) (amended by SI 2009/1307). See further note 7.
10   Compulsory Purchase (Vesting Declarations) Act 1981 s 11(3).
11   Ie under the Compulsory Purchase (Vesting Declarations) Act 1981 Pt III: see PARAS 689, 693–694.
12   As to the meaning of 'tenancy' see PARA 688 note 5.
13   Compulsory Purchase (Vesting Declarations) Act 1981 s 13.

696. Rentcharges apportioned. Subject to any agreement[1], where land specified in a general vesting declaration[2], together with other land not so specified, is charged with a rentcharge, such proportion of the rentcharge as may be apportioned[3] to the land specified in the declaration must be treated as having been extinguished[4] on the vesting of that land in the acquiring authority[5]. Where in such a case a portion of a rentcharge is treated as having been extinguished, the provisions of the Compulsory Purchase Act 1965 as to rentcharges[6] have effect as if the extinguishment had taken place under them[7].

1   If the person entitled to the rentcharge and the owner of the land subject to it enter into an agreement to that effect, the Compulsory Purchase Act 1965 s 18 (see PARAS 709–710) has effect as if at the time the land vested in the acquiring authority under the Compulsory Purchase (Vesting Declarations) Act 1981 Pt III (ss 7–9) (see PARAS 689, 693–694), the person entitled to the rentcharge had released the land from the rentcharge on the condition that the part of land remaining be exclusively subject to the whole of the rentcharge under the Compulsory Purchase Act 1965 s 18(2); and in that case no part of the rentcharge may be treated as having been extinguished as regards the remaining part of the land charged with it: Compulsory Purchase (Vesting Declarations) Act 1981 Sch 1 para 11(3). For these purposes, 'rentcharge' includes any other payment or incumbrance charged on the land not provided for in the Compulsory Purchase Act 1965 ss 1–17: s 18(6) (definition applied by the Compulsory Purchase (Vesting Declarations) Act 1981 Sch 1 para 11(4)). As to the meaning of 'acquiring authority' see PARA 686 note 1. As to the meaning of 'land' see PARA 686 note 2. As to rentcharges see RENTCHARGES AND ANNUITIES.
2   As to the meaning of 'general vesting declaration' see PARA 686 note 4.
3   Ie under the Compulsory Purchase Act 1965 s 18: see PARAS 709–710.
4   Ie by virtue of the Compulsory Purchase (Vesting Declarations) Act 1981 Pt III (ss 7–9): see PARAS 689, 693–694.
5   Compulsory Purchase (Vesting Declarations) Act 1981 Sch 1 para 11(1). As to the relief given where payments are made after such extinguishment see s 13; and PARA 695.
6   Ie the Compulsory Purchase Act 1965 s 18: see PARAS 709–710.
7   Compulsory Purchase (Vesting Declarations) Act 1981 Sch 1 para 11(2).

697.   Rent apportioned.   Where land[1] specified in a general vesting declaration[2], together with other land not so specified, is comprised in a tenancy[3] for a term of years unexpired, the provisions of the Compulsory Purchase Act 1965 for the apportionment of rent[4] have effect as if for the references in them to the time of the apportionment of rent there were substituted references to the time of the vesting of the tenancy in the acquiring authority[5].

1   As to the meaning of 'land' see PARA 686 note 2.
2   As to the meaning of 'general vesting declaration' see PARA 686 note 4.
3   As to the meaning of 'tenancy' see PARA 688 note 5.
4   Ie the Compulsory Purchase Act 1965 s 19: see PARAS 707–708.
5   Compulsory Purchase (Vesting Declarations) Act 1981 Sch 1 para 12. As to the relief given where payments are made after the apportionment see s 13; and PARA 695.

(9) STEPS WHERE LAND UNDER LEASE, SHORT TENANCY, RENTCHARGE OR MORTGAGE

(i) Leases and Short Tenancies

698.   Leases allowed to expire or otherwise terminated.   When undertakers[1] or an acquiring authority[2] require to purchase or take land in the possession of a person under a lease, they may purchase the lessor's interest and allow the lessee's interest to expire; and no compensation will be payable under the Lands Clauses Acts[3] or the Compulsory Purchase Act 1965[4], but the lessee may be entitled to compensation under some other enactment[5]. The same applies if the undertakers or acquiring authority determine the lease by notice and allow him to remain in possession[6] or if they induce the lessor to determine the lease before the acquisition of the lessee's interest[7].

Otherwise, if they require to enter on the lessee's interest, the undertakers or acquiring authority must serve on the lessee a notice to treat for the purchase of his interest[8]; but if he is allowed to remain in possession until his interest expires he will have no right to compensation under that notice[9]. In the case of tenants from year to year, however, the undertakers or authority need not serve a notice to treat but may avail themselves of special statutory provisions[10].

1   As to the meaning of 'undertakers' see PARA 511.
2   As to the meaning of 'acquiring authority' for these purposes see PARA 549 note 5.
3   As to the Lands Clauses Acts see PARA 509 note 1.
4   *Holloway v Dover Corpn* [1960] 2 All ER 193, [1960] 1 WLR 604, CA; *Ex p Nadin* (1848) 17 LJCh 421; *Syers v Metropolitan Board of Works* (1877) 36 LT 277, CA; and see *Re Portsmouth Rly Co, ex p Merrett* (1860) 2 LT 471. As to the application of the Compulsory Purchase Act 1965 in place of the Lands Clauses Acts see PARA 513.
5   Compensation may become payable eg to a tenant whose tenancy is determined by notice to quit under the Landlord and Tenant Acts 1927 and 1954 (see LANDLORD AND TENANT vol 27(2) (2006 Reissue) PARAS 758, 788 et seq), under the Agricultural Holdings Act 1986 or the Agricultural Tenancies Act 1995 (see Pt III (ss 15–27) (see AGRICULTURAL LAND vol 1 (2008) PARAS 606–607)), or under the Allotments Acts 1922 and 1950 (see AGRICULTURAL LAND vol 1 (2008) PARA 566 et seq).
6   *Holloway v Dover Corpn* [1960] 2 All ER 193, [1960] 1 WLR 604, CA.
7   See the cases cited in note 4.
8   See PARAS 616, 619.
9   *Holloway v Dover Corpn* [1960] 2 All ER 193, [1960] 1 WLR 604, CA; *R v Kennedy* [1893] 1 QB 533.
10   See PARAS 699, 702.

699. Notice to tenants from year to year requiring possession. If any of the land subject to compulsory purchase[1] is in the possession of a person having no greater interest in it than as tenant for a year or from year to year[2] and that person is required to give up possession[3] of any land so occupied by him before the expiration of his term or interest in it, he is entitled to compensation for the value of his unexpired term or interest in the land, and for any just allowance which ought to be made to him by an incoming tenant, and for any loss or injury he may sustain[4]. If a part only of the land is required, he is also entitled to compensation for the damage done to him by severing the land held by him, or otherwise injuriously affecting it[5].

1   As to the meaning of 'land' see PARA 549 note 1. See also PARA 511 text to note 7. As to the meaning of 'subject to compulsory purchase' see PARA 549 note 2.
2   As to tenancies within this provision see PARA 700.
3   As to possession being required see PARA 701.
4   Lands Clauses Consolidation Act 1845 s 121 (where that Act is incorporated: see PARA 509); Compulsory Purchase Act 1965 s 20(1) (where that Act applies: see PARA 513).
5   Lands Clauses Consolidation Act 1845 s 121; Compulsory Purchase Act 1965 s 20(2) (amended by the Planning and Compensation Act 1991 s 70, Sch 15 para 4). If the parties differ as to the amount of compensation payable under the Compulsory Purchase Act 1965 s 20(1), (2), the dispute must be referred to and determined by the Upper Tribunal: s 20(3) (amended by SI 2009/1307). As to the Upper Tribunal see PARA 720; and ADMINISTRATIVE LAW. The Compulsory Purchase Act 1965 s 20 has effect subject to the Landlord and Tenant Act 1954 s 39 (see LANDLORD AND TENANT vol 27(2) (2006 Reissue) PARA 701): see the Compulsory Purchase Act 1965 s 20(6). Section 20 is modified in relation to the compulsory acquisition of rights by, inter alia:
     (1)   a local authority (see the Local Government (Miscellaneous Provisions) Act 1976 s 13(3)(b), Sch 1 para 10; and LOCAL GOVERNMENT vol 69 (2009) PARA 511);
     (2)   urban development corporations (see the Local Government, Planning and Land Act 1980 s 144, Sch 28 para 23(5); and TOWN AND COUNTRY PLANNING vol 46(1) (Reissue) PARA 180);
     (3)   highway authorities (see the Highways Act 1980 s 250(5)(a), Sch 19 para 10; and HIGHWAYS, STREETS AND BRIDGES vol 21 (2004 Reissue) PARAS 49 et seq, 85);
     (4)   gas transporters (see the Gas Act 1986 s 9(3), Sch 3 para 11; and FUEL AND ENERGY vol 19(2) (2007 Reissue) PARA 841);

(5)   housing action trusts (see the Housing Act 1988 s 78(2), Sch 10 para 23(3); and HOUSING vol 22 (2006 Reissue) PARA 340);

(6)   licence holders under the Electricity Act 1989 (see s 10(1), Sch 3 para 12; and FUEL AND ENERGY vol 19(2) (2007 Reissue) PARA 1284);

(7)   the Environment Agency (see the Water Resources Act 1991 s 154(5), Sch 18 para 7; the Environment Act 1995 (Consequential Amendments) Regulations 1996, SI 1996/593, reg 2, Sch 1; and WATER AND WATERWAYS vol 101 (2009) PARA 453);

(8)   water and sewerage undertakers (see the Water Industry Act 1991 s 155(5), Sch 9 para 7; and WATER AND WATERWAYS vol 101 (2009) PARA 453);

(9)   regional development agencies (see the Regional Development Agencies Act 1998 s 20, Sch II para 5(3); and TRADE, INDUSTRY AND INDUSTRIAL RELATIONS vol 47 (2001 Reissue) PARA 901); and

(10) universal service providers (see the Postal Services Act 2000 s 95, Sch 5 para 11; and POST OFFICE).

700.   Interests entitled to compensation. The term or interest in respect of which notice requiring possession is given[1] must be a tenancy in law or in equity[2] and mere licensees[3], or persons holding under statutory controlled or regulated tenancies[4], are not included.

A person in possession as the owner of the residue of a long term, but of which less than a year remains, is a person falling within the provisions relating to compensation[5]. If a notice to treat is served in respect of an interest greater than a tenancy from year to year and nothing is done under that notice before the unexpired residue of the term is less than a year, a notice then served requiring possession in respect of the tenancy is effective for these purposes[6], but not if a notice to treat is so served and is not followed by a notice requiring possession[7].

If any person having a greater interest than as tenant at will claims compensation in respect of any unexpired term or interest under any lease[8] or grant of the land subject to compulsory purchase[9], the undertakers[10] or the acquiring authority[11] may require him to produce the lease or grant, or the best evidence of it in his power; and if, after written demand by the undertakers or authority, the lease, grant or best evidence is not produced within 21 days, that person will be considered as a tenant holding only from year to year, and will be entitled to compensation accordingly[12].

1   See PARA 699.

2   *Municipal Freehold Land Co v Metropolitan and District Rlys Joint Committee* (1883) Cab & El 184. As to equitable interests see *Re King's Leasehold Estates, ex p East of London Rly Co* (1873) LR 16 Eq 521; *Sweetman v Metropolitan Rly Co* (1864) 1 Hem & M 543. A schoolmaster in possession of a house under the terms of his appointment which was terminable by three months' notice was held to be a tenant within these provisions: *R v Manchester, Sheffield and Lincolnshire Rly Co* (1854) 4 E & B 88.

3   *Frank Warr & Co Ltd v LCC* [1904] 1 KB 713, CA (licence to use theatre for premises for supplying refreshments); *Bird v Great Eastern Rly Co* (1865) 19 CBNS 268.

4   *Re Dudley and District Benefit Building Society v Emerson* [1949] Ch 707 at 717, [1949] 2 All ER 252 at 257, CA.

5   *R v Great Northern Rly Co* (1876) 2 QBD 151.

6   *R v Kennedy* [1893] 1 QB 533, considered and explained in *Bexley Heath Rly Co v North* [1894] 2 QB 579, CA.

7   Cf *Tyson v London Corpn* (1871) LR 7 CP 18.

8   As to the meaning of 'lease' see PARAS 511 note 7, 682 note 1.

9   As to the meaning of 'land' see PARA 549 note 1. See also PARA 511 text to note 7. As to the meaning of 'subject to compulsory purchase' see PARA 549 note 2.

10 As to the meaning of 'undertakers' see PARA 511.

11 As to the meaning of 'acquiring authority' see PARA 549 note 5.

12 Lands Clauses Consolidation Act 1845 s 122 (where that Act is incorporated: see PARA 509); Compulsory Purchase Act 1965 s 20(5) (where that Act applies: see PARA 513). See *Sweetman v Metropolitan Rly Co* (1864) 1 Hem & M 543 (application to equitable interests).

701. Possession must be required. In order for the provisions relating to compensation[1] to apply, there must be a notice requiring possession; the service of a notice to treat is not in itself such a requiring of possession[2], nor is it constituted by going out of possession on receipt of notice to treat[3], but a person who goes out of possession by agreement with the undertakers[4] or the acquiring authority[5] falls within those provisions[6].

1 See PARA 699.
2 *R v Stone* (1866) LR 1 QB 529; *R v London and Southampton Rly Co* (1839) 10 Ad & El 3; cf *Tyson v London Corpn* (1871) LR 7 CP 18 at 22–23.
3 *Great Northern and City Rly Co v Tillett* [1902] 1 KB 874 at 876. If the lessee receives a notice to treat under the Compulsory Purchase Act 1965 s 11(1) (see PARA 645), to comply with that provision and he is then required to give up possession, his interest must be compensated under s 20 as for a short tenancy: *Newham London Borough Council v Benjamin* [1968] 1 All ER 1195, [1968] 1 WLR 694, CA.
4 As to the meaning of 'undertakers' see PARA 511.
5 As to the meaning of 'acquiring authority' see PARA 549 note 5.
6 *Knapp v London, Chatham and Dover Rly Co* (1863) 32 LJ Ex 236; *R v Great Northern Rly Co* (1876) 2 QBD 151. A mere permission to continue in possession to a given date is not a requirement of possession: *Frisby v Chingford Corpn* (1957) 8 P & CR 423. However, tenants of unfit houses given permission to continue in possession under the Housing Act 1985 s 583 are deemed to have been required to give up possession for the purposes of the Compulsory Purchase Act 1965 s 20: see the Housing Act 1985 s 583(3); and HOUSING vol 22 (2006 Reissue) PARA 582.

702. Delivery of possession. On payment or tender of the amount of the compensation[1], all persons who have been required to deliver up possession as having interests not greater than that of a tenant for a year or from year to year[2] must respectively deliver up to the undertakers[3] or the acquiring authority[4], or to the person appointed by them to take possession, any land subject to compulsory purchase[5] which is in their possession and is required by the undertakers or authority[6]. If this procedure is followed, no conveyance and no notice to treat is necessary in order to enable the undertakers or authority to acquire the tenant's interest[7].

1 As to the power to enter without tender or payment of compensation see PARA 639 et seq.
2 See PARA 699.
3 As to the meaning of 'undertakers' see PARA 511.
4 As to the meaning of 'acquiring authority' see PARA 549 note 5.
5 As to the meaning of 'land' see PARA 549 note 1. As to the meaning of 'subject to compulsory purchase' see PARA 549 note 2.
6 Lands Clauses Consolidation Act 1845 s 121 (amended by the Compulsory Purchase Act 1965 s 39(4), Sch 8 Pt III) (where the Lands Clauses Consolidation Act 1845 is incorporated: see PARA 509); Compulsory Purchase Act 1965 s 20(4) (where that Act applies: see PARA 513). As to the rights of a yearly tenant allowed to continue in possession after notice requiring possession see *Cranwell v London Corpn* (1870) LR 5 Exch 284 at 287, Ex Ch; *R v Rochdale Improvement Act Comrs* (1856) 2 Jur NS 861; *R v London and Southampton Rly Co* (1839) 10 Ad & El 3 (as explained in *Cranwell v London Corpn*).
7 *Syers v Metropolitan Board of Works* (1877) 36 LT 277 at 278, CA, per Jessel MR. See also *London Borough of Newham v Benjamin* [1968] 1 All ER 1195, [1968] 1 WLR 694, CA; and PARA 701 note 3.

703. Counter-notice where possession required of part of agricultural holding by notice of entry after notice to treat. Where an acquiring authority[1] serves notice of entry[2] on the person in occupation of an agricultural holding[3], being a person having no greater interest in it than as tenant for a year or from year to year[4], and the notice relates to part only of that holding[5], the person on whom the notice is served (the 'claimant'), may, within the period of two months beginning with the date of service of the notice of entry, serve on the acquiring authority a counter-notice: (1) claiming that the remainder of the holding is not reasonably capable of being farmed, either by itself or in conjunction with other relevant land[6], as a separate agricultural unit[7]; and (2) electing to treat the notice of entry as a notice relating to the entire holding[8].

A claimant who serves a counter-notice must, within the same period, serve a copy of it on the landlord of the holding, although failure to do so will not invalidate the counter-notice[9].

These provisions have effect, subject to any necessary modifications, in relation to a notice of entry under certain provisions of the New Towns Act 1981[10] and of the Housing Act 1985[11]. They apply in relation to the acquisition of interests in land, whether compulsorily or by agreement, by government departments which are authorities possessing compulsory purchase powers[12] as they apply in relation to the acquisition of interests in land by such authorities which are not government departments[13].

1 As to the meaning of 'acquiring authority' for these purposes see PARA 622 note 1.
2 Ie under the Compulsory Purchase Act 1965 s 11(1): see PARA 645.
3 'Agricultural holding' means the aggregate of the land (whether agricultural land or not) comprised in a contract of tenancy which is a contract for an agricultural tenancy, not being a contract under which that land is let to the tenant during his continuance in any office, appointment or employment held under the landlord: Agricultural Holdings Act 1986 s 1(1) (applied by the Land Compensation Act 1973 s 87(1) (amended for these purposes by the Land Compensation (Scotland) Act 1973 s 81(1), Sch 2 Pt I; and by the Agricultural Holdings Act 1986 s 100, Sch 14 para 56)). 'Tenant' means the holder of land under a contract of tenancy, and includes the executors, administrators, assigns or trustee in bankruptcy of a tenant, or other person deriving title from a tenant; and 'landlord' means any person for the time being entitled to receive the rents and profits of any land: Agricultural Holdings Act 1986 s 1(1) (as so applied). These provisions do not apply to farm business tenancies under the Agricultural Tenancies Act 1995: s 4.
4 As to such an interest see PARA 700.
5 Where, however, an acquiring authority has served a notice to treat in respect of land in the agricultural holding, other than that to which the notice of entry relates, then unless and until that notice to treat is withdrawn, the provisions of the Land Compensation Act 1973 s 55 (see the text and notes 1–13), s 56 (see PARA 704) have effect as if that land did not form part of the holding: s 55(4).
6 'Other relevant land' means (1) land comprised in the same agricultural unit as the agricultural holding (Land Compensation Act 1973 s 55(3)(a)); and (2) land comprised in any other agricultural unit occupied by the claimant on the date of service of the notice of entry, being land in respect of which he is then entitled to a greater interest than as tenant for a year or from year to year (s 55(3)(b)). Where, however, an acquiring authority has served a notice to treat in respect of other relevant land, then, unless and until that notice to treat is withdrawn, the provisions of ss 55, 56 have effect as if that land did not constitute other relevant land: s 55(4). As to the meaning of 'agricultural unit' see PARA 622 note 6.
7 Land Compensation Act 1973 s 55(1)(a).
8 Land Compensation Act 1973 s 55(1)(b).
9 Land Compensation Act 1973 s 55(2).
10 Land Compensation Act 1973 s 57(2) (amended by the New Towns Act 1981 s 81, Sch 12). The notice of entry referred to is a notice under s 14(1), Sch 6 para 4 (provisions applicable to compulsory acquisition under that Act): see TOWN AND COUNTRY PLANNING vol 46(3) (Reissue) PARA 1352.
11 Land Compensation Act 1973 s 57(3) (amended by the Housing (Consequential Provisions) Act 1985 s 4, Sch 2 para 24(7)). The notice of entry referred to is a notice under the Housing Act 1985 s 584 (power to enter and determine short tenancies of land acquired or appropriated for certain purposes of that Act): see further HOUSING vol 22 (2006 Reissue) PARA 583.

12 As to the meaning of 'authority possessing compulsory purchase powers' see PARA 763 note 6; definition applied by the Land Compensation Act 1973 s 87(1).

13 See the Land Compensation Act 1973 s 84(2).

704. Effect of counter-notice where possession required of part of agricultural holding; in general. If the acquiring authority[1] does not, within the period of two months beginning with the date of service of a counter-notice[2], agree in writing to accept it as valid, the claimant[3] or the authority may, within two months after the end of that period, refer it to the Upper Tribunal (the 'Tribunal'); and on any such reference the Tribunal must determine whether the claim in the counter-notice is justified and declare the counter-notice valid or invalid in accordance with its determination of that question[4].

If, before the end of 12 months after a counter-notice has been accepted as, or declared to be, valid, the claimant has given up possession of every part of the agricultural holding[5] to the acquiring authority:

(1)   the notice of entry is deemed to have extended to the part of the holding to which it did not relate; and

(2)   the authority is deemed to have taken possession of that part in pursuance of that notice on the day before the expiration of the year of the tenancy which is current when the counter-notice is so accepted or declared[6].

These provisions have effect, subject to any necessary modifications, in relation to a notice of entry under certain provisions of the New Towns Act 1981[7] and of the Housing Act 1985[8].

1 As to the meaning of 'acquiring authority' for these purposes see PARA 622 note 1.

2 Ie under the Land Compensation Act 1973 s 55: see PARA 703. For exceptions see PARA 703 notes 5–6.

3 Ie the person serving the counter-notice: see the Land Compensation Act 1973 s 55(1); and PARA 703.

4 Land Compensation Act 1973 s 56(1) (amended by SI 2009/1307). As to the Upper Tribunal see PARA 720; and ADMINISTRATIVE LAW.

5 As to the meaning of 'agricultural holding' see PARA 703 note 3.

6 Land Compensation Act 1973 s 56(2). As to notice of entry see PARA 703.

7 Land Compensation Act 1973 s 57(2) (amended by the New Towns Act 1981 s 81, Sch 12). The notice of entry referred to is a notice under Sch 6 para 4 (provisions applicable to compulsory acquisition under that Act): see TOWN AND COUNTRY PLANNING vol 46(3) (Reissue) PARA 1352.

8 Land Compensation Act 1973 s 57(3) (amended by the Housing (Consequential Provisions) Act 1985 s 4, Sch 2 para 24(7)). The notice of entry referred to is a notice under the Housing Act 1985 s 584 (power to enter and determine short tenancies of land acquired or appropriated for certain purposes of that Act): see further HOUSING vol 22 (2006 Reissue) PARA 583.

705. Effect of counter-notice where possession required of part of agricultural holding and entry on land not subject to compulsory purchase. Where the claimant[1] gives up possession of an agricultural holding[2] to the acquiring authority[3] under a notice of entry[4], but the authority has not been authorised to acquire the landlord's[5] interest in, or in any of, the part of the holding to which the notice of entry did not relate (the 'land not subject to compulsory purchase'), neither the claimant nor the authority is under any liability to the landlord by reason of the claimant giving up possession of the land not subject to compulsory purchase or the authority taking or being in possession of it[6], and immediately after the date on which the authority takes possession of that land it must give up to the landlord, and he must take, possession of that land[7].

Accordingly, the tenancy must be treated as terminated on the date on which the claimant gives up possession of the holding to the acquiring authority or, if he gives up possession of different parts at different times, gives up possession of the last part, but without prejudice to any rights or liabilities of the landlord or the claimant which have accrued before that date[8]. Thereafter, any rights of the claimant against, or liabilities of his to, the landlord which arise on or out of the termination of the tenancy by virtue of this provision, whether under the contract of tenancy, under the Agricultural Holdings Act 1986 or otherwise, will be rights and liabilities of the authority, and any question as to the payment to be made in respect of any such right or liability must be referred to and determined by the Upper Tribunal[9].

These provisions have effect, subject to any necessary modifications, in relation to a notice of entry under certain provisions of the New Towns Act 1981[10].

1 Ie the person serving the counter-notice after a notice of entry: see the Land Compensation Act 1973 s 55(1); and PARA 703.
2 As to the meaning of 'agricultural holding' see PARA 703 note 3.
3 As to the meaning of 'acquiring authority' for these purposes see PARA 622 note 1.
4 See PARA 704.
5 As to the meaning of 'landlord' in relation to agricultural holdings see PARA 703 note 3.
6 Land Compensation Act 1973 s 56(3)(a).
7 Land Compensation Act 1973 s 56(3)(b). Any increase in the value of the land not subject to compulsory purchase which is attributable to the landlord's so taking possession must be deducted from the compensation payable in respect of the acquisition of his interest in the remainder of the holding: s 56(3)(e).
8 Land Compensation Act 1973 s 56(3)(c). Where a tenancy is so terminated, the Agricultural Holdings Act 1986 s 72 (landlord's right to compensation for deterioration of holding: see AGRICULTURAL LAND vol 1 (2008) PARAS 461–462) has effect as if s 72(4) required the landlord's notice of intention to claim compensation to be served on the acquiring authority and to be so served within three months after the termination of the tenancy: Land Compensation Act 1973 s 56(4) (amended by the Agricultural Holdings Act 1986 s 100, Sch 14 para 54).
9 Land Compensation Act 1973 s 56(3)(d) (amended by the Agricultural Holdings Act 1986 Sch 14 para 54; and SI 2009/1307). As to the Upper Tribunal see PARA 720; and ADMINISTRATIVE LAW.
10 Land Compensation Act 1973 s 57(2) (amended by the New Towns Act 1981 s 81, Sch 12). The notice of entry referred to is a notice under the New Towns Act 1981 Sch 6 para 4 (provisions applicable to compulsory acquisition under that Act): see TOWN AND COUNTRY PLANNING vol 46(3) (Reissue) PARA 1352. The Land Compensation Act 1973 s 56(3), (4) does not, however, have effect in relation to a notice of entry under the Housing Act 1985 s 584 (power to enter and determine short tenancies of land acquired or appropriated for certain purposes of that Act: see further HOUSING vol 22 (2006 Reissue) PARA 583): see the Land Compensation Act 1973 s 57(3) (amended by the Housing (Consequential Provisions) Act 1985 s 4, Sch 2 para 24(7)).

706. Counter-notice where possession required of part of agricultural holding on deposit of compensation and giving of bond. Before taking possession of part only of an agricultural holding[1] under the power to enter after depositing in court the amount of the compensation and giving a bond[2], or under the statutory provisions relating to vesting declarations[3], the acquiring authority[4] must serve notice of its intention to do so on the person in occupation of the holding; and the provisions relating to the service and the effect of a counter-notice where possession is required by notice of entry after notice to treat[5] have effect, subject to any necessary modifications, as if possession were being obtained pursuant to a notice of entry under the Compulsory Purchase Act 1965[6].

1 As to the meaning of 'agricultural holding' see PARA 703 note 3.
2 Ie under the Lands Clauses Consolidation Act 1845 s 85 or the Compulsory Purchase Act 1965 s 11(2), Sch 3: see PARA 639.

3   Ie under the Compulsory Purchase (Vesting Declarations) Act 1981 Pt III (ss 7–9): see PARAS 689, 693–694.
4   As to the meaning of 'acquiring authority' for these purposes see PARA 622 note 1.
5   Ie the Land Compensation Act 1973 ss 55, 56 (see PARAS 703–705), which apply where notice of entry is given after notice to treat under the Compulsory Purchase Act 1965 s 11(1) (see PARA 645).
6   Land Compensation Act 1973 s 57(1) (amended by the Compulsory Purchase (Vesting Declarations) Act 1981 s 16(1), Sch 3 para 1).

707.   Apportionment of rent under lease. If part only of the land[1] comprised in a lease[2] for an unexpired term of years is required by the undertakers[3] or the acquiring authority[4], the rent payable in respect of the land comprised in the lease must be apportioned between the land so required and the residue of the land[5]. The apportionment may be settled by agreement between the lessor and lessee, on the one part, and the undertakers or the authority, on the other part, and, if not so agreed, must be settled by the Upper Tribunal (the 'Tribunal')[6].

If the undertakers or authority agree with the lessee as to the apportionment, specific performance of an agreement to purchase the land agreed to be sold may be decreed even though the lessor's consent to the apportionment has not been obtained[7], and if he refuses consent the matter must be referred to the Tribunal[8]. The costs of the apportionment are not payable as costs of the conveyance by the undertakers or authority[9], but it is within the court's discretion to order them to pay these costs where money has been paid into court[10]. Costs of proceedings before the Tribunal are in general in its discretion[11].

1   As to the meaning of 'land' see PARA 549 note 1. See also PARA 511 text to note 7.
2   As to the meaning of 'lease' see PARAS 511 note 7, 682 note 1.
3   As to the meaning of 'undertakers' see PARA 511.
4   As to the meaning of 'acquiring authority' see PARA 549 note 5.
5   Lands Clauses Consolidation Act 1845 s 119 (where that Act is incorporated: see PARA 509); Compulsory Purchase Act 1965 s 19(1) (where that Act applies: see PARA 513). The lessee may be entitled to compensation for the value of his lease (see PARAS 715, 799), and also for damage by severance or otherwise by the execution of the works (see PARA 810); and so also may a tenant from year to year (see PARA 813).
6   Lands Clauses Consolidation Act 1845 s 119; Land Compensation Act 1961 s 1 (amended by SI 2009/1307); Compulsory Purchase Act 1965 s 19(2) (amended by SI 2009/1307). As to the effect of the apportionment see PARA 708. As to the apportionment of rent where land is vested in the acquiring authority by a vesting declaration see PARA 697. As to the Upper Tribunal see PARA 720; and ADMINISTRATIVE LAW.
7   *Slipper v Tottenham and Hampstead Junction Rly Co* (1867) LR 4 Eq 112; *Williams v East London Rly Co* (1869) 18 WR 159.
8   *Slipper v Tottenham and Hampstead Junction Rly Co* (1867) LR 4 Eq 112 at 115 per Romilly MR. It would seem to follow that the lessee and lessor together might take the undertakers or authority before the Tribunal to have the rent apportioned.
9   *Re Hampstead Junction Rly Co, ex p Buck* (1863) 33 LJCh 79. As to the obligation to pay costs of the conveyance see PARA 659.
10 See *Re London, Brighton and South Coast Rly Co, ex p Flower* (1866) 1 Ch App 599; and PARA 681.
11 See PARA 746.

708.   Effect of apportionment. After the apportionment[1], the lessee is liable to pay only so much of the future accruing rent[2] as is apportioned in respect of the land[3] not required by the undertakers[4] or acquiring authority[5]. The lessor has all the same rights and remedies against the lessee in respect of the land not so required for the recovery of the portion of rent as, before the apportionment, he had for the recovery of the whole rent reserved by the lease[6]; and all the covenants, conditions and terms of the lease, except as to the amount of rent to be paid, remain in force with regard to that part of the land not so required in the same manner as they would have done if that part only of the land had been included in the lease[7].

The lessee is entitled to receive from the undertakers or the acquiring authority compensation for the damage done to him in his tenancy by reason of the severance of the land required by them from that not required, or otherwise by reason of the execution of the works[8].

Where the land is acquired under an order providing for a vesting declaration, the time of apportionment is the time when the land is vested in the acquiring authority[9].

1   Ie under the Lands Clauses Consolidation Act 1845 s 119 or the Compulsory Purchase Act 1965 s 19(1), (2): see PARA 707.
2   Rents accrue from day to day and are apportionable as to time accordingly in the absence of any express stipulation to the contrary: see the Apportionment Act 1870 ss 2, 7; and LANDLORD AND TENANT vol 27(1) (2006 Reissue) PARA 278.
3   As to the meaning of 'land' see PARA 549 note 1. See also PARA 511 text to note 7.
4   As to the meaning of 'undertakers' see PARA 511.
5   Lands Clauses Consolidation Act 1845 s 119 (where that Act is incorporated: see PARA 509); Compulsory Purchase Act 1965 s 19(3) (where that Act applies: see PARA 513). As to the meaning of 'acquiring authority' see PARA 549 note 5.
6   As to the meaning of 'lease' see PARAS 511 note 7, 682 note 1.
7   Lands Clauses Consolidation Act 1845 s 119; Compulsory Purchase Act 1965 s 19(4). The apportioned rent becomes payable from the date of the apportionment or agreement: see *Ball v Graves* (1886) 18 LR Ir 224; *Re War Secretary and Hurley's Contract* [1904] 1 IR 354.
8   Lands Clauses Consolidation Act 1845 s 120; Compulsory Purchase Act 1965 s 19(5). As to the meaning of 'works' see PARAS 511 text to note 4, 549 note 3.
9   See PARA 697.

(ii) Rentcharges; Release on Payment or Tender

709.   Proceedings preliminary to release from rentcharge.   If any difference arises between the undertakers[1] or the acquiring authority[2] and a person entitled to a rentcharge[3] on any of the land subject to compulsory purchase[4] as to the compensation to be paid for the release of the land from the rentcharge or from the part of it affecting the land, it must be referred to and determined by the Upper Tribunal (the 'Tribunal')[5].

If part only of the land so charged is comprised in the land required by the undertakers or acquiring authority, the apportionment of the rentcharge may be settled by agreement between the party entitled to it and the owner of the land on the one part and the undertakers or the acquiring authority on the other[6]. If not so settled, the apportionment must be referred to and determined by the Tribunal[7]. If, however, the remaining part of the land so charged is a sufficient security for the rentcharge, the person entitled to the rentcharge may, with the consent of the owner of that part of the land, release the land required from it on condition or in consideration of that part of the land remaining exclusively subject to the whole of the rentcharge[8].

1   As to the meaning of 'undertakers' see PARA 511.
2   As to the meaning of 'acquiring authority' see PARA 549 note 5.
3   As to the meaning of 'rentcharge' see PARA 696 note 1.
4   As to the meaning of 'land' see PARA 549 note 1. See also PARA 511 text to note 7. As to the meaning of 'subject to compulsory purchase' see PARA 549 note 2.
5   Lands Clauses Consolidation Act 1845 s 115 (where that Act is incorporated: see PARA 509); Land Compensation Act 1961 s 1 (amended by SI 2009/1307); Compulsory Purchase Act 1965 s 18(1) (amended by SI 2009/1307) (where that Act applies: see PARA 513). In the case of a rentcharge belonging to a person suffering from mental disorder, the court has sanctioned the

release of the rentcharge on the undertakers or authority purchasing, in lieu of it, a government annuity of the same amount: see *Re Brewer* (1875) 1 ChD 409, CA.

6   Lands Clauses Consolidation Act 1845 s 116; Compulsory Purchase Act 1965 s 18(2)(a).
7   Lands Clauses Consolidation Act 1845 s 116 (amended by the Compulsory Purchase Act 1965 s 39(4), Sch 8 Pt II); Land Compensation Act 1961 s 1 (amended by SI 2009/1307); Compulsory Purchase Act 1965 s 18(2)(b) (amended by SI 2009/1307).
8   Lands Clauses Consolidation Act 1845 s 116; Compulsory Purchase Act 1965 s 18(2). For an example of the remaining land being wholly charged by court order see *Powell v South Wales Rly Co* (1855) 1 Jur NS 773.

710.   Release from rentcharge on payment of compensation. If, on payment or tender of the compensation agreed or awarded to the person entitled to the rentcharge[1], he fails to execute a release of the rentcharge in favour of the undertakers[2] or the acquiring authority[3], or if he fails to make out a good title to the rentcharge to their satisfaction, they may pay the amount of the compensation into court[4]. When they have paid the compensation into court, they may execute a deed poll[5], and thereupon the rentcharge, or the part of it in respect of which the compensation was paid ceases and is extinguished[6].

If, however, any of the land subject to compulsory purchase[7] is so released from a rentcharge, or part of a rentcharge, to which it was subject jointly with other land, that other land alone becomes charged with the whole of the rentcharge or with the remainder of it, as the case may be, and the person entitled to the rentcharge has all the same rights and remedies over that other land for the whole or the remainder of the rentcharge as he had previously over the whole of the land subject to the rentcharge[8].

Upon any such rentcharge or part of a rentcharge being so released, the deed or instrument creating or transferring it may be tendered to the undertakers or the acquiring authority, and they must affix their common or official seal to a memorandum of the release indorsed on the deed or instrument, declaring (1) what part of the land originally subject to the rentcharge has been purchased by virtue of the empowering enactment[9]; (2) if the land is released from part of the rentcharge, what part of it has been released, and how much continues payable[10]; and (3) if the land so required has been released from the whole of the rentcharge, then that the remaining land is thenceforward to remain exclusively charged with it[11]. The memorandum must be made and executed at the expense of the undertakers or acquiring authority and is evidence in all courts and elsewhere of the facts stated in it, but not so as to exclude any other evidence of the same facts[12].

Where land is acquired under an order providing for a vesting declaration, special provision is made as to land subject to a rentcharge[13].

1   See PARA 709. As to the meaning of 'rentcharge' see PARA 696 note 1.
2   As to the meaning of 'undertakers' see PARA 511.
3   As to the meaning of 'acquiring authority' see PARA 549 note 5.
4   Lands Clauses Consolidation Act 1845 s 117 (amended by the Administration of Justice Act 1965 s 17(1), Sch 1) (where the Lands Clauses Consolidation Act 1845 is incorporated: see PARA 509); Compulsory Purchase Act 1965 s 18(3) (where that Act applies: see PARA 513). As to payment into court see PARAS 555 note 6, 640, 661. As from 1 October 2009, the reference in the Lands Clauses Consolidation Act 1845 s 117 to the Supreme Court is repealed and a reference to the Senior Courts is inserted instead: see s 117 (prospectively amended by the Constitutional Reform Act 2005 s 59(5), Sch 11 para 9(1), (2)).
5   As to the execution of deeds poll see PARA 663.
6   Lands Clauses Consolidation Act 1845 s 117 (amended by the Compulsory Purchase Act 1965 s 39(4), Sch 8 Pt II); Compulsory Purchase Act 1965 s 18(3).
7   As to the meaning of 'land' see PARA 549 note 1. See also PARA 511 text to note 7. As to the meaning of 'subject to compulsory purchase' see PARA 549 note 2.

8 Lands Clauses Consolidation Act 1845 s 118; Compulsory Purchase Act 1965 s 18(4).
9 Lands Clauses Consolidation Act 1845 s 118; Compulsory Purchase Act 1965 s 18(5)(a).
10 Lands Clauses Consolidation Act 1845 s 118; Compulsory Purchase Act 1965 s 18(5)(b).
11 Lands Clauses Consolidation Act 1845 s 118; Compulsory Purchase Act 1965 s 18(5)(c).
12 Lands Clauses Consolidation Act 1845 s 118; Compulsory Purchase Act 1965 s 18(5).
13 See PARA 696.

(iii) Mortgaged Land

711. Right to treat with mortgagor alone. The mortgagee as well as the mortgagor of land to be taken is entitled to a notice to treat[1]; but if a lump sum is paid into court in respect of both interests the court will apportion the amount between the mortgagee and mortgagor[2]. It is a common practice, however, when the mortgagee is not in possession, for the undertakers or the acquiring authority to treat with the mortgagor for the full value of the land, and to leave him to pay off or otherwise discharge the mortgage out of the purchase money. They are entitled so to proceed, but unless the mortgagee agrees to this procedure, they must take care that his interest is provided for, as otherwise they may be restrained from prosecuting their works on the mortgaged land until the mortgage has been redeemed or provision has been made in accordance with the statutory provisions for payment of compensation to the mortgagee[3].

If the undertakers or authority deal with the mortgagor only in respect both of his interest and of the mortgagee's interest, and the amount assessed is less than the sum due in respect of the mortgage, and if they have entered and destroyed the buildings on the land, they may be treated as being in the same position as the mortgagor, and be ordered to pay the total amount found due in respect of the principal, interest and costs[4]. Nevertheless, the fact that they take possession as against the mortgagor does not deprive them of their statutory right to serve a notice to treat on the mortgagee and to proceed in due course to assess the compensation under that notice[5].

1 *Martin v London, Chatham and Dover Rly Co* (1866) 1 Ch App 501; *R v Metropolitan Rly Co* (1865) 13 LT 444; *Cooke v LCC* [1911] 1 Ch 604. As to persons entitled to a notice to treat see PARA 619. As to the notice to treat see PARA 616 et seq.
2 *Pile v Pile, ex p Lambton* (1876) 3 ChD 36, CA; *Cooper v Metropolitan Board of Works* (1883) 25 ChD 472, CA; and see *Re South City Market Co, ex p Bergin* (1884) 13 LR Ir 245.
3 *Ranken v East and West India Docks and Birmingham Junction Rly Co* (1849) 12 Beav 298; *Spencer-Bell to London and South Western Rly Co and Metropolitan District Rly Co* (1885) 33 WR 771; and see *Re Eastern Counties Rly Co, Re Lands Clauses Consolidation Act 1845, ex p Peyton's Settlement* (1856) 4 WR 380. For the position where the undertakers or authority enter into possession after treating only with the mortgagor and the assessed purchase money is less than the mortgage debt see the text and notes 4–5.
4 *Martin v London, Chatham and Dover Rly Co* (1866) 1 Ch App 501. As to cases of entry where they have not known of the existence of a mortgage see PARA 648.
5 *Cooke v LCC* [1911] 1 Ch 604.

712. Redemption of mortgagee's interest. Special statutory provision is made for the purchase or redemption of the mortgagee's interest by the undertakers[1] or acquiring authority[2], independently of the mortgagor[3]. The undertakers or authority may purchase or redeem the mortgagee's interest in any of the land subject to compulsory purchase[4], whether or not:

(1) they have previously purchased the equity of redemption[5];
(2) the mortgagee is a trustee[6];
(3) the mortgagee is in possession of the land[7];
(4) the mortgage includes other land in addition to the land subject to compulsory purchase[8].

The undertakers or authority may redeem the mortgage by paying or tendering to the mortgagee the principal and interest due on the mortgage, together with his costs and charges, if any, and also six months' additional interest[9]; and thereupon he must immediately convey or release his interest in the land comprised in the mortgage to them or as they may direct[10]. Alternatively, they may give written notice to the mortgagee that they will pay off the principal and interest due on the mortgage at the end of six months, computed from the day of giving the notice; and if they give this notice, or if the person entitled to the equity of redemption gives six months' notice of his intention to redeem the mortgage, then at the expiration of either of these notices, or at any intermediate period, on payment or tender by them to the mortgagee of the principal money due on the mortgage and the interest which would become due at the end of six months from the time of giving either of the notices, together with his costs and expenses, if any, the mortgagee must convey or release his interest in the land comprised in the mortgage to the undertakers or authority or as they may direct[11].

If, in either of the above cases, on such payment or tender the mortgagee fails to convey or release his interest in the mortgage as directed by the undertakers or acquiring authority, or if he fails to make out a good title to that interest to their satisfaction, they may pay into court[12] the sums payable under the above provisions[13] and may then execute a deed poll[14] in the manner provided in the case of a purchase of land[15]. On the execution of the deed poll, as well as upon a conveyance by the mortgagee, all the estate and interest of the mortgagee, and of all persons in trust for him or for whom he may be a trustee, in the land vests in the undertakers or authority and, where he was entitled to possession of the land, they become similarly entitled[16].

1   As to the meaning of 'undertakers' see PARA 511.
2   As to the meaning of 'acquiring authority' see PARA 549 note 5.
3   See the Lands Clauses Consolidation Act 1845 ss 108–114 (where that Act is incorporated: see PARA 509); and the Compulsory Purchase Act 1965 ss 14–17 (where that Act applies: see PARA 513). These groups of sections do not form complete and exhaustive codes dealing with mortgagees' rights, but are supplementary to the general provisions of those Acts; and the Lands Clauses Consolidation Act 1845 ss 108, 110, and the Compulsory Purchase Act 1965 ss 14, 15, therefore, do not exclude mortgagees' rights, as owners, to recover compensation for injury by severance: *R v Clerk of the Peace for Middlesex* [1914] 3 KB 259. See also PARA 810.
4   Lands Clauses Consolidation Act 1845 s 108; Compulsory Purchase Act 1965 s 14(1). However, an acquiring authority is not under a legal obligation either to redeem a mortgage or to discharge an owner's liability to a mortgagee, and compensation is not available on the ground that the authority had not discharged the mortgage: *Shewu v Richmond upon Thames and Hackney London Borough Councils* (1999) 79 P & CR 47, CA. As to the meaning of 'land' see PARA 549 note 1. See also PARA 511 text to note 7. As to the meaning of 'subject to compulsory purchase' see PARA 549 note 2.
5   Lands Clauses Consolidation Act 1845 s 108; Compulsory Purchase Act 1965 s 14(7)(a).
6   Lands Clauses Consolidation Act 1845 s 108; Compulsory Purchase Act 1965 s 14(7)(b).
7   Lands Clauses Consolidation Act 1845 s 108; Compulsory Purchase Act 1965 s 14(7)(c).
8   Lands Clauses Consolidation Act 1845 s 108; Compulsory Purchase Act 1965 s 14(7)(d).
9   If a time was limited in the mortgage deed for payment of the principal secured by it, and the mortgagee has been required under the Lands Clauses Consolidation Act 1845 ss 108–113 or the Compulsory Purchase Act 1965 ss 14–16 to accept payment of the principal at a time earlier than the time so limited, the amounts payable to him will include all costs and expenses incurred by him in respect of, or as incidental to, the reinvestment of the sum so paid off: Lands Clauses Consolidation Act 1845 s 114; Compulsory Purchase Act 1965 s 17(1)(a). In case of difference these costs must be taxed, and their payment may be enforced in the manner provided by the Lands Clauses Consolidation Act 1845 s 83 or the Compulsory Purchase Act 1965 s 23 (see PARA 660), with respect to the costs of conveyances: Lands Clauses Consolidation Act 1845 s 114; Compulsory Purchase Act 1965 s 17(2). Further, if the rate of interest secured by the mortgage is higher than can reasonably be expected to be obtained on reinvestment at the time

the mortgage is paid off, regard being had to the current rate of interest, the amount payable to the mortgagee will include compensation in respect of the loss thereby sustained: Lands Clauses Consolidation Act 1845 s 114; Compulsory Purchase Act 1965 s 17(1)(b). In case of difference the amount of the compensation must be referred to and determined by the Upper Tribunal: Lands Clauses Consolidation Act 1845 s 114; Land Compensation Act 1961 s 1 (amended by SI 2009/1307); Compulsory Purchase Act 1965 s 17(2) (amended by SI 2009/1307). As to the Upper Tribunal see PARA 720; and ADMINISTRATIVE LAW. As to references to the Upper Tribunal see PARA 724 et seq. Entry without payment of the amounts required will be an unauthorised entry: see the Lands Clauses Consolidation Act 1845 s 114. As to unauthorised entry see PARA 644.

10 Lands Clauses Consolidation Act 1845 s 108; Compulsory Purchase Act 1965 s 14(2).
11 Lands Clauses Consolidation Act 1845 s 108; Compulsory Purchase Act 1965 s 14(3).
12 As to payment into court in such cases see PARA 661.
13 Lands Clauses Consolidation Act 1845 s 109 (amended by the Administration of Justice Act 1965 s 17(1), Sch 1); Compulsory Purchase Act 1965 s 14(4). As to payment into court see PARAS 555 note 6, 640, 661. As from 1 October 2009, the reference in the Lands Clauses Consolidation Act 1845 s 109 to the Supreme Court is repealed and a reference to the Senior Courts is inserted instead: see s 109 (prospectively amended by the Constitutional Reform Act 2005 s 59(5), Sch 11 para 9(1), (2)).
14 Ie in the manner provided by the Lands Clauses Consolidation Act 1845 s 77 or the Compulsory Purchase Act 1965 ss 9(3), 28: see PARA 663.
15 Lands Clauses Consolidation Act 1845 s 109; Compulsory Purchase Act 1965 s 14(5).
16 Lands Clauses Consolidation Act 1845 s 109; Compulsory Purchase Act 1965 s 14(6).

713. Mortgage debt exceeding value of land. If the value of any of the mortgaged land[1] is less than the principal, interest and costs secured on it, the value of the land, or the compensation to be paid by the undertakers[2] or acquiring authority[3] in respect of the land, must be settled by agreement between the mortgagee and the person entitled to the equity of redemption, on the one part, and the undertakers or authority, on the other part, or, if they fail to agree, must be determined by the Upper Tribunal[4]. The amount so agreed or awarded must be paid by the undertakers or authority to the mortgagee in satisfaction or part satisfaction of his mortgage debt[5]; and, on payment or tender of that amount[6], the mortgagee must convey or release all his interest in the mortgaged land to them or as they direct[7]. If he fails to do so, or fails to adduce a good title to that interest to their satisfaction, they may pay that amount into court[8].

When the undertakers or acquiring authority have paid the amount agreed or awarded into court, they may execute a deed poll[9] in the manner provided in the case of the purchase of land[10]; and thereupon the land, as to the estate and interest then vested in the mortgagee, or any person in trust for him, becomes absolutely vested in them and, where he was entitled to possession of the land, they become similarly entitled[11]. The payment to the mortgagee, or into court, of the amount agreed or awarded must be accepted by the mortgagee in satisfaction or part satisfaction of his mortgage debt, and is a full discharge of the mortgaged land from all money due on it[12]. Nevertheless all rights and remedies possessed by the mortgagee against the mortgagor by virtue of any bond, covenant or other obligation, other than the right to the land, remain in force in respect of so much of the mortgage debt as has not been satisfied by payment to the mortgagee or into court[13].

1 As to the meaning of 'land' see PARA 549 note 1. See also PARA 511 text to note 7.
2 As to the meaning of 'undertakers' see PARA 511.
3 As to the meaning of 'acquiring authority' see PARA 549 note 5.
4 Lands Clauses Consolidation Act 1845 s 110 (where that Act is incorporated: see PARA 509); Land Compensation Act 1961 s 1 (amended by SI 2009/1307); Compulsory Purchase Act 1965 s 15(1) (amended by SI 2009/1307) (where that Act applies: see PARA 513). As to the position

where the undertakers or authority deal with the mortgagor alone and the mortgage debt exceeds the value of the land see PARA 711. As to the Upper Tribunal see PARA 720; and ADMINISTRATIVE LAW.

5   Lands Clauses Consolidation Act 1845 s 110; Compulsory Purchase Act 1965 s 15(2).
6   If the mortgage is paid off before the time stipulated in the mortgage, the costs and expenses of reinvestment and the loss arising from investment at a lower interest rate must also be paid: see PARA 712 note 9.
7   Lands Clauses Consolidation Act 1845 s 110; Compulsory Purchase Act 1965 s 15(3).
8   Lands Clauses Consolidation Act 1845 s 111 (amended by the Administration of Justice Act 1965 s 17(1), Sch 1); Compulsory Purchase Act 1965 s 15(3). As to payment into court see PARAS 555 note 6, 640, 661. As from 1 October 2009, the reference in the Lands Clauses Consolidation Act 1845 s 111 to the Supreme Court is repealed and a reference to the Senior Courts is inserted instead: see s 111 (prospectively amended by the Constitutional Reform Act 2005 s 59(5), Sch 11 para 9(1), (2)).
9   Ie in the manner provided by the Lands Clauses Consolidation Act 1845 s 77 or the Compulsory Purchase Act 1965 ss 9(3), 28: see PARA 663.
10 Lands Clauses Consolidation Act 1845 s 111; Compulsory Purchase Act 1965 s 15(4).
11 Lands Clauses Consolidation Act 1845 s 111; Compulsory Purchase Act 1965 s 15(5).
12 Lands Clauses Consolidation Act 1845 s 111; Compulsory Purchase Act 1965 s 15(6).
13 Lands Clauses Consolidation Act 1845 s 111; Compulsory Purchase Act 1965 s 15(7).

714.   Part only of mortgaged land taken.   If a part only of any mortgaged land[1] is required by the undertakers[2] or the acquiring authority[3] and:

(1)   that part is of less value than the principal, interest and costs secured on the land; and

(2)   the mortgagee does not consider the remaining part of the land a sufficient security for the money charged on it, or is not willing to release the part so required,

then the value of that part, and also the compensation, if any, to be paid in respect of the severance of it or otherwise, must be settled by agreement between the mortgagee and the person entitled to the equity of redemption, on the one part, and the undertakers or acquiring authority, on the other[4]. If they fail to agree as to the amount, it must be determined by the Upper Tribunal[5].

The amount so agreed or awarded[6] must be paid by the undertakers or authority to the mortgagee in satisfaction, or part satisfaction, of his mortgage debt[7], and on the payment or tender of the amount agreed or awarded the mortgagee must convey or release to them, or as they direct, all his interest in the mortgaged land to be taken[8]. A memorandum of what has been so paid must be indorsed on the deed creating the mortgage and signed by the mortgagee, and a copy of it must at the same time, if required, be furnished by the undertakers or authority at their expense to the person entitled to the equity of redemption of the land comprised in the mortgage[9].

If, upon payment or tender to any such mortgagee of the amount so agreed or determined, the mortgagee fails to convey or release to the undertakers or authority, or as they direct, his interest in the land in respect of which the compensation has been paid or tendered, or if he fails to adduce a good title to it to their satisfaction, they may pay the amount of the compensation into court[10]. When the undertakers or authority have paid the money into court, they may execute a deed poll[11] in the manner provided in the case of purchase of land[12]. Thereupon, all the estate and interest in the land then vested in the mortgagee or in any person in trust for him becomes absolutely vested in the undertakers or the authority; and if the mortgagee was entitled to possession of the land, they become similarly entitled[13].

The payment to the mortgagee, or into court, of the amount agreed or awarded must be accepted by the mortgagee in satisfaction or part satisfaction of his mortgage debt and is a full discharge of the mortgaged land from all money due on it[14]. The mortgagee has, however, the same powers and remedies for recovering and compelling payment of the mortgage money or the residue of it, as the case may be, and the interest on it respectively, as against the remaining land comprised in the mortgage, as he would have had for recovering or compelling payment of it as against the whole of the land originally comprised in the mortgage[15].

1   As to the meaning of 'land' see PARA 549 note 1. See also PARA 511 text to note 7.
2   As to the meaning of 'undertakers' see PARA 511.
3   As to the meaning of 'acquiring authority' see PARA 549 note 5.
4   Lands Clauses Consolidation Act 1845 s 112 (where that Act is incorporated: see PARA 509); Land Compensation Act 1961 s 1; Compulsory Purchase Act 1965 s 16(1) (where that Act applies: see PARA 513).
5   Lands Clauses Consolidation Act 1845 s 112; Land Compensation Act 1961 s 1 (amended by SI 2009/1307); Compulsory Purchase Act 1965 s 16(1) (amended by SI 2009/1307). As to the Upper Tribunal see PARA 720; and ADMINISTRATIVE LAW. As to the determination of disputed compensation see PARAS 753–754, 798 (value of the land), 810 (severance or other injurious affection).
6   If the mortgage is paid off before the time stipulated in the mortgage deed, the cost and expenses of reinvestment and the loss arising from reinvestment at a lower interest rate must also be paid: see PARA 712 note 9.
7   Lands Clauses Consolidation Act 1845 s 112; Compulsory Purchase Act 1965 s 16(2).
8   Lands Clauses Consolidation Act 1845 s 112; Compulsory Purchase Act 1965 s 16(3).
9   Lands Clauses Consolidation Act 1845 s 112; Compulsory Purchase Act 1965 s 16(4).
10 Lands Clauses Consolidation Act 1845 s 113 (amended by the Administration of Justice Act 1965 s 17(1), Sch 1); Compulsory Purchase Act 1965 s 16(5). As to payment into court see PARAS 555 note 6, 640, 661. As from 1 October 2009, the reference in the Lands Clauses Consolidation Act 1845 s 113 to the Supreme Court is repealed and a reference to the Senior Courts is inserted instead: see s 113 (prospectively amended by the Constitutional Reform Act 2005 s 59(5), Sch 11 para 9(1), (2)).
11 Ie in the manner provided by the Lands Clauses Consolidation Act 1845 s 77 or the Compulsory Purchase Act 1965 ss 9(3), 28: see PARA 663.
12 Lands Clauses Consolidation Act 1845 s 113; Compulsory Purchase Act 1965 s 15(4) (applied by s 16(5)).
13 Lands Clauses Consolidation Act 1845 s 113; Compulsory Purchase Act 1965 s 15(5) (applied by s 16(5)).
14 Lands Clauses Consolidation Act 1845 s 113; Compulsory Purchase Act 1965 s 15(6) (applied by s 16(5)).
15 Lands Clauses Consolidation Act 1845 s 113; Compulsory Purchase Act 1965 s 16(6).

4. CLAIMS FOR PURCHASE MONEY OR COMPENSATION

(1) RIGHT TO AND CLAIMS FOR PURCHASE MONEY OR COMPENSATION

715. Persons interested in or having power to sell, convey or release land.
When an acquiring authority[1] requires to purchase any land[2] authorised to be
acquired compulsorily it must give a notice to treat[3] to all the persons interested
in or having power to sell, convey or release the land, stating in it that it is
willing to treat for the purchase of the land and as to the compensation for
damage which may be sustained by reason of the execution of the works[4].

1   As to the meaning of 'acquiring authority' see PARA 549 note 5.
2   As to the meaning of 'land' see PARA 549 note 1. See also PARA 511 text to note 7.
3   See PARA 616 et seq. For the time within which a notice to treat must be served see PARA 617. As
    to withdrawal or abandonment of a notice to treat see PARAS 636–637. See also *Grice v Dudley
    Corpn* [1958] Ch 329, [1957] 2 All ER 673; *Simpsons Motor Sales (London) Ltd v Hendon
    Corpn* [1964] AC 1088, [1963] 2 All ER 484, HL; *R v Carmarthen District Council,
    ex p Blewin Trust Ltd* (1989) 59 P & CR 379.
4   See the Lands Clauses Consolidation Act 1845 s 18 (where that Act is incorporated: see PARA
    509); the Compulsory Purchase Act 1965 s 5(1), (2)(c) (where that Act applies: see PARA 513);
    and see PARAS 616, 715. As to the interests entitled to a notice to treat and claim compensation
    see PARA 619 et seq.

716. Making of claim, giving particulars of interest in land. A notice to treat
must give particulars of the land to which the notice relates and demand from
the party served with it particulars of his estate and interest in the land to be
purchased or taken and of the claims made by him in respect of the land[1], but
there is nothing in the Lands Clauses Acts or the Compulsory Purchase Act 1965
to compel the owner of the land to supply the particulars demanded[2].

    However, if the Upper Tribunal (the 'Tribunal')[3] is satisfied that a claimant
has failed to deliver to the acquiring authority[4], in time to enable that authority
to make a proper offer, a written notice of the amount claimed by him containing
particulars of the exact nature of the interest in respect of which compensation is
claimed, and giving details of the amounts claimed under separate heads and
showing how the amount under each head is calculated[5], then, unless for special
reasons the Tribunal thinks it proper not to do so, it must order the claimant to
bear his own costs and to pay the costs of the acquiring authority so far as they
were incurred after the time when in the Tribunal's opinion the notice should
have been delivered[6].

    Failure to deliver particulars also affects compensation payable where a notice
to treat is withdrawn[7].

1   See the Lands Clauses Consolidation Act 1845 s 18; the Compulsory Purchase Act 1965
    s 5(2)(a), (b); and PARAS 616, 715.
2   *Birch v St Marylebone Vestry* (1869) 20 LT 697. As to the Lands Clauses Acts see PARA 509
    note 1. As to the application of the Compulsory Purchase Act 1965 in place of the Lands
    Clauses Acts see PARA 513.
3   As to the Upper Tribunal see PARA 720; and ADMINISTRATIVE LAW.
4   As to the meaning of 'acquiring authority' for these purposes see PARA 622 note 1.
5   Land Compensation Act 1961 s 4(1)(b), (2).
6   Land Compensation Act 1961 s 4(1) (amended by SI 2009/1307). In any proceedings on a
    question referred to the Upper Tribunal under the Land Compensation Act 1961 s 1: (1) the
    provisions of s 4(1)–(6) apply in addition to the Tribunals, Courts and Enforcement Act 2007
    s 29 (costs or expenses) (see ADMINISTRATIVE LAW) and provisions of the Tribunal Procedure
    Rules relating to costs; and (2) to the extent that the provisions of the Land Compensation

Act 1961 s 4(1)–(6) conflict with that section or those provisions, that section or those provisions do not apply: Land Compensation Act 1961 s 4(1A) (added by SI 2009/1307).

Furthermore, where the particulars did not include a proper claim so that the acquiring authority would not know how much compensation it would have to pay, it was free to withdraw from the acquisition (provided that it had not entered into possession of the land): see *Trustees for Methodist Church Purposes v North Tyneside Metropolitan Borough Council* (1979) 38 P & CR 665. As to withdrawal of notices to treat see PARA 636.

7   See PARA 636.

717. Offers by claimant or acquiring authority. Where a claimant has delivered to the acquiring authority[1] written notice of his interest and claim[2] in time to enable that authority to make a proper offer and has made an unconditional offer in writing to accept any sum as compensation, then, if the sum awarded to him by the Upper Tribunal (the 'Tribunal') is equal to or exceeds that sum, the Tribunal must, unless for special reasons it thinks it proper not to do so, order the authority to bear its own costs and pay the claimant's costs so far as they were incurred after his offer was made[3]. An owner, or the assignee of the original claimant's interest, may withdraw or amend a claim before acceptance[4].

The acquiring authority is not obliged to make an offer of a sum in compensation[5], but it may make such an offer, and if it is an unconditional offer in writing and the sum awarded to the claimant by the Tribunal does not exceed the sum offered[6], the Tribunal must, unless for special reasons it thinks it proper not to do so, order the claimant to bear his own costs and to pay the authority's costs so far as they were incurred after the offer was made[7].

If any party unconditionally offers, or is ready to accept, any sum as compensation or by way of price, or to agree a rent or a rateable value, a copy of the offer or indication of the readiness to accept, enclosed in a sealed cover, may be sent to the registrar[8] or delivered to the Tribunal at the hearing by the party who made the offer or indicated the readiness to accept and must be opened by the Tribunal after it has determined the proceedings[9]. Such an offer or indication of readiness to accept must not be disclosed to the Tribunal until it has decided the amount of such sum, rent or rateable value[10].

1   As to the meaning of 'acquiring authority' see PARA 622 note 1.
2   Ie a notice as required by the Land Compensation Act 1961 s 4(1)(b) containing the particulars set out in s 4(2): see PARA 716.
3   Land Compensation Act 1961 s 4(3) (amended by SI 2009/1307). As to the essentials of an offer see note 7. As to the Upper Tribunal see PARA 720; and ADMINISTRATIVE LAW. With regard to pre-offer costs, the Tribunal has a complete discretion and thus there is nothing to prevent an award of such costs to a claimant who is awarded less than the authority's offer. However, it would be a wrong exercise of this discretion to award such costs to a claimant who eventually failed to establish any claim to compensation: *Pepys v London Transport Executive* [1975] 1 All ER 748, [1975] 1 WLR 234, CA.
4   *Cardiff Corpn v Cook* [1923] 2 Ch 115.
5   *Martin v Leicester Waterworks Co* (1858) 3 H & N 463. As to the withdrawal of an offer and the making of a new one see *Fitzhardinge v Gloucester and Berkeley Canal Co* (1872) LR 7 QB 776; *Gray v North Eastern Rly Co* (1876) 1 QBD 696; *Yates v Blackburn Corpn* (1860) 6 H & N 61; *Lascelles v Swansea School Board* (1899) 69 LJQB 24.
6   Land Compensation Act 1961 s 4(1)(a).
7   Land Compensation Act 1961 s 4(1). In order to affect the incidence of costs, the offer must be made in sufficient time to enable the claimant, before he has incurred any substantial expense, to make up his mind whether or not he will accept it: see *Fisher v Great Western Rly Co* [1911] 1 KB 551 at 555, CA. It must be a clear unconditional offer made in respect of the subject matter alone (see *Miles v Great Western Rly Co* [1896] 2 QB 432, CA; *Fisher v Great Western Rly Co*) and must not include costs (see *Balls v Metropolitan Board of Works* (1866) LR 1 QB 337) or the execution of works (see *Fisher v Great Western Rly Co*). If the claim is divided into parts, but there is really only one matter in dispute, the total of the sums awarded and offered

determine the incidence of costs: see *Re Hayward and Metropolitan Rly Co* (1864) 4 B & S 787; and c f *R v Biram* (1852) 17 QB 969. Where compensation is agreed between the parties and the court merely makes a record of that agreement, the Land Compensation Act 1961 s 4 does not apply, as no award of compensation has been made: *Stanford Marsh Ltd v Secretary of State for the Environment* [1997] 1 EGLR 178, Lands Tribunal. Costs, including the costs of the tribunal hearing, may be awarded against a claimant who delays unreasonably in accepting such an offer, the costs being calculated from the date when the offer ought to have been accepted (ie within five working days of receiving the offer, including the date of despatch): *Stanford Marsh Ltd v Secretary of State for the Environment*.

8   'Registrar' means a member of staff appointed under the Tribunals, Courts and Enforcement Act 2007 s 40(1) and authorised by the Senior President of Tribunals, to exercise the powers or functions of the registrar: Lands Tribunal Rules 1996, SI 1996/1022, r 2(1) (definition amended by SI 2006/680; SI 2009/1307).

9   Lands Tribunal Rules 1996, SI 1996/1022, r 44(1).

10 Lands Tribunal Rules 1996, SI 1996/1022, r 44(2).

718. Reference of disputed claims to the Upper Tribunal.

If a person served with a notice to treat[1] does not within 21 days from the service of the notice state the particulars of his claim in respect of the land[2] to be purchased or taken, or treat with the undertakers[3] or the acquiring authority[4] in respect of his claim, or if he and the authority do not agree as to the amount of the compensation[5] to be paid by the authority for the interest belonging to him, or which he has power to sell[6], or for any damage which may be sustained by him by reason of the execution of the works[7], the question of the disputed compensation must be referred to the Upper Tribunal (the 'Tribunal')[8].

Unless agreed between the parties, any question as to the apportionment of rent under a lease where part only of the land subject to the lease is taken must also be referred to the Tribunal[9] and so also must questions as to the release and apportionment of rentcharges[10]. Where the parties entitled to the purchase money or compensation are absent from the United Kingdom[11] and are prevented from treating or cannot after diligent inquiry be found, the purchase money or compensation must be determined by the valuation of a surveyor selected from the members of the Tribunal who are members of the Royal Institution of Chartered Surveyors[12] and paid into court[13]; but if such a party is later dissatisfied with that valuation he may, before applying for payment out or investment of the sum assessed and paid into court, require the submission to the Tribunal of the question whether the compensation paid into court was sufficient or whether any and what further sum ought to be paid over or paid into court[14]. If the Tribunal awards a further sum, the undertakers or the acquiring authority must pay it over, or pay it into court, as the case may require, within 14 days of the making of the award, and if they fail to do so, that further sum may be recovered in proceedings in the High Court[15].

If any person claims compensation in respect of any land, or any interest in land, which has been taken for, or injuriously affected by, the execution of the works[16], and for which the undertakers or the acquiring authority[17] have not made satisfaction[18], any dispute arising in relation to compensation must also be referred to and determined by the Tribunal[19]. Any such compensation carries interest at the prescribed rate[20] from the date of the claim until payment[21].

1   As to notices to treat see PARA 616 et seq.
2   As to the meaning of 'land' see PARA 549 note 1. See also PARA 511 text to note 7.
3   As to the meaning of 'undertakers' see PARA 511.
4   As to the meaning of 'acquiring authority' see PARA 549 note 5.
5   As to such compensation or purchase money see PARAS 753–754, 797 et seq.
6   As to persons with power to sell see PARA 553 et seq.

7 Ie where compensation in respect of damage by severance or injurious affection arises as part of the purchase money for the land taken: see PARA 810. As to the meaning of 'works' see PARAS 511, 549 note 3. See also PARA 511 text to note 4.

8 Lands Clauses Consolidation Act 1845 s 21 (amended by the Compulsory Purchase Act 1965 s 39(4), Sch 8 Pt III) (where the Act is incorporated: see PARA 509); Compulsory Purchase Act 1965 s 6 (amended by SI 2009/1307) (where the Act applies: see PARA 513). Parties are entitled to advance argument and evidence on all issues which the Tribunal is considering in relation to an award of compensation, even if the Tribunal is considering a matter by its own motion: *Faraday v Carmarthenshire County Council* [2004] EWCA Civ 649, [2004] RVR 236. As to the Upper Tribunal see PARA 720; and ADMINISTRATIVE LAW. As to notice of reference to the Tribunal see PARA 724.

9 See PARA 707.

10 See PARA 709.

11 As to the meaning of 'United Kingdom' see PARA 616 note 22.

12 Lands Clauses Consolidation Act 1845 s 58 (amended by the Compulsory Purchase Act 1965 Sch 8 Pt III); Lands Tribunal Act 1949 s 1(6) (amended by the Land Compensation Act 1961 s 40(2)(b), Sch 4 para 8; the Compulsory Purchase Act 1965 Sch 8 Pt III; and SI 2009/1307) (where the Lands Clauses Consolidation Act 1845 is incorporated: see PARA 509); Compulsory Purchase Act 1965 s 2 para 1(1) (amended by SI 2009/1307) (where that Act applies: see PARA 513). See also PARA 616 text to note 21. The undertakers or the acquiring authority must preserve the valuation and produce it on demand to the owners of the land to which it relates and to all other interested parties: Lands Clauses Consolidation Act 1845 s 61 (amended by the Statute Law (Repeals) Act 1974); Compulsory Purchase Act 1965 Sch 2 para 1(3). All the expenses of and incident to the valuation must be borne by the undertakers or the acquiring authority: Lands Clauses Consolidation Act 1845 s 62; Compulsory Purchase Act 1965 Sch 2 para 1(4). The surveyor appointed may apply for a certificate of appropriate alternative development: see PARA 772 note 3. Payments on account may be made of such compensation: see the Planning and Compensation Act 1991 s 80(2), (3), Sch 18 Pt II; and note 21.

13 See PARAS 661–662.

14 Lands Clauses Consolidation Act 1845 ss 64, 65; Land Compensation Act 1961 s 1; Compulsory Purchase Act 1965 Sch 2 para 4(1).

15 Lands Clauses Consolidation Act 1845 s 66 (amended by the Administration of Justice Act 1965 s 34); Land Compensation Act 1961 s 1 (amended by SI 2009/1307); Compulsory Purchase Act 1965 Sch 2 para 4(2) (amended by SI 2009/1307). If the Tribunal determines that the compensation paid into court was sufficient, the costs of and incident to the tribunal proceedings will be in the Tribunal's discretion in accordance with the Tribunals, Courts and Enforcement Act 2007 s 29 (see PARA 746), but if it determines that a further sum ought to be paid, all the costs of and incident to the proceedings must be paid by the undertakers or the acquiring authority: see the Lands Clauses Consolidation Act 1845 s 67; the Land Compensation Act 1961 s 1 (amended by SI 2009/1307); and the Compulsory Purchase Act 1965 Sch 2 para 4(3) (amended by SI 2009/1307).

16 See *Moto Hospitality Ltd v Secretary of State for Transport* [2007] EWCA Civ 764, [2008] 2 All ER 718, [2008] 1 WLR 2822 ('the works' included the entirety of the works of highway construction and improvement and were not confined to the parts of the works to be carried out on the land acquired under the compulsory purchase order).

17 Where the Compulsory Purchase Act 1965 Pt I (ss 1–32) applies by virtue of the Town and Country Planning Act 1990 Pt IX (ss 226–246), this reference to the acquiring authority is to be construed in accordance with s 245(4)(b) (see TOWN AND COUNTRY PLANNING vol 46(2) (Reissue) PARA 944): Compulsory Purchase Act 1965 s 10(3) (amended by the Planning (Consequential Provisions) Act 1990 s 4, Sch 2 para 13(2)(a), (b)).

18 Ie whether under the provisions of the Lands Clauses Consolidation Act 1845, of the Compulsory Purchase Act 1965, or of the special Act: Lands Clauses Consolidation Act 1845 s 68; Compulsory Purchase Act 1965 s 10(1). As to the meaning of 'special Act' see PARAS 509, 514.

19 Lands Clauses Consolidation Act 1845 s 68 (amended by the Compulsory Purchase Act 1965 Sch 8 Pt III); Compulsory Purchase Act 1965 s 10(1) (amended by SI 2009/1307). As to such rights to compensation and other similar rights see PARA 877. The Compulsory Acquisition Act 1965 s 10 is to be construed as affording in all cases a right to compensation for injurious affection to land which is the same as the right which the Lands Clauses Consolidation Act 1845 s 68 has been construed as affording in cases where the amount claimed exceeds £50: Compulsory Purchase Act 1965 s 10(2). See *Argyle Motors (Birkenhead) Ltd v Birkenhead Corpn* (1971) 22 P & CR 829 (despite the fact that the Lands Tribunal was the proper forum in respect of claims for injurious affection, the court refused to strike out a claim which involved

the construction of a private Act of Parliament and which claimed declarations in respect of such compensation). The Lands Tribunal was abolished on 1 June 2009 and its functions were transferred to the Upper Tribunal: see PARA 720. See also *Moto Hospitality Ltd v Secretary of State for Transport* [2007] EWCA Civ 764, [2008] 2 All ER 718, [2008] 1 WLR 2822 (loss due to the motorway junction improvements as a whole was not a proper subject of claim). As to the application of the Compulsory Purchase Act 1965 s 10(2) to development consent orders relating to nationally significant infrastructure projects see PARA 538.

20   Ie at the rate for the time being prescribed under the Land Compensation Act 1961 s 32: see PARA 641 note 6.

21   Land Compensation Act 1973 s 63(1). Payments on account may be made in respect of such interest, which are recoverable if it is subsequently found that the person making them is not liable to pay interest or that the amount of any payment is excessive: see the Planning and Compensation Act 1991 s 80(2), (3), Sch 18 Pt II.

719. Limitation of time for claim. The Upper Tribunal (the 'Tribunal') has no jurisdiction to decide questions of title[1]; it assesses the amount of the purchase money or compensation irrespective of the title. Not only may no claim be brought for any liquidated sum representing the purchase money prior to the date of the award[2], but it has been held that the provisions of the Limitation Act 1980 apply to the making of the reference to the Tribunal for the purpose of assessing the appropriate purchase money or compensation[3].

Furthermore, in the case of an acquisition of land under the provisions for declaring the land to be vested in the acquiring authority, a question of disputed compensation or purchase money may not be referred to the Tribunal after six years from the date of the vesting of the interest[4].

1   *Brierley Hill Local Board v Pearsall* (1884) 9 App Cas 595, HL; *Horrocks v Metropolitan Rly Co* (1863) 4 B & S 315; *Holt Bros and Whitford v Axbridge RDC* (1931) 95 JP 87; *Mountgarret (Rt Hon Viscount) v Claro Water Board* (1963) 15 P & CR 53, Lands Tribunal. The Lands Tribunal was abolished on 1 June 2009 and its functions were transferred to the Upper Tribunal: see PARA 720.

2   *Turner v Midland Rly Co* [1911] 1 KB 832. Note that this was a case under the Lands Clauses Consolidation Act 1845 s 68 (see PARA 718; cf the Compulsory Purchase Act 1965 s 10), ie a claim for injurious affection where no land was taken; and the applicable Act was the Statute of Limitations 1623 (21 Jac 1 c 16), which did not contain the equivalent of the Limitation Act 1980 s 9 (see note 3).

3   *Hillingdon London Borough Council v ARC Ltd* [1999] Ch 139, (1997) 75 P & CR 346, CA (the quantification of compensation by the Tribunal for the compulsory purchase of an interest in land was an 'action to recover' a sum and as such was subject to the limitation period set down in the Limitation Act 1980 s 9); *BP Oil UK Ltd v Kent County Council* [2003] EWCA Civ 798, [2004] 1 P & CR 416, [2003] All ER (D) 171 (Jun). An action to recover any sum by virtue of any enactment may not be brought after the expiration of six years from the date on which the cause of action accrued (see the Limitation Act 1980 s 9(1)), whether or not the compensation has been assessed. See also *West Riding of Yorks County Council v Huddersfield Corpn* [1957] 1 QB 540, [1957] 1 All ER 669; *Central Electricity Board v Halifax Corpn* [1963] AC 785, sub nom *Central Electricity Generating Board v Halifax Corpn* [1962] 3 All ER 915, HL; *Pegler v Railway Executive* [1948] AC 332, [1948] 1 All ER 559, HL. The six year period would thus appear to run from the date upon which the right to compensation (not the right to any particular amount of compensation) accrued. If the word 'action' in the Limitation Act 1980 s 9(1) is to embrace proceedings which are not actions in the true sense, it seems that for 'cause of action' must be read 'cause of proceeding': *China v Harrow UDC* [1954] 1 QB 178 at 185, [1953] 2 All ER 1296 at 1299, DC, per Lord Goddard. There is no promissory estoppel to prevent the acquiring authority from taking the limitation point in the absence of a clear and unequivocal representation that the claim is valid and that the authority would not rely on the statutory limitation defence; nor is there any estoppel by convention in the absence of a shared common assumption that there is a valid claim and that the limitation period is not to be relied upon: *Hillingdon London Borough Council v ARC Ltd (No 2)* [2000] 3 EGLR 97, [2000] RVR 283, CA. Accordingly, estoppel is not available where negotiations continue between parties who are aware at all material times of the statutory limitation period and do nothing to waive

their rights: *SITA (formerly Ebenezer Mears (Sand Producers) Ltd) v Surrey County Council* [2001] RVR 56, Lands Tribunal. As to estoppel see ESTOPPEL.

4   See PARA 695.

(2) SETTLEMENT OF CLAIMS BY THE UPPER TRIBUNAL

(i) Jurisdiction of the Upper Tribunal

720.   Abolition of the Lands Tribunal and transfer of its functions to the Upper Tribunal. On 1 June 2009 the Lands Tribunal (which had been established in 1949[1]) was abolished[2] as part of the changes introduced by the Tribunals, Courts and Enforcement Act 2007 to create a simplified statutory framework for tribunals in England and Wales[3]. The functions of the Lands Tribunal were transferred to the Upper Tribunal of the new system[4]. In this way the Upper Tribunal inherited the existing jurisdiction of the Lands Tribunal[5].

1   The Lands Tribunal was established (with jurisdiction in England, Wales and Northern Ireland) by the Lands Tribunal Act 1949 s 1(1)(b) (as originally enacted). A separate tribunal was established and continues to operate for Scotland: see s 1 (amended by SI 2009/1307).

2   Transfer of Functions (Lands Tribunal and Miscellaneous Amendments) Order 2009, SI 2009/1307, arts 1, 2(2). See also the Tribunals, Courts and Enforcement Act 2007 ss 30(1), (4), 31(1), (2), (7), (9), 38, 145, Sch 6 Pt 3.

3   See ADMINISTRATIVE LAW.

4   Transfer of Functions (Lands Tribunal and Miscellaneous Amendments) Order 2009, SI 2009/1307, art 2(1). As to the transfer of persons who held office in the Lands Tribunal see art 3. Proceedings are assigned to the Lands Chamber of the Upper Tribunal: see the First-tier Tribunal and Upper Tribunal (Chambers) Order 2008, SI 2008/2684, art 6(c) (art 6 substituted by SI 2009/196; and the First-tier Tribunal and Upper Tribunal (Chambers) Order 2008, SI 2008/2684, art 6(c) added by SI 2009/1021). Any proceedings before the Lands Tribunal which were pending before 1 June 2009 continue as proceedings before the Upper Tribunal, and any decision made by the Lands Tribunal before 1 June 2009 is to be treated as a decision of the Upper Tribunal on or after that date: Transfer of Functions (Lands Tribunal and Miscellaneous Amendments) Order 2009, SI 2009/1307, art 5, Sch 5.

5   As to the constitution of the Upper Tribunal see the Tribunals, Courts and Enforcement Act 2007 Pt 1 (ss 1–49); and ADMINISTRATIVE LAW. As to the jurisdiction of the Upper Tribunal in relation to compulsory acquisition of land see PARA 721.

721.   Jurisdiction of the Upper Tribunal. The jurisdiction conferred on the Upper Tribunal (the 'Tribunal')[1] includes jurisdiction:

(1)   as to any question of disputed compensation where land is authorised to be acquired compulsorily and, where any part of the land to be acquired is subject to a lease which comprises land not acquired, any question as to the apportionment of the rent payable under the lease[2];

(2)   formerly exercised by members of certain panels[3] but now transferred to the Tribunal[4];

(3)   to discharge and modify[5] restrictive covenants[6];

(4)   of statutory tribunals[7] to determine questions under any Act, including a local or private Act, or any instrument under any such Act[8];

(5)   on the application of any person, to certify the value of any land being sold by him to a person possessing compulsory purchase powers[9], the sale of the land to that authority at the certified price being deemed to be a sale at the best price that can reasonably be obtained[10];

(6)   to act as arbitrator under a reference by consent[11].

The jurisdiction of the Tribunal is limited to questions of compensation; questions of title are outside its jurisdiction[12].

1   As to the abolition of the Lands Tribunal and the transfer of its functions to the Upper Tribunal see PARA 720. As to the constitution of the Upper Tribunal see ADMINISTRATIVE LAW.

2   Lands Tribunal Act 1949 s 1(3)(b) (amended by the Land Compensation Act 1961 s 40(3), Sch 5); Lands Tribunal Act 1949 s 1(3)(c) (amended by the Compulsory Purchase Act 1965 s 39(4), Sch 8 Pt III); Land Compensation Act 1961 s 1 (amended by SI 2009/1307). As to the meaning of 'land' see PARA 516 note 2.

3   Ie the power: (1) to determine any question which by any Act, including a local or private Act, is directed, in whatever terms, to be determined by a person or one or more persons selected from the panel of official arbitrators appointed under the Acquisition of Land (Assessment of Compensation) Act 1919 (repealed), or the panel of referees appointed under the Finance (1909–10) Act 1910 s 34 (repealed), or which is so directed to be determined in the absence of agreement to the contrary (Lands Tribunal Act 1949 s 1(3)(a) (amended by SI 2009/1307)); (2) to exercise any other jurisdiction conferred by any Act, including a local or private Act, or instrument made under any such Act, on a person or one or more persons so selected (Lands Tribunal Act 1949 s 1(4)(b) (amended by the Land Compensation Act 1961 s 40(3), Sch 5; and SI 2009/1307)). The panel of official arbitrators formerly determined questions of disputed compensation or apportionment of rent where land was authorised to be acquired compulsorily: see the Acquisition of Land (Assessment of Compensation) Act 1919 s 1 (repealed). Subsequent enactments conferred other powers on the panel: see eg the Atomic Energy Act 1946 s 6(8), Sch 1 para 9; and FUEL AND ENERGY vol 19(3) (2007 Reissue) PARA 1426. All such jurisdiction is now exerciseable by the Upper Tribunal. The principal jurisdiction formerly exercised by the panel of referees, and transferred to the Tribunal, was over disputes concerning the valuation of land for estate duty (now abolished) and as to the valuation of land for mineral rights duty (now abolished) and other matters connected with that duty.

4   Lands Tribunal Act 1949 s 1(3)(a), (4)(b) (as amended: see note 3).

5   Ie under the Law of Property Act 1925 s 84: see EQUITY vol 16(2) (Reissue) PARAS 630–631.

6   Lands Tribunal Act 1949 s 1(4)(a) (amended by SI 2009/1307).

7   'Statutory tribunal' means any government department, authority or person entrusted with the judicial determination as arbitrator or otherwise of questions arising under an Act, but does not include: (1) any of the ordinary courts of law or a tribunal consisting of one or more judges of any of those courts; or (2) an arbitrator unless the person to act as arbitrator is designated, or is to be selected from a class or group of persons designated, by the Act or instrument requiring or authorising arbitration: Lands Tribunal Act 1949 s 4(7).

8   See PARA 722. As to private and local Acts see STATUTES vol 44(1) (Reissue) PARAS 1211–1213. Except in so far as the context otherwise requires, any reference in the Lands Tribunal Act 1949 to an enactment is to be construed as referring to that enactment as amended, extended or applied by any other enactment: s 8(2).

9   As to the meaning of 'authority possessing compulsory purchase powers' see PARA 763 note 6.

10 Land Compensation Act 1961 s 35 (amended by SI 2009/1307). A party may apply in writing to the registrar for such a certificate of value and must provide the registrar, at his request, with the information necessary to enable the certificate to be given: Lands Tribunal Rules 1996, SI 1996/1022, r 40.

11 Lands Tribunal Act 1949 s 1(5) (amended by SI 2009/1307); Lands Tribunal Rules 1996, SI 1996/1022, r 25. As to the application of the Arbitration Act 1996 see the Lands Tribunal Rules 1996, SI 1996/1022, rr 26, 32 (both substituted by SI 1997/1965; and amended by SI 2009/1307). Further, any agreement entered into before 1 January 1950 (ie the commencement date of the Lands Tribunal Act 1949) which provides for referring any matter to arbitration by a person or one or more persons selected as mentioned in note 3 has effect, subject to any subsequent agreement, as if it provided for referring the matter to arbitration by the Upper Tribunal: s 1(5) (amended by SI 2009/1307). Where the Tribunal is acting as arbitrator under a reference by consent, the following provisions of the Arbitration Act 1996 apply (in addition to those referred to in PARA 724 note 11): s 8 (whether agreement discharged by death of a party), s 9 (stay of legal proceedings), s 10 (reference of interpleader issue to arbitration), s 12 (power of court to extend time for beginning arbitral proceedings, etc), s 23 (revocation of arbitrator's authority), s 57 (correction of award or additional award, in so far as it relates to costs and so that the reference to 'award' includes a reference to any decision of the Lands Tribunal), and s 60 (agreement to pay costs in any event): Lands Tribunal Rules 1996, SI 1996/1022, r 26 (as so substituted and amended). Any person referring the matter to the Upper Tribunal must, at the time the reference is made, supply the Tribunal with copies of the arbitration agreement and any other written agreement relevant to the manner of arbitration: Lands Tribunal Rules 1996, SI 1996/1022, r 26A (added by SI 1997/1965; and amended by SI 2009/1307). As to arbitration generally see ARBITRATION.

12 *Mountgarret (Rt Hon Viscount) v Claro Water Board* (1963) 15 P & CR 53, Lands Tribunal.
This limitation might not apply where there is a reference by consent under the Lands Tribunal
Act 1949 s 1(5). For other limitations see *Williams v Secretary of State for the Environment*
(1976) 33 P & CR 131, Lands Tribunal (prior agreement between parties as to amount of
compensation); cf *Cadwallader v Rochdale Metropolitan Borough Council* [1979] RVR 302,
Lands Tribunal. The Tribunal will not investigate a solicitor's express instructions to reach
agreement to settle: *Harford v Birmingham City Council* (1993) 66 P & CR 468, Lands
Tribunal. Where land is owned by two or more persons jointly, any claim must be pursued by all
the joint owners: *Williams v British Gas Corpn* (1980) 41 P & CR 106, Lands Tribunal. The
Tribunal has jurisdiction to determine a claim for compensation arising from the withdrawal of
a notice to treat notwithstanding that the claimant had already recovered the expense of his
professional fees in the county court: *Williams v Blaenau Gwent Borough Council* (1994)
67 P & CR 393, Lands Tribunal. Where the property to be compulsorily acquired is subject to
a mortgage, the Tribunal has no jurisdiction to decide whether the acquiring authority is obliged
to redeem the mortgage: *Shewu v Richmond upon Thames and Hackney London Borough
Councils* (1999) 79 P & CR 47, CA. See also *Union Railways (North) Ltd v Kent County
Council* [2009] EWCA Civ 363, [2009] RVR 146, [2009] All ER (D) 56 (May).

722. Power to add to jurisdiction of the Upper Tribunal. Questions which are
required or authorised by an Act (including a local or private Act)[1], or
instrument made under any such Act, to be determined by any statutory tribunal
may be directed by Order in Council to be determined instead by the Upper
Tribunal (referred to in this context as the 'transferee Tribunal')[2] if it appears to
Her Majesty: (1) that the questions are appropriate for the transferee Tribunal as
involving valuation of land or for other reasons; and (2) that it is desirable to
transfer the jurisdiction to determine those questions from the first-mentioned
tribunal to the transferee Tribunal: (a) to promote uniformity of decision; or (b)
to use economically the services of those having experience in the valuation of
land or other special qualifications; or (c) to make possible the winding up of a
statutory tribunal having little work to do[3]. Jurisdiction conferred on a tribunal
by or under an Act passed after the Lands Tribunal Act 1949 may be so
transferred unless the Act conferring the jurisdiction contains a direction to the
contrary[4]; but where the jurisdiction is first conferred on a tribunal by or under
an Act so passed, heads (a) and (b) above do not apply[5].

The Order in Council transferring jurisdiction may contain supplementary
and consequential provisions which appear to Her Majesty to be expedient, and
any such provisions may be revoked or varied by a subsequent order or, if the
order so provides, by rules made under the Lands Tribunal Act 1949[6]. Without
prejudice to this power, the supplementary and consequential provisions must
include provisions for:

(i)   the enforcement of the transferee Tribunal's decisions in the same way
        as those of the statutory tribunal from which the jurisdiction is
        transferred[7];

(ii)   applying with or without modifications to the exercise of that
        jurisdiction by the transferee Tribunal, or repealing, any procedural
        provisions governing its exercise by the statutory tribunal[8]; and

(iii)   preserving the effect of things done in or for the purpose of the exercise
        of that jurisdiction by the statutory tribunal[9].

The transfer of any jurisdiction to the Upper Tribunal by or under the Lands
Tribunal Act 1949 does not affect the principles on which any question is to be
determined or the persons on whom the determination is binding, or any
provision which requires particular matters to be expressly dealt with or
embodied in the determination, or which relates to evidence[10]; nor is the

transfer[11] of any jurisdiction conferred on some other tribunal or person by an instrument made under any Act to be taken as affecting any power by virtue of which that instrument was made[12].

The Treasury may by regulations provide for the payment of compensation to persons suffering loss of office or employment, or loss or diminution of emoluments, attributable to the transfer of any jurisdiction to the Upper Tribunal[13]. Such regulations may provide for the manner in which, and the persons to whom, compensation claims are to be made, and for the determination of questions arising thereunder[14].

1   As to local and private Acts see STATUTES vol 44(1) (Reissue) PARAS 1211–1213.
2   As to the meaning of 'statutory tribunal' see PARA 721 note 7. As to the abolition of the Lands Tribunal and the transfer of its functions to the Upper Tribunal see PARA 720. As to the constitution of the Upper Tribunal see ADMINISTRATIVE LAW.
3   Lands Tribunal Act 1949 s 4(1) (amended by SI 2009/1307). See the Lands Tribunal (War Damage Appeals Jurisdiction) Order 1950, SI 1950/513; the Lands Tribunal (Statutory Undertakers Compensation Jurisdiction) Order 1952, SI 1952/161. As to the jurisdiction of the Upper Tribunal in relation to compulsory acquisition of land see PARA 721.
4   Lands Tribunal Act 1949 s 4(2). As to application to Northern Ireland see ss 4(2A), 9 (respectively added and substituted by SI 2009/1307). Such Orders in Council are subject to annulment by resolution of either House of Parliament: Lands Tribunal Act 1949 s 4(6).
5   Lands Tribunal Act 1949 s 4(2) proviso.
6   Lands Tribunal Act 1949 s 4(3). Any power to make rules under the Lands Tribunal Act 1949 is exercisable by statutory instrument: s 8(3).
7   Lands Tribunal Act 1949 s 4(4)(a) (amended by SI 2009/1307).
8   Lands Tribunal Act 1949 s 4(4)(c) (amended by SI 2009/1307).
9   Lands Tribunal Act 1949 s 4(4)(d). See also s 4(4A) (added by SI 2009/1307).
10   Lands Tribunal Act 1949 s 7(1) (amended by the Land Compensation Act 1961 s 40(3), Sch 5; and SI 2009/1307). Nothing in the Lands Tribunal Act 1949 affects the operation of any enactment applying or giving power to apply the Acquisition of Land (Assessment of Compensation) Act 1919 (repealed) or any of its provisions in relation to the exercise of a jurisdiction not transferred by or under the Lands Tribunal Act 1949, except that any enactment applying or giving power to apply the Acquisition of Land (Assessment of Compensation) Act 1919 s 5(2) (repealed) has like operation in relation to the Lands Tribunal Act 1949 s 5 (repealed): ss 7(3), 8(1).
11   Ie by the Lands Tribunal Act 1949 s 1(4) (see PARA 721) or by an Order in Council under s 4 (see the text and notes 1–9).
12   Lands Tribunal Act 1949 s 7(2) (amended by SI 2009/1307). The provision conferring that power accordingly has effect as from the transfer as if it directed the jurisdiction to be exercised by the Upper Tribunal as provided by or under the Lands Tribunal Act 1949, except in so far as provision to the contrary is thereafter made in pursuance of that power: s 7(2) (as so amended).
13   Lands Tribunal Act 1949 s 6(1) (amended by SI 2009/1307). Any compensation must be paid out of money provided by Parliament: Lands Tribunal Act 1949 s 6(3).
14   Lands Tribunal Act 1949 s 6(2). Such regulations are not made by statutory instrument, and are not recorded in this work.

723.   Rules of procedure.   Tribunal Procedure Rules govern the practice and procedure to be followed in the Upper Tribunal (the 'Tribunal')[1]. The Lands Tribunal Rules 1996[2], which were made under the Lands Tribunal Act 1949, now have effect as if they were Tribunal Procedure Rules[3]. In addition to general procedural provisions, the rules that have been made make special provision for particular aspects of the Tribunal's jurisdiction[4].

Any failure by any person to comply with the rules does not render the proceedings or anything done in pursuance of them invalid unless the Tribunal so directs[5].

1   Tribunals, Courts and Enforcement Act 2007 s 22(1)(b). See the Tribunal Procedure (Upper Tribunal) Rules 2008, SI 2008/2698 (amended by SI 2009/274); and ADMINISTRATIVE LAW. As

to the abolition of the Lands Tribunal and the transfer of its functions to the Upper Tribunal see PARA 720. As to the constitution of the Upper Tribunal see ADMINISTRATIVE LAW.

2	Ie the Lands Tribunal Rules 1996, SI 1996/1022, which came into force on 1 May 1996 (see r 1(1) (r 1 substituted by SI 2009/1307)) and which now apply to proceedings which have been assigned to the Lands Chamber of the Upper Tribunal by the First-tier Tribunal and Upper Tribunal (Chambers) Order 2008, SI 2008/2684 (see the Lands Tribunal Rules 1996, SI 1996/1022, r 1(2) (as so substituted)). As to the fees payable see the Upper Tribunal (Lands Chamber) Fees Order 2009, SI 2009/1114.

3	Transfer of Tribunal Functions (Lands Tribunal and Miscellaneous Amendments) Order 2009, SI 2009/1307, art 4.

4	This title sets out the effect of the specific provisions relating to the compulsory acquisition of land and associated compensation: see PARAS 721–752. Other procedural provisions are set out elsewhere in this work within the titles on the subject matter to which they relate. The Lands Tribunal Rules 1996, SI 1996/1022, provide for applications to the Upper Tribunal for permission to appeal under the Commonhold and Leasehold Reform Act 2002 s 175 against a decision of the leasehold valuation tribunal, or under the Housing Act 2004 s 231 against a decision of the residential property tribunal: see the Lands Tribunal Rules 1996, SI 1996/1022, rr 5A–5H; and LANDLORD AND TENANT vol 27(1) (2006 Reissue) PARA 72. The rules also provide for appeals against a determination of any question by an authority in respect of whose decision an appeal lies to the Upper Tribunal: see the Lands Tribunal Rules 1996, SI 1996/1022, rr 6–8; and RATING AND COUNCIL TAX vol 39(1B) (Reissue) PARA 166. Such appeals may lie eg from certain decisions and assessments of the Inland Revenue in which the question at issue is the value of any land (see the Taxes Management Act 1970 s 46D). The Upper Tribunal may also hear applications made under the Law of Property Act 1925 s 84 (relief from restrictive covenants affecting land): see the Lands Tribunal Rules, SI 1996/1022, Pt V (rr 12–20); and EQUITY vol 16(2) (Reissue) PARA 633 et seq. It also hears applications made under the Rights of Light Act 1959 s 2: see the Lands Tribunal Rules 1996, SI 1996/1022, Pt VI (rr 21–24); and EASEMENTS AND PROFITS A PRENDRE vol 16(2) (Reissue) PARA 244.

	An appeal from a decision of the Upper Tribunal itself lies to the Court of Appeal: see PARAS 751–752.

5	Lands Tribunal Rules 1996, SI 1996/1022, r 47 (amended by SI 2009/1307). As to the Upper Tribunal's power to correct an award for clerical mistakes or errors, or ambiguities, see PARA 744.

(ii) Notice of Reference

724. Notice of reference instituting proceedings. A reference to the Upper Tribunal (the 'Tribunal')[1] is started by one or other of the parties sending to the registrar[2] a notice of reference together with sufficient copies for service upon every other person named in the notice[3]. The notice of reference must contain: (1) the name and address of the person lodging the reference and, if he is represented, the name, address and profession of the representative; (2) the name and address of every other person with an interest in the land to which the reference relates; (3) the address or description of the land to which the reference relates; (4) the nature of the interest in the land of the person lodging the reference; (5) the statutory provision under which the reference is made; and (6) the signature of the person lodging the reference, or his representative, and the date the reference was signed[4].

Where the matter relates to compensation payable on the compulsory acquisition of land, the person lodging the notice of reference must attach to it a copy of the notice to treat (if one has been served)[5], a copy of the notice of entry (if one has been served)[6], and any notice of claim and amendments of it delivered[7] to the acquiring authority[8]. In any other case, the person lodging the notice of reference must attach a copy of the order or other document in consequence of which proceedings for the determination of the reference are instituted, including a copy of any agreement conferring jurisdiction on the Tribunal[9].

A notice of reference relating to the compensation payable on the compulsory acquisition of land may not be given before the expiration of 28 days from the date of service or constructive service of the notice to treat, or where no such notice is served (or is deemed to be served, in accordance with the appropriate statutory provision) of the notice of claim[10].

Certain provisions of the Arbitration Act 1996 apply to proceedings before the Tribunal[11].

1   Ie any reference to the Upper Tribunal other than an appeal or an application to which the Lands Tribunal Rules 1996, SI 1996/1022, Pt V (rr 12–20) or Pt VI (rr 21–24) applies: r 9 (amended by SI 2009/1307). As to the Upper Tribunal see PARA 720; and ADMINISTRATIVE LAW. The Lands Tribunal was abolished on 1 June 2009 and its functions were transferred to the Upper Tribunal: see PARA 720.

2   Any application or communication to be made to the Upper Tribunal in respect of any case must be addressed to the registrar: Lands Tribunal Rules 1996, SI 1996/1022, r 54(5) (amended by SI 2009/1307).

3   Lands Tribunal Rules 1996, SI 1996/1022, r 10(1). The person lodging the notice of reference and the persons named in that notice become the parties to the proceedings: r 10(2). As to the fees payable see the Upper Tribunal (Lands Chamber) Fees Order 2009, SI 2009/1114.

4   Lands Tribunal Rules 1996, SI 1996/1022, r 10(3).

5   Lands Tribunal Rules 1996, SI 1996/1022, r 10(4)(a)(i). As to notices to treat see PARA 616 et seq.

6   Lands Tribunal Rules 1996, SI 1996/1022, r 10(4)(a)(ii). As to entry on notice after notice to treat see PARA 645.

7   Ie delivered in pursuance of the Land Compensation Act 1961 s 4: see PARAS 716–717.

8   Lands Tribunal Rules 1996, SI 1996/1022, r 10(4)(a)(iii).

9   Lands Tribunal Rules 1996, SI 1996/1022, r 10(4)(b) (amended by SI 2009/1307).

10 Lands Tribunal Rules 1996, SI 1996/1022, r 10(5).

11 See the Lands Tribunal Rules 1996, SI 1996/1022, r 32 (substituted by SI 1997/1965; amended by SI 1998/22; SI 2009/1307). This applies the following provisions of the Arbitration Act 1996 to all proceedings before the Upper Tribunal as they apply to an arbitration: s 47 (awards on different issues, etc), s 49 (interest, subject to any enactment that prescribes a rate of interest), s 57(3)–(7) (correction of award or additional award), and s 66 (enforcement of the award). See further ARBITRATION vol 2 (2008) PARA 1209 et seq.

725.   Case management.   As soon as the Upper Tribunal or registrar has sufficient information to do so, each case will be assigned to one of four possible procedures[1]: (1) the standard procedure[2]; (2) the special procedure[3]; (3) the written representations procedure[4]; or (4) the simplified procedure[5]. In assigning a procedure, the views expressed by the parties will be taken into account[6].

1   Lands Tribunal Practice Directions (2006) para 3.1. The Lands Tribunal was abolished on 1 June 2009 and its functions were transferred to the Upper Tribunal established under the Tribunals, Courts and Enforcement Act 2007: see the Transfer of Tribunal Functions (Lands Tribunal and Miscellaneous Amendments) Order 2009, SI 2009/1307; PARA 720; and ADMINISTRATIVE LAW.

2   As to the standard procedure see PARA 726 et seq.

3   A case is assigned to the special procedure if, in view of its complexity, the amount in issue or its wider importance, it requires case management by a member of the Tribunal, who orders a pre-trial review to be held under the Lands Tribunal Rules 1996, SI 1996/1022, r 39 (see PARA 732): Lands Tribunal Practice Directions (2006) para 3.2.

4   As to the written representations procedure see PARA 736.

5   As to the simplified procedure see PARA 737.

6   Lands Tribunal Practice Directions (2006) para 3.1.

726.   Entry, withdrawal and dismissal of references.   Upon receiving a notice of reference[1], the registrar of the Upper Tribunal (the 'Tribunal')[2] must enter particulars of the reference in the Register of References and send[3] a copy of the notice to every party to the proceedings (other than the party instituting the proceedings)[4]. He must also inform all parties to the proceedings of the number of the reference, which thereafter constitutes the title of the proceedings[5].

A reference[6] may be withdrawn by sending to the registrar a written notice of withdrawal, signed by all the parties or by their representatives[7].

A party may, at any time before the hearing of the proceedings, apply to the Tribunal for an order to dismiss the proceedings and the Tribunal may make such order as it thinks fit[8].

Where any party has failed to pursue any proceedings with due diligence or has failed to comply with any of the rules of procedure, the registrar or the Tribunal, on the application of any party or of his or its own motion and after giving the parties an opportunity to be heard, may: (1) make an order that the proceedings be heard by the Tribunal; or (2) make an order that the proceedings be dismissed or that any party be debarred from taking any further part in the proceedings; or (3) make such other order as may be appropriate for the purpose of expediting or disposing of the proceedings, including an order for costs[9].

1   As to the notice of reference see PARA 724. As to the meaning of 'reference' in this context see PARA 724 note 1.
2   As to the registrar see PARA 717 note 8. As to the Upper Tribunal see PARA 720; and ADMINISTRATIVE LAW. The Lands Tribunal was abolished on 1 June 2009 and its functions were transferred to the Upper Tribunal: see PARA 720.
3   Any document to be served on any person under the Lands Tribunal Rules 1996, SI 1996/1022, is deemed to have been served if it is sent by pre-paid post to that person at his address for service: r 54(3). Every party to proceedings must notify the registrar of an address for service of documents on him: r 54(1). This address may be changed at any time by notice in writing to the registrar and to every other party to the proceedings: r 55.
    If any person to whom any notice or other document is required to be sent:
    (1)   cannot be found after all diligent enquiries have been made; or
    (2)   has died and has no personal representative; or
    (3)   is out of the United Kingdom,
    or if for any other reason service upon him cannot readily be effected in accordance with the rules, the Tribunal may dispense with service upon that person or make an order for substituted service in such other form (whether by advertisement in a newspaper or otherwise) as the Tribunal may think fit: r 56 (amended by SI 2009/1307). As to the meaning of 'United Kingdom' see PARA 616 note 22.
4   Lands Tribunal Rules 1996, SI 1996/1022, r 11(1).
5   Lands Tribunal Rules 1996, SI 1996/1022, r 11(2).
6   This provision applies equally to an appeal or application: Lands Tribunal Rules 1996, SI 1996/1022, r 45(1).
7   Lands Tribunal Rules 1996, SI 1996/1022, r 45(1). Where a reference is conditionally withdrawn it is necessary for the Tribunal to know the facts of the case, and so it may proceed to hear and determine the reference: *Perkins v Central Land Board* (1953) 4 P & CR 162, Lands Tribunal.
8   Lands Tribunal Rules 1996, SI 1996/1022, r 45(2) (amended by SI 2009/1307). Any such application is dealt with as an interim matter: see the Lands Tribunal Rules 1996, SI 1996/1022, r 45(3). The application must be made in writing, stating the title of the proceedings and the grounds upon which the application is made: r 38(2). If it is not made with the consent of every party, then before it is made a copy of the application must be served on every other party and the application must state that this has been done: r 38(4). Any party who objects to the application may within seven days of service of a copy on him send a written notice of objection to the Tribunal: r 38(5) (modified by r 45(3); amended by SI 2009/1307). Before making an order on the application, the Tribunal must consider all the objections that it has received and may allow any party who wishes to appear before it the opportunity to do so: Lands Tribunal Rules 1996, SI 1996/1022, r 38(6) (modified by r 45(3); amended by SI 2009/1307). In dealing with the application, the Tribunal must have regard to the convenience of all the parties and the desirability of limiting, so far as practicable, the costs of the proceedings, and must inform the parties in writing of its decision: Lands Tribunal Rules 1996, SI 1996/1022, r 38(7) (modified by r 45(3); amended by SI 2009/1307).
9   Lands Tribunal Rules 1996, SI 1996/1022, r 46(2). An appeal from any such order made by the registrar is dealt with as an interim matter: r 46(3). See r 38(9), (10); and PARA 730.

727.   Consolidation of references, etc.   Where two or more notices of reference[1] have been made which: (1) are in respect of the same land or buildings; or (2) relate to different interests in the same land or buildings; or (3) raise the same issues, the Upper Tribunal (the 'Tribunal') may, on its own motion or on the application of a party to the proceedings, order that the references be consolidated or heard together[2]. An order for consolidation may be made with respect to some only of the matters to which the references relate[3].

Where the Tribunal is of the opinion that two or more references (or appeals) involve the same issues it may, with the written consent of all the parties to the references (or appeals), select one or more references (or appeals) to be heard in the first instance as a test case (or test cases) and the parties to each reference (or appeal) are bound by the decision of the Tribunal on that reference (or appeal)[4].

1   As to notices of reference see PARA 724. As to the meaning of 'reference' in this context see PARA 724 note 1. These provisions apply to notices of appeal made under the Lands Tribunal Rules 1996, SI 1996/1022, and to applications under Pt V (rr 12–20) or Pt VI (rr 21–24), as they apply to references: r 30(1). The Lands Tribunal was abolished on 1 June 2009 and its functions were transferred to the Upper Tribunal: see PARA 720.
2   Lands Tribunal Rules 1996, SI 1996/1022, r 30(1) (amended by SI 2009/1307).
3   Lands Tribunal Rules 1996, SI 1996/1022, r 30(2).
4   Lands Tribunal Rules 1996, SI 1996/1022, r 31(1).

728.   Disclosure of documents at registrar's request.   The Upper Tribunal (the 'Tribunal') or (subject to any direction given by the Tribunal) the registrar[1] may, on the application of any party to the proceedings or of its or his own motion, order any party:

(1)   to deliver to the registrar any document or other information which the Tribunal may require[2] and which it is in the power of the party to deliver[3];

(2)   to afford to every other party to the proceedings an opportunity to inspect those documents (or copies of them) and to take copies[4];

(3)   to deliver to the registrar an affidavit or make a list stating whether any document or class of document specified or described in the order or application is, or has at any time been, in his possession, custody or power, and stating when he parted with it[5];

(4)   to deliver to the registrar a statement in the form of a pleading setting out further and better particulars of the grounds on which he intends to rely and any relevant facts or contentions[6];

(5)   to answer requests for further information on affidavit relating to any matter at issue between the applicant and the other party[7];

(6)   to deliver to the registrar a statement of agreed facts, facts in dispute and the issue or issues to be tried by the Tribunal[8]; or

(7)   to deliver to the registrar witness statements or proofs of evidence[9].

Where any order is made under heads (1) to (7) above, the Tribunal or registrar may give directions as to the time within which any document must be sent to the registrar (being at least 14 days from the date of the direction) and the parties to whom copies of the document are to be sent[10].

1   As to the registrar see PARA 717 note 8. As to the Upper Tribunal see PARA 720; and ADMINISTRATIVE LAW.
2   As to the Upper Tribunal's power to require documents not supplied see the Lands Tribunal Rules 1996, SI 1996/1022, r 46(1); and PARA 738. The Lands Tribunal was abolished on 1 June 2009 and its functions were transferred to the Upper Tribunal: see PARA 720.
3   Lands Tribunal Rules 1996, SI 1996/1022, r 34(1)(a).
4   Lands Tribunal Rules 1996, SI 1996/1022, r 34(1)(b).

5   Lands Tribunal Rules 1996, SI 1996/1022, r 34(1)(c).
6   Lands Tribunal Rules 1996, SI 1996/1022, r 34(1)(d).
7   Lands Tribunal Rules 1996, SI 1996/1022, r 34(1)(e).
8   Lands Tribunal Rules 1996, SI 1996/1022, r 34(1)(f).
9   Lands Tribunal Rules 1996, SI 1996/1022, r 34(1)(g).
10 Lands Tribunal Rules 1996, SI 1996/1022, r 34(2). Both in relation to applications and where the registrar acts of his own motion, the rule governing interim applications (see r 38; and PARA 730) applies as appropriate: see r 34(3).

729. Consent orders. Where the parties to proceedings have agreed the terms of any order to be made by the Upper Tribunal (the 'Tribunal')[1], particulars of those terms, signed by all the parties or by their representatives[2], must be sent to the registrar[3], and an order may be made by the Tribunal in accordance with those terms in the absence of the parties[4].

1   As to the Upper Tribunal see PARA 720; and ADMINISTRATIVE LAW.
2   As to rights of audience before the Upper Tribunal see PARA 739.
3   As to the registrar see PARA 717 note 8.
4   Lands Tribunal Rules 1996, SI 1996/1022, r 51. As to the fees payable see the Upper Tribunal (Lands Chamber) Fees Order 2009, SI 2009/1114. The Lands Tribunal was abolished on 1 June 2009 and its functions were transferred to the Upper Tribunal: see PARA 720.

(iii) Interim Applications

730. Applications for directions. Except where other provision is made[1], or the Upper Tribunal (the 'Tribunal') otherwise orders, an application for directions of an interim nature in connection with any proceedings in the Tribunal must be made to the registrar[2].

The application must be made in writing, stating the title of the proceedings and the grounds upon which the application is made[3], and, if made with the consent of all parties, must be accompanied by consents signed by or on behalf of the parties[4]. If it is not made with the consent of every party, then, before it is made, a copy of the application must be served on every other party and the application must state that this has been done[5].

Any party who objects to the application may, within seven days of service of a copy on him, send a written notice of objection to the registrar[6], and, before making an order on the application, the registrar must consider all the objections that he has received and may allow any party who wishes to appear before him the opportunity to do so[7].

The parties may appear on the application either in person or be represented by counsel or solicitor or by any other person allowed by permission of the registrar[8]. In dealing with any interim application, the registrar must have regard to the convenience of all the parties and the desirability of limiting the costs of the proceedings so far as practicable[9]. The registrar may, and must if the applicant or any party objecting to an application so requests[10], refer the application to the Tribunal for a decision[11].

The registrar must inform the parties in writing of his decision[12]. Any party may appeal to the Tribunal from the registrar's decision by giving written notice to the registrar within seven days of service of the notice of decision or within such further time as the registrar may allow[13], but any such appeal does not act as a stay of proceedings unless the Tribunal so orders[14].

1   Ie under the Lands Tribunal Rules, SI 1996/1022.
2   Lands Tribunal Rules 1996, SI 1996/1022, r 38(1) (amended by SI 2009/1307). The Lands Tribunal was abolished on 1 June 2009 and its functions were transferred to the Upper Tribunal: see PARA 720. Certain provisions of the Lands Tribunal Rules 1996, SI 1996/1022, r 38

(ie r 38(2), (4)–(7)) apply with modifications to applications for the dismissal of proceedings before the Upper Tribunal: see r 45(3); and PARA 726. Rule 38 also applies to r 34, as appropriate, to applications and in relation to cases where the registrar acts of his own motion: see r 34(3); and PARA 728. Applications for a pre-trial review are conducted under r 38(6)–(11), as if it were an interim application: see r 39(6); and PARA 732. Applications for an order for affidavit evidence, and for the disposal of a preliminary point of law, are made to the Tribunal under r 38(2)–(7) (modified by r 33(3), and by r 43(3) (amended by SI 2009/1307)) (see PARAS 733–734). Where an objection is received by the registrar under the simplified procedure (see PARA 737), the provisions of the Lands Tribunal Rules 1996, SI 1996/1022, r 38(6)–(9), (11) apply: r 28(3). The provisions of r 38(8), (10) apply to any application made as to costs: see r 52(8); and PARA 747. As to the registrar see PARA 717 note 8.

3   Lands Tribunal Rules 1996, SI 1996/1022, r 38(2).
4   Lands Tribunal Rules 1996, SI 1996/1022, r 38(3).
5   Lands Tribunal Rules 1996, SI 1996/1022, r 38(4). As to service see PARA 726 note 3.
6   Lands Tribunal Rules 1996, SI 1996/1022, r 38(5).
7   Lands Tribunal Rules 1996, SI 1996/1022, r 38(6).
8   Lands Tribunal Rules 1996, SI 1996/1022, r 37(1) (amended by SI 2009/1307).
9   Lands Tribunal Rules 1996, SI 1996/1022, r 38(7). As to withdrawal of applications see r 45; and PARA 726.
10   See note 2.
11   Lands Tribunal Rules 1996, SI 1996/1022, r 38(8) (amended by SI 2009/1307).
12   Lands Tribunal Rules 1996, SI 1996/1022, r 38(7).
13   Lands Tribunal Rules 1996, SI 1996/1022, r 38(9).
14   Lands Tribunal Rules 1996, SI 1996/1022, r 38(10) (amended by SI 2009/1307).

731. Alteration of time limits. The time appointed for doing any act or taking any steps in relation to any Upper Tribunal proceedings[1] may be extended by the registrar[2] on application to him[3], upon such terms as he thinks fit; and an extension may be ordered even though the application is not made until after the time limit has expired[4].

1   Ie the time appointed by or under the Lands Tribunal Rules 1996, SI 1996/1022. As to the Upper Tribunal see PARA 720; and ADMINISTRATIVE LAW.
2   As to the registrar see PARA 717 note 8.
3   Ie under the Lands Tribunal Rules 1996, SI 1996/1022, r 38 (see PARA 730): r 35(1).
4   Lands Tribunal Rules 1996, SI 1996/1022, r 35(2). The Lands Tribunal was abolished on 1 June 2009 and its functions were transferred to the Upper Tribunal: see PARA 720. The Upper Tribunal may also make an urgency direction for the shortening of a time limit in relation to appeals to it under the Commonhold and Leasehold Reform Act 2002 s 175 (see LANDLORD AND TENANT vol 27(1) (2006 Reissue) PARA 72) or the Housing Act 2004 (see HOUSING): see the Lands Tribunal Rules 1996, SI 1996/1022, r 35A (added by SI 2006/880).

732. Pre-trial review. The Upper Tribunal (the 'Tribunal') and, subject to any directions given by the Tribunal, the registrar[1] may on the application of a party to the proceedings or of its or his own motion order a pre-trial review to be held[2]. Unless the parties agree otherwise, the review must be held not less than 14 days from the making of the order[3].

The registrar must send to each party a notice informing him of the place and date of the pre-trial review[4]. The provisions relating to interim applications[5] have effect as if the pre-trial review were the hearing of an interim application[6]. Where any party seeks a specific direction he must, so far as practicable, apply for it on the pre-trial review, giving notice of his intention to do so to the registrar and to every other party[7]. On the pre-trial review, the Tribunal or the registrar: (1) must give any direction that appears necessary or desirable for securing the just, expeditious and economical disposal of the proceedings[8]; (2) must endeavour to secure that the parties make all such admissions and agreements as ought reasonably to be made by them in relation to the proceedings[9]; and (3) may record in the order made on the review any admission or agreement so made or any refusal to make one[10]. Where a party fails to appear on a pre-trial review, the Tribunal or the registrar, after giving the parties an opportunity to be heard, may make such order as may be appropriate for the purpose of expediting or disposing of the proceedings[11].

1 As to the registrar see PARA 717 note 8. As to the Upper Tribunal see PARA 720; and ADMINISTRATIVE LAW.
2 Lands Tribunal Rules 1996, SI 1996/1022, r 39(1). The purpose of the pre-trial review is to ensure so far as practicable that all appropriate directions are given for the fair, expeditious and economical conduct of the proceedings. Where appropriate a date for the hearing will be fixed at the pre-trial review and the steps which the parties are required to take, and further pre-trial reviews, will be timetabled by reference to this date: Lands Tribunal Practice Directions (2006) para 3.2. The Lands Tribunal was abolished on 1 June 2009 and its functions were transferred to the Upper Tribunal: see PARA 720.
3 Lands Tribunal Rules 1996, SI 1996/1022, r 39(2).
4 Lands Tribunal Rules 1996, SI 1996/1022, r 39(1).
5 Ie the provisions in the Lands Tribunal Rules 1996, SI 1996/1022, r 38(6)–(10): see PARA 730.
6 Lands Tribunal Rules 1996, SI 1996/1022, r 39(6).
7 Lands Tribunal Rules 1996, SI 1996/1022, r 39(4). Before the pre-trial review, the parties are asked, to the extent that they are able to do so at that stage, to identify the issues in the case, and to state the areas of expertise of each expert witness that they propose to rely on and the general scope of his evidence: Lands Tribunal Practice Directions (2006) para 3.2. Each party must consider whether it is appropriate to make applications for the determination of a preliminary issue under the Lands Tribunal Rules 1996, SI 1996/1022, r 43 (see PARA 733) and permission to call more than the permitted number of expert witnesses under r 42 (see PARAS 734, 742); and it should identify, and where necessary make application for, any other order that it wishes the Tribunal to make at the pre-trial review: Lands Tribunal Practice Directions (2006) para 3.2. If an application which might have been made on the review is made subsequently, the applicant must pay the costs of and occasioned by the application, unless the Tribunal considers that there was sufficient reason for the application not having been made on the review: Lands Tribunal Rules 1996, SI 1996/1022, r 39(5).
8 Lands Tribunal Rules 1996, SI 1996/1022, r 39(3)(a). Because it is for the applicant to make his own case, the test is whether it would be in the interests of securing a just, expeditious and economical disposal of the proceedings for the Tribunal to require the records to be produced: see *Kingsley v IRC* [1987] 2 EGLR 217, Lands Tribunal.
9 Lands Tribunal Rules 1996, SI 1996/1022, r 39(3)(b).
10 Lands Tribunal Rules 1996, SI 1996/1022, r 39(3)(c).
11 Lands Tribunal Rules 1996, SI 1996/1022, r 39(7).

733. Applications for disposal of preliminary points of law. On the application of any party to proceedings before the Upper Tribunal (the 'Tribunal')[1], the Tribunal may order any preliminary issue in the proceedings to be disposed of at a preliminary hearing[2]. If, in the opinion of the Tribunal, the decision on the preliminary issue disposes of the proceedings, it may order that the preliminary hearing is to be treated as the hearing of the case, or may make such other order as it thinks fit[3].

1 As to the Upper Tribunal see PARA 720; and ADMINISTRATIVE LAW.
2 Lands Tribunal Rules 1996, SI 1996/1022, r 43(1) (amended by SI 2009/1307). Any such application is dealt with as an interim matter: see the Lands Tribunal Rules 1996, SI 1996/1022, r 43; and PARA 730. The application must be made in writing, stating the title of the proceedings and the grounds upon which the application is made (r 38(2)) and, if made with the consent of all parties, must be accompanied by consents signed by or on behalf of the parties (r 38(3)). If it is not made with the consent of every party, then before it is made a copy of the application must be served on every other party and the application must state that this has been done: r 38(4). Any party who objects to the application may within seven days of service of a copy on him send a written notice of objection to the Tribunal: r 38(5) (modified by r 43(3) (amended by SI 2009/1307)). Before making an order on the application, the Tribunal must consider all the objections that it has received and may allow any party who wishes to appear before it the opportunity to do so: Lands Tribunal Rules 1996, SI 1996/1022, r 38(6) (modified by r 43(3) (as so amended)). In dealing with the application, the Tribunal must have regard to the convenience

of all the parties and the desirability of limiting, so far as practicable, the costs of the proceedings, and must inform the parties in writing of its decision: r 38(7) (modified by r 43(3) (as so amended)). As to applications for the disposal of preliminary points of law generally see *Western Steamship Co v Amaral Sutherland & Co Ltd* [1914] 3 KB 55, CA; *Windsor Refrigerator Co Ltd v Branch Nominees Ltd* [1961] Ch 375, [1961] 1 All ER 277, CA. The Lands Tribunal was abolished on 1 June 2009 and its functions were transferred to the Upper Tribunal: see PARA 720.
3   Lands Tribunal Rules 1996, SI 1996/1022, r 43(2).

734.   Applications as to evidence. Evidence before the Upper Tribunal (the 'Tribunal')[1] may be given orally and may be on oath or affirmation[2] or, if the parties to the proceedings consent or the Tribunal so orders, by affidavit[3]. Notwithstanding this, the Tribunal may at any stage of the proceedings require the personal attendance of any deponent for examination or cross-examination[4].

Application for permission to call more than the permitted[5] number of expert witnesses may be made either to the registrar as an interim application[6] or to the Tribunal at the hearing[7].

1   As to the Upper Tribunal see PARA 720; and ADMINISTRATIVE LAW.
2   The registrar and the Tribunal have the power to administer oaths and take affirmations for the purpose of affidavits to be used in proceedings before the Tribunal, or for the purpose of the giving of oral evidence at hearings: Lands Tribunal Rules 1996, SI 1996/1022, r 41. As to the registrar see PARA 717 note 8. The Lands Tribunal was abolished on 1 June 2009 and its functions were transferred to the Upper Tribunal: see PARA 720.
3   Lands Tribunal Rules 1996, SI 1996/1022, r 33(1) (amended by SI 2009/1307). An application to the Tribunal for permission to give evidence by affidavit is dealt with as an interim matter: see the Lands Tribunal Rules 1996, SI 1996/1022, r 33(3) (amended by SI 2009/1307); and PARA 730. The application must be made in writing, stating the title of the proceedings and the grounds upon which the application is made (Lands Tribunal Rules 1996, SI 1996/1022, r 38(2)) and, if made with the consent of all parties, must be accompanied by consents signed by or on behalf of the parties (r 38(3)). If it is not made with the consent of every party, then before it is made a copy of the application must be served on every other party and the application must state that this has been done: r 38(4). Any party who objects to the application may within seven days of service of a copy on him send a written notice of objection to the Tribunal: r 38(5) (modified by r 33(3) (as so amended)). Before making an order on the application, the Tribunal must consider all the objections that it has received and may allow any party who wishes to appear before it the opportunity to do so: r 38(6) (modified by r 33(3) (as so amended)). In dealing with the application, the Tribunal must have regard to the convenience of all the parties and the desirability of limiting, so far as practicable, the costs of the proceedings, and must inform the parties in writing of its decision: r 38(7) (modified by r 33(3) (as so amended)).
4   Lands Tribunal Rules 1996, SI 1996/1022, r 33(2). Where an affidavit has been produced by consent in evidence or by order, the Tribunal may at any stage order the personal attendance of the deponent: *Mahboob Hussain v Oldham Metropolitan Borough Council* (1981) 42 P & CR 388, Lands Tribunal.
5   Ie under the rules relating to expert evidence generally: see the Lands Tribunal Rules 1996, SI 1996/1022, r 42; and PARA 742.
6   Ie in accordance with the Lands Tribunal Rules 1996, SI 1996/1022, r 38: see PARA 730.
7   Lands Tribunal Rules 1996, SI 1996/1022, r 42(4).

(iv) The Hearing

735.   Place and notification of hearing. The registrar[1] must, as soon as practicable after the commencement of proceedings before the Upper Tribunal[2], send to each party a notice informing him of the date, time and place of the hearing[3]. Upon receiving notice of intention to respond from a person who is not already a party to the proceedings, the registrar must send to that person a notice informing him of the date, time and place of the hearing[4].

Any hearing in proceedings on a compulsory purchase compensation reference must be in public[5].

1   As to the registrar see PARA 717 note 8.
2   As to the Upper Tribunal see PARA 720; and ADMINISTRATIVE LAW. See the Lands Tribunal
     Practice Directions (2006) para 12.1. The Lands Tribunal was abolished on 1 June 2009 and its
     functions were transferred to the Upper Tribunal: see PARA 720.
3   Lands Tribunal Rules 1996, SI 1996/1022, r 4(1).
4   Lands Tribunal Rules 1996, SI 1996/1022, r 4(2). As to the fees payable see the Upper Tribunal
     (Lands Chamber) Fees Order 2009, SI 2009/1114.
5   Lands Tribunal Rules 1996, SI 1996/1022, r 5(1A) (added by SI 2009/1307). Subject to the
     Lands Tribunal Rules 1996, SI 1996/1022, r 5(1A), however, all hearings must be in public
     except where (1) it is acting as an arbitrator under a reference by consent under the Lands
     Tribunal Act 1949 s 1(5); or (2) it is satisfied that, by reason of disclosure of confidential
     matters or matters concerning national security, it is just and reasonable for the hearing or any
     part of the hearing to be in private: Lands Tribunal Rules 1996, SI 1996/1022, r 5(1) (amended
     by SI 2009/1307). A judge or other member of the Upper Tribunal is entitled to attend a hearing
     whether or not it is in private, notwithstanding that they do not constitute the Tribunal for the
     purpose of the hearing: Lands Tribunal Rules 1996, SI 1996/1022, r 5(2) (substituted by
     SI 2009/1307).

736.   Written representations procedure (contested proceedings without a hearing). The Upper Tribunal (the 'Tribunal')[1] may, with the consent of the parties to the proceedings, order that the proceedings be determined without an oral hearing[2] (referred to as the 'written representations procedure'), and will give such directions relating to the lodging of documents and representations as it considers appropriate[3]. Where the Tribunal makes such an order, any party to the proceedings may submit written representations to the Tribunal[4].

The Tribunal may at any time, on the application of a party to the proceedings or of its own motion, order that the proceedings which are being contested without a hearing should be heard and so give directions for the disposal of those proceedings[5].

1   As to the Upper Tribunal see PARA 720; and ADMINISTRATIVE LAW.
2   Lands Tribunal Rules 1996, SI 1996/1022, r 27(1). The rule relating to expert witnesses (see
     r 42; and PARA 742) applies to contested proceedings without a hearing as if references to the
     calling of witnesses and the hearing of evidence in that rule were references to representations:
     r 27(4). The Lands Tribunal was abolished on 1 June 2009 and its functions were transferred to
     the Upper Tribunal: see PARA 720.
3   Lands Tribunal Rules 1996, SI 1996/1022, r 27(3). Such an order for the written representation
     procedure to be followed will only be made if the Tribunal, having regard to the issues in the
     case and the desirability of minimising costs, is of the view that oral evidence and argument can
     properly be dispensed with: Lands Tribunal Practice Directions (2006) para 3.5.
4   Lands Tribunal Rules 1996, SI 1996/1022, r 27(2).
5   Lands Tribunal Rules 1996, SI 1996/1022, r 27(5).

737.   Simplified procedure. The Upper Tribunal (the 'Tribunal')[1] or the registrar[2] may, with the consent of the appellant, or, in relation to any reference[3] to the Tribunal, with the consent of the person who is claiming compensation, direct that proceedings[4] are to be determined in accordance with the simplified procedure described below[5]. The registrar must send a copy of any such direction to all the parties to the proceedings and any party who objects to the direction may, within seven days of service of the copy on him, send written notice of his objection to the registrar[6].

Where the registrar has made a direction[7], the following procedure applies[8]. The registrar must: (1) give directions concerning the filing and contents of a statement of claim by the appellant and a reply by the other parties to the proceedings[9]; and (2) give the parties not less than 21 days' notice of the day fixed for the hearing of the proceedings[10]. Each party must, not less than 14 days before the date fixed for the hearing, send to every other party copies of all

claims or cross-claims submitted to it for decision[5]. If the Tribunal does so, it must specify in its award the issue, or the claim or part of a claim, which is the subject matter of the award[6].

Where an amount awarded or value determined by the Tribunal is dependent upon its decision on a question of law which is in dispute in the proceedings, the Tribunal must ascertain, and state in its decision, any alternative amount or value which it would have awarded or determined if it had come to a different decision on the point of law[7].

The Tribunal's decision on a reference[8] is normally given in writing, together with a statement of its reasons for its decision[9].

The Tribunal must serve a copy of the decision or, where the decision was given orally, an order stating its effect, on every party who has appeared before the Tribunal in the proceedings[10]. The Tribunal has power to correct an award so as to remove any clerical mistake or error arising from an accidental slip or omission or to clarify or remove any ambiguity in the award[11].

1   As to the Upper Tribunal see PARA 720; and ADMINISTRATIVE LAW.
2   Lands Tribunal Rules 1996, SI 1996/1022, r 50(3). The Lands Tribunal was abolished on 1 June 2009 and its functions were transferred to the Upper Tribunal: see PARA 720; and ADMINISTRATIVE LAW.
3   Arbitration Act 1996 s 47(1); applied by the Lands Tribunal Rules, SI 1996/1022, r 32. See ARBITRATION vol 2 (2008) PARA 1258.
4   Arbitration Act 1996 s 47(2)(a); applied by the Lands Tribunal Rules, SI 1996/1022, r 32. See ARBITRATION vol 2 (2008) PARA 1258.
5   Arbitration Act 1996 s 47(2)(b); applied by the Lands Tribunal Rules, SI 1996/1022, r 32. See ARBITRATION vol 2 (2008) PARA 1258.
6   Arbitration Act 1996 s 47(3); applied by the Lands Tribunal Rules, SI 1996/1022, r 32. See ARBITRATION vol 2 (2008) PARA 1258. See also r 50(7) (added by SI 2009/1307).
7   Lands Tribunal Rules 1996, SI 1996/1022, r 50(4).
8   As to the meaning of 'reference' see PARA 724 note 1.
9   Lands Tribunal Rules 1996, r 50(1) (which applies equally to a decision on an appeal or application). The Tribunal may give its decision orally in cases where it is satisfied that no injustice or inconvenience would result to the parties: r 50(2). The Tribunal may not make an award on a basis not relied on by either of the parties: *Aquilina v Havering London Borough Council* (1992) 66 P & CR 39, CA. The statement of reasons will be part of the 'speaking' record for the purposes of any case stated: *R v Northumberland Compensation Appeal Tribunal, ex p Shaw* [1952] 1 KB 338, [1952] 1 All ER 122, CA. In order to be adequate, reasons must not only be intelligible but must also deal with the substantial points which have been raised: *Re Poyser and Mills' Arbitration* [1964] 2 QB 467, [1963] 1 All ER 612. The Tribunal should not regard itself as bound by its earlier decisions on points of law: *West Midland Baptist (Trust) Association (Inc) v Birmingham Corpn* [1968] 2 QB 188, [1968] 1 All ER 205, CA; affd sub nom *Birmingham Corpn v West Midland Baptist (Trust) Association (Inc)* [1970] AC 874, [1969] 3 All ER 172, HL (case concerning the Lands Tribunal).
10 Lands Tribunal Rules 1996, SI 1996/1022, r 50(5) (amended by SI 1997/1965; SI 2009/1307). As to the service of documents see PARA 726 note 3. In the case of an appeal against the decision of a valuation tribunal, a copy must be sent to the clerk of that tribunal and, if the appeal is a rating appeal, to the valuation officer: Lands Tribunal Rules 1996, SI 1996/1022, r 50(5)(a). In the case of any other appeal under Pt III (rr 6–8), a copy must be sent to the authority from whose decision the appeal was brought: r 50(5)(b).
    As to the power of the Upper Tribunal to review its decisions see the Tribunals, Courts and Enforcement Act 2007 s 10; PARA 750; and ADMINISTRATIVE LAW. As to the right to appeal to the Court of Appeal see s 13; PARA 751; and ADMINISTRATIVE LAW. Where a decision of the Upper Tribunal is appealed to the Court of Appeal, and the Court of Appeal directs that the decision should be amended, the registrar must send copies of the amended decision to every person who was notified of the original decision: r 50(6) (amended by SI 2009/1307).
11 See the Arbitration Act 1996 s 57(3)–(7); Lands Tribunal Rules 1996, SI 1996/1022, r 32; and PARA 724 note 11. See further ARBITRATION vol 2 (2008) PARA 1267.

745. Interest on awards. Where statute provides for interest to be payable on awards, the Upper Tribunal (the 'Tribunal')[1] may, if it thinks fit, direct that any sum awarded by it should carry interest from the date of the award at such rate as may from time to time be prescribed[2] by regulations made by the Treasury[3]. If entry has been made before the date of the award, interest on the award will be payable from the date of entry[4].

Subject to an agreement to the contrary between the parties, the Tribunal has jurisdiction also to award interest on the whole or part of any award made in respect of any period up to the date of the award[5].

1　As to the Upper Tribunal see PARA 720; and ADMINISTRATIVE LAW.
2　Ie prescribed by the Land Compensation Act 1961 s 32: see PARA 641 note 6.
3　See the Acquisition of Land (Rate of Interest after Entry) Regulations 1995, SI 1995/2262; and PARA 641 note 6. The Arbitration Act 1996 s 49 (see ARBITRATION vol 2 (2008) PARA 1260) applies to all proceedings as it applies to an arbitration, subject to any enactment that prescribes a rate of interest: Lands Tribunal Rules, SI 1996/1022, r 32(b) (r 32 substituted by SI 1997/1965). Application must be made at the time of the award, and the direction must be embodied in the decision: *Merediths Ltd v LCC (No 2)* (1957) 9 P & CR 258, Lands Tribunal. The Lands Tribunal was abolished on 1 June 2009 and its functions were transferred to the Upper Tribunal: see PARA 720.
　　As to the Treasury see CONSTITUTIONAL LAW AND HUMAN RIGHTS vol 8(2) (Reissue) PARA 512 et seq.
4　See the Lands Clauses Consolidation Act 1845 s 85; the Compulsory Purchase Act 1965 s 11(1), (2), Sch 3 para 3; and PARAS 639, 645.
5　Arbitration Act 1996 s 49(3)(a).

746. Costs. The costs of and incidental to all proceedings in the Upper Tribunal (the 'Tribunal') are in its own discretion[1]. However, where an unconditional offer in writing to pay compensation has been made and the award does not exceed the offer, or a claimant has failed to make his claim in time to allow the acquiring authority[2] to make a proper offer, the Tribunal must, unless for special reasons it thinks it proper not to do so, order the claimant to bear his own costs and pay the authority's costs incurred after the offer was made or, as the case may be, after the time when, in the Tribunal's opinion, the claim should have been made[3]. Where an unconditional offer to accept compensation has been made and the award exceeds the offer, the Tribunal must, unless for special reasons it thinks it proper not to do so, order the acquiring authority to bear its own costs and pay the claimant's costs incurred after the offer was made[4]. The Tribunal may make an award of costs where, under the simplified procedure[5], either: (1) an offer of settlement has been made by a party and the Tribunal considers it appropriate to have regard to the fact that such an offer has been made[6]; or (2) the Tribunal regards the circumstances as exceptional[7]. If, exceptionally, an award of costs is made under the simplified procedure, the amount must not exceed that which would be allowed if the proceedings had been heard in a county court[8].

The registrar[9] may make an order as to costs in respect of any application or proceedings heard by him[10]. Any party dissatisfied with such an order may, within ten days of it, appeal to the Tribunal which may make such order as to the payment of costs, including the costs of the appeal, as it thinks fit[11].

The Tribunal has full power to determine by whom and to what extent the costs are to be paid[12]. It may in any case before it disallow the costs of counsel[13].

1　See the Tribunals, Courts and Enforcement Act 2007 s 29(1); and ADMINISTRATIVE LAW. The Lands Tribunal was abolished on 1 June 2009 and its functions were transferred to the Upper Tribunal: see PARA 720; and ADMINISTRATIVE LAW. The discretion to award costs must be exercised judicially: see *Gray v Lord Ashburton* [1917] AC 26, HL; *Bradshaw v Air Council*

[1926] Ch 329 at 336; *Lloyd del Pacifico v Board of Trade* (1930) 46 TLR 476 at 477; *P Rosen & Co Ltd v Dowley and Selby* [1943] 2 All ER 172; *Wootton v Central Land Board* [1957] 1 All ER 441, [1957] 1 WLR 424, CA; *Church Cottage Investments Ltd v Hillingdon London Borough Council (No 2)* [1991] 2 EGLR 13, CA. Reasons should be given for any departure from the usual rule that costs follow the event: see *Pepys v London Transport Executive* [1975] 1 All ER 748, [1975] 1 WLR 234, CA. Although the normal rule is that the claimant gets his costs, adverse costs may be awarded against a successful claimant who wastes time with unnecessarily complicated submissions: *Purfleet Farms Ltd v Secretary of State for the Transport, Local Government and the Regions* [2002] EWCA Civ 1430, [2003] 1 P & CR 324, [2003] 1 EGLR 9. As to costs when the Court of Appeal re-submits a dispute back to the Tribunal for re-determination see PARA 752.

2   As to the meaning of 'acquiring authority' see PARA 622 note 1.
3   Land Compensation Act 1961 s 4(1), (A1), (2) (s 4(A1) added by SI 2009/1307); and see PARAS 716–717.

     An offer to settle that was open until the first day of trial and withdrawn on the same day was not relevant to the issue of the costs of a re-hearing some years later, which represented a new start to proceedings with newly-prepared points of claim: *Hepworth Building Products Ltd v Coal Authority* [1999] 3 EGLR 99, [1999] 41 EG 157, CA.
4   Land Compensation Act 1961 s 4(3) (see PARA 717). For a case where the award was above both parties' respective sealed offers see *Toye v Kensington and Chelsea Royal London Borough* [1994] 1 EGLR 204, Lands Tribunal.
5   As to the simplified procedure see PARA 737.
6   Lands Tribunal Rules 1996, SI 1996/1022, r 28(11)(a); and see PARA 737 note 17.
7   Lands Tribunal Rules 1996, SI 1996/1022, r 28(11)(b); and see PARA 737 note 17.
8   See the Lands Tribunal Rules 1996, SI 1996/1022, r 28(11); and PARA 737.
9   As to the registrar see PARA 717 note 8.
10   Lands Tribunal Rules 1996, SI 1996/1022, r 52(2).
11   Lands Tribunal Rules 1996, SI 1996/1022, r 52(3) (amended by SI 2009/1307).
12   See the Tribunals, Courts and Enforcement Act 2007 s 29(2); and ADMINISTRATIVE LAW. See *Goldstein v Conley* [2001] EWCA Civ 637, [2002] 1 WLR 281 (where it was held that the Leasehold Reform, Housing and Urban Development Act 1993 s 60(5) (see LANDLORD AND TENANT vol 27(3) (2006 Reissue) PARA 1724) cannot be applied to deprive the Tribunal of its jurisdiction to make an order for the costs of the appeal). As to costs on a reference by a returned absent owner see PARA 718 note 15. Legal and accountancy costs, like surveyors' and valuers' fees, are recoverable as part of the substantive compensation: see *LCC v Tobin* [1959] 1 All ER 649, [1959] 1 WLR 354, CA. For costs awarded against claimants see *Armstrong v Minister of Transport* (1951) 2 P & CR 36, Lands Tribunal; *Fooks v Minister of Supply* (1951) 2 P & CR 102, Lands Tribunal; *Ford v Hartley Wintney RDC* (1951) 2 P & CR 99, Lands Tribunal; *Church Cottage Investments Ltd v Hillingdon London Borough Council (No 2)* [1991] 2 EGLR 13, CA. As to calculation of surveyors' fees see *Truman v Chatham Borough Council* (1974) 28 P & CR 326, Lands Tribunal.

     Where any costs of a litigant in person are ordered to be paid by any other party to the proceedings or in any other way, there may, subject to the Lands Tribunal Rules 1996, SI 1996/1022, be allowed on the assessment, taxation or other determination of those costs sums in respect of any work done, and any expenses and losses incurred, by the litigant in or in connection with the proceedings before the Upper Tribunal to which the order relates: see the Litigants in Person (Costs and Expenses) Act 1975 s 1(1), (4) (amended by the Tribunals, Courts and Enforcement Act 2007 s 48(1), Sch 8 para 6(1), (2), (3)). As to the assessment of costs generally see PARA 747.
13   Land Compensation Act 1961 s 4(4) (amended by SI 2009/1307).

747. Assessment of costs. The Upper Tribunal (the 'Tribunal') has full power to determine by whom and to what extent the costs are to be paid[1]. Thus it may settle the amount of the costs by fixing a lump sum or may direct that costs be assessed by the registrar[2] on such basis as the Tribunal thinks fit, being a basis that would be applied on an assessment of the costs of High Court or county court proceedings[3]. If any party is dissatisfied with the assessment of costs so directed by the Tribunal, he may within seven days of the assessment serve on the registrar and on any other interested party an objection in writing, specifying the items objected to and applying for the assessment to be reviewed in respect of those items[4]. On such an application, the registrar must review the assessment of the items objected to and state in writing the reasons for his decision[5]. Any party dissatisfied with the registrar's decision given on the review may, within ten days of the decision, apply to the Tribunal to review the assessment, and the Tribunal may thereupon make such order as it thinks fit, including an order as to the payment of the costs of the review[6].

1　See the Tribunals, Courts and Enforcement Act 2007 s 29; PARA 746; and ADMINISTRATIVE LAW. As to the Upper Tribunal see PARA 720; and ADMINISTRATIVE LAW.
2　As to the registrar see PARA 717 note 8.
3　Lands Tribunal Rules 1996, SI 1996/1022, r 52(4). The Lands Tribunal was abolished on 1 June 2009 and its functions were transferred to the Upper Tribunal: see PARA 720; and ADMINISTRATIVE LAW.
4　Lands Tribunal Rules 1996, SI 1996/1022, r 52(5). Any application made as to costs is conducted as an interim matter to the extent that the provisions of r 38(8), (10) (see PARA 730) apply: r 52(8). As to interim applications generally see PARA 730.
5　Lands Tribunal Rules 1996, SI 1996/1022, r 52(6).
6　Lands Tribunal Rules 1996, SI 1996/1022, r 52(7) (amended by SI 2009/1307). See also *Tollemache v Richmond Borough Council* (1953) 4 P & CR 144, Lands Tribunal; *Coon v Diamond Tread Co (1938) Ltd* [1950] 2 All ER 385 (read in the light of and qualified by the note on that case in [1956] 1 All ER 609n); *Madurasinghe v Penguin Electronics* [1993] 3 All ER 20, [1993] 1 WLR 989, CA.

748. Recovery of costs. Where the Upper Tribunal[1] orders the claimant to pay the costs, or any part of the costs, of the acquiring authority[2], the acquiring authority may deduct the amount so payable from the compensation payable to the claimant[3]. The right to costs is independent of the conveyance of the land, and a claimant in good faith may recover them, even though he is unable to make a good title[4].

1　As to the Upper Tribunal see PARA 720; and ADMINISTRATIVE LAW.
2　As to the meaning of 'acquiring authority' see PARA 622 note 1. As to costs generally see PARAS 746–747.
3　Land Compensation Act 1961 s 4(5) (amended by SI 2009/1307).
4　*Capell v Great Western Rly Co* (1883) 11 QBD 345, CA. The vendor has no lien in respect of these costs: *Earl of Ferrers v Stafford and Uttoxeter Rly Co* (1872) LR 13 Eq 524. As to lien generally see LIEN.

749. Enforcement of decision. By permission of the High Court, an award of the Upper Tribunal may be enforced in the same manner as a judgment or order[1] and, where permission is given, judgment may be entered in the terms of the award[2]. However, it is unlikely that permission would be given where a question of title was raised. In such circumstances, the appropriate course would be to bring a claim to enforce the award[3].

1　Arbitration Act 1996 s 66(1); applied by the Lands Tribunal Rules 1996, SI 1996/1022, r 32. The Lands Tribunal was abolished on 1 June 2009 and its functions were transferred to the Upper Tribunal: see PARA 720; and ADMINISTRATIVE LAW.
2　Arbitration Act 1996 s 66(2); applied by the Lands Tribunal Rules 1996, SI 1996/1022, r 32. See further ARBITRATION vol 2 (2008) PARA 1274.
3　See ARBITRATION vol 2 (2008) PARA 1274.

(vi) Review of Decisions and Appeal to Court of Appeal

750. Review of decision of Upper Tribunal. The Upper Tribunal (the 'Tribunal')[1] may review a decision made by it on a matter in a case[2] and this power is exercisable (1) of its own initiative; or (2) on application by a person who[3] has a right of appeal in respect of the decision[4]. Where the Tribunal has reviewed a decision, it may, in the light of the review, do any of the following: (a) correct accidental errors in the decision or in a record of the decision; (b) amend reasons given for the decision; (c) set the decision aside (and therefore re-decide the matter concerned)[5].

On receiving an application for permission to appeal[6] the Tribunal may review the decision[7], but may only do so if (i) when making the decision the Tribunal overlooked a legislative provision or binding authority which could have had a material effect on the decision; or (ii) since the Tribunal's decision, a court has made a decision which is binding on the Tribunal and which, had it been made before the Tribunal's decision, could have had a material effect on the decision[8]. The Tribunal must notify the parties in writing of the outcome of any review and of any rights of review or appeal in relation to the outcome[9]. If the Tribunal decides not to review the decision, or reviews the decision and decides to take no action, the Tribunal must consider whether to give permission to appeal[10]. The Tribunal must send a record of its decision to the parties as soon as practicable[11].

1   As to the Upper Tribunal see PARA 720; and ADMINISTRATIVE LAW.
2   Ie other than a decision that is an excluded decision for the purposes of the Tribunals, Courts and Enforcement Act 2007 s 13(1) (but see s 10(7)): s 10(1). A decision of the Upper Tribunal may not be reviewed under s 10(1) more than once: s 10(8). See note 5.
3   Ie for the purposes of the Tribunals, Courts and Enforcement Act 2007 s 13(2).
4   Tribunals, Courts and Enforcement Act 2007 s 10(2).
5   See the Tribunals, Courts and Enforcement Act 2007 s 10(4)–(7). Where under s 10 a decision is set aside and the matter concerned is then re-decided, the decision set aside and the decision made in re-deciding the matter are for the purposes of s 10(8) (see note 2) to be taken to be different decisions: s 10(9).
6   See the Lands Tribunal Rules 1996, SI 1996/1022, r 58; and PARA 751. The Lands Tribunal was abolished on 1 June 2009 and its functions were transferred to the Upper Tribunal: see PARA 720; and ADMINISTRATIVE LAW.
7   Ie in accordance with the Lands Tribunal Rules 1996, SI 1996/1022, r 60(1)–(3) (added by SI 2009/1307).
8   See the Lands Tribunal Rules 1996, SI 1996/1022, r 59(1) (r 59 added by SI 2009/1307).
9   See the Lands Tribunal Rules 1996, SI 1996/1022, r 60(2) (as added: see note 7).
10   See the Lands Tribunal Rules 1996, SI 1996/1022, r 59(2) (as added: see note 8).
11   See the Lands Tribunal Rules 1996, SI 1996/1022, r 59(3)–(5) (as added: see note 8).

751. Procedure on appeal. Any party to a case has a right to appeal to the Court of Appeal on any point of law arising from a decision made by the Upper Tribunal (the 'Tribunal')[1] (other than an excluded decision)[2]. This right may be exercised only with permission[3]. Permission may be given by the Tribunal or the Court of Appeal, on an application by the party[4], but an application may be made to the Court of Appeal only if permission has been refused by the Tribunal[5].

The application for permission to appeal is made by appellant's notice[6]. The appellant must lodge: (1) sufficient copies of his notice for the appeal court and for each of the respondents; (2) one copy of any skeleton argument (which should contain a numbered list of points which both define and confine the areas of controversy[7]); (3) a sealed copy of the order being appealed; (4) any witness statements or affidavits in support of the application; and (5) any other documents that the appellant reasonably considers necessary to enable the court to reach its decision, including a sealed copy of the Tribunal's reasons for the decision[8].

The grounds of appeal should set out clearly the reasons why (in the appellant's opinion) the appeal should be allowed[9].

The documents relevant to proceedings in the Court of Appeal must be filed in the Civil Appeals Office Registry, but the parties must serve the documents[10]. Service on the respondent takes place as soon as practicable after filing[11], although the respondent need take no action until such time as permission has been given[12].

1   As to the Upper Tribunal see PARA 720; and ADMINISTRATIVE LAW.
2   See the Tribunals, Courts and Enforcement Act 2007 s 13(1), (2); and ADMINISTRATIVE LAW. As to excluded decisions see s 13(8)–(10).
3   See the Tribunals, Courts and Enforcement Act 2007 s 13(3).
4   Tribunals, Courts and Enforcement Act 2007 s 13(4).
5   Tribunals, Courts and Enforcement Act 2007 s 13(5). The Lord Chancellor may make provision for permission not to be granted unless the Upper Tribunal or the Court of Appeal considers (1) that the proposed appeal would raise some important point of principle or practice; or (2) that there is some other compelling reason for the Court of Appeal to hear the appeal: see s 13(6), (7); and ADMINISTRATIVE LAW.
6   CPR 52.4(1). See also the Lands Tribunal Rules 1996, SI 1996/1022, r 58 (added by SI 2009/1307) (application for permission to appeal). The appellant must file the appellant's notice at the Court of Appeal within 28 days after the date of the Tribunal's decision: *Practice Direction—Appeals* PD52 para 21.9. The Tribunal's decision takes effect for this purpose on the day on which it is given unless the decision states otherwise; and usually the decision will state that it will take effect when, and not before, the issue of costs has been determined: Lands Tribunal Practice Directions (2006) para 23.1. The Lands Tribunal was abolished on 1 June 2009 and its functions were transferred to the Upper Tribunal: see PARA 720.
7   *Practice Direction—Appeals* PD52 para 5.10.
8   *Practice Direction—Appeals* PD52 para 5.6.
9   *Practice Direction—Appeals* PD52 para 3.2. The appeal court will allow an appeal where the decision of the Tribunal was wrong on a matter of law: CPR 52.11(3)(a).
10 *Practice Direction—Appeals* PD52 para 15.1.
11 CPR 52.4(3).
12 *Practice Direction—Appeals* PD52 para 5.21–5.22. The respondent need not be given notice of the permission hearing unless the court so directs: *Practice Direction—Appeals* PD52 para 4.15. See also *Practice Direction—Appeals* PD52 para 17.5. Service must be in accordance with CPR 52.4(3) (see the text to note 11).

752.   Powers of the Court of Appeal.   The Court of Appeal has power to affirm, set aside or vary any order or judgment given, and to refer back any claim or issue for determination[1]. If the Court of Appeal directs that any decision of the Upper Tribunal[2] which has been appealed to the Court of Appeal should be amended, the registrar[3] must send copies of the amended decision to every person who was notified of the original decision[4].

1   CPR 52.10(2).
2   As to the Upper Tribunal see PARA 720; and ADMINISTRATIVE LAW.
3   As to the registrar see PARA 717 note 8.
4   Lands Tribunal Rules 1996, SI 1996/1022, r 50(6) (amended by SI 2009/1307). See *Barclays Bank plc v Kent County Council* (1997) 76 P & CR 1, sub nom *Kent County Council v Barclays Bank plc* [1998] RVR 74, CA (where it was held that where the Court of Appeal re-submitted the whole substance of a dispute back to the Lands Tribunal for re-determination, the issue of costs was impliedly also referred back for re-determination; the only effective award for costs was the later award, incorporating the whole period of litigation, and that carried with it the right to interest on costs at the re-determined level). The Lands Tribunal was abolished on 1 June 2009 and its functions were transferred to the Upper Tribunal: see PARA 720.

5. ASSESSMENT OF PURCHASE MONEY OR COMPENSATION

(1) AMOUNT OF COMPENSATION

753. Amount of compensation. The owner whose land is compulsorily acquired is entitled to compensation no less than the loss imposed on him but on the other hand no greater[1], since the purpose of compensation is to provide fair compensation for a claimant whose land has been compulsorily taken from him. This is sometimes described as the principle of equivalence[2]. Compensation or purchase money[3] is assessed upon the basis of the value of the land to the owner[4] and in addition the owner is entitled to compensation for disturbance[5], for severance of his retained land[6] or for other injurious affection[7].

1   *Horn v Sunderland Corpn* [1941] 2 KB 26 at 42, [1941] 1 All ER 480 at 491, CA. See also *Scout Association Trust Corpn v Secretary of State for the Environment* [2005] EWCA Civ 980, [2005] STC 1808 (whether reasonable cost of equivalent reinstatement included VAT paid; Commissioners of Revenue and Customs claimed that VAT should not have been repaid to the claimant but assured they would not seek to recover repayments).
2   *Director of Buildings and Lands v Shun Fung Ironworks Ltd* [1995] 2 AC 111 at 125, [1995] 1 All ER 846 at 852, PC, per Lord Nicholls.
3   Compensation and purchase money are the same thing under different names: see *IRC v Glasgow and South Western Rly Co* (1887) 12 App Cas 315, HL.
4   See PARA 761 et seq. See also *Corrie v MacDermott* [1914] AC 1056, PC; *Cedar Rapids Manufacturing and Power Co v Lacoste* [1914] AC 569, PC; *Fraser v City of Fraserville* [1917] AC 187, PC; *Pastoral Finance Association Ltd v The Minister* [1914] AC 1083, PC; *IRC v Glasgow and South Western Rly Co* (1887) 12 App Cas 315 at 320, HL.
5   See PARA 814 et seq.
6   See PARA 810 et seq.
7   See PARAS 811, 877 et seq.

754. The alternative bases. The owner is entitled to the amount which the land[1] if sold in the open market by a willing seller might be expected to realise[2], no allowance being made on account of the acquisition being compulsory[3] and subject to specific assumptions as to the valuation[4]. As an alternative, however, where the land is, and but for the compulsory acquisition would continue to be, devoted to a purpose of such a nature that there is no general demand or market for land for that purpose, the compensation may, if the Upper Tribunal is satisfied that reinstatement in some other place is bona fide intended, be assessed on the basis of the reasonable cost of equivalent reinstatement[5].

1   As to the meaning of 'land' see PARA 516 note 2.
2   Land Compensation Act 1961 s 5 r 2. In the absence of a market, there will be no compensation: *Thomas's Executors v Merthyr Tydfil County Borough Council* (26 February 2003, unreported), Lands Tribunal. This does not, however, affect the assessment of compensation for disturbance (see PARA 814 et seq) or any other matter not directly based on the value of the land: Land Compensation Act 1961 s 5 r 6. See *Ryde International plc v London Regional Transport* [2004] EWCA Civ 232, [2004] RVR 60.
3   Land Compensation Act 1961 s 5 r 1.
4   See PARA 761 et seq. See also *Windward Properties Ltd v Government of Saint Vincent and the Grenadines* [1996] 1 WLR 279, [1996] RVR 190, PC (where the owner had only recently purchased land, which was now subject to compulsory acquisition under the law of Saint Vincent and the Grenadines, the court was entitled to conclude, in the absence of acceptable evidence to the contrary, that the transaction had been entered into at arm's length in the normal course of the market, and that the actual price paid is the best evidence of its value, to be weighed with any other evidence).
5   Land Compensation Act 1961 s 5 r 5 (amended by SI 2009/1307). See PARA 800. As to the Upper Tribunal see PARA 720; and ADMINISTRATIVE LAW.

(2) DATE FOR ASSESSMENT OF COMPENSATION FOR LAND TAKEN

755. The date for assessment. For the value of land to be assessed[1], the valuation must be made as at the relevant valuation date[2]. If the land is the subject of a notice to treat[3], the relevant valuation date is the earlier of: (1) the date when the acquiring authority enters on and takes possession of the land[4]; and (2) the date when the assessment is made[5]. If the land is the subject of a general vesting declaration[6], the relevant valuation date is the earlier of: (a) the vesting date; and (b) the date when the assessment is made[7].

No adjustment is to be made to the valuation in respect of anything which happens after the relevant valuation date[8].

An assessment by the Upper Tribunal (the 'Tribunal') is treated as being made on the date certified by the Tribunal as the last hearing date before it makes its determination, or in a case to be determined without an oral hearing, the last date for making written submissions before it makes its determination[9].

Nothing in the provisions described above affects any express provision in any other enactment which requires the valuation of land subject to compulsory acquisition to be made at a particular date; nor does it affect the valuation of land for purposes other than the compulsory acquisition of that land[10].

1 Ie where land is to be assessed in accordance with the Land Compensation Act 1961 s 5 r 2: see PARA 754.

2 Land Compensation Act 1961 s 5A(1) (s 5A added by the Planning and Compulsory Purchase Act 2004 s 103).

3 As to the notice to treat see PARA 616 et seq.

4 Land Compensation Act 1961 s 5A(3)(a) (as added: see note 2). As to the meaning of 'acquiring authority' see PARA 622 note 1. If the acquiring authority enters on and takes possession of part of the land (1) specified in a notice of entry under the Compulsory Purchase Act 1965 s 11(1) (see PARA 645); or (2) in respect of which a payment into court under Sch 3 or under the Lands Clauses Consolidation Act 1845 s 85 has been made, the authority is deemed, for the purposes of s 5A(3)(a), to have entered on and taken possession of the whole of that land on that date: s 5A(5), (9) (as so added). Section 5A(5) also applies for the purposes of calculating interest under the Compulsory Purchase Act 1965 s 11(1) (see PARA 645), Sch 3 para 3 (see PARA 639); the Lands Clauses Consolidation Act 1845 s 85 (see PARA 639); the Land Compensation Act 1973 s 52A (see PARA 657), and references there to the date or time of entry are to be construed accordingly: Land Compensation Act 1961 s 5A(6) (as so added). See *Birmingham Corpn v West Midland Baptist (Trust) Association (Inc)* [1970] AC 874, [1969] 3 All ER 172, HL; *Miller & Partners Ltd v Edinburgh Corpn* 1978 SC 1, Ct of Sess; *Washington Development Corpn v Bamlings (Washington) Ltd* (1984) 52 P & CR 267, [1985] 1 EGLR 16, CA. See also *Birmingham Corpn v West Midland Baptist (Trust) Association (Inc)* [1970] AC 874, [1969] 3 All ER 172, HL; *Zoar Independent Church Trustees v Rochester Corpn* [1975] QB 246 at 255, [1974] 3 All ER 5 at 12, CA, per Buckley LJ.

5 Land Compensation Act 1961 s 5A(3)(b) (as added: see note 2).

6 As to the meaning of 'general vesting declaration' see PARA 686 note 4.

7 Land Compensation Act 1961 s 5A(4) (as added: see note 2). As to the meaning of 'vesting date' see PARA 687.

8 Land Compensation Act 1961 s 5A(2) (as added: see note 2).

9 Land Compensation Act 1961 s 5A(7) (as added (see note 2); amended by SI 2009/1307). See *W & S (Long Eaton) Ltd v Derbyshire County Council* (1975) 31 P & CR 99, CA. See also *C & J Seymour (Investments) Ltd v Lewes District Council* [1992] 1 EGLR 237, Lands Tribunal; *Hoveringham Gravels Ltd v Chiltern District Council* (1978) 39 P & CR 414, Lands Tribunal. The Lands Tribunal was abolished on 1 June 2009 and its functions were transferred to the Upper Tribunal: see PARA 720.

10 Land Compensation Act 1961 s 5A(8) (as added: see note 2). This applies even if the valuation is to be made in accordance with the rules in s 5: see s 5A(8) (as so added).

756.   Time for ascertaining the interest acquired. The usual principle is that the nature of the claimant's interest is to be ascertained at the time of (or immediately before or immediately after) the service of the notice to treat[1]. Regard has, however, been had in some circumstances to events occurring after service of the notice to treat which affect the nature of the claimant's interest; for instance, where a lease which subsists at the date of the notice to treat expires before possession is taken and the claim for compensation is made, regard will be had to the fact that the claimant tenant has had the beneficial use of the leasehold land and no land has in fact been compulsorily acquired[2].

1   *Rugby Joint Water Board v Foottit, Rugby Joint Water Board v Shaw-Fox* [1973] AC 202 at 216, [1972] 1 All ER 1057 at 1064, HL, per Lord Pearson; *Penny v Penny* (1867) LR 5 Eq 227; *Re Morgan and London and North Western Rly Co* [1896] 2 QB 469; *Re Rowton Houses Ltd's Leases, Square Grip Reinforcement Co (London) Ltd v Rowton Houses Ltd* [1967] Ch 877, [1966] 3 All ER 996. See also *Lyle v Bexley London Borough Council* [1972] RVR 318, Lands Tribunal; *Runcorn Association Football Club v Warrington and Runcorn Development Corpn* (1982) 45 P & CR 183, Lands Tribunal.

2   *Holloway v Dover Corpn* [1960] 2 All ER 193, [1960] 1 WLR 604, CA; see also *R v Kennedy* [1893] 1 QB 533; *Soper and Soper v Doncaster Corpn* (1964) 16 P & CR 53, Lands Tribunal; *Banham v London Borough of Hackney* (1970) 22 P & CR 922, Lands Tribunal; *Bradford Property Trust Ltd v Hertfordshire County Council* (1973) 27 P & CR 228, Lands Tribunal; *Midland Bank Trust Co Ltd (Executors) v London Borough of Lewisham* (1975) 30 P & CR 268, Lands Tribunal.

(3)   THE LAND AND BUILDINGS TO BE VALUED

(i)   Intrinsic Quality and Circumstances of Land and Buildings

757.   Intrinsic quality and circumstances to be considered unless excluded. Every intrinsic quality of the land and buildings and every intrinsic circumstance must be taken into consideration[1], except so far as any statute requires the buildings or uses to be excluded[2].

The land may be fertile or infertile, cultivated or neglected, and with or without adequate buildings in a proper state of repair or an adequate water supply. It may be crossed by a footpath or liable to flooding, but on the other hand it may be otherwise protected from the hazards of nature, and may have views sufficiently ensured[3].

1   *Robinson Bros (Brewers) Ltd v Houghton and Chester-le-Street Assessment Committee* [1937] 2 KB 445 at 469, [1937] 2 All ER 298 at 307, CA; affd sub nom *Robinson Bros (Brewers) Ltd v Durham County Assessment Committee (Area No 7)* [1938] AC 321, sub nom *Robinson Bros (Brewers) Ltd v Houghton and Chester-le-Street Assessment Committee* [1938] 2 All ER 79, HL. 'No one can suppose, in the case of land which is certain, or even likely, to be used in the immediate or reasonably near future for building purposes but which at the valuation date is waste land, or is being used for agricultural purposes, that the owner, however willing a vendor, will be content to sell the land for its value as waste or agricultural land, as the case may be. It is plain that in ascertaining its value the possibility of its being used for building purposes would have to be taken into account': *Vyricherla Narayana Gajapatiraju Bahadur Garu v Revenue Divisional Officer, Vizagapatam* [1939] AC 302 at 313, [1939] 2 All ER 317 at 322, PC.

2   See PARAS 759–760.

3   Where land has a potential or development value some of the advantages and disadvantages would be ignored and others would become important; however, increases (or decreases) in value on account of the acquisition being compulsory must be ignored: see the Land Compensation Act 1961 s 5 r 1; and PARA 754.

758.   Circumstances affecting quality of the land. On a purchase of licensed premises the owner is entitled to a purchase price as of licensed premises[1];

nevertheless, the purchaser does not purchase the existing licence, although the right or chance of obtaining a similar licence would belong to him[2]. The value of the goodwill of licensed premises is included in the value of the land as licensed premises[3]. In valuing the interest of a lessor the probability of the continuance of the premises as licensed premises must be regarded[4] and, if the house is a tied house, the lessor will be entitled to a payment based on the benefit derived from the tying covenant[5].

The land may be fronting a highway maintainable at the public expense or fronting a private street and liable to street works charges[6] or be with or without services in respect of sewers, water, electricity and gas.

1   *Tadcaster Tower Brewery Co v Wilson* [1897] 1 Ch 705; *Belton v LCC* (1893) 68 LT 411.
2   *Earl Fitzwilliam v IRC* [1914] AC 753 at 757, HL.
3   *Re Kitchin, ex p Punnett* (1880) 16 ChD 226 at 233, CA (ie the goodwill so called arising from the establishment and existence of the business and its situation).
4   *Belton v LCC* (1893) 68 LT 411.
5   *Bourne v Liverpool Corpn* (1863) 33 LJQB 15; *Re Chandler's Wiltshire Brewery Co Ltd and LCC* [1903] 1 KB 569; *Re LCC and City of London Brewery Co* [1898] 1 QB 387. As to tied house covenants see LANDLORD AND TENANT vol 27(1) (2006 Reissue) PARA 546.
6   See HIGHWAYS, STREETS AND BRIDGES. As to market value as affected by development on adjoining land see PARA 787 et seq.

(ii) Works on or Uses of Land to be Disregarded

759.   Works executed with view to compensation.   It has been held that works by the owner of the land altering the land after the notice to treat so as to increase the acquiring authority's burden with respect to the payment of purchase money or compensation must be disregarded[1]. The Upper Tribunal[2] may not take into account any enhancement of the value of any interest in land by reason of any building erected, work done or improvement or alteration made, whether on the land purchased or on any other land[3] with which the claimant is, or was at the time of the erection, doing or making of the building, works, improvement or alteration, directly or indirectly concerned, if it is satisfied that the erection of the building, the doing of the work, the making of the improvement or the alteration, as the case may be, was not reasonably necessary and was undertaken with a view to obtaining compensation or increased compensation[4]. Works carried out after service of the notice to treat may, if they go beyond what is necessary for the owner's continued enjoyment of the land and add to the burden on the acquiring authority, be disregarded in the assessment of compensation[5].

1   See PARA 632.
2   As to the Upper Tribunal see PARA 720; and ADMINISTRATIVE LAW.
3   This provision will therefore affect compensation for severance or other injurious affection of land not taken: see PARA 810.
4   See the Acquisition of Land Act 1981 s 4(2) (amended by SI 2009/1307) (where that Act applies: see PARA 556); and PARA 632.
5   *Cardiff Corpn v Cook* [1923] 2 Ch 115; cf *City of Glasgow Union Rly Co v James McEwen & Co* (1870) 8 M 747.

760.   Uses or works contrary to law.   Where the value of the land[1] is increased by reason of the use of the land or of any premises on it in a manner which could be restrained by any court or is contrary to law[2], or is detrimental to the health of the occupants of the premises or to the public health, the amount of that increase is not to be taken into account in assessing compensation in respect of compulsory acquisition[3]. However, there is no express statutory provision making buildings or works contrary to law liable to proceedings for their demolition or removal[4].

1   As to the meaning of 'land' see PARA 516 note 2.
2   Evidence of legal proceedings in respect of the use, or the possibility of legal proceedings, may be received: cf *Higham v Havant and Waterloo UDC* [1951] 2 KB 527, [1951] 2 All ER 178n, CA.
3   Land Compensation Act 1961 s 5 r 4. See *Hall v Sandwell Metropolitan Borough Council* [2008] RVR 345, Lands Tribunal. As to uses contrary to planning law see TOWN AND COUNTRY PLANNING. As to uses which are a nuisance see NUISANCE. There is no longer a distinction between a use which could not be enforced against (though it was unlawful) and a use which, though not permitted, was not unlawful: see the Town and Country Planning Act 1990 ss 191, 192; and TOWN AND COUNTRY PLANNING vol 46(2) (Reissue) PARAS 586–587. Accordingly the distinction relied on in *Hughes v Doncaster Metropolitan Borough Council* [1991] 1 AC 382, [1991] 1 All ER 295, HL, would no longer appear to be good law.
4   Any purchaser in the market would nevertheless take these matters into account. Buildings may, inter alia, be contrary to planning control (see *Handoll v Warner Goodman and Streat* (1994) 70 P & CR 627, [1995] 1 EGLR 173, CA; and TOWN AND COUNTRY PLANNING vol 46(2) (Reissue) PARA 583) or contrary to building regulations (see BUILDING vol 4(2) (2002 Reissue) PARA 306 et seq).

(4) POTENTIAL USE OF LAND TO BE CONSIDERED

(i) In general

761. The general rule. The owner of land is entitled to its value to him; this comprises all the advantages, present and future, which the land possesses[1]. Nevertheless, it is only the present value of these advantages which fall to be considered, and not the advantages as realised in the hands of the acquiring authority, and there must be disregarded any increase in value due to the scheme underlying the acquisition[2]; although if the land is suitable for some purpose, that purpose is not excluded merely because the authority intends to apply the land to it[3].

If the owner holds the land subject to restrictions in his hands, they must be taken into account[4], but the possibility of the restrictions being discharged must also be kept in view[5]. Examples of restrictions are planning restrictions[6], restrictive covenants[7], and the restrictions which attach to an open space held for amenity[8] or which attach to ecclesiastical land[9].

The general right to the potential value is not limited to that value at the date of the notice to treat but applies at the date of entry or time of valuation[10]; nor is it restricted by assumed permission at the date of the notice to treat except to a limited extent by a certificate of appropriate alternative development[11].

1   *Cedar Rapids Manufacturing and Power Co v Lacoste* [1914] AC 569 at 576, PC; *Re Lucas and Chesterfield Gas and Water Board* [1909] 1 KB 16, CA; *Fraser v City of Fraserville* [1917] AC 187 at 194, PC; and see *R v Brown* (1867) LR 2 QB 630 (value of agricultural land as building land); *Ripley v Great Northern Rly Co* (1875) 10 Ch App 435 (land near a reservoir suitable for cotton mills); *Brown v Railways Comr* (1890) 15 App Cas 240, PC (land suitable for mining); *Bailey v Isle of Thanet Light Rlys Co* [1900] 1 QB 722 (land bought and held by owner for intended school). In *Birmingham District Council v Morris and Jacombs Ltd* (1976) 33 P & CR 27, CA, a strip of land was compulsorily acquired that had been specifically conditioned as an access in a planning permission; compensation was assessed solely on access and not on residential value. These cases must, however, be read subject to restrictions on use but subject to the possibility of removal of those restrictions: see the text and notes 4–5. They must also be read subject to the exclusion from market value of a purchaser for a purpose only attainable by statutory powers or for which there is no market apart from the special needs of a particular purchaser or the requirements of any authority possessing compulsory purchase powers as provided by the Land Compensation Act 1961 s 5 r 3: see PARA 789. In summary, an owner

whose land is acquired compulsorily is entitled to the higher of: (1) its potential value (on the assumption that the present use is abandoned); or (2) its existing use value (together with any relevant compensation for disturbance), but not to both.

2   *Stebbing v Metropolitan Board of Works* (1870) LR 6 QB 37; *IRC v Glasgow and South-Western Rly Co* (1887) 12 App Cas 315, HL; *Cedar Rapids Manufacturing and Power Co v Lacoste* [1914] AC 569 at 576, PC; *Penny v Penny* (1867) LR 5 Eq 227; *Re Lucas and Chesterfield Gas and Water Board* [1909] 1 KB 16, CA; *Re Gough and Aspatria, Silloth and District Joint Water Board* [1904] 1 KB 417 at 423, CA. Since the assessment of compensation is on the same basis as at common law, it would be contrary to public policy to deduct from it the value of eg a regional development grant which was paid under a different statutory code and with different objectives: *Palatine Graphic Arts Co Ltd v Liverpool City Council* [1986] QB 335, [1986] 1 All ER 366, CA; cf *A & B Taxis Ltd v Secretary of State for Air* [1922] 2 KB 328, CA. See also the cases cited in PARA 787 note 1. See also the reservations set out in note 1 above.

3   *Re Riddell and Newcastle and Gateshead Water Co* (1878) Browne and Allan's Law of Compensation (2nd Edn) 672, 90 LT 44n, CA; *Re Countess Ossalinsky and Manchester Corpn* (1883) Browne and Allan's Law of Compensation (2nd Edn) 659, DC; *Re Gough and Aspatria, Silloth and District Joint Water Board* [1904] 1 KB 417, CA; *Cedar Rapids Manufacturing and Power Co v Lacoste* [1914] AC 569 at 579–580, PC; *Trent-Stoughton v Barbados Water Supply Co Ltd* [1893] AC 502, PC; *Re Lucas and Chesterfield Gas and Water Board* [1909] 1 KB 16 at 26, 31, CA. See also the reservations set out in note 1 above.

4   *Corrie v MacDermott* [1914] AC 1056 at 1062, PC.

5   *Corrie v MacDermott* [1914] AC 1056 at 1063–1064, PC; and see *City and South London Rly Co v United Parishes of St Mary, Woolnoth and St Mary, Woolchurch Haw* [1905] AC 1, HL, where, in assessing the value of the subsoil of a church, the fact that the land might be made available for building purposes by an Order in Council under the Union of Benefices Act 1860 (repealed) was held to be rightly taken into account. As to the valuation of a church see also *Hilcoat v Archbishops of Canterbury and York* (1850) 19 LJCP 376; and as to the valuation of a burial ground see *Stebbing v Metropolitan Board of Works* (1870) LR 6 QB 37, considered in *Corrie v MacDermott*. However, such properties will be subject to reinstatement value if there is a genuine intention to reinstate. See also the reservations set out in note 1 above.

6   See PARA 762; and *Birmingham District Council v Morris and Jacombs Ltd* (1976) 33 P & CR 27, CA.

7   As to the possibility of removal or discharge of a restrictive covenant see the Law of Property Act 1925 s 84; and EQUITY. See also *Re Abbey Homesteads (Developments) Ltd's Application, Abbey Homesteads (Developments) Ltd v Northamptonshire County Council* (1986) 53 P & CR 1, [1986] 1 EGLR 24, CA; *Abbey Homesteads (Developments) Ltd v Northamptonshire County Council* (1992) 64 P & CR 377, [1992] 2 EGLR 18, CA (effect on compensation). It has been held that private rights restricting the use of the land that is to be acquired compulsorily cannot be enforced in the courts because Parliament has provided an exclusive remedy by way of statutory compensation, which extends to injurious affection resulting from the use of the land for the statutory purposes: *Brown v Heathlands Mental Health National Health Service Trust* [1996] 1 All ER 133.

8   See *Re Edinburgh Corpn and North British Rly* (unreported arbitration), cited in *Corrie v MacDermott* [1914] AC 1056 at 1064, PC; but see now PARA 800 (reinstatement value).

9   See note 5.

10 See PARAS 635, 755–756.

11 See PARA 762.

762. Actual, possible and assumed planning permission. The enjoyment of the potentialities of land is restricted by the requirement of planning permission[1] for the carrying out of development[2]. The restriction may be removed by actual planning permission at the date of service of the notice to treat or by a permission assumed by statute[3]; and any planning permission which is to be assumed in accordance with the relevant statutory provisions is in addition to any planning permission which may be in force at the date of the service of the notice to treat[4].

The planning permissions which are to be assumed in relation to the relevant land[5] or any part of it in ascertaining the value of the interest in the land for the purpose of assessing compensation in respect of any compulsory acquisition are such one or more of the following as are applicable to that land[6]:

(1)   an assumption of permission such as would permit development in accordance with the acquiring authority's proposals[7];

(2)   an assumption of permission for development[8] included in the existing use of land[9];

(3)   an assumption of permission for development defined or shown in a development plan[10]; and

(4)   an assumption of permission for development certified by a planning authority as permission that would have been granted[11].

The provisions for the statutory assumption of planning permission must not, however, be construed as requiring it to be assumed that planning permission would necessarily be refused for any development which is not development for which the granting of planning permission is to be assumed[12]; but in determining whether planning permission for any development could in any particular circumstances reasonably have been expected to be granted in respect of any land, regard must be had to any contrary opinion expressed in relation to that land in any certificate[13] of appropriate alternative development[14].

1   'Planning permission' means permission under the Town and Country Planning Act 1990 Pt III (ss 55–106B) (see TOWN AND COUNTRY PLANNING): Land Compensation Act 1961 s 39(1); Planning (Consequential Provisions) Act 1990 s 2(4). Whilst development potential must in some circumstances be assumed for the purpose of valuation, it does not follow that any relevant planning permission will automatically enhance the value of the land in the absence of demand: see *Bromilow v Greater Manchester Council* (1974) 29 P & CR 517, Lands Tribunal (affd (1975) 31 P & CR 398, CA); *Davy Ltd v London Borough of Hammersmith* (1975) 30 P & CR 469, Lands Tribunal.

2   'Development' has the meaning assigned to it by the Town and Country Planning Act 1990 s 55 (see TOWN AND COUNTRY PLANNING vol 46(1) (Reissue) PARA 217): Land Compensation Act 1961 s 39(1); Planning (Consequential Provisions) Act 1990 s 2(4).

3   For the statutory assumptions see the Land Compensation Act 1961 ss 15, 16; and PARA 765 et seq.

4   Land Compensation Act 1961 s 14(2). This applies also where a notice to treat is deemed to have been served: see s 39(8). As to the time of the valuation see PARA 635; and as to the notice to treat see PARA 616 et seq. As to the meaning of 'notice to treat' see PARA 636 note 4. For these purposes, and for the purpose of any reference in s 15 to planning permission which is in force on the date of service of the notice to treat, it is immaterial whether the planning permission was granted: (1) unconditionally or subject to conditions; or (2) in respect of the land in question taken by itself or in respect of an area including that land; or (3) on an ordinary application or on an outline application or by virtue of a development order, or is planning permission which, in accordance with any direction or provision given or made by or under any enactment, is deemed to have been granted: s 14(4). 'Development order' means an order under the Town and Country Planning Act 1990 s 59(1) (see TOWN AND COUNTRY PLANNING vol 46(1) (Reissue) PARA 252): Land Compensation Act 1961 s 39(1); Planning (Consequential Provisions) Act 1990 s 2(4). See the Town and Country Planning (General Permitted Development) Order 1995, SI 1995/418; the Town and Country Planning (General Development Procedure) Order 1995, SI 1995/419; and TOWN AND COUNTRY PLANNING. 'Outline application' means an application for planning permission subject to subsequent approval on any matters: Land Compensation Act 1961 s 39(1). As to the meaning of 'enactment' see PARA 501 note 3.

5   As to the meaning of 'land' see PARA 516 note 2. 'Relevant land' means the land in which the relevant interest (ie the interest acquired in pursuance of the notice to treat: see PARA 636 note 4) subsists: Land Compensation Act 1961 s 39(2).

6   Land Compensation Act 1961 s 14(1) (amended by the Planning and Compensation Act 1991 s 70, Sch 15 para 15(1)). See *Greenweb Ltd v Wandsworth London Borough Council* [2008] EWCA Civ 910, [2009] 1 WLR 612, [2008] RVR 294.

7   See the Land Compensation Act 1961 s 15(1), (2); and PARA 764.

8   Ie development of a class specified in the Town and Country Planning Act 1990 s 107(4), Sch 3 para 1 (subject to the condition set out in s 111(5), Sch 10 (see TOWN AND COUNTRY PLANNING vol 46(2) (Reissue) PARAS 918, 921)) and in Sch 3 para 2 (see TOWN AND COUNTRY PLANNING

vol 46(2) (Reissue) PARA 920): Land Compensation Act 1961 s 15(3) (substituted by the
Planning and Compensation Act 1991 s 31(4), Sch 6 para 1(1)(a)).
9 See the Land Compensation Act 1961 s 15(3), (4); and PARA 765.
10 See the Land Compensation Act 1961 s 16; and PARAS 766–770. As to development plans see
TOWN AND COUNTRY PLANNING vol 46(1) (Reissue) PARA 91 et seq.
11 See the Land Compensation Act 1961 ss 15(5), 17–22; and PARAS 771–778.

12 Land Compensation Act 1961 s 14(3) (amended by the Planning and Compensation Act 1991
Sch 15 para 15(2)).
13 Ie any certificate issued under the Land Compensation Act 1961 Pt III (ss 17–22): see PARA 771
et seq.
14 Land Compensation Act 1961 s 14(3A)(a) (added by the Planning and Compensation Act 1991
Sch 15 para 15(2)).

763. Statutory assumption where land required for highway use. If a
determination mentioned in heads (a) and (b) below falls to be made in a case
where: (1) the relevant land[1] is to be acquired for use for or in connection with
the construction of a highway[2]; or (2) the use of the relevant land for or in
connection with such construction is being considered by a highway authority,
that determination must be made on the assumption that, if the relevant land
were not so used, no highway would be constructed to meet the same or
substantially the same need as that highway would have been constructed to
meet[3]. The determinations which must be made on this assumption are:

(a) a determination, for the purpose of assessing compensation in respect of
any compulsory acquisition, whether planning permission[4] might
reasonably be expected to be granted for any development[5] if no part of
the relevant land were proposed to be acquired by an authority
possessing compulsory purchase powers[6]; and

(b) a determination[7] as to the development for which, in the opinion of the
local planning authority[8], planning permission would or would not have
been granted if no part of the relevant land were proposed to be
acquired by any authority possessing such powers[9].

1 As to the meaning of 'relevant land' see PARA 762 note 5. As to the meaning of 'land' see PARA
516 note 2.
2 For these purposes, references to the construction of a highway include references to its
alteration or improvement: Land Compensation Act 1961 s 14(8) (s 14(5)–(8) added by the
Planning and Compensation Act 1991 s 64).
3 Land Compensation Act 1961 s 14(5), (6) (as added: see note 2).
4 As to the meaning of 'planning permission' see PARA 762 note 1.
5 As to the meaning of 'development' see PARA 762 note 2.
6 Land Compensation Act 1961 s 14(7)(a) (as added: see note 2). 'Authority possessing
compulsory purchase powers', where it occurs in the Land Compensation Act 1961 otherwise
than in relation to a transaction, means any person or body of persons who could be or have
been authorised to acquire an interest in land compulsorily, and, in relation to any transaction,
means any person or body of persons who could be or have been so authorised for the purposes
for which the transaction is or was effected, or a parish council, community council or parish
meeting on whose behalf a district council, county council or county borough council could be
or have been so authorised: s 39(1) (definition amended by the Local Government (Wales)
Act 1994 s 66(6), Sch 16 para 17; and SI 1976/315). As to areas and authorities in England and
Wales see LOCAL GOVERNMENT vol 69 (2009) PARA 22 et seq.
7 Ie under the Land Compensation Act 1961 s 17: see PARA 772.
8 'Local planning authority' is to be construed in accordance with the Town and Country
Planning Act 1990 Pt I (ss 1–9) (see TOWN AND COUNTRY PLANNING): Land Compensation
Act 1961 s 39(1); Planning (Consequential Provisions) Act 1990 s 2(4) (definition substituted by
the Environment Act 1995 s 78, Sch 10 para 4(2)).
9 Land Compensation Act 1961 s 14(7)(b) (as added: see note 2).

(ii) Assumed Permission for Development in accordance with Acquiring Authority's Proposals

764. Where at the date of the notice to treat there is no permission already in force. In a case where the relevant interest[1] to be acquired in pursuance of the notice to treat[2] is to be acquired for purposes which involve the carrying out of the acquiring authority's[3] proposals for development[4] of the relevant land or any part of it[5], and on the date of service of the notice to treat there is not in force planning permission[6] for that development which will enure, while it is in force, for the benefit of the land and all persons interested in it[7], then it must be assumed that[8] planning permission would be granted, in respect of that land or that part of it, such as would permit its development in accordance with the authority's proposals[9].

This assumed permission is in addition to any planning permission which may be in force at the date of the service of the notice to treat[10].

1 As to the meaning of 'relevant interest' see PARA 636 note 4.
2 As to the notice to treat see PARA 616 et seq. As to the meaning of 'notice to treat' see PARA 636 note 4.
3 As to the meaning of 'acquiring authority' see PARA 622 note 1.
4 As to the meaning of 'development' see PARA 762 note 2.
5 Land Compensation Act 1961 s 15(1)(a). As to the meaning of 'land' see PARA 516 note 2. As to the meaning of 'relevant land' see PARA 762 note 5.
6 As to the meaning of 'planning permission' for this purpose see PARA 762 note 4; and as to the meaning of 'planning permission' generally see PARA 762 note 1.
7 Land Compensation Act 1961 s 15(1)(b), (2).
8 The Land Compensation Act 1961 is drafted as 'It shall be assumed that ...'. There is no ambiguity in the word 'shall', or in the phrase 'it shall be assumed that ...' The assumption is mandatory: *Greenweb Ltd v Wandsworth London Borough Council* [2008] EWCA Civ 910, [2009] 1 WLR 612, [2008] RVR 294.
9 Land Compensation Act 1961 s 15(1). Thus, as the assumed permission is only permission to develop in accordance with the proposals, it will be sufficient and proper to assume a permission in general terms and not for the actual scheme of the acquiring authority, which must in any case be disregarded: see *Myers v Milton Keynes Development Corpn* [1974] 2 All ER 1096, [1974] 1 WLR 696, CA. In valuing land acquired by the authority for residential and industrial purposes, with the assumed permission, the authority's actual scheme for development of the land must thus be ignored, in accordance with the principle in *Pointe Gourde Quarrying and Transport Co Ltd v Sub-Intendent of Crown Lands* [1947] AC 565, PC. The question is whether any other persons would be likely to want to purchase the land for development to the same or less extent, and if the development by those other persons would not be likely or would be deferred, the land must be valued accordingly: *Abbey Homesteads (Developments) Ltd v Northamptonshire County Council* (1992) 64 P & CR 377, [1992] 2 EGLR 18, CA. Planning permission alone does not raise the value of the land; it merely removes the restrictions on development so that demand for the development must be taken into account: *Viscount Camrose v Basingstoke Corpn* [1966] 3 All ER 161, [1966] 1 WLR 1100, CA. Consequently, if planning permission would have been refused for purposes other than the development scheme, any enhancement of value derived solely from the scheme itself has to be ignored for valuation purposes: *Roberts v South Gloucestershire Council* [2002] EWCA Civ 1568, [2003] 1 P & CR 411, [2003] RVR 43 (no compensation allowed in respect of minerals to be excavated during the construction of a relief road since permission would not have been granted for the excavation alone).
    An assumed permission for industrial purposes is satisfied by an assumed permission for a change of use to industrial purposes, and it must not be assumed that an industrial development certificate necessary for planning permission for building operations would be granted: *Viscount Camrose v Basingstoke Corpn* above. Any increase in the value of the land by reason of development or the prospect of development of other land must also be excluded so far as it is development which would not be likely to be carried out if the authority did not propose to acquire any of that other land, or that other land had not been defined or designated for development as provided in the Land Compensation Act 1961 s 6, Sch 1: *Viscount Camrose v Basingstoke Corpn*.

10 Land Compensation Act 1961 s 14(2). It is not to be assumed that planning permission would necessarily be refused for development which is not development for which the granting of planning permission is assumed: see s 14(3); and PARA 762.

(iii) Assumed Permission included in Existing Use of Land

765. Assumed permission for development included in the existing use of land. For the purpose of assessing compensation in respect of any compulsory acquisition, it must be assumed that[1] planning permission[2] would be granted, in respect of the relevant land[3] or any part of it, for development[4] consisting of: (1) specified rebuilding operations or the maintenance, improvement or alteration of a building[5] subject to the statutory condition[6] relating thereto[7]; and (2) the use as two or more separate dwelling houses of any building which at a material date was used as a single dwelling house[8]. Where, however, at any time before the date of service of the notice to treat[9] an order was made[10] in respect of the relevant land or any part of it requiring the removal of any building[11] or the discontinuance of any use, and compensation became payable in respect of that order[12], it must not be assumed that planning permission would be granted in respect of the relevant land or part of it for the rebuilding of that building or the resumption of that use[13].

1 The Land Compensation Act 1961 is drafted as 'It shall be assumed that …'. There is no ambiguity in the word 'shall', or in the phrase 'it shall be assumed that …' The assumption is mandatory: *Greenweb Ltd v Wandsworth London Borough Council* [2008] EWCA Civ 910, [2009] 1 WLR 612, [2008] RVR 294.
2 As to the meaning of 'planning permission' for these purposes see PARA 762 note 4. As to the meaning of 'planning permission' generally see PARA 762 note 1.
3 As to the meaning of 'land' see PARA 516 note 2. As to the meaning of 'relevant land' see PARA 762 note 5.
4 As to the meaning of 'development' generally see PARA 762 note 2.
5 Ie development of a class specified in the Town and Country Planning Act 1990 s 107(4), Sch 3 para 1: see TOWN AND COUNTRY PLANNING vol 46(2) (Reissue) PARAS 914, 920. As to what amounts to rebuilding see *Re Walker's Settled Estate* [1894] 1 Ch 189; *Re Kensington Settled Estates* (1905) 21 TLR 351; *Re Windham's Settled Estate* [1912] 2 Ch 75; *Re Lord Gerard's Settled Estate* [1893] 3 Ch 252 at 267, CA; *Re Wright's Settled Estates* (1900) 83 LT 159; *Re De Teissier's Settled Estates* [1893] 1 Ch 153. The permission may be subject to any other control apart from the planning permission: cf *Trustees of the Walton-on-Thames Charities v Walton and Weybridge UDC* (1970) 21 P & CR 411, CA.
6 Ie subject to the condition set out in the Town and Country Planning Act 1990 Sch 10: see TOWN AND COUNTRY PLANNING vol 46(2) (Reissue) PARAS 918, 921.
7 Land Compensation Act 1961 s 15(3)(a) (substituted by the Planning and Compensation Act 1991 s 31(4), Sch 6 para 1(1)(a)).
8 Land Compensation Act 1961 s 15(3)(b) (as substituted: see note 7). The development referred to is development of a class specified in the Town and Country Planning Act 1990 Sch 3 para 2: see TOWN AND COUNTRY PLANNING vol 46(2) (Reissue) PARA 920. As to what is a dwelling house see *Gravesham Borough Council v Secretary of State for the Environment* (1982) 47 P & CR 142; cf *Lewin v End* [1906] AC 299 at 302, 304, HL. It should not be assumed that assumed planning permissions under the Land Compensation Act 1961 s 15 and the Town and Country Planning Act 1990 Sch 3 automatically increase the value of the land: *Halliwell and Halliwell v Skelmersdale Development Corpn* (1965) 16 P & CR 305, Lands Tribunal.
9 As to the notice to treat see PARA 616 et seq. As to the meaning of 'notice to treat' see PARA 636 note 4.
10 Ie under the Town and Country Planning Act 1990: see s 102; and TOWN AND COUNTRY PLANNING vol 46(1) (Reissue) PARAS 546–547; TOWN AND COUNTRY PLANNING vol 46(2) (Reissue) PARA 756.
11 As to the meaning of 'building' see PARA 516 note 2.
12 As to compensation see the Town and Country Planning Act 1990 s 115; and TOWN AND COUNTRY PLANNING vol 46(2) (Reissue) PARAS 923, 928–929.
13 Land Compensation Act 1961 s 15(4)(c); Planning (Consequential Provisions) Act 1990 s 2(4).

(iv) Assumed Permission in respect of Certain Land in Development Plan

766. Land allocated for a particular purpose in the development plan. If the relevant land[1] or any part of it, not being land subject to comprehensive development[2], consists or forms part of a site defined in the current development plan as the site of proposed development[3] of a description specified in relation to it in the plan, it must be assumed that planning permission[4] would be granted for that development[5]. In determining whether this assumption is applicable to the relevant land or any part of it, regard must be had to any contrary opinion expressed in relation to that land in any certificate[6] of appropriate alternative development[7].

1   As to the meaning of 'relevant land' see PARA 762 note 5. As to the meaning of 'land' see PARA 516 note 2.
2   'Land subject to comprehensive development' means land which consists or forms part of an area defined in the current development plan as an area of comprehensive development: Land Compensation Act 1961 s 16(8). 'Current development plan', in relation to any land, means a development plan comprising that land, in the form in which, whether as originally approved or made or as for the time being amended, that plan is in force on the date of service of the notice to treat: s 39(1) (definition amended by the Town and Country Planning Act 1968 s 108, Sch 11). A reference to a development plan in the Land Compensation Act 1961 must be construed in accordance with the Planning and Compulsory Purchase Act 2004 s 38(2)–(5): see s 38(1), (7); and TOWN AND COUNTRY PLANNING vol 46(1) (Reissue) PARA 91.
3   As to the meaning of 'development' see PARA 762 note 2.
4   As to the meaning of 'planning permission' see PARA 762 note 1. As to the nature and extent of the assumed permission see PARA 770.
5   Land Compensation Act 1961 s 16(1).
6   Ie any certificate issued under the Land Compensation Act 1961 Pt III (ss 17–22): see PARAS 771–778.
7   Land Compensation Act 1961 s 14(3A)(b) (added by the Planning and Compensation Act 1991 s 70, Sch 15 para 15(2)). As to the effect of a negative certificate see *Pentrehobyn Trustees v National Assembly for Wales* [2003] RVR 140, Lands Tribunal (the use of the word 'regard' in the Land Compensation Act 1961 s 14(3A) means that the Tribunal is not necessarily bound by the view expressed in such a certificate, although it does constitute one of the considerations upon which the Tribunal must come to a view of its own). See also PARA 772 note 5. The Lands Tribunal was abolished on 1 June 2009 and its functions were transferred to the Upper Tribunal: see PARA 720.

767. Land allocated for specified use in development plan. If the relevant land[1] or any part of it (not being land subject to comprehensive development[2]), consists or forms part of an area shown in the current development plan[3] as an area allocated primarily for a use specified in the plan in relation to that area, it must be assumed that planning permission[4] would be granted, in respect of that land or that part of it, as the case may be, for any development[5] which is development: (1) for the purposes of that specified use of that land or part[6]; and (2) for which planning permission might reasonably have been expected to be granted in respect of that land or part[7] if no part of that land were proposed to be acquired by any authority possessing compulsory purchase powers[8].

In determining whether this assumption is applicable to the relevant land or any part of it, regard must be had to any contrary opinion expressed in relation to that land in any certificate[9] of appropriate alternative development[10].

1   As to the meaning of 'relevant land' see PARA 762 note 5. As to the meaning of 'land' see PARA 516 note 2.
2   As to the meaning of 'land subject to comprehensive development' see PARA 766 note 2.
3   As to the meaning of 'current development plan' see PARA 766 note 2.
4   As to the meaning of 'planning permission' see PARA 762 note 1. As to the nature and extent of the assumed permission see PARA 770.

5   As to the meaning of 'development' see PARA 762 note 2.
6   Land Compensation Act 1961 s 16(2)(a). See note 7.
7   Land Compensation Act 1961 s 16(2)(b). The provisions of s 16(2)(a) and (b) must both be satisfied and applied together; it is not a matter of finding under s 16(2)(b) what kind of permission would be granted if s 16(2)(a) is satisfied and, accordingly, if no planning permission might reasonably have been expected, there can be no assumed permission: *Provincial Properties (London) Ltd v Caterham and Warlingham UDC* [1972] 1 QB 453, [1972] 1 All ER 60, CA. On the other hand, the likelihood of a planning permission actually being sought or granted is irrelevant to the making of the assumption: *Sutton v Secretary of State for the Environment* [1984] JPL 648. However, if there is no demand for land with that permission, the value of the land may not be increased: *Bromilow v Greater Manchester Council* (1975) 31 P & CR 398, CA; *Davy Ltd v London Borough of Hammersmith* (1975) 30 P & CR 469, Lands Tribunal.
8   Land Compensation Act 1961 s 16(2), (7). As to the meaning of 'authority possessing compulsory purchase powers' see PARA 763 note 6. If, on considering whether planning permission might reasonably have been expected, there are traffic reasons against permission, but there is a proposal for a by-pass partly on the land to be acquired which has to be ignored under s 16(7), it is not to be assumed that there would be a by-pass elsewhere in relief of traffic, but evidence of the possibility of such a by-pass must be considered: see *Margate Corpn v Devotwill Investments Ltd* [1970] 3 All ER 864, 22 P & CR 328, HL. Any question as to whether planning permission might reasonably have been expected is within the jurisdiction of the Upper Tribunal: *Harrison v Croydon London Borough Council* [1968] Ch 479, [1967] 2 All ER 589. See also *Richardsons Developments Ltd v Stoke-on-Trent Corpn* (1971) 22 P & CR 958, Lands Tribunal; *Menzies Motors Ltd v Stirling District Council* 1977 SC 33, Lands Tribunal for Scotland. The Lands Tribunal was abolished on 1 June 2009 and its functions were transferred to the Upper Tribunal: see PARA 720. A local authority cannot specify a planning permission for a purpose which could only be achieved by an authority possessing compulsory purchase powers: *Scunthorpe Borough Council v Secretary of State for the Environment* [1977] JPL 653.
      Special provisions apply where land is acquired for or in connection with the construction of a highway: see the Land Compensation Act 1961 s 14(5)–(8); and PARA 763.
9   Ie any certificate issued under the Land Compensation Act 1961 Pt III (ss 17–22): see PARAS 771–778.
10 Land Compensation Act 1961 s 14(3A)(b) (added by the Planning and Compensation Act 1991 s 70, Sch 15 para 15(2)).

768. Land allocated for range of specified uses in development plan. If the relevant land[1] or any part of it, not being land subject to comprehensive development[2], consists or forms part of an area shown in the current development plan[3] as an area allocated primarily for a range of two or more uses specified in the plan in relation to the whole of that area, it must be assumed that planning permission[4] would be granted in respect of that land or that part for any development[5] which: (1) is development for the purposes of a use of that land or that part of it which is a use falling within that range of uses[6]; and (2) is development for which planning permission might reasonably have been expected to be granted in respect of that land or part if no part of that land were proposed to be acquired by any authority possessing compulsory purchase powers[7].

In determining whether this assumption is applicable to the relevant land or any part of it, regard must be had to any contrary opinion expressed in relation to that land in any certificate[8] of appropriate alternative development[9].

1   As to the meaning of 'relevant land' see PARA 762 note 5; and as to the meaning of 'land' see PARA 516 note 2.
2   As to the meaning of 'land subject to comprehensive development' see PARA 766 note 2.
3   As to the meaning of 'current development plan' see PARA 766 note 2.
4   As to the meaning of 'planning permission' see PARA 762 note 1. As to the nature and extent of the assumed permission see PARA 770.
5   As to the meaning of 'development' see PARA 762 note 2.
6   Land Compensation Act 1961 s 16(3)(a).

7   Land Compensation Act 1961 s 16(3)(b), (7). Cf PARA 767 notes 7–8. As to the meaning of
    'authority possessing compulsory purchase powers' see PARA 763 note 6.
8   Ie any certificate issued under the Land Compensation Act 1961 Pt III (ss 17–22): see PARAS
    771–778.
9   Land Compensation Act 1961 s 14(3A)(b) (added by the Planning and Compensation Act 1991
    s 70, Sch 15 para 15(2)).

769.   Land allocated for comprehensive development in the development plan.
If the relevant land[1] or any part of it is land subject to comprehensive
development[2], it must be assumed that planning permission[3] would be granted in
respect of that land or part for any development[4] for the purposes of a use of
that land or part falling within the planned range of uses[5], being development for
which planning permission might reasonably have been expected to be granted in
respect of that land or part in the specified circumstances[6]. The specified
circumstances are those which would have existed if:

(1)   no part of that land were proposed to be acquired by any authority
      possessing compulsory purchase powers[7];

(2)   the area in question had not been defined in the current development
      plan as an area of comprehensive development and no particulars or
      proposals relating to any land in that area had been comprised in the
      plan[8]; and

(3)   in a case where, on the date of service of the notice to treat[9], land in that
      area has already been developed in the course of the development or
      redevelopment of the area in accordance with the plan, no land in that
      area had been so developed on or before that date[10].

In determining whether this assumption is applicable to the relevant land or
any part of it, regard must be had to any contrary opinion expressed in relation
to that land in any certificate[11] of appropriate alternative development[12].

1   As to the meaning of 'relevant land' see PARA 762 note 5. As to the meaning of 'land' see PARA
    516 note 2.
2   As to the meaning of 'land subject to comprehensive development' see PARA 766 note 2.
3   As to the meaning of 'planning permission' see PARA 762 note 1. As to the nature and extent of
    the assumed permission see PARA 770.
4   As to the meaning of 'development' see PARA 762 note 2.
5   Ie whether it is the use which, in accordance with the particulars and proposals comprised in the
    current development plan in relation to the area in question, is indicated in the plan as the
    proposed use of the relevant land or that part of it, or is any other use falling within the planned
    range of uses: Land Compensation Act 1961 s 16(4). 'Planned range of uses' means the range of
    uses which, in accordance with the particulars and proposals comprised in the current
    development plan in relation to the area in question, are indicated in the plan as proposed uses
    of land in that area: s 16(5). As to the meaning of 'current development plan' see PARA 766 note
    2.
6   Land Compensation Act 1961 s 16(4).
7   Land Compensation Act 1961 s 16(7). As to the meaning of 'authority possessing compulsory
    purchase powers' see PARA 763 note 6.
8   Land Compensation Act 1961 s 16(5)(a).
9   As to the notice to treat see PARA 616 et seq. As to the meaning of 'notice to treat' see PARA 636
    note 4.
10 Land Compensation Act 1961 s 16(5)(b).
11 Ie any certificate issued under the Land Compensation Act 1961 Pt III (ss 17–22): see PARAS
    771–778.
12 Land Compensation Act 1961 s 14(3A)(b) (added by the Planning and Compensation Act 1991
    s 70, Sch 15 para 15(2)).

770.   Nature and extent of assumed planning permission.   Where in
accordance with the statutory provisions[1] it is to be assumed that planning

permission[2] would be granted, the assumption must be that permission would be granted subject to such conditions, if any, as, in the circumstances mentioned in relation to the assumed permission in question, might reasonably be expected to be imposed by the authority granting the permission[3]. Further, if, in accordance with any map or statement comprised in the current development plan[4], it is indicated that any such planning permission would be granted only at a future time, then, without prejudice to the above assumed conditions, the assumption must be that the planning permission in question would be granted at the time when, in accordance with the indications in the plan, that permission might reasonably be expected to be granted[5], if no part of that land were proposed to be acquired by any authority possessing compulsory purchase powers[6].

1 Ie in accordance with the Land Compensation Act 1961 s 16(1)–(5): see PARAS 766–769.
2 As to the meaning of 'planning permission' see PARA 762 note 1.
3 Land Compensation Act 1961 s 16(6)(a).
4 As to the meaning of 'current development plan' see PARA 766 note 2.
5 Land Compensation Act 1961 s 16(6)(b).
6 Land Compensation Act 1961 s 16(7). As to the meaning of 'authority possessing compulsory purchase powers' see PARA 763 note 6.

(v) Assumed Permission in accordance with Certificate of Appropriate Alternative Development

771. Permission certified subject to conditions including condition as to time.
Where a certificate of appropriate alternative development is issued[1], it must be assumed in the case of a compulsory acquisition[2] or purchase by agreement[3] that any planning permission[4] which, according to the certificate, would have been granted in respect of the relevant land[5] or part of it, if it were not proposed to be acquired by any authority possessing compulsory purchase powers[6], would be so granted[7]. Where, however, any conditions are specified[8] in the certificate, then it must be assumed that the permission would be granted only subject to those conditions and, if any future time is so specified, only at that time[9]. The general principle of the possibility of removal of restrictions is applied by such a certificate[10].

1 Ie under the provisions of the Land Compensation Act 1961 Pt III (ss 17–22): see PARAS 772–778.
2 See the Land Compensation Act 1961 ss 17, 22(2)(a), (b); and PARA 772.
3 See the Land Compensation Act 1961 ss 17(2), 22(2)(c); and PARA 772.
4 As to the meaning of 'planning permission' see PARA 762 note 1.
5 As to the meaning of 'relevant land' see PARA 762 note 5. As to the meaning of 'land' see PARA 516 note 2.
6 As to the meaning of 'authority possessing compulsory purchase powers' see PARA 763 note 6.
7 Land Compensation Act 1961 s 15(5) (amended by the Local Government, Planning and Land Act 1980 s 193, Sch 33 para 5). See *Stevens v Bath and North East Somerset District Council* [2004] RVR 189.
8 Ie in accordance with the provisions of the Land Compensation Act 1961 Pt III: see PARAS 772–778.
9 Land Compensation Act 1961 s 15(5). As to the specification of those matters in the certificate see s 17(5); and PARA 776. See also PARA 772 note 5.
10 See PARAS 761–762.

772. Right to apply for certificate of appropriate alternative development.
Where an authority possessing compulsory purchase powers[1] proposes to acquire an interest in land[2], either of the parties directly concerned[3] may apply to the local planning authority[4] for a certificate of appropriate alternative development[5]. If, however, the authority proposing to acquire the interest has

served a notice to treat[6] in respect of it, or if an agreement has been made[7] for the sale of that interest to the authority, and a reference has been made to the Upper Tribunal (the 'Tribunal')[8] to determine the amount of the compensation payable in respect of that interest, then no such application for a certificate may be made by either of the parties after the date of that reference except either with the consent in writing of the other party or the permission of the Tribunal[9].

1   As to the meaning of 'authority possessing compulsory purchase powers' see PARA 763 note 6.
2   For these purposes, an interest in land is to be taken to be an interest proposed to be acquired by an authority possessing compulsory purchase powers in the following, but no other, circumstances: (1) where, for the purpose of a compulsory acquisition by that authority of land consisting of or including land in which that interest subsists, a notice required to be published or served in connection with that acquisition, either by an Act or by any standing order of either House of Parliament relating to petitions for private Bills, has been published or served in accordance with that Act or order (Land Compensation Act 1961 s 22(2)(a)); or (2) where a notice requiring the purchase of that interest has been served under any enactment, and in accordance with that enactment that authority is deemed to have served a notice to treat in respect of that interest (eg purchase notices, or blight notices: see TOWN AND COUNTRY PLANNING vol 46(2) (Reissue) PARAS 970, 987) (Land Compensation Act 1961 s 22(2)(b); and see *Jelson Ltd v Minister of Housing and Local Government* [1970] 1 QB 243, [1969] 3 All ER 147, CA); or (3) where a written offer has been made by or on behalf of that authority to negotiate for the purchase of that interest (Land Compensation Act 1961 s 22(2)(c)); or (4) where an order has been made under the Local Government, Planning and Land Act 1980 s 141 vesting the land in an urban development corporation (see TOWN AND COUNTRY PLANNING vol 46(3) (Reissue) PARA 1454) (Land Compensation Act 1961 s 22(2)(d) (added as a modification for the purposes of such orders by the Local Government, Planning and Land Act 1980 s 141(5), Sch 27 paras 9, 12)); or (5) where an order has been made under the Housing Act 1988 s 76 vesting the land in a housing action trust (see HOUSING vol 22 (2006 Reissue) PARA 339) (Land Compensation Act 1961 s 22(2)(cc) (added as a modification for the purposes of such orders by the Housing Act 1988 s 76(6), Sch 9 paras 6, 9)). A certificate may be applied for where there is an express power to acquire any interest or right in or over the land without having to acquire the whole land: see PARAS 532–534. As to the meaning of 'land' see PARA 516 note 2. As to the meaning of 'enactment' see PARA 501 note 3.
3   'Parties directly concerned', in relation to an interest in land, means the person entitled to the interest and the authority by whom it is proposed to be acquired: Land Compensation Act 1961 s 22(1). See also PARA 774.
      A surveyor who has to determine the compensation or purchase money under the Lands Clauses Consolidation Act 1845 s 58 or under the Compulsory Purchase Act 1965 s 5(3), Sch 2 (see PARA 718), in respect of an interest in land (1) proposed to be acquired by an authority possessing compulsory purchase powers; and (2) to which a person who is absent from the United Kingdom or who cannot be found is entitled, may apply for a certificate under these provisions before carrying out his valuation: Land Compensation Act 1961 s 19(1) (amended by the Planning and Compensation Act 1991 s 70, Sch 15 para 17; applied by the Compulsory Purchase Act 1965 s 39(3), Sch 7). The provisions of the Land Compensation Act 1961 ss 17, 18 apply in relation to an application so made as they apply in relation to an application made by virtue of s 17(1): s 19(1). As to the meaning of 'United Kingdom' see PARA 616 note 22.
4   As to the meaning of 'local planning authority' see PARA 763 note 8. The Broads Authority is the sole district planning authority in respect of the Broads for these purposes and for the purposes of the Land Compensation Act 1961 ss 18, 19; and 'the Broads' has the same meaning as in the Norfolk and Suffolk Broads Act 1988: Land Compensation Act 1961 s 17(10), (11) (added by the Norfolk and Suffolk Broads Act 1988 s 2(5), Sch 3 para 3). As to district planning authorities see TOWN AND COUNTRY PLANNING vol 46(1) (Reissue) PARA 28. As to the Broads Authority see OPEN SPACES AND ANCIENT MONUMENTS vol 34 (Reissue) PARA 130.
      Wherever possible application under the Land Compensation Act 1961 s 17 for a certificate (and if necessary appeal under s 18: see PARA 777) should be made instead of leaving the self-same question to be determined on a hypothetical basis by the Tribunal: *Williamson and Stevens v Cambridgeshire County Council* [1977] 1 EGLR 165, Lands Tribunal. The Lands Tribunal was abolished on 1 June 2009 and its functions were transferred to the Upper Tribunal: see PARA 720.
5   Land Compensation Act 1961 s 17(1) (substituted by the Planning and Compensation Act 1991 s 65(1)). As to the contents of the certificate see PARA 776. A 'negative certificate' under the Land Compensation Act 1961 s 17 is not necessarily fatal to a claim but the claimant must then

satisfy the Tribunal of his prospects for obtaining planning permission for such use as he claims is appropriate in a 'no-plan' world; and the Tribunal will attach such weight to the certificate as it may in the exercise of its discretion, having regard to the evidence before it on planning matters: *Pentrehobyn Trustees v National Assembly for Wales* [2003] RVR 140, Lands Tribunal. The Land Compensation Act 1961 operates in such a way that, to the extent that a certificate is positive, s 15(5) (see PARA 771) requires the Tribunal to assume that planning permission would be granted for the development specified and, to the extent that a certificate is negative, s 14(3A) (see PARA 766) requires the Tribunal, in determining whether planning permission might reasonably have been expected to be granted, to have regard to the opinion expressed in the certificate that planning permission would not have been granted: *Thomas's Executors v Merthyr Tydfil County Borough Council* (26 February 2003, unreported), Lands Tribunal.

6   As to the notice to treat see PARA 616 et seq. As to the meaning of 'notice to treat' see PARA 636 note 4.

7   The making of a contract means the execution of it or, if it was not in writing, the signing of the memorandum or note by which it was attested: Land Compensation Act 1961 s 39(4). It appears that this provision has not been affected by the Law of Property (Miscellaneous Provisions) Act 1989 s 2 (formalities required on a sale or other disposition of land: see SALE OF LAND vol 42 (Reissue) PARA 29); sed quaere.

8   As to the Upper Tribunal see PARA 720; and ADMINISTRATIVE LAW.

9   Land Compensation Act 1961 s 17(2) (amended by the Planning and Compensation Act 1991 s 70, Sch 15 para 16(a); and SI 2009/1307). The Land Compensation Act 1961 s 17(2) is modified in relation to an order vesting the land in: (1) an urban development corporation, by the Local Government, Planning and Land Act 1980 Sch 27 paras 9, 11; (2) a housing action trust, by the Housing Act 1988 Sch 9 paras 6, 8; and (3) regional development agencies, by the Regional Development Agencies Act 1998 Sch 4 para 3.

773. Power to prescribe relevant matters. The provisions which may be made by a development order[1] include provision for regulating the manner in which applications for certificates of appropriate alternative development[2] and appeals in relation to them[3] are to be made and dealt with respectively[4], and in particular:

(1)   for prescribing[5] the time within which a certificate is required[6] to be issued[7];

(2)   for prescribing the manner in which notices of appeals[8] are to be given, and the time for giving any such notice[9];

(3)   for requiring local planning authorities[10] to furnish the Secretary of State[11], and such other persons, if any, as may be prescribed by or under the order, with such information as may be so prescribed with respect to applications for such certificates, including information whether any such application has been made in respect of any particular land[12] and information as to the manner in which any such application has been dealt with, together, in such cases as may be so prescribed, with copies of certificates issued[13];

(4)   for requiring a local planning authority, on issuing a certificate specifying conditions by reference to general requirements[14], to supply a copy of those requirements, or so much of them as is relevant to the certificate, with each copy of the certificate, unless, before the certificate is issued, the requirements in question have been made available to the public in such manner as may be specified in the development order[15].

1   As to the meaning of 'development order' see PARA 762 note 4.
2   Ie under the Land Compensation Act 1961 ss 17, 19: see PARAS 772–776.
3   Ie under the Land Compensation Act 1961 s 18: see PARA 777.
4   Land Compensation Act 1961 s 20.
5   Ie subject to the provisions of the Land Compensation Act 1961 s 17(4): see PARA 775.
6   Ie under the Land Compensation Act 1961 s 17: see PARA 775.

7   Land Compensation Act 1961 s 20(a). In exercise of the powers conferred, inter alia, by s 20, the Secretary of State has made the Land Compensation Development Order 1974, SI 1974/539: see PARA 774 et seq.
8   See the text to note 3.
9   Land Compensation Act 1961 s 20(b). See note 7.
10 As to the meaning of 'local planning authority' see PARA 763 note 8.
11 As to the Secretary of State see PARA 507 note 1. The functions of the Secretary of State under the Land Compensation Act 1961, so far as they are exercisable in relation to Wales, are now exercisable by the Welsh Ministers: see the National Assembly for Wales (Transfer of Functions) Order 1999, SI 1999/672, art 2, Sch 1; and the Government of Wales Act 2006 s 162(1), Sch 11 para 30. As to the Welsh Assembly Government and the Welsh Ministers see CONSTITUTIONAL LAW AND HUMAN RIGHTS.
12 As to the meaning of 'land' see PARA 516 note 2.
13 Land Compensation Act 1961 s 20(c). See note 7.
14 Ie in accordance with the Land Compensation Act 1961 s 17(6): see PARA 776.
15 Land Compensation Act 1961 s 20(d). See note 7.

774. Application for certificate.   An application for a certificate of appropriate alternative development[1] must be in writing[2] and must include a plan or map sufficient to identify the land[3] to which the application relates[4]. The application must state:

(1)   whether or not there are, in the applicant's opinion, any classes of development[5] which would be appropriate for the land in question[6] if it were not proposed to be acquired by any authority possessing compulsory purchase powers[7] and, if so, must specify the classes of development and the times at which they would be so appropriate[8];
(2)   the applicant's grounds for holding that opinion[9].

It must be accompanied by a statement specifying the date on which a copy of the application has been or will be served on the other party directly concerned[10].

On a written request to the local planning authority[11] by any person appearing to it to have an interest in the land which is the subject of an application for a certificate, that authority must furnish to that person the name and address of the applicant for the certificate and the date of the application and, after it is issued, a copy of the certificate[12]. The persons served with notice of an application may make written representations to the authority with respect to the application[13].

1   Ie a certificate under the Land Compensation Act 1961 s 17: see the text and notes 5–10; and PARAS 772, 775–776.
2   Land Compensation Development Order 1974, SI 1974/539, art 3(1).
3   As to the meaning of 'land' see PARA 516 note 2.
4   Land Compensation Development Order 1974, SI 1974/539, art 3(1).
5   As to the meaning of 'development' see PARA 762 note 2.
6   Ie either immediately or at a future time: Land Compensation Act 1961 s 17(3)(a) (s 17(3) substituted by the Community Land Act 1975 s 47(1), (2); and saved by virtue of the Local Government, Planning and Land Act 1980 s 121(2), Sch 24).
7   As to the meaning of 'authority possessing compulsory purchase powers' see PARA 763 note 6.
8   Land Compensation Act 1961 s 17(3)(a) (as substituted: see note 6).
9   Land Compensation Act 1961 s 17(3)(b) (as substituted: see note 6).
10 Land Compensation Act 1961 s 17(3)(c) (as substituted: see note 6). In the case of an application for a certificate made by virtue of s 19(1) in respect of the interest of a person absent or unknown (see PARA 772), the statement must specify the date on which a copy of the application has been or will be served on each of the parties directly concerned: s 19(3) (amended by the Community Land Act 1975 s 58(2), Sch 10 para 4(3), (5); and saved by virtue of the Local Government, Planning and Land Act 1980 s 193, Sch 33 para 5). As to the meaning of 'parties directly concerned' see PARA 772 note 3.
11 As to the meaning of 'local planning authority' see PARA 763 note 8.

12 Land Compensation Development Order 1974, SI 1974/539, art 5. Alternatively, the authority must pass the written request to the local planning authority whose function it is to issue the certificate, and that authority must then comply with the request: art 5. As to the power to prescribe other information see PARA 773. As to service of a copy of the certificate see PARAS 775–776, 779.

13 See the Land Compensation Development Order 1974, SI 1974/539, art 3(3); and PARA 776.

775. Issue of certificate. Where an application is made to the local planning authority[1] for a certificate of appropriate alternative development in respect of an interest in land[2], the authority must issue a certificate to the applicant[3] not earlier than 21 days after the date specified in the statement accompanying the application[4] and not later than two months after receipt of the application[5]. On issuing a certificate in respect of an interest in land to one of the parties directly concerned[6], the local planning authority must serve a copy of the certificate on the other of those parties[7].

Where a certificate is issued by a county planning authority[8], that authority must send a copy to the district planning authority[9] for the area in which the land or any part of it is situated; and where a certificate is issued by a district planning authority and specifies a class or classes of development[10] relating to a county matter[11], the district authority must send a copy to the county authority[12]. The local planning authority must also, on written request, furnish a copy of the certificate to any person appearing to it to have an interest in the land[13].

1 As to the meaning of 'local planning authority' see PARA 763 note 8.
2 Ie a certificate under the Land Compensation Act 1961 s 17: see the text and notes 3–7; and PARAS 772–774, 776. As to the meaning of 'land' see PARA 516 note 2.
3 Land Compensation Act 1961 s 17(4) (s 17 substituted by the Community Land Act 1975 s 47(1), (3); and saved by virtue of the Local Government, Planning and Land Act 1980 s 121(2), Sch 24). As to applications for certificates see PARA 774.
4 Ie the date specified in the statement mentioned in the Land Compensation Act 1961 s 17(3)(c) (see PARA 774); or, in the case of a certificate applied for by virtue of s 19(1) (ie an application by a surveyor in respect of the interest of a person absent or unknown: see PARA 772), the date specified in the statement in accordance with s 19(3) (see PARA 774) or, where more than one date is so specified, the later of those dates: see s 17(4) (as substituted: see note 3), s 19(3) (amended by the Local Government, Planning and Land Act 1980 s 193, Sch 33 para 5).
5 Land Compensation Act 1961 s 17(4) (as substituted: see note 3); Land Compensation Development Order 1974, SI 1974/539, art 3(2).
6 As to the meaning of 'parties directly concerned' see PARA 772 note 3.
7 Land Compensation Act 1961 s 17(9) (as substituted: see note 3). Where, in pursuance of an application made by virtue of s 19(1), the local planning authority issues a certificate to the surveyor, it must serve copies of the certificate on both the parties directly concerned: s 19(2). Service on a person who is absent or unknown will, however, have to be postponed. As to service see further PARA 779.
8 As to county planning authorities see TOWN AND COUNTRY PLANNING vol 46(1) (Reissue) PARA 28.
9 As to district planning authorities see TOWN AND COUNTRY PLANNING vol 46(1) (Reissue) PARA 28.
10 As to the meaning of 'development' see PARA 762 note 2.
11 As to the meaning of 'county matter' see TOWN AND COUNTRY PLANNING vol 46(1) (Reissue) PARA 38.
12 Land Compensation Development Order 1974, SI 1974/539, art 3(4) (substituted by SI 1986/435).
13 Land Compensation Development Order 1974, SI 1974/539, art 5.

776. Contents of certificate. The certificate of appropriate alternative development[1] issued to the applicant must state that it is the opinion of the local planning authority[2] regarding the grant of planning permission[3] in respect of the land[4] in question, that if it were not proposed to be acquired by an authority possessing compulsory purchase powers[5], either:

(1)   planning permission would have been granted for development[6] of one or more classes specified in the certificate, whether specified in the application or not, and for any development for which the land is to be acquired[7], but would not have been granted for any other development[8]; or

(2)   planning permission would have been granted for any development for which the land is to be acquired, but would not have been granted for any other development[9].

In determining whether planning permission for any particular class of development would have been granted in respect of any land, the local planning authority must not treat development of that class as development for which planning permission would have been refused by reason only that it would have involved development of the land in question, or of that land together with other land, otherwise than in accordance with the provisions of the development plan[10] relating to it[11].

Where, in the local planning authority's opinion, planning permission would have been granted as mentioned in head (1) above, but would only have been granted subject to conditions[12], or at a future time, or both subject to conditions and at a future time, the certificate must specify those conditions or that future time, or both, as the case may be, in addition to the other matters required to be contained in it[13].

If a local planning authority issues a certificate otherwise than for the class or classes of development specified in the application made to it, or contrary to written representations made to it by one of the parties directly concerned[14], it must include in the certificate a written statement of its reasons for doing so and must give particulars of the manner in which and the time within which an appeal may be made[15] to the Secretary of State[16].

In assessing the compensation payable to any person in respect of any compulsory acquisition[17], there must be taken into account any expenses reasonably incurred by him[18] in connection with the issue of a certificate of appropriate alternative development[19].

1   Ie the certificate under the Land Compensation Act 1961 s 17: see the text and notes 2–19; and PARAS 772–775.
2   As to the meaning of 'local planning authority' see PARA 763 note 8.
3   As to the meaning of 'planning permission' see PARA 762 note 1.
4   As to the meaning of 'land' see PARA 516 note 2.
5   Land Compensation Act 1961 s 17(4) (s 17 substituted by the Community Land Act 1975 s 47(1), (3); and saved by virtue of the Local Government, Planning and Land Act 1980 s 121(2), Sch 24). As to the meaning of 'authority possessing compulsory purchase powers' see PARA 763 note 6.
6   As to the meaning of 'development' see PARA 762 note 2.
7   For these purposes, development is development for which the land is to be acquired if the land is to be acquired for purposes which involve the carrying out of proposals of the acquiring authority for that development: Land Compensation Act 1961 s 17(4) (amended by the Planning and Compensation Act 1991 s 65(2)). As to the meaning of 'acquiring authority' see PARA 622 note 1.
8   Land Compensation Act 1961 s 17(4)(a) (s 17(4)(a), (b) substituted by the Planning and Compensation Act 1991 s 65(2)). The local planning authority must determine what planning permission would be granted at the date of an actual notice to treat, or a deemed notice to treat or an offer to negotiate for the purchase of the interest, as the case may be: *Jelson Ltd v Minister of Housing and Local Government* [1970] 1 QB 243, [1969] 3 All ER 147, CA; followed in *Fox v Secretary of State for the Environment and Surrey Heath Borough Council* (1991) 62 P & CR 459, [1991] 2 EGLR 13; cf *Robert Hitchins Builders Ltd v Secretary of State for the*

Environment (1978) 37 P & CR 140. These cases were, however, decided before the Planning and Compensation Act 1991 s 65(2) came into force.

A potentiality may be taken into account under the general principle: see *Sutton v Secretary of State for the Environment* [1984] JPL 648; *ADP & E Farmers v Department of Transport* [1988] 1 EGLR 209, Lands Tribunal; *Corrin v Northampton Borough Council* [1980] 1 EGLR 148, Lands Tribunal; and PARAS 761–762. Where land otherwise available for urban development is taken for a public purpose, the certificate should reflect its urban development value: *Grampian Regional Council v Secretary of State for Scotland* [1983] 3 All ER 673, [1983] 1 WLR 1340, HL, distinguishing *Skelmersdale Development Corpn v Secretary of State for the Environment* [1980] JPL 322. Where a certificate of appropriate alternative development has been granted which enhances a particular site only part of which is subsequently acquired, the landowner may be entitled to additional compensation for severance of the land acquired from that retained: *Hoveringham Gravels Ltd v Chiltern District Council* (1978) 39 P & CR 414, Lands Tribunal; c f *Phipps v Wiltshire County Council* [1983] 1 EGLR 181, Lands Tribunal.

It is wrong for the authority to specify a use, such as public open space, which could be achieved only by an authority possessing compulsory purchase powers: *Scunthorpe Borough Council v Secretary of State for the Environment* [1977] JPL 653. However, the loss of potential public open space may be a material consideration, unless statute provides otherwise, where the owner is a local authority: *Maidstone Borough Council v Secretary of State for the Environment* [1996] RVR 127, CA.

9   Land Compensation Act 1961 s 17(4)(b) (as substituted: see note 8). Where an application is made for a certificate and at the expiry of the prescribed time for its issue (or, if an extended period is at any time agreed upon in writing by the parties and the local planning authority, at the end of that period), no certificate has been issued, s 18 (see PARA 777) applies as if the local planning authority had issued such a certificate containing such a statement as is mentioned in s 17(4)(b): s 18(4).

10 As to development plans see TOWN AND COUNTRY PLANNING vol 46(1) (Reissue) PARA 91 et seq.

11 Land Compensation Act 1961 s 17(7) (as substituted: see note 5). See *Fletcher Estates (Harlescott) Ltd v Secretary of State for the Environment; Newell v Secretary of State for the Environment* [2000] 2 AC 307, [2000] 1 All ER 929, HL (in making assumptions when valuing land for the purpose of the Land Compensation Act 1961 s 17(4), the planning authority must apply ordinary planning principles to the land and to circumstances existing at the date of publication of the notice under s 22(2)(a) (see PARA 772 note 2), but disregard the effects and incidents of the acquiring authority's proposal as a whole, irrespective of whether they had occurred before or after the date of publication).

12 For these purposes, a local planning authority may formulate general requirements applicable to such classes of case as may be described in them; and any conditions required to be specified in the certificate in accordance with these provisions may, if it appears to the local planning authority to be convenient to do so, be specified by reference to those requirements, subject to such special modifications of them, if any, as may be set out in the certificate: Land Compensation Act 1961 s 17(6) (as substituted: see note 5). If a local planning authority, on issuing a certificate, specifies conditions by reference to general requirements so formulated, it must supply with the certificate and every copy of it a copy of those requirements, or so much of them as is relevant to the certificate, unless, before the certificate is issued, the requirements in question have been made available to the public by depositing them for public inspection at all reasonable hours at the authority's office and, where the issuing authority is a district planning authority, at the county planning authority's office, or, where, the issuing authority is a county planning authority, at the office of the district planning authority in whose area the land is situated: Land Compensation Development Order 1974, SI 1974/539, art 6 (amended by SI 1986/435). As to district planning authorities and county planning authorities see TOWN AND COUNTRY PLANNING vol 46(1) (Reissue) PARA 28.

13 Land Compensation Act 1961 s 17(5) (as substituted: see note 5).

14 As to the meaning of 'parties directly concerned' see PARA 772 note 3.

15 Ie under the Land Compensation Act 1961 s 18: see PARA 777.

16 Land Compensation Development Order 1974, SI 1974/539, art 3(3). A failure to include all the particulars so required invalidates the certificate: *London and Clydeside Estates Ltd v Aberdeen District Council* [1979] 3 All ER 876, [1980] 1 WLR 182, HL. As to the Secretary of State see PARA 507 note 1. All functions of a Minister of the Crown under the Land Compensation Act 1961, so far as they are exercisable in relation to Wales, are now exercisable by the Welsh Ministers: see the National Assembly for Wales (Transfer of Functions) Order 1999,

SI 1999/672, art 2, Sch 1; and the Government of Wales Act 2006 s 162(1), Sch 11 para 30. As to the Welsh Assembly Government and the Welsh Ministers see CONSTITUTIONAL LAW AND HUMAN RIGHTS.
17 As to the assessment of compensation see PARAS 761 et seq, 780 et seq.
18 Ie including expenses incurred in connection with an appeal under the Land Compensation Act 1961 s 18 where any of the issues on the appeal are determined in his favour: s 17(9A) (added by the Planning and Compensation Act 1991 s 65(3)).
19 Land Compensation Act 1961 s 17(9A) (as added: see note 18).

777. Appeal to the Secretary of State against certificates. Where the local planning authority[1] has issued a certificate of appropriate alternative development[2] in respect of an interest in land[3], the person for the time being entitled to that interest may appeal to the Secretary of State[4] against that certificate, as may any authority possessing compulsory purchase powers[5] by whom that interest is proposed to be acquired[6]. There is also a right of appeal where the authority has not issued a certificate within the prescribed period or any extended period which may have been agreed and the certificate is deemed to have been issued[7].

The appellant must give the Secretary of State written notice of appeal within one month of the receipt of the certificate or of the date when a certificate is deemed to have been issued, as the case may be[8], and must send a copy of the notice to the local planning authority and to the other of the parties directly concerned[9]. Within one month of giving notice of appeal, or such longer period as the Secretary of State may in any particular case allow[10], the appellant must furnish to him one copy of the application made to the local planning authority for the certificate, and one copy of the certificate, if any, issued by that authority together with a statement of the grounds of appeal[11]. If the appellant does not supply these copies within the time so limited, the appeal will be treated as withdrawn[12].

If any person or authority entitled to appeal so desires, the Secretary of State must, before determining the appeal, afford that person or authority and the local planning authority an opportunity of appearing before, and being heard by, a person appointed by the Secretary of State for the purpose[13].

On the appeal the Secretary of State must consider the matters to which the certificate relates as if the application for the certificate had been made to him in the first instance, and must either confirm the certificate, or vary it, or cancel it and issue a different certificate in its place, as he considers appropriate[14].

The Secretary of State may cause a local inquiry to be held for the purpose of the exercise of any of his functions under the Land Compensation Act 1961[15].

1 As to the meaning of 'local planning authority' see PARA 763 note 8.
2 Ie a certificate under the Land Compensation Act 1961 s 17: see PARAS 772–776.
3 As to the meaning of 'land' see PARA 516 note 2.
4 As to the Secretary of State see PARA 507 note 1. The functions of the Secretary of State under the Land Compensation Act 1961, so far as they are exercisable in relation to Wales, are now exercisable by the Welsh Ministers: see the National Assembly for Wales (Transfer of Functions) Order 1999, SI 1999/672, art 2, Sch 1; and the Government of Wales Act 2006 s 162(1), Sch 11 para 30. As to the Welsh Assembly Government and the Welsh Ministers see CONSTITUTIONAL LAW AND HUMAN RIGHTS.
5 As to the meaning of 'authority possessing compulsory purchase powers' see PARA 763 note 6.
6 Land Compensation Act 1961 s 18(1). Section 18 also applies in relation to an application made by virtue of s 19(1): see PARA 772.
7 See the Land Compensation Act 1961 s 18(4); and PARA 776.
8 Land Compensation Development Order 1974, SI 1974/539, art 4(1), (2).
9 Land Compensation Development Order 1974, SI 1974/539, art 4(2). As to the meaning of 'parties directly concerned' see PARA 772 note 3.

10 Application for any extension of time must be made before expiry of the period: *R v Secretary of State for the Environment, ex p Ward, Ward v Secretary of State for the Environment and Secretary of State for Transport* [1995] JPL B39.
11 Land Compensation Development Order 1974, SI 1974/539, art 4(3).
12 Land Compensation Development Order 1974, SI 1974/539, art 4(4).
13 Land Compensation Act 1961 s 18(3).
14 Land Compensation Act 1961 s 18(2).
15 See the Land Compensation Act 1961 s 37. The provisions of the Local Government Act 1972 s 250 which relate to the giving of evidence at, and defraying the cost of, local inquiries (see LOCAL GOVERNMENT vol 69 (2009) PARA 105) have effect with respect to any such inquiry: Land Compensation Act 1961 s 37; Interpretation Act 1978 s 17(2)(a). See also PARA 587 et seq.

778. Appeal to the High Court from Secretary of State. If the local planning authority[1] or any person aggrieved[2] by a decision of the Secretary of State[3] as to a certificate of appropriate alternative development[4] desires to question the validity of that decision on the ground that it is not within the statutory powers[5] or that any of the requirements of the relevant statutory provisions[6], or of a development order[7], or of the Tribunals and Inquiries Act 1992 or any enactment replaced thereby or rules made thereunder have not been complied with in relation to the decision, that person or authority may, within six weeks from the date of the decision, apply to the High Court[8], which may:

(1) by interim order suspend the operation of the decision until the determination of the proceedings[9];

(2) quash the decision if satisfied that it is not within the statutory powers or that the applicant's interests have been substantially prejudiced by a failure to comply with the relevant requirements[10].

Subject to such an application, the validity of the Secretary of State's decision may not be questioned in any legal proceedings whatsoever[11]; but this does not affect the exercise of the jurisdiction of any court in respect of any refusal or failure on the part of the Secretary of State to give a decision on an appeal[12] to him[13].

1 As to the meaning of 'local planning authority' see PARA 763 note 8.
2 As to the meaning of 'person aggrieved' see ADMINISTRATIVE LAW vol 1(1) (2001 Reissue) PARA 56.
3 As to the Secretary of State see PARA 507 note 1. The functions of the Secretary of State under the Land Compensation Act 1961, so far as they are exercisable in relation to Wales, are now exercisable by the Welsh Ministers: see the National Assembly for Wales (Transfer of Functions) Order 1999, SI 1999/672, art 2, Sch 1; and the Government of Wales Act 2006 s 162(1), Sch 11 para 30. As to the Welsh Assembly Government and the Welsh Ministers see CONSTITUTIONAL LAW AND HUMAN RIGHTS.
4 Ie a decision on an appeal under the Land Compensation Act 1961 s 18: see PARA 777.
5 Ie within the powers of the Land Compensation Act 1961: see Pt III (ss 17–22); and PARAS 772–777.
6 Ie the requirements of the Land Compensation Act 1961: see Pt III; and PARAS 772–777.
7 As to the meaning of 'development order' see PARA 762 note 4.
8 Land Compensation Act 1961 s 21(1) (amended by the Tribunals and Inquiries Act 1992 s 18(1), Sch 3 para 1). As to the procedure on the application see PARA 613.
9 Land Compensation Act 1961 s 21(1)(a).
10 Land Compensation Act 1961 s 21(1)(b).
11 Land Compensation Act 1961 s 21(2). As to the effect of this provision see *Anisminic Ltd v Foreign Compensation Commission* [1969] 2 AC 147, [1969] 1 All ER 208, HL; and ADMINISTRATIVE LAW vol 1(1) (2001 Reissue) PARA 21.
12 See note 4.
13 Land Compensation Act 1961 s 21(3).

779. Service of notices and documents. Any notice or other document required or authorised to be served or given under the statutory provisions relating to certificates of appropriate alternative development[1] or compensation where permission for additional development is granted after acquisition[2] may be served or given either:

(1)   by delivering it to the person on whom it is to be served or to whom it is to be delivered[3]; or

(2)   by leaving it at the usual or last known place of abode of that person or, in a case in which an address for service has been furnished by that person, at that address[4]; or

(3)   by sending it in a prepaid registered letter[5] addressed to that person at his usual or last known place of abode, or, in a case in which an address for service has been furnished by that person, at that address[6]; or

(4)   in the case of an incorporated company or body, by delivering it to the secretary or clerk of the company or body at its registered or principal office, or sending it in a prepaid registered letter addressed to the secretary or clerk of the company or body at that office[7].

Where the notice or document is required or authorised to be served on any person as having an interest in premises, and the name of that person cannot be ascertained after reasonable inquiry, the notice is deemed to be duly served if:

(a)   being addressed to him either by name or by the description of 'the owner' of the premises (describing them) it is delivered or sent in the manner mentioned in head (1), (2) or (3) above[8]; or

(b)   being so addressed, and marked in the prescribed manner[9], it is sent in a prepaid registered letter to the premises and is not returned to the authority sending it, or is delivered to some person on those premises or is affixed conspicuously to some object on those premises[10].

1   Ie under the Land Compensation Act 1961 Pt III (ss 17–22): see PARA 772 et seq.

2   Ie under the Land Compensation Act 1961 Pt IV (ss 23–29): see PARA 781 et seq.

3   Land Compensation Act 1961 s 38(1)(a).

4   Land Compensation Act 1961 s 38(1)(b).

5   References to the registered post include a reference to the recorded delivery service: see the Recorded Delivery Service Act 1962 s 1(1), (2), Schedule para 1. However, any reference in any legislation or legal document to 'Registered Post' or 'the Registered Service' must be taken to be a reference to 'Special Delivery', as it is the same service in all material particulars: see the Successor Postal Services Company Inland Letter Post Scheme 2001 Sch 2; and POST OFFICE vol 36(2) (Reissue) PARAS 116–119. Any enactment which requires or authorises a document or other thing to be sent by post (whether or not it makes any other provision in that respect) is not to be construed as limited to requiring or (as the case may be) authorising that thing to be sent by the postal system of the Post Office company: Postal Services Act 2000 s 127(4), Sch 8 para 1.

6   Land Compensation Act 1961 s 38(1)(c).

7   Land Compensation Act 1961 s 38(1)(d).

8   Land Compensation Act 1961 s 38(2)(a).

9   Ie marked in the manner for the time being prescribed by regulations under the Town and Country Planning Act 1990 for securing that notices thereunder are plainly identifiable as a communication of importance (see TOWN AND COUNTRY PLANNING): Land Compensation Act 1961 s 38(2); Planning (Consequential Provisions) Act 1990 s 2(4).

10 Land Compensation Act 1961 s 38(2)(b).

(5) EFFECT OF PLANNING PERMISSIONS WHERE COMPENSATION FOR GRANT OR REFUSAL OF PERMISSION PAYABLE OR REPAYABLE

(i) Outstanding Right to Compensation for Refusal etc of Planning Permission

780. In general. The Town and Country Planning Act 1947 in effect attempted to nationalise the development value of land[1]. This scheme was abandoned in 1953[2] but there remained an extremely narrow and increasingly anachronistic class of cases where compensation had been paid for a refusal of planning permission in the period between 1947 and 1953 and where there was a possible liability on landowners in respect of certain land to pay a development charge on the enhancement of the value of their land as a result of the obtaining of planning permission. The relevant provisions were continued in effect by Part V of the Town and Country Planning Act 1990[3] but were repealed by the Planning and Compensation Act 1991 in relation to claims made after 25 September 1991[4] and are of historical relevance only.

Statutory provision is, however, still made for cases where there is an outstanding right to compensation for the refusal of planning permission[5]. Where, in the case of any compulsory acquisition, a planning decision[6] or order has been made before the service of the notice to treat[7], and in consequence of the decision or order any person is entitled[8] to compensation for the depreciation of the value of an interest in land[9] which consists of or includes the whole or part of the relevant land[10], then if: (1) no notice stating that the compensation has become payable has been registered[11] before the date of service of the notice to treat, whether or not a claim for compensation has been made; but (2) such a notice is registered on or after that date, the compensation payable in respect of the compulsory acquisition must be assessed as if that notice had been registered before the date of service of the notice to treat and had remained on the register of local land charges on that date[12].

1 The Town and Country Planning Act 1947 imposed restrictions on the development of land by the requirement of planning permission and provided for the payment of compensation for those restrictions to the extent that they had depreciated the value of the land: see ss 58–68 (repealed). The compensation was to be paid out in full in 1953 (see s 65(2) (repealed)) and land was to be sold and acquired at existing use value, ie without the possibility of removal of permission (see s 51 (repealed)). On obtaining planning permission, owners of land were to pay a development charge and, in effect, to buy back the development value for the loss of which they had been compensated: see ss 69–74 (repealed).

2 The development charge was abolished and the compensation was no longer payable: see the Town and Country Planning Act 1953 s 2 (repealed). It was later decided to attach it to the land on 1 January 1955 and to pay it on the refusal or conditional grant of planning permission so far as the value of the land was depreciated thereby (see the Town and Country Planning Act 1954 ss 19, 20 (repealed)), or when the land was acquired by compulsory purchase under the provisions as to sale at existing use, which continued until 30 October 1958 (see s 31 (repealed)): see the Town and Country Planning Act 1959 ss 1–13, 58, Sch 8 (repealed). Meanwhile, before 1 January 1955, the date on which the unexpended balance was to attach to the land, some claim holdings for such depreciation had been reduced or extinguished by pledges of the claim holding in respect of development charges, or payments in respect of war-damaged land, or by way of development charge, or in respect of land compulsorily acquired, or land disposed of by gift, or where claim holdings had been purchased: see the Town and Country Planning Act 1954 ss 1–14 (repealed). If these payments were less than the value of the claim holding before 1 January 1955, and that holding had not been extinguished by compensation payable in respect of refusals of permission or conditional grant or revocation or modification of it, then the claim holding became attached to the land as the unexpended balance of established development value: see s 17 (repealed). The attachment of the balance to

15 Ie under the Welsh Development Agency Act 1975 s 21A (powers of land acquisition): Land Compensation Act 1961s 23(3)(za) (added by the Government of Wales Act 1998 s 128, Sch 14 para 14; amended by SI 2005/3226).

16 Ie under the Local Government, Planning and Land Act 1980 s 142 or s 143: see TOWN AND COUNTRY PLANNING vol 46(3) (Reissue) PARAS 1455–1457.

17 Land Compensation Act 1961 s 23(3)(a) (as revived: see note 6). Nor is such compensation payable by virtue of an order under the Local Government, Planning and Land Act 1980 s 141 vesting land in an urban development corporation: see s 141(5A); and TOWN AND COUNTRY PLANNING vol 46(3) (Reissue) PARA 1454.

18 Land Compensation Act 1961 s 23(3)(b) (as revived (see note 6); and amended by the Leasehold Reform, Housing and Urban Development Act 1993 s 187(2), Sch 22. As to acquisitions by development corporations and highway authorities in connection with new town areas see TOWN AND COUNTRY PLANNING.

19 As to compulsory purchase orders see PARA 557 et seq.

20 Ie under the Planning (Listed Buildings and Conservation Areas) Act 1990 s 50: see TOWN AND COUNTRY PLANNING vol 46(3) (Reissue) PARA 1159.

21 Land Compensation Act 1961 s 23(3)(c) (as revived (see note 6); and amended by the Leasehold Reform, Housing and Urban Development Act 1993 s 181(1), (3)).

22 Ie under the Housing and Regeneration Act 2008 Pt 1 (ss 1–58) (acquisition by the Homes and Communities Agency): see HOUSING.

23 Land Compensation Act 1961 s 23(3)(d) (added by the Leasehold Reform, Housing and Urban Development Act 1993 s 181(1), (3); and amended by the Housing and Regeneration Act 2008 Sch 8 para 2).

24 Land Compensation Act 1961 s 23(4) (as revived: see note 6). Section 23(4) does not apply where Sch 3 para 7(1) applies (see note 9): Sch 3 para 7(2) (as revived: see note 7).

25 Ie the rate prescribed under the Land Compensation Act 1961 s 32: see PARA 641 note 6.

26 Land Compensation Act 1961 s 23(5) (as revived: see note 6).

27 Planning and Compensation Act 1991 s 80(2), Sch 18 Pt II.

28 Planning and Compensation Act 1991 s 80(3).

29 Ie the Land Compensation Act 1961 Pt I (ss 1–4).

30 Ie so far as applicable and subject to the Land Compensation Act 1961 ss 24–29.

31 Land Compensation Act 1961 s 23(6) (as revived: see note 6).

782. Meaning of 'additional development'. For the purposes of the statutory provisions relating to compensation where a planning decision is made after acquisition[1], 'additional development', in relation to an acquisition or sale of an interest in land[2], means any development[3] which is not development:

(1) for the purposes of the functions for which a local authority[4] acquired the interest, when it is the acquiring authority[5] and acquired the interest for the purposes of any of its functions;

(2) for the purposes of the project for which the acquiring authority acquired the interest, when that authority is not a local authority;

(3) for which planning permission[6] was in force on the relevant date[7];

(4) for which it was assumed[8], for the purpose of assessing compensation in the case of compulsory acquisition, that planning permission would be granted; and

(5) for which it would have been so assumed, in the case of a sale by agreement, if the interest had been compulsorily acquired by the acquiring authority in pursuance of a notice to treat[9] served on the relevant date, instead of being sold by agreement[10].

1 Ie the Land Compensation Act 1961 Pt IV (ss 23–29): see PARA 781 et seq.

2 As to the meaning of 'land' see PARA 516 note 2.

3 As to the meaning of 'development' see PARA 762 note 2.

4 For these purposes, 'local authority' means: (1) a charging authority or precepting authority (as defined in the Local Government Finance Act 1988 s 144: see LOCAL GOVERNMENT vol 29(1) (Reissue) PARA 530), or a combined police authority; (2) a fire and rescue authority in Wales constituted by a scheme under the Fire and Rescue Services Act 2004 s 2 (see FIRE SERVICES) or a scheme to which s 4 applies; (3) a levying board within the meaning of the Local Government

Finance Act 1988 s 74 (see LOCAL GOVERNMENT vol 29(1) (Reissue) PARA 530); (4) a body as regards which s 75 applies (see LOCAL GOVERNMENT vol 29(1) (Reissue) PARA 530); (5) any joint board or joint committee if all the constituent authorities are such authorities as are described in heads (1)–(4) above; and (6) the Honourable Society of the Inner Temple or the Honourable Society of the Middle Temple; and includes any internal drainage board under the Land Drainage Act 1991 s 1, Sch 1: Land Compensation Act 1961 s 29(1) (repealed; revived by the Planning and Compensation Act 1991 s 66(1), Sch 14 para 1; amended by the Fire and Rescue Services Act 2004 s 53(1), Sch 1 para 15(1), (2), (3)); Interpretation Act 1978 s 17(2)(a).

5   As to the meaning of 'acquiring authority' see PARA 622 note 1.
6   As to the meaning of 'planning permission' see PARA 762 note 1.
7   As to the meaning of 'relevant date' see PARA 781 note 13.
8   Ie in accordance with the provisions of the Land Compensation Act 1961 ss 14–16: see PARA 762 et seq.
9   As to the notice to treat see PARA 616 et seq. As to the meaning of 'notice to treat' see PARA 636 note 4.
10 Land Compensation Act 1961 s 29(1) (as revived: see note 4).

783.   Special provisions relating to mortgaged and settled land. No compensation is payable[1] where a planning decision is made after acquisition in respect of a compulsory acquisition or sale by agreement where the interest acquired or sold was the interest of a mortgagee, as distinct from an interest subject to a mortgage[2].

Any compensation paid[3] to the trustees of a settlement[4] in respect of a compulsory acquisition or sale by agreement is applicable by the trustees as if it were proceeds of the sale of the interest acquired or sold[5].

1   Ie by virtue of the Land Compensation Act 1961 s 23 (see PARA 781) or by virtue of that provision as applied by s 25 or s 26 (see PARAS 785–786): Sch 3 paras 6, 8 (repealed; revived by the Planning and Compensation Act 1991 s 66(1), Sch 14 paras 1, 2).
2   Land Compensation Act 1961 Sch 3 para 6 (as revived: see note 1).
3   Ie paid by virtue of the Land Compensation Act 1961 s 23 or by virtue of that provision as applied by s 25 or s 26: Sch 3 paras 7(3), 8 (as revived: see note 1).
4   As to the meaning of 'settlement' see PARA 781 note 9. As to settlements see PARA 553 note 11.
5   Land Compensation Act 1961 Sch 3 para 7(3) (as revived: see note 1).

784.   Claims for compensation where planning decision made after acquisition. For the purpose of facilitating the making of claims for compensation where a planning decision is made after acquisition[1], the person entitled to receive the compensation or purchase price in respect of a relevant acquisition or sale[2] or any person claiming under him[3] may give to the acquiring authority[4] an address for service[5]. Where a planning decision is made[6] at any time after a person has so given an address for service and before the end of the specified period[7], the acquiring authority must give notice of the decision in the prescribed form[8] to that person at that address[9].

Where a person has given an address for service to an acquiring authority and that authority, before the end of the specified period, ceases to be entitled to an interest in the whole or part of the land[10] comprised in the acquisition or sale, without remaining or becoming entitled to a freehold interest in, or tenancy[11] of, that land or that part of it, that authority must notify the local planning authority[12]; and after that it is the duty of the local planning authority to give notice to the acquiring authority of any planning decision of which the acquiring authority is required to give notice under the provisions described above[13].

A claim for compensation in respect of a planning decision[14] does not have effect if made more than six months after the date:

(1)   of the decision[15], if the claim is made by a person who has not given the acquiring authority an address for service; or

(amended by SI 2000/253); and the Government of Wales Act 2006 s 162(1), Sch 11 para 30. As to the Welsh Assembly Government and the Welsh Ministers see CONSTITUTIONAL LAW AND HUMAN RIGHTS.

9 As to the meaning of 'local planning authority' see PARA 763 note 8; and TOWN AND COUNTRY PLANNING vol 46(1) (Reissue) PARA 28.

10 Land Compensation Act 1961 s 25(1) (s 25 repealed; revived by the Planning and Compensation Act 1991 s 66(1), Sch 14 para 1).

11 Ie under the Land Compensation Act 1961 s 24(1) (see PARA 784) as applied by s 25(1): s 25(2)(a) (as so revived).

12 As to the meaning of 'acquiring authority' see PARA 622 note 1.

13 Land Compensation Act 1961 s 25(2)(b) (as revived: see note 10).

14 For the prescribed form see the Land Compensation (Additional Development) (Forms) Regulations 1992, SI 1992/271, reg 3(b), Schedule, Form 2.

15 Land Compensation Act 1961 s 25(2) (as revived: see note 10). An acquiring authority is not, however, required to give such notice of proposed development to the entitled person if: (1) an address for service has been given to the authority by such a person as is mentioned in s 24(1)(b) (ie any person claiming under the entitled person as being a person who, if compensation under s 23 became payable, would be entitled to it by virtue of s 23(4) (see PARA 781)); and (2) the authority has reasonable grounds for believing that the entitled person is dead or that any other act or event has occurred as mentioned in s 23(4)(b): s 25(3) (as so revived).

16 Ie under the Land Compensation Act 1961 s 23: see PARA 781.

17 Ie in accordance with the Land Compensation Act 1961 s 25(2): see the text and notes 10–15.

18 Land Compensation Act 1961 s 25(4) (as revived: see note 10).

786. Extension to Crown development. Where:

(1) any interest in land[1] is compulsorily acquired or is sold to an authority possessing compulsory purchase powers[2], and before the end of the period of ten years beginning with the date of completion[3] there is initiated[4] any additional development[5] of any of the land which was comprised in the acquisition or sale[6]; and

(2) the development in question is development for which planning permission[7] is not required because it is initiated by or on behalf of the Crown[8] or there is a Crown or Duchy interest[9] in the land and the development is initiated in right of that interest[10],

the provisions relating to claims for compensation where a planning decision is made after acquisition[11] apply as if a planning decision granting permission for that development had been made at the time when the additional development is so initiated[12].

Where those provisions have effect as so applied in relation to the initiation of any development, and before the development is initiated a person who is entitled[13] to give an address for service has given such an address to the acquiring authority[14], it is the duty of that authority to give notice in the prescribed form[15] of the initiation of the development to the entitled person at the address given by him to the authority[16]. Where, however, this duty to give notice is the duty of a government department, and the Minister in charge of the department certifies that for reasons of national security it is necessary that the nature of the development should not be disclosed, except to the extent specified in the certificate, the department must give notice of development but is not required to give any particulars of the nature of the development except to the extent so specified[17].

A claim for compensation[18] in respect of the initiation of any development does not have effect if made more than six months after:

(a) the date on which notice was given[19] to the person making the claim, if he is a person to whom notice has been given; or

(b) the time the development is initiated, in any other case[20].

1   As to the meaning of 'land' see PARA 516 note 2.
2   As to the meaning of 'authority possessing compulsory purchase powers' see PARA 763 note 6.
3   As to the meaning of 'date of completion' see PARA 781 note 3.
4   As to when development is initiated see PARA 785 note 5. As to the meaning of 'development' see PARA 762 note 2.
5   As to the meaning of 'additional development' see PARA 782.
6   Land Compensation Act 1961 s 26(1)(a) (s 26 repealed; revived by the Planning and Compensation Act 1991 s 66(1), Sch 14 para 1).
7   As to the meaning of 'planning permission' see PARA 762 note 1.
8   Land Compensation Act 1961 s 26(1)(b), (2)(a) (as revived: see note 6).
9   For these purposes, 'Crown or Duchy interest' means an interest belong to Her Majesty in right of the Crown or of the Duchy of Lancaster, or belonging to the Duchy of Cornwall, or belonging to a government department, or held in trust for Her Majesty for the purposes of a government department: Land Compensation Act 1961 s 26(7) (as revived: see note 6).
10 Land Compensation Act 1961 s 26(1)(b), (2)(b) (as revived: see note 6).
11 Ie the provisions of the Land Compensation Act 1961 ss 23, 24(1): see PARAS 781, 784. As to the meaning of 'planning decision' see PARA 781 note 4.
12 Land Compensation Act 1961 s 26(1) (as revived: see note 6).
13 Ie under the Land Compensation Act 1961 s 24(1) (see PARA 784) as that provision is applied by s 26(1): see s 26(3)(b) (as revived: see note 6).
14 As to the meaning of 'acquiring authority' see PARA 622 note 1.
15 For the prescribed form see the Land Compensation (Additional Development) (Forms) Regulations 1992, SI 1992/271, reg 3(c), Schedule, Form 3.
16 Land Compensation Act 1961 s 26(3) (as revived: see note 6). An acquiring authority is not, however, required to give such notice of proposed development to the entitled person if: (1) an address for service has been given to the authority by such a person as is mentioned in s 24(1)(b) (ie any person claiming under the entitled person as being a person who, if compensation under s 23 became payable, would be entitled to it by virtue of s 23(4) (see PARA 781)); and (2) the authority has reasonable grounds for believing that the entitled person is dead or that any other act or event has occurred as mentioned in s 23(4)(b): s 26(5) (as so revived).
17 Land Compensation Act 1961 s 26(4) (as revived: see note 6).
18 Ie under the Land Compensation Act 1961 s 23: see PARA 781.
19 Ie under the Land Compensation Act 1961 s 26(3): see the text and notes 13–16.
20 Land Compensation Act 1961 s 26(6) (as revived: see note 6).

(6) SCHEME FOR WHICH THE LAND IS TAKEN TO BE DISREGARDED

(i) The General Principle

787.   The general principle (the 'Pointe Gourde' principle).   In valuing the land taken there must be disregarded any increase in value which is due to the scheme for which the land is taken; it is well settled that compensation for the compulsory acquisition of land cannot include an increase in value which is entirely due to the scheme underlying the acquisition[1]. The purpose of this principle is to prevent the acquisition of the land being at a price which is inflated by the very project or scheme which gives rise to the acquisition[2]. Conversely, the compensation payable cannot include any decrease in value which is entirely due to this scheme[3]; no account is taken of any depreciation of the value of the relevant interest[4] which is attributable to the fact that (whether by way of allocation or other particulars contained in the current development plan[5] or by any other means[6]) an indication has been given that the relevant land[7] is, or is likely to be, acquired by an authority possessing compulsory purchase powers[8].

1   *Pointe Gourde Quarrying and Transport Co Ltd v Sub-Intendent of Crown Lands* [1947] AC 565, PC (approved in *Davy v Leeds Corpn* [1965] 1 All ER 753, [1965] 1 WLR 445, HL); *Penny v Penny* (1867) LR 5 Eq 227; *Re Lucas and Chesterfield Gas and Water Board* [1909]

1 KB 16, CA; *Cedar Rapids Manufacturing and Power Co v Lacoste* [1914] AC 569, PC; *Fraser v City of Fraserville* [1917] AC 187, PC; *Re Gough and Aspatria, Silloth and District Joint Water Board* [1904] 1 KB 417 at 423, CA; *Vyricherla Narayana Gajapatiraju v Revenue Divisional Officer, Vizagapatam* ('the Indian case') [1939] AC 302 at 313, [1939] 2 All ER 317 at 322, PC. The principle is commonly referred to as the 'Pointe Gourde' principle after *Pointe Gourde Quarrying and Transport Co Ltd v Sub-Intendent of Crown Lands* above. It applies to the value of the interest when ascertained and not to the ascertainment of what is the interest to be valued, and cannot affect the lessor's rights in relation to his lessee: see *Minister of Transport v Pettitt* (1968) 20 P & CR 344 at 355, CA; *Rugby Joint Water Board v Foottit, Rugby Joint Water Board v Shaw-Fox* [1973] AC 202, [1972] 1 All ER 1057, HL; *Abbey Homesteads (Developments) Ltd v Northamptonshire County Council* (1992) 64 P & CR 377, [1992] 2 EGLR 18, CA. As to agricultural holdings see PARA 807 note 8. When valuing the land in relation to other land, the actual scheme of the acquiring authority on that other land must also be disregarded: see the cases cited above; and PARA 790. The exact nature of the scheme could be determined, and any apparent conflict between the Pointe Gourde principle and the Indian case reconciled, if the cases were each seen as turning on their own particular facts: *Waters v Welsh Development Agency* [2004] UKHL 19, [2004] 2 All ER 915, [2004] 1 WLR 1304; affg [2002] EWCA Civ 924, [2003] 4 All ER 384, [2002] RVR 298 (where the Lands Tribunal was entitled to treat the creation of a wetlands nature reserve, intended to mitigate the effects of a large scale river barrage project, as an integral part of the scheme that comprised the barrage project). For a consideration of the case law see *Spirerose Ltd v Transport for London* [2008] EWCA Civ 1230, [2009] 1 P & CR 471, [2008] All ER (D) 128 (Nov) (importance of considering both policy and principle).

    The Lands Tribunal was abolished on 1 June 2009 and its functions were transferred to the Upper Tribunal: see PARA 720.

2   *Wilson v Liverpool City Council* [1971] 1 All ER 628 at 635, [1971] 1 WLR 302 at 310, CA, per Widgery LJ.

3   See the Land Compensation Act 1961 s 9; *Jelson Ltd v Blaby District Council* [1978] 1 All ER 548, [1977] 1 WLR 1020, CA; *Ryde International plc v London Regional Transport* [2001] 1 EGLR 101, [2001] RVR 59, Lands Tribunal; *Ryde International plc v London Regional Transport* [2003] RVR 49, Lands Tribunal.

4   As to the meaning of 'relevant interest' see PARA 636 note 4. The depreciation, for the purposes of the Land Compensation Act 1961 s 9, is that sustained by the acquired land, distinct and separate both from the site as a whole and any land retained: *English Property Corpn plc v Royal Borough of Kingston Upon Thames* [1998] JPL 1158, CA.

5   As to the meaning of 'current development plan' see PARA 766 note 2.

6   An indication given by 'other means' must provide information which is available not merely to the owner but also to a potential purchaser: *Abbey Homesteads (Developments) Ltd v Northamptonshire County Council* (1992) 64 P & CR 377 at 385, [1992] 2 EGLR 18 at 21, CA. See also *Thornton v Wakefield Metropolitan District Council* (1991) 62 P & CR 441, [1991] 2 EGLR 215, Lands Tribunal; *London Borough of Hackney v Macfarlane* (1970) 21 P & CR 342, CA; *Trocette Property Co Ltd v GLC* (1974) 28 P & CR 408, CA. As to the method of assessing the market value of the land acquired see PARAS 797–799.

7   As to the meaning of 'relevant land' see PARA 762 note 5.

8   Land Compensation Act 1961 s 9 (amended by the Town and Country Planning Act 1968 s 108, Sch 11); and see *London Borough of Hackney v Macfarlane* (1970) 21 P & CR 342, CA; *Trocette Property Co Ltd v GLC* (1974) 28 P & CR 408, CA; *Tranter v Birmingham City District Council* (1975) 31 P & CR 327, Lands Tribunal; *London and Provincial Poster Group Ltd v Oldham Metropolitan Borough Council* [1991] 1 EGLR 214, Lands Tribunal; *Thornton v Wakefield Metropolitan District Council* (1991) 62 P & CR 441, [1991] 2 EGLR 215, Lands Tribunal. As to the meaning of 'authority possessing compulsory purchase powers' see PARA 763 note 6.

(ii) Statutory Disregard of Actual or Prospective Development in Certain Cases

788. Statutory disregard of the scheme for which land is acquired. No account is to be taken of any increase or diminution in the value of the relevant interest[1] which is attributable in certain circumstances[2] to the carrying out, or the prospect of, so much of the relevant development[3] as would not have been likely to be carried out if the statutory conditions[4] had been satisfied[5]. This statutory provision does not, however, affect the general principle[6]; both the statutory assumptions and the general principle operate concurrently[7]. Identification of the scheme which must be disregarded will turn on the facts of each case[8], but there is no provision for the disregard of any increase in value due to persons in the market who are prepared to develop the land to the same as, or to a lesser extent than, it would be developed under the acquiring authority's scheme[9].

1   As to the meaning of 'relevant interest' see PARA 636 note 4.
2   Ie the circumstances described in any of the provisions of the Land Compensation Act 1961 s 6(1), Sch 1 paras 1–4B col 1: see PARA 790 et seq.
3   For these purposes, references to 'development' are to be construed as including reference the clearing of the land: Land Compensation Act 1961 s 6(3). As to the meaning of 'development' generally see PARA 762 note 2. The relevant development referred to in the text is the development mentioned (in relation to the circumstances described in any of the provisions of Sch 1 paras 1–4B col 1) in Sch 1 paras 1–4B col 2: see PARA 790 et seq.
4   Ie the conditions mentioned in the Land Compensation Act 1961 s 6(1)(a) (see PARA 790) or, where the circumstances are those described in any of the provisions of Sch 1 paras 2–4B col 1, the condition that the area or areas referred to therein had not been defined or designated as therein mentioned: see s 6(1)(b) (amended by the Housing Act 1988 s 78(4)); and PARA 791 et seq.
5   Land Compensation Act 1961 s 6(1).
6   Ie the Pointe Gourde principle: see PARA 787.
7   *Viscount Camrose v Basingstoke Corpn* [1966] 3 All ER 161, [1966] 1 WLR 1100, CA.
8   *Wilson v Liverpool City Council* [1971] 1 All ER 628 at 635, [1971] 1 WLR 302 at 310, CA, per Widgery LJ.
9   As to market value see further PARAS 797–799.

789. Disregard of special suitability or adaptability of land for certain purposes. The special suitability or adaptability of the land for any purpose[1] must not be taken into account, in assessing compensation in respect of its compulsory acquisition, if that purpose is a purpose to which it could be applied only in pursuance of statutory powers[2], or for which there is no market apart from the requirements of any authority possessing compulsory purchase powers[3].

1   'Purpose' connotes an actual or potential use of the land itself; it cannot be regarded as meaning a purpose which is only concerned with the use of the products of that land elsewhere: see *Pointe Gourde Quarrying and Transport Co Ltd v Sub-Intendent of Crown Lands* [1947] AC 565, PC. See also *Waters v Welsh Development Agency* [2004] UKHL 19, [2004] 2 All ER 915, [2004] 1 WLR 1304; affg [2002] EWCA Civ 924, [2003] 4 All ER 384, [2002] RVR 298 (the 'purpose' of any project may be defined at different levels so that the ultimate purpose may not be left out of consideration for compensation purposes while other more immediate, but lesser, purposes may be). The purchase of the freehold interest in land for the purposes of the merger with the leasehold interest is not a use of the land itself and a purchaser for such a purpose is not excluded: *Lambe v Secretary of State for War* [1955] 2 QB 612, [1955] 2 All ER 386, CA. See *Spirerose Ltd v Transport for London* [2008] EWCA Civ 1230, [2009] 1 P & CR 471, [2008] All ER (D) 128 (Nov).
2   Statutory powers not related to the use of the land proposed to be acquired cannot justify the disregarding of the special suitability or adaptability of that land for the purposes of assessing compensation under this rule: see *Hertfordshire County Council v Ozanne* [1991] 1 All ER 769, (1991) 62 P & CR 1, HL.
3   Land Compensation Act 1961 s 5 r 3 (amended by the Planning and Compensation Act 1991 ss 70, 84(6), Sch 15 para 1, Sch 19 Pt III). For an example where the rule (as originally enacted) did not apply see *Batchelor v Kent County Council* (1989) 59 P & CR 357, [1990] 1 EGLR 32, CA (land comprised in the compulsory purchase order provided the most suitable, but not the only, access to a development site; held that 'most suitable' does not correspond with 'specially suitable'). See also *Blandrent Investment Developments Ltd v British Gas Corpn* [1979] 2 EGLR 18, HL. As to the meaning of 'authority possessing compulsory purchase powers' see PARA 763 note 6.

790.   Development on other land for purposes for which that land and the land to be valued is acquired.   An increase or diminution in the value of the relevant interest which must be disregarded[1] arises where the acquisition is for purposes involving development[2] of any of the land authorised to be acquired[3], if the increase or diminution is attributable to the carrying out, or the prospect, of development of any of the land authorised to be acquired (other than the relevant land[4]) which is development for any of the purposes for which any part of the land (including any part of the relevant land) is to be acquired, so far as that development would not have been likely to be carried out if the acquiring authority[5] had not acquired, and did not propose to acquire, any of the land so authorised[6].

1   Ie an increase or decrease which must be disregarded in accordance with the Land Compensation Act 1961 s 6(1): see PARA 788. As to the meaning of 'relevant interest' see PARA 636 note 4.
2   As to the meaning of 'development' for these purposes see PARA 788 note 3. See also PARA 762 note 2.
3   'Land authorised to be acquired' means: (1) in relation to an acquisition authorised by a compulsory purchase order or a special enactment, the aggregate of the land comprised in the authorisation (Land Compensation Act 1961 s 6(3)(a)); and (2) in relation to a compulsory acquisition not so authorised but effected under powers exercisable by virtue of any enactment for defence purposes, the aggregate of: (a) the land comprised in the notice to treat; and (b) any land contiguous or adjacent to it which is comprised in any other notice to treat served under the like powers not more than one month before and not more than one month after the date of service of that notice (s 6(3)(b)). 'Special enactment' means a local enactment, or a provision contained in an Act other than a local or private Act, being a local enactment or provision authorising the compulsory acquisition of land specifically identified in it; and 'local enactment' means any local or private Act or an order confirmed by Parliament or brought into operation in accordance with special parliamentary procedure: s 39(1). As to local and private Acts see STATUTES vol 44(1) (Reissue) PARAS 1211, 1213. As to special parliamentary procedure see PARA 605; and PARLIAMENT vol 34 (Reissue) PARA 912 et seq; STATUTES vol 44(1) (Reissue) PARA 1514. 'Defence purposes' includes any purpose of any of Her Majesty's naval, military or air forces, the service of any visiting force within the Visiting Forces Act 1952 Pt I (ss 1–12), and any purpose of the Secretary of State connected with the service of any of those forces: Land Powers (Defence) Act 1958 s 25(1) (applied by the Land Compensation Act 1961 s 6(3)). As to the Secretary of State see PARA 507 note 1.
4   As to the meaning of 'relevant land' see PARA 762 note 5.
5   As to the meaning of 'acquiring authority' see PARA 622 note 1. Where the land acquired is included in and is part of a clearance area and is purchased for clearing the area, the clearance would not normally be likely to be carried out if the authority had not acquired or did not propose to acquire the land for the purpose, even though the acquiring authority could have proceeded to exercise its powers to make clearance orders instead of purchasing the land: *Davy v Leeds Corpn* [1965] 1 All ER 753, [1965] 1 WLR 445, HL. As to clearance areas see the Housing Act 1985 ss 289–298; and HOUSING vol 22 (2006 Reissue) PARA 425 et seq.
6   Land Compensation Act 1961 s 6(1)(a), Sch 1 Case 1.

791.   Areas of comprehensive development.   An increase or diminution in the value of the relevant interest which must be disregarded[1] arises where any of the relevant land[2] forms part of an area defined in the current development plan as an area of comprehensive development[3], if the increase is attributable to the carrying out, or the prospect, of development[4] of any land in that area (other than the relevant land) in the course of the development or redevelopment of the area in accordance with the plan, so far as that development would not have been likely to be carried out if the area had not been so defined[5].

1   Ie an increase or decrease which must be disregarded in accordance with the Land Compensation Act 1961 s 6(1): see PARA 788. As to the meaning of 'relevant interest' see PARA 636 note 4.
2   As to the meaning of 'relevant land' see PARA 762 note 5.

3   See PARA 766 note 2.
4   As to the meaning of 'development' for these purposes see PARA 788 note 3. See also PARA 762 note 2.
5   Land Compensation Act 1961 s 6(1)(b) (amended by the Housing Act 1988 s 78(4)); Land Compensation Act 1961 Sch 1 Case 2.

792.   Development in area designated as site, or extension of site, of new town. An increase or diminution in the value of the relevant interest which must be disregarded[1] arises where any of the relevant land[2], on the date of the service of the notice to treat[3], forms part of an area designated as the site of a new town[4] or as an extension of the site of a new town[5], if the increase is attributable to the carrying out, or the prospect, of:

(1)   development[6] of any land in that area (other than the relevant land) in the course of development of that area as a new town, or as part of a new town[7]; or

(2)   any public development[8] specified by direction of the Secretary of State[9] as development in connection with which, or in consequence of which, the provision of housing or other facilities is required and for whose purposes an order designating any area as the site, or an extension of the site, of a new town is proposed to be made[10],

so far as that development would not have been likely to be carried out if the area had not been so designated[11].

1   Ie an increase or decrease which must be disregarded in accordance with the Land Compensation Act 1961 s 6(1): see PARA 788. As to the meaning of 'relevant interest' see PARA 636 note 4.
2   As to the meaning of 'relevant land' see PARA 762 note 5.
3   As to the meaning of 'notice to treat' see PARA 636 note 4. As to the notice to treat see PARA 616 et seq.
4   Ie by an order under the New Towns Act 1946 (repealed) or the New Towns Act 1981: see TOWN AND COUNTRY PLANNING. Land is not to be treated as forming part of such an area if the notice to treat is served on or after the transfer date, ie the date on which, by virtue of any enactment contained in any Act relating to new towns, whenever passed, the development corporation established for the purposes of that new town ceases to act, except for the purposes of or incidental to the winding up of its affairs: Land Compensation Act 1961 s 6(2), Sch 1 paras 5, 6 (Sch 1 para 6 amended by the New Towns Act 1966 s 2, Schedule Pt I). In determining whether the land to be acquired and valued forms part of an area designated as the site of a new town, in the case of an area designated by an order operative on or before 29 October 1958, regard must be had to the order as it was in force on that day, any variation becoming operative after that day being disregarded; and, in the case of an area so designated by an order becoming operative after that day, regard must be had to the order in its original form, any variation of the order being disregarded: Land Compensation Act 1961 Sch 1 para 7.
5   Ie by an order under the New Towns Act 1965 s 1 (repealed) or the New Towns Act 1981 s 1: see TOWN AND COUNTRY PLANNING vol 46(3) (Reissue) PARAS 1315–1317.
6   As to the meaning of 'development' for these purposes see PARA 788 note 3. See also PARA 762 note 2.
7   For the purpose of determining whether any development of which there is a prospect on the date of service of the notice to treat would be such development, it is immaterial whether the time when that development will or may take place is a time before, on or after the date when the development corporation established for the purposes of the new town ceases to act except for the purposes of or incidental to the winding up of its affairs: Land Compensation Act 1961 Sch 1 paras 5, 8 (amended by the New Towns Act 1966 Schedule Pt I).
8   'Public development' means development, whether or not in the area designated under the New Towns Act 1981 s 1, in the exercise of statutory powers by: (1) a government department; (2) any statutory undertakers within the meaning of the Town and Country Planning Act 1990 (see TOWN AND COUNTRY PLANNING vol 46(3) (Reissue) PARA 1009) or any body deemed by virtue of any enactment to be statutory undertakers for the purposes of, or of any provision of, that Act; or (3) without prejudice to head (2), any body having power to borrow money with the consent of a Minister, and it includes such development which has already been carried out

when the direction in respect of it is given, as well as such development which is then proposed: Land Compensation Act 1973 s 51(6) (amended by the New Towns Act 1981 s 81, Sch 12 para 9; and the Planning (Consequential Provisions) Act 1990 s 4, Sch 2 para 29(8)).

9   Ie a direction under the Land Compensation Act 1973 s 51. Where the Secretary of State proposes to make an order under the New Towns Act 1981 s 1 designating any area as the site of a new town, or an extension of the site of a new town, and the purpose or main purpose, or one of the main purposes, for which the order is proposed to be made is the provision of housing or other facilities required in connection with, or in consequence of the carrying out of, any public development, he may, before making the order, give a direction specifying that development for the purposes of the Land Compensation Act 1973 s 51 in relation to that area: s 51(1) (amended by the New Towns Act 1981 Sch 12 para 9). No such direction may be given in relation to any area until the Secretary of State has prepared a draft of the order under the New Towns Act 1981 s 1 in respect of that area and has published the notice required by s 1(4), Sch 1 para 2 (see TOWN AND COUNTRY PLANNING vol 46(3) (Reissue) PARA 1316): Land Compensation Act 1973 s 51(3) (amended by the New Towns Act 1981 Sch 12 para 9). Any direction must be given by order, and any order containing such a direction may be varied or revoked by a subsequent order: Land Compensation Act 1973 s 51(4). The power to make such orders is exercisable by statutory instrument, subject to annulment in pursuance of a resolution of either House of Parliament: s 51(5). As to the Secretary of State see PARA 507 note 1. The functions of the Secretary of State under the New Towns Act 1981, so far as they are exercisable in relation to Wales, are now exercisable by the Welsh Ministers: see the National Assembly for Wales (Transfer of Functions) Order 1999, SI 1999/672, art 2, Sch 1; and the Government of Wales Act 2006 s 162(1), Sch 11 para 30. As to the Welsh Assembly Government and the Welsh Ministers see CONSTITUTIONAL LAW AND HUMAN RIGHTS.

10   Ie an order under the New Towns Act 1981 s 1: Land Compensation Act 1973 s 51(1) (amended by the New Towns Act 1981 Sch 12 para 9).

11   Land Compensation Act 1961 s 6(1)(b) (amended by the Housing Act 1988 s 78(4)); Land Compensation Act 1961 Sch 1 Cases 3, 3A (Sch 1 Case 3A added by the New Towns Act 1966 Schedule Pt I); Land Compensation Act 1973 s 51(2)(a). Where, before the date of service of the notice to treat for the purposes of a compulsory acquisition, the land has been disposed of by an authority or body in circumstances where the Land Compensation Act 1961 Sch 1 Case 3 or Case 3A would have applied if the authority or body had been compulsorily acquiring the land at the time of the disposal, then those Cases do not apply for the purposes of that acquisition: Sch 1 para 9 (added by the Local Government, Planning and Land Act 1980 s 133, Sch 25 para 8). The exclusion, as extended to public development (see the text and notes 8–10), applies also so as to exclude any increase or diminution of value to be disregarded under any rule of law relating to the assessment of compensation (see PARAS 761–786): Land Compensation Act 1973 s 51(2)(a).

793. Development in area defined in development plan as area of town development.

An increase or diminution in the value of the relevant interest which must be disregarded[1] arises where any of the relevant land[2] forms part of an area defined in the current development plan[3] as an area of town development[4], if the increase is attributable to the carrying out, or the prospect, of development[5] of any land in that area (other than the relevant land) in the course of town development so far as that development would not have been likely to be carried out if the area had not been so defined as an area of town development[6].

1   Ie an increase or decrease which must be disregarded in accordance with the Land Compensation Act 1961 s 6(1): see PARA 788. As to the meaning of 'relevant interest' see PARA 636 note 4.

2   As to the meaning of 'relevant land' see PARA 762 note 5.

3   As to the meaning of 'current development plan' see PARA 766 note 2.

4   Ie town development within the meaning of the Town Development Act 1952 (repealed): see s 1(1) (repealed by the Local Government and Housing Act 1989 ss 175, 194(4), Sch 12 Pt II).

5   As to the meaning of 'development' for these purposes see PARA 788 note 3. See also PARA 762 note 2.

6   Land Compensation Act 1961 s 6(1)(b) (amended by the Housing Act 1988 s 78(4)); Land Compensation Act 1961 Sch 1 Case 4.

794. Development in area designated as urban development area. An increase or diminution in the value of the relevant interest which must be disregarded[1] arises where any of the relevant land[2] forms part of an area designated as an urban development area[3], if the increase is attributable to the carrying out, or the prospect, of development[4] of any land (other than the relevant land) in the course of the development or redevelopment of that area as an urban development area[5].

1 Ie an increase or decrease which must be disregarded in accordance with the Land Compensation Act 1961 s 6(1): see PARA 788. As to the meaning of 'relevant interest' see PARA 636 note 4.
2 As to the meaning of 'relevant land' see PARA 762 note 5.
3 Ie by an order under the Local Government, Planning and Land Act 1980 s 134: see TOWN AND COUNTRY PLANNING vol 46(3) (Reissue) PARAS 1426–1427. In assessing the increase or diminution in value to be left out of account, no increase is to be excluded from being left out of account merely because it is attributable: (1) to any development of land which was carried out before the area was designated as an urban development area; (2) to any development or prospect of development of land outside the urban development area; (3) to any development or prospect of development of land by an authority, other than the acquiring authority, possessing compulsory purchase powers: Land Compensation Act 1961 Sch 1 para 10 (Sch 1 paras 10, 11 both added by the Local Government, Planning and Land Act 1980 s 145(2)). As to the meaning of 'authority possessing compulsory purchase powers' see PARA 763 note 6. As to the meaning of 'acquiring authority' see PARA 622 note 1. The Land Compensation Act 1961 Sch 1 para 10 has effect in relation to any increase or diminution in value to be left out of account by virtue of any rule of law relating to the assessment of compensation in respect of compulsory acquisition as it has effect in relation to any increase or diminution in value to be left out of account by virtue of s 6: Sch 1 para 11 (as so added). See PARAS 761–786.
4 As to the meaning of 'development' for these purposes see PARA 788 note 3; and see also PARA 762 note 2.
5 Land Compensation Act 1961 s 6(1)(b) (amended by the Housing Act 1988 s 78(4)), Land Compensation Act 1961 Sch 1 Case 4A (added by the Local Government, Planning and Land Act 1980 s 145(1)).

795. Development in housing action trust area. An increase or diminution in the value of the relevant interest which must be disregarded[1] arises where any of the relevant land[2] forms part of a housing action trust area[3], if the increase is attributable to the carrying out, or the prospect, of development[4] of any land (other than the relevant land) in the course of the development or redevelopment of that area as a housing action trust area[5].

1 Ie an increase or decrease which must be disregarded in accordance with the Land Compensation Act 1961 s 6(1): see PARA 788. As to the meaning of 'relevant interest' see PARA 636 note 4.
2 As to the meaning of 'relevant land' see PARA 762 note 5.
3 Ie a housing action trust area established under the Housing Act 1988 Pt III (ss 60–92): see HOUSING vol 22 (2006 Reissue) PARA 340.
4 As to the meaning of 'development' for these purposes see PARA 788 note 3. See also PARA 762 note 2.
5 Land Compensation Act 1961 s 6(1)(b) (amended by the Housing Act 1988 s 78(4)); Land Compensation Act 1961 Sch 1 Case 4B (added by the Housing Act 1988 s 78(3)).

796. Subsequent acquisition of adjacent land. Where, in connection with the compulsory acquisition of an interest in land[1], a diminution in the value of an interest in other land has been taken into account[2] in assessing compensation for injurious affection[3], then, in connection with any subsequent acquisition where either:

(1)   the interest acquired thereby is the same as the interest previously taken

no general demand or market for land is not satisfied merely because there is no demand for the subject land[9]. Further, the word 'general' in this phrase qualifies only 'demand' and not 'market'; the underlying concept is that there cannot be a market unless both supply and demand exist, but there may be a general demand although there is no supply. In that case the demand will be unsatisfied[10].

The reasonable cost of equivalent reinstatement includes the cost of acquiring substituted premises and the cost of converting the substituted premises so that, in the case of a business, the former purpose may be carried on substantially unaltered and undiminished[11]. The claimant must, however, minimise his loss[12].

1   See the Land Compensation Act 1961 s 5 r 5 (embodying the recommendations of the *Second Report of the Committee Dealing with the Law and Practice relating to the Acquisition of Land for Public Purposes* (Cd 9229) (1918)); and PARA 754.

2   'Devoted' connotes an intention to use the land for that particular purpose: *Aston Charities Trust Ltd v Stepney Borough Council* [1952] 2 QB 642, [1952] 2 All ER 228, CA (land continued to be devoted to purpose notwithstanding de facto use had been interrupted temporarily by bombing).

3   The date of the notice to treat is the date at which it must be shown that the premises are devoted to the purpose for which there is no general demand: *Zoar Independent Church Trustees v Rochester Corpn* [1975] QB 246, [1974] 3 All ER 5, CA. Although there is no requirement that the land must be committed to that purpose for any particular length of time, the probable duration of the continuance of the purpose is a matter which may affect how the Tribunal exercises its discretion whether to apply the Land Compensation Act 1961 s 5 r 5: see *Zoar Independent Church Trustees v Rochester Corpn* above. The Lands Tribunal was abolished on 1 June 2009 and its functions were transferred to the Upper Tribunal: see PARA 720.

4   The question whether there is a general demand or market is to be determined at the time the compensation falls to be assessed: *Harrison & Hetherington Ltd v Cumbria County Council* (1985) 50 P & CR 396, HL.

5   *Zoar Independent Church Trustees v Rochester Corpn* [1975] QB 246, [1974] 3 All ER 5, CA (the fact that the realisation of the intention is dependent upon the receipt of compensation does not deprive the intention of any necessary quality).

6   It is the purpose that needs to be reinstated, not the precise use which had taken place on the acquired land: *Zoar Independent Church Trustees v Rochester Corpn* [1975] QB 246, [1974] 3 All ER 5, CA; *Trustee of the Nonentities Society v Kidderminster Borough Council* (1970) 22 P & CR 224, Lands Tribunal; c f *Edge Hill Light Rly Co v Secretary of State for War* (1956) 6 P & CR 211, Lands Tribunal.

7   Before the Tribunal exercises its discretion, it will require to know what constitutes equivalent reinstatement and its cost and the amount of compensation that would be payable under the Land Compensation Act 1961 s 5 rr 2, 6 (see PARA 754) compared with s 5 r 5: *Harrison & Hetherington Ltd v Cumbria County Council* (1985) 50 P & CR 396 at 397, HL. It would contravene the principle of equivalence to deny compensation under the Land Compensation Act 1961 s 5 r 5 for consequential losses (including loss of profit and disturbance consequent on relocation) when such losses are recoverable under s 5 r 2 for land that is not devoted to a particular purpose: *Eronpark Ltd v Secretary of State for Transport* [2000] 2 EGLR 165, Lands Tribunal. In the case of a business, the relation between the cost of reinstatement and the value of the business may be paramount in considering the question of reasonableness (*Festiniog Rly Co v Central Electricity Generating Board* (1962) 13 P & CR 248, 60 LGR 157, CA); however, the relation between the cost of reinstatement and the value of the undertaking to be reinstated may be of less significance in considering the reinstatement of a social or charitable purpose (see *Sparks v Leeds City Council* (1977) 34 P & CR 234, sub nom *Sparks (Trustees of East Hunslet Liberal Club) v Leeds City Council* [1977] 2 EGLR 163, Lands Tribunal). As to the Upper Tribunal see PARA 720; and ADMINISTRATIVE LAW.

8   *Birmingham Corpn v West Midland Baptist (Trust) Association (Inc)* [1970] AC 874, [1969] 3 All ER 172, HL; and PARA 755. The owner of land acquired under a compulsory purchase order is entitled to recover interest under the Compulsory Purchase Act 1965 s 11(1) on the agreed amount awarded for reinstatement from the time of entry on to the land up to the date when the compensation is paid; the amount of interest depends on the value given to the land under the Land Compensation Act 1961 s 5 r 5, and the length of the period from the time of entry until reinstatement (that is, the length of time during which he has neither the land nor its value): *Halstead v Manchester City Council* [1998] 1 All ER 33, (1997) 96 LGR 711, CA.

9   *Harrison & Hetherington Ltd v Cumbria County Council* (1985) 50 P & CR 396 at 397, HL.
10 *Harrison & Hetherington Ltd v Cumbria County Council* (1985) 50 P & CR 396 at 397, HL;
    Wilkinson v Middlesbrough Borough Council (1981) 45 P & CR 142 at 148, CA.
11 See *A and B Taxis Ltd v Secretary of State for Air* [1922] 2 KB 328 at 344, CA. See also *Trustees
    of Zetland Lodge of Freemasons v Tamar Bridge Joint Committee* (1961) 12 P & CR 326,
    Lands Tribunal; *Trustees of Old Dagenham Methodist Church v Dagenham Borough Council*
    (1961) 179 Estates Gazette 295.
12 See *Service Welding Ltd v Tyne and Wear County Council* (1979) 38 P & CR 352, CA.

801.   Examples of land devoted to a purpose for which there is no market.
Land with churches, schools or hospitals on it, or with buildings devoted to
general religious and charitable purposes[1], or land with a club house[2], or
carrying a light railway[3], or barracks[4], or houses of an exceptional character, or
special business premises[5], provide examples of land which may be within the
rule relating to reinstatement value[6].

Land held under a lease is not excluded[7]. Land is devoted to a purpose even
though the use of that purpose is temporarily interrupted[8].

The land devoted to the purpose must be considered as a whole, and it seems
that there is no right to take parts of the land separately and show that they
could be used for some other purposes[9].

1   See *London School Board v South Eastern Rly Co* (1887) 3 TLR 710, CA; *Zoar Independent
    Church Trustees v Rochester Corpn* [1975] QB 246, [1974] 3 All ER 5, CA.
2   *St John's Wood Working Men's Club Trustees v LCC* (1947) 150 Estates Gazette 213; *Trustees
    of Zetland Lodge of Freemasons v Tamar Bridge Joint Committee* (1961) 12 P & CR 326,
    Lands Tribunal.
3   *Edge Hill Light Rly Co v Secretary of State for War* (1956) 6 P & CR 211, Lands Tribunal.
4   *Territorial Army Association of Devon v Plymouth Corpn* [1928] EGD 195.
5   *A and B Taxis Ltd v Secretary of State for Air* [1922] 2 KB 328 at 336–337, CA.
6   See the Land Compensation Act 1961 s 5 r 5; and PARAS 754, 800.
7   *Territorial Army Association of Devon v Plymouth Corpn* [1928] EGD 195.
8   *Aston Charities Trust Ltd v Stepney Borough Council* [1952] 2 QB 642, [1952] 2 All ER
    228, CA.
9   *London Diocesan Fund v Stepney Corpn* (1953) 4 P & CR 9, Lands Tribunal.

**802.   Application of equivalent reinstatement rule to dwelling specially adapted
for disabled person where disabled person resident.**   In the case of compulsory
acquisition of an interest in a dwelling[1] which: (1) has been constructed or
substantially modified to meet the special needs of a disabled person[2]; and (2) is
occupied by that person as his residence immediately before the date when the
acquiring authority[3] takes possession of the dwelling or was last so occupied
before that date[4], then, if the person whose interest is acquired so elects, the
compensation is to be assessed as if the dwelling were land which is devoted to a
purpose of such a nature that there is no general demand or market for that
purpose[5]. The compensation will accordingly be on the basis of the reasonable
cost of equivalent reinstatement, and the Upper Tribunal has no discretion in
applying the measure of compensation; nor is it required to be satisfied of an
intention to reinstate[6].

1   'Dwelling' means a building or part of a building occupied or, if not occupied, last occupied or
    intended to be occupied as a private dwelling, and includes any garden, yard, outhouses and
    appurtenances belonging to or usually enjoyed with that building or part: Land Compensation
    Act 1973 s 87(1) (definition amended by the Land Compensation (Scotland) Act 1973 s 81(1),
    Sch 2 Pt I; and the Planning and Compulsory Purchase Act 2004 ss 118(2), 120, Sch 7
    para 7(1), (4), Sch 9).
2   Land Compensation Act 1973 s 45(1)(a). 'Disabled person' means a person who is substantially
    and permanently handicapped by illness, injury or congenital infirmity: s 87(1) (definition
    amended by the Land Compensation (Scotland) Act 1973 s 81(1), Sch 2 Pt I).

3   As to the meaning of 'acquiring authority' see PARA 622 note 1.
4   Land Compensation Act 1973 s 45(1)(b).
5   Land Compensation Act 1973 s 45(2).
6   As to land devoted to a purpose for which there is no market see generally PARAS 800–801. As to the Upper Tribunal see PARA 720; and ADMINISTRATIVE LAW.

(8) COMPENSATION WHERE PERSON ENTITLED IS NOT IN OCCUPATION

803.   Expenses of owners not in occupation.   Where, in consequence of any compulsory acquisition of land[1], the acquiring authority[2] acquires an interest of a person who is not then in occupation of the land, and that person incurs incidental charges or expenses in acquiring, within the period of one year beginning with the date of entry, an interest in other land in the United Kingdom[3], the charges or expenses must be taken into account in assessing his compensation as they would be taken into account if he were in occupation of the land[4].

1   As to the meaning of 'land' see PARA 516 note 2.
2   As to the meaning of 'acquiring authority' see PARA 622 note 1.
3   As to the meaning of 'United Kingdom' see PARA 616 note 22.
4   Land Compensation Act 1961 s 10A (added by the Planning and Compensation Act 1991 s 70, Sch 15 para 2).

804.   Effect on value of interest of landlord or tenant.   Where the owner of the interest in the land to be valued is not in occupation at the date of the notice to treat and the land is in the occupation of a tenant[1] or a subtenant, the value of the owner's interest will be affected by the owner's ability, at the time of valuation or date of entry, whichever is the earlier[2], to obtain possession and the time within which possession may be obtained by notice to quit or otherwise, and also by whether the person in occupation has gone out of occupation at the time of valuation or date of entry[3].

The length of the lease for a term of years affects the value of the landlord's interest, and if there is a right to renewal of the lease this must be taken into account[4], but not a mere expectation of renewal[5].

Where a lease contains a proviso for re-entry on any part of the land leased being compulsorily taken, the landlord is entitled to the value of the land free of the lease[6]. An invalid lease would not affect the landlord's compensation[7], and a lease granted after the date of the notice to treat cannot increase the burden on the acquiring authority[8], but in either case the tenant may have a remedy against the landlord.

The values of the interest of the landlord and the tenant are affected by statute; possession by the landlord arising out of the tenant's rehousing by an acquiring authority may fall to be disregarded[9], the right of renewal of a business tenancy is protected[10], and the landlord's right to serve notice to quit an agricultural holding is restricted[11]. These provisions do not, however, prevent a tenant from surrendering his interest after the notice to treat and before the time of valuation or date of entry[12].

1   As to the effect of rehousing tenants see PARA 805.
2   Land is to be valued as at the date of valuation or the date of entry, whichever is the earlier, and not as at the date of the notice to treat: see PARA 635. As to the notice to treat see PARA 616 et seq.
3   As to the statutory modification of rights to obtain possession and value where possession is obtained see PARAS 805–807.

4 *Bogg v Midland Rly Co* (1867) LR 4 Eq 310.
5 *Lynch v Glasgow Corpn* (1903) 5 F 1174, Ct of Sess. Other rights of a lessee must be taken into
   account (see *Re McIntosh and Pontypridd Improvements Co Ltd* (1892) 8 TLR 203, CA); and
   so must restrictions in the lease in favour of the landlord (cf *Priestman Collieries Ltd v
   Northern District Valuation Board* [1950] 2 KB 398, [1950] 2 All ER 129, DC).
6 *Re Morgan and London and North Western Rly Co* [1896] 2 QB 469. The proviso could
   operate as a surrender under the Landlord and Tenant Act 1954 s 24(2): see LANDLORD AND
   TENANT vol 27(2) (2006 Reissue) PARA 713. A proviso in a lease giving the landlord power to
   resume possession for building does not, however, entitle him to resume possession where the
   acquiring authority acquires the land for some other purpose: *Johnson v Edgware, Highgate and
   London Rly Co* (1866) 35 Beav 480, 14 LT 45. Furthermore, an acquiring authority cannot,
   after acquisition, exercise a power of resuming possession reserved in the lease by the landlord
   for the purpose of reducing or taking away the tenant's right to compensation: see *Fleming v
   Newport Rly Co* (1883) 8 App Cas 265, HL, approving *Solway Junction Rly Co v Jackson*
   (1874) 1 R 831, Ct of Sess.
7 Cf *Re North London Rly Co, ex p Cooper* (1865) 34 LJCh 373.
8 See PARA 632.
9 See PARA 805.
10 See PARA 806.
11 See PARA 807.
12 See PARA 799.

**805. Rehousing or prospect of rehousing tenants by acquiring authority not to
enhance landlord's compensation.** In assessing the compensation payable in
respect of the compulsory acquisition of an interest in land which, on the date of
service of the notice to treat[1] or deemed notice to treat[2], is subject to a tenancy[3],
there must be left out of account any part of the value of that interest which is
attributable to, or to the prospect of, the tenant giving up possession after that
date in consequence of being provided with other accommodation by virtue of
the duty[4] of an authority possessing compulsory purchase powers[5] to secure that
a person displaced from residential accommodation on any land acquired by that
authority will, if suitable alternative residential accommodation on reasonable
terms is not otherwise available to that person, be provided with that other
accommodation[6]. Accordingly, for the purpose of determining the date by
reference to which that compensation is to be assessed, the acquiring authority[7]
is to be deemed, where the tenant gives up possession, to have taken possession
on the date on which it is given up by the tenant[8].

   Thus, as compensation in respect of land acquired is to be assessed in respect
of the interests and state of the land at the date of entry by the acquiring
authority, or the date of assessment, whichever is the earlier[9], the removal of the
tenant or the prospect of such removal will not enhance the amount of the
purchase money to which the landlord would otherwise be entitled.

1 As to the notice to treat see PARA 616 et seq.
2 Ie a notice to treat deemed to have been served by virtue of the Compulsory Purchase (Vesting
   Declarations) Act 1981 Pt III (ss 7–9) (general vesting declarations: see PARAS 689, 693–694):
   Land Compensation Act 1973 s 50(4) (amended by the Land Compensation (Scotland)
   Act 1973 s 81(1), Sch 2 Pt I; and by the Compulsory Purchase (Vesting Declarations) Act 1981
   s 16(1), Sch 3 para 1).
3 'Tenancy', otherwise than in relation to an agricultural holding, has the same meaning as in the
   Landlord and Tenant Act 1954 (see LANDLORD AND TENANT vol 27(1) (2006 Reissue) PARA
   455): Land Compensation Act 1973 s 87(1) (definition amended by the Land Compensation
   (Scotland) Act 1973 Sch 2 Pt I). As to the meaning of 'agricultural holding' see PARA 703 note 3.
4 Ie under the Land Compensation Act 1973 s 39(1)(a): see PARA 853; and HOUSING vol 22 (2006
   Reissue) PARA 287.
5 As to the meaning of 'authority possessing compulsory purchase powers' see PARA 763 note 6
   (definition applied by the Land Compensation Act 1973 s 87(1)).
6 Land Compensation Act 1973 s 50(2).

7   As to the meaning of 'acquiring authority' see PARA 622 note 1.
8   Land Compensation Act 1973 s 50(2).
9   See PARA 635.

806.   Compensation of landlord and tenant affected by right to apply for new business tenancy.   Where, in pursuance of any enactment providing for the acquisition or taking of possession of land compulsorily, an acquiring authority[1]: (1) acquires the landlord's interest in any land subject to a tenancy to which Part II of the Landlord and Tenant Act 1954[2] applies; or (2) acquires the tenant's interest in, or takes possession of, that land[3], then the tenant's right to apply under Part II of that Act for the grant of a new tenancy must be taken into account in assessing the compensation payable by the acquiring authority, whether to the landlord or the tenant, in connection with the acquisition of the interest or the taking of possession of the land, and, in assessing that compensation, it must be assumed that neither the acquiring authority nor any other authority possessing compulsory purchase powers[4] has acquired or proposes to acquire any interest in the land[5].

1   As to the meaning of 'acquiring authority' see PARA 622 note 1.
2   Ie the Landlord and Tenant Act 1954 Pt II (ss 23–46) (security of tenure for business tenants): see LANDLORD AND TENANT vol 27(2) (2006 Reissue) PARA 701 et seq. As to the meaning of 'tenancy' see PARA 805 note 3.
3   In the case of a tenancy greater than one for a year or from year to year, the interest would be acquired after a notice to treat (see PARA 616 et seq) and in the case of a tenancy for a year or from year to year or less, the interest would be dealt with by a notice requiring possession under the Lands Clauses Consolidation Act 1845 s 121 or the Compulsory Purchase Act 1965 s 20, or by notice of entry or entry after the deposit of security under s 11 and compensation paid in respect of it accordingly (see PARAS 698 et seq, 819 et seq). Further, where the amount of the compensation which would have been payable under the Landlord and Tenant Act 1954 s 37 (see LANDLORD AND TENANT vol 27(2) (2006 Reissue) PARA 758 et seq), if the tenancy had come to an end in circumstances giving rise to compensation under that provision and the date at which the acquiring authority obtained possession had been the termination of the current tenancy, exceeds the amount of the compensation payable under the Lands Clauses Consolidation Act 1845 s 121 or the Compulsory Purchase Act 1965 s 20, in the case of a tenancy to which the Landlord and Tenant Act 1954 Pt II applies, that compensation will be increased by the amount of the excess: s 39(2) (amended by the Land Compensation Act 1973 s 47(3)); and see LANDLORD AND TENANT vol 27(2) (2006 Reissue) PARA 701.
4   As to the meaning of 'authority possessing compulsory purchase powers' see PARA 763 note 6 (definition applied by the Land Compensation Act 1973 s 87(1)).
5   Land Compensation Act 1973 s 47(1).

807.   Compensation of landlord and tenant affected by restrictions on notices to quit agricultural holdings.   Where, in pursuance of any enactment providing for the acquisition or taking of possession of land compulsorily, an acquiring authority[1]: (1) acquires the landlord's[2] interest in an agricultural holding[3] or any part of it; or (2) acquires the interest of the tenant[4] in, or takes possession of [5], an agricultural holding or any part of it, then compensation is to be assessed as set out below[6].

In assessing the compensation payable by the acquiring authority to the landlord in connection with the acquisition of the landlord's interest in an agricultural holding or any part of it, there must be disregarded the landlord's right to serve a notice to quit, and any notice to quit already served by the landlord, which would not be or would not have been effective if:

(a)   in the statutory provision for a case where notice to quit is given on the ground that the land is required for a use other than agriculture for which planning permission has been granted or is not required[7], the reference to the land being required did not include a reference to its being required by an acquiring authority[8]; and

(b) in the statutory provision[9] relating to the proposed termination of a tenancy for the purpose of the land's being used for a non-agricultural use not falling within head (1) above, the reference to the land's being used did not include a reference to its being used by an acquiring authority[10].

Furthermore, if the tenant has quitted the holding or any part of it by reason of a notice to quit which is to be so disregarded, it must be assumed that he has not done so[11].

In assessing the compensation payable by the acquiring authority to the tenant in connection with the acquisition of the tenant's interest in, or taking of possession of, an agricultural holding or any part of it (the 'tenant's compensation'), there must be disregarded the landlord's right to serve a notice to quit and any notice to quit already served by him which would not be or would not have been effective[12] in the circumstances set out in heads (a) and (b) above[13]. The tenant's compensation must, however, be reduced by an amount equal to any payment which the acquiring authority is liable to make to him in respect of the acquisition or taking of possession in question under the statutory provisions[14] relating to additional payments by an acquiring authority where it acquires the tenant's interest in, or takes possession of, an agricultural holding or any part of it[15].

If the tenant's compensation as determined in accordance with the above provisions[16] is less than it would have been if those provisions had not been enacted, it must be increased by the amount of the deficiency[17]; and in assessing his compensation no account is to be taken of any benefit which might accrue to him by virtue of the statutory provisions[18] relating to additional payments by the landlord for disturbance[19].

The above provisions do not, however, have effect where the tenancy of the agricultural holding is a tenancy to which the Agricultural Holdings Act 1986 does not apply[20] by virtue of the Agricultural Tenancies Act 1995[21].

1 As to the meaning of 'acquiring authority' see PARA 622 note 1.
2 As to the meaning of 'landlord' see PARA 703 note 3.
3 As to the meaning of 'agricultural holding' see PARA 703 note 3.
4 As to the meaning of 'tenant' see PARA 703 note 3.
5 In the case of a tenancy for a year or from year to year or less, the interest is taken possession of and, in the case of a greater interest, the lease is acquired, under a notice to treat: see PARA 806 note 3.
6 Land Compensation Act 1973 s 48(1). Section 48(1) is subject to s 48(1A) (see the text and notes 20–21): s 48(1) (amended by the Agricultural Tenancies Act 1995 s 40, Schedule para 24).
7 Ie in the Agricultural Holdings Act 1986 s 26(2), Sch 3 Pt I Case B: see AGRICULTURAL LAND vol 1 (2008) PARAS 376, 378. For these purposes, 'notice to quit' has the same meaning as in the Agricultural Holdings Act 1986: Land Compensation Act 1973 s 87(1) (definition amended by the Land Compensation (Scotland) Act 1973 s 81(1), Sch 2 Pt I; and by virtue of the Agricultural Holdings Act 1986 s 100, Sch 14 para 56).
8 Land Compensation Act 1973 s 48(2)(a)(i) (amended by the Agricultural Holdings Act 1986 Sch 14 para 53(1), (2)). The landlord is thus prevented from taking advantage of the acquiring authority's special needs as he could have done by virtue of the decision in *Rugby Joint Water Board v Foottit, Rugby Joint Water Board v Shaw-Fox* [1973] AC 202, [1972] 1 All ER 1057, HL, where land was acquired for a reservoir and it was held that the landlords were entitled to be compensated on the basis that they could have served an incontestable notice to quit on the tenants on the ground that the land was required for non-agricultural use for which planning permission had been obtained, although that permission had been obtained by the acquiring authority. A landlord would, however, be entitled to have taken into account his right to serve a notice to quit, or a notice to quit served by him, based on his planning permission, or

based on one obtained by the acquiring authority for a purpose not limited to that authority's special requirements, as e g the special requirements of any government department, local or public authority or statutory undertakers: c f the Land Compensation Act 1961 s 5 r 3 (see PARA 789); and see PARA 787.

9   Ie the Agricultural Holdings Act 1986 s 27(3)(f): see AGRICULTURAL LAND vol 1 (2008) PARA 375.

10 Land Compensation Act 1973 s 48(2)(a)(ii) (amended by the Agricultural Holdings Act 1986 Sch 14 para 53(1), (2); the Agricultural Holdings (Notices to Quit) Act 1977 s 13(1), Sch 1 para 6; and by virtue of the Agricultural Holdings Act 1986 s 101(1), Sch 14 para 53(2), Sch 15 Pt I).

11 Land Compensation Act 1973 s 48(2)(b).

12 Ie if the Agricultural Holdings Act 1986 Sch 3 Pt I Case B and s 27(3)(f) were construed in accordance with heads (1)–(2) in the text: Land Compensation Act 1973 s 48(3) (amended by the Agricultural Holdings Act 1986 Sch 14 para 53(1), (3)).

13 Land Compensation Act 1973 s 48(3) (as amended: see note 12).

14 Ie under the Agriculture (Miscellaneous Provisions) Act 1968 s 12: see AGRICULTURAL LAND vol 1 (2008) PARAS 455, 607–608.

15 Land Compensation Act 1973 s 48(5).

16 Ie determined in accordance with the Land Compensation Act 1973 s 48(3), (5): see the text and notes 12–15.

17 Land Compensation Act 1973 s 48(6).

18 Ie by virtue of the Agricultural Holdings Act 1986 s 60(2)(b) (see AGRICULTURAL LAND vol 1 (2008) PARA 448), but not by virtue of s 60(2)(b) as applied by the Agriculture (Miscellaneous Provisions) Act 1968 s 12: Land Compensation Act 1973 s 48(6A) (added by the Agricultural Holdings Act 1986 Sch 14 para 53(1), (4)).

19 Land Compensation Act 1973 s 48(6A) (as added: see note 18). As to the method of assessment of the compensation payable under s 48 see *Wakerley v St Edmundsbury Borough Council* (1977) 33 P & CR 497, Lands Tribunal; *Dawson v Norwich City Council* (1978) 37 P & CR 516, Lands Tribunal.

20 Ie by virtue of the Agricultural Tenancies Act 1995 s 4: see AGRICULTURAL LAND vol 1 (2008) PARAS 301, 321.

21 Land Compensation Act 1973 s 48(1A) (added by the Agricultural Tenancies Act 1995 Schedule para 24).

(9) OTHER SPECIAL CASES

808.   Measure of compensation to statutory undertakers etc.   Special statutory provision is made with regard to the calculation of compensation to statutory undertakers[1] who are entitled to be compensated as a result of certain planning decisions and orders[2] or in consequence of a compulsory acquisition of land[3]. This special provision may, however, be excluded at the option of those undertakers when the right to compensation arises on a compulsory acquisition[4]; and in that case the normal rules[5] for the assessment of compensation apply[6].

Nothing in the Land Compensation Act 1961 applies to any purchase of the whole or any part of any statutory undertaking[7] under any enactment in that behalf prescribing the terms on which the purchase is to be effected[8].

1   As to the meaning of 'statutory undertakers' in the planning legislation see TOWN AND COUNTRY PLANNING vol 46(3) (Reissue) PARA 1009. The special statutory provision also applies to the operator of a telecommunications code system: see TOWN AND COUNTRY PLANNING vol 46(3) (Reissue) PARA 1376.

2   As to the right to compensation see the Town and Country Planning Act 1990 s 279; and TOWN AND COUNTRY PLANNING vol 46(3) (Reissue) PARA 1027.

3   See the Town and Country Planning Act 1990 s 280; and TOWN AND COUNTRY PLANNING vol 46(3) (Reissue) PARA 1028. As to the procedure for assessing compensation see s 282; and TOWN AND COUNTRY PLANNING vol 46(3) (Reissue) PARA 1030. In relation to compulsory acquisitions of interests in land which has been acquired by statutory undertakers for the purposes of their undertaking, the provisions of the Land Compensation Act 1961 have effect subject to the Town and Country Planning Act 1990 s 280(1) (see TOWN AND COUNTRY PLANNING vol 46(3) (Reissue) PARA 1028): Land Compensation Act 1961 s 11; Planning

(Consequential Provisions) Act 1990 s 2(4). This provision does not, however, apply where the Land Compensation Act 1961 s 36 excludes the provisions of the Land Compensation Act 1961: see the text and notes 7–8.

4	See the Town and Country Planning Act 1990 s 281; and TOWN AND COUNTRY PLANNING vol 46(3) (Reissue) PARA 1029.

5	Ie with the exclusion of the Land Compensation Act 1961 s 5 r 5 (see PARAS 754, 800–801): see the Town and Country Planning Act 1990 s 281(1); and TOWN AND COUNTRY PLANNING vol 46(3) (Reissue) PARA 1029.

6	See the Town and Country Planning Act 1990 s 281(1); and TOWN AND COUNTRY PLANNING vol 46(3) (Reissue) PARA 1029. As to the assessment of compensation under the normal rules see PARAS 753 et seq, 810 et seq.

7	As to the meanings of 'statutory undertaking' and 'enactment' see PARA 501 note 3.

8	Land Compensation Act 1961 s 36(1).

## 809.	Determination of compensation in cases of relevant prohibition orders and demolition orders.

Where a relevant prohibition order[1] becomes operative in respect of any premises[2] or a demolition order[3] is made in respect of any premises[4], the local housing authority must pay to every owner of the premises an amount[5] which is the diminution in the compulsory purchase value[6] of the owner's interest in the premises as a result of the coming into operation of the relevant prohibition order or, as the case may be, the making of the demolition order[7]. That amount is to be determined as at the date of the coming into operation or making of the order in question, and must be determined (in default of agreement) as if it were compensation payable in respect of the compulsory purchase of the interest in question and is dealt with accordingly[8]. In any case where a relevant prohibition order has been made in respect of any premises, and that order is revoked and a demolition order is made in its place, the amount payable to the owner[9] in connection with the demolition order must be reduced by the amount (if any) paid to the owner or a previous owner[10] in connection with the relevant prohibition order[11].

1	'Relevant prohibition order' means a prohibition order under the Housing Act 2004 s 20 or s 21 (see HOUSING vol 22 (2006 Reissue) PARA 387 et seq) which imposes in relation to the whole of any premises a prohibition on their use for all purposes other than any purpose approved by the authority: Housing Act 1985 s 584A(4) (s 584A added by the Local Government and Housing Act 1989 Sch 9 para 75; substituted by the Housing Act 2004 s 265(1), Sch 15 paras 10, 30).

2	'Premises', in relation to a prohibition order, means premises which are specified premises in relation to the order within the meaning of the Housing Act 2004 Pt 1 (ss 1–54): Housing Act 1985 s 584A(4) (as added and substituted: see note 1).

3	Ie under the Housing Act 1985 s 265: see HOUSING vol 22 (2006 Reissue) PARA 415 et seq.

4	'Premises', in relation to a demolition order, has the meaning given by the Housing Act 1985 s 322 (see HOUSING vol 22 (2006 Reissue) PARA 415): s 584A(4) (as added and substituted: see note 1).

5	Housing Act 1985 s 584A(1) (as added and substituted: see note 1).

6	'Compulsory purchase value', in relation to an owner's interest in premises, means the compensation which would be payable in respect of the compulsory purchase of that interest if it fell to be assessed in accordance with the Land Compensation Act 1961: Housing Act 1985 s 584A(4) (as added and substituted: see note 1).

7	Housing Act 1985 s 584A(2) (as added and substituted: see note 1).

8	Housing Act 1985 s 584A(2)(a), (b) (as added and substituted: see note 1).

9	Ie under the Housing Act 1985 s 584A(1): see the text and notes 1–5.

10	See note 9.

11	Housing Act 1985 s 584A(3) (as added and substituted: see note 1). See further HOUSING vol 22 (2006 Reissue) PARA 417.

The normal date for the assessment of compensation for disturbance is the same as the date for the assessment of the value of the land itself, namely the date of entry or the date of the valuation itself, whichever is the earlier[17]; but it is possible, where appropriate, to deal with the assessment of compensation for disturbance after the assessment of the value of the land itself, in order to enable the actual losses to be considered[18].

The amount of compensation payable in respect of the compulsory acquisition of an interest in land must not be subject to any reduction on account of the fact that the acquiring authority[19] has provided, or undertaken to provide, or arranges for the provision of, residential accommodation under any enactment for the person entitled to the compensation, or that another authority will provide such accommodation[20].

1   Ie including a lessee for more than a year: see PARA 619. For special provisions as to lessees see PARA 818.
2   Ie damage suffered consequent upon the acquisition, because the money paid for the land may not compensate the owner for all personal loss suffered as a result of the forced sale.
3   See *Horn v Sunderland Corpn* [1941] 2 KB 26, [1941] 1 All ER 480, CA.
4   The Land Compensation Act 1961 s 5 r 6 merely states that s 5 r 2 (which requires open market value to be paid: see PARAS 754, 798) does not affect the assessment of compensation for disturbance: see PARAS 754, 810. Cf the express provision made for disturbance payments for non-owners without compensatable interests: see the Land Compensation Act 1973 ss 37, 38; and PARAS 838–839.
5   *IRC v Glasgow and South Western Rly Co* (1887) 12 App Cas 315 at 320, HL; *Horn v Sunderland Corpn* [1941] 2 KB 26 at 32–33, 47, 49, [1941] 1 All ER 480 at 484, 495–496, CA. The compensation payable to an owner in respect of disturbance is an element in assessing the value of the land to him and not an independent head of compensation: *Hughes v Doncaster Metropolitan Borough Council* [1991] 1 AC 382 at 390, [1991] 1 All ER 295 at 299, HL, per Lord Bridge.
6   See *Director of Buildings and Lands v Shun Fung Ironworks Ltd* [1995] 2 AC 111 at 125, [1995] 1 All ER 846 at 852, PC.
7   *Horn v Sunderland Corpn* [1941] 2 KB 26 at 42, [1941] 1 All ER 480 at 491, CA.
8   *Hughes v Doncaster Metropolitan Borough Council* [1991] 1 AC 382 at 392, [1991] 1 All ER 295 at 301, HL, per Lord Bridge.
9   See *Harvey v Crawley Development Corpn* [1957] 1 QB 485 at 494, [1957] 1 All ER 504 at 507, CA, per Romer LJ. See also *Judge Lee v Minister of Transport* [1966] 1 QB 111, sub nom *Minister of Transport v Lee* [1965] 2 All ER 986, CA; *London County Council v Tobin* [1959] 1 All ER 649, [1959] 1 WLR 354, CA; *Redfield Hardware Ltd v Bristol Corpn* (1963) 15 P & CR 47; *J Bibby & Sons Ltd v Merseyside County Council* (1979) 39 P & CR 53, CA; *Director of Buildings and Lands v Shun Fung Ironworks Ltd* [1995] 2 AC 111, [1995] 1 All ER 846, PC.
10 *Horn v Sunderland Corpn* [1941] 2 KB 26, [1941] 1 All ER 480, CA. Similarly, compensation will not be payable for disturbance if that disturbance has already been taken into account in assessing the compensation payable in respect of severance and injurious affection: see *Cooke v Secretary of State for the Environment* (1973) 27 P & CR 234, Lands Tribunal.
11 See the Land Compensation Act 1961 s 10A; and PARA 803. An owner who is not in occupation may also claim for other consequential loss: see *Wrexham Maelor Borough Council v MacDougall* (1993) 69 P & CR 109, [1993] 2 EGLR 23, CA (loss of a service contract). As to the meaning of 'United Kingdom' see PARA 616 note 22.
12 *Woolfson v Strathclyde Regional Council* (1978) 38 P & CR 521, HL. Cf *DHN Food Distributors Ltd v Tower Hamlets London Borough Council* [1976] 3 All ER 462, [1976] 1 WLR 852, CA. Where a claimant for compensation does not have a legal or equitable title to the land, all that is needed to ground a compensation claim is possession, meaning physical occupation with the intention to exclude unauthorised intruders: *Wrexham Maelor Borough Council v MacDougall* (1993) 69 P & CR 109, [1993] 2 EGLR 23, CA, per Ralph Gibson LJ (considering the Land Compensation Act 1973 s 37).
13 *Smith, Stone and Knight Ltd v Birmingham Corpn* [1939] 4 All ER 116.
14 *Director of Buildings and Lands v Shun Fung Ironworks Ltd* [1995] 2 AC 111 at 137–138, [1995] 1 All ER 846 at 863–864, PC, approving and extending *Prasad v Wolverhampton Borough Council* [1983] Ch 333, [1983] 2 All ER 140, CA.

15 *Palatine Graphic Arts Co Ltd v Liverpool City Council* [1986] QB 335, [1986] 1 All ER 366, CA.

16 *Hughes v Doncaster Metropolitan Borough Council* [1991] 1 AC 382, [1991] 1 All ER 295, HL, applying the Land Compensation Act 1961 s 5 r 4. An unpermitted use which is immune from enforcement proceedings is not, however, contrary to law for these purposes: *Hughes v Doncaster Metropolitan Borough Council*. See also the Town and Country Planning Act 1990 s 191(2) which does not distinguish between lawful uses and those that are merely immune from enforcement: see TOWN AND COUNTRY PLANNING vol 46(2) (Reissue) PARA 586.

17 See *Birmingham Corpn v West Midland Baptist (Trust) Association (Inc)* [1970] AC 874, [1969] 3 All ER 172, HL.

18 See *Munton v GLC* [1976] 2 All ER 815, [1976] 1 WLR 649, CA.

19 As to the meaning of 'acquiring authority' see PARA 622 note 1.

20 Land Compensation Act 1973 s 50(1). This provision applies also in relation to any payment to which a person is entitled under Pt III (ss 29–43) (home loss payments etc) as it applies in relation to the compensation payable in respect of the compulsory acquisition of an interest in land, taking references to the acquiring authority as references to the authority responsible for making that payment: s 50(3). See also PARAS 829 et seq, 839. As to the provision of housing for persons displaced by statutory works see PARA 853 et seq.

815. Expense of finding new premises and removing goods. Costs incurred in preparing a claim for compensation should be included in the compensation payable, because such costs are incurred as a direct consequence of dispossession[1]. Such costs would not be excluded by any express statutory exclusion of compensation for disturbance, because compensation for such costs is properly described as compensation for 'any other matter not directly based on the value of land' as opposed to compensation for disturbance[2]. Costs reasonably incurred in connection with the issue of a certificate of appropriate alternative development should also be included[3].

The owner disturbed is also entitled to the legal costs and stamp duty on the purchase of a comparable property, to surveyors' fees in relation to it and to travelling expenses in finding such a property[4].

If the claimant has incurred increased operating costs (including an increased rent) after taking new premises, then he is entitled to compensation in respect of those costs if he had no alternative but to incur them and has obtained no benefit as a result of the extra costs which would make them worthwhile[5]. Costs of adaptation of new premises should be treated in a similar manner[6], but in relation to the acquisition or improvement of new premises there is a rebuttable presumption that value for money has been obtained by any extra cost[7].

The costs of removal of fixtures[8], furniture and goods[9] are payable as compensation. This includes depreciation in the value of furniture specially fitted[10] and in the case of a trader it includes the diminution in the value of his stock consequent on its removal or on a forced sale where such a sale is necessary[11]. The fact that a business is being carried on at a loss does not disentitle the claimant from claiming in respect of an increase in that loss caused by the acquisition, provided it is reasonable in the circumstances for the business to be continued[12].

If interest charges are incurred by the claimant in financing the development of new premises, then these will generally be treated as being part of the purchase price of the premises and thus, in view of the rebuttable presumption referred to above, the charges will not normally be payable as part of the compensation[13].

1 *London County Council v Tobin* [1959] 1 All ER 649, [1959] 1 WLR 354, CA (legal and accountancy fees reasonably and properly incurred in preparing the claim for compensation). An interpreter's fees may be included: *Sadik v London Borough of Haringey* (1978) 37 P & CR

the Land Compensation Act 1973 s 48(1A); and PARA 807. As to the method of assessment of the compensation payable to an agricultural tenant see the cases cited in PARA 807 note 19.

(ii) Short Tenancies

819.   Compensation payable on compulsory acquisition of short tenancies. There are special statutory provisions governing the position if any of the land subject to compulsory purchase is in the possession of a person having no greater interest in the land than as a tenant from year to year[1]. The acquiring authority[2] may acquire the landlord's interest and give a notice to quit to the tenant or accept a surrender from the tenant, or persuade the landlord to give a notice to quit before the acquisition[3]. Alternatively it may await the contractual expiry of the tenant's interest. In these cases, there is no compulsory acquisition of the tenant's interest and thus no compensation payable for it[4].

It may be, however, that the acquiring authority is not willing or able to await the termination of the tenant's interest in one of the ways mentioned above. If the tenant is required to give up possession of any of the land occupied by him before the expiration of his term or interest in the land, then he is entitled to compensation for the value of his unexpired term or interest in the land, and for any just allowance which ought to be made to him by an incoming tenant, and for any loss or injury he may sustain[5]. In this way, the tenant may obtain compensation for disturbance[6]. The compensation is assessed when the tenant is required to give up possession[7].

1   See the Compulsory Purchase Act 1965 s 20; and PARA 699 et seq.
2   As to acquiring authorities generally see PARA 519 et seq.
3   See PARA 823. For provisions relating to agricultural tenancies see PARAS 824–825.
4   Even though the tenant has no compensatable interest, he may nonetheless be entitled to a payment for disturbance: see PARAS 838–839.
5   See the Lands Clauses Consolidation Act 1845 s 121; the Compulsory Purchase Act 1965 s 20; and PARA 699 et seq.
6   See eg *Greenwoods Tyre Services Ltd v Manchester Corpn* (1972) 23 P & CR 246, Lands Tribunal.
7   *Newham London Borough Council v Benjamin* [1968] 1 All ER 1195, [1968] 1 WLR 694, CA. Thus the service of a notice to treat is not a requirement for these purposes: see *Newham London Borough Council v Benjamin*. If the tenant gives up possession without a notice of entry he will lose his right to compensation: see *GW Roberts and Midland Bank Ltd v Bristol Corpn* (1960) 11 P & CR 205, Lands Tribunal.

820.   Nature of compensation. Compensation for loss or injury[1] includes compensation for every kind of damage which the tenant may suffer[2]. The amount of any compensation payable in respect of the compulsory acquisition of an interest[3] in land must not be subject to any reduction on account of the fact that the acquiring authority[4] has provided, or undertakes to provide, or arranges for the provision of, or another authority will provide, residential accommodation under any enactment for the person entitled to the compensation[5].

1   See PARA 819.
2   *R v Great Northern Rly Co* (1876) 2 QBD 151 at 156. The compensation therefore may include compensation for disturbance: see PARA 819.
3   The interest of a tenant for a year, or from year to year, is not purchased under a notice to treat (see PARA 619), but it is acquired by a notice requiring possession (see PARAS 699, 702).
4   As to the meaning of 'acquiring authority' see PARA 622 note 1.
5   Land Compensation Act 1973 s 50(1). As to the provision of housing for persons displaced by statutory works see PARA 853 et seq.

821.   Loss of value of unexpired term.   The tenant, when required to give up possession[1], is entitled to compensation for the value of his unexpired term[2]. There are statutory provisions[3] whereby the right of a business tenant to apply for a new tenancy[4] is to be taken into account, and the right of landlords of certain agricultural tenants to serve a notice to quit[5] is to be disregarded[6].

1   *Newham London Borough Council v Benjamin* [1968] 1 All ER 1195, [1968] 1 WLR 694, CA.
2   See the Lands Clauses Consolidation Act 1845 s 121; the Compulsory Purchase Act 1965 s 20; and PARA 699 et seq.
3   Ie the Land Compensation Act 1973 ss 47, 48: see PARAS 806–807.
4   Ie under the Landlord and Tenant Act 1954 Pt II (ss 23–46): see LANDLORD AND TENANT vol 27(2) (2006 Reissue) PARA 701 et seq.
5   Ie under the Agricultural Holdings Act 1986 (see AGRICULTURAL LAND); but not under the Agricultural Tenancies Act 1995: see the Land Compensation Act 1973 s 48(1A); and PARA 807.
6   See note 3.

822.   Other grounds for compensation.   A claim for compensation for the expenses of removal will depend on whether the tenant has given up possession. If he continues in possession, after a notice requiring possession, until the expiration of his fixed term[1], if any, or until the tenancy could have been determined by a notice to quit[2], he will have no claim under that head, except in so far as he has made preparations in good faith to give up possession on receiving the notice requiring possession[3].

Compensation for loss from injury to goodwill and loss of profits pending re-establishment of the business[4] will be restricted by the tenancy being one for a year or from year to year, subject to any right of renewal or other protection of the tenancy[5].

Where it is not reasonably practicable to re-establish the business, and compensation is payable for the extinguishment of the business[6], the amount will be affected by the shortness of the term and any right of renewal or protection[7]. If the statutory conditions are fulfilled it will be assumed that it will not be reasonably practicable to re-establish a business in the case of a person over 60 carrying on the business when possession is given up[8].

In addition to the compensation previously discussed[9], a tenant for a year or from year to year may be entitled to a home loss payment[10].

1   Ie where the unexpired residue of the term is less than a year: see *R v Great Northern Rly Co* (1876) 2 QBD 151.
2   *Watson v Secretary of State for Air* [1954] 3 All ER 582, [1954] 1 WLR 1477, CA; *Pearl v LCC* [1961] 1 QB 287 at 302, [1960] 3 All ER 588 at 592–593, CA.
3   *R v Rochdale Improvement Act Comrs* (1856) 2 Jur NS 861.
4   See PARA 816.
5   See PARA 821.
6   See PARA 817.
7   See PARA 821.
8   See the Land Compensation Act 1973 s 46; and PARA 817. This provision applies also to compensation under the Lands Clauses Consolidation Act 1845 s 121 and the Compulsory Purchase Act 1965 s 20: see PARA 817 note 11.
9   See PARA 819 et seq.
10   As to home loss payments see PARA 827 et seq.

823.   When a notice to quit may be served instead of a notice requiring possession.   Instead of giving a notice requiring possession[1], the acquiring authority[2] may acquire the landlord's interest and give a notice to quit[3], or accept a surrender from the tenant[4]; or, before the acquisition, the landlord may accept a surrender or give a notice to quit, or be persuaded by the acquiring authority to give a notice to quit[5].

Where, however, a notice to quit an agricultural holding, or part of it, is given, the tenant may have additional statutory rights[6]. Those rights do not, however, apply in relation to farm business tenancies under the Agricultural Tenancies Act 1995[7].

1   See PARAS 699, 819.
2   As to acquiring authorities generally see PARA 519 et seq.
3   *Syers v Metropolitan Board of Works* (1877) 36 LT 277, CA.
4   Cf *R v Poulter* (1887) 20 QBD 132, CA.
5   *Ex p Nadin* (1848) 17 LJCh 421; *Re Portsmouth Rly Co, ex p Merrett* (1860) 2 LT 471.
6   See PARAS 824–825.
7   The Land Compensation Act 1973 ss 59, 61 (see PARAS 824–825) apply to agricultural holdings as defined in the Agricultural Holdings Act 1986 s 1: see the Land Compensation Act 1973 s 87(1); and PARA 703 note 3. As to farm business tenancies see generally AGRICULTURAL LAND vol 1 (2008) PARA 301 et seq.

824.   Notice to quit agricultural holding: right to opt for notice of entry compensation. A person in occupation of an agricultural holding[1], having no greater interest in it than as tenant[2] for a year or from year to year, may elect to take compensation for the acquisition of his interest[3] after service of a notice to quit the holding or part of it[4] as if the notice to quit had not been served[5]. These provisions apply where:

(1)   the notice is served after an acquiring authority[6] has served notice to treat, or is deemed to have served such a notice[7], on the landlord of the holding, or, being an authority possessing compulsory purchase powers[8], has agreed to acquire his interest in the holding[9]; and

(2)   either:

(a)   the statutory restriction on the operation of a notice to quit[10] does not apply because the land is required for non-agricultural use for which planning permission has been, or is deemed to have been, granted or is not required[11]; or

(b)   the Agricultural Land Tribunal has consented to the operation of the notice to quit and stated in the reasons for its decision that it is satisfied[12] that the land is required for non-agricultural use[13].

If the person served with the notice to quit elects that these provisions are to apply to the notice and gives up possession of the holding to the acquiring authority on or before the date on which his tenancy terminates in accordance with the notice, then the compensation provisions of the Compulsory Purchase Act 1965[14] and the Agriculture (Miscellaneous Provisions) Act 1968[15] are to have effect as if the notice to quit had not been served and the acquiring authority had taken possession of the holding in pursuance of a notice of entry[16] on the day before that on which the tenancy terminates in accordance with the notice to quit[17]. The provisions of the Agricultural Holdings Act 1986 relating to compensation to a tenant on the termination of his tenancy[18] do not, however, have effect in relation to the termination of the tenancy by reason of the notice to quit[19].

The election must be made by notice in writing served on the acquiring authority not later than the date on which possession of the holding is given up[20]. No such election may, however, be made or, if already made, continue to have effect in relation to any land[21] if, before the expiration of that notice, an acquiring authority takes possession of that land in pursuance of an enactment providing for the taking of possession of land compulsorily[22].

These provisions do not apply in relation to farm business tenancies under the Agricultural Tenancies Act 1995[23].

1   As to the meaning of 'agricultural holding' see PARA 703 note 3.

2   As to the meaning of 'tenant' see PARA 703 note 3.

3   A person served with a notice to quit part of an agricultural holding is not entitled, in relation to
    that notice, both to make an election under the Land Compensation Act 1973 s 59 (see the text
    and notes 4–22) and to give a counter-notice under the Agricultural Holdings Act 1986 s 32
    (tenant's right to cause notice to quit part of holding to operate as notice to quit entire holding:
    see AGRICULTURAL LAND vol 1 (2008) PARA 398): Land Compensation Act 1973 s 59(6)
    (amended by the Agricultural Holdings Act 1986 s 100, Sch 14 para 55). As to the meaning of
    'notice to quit' see PARA 807 note 7.

4   The Land Compensation Act 1973 s 59 has effect in relation to a notice to quit part of an
    agricultural holding as it has effect in relation to a notice to quit an entire holding, and
    references to a holding and the termination of the tenancy are to be construed accordingly:
    s 59(5).

5   See the Land Compensation Act 1973 s 59(1), (2); and the text and notes 6–19.

6   As to the meaning of 'acquiring authority' see PARA 622 note 1.

7   This reference to a notice to treat served by an acquiring authority includes a reference to a
    notice to treat deemed to have been so served under any of the provisions of the Compulsory
    Purchase (Vesting Declarations) Act 1981 Pt III (ss 7–9) (see PARA 689 et seq): Land
    Compensation Act 1973 s 59(7) (applying s 53(5) (see PARA 622)).

8   This reference to an authority possessing compulsory purchase powers includes a person or
    body of persons who would be an authority possessing compulsory purchase powers if the
    landlord's interest were not an interest in Crown land as defined by the Town and Country
    Planning Act 1990 s 293 (see TOWN AND COUNTRY PLANNING vol 46(1) (Reissue) PARAS 11, 14,
    239; TOWN AND COUNTRY PLANNING vol 46(2) (Reissue) PARA 555): Land Compensation
    Act 1973 s 59(7) (amended by the Planning and Compensation Act 1991 s 70, Sch 15 para 7).
    See also the Land Compensation Act 1973 s 84(2); and PARA 811. As to the meaning of
    'authority possessing compulsory purchase powers' see PARA 763 note 6 (definition applied by
    s 87(1)). See also *Dawson v Norwich City Council* (1978) 37 P & CR 516, Lands Tribunal.

9   Land Compensation Act 1973 s 59(1)(a).

10 Ie the Agricultural Holdings Act 1986 s 26(1): see AGRICULTURAL LAND vol 1 (2008) PARA 374.

11 Land Compensation Act 1973 s 59(1)(b)(i) (s 59(1)(b) amended by the Agricultural Holdings
    (Notices to Quit) Act 1977 s 13(1), Sch 1 para 6; and by the Agricultural Holdings Act 1986
    Sch 14 para 55). The Agricultural Holdings Act 1973 s 26(1) does not apply by virtue of s 26(2),
    Sch 3 Pt I Case B: see AGRICULTURAL LAND vol 1 (2008) PARAS 376, 378.

12 Ie satisfied as to the matter mentioned in the Agricultural Holdings Act 1986 s 27(3)(f): see
    AGRICULTURAL LAND vol 1 (2008) PARA 375.

13 Land Compensation Act 1973 s 59(1)(b)(ii) (as amended: see note 11).

14 Ie the Compulsory Purchase Act 1965 s 20 (compensation for tenants from year to year etc): see
    PARAS 699 et seq, 819.

15 Ie the Agriculture (Miscellaneous Provisions) Act 1968 s 12: see AGRICULTURAL LAND vol 1
    (2008) PARAS 455, 607–608.

16 Ie under the Compulsory Purchase Act 1965 s 11(1): see PARA 645.

17 Land Compensation Act 1973 s 59(2)(a).

18 As to the statutory right to compensation under the Agricultural Holdings Act 1986 see
    AGRICULTURAL LAND vol 1 (2008) PARA 414 et seq.

19 Land Compensation Act 1973 s 59(2)(b) (amended by the Agricultural Holdings Act 1986
    Sch 14 para 55).

20 Land Compensation Act 1973 s 59(4).

21 Ie whether the whole or part of the land to which the notice to quit relates: Land Compensation
    Act 1973 s 59(3).

22 Land Compensation Act 1973 s 59(3). As to that power of taking possession see the
    Compulsory Purchase Act 1965 s 11(1); and PARA 645.

23 See PARA 823 text and note 7.

**825.   Notice to quit part of agricultural holding by landlord after notice to
treat; counter-notice to acquiring authority to take the whole.**   Where a notice to
quit part only of an agricultural holding[1] is served by the landlord on the tenant
in circumstances where the tenant is entitled to make an election to take
compensation as if a notice of entry has been served[2], and the tenant makes that
election within the period of two months beginning with the date of the service
of the notice to quit, or, if later, the decision of the Agricultural Land Tribunal[3],

then the tenant may also within that period serve a notice on the acquiring authority[4] claiming that the remainder of the holding is not reasonably capable of being farmed, either by itself or in conjunction with other relevant land[5], as a separate agricultural unit[6]. If, within the period of two months beginning with the date of service of the notice by the claimant, the acquiring authority does not agree in writing to accept the notice as valid, the claimant or the authority may refer it to the Upper Tribunal within two months after the end of that period, and on that reference the Upper Tribunal must determine whether the claim in the claimant's notice is justified and declare the notice valid or invalid in accordance with its determination of that question[7].

Where the claimant's notice is accepted as, or is declared to be, valid, then, if before the end of 12 months after it has been so accepted or declared valid, the claimant has given up possession of part of the holding to which the notice relates to the acquiring authority, the provisions of the Compulsory Purchase Act 1965, relating to compensation to tenants for a year or from year to year[8], and the provisions of the Agriculture (Miscellaneous Provisions) Act 1968 giving compensation to tenants[9] have effect as if the acquiring authority had taken possession of that part in pursuance of a notice of entry[10] on the day before the expiration of the year of the tenancy which is current when the notice is so accepted or declared to be valid[11].

Under these provisions the acquiring authority may be compelled to take possession of part of an agricultural holding in land where it has not been authorised to acquire the landlord's interest in or in any part of that land[12], and, accordingly, where the claimant gives up possession of an agricultural holding to the acquiring authority, but the authority has not been authorised to acquire the landlord's interest in, or in any of, the part of the holding to which the notice to quit did not relate ('the land not subject to compulsory purchase'), neither the claimant nor the authority is to be under any liability to the landlord by reason of the claimant giving up possession of the land not subject to compulsory purchase or the authority taking or being in possession of it[13]. Furthermore, immediately after the date on which the authority takes possession of the land not subject to compulsory purchase, it must give up to the landlord, and he must take, possession of that land[14]; and any increase in the value of that land which is attributable to the landlord's taking possession of it must be deducted from the compensation payable in respect of the acquisition of his interest in the remainder of the holding[15].

The tenancy must also be treated as terminated on the date on which the claimant gives up possession of the holding to the acquiring authority, or, if he gives up possession of different parts at different times, gives up possession of the last part, but without prejudice to any rights or liabilities of the landlord or the claimant which have accrued before that date[16]; and any rights of the claimant against, or liabilities of the claimant to, the landlord, which arise on or out of the termination of the tenancy, whether under the contract of tenancy, under the Agricultural Holdings Act 1986[17] or otherwise, will be the rights and liabilities of the authority, and any question as to the payment to be made in respect of any such right or liability must be referred to and determined by the Upper Tribunal[18].

Where an election to take notice of entry compensation[19] ceases to have effect in relation to any land by virtue of the acquiring authority having taken possession of the land compulsorily[20], any counter-notice served by the claimant by virtue of the above provisions will also cease to have effect in relation to that land[21].

These provisions do not apply in relation to farm business tenancies under the Agricultural Tenancies Act 1995[22].

1   As to the meaning of 'agricultural holding' see PARA 703 note 3.
2   Ie under the Land Compensation Act 1973 s 59: see PARA 824.
3   Ie the decision to consent to the notice to quit under the Agricultural Holdings Act 1986 s 27: see PARA 824.
4   As to the meaning of 'acquiring authority' see PARA 622 note 1.
5   As to the meaning of 'other relevant land' see the Land Compensation Act 1973 s 55(3), (4) (applied by s 61(4) as if references to the notice of entry were references to the notice to quit); and PARA 703 note 6.
6   Land Compensation Act 1973 s 61(1). As to the meaning of 'agricultural unit' see PARA 622 note 6. The claimant must also within the same period serve a copy of the notice on the landlord of the holding, but failure to do so will not invalidate the claimant's notice: see s 55(2) (applied by s 61(4)); and PARA 703.
7   Land Compensation Act 1973 s 61(2) (amended by SI 2009/1370). As to the Upper Tribunal see PARA 720; and ADMINISTRATIVE LAW.
8   Ie the provisions of the Compulsory Purchase Act 1965 s 20: see PARAS 699 et seq, 819.
9   Ie the provisions of the Agriculture (Miscellaneous Provisions) Act 1968 s 12: see AGRICULTURAL LAND vol 1 (2008) PARAS 455, 607–608.
10 Ie under the Compulsory Purchase Act 1965 s 11(1): see PARA 645. On such entry the tenant is entitled to compensation under s 20: see PARA 819.
11 Land Compensation Act 1973 s 61(3).
12 The acquiring authority is not authorised to acquire that land because it does not need it.
13 Land Compensation Act 1973 s 56(3)(a) (applied by s 61(4)).
14 Land Compensation Act 1973 s 56(3)(b) (applied by s 61(4)).
15 Land Compensation Act 1973 s 56(3)(e) (applied by s 61(4)).
16 Land Compensation Act 1973 s 56(3)(c) (applied by s 61(4)).
17 See AGRICULTURAL LAND vol 1 (2008) PARA 607 et seq.
18 Land Compensation Act 1973 s 56(3)(d) (amended by SI 2009/1307) (applied by the Land Compensation Act 1973 s 61(4); and amended by the Agricultural Holdings Act 1986 s 100, Sch 14 para 54).
19 Ie under the Land Compensation Act 1973 s 59: see PARA 824.
20 Ie under the Land Compensation Act 1973 s 59(3): see PARA 824.
21 Land Compensation Act 1973 s 61(5).
22 See PARA 823 text and note 7.

8. PAYMENTS FOR DISTURBANCE APART FROM COMPENSATION

(1) CLASSES OF PAYMENTS AND PERSONS ENTITLED

826.   Payments additional to purchase money and compensation and payments where interests not acquirable.   An owner of land who has an interest greater than a tenancy for a year or from year to year is entitled to compensation for disturbance as part of his purchase money[1] but, in addition and apart from it, he may be entitled to a home loss payment or occupier's loss payment[2].

A tenant for a year or from year to year or less is not entitled to a notice to treat and his interest is not purchased[3], but he is entitled to compensation for disturbance if he is required to give up possession and does so[4], and in addition to his compensation he may be entitled to a home loss payment[5].

Some occupiers of the land compulsorily acquired have no interest which gives a right to compensation under the above provisions, but certain of them may be entitled to payments for disturbance if they qualify by complying with certain statutory conditions[6], and in the case of others who do not so qualify the acquiring authority may make a voluntary payment[7]. Some occupiers in either class may be entitled to a home loss payment[8].

1   See PARA 814 et seq.
2   See PARA 827 et seq.
3   See PARA 699.
4   See PARAS 702, 819 et seq.
5   See PARA 827.
6   See PARA 838.
7   See PARA 838 text to notes 13–15.
8   See PARA 827.

(2) HOME LOSS PAYMENTS

827.   Right to home loss payment.   Where a person is displaced[1] from a dwelling on any land in consequence of the compulsory acquisition of an interest in the dwelling or some other specified event[2] he will be entitled to receive a payment (a 'home loss payment') from the acquiring authority[3] or other specified authority or body[4] provided that the statutory conditions have been satisfied throughout the period of one year ending with the date of displacement[5]. Those conditions are that:

(1)   he has been in occupation of the dwelling, or a substantial part of it, as his only or main residence[6]; and

(2)   he has been in such occupation by virtue of any of the following interests or rights:

(a)   any interest[7] in the dwelling[8];

(b)   a right to occupy the dwelling as a statutory tenant[9] or under a restricted[10] contract[11];

(c)   a right to occupy the dwelling under a contract of employment[12];

(d)   a right to occupy the dwelling under a licence where either it is a right to occupy as a protected occupier[13], or the statutory provisions relating to secure tenancies apply to the licence[14], or the licence is an assured agricultural occupancy[15] or where the statutory provisions relating to introductory tenancies apply to the licence[16].

If these conditions have not been so satisfied throughout that period but are satisfied on the date of displacement, a discretionary payment may be made to that person of an amount not exceeding the amount to which he would have been entitled if he had satisfied those conditions throughout that period[17].

Where an authority possessing compulsory purchase powers acquires the interest of any person in a dwelling by agreement, then, in relation to any other person who is displaced from the dwelling in consequence of the acquisition, the above provisions have effect as if the acquisition were compulsory and the authority (if not authorised to acquire the interest compulsorily) had been so authorised on the date of the agreement[18].

Where by reason of the entitlement of one spouse or civil partner ('A') to occupy a dwelling[19] by virtue of any such interest or right as is mentioned in heads (1) and (2) above, the other spouse or civil partner ('B') acquires home rights[20], then so long as:

(i)   those home rights continue;

(ii)   B is in occupation of the dwelling and A is not; and

(iii)   B is not otherwise treated as occupying the dwelling by virtue of such an interest or right,

then B is to be treated for the purposes of the above provisions as occupying the dwelling by virtue of such an interest[21].

A person residing in a caravan on a caravan site[22] who is displaced from that site may also be entitled to a home loss payment or discretionary payment[23], but no such payment may be made to any person by virtue of this provision except where no suitable alternative site for stationing a caravan is available to him on reasonable terms[24].

These provisions[25] apply in relation to the acquisition of interests in land, whether compulsorily or by agreement, by government departments which are authorities possessing compulsory purchase powers as they apply in relation to the acquisition of interests in land by such authorities which are not government departments[26].

1   For these purposes, a person is not to be treated as displaced from a dwelling in consequence of the compulsory acquisition of an interest in it if he gives up his occupation of it before the date on which the acquiring authority was authorised to acquire that interest, but, subject to that, it is not necessary for the authority to have required him to give up his occupation of the dwelling: Land Compensation Act 1973 s 29(3). A voluntary move does not amount to 'displacement', which has overtones of compulsion requiring sufficient action or persuasion operating upon the occupier, apart from the mere fact of redevelopment itself: *Ingle v Scarborough Borough Council* [2002] EWCA Civ 290, [2003] RVR 177. Nor is a person to be treated as displaced from a dwelling in consequence of the carrying out of any improvement to the dwelling unless he is permanently displaced from it in consequence of the carrying out of that improvement: Land Compensation Act 1973 s 29(3A) (added by the Housing Act 1974 s 130, Sch 13 para 38(3); amended by the Planning and Compensation Act 1991 ss 70, 84(6), Sch 15 para 22(1), (3), Sch 19 Pt III; and Housing Act 2004 s 265(1), Sch 15 paras 2, 3(1), (3)). 'Improvement' includes alteration and enlargement: Land Compensation Act 1973 s 29(7A) (added by the Housing Act 1974 Sch 13 para 38(3)). A person must not be treated as displaced from a dwelling in consequence only of the compulsory acquisition of part of a garden or yard or of an outhouse or appurtenance belonging to or usually enjoyed with the building which is occupied or is intended to be occupied as the dwelling: Land Compensation Act 1973 s 29(3B) (added by the Planning and Compulsory Purchase Act 2004 s 118(2), Sch 7 para 7(1), (2)). The Land Compensation Act 1973 s 29 applies if the date of displacement is on or after 17 October 1972: s 29(9). As to the meaning of 'dwelling' see PARA 802 note 1. As to the meaning of 'acquiring authority' see PARA 622 note 1.

2   Land Compensation Act 1973 s 29(1)(a). The other specified events are:

    (1)   the making of a housing order in respect of the dwelling (s 29(1)(b) (substituted by the Housing Act 2004 s 265(1), Sch 15 paras 2, 3(1), (2)(a)));

(2)   where the land has been previously acquired by an authority possessing compulsory purchase powers or appropriated by a local authority and is for the time being held by the authority for the purposes for which it was acquired or appropriated, the carrying out of any improvement to the dwelling or of redevelopment on the land (Land Compensation Act 1973 s 29(1)(c) (amended by the Housing Act 1974 Sch 13 para 38(3)));

(3)   the carrying out of any improvement to the dwelling or of redevelopment on the land by a housing association which has previously acquired the land and at the date of the displacement is a registered social landlord within the meaning of the Housing Act 1985 (see s 5(4), (5); and HOUSING vol 22 (2006 Reissue) PARA 67) (Land Compensation Act 1973 s 29(1)(d) (substituted by the Housing (Consequential Provisions) Act 1985 s 4, Sch 2 para 24(2)(b); and amended by SI 1996/2325));

(4)   the making of an order for possession on the grounds set out in the Housing Act 1985 s 84, Sch 2 Pt II Ground 10 or Ground 10A (see LANDLORD AND TENANT vol 27(2) (2006 Reissue) PARAS 1367–1368) (Land Compensation Act 1973 s 29(1)(e) (added by the Housing and Planning Act 1986 s 9(3))).

For these purposes, a 'housing order' means (a) a prohibition order under the Housing Act 2004 s 20 or s 21; or (b) a demolition order under the Housing Act 1985 s 265 (see HOUSING vol 22 (2006 Reissue) PARAS 387 et seq, 414 et seq): Land Compensation Act 1973 s 29(7) (substituted by the Housing Act 2004 s 265(1), Sch 15 paras 2, 3(1), (4)).

'Redevelopment' includes a change of use: Land Compensation Act 1973 s 29(7A) (as added: see note 1). It has also been held to include demolition preceding the substitution of new buildings: see *R v Corby District Council, ex p McLean* [1975] 2 All ER 568, [1975] 1 WLR 735; *Follows v The Peabody Trust* (1983) 10 HLR 62, CA; *GLC v Holmes* [1986] QB 989, [1986] 1 All ER 739, CA. As to the meaning of 'authority possessing compulsory purchase powers' see PARA 763 note 6 (definition applied by the Land Compensation Act 1973 s 87(1)).

3   Ie where the Land Compensation Act 1973 s 29(1)(a) (compulsory acquisition of an interest in the dwelling) applies: s 29(1)(i) (s 29(1)(i)–(iv) substituted by the Housing Act 1974 Sch 13 para 38(1)(c)).

4   The specified authorities and bodies are as follows:

(1)   where the Land Compensation Act 1973 s 29(1)(b) applies (see note 2 head (1)), the authority who made the housing order (s 29(1)(ii) (as substituted (see note 3); and amended by the Planning and Compensation Act 1991 Sch 15 para 22(1), (2), Sch 19 Pt III; and the Housing Act 2004 Sch 15 paras 2, 3(1), (2)(b)));

(2)   where the Land Compensation Act 1973 s 29(1)(c) applies (see note 2 head (2)), the authority carrying out the improvement or redevelopment (s 29(1)(iii) (as substituted (see note 3); and amended by the Planning and Compensation Act 1991 Sch 15 para 22(1), (2), Sch 19 Pt III));

(3)   where s 29(1)(d) applies (see note 2 head (3)), the housing association carrying out the improvement or redevelopment (s 29(1)(iv) (as substituted (see note 3); and amended by the Planning and Compensation Act 1991 Sch 15 para 22(1), (2))); and

(4)   where the Land Compensation Act 1973 s 29(1)(e) applies (see note 2 head (4)), the landlord (s 29(1)(v) (added by the Housing and Planning Act 1986 s 9(3); and amended by the Planning and Compensation Act 1991 Sch 15 para 22(1), (2))).

5   Land Compensation Act 1973 s 29(2) (substituted by the Planning and Compensation Act 1991 s 68(1)). Where the claimant has satisfied, throughout any period, the conditions mentioned in the Land Compensation Act 1973 s 29(2), that period is treated for these purposes as including any immediately preceding period throughout which:

(1)   he has resided in the dwelling as his only or main residence but without satisfying those conditions; and

(2)   another person or other persons have satisfied those conditions,

and references to a dwelling include a reference to a substantial part of it: s 32(3) (substituted by the Planning and Compensation Act 1991 s 68(4)). Where he has satisfied those conditions throughout any period, that period (or that period as so extended) is treated for these purposes as including any immediately preceding period, or successive periods, throughout which he satisfied those conditions in relation to another dwelling or, as the case may be, other dwellings, applying heads (1)–(2) to determine the length of any period or periods: Land Compensation Act 1973 s 32(3A) (added by the Planning and Compensation Act 1991 s 68(4)). Where the claimant has successively been in occupation of or resided in different dwellings in the same building, being dwellings consisting of a room or rooms not structurally adapted for use as a separate dwelling, the Land Compensation Act 1973 ss 29(2), 32(3), (3), (3A) have effect as if those dwellings were the same dwelling: s 32(5) (amended by the Planning and Compensation Act 1991 s 68(6)).

6   There is no statutory definition of 'only or main residence' for these purposes; but cf CAPITAL GAINS TAXATION vol 5(1) (2004 Reissue) PARA 351.

7   Where an interest in a dwelling is vested in trustees (other than a sole tenant for life within the meaning of the Settled Land Act 1925) and a person beneficially entitled, whether directly or derivatively, under the trusts is entitled or permitted by reason of his interest to occupy the dwelling, he is to be treated for these purposes as occupying it by virtue of an interest in the dwelling: Land Compensation Act 1973 s 29(8) (amended by the Land Compensation (Scotland) Act 1973 Sch 2).

8   Land Compensation Act 1973 s 29(4)(a).

9   Ie within the meaning of the Rent (Agriculture) Act 1976 (see LANDLORD AND TENANT vol 27(2) (2006 Reissue) PARA 1146 et seq) or the Rent Act 1977 (see LANDLORD AND TENANT vol 27(2) (2006 Reissue) PARA 831 et seq).

10   Ie under a contract to which the Rent Act 1977 s 19 (repealed with savings by the Housing Act 1988 s 140(2), Sch 18 para 1) applies or would apply if the contract or dwelling were not excluded by s 19(3)–(5) (repealed) or s 144: see LANDLORD AND TENANT vol 27(2) (2006 Reissue) PARAS 986–987.

11   Land Compensation Act 1973 s 29(4)(b) (substituted by the Planning and Compensation Act 1991 Sch 15 para 22(1), (4)).

12   Land Compensation Act 1973 s 29(4)(d).

13   Ie within the meaning of the Rent (Agriculture) Act 1976 (see LANDLORD AND TENANT vol 27(2) (2006 Reissue) PARA 1144).

14   Ie the Housing Act 1985 Pt IV (ss 79–117) (see LANDLORD AND TENANT vol 27(2) (2006 Reissue) PARA 1300 et seq).

15   Ie within the meaning of the Housing Act 1988 Pt I (ss 1–45) (see LANDLORD AND TENANT vol 27(2) (2006 Reissue) PARA 1037 et seq).

16   Land Compensation Act 1973 s 29(4)(e) (added by the Housing and Planning Act 1986 s 9(3); substituted by the Planning and Compensation Act 1991 Sch 15 para 22(1), (4); and amended by SI 1997/74). The reference in the text to the statutory provisions relating to introductory tenancies is to the Housing Act 1996 Pt V Ch 1 (ss 124–143) (see HOUSING vol 22 (2006 Reissue) PARA 266 et seq).

17   Land Compensation Act 1973 s 29(2) (as substituted: see note 5).

18   Land Compensation Act 1973 s 29(6).

19   For these purposes, references to a dwelling include a reference to a substantial part of it: Land Compensation Act 1973 s 29A(3) (s 29A added by the Planning and Compensation Act 1991 s 69).

20   Ie within the meaning of the Family Law Act 1996 Pt IV (ss 30–63) (see MATRIMONIAL AND CIVIL PARTNERSHIP LAW vol 72 (2009) PARA 285 et seq).

21   Land Compensation Act 1973 s 29A(1), (2) (as added (see note 19); and amended by the Civil Partnership Act 2004 s 82, Sch 9 Pt 2 para 17).

22   For these purposes, 'caravan site' means land on which a caravan is stationed for the purpose of human habitation and land which is used in conjunction with land on which a caravan is so stationed: Land Compensation Act 1973 s 33(7).

23   See the Land Compensation Act 1973 s 33(1), applying ss 29–32 subject to certain modifications. For these purposes, ss 29–32 are modified so as to refer to a caravan on a caravan site instead of to a dwelling: see s 33(3) (amended by the Planning and Compensation Act 1991 s 68(8)(b)); the Land Compensation Act 1973 s 33(5) (amended by the Planning and Compensation Act 1991 s 68(8)(d)); and the Land Compensation Act 1973 s 33(6).

24   Land Compensation Act 1973 s 33(2) (amended by the Planning and Compensation Act 1991 s 68(8)(a)).

25   Ie the Land Compensation Act 1973 Pt III (ss 29–43): see PARA 828 et seq.

26   Land Compensation Act 1973 s 84(2).

828.   Claim for home loss payment.   No home loss payment[1] or discretionary payment[2] may be made except on a claim in writing made by the claimant within six years of the date of displacement[3]. The claim must give such particulars as the authority responsible for making the payment[4] may reasonably require for the purpose of determining whether the payment should be made and, if so, its amount[5].

Where a person (the 'deceased') entitled to a home loss payment dies without having claimed it, a claim to the payment may be made by any person who is not a minor and who (1) throughout a period of not less than one year ending with the date of displacement of the deceased, has resided in the dwelling[6], or a substantial part of it, as his only or main residence[7]; and (2) is entitled to benefit by virtue of testamentary dispositions taking effect on the death of the deceased, or by virtue of the law of intestate succession or the right of survivorship between joint tenants as applied to that death[8].

A person residing in a caravan on a caravan site[9] who is displaced from that site may also make a claim for a home loss payment or discretionary payment[10], but no such payment may be made to any person by virtue of this provision except where no suitable alternative site for stationing a caravan is available to him on reasonable terms[11].

1   As to the meaning of 'home loss payment' see PARA 827.
2   As to the meaning of 'discretionary payment' see PARA 827.
3   Land Compensation Act 1973 s 32(1) (substituted by the Planning and Compensation Act 1991 s 68(4)); Land Compensation Act 1973 s 32(7A) (added by the Local Government, Planning and Land Act 1980 s 114; applying the Limitation Act 1980 by virtue of the Interpretation Act 1978 s 17(2)(a)). As to the date of displacement see PARA 827.
4   As to the authorities responsible for making the payment see PARA 827 note 4. As to the application of these provisions to the Crown see PARA 827 text and notes 25–26.
5   Land Compensation Act 1973 s 32(1). As to the amount of the payment see PARA 829.
6   As to the meaning of 'dwelling' see PARA 802 note 1. Where the claimant has successively been in occupation of or resided in different dwellings in the same building, being dwellings consisting of a room or rooms not constructed or structurally adapted for use as a separate dwelling, the Land Compensation Act 1973 s 32(4) (see heads (1)–(2) in the text, and note 8) has effect as if those dwellings were the same dwelling: s 32(5) (amended by the Planning and Compensation Act 1991 s 68(6)).
7   See PARA 827 note 6.
8   Land Compensation Act 1973 s 32(4) (amended by the Local Government, Planning and Land Act 1980 s 114; and by the Planning and Compensation Act 1991 s 68(5)).
9   As to the meaning of 'caravan site' see PARA 827 note 22.
10 See the Land Compensation Act 1973 s 33(1), applying s 32 with certain modifications.
11 See the Land Compensation Act 1973 s 33(2) (amended by the Planning and Compensation Act 1991 s 68(8)(a)). For these purposes, the Land Compensation Act 1973 s 32 is modified so as to refer to a caravan on a caravan site instead of to a dwelling: see s 33(5)(b). See also s 33(6); and PARA 827 note 23.

829.   Payments for home loss.   In the case of a person who on the date of displacement[1] is occupying, or is treated[2] as occupying, the dwelling[3] by virtue of an interest in it which is an owner's interest[4], the amount of the home loss payment[5] is 10 per cent of the market value of his interest in the dwelling[6] or, as the case may be, the interest in the dwelling vested in trustees, subject to a maximum of £47,000 and a minimum of £4,700[7]. In any other case, the amount of the home loss payment is £4,700[8].

Where a person is entitled to a home loss payment, the payment must be made on or before the latest of the following dates:

(1)   the date of displacement[9];

(2)   the last day of the period of three months beginning with the making of the claim[10]; and

(3)   where the amount of the payment is to be determined on the basis that the interest in the dwelling is an owner's interest[11], the day on which the market value of the interest in question is agreed or finally determined[12].

Where the amount of the payment is to be determined as mentioned in head (3) above, the acquiring authority[13] may at any time make a payment in advance[14] and if, on the later of the dates referred to in heads (1) and (2) above, the market value of the interest in question has not been agreed or finally determined, the acquiring authority must make a payment in advance where it has not already done so[15]. Where the amount of a payment in advance differs from the amount of the home loss payment, the shortfall or excess must be paid by or, as the case may be, repaid to the acquiring authority when the market value of the interest in question is agreed or finally determined[16].

Where there are two or more persons entitled to make a claim to a home loss payment in respect of the same dwelling[17] the payment to be made on each claim is equal to the whole amount of the home loss payment divided by the number of such persons[18].

Where an interest in a dwelling is acquired by agreement by an authority possessing compulsory purchase powers[19], the authority may, in connection with the acquisition, make to the person from whom the interest is acquired a payment corresponding to any home loss payment or discretionary payment which it would be required or authorised to make to him if the acquisition were compulsory and the authority had been authorised to acquire that interest before he gave up occupation of the dwelling[20]. Where a landlord obtains possession by agreement of a dwelling subject to a secure tenancy[21] and either (a) notice of proceedings for possession of the dwelling has been, or might have been, served specifying certain grounds[22]; or (b) the landlord has applied, or could apply, to the Secretary of State or the Regulator of Social Housing for approval[23] of a redevelopment scheme including the dwelling, or part of it, the landlord may make to any person giving up possession or occupation a payment corresponding to any home loss payment or discretionary payment which it would be required or authorised to make to him if an order for possession had been made on either of those grounds[24].

The amount of any home loss payment or discretionary payment must not be subject to any reduction on account of the fact that the authority responsible for making that payment has provided, or undertakes to provide, or arranges for the provision of, or another authority will provide, residential accommodation under any enactment for the person entitled to the payment[25].

Where a person residing in a caravan on a caravan site[26] who is displaced from that site is entitled to a home loss payment or discretionary payment[27], the statutory provisions relating to the amount of the payment[28] have effect as if the references to a person occupying a dwelling by virtue of an interest in it and to his interest in the dwelling were to a person occupying a caravan site by virtue of an interest in it and to that interest[29], and the statutory provisions relating to the date and method of payment[30] have effect with specified modifications[31].

1   As to the date of displacement see PARA 827.
2   Ie for the purposes of the Land Compensation Act 1973 s 29: see PARA 827.
3   As to the meaning of 'dwelling' see PARA 802 note 1.
4   For these purposes, 'owner's interest' means the interest of a person who is an owner as defined in the Acquisition of Land Act 1981 s 7 (see PARA 560 note 3): Land Compensation Act 1973 s 30(7) (s 30 substituted by the Planning and Compensation Act 1991 s 68(3)). A spouse or civil partner with a statutory right of occupation is not treated as occupying the dwelling by virtue of an owner's interest: see the Land Compensation Act 1973 s 29A(2); and PARA 827.
5   As to home loss payment see PARA 827.
6   For these purposes, the market value of an interest in a dwelling is: (1) in a case where the interest is compulsorily acquired, the amount assessed for the purposes of the acquisition as the value of the interest; and (2) in any other case, the amount which, if the interest were being compulsorily acquired in pursuance of a notice to treat served on the date of displacement, would be assessed for the purposes of the acquisition as the value of the interest, and any dispute as to the latter amount must be determined by the Upper Tribunal: Land Compensation Act 1973 s 30(3) (as substituted (see note 4); amended by SI 2009/1307). In determining the market value of an interest in a dwelling, the dwelling must be taken to include any garden,

yard, outhouses and appurtenances belonging to or usually enjoyed with that dwelling: Land Compensation Act 1973 s 30(4) (as so substituted). As to the Upper Tribunal see PARA 720; and ADMINISTRATIVE LAW.

7   Land Compensation Act 1973 s 30(1) (as substituted (see note 4); amended by virtue of SI 2008/1598; SI 2008/2845). The amounts quoted in the text are applicable where the date of displacement is on or after 1 September 2008: see the Home Loss Payments (Prescribed Amounts) (England) Regulations 2008, SI 2008/1598; and the Home Loss Payments (Prescribed Amounts) (Wales) Regulations 2008, SI 2008/2845. For amounts applicable to displacements before that date see the Home Loss Payments (Prescribed Amounts) (England) Regulations 2007, SI 2007/1750; and the Home Loss Payments (Prescribed Amounts) (Wales) Regulations 2007, SI 2007/2372. The Secretary of State may from time to time by regulations prescribe a different maximum or minimum for these purposes and a different amount for the purposes of the Land Compensation Act 1973 s 30(2) (see the text and note 8): s 30(5), (6) (as so substituted). As to the Secretary of State see PARA 507 note 1. The functions of the Secretary of State under the Land Compensation Act 1973, so far as they are exercisable in relation to Wales, are now exercisable by the Welsh Ministers: see the National Assembly for Wales (Transfer of Functions) Order 1999, SI 1999/672, art 2, Sch 1; and the Government of Wales Act 2006 s 162(1), Sch 11 para 30. As to the Welsh Assembly Government and the Welsh Ministers see CONSTITUTIONAL LAW AND HUMAN RIGHTS.

8   Land Compensation Act 1973 s 30(2) (as substituted: see note 4). See also note 7.
9   Land Compensation Act 1973 s 32(2)(a) (s 32(2) substituted by the Planning and Compensation Act 1991 s 68(4)).
10 Land Compensation Act 1973 s 32(2)(b) (as substituted: see note 9). As to making the claim see PARA 828.
11 Ie determined in accordance with the Land Compensation Act 1973 s 30(1): see the text and notes 1–7.
12 Land Compensation Act 1973 s 32(2)(c) (as substituted: see note 9).
13 As to the meaning of 'acquiring authority' see PARA 622 note 1.
14 Land Compensation Act 1973 s 32(2A)(a) (s 32(2A)–(2C) added by the Planning and Compensation Act 1991 s 68(4)). The amount of the payment in advance is the lesser of: (1) the maximum amount for the purposes of the Land Compensation Act 1973 s 30(1) (see the text and notes 1–7); (2) 10% of the amount agreed to be the market value of the interest in question or, if there is no such agreement, 10% of the acquiring authority's estimate of that amount: s 32(2B) (as so added).
15 Land Compensation Act 1973 s 32(2A)(b) (as added: see note 14).
16 Land Compensation Act 1973 s 32(2C) (as added: see note 14).
17 Ie whether by virtue of joint occupation or by virtue of the Land Compensation Act 1973 s 32(4) (see PARA 828): s 32(6).
18 Land Compensation Act 1973 s 32(6).
19 As to the meaning of 'authority possessing compulsory purchase powers' see PARA 763 note 6 (definition applied by the Land Compensation Act 1973 s 87(1)).
20 Land Compensation Act 1973 s 32(7) (amended by the Planning and Compensation Act 1991 s 68(7)). As to discretionary payments see further PARA 827.
21 Ie within the meaning of the Housing Act 1985 Pt IV (ss 79–117): see LANDLORD AND TENANT vol 27(2) (2006 Reissue) PARA 1300 et seq.
22 Ie specifying the Housing Act 1985 s 84, Sch 2 Pt II Ground 10 or Ground 10A: see LANDLORD AND TENANT vol 27(2) (2006 Reissue) PARAS 1367–1368.
23 Ie for the purposes of the Housing Act 1985 Sch 2 Pt II Ground 10A: see LANDLORD AND TENANT vol 27(2) (2006 Reissue) PARA 1368. The functions of the Secretary of State under the Housing Act 1985, so far as they are exercisable in relation to Wales, are now exercisable by the Welsh Ministers: see the National Assembly for Wales (Transfer of Functions) Order 1999, SI 1999/672, art 2, Sch 1; and the Government of Wales Act 2006 s 162(1), Sch 11 para 30.
24 Land Compensation Act 1973 s 32(7B) (added by the Housing and Planning Act 1986 s 9(4); amended by the Planning and Compensation Act 1991 s 68(7); and the Government of Wales Act 1998 s 152, Sch 18 Pt VI; and by virtue of SI 2008/2839).
25 See the Land Compensation Act 1973 s 50(1), (3); and PARA 814. See also *Khan v Islington London Borough Council* [2000] LGR 1, CA (local authority permitted to set off rent arrears against home loss payment, the right being based in equity, as both the duty to pay rent and the obligation to make a home loss payment derived from the same relationship).
26 As to the meaning of 'caravan site' see PARA 827 note 22.
27 No such payment may be made to any person except where no suitable alternative site for stationing a caravan is available to him on reasonable terms: see the Land Compensation Act 1973 s 33(2); and PARA 827.

28 Ie the Land Compensation Act 1973 s 30: see the text and notes 1–8.
29 Land Compensation Act 1973 s 33(4) (substituted by the Planning and Compensation Act 1991 s 68(8)(c)).
30 Ie the Land Compensation Act 1973 s 32: see the text and notes 9–24.
31 See the Land Compensation Act 1973 s 33(5); and PARAS 827 note 23, 828 note 11. See also s 33(6); and PARA 827 note 23.

(3) OTHER LOSS PAYMENTS

830. Basic loss payment. Where a person has a qualifying interest in land[1] which is acquired compulsorily[2] (and he is not entitled to a home loss payment[3] in respect of any part of the interest) he is entitled to payment of whichever is the lower of 7·5 per cent of the value of his interest[4] or £75,000[5]. Such a payment must be made by the acquiring authority[6].

1 An interest in land is a qualifying interest if it is a freehold interest or an interest as tenant and (in either case) it subsists for a period of not less than one year ending with whichever is the earliest of (1) the date on which the acquiring authority takes possession of the land under the Compulsory Purchase Act 1965 s 11 (see PARA 638 et seq); (2) the date on which the acquiring authority enters the land if it proceeds under Sch 3 (see PARA 639); (3) the vesting date (within the meaning of the Compulsory Purchase (Vesting Declarations) Act 1981: see PARA 687) if a declaration is made under s 4 (general vesting declaration: see PARAS 686–687); (4) the date on which compensation is agreed between the person and the acquiring authority; (5) the date on which the amount of compensation is determined by the Upper Tribunal: Land Compensation Act 1973 s 33A(4) (s 33A added by the Planning and Compulsory Purchase Act 2004 s 106(1); the Land Compensation Act 1973 s 33A(4) amended by SI 2009/1307). As to the Upper Tribunal see PARA 720; and ADMINISTRATIVE LAW.
2 The compulsory acquisition of an interest in land includes acquisition of the interest in consequence of the service of a purchase notice under the Town and Country Planning Act 1990 s 137 (right to require purchase of certain interests: see TOWN AND COUNTRY PLANNING vol 46(2) (Reissue) PARA 966), or a notice under s 150 (purchase of blighted land: see TOWN AND COUNTRY PLANNING vol 46(2) (Reissue) PARA 992): Land Compensation Act 1973 s 33A(5) (as added: see note 1).
3 As to home loss payment see PARA 827.
4 The 'value of an interest' is its value for the purpose of deciding the amount of compensation payable in respect of the acquisition: Land Compensation Act 1973 s 33A(6) (as added: see note 1). If an interest consists partly of a dwelling in respect of which the person is entitled to a home loss payment the value of the interest is the value of the whole interest less the value of so much of the interest as is represented by the dwelling: s 33A(7) (as so added). If the Land Compensation Act 1961 s 5 r 5 (equivalent reinstatement) applies for the purpose of assessing the amount of compensation the value of the interest is nil: Land Compensation Act 1973 s 33A(8) (as so added).
5 Land Compensation Act 1973 s 33A(1), (2) (as added: see note 1). The Secretary of State may by regulations substitute for any amount or percentage figure specified such other amount or percentage figure (as the case may be) as he thinks fit: s 33K(2) (s 33K added by the Planning and Compulsory Purchase Act 2004 s 109).
6 Land Compensation Act 1973 s 33A(3) (as added: see note 1). As to the meaning of 'acquiring authority' see PARA 622 note 1.

831. Occupier's loss payment. Where: (1) a person has a qualifying interest in land[1]; (2) the land is agricultural land; (3) the interest is acquired compulsorily; and (4) the person has occupied the land for a specified period[2], he is entitled to a payment of whichever is the greatest of 2·5 per cent of the value of his interest[3], or the land amount[4], or the buildings amount[5]. Similarly, where: (a) a person has a qualifying interest in land; (b) the land is not agricultural land; (c) the interest is acquired compulsorily; and (d) the person has occupied the land for a specified period[6], he is entitled to a payment of whichever is the greatest of 2·5 per cent of the value of his interest[7], the land amount[8] or the buildings amount[9]. However, the land amount is calculated differently[10]. In either case the maximum amount which may be paid to a person in respect of an interest in land is £25,000[11]. The payment must be made by the acquiring authority[12].

If a person is entitled in respect of the same interest in agricultural land to both an occupier's loss payment[13] and an additional payment in consequence of compulsory acquisition of agricultural holding[14], then payment may be made in respect of only one entitlement[15]. If the person makes a claim under both provisions he must be paid in respect of the entitlement which produces the greater amount[16].

1 As to the meaning of 'qualifying interest in land' see PARA 830 note 1.
2 Ie the period specified in the Land Compensation Act 1973 s 33A(4): see PARA 830 note 1.
3 The value of an interest is its value for the purpose of deciding the amount of compensation payable in respect of the acquisition: Land Compensation Act 1973 s 33B(5) (ss 33B, 33C added by the Planning and Compulsory Purchase Act 2004 s 107(1)). If an interest consists partly of a dwelling in respect of which the person is entitled to a home loss payment (see PARA 827) the value of the interest is the value of the whole interest less the value of so much of the interest as is represented by the dwelling: Land Compensation Act 1973 s 33B(6) (as so added). If the Land Compensation Act 1961 s 5 r 5 (see PARA 800) applies for the purpose of assessing the amount of compensation the value of the interest is nil: Land Compensation Act 1973 s 33B(7) (as so added).
4 The 'land amount' is the greater of £300 and the following amounts. Where the area of the land does not exceed 100 hectares then the amount is £100 per hectare or part of a hectare. Where the area of the land exceeds 100 hectares then the amount is £100 per hectare for the first 100 hectares and £50 per hectare for the next 300 hectares or part of a hectare: Land Compensation Act 1973 s 33B(8) (as added: see note 3).
5 The 'buildings amount' is £25 per square metre (or part of a square metre) of the gross floor space (measured externally) of any buildings on the land: Land Compensation Act 1973 s 33B(9), (10) (as added: see note 3). The Secretary of State may by regulations substitute for any amount or percentage figure specified such other amount or percentage figure (as the case may be) as he thinks fit: see s 33K (added by the Planning and Compulsory Purchase Act 2004 s 109). At the date at which this volume states the law no such regulations had been made.
6 See note 2.
7 The value of an interest is its value for the purpose of deciding the amount of compensation payable in respect of the acquisition; but if an interest consists partly of a dwelling in respect of which the person is entitled to a home loss payment the value of the interest is the value of the whole interest less the value of so much of the interest as is represented by the dwelling, and if the Land Compensation Act 1961 s 5 r 5 (equivalent reinstatement) applies for the purpose of assessing the amount of compensation the value of the interest is nil: Land Compensation Act 1973 s 33C(5)–(7) (as added: see note 3).
8 The 'land amount' is the greater of £2,500 and £2·50 per square metre (or part of a square metre) of the area of the land, but if only part of land in which a person has an interest is acquired the sum is £300: Land Compensation Act 1973 s 33C(8), (9) (as added: see note 3).
9 Land Compensation Act 1973 s 33C(1), (2) (as added: see note 3). The 'buildings amount' is £25 per square metre (or part of a square metre) of the gross floor space (measured externally) of any buildings on the land: s 33C(10), (11) (as so added).
10 See note 8.
11 Land Compensation Act 1973 ss 33B(3), 33C(3) (both as added: see note 3). The Secretary of State may by regulations substitute for any amount or percentage figure specified such other amount or percentage figure (as the case may be) as he thinks fit: s 33K(2) (as added: see note 5).
12 Land Compensation Act 1973 ss 33B(4), 33C(4) (both as added: see note 3). As to the meaning of 'acquiring authority' see PARA 622 note 1.
13 Ie under the Land Compensation Act 1973 s 33B: see the text and notes 1–12.
14 Ie by virtue of the Agriculture (Miscellaneous Provisions) Act 1968 s 12(1): see AGRICULTURAL LAND vol 1 (2008) PARAS 607–608.
15 Land Compensation Act 1973 s 33H(1), (2) (s 33H added by the Planning and Compulsory Purchase Act 2004 s 109).
16 Land Compensation Act 1973 s 33H(3) (as added: see note 15).

832. Exclusions. If (1) a person who qualifies for a basic loss payment or an occupier's loss payment[1] has been served with a notice[2] at the relevant time[3], and the notice has effect or is operative, and he has failed to comply with any requirement of the notice; or (2) that person has been served with a copy of an order[4], and the order has not been quashed on appeal, then no payment may be made[5] to that person[6].

1   Ie a person to whom the Land Compensation Act 1973 s 33A (basic loss payments: see PARA 830), or s 33B or s 33C (occupier's loss payments: see PARA 831) applies: s 33D(1)(a) (s 33D added by the Planning and Compulsory Purchase Act 2004 s 108(1)).

2   Ie (1) notice under the Town and Country Planning Act 1990 s 215 (power to require proper maintenance of land: see TOWN AND COUNTRY PLANNING vol 46(2) (Reissue) PARA 887); (2) notice under the Housing Act 2004 s 11 (improvement notice relating to category 1 hazard: see HOUSING vol 22 (2006 Reissue) PARA 368); (3) notice under s 12 (improvement notice relating to category 2 hazard: see HOUSING vol 22 (2006 Reissue) PARA 369); (4) notice under the Planning (Listed Buildings and Conservation Areas) Act 1990 s 48 (repairs notice prior to compulsory notice of acquisition of listed building: see TOWN AND COUNTRY PLANNING vol 46(3) (Reissue) PARA 1156): see the Land Compensation Act 1973 s 33D(4) (s 33D as added (see note 1); s 33D(4) amended by the Housing Act 2004 s 265(1), Sch 15 paras 2, 4). The Secretary of State may by regulations amend the Land Compensation Act 1973 s 33D(4): see s 33D(7) (as so added). As to the Secretary of State see PARA 507 note 1.

3   The 'relevant time' is the time at which the compulsory purchase order in relation to the person's interest in the land (1) is confirmed, in the case of an order falling within the Acquisition of Land Act 1981 s 2(2) (see PARA 557); (2) is made, in the case of an order falling within s 2(3): Land Compensation Act 1973 s 33D(6) (as added: see note 1).

4   Ie (1) an order under the Housing Act 2004 s 20 (prohibition order relating to category 1 hazard: see HOUSING vol 22 (2006 Reissue) PARA 387); (2) an order under s 21 (prohibition order relating to category 2 hazard: see HOUSING vol 22 (2006 Reissue) PARA 388); (3) an order under s 43 (emergency prohibition order: see HOUSING vol 22 (2006 Reissue) PARA 410); (4) an order under the Housing Act 1985 s 265 (demolition order relating to category 1 or 2 hazard: see HOUSING vol 22 (2006 Reissue) PARA 415): see the Land Compensation Act 1973 s 33D(5) (s 33D as added (see note 1); and substituted by the Housing Act 2004 Sch 15 paras 2, 4). The Secretary of State may by regulations amend the Land Compensation Act 1973 s 33D(5): see s 33D(7) (as so added).

5   Ie under the Land Compensation Act 1976 s 33A, s 33B or s 33C: see PARA 830 et seq.

6   Land Compensation Act 1973 s 33D(1)–(3) (as added: see note 1).

833.   Claims for loss payments.   A claim for basic loss payment[1] or occupier's loss payment[2] must be made in writing to the acquiring authority[3]. The claim must give such particulars as the authority may reasonably require for the purpose of deciding whether a payment is to be made and the amount of any such payment[4].

For the purposes of the Limitation Act 1980 a person's right of action to recover a payment is taken to have accrued, in the case of a claim for basic loss payment[5], on the last day of the specified period[6], and in the case of a claim for occupier's loss payment[7], on the date of his displacement from the land[8].

1   As to basic loss payment see PARA 830.

2   As to occupier's loss payment see PARA 831.

3   Land Compensation Act 1973 s 33E(1), (2) (s 33E added by the Planning and Compulsory Purchase Act 2004 s 109). As to the meaning of 'acquiring authority' see PARA 622 note 1.

4   Land Compensation Act 1973 s 33E(3) (as added: see note 3).

5   Ie under the Land Compensation Act 1973 s 33A: see PARA 830.

6   Ie the period specified in the Land Compensation Act 1973 s 33A(4): see PARA 830.

7   Ie under the Land Compensation Act 1973 s 33B or s 33C: see PARA 831.

8   Land Compensation Act 1973 s 33E(4) (as added: see note 3). As to limitation periods see further LIMITATION PERIODS.

834.   Effect of insolvency before claim is made.   If a person is entitled to a basic loss payment[1] or an occupier's loss payment[2] but before a claim is made[3] insolvency proceedings are started in relation to the person, then the following persons may make a claim instead[4]. In the case of an individual, a receiver, trustee in bankruptcy or the official receiver may make the claim[5]. In the case of a company or a partnership, an administrator, administrative receiver, liquidator or provisional liquidator or the official receiver may make the claim[6].

1 Ie under the Land Compensation Act 1973 s 33A: see PARA 830.
2 Ie under the Land Compensation Act 1973 s 33B or s 33C: see PARA 831.
3 Ie under the Land Compensation Act 1973 s 33E: see PARA 833.
4 Land Compensation Act 1973 s 33F(1), (2) (s 33F added by the Planning and Compulsory Purchase Act 2004 s 109). Insolvency proceedings are: (1) proceedings in bankruptcy; (2) proceedings under the Insolvency Act 1986 for the winding up of a company or an unregistered company (including voluntary winding up of a company under Pt 4); (3) proceedings for the winding up of a partnership: Land Compensation Act 1973 s 33F(3) (as so added). See further COMPANY AND PARTNERSHIP INSOLVENCY.
5 Land Compensation Act 1973 s 33F(2)(a) (as added: see note 4).
6 Land Compensation Act 1973 s 33F(2)(b) (as added: see note 4).

835. Death before claim is made. If a person is entitled to a basic loss payment[1] or an occupier's loss payment[2] but dies before a claim[3] is made, then a claim may be made by a person who:

(1) occupied the land for a period of not less than one year ending with the date on which the deceased is displaced from the land[4]; and

(2) is entitled to benefit on the death of the deceased by virtue of: (a) a testamentary disposition[5]; (b) the law of intestate succession[6]; or (c) the right of survivorship between joint tenants[7].

1 Ie under the Land Compensation Act 1973 s 33A: see PARA 830.
2 Ie under the Land Compensation Act 1973 s 33B or s 33C: see PARA 831.
3 Ie under the Land Compensation Act 1973 s 33E: see PARA 833.
4 Land Compensation Act 1973 s 33G(1), (2)(a) (s 33G added by the Planning and Compulsory Purchase Act 2004 s 109).
5 Land Compensation Act 1973 s 33G(2)(b), (3)(a) (as added: see note 4). As to testamentary dispositions see WILLS vol 50 (2005 Reissue) PARA 301 et seq.
6 Land Compensation Act 1973 s 33G(2)(b), (3)(b) (as added: see note 4). As to intestate succession see EXECUTORS AND ADMINISTRATORS vol 17(2) (Reissue) PARA 583 et seq.
7 Land Compensation Act 1973 s 33G(2)(b), (3)(c) (as added: see note 4).

836. Payment. Any dispute as to the amount of a payment to be made[1] must be determined by the Upper Tribunal[2]. The acquiring authority[3] must make any basic loss payment[4] not later than whichever is the latest of (1) the last day of the specified period[5]; (2) the last day of the period of three months beginning with the day the claim is made; and (3) the day on which the amount of the payment is determined[6]. The authority must make any occupier's loss payment[7] not later than whichever is the latest of: (a) the date the person is displaced from the land; (b) the last day of the period of three months beginning with the day the claim is made; (c) the day on which the amount of the payment is determined[8].

If in either case the latest date is the date on which the amount of the payment is determined, then the authority may at any time make a payment in advance to the person entitled to a payment (the 'claimant')[9].

The acquiring authority must pay interest at the prescribed rate on the amount required to be paid[10]. In the case of basic loss payment interest accrues from the last day of the specified period, and in the case of occupier's loss payment the interest accrues from the date on which the person is displaced from the land[11]. The authority may, at the request of the person entitled to the payment, make a payment on account of the interest[12].

1 Ie under the Land Compensation Act 1973 s 33A, s 33B or s 33C: see PARAS 830–831.

2   Land Compensation Act 1973 s 33I(1) (s 33I added by the Planning and Compulsory Purchase Act 2004 s 109; the Land Compensation Act 1973 s 33I(1) amended by SI 2009/1307). As to the Upper Tribunal see PARA 720; and ADMINISTRATIVE LAW.
3   As to the meaning of 'acquiring authority' see PARA 622 note 1.
4   Ie under the Land Compensation Act 1973 s 33A: see PARA 830.
5   Ie the period specified in the Land Compensation Act 1973 s 33A(4): see PARA 830.
6   Land Compensation Act 1973 s 33I(2) (as added: see note 2).
7   Ie any payment required by the Land Compensation Act 1961 s 33B or s 33C: see PARA 831.
8   Land Compensation Act 1973 s 33I(3) (as added: see note 2).
9   Land Compensation Act 1973 s 33I(4) (as added: see note 2). If when the value of the interest is agreed or determined the amount of a payment made under s 33I(4) differs from the payment required by s 33A, s 33B or s 33C then the amount by which the advance payment exceeds the payment required must be repaid by the claimant to the authority, and the amount by which the payment required exceeds the advance payment must be paid by the authority to the claimant: s 33I(5) (as so added).
10   Land Compensation Act 1973 s 33I(6) (as added: see note 2). The interest rate is prescribed by regulations under the Land Compensation Act 1961 s 32: see the Acquisition of Land (Rate of Interest after Entry) Regulations 1995, SI 1995/2262; and PARA 641.
11   Land Compensation Act 1973 s 33I(7) (as added: see note 2).
12   Land Compensation Act 1973 s 33I(8) (as added: see note 2).

837. Acquisition by agreement. If a qualifying interest in land for the purpose of basic loss payment[1] is acquired by agreement by an authority which has power to acquire the interest compulsorily, and the interest is acquired from a person who would be entitled to a basic loss payment[2] or an occupier's loss payment[3] if the interest is acquired compulsorily, then the authority may make a payment to the person of an amount equal to the amount they would be required to pay if the interest is acquired compulsorily[4].

1   Ie an interest in land which is a qualifying interest for the purpose of the Land Compensation Act 1973 s 33A: see PARA 830.
2   Ie under the Land Compensation Act 1973 s 33A: see PARA 830.
3   Ie under the Land Compensation Act 1973 s 33B or s 33C: see PARA 831.
4   Land Compensation Act 1973 s 33J(1), (2) (s 33J added by the Planning and Compulsory Purchase Act 2004 s 109).

(4) PAYMENTS FOR DISTURBANCE TO PERSONS WITHOUT COMPENSATABLE INTERESTS

838. Right to disturbance payment. Where a person is displaced[1] from any land, other than land used for the purposes of agriculture[2], in consequence of the acquisition of the land by an authority possessing compulsory purchase powers[3] or some other specified event[4], he is entitled to receive a payment (a 'disturbance payment') from the acquiring authority[5] or other specified authority or body[6] if he fulfils the required conditions as to his displacement[7], possession and interest[8]. A disturbance payment is primarily intended to benefit those who do not otherwise qualify for compensation because they have no interest requiring to be purchased[9].

A person is not entitled to a disturbance payment unless he was in lawful possession of the land[10].

Where a person is displaced from land in such circumstances that he would otherwise be entitled to a disturbance payment from any authority and also to compensation from that authority where an order for a new tenancy of business premises is precluded on certain grounds[11], he will be entitled, at his option, to one or the other but not to both[12].

Where a person is displaced from any land in consequence of the acquisition of the land by an authority possessing compulsory purchase powers or some other specified event[13] but is not entitled as against the relevant authority to a disturbance payment, or to compensation for disturbance under any other enactment, the authority if it thinks fit may make a payment to him determined in accordance with the statutory provisions[14] determining the amount of a disturbance payment[15].

These provisions[16] apply in relation to the acquisition of interests in land, whether compulsorily or by agreement, by government departments which are authorities possessing compulsory purchase powers as they apply in relation to the acquisition of interests in land by such authorities which are not government departments[17].

1   As to when a person is treated as displaced for these purposes see note 7. See also *Prasad v Wolverhampton Borough Council* [1983] Ch 333, [1983] 2 All ER 140, CA (a person is displaced in consequence of the acquisition if, under the threat of dispossession by virtue of a compulsory purchase order, he reasonably moves to other accommodation before the service of any notice to treat); approved in *Director of Buildings and Lands v Shun Fung Ironworks Ltd* [1995] 2 AC 111, [1995] 1 All ER 846, PC. If, however, a tenancy is surrendered to the authority, the interest created by it is extinguished and not acquired, so that nothing is payable by virtue of the Land Compensation Act 1973 s 37: *R v Islington London Borough Council, ex p Knight* [1984] 1 All ER 154, [1984] 1 WLR 205.

2   Land Compensation Act 1973 s 37(7). As to the meaning of 'agriculture' see PARA 622 note 3.

3   Land Compensation Act 1973 s 37(1)(a). As to the meaning of 'authority possessing compulsory purchase powers' see PARA 763 note 6 (definition applied by s 87(1)).

4   The specified events are:
      (1)   the making of a housing order in respect of a house or building on the land (Land Compensation Act 1973 s 37(1)(b) (substituted by the Housing Act 2004 s 265(1), Sch 15 paras 2, 5(1), (2)));
      (2)   where the land has been previously acquired by an authority possessing compulsory purchase powers or appropriated by a local authority and is for the time being held by the authority for the purposes for which it was acquired or appropriated, the carrying out of any improvement to a house or building on the land or of redevelopment on the land (Land Compensation Act 1973 s 37(1)(c) (amended by the Housing Act 1974 Sch 13 para 39));
      (3)   the carrying out of any improvement to a house or building on the land or of redevelopment on the land by a housing association which has previously acquired the land and at the date of the displacement is a registered social landlord within the meaning of the Housing Act 1985 (see s 5(4), (5); and HOUSING vol 22 (2006 Reissue) PARA 66 et seq) (Land Compensation Act 1973 s 37(1)(d) (added by the Housing Act 1974 Sch 13 para 39; substituted by the Housing (Consequential Provisions) Act 1985 s 4, Sch 2 para 24; and amended by SI 1996/2325)).
      For these purposes, 'housing order', 'improvement' and 'redevelopment' have the same meanings as in the Land Compensation Act 1973 s 29 (see PARA 827 notes 1–2): s 37(9) (amended by the Land Compensation (Scotland) Act 1973 Sch 3 para 39(4); the Housing Act 1974 Sch 13 para 39(4); and the Housing Act 2004 Sch 15 paras 2, 5(1), (6), Sch 16).

5   Land Compensation Act 1973 s 37(1)(i) (s 37(1)(i)–(iv) added by the Housing Act 1974 Sch 13 para 39).

6   The authorities and bodies are as follows:
      (1)   where the Land Compensation Act 1973 s 37(1)(b) applies (see note 4 head (1)), the authority who made the housing order (s 37(1)(ii) (as added (see note 5); and amended by the Housing Act 2004 Sch 15 paras 2, 5(1), (2)));
      (2)   where the Land Compensation Act 1973 s 37(1)(c) applies (see note 4 head (2)), the authority carrying out the improvement or redevelopment (s 37(1)(iii) (as so added)); and
      (3)   where s 37(1)(d) applies (see note 4 head (3)), the housing association carrying out the improvement or redevelopment (s 37(1)(iv) (as so added)).

7   A person is not to be treated as displaced in consequence of any such acquisition, improvement or redevelopment as is mentioned in the Land Compensation Act 1973 s 37(1)(a) (see the text and notes 1–3), s 37(1)(c) (see note 4 head (2)) or s 37(1)(d) (see note 4 head (3)) unless he was in lawful possession of the land:

(1)   in the case of land acquired under a compulsory purchase order, at the time when notice
       was first published of the making of the compulsory purchase order prior to its
       submission for confirmation or, where the order did not require confirmation, of the
       preparation of the order in draft;
(2)   in the case of land acquired under an Act specifying the land as subject to compulsory
       acquisition, at the time when the provisions of the Bill for that Act specifying the land
       were first published;
(3)   in the case of land acquired by agreement, at the time when the agreement was made,
and a person is not treated as displaced in consequence of a housing order within s 37(1)(b) (see
note 4 head (1)) unless he was in lawful possession of the land at the time when the order was
made: s 37(3) (amended by the Land Compensation (Scotland) Act 1973 Sch 3; the Housing
Act 1974 Sch 13 para 39; and the Housing Act 2004 Sch 15 paras 2, 5(1), (4)). Nor is a person
treated as displaced in consequence of the carrying out of any improvement to a house or
building unless he is permanently displaced in consequence of the carrying out of that
improvement: Land Compensation Act 1973 s 37(3A) (added by the Housing Act 1974 Sch 13
para 39; and amended by the Housing Act 2004 Sch 15 paras 2, 5(1), (5)).

8   Land Compensation Act 1973 s 37(1). A person is not entitled to a disturbance payment: (1) in
      a case within s 37(1)(a) (see the text and notes 1–3) unless he has no interest in the land for the
      acquisition or extinguishment of which he is, or if the acquisition or extinguishment were
      compulsory would be, entitled to compensation under any other enactment; (2) in a case within
      s 37(1)(b) (see note 4 head (1)), if he is entitled to a payment under the Housing Act 1985
      s 584A(1) (compensation payable in cases of prohibition and demolition orders: see PARA 809;
      and HOUSING vol 22 (2006 Reissue) PARA 414 et seq); (3) in a case within the Land
      Compensation Act 1973 s 37(1)(d) (see note 4 head (3)) unless the displacement occurred on or
      after 31 July 1974: s 37(2)(b)–(d) (amended by the Housing Rents and Subsidies Act 1975
      s 17(4), Sch 5; the Housing (Consequential Provisions) Act 1985 ss 3, 4, Sch 1 Pt I, Sch 2
      para 24(3); the Local Government and Housing Act 1989 s 194, Sch 11 para 31, Sch 12 Pt II;
      and the Housing Act 2004 Sch 15 paras 2, 5(1), (3)).

9   See *Prasad v Wolverhampton Borough Council* [1983] Ch 333 at 353, [1983] 2 All ER 140 at
      152, CA, per Stephenson LJ.

10   Land Compensation Act 1973 s 37(2)(a). In this context, 'lawful possession' means physical
      occupation with the intention to exclude unauthorised intruders, with the permission of the
      person who has the legal right to possession, so that a licensee who does not have exclusive
      possession may have a claim under these provisions: *Wrexham Maelor Borough Council v
      MacDougall* (1993) 69 P & CR 109, [1993] 2 EGLR 23, CA.

11   Ie where he is entitled to compensation under the Landlord and Tenant Act 1954 s 37: see
      LANDLORD AND TENANT vol 27(2) (2006 Reissue) PARA 759.

12   Land Compensation Act 1973 s 37(4).

13   Ie where a person is displaced as mentioned in the Land Compensation Act 1973 s 37(1): see the
      text and notes 1–8.

14   Ie determined in accordance with the Land Compensation Act 1973 s 38(1)–(3): see PARA 839.

15   Land Compensation Act 1973 s 37(5). Any dispute as to the amount of such a discretionary
      payment, if the authority exercises its discretion to make it, must be determined by the Upper
      Tribunal under s 38(4) (see PARA 839): *Gozra v Hackney London Borough Council* (1988)
      57 P & CR 211, CA. As to the Upper Tribunal see PARA 720; and ADMINISTRATIVE LAW.

16   Ie the Land Compensation Act 1973 Pt III (ss 29–43).

17   Land Compensation Act 1973 s 84(2).

839.   Payments for disturbance.   The amount of a disturbance payment[1] must
be equal to the reasonable expenses of the person entitled to the payment in
removing from the land from which he is displaced[2], and, if he was carrying on a
trade or business on that land, the loss he will sustain by reason of the
disturbance of that trade or business consequent upon his having to quit the
land[3]. In estimating that loss, regard must be had to the period for which the
land occupied by him may reasonably have been expected to be available for the
purposes of his trade or business and to the availability of other land suitable for
that purpose[4]. In the case of a person over 60 who is displaced, it must be
assumed that it is not reasonably practicable to carry on the trade or business

...ctural ... of a disabled ... disturbance payment, ... functions[8] provided assistance ..., have provided assistance for making ... of the disturbance payment must include an ... reasonable expenses incurred by the person entitled to the ... making, in respect of a dwelling to which the disabled person ... es, comparable modifications which are reasonably required for meeting the disabled person's special needs[9].

Any dispute as to the amount of a disturbance payment must be referred to and determined by the Upper Tribunal[10]. A disturbance payment carries interest at the prescribed rate[11] from the date of displacement until payment[12]. Payments on account of the disturbance payment or interest may be made, on written request by the person entitled to the payment; and if it is subsequently agreed or determined that the person who made the payment is not liable to pay the compensation or interest, or that any such payment is excessive, the payment or the excess is recoverable by him[13].

The amount of any payment to persons without compensatable interests must not be subject to any reduction on account of the fact that the authority responsible for making that payment has provided, or undertakes to provide, or arranges for the provision of, or another authority will provide, residential accommodation under any enactment for the person entitled to the payment[14].

1   As to the meaning of 'disturbance payment' see PARA 838.
2   Land Compensation Act 1973 s 38(1)(a). The reasonable expenses of removal include all reasonable expenses flowing from the need to move as a direct and natural consequence of it: see *Nolan v Sheffield Metropolitan District Council* (1979) 38 P & CR 741, Lands Tribunal. They may include expenses reasonably incurred before the notice to treat (see PARA 838 note 1).
3   Land Compensation Act 1973 s 38(1)(b). This may include compensation for the total extinguishment of a business: see *Wrexham Maelor Borough Council v MacDougall* (1993) 69 P & CR 109, [1993] 2 EGLR 23, CA; and see PARA 820.
4   Land Compensation Act 1973 s 38(2).
5   See the Land Compensation Act 1973 ss 38(2), 46(7); and PARA 817.
6   As to the meaning of 'dwelling' see PARA 802 note 1.
7   As to the meaning of 'disabled person' see PARA 802 note 2.
8   Ie under the National Assistance Act 1948 s 29 (which relates to welfare arrangements for disabled persons): see SOCIAL SERVICES AND COMMUNITY CARE vol 44(2) (Reissue) PARAS 1020–1021.
9   Land Compensation Act 1973 s 38(3) (amended by the Land Compensation (Scotland) Act 1973 s 81(1), Sch 2 Pt I).
10 Land Compensation Act 1973 s 38(4) (amended by the Land Compensation (Scotland) Act 1973 Sch 2 Pt I; and SI 2009/1307). As to the Upper Tribunal see PARA 720; and ADMINISTRATIVE LAW.
11 Ie the rate prescribed under the Land Compensation Act 1961 s 32: see PARA 641 note 6.
12 Land Compensation Act 1973 s 37(6) (amended by the Land Compensation (Scotland) Act 1973 Sch 3).
13 See the Planning and Compensation Act 1991 s 80(2), (3), Sch 18 Pt II.
14 See the Land Compensation Act 1973 s 50(1), (3); and PARA 814.

circ...
much o...
out if the s...
any compulso...
subject to the p...
compulsory acquisitio...
to the provisions of any...
that, in assessing compensa...
thereunder account must be taken...
contiguous or adjacent land which is a...   in
by that enactment[14].   sed

1   As to the meaning of 'notice to treat' see PARA 636...   ...see PARAS
    616–620.
2   As to the meaning of 'relevant interest' see PARA 636 note 4.
3   A person entitled to two interests in land is to be taken to be ... ...n in the same
    capacity if, but only if, he is entitled (1) to both of them beneficially; ... both of them as
    trustee of one particular trust; or (3) to both of them as personal represent... ...of one particular
    person: Land Compensation Act 1961 s 39(6). A person will not be 'entitled' if his title is statute
    barred: C & M Matthews Ltd v Marsden Building Society [1951] Ch 758, sub nom Re Martin's
    Mortgage Trusts [1951] 1 All ER 1053, CA; cf Re The Statutory Trusts Declared by Section 105
    of the Law of Property Act 1925 Affecting the Proceeds of Sale of Moat House Farm, Thurlby
    [1948] Ch 191, sub nom Young v Clarey [1948] 1 All ER 197.
4   As to the meaning of 'land' see PARA 516 note 2.
5   As to the meanings of 'contiguous' and 'adjacent' see PARA 781 note 7.
6   As to the meaning of 'relevant land' see PARA 762 note 5.
7   Ie the circumstances described in any of the Land Compensation Act 1961 s 7(2), Sch 1
    paras 1–4B col 1: see PARA 843 et seq.
8   For these purposes, 'relevant development', in relation to the circumstances mentioned in note 7,
    is that mentioned in relation thereto in the Land Compensation Act 1961 Sch 1 paras 1–4B col
    2, but modified, as respects the prospect of any development, by the omission of the words
    'other than the relevant land' wherever they occur: s 7(2). As to the meaning of 'development'
    see PARA 762 note 2.
9   Ie the conditions mentioned in the Land Compensation Act 1961 s 6(1)(a), (b): see PARA 788 et
    seq.
10 Land Compensation Act 1961 s 7(1). Apart from the statutory provisions discussed in this part
    of the title (see PARAS 840–849), and the Land Compensation Act 1973 s 6 (see PARA 897), there
    is no general power to set off against an owner's compensation any increased value to other land
    in his ownership: Re South Eastern Rly Co and LCC's Contract, South Eastern Rly Co v LCC
    [1915] 2 Ch 252 at 259–260, CA (see PARA 812); cf Melwood Units Property Ltd v Comr of
    Main Roads [1979] AC 426, [1979] 1 All ER 161, PC.
11 The rule may apply unfairly as between two owners who benefit from a scheme of public works,
    but only one of whom has any land taken. Furthermore, the enhancement in value of an owner's
    remaining land may be such that the compensation for the land taken is nil: Cotswold Trailer
    Parks Ltd v Secretary of State for the Environment (1972) 27 P & CR 219, Lands Tribunal.
    However, for the set-off provisions to apply it must be shown that the increase in value of the
    remaining land would not have occurred but for the scheme: Laing Homes Ltd v Eastleigh
    Borough Council [1979] 1 EGLR 187, Lands Tribunal.

12 As to the meaning of 'corresponding enactment' see PARA 796 note 11. See further PARA 841.
13 As to the meaning of 'local enactment' see PARA 790 note 3. Where any such local enactment includes a provision restricting the assessment of the increase in value thereunder by reference to existing use (ie, by providing, in whatever terms, that the increase in value is to be assessed on the assumption that planning permission in respect of the contiguous or adjacent land in question would be granted for development of any class specified in the Town and Country Planning Act 1990 s 107(4), Sch 3 (see TOWN AND COUNTRY PLANNING vol 46(2) (Reissue) PARAS 914, 920) but would not be granted for any other development of that land), the enactment is to have effect as if it did not include that provision: Land Compensation Act 1961 s 8(6); Planning (Consequential Provisions) Act 1990 s 2(4). As to the meaning of 'planning permission' see PARA 762 note 1.
14 Land Compensation Act 1961 s 8(5).

841. Purchases under the Light Railways Act 1896 and the Highways Act 1980. There are two cases where specific provision is made by enactments corresponding to the deduction provisions of the Land Compensation Act 1961[1]; here the general power of deduction under that Act does not apply[2] but the provisions as to the protection of owners on any subsequent acquisition of the land benefited[3] do apply.

In determining the amount of compensation where land is acquired under the Light Railways Act 1896, the arbitrator must have regard to the extent to which the remaining and contiguous land and hereditaments belonging to the same proprietor may be benefited by the proposed light railway[4].

In assessing the compensation payable in respect of the compulsory acquisition of land by a highway authority[5] under certain provisions of the Highways Act 1980[6], the Upper Tribunal (the 'Tribunal') must have regard to the extent to which the remaining contiguous land belonging to the same person may be benefited by the purpose for which the land is authorised to be acquired[7]. Without prejudice to the generality of this duty, in the case of land authorised to be acquired for widening a highway, the Tribunal must also set off against the value of the land to be acquired any increase in the value of other land belonging to the same person which will accrue to him by reason of the creation of a frontage to the highway as widened[8]. The Tribunal must also take into account, and embody in its award, any undertaking given by the highway authority as to the use to which the land, or any part of it, will be put[9].

1 Ie the Land Compensation Act 1961 s 7: see PARA 840. As to the meaning of 'corresponding enactment' see PARA 796 note 11.
2 See the Land Compensation Act 1961 s 8(5); and PARA 840 text and notes 11–14. As to the general power of deduction see PARA 840.
3 See PARA 849.
4 Light Railways Act 1896 s 13 (repealed with transitional provisions; see the Transport and Works Act 1992 (Commencement No 3 and Transitional Provisions) Order 1992, SI 1992/2784).
5 As to highway authorities see HIGHWAYS, STREETS AND BRIDGES vol 21 (2004 Reissue) PARA 49 et seq.
6 Ie the Highways Act 1980 ss 239(1)–(5), 240, 246, 250(2): see HIGHWAYS, STREETS AND BRIDGES.
7 Highways Act 1980 s 261(1)(a) (s 261(1) amended by SI 2009/1307). For the way in which these provisions have been applied see *Cooke v Secretary of State for the Environment* (1973) 27 P & CR 234, Lands Tribunal; *Portsmouth Roman Catholic Diocesan Trustees v Hampshire County Council* (1979) 40 P & CR 579, Lands Tribunal; *Leicester City Council v Leicestershire County Council* (1995) 70 P & CR 435, Lands Tribunal. The Lands Tribunal was abolished on 1 June 2009 and its functions were transferred to the Upper Tribunal: see PARA 720; and ADMINISTRATIVE LAW.
8 Highways Act 1980 s 261(1)(b) (as amended: see note 7).
9 Highways Act 1980 s 261(1)(c) (as amended: see note 7); and see HIGHWAYS, STREETS AND BRIDGES vol 21 (2004 Reissue) PARA 104.

842. Purchases under the Highways Act 1980 of land between street and improvement line. Any person whose property is injuriously affected by the prescribing of an improvement line[1] is entitled to recover from the authority which prescribed the line compensation for the injury sustained[2]. In assessing the compensation payable in respect of the compulsory acquisition by a highway authority of land[3] lying between an improvement line and the boundary of a street, the Upper Tribunal[4] must take into account any benefit accruing to the vendor by reason of the improvement of the street except in so far as it may have been previously taken into account in the assessment of compensation[5] payable under the above provisions[6].

1 As to improvement lines see HIGHWAYS, STREETS AND BRIDGES vol 21 (2004 Reissue) PARA 491 et seq.
2 Highways Act 1980 s 73(9).
3 Ie under the Highways Act 1980 s 241: see HIGHWAYS, STREETS AND BRIDGES vol 21 (2004 Reissue) PARA 80.
4 As to the Upper Tribunal see PARA 720; and ADMINISTRATIVE LAW.
5 Ie under the Highways Act 1980 s 73(9): see the text and notes 1–2.
6 Highways Act 1980 s 261(5) (amended by SI 2009/1307).

(2) CIRCUMSTANCES INVOLVING INCREASE IN VALUE OF OTHER LAND

843. Development of land authorised to be acquired. An increase in the value of the interest in the other land to be deducted from compensation[1] arises where the acquisition is for purposes involving development[2] of any of the land authorised to be acquired[3], if the increase is attributable to the carrying out, or the prospect, of development of any of the land authorised to be acquired which is development for any of the purposes for which any part of the land (including any part of the relevant land[4]) is to be acquired, so far as that development would not have been likely to be carried out if the acquiring authority[5] had not acquired, and did not propose to acquire, any of the land so authorised[6].

1 Ie an increase which must be deducted from compensation under the Land Compensation Act 1961 s 7(1): see PARA 840. As to the meaning of 'land' see PARA 516 note 2.
2 For these purposes, 'development' is to be construed as including the clearing of land: Land Compensation Act 1961 ss 6(3), 7(2). As to the meaning of 'development' generally see PARA 762 note 2. See also *Cambridge City Council v Secretary of State for the Environment* (1992) 64 P & CR 257, CA.
3 As to the meaning of 'land authorised to be acquired' see PARA 790 note 3.
4 As to the meaning of 'relevant land' see PARA 762 note 5.
5 As to the meaning of 'acquiring authority' see PARA 622 note 1.
6 Land Compensation Act 1961 ss 6(1)(a), 7(2), Sch 1 Case 1. It is the increase in value of the other land which is material; that increase in value must arise as the product of the development of the land for the purpose for which it is authorised to be acquired, and not from any alteration of the state of the other land or its profitability arising not as the product of the development but arising incidentally or by chance in the course of works for the development of the land for the purpose for which it is authorised to be acquired: see *Cooke v Secretary of State for the Environment* (1973) 27 P & CR 234, Lands Tribunal; cf *Marriage v East Norfolk Rivers Catchment Board* [1950] 1 KB 284 at 308–309, [1949] 2 All ER 1021 at 1035, CA. In valuing an increase from the prospects of development, only an increase in value from the product of the authorised development could be ascertained, and any incidental increase would be pure speculation. There may, however, be special statutory provision for accommodation works on the other land to reduce injury to it, and this may affect compensation.

844. Areas of comprehensive development. An increase in the value of the interest in the other land to be deducted from compensation[1] arises where any of

...tion under the Land Compensation ...ing of 'land' see PARA 516 note 2.

...see PARA 762 note 5.

...TOWN AND COUNTRY PLANNING vol 46(1) (Reissue) PARAS 151, 195

...the meaning of 'development' for these purposes see PARA 843 note 2. See also PARA 762 note 2.

5   Land Compensation Act 1961 s 6(1)(b) (amended by the Housing Act 1988 s 78(4)); Land Compensation Act 1961 s 7(2), Sch 1 Case 2.

845. Development in area designated as site of or extension of site of new town. An increase in the value of the interest in the other land to be deducted from compensation[1] arises where any of the relevant land[2], on the date of the service of the notice to treat[3] for that interest, forms part of an area designated as the site of a new town[4] or as an extension of the site of a new town[5], if the increase is attributable to the carrying out, or the prospect, of:

(1)   development[6] of any land in that area in the course of development of that area as a new town, or as part of a new town[7]; or

(2)   any public development[8] specified by direction of the Secretary of State[9] as development in connection with which, or in consequence of which, the provision of housing or other facilities is required and for whose purposes an order designating any area as the site, or an extension of the site, of a new town is proposed to be made[10],

so far as that development would not have been likely to be carried out if the area had not been so designated[11].

1   Ie an increase which must be deducted from compensation under the Land Compensation Act 1961 s 7(1): see PARA 840. As to the meaning of 'land' see PARA 516 note 2.

2   As to the meaning of 'relevant land' see PARA 762 note 5.

3   As to the meaning of 'notice to treat' see PARA 636 note 4. As to notices to treat see PARAS 616–620.

4   Ie by an order under the New Towns Act 1946 (repealed) or the New Towns Act 1981: see TOWN AND COUNTRY PLANNING. As to determining whether the relevant land forms part of an area designated as the site of a new town see further PARA 792.

5   Ie by an order under the New Towns Act 1965 s 1 (repealed) or the New Towns Act 1981 s 1: see TOWN AND COUNTRY PLANNING vol 46(3) (Reissue) PARAS 1315–1317.

6   As to the meaning of 'development' for these purposes see PARA 843 note 2. See also PARA 762 note 2.

7   For the purpose of deciding whether any development of which there is a prospect on the date of service of the notice to treat would be such development, it is immaterial whether the time when that development will or may take place is a time before, on or after the date when the development corporation established for the purposes of the new town ceases to act except for the purposes of or incidental to the winding up of its affairs: Land Compensation Act 1961 s 6(1)(b) (amended by the Housing Act 1988 s 78(4)); Land Compensation Act 1961 ss 6(2), 7(2), Sch 1 paras 5, 8 (s 6(2), Sch 1 para 8 amended by the New Towns Act 1966 s 2, Schedule Pt I).

8   As to the meaning of 'public development' see PARA 792 note 8.

9   Ie a direction under the Land Compensation Act 1973 s 51: see PARA 792. As to the Secretary of State see PARA 507 note 1. The functions of the Secretary of State under the Land Compensation Act 1961 and the Land Compensation Act 1973, so far as they are exercisable in relation to Wales, are now exercisable by the Welsh Ministers: see the National Assembly for Wales

846.
developm
deducted from
of an area defin
development[4], if the n
of development[5] of any la
far as that development would
had not been so defined as an area

1 Ie an increase which must be deducted from
   Act 1961 s 7(1): see PARA 840. As to the meaning o
2 As to the meaning of 'relevant land' see PARA 762 note 5.
3 As to the meaning of 'current development plan' see PARA 76
4 Ie town development within the meaning of the Town Developm   ealed): see
   s 1(1) (repealed, subject to a transitional provision, by the Local G   d Housing
   Act 1989 ss 175, 194(4), Sch 12 Pt II).
5 As to the meaning of 'development' for these purposes see PARA 843 note 2. See also PARA 762
   note 2.
6 Land Compensation Act 1961 s 6(1)(b) (amended by the Housing Act 1988 s 78(4)); Land
   Compensation Act 1961 s 7(2), Sch 1 Case 4.

847. **Development in area designated as urban development area.** An increase
in the value of the interest in the other land to be deducted from compensation[1]
arises where any of the relevant land[2] forms part of an area designated as an
urban development area[3], if the increase is attributable to the carrying out, or the
prospect, of development[4] of any land in the course of the development or
redevelopment of that area as an urban development area[5].

1 Ie an increase which must be deducted from compensation under the Land Compensation
   Act 1961 s 7(1): see PARA 840. As to the meaning of 'land' see PARA 516 note 2.
2 As to the meaning of 'relevant land' see PARA 762 note 5.
3 Ie by an order under the Local Government, Planning and Land Act 1980 s 134: see TOWN AND
   COUNTRY PLANNING vol 46(3) (Reissue) PARAS 1426–1427. In assessing the increase in value to
   be taken into account, no increase is to be excluded from being taken into account merely
   because it is attributable: (1) to any development of land which was carried out before the area
   was designated as an urban development area; (2) to any development or prospect of
   development of land outside the urban development area; (3) to any development or prospect of
   development of land by an authority, other than the acquiring authority, possessing compulsory
   purchase powers: Land Compensation Act 1961 s 6(1)(b) (amended by the Housing Act 1988
   s 78(4)), Land Compensation Act 1961 s 6(2) (amended by the Local Government, Planning and
   Land Act 1980 s 145(3)), Land Compensation Act 1961 s 7(2), Sch 1 para 10 (added by the
   Local Government, Planning and Land Act 1980 s 145(2)).
4 As to the meaning of 'development' for these purposes see PARA 843 note 2. See also PARA 762
   note 2.
5 Land Compensation Act 1961 s 6(1)(b) (as amended: see note 3), s 7(2), Sch 1 Case 4A (added
   by the Local Government, Planning and Land Act 1980 s 145(1)).

848. Development in housing action trust area. An increase in the value of the interest in the other land to be deducted from compensation[1] arises where any of the relevant land[2] forms part of a housing action trust area[3], if the increase is attributable to the carrying out, or the prospect, of development[4] of any land in the course of the development or redevelopment of that area as a housing action trust area[5].

1 Ie an increase which must be deducted from compensation under the Land Compensation Act 1961 s 7(1): see PARA 840. As to the meaning of 'land' see PARA 516 note 2.
2 As to the meaning of 'relevant land' see PARA 762 note 5.
3 Ie a housing action trust area established under the Housing Act 1988 Pt III (ss 60–92): see HOUSING vol 22 (2006 Reissue) PARA 322.
4 As to the meaning of 'development' for these purposes see PARA 843 note 2. See also PARA 762 note 2.
5 Land Compensation Act 1961 s 6(1)(b) (amended by the Housing Act 1988 s 78(4)); Land Compensation Act 1961 s 7(2), Sch 1 Case 4B (added by the Housing Act 1988 s 78(3)).

849. No further deduction on subsequent purchase of other land. Where, for the purpose of assessing compensation in respect of a compulsory acquisition of an interest in land[1], an increase in the value of an interest in other land has been taken into account[2], then, in connection with any subsequent acquisition where either:

(1)   the interest acquired thereby is the same as the interest previously taken into account[3] (whether the acquisition extends to the whole of the land in which that interest previously subsisted or only to part of that land)[4]; or

(2)   the person entitled to the interest acquired is, or derives title[5] to that interest from, the person who at the time of the previous acquisition was entitled to the interest previously taken into account[6],

that increase is not to be taken into account[7] in so far as it was taken into account in connection with the previous acquisition[8].

Where, in connection with a sale of an interest in land by agreement, the circumstances are such that, if it had been a compulsory acquisition, an increase in value would have fallen to be taken into account as mentioned above, the same protection applies, with the necessary modifications, as if that sale had been a compulsory acquisition and that increase in value had been taken into account accordingly[9].

1 As to the interests entitled to compensation see PARAS 616, 619. As to the meaning of 'land' see PARA 516 note 2.
2 Ie by virtue of the Land Compensation Act 1961 s 7 or any corresponding enactment and in any of the circumstances mentioned in s 7(2), Sch 1 Pt I col 1 (see PARA 840 et seq): see s 8(1). As to the meaning of 'corresponding enactment' see PARA 796 note 11. See also PARA 841.
3 For these purposes, any reference to the interest previously taken into account is a reference to the interest whose increased value was taken into account as mentioned in the Land Compensation Act 1961 s 8(1) (see note 2): s 8(3).
4 Land Compensation Act 1961 s 8(3)(a).
5 See PARA 796 note 6.
6 Land Compensation Act 1961 s 8(3)(b).
7 Ie by virtue of the Land Compensation Act 1961 s 7 or any corresponding enactment: s 8(1).
8 Land Compensation Act 1961 s 8(1).
9 Land Compensation Act 1961 s 8(4).

10. USE OF LAND ACQUIRED AND COMPENSATION FOR INJURY

(1) PERMISSIBLE WORKS ON AND USES OF LAND ACQUIRED

850. Authorised works and uses. The works which may be executed on the land acquired are works for the purposes for which the land was authorised to be acquired by the special Act or empowering enactment[1].

The works may be specified in the empowering enactment by plans, description and location and uses defined and limited, in which case there will be no power to construct works beyond those specified or beyond the limits, nor any power to use the works for purposes other than those defined[2], except for purposes fairly regarded as incidental to or consequential upon those purposes[3].

The works and uses for which land is acquired by local authorities are often specified in general terms. An object not expressly sanctioned but fairly derivable from the statutory powers is authorised by implication[4], and power is implied to do what is necessarily and properly required for carrying into effect the authorised purposes[5], or which may fairly be regarded as incidental to or consequential upon those things which the empowering enactment has authorised[6], but not works for collateral objects, however convenient they may be for carrying out the authorised purposes[7]. Where an authority had two purposes, one of which was within its powers and the other of which was not, its action is lawful only if the intra vires purpose is the dominant reason and the other purpose has not materially influenced its conduct[8].

An acquiring authority may not enter into a contract or undertaking not to use the land in accordance with its statutory powers[9] and, if it does so, the contract or undertaking will be void[10], but it may give an undertaking not inconsistent with the carrying out of the statutory powers[11], and may enter into restrictive covenants so long as it is not precluded by them from using the land for the purposes for which it was acquired[12].

If the acquiring authority executed works beyond its powers formerly it could be restrained by a claim brought in the name of the Attorney General at the relation of a relator[13]. Nowadays it may be dealt with by judicial review[14], or a claim may be brought by a person suffering special damage without involving the Attorney General, whether or not a private right of the individual is interfered with[15].

Where the carrying out of statutory purposes and the execution of works is permissive, no liability attaches for not exercising the power[16], and, where land has been acquired with a genuine intention to carry out works, the authority is not bound to complete the works if circumstances arise which make completion inadvisable[17]. Where, however, there is a duty to carry out the statutory purposes and execute the works in furtherance of them, a mandatory order may issue to compel the acquiring authority to carry out the duties imposed upon it[18]; but the court will usually refuse such an order where there is an alternative remedy which is not less convenient, beneficial and effective[19]. If the duty is owed to any individual or class of individuals, the individual or one of the class may bring a claim in respect of the failure to perform the duty[20].

1 *A-G v Manchester Corpn* [1906] 1 Ch 643 at 651; *Baroness Wenlock v River Dee Co* (1883) 36 ChD 675n at 685n, CA; on appeal (1885) 10 App Cas 354, HL; *Bayley v Great Western Rly Co* (1884) 26 ChD 434, CA. As to the meaning of 'special Act' see PARAS 509, 514.

carrying out of that improvement: s 39(6A) (added by the Housing Act 1974 Sch 13 para 40; and amended by the Housing Act 2004 Sch 15 paras 2, 6(1), (4)).

18   *Bradford Property Trust Ltd v Hertfordshire County Council* (1973) 27 P & CR 228, Lands Tribunal.

854. Advances by relevant authorities to displaced residential owner-occupiers including certain lessees. Where a person displaced from a dwelling[1] in consequence of the acquisition of land by an authority possessing compulsory purchase powers[2]: (1) is an owner-occupier[3] of the dwelling; and (2) wishes to acquire or construct another dwelling in substitution for that from which he is displaced, the relevant authority[4] liable to rehouse the person displaced[5] may advance money to him for the purpose of enabling him to acquire or construct the other dwelling[6].

This power to advance money is without prejudice to any power to advance money exercisable by the authority under any other enactment[7]. It is only exercisable subject to such conditions as may be approved by the Secretary of State, and the following provisions also apply with respect to any advance made in the exercise of that power[8]. The advance may be made: (a) on terms providing for the payment of the principal at the end of a fixed period, with or without a provision allowing the authority to extend that period, or upon notice given by the authority, subject, in either case, to a provision for earlier repayment on the happening of a specified event[9]; (b) on such other terms as the authority may think fit having regard to all the circumstances[10]. An advance for the construction of a dwelling may be made by instalments from time to time as the works of construction progress[11].

Before advancing money under the above provisions the authority must satisfy itself that the dwelling to be acquired is or will be made, or that the dwelling to be constructed will on completion be, in all respects fit for human habitation[12].

The principal of the advance, together with interest on it, must be secured by a mortgage of the borrower's interest in the dwelling, and the amount of the principal must not exceed the value which, in accordance with a valuation duly made on behalf of the relevant authority, it is estimated that the borrower's interest will bear, or, as the case may be, will bear when the dwelling has been constructed[13].

1   As to the meaning of 'dwelling' see PARA 802 note 1.
2   Ie under the Land Compensation Act 1973 s 39(1)(a): see PARA 853. Section 41 (see the text and notes 3–13) also applies where a person is displaced in consequence of any other event specified in s 39(1) (see PARA 853 note 3): see s 41. As to the application of s 39 to persons displaced from caravan sites see s 40; and PARA 853.
3   In relation to any dwelling, 'owner-occupier' for this purpose means a person who occupies it on the date of displacement either in right of a freehold interest in it or a tenancy of it granted or extended for a term of years certain of which not less than three years remain unexpired: Land Compensation Act 1973 s 41(9)(a).
4   As to the meaning of 'relevant authority' see PARA 853 note 2. Local authorities may no longer make advances under the Land Compensation Act 1973 s 41, but the powers of development corporations and the new town residuary bodies (as to which see PARA 853 note 11) are unaffected: see PARA 853 note 9. As to local authorities' powers to advance money for certain housing purposes see HOUSING vol 22 (2006 Reissue) PARA 686 et seq. As to the development corporations and the new town residuary bodies see TOWN AND COUNTRY PLANNING vol 46(3) (Reissue) PARA 1428 et seq. The relevant authority's functions may be conferred on a housing action trust: see the Housing Act 1988 s 65(2)(c); and HOUSING vol 22 (2006 Reissue) PARA 330.
5   Ie under the Land Compensation Act 1973 s 39(1): see PARA 853.
6   Land Compensation Act 1973 s 41(1). References in s 41 to the construction of a dwelling include references to the acquisition of a building and its conversion into a dwelling and to the conversion into a dwelling of a building previously acquired: s 41(10).

7 Land Compensation Act 1973 s 41(7), (8).
8 Land Compensation Act 1973 s 41(2). As to the Secretary of State see PARA 507 note 1. The functions of the Secretary of State under the Land Compensation Act 1973, so far as they are exercisable in relation to Wales, are now exercisable by the Welsh Ministers: see the National Assembly for Wales (Transfer of Functions) Order 1999, SI 1999/672, art 2, Sch 1; and the Government of Wales Act 2006 s 162(1), Sch 11 para 30. As to the Welsh Assembly Government and the Welsh Ministers see CONSTITUTIONAL LAW AND HUMAN RIGHTS.
9 Land Compensation Act 1973 s 41(3)(a).
10 Land Compensation Act 1973 s 41(3)(b).
11 Land Compensation Act 1973 s 41(4).
12 Land Compensation Act 1973 s 41(6).
13 Land Compensation Act 1973 s 41(5).

855. Acquiring authority's duty to indemnify local authority in respect of losses on rehousing and advances to persons displaced. Where a relevant authority[1] provides or secures the provision of accommodation for any person displaced in consequence of a compulsory acquisition[2], then, if: (1) the authority providing the accommodation (the 'rehousing authority') is not the same as the authority by which the land in question is acquired (the 'displacing authority')[3]; and (2) the displacing authority is not an authority having functions under Part II of the Housing Act 1985[4] or (if it is such an authority) the land is acquired or redeveloped by it otherwise than in the discharge of those functions[5], the displacing authority must make to the rehousing authority periodical payments, or, if the rehousing authority so requires, a lump sum payment, by way of indemnity against any net loss in respect of the rehousing authority's provision of that accommodation which may be incurred by that authority in any year during the period of ten years commencing with the year in which the accommodation is first provided[6].

For this purpose a local authority incurs a net loss in respect of its provision of accommodation for a person whom it is rehousing: (a) if it rehouses him in a dwelling provided by it under Part II of the Housing Act 1985 for the purpose of rehousing him[7]; or (b) if it rehouses him in a housing revenue account dwelling[8] not so provided, and provides under Part II of the Housing Act 1985, in the financial year immediately preceding that in which he first occupies it, or in the period of three financial years commencing with the financial year in which he first occupies it, a dwelling of a similar type or size[9].

Losses by authorities making advances to persons displaced are also provided for, and where money has been advanced to a person displaced for the purpose of enabling him to obtain accommodation[10], then if (i) the authority making the advance (the 'lending authority') is not the same as the displacing authority[11]; and (ii) the lending authority incurs a net loss in respect of the making of the advance[12], the displacing authority must make to the lending authority a lump sum payment by way of indemnity against that loss[13]. For this purpose a lending authority incurs a net loss in respect of the making of an advance to any person if he does not fully discharge his liability to the authority in respect of principal, interest and costs or expenses in accordance with the terms on which the advance is made[14] and the deficiency exceeds the net proceeds arising to the authority on a sale of the interest on which the principal and interest is secured[15].

1 As to the meaning of 'relevant authority' see PARA 853 note 2.
2 Ie in pursuance of the Land Compensation Act 1973 s 39(1)(a): see PARA 853. As to the application of s 39 to persons displaced from caravan sites see s 40; and PARA 853. Section 42 (see the text and notes 3–15) also applies where a person is displaced as a result of an event specified in s 39(1)(c) (see PARA 853 note 3): see s 42(1).
3 Land Compensation Act 1973 s 42(1)(a).

4   Ie functions under the Housing Act 1985 Pt II (ss 8–57) (provision of housing accommodation and related matters): see HOUSING vol 22 (2006 Reissue) PARA 224 et seq.
5   Land Compensation Act 1973 s 42(1)(b) (amended by the Housing Act 1980 s 138; and the Housing (Consequential Provisions) Act 1985 s 4, Sch 2 para 24).
6   Land Compensation Act 1973 s 42(1).
7   Land Compensation Act 1973 s 42(2)(a) (s 42(2)(a), (b) amended by the Land Compensation (Scotland) Act 1973 s 81(1), Sch 2 Pt I; and the Housing (Consequential Provisions) Act 1985 Sch 2 para 24).
8   'Housing revenue account dwelling' means a dwelling which is within the authority's housing revenue account within the meaning of the Local Government and Housing Act 1989 Pt VI (ss 74–88) (see HOUSING vol 22 (2006 Reissue) PARA 127 et seq): Land Compensation Act 1973 s 42(6) (substituted by the Housing (Consequential Provisions) Act 1985 s 4, Sch 2 para 24(5); and amended by the Local Government and Housing Act 1989 s 194, Sch 11 para 32(1)).
9   Land Compensation Act 1973 s 42(2)(b) (as amended: see note 7), s 42(6) (as substituted: see note 8). The Secretary of State may (1) for the purposes of s 42(1) from time to time determine a method to be used generally in calculating net losses incurred by rehousing authorities (s 42(5)(a)); (2) for the purposes of s 42(1) or s 42(3), determine the net loss incurred by a rehousing authority, or by a lending authority (see head (i) in the text) in any particular case (s 42(5)(b)); and (3) give directions as to the manner in which any payment is to be made (s 42(5)(c)). As to the Secretary of State see PARA 507 note 1. The functions of the Secretary of State under the Land Compensation Act 1973, so far as they are exercisable in relation to Wales, are now exercisable by the Welsh Ministers: see the National Assembly for Wales (Transfer of Functions) Order 1999, SI 1999/672, art 2, Sch 1; and the Government of Wales Act 2006 s 162(1), Sch 11 para 30. As to the Welsh Assembly Government and the Welsh Ministers see CONSTITUTIONAL LAW AND HUMAN RIGHTS.
10 Ie as mentioned in the Land Compensation Act 1973 s 39(4): see PARA 853.
11 Land Compensation Act 1973 s 42(3)(a).
12 Land Compensation Act 1973 s 42(3)(b).
13 Land Compensation Act 1973 s 42(3). As to the determination of a net loss by the Secretary of State and payment under his direction see s 42(5); and note 9.
14 Land Compensation Act 1973 s 42(4)(a).
15 Land Compensation Act 1973 s 42(4)(b).

856.   Acquiring authority's power to pay expenses of displaced persons in acquiring another dwelling.   Where a person displaced from a dwelling[1] in consequence of certain specified events[2] has no interest in the dwelling (or no greater interest in it than as tenant for a year or from year to year) and wishes to acquire another dwelling in substitution for that from which he is displaced, then, according to the nature of the event in consequence of which he was displaced, the acquiring authority[3] which made the order, passed the resolution, accepted the undertaking or served the notice or the authority carrying out the improvement or the redevelopment may pay any reasonable expenses incurred by him in connection with the acquisition, other than the purchase price[4].

This power does not apply to any person who is a trespasser on the land, or who has been permitted to reside in any house or building on the land pending its demolition or improvement[5]; and no payment may be made under this power in respect of expenses incurred by any person in connection with the acquisition of a dwelling unless the dwelling is acquired not later than one year after the displacement and is reasonably comparable with that from which he is displaced[6].

1   As to the meaning of 'dwelling' see PARA 802 note 1.
2   Ie in consequence of any of the events specified in the Land Compensation Act 1973 s 39(1)(a)–(c): see PARA 853. Section 43(1) also refers to an event specified in s 39(1)(d) (repealed). As to when a person is to be treated as displaced see s 39(6) (see PARA 853); applied by s 43(4).
3   As to the meaning of 'acquiring authority' see PARA 622 note 1.
4   Land Compensation Act 1973 s 43(1) (amended by the Housing Act 1974 s 130(1), Sch 13 para 41).

5 Land Compensation Act 1973 s 39(3) (amended by the Housing Act 1974 Sch 13 para 40); applied by the Land Compensation Act 1973 s 43(4).
6 Land Compensation Act 1973 s 43(2). A dwelling acquired pursuant to a contract must be treated as acquired when the contract is made: s 43(3).

857.   Acquiring authority's liability to make good rate deficiency during construction of works.   If the undertakers[1] or the acquiring authority[2] became possessed, by virtue of the special Act[3], or of any incorporated Act, or of the Compulsory Purchase Act 1965, of any land[4] liable to be assessed to the general rate (now abolished)[5] then, in respect of any period up to the time the works were completed and assessed to the general rate, they were liable, under the Lands Clauses Consolidation Act 1845[6], if incorporated[7], or in respect of certain acquisitions under the Compulsory Purchase Act 1965[8], to make good the deficiency in the assessments for the general rate by reason of the taking or use of the land for the purpose of the works[9]. The repeal of the relevant statutory provisions does not affect any liability, whenever incurred, to make good a deficiency in respect of any period ending before 1 April 1990[10]. The statutory provisions regarding deficiency of general rates do not apply to non-domestic rates, community charge or council tax; but subject to the operation of the limitation period, arrears in respect of a deficiency of general rates remain recoverable[11].

1 As to the meaning of 'undertakers' see PARA 511.
2 As to the meaning of 'acquiring authority' see PARA 549 note 5.
3 As to the meaning of 'special Act' see PARAS 509, 514.
4 As to the meaning of 'land' see PARA 549 note 1. See also PARA 511.
5 This was formerly the poor rate: see the Rating and Valuation Act 1925 s 2(1), (2) (repealed). The general rate was, in turn, abolished with effect from 1 April 1990: see the Local Government Finance Act 1988 ss 117(1), 149, Sch 13. For non-domestic property it was replaced by the non-domestic rate, and for domestic property it was replaced initially by the community charge under the Local Government Finance Act 1988, and subsequently by the council tax under the Local Government Finance Act 1992: see RATING AND COUNCIL TAX vol 39(1B) (Reissue) PARA 2.
6 Ie under the Lands Clauses Consolidation Act 1845 s 133 (repealed with savings: see the text and note 10).
7 As to the Lands Clauses Acts see PARA 509 note 1. As to incorporation of the Lands Clauses Acts see PARAS 509–510.
8 See the Compulsory Purchase Act 1965 s 27(1) (repealed with savings: see the text and note 10).
9 See the Lands Clauses Consolidation Act 1845 s 133; the Compulsory Purchase Act 1965 s 27 (both repealed with savings: see the text and note 10).
10 Local Government Finance (Repeals, Savings and Consequential Amendments) Order 1990, SI 1990/776, art 3(1), (3), Sch 1.
11 As to the abolition and replacement of the general rate see note 5. In *Stratton v Metropolitan Board of Works* (1874) LR 10 CP 76 it was held that a deficiency of assessment for 1865–71 was recoverable although not demanded until 1871–72. For the former general rate, recovery proceedings were to be commenced within six years of the first demand: *China v Harrow UDC* [1954] 1 QB 178, [1953] 2 All ER 1296, DC. Although the general rate was due and payable when made and published (*Thomson v Beckenham Borough Rating Authority* [1947] KB 802, [1947] 2 All ER 274) there was no statutory time limit on the issue of the demand; but enforcement sometimes failed due to lapse of time (*R v Lambeth London Borough Council, ex p Ahijah Sterling* [1986] RVR 27, CA).

(3) RIGHTS TO FACILITATE WORKS

858.   Extinguishment of rights to facilitate works.   Where a statute gives power to execute works and there is power to do the works even though they may injure the rights of others[1], those rights are not extinguished by the injurious works, but continue to exist as adversely affected[2].

However, provision is made for the stopping up or diversion of non-vehicular public rights of way where land is acquired compulsorily by a compulsory purchase order under the Acquisition of Land Act 1981 or by agreement[3], and several statutes make provision for extinguishing other public rights of way and also statutory rights on land acquired for the purpose of enabling the carrying into effect of the statutory purposes for which the land was acquired[4]. There is also statutory power to stop up and divert highways for the purpose of enabling the carrying out of development for which planning permission has been given under the Town and Country Planning Act 1990[5]. There are various other statutory powers to stop up and divert highways, to stop up means of access to highways, and to extinguish a right for vehicles to use a highway[6].

1   See PARA 859.
2   *Ellis v Rogers* (1885) 29 ChD 661 at 670, 672, CA: see PARAS 879, 906.
3   See the Acquisition of Land Act 1981 ss 32, 33; and HIGHWAYS, STREETS AND BRIDGES vol 21 (2004 Reissue) PARA 806.
4   See eg the Housing Act 1985 ss 294–297, 611 (see HOUSING vol 22 (2006 Reissue) PARA 429); the Town and Country Planning Act 1990 ss 236, 237 (see TOWN AND COUNTRY PLANNING vol 46(2) (Reissue) PARAS 954–955); Pt X (ss 247–261) (see HIGHWAYS, STREETS AND BRIDGES vol 21 (2004 Reissue) PARA 791 et seq; TOWN AND COUNTRY PLANNING).
5   See the Town and Country Planning Act 1990 s 247; and HIGHWAYS, STREETS AND BRIDGES vol 21 (2004 Reissue) PARA 791.
6   See eg the Highways Act 1980 Pt VIII (ss 116–129) (see HIGHWAYS, STREETS AND BRIDGES); and the Town and Country Planning Act 1990 s 249 (see HIGHWAYS, STREETS AND BRIDGES vol 21 (2004 Reissue) PARA 794). This may give rise to an entitlement to compensation if it can be proved that the extinguishment of the right caused loss: *Saleem v Bradford Metropolitan Borough Council* [1984] 2 EGLR 187, Lands Tribunal (where on the facts no compensation was payable).

(4) INJURIOUS WORKS

859.   Power to execute injurious works.   Where a public body is authorised by statute to exercise powers or execute works, whether for profit or not, it is subject to the same liabilities as an ordinary person[1] unless absolved by the terms of its statute or some other statute[2]. If the public body claims that its powers enable it to take away the common law rights of any person, it is bound to show that the statute clearly authorises it to do so, so as to make lawful that which would otherwise have been unlawful and to remove the remedy by action otherwise available[3].

A public body may be absolved from liability where Parliament has indicated that the works may be done notwithstanding injury to others, for example where there is a duty to do the works[4], or by the specification of the works in the statute by plans and sections[5], or where the works, although not prescribed by plans and sections, are of such a nature that in whatever form, as prescribed, they will inevitably cause injury[6], or by inference from special protective sections in the statute[7]. If the works do not fall clearly within this category, an implication of a power to do an act to the injury of the rights of others may be drawn from the provision of compensation for certain acts[8]. The implication is that Parliament contemplated that it was not feasible or practicable to do those acts for which compensation is provided without injury to the rights of others[9].

Where an Act authorises the acquisition of land for the construction of works, it may be a necessary implication that the Act authorised the operation of the completed works, with the result that there is no remedy so far as nuisance was the inevitable result of the authorised operation[10]. A nuisance clause providing that statutory powers may not be exercised so as to cause a nuisance may exclude an intention that an act may be done notwithstanding that it may cause injury to others[11]; but that clause cannot frustrate the discharge of a duty where the works will inevitably cause injury[12], or where the power to do works is prescribed as to place or manner[13], or, it seems, where the works are of such a nature with such a restricted area of execution that they will cause some injury whatever the case[14]. The body executing the works will only be liable in these cases if it is negligent in doing the works[15]. An injury will not be lawful unless it arises out of an authorised act and is one contemplated by the statute at the time when it was passed[16].

Where no provision is made for compensation, the question whether the person doing the works is acting strictly within his powers requires detailed consideration in order to establish liability for injury[17]; but where full compensation is provided for an injury it is questionable how far it is worthwhile going into matters of negligence[18]. However, in some cases an injunction may be proper even if provision is made for full compensation[19].

The standard of care is what is possible within practical feasibility and expense[20], but, to that extent, all statutory and common law powers must be used to avoid injury[21] unless the statute provides otherwise[22]; and, whether or not provision is made for compensation, the duty to take care applies both to the original construction and to subsequent maintenance, user and improvement, and if new practical means of preventing injury are discovered those means must be adopted[23].

Further powers and duties to mitigate injury by the effect of statutory works are now given whether compensation is provided or not[24].

There may also be negligence in the actual construction or use of the works, and if the undertakers carry out their authorised works without negligence in the choice of place or manner, but fail to take sufficient care to prevent damage in the course of the execution of the works, or their user, and cause injury which is not the product of the authorised works, they will be liable to a claim in respect of that injury[25] and also to pay compensation for the damage caused by their authorised act[26].

If an act of God or of third parties makes injurious statutory works which would otherwise be innocuous, the undertakers are under the same liability as ordinary persons at common law and may be liable for continuing the nuisance on their land[27], but they will not be liable until they know or ought to have known of the nuisance[28] and have had a reasonable time to take steps to abate it[29]. However, the statutory works, in some cases, may not be the nuisance and the nuisance, in fact, may be the condition of the land arising from the failure of some person or body to perform a duty, in which case no liability will rest on the undertakers[30].

1 Ie an ordinary person with power to do no more than that authorised by the statute. The liability under a statutory power (eg to break open a street) cannot be compared with a common law power to do so with no liability if done in a reasonable manner and in a reasonable time. Without the statutory authorisation the public body would be liable for the act whatever the care.

2 See *Mersey Docks and Harbour Board Trustees v Gibbs* (1866) LR 1 HL 93 at 107, 110; *Gibraltar Sanitary Comrs v Orfila* (1890) 15 App Cas 400 at 412, PC; *Sharpness New Docks and Gloucester and Birmingham Navigation Co v A-G* [1915] AC 654 at 662, 665, HL. For example, the Planning Act 2008 s 158 (not yet in force) confers statutory authority for (1) carrying out development for which consent is granted by an order granting development

consent; (2) doing anything else authorised by an order granting development consent, for the purpose of providing a defence in civil or criminal proceedings for nuisance: see TOWN AND COUNTRY PLANNING.

3   *Clowes v Staffordshire Potteries Waterworks Co* (1872) 8 Ch App 125 at 139; *Metropolitan Asylum District Managers v Hill* (1881) 6 App Cas 193 at 203, 208, 212, HL; *Caledonian Rly Co v Walker's Trustees* (1882) 7 App Cas 259 at 293, HL; *T Tilling Ltd v Dick, Kerr & Co Ltd* [1905] 1 KB 562 at 568, 570; *Vernon v St James' Westminster Vestry* (1880) 16 ChD 449, CA.

4   *Metropolitan Asylum District Managers v Hill* (1881) 6 App Cas 193 at 203, 212, HL.

5   *Metropolitan Asylum District Managers v Hill* (1881) 6 App Cas 193, at 211–212, HL; *Manchester Corpn v Farnworth* [1930] AC 171 at 183, HL.

6   *Edgington v Swindon Corpn* [1939] 1 KB 86, [1938] 4 All ER 57; *WH Chaplin & Co Ltd v Westminster Corpn* [1901] 2 Ch 329; *Goldberg & Son Ltd v Liverpool Corpn* (1900) 82 LT 362, CA.

7   *Edgington v Swindon Corpn* [1939] 1 KB 86 at 90–91, [1938] 4 All ER 57 at 62–63.

8   'The legislature has very often interfered with the rights of private persons, but in modern times it has generally given compensation to those injured; and if no compensation is given it affords a reason, though not a conclusive one, for thinking that the intention of the legislature was, not that the thing should be done at all events, but only that it should be done, if it could be done, without injury to others. What was the intention of the legislature in any particular Act is a question of construction of the Act': see *Metropolitan Asylum District Managers v Hill* (1881) 6 App Cas 193 at 203, HL, per Lord Blackburn; *Price's Patent Candle Co Ltd v LCC* [1908] 2 Ch 526, CA; affd sub nom *LCC v Price's Candle Co Ltd* (1911) 75 JP 329, HL.

9   See note 8.

10   *Allen v Gulf Oil Refining Ltd* [1981] AC 1001, [1981] 1 All ER 353, HL (the defence of statutory authority was available to an oil company seeking to resist a claim for nuisance from the operation of the company's oil refinery constructed on land compulsorily acquired under a private Act which expressly authorised the compulsory acquisition of land for that purpose. The Act contained no provision for compensation for nuisance arising from the operation of the refinery. The statutory powers must, however, be exercised without negligence, that word being used in a special sense so as to require the undertaker, as a condition of obtaining immunity from action, to carry out the work and conduct the operation with all reasonable regard and care for the interests of other persons). As to negligence see generally NEGLIGENCE. As to nuisance see generally NUISANCE.

11   *A-G v Gaslight and Coke Co* (1877) 7 ChD 217.

12   *Smeaton v Ilford Corpn* [1954] Ch 450 at 477, [1954] 1 All ER 923 at 936. A provision that nothing in a statute shall exonerate the undertakers from an action or suit does not render them liable, in the absence of negligence, for nuisance attributable to the performance of a statutory duty: *Department of Transport v North West Water Authority* [1984] AC 336, [1983] 3 All ER 273, HL.

13   *Jordeson v Sutton, Southcoates and Drypool Gas Co* [1899] 2 Ch 217 at 237, 257, CA.

14   Cf *Edgington v Swindon Corpn* [1939] 1 KB 86, [1938] 4 All ER 57.

15   See note 12.

16   *Fisher v Ruislip-Northwood UDC and Middlesex County Council* [1945] KB 584 at 596, [1945] 2 All ER 458 at 463, CA; *R v Bradford Navigation Co* (1865) 34 LJQB 191 at 199–200.

17   *Southwark and Vauxhall Water Co v Wandsworth District Board of Works* [1898] 2 Ch 603, CA.

18   *Marriage v East Norfolk Rivers Catchment Board* [1950] 1 KB 284 at 299–300, [1949] 2 All ER 1021 at 1030, CA; *Colac Corpn v Summerfield* [1893] AC 187, PC.

19   *Jordeson v Sutton, Southcoates and Drypool Gas Co* [1899] 2 Ch 217, CA; *A-G v Metropolitan Board of Works* (1863) 1 Hem & M 298; *Holyoake v Shrewsbury and Birmingham Rly Co* (1848) 5 Ry & Can Cas 421; *Wintle v Bristol and South Wales Union Rly Co* (1862) 10 WR 210; *Ware v Regent's Canal Co* (1858) 3 De G & J 212 at 228; *Webster v Bakewell Rural Council (No 2)* (1916) 86 LJCh 89. See also note 18.

20   The test of injury without negligence is not what is theoretically possible, but what is possible according to the state of scientific knowledge at the time, having also in view a certain common sense appreciation, which cannot be rigidly defined, of practical feasibility in view of the situation and expense: *Manchester Corpn v Farnworth* [1930] AC 171 at 183, HL, per Viscount Dunedin. If the choice of the place or manner of doing an act is made with skill, diligence and caution on proper advice, and is made reasonably and in good faith, the court will not hold that there is negligence: *Raleigh Corpn v Williams* [1893] AC 540 at 550, PC; *Marriage v East Norfolk Rivers Catchment Board* [1950] 1 KB 284 at 299, 309, [1949] 2 All ER 1021 at 1029, 1035, CA. The undertakers will not be liable in negligence for a genuine error of judgment or

lack of foresight: *Marriage v East Norfolk Rivers Catchment Board* at 310 and 1036; *Sutton v Clarke* (1815) 6 Taunt 29. Cf *Tate & Lyle Industries Ltd v GLC* [1983] 2 AC 509, [1983] 1 All ER 1159, HL (held that damages were recoverable in respect of nuisance by the siltation of a river due to the construction of ferry terminals which restricted access to jetties and made dredging necessary; no immunity in respect of damage that was avoidable by taking all reasonable care for the interests of other persons).

21 *Geddis v Bann Reservoir Proprietors* (1878) 3 App Cas 430 at 456, HL; *Bond v Nottingham Corpn* [1940] Ch 429, [1940] 2 All ER 12, CA; but not where no right would otherwise be infringed: see *Southwark and Vauxhall Water Co v Wandsworth District Board of Works* [1898] 2 Ch 603 at 612, CA.

22 Eg by specifying the works by plans and sections or provision for compensation.

23 *Manchester Corpn v Farnworth* [1930] AC 171 at 202, HL; *Fisher v Ruislip-Northwood UDC and Middlesex County Council* [1945] KB 584 at 595–598, [1945] 2 All ER 458 at 462–464, CA; *Fremantle v London and North-Western Rly Co* (1860) 2 F & F 337 at 340 (approved (1861) 10 CBNS 89); *Dimmock v North Staffordshire Rly Co* (1866) 4 F & F 1058; *Groom v Great Western Rly Co* (1892) 8 TLR 253.

24 See PARA 860 et seq.

25 *Clothier v Webster* (1862) 12 CBNS 790; *Biscoe v Great Eastern Rly Co* (1873) LR 16 Eq 636; *Hall v Batley Corpn* (1877) 47 LJQB 148; *Fairbrother v Bury Rural Sanitary Authority* (1889) 37 WR 544; *Marriage v East Norfolk Rivers Catchment Board* [1950] 1 KB 284 at 309, [1949] 2 All ER 1021 at 1035, CA.

26 *Uttley v Todmorden Local Board of Health* (1874) 44 LJCP 19.

27 *A-G and Dommes v Basingstoke Corpn* (1876) 45 LJCh 726; *A-G v Tod Heatley* [1897] 1 Ch 560, CA; *Barker v Herbert* [1911] 2 KB 633, CA; *R v Bradford Navigation Co* (1865) 34 LJQB 191.

28 *Wringe v Cohen* [1940] 1 KB 229, [1939] 4 All ER 241, CA; *Mersey Docks and Harbour Board Trustees v Gibbs* (1866) LR 1 HL 93; *Lambert v Lowestoft Corpn* [1901] 1 KB 590.

29 *Barker v Herbert* [1911] 2 KB 633, CA; *Maitland v RT and J Raisbeck and Hewitt Ltd* [1944] KB 689 at 691–692, [1944] 2 All ER 272 at 272–273, CA; *Fisher v Ruislip-Northwood UDC and Middlesex County Council* [1945] KB 584 at 607–608, [1945] 2 All ER 458 at 468–469, CA; *Longhurst v Metropolitan Water Board* [1948] 2 All ER 834, HL.

30 *Thompson v Brighton Corpn* [1894] 1 QB 332, CA; *Moore v Lambeth Waterworks Co* (1886) 17 QBD 462, CA; *Railway Executive v West Riding of York County Council* [1949] Ch 423, [1949] 1 All ER 836, CA; *West Lancashire RDC v Lancashire and Yorkshire Rly Co* [1903] 2 KB 394.

860. Mitigation of injurious effect. Where public bodies are authorised by statute to exercise powers or execute works, other than works prescribed by plans and sections, they must use all statutory and common law powers to avoid injury to the rights of others where it is possible to do so within practical feasibility and expense[1].

In addition to this duty and also where no such duty arises, regulations may impose on a highway authority and the person managing public works a duty to mitigate the injury caused by a highway or public works and may give them various powers to effect that purpose[2].

Highway authorities are given power to acquire land to mitigate the adverse effect of the use of a highway constructed or improved by them, or proposed to be constructed or improved, and to acquire land so adversely affected[3] and are also given power to execute works to effect that mitigation[4]. They may enter into agreements with respect to the use of land adjoining a highway so that the highway cannot now or in the future have an adverse effect on the use of that land[5]. Persons managing public works other than a highway may also acquire land to mitigate the adverse effect of the existence or use of their works and acquire land adversely affected[6], and are given power to execute works to effect that mitigation[7].

1   See PARA 859.
2   See the Land Compensation Act 1973 s 20; and PARA 861 et seq.

s 264(4) (repealed) or s 368(2) (repealed) (see now the Housing Act 2004; and HOUSING) (Noise Insulation Regulations 1975, SI 1975/1763, reg 7(2)(c) (substituted by SI 1988/2000));

(4)   any building within an area declared to be a clearance area by a resolution under the Housing Act 1985 s 289 (see HOUSING vol 22 (2006 Reissue) PARA 426) (Noise Insulation Regulations 1975, SI 1975/1763, reg 7(2)(d) (amended by SI 1988/2000));

(5)   any building which was first occupied after the relevant date (Noise Insulation Regulations 1975, SI 1975/1763, reg 7(2)(e));

(6)   any part of a building in respect of which part of a grant has been paid or is payable in respect of the carrying out of insulation work under any enactment other than the Land Compensation Act 1973 or any instrument made under any such enactment (Noise Insulation Regulations 1975, SI 1975/1763, reg 7(2)(f)).

'Relevant date' means the date on which a highway or additional carriageway was first open to public traffic or, in the case of an altered highway, the date on which it was first open to public traffic after completion of the alteration: reg 2(1).

6   Ie (1) a highway, and a highway for which an additional carriageway has been or is to be constructed if the highway or additional carriageway was first open to public traffic after 16 October 1969 and before 17 October 1972; or (2) an altered highway and a highway to which the Noise Insulation Regulations 1975, SI 1975/1763, reg 3 applies before any duty under reg 8 (see PARA 867) has arisen: reg 4(2). 'Altered highway' means a highway of which the location, width or level of the carriageway has been or is to be altered, other than by resurfacing, after 16 October 1969: reg 2(1). See also the Land Compensation Act 1973 s 20(2)(b); and PARA 861.

7   Noise Insulation Regulations 1975, SI 1975/1763, reg 4(1). Where the authority is required by reg 3 or is empowered by reg 4(1) or reg 4(3) to carry out work or make a grant in respect of an eligible building it may also carry out work or make a grant in respect of the cost of carrying out insulation work in or to an eligible building in respect of which no duty under reg 3 or power under reg 4(1) or reg 4(3) has arisen if the facades of both buildings are contiguous or form part of a series of contiguous facades: reg 4(4). 'Facade' means a side of a building: reg 2(1).

8   Ie the duty under the Noise Insulation Regulations 1975, SI 1975/1763, reg 3(1) or the power under reg 4(1): see the text and notes 1–7.

9   Noise Insulation Regulations 1975, SI 1975/1763, reg 4(3).

10   Ie the duty under the Noise Insulation Regulations 1975, SI 1975/1763, reg 3(1) or the power under reg 4(1): see the text and notes 1–7.

11   Noise Insulation Regulations 1975, SI 1975/1763, reg 5(1).

12   See the Highways Act 1980 s 272(1)(k); and HIGHWAYS, STREETS AND BRIDGES vol 21 (2004 Reissue) PARA 70. As to the Secretary of State see PARA 507 note 1. This function of the Secretary of State under the Highways Act 1980, so far as it is exercisable in relation to Wales, is now exercisable by the Welsh Ministers: see the National Assembly for Wales (Transfer of Functions) Order 1999, SI 1999/672, art 2, Sch 1; and the Government of Wales Act 2006 s 162(1), Sch 11 para 30. As to the Welsh Assembly Government and the Welsh Ministers see CONSTITUTIONAL LAW AND HUMAN RIGHTS.

864. Ascertainment of eligible buildings. The appropriate highway authority[1] for a highway[2] in respect of which it is under a duty to carry out insulation work[3] or make grants[4] must ascertain every eligible building[5] in respect of which that duty has arisen and must prepare a map or list, or both, identifying every such building[6]. Any such map or list must be deposited at the office of the appropriate highway authority or its agent[7] nearest to the building identified in it and made available for public inspection during the hours when the office is open, not later than six months after the relevant date[8] or, if the relevant date was before 7 November 1975, not later than six months after that date[9]. However, where the appropriate highway authority has merely the power and not the duty to carry out such insulation work and make such grants[10] there is no requirement for the preparation of any map or list or to require any map or list which is prepared to identify any building other than a building in respect of which an offer[11] is to be made; neither is there any requirement for such a map or list to be prepared before any date[12].

1   As to the meaning of 'appropriate highway authority' see PARA 863 note 3.

2   As to the meaning of 'highway' see PARA 863 note 1.
3   As to the meaning of 'insulation work' see PARA 863 note 4.
4   Ie the duty under the Noise Insulation Regulations 1975, SI 1975/1763, reg 3(1): see PARA 863.
5   As to the meaning of 'eligible building' see PARA 863 note 5.
6   Noise Insulation Regulations 1975, SI 1975/1763, reg 6(2).
7   As to appropriate highway authorities and their agents see PARA 866.
8   As to the meaning of 'relevant date' see PARA 863 note 5.
9   Noise Insulation Regulations 1975, SI 1975/1763, reg 6(3).
10   Ie under the Noise Insulation Regulations 1975, SI 1975/1763, reg 4(1): see PARA 863.
11   Ie an offer made under the Noise Insulation Regulations 1975, SI 1975/1763, reg 8: see PARA 867.
12   See the Noise Insulation Regulations 1975, SI 1975/1763, reg 4(5).

865.   Ascertainment of noise level.   The ascertainment of the prevailing noise level, the relevant noise level and the effective contribution to the relevant noise level made by noise caused or expected to be caused by traffic using or expected to use a highway is to be made in accordance with the technical memoranda entitled 'Calculation of Road Traffic Noise' of 1975 or 1988, as applicable[1].

1   See the Noise Insulation Regulations 1975, SI 1975/1763, reg 6(1) (amended by SI 1988/2000), Noise Insulation Regulations 1975, SI 1975/1763, reg 15 (added by SI 1988/2000). In relation to any offer made on or after 1 December 1988 by the appropriate highway authority in pursuance of any duty or power under the Noise Insulation Regulations 1975, SI 1975/1763, reg 3, 4 or 13 as provided in reg 8 (see PARA 867), the matter must be determined in accordance with *'Calculation of Road Traffic Noise'* (HMSO) (1988): Noise Insulation Regulations 1975, SI 1975/1763, reg 15(3). As to the meaning of 'appropriate highway authority' see PARA 863 note 3.

866.   Local authorities as agents of highway authorities.   A local authority[1] may act as agent[2] for the appropriate highway authority[3] in the discharge and exercise of its duties and powers under the Noise Insulation Regulations 1975[4]. The appropriate highway authority alone, and not the agent local authority, unless that authority is also acting as agent of the appropriate highway authority in the construction or alteration of the highway[5] or carriageway in relation to which the functions are exercisable: (1) must determine the buildings in respect of which insulation work[6] or a grant in respect of such work will be offered[7]; and (2) must consider and determine applications for reconsideration of buildings[8]. The appropriate highway authority must reimburse to each local authority the amounts paid by the local authority as agent[9] and such sums as may be reasonable in respect of the services rendered to the highway authority by that local authority[10].

1   For these purposes, 'local authority' means: (1) elsewhere than in Greater London, the council of a county or a district within the meaning of the Local Government Act 1972; (2) in Greater London, the council of a London borough and the Common Council of the City of London: Noise Insulation Regulations 1975, SI 1975/1763, reg 14(5) (amended by SI 1988/2000). As to areas and authorities in England and Wales see LOCAL GOVERNMENT vol 69 (2009) PARA 22 et seq; LONDON GOVERNMENT vol 29(2) (Reissue) PARA 29 et seq.
2   As to agency generally see AGENCY.
3   As to the meaning of 'appropriate highway authority' see PARA 863 note 3.
4   See the Land Compensation Act 1973 s 20(5); the Noise Insulation Regulations 1975, SI 1975/1763, reg 14(1); and PARA 861 text and note 14.
5   As to the meaning of 'highway' see PARA 863 note 1.
6   As to the meaning of 'insulation work' see PARA 863 note 4.
7   Noise Insulation Regulations 1975, SI 1975/1763, reg 14(2)(a).
8   Ie applications made under the Noise Insulation Regulations 1975, SI 1975/1763, reg 13(1) (see PARA 872): reg 14(2)(b).
9   Noise Insulation Regulations 1975, SI 1975/1763, reg 14(3).
10   Noise Insulation Regulations 1975, SI 1975/1763, reg 14(4).

months after the relevant date[13], provided that the appropriate highway authority may extend the time limit whether before or after its expiration[14].

Where the noise is created by works for the construction of a highway or additional carriageway or the alteration of a highway[15], an offer to carry out insulation work or make grants may not be accepted after the expiration of two months after the date of the offer or of such longer period as the appropriate highway authority may by extension at any time allow[16].

Where insulation work has been carried out in or to an eligible building and completed in accordance with the relevant specifications before the offer is made, an offer is deemed to be an offer of grant only, and may be accepted only by the person who incurred the cost of the work[17].

1   As to the meaning of 'appropriate highway authority' see PARA 863 note 3.
2   Ie an offer made under the Noise Insulation Regulations 1975, SI 1975/1763, reg 8: see PARA 867. As to the meaning of 'insulation work' see PARA 863 note 4.
3   See the Noise Insulation Regulations 1975, SI 1975/1763, reg 8(5).
4   Noise Insulation Regulations 1975, SI 1975/1763, reg 8(5).
5   Noise Insulation Regulations 1975, SI 1975/1763, reg 8(6)(a). As to the meaning of 'claimant' see PARA 868 note 2.
6   Noise Insulation Regulations 1975, SI 1975/1763, reg 8(6)(b). As to the meaning of 'eligible building' see PARA 863 note 5.
7   Noise Insulation Regulations 1975, SI 1975/1763, reg 8(6)(c).
8   Ie pursuant to the Noise Insulation Regulations 1975, SI 1975/1763, reg 8(3)(d) or (e): see PARA 867 heads (d) and (e).
9   Noise Insulation Regulations 1975, SI 1975/1763, reg 8(6)(d).
10 Noise Insulation Regulations 1975, SI 1975/1763, reg 8(6)(e).
11 Noise Insulation Regulations 1975, SI 1975/1763, reg 8(6)(f).
12 Noise Insulation Regulations 1975, SI 1975/1763, reg 8(4). This provision does not apply so as to limit the period within which any person may accept an offer where the noise is created by works for the construction of a highway or additional carriageway or the alteration of a highway: reg 5(2)(b). As to the meaning of 'additional carriageway' see PARA 863 note 1.
13 As to the meaning of 'relevant date' see PARA 863 note 5.
14 Noise Insulation Regulations 1975, SI 1975/1763, reg 8(7).
15 Ie under the Noise Insulation Regulations 1975, SI 1975/1763, reg 5(1): see PARA 863.
16 Noise Insulation Regulations 1975, SI 1975/1763, reg 5(2)(a).
17 Noise Insulation Regulations 1975, SI 1975/1763, reg 8(8).

870.   Nature and extent of work to be undertaken.   Insulation work[1] carried out must be in accordance with the relevant specifications[2]. Notwithstanding anything in the Noise Insulation Regulations 1975, no insulation work must be carried out and no grant in respect of the cost of carrying out insulation work must be made in or to any eligible room[3] in which there is installed any flueless combustion appliance other than a gas cooker, unless there will be in that room, after completion of the insulation work in or to that room in accordance with the relevant specifications, an uninsulated window capable of being opened[4]. Nothing in the regulations requires an authority to carry out work or to make a grant in respect of the carrying out of work required to remedy a defect in a building or to maintain or repair any equipment or apparatus installed in or on any building pursuant to the regulations[5].

1   As to the meaning of 'insulation work' see PARA 863 note 4.
2   Noise Insulation Regulations 1975, SI 1975/1763, reg 9(1). The relevant specifications are set out in Sch 1. This sets out the items required to be included in the insulation work (see Sch 1 para 2), the items which may be included (see Sch 1 para 3) as well as the specifications for windows (see Sch 1 para 4), venetian blinds (see Sch 1 para 5), ventilation systems (see Sch 1 para 6) and permanent vents (see Sch 1 para 7). Where alternative methods are specified the most practicable method in the circumstances of the case must be adopted: see Sch 1 para 8.
3   As to the meaning of 'eligible room' see PARA 867 note 6.

4   Noise Insulation Regulations 1975, SI 1975/1763, reg 9(2).
5   Noise Insulation Regulations 1975, SI 1975/1763, reg 9(3).

871.   Amount of grant.   The amount of noise insulation grant must be equal to the actual cost incurred by the claimant[1] in carrying out (in accordance with the relevant specifications[2]) the insulation work[3] in respect of which the claimant has accepted an offered grant, or to the reasonable cost of carrying out that work in accordance with those specifications, whichever is the less[4].

1   As to the meaning of 'claimant' see PARA 868 note 2.
2   As to the relevant specifications see the Noise Insulation Regulations 1975, SI 1975/1763, reg 9, Sch 1; and PARA 870 note 2.
3   As to the meaning of 'insulation work' see PARA 863 note 4.
4   Noise Insulation Regulations 1975, SI 1975/1763, reg 11.

872.   Applications for reconsideration of building.   Where there is a highway[1] to which the duty to carry out insulation work[2] or to make grants[3] applies and no offer[4] has been made in relation to an eligible building[5], any person[6] who claims that a duty has arisen with respect to the building may apply in writing to the appropriate highway authority[7], setting out the facts on which he relies, and may request the authority to make him an offer in accordance with the regulations[8]. Such an application must be made within six months after either: (1) the date of depositing the map or list or both for public inspection[9]; or (2) the date six months after whichever is the later of the commencement date[10] and the relevant date[11]. On the commencement of each period within which applications may be made, the appropriate highway authority must publish once in a local newspaper circulating in the area of the highway a notice setting out particulars of the right to make an application, including particulars of the time within which, and the authority to which, such an application must be made[12].

On receiving an application the authority must review its noise level calculations[13] or make such calculations and, if it finds that a duty to carry out insulation work or to make grants[14] has arisen with respect to the building, it must comply with the request, but otherwise it must refuse it[15] and furnish the applicant with a written statement of its reasons for refusing[16].

1   As to the meaning of 'highway' see PARA 863 note 1.
2   As to the meaning of 'insulation work' see PARA 863 note 4.
3   Ie the duty under the Noise Insulation Regulations 1975, SI 1975/1763, reg 3: see PARA 863.
4   Ie an offer under the Noise Insulation Regulations 1975, SI 1975/1763, reg 8(2): see PARA 867.
5   As to the meaning of 'eligible building' see PARA 863 note 5.
6   Ie (1) the person who is the occupier of the building (or if the building is unoccupied, the person who is entitled to occupy the building); or (2) the immediate landlord or licensor of that person: Noise Insulation Regulations 1975, SI 1975/1763, reg 13(2).
7   As to the meaning of 'appropriate highway authority' see PARA 863 note 3.
8   Noise Insulation Regulations 1975, SI 1975/1763, reg 13(1).
9   See the Noise Insulation Regulations 1975, SI 1975/1763, reg 6; and PARA 864.
10   The 'commencement date' means the date on which the Noise Insulation Regulations 1975, SI 1975/1763, came into force, ie 7 November 1975: see reg 2(1).
11   Noise Insulation Regulations 1975, SI 1975/1763, reg 13(3). As to the meaning of 'relevant date' see PARA 863 note 5.
12   Noise Insulation Regulations 1975, SI 1975/1763, reg 13(6).
13   See the Noise Insulation Regulations 1975, SI 1975/1763, reg 6; and PARA 865.
14   See note 3.
15   Noise Insulation Regulations 1975, SI 1975/1763, reg 13(4). For transitional provisions see Sch 2.
16   Noise Insulation Regulations 1975, SI 1975/1763, reg 13(5).

surroundings of public works in any manner which it thinks desirable by reason of the construction, alteration, existence or use of the works[8]; and (b) dispose of any land acquired[9] by it[10].

1   For these purposes, 'responsible authority' means the person managing the public works but does not include a highway authority: Land Compensation Act 1973 s 1(4); definition modified and applied by s 27(5). 'Public works' means: (1) any aerodrome; and (2) any works or land (not being a highway or aerodrome) provided or used in the exercise of statutory powers: s 1(3)(b), (c) (as so applied). 'Public works' does not, however, include a highway: s 27(5) (amended by the Land Compensation (Scotland) Act 1973 s 81(1), Sch 2 Pt I). The power applies only where the responsible authority is a body incorporated by or under any enactment and has effect only for extending the corporate powers of any such authority: Land Compensation Act 1973 s 27(4). As to the meaning of 'highway' see PARA 861 note 4. As to the meaning of 'aerodrome' see PARA 861 note 1. As to the application of these provisions to the Crown see PARA 874 note 1.

2   Ie under the Land Compensation Act 1973 s 26: see PARA 874.
3   Land Compensation Act 1973 s 27(1)(a).
4   Land Compensation Act 1973 s 27(1)(b).
5   Land Compensation Act 1973 s 27(1).
6   Land Compensation Act 1973 s 27(2).
7   Ie under the Land Compensation Act 1973 s 26: see PARA 874.
8   Land Compensation Act 1973 s 27(3)(a).
9   Ie land acquired under the Land Compensation Act 1973 s 26: see PARA 874.
10   Land Compensation Act 1973 s 27(3)(b).

876. Expenses of persons moving temporarily during construction works etc.
Where works are carried out by a highway authority[1] for the construction or improvement of a highway, or by a responsible authority[2] for the construction or alteration of any public works other than a highway, and the carrying out of those works affects the enjoyment of a dwelling[3] adjacent to the site on which they are being carried out to such an extent that continued occupation of the dwelling is not reasonably practicable[4], the highway authority or responsible authority, as the case may be, may pay any reasonable expenses incurred by the occupier of the dwelling in providing suitable alternative residential accommodation for himself and members of his household for the whole or any part of the period during which the works are being carried out[5].

No such payment may, however, be made to any person in respect of any expenses except in pursuance of an agreement made between that person and the authority concerned before the expenses are incurred; and no payment may be so made except in respect of the amount by which the expenses exceed those which that person would have incurred if the dwelling had continued to be occupied[6].

1   As to highway authorities see the Highways Act 1980 ss 1–3; and HIGHWAYS, STREETS AND BRIDGES vol 21 (2004 Reissue) PARA 49 et seq.
2   In relation to a highway, 'responsible authority' means the appropriate highway authority (see PARA 861 note 4) and, in relation to other public works, the person managing those works: Land Compensation Act 1973 ss 1(4), 28(4). 'Public works' means any highway, any aerodrome and any works or land, not being a highway or aerodrome, provided or used in the exercise of statutory powers: ss 1(3), 28(4). As to the meaning of 'aerodrome' see PARA 861 note 1.
3   As to the meaning of 'dwelling' see PARA 802 note 1.
4   Land Compensation Act 1973 s 28(1).
5   Land Compensation Act 1973 s 28(2).
6   Land Compensation Act 1973 s 28(3).

(5) COMPENSATION FOR INJURY BY AUTHORISED WORKS

877. Compensation where statutory provision is made. Compensation for injury by the execution of statutory powers may be given by express provision in the special Act[1], or a public general Act[2], but if the special Act makes no such express provision, there will nevertheless be a right to compensation[3] if certain provisions of the Lands Clauses Consolidation Act 1845 are incorporated[4] or certain provisions of the Compulsory Purchase Act 1965 apply[5].

Where the special Act gives compensation for injury by works authorised by the statute, then injury by works on land already acquired or to be acquired by the acquiring authority, or on land which need not be acquired, may be the subject of compensation[6]; but if the provision of compensation is only by incorporation of the 1845 Act or application of the 1965 Act in, or to a compulsory purchase order as part of, the special Act for the purchase of specific land only, then the compensation provisions will apply only with respect to works on that land[7].

Activities authorised by another statute[8] will not be the subject of compensation under the special Act; but where the activity authorised by the other statute is in consequence of the injury or probability of it and a special power to do that which could be effected at common law, there would appear to be no reason to deprive the person suffering injury of his right to compensation[9].

The compensation is in lieu of a right of action which would lie but for the statutory authorisation of the works causing injury[10], but even when there would have been that right of action, compensation may be limited by the special Act to injury by construction and not by user[11]. However, other provision is made in these cases for compensation in respect of injury by noise, vibration, smell, fumes, smoke, artificial lighting and the discharge of any solid or liquid substances and also, in the case of highways, for that injury where there would not otherwise have been a right of action[12].

Where certain local councils[13] are authorised to acquire land by agreement[14], the provisions of Part I of the Compulsory Purchase Act 1965[15] apply[16]. Where an interest in land is held by a local authority[17] for a purpose for which the authority can by virtue of an enactment be authorised to acquire land compulsorily and: (1) the interest was acquired by agreement by the authority or another body before 1 April 1974 and, where it was acquired by another body, has not since the acquisition been transferred otherwise than by an Act or an order made under an Act; and (2) the Lands Clauses Acts or the Compulsory Purchase Act 1965 apply with the exception of certain provisions[18] to the acquisition, the authority may by resolution provide that, on and after the date when the resolution comes into force, those excluded provisions will be included among the statutory provisions which apply to the acquisition[19].

1   As to the meaning of 'special Act' see PARAS 509, 514.
2   See eg the Public Health Act 1936 s 278; and PROTECTION OF ENVIRONMENT AND PUBLIC HEALTH vol 38 (2006 Reissue) PARA 105.

3   *R v St Luke's, Chelsea* (1871) LR 6 QB 572 (affd (1871) LR 7 QB 148, Ex Ch); *Wright v President of the Air Council* (1929) 143 LT 43.
4   Ie the provisions of the Lands Clauses Consolidation Act 1845 s 68: see PARA 878. As to the Lands Clauses Acts see PARA 509 note 1. Whether s 68 is incorporated depends on the construction of the Act incorporating the Lands Clauses Consolidation Act 1845: see *Ferrar v London Sewers Comrs* (1869) LR 4 Exch 227, Ex Ch; *Dungey v London Corpn* (1869) 38 LJCP 298; *Broadbent v Imperial Gaslight Co* (1857) 26 LJCh 276, CA (on appeal sub nom *Imperial*

Gas Light and Coke Co v Broadbent (1859) 7 HL Cas 600); *Kirby v Harrogate School Board* [1896] 1 Ch 437, CA. Some special Acts give an express right to compensation and apply the Lands Clauses Consolidation Act 1845 s 68 (see eg the Land Drainage Act 1991 s 14(5), (6); the Water Resources Act 1991 s 177, Sch 21 para 5(1), (2)), and some give no right to compensation and do not incorporate the Lands Clauses Consolidation Act 1845 s 68 (see *Dungey v London Corpn* above; *Baker v St Marylebone Vestry* (1876) 35 LT 129; *Burgess v Northwich Local Board* (1880) 6 QBD 264, DC).

5   Ie the provisions of the Compulsory Purchase Act 1965 s 10: see PARA 878.
6   See *Lingké v Christchurch Corpn* [1912] 3 KB 595, CA.
7   *Jolliffe v Exeter Corpn* [1967] 2 All ER 1099, [1967] 1 WLR 993, CA.
8   See eg the Road Traffic Regulation Act 1984 ss 14, 15, 16A–16C; and ROAD TRAFFIC vol 40(2) (2007 Reissue) PARA 755 et seq.
9   See note 7.
10 See PARA 879.
11 See PARA 880.
12 See the Land Compensation Act 1973 Pt I (ss 1–19); and PARA 883 et seq.
13 Ie councils which are principal councils within the meaning of the Local Government Act 1972 s 270(1) (ie a council elected for a non-metropolitan county, a district or a London borough and, by virtue of the Local Government (Wales) Act 1994 s 1(8), in relation to Wales, a county or county borough): see LOCAL GOVERNMENT vol 69 (2009) PARA 37 et seq.
14 Ie under the Local Government Act 1972 s 120: see LOCAL GOVERNMENT vol 69 (2009) PARA 509.
15 Ie the provisions of the Compulsory Purchase Act 1965 Pt I (ss 1–32) (see PARA 549 et seq) other than s 31 (see PARA 668): Local Government Act 1972 s 120(3).
16 Local Government Act 1972 s 120(3). This provision came into force on 1 April 1974: see s 273. In relation to acquisitions made before that date see the text and notes 17–19.
17 As to the meaning of 'local authority' see PARA 532 note 7.
18 The provisions specifically excluded are the Lands Clauses Consolidation Act 1845 s 68 (see PARA 878) under which there is among other things a right to compensation in respect of land injuriously affected by certain works, and the Compulsory Purchase Act 1965 s 10 (see PARA 878) which re-enacts the Lands Clauses Consolidation Act 1845 s 68: see the Local Government (Miscellaneous Provisions) Act 1976 s 14(1).
19 Local Government (Miscellaneous Provisions) Act 1976 s 14(1); and see LOCAL GOVERNMENT vol 69 (2009) PARA 509. In relation to acquisitions before 1 April 1974 see the text and notes 17–18.

878.   Statutory provisions for compensation; parties entitled. Provision is made by the Lands Clauses Consolidation Act 1845, if incorporated[1], that if any party is entitled to compensation in respect of any land[2], or of any interest in it, which has been taken for or injuriously affected by the execution of the works, and for which the undertakers[3] have not made satisfaction under the provisions of that Act or the special Act[4], or any Act incorporated with it, that party may have the compensation settled[5].

An owner of land who has had land taken will have received compensation under the 1845 Act as part of his purchase money[6] for injury by works:

(1)   on the land taken from him; and
(2)   on the land taken from other persons,

to land not taken from him but held with land taken from him[7]; but not for injury by works to his land not held with land taken from him, either from works on the land taken from him or works on the land taken from other persons[8]. He is, therefore, entitled in respect of it to compensation under certain provisions of the 1845 Act[9]. Persons who have had no land taken are also entitled to compensation under those provisions because they are not entitled to compensation under the provisions relating to purchase money[10].

Provision is made by the Compulsory Purchase Act 1965, where it applies[11], that if any person claims compensation in respect of any land[12] or any interest in land which has been taken for, or injuriously affected by, the execution of the works and for which the acquiring authority[13] has not made satisfaction under the provisions of that Act or of the special Act, any dispute arising in relation to it must be referred to and determined by the Upper Tribunal[14]. This provision is to be construed as affording, in all cases, a right to compensation for injurious affection to land which is the same as the right which certain provisions of the Lands Clauses Consolidation Act 1845[15] have been construed as affording in cases where the amount claimed exceeds £50[16].

A person with a qualifying interest[17] may claim compensation in respect of injury by noise, vibration, smell, fumes, smoke, artificial lighting and the discharge of any solid or liquid substances and also, in the case of highways, for that injury where there would not otherwise have been a right of action[18].

1   As to the Lands Clauses Acts see PARA 509 note 1. See also PARA 877 note 4.
2   Compensation is limited to injury to land: see PARA 881. As to the meaning of 'lands' see PARA 511.
3   As to the meaning of 'undertakers' see PARA 511. As to the meaning of 'works' see PARA 511.
4   As to the meaning of 'special Act' see PARAS 509, 514.
5   Lands Clauses Consolidation Act 1845 s 68 (amended by the Compulsory Purchase Act 1965 s 39(4), Sch 8 Pt III). This provision has long been construed as giving compensation for injury to the value of land by the execution of works in lieu of the right of action which would have lain but for the statutory authorisation of the works: see *Horn v Sunderland Corpn* [1941] 2 KB 26 at 42–43, [1941] 1 All ER 480 at 491–492, CA; and PARA 879 et seq. As to the claim for and settlement of the compensation see PARA 882.
6   Ie under the Lands Clauses Consolidation Act 1845 s 63: see PARA 810.
7   See the Lands Clauses Consolidation Act 1845 s 63; the Compulsory Purchase Act 1965 s 7; and PARA 810.
8   Ie under the Lands Clauses Consolidation Act 1845 s 63: see PARA 810.
9   Ie under the provisions of the Lands Clauses Consolidation Act 1845 s 68. See also PARA 718.
10 Ie under the provisions of the Lands Clauses Consolidation Act 1845 s 63: see PARA 810.
11 As to the compulsory purchase orders to which the Compulsory Purchase Act 1965 applies see PARAS 513–514.
12 As to the meaning of 'land' see PARA 549 note 1.
13 As to the meaning of 'acquiring authority' see PARA 549 note 5.
14 Compulsory Purchase Act 1965 s 10(1) (amended by SI 2009/1307). See further PARA 718. As to claims for and the settlement of compensation see PARA 882. As to the Upper Tribunal see PARA 720; and ADMINISTRATIVE LAW.
15 Ie the provisions of the Lands Clauses Consolidation Act 1845 s 68: see PARA 718.
16 Compulsory Purchase Act 1965 s 10(2). Section 10 can be construed as allowing compensation to be calculated in respect of either a permanent interference or a temporary interference with land: *Wildtree Hotels Ltd v Harrow London Borough Council* [2001] 2 AC 1, [2000] 3 All ER 289, HL (accordingly, compensation is payable for a reduction in letting value arising from the temporary obstruction of access to a hotel). See also *Ocean Leisure Ltd v Westminster City Council* [2004] EWCA Civ 970, [2004] 3 EGLR 9, [2004] All ER (D) 368 (Jul) (compensation payable for diminution in value of commercial premises arising from significant temporary interference with access); *Moto Hospitality Ltd v Secretary of State for Transport* [2007] EWCA Civ 764, [2008] 2 All ER 718, [2008] 1 WLR 2822 (damage was not sufficiently direct to establish a claim for compensation under the Compulsory Purchase Act 1965 s 10 as immediate access to the motorway service station remained unaffected).
17 As to the meaning of 'qualifying interest' see PARA 874 note 7.
18 See the Land Compensation Act 1973 Pt I (ss 1–19); and PARA 884 et seq.

879.   Damage from authorised works which would have been actionable.   The person whose rights have been injured can recover compensation for injury by authorised works[1] only in respect of losses sustained in consequence of what the undertakers or the acquiring authority have lawfully done under their statutory powers[2]. The damage must arise from something which would, if done without statutory authority, have given rise to a cause of action[3]. In other words, in order to have a right to compensation against the undertakers or the acquiring authority in respect of any act done under their statutory powers, the person claiming must have had a good cause of action in respect of that act, if it had been done by any person not so authorised[4]. The undertakers or the acquiring authority, having acquired land, may therefore use it in any way in which an ordinary owner might have lawfully used it without conferring any right to compensation, apart from any specific provision for compensation in a particular case, for example in respect of highways constructed by the highway authority[5].

Thus the undertakers or the acquiring authority may:

(1)   erect an embankment on the land acquired and destroy the amenity of adjoining property[6];

(2)   block up access to light and air so long as no right of easement is interfered with[7];

(3)   remove the support of buildings where no right of support has been acquired[8];

(4)   draw off underground water[9];

(5)   build a bridge and by doing so injure a ferry undertaking[10];

(6)   cause loss of business to shops by pulling down neighbouring houses[11], or by demolishing and re-erecting party walls in accordance with requirements of building regulations[12];

(7)   exercise the rights of ordinary riparian owners, if they are such owners[13]; and

(8)   block up private roads on building estates unless the persons damaged can show they have a right to those roads[14].

Damage which would be too remote to be recovered by a claim cannot be recovered as compensation[15].

The obstruction of a public way gives rise to no cause of action to a person unless he suffers special damage different from that suffered by the public generally[16]. However, interference with an adjoining owner's right of access from his premises to the highway, including a highway by water[17], is interference with a private right, which is distinct from the owner's right to use the highway which he enjoys as a member of the public[18]. If unauthorised, the interference will be actionable[19] and so, if authorised, it may be the subject of compensation for injurious affection, as for example where the interference makes access less convenient by the alteration of the level of the roadway[20], or by the blocking up of one of two means of access, whether by river or land[21].

The obstruction of easements, such as rights of way[22], of light[23], of obtaining a water supply[24], or of support[25] will also entitle the owner of the dominant tenement to compensation for any loss he may suffer as a result of it[26].

If land taken or used by the undertakers or the acquiring authority has been subject to restrictive covenants for the benefit of other land, the breach of such a covenant by the undertakers or the authority will confer upon the owner of that other land a right to compensation for injurious affection[27]. If acts done by the undertakers or the authority prevent covenants relating to land from being carried out, the undertakers or the authority will be liable in respect of those acts[28].

Rights over the land under licence may be the subject of compensation if coupled with an interest in land[29].

1   See PARAS 877–878.
2   *Caledonian Rly Co v Colt* (1860) 3 Macq 833, HL; *Imperial Gas Light and Coke Co v Broadbent* (1859) 7 HL Cas 600. As to the authorised works see PARA 850. This rule does not apply where the effects complained of are caused by activities on land taken from the claimant: *Re Stockport, Timperley and Altrincham Rly Co* (1864) 33 LJQB 251; *Cowper Essex v Acton Local Board* (1889) 14 App Cas 153, HL. See the Compulsory Purchase Act 1965 s 7; and PARA 810. If the powers are exceeded there will be a remedy by action: see PARA 850.

3　*Glover v North Staffordshire Rly Co* (1851) 16 QB 912; *Ricket v Metropolitan Rly Co* (1867) LR 2 HL 175; *Metropolitan Board of Works v McCarthy* (1874) LR 7 HL 243; *Caledonian Rly Co v Walker's Trustees* (1882) 7 App Cas 259, HL; *Marriage v East Norfolk Rivers Catchment Board* [1949] 2 KB 456, [1949] 2 All ER 50 (affd [1950] 1 KB 284, [1949] 2 All ER 1021, CA) (applied e g in *Thameside Estates Ltd v GLC* [1979] 1 EGLR 167, Lands Tribunal). See also *R v Bristol Dock Co* (1810) 12 East 429 (interference with right to water enjoyed in common with the rest of the public); *Day & Sons v Thames Water Authority* [1984] 1 EGLR 197, Lands Tribunal; *Clift v Welsh Office* [1998] 4 All ER 852, [1999] 1 WLR 796, CA (the actual physical damage caused by the effect of dust and mud to the exterior and interior decoration of a house gave rise to compensation, separate from the structural damage already assessed).

4　It is immaterial whether the right interfered with would be enforceable at law or in equity: *Furness Rly Co v Cumberland Co-operative Building Society* (1884) 52 LT 144, HL. See also PARA 859 note 1.

5　See the Land Compensation Act 1973 Pt I (ss 1–19); and PARA 884 et seq.

6　*Re Penny* (1857) 7 E & B 660.

7　*Butt v Imperial Gas Co* (1866) 2 Ch App 158; *Eagle v Charing Cross Rly Co* (1867) LR 2 CP 638.

8　*Metropolitan Board of Works v Metropolitan Rly Co* (1868) LR 3 CP 612; affd (1869) LR 4 CP 192, Ex Ch.

9　*New River Co v Johnson* (1860) 29 LJMC 93; *R v Metropolitan Board of Works* (1863) 32 LJQB 105; and cf *Bradford Corpn v Pickles* [1895] AC 587, HL.

10　*Hopkins v Great Northern Rly Co* (1877) 2 QBD 224, CA; cf *R v Cambrian Rly Co* (1871) LR 6 QB 422; and see *Dibden v Skirrow* [1908] 1 Ch 41, CA.

11　*R v Vaughan* (1868) LR 4 QB 190; *R v London Dock Co* (1836) 5 Ad & El 163.

12　*R v Hungerford Market Co, ex p Yeates* (1834) 1 Ad & El 668; *R v Hungerford Market Co, ex p Eyre* (1834) 1 Ad & El 676.

13　*Rhodes v Airedale Drainage Comrs* (1876) 1 CPD 402, CA.

14　*Fleming v Newport Rly Co* (1883) 8 App Cas 265, HL; *Furness Rly Co v Cumberland Co-operative Building Society* (1884) 52 LT 144, HL.

15　*R v Poulter* (1887) 20 QBD 132, CA; *Re Clarke and Wandsworth District Board of Works* (1868) 17 LT 549; *Birkenhead Corpn v London and North Western Rly Co* (1885) 15 QBD 572, CA; and cf *Knock v Metropolitan Rly Co* (1868) LR 4 CP 131; *Sydney Municipal Council v Young* [1898] AC 457, PC. Thus an occupier of a public house situated by the side of a public footway was held not to be entitled to recover compensation for loss of business caused by certain streets which led to the footway being temporarily obstructed, whereby the access to the house was rendered inconvenient: *Ricket v Metropolitan Rly Co* (1867) LR 2 HL 175; and see *Bigg v London Corpn* (1873) LR 15 Eq 376. As to remoteness of damage see generally DAMAGES vol 12(1) (Reissue) PARA 851 et seq.

16　See e g *Vanderpant v Mayfair Hotel Co Ltd* [1930] 1 Ch 138; *Harper v GN Haden & Sons Ltd* [1933] Ch 298, CA; *Ricket v Metropolitan Rly Co* (1867) LR 2 HL 175. See also *Ocean Leisure Ltd v Westminster City Council* [2004] EWCA Civ 970, [2004] 3 EGLR 9, [2004] All ER (D) 368 (Jul).

17　See *Lyon v Fishmongers' Co* (1876) 1 App Cas 662, HL; *North Shore Rly Co v Pion* (1889) 14 App Cas 612, PC (rivers); *R v Rynd* (1863) 16 ICLR 29; *A-G of Straits Settlement v Wemyss* (1888) 13 App Cas 192 at 195, PC (sea).

18　*A-G v Thames Conservators* (1862) 1 Hem & M 1 at 31–32; *Lyon v Fishmongers' Co* (1876) 1 App Cas 662, HL; *Marshall v Blackpool Corpn* [1935] AC 16 at 22, HL; *Rose v Groves* (1843) 5 Man & G 613. See further HIGHWAYS, STREETS AND BRIDGES.

19　See PARA 850.

20　*Moore v Great Southern and Western Rly Co* (1858) 10 ICLR 46, Ex Ch (lowering level of road alongside premises); *Tuohey v Great Southern and Western Rly Co* (1859) 10 ICLR 98 (raising level of road); *R v Eastern Counties Rly Co* (1841) 2 QB 347 (lowering level of road); *Caledonian Rly Co v Walker's Trustees* (1882) 7 App Cas 259, HL (access made steeper); *Beckett v Midland Rly Co* (1867) LR 3 CP 82; *Chamberlain v West End of London and Crystal Palace Rly Co* (1862) 2 B & S 605 (affd (1863) 2 B & S 617, Ex Ch) (access made narrower). See also *Wedmore v Bristol Corpn* (1862) 7 LT 459; *R v Wallasey Local Board of Health* (1869) LR 4 QB 351; *R v St Luke's, Chelsea* (1871) LR 7 QB 148, Ex Ch; *Pearsall v Brierley Hill Local Board* (1883) 11 QBD 735, CA (affd sub nom *Brierley Hill Local Board v Pearsall* (1884) 9 App Cas 595, HL); and see *R v Eastern Counties Rly Co* (1841) 2 QB 347; *Arnott v Whitby UDC* (1909) 101 LT 14; *Re McMullen and Ulster Rly Co* (1863) Ir Reserved Cas 35.

21　*Metropolitan Board of Works v McCarthy* (1874) LR 7 HL 243; *Macey v Metropolitan Board of Works* (1864) 33 LJCh 377; *Re Wadham and North Eastern Rly Co* (1884) 14 QBD 747 (on appeal (1885) 16 QBD 227, CA); and cf *R v Metropolitan Board of Works* (1869) LR 4 QB 358; *Duke of Buccleuch v Metropolitan Board of Works* (1872) LR 5 HL 418; *Bell v Hull and Selby Rly Co* (1840) 6 M & W 699; *A-G of-Southern Nigeria v John Holt & Co (Liverpool) Ltd* [1915] AC 599, PC; *Hewett v Essex County Council* (1928) 138 LT 742; *Blundy, Clarke & Co v London and North Eastern Rly Co* [1931] 2 KB 334, CA; and see note 14.

22 *Glover v North Staffordshire Rly Co* (1851) 16 QB 912; *Furness Rly Co v Cumberland Co-operative Building Society* (1884) 52 LT 144, HL; *Ford v Metropolitan and Metropolitan District Rly Companies* (1886) 17 QBD 12, CA; *Barnard v Great Western Rly Co* (1902) 86 LT 798; *London School Board v Smith* [1895] WN 37; and cf *Great Central Rly Co v Balby-with-Hexthorpe UDC, A-G v Great Central Rly Co* [1912] 2 Ch 110. As to blocking up access to a ferry see *R v Great Northern Rly Co* (1849) 14 QB 25. However, rights of way and statutory rights over land may be subject to special provisions for their extinguishment or special provision enabling them to be overridden: see eg the Town and Country Planning Act 1990 ss 236, 237, 251; and TOWN AND COUNTRY PLANNING vol 46(2) (Reissue) PARAS 954–955. See also HIGHWAYS, STREETS AND BRIDGES.

23 *Eagle v Charing Cross Rly Co* (1867) LR 2 CP 638; *Clark v London School Board* (1874) 9 Ch App 120; *R v Poulter* (1887) 20 QBD 132, CA; *Wigram v Fryer* (1887) 36 ChD 87; *Re London, Tilbury and Southend Rly Co and Trustees of Gower's Walk Schools* (1889) 24 QBD 326, CA; *Courage & Co v South Eastern Rly Co* (1902) 19 TLR 61; *Emsley v North Eastern Rly Co* [1896] 1 Ch 418, CA.

24 See *Re Simeon and Isle of Wight RDC* [1937] Ch 525, [1937] 3 All ER 149.

25 See *Metropolitan Board of Works v Metropolitan Rly Co* (1868) LR 3 CP 612 (affd (1869) LR 4 CP 192, Ex Ch), explained in *Roderick v Aston Local Board* (1877) 5 ChD 328, CA.

26 Riparian owners will be similarly entitled to compensation for interference with the natural flow of water (*R v Nottingham Old Waterworks Co* (1837) 6 Ad & El 355), as where part of the water is diverted, but where the whole of a stream was appropriated for waterworks under the Water Act 1945 s 24, Sch 3 (now repealed), it was deemed to be a taking and not merely an injurious affection, for the purposes of compensation (see *Ferrand v Bradford Corpn* (1856) 21 Beav 412; *Bush v Trowbridge Waterworks Co* (1875) 10 Ch App 459; *Stone v Yeovil Corpn* (1876) 2 CPD 99, CA; *Page v Kettering Waterworks Co* (1892) 8 TLR 228; and see *Stainton v Woolrych, Stainton v Metropolitan Board of Works and Lewisham District Board of Works* (1857) 26 LJCh 300). See also WATER AND WATERWAYS vol 100 (2009) PARA 84. As to compensation for the occasional flooding of land even though the works were properly executed see *Ware v Regent's Canal Co* (1858) 3 De G & J 212 at 227; *Marriage v East Norfolk Rivers Catchment Board* [1950] 1 KB 284, [1949] 2 All ER 1021, CA.

27 *Kirby v Harrogate School Board* [1896] 1 Ch 437, CA; *Long Eaton Recreation Grounds Co v Midland Rly Co* [1902] 2 KB 574, CA; cf *Baily v De Crespigny* (1869) LR 4 QB 180 at 189. Thus, if land taken has been subject to a covenant restricting the class of buildings which may be erected, the erection by the undertakers or the acquiring authority of a different class will render them liable to pay compensation to the covenantee, and so will the breach by them of the covenant against carrying on a noisy and offensive trade (*Long Eaton Recreation Grounds Co v Midland Rly Co* above), or of a covenant for quiet enjoyment (*Manchester, Sheffield and Lincolnshire Rly Co v Anderson* [1898] 2 Ch 394 at 401, CA). Breach of a covenant not to interfere with the water supply from the land taken to the adjoining land may give rise to a claim for compensation: see *Re Simeon and Isle of Wight RDC* [1937] Ch 525, [1937] 3 All ER 149.

28 *Furness Rly Co v Cumberland Co-operative Building Society* (1884) 52 LT 144, HL (duty to lay out streets); and see *Re Masters and Great Western Rly Co* [1901] 2 KB 84, CA. As to the undertakers' duty to enter into a covenant to indemnify the lessee against breaches see *Harding v Metropolitan Rly Co* (1872) 7 Ch App 154. As to the effect of taking part of land let on a building agreement see *Re Furness and Willesden UDC* (1905) 70 JP 25.

29 As to sporting rights see *Bird v Great Eastern Rly Co* (1865) 34 LJCP 366; *Webber v Lee* (1882) 9 QBD 315, CA. However, these rights may be subject to acquisition as interests in land: see the National Parks and Access to the Countryside Act 1949 s 103(6) (amended by the Acquisition of Land Act 1981 s 34, Sch 6 Pt I).

880. Injury from construction or user of works. Where the special Act[1] provides for compensation for injury from construction of works, a claim for injury caused by the execution of works under the applicable provision of the Lands Clauses Consolidation Act 1845[2] or of the Compulsory Purchase

Act 1965[3] is limited to injury from construction of works[4] and no claim will lie for injury by user[5], for example by noise, vibration and smoke[6], except under other statutory provisions for compensation[7].

In Acts authorising underground railways in London a clause providing for compensation for injurious affection by reason of vibration caused by the working of the railway has been inserted, and clauses with a similar object are commonly inserted in special Acts for the protection of individual owners[8].

Where an Act authorises the acquisition of land for the construction of works, it may be a necessary implication that the Act authorised the operation of the completed works, with the result that there is no remedy so far as nuisance was the inevitable result of the authorised operation[9].

1   As to the meaning of 'special Act' see PARAS 509, 514.
2   Ie under the Lands Clauses Consolidation Act 1845 s 68: see PARAS 718, 878.
3   Ie under the Compulsory Purchase Act 1965 s 10: see PARAS 718, 878.
4   Injury to the trade of a ferry by the opening and use of a bridge constructed under statutory powers is not an injury by construction: see *Hopkins v Great Northern Rly Co* (1877) 2 QBD 224, CA, overruling *R v Cambrian Rly Co* (1871) LR 6 QB 422.
5   *Hammersmith and City Rly Co v Brand* (1868) LR 4 HL 171 (decided with respect to the Railways Clauses Consolidation Act 1845 s 6, which incorporates the Lands Clauses Acts and requires compensation to be paid in respect of injurious affection by the 'construction' of the railway). As to the Lands Clauses Acts see PARA 509 note 1.
6   See *A-G v Metropolitan Rly Co* [1894] 1 QB 384, CA; *Caledonian Rly Co v Ogilvy* (1855) 2 Macq 229, HL; *Holditch v Canadian Northern Ontario Rly Co* [1916] 1 AC 536, PC.
7   See the Land Compensation Act 1973 Pt I (ss 1–19); and PARA 883 et seq. Where, however, the special Act provides for compensation in respect of construction and maintenance there is a right to compensation for construction and user: *Fletcher v Birkenhead Corpn* [1907] 1 KB 205, CA (distinguishing *Hammersmith and City Rly Co v Brand* (1868) LR 4 HL 171); applied in *Re Simeon and Isle of Wight RDC* [1937] Ch 525 at 539, [1937] 3 All ER 149 at 155–156 per Luxmoore J.
8   See eg *Re London and North Western Rly Co and Reddaway* (1907) 71 JP 150. In Acts authorising railway works the undertakers may be required to underpin or strengthen nearby houses or buildings at the request of owners and lessees to avoid injury in the execution and maintenance of the works, and are liable to compensate for loss or damage resulting from this power to underpin and strengthen: see eg the British Transport Commission Act 1949 s 17 (repealed). See also the Crossrail Act 2008 s 2, Sch 2 paras 5, 6.
9   *Allen v Gulf Oil Refining Ltd* [1981] AC 1001, [1981] 1 All ER 353, HL; and see PARA 859. Note that the Planning Act 2008 s 158 (not yet in force) confers statutory authority for (1) carrying out development for which consent is granted by an order granting development consent; (2) doing anything else authorised by an order granting development consent, for the purpose of providing a defence in civil or criminal proceedings for nuisance: see TOWN AND COUNTRY PLANNING.

881. Injury to the value of land. Where the right to compensation is derived only from the Lands Clauses Acts or the Compulsory Purchase Act 1965, compensation may be claimed only in respect of injury to the value of the land or an interest in land[1]. If there is a physical interference with some right, public or private, which the owners or occupiers of property are by law entitled to make use of in connection with that property, and which right gives an additional market value to that property apart from the uses to which any particular owner or occupier might put it, and by reason of that interference the property is lessened in value, there will be a right to compensation[2].

Where the interference is only temporary but is such that, if perpetual, it would give a ground for compensation, it will attract compensation[3].

1   As to the terms of that compensation see PARAS 877–878. See also *Caledonian Rly Co v Walker's Trustees* (1882) 7 App Cas 259 at 276, HL, per Lord Selborne LC. Under other Acts, such as the Public Health Act 1936 s 278 (see PROTECTION OF ENVIRONMENT AND PUBLIC

HEALTH vol 38 (2006 Reissue) PARA 105), compensation may be claimed for losses of a personal nature. See eg *Re Bater and Birkenhead Corpn* [1893] 1 QB 679 (affd [1893] 2 QB 77, CA); *Lingké v Christchurch Corpn* [1912] 3 KB 595, CA. However, the only compensation which can be awarded under the Lands Clauses Consolidation Act 1845 s 68 is compensation in respect of some loss of value of the land; compensation cannot be awarded for loss which is personal to the owner of the land or which is related to some particular user of the land: *Argyle Motors (Birkenhead) Ltd v Birkenhead Corpn* [1975] AC 99, [1974] 1 All ER 201, HL. As to the Lands Clauses Acts see PARA 509. As to the application of the Compulsory Purchase Act 1965 in place of the Lands Clauses Acts see PARA 513.

2   *Metropolitan Board of Works v McCarthy* (1874) LR 7 HL 243 at 253, 256. Personal inconvenience caused by a level crossing near a house will not furnish a ground for compensation if the property itself is not depreciated in value (*Caledonian Rly Co v Ogilvy* (1855) 2 Macq 229, HL; *Wood v Stourbridge Rly Co* (1864) 16 CBNS 222), nor will loss of trade or custom occasioned by a work not otherwise directly affecting the house or land in or upon which the trade has been carried on, or any right properly incident to that house or land (*Caledonian Rly Co v Walker's Trustees* (1882) 7 App Cas 259 at 276, HL, per Lord Selborne LC), unless the interference depreciates the value of the land (see *Metropolitan Board of Works v Howard* (1889) 5 TLR 732, HL (diversion of traffic by erection of new bridge)). See also *Hewett v Essex County Council* (1928) 138 LT 742 (interference with access to a wharf where all loss, apart from depreciation of the value of the wharf was excluded). Further, loss of trade or diminution in the value of goodwill is excluded unless it affects the market value of the premises: see *Re Harvey and LCC* [1909] 1 Ch 528; *Eagle v Charing Cross Rly Co* (1867) LR 2 CP 638; *Hammersmith and City Rly Co v Brand* (1869) LR 4 HL 171 at 198; *Argyle Motors (Birkenhead) Ltd v Birkenhead Corpn* [1975] AC 99 at 114, [1973] 1 All ER 866 at 877, CA (affd [1975] AC 99, [1974] 1 All ER 201, HL).

3   *Ford v Metropolitan and Metropolitan District Rly Companies* (1886) 17 QBD 12, CA; *Lingké v Christchurch Corpn* [1912] 3 KB 595 at 607, CA.

882.   Claim for compensation.   A claim for compensation may be made when the injury by the works has occurred[1], but no claim lies for an injury which is merely prospective[2]. The claim must then be made for all damage which is capable of being foreseen, and the compensation must be assessed once and for all; no further claim may be made in respect of that injury[3], but new acts which would otherwise give rise to a further cause of action will be ground for a new claim[4].

The period of limitation is six years from the time when the cause of claim for compensation arose[5]. Any question of disputed compensation is within the jurisdiction of the Upper Tribunal[6].

If the right to compensation is established, the amount of compensation under the Lands Clauses Acts is commonly determined by the ordinary rules applicable to damages in actions in tort[7]. The compensation is for injury to the market value of the land as it is, and also in respect of any use to which the land may be put in its existing state[8]; it is the difference between the market value before injury and the market value after injury[9], and in assessing the value after injury there is no right to take into account a general increase in the value of property by reason of the works or their imminence[10]. When, under a statute, a person is entitled to full compensation for all damage, once the right to it is established, the amount of compensation may properly include a sum for damage caused by acts in themselves legal, but which could not have been committed had there been no interference with the claimant's legal rights[11].

Compensation[12] carries interest at the rate for the time being prescribed[13] from the date of the claim until payment[14]. There is provision for advance payments on account of compensation and accrued interest[15].

1   *Macey v Metropolitan Board of Works* (1864) 33 LJCh 377; *Stone v Yeovil Corpn* (1876) 2 CPD 99, CA; *Chamberlain v West End of London and Crystal Palace Rly Co* (1863) 2 B & S 617 at 638, Ex Ch.
2   *R v Poulter* (1887) 20 QBD 132, CA.

3   See the cases cited in note 1.
4   *Stone v Yeovil Corpn* (1876) 2 CPD 99, CA; and cf *Darley Main Colliery Co v Mitchell* (1886) 11 App Cas 127, HL.
5   *Pegler v Railway Executive* [1948] AC 332, [1948] 1 All ER 559, HL; *Vincent v Thames Conservancy* (1953) 4 P & CR 66, Lands Tribunal. See now the Limitation Act 1980 s 9; the Arbitration Act 1996 ss 13, 14; and ARBITRATION vol 2 (2008) PARAS 1219–1220; LIMITATION PERIODS vol 68 (2008) PARA 917.
6   See the Lands Tribunal Act 1949 s 1(3)(b) (amended by the Land Compensation Act 1961 s 40(3), Sch 5; and SI 2009/1307); and PARA 721. As to the Upper Tribunal see PARA 720; and ADMINISTRATIVE LAW.
7   *Re London, Tilbury and Southend Rly Co and Trustees of Gower's Walk Schools* (1889) 24 QBD 326 at 329, CA, per Lord Fisher; *Re Clarke and Wandsworth District Board of Works* (1868) 17 LT 549; cf *R v Thames and Isis Navigation Comrs* (1836) 5 Ad & El 804; and see DAMAGES vol 12(1) (Reissue) PARA 851 et seq. As to the Lands Clauses Acts see PARA 509 note 1.
8   *Beckett v Midland Rly Co* (1867) LR 3 CP 82 at 95; *Re Wadham and North Eastern Rly Co* (1884) 14 QBD 747 (on appeal (1885) 16 QBD 227, CA); and see *Metropolitan Board of Works v Howard* (1889) 5 TLR 732, HL; *Hewett v Essex County Council* (1928) 138 LT 742.
9   *Re Wadham and North Eastern Rly Co* (1884) 14 QBD 747 (on appeal (1885) 16 QBD 227, CA).
10 See *Eagle v Charing Cross Rly Co* (1867) LR 2 CP 638; *Senior v Metropolitan Rly Co* (1863) 32 LJ Ex 225.
11 *Re London, Tilbury and Southend Rly Co and Trustees of Gower's Walk Schools* (1889) 24 QBD 326, CA, where a railway company had erected a warehouse which obstructed some ancient lights of the claimants and also some other lights in respect of which no right existed, which latter could not have been interfered with but for the interference with the former; the company was held liable to pay for all the damage occasioned to the property. However, see *Horton v Colwyn Bay and Colwyn UDC* [1907] 1 KB 14 at 22–23 (on appeal [1908] 1 KB 327 at 339, 343, CA), where it was held that the owner who received compensation in respect of land taken and land held with it injuriously affected was not entitled to compensation for injury to other land of his by works on the land taken from him because he would not have had a right of action for that injury but for the statutory powers. The measure of compensation may be given by express enactment as in the Railway Fires Act 1905 s 2(3). As to the meaning of 'full compensation' in relation to costs see *Barnett v Eccles Corpn* [1900] 2 QB 423, CA.
12 Ie under the Lands Clauses Consolidation Act 1845 s 68 or the Compulsory Purchase Act 1965 s 10: see PARAS 718, 878.
13 Ie under the Land Compensation Act 1961 s 32: see PARA 641 note 6.
14 See the Land Compensation Act 1973 s 63(1); and PARA 718.
15 See the Land Compensation Act 1973 ss 52, 52A; and PARAS 652–657. Payments on account may be recoverable where it is subsequently agreed or determined that there was no liability to pay the compensation or interest or that the payment on account was excessive: see the Planning and Compensation Act 1991 s 80(2), (3), Sch 18 Pt II; and PARA 718.

(6) COMPENSATION FOR INJURY BY NOISE, VIBRATION ETC

(i) Right to Compensation

883.   Extension of rights to compensation.   Some special Acts[1] and some public general Acts which give powers and authorise works contain a compensation clause of the widest kind, not limited to injury to the value of the land[2]. In most modern statutes compensation for injury to land by the execution of statutory powers is provided for by the incorporation in the special Act of certain provisions of the Lands Clauses Consolidation Act 1845[3] or by the application to the empowering enactment of certain provisions of the Compulsory Purchase Act 1965[4], and the compensation may by virtue of the empowering enactment be applicable to injury by the construction and maintenance of works, so that there will be a right to compensation for such things as noise and vibration in use and construction[5]. In some cases, however, the right to compensation is limited to injury by construction, and then there can be no compensation for injury by such things as noise and vibration except during the period of construction[6].

However, the Land Compensation Act 1973, where it applies[7], gives a right to compensation for injury to the value of land by noise, vibration, smell etc by the use of public works for which there would otherwise be a right of action arising after the first use of the works after completion, or alteration, or change of use after construction[8], and there may be a claim under that Act and under the statutes mentioned above, but compensation is not payable twice in respect of the same depreciation[9]. Moreover, that first use must have occurred after 17 October 1969[10].

In the case of highways, anyone may dedicate a highway and if the public accepts it by user there is no right of action for injury to the value of land by the user by the public, except in the case of special damage by excessive or negligent user by a member of the public using the highway[11]. The construction and dedication of a highway under statute by the highway authority opening it to the public is not, therefore, a statutory authorisation of that which would otherwise be unlawful, and no compensation for injury by user of the highway is payable, even where the provisions of the Lands Clauses Consolidation Act 1845[12] or of the Compulsory Purchase Act 1965[13] are applicable; but a right to compensation for injury to the value of land by the use of a highway is given under the Land Compensation Act 1973[14] in the case of a highway maintainable at the public expense when constructed or where the carriageway of the highway is altered[15] if the highway is first open to public traffic after 17 October 1969[16]; and such a claim is not subject to the limitation that compensation is only payable where there would otherwise be a right of action[17].

1   As to the meaning of 'special Act' see PARAS 509, 514.
2   See eg the Public Health Act 1936 s 278; and PROTECTION OF ENVIRONMENT AND PUBLIC HEALTH vol 38 (2006 Reissue) PARA 105. In *George Whitehouse Ltd (t/a Clarke Bros (Services)) v Anglian Water Authority* [1978] 2 EGLR 168, Lands Tribunal, claimants were held entitled under the Public Health Act 1936 s 278 for losses caused by the laying in the highway of a public sewer, including damage caused by the breaking open of the street, the cost of removing mud and dust from cars displayed for sale, and for loss of profits due to obstruction of the road during the works.
3   Ie the Lands Clauses Consolidation Act 1845 s 68: see PARAS 718, 878. As to the Lands Clauses Acts see PARA 509 note 1.
4   Ie by the Compulsory Purchase Act 1965 s 10: see PARAS 718, 878. As to the application of the Compulsory Purchase Act 1965 in place of the Lands Clauses Acts see PARA 513.
5   See PARA 878.
6   See PARA 880.
7   Ie the Land Compensation Act 1973 Pt I (ss 1–19): see PARA 884 et seq.
8   See the Land Compensation Act 1973 ss 1, 9; and PARAS 884–885.
9   See the Land Compensation Act 1973 s 8(7); and PARA 888.
10   See the Land Compensation Act 1973 s 1(8); and PARA 891.
11   See HIGHWAYS, STREETS AND BRIDGES vol 21 (2004 Reissue) PARA 325.
12   Ie the provisions of the Lands Clauses Consolidation Act 1845 s 68: see PARA 878.
13   Ie the provisions of the Compulsory Purchase Act 1965 s 10: see PARA 878.
14   Ie under the Land Compensation Act 1973 Pt I: see PARA 884 et seq.
15   See the Land Compensation Act 1973 ss 1, 9; and PARAS 884–885.
16   See the Land Compensation Act 1973 s 1(8); and PARA 891.
17   See the Land Compensation Act 1973 s 1(6); and PARA 884.

884. Compensation after construction and use of public works. Where the value of an interest in land[1] is depreciated by physical factors[2] (other than those which are caused by accidents involving vehicles on a highway[3] or accidents involving aircraft[4]), caused by the use of public works[5], then, if: (1) the interest qualifies for compensation[6]; and (2) the person entitled to the interest makes a claim after the time provided by, and otherwise in accordance with, the appropriate provisions[7], compensation for that depreciation may be payable by the responsible authority[8] to the person making the claim (the 'claimant')[9].

No compensation is payable on any claim unless the relevant date[10] in relation to the claim falls on or after 17 October 1969[11].

Compensation is not payable in respect of physical factors caused by the use of any public works other than a highway unless immunity from actions for nuisance in respect of that use is conferred, whether expressly or by implication, by an enactment relating to those works[12], or, in the case of an aerodrome and physical factors caused by aircraft, the aerodrome is one in respect of which the Civil Aviation Act 1982[13] gives immunity from actions for nuisance in respect of noise and vibration caused by aircraft on an aerodrome[14].

There is no right to compensation under these provisions in respect of any aerodrome in the occupation of a government department[15].

1	'Land' includes messuages, tenements and hereditaments, houses and buildings of any tenure: Interpretation Act 1978 ss 5, 22, Sch 1, Sch 2 para 5(b).

2	'Physical factors' means noise, vibration, smell, fumes, smoke, artificial lighting or the discharge on to the land in respect of which the claim is made of any solid or liquid substance: Land Compensation Act 1973 s 1(2). Physical factors caused by all aircraft arriving at or departing from an aerodrome must be treated as caused by the use of the aerodrome, but, otherwise, the source of the physical factors must be situated on or in the public works the use of which is alleged to be their cause: s 1(5). 'Claim' means a claim under Pt I (ss 1–19): s 19(1). As to the meaning of 'public works' see note 5. As to the meaning of 'aerodrome' see PARA 861 note 1. Danger and appreciation of danger are not physical factors; nor are they expressly covered in s 1(2): *Hickmott v Dorset County Council* (1975) 30 P & CR 237, [1975] 1 EGLR 166, Lands Tribunal (affd (1977) 35 P & CR 195, [1977] 2 EGLR 15, CA); *Stuart and Stuart v British Airports Authority* [1983] RVR 161, Lands Tribunal for Scotland. In *Barb v Secretary of State for Transport, Rigby v Secretary of State for Transport* [1978] 2 EGLR 171, Lands Tribunal, depreciation to the value of two residential properties by traffic noise from a nearby motorway was held to be 7.5% of value, the properties being 620 metres and 730 metres from the motorway. Compensation of £1,000 was awarded for motorway traffic noise in *Marchant v Secretary of State for Transport* [1979] 1 EGLR 194, Lands Tribunal; and £2,000 in *Maile and Brock v West Sussex County Council* [1984] 1 EGLR 194, Lands Tribunal; but nil eg in *Hallows v Welsh Office* [1995] 1 EGLR 191, Lands Tribunal. As to the effect of physical factors generally see *Arkell v Department of Transport* [1983] 2 EGLR 181, Lands Tribunal; *Fallows v Gateshead Metropolitan Borough Council* (1993) 66 P & CR 460, Lands Tribunal. The upgrading of an existing road was the cause of the physical factors in *Broom and Broom v Department of Transport* [1993] RVR 218, Lands Tribunal. Compensation for the effect of aircraft noise was assessed at 10% for a house situated near a new runway constructed at Turnhouse Airport, Edinburgh: see *Inglis v British Airports Authority (No 2)* [1979] RVR 266, Lands Tribunal. Work carried out in three phases to Cardiff (South Wales) Airport was held a single project and compensation of £1,600 was payable to the owner of a nearby house: *Davies v Mid-Glamorgan County Council* [1979] 2 EGLR 158, Lands Tribunal. Compensation for loss in value of a house caused by noise and fumes from traffic on a length of highway which had undergone minor alterations as part of a larger scheme, including a new river bridge, could take into account the increase in traffic on the altered highway due to the bridge: *Williamson v Cumbria County Council* [1995] RVR 102, Lands Tribunal. No compensation is payable in respect of the psychological effect of a rubbish tip: *Shepherd v Lancashire County Council* (1976) 33 P & CR 296, Lands Tribunal. Artificial lighting refers to illumination caused by street lighting (even if that illumination is of low intensity) and not to the lighting structures themselves: *Blower v Suffolk County Council* (1994) 67 P & CR 228, Lands Tribunal.

3	As to the meaning of 'highway' see PARA 861 note 4.

4	Land Compensation Act 1973 s 1(7).

5	For these purposes, 'public works' means any highway, any aerodrome, and any works or land (not being a highway or aerodrome) provided or used in the exercise of statutory powers: Land Compensation Act 1973 s 1(3). See also note 15.

6   Ie under the Land Compensation Act 1973 Pt I: s 1(1)(a). As to interests which qualify see PARA 886.
7   Land Compensation Act 1973 s 1(1)(b) (amended by the Local Government, Planning and Land Act 1980 s 112(1), (3)). As to the appropriate procedures see PARAS 890–891.
8   In relation to a highway, 'responsible authority' means the appropriate highway authority and in relation to other public works it means the person managing those works: Land Compensation Act 1973 s 1(4). See also note 15. As to the meaning of 'appropriate highway authority' see PARA 861 note 4.
9   Land Compensation Act 1973 s 1(1). As to claims see PARAS 889–891.
10   'Relevant date' means: (1) in relation to a claim in respect of a highway, the date on which it was first open to public traffic (Land Compensation Act 1973 s 1(9)(a)); or, in the case of a highway which has not always since 17 October 1969 been a highway maintainable at the public expense, the date on which it was first so open whether or not as a highway so maintainable (s 19(3)(a)), and no claim may be made if the relevant date falls at a time when the highway was not so maintainable and the highway does not become so maintainable within three years of that date (s 19(3) (amended by the Local Government, Planning and Land Act 1980 s 112(1), (8), Sch 34 Pt XII)); and (2) in relation to a claim in respect of other public works, the date on which they were first used after completion (Land Compensation Act 1973 s 1(9)(b)).
     The responsible authority must keep a record and, on demand, furnish a statement in writing of the date on which the highway was first open to public traffic and of the date when public works were first used after completion: see s 15(1)(a), (b); and PARA 885.
11   Land Compensation Act 1973 s 1(8).
12   As to immunity from claims for nuisance by implication (ie by a statute making lawful that which would otherwise be unlawful) see PARAS 877–882. In *Vickers v Dover District Council* [1993] 1 EGLR 193, Lands Tribunal, a claim under the Land Compensation Act 1973 s 1 for depreciation in the value of land by physical factors caused by the use of public works was dismissed; the Tribunal held that the Road Traffic Regulation Act 1984 s 32 was entirely permissive and therefore did not, either expressly or by implication, confer on the council immunity from actions for nuisance within the meaning of the Land Compensation Act 1973 s 1(6) (see the text and note 14). Similarly, in *Marsh v Powys County Council* (1997) 75 P & CR 538, [1997] RVR 283, Lands Tribunal, a local authority's duty under the Education Act 1944 to provide primary schools was held to be permissive with regard to the location, erection and management of such schools, and did not confer immunity upon the local authority from a nuisance action in respect of the use of the school, so a claim under the Land Compensation Act 1973 s 1(6) could not be maintained in respect of any depreciation caused by the school.
13   Ie the Civil Aviation Act 1982 s 77(2): see AIR LAW vol 2 (2008) PARAS 259, 656.
14   Land Compensation Act 1973 s 1(6) (amended by the Civil Aviation Act 1982 s 109(2), Sch 15 para 12(1)). The Land Compensation Act 1973 s 1(6) does not apply to development consent orders relating to nationally significant infrastructure projects: see the Planning Act 2008 s 152; and PARA 538.
15   Land Compensation Act 1973 s 84(1). Subject to that, references in Pt I to public works and responsible authorities include references to any works or authority which, apart from any Crown exemption, would be public works or a responsible authority: s 84(1).

885. Alterations to and changes of use of public works. Where[1]:

(1)   the carriageway of a highway[2] has been altered[3] after the highway has been open to public traffic[4];

(2)   any public works[5] other than a highway have been reconstructed, extended or otherwise altered after they have been first used[6]; or

(3)   there has been a change of use[7] in respect of any public works, other than a highway or aerodrome[8],

then if and so far as a claim[9] in respect of the highway or other public works relates to depreciation that would not have been caused but for the alterations[10] or change of use, the relevant date for the purposes of a claim will be:

(a)   the date on which the highway was first open to public traffic after completion of the alterations to the carriageway[11];

(b)   the date on which the other public works were first used after completion of the alterations[12]; or

(c)   the date of the change of use[13],

as the case may be[14].

1   The Land Compensation Act 1973 s 9 (see the text and notes 2–14) applies at any time, whether before, on or after 23 June 1973 (ie the commencement date of Pt I (ss 1–19): see ss 19(1), 89(2)): s 9(1).
2   As to the meaning of 'highway' see PARA 861 note 4.
3   For these purposes, the carriageway of a highway is altered if, and only if: (1) the location, width or level of the carriageway is altered otherwise than by resurfacing; or (2) an additional carriageway is provided for the highway beside, above or below an existing one: Land Compensation Act 1973 s 9(5)(a), (b).
4   Land Compensation Act 1973 s 9(1)(a). As to compensation for injury after the first opening for public traffic by use after construction of a highway see s 1; and PARA 884.
5   As to the meaning of 'public works' see PARA 884 note 5.
6   Land Compensation Act 1973 s 9(1)(b). As to compensation for injury after the date of the first use after completion of the works see s 1; and PARA 884.
7   References to a change of use do not include references to the intensification of an existing use: Land Compensation Act 1973 s 9(7).
8   Land Compensation Act 1973 s 9(1)(c). As to the meaning of 'aerodrome' see PARA 861 note 1.
9   As to the meaning of 'claim' see PARA 884 note 2. As to claims see PARAS 889–891.
    The responsible authority in relation to a highway or other public works must keep a record and, on demand, furnish a written statement of: (1) the date on which the highway was first open to public traffic after completion of any particular alterations to the carriageway of the highway; (2) the date on which the public works were first used after completion of any particular alterations to those works; (3) in the case of public works other than a highway or aerodrome, the date on which there was a change of use in respect of the public works: s 15(1). However, this duty will apply only in respect of the dates mentioned in heads (1)–(3) which fall on or after 23 June 1973: s 15(3). References to alterations to the carriageway of a highway, to runway or apron alterations and to a change of use must be construed in the same way as in s 9: see s 15(3); and notes 7–8, 10. A certificate by the Secretary of State stating that runway or apron alterations (see note 10) have or have not been carried out at an aerodrome and the date on which an aerodrome at which any such alterations have been carried out was first used after completion of the alterations is conclusive evidence of the facts stated: s 15(2). As to the Secretary of State see PARA 507 note 1. The functions of the Secretary of State under the Land Compensation Act 1973, so far as they are exercisable in relation to Wales, are now exercisable by the Welsh Ministers: see the National Assembly for Wales (Transfer of Functions) Order 1999, SI 1999/672, art 2, Sch 1; and the Government of Wales Act 2006 s 162(1), Sch 11 para 30. As to the Welsh Assembly Government and the Welsh Ministers see CONSTITUTIONAL LAW AND HUMAN RIGHTS.
10 The Land Compensation Act 1973 s 9(2) (see the text and notes 11–14) does not, by virtue of any alterations to an aerodrome, apply to a claim in respect of physical factors caused by aircraft, unless the alterations are runway or apron alterations: s 9(3). 'Runway or apron alterations' means: (1) the construction of a new runway, the major realignment of an existing runway or the extension or strengthening of an existing runway; or (2) a substantial addition to, or alteration of, a taxiway or apron, being an addition or alteration whose purpose or main purpose is the provision of facilities for a greater number of aircraft: s 9(6). As to the meaning of 'physical factors' see PARA 884 note 2.
11 Land Compensation Act 1973 s 9(2)(a). The reference to depreciation that would not have been caused but for alterations to the carriageway of a highway is a reference to such depreciation by physical factors which are caused by the use of, and the source of which is situated on, the length of carriageway which has been altered as mentioned in s 9(5)(a) (see note 3 head (1)) or, as the case may be, the additional carriageway and the corresponding length of the existing one mentioned in s 9(5)(b) (see note 3 head (2)): s 9(5).
12 Land Compensation Act 1973 s 9(2)(b).
13 Land Compensation Act 1973 s 9(2)(c).
14 Land Compensation Act 1973 s 9(2). As to the time for claims in relation to the relevant date see s 1(8), (9); and PARA 884.

886.   Interests qualifying for compensation; in general.   An interest which is an owner's interest[1] or an owner-occupier's interest[2] qualifies for compensation if it was acquired[3] by the claimant before the relevant date[4]. However, this does not apply to any interest acquired by the claimant by inheritance[5] from a person who acquired that interest, or a greater interest out of which it is derived, before the relevant date[6].

On the date on which notice of claim for compensation in respect of an interest is served, the claimant, if and so far as the interest is in land which is a dwelling[7], must have an owner's interest[8]; and where the interest carries the right to occupy the land, the land must be occupied by the claimant in right of that interest as his residence[9]. If and so far as the interest is not in land which is a dwelling, the claimant must have an interest which is that of an owner-occupier[10] and the land must be or form part of either a hereditament, the annual value[11] of which does not exceed the prescribed amount[12], or an agricultural unit[13].

1   In relation to any land, 'owner's interest' means the legal fee simple in the land, or a tenancy of it granted or extended for a term of years certain of which, on the date of service of the notice of claim in respect of it, not less than three years remain unexpired: Land Compensation Act 1973 s 2(4). As to tenancies treated as owner's interests for these purposes see PARA 887. As to the situation where a potential claimant has disposed of a qualifying interest see PARA 889.
2   In relation to land in a hereditament, 'owner-occupier' means a person who occupies the whole or a substantial part of the land in right of an owner's interest in it and, in relation to land in an agricultural unit, means a person who occupies the whole of that unit and is entitled, while so occupying it, to an owner's interest in the whole or any part of that land: Land Compensation Act 1973 s 2(5). 'Hereditament' has the meaning given in the Town and Country Planning Act 1990 s 171 (see TOWN AND COUNTRY PLANNING vol 46(2) (Reissue) PARA 987): Land Compensation Act 1973 s 2(6) (amended by the Planning (Consequential Provisions) Act 1990 s 4, Sch 2 para 29(1)). As to the meaning of 'agricultural unit' see PARA 622 note 6.
3   An interest acquired pursuant to a contract must be treated as acquired when the contract was made: see the Land Compensation Act 1973 s 19(2).
4   See the Land Compensation Act 1973 s 2(1). As to the meaning of 'relevant date' see PARA 884 note 10.
5   An interest is acquired by a person by inheritance if it devolves on him by virtue only of testamentary dispositions taking effect on, or the law of intestate succession or the right of survivorship between joint tenants as applied to, the death of another person or the successive deaths of two or more other persons: Land Compensation Act 1973 ss 2(7), 11(2). A person who acquires an interest by appropriation of it in or towards satisfaction of any legacy, share in residue or other share in the estate of a deceased person must be treated as a person on whom the interest devolves by direct bequest: ss 2(7), 11(3).
    Where an interest is settled land for the purposes of the Settled Land Act 1925 and on the death of a tenant for life within the meaning of that Act a person becomes entitled to the interest in accordance with the settlement, or by any appropriation by the personal representatives in respect of the settled land, the Land Compensation Act 1973 s 11(2) applies as if the interest had belonged to the tenant for life absolutely and the trusts of the settlement taking effect after his death had been the trusts of his will: ss 2(7), 11(4). This provision as to settled land applies, with any necessary modifications, where a person becomes entitled to an interest on the termination of a settlement as it would apply if he had become entitled in accordance with the terms of the settlement: ss 2(7), 11(5). As to settlements see PARA 553 note 11; and SETTLEMENTS.
6   Land Compensation Act 1973 ss 2(7), 11(1).
7   As to the meaning of 'dwelling' see PARA 802 note 1.
8   Land Compensation Act 1973 s 2(1), (2)(a).
9   Land Compensation Act 1973 s 2(1), (2)(b). Where an interest in land is vested in trustees other than a sole tenant for life within the meaning of the Settled Land Act 1925 and a person beneficially entitled, whether directly or derivatively, under the trusts is entitled or permitted by reason of his interest to occupy the land, these provisions have effect as if occupation by that person were occupation by the trustees in right of the interest vested in them: Land Compensation Act 1973 ss 2(7), 10(4).
10 Land Compensation Act 1973 s 2(1), (3)(a).
11 'Annual value' has the meaning given in the Town and Country Planning Act 1990 s 171 (see TOWN AND COUNTRY PLANNING vol 46(2) (Reissue) PARA 987), taking references to the date of service of a notice under s 150 as references to the date on which notice of the claim is served: Land Compensation Act 1973 s 2(6) (as amended: see note 2).
12 'Prescribed amount' means the amount prescribed for the purposes of the Town and Country Planning Act 1990 s 149(3)(a) (see TOWN AND COUNTRY PLANNING vol 46(2) (Reissue) PARA

987): Land Compensation Act 1973 s 2(6) (as amended: see note 2). At the date at which this volume states the law, the prescribed amount is £29,200: Town and Country Planning (Blight Provisions) (England) Order 2005, SI 2005/406, art 2; Town and Country Planning (Blight Provisions) (Wales) Order 2005, SI 2005/367, art 2.

13 Land Compensation Act 1973 s 2(1), (3)(b).

887. Interests qualifying for compensation; qualifying tenancies. Certain qualifying tenancies are treated as owner's interests for the purposes of the statutory provisions relating to compensation for injury by noise or other physical factors[1] whether or not the unexpired term on the date of service of the notice of claim[2] is of the specified[3] length[4]. Such qualifying tenancies are:

(1) any tenancy by virtue of which a person is entitled under Part I of the Leasehold Reform Act 1967[5] to acquire the freehold or an extended lease of a house, where that person has on or before the relevant date[6] given the landlord notice under that Act of his desire to have the freehold or an extended lease, and has not acquired the freehold or an extended lease before that date[7];

(2) a tenancy where on the relevant date the tenant:

    (a) is a qualifying tenant in respect of the tenancy for the purposes of the provisions of the Leasehold Reform, Housing and Urban Development Act 1993 relating to collective enfranchisement[8];

    (b) is by virtue of the tenancy either a participating tenant in relation to a claim to exercise the right to collective enfranchisement under those provisions, or is one of the participating tenants on whose behalf the acquisition by the nominee purchaser has been made in pursuance of such a claim[9];

(3) a tenancy where, on the relevant date and in respect of the tenancy, the tenant is a qualifying tenant for the purposes of the provisions of the Leasehold Reform, Housing and Urban Development Act 1993 conferring the individual right to acquire a new lease[10] who has given notice of a claim to exercise that right on or before the relevant date and who has not acquired a new lease before that date[11].

1 Ie owner's interests as defined in the Land Compensation Act 1973 s 2(4): see PARA 886.
2 As to the notice of claim see PARA 890. As to the meaning of 'claim' see PARA 884 note 2.
3 Ie the length specified in the Land Compensation Act 1973 s 2(4): see PARA 886.
4 Land Compensation Act 1973 ss 12(2), 12A(1) (s 12A added by the Leasehold Reform, Housing and Urban Development Act 1993 s 187(1), Sch 21 para 5).
5 Ie under the Leasehold Reform Act 1967 Pt I (ss 1–37): see LANDLORD AND TENANT vol 27(3) (2006 Reissue) PARA 1389 et seq.
6 As to the relevant date see PARA 884 note 10.
7 Land Compensation Act 1973 s 12(1). If no claim is made in respect of the qualifying tenancy before the claimant has ceased to be entitled to it by reason of his acquisition of the freehold or an extended lease, he may claim in respect of the qualifying tenancy as if he were still entitled to it: s 12(3). As to the time for that claim see s 12(4), (5); and PARA 889. As to notice of claim see s 12(6); and PARA 890. As to assessment of the claim see ss 4(4), 12(7); and PARA 895.
8 Land Compensation Act 1973 s 12A(1), (2)(a) (as added: see note 4). The provisions relating to collective enfranchisement are those in the Leasehold Reform, Housing and Urban Development Act 1993 Pt I Ch I (ss 1–38): see LANDLORD AND TENANT vol 27(3) (2006 Reissue) PARA 1552 et seq.
9 Land Compensation Act 1973 s 12A(1), (2)(b) (as added: see note 4). The terms 'participating tenant', 'nominee purchaser' and 'the acquisition by the nominee purchaser' are to be construed in accordance with the Leasehold Reform, Housing and Urban Development Act 1993 ss 14, 15 (both prospectively repealed), s 38(2) (prospectively amended): Land Compensation Act 1973 s 12A(9)(b) (as so added). As from a day to be appointed, s 12A(2)(b) (see head (2)(b) in the text) is amended so that a qualifying tenancy is a tenancy where on the relevant date the tenant is a participating member of an RTE company which is making a claim to exercise the right to

collective enfranchisement under the Leasehold Reform, Housing and Urban Development Act 1993 Pt I Ch I; or is a member of an RTE company which has made an acquisition in pursuance of such a claim: Land Compensation Act 1973 s 12A(2)(b) (prospectively amended by the Commonhold and Leasehold Reform Act 2002 s 124, Sch 8 para 1, Sch 14). In relation to the amended wording, the terms 'participating member' and 'RTE company' have the same meanings as in the Leasehold Reform, Housing and Urban Development Act 1993 Pt I Ch I: see the Land Compensation Act 1973 s 12A(9)(b) (prospectively amended by the Commonhold and Leasehold Reform Act 2002 Sch 8 para 1). A reference to the making of an acquisition by an RTE company will be construed in accordance with the Leasehold Reform, Housing and Urban Development Act 1993 s 38(2): see the Land Compensation Act 1973 s 12A(9)(c) (prospectively added by the Commonhold and Leasehold Reform Act 2002 Sch 8 para 1). At the date at which this volume states the law no such day had been appointed for these amendments to be brought into force.

10   Ie the Leasehold Reform, Housing and Urban Development Act 1993 Pt I Ch II (ss 39–62): see LANDLORD AND TENANT vol 27(3) (2006 Reissue) PARA 1671 et seq.

11   Land Compensation Act 1973 s 12A(1), (3) (as added: see note 4). Section 12A only applies where the relevant date occurs after 1 November 1993: Leasehold Reform, Housing and Urban Development Act 1993 (Commencement and Transitional Provisions No 1) Order 1993, SI 1993/2134, Sch 1 para 9. If no claim is made in respect of the qualifying tenancy before the claimant has ceased to be entitled to it in consequence of a lease being granted to him by the nominee purchaser or, as the case may be, under the Leasehold Reform, Housing and Urban Development Act 1993 Pt I Ch II, he may make a claim in respect of the qualifying tenancy as if he were still entitled to it: Land Compensation Act 1973 s 12A(4) (as so added). As from a day to be appointed the reference to the 'nominee purchaser' is repealed and a reference to the 'RTE company' is inserted instead: s 12A(4) (prospectively amended by the Commonhold and Leasehold Reform Act 2002 Sch 8 para 1). At the date at which this volume states the law no such day had been appointed. As to the time for that claim see the Land Compensation Act 1973 s 12A(5), (6); and PARA 889. As to notice of claim see s 12A(7); and PARA 890. As to assessment of the claim see ss 4(4), 12A(8); and PARA 895.

888. Limitation on right to compensation. Compensation is not payable in respect of the same depreciation both under the provisions relating to compensation for noise and other physical factors[1] and under any other enactment, except to the extent provided below[2].

Where a claim has been made in respect of depreciation of the value of an interest in land caused by the use of any public works[3] and compensation has been paid or is payable on that claim, compensation is not payable on any subsequent claim in relation to the same works and the same land or any part of it, whether in respect of the same or a different interest, except that, in the case of land which is a dwelling[4], this provision does not preclude the payment of compensation both on a claim in respect of the fee simple and on a claim in respect of a tenancy[5]. Furthermore, in the case of a claim for compensation for depreciation in the value of land after alterations of a highway or other public works or the change of use of public works other than a highway or aerodrome[6], these provisions do not preclude the payment of compensation unless the previous claim was in respect of depreciation that would not have been caused but for the same alterations or change of use[7]. Where a person is entitled to compensation in respect of the acquisition of an interest in land by an authority possessing compulsory purchase powers[8], or would be so entitled if the acquisition were compulsory, and:

(1)   the land is acquired for the purposes of any public works; and

(2)   that person retains land which, in relation to the land acquired, constitutes other land within the meaning of the Lands Clauses Consolidation Act 1845[9] or the Compulsory Purchase Act 1965[10], so that the compensation for the acquisition will include compensation for injurious affection of that other land retained,

then, whether or not any sum is paid or payable in respect of injurious affection of the land retained, compensation is not payable under the provisions relating to noise or other physical factors[11] on any claim in relation to those works made after the date of service of the notice to treat[12], or, if the acquisition is by agreement, the date of the agreement, in respect of any interest in the land retained[13]. The provisions described above do not, however, preclude the payment of compensation in the case of a claim for compensation for depreciation in the value of land after alterations of a highway or other public works or the change of use of public works other than a highway or aerodrome[14], unless the works for which the land was acquired were works resulting from the alterations, or works used for the purpose, to which the claim relates[15].

Where on or after 23 June 1973[16] an authority possessing compulsory purchase powers acquires land for the purposes of any public works and the person from whom the land is acquired retains land which, in relation to the land acquired, constitutes other land or lands within the meaning of the statutory provisions relating to injurious affection[17], the authority must deposit particulars of the land retained and the nature and extent of those works with the council of the district or London borough or the Welsh county or county borough in which the land retained is situated[18]. Any particulars so deposited are a local land charge and for the purposes of the Local Land Charges Act 1975 the council with which any such particulars are deposited is treated as the originating authority as respects the charge thereby constituted[19]. Where the acquisition is on or after 23 June 1973, the public works for the purposes of which the land is acquired must be taken to be those specified in the relevant particulars registered as set out above[20].

1 Ie under the Land Compensation Act 1973 Pt I (ss 1–19): see PARA 883 et seq. As to the meaning of 'physical factors' see PARA 884 note 2.
2 Land Compensation Act 1973 s 8(7).
3 As to such claims see the Land Compensation Act 1973 ss 1, 9; and PARAS 884–885. As to particulars of claim and service see s 3; and PARA 890. As to the meaning of 'public works' see PARA 884 note 5.
4 As to the meaning of 'dwelling' see PARA 802 note 1.
5 Land Compensation Act 1973 s 8(1); and see *Bannocks v Secretary of State for Transport* [1995] RVR 57, Lands Tribunal.
6 See Land Compensation Act 1973 s 9(1)–(3); and PARA 885. As to the meaning of 'aerodrome' see PARA 861 note 1.
7 Land Compensation Act 1973 s 9(4)(b).
8 As to the meaning of 'authority possessing compulsory purchase powers' see PARA 763 note 6; definition applied by the Land Compensation Act 1973 s 87(1).
9 Ie within the meaning of the Lands Clauses Consolidation Act 1845 s 63: see PARA 810.
10 Ie within the meaning of the Compulsory Purchase Act 1965 s 7: see PARA 810.
11 See note 1.
12 As to the notice to treat see PARA 616 et seq.
13 Land Compensation Act 1973 s 8(2). Section 8(2) applies whether the acquisition is before, on or after 23 June 1973: s 8(3). The right to compensation under the Lands Clauses Consolidation Act 1845 s 63 or the Compulsory Purchase Act 1965 s 7 for injurious affection to the land retained is in respect of any works on the land taken from the owner and held with the land retained and also in respect of the statutory works partly on the land taken from the owner and partly elsewhere: see PARA 811. Furthermore, the owner of the land taken may have other land not held with the land taken but injuriously affected by statutory works on land taken from him and on the land of others and for the injurious affection he may have a claim under the Lands Clauses Consolidation Act 1845 s 68 or the Compulsory Purchase Act of 1965 s 10 (see PARAS 718, 878), and he is not precluded from the payment of compensation under the Land Compensation Act 1973 Pt I in respect of depreciation by public works so far as situated elsewhere than on the land acquired (s 8(5)); nor would it seem that s 8(2) can operate to

preclude a claim under Pt I in respect of injury by works on the land acquired where the claim is not in respect of land severed and retained. However, compensation is not payable in respect of the same depreciation both under Pt I and under any other enactment: see s 8(7); and the text and notes 1–2.

14 See the Land Compensation Act 1973 s 9(1), (3); and PARA 885.
15 Land Compensation Act 1973 s 9(4)(b).
16 Ie the commencement date of the Land Compensation Act 1973 Pt I (ss 1–19): see ss 19(1), 89(2).
17 Ie the Lands Clauses Consolidation Act 1845 s 63 or the Compulsory Purchase Act 1965 s 7: see PARA 810.
18 Land Compensation Act 1973 s 8(2)(b), (4) (s 8(4) amended by the Local Land Charges Act 1975 ss 17(2), 19(2)–(4), Sch 1; and the Local Government (Wales) Act 1994 s 66(6), Sch 16 para 40(1)).
19 Land Compensation Act 1973 s 8(4A) (added by the Local Land Charges Act 1975 ss 17(2), 19(2)–(4), Sch 1).
20 Land Compensation Act 1973 s 8(3).

(ii) Claims for Compensation

889. Persons entitled to claim. The persons who may claim compensation are those who have a qualifying interest[1].

Where an interest is subject to a mortgage, a claim may be made by any mortgagee of the interest as if he were the person entitled to that interest but without prejudice to the making of a claim by that person[2] and no compensation is payable in respect of the interest of the mortgagee, as distinct from the interest which is subject to the mortgage[3].

In the case of a person who is entitled by virtue of a qualifying tenancy to claim as having an owner's interest[4], but who has not made a claim in respect of the qualifying tenancy before he has ceased to be entitled to it by reason of his acquisition of the freehold or an extended lease[5], a lease granted by the nominee purchaser[6] or a new lease[7], he may make a claim in respect of the qualifying tenancy as if he were still entitled to it[8]. He may not, however, make that claim after he has ceased to be entitled to the freehold, extended lease, lease granted by the nominee purchaser or new lease, as the case may be, but he may make the claim before the first claim day[9] if it is made before the claimant has disposed of the freehold or of the lease in question and after he has made a contract for disposing of it[10]. No compensation is payable before the first claim day on any claim made by virtue of these provisions[11].

1 See the Land Compensation Act 1973 ss 1, 2; and PARAS 884, 886.
2 Land Compensation Act 1973 s 10(1)(a). As to mortgage generally see MORTGAGE.
3 Land Compensation Act 1973 s 10(1)(b). As to the payment of the compensation to the mortgagee and the application by him see s 10(1)(c); and PARA 898.
4 As to that entitlement see the Land Compensation Act 1973 ss 12(1), (2), 12A(1)–(3); and PARA 887.
5 Ie under the Leasehold Reform Act 1967 Pt I (ss 1–37): see LANDLORD AND TENANT vol 27(3) (2006 Reissue) PARA 1389 et seq.
6 As from a day to be appointed the reference to 'the nominee purchaser' is repealed and a reference to 'the RTE company' is inserted instead: see the Land Compensation Act 1973 s 12A(4) (prospectively amended by the Commonhold and Leasehold Reform Act 2002 s 124, Sch 8 para 1). At the date at which this volume states the law no such day had been appointed. See PARA 887 note 9; and LANDLORD AND TENANT vol 27(3) (2006 Reissue) PARA 1581 et seq.
7 Ie under the Leasehold Reform, Housing and Urban Development Act 1993 Pt I Ch II (ss 39–62): see LANDLORD AND TENANT vol 27(3) (2006 Reissue) PARA 1671 et seq.
8 Land Compensation Act 1973 ss 12(3), 12A(4) (s 12A added by the Leasehold Reform, Housing and Urban Development Act 1993 s 187(1), Sch 21 para 5).
9 As to the first claim day see PARA 891.

10 Land Compensation Act 1973 s 12(4) (amended by the Local Government, Planning and Land
    Act 1980 s 112); Land Compensation Act s 12A(5) (as added: see note 8). As to notice of the
    claim see ss 3, 12(6), 12A(7); and PARA 890. As to the assessment see ss 4(4)(a), 12(7), 12A(8);
    and PARA 895.
11 Land Compensation Act 1973 s 12(5) (amended by the Local Government, Planning and Land
    Act 1980 s 112(1), (4)); Land Compensation Act 1973 s 12A(6) (as added: see note 8).

890.   Notice of claim and service.   A claim for compensation in respect of
noise and other physical factors[1] is made by serving on the responsible authority[2]
a notice containing particulars[3] of:

(1)   the land in respect of which the claim is made[4];
(2)   the claimant's interest and the date on which, and the manner in which,
       it was acquired[5];
(3)   the claimant's occupation of the land, except where the interest qualifies
       for compensation without occupation[6];
(4)   any other interests in the land so far as known to the claimant[7];
(5)   the public works[8] to which the claim relates[9];
(6)   the amount of compensation claimed[10];
(7)   any land contiguous or adjacent to the land in respect of which the
       claim is made, being land to which the claimant was entitled in the same
       capacity[11] on the relevant date[12];
(8)   in the case of a claim relating to the depreciation in the value of land
       after the alteration of a highway or other public works or the change of
       use of public works other than a highway or aerodrome[13], the
       alterations or change of use alleged to give rise to the depreciation[14].

In the case of a person who is entitled by virtue of a qualifying tenancy to
claim as having an owner's interest[15], the notice of claim must state that he
makes his claim in respect of that qualifying tenancy[16]; and if he claims after he
has ceased to be entitled to the qualifying tenancy[17], or if, having disposed of the
freehold or extended lease acquired by him[18] or of the lease granted to him[19], he
has made a claim before that disposal[20], he must include sufficient particulars in
the notice of claim to show that he has the right to make that claim[21].

1 Ie a claim under the Land Compensation Act 1973 Pt I (ss 1–19): see PARA 884 et seq. As to the
   meaning of 'physical factors' see PARA 884 note 2.
2 As to the meaning of 'responsible authority' see PARA 884 note 8.
3 Land Compensation Act 1973 s 3(1). In the absence of waiver or estoppel, a notice of reference
   to the Upper Tribunal which does not contain the particulars required by s 3 does not constitute
   a notice of claim and is ineffective for the making of a claim under the Act: see *Donaldson v
   Hereford and Worcester County Council* (1997) 76 P & CR 93, Lands Tribunal. The Lands
   Tribunal was abolished on 1 June 2009 and its functions were transferred to the Upper Tribunal:
   see PARA 720.
4 Land Compensation Act 1973 s 3(1)(a).
5 Land Compensation Act 1973 s 3(1)(b). See also ss 2, 10(4), 11; and PARA 886.
6 Land Compensation Act 1973 s 3(1)(c). See also ss 2, 10(4), 11; and PARA 886.
7 Land Compensation Act 1973 s 3(1)(d).
8 As to the meaning of 'public works' see PARA 884 note 5.
9 Land Compensation Act 1973 s 3(1)(e).
10 Land Compensation Act 1973 s 3(1)(f).
11 Ie within the meaning of the Land Compensation Act 1973 s 6: see PARA 897.
12 Land Compensation Act 1973 s 3(1)(g). As to the relevant date, which for compensation to be
    payable must fall on or after 17 October 1969 (s 1(8)), see PARA 884 note 10.
13 See the Land Compensation Act 1973 s 9(1)–(3); and PARA 885. As to public works other than
    a highway see PARA 885. As to the meaning of 'aerodrome' see PARA 861 note 1. As to the
    meaning of 'highway' see PARA 861 note 4.
14 Land Compensation Act 1973 s 9(4).
15 See PARA 887.

16 Land Compensation Act 1973 ss 12(6), 12A(7) (s 12A added by the Leasehold Reform, Housing and Urban Development Act 1993 s 187(1), Sch 21 para 5).

17 Ie if he claims under the Land Compensation Act 1973 s 12(3) or s 12A(4): see PARA 887.

18 Ie acquired by him under the Leasehold Reform Act 1967 Pt I (ss 1–37): see LANDLORD AND TENANT vol 27(3) (2006 Reissue) PARA 1389 et seq.

19 Ie granted to him under the Leasehold Reform, Housing and Urban Development Act 1993 Pt I Ch I (ss 1–38) (collective enfranchisement) or under Pt I Ch II (ss 39–62) (individual right to new lease): see LANDLORD AND TENANT vol 27(3) (2006 Reissue) PARAS 1552 et seq, 1671 et seq.

20 Ie if he claims under the Land Compensation Act 1973 s 12(4) or s 12A(5): see PARA 889.

21 Land Compensation Act 1973 s 12(6), s 12A(7) (as added: see note 16).

891. Time for claim. No claim may be made before the expiration of 12 months from the relevant date[1]. The day next following the expiration of the 12 months is referred to as the first claim day[2].

However, this will not preclude the making of a claim in respect of an interest in land before the first claim day if[3]: (1) the claimant has during the 12 months after the relevant date made a contract for disposing of that interest, or, in so far as the interest is in land which is not a dwelling[4], for the grant of a tenancy[5] of that land[6]; and (2) the claim is made before the interest is disposed of or the tenancy is granted[7]; but compensation is not payable before the first claim day on any claim so made[8].

Claims before the first claim day may also be made by persons having a qualifying tenancy under the Leasehold Reform Act 1967 or the Leasehold Reform, Housing and Urban Development Act 1993[9].

Provision was made by the Local Government, Planning and Land Act 1980 to extend the claim period for certain claims which were out of time on 13 November 1980[10]. A person's right of action to recover compensation on a claim made by virtue of that special provision is, however, deemed to have accrued on that date for the purposes of the limitation period[11].

1 As to the relevant date, which in any case must fall on or after 17 October 1969 (Land Compensation Act 1973 s 1(8)), see ss 1(9), 9(2); and PARAS 884 note 10, 885.

2 Land Compensation Act 1973 s 3(2) (amended by the Local Government, Planning and Land Act 1980 s 112(1), (2)). This provision is subject to the Land Compensation Act 1973 s 12: see s 3(2); and the text and note 9. For the purposes of the Limitation Act 1980 a person's right of action to recover compensation under the Land Compensation Act 1973 Pt I (ss 1–19) is deemed to have accrued on the first claim day: s 19(2A) (added by the Local Government, Planning and Land Act 1980 s 112(1), (6)); Interpretation Act 1978 s 17(2)(a). The limitation period is six years: see the Limitation Act 1980 s 9(1).

3 Land Compensation Act 1973 s 3(3) (amended by the Local Government, Planning and Land Act 1980 s 112(1), (4)).

4 As to the meaning of 'dwelling' see PARA 802 note 1.

5 As to the meaning of 'tenancy' see PARA 805 note 3.

6 Land Compensation Act 1973 s 3(3)(a). See *Dodd v Stansted Airport* (1998) 76 P & CR 456, [1998] RVR 107 (although the claim was made before the contract actually bound the vendor and purchaser, compensation was payable due to estoppel by convention, created by both parties having proceeded for five years on the shared assumption that the claim was validly made under the Land Compensation Act 1973 s 3(3)(a)).

7 Land Compensation Act 1973 s 3(3)(b).

8 Land Compensation Act 1973 s 3(3) (as amended: see note 3).

9 See the Land Compensation Act 1973 ss 12(4), 12A(5); and PARA 889. As to the treatment of qualifying tenancies as owner's interests see PARA 887.

10 See the Local Government, Planning and Land Act 1980 s 113.

11 Local Government, Planning and Land Act 1980 s 113(10); Interpretation Act 1978 s 17(2)(a). See also note 2.

(iii) Assessment of Compensation

892. Entry to survey and value. Where notice of a claim[1] has been served on a responsible authority[2], any person authorised by that authority, on giving reasonable notice, may enter the land to which the claim relates for the purpose of surveying it and ascertaining its value in connection with the claim; and any person who wilfully obstructs[3] a person in the exercise of the powers so conferred is guilty of an offence[4].

1 As to the notice of claim see PARA 890. As to the meaning of 'claim' see PARA 884 note 2.
2 As to the meaning of 'responsible authority' see PARA 884 note 8.
3 In order to be wilful, obstruction must be deliberate and intentional: *R v Senior* [1899] 1 QB 283 at 290–291. It is therefore necessary for the prosecution to prove that the act was done with the intention of obstructing: *Willmott v Atack* [1977] QB 498, [1976] 3 All ER 794, DC. It is immaterial that the person prosecuted did not appreciate that what he did amounted in law to obstruction or that his actions were not aimed primarily at the person obstructed: see eg *Hills v Ellis* [1983] QB 680, [1983] 1 All ER 667; *Lewis v Cox* [1985] QB 509, [1984] 3 All ER 672. See also *Department of Transport v Williams* (1993) 138 Sol Jo LB 5, CA.
4 Any person guilty of such an offence is liable on summary conviction to a fine not exceeding level 1 on the standard scale: Land Compensation Act 1973 s 3(4) (amended by virtue of the Criminal Justice Act 1982 ss 38, 46). As to the standard scale see PARA 522 note 9.

893. Upper Tribunal's jurisdiction. Any question of disputed compensation must be referred to and determined by the Upper Tribunal (the 'Tribunal')[1], but no such question arising out of a claim[2] made before the first claim day[3] may be referred to the Tribunal before the beginning of that day[4].

1 Land Compensation Act 1973 s 16(1) (amended by the Land Compensation (Scotland) Act 1973 s 81(1), Sch 2; and SI 2009/1307). As to the Upper Tribunal see PARA 720; and ADMINISTRATIVE LAW.
2 As to the meaning of 'claim' see PARA 884 note 2.
3 As to the first claim day see PARA 891.
4 Land Compensation Act 1973 s 16(2) (amended by the Land Compensation (Scotland) Act 1973 Sch 2; and by the Local Government, Planning and Land Act 1980 s 112(1), (4)).

894. Action for nuisance where responsible authority has disclaimed statutory immunity. Where, in resisting a claim[1], a responsible authority[2] contends that no enactment relating to the works in question confers immunity from actions for nuisance[3] in respect of the use to which the claim relates so as to give a ground for compensation[4], then if: (1) compensation is not paid on the claim; and (2) an action for nuisance in respect of the matters which were the subject of the claim is subsequently brought by the claimant against the authority, no enactment relating to those works, being an enactment in force when the contention was made, affords a defence to that action in so far as it relates to those matters[5].

1 As to the meaning of 'claim' see PARA 884 note 2.
2 As to the meaning of 'responsible authority' see PARA 884 note 8.
3 As to nuisance generally see NUISANCE.
4 See the Land Compensation Act 1973 s 1(6); and PARA 884.
5 Land Compensation Act 1973 s 17. The Land Compensation Act 1973 s 17 does not apply to development consent orders relating to nationally significant infrastructure projects: see the Planning Act 2008 s 152 (not yet in force); and PARA 538.

895. Relevant matters in assessing compensation. The compensation payable on any claim[1] must be assessed by reference to prices current on the first claim day[2].

In assessing depreciation due to the physical factors[3] caused by the use of any public works[4], account must be taken of the use of those works as it exists on the first claim day, and of any intensification that may then be reasonably expected of the use of those works in the state in which they are on that date[5]. In assessing the extent of the depreciation, there must be taken into account the benefit of any relevant works: (1) which have been carried out, or in respect of which a grant has been paid, under the statutory powers for sound-proofing of buildings affected by public works[6] or by aerodromes[7], or any corresponding local enactment or under any provision of a scheme operated by a person managing an aerodrome which provides for the payment of sound-proofing grants[8] in respect of buildings near the aerodrome[9]; and (2) which have been carried out[10] to mitigate any adverse effect of the construction, improvement, existence or use of a highway or other public works on the land surrounding the highway or public works[11].

The value of the interest in respect of which the claim is made must be assessed:

(a)　　by reference to the nature of the interest and the condition of the land as it subsisted on the date of service of notice of the claim[12], subject to certain exceptions[13];

(b)　　in accordance with certain rules set out in the Land Compensation Act 1961[14], subject to certain exceptions[15];

(c)　　if the interest is subject to a mortgage, to a contract of sale or to a contract made after the relevant date for the grant of a tenancy[16], as if it were not subject to the mortgage or contract[17].

However, in assessing the value of the interest in respect of which the claim is made there must be left out of account any part of that value which is attributable to any building, or improvement or extension of a building, on the land if the building or, as the case may be, the building as improved or extended, was first occupied after the relevant date[18], and any change in the use of the land made after that date[19].

1　As to the meaning of 'claim' see PARA 884 note 2.
2　Land Compensation Act 1973 s 4(1) (amended by the Local Government, Planning and Land Act 1980 s 112(1), (4)). As to the first claim day see PARA 891.
3　As to the meaning of 'physical factors' see PARA 884 note 2.
4　As to the meaning of 'public works' see PARA 884 note 5.
5　Land Compensation Act 1973 s 4(2) (amended by the Local Government, Planning and Land Act 1980 s 112(1), (4)).
6　Ie under the Land Compensation Act 1973 s 20: see PARA 861.
7　Ie under the Airports Authority Act 1965 s 15 (repealed), the Civil Aviation Act 1971 s 29A (repealed) and the Civil Aviation Act 1982 s 79: see AIR LAW vol 2 (2008) PARA 264. As to the meaning of 'aerodrome' see PARA 861 note 1.
8　'Sound-proofing grants' in relation to any buildings, means grants towards the cost of insulating those buildings or parts of those buildings against noise: Land Compensation Act 1973 s 4(3) (definition added by the Civil Aviation Act 1980 s 20(1)).
9　Land Compensation Act 1973 s 4(3)(a) (amended by the Airports Authority Act 1975 s 25(2), Sch 5 Pt II; the Civil Aviation Act 1980 s 20(1); and the Civil Aviation Act 1982 s 109(2), Sch 15 para 12(2)). It must be assumed that any relevant works which could be or could have been carried out, or in respect of which a grant could be or could have been paid, have been carried out, but, in a case where the authority having functions has a discretion whether or not to carry out the works or pay the grant, only if it has undertaken to do so: Land Compensation Act 1973 s 4(3).
10　Ie under the Highways Act 1980 s 282 (see HIGHWAYS, STREETS AND BRIDGES vol 21 (2004 Reissue) PARA 91); or the Land Compensation Act 1973 s 27 (see PARA 875).
11　Land Compensation Act 1973 s 4(3)(b).

12 As to the notice of claim see the Land Compensation Act 1973 s 3; and PARA 890. In the case of
    a person claiming in respect of a qualifying tenancy (see PARA 887), the reference to the date of
    service of the notice of claim is to have effect as if it were a reference to the relevant date:
    s 12(7), s 12A(8) (added by the Leasehold Reform, Housing and Urban Development Act 1993
    s 187(1), Sch 21 para 5). As to the relevant date see PARA 884 note 10.

13 Land Compensation Act 1973 s 4(4)(a). This excludes value attributable to certain buildings and
    uses under the Land Compensation Act 1973 s 4(5) (see the text and notes 18–19): see s 4(4)(a).

14 Ie under the rules set out in the Land Compensation Act 1961 s 5 rr 2–4: see PARAS 754, 760,
    789, 798.

15 Land Compensation Act 1973 s 4(4)(b). This is subject to s 5 (see PARA 896): see s 4(4)(b).

16 As to the meaning of 'tenancy' see PARA 805 note 3.

17 Land Compensation Act 1973 s 4(4)(c).

18 Land Compensation Act 1973 s 4(5)(a).

19 Land Compensation Act 1973 s 4(5)(b).

896. Assumptions as to planning permission in assessing value. The following
assumptions must be made in assessing the value of the interest in respect of
which the claim is made[1].

It must be assumed that planning permission[2] would be granted in respect of
the land in which the interest subsists (the 'relevant land') or any part of it, for
any development[3] consisting of: (1) specified rebuilding operations or the
maintenance, improvement or alteration of a building[4] subject to the statutory
condition[5] relating thereto[6]; and (2) the use as two or more separate dwelling
houses of any building which at a material date was used as a single dwelling
house[7]. Where, however, an order has been made[8] in respect of the relevant land
or any part of it requiring the removal of any building or the discontinuance of
any use[9], and compensation has become payable in respect of that order[10], it
must not be assumed that planning permission would be granted in respect of the
relevant land or any part of it for the rebuilding of that building or the
resumption of that use[11].

It must be assumed that planning permission would not be granted in respect
of the relevant land or any part of it for any development other than the
development mentioned above; and, if planning permission has been granted in
respect of the relevant land or any part of it for that other development, it must
be assumed that the planning permission has not been granted in so far as it
relates to development that has not been carried out[12].

1 Land Compensation Act 1973 s 5(1). As to the meaning of 'claim' see PARA 884 note 2.

2 For these purposes, 'planning permission' has the same meaning as in the Town and Country
   Planning Act 1990 (see TOWN AND COUNTRY PLANNING vol 46(1) (Reissue) PARA 43): see the
   Land Compensation Act 1973 s 5(5) (amended by the Planning (Consequential Provisions)
   Act 1990 s 4, Sch 2 para 29(2)(c)).

3 For these purposes, 'development' has the same meaning as in the Town and Country Planning
   Act 1990 (see TOWN AND COUNTRY PLANNING vol 46(1) (Reissue) PARA 217): see the Land
   Compensation Act 1973 s 5(5) (as amended: see note 2).

4 Ie development of a class specified in the Town and Country Planning Act 1990 s 107(4), Sch 3
   para 1: see TOWN AND COUNTRY PLANNING vol 46(2) (Reissue) PARA 914. See also PARA 765
   note 5.

5 Ie subject to the condition set out in the Town and Country Planning Act 1990 s 111(5), Sch 10:
   see TOWN AND COUNTRY PLANNING vol 46(2) (Reissue) PARA 918.

6 Land Compensation Act 1973 s 5(2)(a) (s 5(2) substituted by the Planning and Compensation
   Act 1991 s 31(4), Sch 6 para 5).

7 Land Compensation Act 1973 s 5(2)(b) (as substituted: see note 6). The development referred to
   in the text is development of a class specified in the Town and Country Planning Act 1990 Sch 3
   para 2: see TOWN AND COUNTRY PLANNING vol 46(2) (Reissue) PARA 920. See also PARA 765
   note 8.

8   Ie an order under the Town and Country Planning Act 1990 s 102 or Sch 9 para 1: see TOWN
    AND COUNTRY PLANNING vol 46(1) (Reissue) PARAS 546–547; TOWN AND COUNTRY PLANNING
    vol 46(2) (Reissue) PARAS 756–758.
9   For these purposes, 'use' has the same meaning as in the Town and Country Planning Act 1990
    (see TOWN AND COUNTRY PLANNING vol 46(1) (Reissue) PARA 221): see the Land
    Compensation Act 1973 s 5(5) (as amended: see note 2).
10 Ie under the Town and Country Planning Act 1990 s 115: see TOWN AND COUNTRY PLANNING
    vol 46(2) (Reissue) PARAS 923, 928–929.
11 Land Compensation Act 1973 s 5(3)(c) (amended by the Planning (Consequential Provisions)
    Act 1990 Sch 2 para 29(2)(b)(iii)). Any expression which is also used in the Town and Country
    Planning Act 1990 has the same meaning for these purposes as in that Act and references to any
    provision of that Act include references to any corresponding provision previously in force:
    Land Compensation Act 1973 s 5(5) (as amended: see note 2).
12 Land Compensation Act 1973 s 5(4).

897. Compensation reduced by betterment of claimant's land. The
compensation payable on a claim[1] must be reduced by an amount equal to any
increase in the value of: (1) the claimant's interest in the land in respect of which
the claim is made[2]; and (2) any interest in other land contiguous or adjacent[3] to
that land to which the claimant was entitled in the same capacity[4] on the relevant
date[5], if, in either case, that increase is attributable to the existence of, or the use
or prospective use of, the public works[6] to which the claim relates[7]. In the case of
a claim for compensation for depreciation in the value of land after alterations of
a highway or other public works or the change of use of public works other than
a highway or aerodrome[8], the increase in value to be taken into account is any
increase that would not have been caused but for the alteration or change of use
in question[9].

Where, however, an increase in the value of an interest in other land has been
taken into account under the provisions described above, then, in connection
with any subsequent acquisition of that other land[10], that increase must not be
left out of account by virtue of the provisions of the Land Compensation
Act 1961[11] which require increases in value of the land compulsorily acquired
arising from development or prospective development of certain areas to be
disregarded on assessing the value of that land, or be taken into account by
virtue of the provisions of that Act[12] which require the deduction from the value
of land compulsorily acquired of any increase in the value of other adjacent or
contiguous land owned by the same owner arising from development or
prospective development of certain areas, or any corresponding enactment[13], in
so far as it was taken into account in connection with that claim[14].

1   As to the meaning of 'claim' see PARA 884 note 2.
2   Land Compensation Act 1973 s 6(1)(a). Sections 4 and 5 (see PARAS 895–896), which apply to
    the assessment of the depreciation in the value of the land to which the claim relates, do not
    apply to the assessment for these purposes of the value of the interest mentioned in head (1) in
    the text: s 6(2). As to the consideration by the Upper Tribunal of the deductions for benefits due
    to the scheme in highways cases see PARA 841 note 7. See also *Hallows v Welsh Office* [1995]
    1 EGLR 191, Lands Tribunal. The Lands Tribunal was abolished on 1 June 2009 and its
    functions were transferred to the Upper Tribunal: see PARA 720.
3   As to the meanings of 'adjacent' and 'contiguous' see PARA 781 note 7.
4   A person entitled to two interests in land must be taken to be entitled to them in the same
    capacity if, but only if, he is entitled: (1) to both of them beneficially; or (2) to both of them as
    trustee of one particular trust; or (3) to both of them as personal representative of one particular
    person: Land Compensation Act 1973 s 6(5).
5   Land Compensation Act 1973 s 6(1)(b). As to the relevant date see PARA 884 note 10.
6   As to the meaning of 'public works' see PARA 884 note 5.
7   Land Compensation Act 1973 s 6(1).
8   See the Land Compensation Act 1973 s 9(1)–(3); and PARA 885. As to the meanings of
    'aerodrome' and 'highway' see PARA 861 notes 1, 4. Compensation for loss in value of a house

caused by noise and fumes from traffic on a length of highway which had undergone minor alterations as part of a larger scheme including a new river bridge, could take into account the increase in traffic on the altered highway due to the bridge: *Williamson v Cumbria County Council* [1995] RVR 102, Lands Tribunal.

9   Land Compensation Act 1973 s 9(4)(a).
10 Ie where either: (1) the interest acquired by the subsequent acquisition is the same as the interest the increased value of which was previously taken into account as mentioned in the Land Compensation Act 1973 s 6(3), whether the acquisition extends to the whole of the land in which that interest previously subsisted or only to part of that land; or (2) the person entitled to the interest acquired is, or directly or indirectly derives title to that interest from, the person who at the time of the claim mentioned was entitled to the interest the increased value of which was previously so taken into account: s 6(4). A reference to a person deriving title from another person includes a reference to any successor in title of that other person: s 6(5).
11 Ie by virtue of the Land Compensation Act 1961 s 6: see PARA 788 et seq. Cf s 8(1); and PARAS 796, 849.
12 Ie by virtue of the Land Compensation Act 1961 s 7: see PARA 840 et seq. Cf s 8(1); and PARAS 796, 849.
13 'Corresponding enactment' has the same meaning as in the Land Compensation Act 1961 s 8 (see PARA 796 note 11): Land Compensation Act 1973 s 6(6).
14 Land Compensation Act 1973 s 6(3).

(iv) Payment of Compensation

898. Persons to whom compensation is payable, and limits and extent of compensation. Where an interest is subject to a mortgage, any compensation which is payable in respect of the interest which is subject to the mortgage must be paid to the mortgagee or, if there is more than one mortgagee, to the first mortgagee, and must in either case be applied by him as if it were proceeds of sale[1].

Where the interest is subject to a trust of land, the compensation must be dealt with as if it were proceeds of sale arising under the trust[2]; and where it is settled land for the purposes of the Settled Land Act 1925, the compensation must be treated as capital money arising under that Act[3].

Any compensation payable in respect of land which is ecclesiastical property[4] must be paid to the Diocesan Board of Finance for the diocese in which the land is situated and it must be applied for the purposes for which the proceeds of a sale by agreement of the land would be applicable under any enactment or Measure authorising, or disposing of the proceeds of, such a sale[5].

Compensation is not payable on any claim unless the amount of the compensation exceeds £50[6]. Where compensation is payable by a responsible authority[7] on a claim[8], the authority must pay, in addition to the compensation, any reasonable valuation or legal expenses incurred by the claimant for the purposes of the preparation and prosecution of the claim, but without prejudice to the power of the Upper Tribunal in respect of costs of and incidental to proceedings in the Upper Tribunal[9].

1   Land Compensation Act 1973 s 10(1)(c). As to mortgage generally see MORTGAGE.
2   Land Compensation Act 1973 s 10(2) (amended by the Trusts of Land and Appointment of Trustees Act 1996 s 25(1), Sch 3 para 13). As to trusts of land see SETTLEMENTS vol 42 (Reissue) PARA 897.
3   Land Compensation Act 1973 s 10(3). See SETTLEMENTS vol 42 (Reissue) PARA 795. As to settled land see PARA 553 note 11; and SETTLEMENTS.
4   For these purposes, 'ecclesiastical property' means land belonging to an ecclesiastical benefice of the Church of England, or being or forming part of a church subject to the jurisdiction of a bishop of any diocese of the Church of England or the site of such a church, or being or forming part of a burial ground subject to such jurisdiction: Land Compensation Act 1973 s 13(2) (amended by the Church of England (Miscellaneous Provisions) Measure 2006 s 14, Sch 5 para 18(2)). See ECCLESIASTICAL LAW vol 14 PARAS 517–518.

5 Land Compensation Act 1973 s 13(1) (amended by the Planning and Compensation Act 1991 s 70, Sch 15 para 20; and the Church of England (Miscellaneous Provisions) Measure 2006 Sch 5 para 18(1)).
6 Land Compensation Act 1973 s 7. As to the limits on the right to compensation see PARA 888.
7 As to the meaning of 'responsible authority' see PARA 884 note 8.
8 As to the meaning of 'claim' see PARA 884 note 2.
9 Land Compensation Act 1973 s 3(5) (amended by the Land Compensation (Scotland) Act 1973 s 81(2), Sch 2 Pt I; and SI 2009/1307). The text refers to the power under the Tribunals, Courts and Enforcement Act 2007 s 29 (costs or expenses): see PARA 746; and ADMINISTRATIVE LAW. As to the Upper Tribunal see PARA 720; and ADMINISTRATIVE LAW.

899. Effect of payment when land is compulsorily acquired after claim. Where, after a claim[1] has been made in respect of any interest in land, the whole or part of the land in which that interest subsists is compulsorily acquired, then, if the value of that land has been diminished by the public works[2] to which the claim relates, but the compensation in respect of the compulsory acquisition falls to be assessed without regard to the diminution[3], the compensation in respect of the acquisition must be reduced by an amount equal to the compensation paid or payable on the claim, or, if the acquisition extends only to part of the land, to so much of that compensation as is attributable to that part[4].

1 As to the meaning of 'claim' see PARA 884 note 2.
2 As to the meaning of 'public works' see PARA 884 note 5.
3 As to these cases see the Land Compensation Act 1973 s 6(3); and PARA 897. See also the Land Compensation Act 1961 s 8(1); and PARAS 796, 849.
4 Land Compensation Act 1973 s 8(6).

900. Interest on compensation. Compensation[1] carries interest at the rate for the time being prescribed under the Land Compensation Act 1961[2] from: (1) the date of service of the notice of claim[3]; or (2) if that date is before the first claim day[4], the beginning of the claim period, until payment[5]. If it appears to any person that he may become liable to pay to another compensation or interest thereon under this provision he may, if the other person requests him in writing to do so, make one or more payments on account of such compensation or interest[6]. If after payment has been made by such person it is agreed or determined that he is not liable to pay the compensation or interest or, by reason of any agreement or determination, any such payment is shown to have been excessive, the payment or excess is recoverable by that person[7].

1 Ie compensation under the Land Compensation Act 1973 Pt I (ss 1–19): see PARA 883 et seq.
2 Ie at the rate prescribed under the Land Compensation Act 1961 s 32: see PARA 641 note 6.
3 As to service of the notice of claim see PARA 890.
4 As to the first claim day see PARA 891.
5 Land Compensation Act 1973 s 18(1) (amended by the Local Government, Planning and Land Act 1980 s 112(1), (4)).
6 Planning and Compensation Act 1991 s 80(2), Sch 18 Pt II.
7 Planning and Compensation Act 1991 s 80(3), Sch 18 Pt II.

(7) DISPOSAL OF SUPERFLUOUS LAND

901. Various powers of disposal. Where land is compulsorily acquired under an empowering enactment by an authority to which the Compulsory Purchase Act 1965 applies[1], there is no provision for the disposal of superfluous land unless it is made by the empowering enactment or special Act[2] or the authority has power to appropriate superfluous land to other statutory purposes[3]. Where, however, there is a compulsory purchase of land by an authority under a special

Act incorporating certain provisions of the Lands Clauses Consolidation
Act 1845[4], or those provisions are specially applied[5], the disposal of superfluous
land is controlled by those provisions[6].

1   See PARA 513.
2   Ie by special provisions for sale or exchange or letting (see eg the Local Government Act 1972
    ss 123, 127) or by specific incorporation or application of the Lands Clauses Consolidation
    Act 1845 ss 127–132 (see eg the incorporation of those sections in the Pipe-lines Act 1962 by
    the Compulsory Purchase Act 1965 s 37(3)). As to the incorporation of the Lands Clauses Acts
    see PARA 509. As to the meaning of 'special Act' see PARAS 509, 514.
3   See eg the Town and Country Planning Act 1990 s 232 (see TOWN AND COUNTRY PLANNING
    vol 46(2) (Reissue) PARAS 945–946); and the Local Government Act 1972 ss 122, 123, 126, 127
    (see LOCAL GOVERNMENT vol 69 (2009) PARA 513 et seq).
4   Ie the Lands Clauses Consolidation Act 1845 ss 127–132: see PARA 902 et seq.
5   See note 2.
6   See PARA 902 et seq.

902. Superfluous land under the Lands Clauses Acts. The Lands
Clauses Consolidation Act 1845 makes provision with respect to superfluous
land[1]. This is land acquired under the provisions of the special Act[2], either
compulsorily or by negotiations undertaken by virtue of the compulsory powers,
but subsequently found not to be required for the purposes of the undertaking[3].
These provisions[4] are deemed to be incorporated unless expressly or impliedly
excluded[5].

The object of the relevant provisions is to secure to the landowners from
whom land is taken by compulsion a reversion, as nearly as the legislature can
accomplish it, of all land which is not required for the undertaking[6]. When
incorporated, those provisions apply to all land acquired directly or indirectly
under compulsory powers, but they do not apply to land bought under mere
powers of purchase by agreement[7], among which is included land bought for
extraordinary purposes[8], nor do they apply to cases where the land ceases to be
required because of the partial or total abandonment of the undertaking[9]. In the
case of abandonment, the Act authorising the abandonment usually makes
provision as to the disposal of the land[10].

1   See the Lands Clauses Consolidation Act 1845 ss 127–132. As to the incorporation of these
    provisions see PARAS 509–510. As to their exclusion in the case of acquisitions to which the
    Acquisition of Land Act 1981 applies by the re-enactment of the Lands Clauses Acts in the
    Compulsory Purchase Act 1965 in substitution for those Acts and omitting provisions as to
    superfluous land see the Compulsory Purchase Act 1965 s 1(1); and PARA 513.
2   As to the meaning of 'special Act' see PARAS 509, 514.
3   See the introductory words to the Lands Clauses Consolidation Act 1845 ss 127–132; and see
    Great Western Rly Co v May (1874) LR 7 HL 283 at 292 per Lord Cairns LC; *Hooper v
    Bourne* (1877) 3 QBD 258 at 272, CA, per Bramwell LJ (affd (1880) 5 App Cas 1, HL). As to
    the meaning of 'undertaking' see PARA 511.
4   Ie the Lands Clauses Consolidation Act 1845 ss 127–132.
5   See note 1.
6   *Great Western Rly Co v May* (1874) LR 7 HL 283 at 295 per Lord Cairns LC. For the causes of
    land becoming superfluous see *Great Western Rly Co v May* at 292–293.
7   *Horne v Lymington Rly Co* (1874) 31 LT 167.
8   *City of Glasgow Union Rly Co v Caledonian Rly Co* (1871) LR 2 Sc & Div 160, HL; *Hooper v
    Bourne* (1877) 3 QBD 258, CA (affd (1880) 5 App Cas 1, HL).
9   *Astley v Manchester, Sheffield and Lincolnshire Rly Co* (1858) 27 LJCh 478; *Smith v Smith*
    (1868) LR 3 Exch 282; *Re Duffy's Estate* [1897] 1 IR 307 at 315, CA.
10 See eg the Transport Act 1962 s 14(1)(e); and RAILWAYS, INLAND WATERWAYS AND
    CROSS-COUNTRY PIPELINES vol 39(1A) (Reissue) PARA 460.

903. Evidence that land is superfluous. It would be cogent evidence that land
had become superfluous if it had been permanently devoted to some object

which was not a purpose of the undertaking, such as the making of a highway[1], or if the undertakers had sold it[2] or advertised it for sale and described it as surplus land[3], but even these facts are not conclusive, as the acts of the undertakers may have been ultra vires[4]. The compulsory purchase by another company is not evidence that the land was superfluous[5]. On the other hand, land above a tunnel[6] or underneath an archway[7] is not superfluous land, because the term 'land' in that case is not considered to include a horizontal stratum, and that land might also be required for repairs. It is immaterial that the land is let to tenants or used for other purposes, because undertakers may use their land in any way not inconsistent with their statutory powers or contrary to the rights of others[8].

1   *Lord Beauchamp v Great Western Rly Co* (1868) 3 Ch App 745.

2   *Lord Carington v Wycombe Rly Co* (1868) 3 Ch App 377 at 384.

3   *London and South Western Rly Co v Blackmore* (1870) LR 4 HL 610.

4   *Macfie v Callander and Oban Rly Co* [1898] AC 270 at 284, HL; *Hobbs v Midland Rly Co* (1882) 20 ChD 418.

5   *Dunhill v North Eastern Rly Co* [1896] 1 Ch 121, CA. Land acquired for spoilbanks and no longer required for that or any fresh purpose is superfluous: *Great Western Rly Co v May* (1874) LR 7 HL 283. See also *Moody v Corbett* (1865) 5 B & S 859; affd in part (1866) LR 1 QB 510, Ex Ch. Land between a decayed fence and ditch alongside a railway, which had been cultivated by the adjoining owner, has been held to be superfluous: *Norton v London and North Western Rly Co* (1879) 13 ChD 268, CA; and see *Ware v London, Brighton and South Coast Rly Co* (1882) 52 LJCh 198.

6   *Re Metropolitan District Rly Co and Cosh* (1880) 13 ChD 607, CA; *Rosenberg v Cook* (1881) 8 QBD 162, CA; and see *Hooper v Bourne* (1877) 3 QBD 258, CA; *Re Lancashire and Yorkshire Rly Co and Earl of Derby's Contract* (1908) 100 LT 44. A good possessory title to such land may be acquired by adverse possession: *Midland Rly Co v Wright* [1901] 1 Ch 738. See further LIMITATION PERIODS vol 68 (2008) PARA 1083.

7   *Mulliner v Midland Rly Co* (1879) 11 ChD 611.

8   *Bostock v North Staffordshire Rly Co* (1855) 4 E & B 798; *Grand Junction Canal Co v Petty* (1888) 21 QBD 273, CA; *Teebay v Manchester, Sheffield and Lincolnshire Rly Co* (1883) 24 ChD 572; *Foster v London, Chatham and Dover Rly Co* [1895] 1 QB 711, CA; *Onslow v Manchester, Sheffield and Lincolnshire Rly Co* (1895) 64 LJCh 355; *Great Western Rly Co v Solihull RDC* (1902) 86 LT 852, CA; *Lancashire and Yorkshire Rly Co v Davenport* (1906) 70 JP 129, CA.

904.   Obligation to sell superfluous land.   The undertakers[1] are required under the provisions of the Lands Clauses Acts[2] to sell and dispose absolutely[3] of all superfluous land[4] within the period prescribed in the special Act[5] or, if no period is so prescribed, within ten years after the expiration of the time limited in the special Act for the completion of works[6], and apply the purchase money arising from the sale to the purposes of the special Act[7].

1   As to the meaning of 'undertakers' see PARA 511.

2   As to the Lands Clauses Acts see PARA 509 note 1.

3   A conditional sale providing for repurchase by the undertakers has been held to be void (see *London and South Western Rly Co v Gomm* (1882) 20 ChD 562, CA; *Ray v Walker* [1892] 2 QB 88); and a sale providing a lien on the land for unpaid purchase money might also be void (see *Re Thackwray and Young's Contract* (1888) 40 ChD 34). However, the undertakers could impose restrictive covenants on the land: see *Re Higgins and Hitchman's Contract* (1882) 21 ChD 95.

4   As to superfluous land see PARA 902.

5   As to the meaning of 'special Act' see PARAS 509, 514.

6   As to the meaning of 'works' see PARA 511. As to when a time for completion of works is prescribed see PARA 852.

7   Lands Clauses Consolidation Act 1845 s 127.

905. Right of pre-emption. Before the undertakers[1] dispose of any superfluous land[2], either by sale or by applying it to some purpose not a purpose of the undertaking[3], then unless the land is situated within a town or built upon[4] or used for building purposes[5], they must first offer to sell it to the person then entitled to the land, if any, from which it was originally severed[6]. This right of pre-emption arises whenever the undertakers decide that the land is superfluous and proceed to dispose of it, and it is not necessary that the prescribed period should have elapsed[7]. If the person entitled refuses to purchase the land, or cannot after diligent inquiry be found, then a similar offer must be made to the person or to the several persons[8] whose land immediately adjoins the land so proposed to be sold[9], provided those persons are capable of entering into a contract for the purchase of the land[10].

This right of pre-emption must be claimed within six weeks after the offer, and ceases if not accepted within that time[11]. The right of pre-emption may be released, and if not released remains in force as an equitable interest only[12]. In the absence of agreement the price of the land must be ascertained by arbitration and the costs of the arbitration are in the discretion of the arbitrators[13].

1   As to the meaning of 'undertakers' see PARA 511.
2   An agreement for sale is not in itself a disposal of the land: *London and Greenwich Rly Co v Goodchild* (1844) 3 Ry & Can Cas 507 at 511. As to superfluous land see PARA 902.
3   *London and South Western Rly Co v Blackmore* (1870) LR 4 HL 610; *Lord Carington v Wycombe Rly Co* (1868) 3 Ch App 377; *Lord Beauchamp v Great Western Rly Co* (1868) 3 Ch App 745. Applying the land to an extension of the undertaking sanctioned by another Act is not a disposal (*Astley v Manchester, Sheffield and Lincolnshire Rly Co* (1858) 27 LJCh 478); nor is a compulsory purchase by other promoters (*Dunhill v North Eastern Rly Co* [1896] 1 Ch 121, CA).
4   As to the meanings of 'town' and 'land built upon' see PARA 629 note 2.
5   'Used for building purposes' means actually used, or at least laid out and sold or leased as building land: see *Lord Carington v Wycombe Rly Co* (1868) 3 Ch App 377; *Directors etc of the London and South Western Rly Co v Blackmore* (1870) LR 4 HL 610; *R v Cottle* (1851) 16 QB 412 at 421–422; *Elliott v South Devon Rly Co* (1848) 2 Exch 725; *Coventry v London, Brighton and South Coast Rly Co* (1867) LR 5 Eq 104.
6   Lands Clauses Consolidation Act 1845 s 128. As to the meaning of 'severed' see *Hobbs v Midland Rly Co* (1882) 20 ChD 418 at 429; and see PARA 810.
7   *Great Western Rly Co v May* (1874) LR 7 HL 283 at 295 per Lord Cairns LC; *Lord Carington v Wycombe Rly Co* (1868) 3 Ch App 377; *London and South Western Rly Co v Gomm* (1882) 20 ChD 562 at 584, CA, per Jessel MR. As to the prescribed period see PARA 904.
8   Where more than one person is entitled the offer has to be made to each in succession in such order as the undertakers think fit: Lands Clauses Consolidation Act 1845 s 128.
9   As to the meaning of 'adjoining' see *Coventry v London, Brighton and South Coast Rly Co* (1867) LR 5 Eq 104 (in which lessees were held entitled to a right of pre-emption); *London and South Western Rly Co v Blackmore* (1870) LR 4 HL 610; *Re Baroness Bateman and Parker's Contract* [1899] 1 Ch 599.
10 Lands Clauses Consolidation Act 1845 s 128. As to enforcing this right and for the form of order see *London and South Western Rly Co v Blackmore* (1870) LR 4 HL 610 at 627.
11 Lands Clauses Consolidation Act 1845 s 129. A declaration in writing made before a justice by some person not interested in the matter in question, stating that: (1) such an offer was made and was refused or not accepted within six weeks from the time of making the offer; or (2) the person or all the persons entitled to the right of pre-emption were out of the country, or could not after diligent inquiry be found, or were not capable of entering into a contract for the purchase of such lands, is sufficient evidence in all courts of the facts stated: s 129.
12 Law of Property Act 1925 s 186. Contracts by estate owners conferring by statutory implication a right of pre-emption are registrable as estate contracts under the Land Charges Act 1972 s 2(1), (4), Class C(iv): see LAND CHARGES vol 26 (2004 Reissue) PARA 632. A right of pre-emption in relation to registered land has effect from the time of creation as an interest capable of binding successors in title (subject to the rules about the effect of dispositions on priority): Land Registration Act 2002 s 115; and LAND REGISTRATION vol 26 (2004 Reissue) PARA 939.

13 Lands Clauses Consolidation Act 1845 s 130. The arbitration provisions of the Lands Clauses Consolidation Act 1845 are not applicable to the arbitration, but those of the Arbitration Act 1996 Pt I (ss 1–84) are: see s 94; and ARBITRATION vol 2 (2008) PARA 1209.

906. Conveyance of land. Upon payment or tender to the undertakers[1] of the purchase money agreed or determined for the sale of superfluous land[2], the undertakers must convey the land to the purchaser by deed under the common seal of the undertakers if they are a corporation, or if they are not a corporation under the hands and seals of the undertakers or any two of the directors or managers acting by the authority of the body; and a deed so executed is effectual to vest the lands in the purchaser and a receipt under such a common seal or under the hands of two of the directors or managers of the undertaking is a sufficient discharge to the purchaser for the purchase money[3]. The purchaser will acquire no greater right than that of the undertakers[4], and restrictions existing before the land was taken compulsorily are revived[5].

In the absence of express limitations in the conveyances the use of the word 'grant' in conveyances by the undertakers operates as the following express covenants: (1) a covenant that, notwithstanding any act or default done by the undertakers, they were at the time of the execution of the conveyance seised or possessed of the lands or premises thereby granted for an indefeasible estate of inheritance in fee simple, free from all incumbrances done or occasioned by them, or otherwise for such estate or interest as therein expressed to be thereby granted, free from incumbrances done or occasioned by them; (2) a covenant that the grantee of such lands and all his heirs, successors, executors, administrators and assigns (as the case may be) will quietly enjoy the lands against the undertakers and their successors and all other persons claiming under them, and be indemnified by the undertakers and their successors from all incumbrances created by the undertakers; and (3) a covenant for further assurance of such lands, at the expense of such grantee, his heirs, successors, executors, administrators or assigns (as the case may be) by the undertakers, or their successors and all other persons claiming under them[6].

All such grantees and their successors, heirs, executors, administrators and assigns, according to their respective quality or nature and the estate or interest in the conveyance, may in all claims brought by them assign breaches of covenants as they might do if such covenants were expressly inserted in the conveyance[7].

1　As to the meaning of 'undertakers' see PARA 511.

2　As to superfluous land see PARA 902.

3　Lands Clauses Consolidation Act 1845 s 131. Any rule of law which required a seal for the valid execution of an instrument as a deed by an individual has, however, been abolished, except in relation to a corporation sole: see the Law of Property (Miscellaneous Provisions) Act 1989 s 1(1)(b), (10); and DEEDS AND OTHER INSTRUMENTS vol 13 (2007 Reissue) PARA 7. See also CORPORATIONS vol 9(2) (2006 Reissue) PARA 1261 et seq.

4　*Pountney v Clayton* (1883) 11 QBD 820, CA; *Myers v Catterson* (1889) 43 ChD 470, CA.

5　*Ellis v Rogers* (1885) 29 ChD 661; *Pountney v Clayton* (1883) 11 QBD 820, CA; *Bird v Eggleton* (1885) 29 ChD 1012.

6　Lands Clauses Consolidation Act 1845 s 132. The use of the word 'grant' is no longer necessary in conveyances; and does not imply any covenant in law except where otherwise provided by statute (such as the provision in s 132): see the Law of Property Act 1925 ss 51(2), 59(2). As to the covenants for title implied by statute on the disposition of a property see the Law of Property (Miscellaneous Provisions) Act 1994 Pt I (ss 1–13); and SALE OF LAND vol 42 (Reissue) PARAS 336–337, 349 et seq.

7　Lands Clauses Consolidation Act 1845 s 132.

907. Default in disposal of superfluous land. If the undertakers[1] make default in disposing of superfluous land, the land remaining unsold at the expiration of the prescribed period vests in and becomes the property of the adjoining owners in proportion to the extent of their lands respectively adjoining the land[2]. The land has to be superfluous at the expiry of the statutory period[3]. If it becomes superfluous afterwards these clauses do not apply[4].

The question whether at the expiration of the ten years or other specified period land was superfluous or not is a mixed question of law and fact[5]. The issue to be determined is whether at the expiration of the period the land had become either requisite for the undertaking or would in all probability become requisite within a reasonable time after that date; if it may be so requisite, it is not superfluous[6].

1 As to the meaning of 'undertakers' see PARA 511.
2 Lands Clauses Consolidation Act 1845 s 127. Where several properties are in contact with the superfluous land, that land will be divided in proportion to the frontage of each: *Moody v Corbett* (1866) LR 1 QB 510, Ex Ch; and see *Smith v Smith* (1868) LR 3 Exch 282 at 287; *Great Western Rly Co v May* (1874) LR 7 HL 283 at 303. If the undertakers continue to occupy the land and let it to a tenant, he cannot raise the question as to its being superfluous land: *London and North Western Rly Co v West* (1867) LR 2 CP 553. As to superfluous land see PARA 902. As to the meaning of 'adjoining' see PARA 905 note 9.
3 *Great Western Rly Co v May* (1874) LR 7 HL 283 at 294 per Lord Cairns LC; *Macfie v Callander and Oban Rly Co* [1898] AC 270 at 276, 278, HL; *Hooper v Bourne* (1880) 5 App Cas 1 at 9, 11, HL; *Re Metropolitan District Rly Co and Cosh* (1880) 13 ChD 607 at 615, CA. A subsequent extension by an Act, passed at the time of vesting, of the time for disposing of superfluous land does not affect the vesting: *Great Western Rly Co v May*; *London and South Western Rly Co v Gomm* (1882) 20 ChD 562 at 584, CA, per Jessel MR; *Moody v Corbett* (1865) 5 B & S 859 (affd on this point (1866) LR 1 QB 510, Ex Ch). As to the statutory period see PARA 904.
4 *Macfie v Callander and Oban Rly Co* [1898] AC 270, HL.
5 *Smith v North Staffordshire Rly Co* (1880) 44 LT 85.
6 *Macfie v Callander and Oban Rly Co* [1898] AC 270 at 284, HL, per Lord Watson; *Hooper v Bourne* (1877) 3 QBD 258 at 274–275, CA, per Bramwell LJ (affd (1880) 5 App Cas 1, HL).

908. Disposal of surplus land by government departments: the 'Crichel Down Rules'. In addition to the statutory requirements regarding an undertaker's obligation to sell superfluous land[1], non-statutory arrangements (referred to as the 'Crichel Down Rules'[2]) govern the disposal of government land[3] which has become surplus and should be offered back to former owners, their successors, or to sitting tenants[4]. The rules apply to: (1) all freehold disposals and to the creation and disposal of a lease of more than seven years[5]; (2) land that was acquired by, or under threat of, compulsion[6]; and (3) land acquired under the blight provisions in the Town and Country Planning Act 1990[7]. The rules do not apply to: (a) agricultural land acquired before 1 January 1935[8]; or (b) agricultural land acquired on and after 30 October 1992 which becomes surplus and available for disposal more than 25 years after the date of acquisition[9]; or (c) non-agricultural land which becomes surplus and available for disposal more than 25 years after the date of acquisition[10].

The general rule, which is subject to certain exceptions[11], is that, where a government department wishes to dispose of land to which the rules apply, former owners will be given a first opportunity to repurchase the land previously in their ownership, provided that its character has not materially changed[12] since acquisition[13]. Where only part of the land for disposal has been materially changed in character, the general obligation to offer back will apply only to the part that has not been changed[14].

Land will normally be offered back to the former freeholder[15]. If the land was, at the time of acquisition, subject to a long lease and more than 21 years of the term would have remained unexpired at the time of disposal, departments may, at their discretion, offer the freehold to the former leaseholder if the freeholder is not interested in buying back the land[16]. In the case of a tenanted dwelling, any pre-emptive right of the former owner[17] is subject to the prior right of the sitting tenant[18]. Where a dwelling, whether acquired compulsorily or under statutory blight provisions, has a sitting tenant at the time of the proposed disposal, the freehold should first be offered to the tenant; and if the tenant declines to purchase the freehold, it should then be offered to the former owner, although this may be subject to the tenant's continued occupation[19].

Where it is decided, in accordance with the Crichel Down Rules, that surplus land is to be disposed of subject to the obligation to offer back, government departments must follow the appropriate administrative procedures which are also set out in the Crichel Down Rules[20].

Disposals to former owners under these arrangements are at current market value, as determined by the disposing department's professionally qualified, appointed valuer[21].

As a general rule, departments must obtain planning consent before disposing of properties which have potential for development[22]. However: (i) where it would not be practicable or appropriate for departments to take action to establish the planning position at the time of disposal; or (ii) where it seems that the likelihood of obtaining planning permission (including a more valuable permission) is not adequately reflected in the current market value, the terms of sale must include clawback provisions[23], the precise terms of which are a matter for negotiation in each case[24].

1   Ie the requirements of the Lands Clauses Consolidation Acts 1845 ss 127–132 (see PARA 902 et seq). As to the meaning of 'undertakers' see PARA 511. As to superfluous land see PARA 902.

2   Ie the Office of the Deputy Prime Minister Circular 06/2004 (31 October 2004) *Compulsory Purchase and the Crichel Down Rules*. The Office of the Deputy Prime Minister became Communities and Local Government on 5 May 2006 and all such references in the Circular now refer to Communities and Local Government. The Crichel Down Rules have been revised and restated by the government at various times since 1954 and the current Circular supersedes the Department of the Environment and Welsh Office Circular *Disposal of Surplus Government Land: Obligation to Offer Land Back to Former Owners or their Successors – The 'Crichel Down Rules'* (30 October 1992). As to the circumstances that led to the development (and the nomenclature) of the rules see *Public Inquiry ordered by the Minister of Agriculture into the disposal of Land at Crichel Down* (Cmd 9176) (1954); and 530 HC Official Report (5th series), 20 July 1954, cols 1189–1194.

3   The Crichel Down Rules apply to land in England. They also apply to land in Wales acquired by and still owned by a United Kingdom government department. Similar rules have been issued by the National Assembly for Wales: Crichel Down Rules para 2. For the sake of brevity, all bodies to whom the Crichel Down Rules may apply are referred to as 'departments', whether they are Government Departments, including Executive Agencies, other non-departmental public bodies ('NDPBs'), local authorities or other statutory bodies: Crichel Down Rules para 1. Local authorities, statutory bodies and bodies in the private sector to which public sector land holdings have been transferred (eg on privatisation) are recommended to follow the rules: see Crichel Down Rules paras 3, 4. However, the rules are not relevant to land transferred to the National Rivers Authority (now abolished) or land acquired compulsorily by its successor the Environment Agency or to the water and sewerage service companies in consequence of the Water Act 1989 or subsequently acquired by them compulsorily, as such land is governed by the statutory restrictions on disposal under the Water Resources Act 1991 s 157 and the Water Industry Act 1991 s 156 and the consents or authorisations given by the Secretary of State under those provisions: see the Crichel Down Rules para 6. As to the transfer of functions from the National Rivers Authority to the Environment Agency see PROTECTION OF ENVIRONMENT AND PUBLIC HEALTH vol 38 (2006 Reissue) PARA 54. See also WATER AND WATERWAYS vol 100

(2009) PARA 17. As to the Secretary of State see PARA 507 note 1. The functions of the Secretary of State under the Water Resources Act 1991 s 157 and the Water Industry Act 1991 s 156, in so far as they are exercisable in relation to Wales, are now exercisable by the Welsh Ministers (but, in the case of the Water Industry Act 1991 s 156, only in relation to any water or sewerage undertaker whose area is wholly or mainly in Wales): see the National Assembly for Wales (Transfer of Functions) Order 1999, SI 1999/672, art 2, Sch 1; and the Government of Wales Act 2006 s 162(1), Sch 11 para 30. As to the Welsh Assembly Government and the Welsh Ministers see CONSTITUTIONAL LAW AND HUMAN RIGHTS.

    Where land is to be transferred to another body which is to take over some or all of the functions or obligations of the department that currently owns the land, the transfer itself does not constitute a disposal for the purpose of the Rules. Disposals for the purposes of PFI/PPP projects do not fall within the rules: Crichel Down Rules para 5.

4   Crichel Down Rules para 1. For further provisions regarding sitting tenants see Appendix A.

5   Crichel Down Rules para 9. Sale is normally preferable to lease but there may be cases where a short-term lease is appropriate if there is little prospect of an early sale: see the Crichel Down Rules Annex para 7.

6   Crichel Down Rules para 7. A threat of compulsion will be assumed in the case of a voluntary sale if power to acquire the land compulsorily existed at the time unless the land was publicly or privately offered for sale immediately before the negotiations for acquisition: para 7. This means that the acquiring department did not need to have instituted compulsory purchase procedures or even to have actively 'threatened' to use them for the Crichel Down Rules para 7 to apply. It is enough for the acquiring authority to have statutory powers available if it wished to invoke them. For example, land acquired by a highway authority for the purposes of building a road is acquired under the threat of compulsion because such an authority could use its powers under the Highways Act 1980 to make a compulsory purchase order. The only exception is where the land was publicly or privately offered for sale immediately before the negotiations for acquisition: see the Crichel Down Rules Annex para 6.

7   Ie under the Town and Country Planning Act 1990 Pt VI Ch II (ss 149–171), Sch 13 (see PARA 547 et seq; and TOWN AND COUNTRY PLANNING vol 46(2) (Reissue) PARA 978 et seq): Crichel Down Rules para 8. The rules do not apply to land acquired by agreement in advance of any liability under these provisions: para 8.

8   Crichel Down Rules para 14(1). The date of acquisition is the date of the conveyance, transfer or vesting declaration: Crichel Down Rules para 14.

9   Crichel Down Rules para 14(2). See note 8.

10   Crichel Down Rules para 14(3). see note 8.

11   As to the exceptions see PARA 909.

12   The character of the land may be considered to have 'materially changed' where, for example, dwellings or offices have been erected on open land, mainly open land has been afforested, or where substantial works to an existing building have effectively altered its character: Crichel Down Rules para 10. The erection of temporary buildings on land, however, is not necessarily a material change. When deciding whether any works have materially altered the character of the land, the disposing department should consider the likely cost of restoring the land to its original use: Crichel Down Rules para 10.

13   Crichel Down Rules para 10. This provision requires consideration to be given to the whole of the land being sold so that the Secretary of State may sell land as a single lot even if each part had been acquired separately: *R v Secretary of State for Defence, ex p Wilkins* [2000] 3 EGLR 11. Cf *R v Trent Regional Health Authority and Secretary of State for Health, ex p Westerman Ltd and Erewash Borough Council* (1995) 72 P & CR 448, [1995] EGCS 175.

    Disposing departments must maintain a central record or file of all transactions covered by the Crichel Down Rules (including those cases that fall within the Crichel Down Rules paras 10 and 15): Crichel Down Rules para 28. Disposing departments should include on each disposal file a note of its consideration of the Crichel Down Rules, including whether they applied (and if not, why not), the subsequent action taken and whether it was possible to sell to the former owner: Crichel Down Rules Annex para 19.

14   Crichel Down Rules para 11.

15   Crichel Down Rules para 12.

16   Crichel Down Rules para 12. If neither the former freeholder nor former leaseholder is identifiable or interested in buying the land back then the freehold freed from any lease can be disposed of on the open market: Crichel Down Rules Annex para 9.

17   'Former owner' may, according to the circumstances, mean former freeholder or former long leaseholder, and his successor. 'Successor' means the person on whom the property, had it not been acquired, would clearly have devolved under the former owner's will or intestacy; and may include any person who has succeeded, otherwise than by purchase, to adjoining land from

which the land was severed by that acquisition: Crichel Down Rules para 13. A successor under a will includes those who would have succeeded by means of a second or subsequent will or intestacy. The qualification 'otherwise than by purchase' may be relaxed if the successor to adjoining land acquired it by means of transfer within a family trust, including a transfer for monetary consideration: Crichel Down Rules Annex para 10.

18 Crichel Down Rules para 17.

19 Crichel Down Rules para 18. See also Appendix A. This rule does not apply where a dwelling with associated land is being sold as an agricultural unit; or where a dwelling was acquired with associated agricultural land but is being sold in advance of that land: Crichel Down Rules para 18. For these purposes, a 'dwelling' includes a flat: Crichel Down Rules Annex para 16.

20 Crichel Down Rules para 19. As to the procedure see the Crichel Down Rules paras 20–25. There is a special procedure (applying where boundaries of agricultural land have been obliterated) set out in the Crichel Down Rules para 25, Appendix B. Although transparency is required in the handling of the sale, the Secretary of State is not required to enter into formal consultations with the previous owners of surplus land in advance of any announcement of an intention to sell: *R v Secretary of State for Defence, ex p Wilkins* [2000] 3 EGLR 11 (it was sufficient that the ministry had given advance public notice of the intention to dispose of the land).

21 Crichel Down Rules para 26. 'Market value' means 'the best price reasonably obtainable for the property': Crichel Down Rules Annex para 18. 'Current market value' means the market value on the date of the receipt by the disposing department of the notification of the former owner's intention to purchase: Crichel Down Rules para 18.

    However, the duty placed upon a statutory authority to obtain the best price for land sold takes priority over any less formal obligation such as the obligation to former owners under the Crichel Down Rules: *R v Commission for New Towns, ex p Tomkins* (1988) 58 P & CR 57, [1989] 1 EGLR 24, CA.

    There can be no common practice in relation to sales to sitting tenants because of the diversity of interests for which housing is held. Government departments will, nonetheless, have regard to the terms set out in the Housing Act 1985 under which local authorities are obliged to sell houses to tenants with the right to buy: Crichel Down Rules para 26.

22 Crichel Down Rules para 27.

23 Ie in order to fulfil the government's or public body's obligation to the taxpayer to obtain the best price: Crichel Down Rules para 27.

24 Crichel Down Rules para 27.

909. Exceptions to the Crichel Down Rules. The general obligation imposed on government departments by the Crichel Down Rules in relation to the disposal of surplus land[1] does not apply in the following circumstances[2]:

(1)   where it is decided on specific ministerial authority that the land is needed by another department (that is to say, where the land is not surplus to the general requirements of the government)[3];

(2)   where it is decided on specific ministerial authority that for reasons of public interest the land should be disposed of as soon as practicable to a local authority or other body with compulsory purchase powers[4];

(3)   where, in the opinion of the disposing body, the area of land is so small that its sale would not be commercially worthwhile[5];

(4)   where it would be mutually advantageous to the department and an adjoining owner to effect minor adjustments in boundaries through an exchange of land[6];

(5)   where it would be inconsistent with the purpose of the original acquisition to offer the land back[7];

(6)   where a disposal is in respect of either: (a) a site for development or redevelopment which comprises two or more previous land holdings; or (b) a site which consists partly of land which has been materially changed in character and part which has not, and there is a risk of a

fragmented sale of such a site realising substantially less than the best price that can reasonably be obtained for the site as a whole (that is to say, its market value)[8];

(7)   where the market value of land is so uncertain that clawback provisions would be insufficient to safeguard the public purse and where competitive sale is advised by the department's professionally qualified appointed valuer and specifically agreed by the responsible Minister[9].

Where it is decided that a site does fall within any of these exceptions or the general exception relating to material change[10] the former owner will be notified of this decision[11].

1   Ie the Office of the Deputy Prime Minister Circular 06/2004 (31 October 2004) *Compulsory Purchase and the Crichel Down Rules*: see PARA 908.

2   Crichel Down Rules para 15.

3   Crichel Down Rules para 15(1).

4   Crichel Down Rules para 15(2). However, transfers of land between bodies with compulsory purchase powers will not be regarded as exceptions unless at the time of transfer the receiving body could have bought the land compulsorily if it had been in private ownership: Crichel Down Rules para 15(2). Appropriations of land within bodies such as local authorities for purposes different to that for which the land was acquired are exceptions if the body has compulsory purchase powers to acquire land for the new purpose: Crichel Down Rules para 15(2). The courts have held that this provision does not require the reasons to be matters where life or limb are at risk: see *R v Secretary of State for the Environment, Transport and the Regions, ex p Wheeler* (2000) 82 P & CR 1. In practice, this exception may be invoked where the body to which the land is to be sold could have made a compulsory purchase order to obtain it had it been owned by a third party: Crichel Down Rules Annex para 12.

5   Crichel Down Rules para 15(3). This exception provides government departments with discretion as to whether to offer land back when the administrative costs in seeking to offer land back are out of proportion to the value of the land. It will also cover cases where there is a disposal of a small area of land without a sale: Crichel Down Rules Annex para 13.

6   Crichel Down Rules para 15(4).

7   Crichel Down Rules para 15(5). The following examples are given in the rules: (1) land acquired under the Agriculture Act 1947 s 16, s 84 or s 85 (now repealed); (2) land which was acquired under the Distribution of Industry Acts or the Local Employment Acts (now repealed), or under any legislation amending or replacing those Acts, and which is resold for private industrial use; (3) where dwellings are bought for onward sale to a Registered Social Landlord; and (4) sites purchased for redevelopment by English Partnerships or a regional development agency: Crichel Down Rules para 15(5). In addition to these statutory examples, the general rule is that land purchased with the intention of passing it on to another body for a specific purpose is not surplus and therefore not subject to the Crichel Down Rules (eg sites of special scientific interest (SSSIs) purchased for management reasons; a listed building purchased for restorations; properties purchased by a local authority for redevelopment which are sold to a private developer partner; or land purchased by English Partnerships or a regional development agency and sold for reclamation and redevelopment). This exception will apply to disposals by statutory bodies with specific primary rather than incidental functions to develop or redevelop land, and to disposals by their successor bodies. In such cases, land would only be subject to the Crichel Down Rules where it was without development potential and, therefore, genuinely surplus in relation to the purpose for which it was originally acquired: see the Crichel Down Rules Annex para 14.

8   Crichel Down Rules para 15(6). In such cases, however, any former owner who has remained in continuous occupation of the whole or part of his former property (by virtue of tenancy or licence) must be given a right of first refusal of that property. or part of property, as the case may be. In the case of land to which head (a) in the text applies, special consideration will be given where a consortium of former owners has indicated a wish to purchase the land collectively: see the Crichel Down Rules para 15(6); and *R v Trent Regional Health Authority and Secretary of State for Health, ex p Westerman Ltd and Erewash Borough Council* (1995) 72 P & CR 448 (the existence of a consortium is a special consideration for the purposes of the Crichel Down Rules para 14(7) and a joint offer made by such a consortium for land which had been acquired discretely as parcels under compulsory purchase powers had to be accepted by the Secretary of State). However, if there are competing bids for a site, it will be disposed of on the open market: Crichel Down Rules para 15(6).

9   Crichel Down Rules para 15(7).
10   See the Crichel Down Rules para 10; and PARA 908.
11   Crichel Down Rules para 16. The former owner will be notified using the same procedures for contacting former owners as indicated in the Crichel Down Rules paras 20–22: Crichel Down Rules para 16.

910.   Letting superfluous land.   Land held by undertakers[1] until the time arrives for deciding whether or not it is superfluous[2] may also be let or used for purposes other than those directly connected with the undertaking[3].

1   As to the meaning of 'undertakers' see PARA 511.
2   As to superfluous land see PARA 902.
3   *Bayley v Great Western Rly Co* (1884) 26 ChD 434, CA. See also *Bostock v North Staffordshire Rly Co* (1855) 4 E & B 798; *Grand Junction Canal Co v Petty* (1888) 21 QBD 273, CA; *Teebay v Manchester, Sheffield and Lincolnshire Rly Co* (1883) 24 ChD 572; *Foster v London, Chatham and Dover Rly Co* [1895] 1 QB 711, CA; *Onslow v Manchester, Sheffield and Lincolnshire Rly Co* (1895) 64 LJCh 355; *Great Western Rly Co v Solihull RDC* (1902) 86 LT 852, CA; *Lancashire and Yorkshire Rly Co v Davenport* (1906) 70 JP 129, CA.

INDEX

Competition

References are to paragraph numbers; superior figures refer to notes

References are to paragraph numbers; superior figures refer to notes

References are to paragraph numbers; superior figures refer to notes

References are to paragraph numbers; superior figures refer to notes

PARTNERSHIP
  agreement in restraint of trade,
    consideration for, 416
POSTAL SERVICES
  statutory monopoly over, 364
PROCUREMENT
  European competition law, 27
RESTRAINT OF TRADE
  acquiescence, effect of, 437
  affirmation of contract, 437
  agreement, by—
    principle, development of, 386
    professional or other bodies, imposed
      by, 382
  agreements subject to doctrine, 388
  area of operation—
    distance, measurement of, 402
    outside United Kingdom, 401
    prohibited, carrying on business
      within, 431
    reasonableness, 399
    residence, restraint of, 400
  breach of covenant, remedies for—
    affirmation and acquiescence, effect
      of, 437
    alternative remedies, election
      between, 435
    injunction, 435
    interim injunction, 440
    liquidated sum—
      contract, fixed by, 438
      entitlement to, 438
      offer to pay, effect of, 439
    mutuality of performance, 436
  business from which covenantor
    restrained—
    covenantor, status and occupation
      of, 398
    locality, change of, 397
    nature of, 396
    scope of, 396
  classification of, 378
  commercial agents, agreements with,
    395
  competition law, application of, 385
  confidential information—
    obligation not to disclose, 410
    restricting use of, 381
  conflict of laws, 441
  consideration for agreement—
    legality of, 414
    partnership as, 416
    sufficiency of, 415
    valuable, necessity for, 413
  construction of contract—
    certainty, 423

RESTRAINT OF TRADE—*continued*
  construction of contract—*continued*
    context, by, 421
    husband or wife, business carried on
      by, 429
    ordinary meaning of words, 422
    ordinary rules, application of, 420
    particular description, business falling
      within, 430
    person interested in business, 427
    prohibited area, carrying on business
      within, 431
    similar business: *meaning*, 426
    solicitor, person practising as, 428
    surgeon, person practising as, 428
  creditor, interest of, 427
  custom, by, 382n[1]
  customers, as to, 407
  director of business, interest of, 427
  duration—
    lease, term of, 406
    period of employment, during, 404
    termination of employment, after,
      404
    time in general, as to, 403
    transfer of undertakings, effect of,
      405
  freedom of trade, principle of, 377
  general, 386
  general and partial, repudiation of
    distinction between, 387
  husband or wife, business carried on
    by, 429
  instances of covenants affecting
    particular trades, etc, 432
  judicial notice of, 384
  knowledge and skill acquired during
    employment, no restraint of use,
    411
  legitimate concerns meriting protection,
    389
  legitimate interest, protecting, 389
  manager of business, interest of, 427
  mutuality of performance of covenants,
    436
  name, as to, 408
  operation of law, by, 381
  particular description, business falling
    within, 430
  parties to agreement—
    assignees, 419
    general principles, 417
    minors, 418
    representatives, 419
    rules applying, 417
  person interested in business, 427

RESTRAINT OF TRADE—*continued*
  professional or other bodies, by, 382
  public policy, contrary to, 383
  reasonableness—
    area of operation, as to, 399
    commercial agents, agreements with, 395
    confidential information, obligation not to disclose, 410
    consideration of agreement as a whole, 393
    courts, function of, 390
    customers, as to, 407
    employment and sale of business, difference between, 394
    knowledge and skill acquired during employment, no restraint of use, 411
    name, as to, 408
    public interest, in, 412
    test of, 391
    time for determining, 392
    trade secrets, contract not to disclose, 409
  scope of application, 388
  settlement of disputes, 388
  severance of contract—
    conditions for, 434
    unenforceable part, of, 433
    vendor and purchaser, between, 433
  similar business: *meaning*, 426
  solicitor, person practising as, 428
  statute, by—
    cases of, 379
    law imposing burdens, imposition of, 380
    proper standard of competence, maintenance of, 379
    regulatory reform, 380
    scope of, 379
  surgeon, person practising as, 428
  trade secrets, contract not to disclose, 409

RESTRAINT OF TRADE—*continued*
  unlimited scope of, 386
  usual covenants, not, 424
  void contracts, 383
  waiver and release of covenant, 425
RESTRICTIVE TRADE PRACTICES
  restrictions on, 365
SECRETARY OF STATE
  functions of, 5
SECTORAL REGULATORS
  concurrent powers, 147
  list of, 147
  role of, 18
SPORT
  European competition law, application of, 49
TRADE
  meaning, 369
  exercise of, 372
  freedom, principle of, 377
  manufacture, as, 369
  profit, disregard of, 371
  restraint. *See* RESTRAINT OF TRADE
  trade: *meaning*, 369
TRADE SECRET
  contract not to disclose, 409
TRANSPORT
  European competition law, application of, 52
WATER
  universal service obligation, 18
WATER SERVICES REGULATION AUTHORITY (OFWAT)
  establishment of, 21
  functions, 21
  sectoral regulator, as, 18, 147
WEIGHTS AND MEASURES AUTHORITY
  enforcer of consumers' interests, as, 342
  intended prosecution, notice to OFT, 359

Compulsory Acquisition of Land

ACQUIRING AUTHORITY
  compulsory purchase order. *See* COMPULSORY PURCHASE ORDER
  contract not to use land in accordance with statutory powers, 850

ACQUIRING AUTHORITY—*continued*
  expenses of displaced persons, payment of, 856
  government department, 519
  information, power to require, 522

References are to paragraph numbers; superior figures refer to notes

DISTURBANCE FROM
   LAND—*continued*
   loss payments—*continued*
      occupier's—*continued*
         claim for, 833
         death before claim, effect of, 835
         entitlement to, 831
         insolvency before claim, effect of,
            834
         payment, 836
      payments for apart from
         compensation—
         additional, 826
         classes of, 826
         persons entitled to, 826
      persons without compensatable
         interests, payments to—
         amount of, 839
         payment of, 839
         right to, 838

EASEMENTS
   acquisition of, 532

ECCLESIASTICAL LAND
   compulsory purchase, payment for, 668
      application for payment out, costs
         of, 680
      application of, 674
      costs of person served, payment of,
         676
      discharge of debts, costs of, 677
      disposal and payment out, application
         for, 675
      leases and reversions, money paid into
         court for, 682
      purchase, costs of, 677
      purchase of other land, costs of, 678
      purchasing and taking land, costs of,
         681
      removal or replacement of buildings,
         costs of, 679
      tenants for life and limited owners,
         discretionary payments to, 683

ECCLESIASTICAL PROPERTY
   meaning, 518n^1, 560n^6
   compulsory purchase order, notice of,
      560
   Land Compensation Act 1961,
      application of, 518
   notice to treat, service of, 619

GAS
   underground storage—
      acquisition of rights, 611
      facilities, development consent, 541

GOODWILL
   injury to, compensation for, 816

GOVERNMENT DEPARTMENT
   compulsory acquisition by, 519
   surplus land, disposal of, 908–909

HIGHWAYS
   adverse effect, acquisition of land and
      execution of works to mitigate,
      873
   injurious works—
      buildings affected by public works,
         sound-proofing—
      acceptance of offer, 869
      conditions for carrying out work or
         making grants, 868
      eligible buildings, ascertainment
         of, 864
      grant, amount of, 871
      highway authorities, agents of, 866
      highways, use of, 863
      insulation work or grant, offer of,
         867
      nature and extent of work, 870
      noise level, ascertainment of, 865
      reconsideration, application for,
         872
      regulations, 861
   compensation for. *See* COMPENSATION
   noise, payments in respect of caravans
      and other structures affected,
      862
   persons moving temporarily, expenses
      of, 876

HOME LOSS PAYMENT
   meaning, 827
   amount of, 829
   claim for, 828
   conditions for, 827
   payment of, 829
   right to, 827

HOUSING ACTION TRUST
   area, development in—
      betterment, 848
      disregard in assessing compensation
         or purchase money, 795

LAND SUBJECT TO ACQUISITION
   ancient monuments, 528
   authorised purposes, for, 526
   exclusion and protection—
      allotments, 531
      commons, 531
      generally, 529
      inalienable land, 530
      local authority land, 531
      National Trust land, 531
      open spaces, 531
      statutory undertakers, of, 531

References are to paragraph numbers; superior figures refer to notes

NOTICE TO TREAT—*continued*
further, service of, 620
interest in land under building
agreement, effect on, 633
lease, re-entry and repossession by
lessor, 633
mortgagee, entitlement of, 711
owner's rights and duties, effect on, 632
part of land, for—
agricultural land, counter-notice in
case of—
land outside compulsory purchase
powers, compelling purchase
of, 623
lessee's interest in land outside
compulsory purchase powers,
compelling purchase of, 624
service of, 622
building: *meaning*, 626
counter-notice—
agricultural land, in case of, 622–
624
invalid case, in, 627
part of premises, in case of, 625,
628
expensive communications, intersected
land requiring, 630
house: *meaning*, 626
injunction to restrain, 627
intersected land not built on, 629
Land Clauses Act, under—
effect of, 627
part of premises, in case of, 625
manufactory: *meaning*, 626
restriction on, 621
town, intersected land not in, 629
period of execution of works, 617
persons to whom given, 715
price, ascertainment of, 634
service—
freehold owner, on, 619
lessee, on, 619
mode of, 618
persons entitled to, 619
time for, 617
subsequent steps, failure to take, 637
valuation of land, time of, 635
vendor and purchaser, relation of parties
as after, 631
vesting declaration, effect of, 689
withdrawal of, 636, 716

OPEN SPACES
acquisition of—
generally, 531
nationally significant infrastructure
projects, for, 541

OPEN SPACES—*continued*
acquisition of—*continued*
special Parliamentary procedure,
confirmation of compulsory
purchase order by, 604
new rights over, acquisition of, 542,
609
PLANNING BLIGHT
blight notice, service of, 547
compensation for, 548
interests affected by, blighted land, 547
PLANNING DECISION
interests affected by, right of owner to
require purchase of—
compensation for, 546
purchase notice, 545
response notice, 545
PLANNING ORDER
interests affected by, right of owner to
require purchase of—
purchase notice, 545
response notice, 545
PLANNING PERMISSION
assumed, effect as to potential use of
land—
certificate of appropriate alternative
development, in accordance
with—
appeals, 777–778
application for, 774
contents of, 776
issue of, 775
notices and documents, service of,
779
permission certified subject to
conditions, 771
relevant matters, powers to
prescribe, 773
right to apply for, 772
development in accordance with
acquiring authority's proposals,
for, 764
development plan, land allocated in—
comprehensive development, for,
769
particular purpose, for, 766
range of specific uses, for, 768
specific use, for, 767
existing use, included in, 765
land required for highway use,
statutory assumption, 763
nature and extent of, 770
restriction of use, 762
certificate of appropriate alternative
development—
appeals, 777–778

VESTING DECLARATION—*continued*
  vesting date, 687
  vesting of land, 693
WORKS
  acquired land, on—
    authorised, 850
    execution, time for, 852
    rate deficiency during construction of
      works, liability to make good,
      857
  compensation for, 521
  execution, time for, 852
  extinguishment of right to facilitate,
    858
  injurious—
    adverse effect of highways, acquisition
      of land and execution of works
      to mitigate, 873
    buildings affected by public works,
      sound-proofing—
      acceptance of offer, 869
      conditions for carrying out work or
        making grants, 868
      eligible buildings, ascertainment
        of, 864
      grant, amount of, 871
      highway authorities, agents of, 866

WORKS—*continued*
  injurious—*continued*
    buildings affected by public works,
      sound-proofing—*continued*
      highways, use of, 863
      insulation work or grant, offer of,
        867
      nature and extent of work, 870
      noise level, ascertainment of, 865
      reconsideration, application for,
        872
      regulations, 861
    compensation for. *See* COMPENSATION
    effect of public works, acquisition of
      land to mitigate effect of, 874
    mitigation of effect, 860
    noise, payments in respect of caravans
      and other structures affected,
      862
    persons moving temporarily, expenses
      of, 876
    power to execute, 859
    responsible authority, execution by,
      875
  land acquired, on, 850
WORKS ORDER
  transport systems, for, 507

Words and Phrases

Words in parentheses indicate the context in which the word or phrase is used

References are to paragraph numbers; superior figures refer to notes